modern Cabinetmaking

by

William D. Umstattd

South Holland, Illinois

THE GOODHEART-WILLCOX COMPANY, INC.

Publishers

Library of Congress Catalog Card Number 88-11308
International Standard Book Number 0-87006-697-8

234567890-90-87654321

Library of Congress Cataloging in Publication Data

Umstattd, William D.
  Modern cabinetmaking.

  Includes index.
  Summary: A textbook for assisting students in
acquiring the skills necessary to enter cabinetmaking
and woodworking occupations.
  1. Cabinet-work. [1. Cabinetwork. 2. Woodwork]
I. Title.
TT197.U47 1988   684.1′04   88-11308
ISBN 0-87006-697-8

INTRODUCTION

MODERN CABINETMAKING is a comprehensive text which explains and illustrates all aspects of fine woodworking. It is written for anyone with an interest in the subject from either a vocational or hobbyist viewpoint. MODERN CABINETMAKING teaches the skills and techniques practiced by the cabinetmaker, finish carpenter, millworker, or serious hobbyist. Others such as the architect, interior designer, and those in furniture design, manufacturing, and sales will find this book to be a valuable guide and reference.

MODERN CABINETMAKING starts you off with an overview of the entire text. You will next find a study of furniture styles and designs which will support an orderly approach to the design/construction process. You will learn how to prepare sketches or drawings and how to prepare a plan before beginning work. The beginner usually adopts drawings or plans prepared by others. The more advanced cabinetmaker or woodworker may alter or adapt plans to suit individual needs or taste. The most experienced individuals may create their own designs and plans. The study of the design units in this book should provide you with an appreciation of good design principles.

MODERN CABINETMAKING also provides you with a thorough understanding of the technology of woodworking. You will be led through a discussion of choices and alternatives which will affect the final product. You will learn the ''How, What, Why, and When'' of selecting the appropriate materials whether they are fine hardwoods, manufactured panel products, plastics, glass, or ceramics. Hardware, abrasives, adhesives, and finishing supplies are discussed in appropriate detail.

Of primary importance is the study of the procedures and techniques of fine cabinet and furniture making. MODERN CABINETMAKING provides complete coverage of modern processes using both hand and power tools and machines. As the book guides you through the processes, it shows how your decisions will affect the final product. You will study the three types of processes: separating, forming, and combining. First, you will learn how to change standard stock into workpieces by sawing, surfacing, drilling, turning, and abrading. Then, you will learn how to form wood and other products using the proper tools and techniques. You will then learn how to assemble individual parts using fasteners and adhesives. Detailed information about finishing materials and processes will help you create products with lasting beauty.

Cabinets and furniture can be intensely important as personal possessions or as an expression of style. You sit on, stand at, lie upon, and display or store items in or on your cabinets and furniture. MODERN CABINETMAKING will assist you in meeting the very personal needs and preferences for furniture and cabinets to be used by children, adults, or the handicapped.

As you study and practice your techniques, you will increase your woodworking and cabinetmaking skills. You will learn to reach make-buy decisions based on your own experience and skill. You will understand how available hand, portable, and stationary tools and machines are influencing factors in your decisions.

Whether you work at home, in industry, or in a school, your activities should focus on your own safety, the safety of your co-workers, and the effects of the process on the environment. Throughout this book, you will receive THINK SAFETY—ACT SAFELY reminders. Always try to protect yourself and others around you against risk of accidents and injuries. Pay special attention to this safety information.

Nearly everyone has an appreciation for fine cabinets and furniture—some as consumers and others as builders. Your personal motivation for reading this book may be for self-satisfaction or to learn some new technique or to earn a living. Hopefully, the information you find in MODERN CABINETMAKING, along with the experience and skills you develop, will help you become successful in cabinetmaking and woodworking.

William D. Umstattd

CONTENTS

Well designed and crafted cabinetwork gives an owner great satisfaction and years of service.
(Quaker Maid)

Chapter 1
INTRODUCTION TO CABINETMAKING

After studying this chapter, you will be able to:
- □ Identify the needs and wants for cabinets in everyday living.
- □ Discuss the importance of function and form for furniture and cabinetry.
- □ Explain the decision-making process for cabinetry production.
- □ Describe the processes of production and management technology.

Throughout history, people have created products with wood. Even with the influx of plastics, wood continues to play an important role in our everyday living. We store food, utensils, and personal belongings in or on wood cabinets. We sit on chairs and sleep on beds supported by wooden frames. We shop from store fixtures, work at desks, prepare food on counters, and pull books from shelves. All of these storage areas, work surfaces, and decorative products might be made of wood, Fig. 1-1.

Every product you see was once a need that an individual set out to meet. Ideas first put on paper later became a design that had to be developed. Decisions were made. Problems, such as acquiring materials and operating tools or machines, were solved. Processes of cutting, shaping, assembling,

Fig. 1-1. These products show the many uses of wood to meet our needs and wants for cabinets and furniture.
(Craft Products, O'Sullivan, Thomasville, Golden Bond Building Products)

and finishing were chosen to bring the design idea to reality.

This book covers the decision-making practices for producing fine cabinets and furniture. The topics focus on the many methods, materials, and machines that create these products. This chapter presents an overview of cabinetmaking and identifies the relationship of various steps, including design, materials, production, and management.

DESIGN DECISIONS

Consider yourself a designer. Your responsibility is to help people meet their needs and wants for furniture and cabinets, Fig. 1-2. The product design you create might be original or influenced by an existing style.

Design decisions must be made before work begins. "As-you-work" decisions about cabinetry needs, sizes, and shapes are very costly. Without a documented plan of attack, you will likely be wasting time and materials.

All design decisions are based on two factors: function and form. Consider these topics as you begin to generate ideas for a product.

FUNCTION AND FORM

Function describes the reason for having the cabinet or piece of furniture. Note the custom-made beauty salon cabinet in Fig. 1-3. When closed, there are few corners to bump against. When open, its contents are displayed and within easy reach. This represents efficient planning and production. Another example of function is the attractive clothes display case shown in Fig. 1-4. Movable shelving makes this product flexible enough to store clothing for any season. As a designer, you must see that every product meets the needs and wants of the user.

Form is the appearance of the cabinet. What will the piece look like? Is there a particular style you want to copy, such as French Provincial, Early American, or Scandinavian? The appearance of the product must fit with the surrounding furniture.

```
NEEDS AND WANTS
      │
   ◇ DESIGN
     DECISIONS ◇
   ┌──┴──┐
FUNCTION   FORM
   └──┬──┘
    IDEAS
   ┌──┴──┐
VARIABLES  STANDARDS
   └──┬──┘
  SKETCHING
      │
  MATERIAL
  CONSIDERATIONS
      │
  WORKING
  DRAWINGS
```

Fig. 1-2. A series of decisions and considerations are made during the design stage.

Fig. 1-3. A styling salon cabinet having excellent function and form. Top—When closed, the cabinet has an attractive appearance. Bottom—When open, the cabinet's contents are within easy reach. (Fox Floor and Cabinet Co.)

Fig. 1-4. Clothes display cabinet. (Fox Floor and Cabinet Co.)

Experienced designers say that form follows function. The cabinetry must first serve a purpose. If the product is not functional, even careful styling will not make it desirable.

DESIGN IDEAS

Once you consider the form and function of a product, sketch your ideas. These quickly-made pictures document your thoughts, and allow you to compare alternate designs. Production cabinet shops often create their designs with the help of a computer-aided design system, Fig. 1-5.

DESIGN VARIABLES

Products vary in size depending on their intended use. A trophy case with 12 in. (300 mm) between shelves obviously will not hold a 14 in. (350 mm) trophy. You must take into account the size of objects to be stored. Furthermore, there are human factors to consider. A chair for a child will have different dimensions than that for an adult. A table or counter designed for a person in a wheel chair must be a different height than standard cabinets and furniture.

DESIGN STANDARDS

Many types of cabinetry are designed and produced based on standards. Kitchen cabinets are one example. There are standards for countertop height, distance between base and wall units, and unit sizes. Widths for factory produced units are established in modules of 3 in. (75 mm). This is further discussed in Chapter 49. When making a custom cabinet, set dimensions to meet customer needs.

Another measurement standard, the 32 mm system, applies to case construction and hardware installation. Holes are drilled 32 mm apart at 37 mm from the edge of the cabinet front. "European" hardware mounting holes are also spaced this distance, making the hinge, pull, or fastener easier to install.

NEW DESIGN CONCEPTS

A fairly new design concept is ready-to-assemble (RTA) cabinets. The product is purchased unassembled in a neatly packaged compact carton. In this form, even a large furniture item can be moved through small doors and narrow stairways. The consumer then assembles the cabinet with special RTA fasteners. The assembled product often

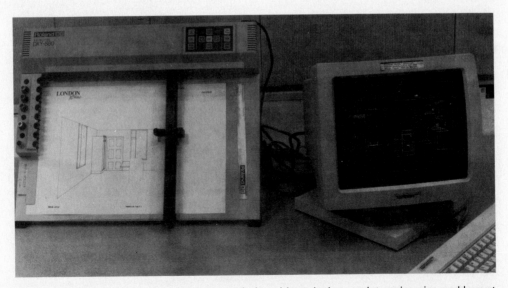

Fig. 1-5. Computer-aided design systems help cabinet designers determine size and layout of cabinetry. (London Kitchens)

looks no different than preassembled-and-finished furniture, Fig. 1-6.

Ready-to-assemble cabinets and furniture came about after World War II when Europe was faced with a severe shortage of home furnishings. Furniture factories appeared nearly overnight to meet the demand for furniture. They began replacing solid wood with newly introduced panel products and plastic laminates. This decreased the cost per item and increased production quantities. However, since plywood, particleboard, and other panel products held nails and screws poorly, manufacturers set out to design new assembly methods. This led to the introduction of RTA fasteners.

RTA fasteners, discussed in Chapter 16, do not create a ''permanent'' joint. They connect and disconnect with ease. Yet, despite making assembly much easier, they hold with great strength, in both solid wood and composite materials.

European manufacturers learned two important lessons about consumers with the introduction of RTA cabinet fasteners.
1. Consumers who previously had difficulties moving large furniture enjoyed being able to disassemble furniture and reassemble it in a new location.
2. Consumers did not mind buying furniture disassembled and assembling it themselves, provided that simple-to-follow instructions were included.

Initially, assemble-it-yourself cabinets were known as knock-down (KD) furniture and the fasteners were known as KD fittings. However, the name ''ready-to-assemble'' has gained wider use because ''knock down'' gives the impression of an unsturdy product.

MATERIAL DECISIONS

There are many materials available for producing cabinets and fine furniture. These should be considered carefully throughout the design and production process. Materials you might consider include lumber, veneer, manufactured panel products, plastic laminates, plastic, ceramic, and glass. To assemble these materials, you will also choose among adhesives, mechanical fasteners, or joinery. Either before or after assembly, a clear or opaque finish is applied. Hardware, such as hinges, pulls, and knobs, add the final touches to the product.

Lumber will be either softwood or hardwood. Softwood identifies lumber from cone-bearing trees that is typically used as a construction material. Hardwood describes lumber from leaf-bearing trees that is usually selected for making cabinets and furniture. Each specie has unique properties affecting appearance and workability.

Trees also are made into wood products such as plywood, particleboard, and veneer. Veneer is a sheet of thinly sliced hardwood or softwood. Use it to cover poor quality lumber or manufactured panel products. Veneer is especially effective when inlaying or overlaying decorative designs.

Manufactured panel products certainly have a place in cabinetmaking today. MDF (medium density fiberboard) has become as popular as particleboard for kitchen cabinets and RTA products. These may be covered with enamel, plastic laminate, or veneer for appearance purposes.

Glass, plastic, and ceramic materials create durable surfaces. They are often applied to table or countertops and edges. Plastic laminates are extremely popular for durable, nonfading surfaces.

Fig. 1-6. This ready-to-assemble computer console was assembled by a consumer. (O'Sullivan)

Some have patterns which look exactly like wood grain.

Cane, a form of grass, is woven to provide patterns and texture. A cane seat can be more comfortable than solid wood. Cane also decorates cabinet door fronts and other surfaces.

Once cabinet components have been cut to size, they are assembled with adhesives or mechanical fasteners. You must select the proper type of adhesive, cement, glue, or mastic for bonding similar and dissimilar materials. If mechanical fasteners are used, you must also carefully choose the type. A screw holds well in solid wood, but poorly in particleboard. Select assembly materials based on the design and material of which the product is made.

At some point in the cabinetmaking process, you must smooth the components. Sanding is done before assembly to components which will be hard to reach after assembly. Exterior surfaces are typically smoothed after assembly.

Finishing materials are coatings which provide color and protection to the wood. Natural and synthetic products are available. Some finishes build up on top of the wood and others penetrate into the wood grain. Carefully select finishes. A poorly chosen or applied finish can ruin hours or days of production time.

PRODUCTION DECISIONS

Production decisions relate to making any product become a reality. They include choosing the tools and procedures necessary to build the product in the most efficient manner, Fig. 1-7. Design and material decisions greatly affect production decisions. A piece of furniture designed with many curves will likely be more difficult to produce than one with only straight surfaces. A cabinet which includes stained glass doors is more difficult to create than one having solid wood doors. Make all decisions in an organized manner and, more importantly, plan each step.

TOOLS

There are many types of tools used in cabinetmaking. Most processing is done with stationary power tools, such as belt sanders, table saws, planers, and shapers. These reduce heavy and bulky materials, such as long lengths of lumber and plywood, into component sizes, Fig. 1-8. Portable

PRODUCT DEMANDS

ANALYZING CURRENT PRACTICES

PRODUCTION

MANAGING WORK

PRE-PROCESSING

PLANNING PRODUCTION

PROCESSING

ORGANIZING MATERIAL, PEOPLE, TOOLS

POST-PROCESSING

DIRECTING ACTIVITIES

CONTROLLING QUALITY

QUALITY PRODUCTS READY FOR USE

Fig. 1-7. A series of factors are involved with producing a product.

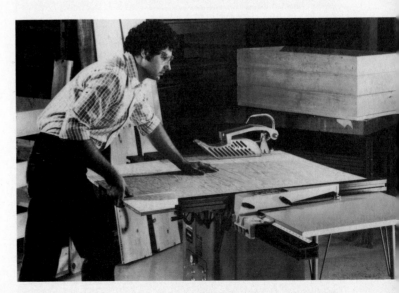

Fig. 1-8. Reducing sheets of plywood to component sizes with a table saw. (Delta)

power tools, such as orbital sanders, screw guns, and jig saws, are easy to handle and often more appropriate than stationary tools for small parts. Hand tools are generally used for minor operations, where set-up time for a stationary machine may be wasteful.

PROCESSES

Material processing for cabinetmaking fits into three categories: separating, forming, and combining. *Separating* refers to cutting or removing material. Cutting stock on a table saw or turning a spindle on a lathe are separating operations. Some machines are automated; the cutting tool is controlled by computer code. The lathe in Fig. 1-9 is called a *numerically controlled* machine. *Forming* includes all operations where material is bent, or formed, into a shape using a mold or form, Fig. 1-10. No material is removed or added. *Combining*

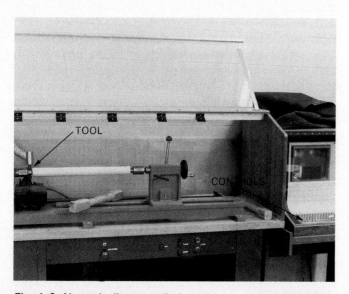

Fig. 1-9. Numerically controlled machines, such as this lathe, reduce the amount of human labor needed to process a part.

Fig. 1-10. Forming wood with a mold and clamps.

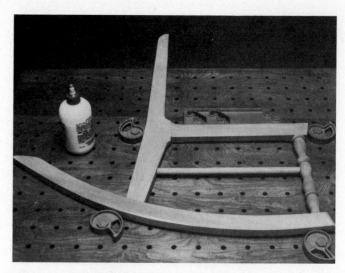

Fig. 1-11. Assembling components with adhesive is one form of combining. (Meyer-Vise)

involves bonding, mechanical fastening, and coating, Fig. 1-11. Each of these processes involves assembling or joining two materials.

PRODUCING CABINETRY

Planning for production involves making efficient and effective decisions related to materials, tools, and processes. Today, most cabinetry is mass-produced by cabinetmaking industries using sophisticated machinery. You will make decisions based on simpler tools found in small- and medium-sized cabinet shops. First, the equipment has to be selected and set up. This is called preprocessing. Then you actually saw, shape, sand, assemble, and finish. This is processing. Transporting and installing the finished product is called postprocessing.

PREPROCESSING

Preprocessing includes all activities prior to building a product. Designs are finished and mock-ups may be built. Mock-ups help you decide if the product will be functional and have a pleasing appearance. Materials are purchased as standard stock items. This includes full lengths of lumber, sheets of plywood, boxes of screws, and containers of finish. They have to be received, stored, and marked as inventory. Storing materials in set locations helps you work more efficiently, Fig. 1-12.

PROCESSING

Processing includes all tasks from cutting standard stock to finishing the product. You need to cut components, such as cabinet doors, drawers, legs, bases, cases, shelves, and tops. Work progresses by cutting and shaping workpieces to size. Then,

Fig. 1-12. Store materials and work in progress in an organized manner. (Craft Products)

joints are made to hold the pieces in place. Holes may be drilled and bored for various mechanical fasteners. Then the components are sanded. A sampling of these processes is found in Fig. 1-13.

Once cut to size and smoothed, parts are bonded together to give strength and structure to the product. Finally, a topcoating is applied by brushing, dipping, rolling, spraying, or wiping. This coating protects the product from moisture and wear.

POSTPROCESSING

Postprocessing includes transporting, installing, and maintaining products. For example, desks you build in a home workshop might then be boxed and transported to an office. Installing refers to setting up the product, such as placing store fixtures, Fig. 1-14, or attaching cabinets to floors and walls, Fig. 1-15. Maintenance is necessary for cabinets and furniture. You maintain a product by waxing it and repairing scratches to protect the product and restore its appearance.

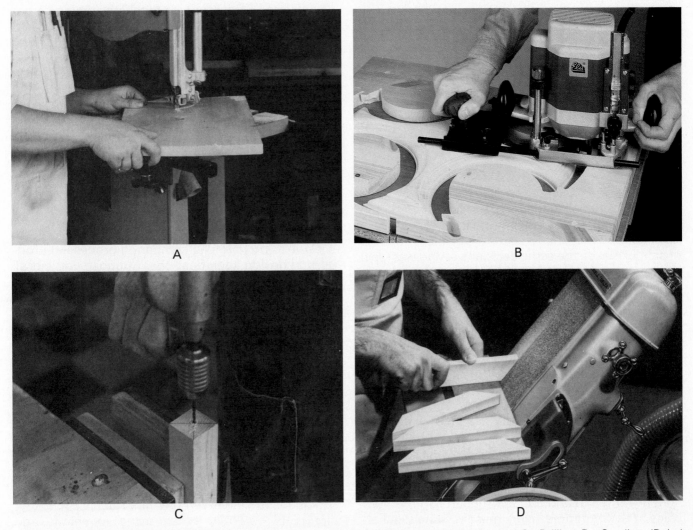

A

B

C

D

Fig. 1-13. Typical processes in cabinetmaking. A—Sawing. (Delta) B—Shaping. (Black & Decker) C—Drilling. D—Sanding. (Delta)

Fig. 1-14. Postprocessing includes setting up products. Top— This finished display case awaits transportation to the store. Bottom—Case installed in a clothing store. (Fox Floor and Cabinet Co.)

Fig. 1-15. Installing kitchen cabinets is a postprocessing task you might do yourself.

MANAGING WORK

Work has to be planned, organized, directed, and controlled to progress smoothly. These activities are *management* responsibilities. An individual at home or school makes the same decisions as the well-paid business manager.

PLANNING

Planning involves establishing goals and deciding how they will be accomplished. Study alternative designs and processes to learn how others have solved similar problems. Experience with various functions, forms, materials, tools, and processes allows you to make sound management decisions.

ORGANIZING FOR EFFICIENCY AND SAFETY

Organizing involves the four "rights." Have the *right* information and the *right* material in the *right* place at the *right* time. Work must be scheduled efficiently to prevent wasting material and time.

Undelivered equipment, or machines which do not operate properly, slows progress. Work is often delayed if adhesives or screws are not on hand when needed.

DIRECTING DAILY ACTIVITIES

Supervisors in industry see that planned and organized tasks are performed on schedule. When working alone, you should still have a schedule. Set guidelines are also valuable if people face an unpopular decision.

CONTROLLING WORK QUALITY

Controlling involves comparing processed products to design specifications. Suppose you cut all joints to size, but later find they do not fit. What should you have done? Trying a test joint could have prevented this problem.

Quality also involves productivity. When work falls short of the goals, corrective action must be taken. Reports and schedules are made to assist in monitoring work activities.

In industry, all management decisions should show concern for and involve employees. This helps build decision-making abilities and self-confidence. In every shop, workers risk exposure to toxic substances, accidents, and injuries. People may be allergic to dust or finishing materials. Some solvents are toxic and flammable. Remember that hazardous conditions exist everywhere. Read labels and follow directions carefully when using machines and materials.

SUMMARY

Cabinetmaking is both an art and a science. You can see the artistic and creative talents of the cabinetmaker in subtle curves, precise joints, suitable coloring, and flawless finish of a product. The cabinetmaking process begins with the designer's goal of meeting a need. Once the design is finished, fine woods and other materials are chosen to make the design become a completed product.

The science of cabinetmaking relates to production decisions. They involve the proper application of materials, tools, and processes in factories, schools, and homes. In this book, hand tool, portable power tool, and stationary power tool operations are explained.

Workpiece assembly and finishing control the final appearance of the product. Joinery determines how well workpieces will fit together. Abrasives help smooth surfaces. Finishing involves adding color and a protective topcoating. The quality of assembly and finishing can make the difference between a poor product and a well-crafted piece of furniture.

The following chapters trace cabinetmaking from selecting or creating designs to applying the final finish. Careful study of these topics will provide you the skills needed to ''think and work safely'' to design and create high quality cabinets and furniture.

CABINETMAKING TERMS

Design decisions, function, form, material decisions, production decisions, separating, forming, combining, preprocessing, processing, postprocessing, management, planning, organizing, controlling.

TEST YOUR KNOWLEDGE

1. Cabinetry should meet the _____ and _____ of those who use it.
2. Adapting cabinetry for children and adults involves:
   a. Size charts.
   b. Human factors.
   c. Disabling injuries.
   d. Identifying needs.
3. Production kitchen cabinet widths vary in _____ in. modules.
4. ''European'' hardware is based on a 32 mm screw hole diameter. True or false?
5. RTA stands for _____.
6. Design for function first, then for form. True or false?
7. Major decisions about production relate to _____, _____, and _____.
8. Planning involves what two steps?
9. Organizing involves what four ''rights?''
10. Hazardous conditions must be taken into consideration for all management and production decisions. True or false?

Fine quality is apparent in these teak cabinets. (Dyrlund-Smith)

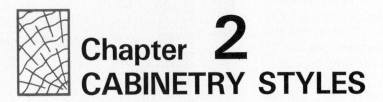

Chapter 2
CABINETRY STYLES

After studying this chapter, you will be able to:
- Explain the progress of cabinetry styles from the 17th century to today.
- Describe the differences between traditional, provincial, and contemporary designs.
- List characteristics of the styles which belong to traditional, provincial, and contemporary designs.

Cabinets and fine furniture are often built to match a style. *Style* refers to the features of the cabinet that distinguish it from other pieces. Some of these features include the color, moulding, and shape of the cabinet.

Many styles originated in 17th and 18th century Europe. Early styles were named after kings, queens, countries, or designers. Many people had pieces designed for them or did the designing themselves. The earlier styles have been ''handed down'' and modified over the years. However, the influence of European, Asian, and early American designers can still be seen.

PROGRESSION OF STYLES

Cabinetry is one way to express individual differences. Most early pieces were highly carved and very heavy, Fig. 2-1. By contrast, some had spindly legs and appeared that they would break if moved, Fig. 2-2. Both of these styles are typically identified as *traditional cabinetry*.

Fig. 2-1. This Sheraton style bookcase is an example of early cabinetwork.   (Thomasville)

Fig. 2-2. Queen Anne style highboys had fragile cabriole legs. (Thomasville)

As time passed, traditional designs were copied. The technology advanced. Less carving was done. Ways were found to reduce the weight of some styles. Products were made to look stronger. More average people, or peasants, could then afford the cabinetry. These products were called *provincial,* which meant ''for people across the countryside,'' Fig. 2-3.

The next transition in cabinetry saw curves replaced by straight line designs. This further reduced the cost of the product. The term *contemporary* was given to this style of cabinetry and furniture, Fig. 2-4.

EARLY CABINETMAKING

You have to admire the early manufacturers. Prior to the early 1800s, neither steam nor electricity was available. Pieces were produced with hand tools like shaper planes and shaped scrapers. Machines, like wood turning lathes and saws, relied on foot or hand power. Lathes and scroll saws had foot treadles. The cabinetmaker pressed the treadle with one foot which turned the piece or the saw blade. On other saws, an apprentice turned a handle to create the power while the master performed the operations.

Fig. 2-3. Provincial furniture had less carving than traditional pieces. (Thomasville)

Fig. 2-4. Contemporary furniture uses straight lines with very little carving. These pieces are easier to produce with modern machinery. (Thomasville)

In early America, handmade products were crude and plain, Fig. 2-5. As people moved westward, they loaded and unloaded their belongings. Many times cabinets had to pass through small doorways. Furnishings were assembled with mechanical fasteners such as wedges, square pegs or round pins. These fasteners could be removed quickly to disassemble the furniture. To have carved, fragile furniture in this environment was not practical.

Built-in closets and storage areas were unknown at this time. Clothing would hang on pegs on the walls or be placed inside movable cabinets.

MODERN CABINETMAKING

Today, people remain mobile. However, few pegs and pins are still used. Modern products include hinges, bolts, nuts, and screws. This hardware simplifies disassembly, reassembly, and provides space-saving features.

Powerful machines in operation today simplify the cabinetmaking process. Modern production practices involve jigs and fixtures to hold the work while the cabinetmaker performs the operation. In more automated facilities, the machine holds the work and performs the operation.

Because of mass production techniques, little free-hand surface carving is done today. Templates used with routers or shapers create the carved look. The same appearance can be achieved with molded or carved accessories.

TRADITIONAL STYLES

Names associated with cabinetry can be traced back hundreds of years. Some of the earliest periods date back to 16th century medieval Europe. The furniture of this era was made of oak which made it very sturdy and bulky. This style was imitated by the early American colonists.

During the 17th century, heavy oak furniture gave way to lighter, more elaborately carved walnut pieces. This furniture became known as traditional cabinetry. Each traditional style claims one or more unique features. Many of these features involve intricate carvings. These pieces would be too expensive to produce today in their original form. However, the influence of traditional styles still affects modern furniture.

WILLIAM AND MARY

Mary, Queen of England, and her husband, William, reigned in the latter 1600s and early 1700s. The *William and Mary style* introduced the *gate leg table*, Fig. 2-6, and the highboy. Gate legs

Fig. 2-6. Gate leg table. Legs swung out to support hinged table leaves. (Thomasville)

supported hinged table leaves that folded down. The *highboy* is a drawered cabinet on legs, Fig. 2-7.

The legs on William and Mary cabinets, tables, and chairs were turned. Sections often looked like upside down cups. Curved stretchers connected the legs for stability, Fig. 2-8.

Other distinctive features were curved, decorative edges and archlike sections. Veneering and marquetry (fitting veneer to form a picture or design) were also used.

Fig. 2-5. Early American furniture was plain. Parts were held together by wood pins for easy disassesmbly. (Ethan Allen)

Fig. 2-7. Highboy of the William and Mary style.
(Colonial Homes)

Fig. 2-9. The cabriole leg was a principal feature of the Queen
Anne style. It was designed after the leg of an animal. The leg
often ended in a carved foot.   (Otto Gerdau Co.)

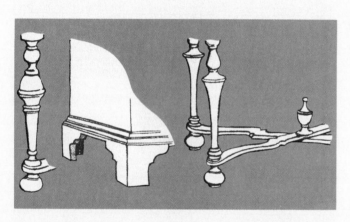

Fig. 2-8. Left. Cabinet legs of William and Mary style were
shaped like inverted cups. Middle. A bracket foot. Right.
Example of trumpet turnings on legs. Shaped stretchers
connected legs diagonally. (Colonial Homes)

QUEEN ANNE

The new elegance in English furniture brought
refinements in design and joinery in the 18th century. Cabinetmaking became a high art in both
England and the American colonies. *Queen Anne
furniture* evolved during this time. The style is best
known for the *cabriole leg,* Fig. 2-9, and carved
surfaces.

Carvings that looked like scalloped shells were
distinctive features. Queen Anne furniture also
adapted the William and Mary arches. Some products had turned spindles attached. Chair splats
(backs) generally were solid vertical components.

Fig. 2-10. Left. A highboy in the Queen Anne style had cabriole
legs, arches, and intricate carvings. Right. This lowboy also
had cabriole legs. (Thomasville)

Popular pieces of this style were highboys, lowboys, wardrobes, chairs, and desks, Fig. 2-10.

CHIPPENDALE

The *Chippendale style* evolved during the last half of the 18th century. Thomas Chippendale designed and built furniture of highly carved mahogany and walnut lumber. Rarely was veneer used nor did he use inlays of any kind.

In 1754, Chippendale published the three volume "Gentlemen and Cabinetmakers Directory." The book brought him much fame in America and Europe, yet Chippendale was not an innovator. He borrowed characteristics from Chinese, French, and English designs.

Of his work, chairs were very distinctive. Cabriole shapes remained popular for front legs on chairs. However, the back legs were straight. Occasionally, all legs were straight. Cabriole legs ended with feet shaped as claws or paws. Chair backs were shaped in open loop sections or resembled the Queen Anne style, Fig. 2-11.

On tables and other pieces, Chippendale cut openings in the aprons. This feature is called *a lattice,* Fig. 2-12. On other pieces, he only carved geometric shapes called *fretwork,* Fig. 2-13.

Chippendale was influenced by Chinese furniture, often made of bamboo. Notice the bamboo-like turnings on the diagonal stretchers in Fig. 2-12. These products are referred to as *Chinese Chippendale.*

HEPPLEWHITE

George Hepplewhite was a designer and builder about the same time as Chippendale. *Hepplewhite* designed mahogany cabinet fronts, including curved doors and drawers, Fig. 2-14. His unique styling

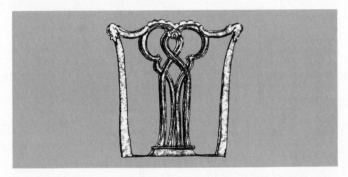

Fig. 2-11. Chippendale chair backs were shaped in open loop sections. (Colonial Homes)

Fig. 2-13. Notice the fretwork on the legs of this Chippendale table. (Drexel)

Fig. 2-12. Chippendale features included lattice work (geometric shapes cut through wood) on table aprons (sides). Also note the diagonal bamboo stretchers between legs. (Thomasville)

Fig. 2-14. George Hepplewhite often made the fronts of his cabinets curved. (Drexel)

included spindly, square, straight legs or fluted round legs. Chair backs often looked like open shields or loops. Carved feathers, ferns, rosettes and urns also were distinctive of his work, Fig. 2-15. Hepplewhite applied veneers extensively. This provided contrasting color and grain patterns.

SHERATON

Thomas Sheraton was a designer with many skilled cabinetmakers working for him. *Sheraton* influenced furniture designs in the late 1700s and early 1800s. It is easy to see how his designs adapted other styles: William and Mary's turned legs and arches; Queen Anne's carving; Chippendale's fretwork; and variations of Hepplewhite's open chair backs. Sheraton also introduced several products such as twin beds, drop leaf tables, roll top desks, and kidney-shaped tables, Fig. 2-16.

Sheraton used characteristics like Prince of Wales feathers along with carved drapery and flowers. His chair backs were filled with intricate carving and tracery, Fig. 2-16.

Dual purpose cabinetry was another Sheraton contribution. Lowboys in dining rooms had door and drawer sections. Tableware (napkins, silverware, table cloths, etc.) was stored in the drawers. Dishes and stemmed glassware were placed behind the doors.

Sheraton also introduced the *secretary,* Fig. 2-17. It was a bookcase with a hinged front door. This door opened downward for a writing surface. Inside were compartments to organize small items.

PROVINCIAL STYLES

Simplified versions of European traditional styles were labeled *provincial.* Typically, they were for average people. In early America, provincial style products were called Colonial. The Colonial name was derived from furniture used in the colonies.

However, many of these products took on traditional features. American colonists wished to remember styles from their European homeland. Other provincial styles are French Provincial,

Fig. 2-16. Top. Thomas Sheraton introduced the kidney-shaped table. Bottom. His chair backs were intricately carved and abounded in tracery. (Colonial Homes)

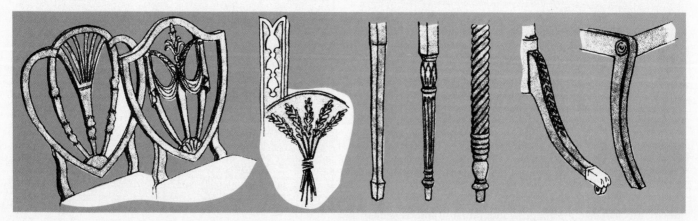

Fig. 2-15. Hepplewhite features. Left. Chair backs looked like open shields or loops. Middle. Carvings of ferns and urns. Right. Legs took on many shapes including flutes and spirals. (Colonial Homes)

Pennsylvania Dutch, Shaker, Windsor, and Duncan Phyfe.

FRENCH PROVINCIAL

French Provincial styles come from the middle 1600s to about 1900. Furniture was noted for having graceful curved edges. The cabriole leg was included in the design after it was introduced in the Queen Anne era, Fig. 2-18. Early pieces included

bunk beds, stools, benches, and wardrobes. They were made by craftspersons using fruitwood and walnut. The pieces were imitations of more elaborate traditional designs. In the 1800s, chairs, tables, desks, chests, and clocks were produced, Fig. 2-19.

AMERICAN COLONIAL

The *American Colonial* period lasted from 1620 to about 1790. Most of the products were very crude. Others were somewhat refined with European influences. Popular pieces included chests, benches, cupboards, gate leg tables, chairs, rockers, and cradles, Fig. 2-20. Ladder back chairs

Fig. 2-17. A secretary had a fold down lid used as a desktop. (Thomasville)

Fig. 2-18. French Provincial furniture had graceful curves. The round chair was a mark of this style. (Thomasville)

Fig. 2-19. Top. Bedroom footstool in French Provincial style. Bottom. Notice the curves of the French table. (Thomasville)

Fig. 2-20. Left. Pins were used in this American Colonial corner cabinet. Middle. The end table has a simple design cut into the apron. Right. Frames and panels were used on the door of this washstand.   (Thomasville)

had a Chippendale influence, Fig. 2-21. Turned spindle backs showed a likeness to the Sheraton style. Turned legs and curved edges illustrated provincial styling. Cane seats were woven for some added comfort.

PENNSYLVANIA DUTCH

Many people from Germany and Switzerland (1680 to 1850) brought ideas from their homelands. Their furniture became known as the *Pennsylvania Dutch* style. Most products were straightline and square-edge designs. Some curved edges were used but most decorations were done freehand. Cabinets were often painted with animals, fruits, people, and flowers, Fig. 2-22. Most products were cupboards, benches, tables, desks, and stacked chests called *chests-on-chests*, Fig. 2-23.

SHAKER

Shaker is a plain style produced from 1776 to the mid 1800s. The term Shaker refers to a religious group originating from the Quakers of England who immigrated to America. These pieces were extremely plain with very few decorations. Some sample products include chairs, tables (some with drop leaves), chests, and desks, Fig. 2-24.

Fig. 2-21. American Colonial chairs had ladderbacks with turned spindle back posts. (Thomasville)

Fig. 2-22. Pennsylvania Dutch cabinets were often painted with flowers or animals. (Thomasville)

Fig. 2-23. This chest-on-chest cabinet came from the Pennsylvania Dutch style. (Thomasville)

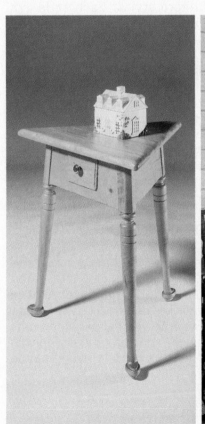

Fig. 2-24. Shaker products were very plain as shown here. Left. Triangle table. Middle. China cabinet. (Thomasville) Right. Fold down desk. (Craft Products)

The ingenuity of the Shaker designers became apparent in later products. Shaker designers introduced the swivel and tilt-back chairs.

WINDSOR

The Windsor Castle in England was the model for the *Windsor style* of chairs and rockers. The chairs were originally manufactured by *wheelwrights.* These individuals were skilled at bending wood for wagon and carriage wheels. They also turned wagon wheel spokes.

The style involved bent wood arm rests, backs, and rockers. Turned legs, stretchers, rungs, and spindles were also used, Fig. 2-25.

Fig. 2-25. Windsor chairs were finely crafted by wheelwrights. Many turned wood spindles were used. (Thomasville)

DUNCAN PHYFE

The first American designer to adapt European and Asian styles was *Duncan Phyfe* (1790 to 1830). He loosely followed the Sheraton and Hepplewhite styles. However, Phyfe designs featured more fine carving. Phyfe also introduced the *lyre-back* chair. The chair back was carved into the shape of a harp.

Another distinctive Duncan Phyfe contribution is the column pedestal. The *pedestal,* with its curved legs, is used as the support for many modern tables, Fig. 2-26.

Fig. 2-26. Pedestals were used instead of four legs on Duncan Phyfe tables. (Drexel)

CONTEMPORARY

Contemporary cabinetry has existed since about 1925. It is not an individual style with specific features. Rather, the term contemporary includes all of the current furniture styles. Each style is a slight adaptation from another. Some pieces are simply copies of former styles with the word *modern* attached.

Modern styling is an influence rather than a style. It applies mostly straight lines to create geometric forms. This type of construction lends itself well to modern production techniques. Changes occur in modern styles as contemporary designers test new markets for their products.

The most common contemporary styles include Early American, American Modern, Oriental Modern, Scandinavian Modern and Shaker Modern.

EARLY AMERICAN

Early American furnishings combine colonial and plain styles. Curved edges, turnings, and bent wood are common features, Fig. 2-27. Many pieces have mechanical components like the Shaker swivel chair and tilt-back chair. On some pieces, pegs and pins are visible for appearance. They are usually permanent, unlike colonial furniture pegs which could be disassembled.

AMERICAN MODERN

American Modern cabinetry usually means clean, undecorated products. Flat surfaces with straight

Fig. 2-27. Much Early American furniture decorates homes today. (Thomasville)

or gracefully curved lines have eye appeal. Textures from cane or fabric provide accents. Legs are straight or slightly tapered. They may be either round or square, Fig. 2-28. There are no carvings to collect dust. Pieces are free of small decorative parts to get broken. The design reflects an on-the-move family lifestyle, Fig. 2-29.

Fig. 2-28. American Modern furniture has straight lines. It is rarely carved or decorated. (Thomasville)

Fig. 2-29. American Modern designs reflect an active, mobile lifestyle. (Sauder)

ORIENTAL MODERN

Oriental styles date back hundreds of years. Once they were highly carved and decorative. Today's *Oriental Modern* pieces combine straight lines and curved geometric shapes. Curved legs and wide feet are typical, Fig. 2-30. Stenciled or hand-painted copies of art remain on lacquered surfaces, Fig. 2-31.

SCANDINAVIAN MODERN

Styles from Swedish and Danish designers are recognized by their sculptured look. *Scandinavian Modern* furniture has gentle curves, especially on stretchers and tapered legs, Fig. 2-32.

SHAKER MODERN

Shaker Modern is an updated version of the original Shaker features. Various parts, legs in particular, remain slim and appear weak. Pin and peg ends may be visible. Most often these pin and peg ends are wood plugs over metal fasteners.

COORDINATING STYLES

Most of the discussion of style has focused on individual pieces of furniture. Often it is desirable that furniture within rooms be coordinated. Coordination of entire home interiors can be attractive. Coordination of style may even be applied to the interior/exterior match of the home.

Fig. 2-31. Often Chinese Modern pieces are finished with black or green lacquer. (Thomasville)

SINGLE ROOMS

Furniture within a single room should have the same style. This gives authenticity to the environment. *Authenticity* refers to how well the room matches the historic original room. For example, to make the atmosphere of a room feel colonial, all of the furniture and decoration should be colonial. Other rooms could have a different style. You might have a Queen Anne bedroom, a Sheraton dining room, and a Hepplewhite living room.

In contemporary design, there is no historic precedent to follow. Here, matching furniture creates harmony. Each piece of furniture fits well with the overall style of the room and furnishings.

MULTIPLE ROOMS

Matching styles of multiple rooms increases the effect of authenticity. Harmony of the entire house is also achieved. Design characteristics of the furniture will apply to doors and door and window mouldings. Wall and floor coverings are finished according to the overall style. Both built-in and free-standing cabinetry and furniture can be coordinated to achieve harmony, Fig. 2-33.

Fig. 2-30. Curved geometric shapes are typical of Oriental Modern furniture. Note the feet turned inward. (Thomasville)

Fig. 2-32. Scandinavian Modern furniture is distinguished by gentle curves and smooth texture. (Dyrlund-Smith)

BEDROOM

FAMILY ROOM

DINING ROOM

Fig. 2-33. Coordination of furniture styles creates harmony of the interior of the home. (Thomasville)

CHANGING AND CREATING A STYLE

The following examples describe how a room may be adapted to match a style. The room to be changed is a kitchen.

First begin with a basic floor plan and layout sketch of a room, Fig. 2-34. From this sketch, you can adapt the styles covered in this chapter to fit the room.

During the Hepplewhite, Sheraton, and Duncan Phyfe eras, raised panels were popular. These panel assemblies, along with combinations of furniture, illustrate the traditional style, Fig. 2-35A.

French Provincial was identified with graceful curved edges. These were placed on the doors and drawers of cabinets. Change the basic cabinet fronts and mouldings to have a French Provincial kitchen, Fig. 2-35B.

Colonial furniture was crude and bulky. To reduce weight, cabinetmakers would set thin panels inside thick frames to build doors. The colonial kitchen in Fig. 2-35C uses plain, bulky cabinet fronts. Brick was common in colonial times. It is placed in the kitchens to surround cooking areas.

Shaker furniture is noted for smooth, undecorated, simplistic features. Cabinet doors had inset

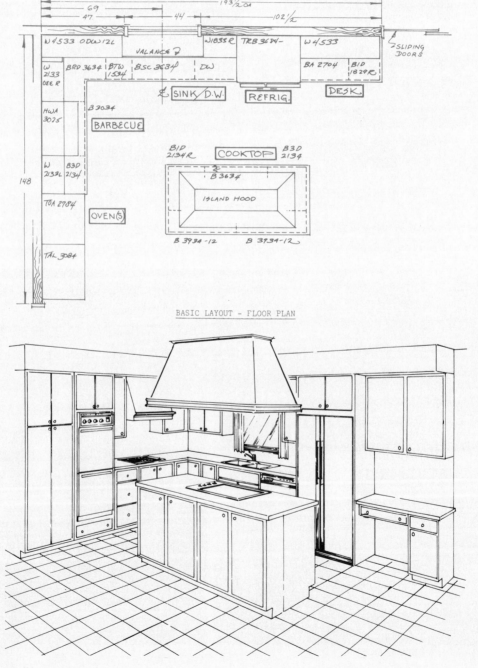

Fig. 2-34. Sketches assist in determining how to change the style of a room. (Wood-Mode)

panels. Inset panels are shallower than the frame that surrounds them. The Shaker kitchen in Fig. 2-35D is very simplistic. Even the rivets to hold overhead vent pieces together are shown.

Scandinavians used smooth surfaces with rounded corners. These are reflected in the Scandinavian kitchen, Fig. 2-35E.

Oriental furniture of Chippendale and Oriental Modern influence used geometric shapes. Chippendale carved lattices into the furniture. Oriental Modern furniture often uses straightline designs.

Many oriental designs include louvers. Louvers are frames of slanted rectangular slats of wood closely spaced in a frame. You cannot see through the louvers, but the slant allows openings for ventilation. The Oriental kitchen in Fig. 2-35F uses repetition of louvers to form the cabinet front.

COORDINATING INTERIORS AND EXTERIORS

Many homes coordinate the interior style of furniture with the exterior of the house. To coordinate

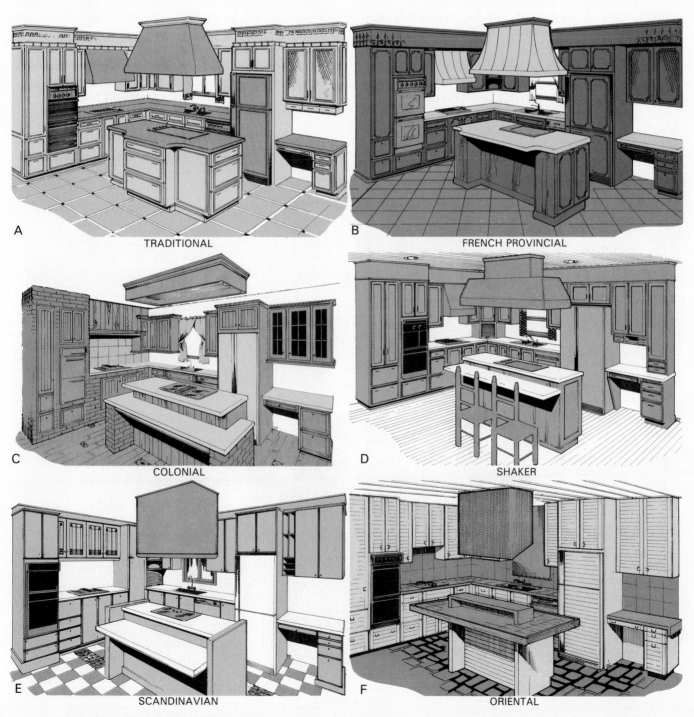

A TRADITIONAL

B FRENCH PROVINCIAL

C COLONIAL

D SHAKER

E SCANDINAVIAN

F ORIENTAL

Fig. 2-35. Many different styles can be created from the original room without much alteration. (Wood-Mode)

styles, you must look at homes of the period. You must also determine the furniture style of that period.

Home styles often are classified differently than furniture styles. Using the familiar kitchen layout, Fig. 2-36 gives some examples of interior/exterior coordination for Georgian Colonial, Victorian, English Tudor, Spanish, and Contemporary homes.

Georgian Colonial homes were usually rectangular, and windows were placed in perfect symmetry. Interior rooms were arranged to allow for the symmetrical exterior. The entrance was placed in the center of the front of the house. The front door had a small entrance portico with pilasters and a pediment above. The Georgian colonial kitchen is designed with symmetry. The doors are also designed with arches on the top of cabinet doors, Fig. 2-36A.

Victorian homes were large and heavily ornamented. Carvings and turnings were fastened to the underside of porch roofs. The homes were typically two story and irregular in shape. Designers paid little attention to harmony or pleasing proportions of the house. This Victorian kitchen is a toned down version of Victorian styling. Curved air vents cover the stove. Much of the ornamentation in modern Victorian rooms is left out, Fig. 2-36B.

English Tudor homes are noted for their timber-like decorations. Solid thin boards surrounding wood panels are most often used. These characteristics are reflected in the cabinet fronts and soffits over the cabinetry, Fig. 2-36C.

Spanish homes are usually single story brick homes with low pitch hip roofs. Architecturally, the houses are very simple. The floor plan usually is a U shape, with an open patio on the front side of the house. The entrance into the patio has multiple arches. The garage doors also have arched tops. The Spanish kitchen reflects this style. Brick is

A

COLONIAL

B

VICTORIAN

Fig. 2-36. Interiors and exteriors of homes may be coordinated. (Wood-Mode)

applied on the interior as it was on the exterior. Arches over certain food preparation areas are formed by bricks. Either real or imitation beams run across the ceiling to replicate earlier Spanish homes built of beams and clay, Fig. 2-36D.

Contemporary homes include straight lines and simple geometric shapes. The home in Fig. 2-36e is almost entirely made up of straight lines. An arc on one window is used to break monotony. The kitchen also follows the clean-cut, straight line design. Subtle geometric forms break the straight lines, Fig. 2-36E.

C

ENGLISH TUDOR

D

SPANISH

E

CONTEMPORARY

(Fig. 2-36. continued)

SUMMARY

For many early kings, queens, and designers, having a cabinetry style named after them was a form of recognition. These people dictated the various features of the piece. Some products were heavy and highly carved. Others appeared weak and top heavy. These styles are classified as traditional.

People of less prominence began to copy traditional products. They simplified some of the design features which affected cost. These products were called provincial.

Since the early 1900s, a contemporary styling trend has gained popularity. In some cases, this represents further simplification of former designs. Style has been altered due to advancing technology in production processes.

Contemporary cabinetry is a broad classification of designs. Earlier designs were modified with the term "modern." Some have been created using other names. Simple straight and curved lines creating geometrical forms are used almost exclusively.

Design coordination often may be desired. Single rooms, multiple rooms, and home exteriors and interiors can be coordinated.

CABINETMAKING TERMS

Style, traditional cabinetry, provincial cabinetry, contemporary cabinetry, William and Mary style, gate leg table, highboy, Queen Anne style, Cabriole leg, Chippendale, lattice, fretwork, Chinese Chippendale, Hepplewhite, Sheraton, secretary, French Provincial, American Colonial, Pennsylvania Dutch, chests-on-chests, Shaker, Windsor, wheelwrights, Duncan Phyfe, lyre-back chair, column pedestal, contemporary, Early American, Modern, American Modern, Oriental Modern, Scandinavian Modern, Shaker Modern, authenticity, Georgian Colonial, Victorian, English Tudor, Spanish homes, contemporary homes.

TEST YOUR KNOWLEDGE

1. Three terms to classify cabinetry designs are _____, _____, and _____.
2. A reason why contemporary designs have less carving than early traditional designs is _____.
3. Describe early cabinetmaking facilities and techniques.
4. Two products introduced by the William and Mary style were _____ and _____.
5. Arches are associated with _____ and _____ styles.
6. The Queen Anne style is best known for:
   a. Bamboo stretchers.
   b. Cabriole legs.
   c. Fluted legs.
   d. Fretwork.
7. Common Chippendale features were _____ and _____.
8. Chinese Chippendale used _____ between table legs.
9. The open shield chair back was associated with what style?
   a. Hepplewhite.
   b. Queen Anne.
   c. Sheraton.
   d. Windsor.
10. What new pieces of furniture did Sheraton introduce?
11. What style first used the column pedestal to support tables?
   a. Duncan Phyfe.
   b. Early American.
   c. Pennsylvania Dutch.
   d. Scandinavian Modern.
12. A distinctive feature of French Provincial furniture was _____.
13. In early America, products were held together with _____.
14. What features did American Colonial furniture borrow from other styles?
15. A common characteristic of Pennsylvania Dutch furniture was:
   a. Cabriole legs.
   b. Carved decorations.
   c. Lattices.
   d. Painted decorations.
16. The chest-on-chest was common in the _____ style.
17. Swivel and tilting chairs were created by the _____.
18. Windsor chairs were originally produced by _____.
19. Shaker designs were often carved. True or False?
20. Two Duncan Phyfe contributions are the _____ and _____.
21. Modern is a provincial style. True or False?
22. Bent wood furniture was originally produced by:
   a. Duncan Phyfe.
   b. George Hepplewhite.
   c. Thomas Sheraton.
   d. Wheelwrights.
23. How does the finish on most Oriental Modern furniture differ with other cabinet styles?
24. Contemporary cabinetry with graceful curves is _____.
25. Describe four home styles and features used on the interior of the home.

Chapter 3
COMPONENTS OF DESIGN

After studying this chapter, you will be able to:
☐*Describe the difference between the function and form of a cabinet.*
☐*Apply design elements and principles to create functional and attractive cabinets.*
☐*Identify alternative designs with convenience and flexibility.*

Designing is the most creative practice in cabinetmaking technology. As the designer, your activities and decisions will affect the outcome of the product. Two factors which guide the development of the product during design are function and form.

FUNCTION

Cabinetry is designed to meet people's needs. A *functional design* serves a purpose, Fig 3-1. The product may store clothes, recreational equipment, or dishes. It might house appliances or electronic devices, or be used to display trophies. Other functions could be supporting lamps, game boards, or work tables.

A functional design should be efficient and effective to meet the needs of the user. Your creative ability as a designer will determine how well the finished product meets these needs.

FORM

Form refers to the style and appearance of the product. The form of the finished product should be pleasing to look at. The product must be large enough and strong enough to serve its intended purpose. It also should fit in with the style of nearby furnishings, Fig. 3-2.

LEVELS OF DESIGN

Achieving a final design solution is challenging. The product must serve its purpose and be visually pleasing. As a designer, you are responsible to meet this challenge.

Fig. 3-1. This functional design is used for storage, display, and as a serving counter. (Thomasville)

Fig. 3-2. Furniture in a room should blend together. (Thomasville)

There are three different ability levels among designers; *copying, adapting,* and *creating.* Beginners often copy a design from prepared drawings and specifications. As their knowledge and skill increases, they begin adapting. Designers at this level remember design features they have seen. Then they might adapt these ideas as they design products. Fully experienced designers should be able to create an original product. Regardless of your artistic ability, all levels of design use the same elements and principles.

DESIGN ELEMENTS

The elements which you will apply are:
1. Lines
2. Shapes
3. Colors
4. Textures

Individually, these elements describe specific details for a design. Combined, they form the overall visual appearance of the product.

LINES

Lines are the basic element in visual communication. Your eyes tend to follow the path of a line, Fig. 3-3. Straight lines lead your eyes in one direction, whether it be horizontal, vertical, or diagonal. Curved lines cause your vision to change direction.

Lines can accent a design. Vertical lines accent a tall, narrow shape such as a curio cabinet. Horizontal lines dominate the design of a wide, low product such as a chest, Fig. 3-4. Diagonal, or inclined, lines draw attention to a focal point.

Straight lines and square corners are the easiest to produce in cabinetry design. However, shaped curves and turnings are also simple to create. Lines and simple curves satisfy most needs for modern and contemporary products. Complex curves, such as those found in French provincial furniture, are harder to put into a modern design.

Fig. 3-3. Lines will lead your eyes from one end to the other.

Fig. 3-4. Top. Vertical lines enhance tall furniture like this curio cabinet. Bottom. Horizontal lines enhance wide furniture like this chest. (Thomasville)

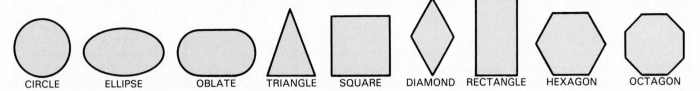

CIRCLE ELLIPSE OBLATE TRIANGLE SQUARE DIAMOND RECTANGLE HEXAGON OCTAGON

Fig. 3-5. Single lines will enclose circular or elliptical shapes. Multiple lines enclose triangles, rectangles, and other polygons.

SHAPES

Designs rely on lines to form shapes. *Shapes* represent masses or spaces and are described by the lines that enclose them, Fig. 3-5. A shape that is narrower than it is high is called a *primary vertical mass*. A shape that is wider than it is high is called a *primary horizontal mass*, Fig. 3-6.

Large primary masses should be divided into *major areas* and *minor areas* of different sizes. These areas may also be subdivided. A number of rules guide the designer in dividing spaces, both vertically or horizontally.

Vertical division

The rules of *vertical division*, Fig. 3-7, suggest:
1. Two parts of unequal sizes (major and minor).
2. Three parts of unequal areas.
   a. From bottom to top, the areas will be progressively smaller.
   b. For other arrangements, the major area should be between the other two minor areas.
3. More than three vertical division.
   a. First separate them according to rules one and/or two.
   b. Then subdivide these masses independently as needed.

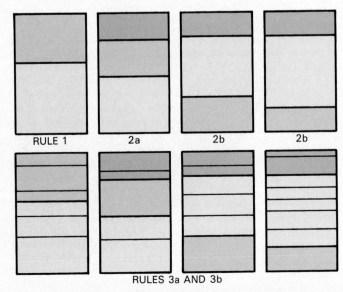

RULE 1   2a   2b   2b

RULES 3a AND 3b

Fig. 3-7. There are many ways to divide tall cabinets.

Fig. 3-6. Top. A primary vertical mass is taller than it is wide. (Butler Specialty Co.) Bottom. A primary horizontal mass is wider than it is tall. (Ethan Allen)

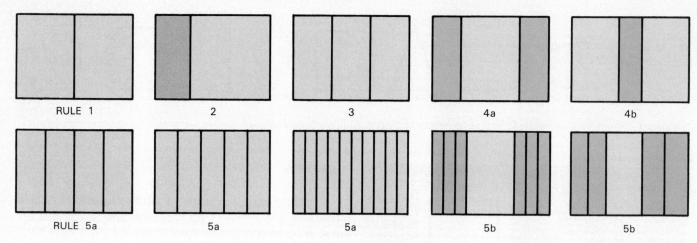

RULE 1 2 3 4a 4b

RULE 5a 5a 5a 5b 5b

Fig. 3-8. Horizontal masses should be divided according to these rules.

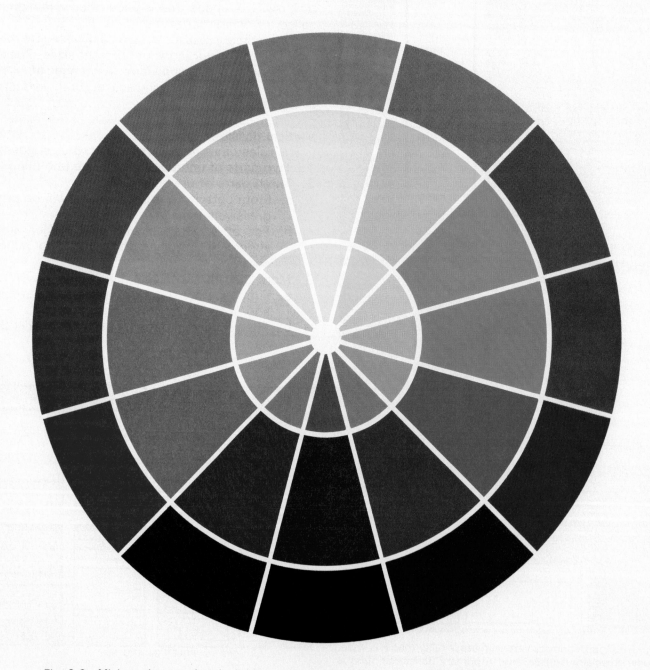

Fig. 3-9. Mixing primary colors (red, blue, yellow) will produce secondary colors (violet, green, orange).

Horizontal division

The rules of *horizontal division*, Fig. 3-8, suggest:
1. Two equal areas.
2. A major and a minor area but retain balance (informal).
3. Three equal areas.
4. Three divisions with major and minor areas.
   a. One major area between two equal minor areas.
   b. One minor area between two equal major areas.
5. More than three areas.
   a. Areas of equal size and importance.
   b. A large area with a number of smaller equal areas on each side.

These rules represent practices for dividing primary masses. The divisions may be accented with textures and colors.

TEXTURE

Texture refers to the contour and feel of the surface of the product. You can specify woven cane (type of grass) to give a rough texture. Moulding and trim is used to give texture to corners of cabinets. Texture can also refer to the quality of the surface finish. The texture could be rough or smooth; high, medium or low luster. Whatever material or method is used, it must blend with the style of the product.

COLORS

There is an infinite number of colors in the color spectrum. However, all are produced from three primary colors; red, yellow, and blue. When these three are mixed with one another, three additional colors are created. They are called secondary colors and include orange (from red and yellow), green (from yellow and blue), and violet (from blue and red). A primary and secondary color mixture adds six tertiary colors. A color wheel shows these combinations, Fig. 3-9. Colors on the opposite side of the color wheel are called complimentary colors.

Color has three distinct properties; hue, value, and intensity. *Hue* refers to any color in its pure form. Each hue has value. *Value* refers to the lightness or darkness of the hue. A pure hue can be tinted to produce a lighter value to near white. A pure hue can also be shaded to produce a darker value to near black, Fig. 3-10.

The third property of color is intensity. *Intensity*

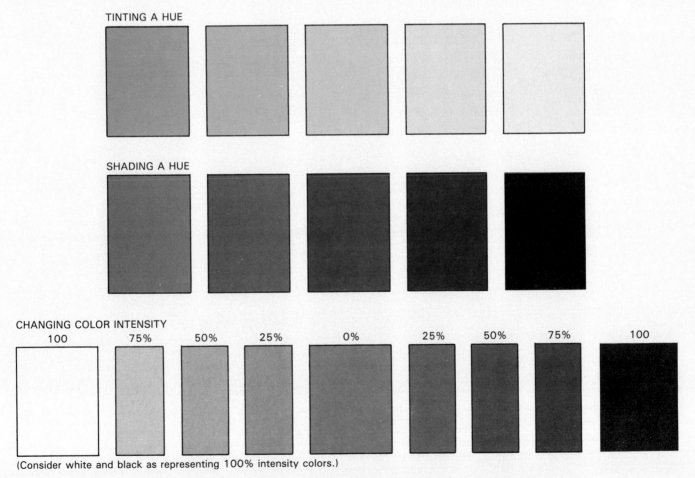

TINTING A HUE

SHADING A HUE

CHANGING COLOR INTENSITY

100   75%   50%   25%   0%   25%   50%   75%   100

(Consider white and black as representing 100% intensity colors.)

Fig. 3-10. Tint, shade, and intensity change the appearance of a color.

refers to the brilliance of the color. Intensity also is called chroma. Any hue can be made less brilliant by mixing it with its complimentary color. For example, small amounts of green added to red dulls the color. The more green added, the more gray the original red color will become, Fig. 3-10.

Color on cabinetry results from painted or stained surfaces. *Paints* contain color pigments which makes an opaque finish. *Opaque finishes* hide the grain and provide a protective topcoating. *Stains* color the wood and enhance the grain pattern. They contain dyes and sometimes pigments.

Hardware (hinges, pulls) of various colors can be installed on cabinets. Such items may be black, white, gray, silver, brown, and gold. These are considered neutral colors and will accent any painted or stained surface. Other colors will need to be selected more carefully. Hardware should be the

same or a complimentary hue as the surface where it is attached.

DESIGN PRINCIPLES

The *principles of design* describe how the design elements apply to cabinetry.
They are:
1. Harmony
2. Repetition
3. Balance
4. Proportion

HARMONY

Harmony is the pleasing relationship of all elements in a given product design. There should be harmony among the masses and the shapes.

REPETITION—1. Headboard posts, spindles, and panels. 2. Chest and dresser drawers.

FORMAL BALANCE—1. Equal vertical spindles and panels on each side of a center line. 2. Drawers in chest and dresser.

INFORMAL BALANCE—1. Night stand. 2. Upper section of the dresser.

Fig. 3-11. Repetition is produced by multiple use of spindles on this headboard and footboard. The chest of drawers is also an example. Formal balance is seen in the dresser drawers and chest of drawers. Informal balance is seen in the night stand and upper part of the dresser. (Unfinished Furniture)

Create this feeling by following the rules dealing with shapes. Harmony of textures includes using compatible surface contours. Harmony of colors follows three basic rules:

1. Less intense colors should be used on large areas.
2. Bright colors are attractive in small areas.
3. Complimentary colors should be used. One hue may be the small intense accent of one color on a tinted or shaded color (such as solid red on green tint).

REPETITION

Repetition means using an element or elements more than once. This creates a rhythm in the design and attracts interest, Fig. 3-11. Straight lines, curved lines, spaces, textures, and colors are effective for this purpose. Experienced designers know when repetition is pleasing. On the other hand, you must recognize when repetition has been used excessively. Too many similar lines, masses, and other elements are boring.

BALANCE

Balance is the use of space and mass to give a feeling of stability or equality to a design. Balance may be either formal or informal, Fig. 3-11.

Formal balance means equality on each side of a center line in the design. Center lines may run horizontally and/or vertically. One half of the product will be the mirror image of the other. For a square mass, balance means repeating a detail in any direction from the center. For a vertical rectangular mass, left and right halves are symmetrical. There may be a center of interest included on the surface. The center may include a decorative detail. It would be above or below the center. Placing a detail above the center is preferred. For a horizontal rectangular mass, the top and bottom halves are equal. Here the detail of interest is below the center line.

Informal balance is more difficult to describe. It is a feeling of balance in the design even though the design is not symmetrical. Usually, one side of the design is more solid than the other. However, to maintain balance, the open side is larger.

PROPORTION

Proportion is a relationship between the height and width or height and length of a product. Generally, a 2:3, 3:5, or 5:8 relationship is more pleasing than a square. The ancient Greeks arrived at a ratio of 1:1.618 which they called the *golden mean* or the perfect proportion, Fig. 3-12.

Proportion is a subtle relationship among elements and principles. The relationship may relate to the function and convenience of the product. When the function of the product requires greater ratios, major and minor masses should be created. For example, a gun cabinet requires extra height, Fig. 3-13. Separating the cabinet with texture or

Fig. 3-13. The use of curves and a drawer keep this gun cabinet from appearing too tall. (Mersman Brothers)

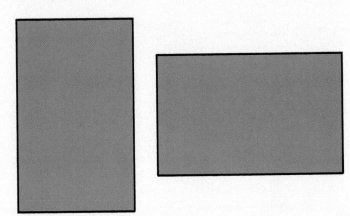

Fig. 3-12. The Greek perfect proportion or "golden mean" was a 1 to 1.618 height to width (or height to length) ratio.

color will make the height of the cabinet appear more in proportion with the width.

DESIGN ALTERNATIVES

Designing can be a challenge for even the most creative cabinetmaker. Making the function and form blend together is the most critical factor.

The pace of people's lifestyles creates problems for a designer. People would like to find items quickly and be able to reach them easily. They dislike unloading a cabinet to get the pot or pan way in back. They would like to place rarely used items higher, lower, or farther from the center of activity.

People are relocating more often. This suggests that cabinetmakers should create light, sturdy cases which can pass through doorways or up and down stairs. Also, items of this nature are easily moved when rearranging room furniture.

During planning, you must consider the person who will use the product. Design elements and principles are the first factors to be addressed. However, convenience and flexibility play a big role in designing a satisfying product.

CONVENIENCE

Convenience is the ease with which a person can use, move, or locate objects in a cabinet. Special cabinet hardware and careful design of cabinet space provides for convenience.

One way to achieve convenience is with hardware. Racks can be put on the inside of doors for condiments. Cups can be suspended from the bottom of a shelf with hooks. Pullout drawers or trays are especially helpful for storage of supplies, Fig. 3-14. Plan for these items during design and not after the cabinet has been built.

The selective use of space increases convenience. Deep drawers store sweaters better than handkerchiefs, socks, etc. Wide shelf spacing is best for blankets and sheets. Shelves for wash cloths and hand towels may be narrower and closer together in a closet because these items do not stack well.

Convenience can be increased in furniture as well as cabinets. For example, nested tables occupy the same space as a single table, Fig. 3-15. Folding chairs can be easily stored for occasional use.

Increasing the use of room corners is a form of convenience. Some items, particularly if they are small, can be displayed or stored in triangular corner cabinets. Other corner cabinets, such as in the kitchen, may be designed with revolving shelves. These methods make good use of space which was formerly wasted.

FLEXIBILITY

Flexibility refers to how many uses your product will have. Adjustable shelving is flexible. It can be made to store very large or very small items. More shelves can be added when needed. When designing for flexibility, convenience may increase or decrease. You may have to choose between them. Adjustable shelving is an example. More shelves, closely spaced, store items that are difficult to stack, such as canned and bottled goods. However, this plan may not work when you want a pullout

Fig. 3-14. This convenient utility room has racks, trays, baskets, and other useful storage areas. (Wood-Mode)

Fig. 3-15. Nested tables take up less space than would a larger table. (Dyrlund-Smith)

shelf for an item. The hardware for it must be permanently mounted.

Modular furniture is a different form of flexibility, Fig. 3-16. It helps meet the needs of people who are mobile. Pieces can be arranged and rearranged as desired.

A drop leaf extension table is another example of flexibility. It occupies little space when closed but can be opened to serve a large group for dinner.

Flexibility and convenience must be considered as well as the elements and principles of design. A final design solution should include all of these fundamentals. Remember, the product built from your design has to be pleasing, both visually and functionally.

DESIGN APPLICATIONS

As a designer, you try very hard to meet the needs of people of all ages and physical conditions. Take pride in creating functional, tasteful cabinetry.

Your designs will frequently fit the architecture of a home. Consider a home style such as Colonial. Early American case goods, tables, and chairs may be found in various rooms. Built-in cabinets may use mounted hardware items of the same style. Home and furniture designs often are matched to give authenticity to the home. Pay close attention to the components of design when coordinating rooms or interiors and exteriors.

Traditional split level ranch homes and townhouses may be furnished differently. You could use traditional or modern furnishings. It might be formally or informally decorated. There may be decor combinations of Oriental, Spanish, or Mediterranean furniture and cabinets.

There are no hard and fast rules for cabinetry styles. The design of cabinetry and its match to the home is a matter of taste. A single style might be desired throughout. If contrasts are desired, you might incorporate different colors and styles. It is your job to plan for the wants and needs of the person who will use your product.

SUMMARY

Efforts to design cabinetry are based on experience. Some designers copy. Others adapt. Still

Fig. 3-16. Modular furniture has individual cabinets which can be rearranged as needed. (Bernhardt)

others create design solutions. Knowing how to adapt or create requires understanding the components of design.

The elements of design include lines, shapes, colors, and textures. They must be coordinated to produce pleasing products.

Principles of design guide the use of design elements. Principles include harmony, repetition, balance, and proportion. These help the elements blend together. Masses and spaces may appear once or be repeated. Harmonious masses and spaces can be formally or informally balanced. You can proportion elements by using the golden mean ratio. It has been in use for many years.

An experienced designer will create alternative designs. Two factors to be considered for these designs are convenience and flexibility. Convenience refers to ease of locating, using, and moving objects. Flexibility refers to the product's ability to be rearranged for different purposes.

Cabinet and furniture designs should fit with their surroundings. Considerations may include how the design blends with the style of the home. Careful consideration of the components of design must be given when coordinating styles.

CABINETMAKING TERMS

Design, functional design, form, copying, adapting, creating, design elements, lines, shapes, primary vertical mass, primary horizontal mass, major area, minor area, vertical division, horizontal division, texture, primary colors, secondary colors, tertiary colors, color wheel, complimentary colors, hue, value, intensity, paint, opaque finishes, stain, design principles, harmony, repetition, balance, formal balance, informal balance, proportion, golden mean, design alternatives, convenience, flexibility.

TEST YOUR KNOWLEDGE

1. The two primary concerns when designing cabinetry are _____ and _____.
2. Name the four elements of design.
3. Give an example of a primary vertical mass.
4. Give an example of a primary horizontal mass.
5. How can texture be applied to a cabinet.
6. List the primary colors.
7. Pure color is also called a _____.
8. Making a color lighter changes its _____.
9. Adding a complimentary color changes a color's _____.
10. List the four design principles.
11. How is harmony different from balance? How are they the same?
12. Rhythm means the same as _____.
13. The relationship between height and width is called _____.
14. When you include design alternatives, be sure to consider _____ and _____.

Chapter 4
DESIGN DECISIONS

After studying this chapter, you will be able to:
☐ *Identify needs and wants for a cabinet.*
☐ *Follow the steps of the decision-making process.*
☐ *Choose materials which will satisfy the design.*
☐ *Design cabinetry which is convenient and flexible.*

The *decision-making process* directs your activities during design, Fig. 4-1. It guides your thoughts and actions through the many steps involved in creating a cabinet design.

The decision-making process allows for flexibility. You are not bound to one design idea. The design that is the most functional may not be the most attractive. The design that is the most attractive may not be the most functional. A good design is a balance of all factors.

IDENTIFYING NEEDS AND WANTS

Designing begins by assessing the needs and wants for a cabinet. A *need* refers to function. You might ''need'' a cabinet that will store food and spices. A *want* refers to added conveniences in the cabinet. You might ''want'' a cabinet on rollers, or one with racks on the doors. Another want may be the cabinet style.

Suppose you are planning to design a new kitchen layout. Every home needs a place for preparing and serving meals. Kitchen cabinets must be designed with the appliances in mind. Items include a range, refrigerator, sink, counter area, service area, and storage space, Fig. 4-2a. Utilities for the appliances include gas, water, electricity, and drains. You might want a built-in microwave oven or dishwasher. Will they be purchased now? If so, the cabinet design will include the appliance. If not, will you allow space now and install them later?

You may also wish to design an entertainment center. Will the cabinet require room for both video and audio equipment? See Fig. 4-2b.

GATHERING INFORMATION

The next step in making design decisions is to obtain *information.* For this discussion, the need is a

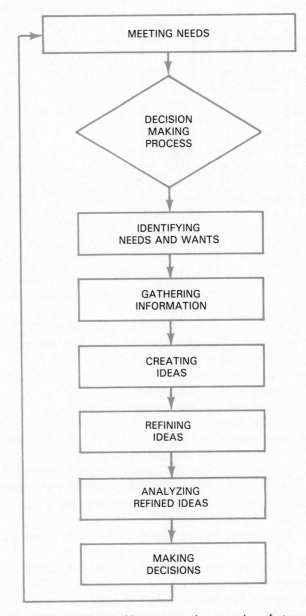

Fig. 4-1. The decision-making process has a series of steps. The final decisions should meet the needs of the user.

home entertainment center. Information must be gathered which relates to function and form.

Think of all situations where the product will be be used. Every question listed below should be

Fig. 4-2. Identify what the cabinet or furniture will be used for.   (NKBA and O'Sullivan)

answered. More concerns may arise when creating preliminary ideas.
- What components (T.V., stereo, VCR) will be stored in this cabinet?
- How large are the components?
- Where will this cabinet be used?
- How much space is available in the room where this entertainment center will be?
- Should the cabinetry be permanently attached or be movable? Remember, built in cabinetry establishes a traffic pattern (people walking around the cabinet) that cannot be changed.
- Should the cabinet be modular? Modular pieces allow for flexibility in arrangements.
- What utilities (electricity, antenna, cable jack) are required for the components?
- Where are the utilities located?
- What cabinet style do you want?
- How much do you wish to spend?

One process for gathering information is called *brainstorming*. When brainstorming, you write down every idea or question which comes into your mind. Don't worry whether the idea is practical. The object is to think of as many options as possible. You will sort through them later.

CREATING IDEAS

Preliminary ideas are made with the collected information. This stage of design allows for much creativity. Use your knowledge of style, design elements, and design principles to develop ideas. Adapt the most practical and pleasing features to your design.

Begin by making sketches. *Sketches* show how space will be arranged. Do not worry about finer details such as dimensions or jointwork. Review all of the questions, answers, and information you have accumulated. Consider the function of the product and who will be using it. Also note how the person will use it (sitting, standing, etc.). Sketch all of your ideas as you think of them. Develop as many as possible and keep all of them until the final decision is made. The sketchs can be cut out and moved around like pieces of a jigsaw puzzle. Use them to arrange a variety of designs.

Your sketches might be *two* or *three dimensional*. Those with two dimensions show only length and height, Fig. 4-3. Some designers find these inadequate. They prefer to see three dimensions. Three dimensional drawings have an advantage

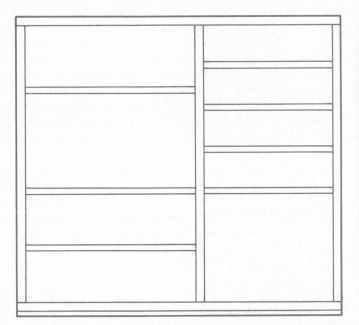

Fig. 4-3. Two-dimensional sketches represent the height and width of a product.

Fig. 4-4. Three-dimensional sketches add depth to the design. They give a realistic view of the product. (O'Sullivan)

over two dimensional. The depth, as well as length and height, of the sides can be seen in one view, Fig. 4-4.

Eventually you will run out of ideas. Be sure you have kept them all. Now begin refining them.

REFINING IDEAS

Refined designs begin to include details. You may combine different features of your first ideas. Pick the best ideas from your sketches and put those together. The combined design should represent the proposed product very accurately.

Dimensions

At some point you must provide dimensions for the cabinet. Measurements will be determined by the size of what will go in or on the cabinet. For an entertainment center, measure the components. Then size the cabinet accordingly, Fig. 4-5.

If you will be designing kitchen cabinets or furniture, there are standard dimensions you will follow. These include heights and widths for tables, chairs, and certain case goods. Standard dimensions are based on the average size of humans. These dimensions, and other considerations for humans, are discussed in the next chapter.

Add the dimensions to the refined sketches. Use a scale to draw the refined design. You can also make the sketch on graph paper. Let each square on the graph paper represent distance of the product. It might be one square equals 1/4 in. (6 mm). The same square could represent 1 ft. for another product.

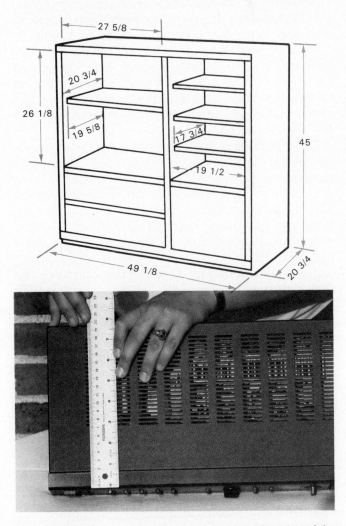

Fig. 4-5. Dimensions are based on the intended function of the cabinet. (O'Sullivan)

Materials

Determine the *materials* you need for the product, Fig. 4-6. Materials for cabinets are classified as:

- Wood — Hardwood and softwood lumber, veneer, cane, wood products (panels, moulding).
- Metals — Steel, brass, aluminum, and copper edging and hardware.
- Plastics — Sheets, edging, laminated tops, hardware, etc.
- Glass — Sheet, pattern, mirror, stained.
- Ceramic tile — Different colors and shapes are available.
- Adhesives — Cements, glues, mastics.
- Hardware — Screws, nails, bolts, hinges, pulls.
- Finishes — Paint, enamel, stain, filler, oil, lacquer, shellac, varnish, urethane, etc.

This list suggests decisions about materials. It does not include every material you might choose in building a cabinet. Later chapters will further examine materials used in cabinetmaking.

The materials you choose greatly affect the appearance of the product. Different woods produce different surface texture and color. Some are stronger than others. Some also cost more than others. You may decide to use manufactured panel products, such as plywood, instead of lumber.

Different woods have similar grain characteristics. You may wish to stain a cheaper wood to appear as a more expensive wood. Veneer can also be used to make a manufactured panel product look like lumber. There are many options which will achieve the desired outcome.

Other materials, such as metal, glass, and plastic also affect the appearance. Hinges, pulls, and knobs made of these materials vary greatly in color, shape, and texture. Choose those which fit the style of the cabinet. When selecting hinges, you must also consider strength of the material. Use metal hinges if supporting heavy doors, such as those with leaded glass panels.

If you are working for a cabinet manufacturer, the materials may be specified. They are purchased in large quantities for mass production of products. In this case, you do not have the option of choosing materials. Company designers set the specifications.

ANALYZING THE REFINED IDEAS

After refining your ideas, you still may have more than one design idea. Check each design to see if it meets your needs and wants. Look at the cost, materials, and function of each of the products. Eventually a final decision will have to be made. Changes can be made after you start building the cabinet. However, later changes will be time consuming and wasteful of material and money.

Three methods of analyzing your ideas are: functional analysis, strength test, and cost analysis.

Functional analysis

In *functional analysis*, you check to see whether the product you have designed meets your needs. Refer back to the information collecting stage. Have you overlooked anything? Are estimated space and size requirements correct? Recheck your measurements. Will the doors and lids move freely? Will they close correctly? Will the cabinet hold the contents with ample room?

If you are unsure about any detail, make a mock-up. A *mock-up* is a full size, working model of your design. It is made of paper, cardboard, or styrofoam. Construct a mock-up of the cabinet. Also construct a model of the components to be placed in the cabinet if they are heavy. This process will verify that the design will work once it is built.

Strength test

You might perform a *strength test* on your design. Will the legs be strong enough? Will a shelf made of a specific material sag? Will the glue hold? Are screws needed for reinforcement?

The extent of the analysis will vary. If you copied a cabinet already in use, little or no testing is necessary. If your design is original, you may want to test the materials. Make sample glue joints and test the strength. You might cut a piece of shelf material to length. Test the shelf with weight to see if it will resist bending.

Cost analysis

The third kind of analysis deals with *cost.* Cost analysis concerns money for equipment, materials, time and space. Here again, many questions must be answered. Will additional tools and machines have to be purchased? Can you adapt available equipment safely? Is lumber available at a reasonable price? How does the cost of plywood compare with the cost of lumber? How expensive are hardware items such as hinges, pulls, and movable shelf supports? From the choices, which will be the most serviceable at the least cost?

Cost factors also influence *make-buy* decisions. Should you make or buy drawer guides? Will you make permanent joints for shelves or buy adjustable shelf supports? Frequently, completed parts are purchased to speed cabinet production. Examples are legs, spindles, shelf supports, etc.

Space in the working area may be a concern. Is the work area large enough to accommodate the cabinetmaker, tools, and materials? Is the area free of health and safety hazards?

MAKING DECISIONS

The *decision-making stage* is the most important. You reach this stage after creating, refining, and analyzing all of the design factors. Accurately scaled

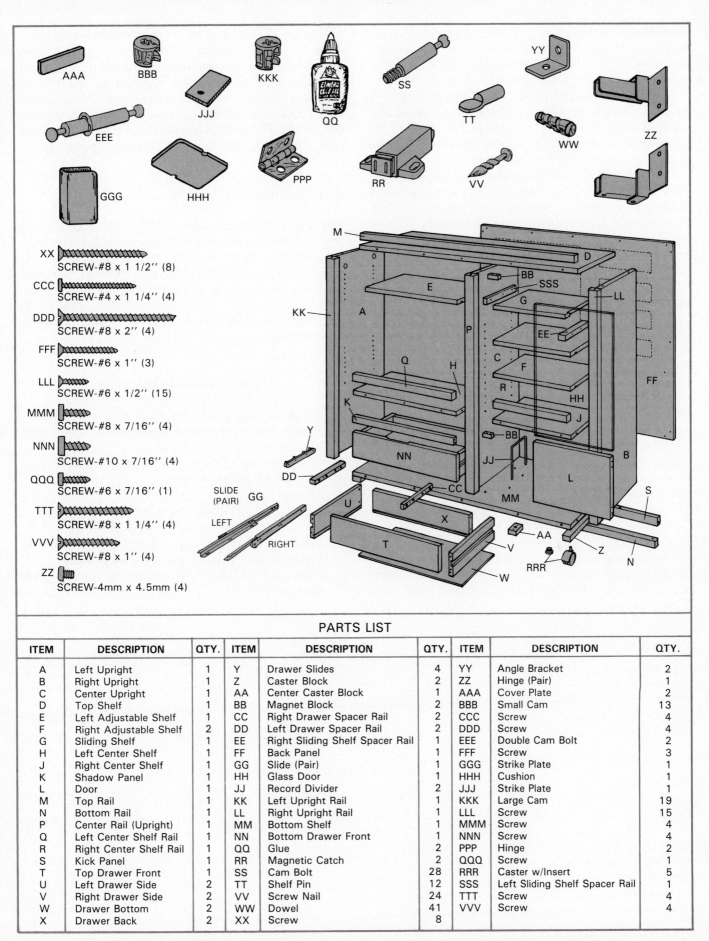

XX ▷▷▷▷▷▷▷▷▷
SCREW-#8 x 1 1/2'' (8)

CCC ▷▷▷▷▷▷▷▷▷
SCREW-#4 x 1 1/4'' (4)

DDD ▷▷▷▷▷▷▷▷▷▷▷
SCREW-#8 x 2'' (4)

FFF ▷▷▷▷▷▷▷
SCREW-#6 x 1'' (3)

LLL ▷▷▷
SCREW-#6 x 1/2'' (15)

MMM ▷▷▷
SCREW-#8 x 7/16'' (4)

NNN ▷▷▷
SCREW-#10 x 7/16'' (4)

QQQ ▷▷▷
SCREW-#6 x 7/16'' (1)

TTT ▷▷▷▷▷▷▷
SCREW-#8 x 1 1/4'' (4)

VVV ▷▷▷▷▷▷▷
SCREW-#8 x 1'' (4)

ZZ ▷▷
SCREW-4mm x 4.5mm (4)

PARTS LIST

ITEM	DESCRIPTION	QTY.	ITEM	DESCRIPTION	QTY.	ITEM	DESCRIPTION	QTY.
A	Left Upright	1	Y	Drawer Slides	4	YY	Angle Bracket	2
B	Right Upright	1	Z	Caster Block	2	ZZ	Hinge (Pair)	1
C	Center Upright	1	AA	Center Caster Block	1	AAA	Cover Plate	2
D	Top Shelf	1	BB	Magnet Block	2	BBB	Small Cam	13
E	Left Adjustable Shelf	1	CC	Right Drawer Spacer Rail	2	CCC	Screw	4
F	Right Adjustable Shelf	2	DD	Left Drawer Spacer Rail	2	DDD	Screw	4
G	Sliding Shelf	1	EE	Right Sliding Shelf Spacer Rail	1	EEE	Double Cam Bolt	2
H	Left Center Shelf	1	FF	Back Panel	1	FFF	Screw	3
J	Right Center Shelf	1	GG	Slide (Pair)	1	GGG	Strike Plate	1
K	Shadow Panel	1	HH	Glass Door	1	HHH	Cushion	1
L	Door	1	JJ	Record Divider	2	JJJ	Strike Plate	1
M	Top Rail	1	KK	Left Upright Rail	1	KKK	Large Cam	19
N	Bottom Rail	1	LL	Right Upright Rail	1	LLL	Screw	15
P	Center Rail (Upright)	1	MM	Bottom Shelf	1	MMM	Screw	4
Q	Left Center Shelf Rail	1	NN	Bottom Drawer Front	1	NNN	Screw	4
R	Right Center Shelf Rail	1	QQ	Glue	2	PPP	Hinge	2
S	Kick Panel	1	RR	Magnetic Catch	2	QQQ	Screw	1
T	Top Drawer Front	1	SS	Cam Bolt	28	RRR	Caster w/Insert	5
U	Left Drawer Side	2	TT	Shelf Pin	12	SSS	Left Sliding Shelf Spacer Rail	1
V	Right Drawer Side	2	VV	Screw Nail	24	TTT	Screw	4
W	Drawer Bottom	2	WW	Dowel	41	VVV	Screw	4
X	Drawer Back	2	XX	Screw	8			

Fig. 4-6. Design includes deciding what materials will be used to construct the cabinet. (O'Sullivan)

sketches of various designs have been developed. Alternatives have been analyzed in terms of function, form, and cost. Remember, the finished product must satisfy the person who will be using it.

At this time, you have narrowed the alternatives to ONE. This final design satisfies the needs and wants of the user. It is functional. The form is attractive. It is structurally sound. Finally, it blends with the style of its surroundings.

All of this design information must be recorded. This involves working drawings and specifications (Chapters 7 and 9). *Working drawings* accurately communicate your design to the builder. One or more views are drawn to describe the shape of the product. Dimensions show length, width, and height. Notes are included to relate special information. This could include certain ways to process the material.

Specifications provide information on materials and tools. Information will cover materials as wood and wood products, plastic laminates, adhesives, hardware, and finishing materials. The list should include quantity, size, and quality descriptions. You might include the manufacturer's name and stock number for purchased items. A special tools and equipment list may be desirable. This list identifies items such as router bits, shaper cutters, and hole saws. These items may have to be ordered. Try to have tools, materials, and supplies in place before you begin working.

SUMMARY

The decision-making process guides you when designing cabinetry. It is a logical way to make decisions when creating products. First, the needs and wants are identified. The problem might be that you need an entertainment center. Information is then gathered about the problem. Every question should be answered. Should the product be built-in or movable? Does it need doors to protect it from dust? Once all of the questions are answered, designing can begin. The design should meet the needs of the user. It should also have a pleasing appearance.

CABINETMAKING TERMS

Decision-making process, need, want, identifying the problem, gathering information, brainstorming, preliminary plan, sketch, two dimensional, sketches, three dimensional sketches, refined design, material, dimension, analysis, functional analysis, mock-up, strength test, cost analysis, make-buy decision, decision-making stage, working drawing, specification.

TEST YOUR KNOWLEDGE

1. What directs your activities during design?
2. Problem statements should include both needs and wants. True or False?
3. One method of producing questions during information gathering is _____.
4. When creating preliminary plans, use _____ to draw the product.
5. Refined designs include what information?
6. When analyzing your refined designs, what types of analysis should be used? Why?
7. How are working drawings different from specifications?

Chapter 5
HUMAN FACTORS

After studying this chapter, you will be able to:
☐ *Describe the human factors which affect cabinet design.*
☐ *List standard dimensions for common cabinets and furniture.*
☐ *Identify safety factors which affect cabinet design.*

Cabinetry must fit the needs of the people who use it. They may be children, adults, the elderly, or disabled persons, Fig. 5-1. Even though a product may be functional and attractive, it may not be the right size for every person. Body measurements and other distances should be known. Then, the product can be designed with the user in mind. These considerations are called *human factors*.

When you design cabinetry, you should consider:
1. How far people can reach while sitting or standing.
2. People's limits on stooping or bending.
3. Space problems confronting the elderly and disabled.

When building customized cabinets and furniture, the dimensions can vary. Altering height, width, and depth helps "fit" products to people. Other times, you may not want to alter dimensions. Consider built-in cabinetry. If the design is altered too much, it may affect the resale value of the home.

Knowing the human factors involved helps designers adapt products to people. Furniture manufacturers establish sizes based on human factors. Many of these measurements have become standards for cabinetmaking.

STANDARD DIMENSIONS

Standard dimensions are based on average sizes for children and adults. These dimensions are referred to as *architectural standards* because they involve residential design.

HEIGHT

Kitchen dimensions are given for average size adults. Countertops are 36 in. (900 mm) above the floor. Ranges for cooking are the same height. Both normally extend 24 in. (600 mm) from the wall. The space between the top of the base (lower) cabinet and the bottom of wall cabinets is usually 16 in. (400 mm), Fig. 5-2. Most countertop appliances, such as toasters and blenders, will fit in this space conveniently. Appliance manufacturers are very concerned with standards. People might not buy a blender that cannot fit on the countertop.

At times, these dimensions are inconvenient for children and short adults. They might need a stool

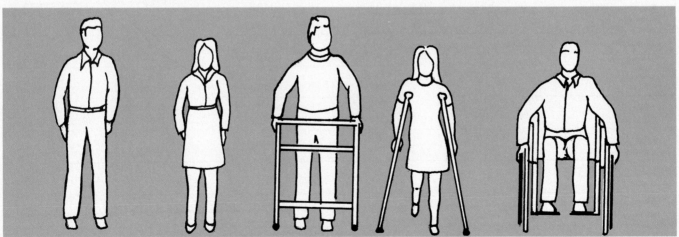

Fig. 5-1. Your designs will have to accommodate many different people.

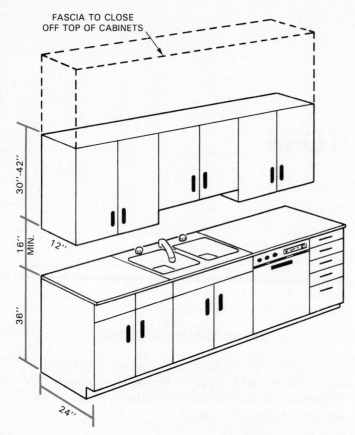

FASCIA TO CLOSE
OFF TOP OF CABINETS

30"-42"

16" MIN.

12"

36"

24"

Fig. 5-2. These are standard dimensions for kitchen cabinets.

A 30 in. (760 mm) to 33 in. (840 mm) cooktop and counter height is preferred for handicapped persons. However, the standard height may be used if a pull-out work shelf is provided at the lower height.

WIDTH AND LENGTH

The width and length of large appliances, tables, etc. vary in size. Range and refrigerator widths vary from 24 in. (600 mm) to 48 in. (1200 mm). Tables are available in different widths, lengths, and shapes. Availabe space, comfort, and convenience will influence choices in these cases. The cabinet-maker will apply standards to provide ample space for the user.

STANDING

Many activities require the user to stand while using a cabinet, Fig. 5-3. When standing, people perform three movements:
1. Reach out in all directions.
2. Bend at the waist.
3. Stoop using knee and hip joints.

These body movements occur at counters, work surfaces, and machines. Usually, movements are restricted for people with canes, crutches, or walkers. These disabilities must be thought of when designing the product.

to reach upper shelves of conventional cabinets. A convenient step might be designed into the base cabinet.

STANDING		AVG. MALE		AVG. FEMALE		AGE 10		AGE 5		ELDERLY (Avg. Adult)	
		in.	mm	in.	mm	in.	mm	in.	mm	in.	mm
Height		69	1725	63.5	1590	50	1250	45	1125	64.5	1610
Eye level		64.5	1612	60	1500	46	1150	41	1025	60.5	1512
Easy Reach	up	77	1925	71.5	1787	55	1375	49	1225	70	1750
	fwd.	21.5	537	20.5	512	16.5	412	15.5	387	20	500
	side	25.5	637	23.5	587	18.5	462	17	425	22.5	562
Shoulder width		18	450	16	400	11.5	287	10	250	16	400
Elbow height		42	1050	39	975	29.5	737	26.5	662	39	975
High counter		44	1100	40.5	1012	30.5	762	27	675	38.5	962
Low counter		38	950	34.5	862	26	650	23.5	587	32.5	812
Low reach		N/A		N/A		N/A		N/A		24	600
Kitchen aisle width		42	1050	42	1050	N/A		N/A		42	1050

Fig. 5-3. These are average dimensions for people when standing.

COUNTERS

There are many kinds of built-in and movable cabinets which have counters. The counter is the top surface of the cabinet. *Counter heights* may be standard or adapted to human factors. An accepted average height of 36 in. is most often used for built-in units.

Low counters may be built for kitchens and other rooms. A 36 in. (900 mm) standard counter height might be too high for an elderly person. This dimension could be lowered to 32 in. (800 mm).

Lavatories normally are 32 in. (800 mm) high. For the elderly, this distance could be raised to 33 in. (825 mm) to reduce bending.

High counters refer to built-in cabinets such as bars. These generally are 42 in. (1050 mm) high. This height fits the person serving from behind the bar. People being served in front can stand comfortably. However, seats at a high counter must be above normal height.

MACHINES

Machine heights follow standards based on human factors. Some examples are: 33 in. (825 mm) jointers; 36 in. (900 mm) table saws, sanders and shapers; 39 in. (1000 mm) radial arm saws; and 46 in. (1170 mm) band saws.

WORK TABLES

Work tables and work benches vary from 32 in. (800 mm) to 40 in. (1000 mm). The type of work (woodworking, appliance repair) and the user's height may change this dimension.

WALKING SPACE

Space is needed for people to move between and around furniture. Even more space is needed for people with canes, crutches, or walkers, Fig. 5-4. For wheelchairs, a five ft. minimum turning radius is required.

SITTING

When seated, people and chairs occupy space. They may be sitting around a table which also occupies space. People may be dining, working, or relaxing while seated. Fig. 5-5 indicates human factors for people when seated. Seat heights are measured from the floor to the top of the compressed seat cushion.

HANDICAPPED	AVG. MALE		AVG. FEMALE		AGE 10		AGE 5	
	in.	mm	in.	mm	in.	mm	in.	mm
Crutch space (max.)	33	825	32	800	28	700	21.5	537
Cane or one crutch (max.)	27.5	687	25	625	22	550	17	425
Doorway clearances (min.)	crutches 26.5	662	canes 22	550	walker 28	700		

Fig. 5-4. People who walk with assistance need additional space.

SITTING		AVG. MALE		AVG. FEMALE		AGE 10		AGE 5		ELDERLY (Avg. Adult)	
		in.	mm	in.	mm	in.	mm	in.	mm	in.	mm
Eye level		50.5	1262	45	1125	36	900	30.5	762	28	700
Easy reach (upward)		61	1525	56.5	1412	48.5	1212	45	1125	50	1250
S e a t	height	17	425	16	400	16	400	13.5	337	16	400
	width (min.)	16	400	16	400	13.5	337	11.5	287	16	400
	length (max.)	18	450	17	425	12.5	312	10.5	262	16	400
Armrest height (above seat)		8.5	212	8	200	7	187	6	150	8	200
Table height		29	725	28	700	22	550	18	450	27.5	687
Leg room		18	450	16	400	16.5	412	13	325	21	525

Fig. 5-5. These are average distances for people when sitting.

CHAIRS

Chairs should be designed for comfort and convenience. There are two general classifications for chairs: straight and lounge. *Straight chairs* position the person upright for dining or working. *Lounge chairs* recline and are used for relaxing. Certain dimensions are helpful when designing chairs, Fig. 5-6.

Standard chair dimensions describe heights to accommodate average males and females. Standard *seat height* is 17 in. However, seat height (height at front edge of seat) for a short person may be reduced to 15 in. (375 mm). If seat height is much below 15 in. (375 mm), getting out of the seat may be difficult. The height can be increased to 18 in. (450 mm) for a tall person. Seat length may be varied. Also, note that the backrest angle and height are variable for lounge chairs, Fig. 5-6. At angles greater than 30 degrees, the head must be supported.

Many chairs have armrests. *Armrests* aid people when rising from a chair. They also support the arm while working or relaxing in a chair. Refer to Fig. 5-6 for suggested dimensions where armrests should be attached. Spacing varies from 19 in. (480 mm) to 22 in. (550 mm) between the armrests. Armrest lengths, from the seat back, are 12 in. (300 mm) for arm and hand support. When working at a table, 8½ in. (210 mm) is sufficient since part of the persons arm can rest on the work table. For elbow support only, 6½ in. (150 mm) is sufficient.

Seating at low and high counters applies similar standards. At a 36 in. (900 mm) counter, use a 24 in. (600 mm) chair or stool. Similarly, at a 42 in. (1050 mm) bar use 36 in. (900 mm) stools.

TABLES AND DESKS

There is a close relationship between chairs and tables or desks. The heights must allow room for the person to move. They must also prevent the user from being pinched between the chair and desk. Maximum table heights and average chair heights appear in Fig. 5-5. Chairs will vary about one in. (250 mm) for each table height. The difference between the table and compressed chair should be 11 in. (275 mm). This allows for the user's thighs to fit under the table. It also allows for drawer space under the table. Chairs could have armrests and the table might not have a drawer. In this case there should be a 1½ in. (40 mm) finger clearance.

Table heights vary with different purposes. Desk and dining tables are approximately the same height, 29 in. to 30 in. (725 mm to 750 mm). Card tables and sewing cabinets are 28 in. (700 mm) high. Surfaces for typewriters are 25 in. to 26 in.

0°-5°	Seat angle from horizontal	5°-25°
95°-98°	Seat to back rest angle	95°-120°
5°-10°	Backrest angle from vertical	10°-45°
15'' (375 mm)	Backrest height from seat	21''-28'' (525-700 mm)
16''-17'' (400-425 mm)	Seat Reference Point (SRP)	11''-12'' (275-300 mm)

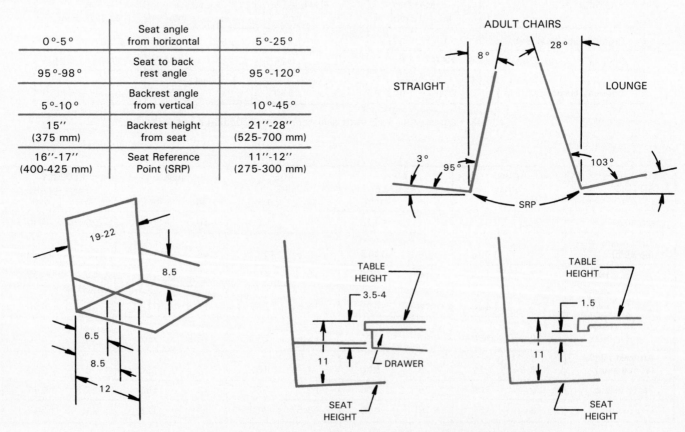

Fig. 5-6. Straight chairs and lounge chairs use different standard dimensions.

Fig. 5-7. Monitor and keyboard heights are factors in computer cabinet design. (Sauder)

(625 mm to 650 mm). End tables and night tables are 18 in. to 24 in. (450 mm to 600 mm) high. Heights for these tables depend on the size of lamps used on them. Coffee tables vary from 11 in. to 18 in. (275 mm to 450 mm). Coffee tables can be raised for the elderly. Tables which are 24 in. (600 mm) high reduce the amount an elderly person must bend.

Computer consoles need work surfaces at various heights, Fig. 5-7. The keyboard should be at typing table height. The monitor should be placed at the line-of-sight level for a sitting person. The monitor can be placed lower for people who wear bifocal glasses. Disk drives and printers should be located at the side within reach.

WHEELCHAIRS

Wheelchairs present a special concern for designers. Space must be made available for mobility. Counters must be within reach of the person. The space requirements for wheelchairs is shown in Fig. 5-8.

WHEELCHAIR		AVG. MALE		AVG. FEMALE		AGE 10		AGE 5	
		in.	mm	in.	mm	in.	mm	in.	mm
Eye level		48.5	1212	46.5	1162	42	1050	39	975
	up	64.5	1612	59	1475	53.5	1337	46	1150
Easy reach	fwd.	21.5	537	20	500	18	450	13.5	337
	side	20	500	17.5	437	14.5	362	10.5	262
	down	13	325	17.5	437	14.5	362	24.5	612
Table height		31	775	31	775	31	775	31	775
Leg room (chair arm to toe)		16.5	412	14.5	362	13.5	337	10	250
Seat	height	19.5	487	19.5	487	19.5	487	19.5	487
	width	18	450	18	450	16	400	12	300
	length	16	400	16	400	13	325	11	275
Clearances		Doorway		32	800	Passageway		36	900

Fig. 5-8. People in wheelchairs require special space consideration.

RECLINING

Human factors for people who are reclining involve height and weight. These factors are most important in mattress manufacturing. If you build a bed, do so after determining mattress size specifications, Fig. 5-9.

Mattress sizes are standardized by manufacturers. However, custom-made mattresses can be made longer for tall people.

Beds often have headboards. They may be plain or may hold books, clocks, and radios. They might support reading lamps. Locate shelves so the user can see and reach objects on the shelves. These same conveniences should be designed into night tables.

LINE OF SIGHT

Line of sight is an important factor in cabinet design. A person's line of sight is the area which they can see. Any television or computer display should be placed where viewers can see it without turning their heads.

STANDING

People stand while tuning a stereo, reading a bulletin board, or looking at trophies. Eye movement is in a vertical arc. From eye level, the normal line of sight (head erect) is 10 degrees downward. There is a convenient and maxium arc of eye movement, Fig. 5-10. This arc can be raised or lowered by moving the head.

SITTING

Sitting restricts the line of sight. The normal line of sight downward is lessened to 15 degrees below eye level. The primary display area would receive the most concentration. This range would be within 15 degrees left, right, above, and below the line of sight. A larger secondary display area lies an added 15 degrees in all directions. However, the outer range is uncomfortable. It is beyond the person's normal focus.

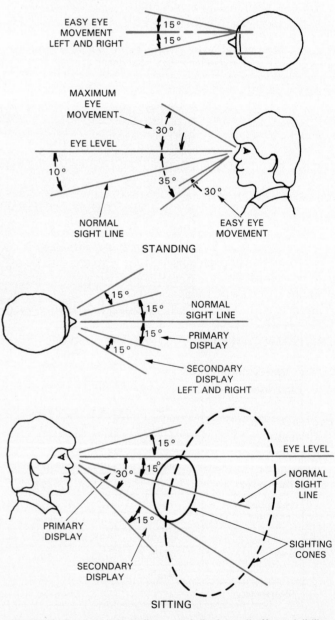

Fig. 5-10. Eye level, sight lines, and displays all affect visibility.

MATTRESS SIZES			
Crib	22¼ x 38¾	Twin	39 x 74, 80, 84
	25¼ x 50¾	Double	54 x 75, 80, 84
	31¼ x 56¾	Queen	60 x 80, 84
Single	30 x 75	King	72, 76 x 80, 84

Fig. 5-9. There are several standard mattress sizes. (Trendwest)

HUMAN FACTORS AND SAFETY

More accidents and injuries occur in the home than anywhere else. There is an endless list of potential hazards. You could walk into something. You might be struck by an object. For a child, chances for possible accidents and injuries are increased.

SHARP EDGES AND CORNERS

Striking the corner or edge of a cabinet can be painful. It may cause temporary or permanent injury especially at head and eye level. Wall cabinet corners, cabinet doors standing open, and pull-out racks are very unsafe.

Other hazards include walking into desks, coffee tables, and other furniture. This represents a special problem for blind and partially sighted individuals. People with normal vision can be injured in a dark room. Eliminate as many sharp edges as possible.

Furniture that is safe for adults may be hazardous for children. A child, at age two, is about 34 in. (850 mm) tall. This is half the height of an average adult. A child might strike a cabinet corner. This same corner causes no problems for adults.

As a designer, you must take into account these factors. Cabinets must be made as safe as possible for adults and children.

FALLING OBJECTS

Falling objects can cause cuts, bruises, or more serious injuries. Cups and cooking utensils are examples of potential problems if stored overhead. Adjustable shelves help guard against excessive stacking. Retaining rails or ledges keep objects from sliding off of a shelf.

CHILDREN'S REACH

Children are attracted by colorful, shiny objects. In addition, they cannot read, nor can they realize where hazards exist. The child might pull a portable appliance from a counter or enter cabinets where toxic substances are kept. Make sure your design eliminates these hazards where possible.

Design lockable compartments for poisonous materials. Make sure power cords do not hang over the counter edge. Consider all situations which are hazardous for children.

SUMMARY

Comfort, convenience, and safety often are overlooked by designers. Many times, cabinetry and furniture products do not serve their intended purpose. The problems are especially true for children, elderly persons, and disabled persons or persons in wheelchairs. Alter dimensions of cabinets to fit the user.

People stand at countertops, tables, machines, and similar surfaces. They may stand alone or with support, such as a crutch. People sit on chairs while relaxing or while working at a desk. Chairs and desks or tables should allow the user freedom to move.

Individuals in wheelchairs have special problems. Adapt counter heights for their reach. Space also must be allowed for wheelchair movement.

Standards exist for many of the dimensions discussed. Standard dimensions will meet the needs of a majority of people. Comply with them unless you are adapting for the elderly and handicapped. If too many deviations are used for built-in cabinets, the resale value of the home may be affected.

CABINETMAKING TERMS

Human factors, standard dimensions, architectural standards, counter height, machine height, work table height, straight chair, lounge chair, standard chair dimensions, seat height, armrests, table height, computer console, wheelchair, mattress sizes, line of sight.

TEST YOUR KNOWLEDGE

1. Describe five human factors.
2. Standard dimensions specify _____, _____, _____, and _____.
3. Standard dimensions are based on what sizes of children and adults?
   a. Average size child or adult.
   b. Largest child or adult.
   c. Smallest child or adult.
4. The standard cabinet height is _____.
5. List four dimensions concerning chair size.
6. Why do wheelchairs present design problems?
7. What dimensions control the size of a bed frame?
   a. Height of a person.
   b. Mattress size.
   c. Size of the bedroom.
   d. Weight of a person.
8. The angle of your line of sight is different when sitting than when standing. True or False?
9. As a designer, how can you make cabinets more safe for children and adults?

Chapter 6
PRODUCTION DECISIONS

After studying this chapter, you will be able to:
☐*Identify the need for a plan of procedure.*
☐*List the steps in making production decisions.*
☐*Describe alternative tools for completing cabinet-making processes.*

Preparing to build cabinetry involves research and planning. Previous chapters dealt with design problems, or those ''what to do'' decisions. *Production decisions* guide you in ''how to do it'' and ''why to do it this way.'' All are essential decision-making phases in the cabinetmaking process, Fig. 6-1.

Production decisions relate very closely to design decisions. When designing, you develop your own working drawings. You might also choose to use someone else's drawings. The drawings specify the shapes, dimensions, and joinery for the product. They also list each part of the cabinet in a bill of materials. Once you have working drawings, you

need to decide how to complete the product. This involves selecting tools, materials, and processes.

Making production decisions means solving problems. You confront problems and choices at each stage of completing your product. Decisions include how to cut, surface, form, assemble, and finish the cabinet. By making these decisions, you form a plan of procedure.

PLANNING YOUR WORK

Planning is essential so that you do not waste time and materials. Each step builds on previous tasks. For example, you cannot cut lumber to length accurately unless one end has been squared. Yet, before you can square one end, you have to square the faces and edges. This is one example where planning your work beforehand can save time and reduce problems. Having a written *plan of procedure* prevents you from missing a crucial step. Some working drawings you buy may have a plan of procedure included, Fig. 6-2. However, you must develop a plan for your own working drawings.

PLAN OF PROCEDURE

The ''what to do'' steps in a plan of procedure usually remain the same for different products. However, you will alter them according to available equipment and your skills. Generally, the plan will follow these steps in production:
1. Identify appropriate tools.
2. Obtain materials and supplies.
3. Lay out and rough cut standard stock.
4. Square workpieces and components accurately to size.
5. Prepare joints.
6. Create holes and other openings.
7. Shape components.
8. Smooth components.
9. Assemble components.
10. Apply finish.
11. Install hardware.

You will notice the terms workpiece, component, and stock have been mentioned. They will be used

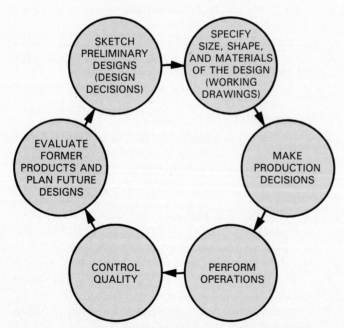

Fig. 6-1. The cabinetmaking process is a series of phases. Production decisions are the link between working drawings and the operations needed to build a cabinet.

PLAN OF PROCEDURE

1. Cut stock to 1/16'' over finished dimension.
2. Glue up 3/4'' workpieces to make a table top 18'' wide and 20'' long. NOTE: Alternate direction of growth rings for each successive board.
3. When the top has dried, smooth the surface with a scraper, then sandpaper.
4. Shape the edge with a rounding-over bit.
5. Cut 3 1/2'' long x 3/8'' wide x 7/8'' deep mortises in the legs with either a 3/8'' mortising chisel or a 3/8'' straight router bit.
6. Cut tenons on the front, back, and sides 3 1/2'' wide x 3/8'' thick x 3/4'' long. Cut them slightly oversize, then fit them in the mortises.
7. Shape the bottom edges of the front, sides, and back with a small bead.
8. Rough-shape the legs on a lathe. Leave 6'' at the top (with the mortises) square. Don't turn this portion at all.
9. Decide on an inside corner of the legs. Offset the foot of the legs 3/8'' in the direction of the inside corner.
10. Attach cleats to the inside of sides, front, and back with 1 1/4''-#8 wood screws. Position these 1/32'' away from the top edge of the sides, back, and front.
11. Assemble the sides, front, and back to the legs with glue. Clamp and let dry.
12. Assemble the leg assembly to the top from underneath with wood screws.
13. Sand the table with garnet paper. Be careful not to sand away the shaped edges.
14. Stain and finish as desired.

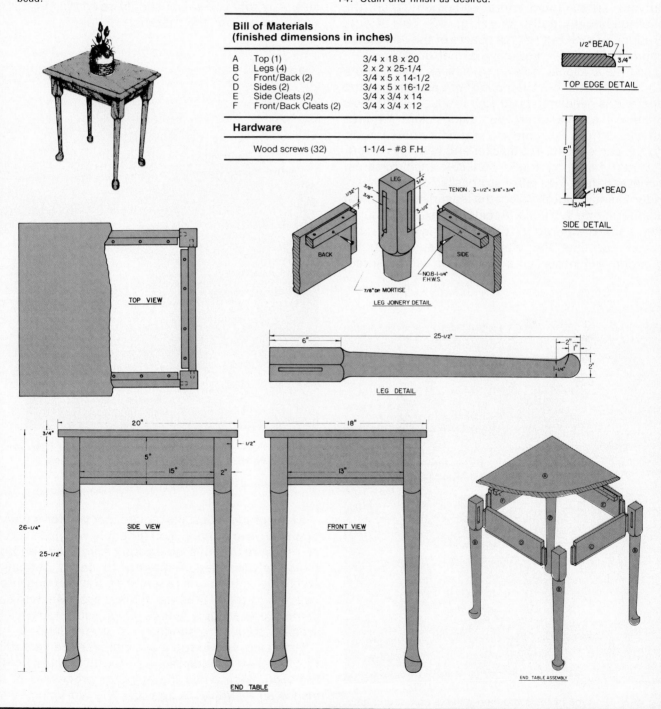

Bill of Materials
(finished dimensions in inches)

A	Top (1)	3/4 x 18 x 20
B	Legs (4)	2 x 2 x 25-1/4
C	Front/Back (2)	3/4 x 5 x 14-1/2
D	Sides (2)	3/4 x 5 x 16-1/2
E	Side Cleats (2)	3/4 x 3/4 x 14
F	Front/Back Cleats (2)	3/4 x 3/4 x 12

Hardware

Wood screws (32)	1-1/4 – #8 F.H.

Fig. 6-2. The plan of procedure for this end table is included in working drawings you purchase. (Shopsmith, Inc.)

throughout the text and are defined as follows:

1. *Stock.* Material in its unprocessed form: a full-length board, a sheet of plywood, and so forth.
2. *Workpiece.* A workpiece is rough cut stock being sized.
3. *Component.* One or more workpieces being processed into a bill of materials item.

IDENTIFYING TOOLS

The tools you have will determine how you process workpieces and components. Well equipped cabinet shops have more equipment than the average home woodworker, Fig. 6-3. This affects production time but not the quality of the completed cabinet. The skills you have affect quality.

List the available tools and machines in your shop. There may be more than one that can perform the operations needed to build your product. Hand tools generally are versatile, but using them requires physical effort. Portable and stationary power tools do the same tasks, but quicker and with less effort.

When selecting tools, consider their hazards. Tools and machines differ as possible causes for accidents and injuries. Select the least risky, but most accurate, one available. Accidents usually occur at the point-of-operation (PO). This is where the cutter contacts the workpiece. Having the PO guarded will lessen your chance of being injured,

Fig. 6-4. Using a pushing device can keep your hands and arms away from the cutter.

Selecting the proper blades, cutters, bits, and drills is an important decision. For example, suppose you are selecting a circular saw blade for a table saw. Rip and crosscut blades leave blade marks on the kerf sides. Hollow ground blades leave a smoother edge. However, they can heat and warp if the lumber is dense. For dense lumber or manufactured panels such as particleboard and fiberboard, you must use carbide-edged blades. Here again the tooling you select depends on the materials and their size. Any tool you select should be sharp. Dull tools will burn or tear the material.

Fig. 6-4. Point-of-operation guards protect you from areas where the cutter contacts the workpiece. (Rockwell International)

Many product designs require that you form wood or plastic into curves. You probably will need force or pressure for this operation. Also, heat and/or moisture are used frequently to assist bending. Available equipment determines the forming process. Hydraulic presses work best. Mechanical clamps are a good source of pressure. Applying weight, such as a sandbag, is often adequate.

Using jigs and fixtures can increase the versatility of tools and equipment. A fixture simply holds the workpiece while the operator processes it. A vise is an example. A jig holds the workpiece and also guides the tool. A dovetail jig is an example, Fig. 6-5.

Fig. 6-3. The type of tools you have affects production time, but not necessarily the quality of the completed cabinet. (Vermont American Tool Company)

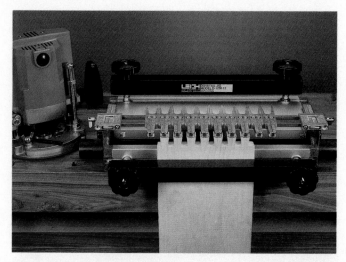
Fig. 6-5. A dovetail jig both holds the workpiece and guides the router to make a dovetail joint. (The Fine Tool Shops)

OBTAINING MATERIALS AND SUPPLIES

Have materials and supplies on hand before beginning production. Materials include any wood, metal, plastic, etc. that will become a part of the finished product, Fig. 6-6. Supplies include abrasives, adhesives, rags, or other consumable items which are not part of the finished product.

Check the amount of materials and supplies you have in stock. Also note their condition. Wood stored in a moist environment may be water marked or warped. Adhesives might not be effective if they have been stored too long. You may not have one grit size of sheet abrasive. Before ordering, compare materials in stock with the bill of materials.

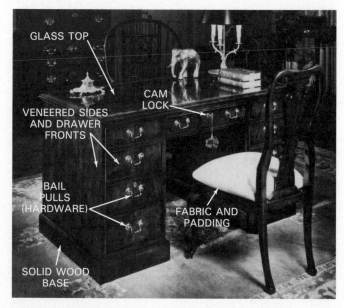

GLASS TOP

CAM LOCK

VENEERED SIDES AND DRAWER FRONTS

BAIL PULLS (HARDWARE)

FABRIC AND PADDING

SOLID WOOD BASE

Fig. 6-6. A number of different materials are visible on a completed cabinet. Those you do not see include fasteners and drawer slides.

There are many options when ordering material. For example, lumber is available rough or surfaced. Do you buy it rough and surface it yourself or do you buy it already smooth? You typically will pay extra if the seller surfaces the material. However, this may be worth the money if you do not own a power planer or jointer, Fig. 6-7.

Another aspect of obtaining materials is make-buy decisions. The design may specify turned chair legs. Do you have a lathe and the time to make them? If not, you will have to buy legs ready-made.

Fig. 6-7. You might choose to buy boards already surfaced if you do not have a power planer. (Makita U.S.A., Inc.)

LAYING OUT AND ROUGH CUTTING STOCK

Stock is measured, laid out, and rough cut larger than workpiece dimensions shown on the working drawings. The extra material allows you to square the workpiece to its finished dimension.

When laying out workpieces, be aware of grain direction (pattern of the wood) and wood defects (knots, splits, etc.). Grain direction may or may not be specified on the design. For example, drawer fronts might have horizontal or vertical grain. Usually, cabinet sides have vertical grain. Laying out and cutting a workpiece the wrong grain direction results in lost material and time. Wood defects can cause problems and should be avoided. Knots may fall out. Weather checks may cause splitting. Work around visible defects as much as possible. This is one reason to order extra materials.

After layout, cut out the materials. You will likely use a hand saw or portable power saw for this operation. Make cuts from 1/4 in. to 1/2 in. (6 to 12 mm) oversize. If the workpiece is roughed out to the finished dimension, sanding it may make it undersize.

Some machine surfacing may be done before layout. When you have many small parts, you may first surface the faces of a larger board. Then lay out each individual workpiece. Do this when the parts will be too small to be passed through the planer. Most planers have a minimum workpiece length. Short lengths can get caught in the machine.

SQUARING WORKPIECES TO SIZE

Begin production by making workpieces from standard stock. If you buy rough lumber, this includes a series of surfacing and sawing steps. The steps listed here are done on stationary power equipment.
1. Surface one face on the jointer.
2. Smooth one edge with the jointer.
3. Surface the second face using the planer.
4. Rip the lumber to width on a table saw or radial arm saw. Have the jointed edge against the rip fence. NOTE: You could make this 1/16 in. (2 mm) oversize. Then return to the jointer and smooth the ripped edge. This removes saw marks and achieves accurate width. Do so on edges that will be visible or bonded together.
5. Square one end on a table or radial arm saw.
6. Crosscut the workpiece to length.
You eliminate the first three steps if you buy surfaced face (S4S) lumber.

The order of steps for squaring workpieces with hand tools is no different. However, you may reduce the accuracy of squared stock. Use a framing square, hand plane of the proper size, and rip and crosscut saws. You may want to use a miter box to make accurate crosscuts.

Portable power tools will square workpieces. Portable power planes work well for edges and narrow-faced workpieces, usually those under 3 in. (75 mm) wide, Fig. 6-8. Portable circular and cutoff saws work well for ripping and crosscutting stock. Power miter saws will square ends.

Check machine setups frequently. Be sure angles of saw blades, fences, and other machine parts are square (90° angle). Before squaring your workpieces, you might cut or surface a piece of scrap wood and inspect it. Do not assume scales printed on the machines are accurate.

PREPARING JOINTS

Joinery is a very important part of the cabinetmaking process. A well made joint will make

Fig. 6-8. A portable power planer works well for narrow faces and edges. (Makita U.S.A., Inc.)

assembly easier and the finished product stronger and more attractive. There are more than 30 different types of joints. Each can be made with various hand and power tools. For example, a groove can be made with a hand saw and chisel, hand router plane, table saw, radial arm saw, shaper, router, etc. Each varies in joint quality depending on the cabinetmaker's skill.

Consider the sequence of steps for making the joint. On some joints, one part should be made before another. For example, the mortise of a mortise and tenon joint should be made first. The tenon then can be cut to fit snugly, Fig. 6-9. For a dovetail joint, you can cut both pieces separately. However, with a dovetail jig, template, dovetail bit, and router, you cut matching workpieces at the same time. This process is quicker and much more accurate. Yet, skill is needed to set the precise depth of cut for the dovetail router bit.

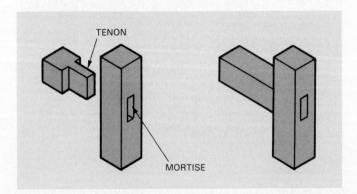

TENON

MORTISE

Fig. 6-9. Cutting the mortise first allows you to cut and fit the tenon accurately.

CREATING HOLES AND OTHER OPENINGS

Holes, such as for installing hardware, are drilled after the stock is squared. This step generally preceeds cutting curves and shaping edges because you need square corners and edges as reference points for locating holes. Also, you may need a straight edge to align a row of holes, such as the holes inside an adjustable shelf book case.

Holes may be made by hand tools or with portable and stationary power drills. Use a brace and bit or hand drill and twist drill bit for hand operations. Portable power drills are versatile. You can make holes almost anywhere and at any given angle, Fig. 6-10. Stationary power drills, such as the drill press, are less versatile. However, you can set them more accurately for hole depths and angles.

Large and irregularly shaped holes are made with a saw or router. By hand, use a compass, keyhole, or coping saw. With power tools, select a scroll saw, saber saw, or router. A scroll saw, also known as a jig saw, is stationary. A saber saw or router is portable. With a router, you can cut your workpiece freehand or with a template as a guide. Sometimes you mount routers and saber saws upside down under an accessory table. Instead of holding the portable tool, you guide the workpiece over table.

SHAPING COMPONENTS

Shaping means creating a curved face, edge, or end on a workpiece. The desired shape is shown on the working drawings. Shaping before making joints could result in poor joints because joinery generally requires square edges and ends. For example, suppose you are making a picture frame. First cut the miter joints that hold the frame together; then shape the edges.

Shaping the face of the workpiece can be done with a saber saw, scroll saw, or band saw. Edge shaping is usually done with a router or shaper, Fig. 6-11. Choose the right router bit or shaper cutter to make the desired design.

SMOOTHING COMPONENTS

Smoothing a surface often is the most time consuming part of the cabinetmaking process. You do this once you have cut and shaped each workpiece. The goal is to produce smooth surfaces. Hand planes and jointers take away saw kerf marks on straight edges. Spokeshaves and cabinet files do the same on curves. Hand and cabinet scrapers are valuable to smooth rough areas around knots on surfaces and edges. Then you will likely use sheet abrasives to finish the process.

Fig. 6-10. The versatility of a portable power drill makes it a needed tool in the shop. (Black and Decker)

Fig. 6-11. Edge designs are created with a portable router and bit. (Robert Bosch Power Tool Corp.)

There are many types of natural and synthetic abrasives. Some remain sharp and will clog less than others. For example, garnet lasts several times longer than flint abrasive. Synthetics, such as silicon carbide and aluminum oxide, are effective longer than garnet.

Abrasives come in many forms: sheets, disks, belts, sleeves, sharpening stones, and grinding wheels. The fine or coarse texture of the abrasive is rated by grit size. The larger the grit size number, the finer the grains of abrasives.

Sanding machines decrease the amount of time spent preparing components for finish. Stationary belt and disk sanders are used to smooth component ends and edges. Portable belt and disk sanders are used to smooth surfaces, Fig. 6-12. Wide belt sanders smooth larger surfaces.

Abrasives leave scratches in the wood's surface. Coarse or medium abrasives remove machine and scraper marks. However, they leave visible scratches. Finer abrasives remove these. Always sand with the grain of the wood. This way, the abrasive marks blend in with the grain lines. Any cross grain scratches will become apparent when finishing the product. Work until you achieve the surface quality you desire.

Using a series of abrasive grit sizes will smooth the wood in the least amount of time. First you start with 80 or 100 grit abrasive, then use 150 grit. At this point you "raise the grain" (expand the wood pores) with water by dampening the surface with a moist sponge. Expanding the grain lifts wood fibers which might raise later during finish. Smooth the roughened surface with 180 to 220 grit paper.

Starting with a high grit size abrasive wastes time. Not using the fine grit leaves too many noticeable scratches. These may be hard to see until the finish is applied. Then you will wish you had followed the recommended smoothing sequence.

ASSEMBLING COMPONENTS

Assembly usually occurs after all components have been cut to size and smoothed. However, occasionally you may make a component after assembling other parts. For example, suppose you are going to produce a desk. You would first complete the assembly of the desk body. Then you could measure, cut, and fit the drawers. After the finish is applied, you reinstall drawer slide hardware.

You can assemble the product with mechanical fasteners, hardware, and/or adhesives. For years, typical fasteners such as screws, nails, and staples have been used. You might consider newly developed fasteners for "ready-to-assemble" cabinetry. These permit quick disassembly and reassembly. You attach doors using hinges or sliding tracks. Some fasteners require that you create holes or

Fig. 6-12. Smoothing a surface with a portable belt sander. (Robert Bosch Power Tool Corp.)

mortise openings in the cabinet.

Adhesives include glues, cements, and mastics. If you plan to use adhesive, research various features which affect assembly time. There are terms like pot life, set time, curing time, and drying time. Pot life of an adhesive is the time you can use it before setting starts. By that time, the assembly must be clamped. If this time is short, you must assemble your product quickly. Set time and curing time equal the drying time. Set time identifies minutes or hours before the water or thinner in the adhesive evaporates. Curing time, usually hours, is the time until the adhesive reaches its full strength.

You should assemble the product without adhesive first. This is called a "dry run." Clamp the assembly to see if all joints fit, dimensions are correct, and corners are square. You might select bar clamps, hand screws, spring clamps, band clamps, or any number of clamp types, Fig. 6-13. Determine which clamping procedure insures that corners are square. Prevent clamps from marring the the wood surface with pads or backing blocks (pieces of soft wood). Preset the opening of the clamps, especially if the adhesive will set quickly. Lay them aside in a precise order. That way you know which to position first, second, etc., after the glue is spread.

If an adhesive is not specified in the working drawings, consider the intended use of the cabinet. If it will be outside, select a waterproof adhesive.

APPLYING FINISH

Finishing affects the quality of any product, no matter how well it was designed and constructed.

Fig. 6-13. This universal clamp consists of threaded rods and jaws which adapt to various clamping situations. (Shopsmith)

There are many decisions to make before applying finish to the product. Included are material selection, application procedure, health considerations, and environmental decisions.

MATERIALS

There are a number of finishing materials on the market. Each one has a different affect on the appearance of the product. Stain will change the color of the wood. Bleach will lighten the wood, yet retain the same color tone. Filler will fill in the open pores of the wood, making the surface smoother.

Most people think of finishing materials as the topcoating, the final layer of finish. There are natural and synthetic topcoatings. Many natural materials, such as linseed oil, varnish, and shellac are being replaced by synthetic finishes. The new materials, such as polyurethane, synthetic lacquer, and other resin-base materials are easier to use and more durable.

Finishing products will either build-up on or penetrate the wood surface. Built-up finishes form a film on the surface of the wood. The film resists scratches, dents, and some liquids. However, if damage occurs it is more difficult to repair. Often, you must remove the coating material and refinish the product.

Penetrating finishes are absorbed into the surface. They include oil-resin finishes, linseed oil, and tung oil. They are best for products exposed to minimum handling because the finish provides little protection from damage. However, penetrating finishes allow you to feel the wood texture. Also, they can be easily repaired by simply wiping additional finish on the wood.

APPLICATION PROCEDURE

The procedure for applying a built-up finish includes preparing the product surface, bleaching, wash coating, staining, sealing, and topcoating. For a penetrating finish, you need only prepare the surface, then apply the finish.

Before applying any finishing material, inspect the surfaces. Remove any dried adhesive with a sharp chisel, hand scraper, or cabinet scraper. Dried glue does not accept stain. Raise dents by placing a wet rag and a warm iron over the dent. If the wood has been chipped away, make repairs with wood putty, colored shellac sticks, or similar materials. Leave tiny defects if you will be using filler on an open grain wood. This material will fill and hide them.

Lightly sand the product where glue was removed or where marks and dents were repaired. Then remove dust from the surface with a fine bristle brush, vacuum cleaner, or clean, dry rag. Now the surface should be ready for finish.

There are several methods to apply liquid coating materials. They are brushing, dipping, rolling, spraying, and wiping. Available equipment usually determines which method you select. Brushing is common for stains, sealers, and almost all built-up topcoatings. Dipping is a quick way to coat small components. Rolling covers large surfaces quickly. Spraying is often used because it gives a quality finish while, at the same time, allowing you to cover large areas quickly, Fig. 6-14. Wiping is done by hand with a lintless cloth pad. Bleaches, stains, and penetrating finishes are often applied by this method.

HEALTH CONSIDERATIONS

Concern for personal health should be given throughout the cabinetmaking process. The finishing process presents some special concerns. Are the vapors toxic? Are they flammable? If they are toxic, you should wear a respirator and possibly rubber gloves and protective clothing. If the finishing materials are toxic, you should use them in a finishing room or in a ventilated area free from heat and open flames.

Fig. 6-14. Spraying is an efficient method of applying finishing materials. (DeVILBISS)

ENVIRONMENTAL DECISIONS

Several finishing conditions relate to the environment. The area should be well ventilated to exhaust fumes and dust. Dust can settle on the wet surface and cause roughness. Try to control the temperature where the work is to be done. Some materials have a minimum and maximum range, such as 65° to 75°. This information is found on the container label. Also have adequate lighting so you can tell whether the finish covers evenly or has dry spots, sags, or runs.

INSTALLING HARDWARE

The last step in the cabinetmaking procedure is installing hardware. Much of the hardware should have been fitted before finishing. This way screw holes will have been drilled during assembly. Marking on and drilling through a finish can crack or peel it. If drilling holes and aligning hardware is necessary, apply masking tape first. Then mark hole centers on the tape. Next, drill through the tape along with the wood. If a hinge or lock must be mortised, lay that out on tape also. If sawing is required, tape helps prevent chipping the wood fibers.

WORKING YOUR PLAN

Working to complete a high quality cabinet is your goal. Following the set plan of procedure is the means to achieving your goal. Safety, health, and efficiency are major concerns while processing materials.

The environment in which you work should be safe. It must be ventilated well and have a dust collection system. Approved fire extinguishers should be nearby. Temperature and humidity should be controlled as they affect the setting and curing time of adhesives and finishes. Excessive moisture can also cause lumber to warp. Leftover materials must be disposed of or stored in containers meeting OSHA (Occupational Safety and Health Administration) standards.

Protect yourself as well. Wear gloves when working with irritating substances or hot materials. Wear a respirator when finishing or creating dust. Always wear safety eyewear when operating machines.

SUMMARY

This chapter has summarized the topics you will discover in the remainder of the text, especially those which concern procedures for making production decisions. It serves to acquaint you to the problems of production and considerations made during the cabinetmaking process.

The plan of procedure is your guide for making production decisions. A well thought out and documented plan will save you hours of frustration and wasted materials. It will also challenge you to find new uses for available tools.

CABINETMAKING TERMS

Production decisions, plan of procedure, stock, workpiece, component.

TEST YOUR KNOWLEDGE

1. Planning is essential so you do not waste _____ and _____.
2. The "what to do" steps are listed in the _____.
3. List the production steps and provide a sample decision you must make in each of those steps.
4. Workpiece sizes are likely to be listed in the bill of materials. True or False?
5. A cabinet produced in a well equipped shop is higher in quality than one produced with limited tools. True or False?
6. In cabinetmaking, PO means:
   a. Plane off.
   b. Point-of-operation.
   c. Put into operation.
   d. Portable tools only.
7. The most common indication of a dull tool is:
   a. Burn marks.
   b. Planer marks.
   c. Rough knots.
   d. Saw tooth marks.

8. Carbide-edged tools are recommended for cutting _____ and _____.
9. Supplies refers to any material that will become part of the finished product. True or False?
10. When rough cutting stock to make cabinet parts, you should:
    a. Cut the workpieces the exact dimension of the finish part.
    b. First surface the lumber.
    c. Cut the workpieces oversize.
    d. Cut the workpieces undersize.
11. Why does S4S lumber save time in squaring workpieces to size?
12. It is just as easy to square wide boards using portable power tools as it is using stationary power tools. True or False?
13. It is easier to make joints after shaping the workpiece than it is to make them before shaping. True or False?
14. Why should you use a medium abrasive before a fine abrasive?
15. Explain how a built-up finish is different from a penetrating finish.

Provide brief answers to the next five questions based on your understanding of this chapter.
16. Generally, why would you not finish the individual parts of a cabinet before assembling them with glue?
17. Why is it, in most cases, desirable to use stationary power tools rather than portable power tools?
18. What factors should you consider when deciding whether to make or buy a certain part of the cabinet?
19. In what case would you cut, assemble, and smooth components, but not apply a finish?
20. What factors affect the time you must spend to develop a plan of procedure?

Chapter 7
USING WORKING DRAWINGS

After studying this chapter, you will be able to:
☐ Describe the types of working drawings used by cabinetmakers.
☐ List the parts of a working drawing.
☐ Identify the importance of specifications.

Working drawings are the link between designing and building a product, Fig. 7-1. A set of *working drawings* contains both drawings and specifications. The *drawings* illustrate the product. The *specifications* list the materials and supplies. Working drawings should be prepared for every product.

A complete set of working drawings has all the necessary information to produce the cabinet. This will include views of the product showing style and features. These views will detail the size and jointwork required for different parts of the cabinet.

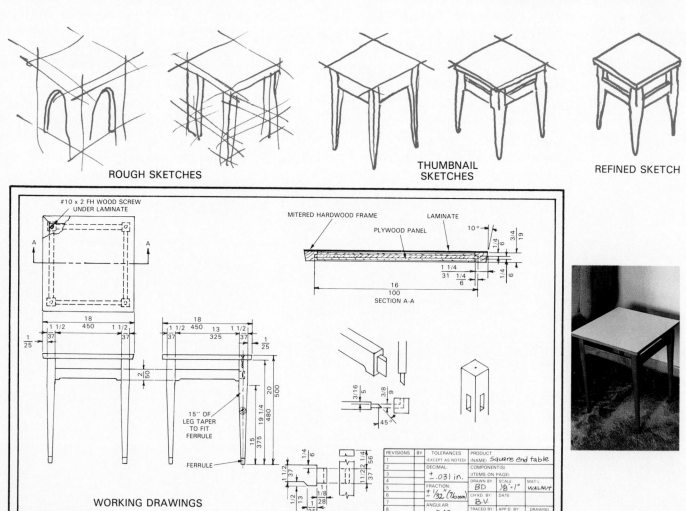

ROUGH SKETCHES   THUMBNAIL SKETCHES   REFINED SKETCH

WORKING DRAWINGS

Fig. 7-1. Working drawings made to accurately show size and features of the product. The product is then built using specifications of the drawing.

Working drawings also include dimensions, materials, supplies, and a plan of procedure.

Working drawings record decisions made during the design process. They also standardize the building of a certain cabinet. For example, two cabinets produced from the same set of drawings should be identical. This occurs if the builders have equal amounts of cabinetmaking skill.

Commercial drawings of cabinet products can be purchased. These would only be used if the drawings meet your design needs. Using purchased drawings will eliminate the time consuming design process. They are pretested for function, strength and appearance. You can modify these drawings if they do not exactly fit your design needs. However, be careful not to alter parts which are essential for the strength of the product.

TYPES OF DRAWINGS

Cabinetmakers work from prints or original drawings. The prints are copies call whiteprints or blueprints. *Whiteprints* are white with blue lines to show the drawings. *Blueprints* use a blue background with white lines for the drawing.

There are two types of drawings the cabinetmaker commonly uses. They are architectural drawings and shop drawings.

ARCHITECTURAL DRAWINGS

Architectural drawings are used by contractors to construct the home. They are also used by interior designers to plan for furnishings. The cabinetmaker needs floor plans, elevations, material specifications, and work schedules shown on the architectural drawings. These drawings will determine the size and style of cabinets to be built.

Floor plans

Floor plans explain where built-in cabinetry is to be located. In a kitchen, placement of the sink, cooking unit, refrigerator, and other major appliances are given. Utilities, such as electricity, gas, and plumbing for major appliances are shown as symbols, Fig. 7-2.

Elevations

Elevations are used to represent vertical views of built-in cabinetry. They show the view you would see when positioned in front of the cabinet, Fig. 7-3. Elevations are used primarily for kitchens. They may be used for bathrooms, utility rooms, recreational rooms, or any other room with built-in cabinetry.

Material specifications

Material specifications list the types of lumber, moulding, or paneling to use. They will also identify styles of hinges, pulls, catches, and other hardware. Finishing materials, such as stain, varnish, and countertop laminate also would be prescribed.

Work schedule

The suggested *work schedule* tells the cabinetmaker when to install built-in cabinetry. This is essential for new construction due to the many per-

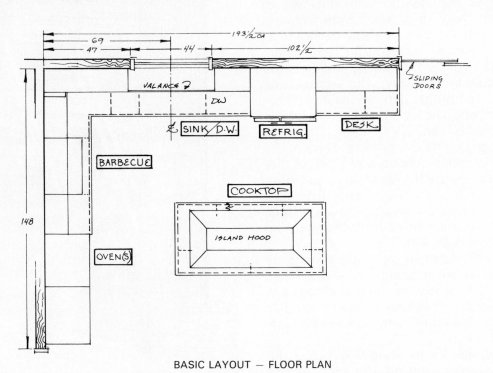

BASIC LAYOUT — FLOOR PLAN

Fig. 7-2. A floor plan shows layout of utilities, cabinets, and major appliances.   (Wood-Mode)

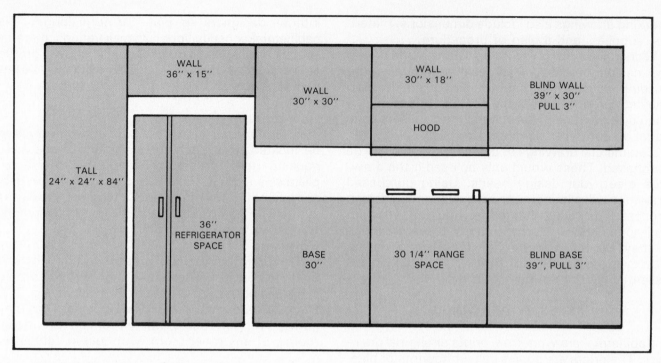

Fig. 7-3. An elevation shows a "real life" view of the structure when finished. (American Woodmark Corp.)

sons working at the same time. Plumbers and electricians may need to install utilities before the cabinets are installed. The work schedule may also call for wall finishings to be done before cabinets are installed.

SHOP DRAWINGS

Shop drawings are used by cabinetmakers to build a product. They are different from architectural drawings in that they only show the product. They do not show the surrounding furnishings. Shop drawings usually accompany architectural drawings for built-in cabinetry. The architectural drawing shows the proper dimensions and placement of the cabinets. The shop drawings detail how the cabinet is to be built.

Shop drawings include one or more *views* of the product, material specifications, and a plan of procedure. The views show details of sizes and jointwork necessary to produce the product. Individual parts and their dimensions are also shown. A three dimensional view is frequently included to represent the assembled product, Fig. 7-4.

The *material specifications* on shop drawings are similar to those used in architectural drawings. However, the material specifications in shop drawings cover specific pieces and hardware used to build the product. Individual manufacturers for parts are sometimes noted.

The *plan of procedure* for shop drawings is different than the work schedule for architectural drawings. The shop plan lists, in order, the separate

operations to construct the cabinet. Each part and the machine used to produce it is given.

Fig. 7-5 shows a set of shop drawings including views, materials, supplies, and plan of procedure.

Fig. 7-4. A pictorial view of the cabinet is often included in shop drawings. (Sauder)

Supplies

Assorted abrasives
Adhesive
Filler (for countersunk nail holes)
Stain (if desired for natural finish)
Sealer*
Top coating* (clear or opaque)
*If opaque paint is used, eliminate stain and sealer and apply primer and paint.

Plan of Procedure

Cabinet body sub-assembly
1. Square all components to size.
2. Saw 45° corners on A and G.
3. Make dado cuts in B, C, and D.
4. Make rabbet cuts in C, D, and J.
5. Bevel C and D.
6. Drill 1/4'' dowel holes 9/16'' deep in E and F. (Two are needed in each joint.)
7. Angle drill 1/4'' holes 9/16'' deep in D and E. (Five are needed for each joint.)
8. Make a dry run assembly (no adhesive) of B, C, D, E, F, and G. Use 10 V dowels between D and E. Use 4 U dowels between E and F.
9. Check for squareness.
10. Disassemble and smooth surface, edge, and end grain except where glue will be applied.
11. Glue B, C, D, E, F, and G with appropriate dowels. Drive nails through B and C into the edges of both G shelves.
12. Remove excess adhesive from the cabinet body sub-assembly before it begins to set.
13. Cut, shape, fit, and install mouldings L and M with glue and brads.

Knickknack shelf sub-assembly
14. Saw H, J, and K to shape.
15. Smooth the grain on the irregular edges and surfaces of H, J, and K.
16. Glue, nail, and remove excess adhesive on H, J, and K knickknack shelf sub-assembly.

17. Align knickknack shelf in the corner under the A bottom.
18. Drill 1/4'' dowel holes through A and 1 3/8'' into H and J.
19. Glue, nail, and remove excess adhesive from sub-assembly.

Cabinet top and bottom installation
20. Shape the visible edges of both A components.
21. Glue, nail, countersink, and remove excessive adhesive from joints where the A components are installed.

Panel door sub-assembly
22. Make rabbet joints on both Q components.
23. Make blind rabbet joints on both P components.
24. Drill U dowel holes 1 1/16'' deep in P and Q.
25. Assemble door without adhesive.
26. Inspect for squareness.
27. Glue door frame sub-assembly together.
28. Remove any excess for the corners of the blind rabbets as needed to allow for the door panel.
29. Fit the door frame sub-assembly in the door opening with 1/16'' space on each side.
30. Install the door on its hinges.
31. Position the latch mechanism.
32. Remove the hinges and latch.
33. Make 8° bevels on edges and ends of N.
34. Abrade and fit panel into door frame sub-assembly with 1/32'' space on the sides and ends. This allows for expansion and contraction.
35. Remove the panel.
36. Inspect all surfaces of sub-assemblies and remove blemishes.

Disassemble and finish
37. Apply the desired finish to all sub-assemblies and the latch if it is wood.

Final assembly
38. Install the door panel with two wood screws and washers on the panel ends near the corners. (Mechanical fasteners allow for panel expansion and contraction due to humidity.)
39. Reinstall the latch.
40. Rehang the door.

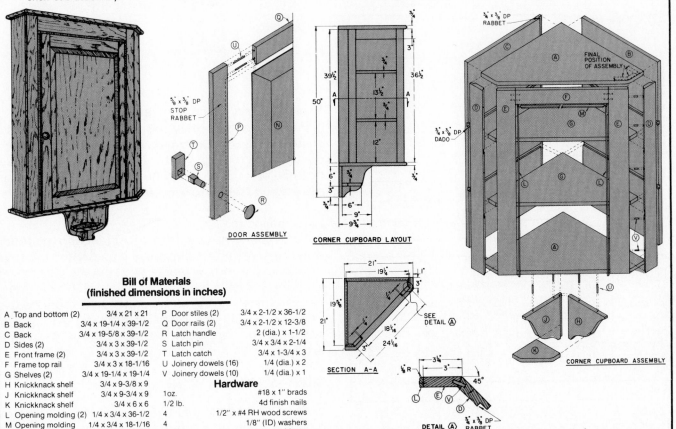

DOOR ASSEMBLY

CORNER CUPBOARD LAYOUT

SECTION A-A

DETAIL A

CORNER CUPBOARD ASSEMBLY

Bill of Materials
(finished dimensions in inches)

A Top and bottom (2)	3/4 x 21 x 21
B Back	3/4 x 19-1/4 x 39-1/2
C Back	3/4 x 19-5/8 x 39-1/2
D Sides (2)	3/4 x 3 x 39-1/2
E Front frame (2)	3/4 x 3 x 39-1/2
F Frame top rail	3/4 x 3 x 18-1/16
G Shelves (2)	3/4 x 19-1/4 x 19-1/4
H Knickknack shelf	3/4 x 9-3/8 x 9
J Knickknack shelf	3/4 x 9-3/4 x 9
K Knickknack shelf	3/4 x 6 x 6
L Opening molding (2)	1/4 x 3/4 x 36-1/2
M Opening molding	1/4 x 3/4 x 18-1/16
N Door panel	3/4 x 32-1/2 x 13-3/8

P Door stiles (2)	3/4 x 2-1/2 x 36-1/2
Q Door rails (2)	3/4 x 2-1/2 x 12-3/8
R Latch handle	2 (dia.) x 1-1/2
S Latch pin	3/4 x 3/4 x 2-1/4
T Latch catch	3/4 x 1-3/4 x 3
U Joinery dowels (16)	1/4 (dia.) x 2
V Joinery dowels (10)	1/4 (dia.) x 1

Hardware

1oz.	#18 x 1'' brads
1/2 lb.	4d finish nails
4	1/2'' x #4 RH wood screws
4	1/8'' (ID) washers
1 pair	hinges

Fig. 7-5. Most shop drawings include a plan of procedure to assist the cabinetmaker during construction. (Shopsmith)

READING SHOP DRAWINGS

There is a logical order to follow when reading shop drawings.
1. Note the information in the title block.
2. Look at the views (pictorial, multiview, section, and details).
3. Check the list of materials.
4. Review the plan of procedure.

TITLE BLOCK

The *title block* is a rectangular space on each page of the set of drawings, Fig. 7-6. It provides information on the product such as:
1. Product, or project name (building name for architectural drawings).
2. Scale of the drawing.
3. A page or drawing number along with the total number of sheets.
4. Revisions of the original drawings.

The title block is essential in shop drawings. It specifies the name of the drawings and number of sheets as well as other identifying information. These items are used to determine which project the drawings are for, who drew them, and the scale of the drawings. The scale indicated on the title block can be used if a critical dimensional is missing. A rule can be used to measure the part.

REVISIONS	BY	(BLDG. NAME AND/OR ADDRESS)		
1				
2		SCALE:	DRAWN BY:	APPROVED BY:
3		DATE		
4		(INFORMATION ON THIS PAGE)		
5				
6				
7				
8			DRAWING NO.	
9			OF	

REVISIONS	BY	TOLERANCES	PRODUCT		
1		(EXCEPT AS NOTED)	(NAME)		
2		DECIMAL:	COMPONENT(S)		
3			(ITEMS ON PAGE)		
4			DRAWN BY:	SCALE:	MAT'L.
5		FRACTION:			
6			CH'KD. BY:	DATE:	
7					
8		ANGULAR:	TRACED BY:	APP'D. BY:	DRAWING
9					OF

SHOP DRAWING

Fig. 7-6. The title block identifies the product, designer, and important information about the drawings.

PICTORIAL VIEWS

A *pictorial view* may be either a photograph or a line drawing. It represents a picture of the final product. More than one surface is usually shown. Dimensions are added if no other views are included in the set of shop drawings. If dimensions are included, they are overall dimensions of the product, Fig. 7-7.

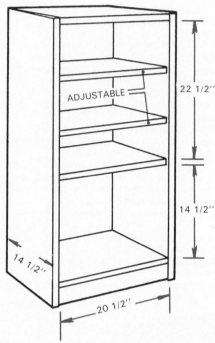

Fig. 7-7. Dimensions may be included on the pictorial view. (Sauder)

Exploded and assembly views

Pictorial views may be exploded views and assembly views. *Exploded views* show the product disassembled, Fig. 7-8. *Assembly views* have dotted lines which show how the product is to be assembled. Refer to Fig. 7-5.

Parts balloons

Parts balloons are often included on pictorial drawings. A parts balloon is a circle with an arrow attached. The arrow points to a specific part of the product. Inside the balloon, a symbol (letter, number) is written which corresponds to a separate list of parts. Using the pictorial drawing with parts balloons, you can see where a part fits in the overall product.

MULTI-VIEW DRAWING

Multi-view drawings use two or more views to describe the product. It provides most of the information necessary to plan and build the cabinet.

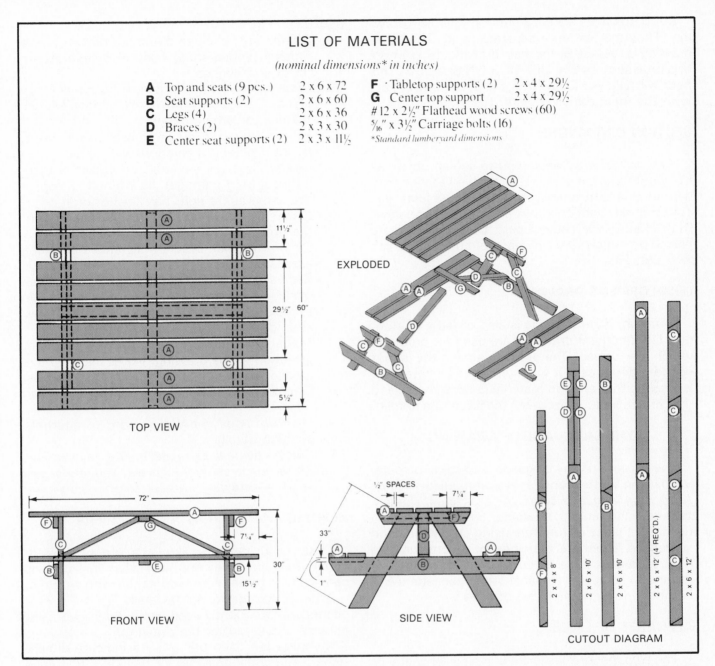

LIST OF MATERIALS
(nominal dimensions* in inches)

A Top and seats (9 pcs.)   2 x 6 x 72
B Seat supports (2)   2 x 6 x 60
C Legs (4)   2 x 6 x 36
D Braces (2)   2 x 3 x 30
E Center seat supports (2)   2 x 3 x 11½

F · Tabletop supports (2)   2 x 4 x 29½
G Center top support   2 x 4 x 29½
#12 x 2½" Flathead wood screws (60)
5⁄16" x 3½" Carriage bolts (16)
*Standard lumberyard dimensions

EXPLODED

TOP VIEW

FRONT VIEW

SIDE VIEW

CUTOUT DIAGRAM

Fig. 7-8. A three view drawing is the most important part of shop drawings. Exploded views and cutout diagrams assist the cabinetmaker. Parts balloons help relate component parts in each view. (Shopsmith)

Multi-view drawings include two-view and three-view drawings.

Two-view drawing

Two-view drawings are used for cylindrical objects, such as those turned on a lathe. Examples are lamp stems, chair spindles, and round table legs. On these objects, a top view of the object would be the same as a front view. Therefore, only a side or end view and a front view are shown.

Three-view drawing

The *three-view drawing* is the most common shop drawing, Fig. 7-8. Typically, the front, side, and top views are shown. Lines which can be seen are called visible lines and are drawn solid. Lines which cannot be seen (joints, inside shelves) are shown by a series of dashes called hidden lines. With so many lines representing the product, detail drawings are often included. They reduce congestion or confusion in a multi-view drawing.

DETAIL DRAWINGS

Detail drawings are used as helping drawings. Individual components or joints are drawn separately. Notes are included to describe special features or procedures.

Detail drawings are separate from the main drawing. They may be on a separate page. The detail drawing is referred to the main drawing using letters or a note such as SEE DETAIL 3 ON SHEET 2. This note will help you locate how the detail drawing fits with the main drawing. Refer to Fig. 7-5.

SECTION DRAWINGS

Section drawings allow you to see an object as if material was cut away. The removed section may be part of a joint to let you see how the joint was constructed. Section views are also used to show the material of a cabinet part. Diagonal lines are placed in section views to represent material which was cut, Fig. 7-9.

DEVELOPMENT DRAWING

A *development drawing* is also called a stretch-out. Development drawings are used for products which are formed. The drawing shows the layout of the product as if it were unfolded or flattened. It assures that enough material is used to achieve the correct produce size when the pieces are formed.

THE LANGUAGE OF DRAWING

The purpose of any language is to communicate. Verbal and written languages communicate ideas. A *drawing language* communicates lines, shapes, texture, and color. It would be impossible to describe a piece of furniture using only words and sentences. Therefore, drawings must communicate how a product is to be built. Drawing languages include an additional alphabet other than letters and numbers. It is the alphabet of lines.

ALPHABET OF LINES

The *alphabet of lines* is the universal language of drafting. Each line communicates by its form and thickness, Fig. 7-10.

1. *Border lines* enclose the entire drawing for a finished appearance. They also separate individual drawings.
2. *Visible lines* form the outline of the object they enclose. They may form circles, triangles, rectangles, or other shapes.
3. *Hidden lines* illustrate an edge or corner which is not visible in a given view.
4. *Center lines* tell you that an object is symmetrical (mirror image). Its left half (or top) is the same as its right half (or bottom).
5. *Extension lines* mark the edges or corners of the product which must be dimensioned.
6. *Dimension lines* describe distances between extension lines.
7. *Radius lines* show dimensions of arcs and circles. An arrow points from the dimension to the edge of the arc or circle. Another arrow extends from the center to the edge.
8. *Leader lines* have one arrowhead. They direct attention to the drawing. Notes usually have a leader line to point to the object they discuss.
9. *Section lines* indicate material in a section view.
10. *Phantom lines* show alignment or alternate position details.
11. *Cutting plane lines* reveal a cutaway section. Arrowheads show which way the reader will see the cutaway surface (section view).

ALPHABET OF LETTERS AND NUMBERS

Letters and numbers, like lines, are symbols of communication. They are used when instructions can be given better with words than with pictures.

At times, words are abbreviated, Fig. 7-11. This occurs with frequently used terms. Entire words or phrases would clutter the drawing.

Numbers are used primarily to indicate dimensions. Critical dimensions will include a tolerance distance. On some shop drawings a global tolerance

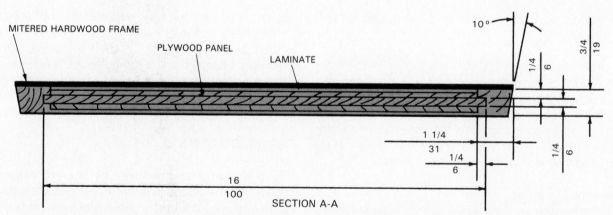

Fig. 7-9. A section view is a cutaway view. It shows the materials of which the part is made.

	MM	TECHNICAL FOUNTAIN PEN	NO.	INCHES	
	0.8	0.8	3	.030	BORDER LINE
THICK	0.5	0.5	2	.020	VISIBLE OUTLINE
MEDIUM	0.4	0.4	1	.015	HIDDEN OUTLINE
THIN	0.3	0.3	0	.011	CENTER LINE
THIN	0.3	0.3	0	.011	EXTENSION, DIMENSION, CROSS SECTION LINES
THICK	0.5	0.5	2	.020	CUTTING PLANE LINE

Fig. 7-10. Line styles are used to represent different aspects of the drawing.

is given in the title block. This tolerance refers to all dimensions in the drawing. Individual tolerances are given as: 3 1/2 in. ± 1/64 in. Therefore, the dimension can range from 3 31/64 to 3 33/64. Tolerances are widely used for mass production of cabinets. The tolerance assures quality control in the product. For custom, or limited production, cabinetry tolerances are not necessary.

The alphabet of lines and alphabet of letters and numbers are essential when reading working drawings. In addition, you must be able to read specifications. This must be done before starting to work on a product.

ABBREVIATIONS			
Architectural Drawings			
CLG	—ceiling	MIN	—minimum
FLR	—flooring	MAX	—maximum
BC, OC	—between or on center	LG	—length
CAB	—cabinet	HGT	—height
CLO	—closet	DW	—dishwasher
CL, C	—center line	REFR	—refrigerator
CTR	—counter	VAN	—vanity
Shop Drawings			
CL, C	—center line	CTR	—counter
R	—radius	FIN	—finish
DIA	—diameter	LAM	—laminate
ASSY	—assembly	MAX	—maximum
AVG	—average	MIN	—minimum
DIM	—dimension	NO, #	—number
DWG	—drawing	RD	—round
ID	—inside diameter	W/	—with
OD	—outside diameter	WO/	—without

Fig. 7-11. Abbreviations reduce the text required in a drawing.

READING SPECIFICATIONS

Specifications list the materials and supplies for producing the product. Architectural drawing specifications are general. They include kind of wood, stain, color, etc. Shop drawings include precise material specifications. The individual manufacturer of the product is often noted. Some items found in specifications include:
1. Solid lumber (kind, size, quality).
2. Wood products (plywood, hardboard).
3. Specialty woods (veneers, inlays, overlays).
4. Hardware (hinges, catches, pulls).
5. Fasteners (adhesives, nails, screws).
6. Finishing materials (abrasives, stain type and manufacturer, top coat).
7. Other components (dowel rods, glass, ceramics, plastic).

Supplies include all items needed to build the cabinet. They should be acquired before work begins. The supplies a cabinetmaker should acquire include machines, abrasives, and special tools. Having to find or buy supplies after work begins can result in wasted material and time.

PLAN OF PROCEDURE

The *plan of procedure* generally is included in shop drawings. It provides a sequence of steps to build a product, refer to Fig. 7-6. Some operations do not have to follow a sequence. Other operations can be accomplished only after a previous operation is complete.

SUMMARY

Working drawings are the link between design and completion of the product. A cabinetmaker must be able to interpret the information found on working drawings.

The two categories of working drawings are architectural and shop drawings. Architectural drawings include floor plans, elevations, specifications, and work schedule. Shop drawings contain pictorial drawings, orthographic drawings, details, specifications, and a plan of procedure.

Working drawings communicate a product with the alphabet of lines, letters, and numbers. The alphabet of lines is the universal language for illustrating a product. Letter or number abbreviations specify different materials needed to build a product.

Working drawings include both drawings and specifications. Specifications list materials and supplies. Architectural specifications are more general. Shop specifications give a precise list of material and supply types, quantities, and often their manufacturer.

A plan of procedure guides the cabinetmaker in building the product. It lists the machines and operations used to shape the various parts.

CABINETMAKING TERMS

Working drawings, specifications, whiteprint, blueprint, architectural drawings, floor plan, elevations, material specifications, work schedule, shop drawings, views, plan of procedure, title block, pictorial view, exploded view, parts balloon, multiview drawing, two-view drawing, three-view drawing, detail drawings, component details, section drawing, development drawing, drawing language, alphabet of lines, border lines, visible lines, hidden lines, center lines, extension lines, dimension lines, radius lines, leader lines, section lines, phantom lines, cutting-plane lines, supplies.

TEST YOUR KNOWLEDGE

1. Prints of working drawings can be either _____ or _____.
2. The two types of drawings used by the cabinetmaker to produce built-in cabinets are _____ and _____.
3. Material specifications for architectural drawings contain what information?
4. How is a work schedule for architectural construction different than the plan of procedure used in shop drawings?
5. What information is found in a shop drawing?
6. The title block of a working drawing contains:
    a. Alphabet of lines.
    b. Name of the designer.
    c. Parts balloons.
    d. Material specifications.
7. Why is a two-view drawing made for cylindrical parts rather than a three-view drawing?
8. Sketch the following lines.
    a. Visible line.
    b. Center line.
    c. Hidden edge line.
    d. Extension and dimension lines.
9. The minimum size of part dimensioned 4 1/4 ± 1/8 would be:
    a. 4 3/8.
    b. 4 1/8.
    c. 4 15/64.
    d. 4 15/32.
10. Shop specifications list _____ and _____.

Chapter 8
MAKING SKETCHES AND MOCK-UPS

After studying this chapter, you will be able to:
☐ Identify the types of sketches used to design cabinetry.
☐ Describe how mock-ups are used to analyze a design.
☐ Apply the techniques of sketching to draw isometric, cabinet, and perspective sketches.

Sketches and mock-ups are useful aids when designing, laying out, and producing cabinetry. The old saying that a picture is worth a thousand words is very appropriate to sketching. A quickly made sketch conveys information which would be difficult to describe otherwise. A *sketch* records your ideas and makes communications easier.

Sketching is part of the design process. Sketches are made to record ideas for a product. Later, they are relied upon for preparing working drawings. During production, sketches are made also. They may show changes in the original design. Some might refer to machine or equipment setups.

Mock-ups are three dimensional replicas of your design made of convenient inexpensive materials. They could be paper, cardboard, or scrap wood. They are used for analysis of your design before the product is built. The mock-up may be a full scale replica or a scaled-down version of the product.

TYPES OF SKETCHES

Sketches may be either rough, thumbnail, or refined sketches. The kind you choose depends on the desired accuracy of the sketch. *Rough sketches* provide simple outlines and very little detail. *Thumbnail sketches* represent the product with more accuracy. Refined sketches add specific details, such as dimensions and materials, Fig. 8-1.

SKETCHING

Sketching communicates ideas with a drawing. Some sketches show several surfaces of an object. Most are drawn in three dimensions. Suppose you are planning to build a small table. You first get a picture of it in your mind. Then you draw the front,

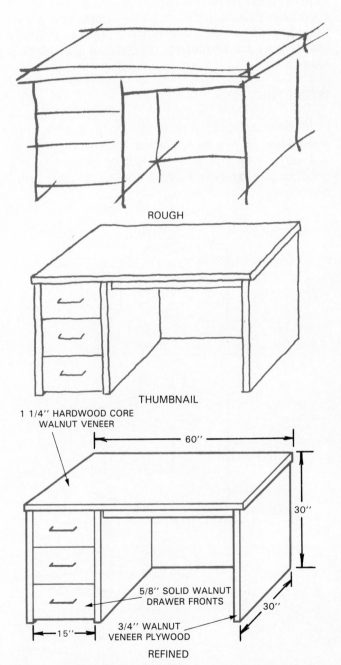

ROUGH

THUMBNAIL

1 1/4'' HARDWOOD CORE WALNUT VENEER

60''

30''

5/8'' SOLID WALNUT DRAWER FRONTS

30''

15''

3/4'' WALNUT VENEER PLYWOOD

REFINED

Fig. 8-1. Top. Rough sketches only show outlines of a design. They have very little detail. Middle. Thumbnail sketches add details to accurately show the product. Bottom. Refined sketches include most information to be put on a working drawing.

top, and side views. These three views come together to show what the product will look like when it is finished. Three dimensional sketches are called pictorial sketches.

PICTORIAL SKETCHES

Three dimensional sketches, called *pictorial views*, are best suited for cabinetry and furniture. How the product is drawn depends on your eye level. A product which sits on the floor would likely show the top, front, and side views. A product which hangs from the ceiling would be drawn as if you were viewing it from below. Here, you would include front, side, and bottom views. Pictorial views may be isometric, cabinet, or perspective sketches.

ISOMETRIC

An *isometric sketch* represents a product as seen from a corner, Fig. 8-2. Vertical lines of the product are vertical on the sketch. Horizontal lines of the product are shown in true length at 30° from horizontal in the drawing.

CABINET

A *cabinet drawing sketch* represents a product if it was viewed from the front. The front view will be a true shape. To add depth, lines representing the side of the object are drawn half length at a 45° angle, refer to Fig. 8-2.

PERSPECTIVE

Perspective sketches rarely are used in cabinet-making. They represent a true view of an object, yet they are hard to sketch. The farther objects are away from you, the smaller they appear to be. On paper, this is accomplished with vanishing lines. Increased depth will be smaller in size, Fig. 8-2.

TECHNIQUES OF SKETCHING

There are four skills for successful sketching. The first is to grip the pencil with the fingers as though you were writing. The second is to keep your wrist flexible. The third is to maintain free arm movement. The fourth skill is coordination of the grip, wrist, and arm to create straight and curved lines.

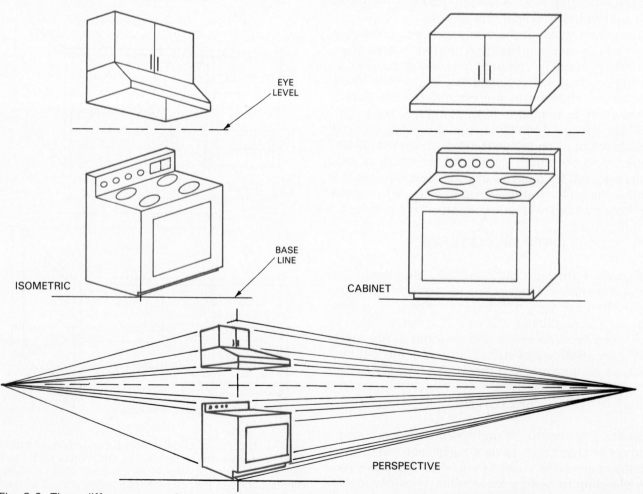

Fig. 8-2. Three different types of pictorial sketches. Notice how the isometric and cabinet sketches distort the object.

All lines are drawn lightly at first. Then darken those lines which best enclose the object.

STRAIGHT LINES

As you have seen in the previous figures, horizontal, vertical, and diagonal lines are used in most sketches. Sketching should illustrate an object as you would see it. With nine straight lines, the surfaces of a cube can be enclosed, Fig. 8-3.

When learning to sketch, *graph paper* or *isometric grid paper* is helpful. Follow the printed lines of the paper to keep your lines parallel, Fig. 8-4. Practice

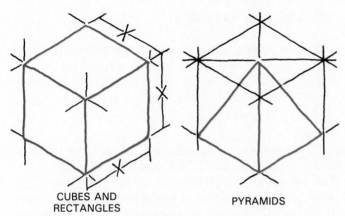

CUBES AND
RECTANGLES   PYRAMIDS

Fig. 8-3. Straight lines sketches are easiest to create.

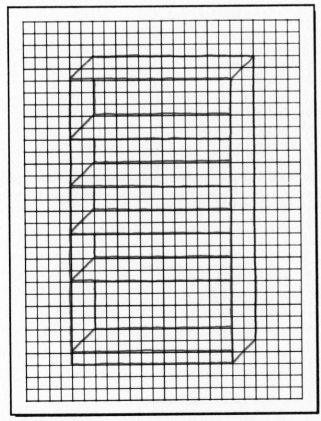

Fig. 8-4. Grid paper is used to help keep sketched lines straight.

will help you to develop coordination of your fingers, wrist, and arm.

For the beginner, horizontal lines are the easiest to control. Each line of the object can be drawn horizontally by turning the paper as the angles of lines change. As you gain experience, vertical and angled lines can be drawn without moving the paper.

With experience, you can use unlined paper. First, mark the end points of the lines. Then add short line segments between the two points, guiding the pencil between starting and stopping points. Reposition your hand for each segment until the desired length is reached.

Cabinet sketches

When creating a cabinet drawing, first sketch the horizontal line of the base, Fig. 8-5. Then cross the horizontal line with light vertical lines indicating the sides and important front features of the cabinet. Then complete the front, darkening the lines which

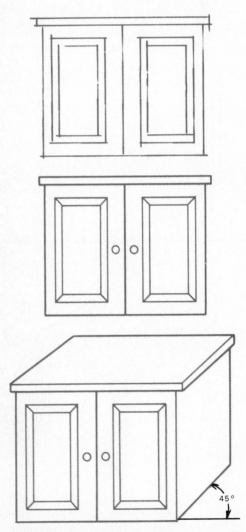

Fig. 8-5. The steps in sketching a cabinet drawing. Top. Light outlines. Middle. Darken lines which accurately outline the object. Bottom. Lines are added to show depth.

enclose parts of the cabinet. You can then draw lines to indicate depth. Remember, depth lines are half length at a 30° to 60° angle.

Isometric sketches

To sketch an isometric drawing, first sketch a horizontal line. Next, cross the horizontal line with a light vertical line. From the intersection of these two lines, draw lines at a 30° angle from horizontal, Fig. 8-6. The intersection of these five lines

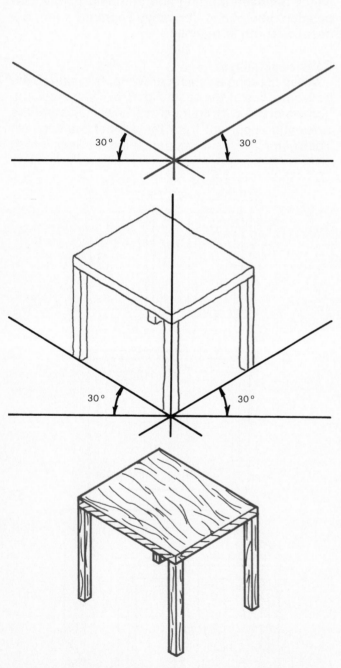

Fig. 8-6. The steps in sketching an isometric drawing. Top. One vertical and two 30° lines make up the front corner of the object. Middle. All horizontal lines of the product are drawn at 30° on an isometric sketch while vertical lines remain vertical. Bottom. The final drawing with unnecessary lines erased.

forms the lower front corner of your design. From here, other lines can be added to complete the drawing.

CURVED LINES

Curved lines are more difficult to sketch than straight lines. A good method is to lightly sketch different points which the curve will pass through. Then sketch light, curved lines to connect these points. Make sure the transition from point to point is smooth. It should not look like a "connect-the-dots" puzzle.

CIRCLES AND ELLIPSES

Circles appear on views which are seen by looking straight at the front, top, or side of an object. An *ellipse* is used to represent circles viewed at an angle. The ellipse appears to be an egg shape.

Circles

The easiest way to create a circle is to trace it. Draw around a coin of the approximate diameter. You can also sketch a circle within a square. First draw a square the size of the diameter of the circle. Then draw diagonals between corners of the square. Mark the radius measurement from the intersection of the diagonals toward each corner. Then draw a circle using the radius marks and the sides of the square, Fig. 8-7.

Ellipses

Ellipses represent circles viewed at an angle. They will be found on all sides of isometric or perspective sketches. On cabinet drawing sketches, ellipses are used on the top and side views.

To sketch an ellipse, first draw an isometric square the size of the diameter of the circle. The isometric square will appear as a diamond shape. Locate the center of the circle and draw isometric center lines. Now draw arcs between the center lines to complete the ellipse, Fig. 8-8.

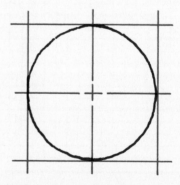

Fig. 8-7. Circles are best sketched within a square.

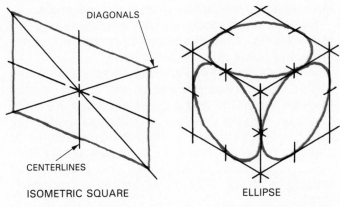

Fig. 8-8. Ellipses are drawn in an isometric square which resembles a diamond.

PERSPECTIVES

Perspective sketches are more difficult to prepare. Only vertical lines are parallel to each other. Horizontal lines all are aimed at a vanishing point. Equally spaced vertical distances get closer as they approach the vanishing points, Fig. 8-9.

The size of objects in perspective sketches can only be estimated. First identify two vanishing points on each side of the object. Draw a vertical line at the intersection of two lines. All horizontal lines lead to these vanishing points. The horizontal lines are drawn less than actual size. The only vertical part of the drawing with true length is the vertical line at the intersection. The height of each part of the object is measured on this vertical line.

DIMENSION LINES

Dimensioning on sketches is relatively simple. Be sure that extension lines are made in the intended direction. Keep dimension lines parallel to the edge being measured. Adding overall width, length, and height dimensions to a sketch may be very useful.

DEVELOPING MOCK-UPS

A *mock-up* is used to represent a product without wasting expensive wood or other materials. Decisions based on a working drawing may not be adequate. Mock-ups help solve design and building problems. With a mock-up, the product can be seen in three-dimensional form. It is built of paper, cardboard, foam board, and glue or tape. There are two kinds of mock-ups: appearance mock-ups and hard mock-ups.

APPEARANCE MOCK-UP

An *appearance mock-up* looks like the final product; however, it is not functional. For example, a

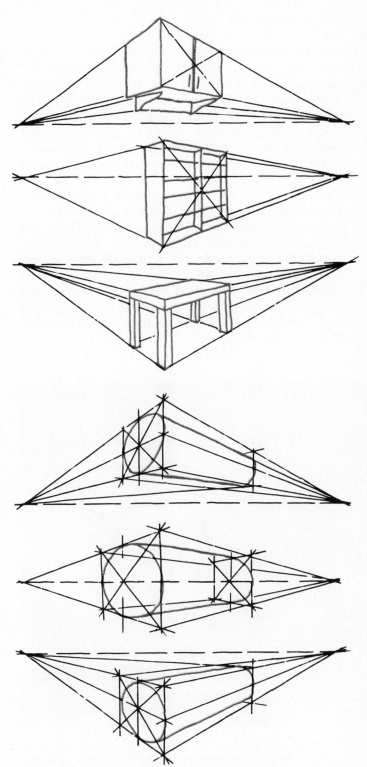

Fig. 8-9. Perspective sketches are the most difficult to draw; yet, they most accurately show the product.

cardboard box may be covered with wood grain contact paper to make it resemble a silverware chest. Handles and knobs could be attached to make it more realistic. This three-dimensional representation of the product lets you see its final appearance. To analyze function, a hard mock-up is made.

HARD MOCK-UP

Hard mock-ups are working models of the product. They may be fully or partially functional. For example, the cardboard lid and drawer of the silverware chest mentioned above would move. The silverware could be placed inside to see if it fits. You could also determine the final arrangement of pieces. This is a fully functional hard mock-up.

Hard mock-ups also are used to adapt products to people. For example, a mock-up might be built to test the use of a product with a person in a wheelchair. Can the person reach objects in or on the cabinet? Do the doors open easily? These are human factors. The mock-up may not be fully functional. It may not have dividers in the drawers for silverware. However, the major parts of the product are functional to test reach, space, and comfort. Mock-ups are often used in the automotive and aerospace industries to test human factors. Refer to Fig. 8-10.

Fig. 8-10. Hard mock-ups have movable parts to test for human comfort. Here, a research pilot checks line of sight to instrument panel and reach to controls.

SUMMARY

The value of sketches and mock-ups is to present a design solution. A sketch might illustrate a product to be built. It could describe a jig or fixture for production. A mock-up may represent the basic shape of a product. It might illustrate how a product looks or how it works. Any or all these prac-tices can prevent wasted time and materials.

Sketches and mock-ups can save time in communications. They allow you to record and communicate ideas quickly and clearly.

Sketches generally illustrate three views of an object. Most people visualize an object in this manner. Isometric and cabinet sketches are quite common. Perspectives are not used as much. They take longer to prepare. Sketching is simple to master. You must first learn to create simple lines and circles. Practice will make you proficient at sketching these and more complex geometric forms.

Mock-up building is more involved. You must measure, cut, and assemble components made of inexpensive material. Appearance mock-ups look like the final product but are not functional. Hard mock-ups may not be finished like the final product, but they are scaled, functional models used to analyze how the product will work.

CABINETMAKING TERMS

Sketches, mock-ups, rough sketches, thumbnail sketches, detail sketches, pictorial view, isometric sketch, cabinet drawing sketch, perspective sketch, graph paper, isometric grid paper, ellipse, appearance mock-up, hard mock-up.

TEST YOUR KNOWLEDGE

1. The purpose for making sketches and mock-ups is to save _____ and _____.
2. Sketches are used during both design and production. True or False?
3. What makes rough, thumbnail, and refined sketches different? When would you use each of them?
4. Why are most sketches made in three dimensions (pictorial views) instead of being drawn as a three-view drawing?
5. Name the three types of pictorial sketches.
6. Isometric views are drawn with:
   a. All three views with true shape and size.
   b. No views with true shape and size.
   c. One view true shape and size.
   d. Two views with true shape and size.
7. Cabinet drawings have:
   a. All three views with true shape and size.
   b. No views with true shape and size.
   c. One view true shape and size.
   d. Two views with true shape and size.
8. What type of pictorial view uses vanishing points?
9. What is the method for sketching a line? A circle? An ellipse?
10. Name the two types of mock-ups. What is the difference between them?

Chapter 9
PRODUCING WORKING DRAWINGS

After studying this chapter, you will be able to:
□ Identify the equipment and supplies used to produce working drawings.
□ Explain the activities leading to a finished drawing.
□ Describe how to generate a bill of materials.

Creating an original design challenges even the most experienced cabinetmaker. Begin by making decisions about the features you wish in the product. Then decide on the best way to produce the product. Make sketches which show this information. From these sketches you will prepare working drawings. Working drawings contain the graphics, measurements, and notes needed to build the product.

Producing working drawings for cabinets, case goods, chairs, and tables is part of drafting technology. Activities include laying out geometric forms, transferring designs, and providing details. Equipment and supplies are needed to construct these components of working drawings.

DRAWING EQUIPMENT

Several pieces of equipment are needed for drawing. They include straightedges, drawing boards, pencils, pens, compasses, dividers, scales, templates, and irregular curves.

STRAIGHTEDGES

Straightedges are used to draw straight lines. The simplest straightedge equipment is a T-square and triangle, Fig 9-1.

T-squares are placed with the head against the end of the drafting board. The blade is then horizontal. A right handed drafter places the head against the left side of the board. A left handed drafter places the head against the right side of the board. Then it does not interfere with arm movement.

A *triangle* placed on the blade of the T-square allows for drawing lines other than horizontal. Triangles are specified by their three angles. The

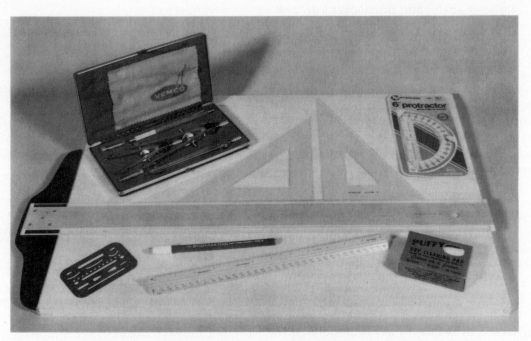

Fig. 9-1. T-square, triangles, and necessary drafting equipment. (Hearlihy & Co.)

two most common triangles are the 30°-60°-90° and the 45°-45°-90°. An adjustable triangle is used to obtain other angles.

Although the T-square and triangle are suitable for most drawings, more accurate drafting straightedges are being used. These are drafting machines, parallel bars, and computer-aided drafting systems.

A *parallel bar* is much like a T-square; however, it is constantly held horizontal by a series of wires or tracks on the edge of the board, Fig. 9-2. The bar moves up and down the board while remaining horizontal. A triangle is used in conjunction with a parallel bar to draw vertical and angled lines.

Fig. 9-3. Drafting machines combine the functions of a T-square, triangle, and scale. (Vemco)

Fig. 9-2. Parallel bars make horizontal lines. This one is portable. (Hearlihy & Co.)

The *drafting machine* combines the functions of a T-square, triangle, scale, and protractor into one tool. One end of the arm is clamped to the table. The other end contains two rules at right angles attached to a mechanism for indexing angles, Fig. 9-3. Even when moving the drafting machine the rules remain at the same angle. The angle is changed by rotating the base plate mechanism.

Modern advances in electronics technology permit drafting to be done by computer, Fig. 9-4. The pencil is replaced by an input device. The drafting board is replaced by a display screen (much like a T.V. screen) and plotter.

There are several advantages for using *computer-aided design* (CAD). With practice, the drawing time may be shortened. Drawings can also be modified easily because they are stored in computer memory, not on paper. The result is a better quality drawing.

DRAWING BOARDS

A *drafting board* provides a flat rectangular surface for drawing. The surface and edges of a draw-

ing board should be straight and smooth. Boards are commonly made out of basswood. This specie of lumber is almost free of visible grain which causes hard and soft spots on the surface of the board. A metal edge is inlayed on most boards to provide a true surface for the T-square to ride against. Some modern drawing boards are made of hard plastic. They resist warping which can occur in wood boards.

A sheet of vinyl often is placed on the surface of the board to reduce damage from pencil, compass,

Fig. 9-4. Computer-aided design systems are being used in modern engineering companies. (Prime Computer, Inc.)

and divider points. The surface remains smooth, even if punctured. The vinyl material expands to close the hole.

LEAD HOLDERS AND PENCILS

Mechanical lead holders are the most popular drawing tool. There are two types of lead holders. One holder uses thick leads which must be sharpened; the other uses thin leads, Fig. 9-5. Different size leads are not interchangeable between these two types of holders.

The so-called "lead" is actually graphite. The graphite comes in varying hardnesses so you can alter line weight. Hardnesses range from 8B (very soft) to B and H (medium hardnesses) to 10H (very hard). In between B and H are HB and F hardness leads. The harder the graphite, the lighter the line. A 4H pencil is relatively hard and used to make light construction, extension, and dimension lines. A 2H lead has medium hardness and is used for object lines. An H pencil is softer and used for dark border lines. The F lead, still softer, is used for lettering.

When drawing, always use the same hand pressure. Change the line weight by changing lead.

A set of pencils is an alternative to mechanical lead holders, Fig. 9-6. They also come with varying hardnesses of graphite.

DRAWING PENS

Drawing pens perform much like lead holders. Each pen tip produces a different line thickness.

Inked lines can be made over pencil lines to produce a finished drawing. However, inked drawings cannot be modified easily. Thus, if you plan to ink a drawing to produce better whiteprints or blueprints, make sure the original pencil drawing is complete.

COMPASSES

Compasses are used for making circles and arcs. Like the mechanical lead holders above, different lead hardnesses are used for thin, medium, and thick lines. The compass includes a lead holder on one side and a point on the other side. An adjusting wheel alters the radius of the compass, Fig. 9-7. The lead is rotated around the point to produce circles and arcs.

DIVIDERS

The *divider* is used to transfer distances without marking the paper. Dividers look somewhat like compasses; however, instead of a steel point and a lead point, there are two steel points. The distance between divider points is maintained by a thumbscrew lock, Fig. 9-7.

SCALES

Scales allow you to control the amount of space covered by pictorial, multiview, and detail drawings. For example a scale may indicate that 1/4 in. = 1 ft.-0 in. Therefore, a 40 ft. wide house would only occupy 10 in. on the drawing. There are three

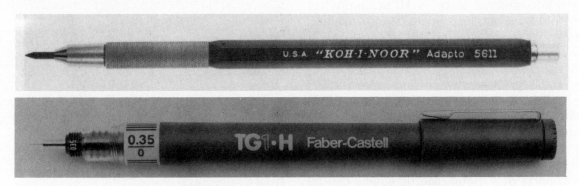

Fig. 9-5. Leadholders. Top. Thick leads must be sharpened. (Hearlihy & Co.) Bottom. Thin leads maintain a fine line. (Utley)

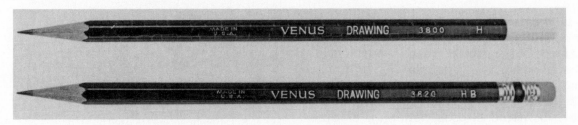

Fig. 9-6. Pencils are still being used by some drafters. (Utley)

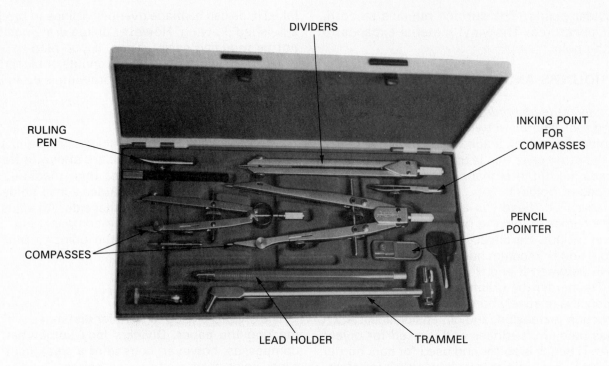

DIVIDERS

RULING PEN

INKING POINT FOR COMPASSES

COMPASSES

PENCIL POINTER

LEAD HOLDER

TRAMMEL

Fig. 9-7. A drafting set contains equipment for laying out lines, circles, and distances. (Hearlihy & Co.)

scales used by cabinetmakers: architect's scale, engineer's scale, and metric scale, Fig. 9-8.

An *architect's scale* permits various scale factors, including 3/32, 1/8, 1/4, 3/8, 1/2, 3/4, 1 1/2, and 3 in. equal to one foot. The scale is triangular; each of the scale factors is found on one of the six different sides.

An *engineer's scale* is divided differently. Inches are divided into decimal parts. A 10 scale divides an inch into 10 units. A 50 scale divides an inch into 50 units. When measuring, the 10 scale could equal 10 feet, 100 feet, or 1000 feet. Engineers' scales are usually flat with a beveled drawing edge. Most are made to fit into a drafting machine.

Metric scales are divided into ratios such as 1:20. This means the drawing is one-twentieth the size of the actual object. Thus, one meter divided by 20 equals 5 centimeters, and the scale is 5 cm ^{5} 1 m. Other ratios are 1:10, 1:25, 1:50, 1:100, 1:150 and 1:200 parts of a meter. Metric scales can be triangular or flat.

TEMPLATES

Templates aid when drawing common shapes. There are hundreds of different kinds of templates. Most are made of transparent plastic. Architects use certain templates to trace symbols (plumbing, electrical) on floor plans. Cabinetmakers would use templates for constructing geometric shapes such as circles, isometric ellipses, lettering, or other specific purposes, Fig. 9-9.

To use a template, first find the desired shape on the template and align it on the drawing. Then trace around the inside of the opening to transfer the symbol to your drawing.

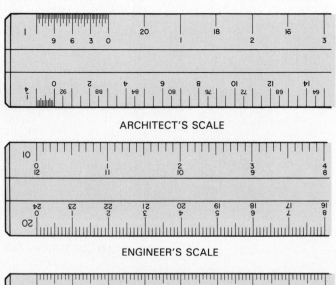

ARCHITECT'S SCALE

ENGINEER'S SCALE

METRIC SCALE

Fig. 9-8. Different scales are used by architects and mechanical engineers.

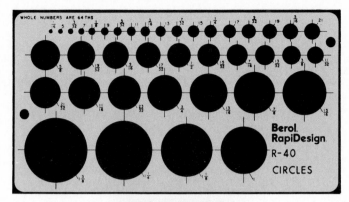

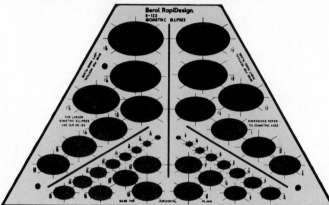

Fig. 9-9. Templates reduce the time it takes to draw circles and ellipses. (Hearlihy & Co.)

IRREGULAR CURVES

Irregular curves are made using templates or flexible curves, Fig. 9-10. *French curves* are clear plastic templates for drawing curves. They create arcs where the center of the arc is unknown or not important. These templates help to create smooth, flowing lines. There are many sizes and styles of irregular curves and you likely will need several.

You might find that a *flexible curve* is useful. It is made out of pliable lead in a plastic casing. Just bend it to the proper form and it remains in that position while drawing the curve.

DRAWING MATERIALS

The material you draw on may be paper, vellum, or polyester (plastic) film. Quality is based on strength, surface stability, erasability, and resistance to brittleness, caused by aging.

PAPER

Drawing paper is opaque (non-transparent) with the qualities noted above. It is three to four times as thick as a sheet of typing paper of the same size. It may be white or tinted light green, blue, or cream color. Tinting reduces eye strain.

Paper can be puchased in a roll or by sheets. Sheet sizes are 9 in. x 12 in. (A size), 12 in. x 18 in. (B size), 18 in x 24 in. (C size), and 24 in. x 36 in. (D size).

VELLUM

Vellum is a translucent (almost clear) paper. Vellum is often used as a tracing paper. A sheet of vellum is placed over a drawing and traced on to produce a master copy for blueprints or whiteprints.

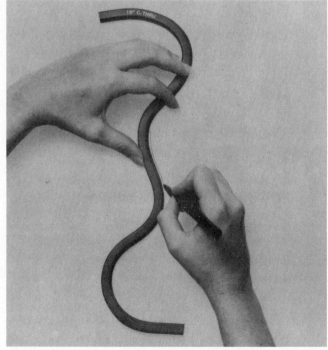

Fig. 9-10. Top. A French curve can be used to draw any irregular curve. Bottom. A flexible curve will bend to trace long curves. (Hearlihy & Co.)

Polyester plastic film probably is the highest quality material for drawing and copying. You mark on it with pencils or pens. Marks can be erased up to 10 times without marring the paper. The result is an excellent master for making prints.

An almost endless list of supplies is available to the drafter. Some items for general use are:
1. A roll of drafting tape to secure paper or film to the board or vinyl board cover.
2. A special pencil sharpener for wood pencils.

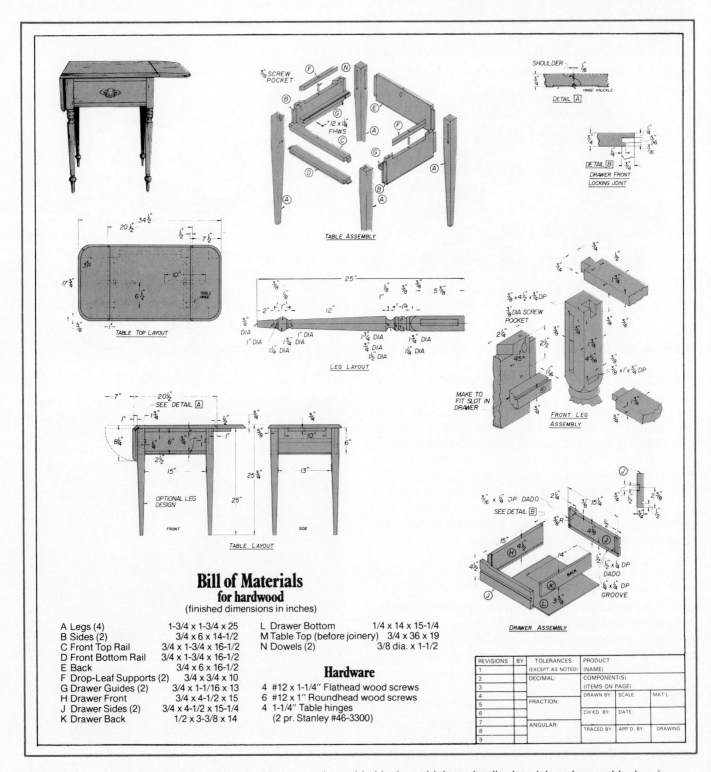

Bill of Materials
for hardwood
(finished dimensions in inches)

A Legs (4)	1-3/4 x 1-3/4 x 25
B Sides (2)	3/4 x 6 x 14-1/2
C Front Top Rail	3/4 x 1-3/4 x 16-1/2
D Front Bottom Rail	3/4 x 1-3/4 x 16-1/2
E Back	3/4 x 6 x 16-1/2
F Drop-Leaf Supports (2)	3/4 x 3/4 x 10
G Drawer Guides (2)	3/4 x 1-1/16 x 13
H Drawer Front	3/4 x 4-1/2 x 15
J Drawer Sides (2)	3/4 x 4-1/2 x 15-1/4
K Drawer Back	1/2 x 3-3/8 x 14
L Drawer Bottom	1/4 x 14 x 15-1/4
M Table Top (before joinery)	3/4 x 36 x 19
N Dowels (2)	3/8 dia. x 1-1/2

Hardware

4 #12 x 1-1/4" Flathead wood screws
6 #12 x 1" Roundhead wood screws
4 1-1/4" Table hinges
   (2 pr. Stanley #46-3300)

REVISIONS	BY	TOLERANCES	PRODUCT		
1		(EXCEPT AS NOTED)	(NAME)		
2		DECIMAL:	COMPONENT(S)		
3			(ITEMS ON PAGE)		
4			DRAWN BY:	SCALE:	MAT'L.
5		FRACTION:			
6			CH'KD. BY:	DATE:	
7		ANGULAR:			
8			TRACED BY:	APP'D. BY:	DRAWING
9					

Fig. 9-11. A complete set of working drawings contains a title block; multiview, detail, pictorial, and assembly drawings; bill of materials, and plan of procedure. (Shopsmith)

Plan of Procedure	

Legs (A)
1. Square to size.
2. Cut mortises in all legs (six of one size and two of another).
3. Saw and chisel single dovetails on front legs.
 	
Drop-Leaf Supports (F)
1. Square to size.
2. Bevel the ends.
 	
Sides (B) and back (E)
1. Square to size.
2. Drill screw pockets.
3. Saw recesses for drop leaf supports (F).
4. Prepare tenons on all ends of (B) and (E).
5. Drill for dowels (N) in parts (B).
 	
Front top rail (C) and bottom rail (D)
1. Square to size.
2. Saw tenons on (C).
3. Prepare dovetails on (F).
 	
Assembly of components (A), (B), (C), (D), and (E)
1. Smooth all surfaces that will receive finish.
2. Glue dowels (N) in sides (B).
3. Assemble and clamp (A), (B), (C). (D), and (E) without adhesive.
4. Inspect for squareness.
5. Disassemble components and lay clamps aside.
6. Coat every surface to be bonded with adhesive.
7. Reassemble, reclamp, and square the assembly.
 	
Decide to make or buy drawer glides (G)
1. If you buy:
  a. Install them on sides (B).
  b. Change dimensions for the width of the drawer as needed.
	Drawer
	1. Square drawer front (H), sides (J), back (K) and bottom (L) to size.
	2. Saw locking rabbet joints on (H).
	3. Saw dadoes in (J) to fit the rabbets on (H).
	4. Saw dadoes in (J) of (K).
	5. Saw grooves in (J) for (L).
	6. Assemble the drawer without adhesive.
	7. Inspect for squareness.
	8. Disassemble the drawer.
	9. If you make drawer glides:
	  a. Route the dovetail groove in (J).
	  b. Square drawer guides (G).
	  c. Route the edges of (G) to fit the groove in (J).
	  d. Drill screw holes in (G).
	10. Smooth all drawer components as necessary.
	11. Coat joints (except the groove for [L]) with adhesive.
	12. Reassemble with clamps and check for squareness.
	13. Allow adhesive to cure and remove clamps.
	14. Install the drawer with screws in (G).
	Top (M)
	1. Square glued workpieces to size.
	2. Saw the radii on the four corners.
	3. Smooth any rough saw marks.
	4. Shape or rout all edges and corners with decorative router bit.
	5. Make cuts to separate the drop leaves.
	6. Shape or rout the table joint with matched cutters or bits.
	7. Smooth all surfaces as necessary.
	8. Install the table hinges with 1/16 in. between the leaves and top.
	9. Install the drop-leaf supports (F).
	10. Attach (M) to the table assembly with screws in the screw pockets in (B) and (E).
	Finish as desired.

Fig. 9-11 continued.

It removes only the wood from around the lead.

3. A pencil pointer to form the tip of the lead. A sheet of sandpaper can be used also.
4. A soft rubber eraser to remove unnecessary lines.
5. An art gum eraser to remove smudges.
6. An erasing shield.
7. A protractor for measuring angles.
8. A cleaning pad.
9. A dusting brush.

Other items, used in inking, are:

1. A container of the recommended ink.
2. A supply of ink-erasing fluid for film.
3. A sharp knife or single-edge razor blade to scrape away dried ink errors on paper.
4. A bottle of recommended pen cleaning fluid.

These materials, equipment, and supplies help you become a more productive drafter.

PRODUCING SHOP DRAWINGS

Shop drawings can be created several different ways. No method is right or wrong, but the drawing must contain essential parts: a title block, a multiview drawing, details, and notes. If needed, a pictorial assembly or exploded view can be added, Fig. 9-11.

PREPARING THE TITLE BLOCK

A *title block* is necessary to identify your drawing. It should contain the name of the product, drafter, and drawing checker. Scale of the drawing, sheet number of the drawing (if more than one), general tolerances, material specifications are also included. Sample title blocks were shown in Chapter 7. When drawing a title block, leave at least 1/4 in. between horizontal lines for lettering height. Also be sure to make the title block sections wide enough to hold the information.

CREATING MULTIVIEW DRAWINGS

A *multiview drawing* is the most accurate description of design features. When creating views, refer to the alphabet of lines to determine characteristics and weight for different line types. A typical procedure for completing a multiview drawing is as follows:

1. Decide what views describe the product totally.
2. Select an appropriate scale so that the drawing will fit on your paper.
3. Establish view placement.
   a. The front view should be the face of the product with the most features. This view

is located at the lower left portion of the drawing.

 b. A top view is directly above front view.
 c. A right side view is placed to the right of the front view.
 d. Include other views as needed. If a left side view is required, the front view is placed in the center of the paper. Left and right side views are placed on the appropriate side.
4. Leave adequate spacing between and around the views for dimensions and notes. A space of two in. (50 mm) is recommended.
5. Enclose necessary views with light contruction lines using a straightedge. Be sure to use the proper scale.
6. Measure necessary distances to lay out joints and other details. Geometric forms, such as lines, rectangles, circles, and arcs describe your design.
7. Transfer all visible and hidden edge or surface lines from one view to another.
8. Add extension, dimension, and leader lines as explained below.
9. Erase any unnecessary lines. Use an erasing shield to prevent removal of dimension or object lines.
10. Add notes where needed to explain part of the design. These should be 1/8 in. (3mm) high.
11. Develop detail drawings for portions of the multiview drawing which are unclear. Details are usually enlarged to provide a precise view of an intricate parts of the product.

DIMENSIONING

Dimensioning includes both linear and radial distances using extension, dimension, leader, and radius dimension lines, Fig. 9-12.

Linear Dimensioning

Linear dimensions note measurement of a straight surface. It could be horizontal, vertical, or inclined.

Extension lines mark the edges to be measured. Extension lines start 1/16 in. (1.5 mm) from the object and extend 1/8 in (3 mm) past the farthest dimension line.

Dimension lines show the distance being measured. The lines should start at least 3/8 in. (10 mm) away from visible edge lines. Short distances are dimensioned nearest the view. Additional dimension lines are 1/4 in. (6 mm) apart. Overall sizes of the object are furthest from the views. Put an arrow where a dimension line meets an extension line.

You must add numbers to show distance. Measurements are given in one of two ways. *Customary dimensioning* requires that you leave a break in the dimension line. The number is placed in the space. It may be in fractions, decimal, or metric units. In

dual dimensioning, there is no break in the dimension line. The decimal dimension is placed above the line. The metric dimension is placed below the line.

Leader lines

Leader lines direct the readers' attention to some point. A common practice is to point from a note to where it is applied.

Radial dimensioning

Radius dimensions note measurements for circles and arcs. They include a line which extends from the center to the edge of the circle or arc. They terminate with an arrow. A leader line extends from a point outside the arc or circle to the edge. The dimension figure is placed at the outer end of the leader line. The leader line can also be placed to point at the center of the circle if it would interfere with other dimensions.

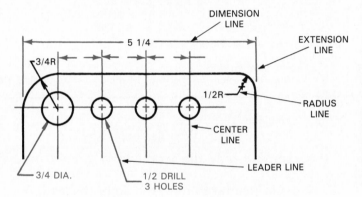

Fig. 9-12. Method of dimensioning lines and circles is different. Leader lines point out important information.

LETTERING

Lettering on shop drawings is *Gothic;* only capitals are used. Letters and numbers are vertical or slightly slanted to the right. The letters are produced either by using a lettering guide or freehand. When using a lettering guide, align it with the straightedge. For freehand lettering, draw two guidelines 1/8 in. (3 mm) apart. Letter and numbers are formed within these guidelines, except for fractions which extend slightly above and below. If you are using tracing paper, draw guidelines on a separate sheet of paper and slide it under the tracing paper. This eliminates having to erase guidelines when finished with lettering.

DEVELOPING DETAILS

Details serve many purposes. You can enlarge and illustrate contours, joints, assemblies, etc. As explained in Chapter 7, details usually are separated from the multiview drawings. They may be pictorial assembly or exploded views, section views, or simply enlarged isometric views. Details are referenced using notes such as SEE DETAIL 1, SHEET 2.

Saving time with details

Notice on Fig. 9-13 that the balcony rail spindles are not fully drawn except the first one. This procedure saves time during drafting and does not hinder production of the rail. Commonly used parts can be drawn once with contours as a detail drawing. Block in the space on the multiview and pictorial drawings where the part is located.

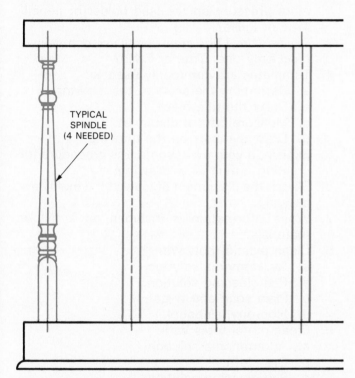

TYPICAL SPINDLE (4 NEEDED)

Fig. 9-13. When drawing details of repeated objects, such as a balcony rail, only draw one object complete. Block in the others.

CREATING A BILL OF MATERIAL

On shop drawings, all components must be identified. Parts can be named or given numbers. These parts are listed in a bill of materials (BOM) during or after the drawing is finished. A *BOM* assists you in ordering materials, refer to Fig. 9-10. It also provides a record in case a substitution is necessary. For example if a part were out of stock, you could check the bill of materials to determine the size of the part desired. Another suitable part can then be substituted.

The bill of materials contains the:
1. Name and/or part number of all parts visible in the multiview, detail, or pictorial drawings.
2. Quantity.

3. Manufacturer of part, including code or identification numbers.
4. Dimensions of the part.
5. Additional notes or comments.

LISTING STANDARD STOCK

Standard stock refers to quantities of materials and supplies as you buy them. For example, your bill of materials specifies a top, two sides, and five shelves for a bookcase to be made out of 1 x 10 in. lumber. This lumber dealer sells in even lengths from 8 ft. to 16 ft. Determine the length of board and the number you need.

Hardware is sold in standard stock quantities, such as each, pair, dozen, hundred, or pound. For example, drawer pulls and catches may be obtained individually or in boxes containing 10 or 12 pulls. Hinges are sold in pairs and in boxes or cases of larger quantities. Nails are usually sold by the pound. Screws may be obtained individually, in display packages of variable quantities, or in boxes of one hundred. Often a box of 100 is less expensive than six or seven packages of 10. Thus, larger quantities generally reduce the cost per piece. However, the extra quantity may become a storage problem.

Standard container sizes exist for adhesives and finishing materials. These are found in pints, quarts, and gallons.

EQUIPMENT MAINTENANCE

There are two major areas of concern for maintaining drawing equipment. One is keeping pencil and compass points sharp. The other is keeping equipment clean.
1. Sharpen drafting pencils with a drafting pencil sharpener. It removes only the wood casing and does not shape a point.
2. Point drafting pencils with an abrasive pad or a mechanical pointer. Mechanical pointers create cone shaped points. This same shape can be placed on a pencil by rotating the pencil while rubbing the lead on an abrasive pad. Some drafters prefer a wedge shaped point.
3. Sharpen a compass lead by rubbing it with an abrasive pad on the outside edge of the lead.
4. Remove any loose graphite from a pencil or compass after pointing it. Wipe the lead with a dry cloth or press the point into a scrap piece of foam plastic. This removes graphite dust.
5. Avoid denting or nicking straightedges. They are ruined once this happens.
6. Store T-squares upside down and flat. This prevents warpage.
7. Wash plastic and vinyl tools with warm water and detergent.

8. Wipe metal tools with a cloth before storing to remove finger prints which might etch the metal.
9. Remove dried ink from plastic tools with a dilluted ammonia solution (window cleaner).
10. Remove dried ink from drawing pens and plated metal tools with pen cleaning solution.
11. Empty the liquid ink and clean the points if you will not use them for several days.

SUMMARY

Cabinetmakers who design as well as build products have to prepare working drawings. Use the appropriate supplies to produce accurate work. Equipment includes a straightedge, drawing board, triangle, lead holder, paper, compass, scale, and templates.

Working drawings contain information essential in describing the product. Title blocks identify the product, scale, drafter, and other details. Multiview drawings show the layout of all parts of the design. Dimensions give measurements of each part. Detail drawings further explain intricate features of the design.

The bill of materials lists the materials needed to produce the product. This table includes part name or number, quantity, dimensions, manufacturer, and other important characteristics of the material. Items to be purchased often are listed in standard stock quanities.

CABINETMAKING TERMS

Straightedge, T-square, parallel bar, drafting machine, computer-aided deisgn, drafting board, mechanical lead holder, drawing pen, compasses, divider, scale, architect's scale, engineer's scale, metric scale, template, French curve, flexible curve, drawing paper, vellum, polyester film, extension line, dimension line, leader line, radius line, Gothic lettering, bill of materials, standard stock.

TEST YOUR KNOWLEDGE

1. Pencils are composed of wood surrounding writing material made of what materials?
   a. Charcoal.
   b. Graphite.
   c. Hardened clay.
   d. Lead.
2. The proper way to make lines darker is to apply more pressure on the lead holder or pencil. True or False?
3. Dividers have two steel points and compasses have only one. True or False?
4. Templates are commonly used to:
   a. Determine the scale of the drawing.
   b. Draw the title block.
   c. Measure critical distances.
   d. Draw symbols on the drawing.
5. Explain, in your own words, the procedure for creating a multiview drawing.
6. Sketch the placement of views for a multiview drawing.
7. What information is included on a bill of materials?
8. Clean plastic tools with:
   a. An ammonia solution.
   b. Pen cleaning solution.
   c. Plain soap and water.
   d. Isopropyl alchohol.
9. Clean metal tools with:
   a. An ammonia solution.
   b. Dry cloth.
   c. Pen cleaning solution.
   d. Isopropyl alchohol.

Chapter 10
WOOD CHARACTERISTICS

After studying this chapter, you will be able to:
☐*Describe the common growth pattern of all trees.*
☐*Explain the difference between hardwood and soft-wood cell structure.*
☐*Determine the moisture content and specific gravity of a particular wood.*
☐*Describe the mechanical properties of wood.*

Cabinetmakers who produce high quality cabinetry understand wood characteristics. They are very careful about selecting, storing, handling, and processing wood to retain its desirable qualities. These include natural beauty, strength, durability, elasticity, and easy maintenance.

Because of its varying color and pattern, wood has natural beauty. Cabinetmakers enhance this beauty through shaping and finishing wood products.

The structural qualities of wood make it a desirable building product. Pound for pound, some wood species are as strong as steel. Most will last for centuries with regular maintenance. If a wood product is marred, it can be resurfaced and refinished to restore the original beauty.

Wood is an elastic material. It will ''bounce back'' to its original shape after being bent. This property is applied in the construction industry where wood beams are used as floor joists.

TREE PARTS

A tree is nature's largest self-supporting plant. It obtains water and food through a complex system of roots, branches, and leaves.

A tree is held upright and nourished by either a tap root or fibrous root system, Fig. 10-1. A tap root is one long tapered vertical root with small hairs. It extends deep into the ground. The fibrous root system consists of many roots and root hairs spread out close to the ground surface. Both systems absorb water and minerals. These are carried by the trunk to the crown where they are processed into food.

The trunk extends up from the ground and supports the crown. The trunk transports the water and minerals to the crown through an internal pipeline of cells. The crown converts nutrients, by photosynthesis, to food (carbohydrates). This food is then carried to the various parts of the tree for nourishment and growth.

Tree growth depends on the addition of millions of cells annually. Their development extends the lengths of the branches and the roots. It also increases the diameter of the roots, trunk, and limbs during each growing season. Thus, a tree not only grows upward, but also downward and outward.

GROWTH CHARACTERISTICS

A cross-section of a log, Fig. 10-2, reveals the layers of a tree.

BARK

The tree is protected from weather, insects, and disease by an outer layer of dead wood cells called *bark.* Its texture and thickness range from smooth and thin to rough, corky, and thick, depending on the tree specie.

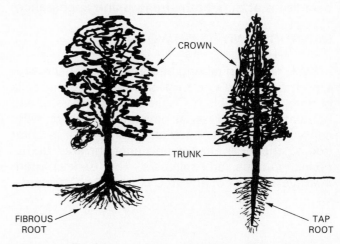

Fig. 10-1. Tree growth occurs in the roots, trunk, and crown. Each part serves a different purpose for the tree.

CAMBIUM

Beneath the bark is a layer of cell production called the *cambium.* The outer part of the cambium, called phloem, generates new cells for the bark. It is often called the inner bark. Besides creating new bark, phloem carries food from the leaves to feed the branches, trunk, and roots. The inner part of the cambium creates new cells for tree growth. It is a two-cell thick layer called xylem. Cells developed by the xylem become sapwood which carries water and nutrients to the leaves.

EARLYWOOD AND LATEWOOD

The cambium produces new cells at different rates, depending on the time of year. In spring there is plenty of moisture. Cells develop quickly and are larger, lighter colored, and have thinner walls. This is *earlywood,* also called *springwood.* The available moisture decreases during the summer. Cells continue to be added. However, they are smaller, darker colored, and have thicker walls. This is *latewood,* also called *summerwood.*

ANNUAL RINGS

The combination of earlywood and latewood growth creates light and dark colored rings, called *annual rings.* The age of the tree can be estimated by counting the rings. (A light ring and dark ring count as one growing season.) More than one ring is possible in a given year. The tree might be affected by drought or insects during the growing season. This would cause temporary slow growth. When moisture is available and growth resumes, earlywood is again created.

When the sawmill produces lumber, logs are cut through the annual rings. This forms a light and dark pattern called the grain. When cabinetmakers work with wood, the *grain pattern* is very important because it affects both strength and appearance.

SAPWOOD AND HEARTWOOD

Each new annual ring becomes part of the sapwood. *Sapwood* is a thick section of young cells beneath the cambium. These cells carry water and nutrients to the leaves. As new growth occurs, older sapwood becomes inactive. It turns dark in color due to chemical change and concentrated gums, resins, tannins, and minerals. This dark colored, inactive section of the tree is called *heartwood.*

PITH

At the center of the tree is the pith. The *pith* is a thin, round, spongy core where the young tree began to grow. Nearly all branches grow from the pith.

WOOD RAYS

Water and nutrients are carried outward from the center of the tree by *wood rays.* Rays are several cells high, several cells wide, and extend horizontally to the outer part of the tree.

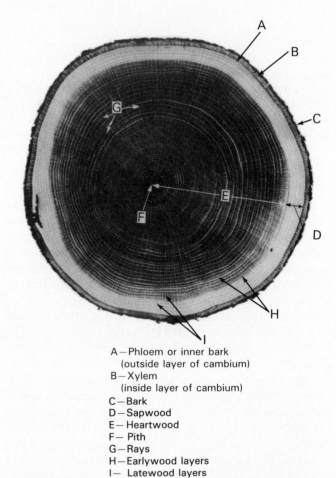

A—Phloem or inner bark
    (outside layer of cambium)
B—Xylem
    (inside layer of cambium)
C—Bark
D—Sapwood
E—Heartwood
F— Pith
G—Rays
H—Earlywood layers
I— Latewood layers

Fig. 10-2. This cross-section of a tree shows the different layers associated with tree growth and function. (Forest Products Laboratory)

TREE IDENTIFICATION

Trees are classified as either deciduous or coniferous. *Deciduous trees* are broadleaved trees which usually drop their leaves in the fall. Examples include oaks, ashes, birches, and maples. Wood from deciduous trees is called *hardwood.*

Coniferous trees have needles or very small scale-like leaves which remain green throughout the year. We commonly refer to them as evergreens. The word conifer means "cone bearing," which is another identifying characteristic of evergreens. Trees include pines, spruces, and firs. Wood from conifers is called *softwood.*

WOOD CLASSIFICATION

The terms "hardwood" and "softwood" classify trees according to their characteristics. It does not mean that all deciduous trees are harder than conifers, nor that all conifers are softer than deciduous trees. They are named because the cell structure of hardwood and softwood trees have noticeable differences.

WOOD CELL STRUCTURE

There are about three million cells per cubic in. (645 cu. mm) of wood. Enlarged sections of a softwood (white pine) and a hardwood (American tulip) show the difference in cell structure. In examining cell structure, there are three viewing angles noted, Fig. 10-3.

• *Cross sectional face.* Seen when you cut across the annual rings. An example is the top of a stump.

• *Radial face.* Seen when the tree is cut through the center. This cut is nearly perpendicular to the growth rings.

• *Tangential face.* Seen by slicing an edge off the section of trunk. The surface of the cut is tangent to the annual rings. On a larger section of log the annual rings appear as arrows. Each corresponds to a new layer or growth.

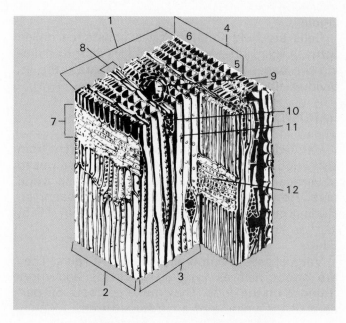

SOFTWOOD CELL STRUCTURE

1. Cross-sectional face
2. Radial face
3. Tangential face
4. Annual ring
5. Earlywood
6. Latewood
7. Wood ray
8. Fusiform ray
9. Vertical resin duct
10. Horizontal resin duct
11. Bordered pit
12. Simple pit

Fig. 10-4. Cell structure of a softwood. Note how rays extend across the radial face and cell length is in the longitudinal direction. Also note the fusiform rays and resin ducts which are not found on the hardwoods. (Forest Products Laboratory)

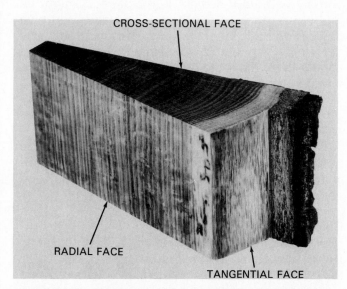

Fig. 10-3. The three faces of wood. Cutting across each face produces a different grain pattern and different strength. (Forest Products Laboratory)

SOFTWOOD CELL STRUCTURE

Softwood cells are composed of vertical earlywood and latewood cells, horizontal rays, and ducts, Fig. 10-4.

Tracheids

Vertical cells, called *tracheids,* are about 1/8 in. (3 mm) long with pointed ends. They develop in fairly uniform rows and make up about 90 percent of the tree's cells. Liquids transported from the roots to the crown pass through tracheids.

Rays

Rays carry nutrients to outer portions of the tree. There are wood rays and fusiform rays. Wood rays are one cell wide and transport sap across the radial face. *Fusiform rays* are several cells wide and are noted by horizontal resin ducts imbedded in the ray.

Resin ducts

Horizontal and *vertical resin ducts* are formed when a space between cells expands. The ducts fill with sticky resin which is released by cells surrounding the duct.

Pits

Passageways among tracheids and rays are called pits. They allow solutions to be passed from cell to cell. Pits between two tracheids have a ring around them; they are called *border pits.* Pits between rays and tracheids are called *simple pits;* they do not have a ring.

Lignin

Cells are held together by a substance called *lignin.* It is an adhesive resin. Lignin is dissolved during the paper making process to separate the individual fibers (cells).

HARDWOOD CELL STRUCTURE

Hardwood cells are both similar and different from softwood cells. Hardwood cells also are composed of vertical earlywood and latewood cells and wood rays. However, additional cells can be seen, including parenchyma cells and vessels, Fig. 10-5.

Fibers

Vertical cells of hardwoods are called *fibers.* They are about half as long as tracheids and more rounded on the ends. They make up about 50 percent of the volume of a hardwood tree.

Rays

Wood rays again are the horizontal food and liquid passages. They are similar to softwood wood rays but do not contain ducts as do fusiform rays.

Parenchyma cells

Parenchyma cells are smaller than normal fibers and rays. They are used for additional food storage.

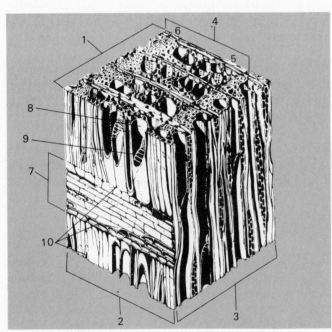

HARDWOOD CELL STRUCTURE

1. Cross-sectional face
2. Radial face
3. Tangential face
4. Annual ring
5. Earlywood
6. Latewood
7. Wood ray
8. Vessel
9. Sieve plate
10. Parenchyma cells

Fig. 10-5. Cell structure of a hardwood. Note how large open vessels replace the tracheids of softwood.
(Forest Products Laboratory)

Vessels

Vessels are elongated cells serving as the main passage for liquid moving from the roots to the crown. They are joined end to end, and separated by grill-like sieve plates. The size and length of vessels look like pores (openings) in finished lumber. This is why hardwoods are referred to as porous.

DIFFUSE AND RING-POROUS HARDWOODS

Hardwoods are classified as *diffuse-porous* and *ring-porous.* The hardwood shown in Fig. 10-6A (Bigtooth Aspen) has vessels which are about the same size in earlywood and latewood. Wood with this structure is called diffuse-porous because the vessels are diffused (scattered) throughout the annual ring.

Other hardwoods, such as oak, are called ring-porous. The vessels in earlywood are considerably larger than those produced in latewood. The arrangement of large to small vessels forms rings which coincide with the annual rings, Fig. 10-6B.

PROPERTIES OF WOOD

Both hardwood and softwood trees have variations in characteristics such as color, weight, density, moisture content, and specific gravity. These terms describe the properties of the wood specie.

Choose the wood with physical properties that comply with your design. Some aspects might be more important than others. The value you give these properties, or any other wood features, helps determine the wood you select. These include appearance, moisture content, shrinkage, weight, working qualities, and mechanical properties.

APPEARANCE

The appearance of the wood determines the decorative effect of your product. Appearance includes color, grain pattern, surface texture, and natural defects.

Color

Wood is primarily brown in color. It might range from a light tan to a dark, reddish brown, Fig. 10-7. Most color comes from chemical pigments and minerals in the cells. The darkest colors are found in the heartwood where these materials are concentrated.

The difference between sapwood and heartwood colors is dramatic. Some cabinetmakers choose only heartwood or softwood to eliminate this contrast. Others like contrast and choose lumber which is cut across both.

Another color change occurs after wood is cut. The chemicals in the cells combine with oxygen in

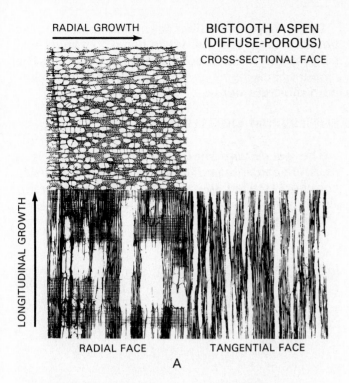

RADIAL GROWTH →

BIGTOOTH ASPEN
(DIFFUSE-POROUS)
CROSS-SECTIONAL FACE

LONGITUDINAL GROWTH

RADIAL FACE   TANGENTIAL FACE

A

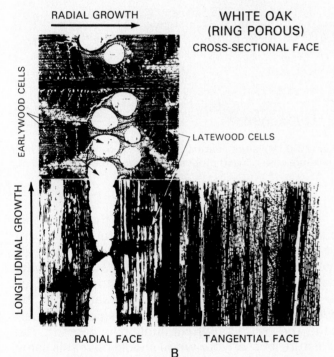

RADIAL GROWTH →

WHITE OAK
(RING POROUS)
CROSS-SECTIONAL FACE

EARLYWOOD CELLS

LATEWOOD CELLS

LONGITUDINAL GROWTH

RADIAL FACE   TANGENTIAL FACE

B

Fig. 10-6. Top. There is little difference between the size of earlywood and latewood cells in diffuse-porous hardwood. Bottom. Cell size is clearly different in ring-porous hardwood. (Forest Products Laboratory)

a process called oxidation. This causes the wood to darken. On the other hand, exposure to the sun causes the wood pigments to lighten.

Cabinetmakers frequently color wood with stain or oil. This helps to achieve a desired color or to enhance the grain pattern. Wood also can be bleached to remove color.

Fig. 10-7. Different wood color gives an attractive appearance to this room.

GRAIN PATTERN

The pattern of lines visible in sawn lumber is formed by the annual rings. It is called *grain.* The grain pattern forms a shape according to the cutting method. Generally, wood cut tangent to the annual rings (see tangential face, Fig. 10-8A) has a "V" effect. Wood cut perpendicular to the annual rings (see radial face, Fig. 10-8B) will have straight grain. These cutting methods will be discussed in Chapter 11.

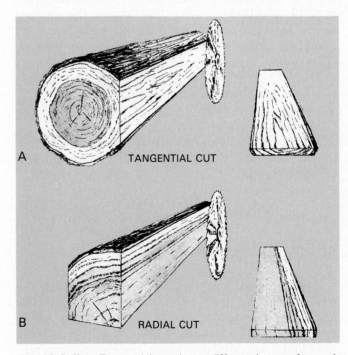

A   TANGENTIAL CUT

B   RADIAL CUT

Fig. 10-8. Top. Tangential cut shows different layers of growth which look like "V" lines. Bottom. Radial cut is perpendicular to annual rings producing straight lines.

SURFACE TEXTURE

The texture of cut lumber is determined by the cell structure of the wood. Large, open cells or pores in some woods, like ring-porous hardwoods, look like small pits in surfaced lumber. These woods are considered *open grain.* Even after finishing, these pits can be seen. You can smooth the texture by filling pores with wood filler. Woods with smaller pores are called *closed grain.* They do not require filler to achieve a smooth surface.

MOISTURE CONTENT

The most significant physical property of wood for cabinetmaking is moisture content. *Moisture content (MC)* describes the amount of water in the wood cells. It is a percent of the oven-dry weight of a wood sample. The oven-dry weight is obtained by removing most moisture by air or kiln drying. These processes, referred to as seasoning, are discussed in the next chapter.

The final MC level may vary from five percent for hardwoods and up to 20 percent for construction grade softwoods.

TESTING MOISTURE CONTENT

Moisture content can be measured quickly with a *moisture meter,* Fig. 10-9. You can test MC levels in a sample of fresh wood without a moisture meter. First weigh a sample of *green wood* (freshly cut lumber). The weight of the sample is called the *wet weight.* Then place the sample in an oven at 214° to 221°F. (101° to 105°C). When the sample stops losing weight, you weigh it again. The sample's weight at this time is the *oven-dry weight.* This drying process may take from 12 to 48 hours.

The following procedure is followed to calculate the MC using the two measured weights:
1. Subtract the final oven-dry weight (DW) from the wet weight (WW).
2. Divide the answer by the oven-dry weight.
3. Multiply the quotient by 100 to get the MC percentage.

$$MC(\%) = \frac{WW - DW}{DW} \times 100$$

REMOVING WATER

The water in green wood is located in both the cell cavity and cell walls. In the cell cavity it is known as *free water.* In the cell walls, it is called *bound water.* As the wood dries, the free water is removed first. When the free water has evaporated, the wood is at its fiber saturation point. The MC is 25 to 30 percent depending on the wood species.

Drying beyond the fiber saturation point removes bound water. The cell walls begin to shrivel and harden. The piece of wood shrinks and distorts. The amount of drying necessary depends on the equilibrium moisture content.

EQUILIBRIUM MOISTURE CONTENT

The *equilibrium moisture content (EMC)* is a moisture percentage of interior woodwork. It is also commonly called the *average moisture content.* When processing any wood, its moisture level should be at the EMC.

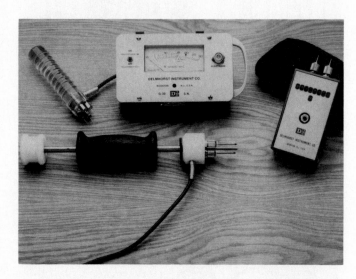

Fig. 10-9. Moisture content of wood can be determined by a moisture meter. Insert probes in the wood to obtain a reading. (Woodcraft)

The EMC percentage depends on the geographic part of the country. It is approximately 18 percent of the average relative humidity of a region when the temperature is 72°F. The EMC represents balance of moisture content which the air will give or remove from the wood. For example, if the average relative humidity of your region is 49 percent, the EMC is approximately nine percent. The moisture level of your wood should have this same percentage. If the MC of your wood cabinet is six percent, your cabinet will take on moisture from the air. The wood might swell and warp. If the moisture of your cabinet is 12 percent, the wood loses moisture to the air. This would cause it to shrink and crack the joints.

The EMC remains fairly stable, changing only slightly with the seasons. These changes affect the surface cells of wood.

The critical time to maintain the wood's moisture content with the EMC is during production, before the finish is applied. The finish will limit the amount of moisture absorbed or lost. To assure that your wood is the same moisture content as the EMC, store it awhile. It is advisable to purchase the wood at a lower moisture content. During storage, it absorbs moisture from the air to attain the EMC percentage.

The results of processing wood not at the EMC level is most apparent in wood joints, Fig. 10-10. If the wood takes on moisture, the joint will tighten. If it loses moisture content, the joint will loosen.

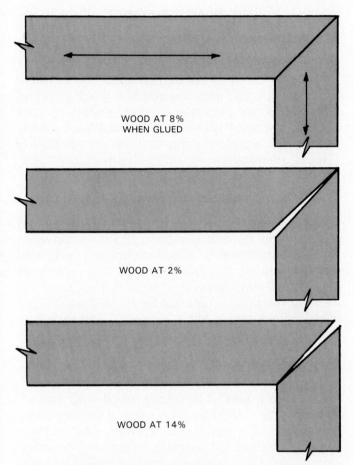

Fig. 10-10. Changes in moisture content have harsh effects on wood joints. (Forest Products Laboratory)

The equilibrium moisture content for most of the United States is eight percent. It is lowest in the southwestern states at 6 percent. Along the southeast and southwest coasts, and gulf states it may be 11 percent.

The moisture content of dried lumber ranges from 6 to 13 percent. It can be several percentage points higher when the lumber is used and stored outside. Be careful of using construction grade lumber. The moisture content is often as high as 20 percent.

SHRINKAGE

Wood shrinks when the moisture level is below the fiber saturation point (25 to 30 percent mois-

ture). The wood cells begin to shrivel up. The wood will shrink in size 1/30 in. for every percentage point of moisture lost. The exact amount of shrinkage of a sample can be calculated by:

$$\text{Shrinkage (\%)} = \frac{\text{Wet dimension} - \text{Dry dimension}}{\text{Wet dimension}} \times 100$$

RATE OF SHRINKAGE

Wood shrinks at different rates in different directions, Fig. 10-11. This is mainly due to the high amount of earlywood compared to latewood. Shrinkage is greatest in the tangential direction. The annual rings attempt to straighten out. Tangential shrinkage in hardwood is 4 to 12 percent; in softwood, it is 4 to 8 percent. Radial shrinkage is about half as much and longitudinal (length) shrinkage is insignificant. Usually, it is less than .3 percent.

Lumber cut from sapwood shrinks more than heartwood because of its high moisture content. The method of cutting also affects the rate of shrinkage. Plain-sawed lumber shrinks twice as much across the face of the board than does quarter-sawed lumber.

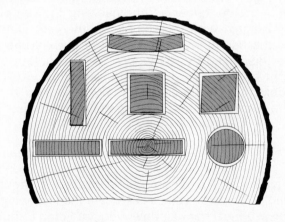

Fig. 10-11. Shrinkage occurs in all directions. Note severe warp of tangentially-cut piece. (Forest Products Laboratory)

WEIGHT

Weight can influence the decision to use a given species of wood. If you move often, build furniture with lighter wood.

Weight is controlled by three factors:
1. Moisture content.
2. Density.
3. Stored minerals and other materials.

All of these factors vary. However, the weight of stored minerals is minimal and the moisture content is relatively stable. The primary factor for weight is the density of the wood.

DENSITY

Density describes weight per unit of volume. For example, obtain samples of different wood species. Cut them to the same size. Be sure that they have the same moisture content, then weigh them. The heavier pieces are more dense than the lighter ones. Most species weigh between 20 and 45 pounds per cubic foot.

The standard measure of density is *specific gravity (SG).* This unit compares the weight of a volume of any substance with an equal volume of water at 4 °C. The volume of water has a constant of 1 SG. For example, the SG of ash is .50; thus, a cubic foot of ash weighs .50 (one-half) as much as a cubic foot of water.

Wood is lighter than water. This is because of air inside dried wood cells. However, the cell wall material actually is heavier, or more dense, than water. If the cell structure is smaller, it will have heavier cell walls. There will also be less trapped air. Thus the specific gravity will be higher. Besides being heavy, a high specific gravity usually means the wood is strong. Lighter woods have larger, thin-walled cells.

There is a quick way to determine specific gravity of a wood. First weigh an oven-dry sample. Then submerge it in a container of water. Mark the water level in the container before inserting the sample. Mark it again with the sample submerged. Determine the rise in water to calculate the volume of water displaced by the wood. Then calculate the weight of the amount of water displaced. NOTE: A cubic foot of water weighs 62.4 pounds.

The formula to compute specific gravity is:

$$SG = \frac{\text{Oven dry weight}}{\text{Weight of displaced volume of water}}$$

If you know a wood specie's specific gravity (found on a chart), you can estimate the final weight of the product. For example, you are going to build a cabinet out of white oak which has a specific gravity of .56. The project requires six pieces, one foot wide, eight feet long, and one inch thick. To calculate the weight of the project, first calculate the number of cubic feet of wood needed. Follow this formula:

$$\text{cu.ft.} = \frac{6 \ (\text{pieces}) \times 12 \ (\text{width}) \times 96 \ (\text{length}) \times 1 \ (\text{thickness})}{1728 \ (\text{cubic in. in a cubic ft.})}$$

$$= \frac{6912}{1728} = 4 \ \text{cu. ft.}$$

Now calculate the weight of a cubic foot of white oak. It is .56 (SG of oak) × 62.4 (the weight of a cubic foot of water). The result is 34.94 pounds.

The final weight of the project is the number of cubic feet of wood multiplied by the weight per cubic foot of wood, 4 × 34.94. The example project will weigh approximately 139.76 pounds. Hardware, finishing products, and other materials add additional weight.

Specific gravity varies among species of wood. Each species has a slightly different cell size and structure. The more condensed the cell structure, the higher the specific gravity.

WORKING QUALITIES

Working qualities describe how a wood will act during processing. Will it splinter? Will it dull tools? How easily can it be sanded smooth? These qualities vary according to the specific gravity. Wood with low specific gravity is easier to process. Woods with high specific gravity tend to dull tools faster.

Other factors of working qualities include dulling effects, reaction wood, and cell structure.

DULLING EFFECT

The *dulling effect* is how the density of wood and stored minerals dull the tool. It varies between woods with different specific gravities. It is also different among the same species due to mineral deposits. During growth, a tree is contantly extracting water and minerals from the ground. One of these minerals is silica, similar to tiny sand particles. Large deposits of silica wear tools quicker.

REACTION WOOD

As a tree grows, it develops wood with distinctive properties called *reaction wood.* Reaction wood is divided into compression wood and tension wood. *Compression wood* is found on the underside of limbs and leaning trunks. *Tension wood* is found on the upper side of limbs and leaning trunks.

Reaction wood tends to expand and twist as it is cut, Fig. 10-12. This causes two problems. First, the surface of reaction wood might feel rough after planing. A smooth finish may be hard to achieve.

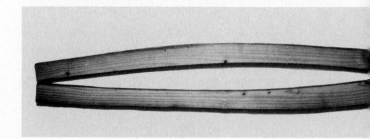

Fig. 10-12. The distortion of reaction wood during cutting can be dramatic. (Forest Products Laboratory)

This occurs more often in low specific gravity (lighter weight) wood.

The second problem of reaction wood is it may pinch the blade during sawing. Sawing relieves internal stress. Reactions to stress relief cannot be predicted. The wood might twist and close the kerf on the blade. This is a serious hazard because the wood could be thrown toward you.

CELL STRUCTURE

The size and bond of cells for different wood species varies. Woods with small, tightly bonded cell structure (usually having high specific gravity) tend to chip and tear. The bond is produced by overlapping fibers held together with the tree's own "glue," called lignin. Chipping can be reduced somewhat by using extremely sharp tools.

MECHANICAL PROPERTIES

The mechanical properties of wood include strength and elasticity. These are partially affected by the moisture content in the wood which decreases strength and increases elasticity.

STRENGTH

A number of properties affect strength. One is the *anisotropic* nature of wood. In other words, it is not equally strong in every direction. Its greatest strength is with the grain (longitudinal), not across the grain (tangential or radial). Long boards, such as shelves, should have the grain in lengthwise direction.

The specific gravity is also another strength factor. Generally, denser woods will be stronger.

ELASTICITY

Elasticity is the capability for the wood to spring back after being bent. Not all woods allow for bending without damaging the cell structure. Moisture permits wood to be bent into a permanent position. Wood is like a sponge. When moistened, it expands and becomes flexible. Remove the water and it shrinks and becomes rigid.

Moisture can expand the wood to remove dents. For example, suppose you dented a piece while processing it. You can remove the dent with a wet cloth and iron. Place the wet cloth over the dent and gently rub with a warm iron. The moisture will enter the cells and expand them to their original position.

Moisture also assists bending wood pieces, such as chair backs. Soak the wood for a period of time until it becomes supple. Then place it in a form and clamp it. When dry, the wood will retain the new shape.

SUMMARY

Wood has a natural beauty which makes it desirable for cabinetmaking and interior design. Wood also has structural qualities which meet the needs of construction.

Wood from deciduous trees is called hardwood. Wood from conifer trees is named softwood. This nomenclature does not refer to the actual density or weight of the wood.

Growth in a tree occurs in the cambium. The cambium produces both bark cells and cells which carry nutrients to the tree. Growth in springtime is earlywood; growth in summer is called latewood. Each growing season produces an annual ring.

The physical properties of wood include color, grain pattern, and surface defects. Most of these qualities are not seen until the tree has been cut into lumber.

The moisture content of wood has significant effect on it. When the moisture content goes below fiber saturation point the wood begins to shrink. Shrinkage in lumber varies according to the section of the tree and how it was cut. The critical time to maintain an even moisture content is during processing.

Working qualities include dulling effect, reaction wood, and the density. The density of a wood describes weight per unit of volume. The more dense a wood is the heavier it will be. It will also be stronger. Woods laden with minerals, dense woods, and tension and compression woods are harder to work.

CABINETMAKING TERMS

Tap root, fibrous root, trunk, crown, photosynthesis, bark, cambium, phloem, inner bark, xylem, sapwood, earlywood, springwood, latewood, summerwood, annual ring, grain pattern, heartwood, pith, wood ray, deciduous tree, hardwood, conifer tree, softwood, cross-sectional face, radial face, tangential face, longitudinal, tracheids, fusiform ray, horizontal resin duct, vertical resin duct, border pit, simple pit, lignin, fiber, parenchyma cell, vessel, pore, diffuse-porous, ring-porous, open grain, closed grain, moisture content, moisture meter, green wood, wet weight, oven-dry weight, free water, bound water, equilibrium moisture content, average moisture content, shrinkage, density, specific gravity, working qualities, dulling effect, reaction wood, compression wood, tension wood, anistropic, elasticity.

TEST YOUR KNOWLEDGE

1. Diagram the structure of tap and fibrous root systems.

2. New cells are produced by the springwood layer of a tree. True or False?
3. Both earlywood and latewood cells are developed in a single growing season. True or False?
4. The leaves of a deciduous tree will drop:
    a. In the fall.
    b. In the spring.
    c. Not at all. They remain green all year.
    d. Only during drought.
5. The difference between hardwoods and softwoods is:
    a. Hardwoods are harder than softwoods.
    b. Softwoods are harder than hardwoods.
    c. Softwoods dent easier than hardwoods.
    d. Hardwood has more cells per inch.
6. Describe the layers seen in a cross-section of a tree.
7. The three terms that identify faces of wood are _____, _____, and _____.
8. List five physical characteristics of wood.
9. Both oxidation of wood cells and springwood becoming inactive cause the wood to _____.
10. What is the difference between free water and bound water in a wood cell?
11. What happens when free water is removed from a piece of wood?
12. What happens when bound water is removed from a piece of wood?
13. Construction grade lumber is adequate for cabinetmaking. True or False?
14. The direction wood shrinks is:
    a. Mostly longitudinal direction.
    b. Mostly in the radial direction.
    c. Mostly in the tangential direction.
    d. Equal in all directions.
15. Sketch the four different samples of shrinkage.
16. Specific gravity is a measure of _____.
17. _____ _____ is caused by compression and tension in the tree as it grows. It (does/does not) cause problems in working wood.
18. What is the difference between open grain and closed grain wood species?
19. Two mechanical properties of wood are _____ and _____.
20. What is the method of removing dents in wood?

Chapter 11

After studying this chapter, you will be able to:
☐ *Explain the sequence of steps used to convert trees to usable lumber.*
☐ *Describe the three methods of sawing.*
☐ *Explain hardwood and softwood grading practices.*
☐ *Order lumber and millwork.*
☐ *Identify various lumber defects.*

Wood is a world-wide resource for cabinetmaking and construction materials. From wood comes lumber, millwork, and manufactured wood products. Lumber is purchased in two ways. One is by nominal size boards (1'' x 3'', 2'' x 4'', etc.). The other is random widths and lengths (RWL). Millwork includes manufactured dowels, mouldings, and decorative wood pieces. Manufactured wood products include plywood, particleboard, and fiberboard.

All wood species are brought to market as lumber through a sequence of steps. These include harvesting, sawing, drying, and grading. Individuals or industries then order lumber and millwork to meet their needs.

HARVESTING

Lumber begins its journey to you as a mature tree being *harvested.* Logging industries select and fell (cut) trees for market by two methods, sectional felling and systematic felling.

SECTIONAL FELLING

Tree farmers using *sectional felling* cut large sections of a forest at one time with heavy machinery, Fig. 11-1. Clearing large portions of a forest is less expensive than cutting individual trees. Sectional felling occurs most often in softwood harvesting. These trees grow faster and mature quicker than hardwoods. The cleared sections are replanted and will reach maturity within a person's lifetime. Seedlings are grown at tree farms and later transported to planned forests. Replenishing wood resources is

Fig. 11-1. Sectional felling of softwood forests. Once logs are cleared, new seedlings will be replanted. (Southern Forest Products Assoc.)

directed under the American Tree Farm System. This system assures wood will remain a renewable resource.

SYSTEMATIC FELLING

Using *systematic felling,* loggers single out trees to be harvested. They may be selected because wood of that specie is needed. They also may be cut because they are diseased or infested with insects. Removal of these trees will allow those nearby to grow quicker and healthier.

Trees marked for systematic felling are notched and cut with a saw, Fig. 11-2. The trees are cut near the ground.

Selective removal of smaller trees is done by hydraulic machines which both cut and transfer the tree. Single trees are difficult and more costly to harvest. Nearby small trees may be destroyed in the process. Large scale replanting is impossible.

Once the trees are felled, small branches are trimmed from the main trunk. The trunk is cut into logs suitable for transporting; this process is called

Fig. 11-2. Systematic felling requires trees be cut individually. (Weyerhauser)

bucking. Logs are then transported to the saw mill by truck or railroad cars.

Most lumber mills are located within short distances from harvestable forests. They are also located near a body of water. Logs can be stored in the water until sawing. Water prevents insect damage and end checking due to premature drying. Denser species which might not float are stacked and sprayed with water, Fig. 11-3.

Fig. 11-3. Logs stored on land are stacked and kept moist to prevent premature drying. (Hoge Lumber Co.)

SAWING

At the lumbermill, logs are loaded onto a jack ladder and transported to a preparation area. There, they are washed and sometimes debarked in preparation for sawing, Fig. 11-4. Each log is placed on a carriage which moves it through a large band saw or circular saw, Fig 11-5. The saw creates rough-edged planks. The angle at which the saw cuts through the log determines the grain pattern, amount of shrinkage during seasoning, and cost of the lumber. Lumber is sawed by three methods: plain sawing, quarter sawing, and rift sawing.

Fig. 11-4. Bark is removed before sawing. It will be used to make other products. (Southern Forest Products Assoc.)

Plain sawing

The most common method of sawing is *plain sawing.* Logs are cut tangent to the annual rings, Fig. 11-6A. Softwood cut by this method is called flat-grained; hardwood lumber is called plain-sawed.

Plain sawing is less costly and wasteful than any other method. The average width of the plank is greater. More nominal or RWL lumber can be produced per log. The wood is also easier to kiln dry.

Plain-sawed lumber is most likely to be lower quality. It is apt to warp. Annual rings attempt to straighten during drying. Plain-sawed lumber also tends to check and split more than lumber sawn by quarter and rift methods. Knots often appear round, caused by saw cuts across branches.

The grain pattern appears as multiple "Vs" because the saw is cutting through successive layers of growth. Each V-shape represents the earlywood and latewood of a single growing season.

Quarter sawing

For *quarter-sawed* lumber, logs are cut into four sections, called quarters. Each quarter is then sawn

Fig. 11-5. Logs are mounted on a carriage to be sawn. Top. Using a band saw. (Forest Products Laboratory) Bottom. Using a circular saw. (Hoge Lumber Co.)

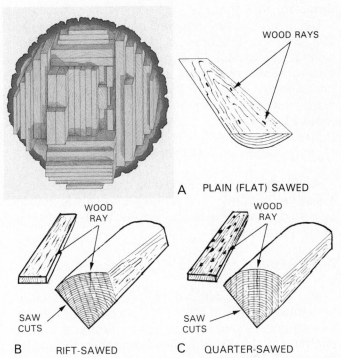

Fig. 11-6. Each method of sawing produces different appearance and structural qualities. (Georgia-Pacific Corp.)

Quarter-sawn and rift-sawn lumber are more costly because of increased handling time. Once the log is quartered, each piece must be loaded onto the carriage and positioned for sawing. In plain sawing, the log only needs to be rotated.

Once the logs are sawn, the flitches are ripped to width and crosscut to length, Fig. 11-7. Each cut must be determined by the sawyer to achieve the longest and widest possible board. The boards will have random lengths and widths.

at a angle between 65° and 90° to the annual rings, Fig. 11-6B. The grain pattern, for the most part will be straight lines. Cuts farthest from the center of the log will produce the most figured grain. Cuts near the center are perpendicular to the annual rings and will produce straight grain.

Quarter-sawed lumber twists and cups less than plain-sawed lumber. There are fewer checks and splits because cuts are parallel with wood rays. The rays appear as flakes running along the length of the board.

Rift sawing

Lumber is also quartered in preparation for *rift sawing.* Saw cuts are made at approximately a 45° angle to the annual rings, Fig. 11-6C. The advantages gained by rift sawing over plain sawing are the same as those gained by quarter sawing. However, the straight grain pattern runs lengthwise and is very thin and decorative. Wood rays are apparent, as in quarter sawn, but are much longer.

Fig. 11-7. Flitches are ripped manually to maximize width. (Forest Products Laboratory)

Saw, dry, rip, process

Using newer sawing techniques such as the *Saw, Dry,* and *Rip* (SDR) process, flitches are ripped after drying. The SDR approach is used to make structural grade lumber from low to medium density hardwoods. Using SDR and controlled drying, both warp and internal stress levels of the wood are reduced.

DRYING

After sawing, lumber must be dried to reduce the moisture content. The drying process is called *seasoning.* Wood is seasoned either by air drying or by kiln drying.

AIR DRYING

Air drying (AD) requires that boards are *sticked* (separated by wood strips) and stacked for free air movement. Drying is done either outdoors or in a shelter, Fig. 11-8. When dried outdoors, the top of the stack is covered to prevent rain water from entering the wood.

Beware of air-dried lumber. Even after years of sheltered protection, the moisture content may remain at 15 to 19 percent. Cabinetmaking woods should have approximately an 8 percent moisture content.

TIME-TABLE FOR AIR-SEASONING (IN DAYS)			
HARDWOODS		**SOFTWOODS**	
Ash	70-110	Red cedar	50-140
Basswood	30-60	Cypress	200-275
Beech	150-200	White pine	45-150
Birch	150-200	Redwood	60-180
Cherry	150-200		
Chestnut	85-125		
Elm	80-130		
Gum	70-160		
Hickory	150-200		
Mahogany	70-110		
Maple	150-200		
Oak	180-300		
Walnut	120-170		

Fig. 11-8. Reducing moisture content by air drying requires many days. (Hoge Lumber Co., Hoadley)

KILN DRYING

The moisture content of *kiln-dried* (KD) *lumber* is reduced using large ovens, called kilns. Circulating air passes through the lumber which, like air-dried lumber, is sticked, Fig. 11-9. The temperature and humidity of the air are controlled to promote gradual, even drying. Steam is added at first to increase humidity. This prevents sudden surface drying which would cause checks and splits. The humidity is then reduced and the temperature gradually increased to a constant level until drying is complete. The time required to complete this process depends on the type of wood, efficiency of the kiln, and amount of wood to be seasoned. Most kiln drying is complete within 24 hours.

For many commercial purposes, lumber is air-dried and then kiln dried. Air drying removes the free water to reach the fiber saturation point; no shrinkage occurs. Controlled kiln drying then removes the bound water. During this time the lumber shrinks. For construction grade lumber, the moisture content is reduced to about 19 percent. For cabinet lumber, the content is reduced to 5 to 10 percent. This lumber is stamped PKD (partially kiln-dried).

IDENTIFYING LUMBER DEFECTS

Lumber defects detract from the appearance and workability of the wood. The Wood Handbook, published by the Forest Products Laboratory, contains information about the formation and nature of defects. Cabinetmakers need to know how defects affect both the aesthetic and structural properties of the wood. There are three categories of defects: natural defects, defects caused by improper seasoning or storage, and defects caused by machining.

NATURAL DEFECTS

Wood contains various natural defects. Most are not seen until the wood has been cut and seasoned. Some affect the strength of the wood, while others make the appearance unique and are desirable. Defects include knots, pitch pockets, bark pockets, and peck.

Knots
Knots are encountered by sawing across part of a log which had a branch. Branches grow from the pith across the trunk or stem. During growth, the tree stem forms around the branch. Although the knot itself is as strong as a piece of wood, the grain pattern surrounding it weakens the lumber. The wood dries, shrinks, and may split. Wood fibers can separate and cause loose knots.

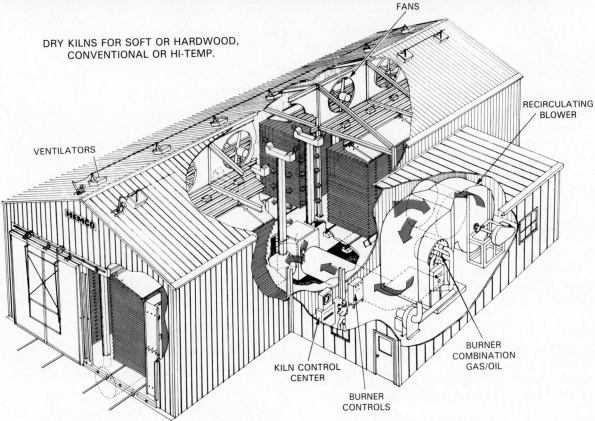

DRY KILNS FOR SOFT OR HARDWOOD,
CONVENTIONAL OR HI-TEMP.

FANS

RECIRCULATING
BLOWER

VENTILATORS

KILN CONTROL
CENTER

BURNER
CONTROLS

BURNER
COMBINATION
GAS/OIL

Fig. 11-9. Kiln drying. Lumber is transported into kiln on rails and dried using circulating, heated air.
(Harvey Engineering and Manufacturing Corp.)

There are different shapes and types of knots, Fig. 11-10. *Round knots*, called branch knots, are found in wood that was cut tangential to the annual rings. The cut gives a cross-section view of the branch. *Spike knots* are found in wood cut radially. The saw splits the branch through the center. *Oval knots* are found when the wood was cut at an angle to the branch.

Knots are further described as intergrown or encased. As long as a branch is alive, there is continuous growth at the intersection of the limb and trunk. Knots cut from live branches are called *intergrown*. They retain their contact with the surrounding wood and are called *tight knots*. If a branch dies, additional growth on the trunk will surround the branch. Knots cut from this area are

INTERGROWN KNOT

ENCASED LOOSE KNOT

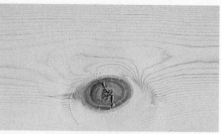
CHECKED KNOT

SPIKE KNOT

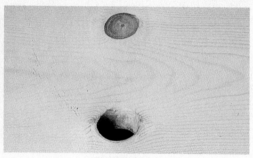
KNOT HOLE

Fig. 11-10. Knot defects come in all shapes and sizes. Intergrown knots are more stable than encased knots. (Western Wood Products Assoc.)

encased by surrounding growth. They often become *loose knots* when they lose contact with the wood surrounding them.

A *checked knot* contains a split in the knot caused by seasoning. A *knot hole* results from a loose, encased knot which has been knocked out during seasoning or by rough handling or machining.

Pitch pocket

Pitch pockets are openings in the wood which contain solid or liquid resins, called pitch, Fig. 11-11. The pocket is formed by resin ducts. Pitch pockets are found in various softwoods such as pine, spruce, and fir.

Bark pocket

Bark pockets contain bark material which was enclosed during growth, Fig. 11-12. This barky section is undetected until the log is sawed. These sections are very weak and unattractive.

Other natural defects

Heartrot, peck, and *grub holes* are other natural defects. Heartrot is a form of decay which occurs while the tree is still alive. Certain decay fungi attack the heartwood (rarely the sapwood), but cease after the tree has been cut. The cypress family is especially susceptible. Fungi attacking bald cypress cause brown pockets, called *peck,* Fig. 11-13. Those attacking Douglas-fir cause *white pockets.*

Grub holes are voids in the wood left by insects. The insects burrowed through the wood while the tree was alive. Residue from the insect may also be found in the holes.

Fig. 11-11. Pitch pockets include hardened resins. (Western Wood Products Assoc.)

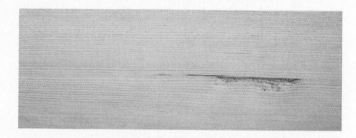
Fig. 11-12. Bark pockets are formed when bark cells are enclosed during growth. (Western Wood Products Assoc.)

DEFECTS CAUSED BY IMPROPER SEASONING OR STORAGE

Improper seasoning and the resulting shrinkage cause various lumber defects. These include warp, splits, checks, shakes, honeycomb, blue stain, decay, and insect damage.

Warp

Warp refers to curving of the wood either on the face, edge, or length of the board. Five types of

Fig. 11-13. Peck is caused by fungus. Grub holes are caused by insects. (Western Wood Products Assoc.)

warp are: bow, crook, twist, kink, and cup, Fig. 11-14. A *bow* is a curve lengthwise along the face of the board from end to end. A *crook* is curve along the edge of a board from end to end. A *twist* is a corkscrew effect. A *kink* is a deviation along the board caused by a knot or irregular grain pattern.

A *cup* is a curve across the face of the board from edge to edge.

Various types of warp occur during seasoning. Most are caused by the shrinkage of the wood cells. Internal stress in the wood is another cause of warping. Constant pressure from weight of a limb or leaning trunk causes reaction wood. The growth rings are compressed or spread apart. Natural irregularities during growth can also cause eccentric annual rings.

Warp also occurs as a result of improper storage. As different surfaces are exposed to moisture, the grain (wood cells) expands. Warp caused by improper storage can be minimized by stacking the lumber neatly and maintaining the average moisture content of the room. Wood is best stacked flat with ample sticking to prevent bowing. The weight of the wood minimizes cupping. If the wood must be stored outdoors, put it on a level foundation above the ground. Also cover it with tarpaulins or plastic.

The amount of warp is related to the wood species, Fig. 11-15. The grain patterns of some wood are more apt to cause warp than others.

Checks and splits

Checks and splits are separations of the wood fibers along the grain and across the annual rings, Fig. 11-16. *Splits* travel the length of the wood. *Checks* are short separations, found in the end of seasoned boards. Checks and splits are caused when wood rays separate during seasoning.

Fig. 11-14. Warp is the result of uneven shrinkage. (Forest Products Laboratory).

TENDENCY TO WARP

SOFTWOODS	
Low	**Intermediate**
Cedars	Bald cypress
Pine, ponderosa	Douglas fir
Pine, sugar	Firs, true
Pine, white	Hemlocks
Redwood	Larch, western
Spruce	Pine, jack
	Pine, lodgepole
	Pine, red
	Pine, southern

HARDWOODS		
Low	**Intermediate**	**High**
Alder	Ash	Beech
Aspen	Basswood	Cottonwood
Birch, paper,	Birch, yellow	Elm, American
and sweet	Elm, rock	Sweetgum
Butternut	Hackberry	Sycamore
Cherry	Hickory	Tanoak
Walnut	Locust	Tupelo
American tulip	Magnolia, southern	
	Maples	
	Oaks	
	Pecan	
	Willow	

Fig. 11-15. Warp is a major factor in the wood you choose.

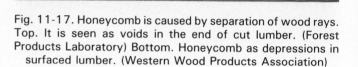

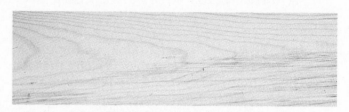

Fig. 11-17. Honeycomb is caused by separation of wood rays. Top. It is seen as voids in the end of cut lumber. (Forest Products Laboratory) Bottom. Honeycomb as depressions in surfaced lumber. (Western Wood Products Association)

Fig. 11-16. Top. Splits run the length of the board. Bottom. Checks are only found in the ends of the board. (Forest Products Laboratory)

Shake

Shakes are separations of the wood between two growth rings. Separation occurs while the tree is standing or when it is felled. *Ring failure* is also a separation of growth rings, but occurs during seasoning. It is caused by the weakening of the bond between rings because of high heat during seasoning.

Honeycomb

Honeycomb refers to internal voids in the wood rays, Fig. 11-17. It is caused by using too high of heat during seasoning while free water is still present in the wood cells. This usually is not detected until the lumber is being machined.

Blue stain

Blue stain is discoloration of the wood caused by a mold or fungus, Fig. 11-18. It occurs after the wood has been cut and left in an area of high humidity.

Fig. 11-18. Abnormal coloring known as blue stain. (Western Wood Products Assoc.)

Blue stain is found mostly in sapwood and ranges from a bluish-black to brown in color. The mold or fungus causing blue stain penetrates into the sapwood and cannot be removed by surfacing. It doesn't affect the strength of the wood; however, it can detract from the appearance. The stain may completely cover the sapwood or may be specks, spots, streaks, or patches of different shades.

Decay

Decay is the disintegration of the wood fibers due to decay-producing fungi. It is found in both heartwood and sapwood. Decay causes the wood to become spongy and unsuitable for use, Fig. 11-19.

Fig. 11-19. Decay ends the useful purpose of wood. (Forest Products Laboratory)

There are two types of decay: brown rot and white rot. In *brown rot*, only the cellulose (material making up wood cells) is removed. The wood becomes brown in color and tends to crack across the grain. Brown rot which has dried is commonly called *dry rot*. With *white rot*, both the cellulose and lignin, which holds cells together, deteriorates. The wood loses color, but does not crack until the white rot is severe.

Serious decay occurs when the wood moisture content is above the fiber saturation point (30 percent). Wood exposed to rain, or in contact with the ground, typically decays very rapidly.

A less common form of decay is soft rot. *Soft rot* is caused by molds and not decay-producing fungi. It only affects the surface and can be removed by planing. It is found on wood exposed to both constant and intermittent moisture levels above 20 percent.

Insect damage

Worms and other insects bore into wood leaving small holes, called *worm holes. Pin holes* (worm holes less than 1/4 in. [6 mm]) are often left to enhance appearance of the wood. Minor defects in the wood make it unique. You can cover unwanted wormholes with wood filler.

Preventing stain, decay, and insect damage

Wood which is consistently exposed to insects or moisture levels above 20 percent should be protected. Chemical preservatives which poison the food supply for both insects and fungi are used to treat more susceptible woods. Commonly used chemicals are listed in Fig. 11-20.

Preservatives can be applied by pressure treatment, hot-cold bath, cold-soaking, and brushing or spraying. Pressure treatment is the most effective because chemicals penetrate deep into the wood.

WOOD PRESERVATIVES

Common wood preservatives are rated here according to various characteristics. Symbols are:

★ = Usable
★ ★ = Better
★ ★ ★ = Best

PRESERVATIVE	Toxicity	Odor	Color	Paintability	Soil contact	Permeability
Creosote	★ ★ ★	★	★	★	★ ★ ★	★ ★ ★
Penta	★ ★ ★	★ ★	★ ★ ★	★ ★ ★	★ ★ ★	★ ★ ★
Water soluble preservatives†	★ ★ ★	★ ★ ★	★ ★	★ ★ ★	★ ★	★ ★

†Containing fluor-chrome-arsenate-phenol, or chromated zinc chloride.

Fig. 11-20. Wood preservatives can be used to prevent decay.

DEFECTS CAUSED BY MACHINING

Lumber defects or blemishes may appear during the manufacturing process. Most occur during surfacing. They are machine burn, raised grain, torn again, wavy dressing, skip, and dog holes, Fig. 11-21.

Machine burn

Machine burn is a darkening of the wood caused by heat. It occurs when dull tools are used. If the board stops during surfacing and the cutter head rubs in one place, a burn may occur. Too slow of feed can also cause burn.

Raised grain

Raised grain is a variation in surface texture caused by machining wood of high moisture content. As the cutter knives smooth the face, they press latewood into the softer earlywood. After leaving the surfacer, the earlywood recovers and expands, causing the grain to lift. Raised grain is most apparent in construction grade softwoods.

Torn grain

Torn grain occurs when wood fibers are torn from the board by the saw, shaper, jointer, or planer. Torn grain occurs most in softer wood and around knots where the grain pattern is irregular.

Wavy dressing

Wavy dressing results when boards are fed into the surfacer faster than the knives can cut. Each knife makes a small arc in the wood. You can feel a slight rippled texture even though rough sawn spots have all been removed.

Skip

A *skip* is a section of a board which is unsurfaced. Skips appear when the board is not flat. The sawyer may not cut the board straight. The board may also warp. Slight depressions are formed. These areas are not hit by the surfacer and the texture remains rough.

Dog hole

A *dog hole* is a scar in the board caused by the metal hook (dog) that grips a log while it is sawed. It is different than torn grain because of the amount of wood removed. A dog hole may be 1/4 in. (6 mm) deep; torn grain is only a surface blemish.

GRADING

After seasoning, lumber is *graded* according to quality. Lumber grading is a matter of judgement and experience, Fig. 11-22. Graders rate each piece according to the size of board and amount of defect-

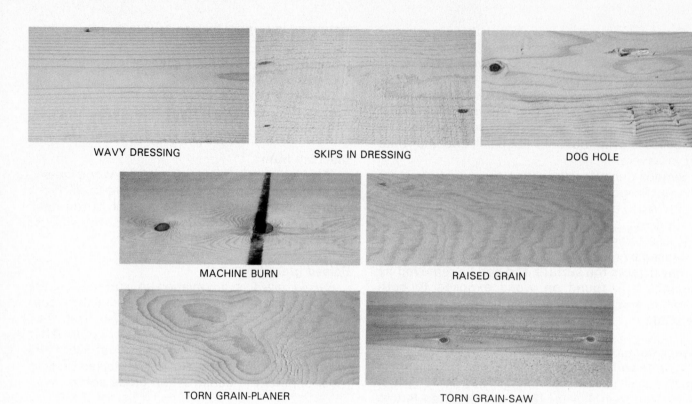

WAVY DRESSING   SKIPS IN DRESSING   DOG HOLE

MACHINE BURN   RAISED GRAIN

TORN GRAIN-PLANER   TORN GRAIN-SAW

Fig. 11-21. Various machine-caused defects occur during surfacing. (Western Wood Products Assoc.)

Fig. 11-22. Graders inspect each board for size and clearness. (Southern Forest Products Assoc.)

free lumber in it. The clear cuttings, or yield, of a board needed to achieve a certain grade will differ between hardwood and softwood. It also can differ between species.

HARDWOOD GRADING

Hardwood is graded as factory, dimension, or finished market lumber. *Factory grades,* also called cutting grades, specify the amount of clear lumber that can be cut from a board. They are established by the National Hardwood Lumber Association. These pieces will have random lengths and widths and slight variations in thickness. However, the wider and longer the board, the better the grade. *Dimension grades* are surfaced to specific thickness and/or cut to specific lengths and widths. They are more expensive, thus, specified less frequently. Factory grades are quality lumber for mouldings and trim. See Fig. 11-31.

FACTORY GRADES

Factory grades are based on the amount of clear wood that can be cut in given lengths from a single board. Each grade requires that the board be at least 3 in. (75 mm) in width. Smaller boards are used for making mouldings. Smaller scraps are processed into particleboard and fiberboard. Fig. 11-23 shows a large board with three cuttings. Since the board exceeds the minimum percentage of clear wood and minimum dimension of boards cut, it is graded as *FAS* (Firsts And Seconds). The different grades and minimum specifications are indicated on Fig. 11-24.

FAS is the top grade for hardwoods. The board must be at least 84 percent clear. It is graded on the poorer face of the board so that you know the other side is as good or better. *FAS 1-Face* lumber maintains the same specifications as FAS. However, it is graded on the better surface of the board. It may contain some pitch pockets or wane. *Wane* is bark incorporated in the wood or on the edge of the board. Lumber graded as *Selects* is the same as FAS 1-Face except the minimum length is reduced by 2 ft. (600 mm) and the minimum width is reduced by 2 in. (50 mm).

FAS 1-Face and Selects lumber are used in products where only one face of the board will be seen. Chests, dressers, and other storage cabinets require only the outer face to be free from defects.

The *No. 1 Common grade* is also called the *Thrift grade* because you get the most clear lumber for your money. However, clear cut lengths can be as short as 2 ft. (600 mm). The board must be 66 percent clear, yet most exceed 75 percent clear. Thrift grade is an excellent choice for small to medium size projects.

Grades not listed on the table include No. 2 Common and No. 3 Common. The *No. 2 Common grade* has the same dimensions as No. 1 Common lumber but requires only 50 percent clear wood. The *No. 3 Common* requires only 25 percent clear wood. These lumber grades are unsuitable for cabinet-making purposes.

The specifications listed in Fig. 11-12 can vary according to specie. The percentage of clear wood may differ. Check with your lumber company first to determine the specifications for the specie you plan to purchase.

Combination grades

Most lumber companies have *combined grades* to sell lumber which is not often requested. For example, people shy away from FAS grades because of price. The *FAS 1-Face and Better* combination grade includes FAS 1-Face and FAS grade boards but is sold at a price lower than the FAS grade. Consumers purchase this combination grade knowing that they are getting better grade lumber along with FAS 1-Face wood. The *Selects and Better* grades include shorter length boards along with higher grades.

DIMENSION GRADES

Dimensioned hardwoods are flats and squares. *Flats* refer to nominal, surfaced standard sizes which are wider than they are thick. Examples are 1 x 2, 1 x 4, 2 x 4, etc. *Squares* are 2 x 2, 3 x 3, etc. Dimension grade hardwoods are graded according to appearance:
• Clear—two sides.
• Clear—one side.
• Paint. May consist of two pieces attached by finger joints.
• Core. Used between veneers for lumber core plywood.
• Sound. Includes defects.

Rough sawn squares are clear, select, or sound grades. Surfaces on squares are clear, select, paint, or second grades.

Few cabinetmakers specify dimension grade hardwood because it is expensive. You might use clear squares for turning on a lathe.

SOFTWOOD GRADING

Softwood grading also applies to appearance. In addition, softwoods are graded according to use and moisture content, Fig. 11-25. The two categories are construction and remanufacture grades.

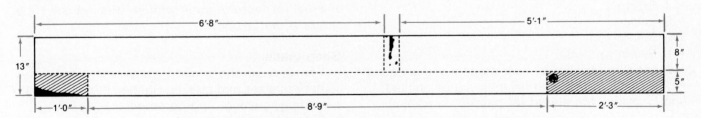

Fig. 11-23. Size of clear cuttings determine the grade of the board.

Generalized NHLA Hardwood Grade Minimums (Does not show species variations.)						
Grade	Side Graded	Minimum Size Length	Width	Minimum Cutting Sizes	Maximum Waste in Board	Price Estimate
FAS	Poorer	8'+	6"+	4" x 5' or 3" x 7'	Up to 16%	Highest
FAS 1-Face	Better	8'+	6"+		Up to 16%	– 5%
Selects	Better	6'+	4"+		Up to 16%	– 10%
#1 Common (Thrift)	Poorer	4'+	3"+	4" x 2' or 3" x 3'	Up to 34%	– 30%

Fig. 11-24. General hardwood grading rules. Some species vary in clear cutting sizes.

Fig. 11-25. Boards are sorted according to grade. (Southern Forest Products Assoc.)

CONSTRUCTION GRADES

Construction grade lumber is the least expensive and most available. It is also called *yard lumber.* The moisture content is 19 percent making it likely to warp, split, and check when it further dries. It will also bleed liquid sap which did not harden during seasoning. Construction grade lumber has a variety of building construction applications.

Construction grades are classified as finish, board, or dimension lumber.

Finish lumber
Finish lumber is less than 3 in. (75 mm) thick and 12 in. (300 mm) or less in width. Use it where appearance is important, such as: floors, siding, wall covering, etc. Grades are:
• A Select.
• B Select.
• C Select.
• D Select.

A and B grades have fewer defects and are used where clear and stained finishes will be applied. C and D grades are suited for painted finishes.

Board lumber
Board lumber is less than 2 in. (50 mm) thick and 2 in. (50 mm) to 12 in. (300 mm) wide. It is used for general construction. Boards are graded from No. 1 board to No. 5 board. Inspect them closely to determine finishing capabilities. Higher numbered grades contain additional knots and pitch pockets.

Dimension lumber
Dimension lumber is used for structural framing. Nominal size is 2 in. thick by 2 in. (50 mm x 50 mm) wide. Dimension lumber is divided into three areas: light framing, structural light framing, and structural joists and planks. Install light framing grades where high strength is not required. They are:
• Construction.
• Standard.
• Utility.
• Economy.

Grades for *structural framing* are:
• Select structural.
• No. 1.
• No. 2.
• No. 3.
• Economy.

The nominal size of structural joist and plank lumber is 2 in. (50 mm) to 4 in. (100 mm) thick and 6 in. (150 mm) wide.

REMANUFACTURE GRADES

Remanufacture grade lumber is divided into factory and shop grades. The moisture content ranges from 6 to 12 percent. This lumber is more suited to cabinetmaking than construction grade materials.

Factory grade
Factory grade lumber is 1 in. (25 mm) to 4 in. (100 mm) thick and 5 in. (125 mm) or more in width. It is used for sash and door construction. It has good appearance for any type of finish. The grades are:
• No. 1 and No. 2 Clear Factory.
• No. 3 Clear Factory.
• No. 1 Shop.
• No. 2 Shop.
• No. 3 Shop.

Note that the word shop is used. This is a quality level for factory grade lumber. It is not the shop grade of softwood.

Shop grade
You can purchase *shop grade* softwoods in a variety of sizes and quality. Ratings include Select, moulding, cutting, and common grades.

Select grades include A through D Select. They are more often specified as:
• B and Better. Clear on both sides.
• C Select and Better. Clear on one side.
• D Select. Contains numerous small, tight, knots.

Grade D is recommended for painting. Others may be finished as desired.

Moulding grade exhibits characteristics of both Select and Shop grades. Pieces are long, narrow, and clear strips used for trim and moulding.

Cutting grades fall in sequence below Select grades. They contain a few too many small knots. Grades, as for hardwoods, depend on the amount of clear lumber that can be cut from a board. Cutting grades are:

- Third Clear. A few small knots.
- No. 1 Shop. More hard knots and smaller cutting yields.
- No. 2 Shop. Not recommended for cabinetry.
- No. 3 Shop. Not recommended for cabinetry.

Common grades contain knots. They are for knotty furniture or paneling and utility purposes such as shelving. They are graded No. 1 Common through No. 5 Common. Combination grades are usually marketed for Common grade softwoods. They include:

- No. 2 Common and Better. Tight knots.
- No. 3 Common. Larger defects including spike knots, pith, and shakes.
- No. 4 and No. 5 Common. These contain many defects.

Local lumber yards typically supply only construction grade softwoods. Few handle remanufacture grades. Their open sheds are not suitable for remanufacture lumber which must maintain a low moisture content. Heated sheds would add to lumber cost. Although not recommended for cabinetmaking, construction grades can be used if left to dry indoors for some time. Before using, check the moisture content to see if it meets the equilibrium moisture content.

ORDERING LUMBER

Ordering hardwood and softwood lumber involves specifications. You have to deal with qualities, quantities, conditions, and species.

QUALITIES

Quality refers to hardwood and softwood grades. Be familiar with grading policies of the National Hardwood Lumber Association and Western Wood Products Association (softwood). Before ordering, check with your lumber company for any special grading practices.

QUANTITIES

Most lumber used in cabinetmaking is sold by quantity, not by single boards. Only construction grade softwoods, dimension grade hardwoods, and some shop grade remanufacture softwoods are sold by nominal widths and lengths. Unless you specify width and length, lumber will be sent in *random widths and lengths* (RWL).

Because boards are sawn in random widths and lengths to minimize waste, boards may not be the same size. Thus, the measure for quantities of lumber is not based on board size, but by volume. This measure is the *board foot* or *cubic meter*.

Board feet

A board foot is 12 in. long by 12 in. wide by 1 in. thick. The total volume is 144 cubic inches. The board footage of any piece of lumber can be determined by multiplying the thickness, width, and length in inches, then divide by 144. You can also multiply the thickness and width in inches, the length in feet, and divide by 12. However, there are some rules to follow.

1. Board thickness under 3/4 in. is figured as square foot measure (multiply width times length). Thickness is not taken into account.
2. Thicker boards, 1 in. or over, are marked to the nearest 1/4 in. It is a practice to express the thickness of cabinet grade lumber in quarters of an inch. For example, 1 1/4 in. = 5/4 in.
3. Thickness is based on measurement before surfacing.

The general formula for board footage is:

$$\text{Bd. ft.} = \frac{N \times T(\text{in.}) \times W(\text{in.}) \times L(\text{ft. or in.})}{144 \text{ (or 12 if L is in feet)}}$$

where:

N = number of pieces of that size
T = rough thickness in inches (1 in. for pieces less than 1 in.)
W = rough width in inches
L = length in inches

Examples:

How many board feet are in one piece of 1 in. rough cherry 6 in. wide and 48 in. long?

$$\text{Bd. ft.} = \frac{1 \times 1 \times 6 \times 48}{144} = \frac{288}{144} = 2 \text{ bd. ft.}$$

How many board feet are in four pieces of 6/4 in. × 12 in. × 8 ft. rough sawn oak?

$$\text{Bd. ft.} = \frac{4 \times 4 \times 12 \times 12 \times 8}{4 \times 12} = \frac{2304}{48} = 48 \text{ bd. ft.}$$

How many board feet are in three pieces of 3/4 in. surfaced cherry 5 1/2 in. × 4 ft.?

$$\text{Bd. ft.} = \frac{3 \times 1 \times 6 \times 4}{12} = \frac{72}{12} = 6 \text{ bd. ft.}$$

Cubic meter

Countries following the metric system use the *cubic meter* for volume measurements of random widths and lengths lumber. A cubic meter contains 423.77 board feet. For those accustomed to the board foot, it is best to convert metric measurements. For example:

Suppose you purchase plans that call for .12m³ of oak. A local lumber yard states the price for that amount will be $86.50. How much is that per board foot?

.12m³ lumber × 423.77 = total bd. ft. = 50.86

$$\text{price per bd. ft.} = \frac{\$86.50}{50.86} = \$1.70 \text{ per bd. ft.}$$

SPECIAL LUMBER PROCESSES

Special lumber processes include the surfacing performed, type of seasoning, preservatives, and milled pattern lumber.

Surfacing

Lumber is either rough or surfaced when you buy it. *Surfacing* removes from 1/8 in. to 1/4 in. from the nominal (rough) size. Standard surfaced thicknesses are shown in Fig. 11-26.

STANDARD SURFACED THICKNESSES			
Rough Thickness	S2S Plain Hardwoods	S2S Quartered Hardwoods	S2S Softwoods
1/2″	5/16″	5/16″	3/8″
5/8″	7/16″	7/16″	1/2″
3/4″	9/16″	9/16″	9/16″
1″	*25/32″	*25/32″	25/32″
1″ Pine S4S	—	—	3/4″
1-1/4″	1-1/16″	1-1/32″	1-5/32″
1-1/2″	1-5/16″	1-9/32″	1-13/32″
2″	1-3/4″	1-11/16″	1-13/16″
2-1/2″	2-1/4″	2-1/4″	2-3/8″
3″	2-3/4″	2-3/4″	2-3/4″
4″	3-3/4″	3-3/4″	3-3/4″

Fig. 11-26. Nominal (rough) and standard surfaced thicknesses.

Lumber is surfaced on the sides you specify, Fig. 11-27. It can be left rough or have one edge sawed straight. Several codes for condition are:
• S1S. Surfaced one side; edges and back rough.
• S2S. Surfaced two sides; edges rough.
• S4S. Surfaced both sides and both edges.
• Rgh. No surfacing.
• SLR1E, Straight-Line Ripped One Edge. In addition to surfacing, the SLR1E process rips a straight edge. This might save you time when gluing boards edge to edge because you do not have to joint the edge first.
Keep in mind that you pay for surfacing. Order only the surfacing services you cannot perform.

Seasoning

Another condition which is always specified on the order form is the type of seasoning. As a cabinetmaker, you will always want to specify KD (kiln dried). If you do not, you might receive air dried (AD) lumber with high moisture content.

Preservatives

Wood subject to excessive moisture or insects is frequently impregnated with preservatives. Oil or water base *preservatives* are used to prevent decay

Fig. 11-27. Lumber is surfaced on one, two, or four sides. (Hoge Lumber Co.)

and repel insects. Most are applied under high pressure to penetrate layers of wood cells, Fig. 11-28. Window sash, stair treads, and other millwork exposed to moisture are usually dipped or sprayed with chemicals.

Fig. 11-28. Wood preservatives are applied in a high pressure container. (Georgia-Pacific Corp.)

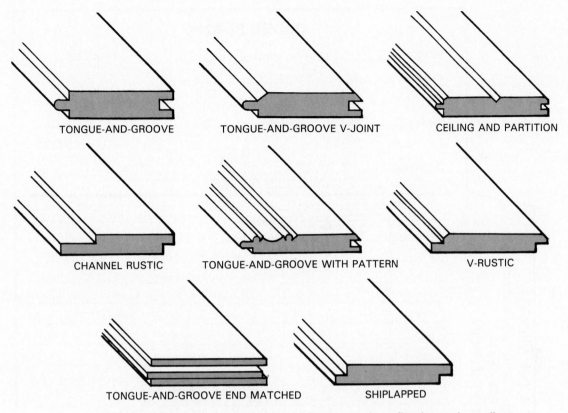

TONGUE-AND-GROOVE   **TONGUE-AND-GROOVE V-JOINT**   **CEILING AND PARTITION**

CHANNEL RUSTIC   **TONGUE-AND-GROOVE WITH PATTERN**   **V-RUSTIC**

TONGUE-AND-GROOVE END MATCHED   **SHIPLAPPED**

Fig. 11-29. Pattern lumber is shaped for special uses, such as flooring and paneling.

Pattern lumber

Beyond surfacing and seasoning, lumber can be specified with milled ends and edges, such as tongue and groove or rabbet joints. Milled boards are referred to as *pattern lumber* and used for floors, siding, and decorative purposes.

Lumber with a tongue and groove on the edges is marked T & G. To specify tongue and groove on both ends and edges, as found in oak flooring, mark T & G & E-M. This lumber often is referred to as matched or *end-matched.* Lumber with rabbet joints to permit accurate edge fitting is called *shiplapped.*

Other effects are available to decorate both interiors and exteriors, Fig. 11-29.

SPECIES

There are hundreds of *species* of trees from which lumber is obtained. Each has different physical and mechanical properties.

Some trees are more abundant than others. Many grow in North America. Others grow on continents around the world.

Tree species have both common and botanical names. For example, ash is a common name for a familiar tree. There are six common species within the ash family. They are white ash, green ash, blue ash, black ash, pumpkin ash, and Oregon ash. Except for Oregon ash, most grow in the eastern half of the country.

The species of wood you choose depends on many factors including color, grain pattern, and strength. You might choose a wood to match other furniture or to fulfill a structural requirement. The various wood species are covered in the next chapter.

WRITTEN ORDERS

A typical lumber company order blank is shown in Fig. 11-30. Note the categories for board feet, thickness, etc. Both single grades and combination grades are specified. Dimensions are specified for several.

MILLWORK

Millwork consists of specialty items frequently processed from moulding grade lumber. Example items are moulding, trim, and specialty items. Only a few wood species are processed into millwork items. They have excellent machining properties and are less likely to warp. Matching colors of millwork to lumber is sometimes a problem because not every species is produced as millwork. You may wish to produce millwork of the same wood species or to fit a particular design.

MOULDING AND TRIM

Moulding and *trim* decorates the edges of most cabinetry, furniture, doorways, and windows. Each

ORDER BLANK

DATE 10 May 1982 SCHOOL DISTRICT No. 213 ORDER No. 369

CHARGE TO Board of Education

CITY Anytown STATE Kansas 66132

SHIP TO Anytown High School 220 Main Street

CITY Anytown STATE Kansas 66132

ORDERED BY John Doe (913) 545-1234 TITLE I.A.I.

TERMS OF SALE: WE SELL OPEN ACCOUNT TO BOARDS OF EDUCATION
AND TO MEMBERS OF SCHOOL FACULTIES

LUMBER

FEET	THICKNESS	CHECK ONE	GRADE AND KIND OF LUMBER
200	1"	RGH ☒ / S2S ☐	No. 1 Com. (Thrift Grade), Basswood, K-D
250	1"	RGH ☐ / S2S ☒	No. 1 Com. & Btr. Aromatic Red Cedar, K-D
100	1"	RGH ☐ / S2S ☒	Selects & Better Cherry, SLR1E, K-D
400	1"	RGH ☐ / S2S ☒	Selects Pin Mark Natural Philippine Mahogany, K-D
300	5/8"	RGH ☐ / S2S ☒	3rd Clear (Thrift Grade) Ponderosa Pine, K-D
200	1"	RGH ☐ / S2S ☒	Same
150	1x12"	RGH ☐ / S2S ☒	No. 2 Com. & Btr. Ponderosa Pine, S4S, K-D
100	1"	RGH ☐ / S2S ☒	No. 1 Com. & Selects (Thrift Grade) Pecan, K-D
100	5/8"	RGH ☐ / S2S ☒	Clear 1 Face Steamed Walnut 4' & 5', S2S to 1/2", K-D
100	1"	RGH ☐ / S2S ☒	FAS 1 Face & Btr. Steamed Walnut 6' & Lgr., K-D
150	1"	RGH ☐ / S2S ☒	No. 1 Com. (Thrift Grade) Steamed Walnut, K-D
200	1"	RGH ☒ / S2S ☐	No. 1 Com. & Selects (Thrift Grade) Willow, K-D
100	1"	RGH ☐ / S2S ☒	Selects & Btr. Northern Birch, 6' to 11', K-D
50	1"	RGH ☐ / S2S ☒	Sel. & Btr. Birdseye Hard Maple, S2S to 7/8", K-D

PLYWOOD — SQUARES — DOWELS — ETC.

PIECES	SIZE	DESCRIPTION OF WOOD	GOOD 1 SIDE OR GOOD 2 SIDES (PLYWOOD ONLY)
4	1/4x48x96"	Natural Birch Plywood	G1S
2	3/4x48x96"	Premium Walnut, Sound Walnut Back, Solid Jointed Veneer Core	G1S-So.Bk.
12	2x2x30"	Walnut Furniture Squares	Clear
20	3/8x36"	Hardwood Dowel Rods	
1-Pkg.	9x11" Sheets	Garnet Finishing Paper	220-A
1	1-Gallon	Paxbond Liquid White Glue	
1	1-Gallon	Clear Deft Wood Finish, Semi-Gloss	

☐ CHECK HERE IF YOU WOULD LIKE FREIGHT PREPAID AND ADDED TO INVOICE

FRANK PAXTON LUMBER COMPANY
... serving the schools since 1914.

HAVE YOU SHOWN
QUANTITY—GRADE—KIND OF WOOD—THICKNESS
RGH OR S2S
THANK YOU

Fig. 11-30. Filling out the order form properly saves time and confusion.

shape has its own name and varies in size, Fig. 11-31. Typical uses for moulding are shown in Figs. 11-32 and 11-33.

MOULDING GRADES

Wood mouldings are available in two grades. *"N-Grade"* is suitable for natural or clear finishes. The exposed face must be one continuous piece of wood. *"P-Grade"* is intended for paint finishes or veneering. P-Grade mouldings may contain two pieces of wood. Finger joints are used for edge gluing.

N-Grade moulding may have the following defects. (Based on one 2 in. face by 12 ft. [3 600 mm] long piece.)

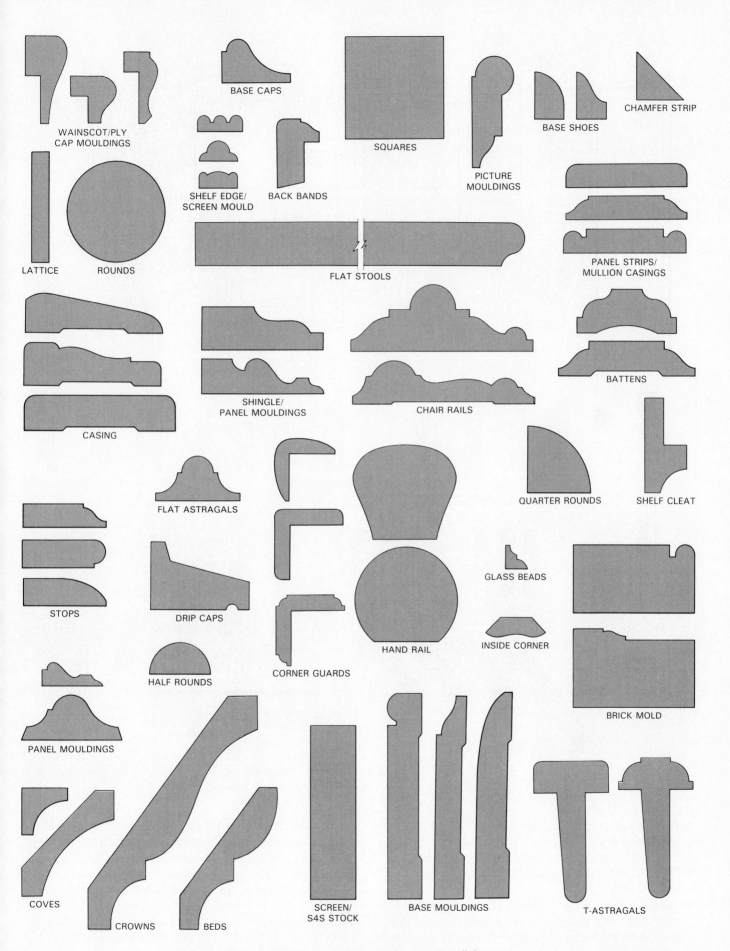

WAINSCOT/PLY CAP MOULDINGS

BASE CAPS

SQUARES

PICTURE MOULDINGS

BASE SHOES

CHAMFER STRIP

SHELF EDGE/ SCREEN MOULD

BACK BANDS

LATTICE

ROUNDS

FLAT STOOLS

PANEL STRIPS/ MULLION CASINGS

CASING

SHINGLE/ PANEL MOULDINGS

CHAIR RAILS

BATTENS

FLAT ASTRAGALS

QUARTER ROUNDS

SHELF CLEAT

STOPS

DRIP CAPS

GLASS BEADS

HAND RAIL

INSIDE CORNER

HALF ROUNDS

CORNER GUARDS

BRICK MOLD

PANEL MOULDINGS

COVES

CROWNS

BEDS

SCREEN/ S4S STOCK

BASE MOULDINGS

T-ASTRAGALS

Fig. 11-31. Many moulding shapes are availabe.

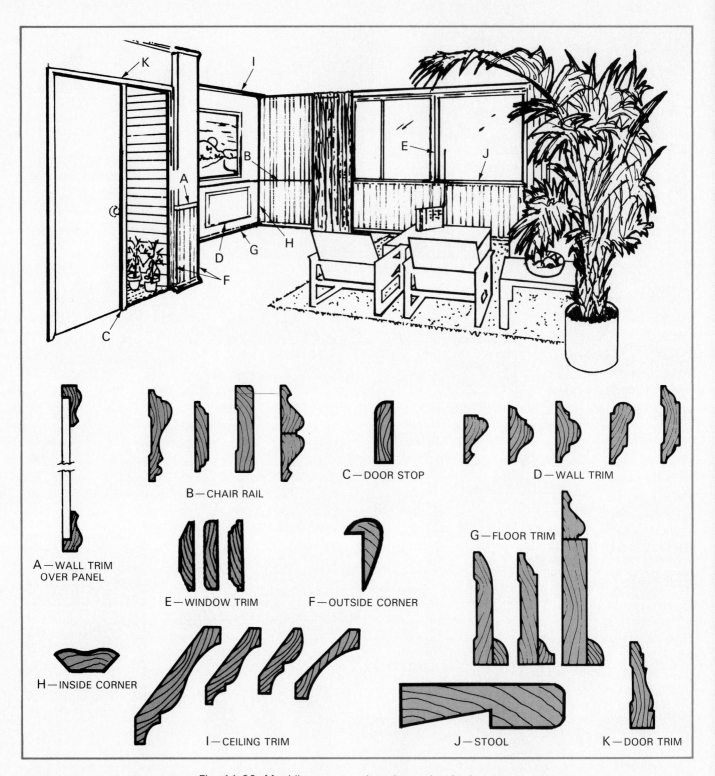

Fig. 11-32. Mouldings are used as decoration for interiors.

- A small spot of torn grain, one foot of medium pitch, light skip in dressing on back.
- One small and one very small pitch pocket.
- One short tight, seasoned check and a light snipe at one end.
- Medium stain in occasional (10%) pieces for one-third the area in an otherwise perfect surface.

P-Grade moulding should be the same quality as N-Grade, except that stain is not a defect. Glue joints (laminated or finger joints) must be precision machined and assembled with tight joints. Patching, filling, or plugging is permitted as long as the moulding still has a paintable surface.

When ordering millwork, you will specify the type, grade, size, and length. Lengths begin at 4 ft. and continue in 2 ft. increments. An example order for moulding might be: 4 pcs. cove moulding—3/4 in. × 1 3/4 in. × 12 ft.

Fig. 11-33. Mouldings are used in this room to accent the walls and ceiling. (Wood Moulding and Millwork Producers Assoc.)

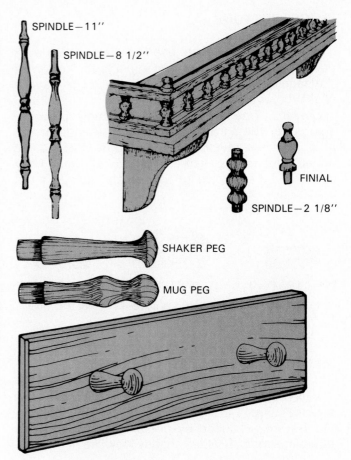

Fig. 11-34. Finials add decoration. Spindles add to the appearance, but also perform a structural function.

SPECIALTY ITEMS

There are a number of millwork items you can make or buy. Those you buy can save production time. However, they may not be of the specie of wood you are using. Some of these items are: legs, spindles, finials, dowels, plugs, buttons, and carvings.

LEGS, SPINDLES, FINIALS

The *legs* on most tables are produced by millwork companies. *Spindles,* used as both support and decoration on stair rails, baby cribs, etc., are examples, Fig. 11-34. A sample order might read: 1 set (4 per set)—#5936 spindles, 24 in.

Finials are ornaments, such as decorative knobs. William and Mary furniture had finials at the top of arches. Finials are inserted into a hole usually at a peak or on a post for ornamentation.

DOWELS

Dowels are round stock used primarily to strengthen joints. A short piece of dowel is glued into two matching holes. Sizes range from 1/8 in. in diameter to 1 in., and are usually 36 in. long.

Dowels are ordered in bundles of 25 to 1000, depending on diameter size. The ends are usually color coded according to size to prevent mixup, Fig. 11-35.

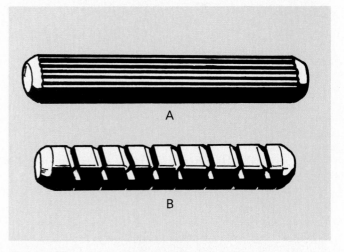

Fig. 11-35. A—Dowels are made in varying diameters and lengths. B—Dowels may be straight or spiral fluted.

Precut dowels come in *straight flutes* or *spiraled grooves.* These permit glue to spread evenly inside the hole. Diameters range from 1/4 in. to 1/2 in. and lengths from 1 1/4 in. to 2 in.

A longer form of round stock is available to use in a closet as a clothes rod. It is called *drapery rod.* The diameter is over 1 in., most often 1 1/4 in. Lengths vary in feet like moulding.

PLUGS, BUTTONS

Plugs and buttons are used to cover holes over countersunk screws. *Flat-head plugs* fit flush with the face of the wood. *Round-head plugs* have a slightly curved surface, Fig. 11-36.

Buttons, frequently called screwhole buttons, also cover the screw but overlap the edge of the hole. This has advantages over plugs. Buttons will cover chipped edges of a countersunk hole. They can also be removed to tighten the screw if the wood shrinks.

FLAT-HEAD PLUG   BUTTON   ROUND-HEAD PLUG

Fig. 11-36. Plugs and buttons cover counterbored holes.

MANUFACTURED WOOD CARVINGS

Wood carvings can decorate an otherwise plain surface, Fig. 11-37. Some are actually carved. Others are produced by pressing wood or wood fibers in a mold. Molded shapes look like hand carved decorations. Carvings will accept both stain and filler.

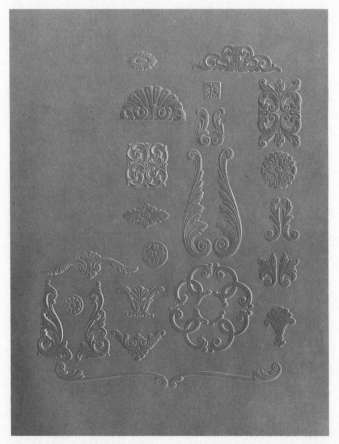

Fig. 11-37. Manufactured wood carvings include many shapes and sizes. (The Woodworker's Store)

CABINETMAKING TERMS

Harvesting, sectional felling, systematic felling, bucking, flitch, plain sawing, quarter sawing, rift sawing, SDR process, seasoning, air drying, sticking, kiln drying, lumber defect, round knot, spike knot, oval knot, intergrown knot, encased knot, checked knot, pitch pocket, bark pocket, peck, grub hole, warp, cup, bow, crook, twist, kink, split, check, shake, ring failure, honeycomb, blue stain, decay, brown rot, dry rot, white rot, soft rot, worm hole, pin hole, machine burn, raised grain, torn grain, wavy dressing, dog hole, grade, factory grade, cutting grade, dimension grade, finished market grade, FAS, FAS 1-Face, wane, Selects, No. 1 Common Grade, Thrift Grade, combined grade, FAS 1-Face and Better, Selects and Better, squares, flats, construction grade, yard lumber, finish lumber, board lumber, dimension lumber, light framing grade, structural framing grade, remanufacture grade, factory grade (softwood), shop grade, select grade (softwood), moulding grade, cutting grade (softwood), common grade, RWL, board foot, square foot, lumber condition, surfacing, preservatives, pattern lumber, milled end, end-matched, shiplapped, species, tree families, millwork, moulding, spindle, finial, dowel, straight flute, spiral groove, drapery rod, plug, button, wood carving.

TEST YOUR KNOWLEDGE

1. Why is wood considered a renewable resource?
2. Two methods of harvesting are _____ and _____.
3. List the three methods of sawing logs. Give advantages and disadvantages of the boards produced by each.
4. Moisture content is easier to control by kiln drying than by air drying. True or False?
5. The moisture content of construction grade lumber is approximately what percent?
   a. 2.
   b. 10.
   c. 20.
   d. 30.
6. List five classifications of knots.
7. Three defects caused by mold and fungus are _____, _____, and _____.
8. Illustrate five types of warp.
9. List three wood defects caused by improper seasoning.
10. Describe the lumber defects often incurred during surfacing.

11. Identify four hardwood factory grades for cabinetmaking lumber.
12. An example of finished market grade lumber is:
    a. A surfaced 2 x 4.
    b. RWL hardwood.
    c. Dimension grade hardwood.
    d. Moulding.
13. Two grading systems for softwoods are _____ and _____.
14. What is the difference between factory grade hardwood and factory grade softwood?
15. Remanufacture grade softwood is readily available in local lumber yards. True or False?
16. Lumber grading systems are established by _____ and _____.
17. Random Widths and Lengths (RWL) lumber is sold by _____.
18. Determine the board feet in two pieces of 1/2 in. by 8 in. by 6 ft. of rough sawn, kiln-dried Willow which is FAS grade. Write an order for the wood.
19. Determine the board feet in three pieces of 1 1/32 in. thick by 9 1/2 in. by 10 ft. kiln-dried White Pine which is surfaced on two sides and A Select finish grade. Write an order for the wood.
20. Explain the difference between spindles, finials, and dowels.

Chapter 12
CABINET AND FURNITURE WOODS

After studying this chapter, you will be able to:
☐ *Identify wood species based on viewing a sample.*
☐ *Classify woods according to certain characteristics, such as color, hardness, texture, and grain pattern.*
☐ *Describe present and potential applications for each wood species.*
☐ *Select woods which may be substituted for another, more expensive wood.*

Wood is the most versatile material used by humans when shaping their living environment. In an age of synthetic and metal surroundings, wood still serves many needs. It forms the shape of our houses and decorates our interiors. It provides structure for case goods that store our belongings.

In addition to being a structural material, wood conveys an aesthetic beauty which few materials can match. Today, as in centuries past, hardwood furnishings are preferred by those who want the finest that nature can offer. Although wood grain plastics may cover much of today's furniture, they cannot fully imitate solid wood.

Various species of wood grow in all parts of the world, Fig. 12-1. Each has different properties, including color, density, flexibility, etc. Woods of the same species even may differ in color and hardness. Identifying wood species requires careful analysis. You must look at grain pattern, pores, color, odor, weight, and hardness. Wood for furniture should be less likely to warp or shrink and have a pleasing appearance.

TERMS

Some of the terms you will need to remember when reading this chapter are:
• *Common name.* The general name given to one or a group of tree species. The heading for each of the woods discussed in this chapter is the common name.
• *Genus/species:* Classification of the tree. This is the botanical name, given in Latin, which groups trees according to their characteristics. Only the most used species are listed. Most genera have more species than can be covered here.

• *Hardwood.* Wood cut from deciduous (broad-leafed) trees.
• *Softwood.* Wood cut from coniferous (pine and evergreen) trees.
• *Earlywood.* Growth which occurs in the spring.
• *Latewood.* Growth which occurs in the summer.
• *Annual ring.* A ring caused by the addition of earlywood and latewood growth to the trunk of a tree.
• *Open grain.* Wood which has large pores which are cut open during machining.
• *Closed grain.* Wood which has small pores.
• *Cross grain.* Growth which occurs across the normal grain direction. Cross grain is difficult to surface.
• *Texture.* The smooth or rough feel of the wood surface. Wood with open grain is usually more coarse than that with closed grain.
• *Dimensional stability.* A measure of how likely the wood is to swell or shrink when exposed to moisture. A high level of dimensional stability is preferred.
• *Density.* Discussed in Chapter 10, density is a measure of the mass of the wood.
• *Luster.* Woods with high luster appear shiny when sanded smooth.
• *Heartwood.* The inner layers of a tree which consist of inactive cells.
• *Sapwood.* The outer layers of a tree which carry food and water.
• *Color.* Color is always associated with the heartwood, as it is preferred by cabinetmakers. The color of sapwood may also be given.
• *Machining/working qualities.* Tells how easily the wood can be cut, surfaced, sanded, or processed by other means.

WOOD SPECIES

There are well over 100,000 species of wood in the world. More than 4,000 have been put to use. The most popular species found in cabinets, furniture, moulding, and paneling are discussed in this chapter. Most of those listed are hardwoods. Selected softwoods are covered because they are

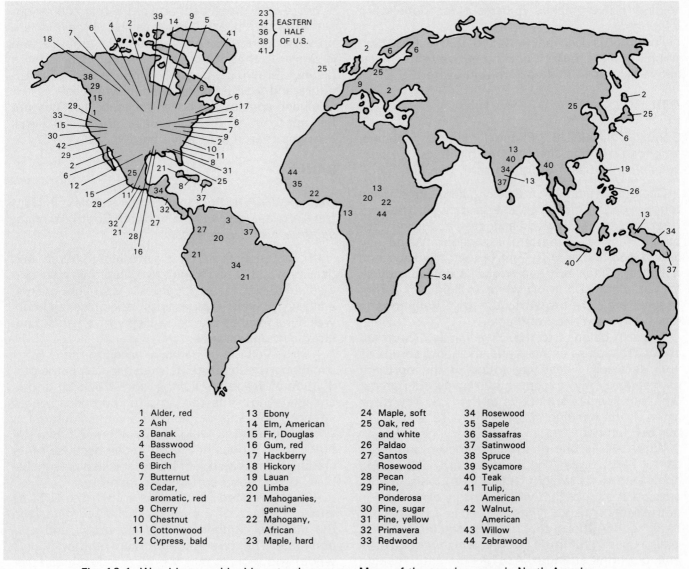

1	Alder, red	13	Ebony	24	Maple, soft	34	Rosewood
2	Ash	14	Elm, American	25	Oak, red	35	Sapele
3	Banak	15	Fir, Douglas		and white	36	Sassafras
4	Basswood	16	Gum, red	26	Paldao	37	Satinwood
5	Beech	17	Hackberry	27	Santos	38	Spruce
6	Birch	18	Hickory		Rosewood	39	Sycamore
7	Butternut	19	Lauan	28	Pecan	40	Teak
8	Cedar,	20	Limba	29	Pine,	41	Tulip,
	aromatic, red	21	Mahoganies,		Ponderosa		American
9	Cherry		genuine	30	Pine, sugar	42	Walnut,
10	Chestnut	22	Mahogany,	31	Pine, yellow		American
11	Cottonwood		African	32	Primavera	43	Willow
12	Cypress, bald	23	Maple, hard	33	Redwood	44	Zebrawood

Fig. 12-1. Wood is a world-wide natural resource. Many of the species grow in North America.

used for various millwork or specialty products. A summary of the characteristics of each wood species is included at the end of the chapter.

RED ALDER

Genus: ALNUS. Principal lumber species: *rubra.* See Fig. 12-2.

Characteristics: Red alder is relatively light weight for a hardwood. Yet, it has fine texture and good impact resistance. There is no apparent difference in earlywood and latewood. The heartwood is a pale roseate color and the luster is low. The sapwood is a slightly lighter color. Red Alder has fine machining and finishing qualities and will stain easily to blend with more expensive woods.

Red Alder is a member of the birch family found from Alaska to southern California. It grows mainly in moist areas of Oregon and Washington. It is

Fig. 12-2. Red alder. (Fine Hardwood Veneer Assoc.)

a good utility furniture wood. Exposed parts are typically stained to blend with walnut, mahogany, or cherry veneers. Its stability and superior tack holding power makes it perfect for upholstery framing.

The wood is used mainly west of the Rockies. High shipping costs make it uncompetitive with similar native woods in midwestern and eastern U.S.

ASH

Genus: FRAXINUS. Principal lumber species: *americana* (white ash); *nigra* (black ash); *pennsylvanica* (red ash) or (green ash). See Fig. 12-3.

Characteristics: Ash is a heavy, hard, strong, and tough wood. It machines and bends well. The contrast between earlywood and latewood is very apparent. The grain pattern is straight. White ash heartwood is cream to light brown; the sapwood is lighter. Black ash heartwood is dull to greyish brown. Sapwood is off-white to light tan. Other species are light brown to tan with variations in heartwood and sapwood color.

The ash belongs to the Olive family. There are about 70 species in the genus, including shrubs as well as trees. These are found in the northern hemisphere only, except in extremely cold areas. Eighteen species are native to the U.S. The three listed in the heading supply nearly 98 percent of our ash lumber.

White ash is one of the best known and most useful hardwoods. The wood is hard, and strong compared to its weight. It is able to resist a succession of shocks that would destroy other woods of the same density. White ash can be found as ball bats, hockey sticks, tool handles, and boat oars. It is also used in furniture designs which require little bulk but great strength. Ash has no taste, making it useful for food containers.

White ash, green ash, and red ash are commonly sold as "white ash." Black ash is sold as northern brown ash or brown cabinet ash. The grain pattern is similar to that of the white ash but color is more distinct. Brown cabinet ash is more beautiful in furniture and wall paneling than is white ash.

All ash species are noted for stability. They are less apt to warp, shrink, or make other dimensional changes than most native hardwoods.

BANAK

Genus: VIROLA. Principal lumber species: in Central America, *koschnyi*; in northern South America, *sebifera and surinamensis*.

Characteristics: Banak is a medium textured, low density wood. It has a light, pinkish-brown color and medium to high luster. It generally is straight-grained and easy to work. It glues easily and holds fasteners well. Fine finishes can be applied with a handsome, but plain, appearance.

A large volume of banak is entering the U.S. as a mahogany substitute. It is used widely in the production of wood mouldings, core stock for doors, and paneling. It is too soft for purposes where strength and impact damage are considerations. When kiln-dried, it weighs only about 2.5 lbs. per board foot. It does not resist decay because of its starchy composition, but is available at a reasonable cost. It is a good softwood substitute.

A wood related to banak is sold in the U.S. as virola. Virola is of the genus Dialanyanthera, and the principal lumber species are *otoba* and *gordonifolia*. The two genera, Dianlyanthera (viola wood) and Viola (banak wood) are closely related. Both are members of the nutmeg family. The woods

Fig. 12-3. Left. Ash has a fairly straight grain pattern. Right. This contemporary style with European influence uses ash solids and veneers. (Fine Hardwood Veneer Assoc.)

are similar in characteristics, except that banak is slightly firmer in texture. It also has somewhat better machining characteristics.

BASSWOOD

Genus: TILIA. Principal lumber species: *Americana.* See Fig. 12-4.

Characteristics: Basswood is one of the softest and lightest hardwoods in regular commercial use. It has fine, even grain, and exceptional stability. It is has little contrast between earlywood and latewood. Heartwood is a very light brown and sapwood is nearly white. Basswood has good machining and sanding characteristics.

Basswood is a member of the linden family, and is sometimes called linn. It is favored for technical uses, including venetian blinds, drawing boards, picture frame mouldings, and wooden toys. These items favor basswood's clean looking, attractive, lightweight qualities. Machining must be done carefully as the wood is apt to split. Like ash, it has no taste, making it suitable for food containers. It is largely used as veneer core stock for plywood.

Basswood is found in the eastern U.S., half of which is located in the Lake Superior region. Northern basswood has some advantages over southern lumber, probably due to slower growth. It is soft, even textured, and relatively free from internal stress.

Fig. 12-4. Basswood is a widely used soft hardwood.

BEECH

Genus: FAGUS. Principal lumber species: *grandifolio*; only one in U.S. and Canada. See Fig. 12-5.

Characteristics: Beech is a heavy, hard, strong wood with good resistance to abrasive wear. Beech bends easily and is not apt to split. It is a good substitute for hard maple, although the surface is slightly coarser in texture and darker in color. Beech

Fig. 12-5. Beech. (Fine Hardwood Veneer Assoc.)

machines cleanly, and can be abraded smoothly to a medium luster. It can be finished comparable to more expensive woods. It has a pale to rich reddish-brown heartwood and lighter sapwood. It is odorless and tasteless.

There are seven or eight species in the world, only one of which is grown in America. Beech is related to oak and chestnut and grows in the eastern one-third of the U.S. and adjacent Canadian provinces. The greatest production is in the Central and Middle Atlantic states. Beech also is popular in Europe and Japan.

Some users feel that northern beech machines and finishes more beautifully than southern specimens. The difference, although small, may be due to different soil and climate.

Beech is used for a number of purposes. These include: flooring, furniture (especially provincial styles), crates, boxes, millwork, turnings, handles, and food containers. Like hard maple, but less costly, beech is valuable as flooring. It is able to withstand heavy foot traffic. It accepts a variety of stains and is well suited to lacquer or varnish finishes.

BIRCH

Genus: BETILA. Principal lumber species: *alleghaniensis* (yellow birch); *lenta* (sweet, black, or cherry birch); and *papyrifera* (paper, canoe, or white birch). See Fig. 12-6.

Characteristics: Birch is a moderately heavy, hard, and strong wood. It has excellent machining, bending, and finishing characteristics. Birch has reddish-brown heartwood and yellowish-white sapwood which often has a trace of pink tint.

Yellow birch grows in southeastern Canada, the Great Lake States, New England, and the Appalachian region as far south as Georgia. Commercially, it is the most important of the birches.

Sweet birch is found from Newfoundland and Ontario, through New England, to the southern

Appalachians. It is a little denser and deeper in color than yellow birch. Where the two are cut together, they are sold simply as birch.

Birch species are decorative, except for paper birch which grows in much the same range as sweet birch (in Maine). Sapwood makes up the greater portion of the tree. It is ideal for turning. Paper birch is somewhat hard, uniform in texture, with fine grain. It is one of the best woods for dowels, spools, handles, etc. Other turned products include toothpicks, clothespins, and shoepegs.

Fig. 12-6. Top. Yellow birch. Bottom. Paper birch is less decorative than other related species. (Fine Hardwood Veneer Assoc.)

Birch is particularly popular for furniture, flooring, doors, and interior trim. It is a good cabinet wood when strength and hardness are desired. It is sometimes available as ''selected white birch'' (all sapwood one face), and ''selected red birch'' (all heartwood one face). Most users prefer birch which contains portions of both heartwood and sapwood.

Birch also is the most popular of the decorative plywood veneer faces. Vast amounts of birch plywood are consumed every year, much of which is imported from Japan. Japanese birch looks the same as American birch.

BUTTERNUT

Genus: JUGLANS. Lumber species: *cinerea*; only species. See Fig. 12-7.

Characteristics: Butternut is relatively soft and weak. It does not bend well and is likely to split. The texture is rather coarse, but it sands well and can be polished to a satin luster. Because of its low density, it is easy to work and will machine well. Butternut has light brown or fawn heartwood and slightly lighter sapwood.

Butternut is a member of the walnut family. It is better known for its edible nuts than its lumber. The tree grows from southern New Brunswick and Maine, through the upper peninsula of Michigan, to eastern South Dakota. It is then found southward into northern Arkansas and the mountains of Alabama and Georgia.

When butternut grows in open spaces, the trunk is short. It branches out just above the ground. Occasionally found in forests, the tree may reach heights of 100 ft. (30 m) and diameters of 4 ft. (1.2 m). The supply of butternut is diminishing. The tree is short lived as the widely branched crown is weak and susceptible to breakage by storms or heavy loads of snow. Injuries leave the trees open to fungus diseases and insects.

Fig. 12-7. Butternut has a light brown heartwood. It is easy to work and machines well. (Fine Hardwood Veneer Assoc.)

The grain pattern of butternut closely resembles that of its relative, black walnut. Yet, butternut is much softer and lighter in color. It is sometimes called white walnut. Butternut is a good cabinet wood, although relatively weak. It is used for interior trim, boat trim, and cabinets. It is preferred over black walnut for wall paneling because of its light, cheery color.

AROMATIC RED CEDAR

Genus: JUNIPERUS. Principal lumber species: *virginiana.* See Fig. 12-8.

Characteristics: Aromatic red cedar trees are softwoods. The tree is an evergreen, with closed-grain wood. It has medium density and is brittle, yet very durable. The wood has a pleasing and lasting scent. The heartwood is red and the sapwood is white.

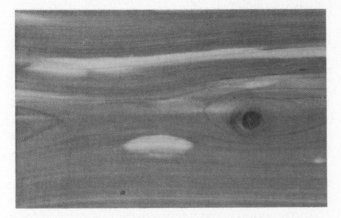

Fig. 12-8. Aromatic red cedar serves as a liner for chests and closets.

Red cedar, or aromatic cedar, is not actually part of the cedar family. It belongs to the cypress family. In fact, the wood we call cypress does not belong to the cypress family. This shows how names and families do not always match.

Red cedar is cut from small timber. The lumber is therefore small in width and only average in length. It is very knotty and contains a great deal of sapwood. Red cedar cannot be purchased as clear lumber, heartwood, or in wide widths.

Aromatic cedar gives off a unique scent. Most persons have smelled it when opening a cedar chest or cedar-lined closet. In spite of popular belief, the aroma does not repel moths. Cedar is also used for novelty furniture, wall paneling, and pencil slats. The sawdust is distilled for the aromatic oils.

CHERRY

Genus: PRUNUS. Lumber species: *serotina.* See Fig. 12-9.

Characteristics: Cherry is a medium weight, hard and stable wood. It is closed grain with visible annual growth. Cherry machines and sands to a glasslike smoothness. It can be bent when moistened. The heartwood is reddish-brown, sometimes with greenish cast; the sapwood is yellowish-white.

Like all our fruit trees, cherry belongs to the rose family. Under poor growing conditions Prunus serotina is a small, scrubby tree. In the rich moist soil of the Appalachian regions it may reach heights of 100 ft. (30 m) or more. Diameters of 4 to 5 ft. (1.2 m to 1.5 m) are fairly common.

Cherry is regarded as one of the top furniture hardwoods. In this country, it is second only to walnut. Although one of the finest cabinet woods, cherry is relatively scarce. The once large timber resource has been cut. Top quality cherry is rarely found. Woodworkers face having to dispose of knots and other defects.

Lumber from any of our fruit trees is commonly called "fruitwood." Cherry falls into this category.

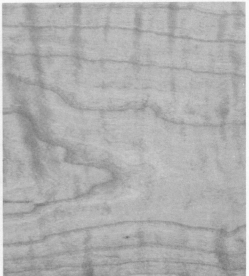

Fig. 12-9. Cherry is one of the most popular hardwoods. It sands exceptionally smooth and has a high luster. (Fine Hardwood Veneer Assoc.)

CHESTNUT

Genus: CASTANEA. Principal lumber species: *dentata*. See Fig. 12-10.

Characteristics: Chestnut is a low density, coarse-textured, durable hardwood. It machines easily. The wood has prominent open-grained annual growth rings.

Chestnut was once an important timber tree of the Appalachian region. Due to the chestnut blight, a parasitic fungus, the specie has been almost entirely destroyed. The remaining timber, standing dead for several decades, is quite wormy.

The wood is still used for wall paneling, chests, etc. It gives a distinctly rustic effect. At one time, it provided material for interior trim, furniture, shingles, and fence posts. It is one of the most durable of our native hardwoods.

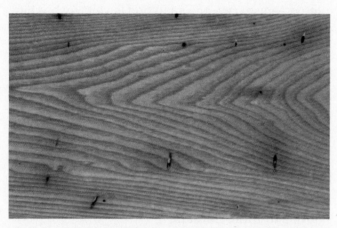

Fig. 12-10. Most chestnut trees were killed by fungus. Wood which is left is quite wormy. (Fine Hardwood Veneer Assoc.)

COTTONWOOD

Genus: POPULUS. Principal lumber species: *deltoides* (eastern cottonwood); *heterophylla* (swamp or river cottonwood); *trichorcarpa* (black cottonwood); and *balsamifera* (balsam poplar or Balm of Gilead). See Fig. 12-11.

Characteristics: Cottonwood is soft and lightweight. It is a close-grained hardwood which is coarse in texture and difficult to split. It machines easily but contains minerals which dull cutting edges on most tools. Carbide-tipped tools are used with cottonwood. Cottonwood is low in luster and finishes poorly because of the minerals. The heartwood is very light brown, often with a grayish tint. The sapwood is lighter. The annual rings are hardly visible.

Eastern cottonwood is scattered over the entire eastern half of the U.S. Swamp or river cottonwood

Fig. 12-11. Cottonwood is soft and light in weight, but difficult to split. (Fine Hardwood Veneer Assoc.)

is abundant in the south Atlantic and Gulf regions of the Mississippi Valley. Black cottonwood is the largest hardwood tree of the West Coast. It grows from southern Alaska to southern California. It is sometimes called western poplar. It is also called balsam poplar in Canada, Alaska, and along the northern border of the U.S.

Cottonwood is used primarily for boxes and food crates. Resistance to splitting and little taste or odor are important for these uses. Other uses include mill products, woodenware, core stock for plywood, and pulp for paper. Cottonwood is hard to finish with beauty.

Cottonwoods are in the true poplar family, a branch of the willow family. The tree we commonly know as ''yellow poplar'' is really a magnolia. Its name has recently been changed to American tulipwood. Cottonwoods are in the same genus as the aspens and poplars. Cottonwood and aspen are almost identical. Aspen is used only as pulp in papermaking.

CYPRESS

Genus: TAXODIUM. Principal lumber species: *distichum*. See Fig. 12-12.

Characteristics: Cypress is lightweight, soft, and easily worked. It is rather coarse in texture. The heartwood of deep swamp and yellow cypress is a light orange-brown color. Tidewater cypress is darker and redder. The heartwood of cypress, particularly tidewater cypress, has a reputation for durability. However, careful seasoning is necessary to prevent hairline checking.

Bald cypress is the name commonly given to this species, yet it is not a true cypress. Actually, it belongs to as family which include redwood. It grows in swamps and streams. You find it from southern New Jersey to Texas in a wide coastal strip. From there, growth is found up the Missis-

Fig. 12-12. Cypress is very durable when placed in a decay-promoting environment.

sippi Valley to southern Indiana and Illinois. The most valuable timber, tidewater cypress, grows along the gulf swamps close to the sea.

Durability when exposed sets cypress apart from most other American woods. Cypress is excellent for exterior use as siding, water tanks, small boats, etc. In the areas which produce cypress, it is widely used for millwork of all kinds. It is somewhat weak for furniture, but is attractive as wall paneling.

Cypress trees over 200 years old are subject to attack by fungus. The fungus produces the lumber defect known as ''peck.'' The fungus dies when the tree is cut, leaving residue and holes. Pecky cypress is widely used for greenhouse benches because it is not affected by soil organisms. It is also used as paneling to give a rustic effect.

EBONY

Genus: DIOSPYROS. Principal lumber species: *celebica* (macassar ebony). See Fig. 12-13.

Characteristics: Ebony is a dense, closed-grain hardwood with very distinct grain pattern. Its color is dark brown to black with large portions streaked

with yellowish-brown or gray. The density of ebony makes it very hard to work.

Several species of the Diospyros genus are available. Macassar ebony, from the East Indies, is the most common because of its pronounced grain pattern. Solid black ebonies are found in Gaboon, Central West Africa, and Ceylon.

Ebony is commonly used for inlays and marquetry. It also is turned into decorative handles and other ornamental work.

ELM

Genus: ULMUS. Principal lumber species: *fulva* (slippery elm or red elm); *racemosa* (rock, cork, or hickory elm); *americana* (American or white elm). See Fig. 12-14.

Characteristics: Elm is very strong and tough for its weight. A medium density wood, elm is both elastic and shock resistant. It machines well, but the texture is rather coarse. Annual rings are clearly defined. Elm stains and fills well. The heartwood color is pale brown, and occasionally dark brown. Slippery or red elm wood is light with a grayish hue.

White elm is the most known elm species. It once lined streets of most cities from the Midwest

Fig. 12-14. Top. American elm. Bottom. Red elm. Both are scarce due to Dutch elm disease.
(Fine Hardwood Veneer Assoc.)

Fig. 12-13. Ebony is a very dark, dense hardwood.

eastward. The wood is used in manufacture of baskets, particularly rims and bent handles.

In recent years, the white elm has been subject to "Dutch elm disease." The disease kills all growth of the tree.

Slippery elm or red elm is sold as "northern gray elm." It is the best elm for cabinet work. This is due to its soft and even texture. It is also light and uniform in color.

Rock elm is more dense and shock resistant than other elm species. It is used mainly for industrial purposes requiring strength.

DOUGLAS FIR

Genus: PSEUDOTSUGA. Principal lumber species: *taxifolio*. See Fig. 12-15.

Characteristics: Douglas fir is a soft, coarse-textured, non-porous softwood. The annual rings are clearly marked by the color of earlywood and latewood. It works easily, but has low luster. Heartwood color varies from pinkish-yellow to reddish-brown depending on conditions of growth. The sapwood is lighter.

Fig. 12-15. Douglas fir has widespread use for plywood and mill products.

Douglas fir is a valuable timber tree. It produces large amounts of softwood lumber and veneer. Inland growth produces smaller timber which is harder and redder in color. It tends to have cross grain in it and is knotty.

Coastal timber grows up to 325 ft. (97 m) high and 17 ft. (5 m) in diameter. It produces most of the lumber known as Douglas fir or Oregon pine. Timber size permits the manufacture of vast amounts of lumber in a variety of grades. The best logs are cut into veneer for use as Douglas fir plywood. Lumber is widely used for mill products including doors, sash, interior trim, and mouldings.

Inland California Douglas fir grows in the moun-

tains and tends to be softer and of more even growth than coastal timber. It is redder in color and marketed as California red fir.

RED GUM

Genus: LIQUIDAMBAR. Principal lumber species: *styraciflua* (red or sweet gum, sap gum); only species. See Fig. 12-16.

Characteristics: Red gum is moderately hard and strong. It has closed grain and will finish with beauty. It is easily machined, but has poor dimensional stability. Red gum heartwood is brown or reddish-brown, sometimes figured with dark markings. Sapwood is an off-white color.

Fig. 12-16. Red gum is often figured with dark markings. (Fine Hardwood Veneer Assoc.)

Gum is one of the most important timber trees of the southern U.S. It is an example of the change brought by advances in technology. Seventy-five years ago the sweet gum was regarded as having little or no value. It was difficult to season. Newer drying techniques permit gum to be processed into furniture and other products. It is one of our most used hardwoods.

Gum has a wide band of sapwood in the trunk. Only mature trees have any heartwood at all. Very large trees can produce the clear, selected red wood favored by woodworkers. In general, however, you must cut out knots and other defects.

Sap gum is not another species. It is red gum with too much sapwood to qualify as selected red gum. Occasionally, you find boards that are all sapwood, but most contain heartwood and sapwood. Selected red gum is all or nearly all heartwood on one face.

Gum is grown across the entire southeastern U.S. It favors moist, rich soil and grows best in river bottoms close to the Gulf, southern Atlantic regions, and the Mississippi Valley. Maximum size is about 150 ft. (45 m) high and 5 ft. (1.5 m) in diameter.

Gum stains well to match other lumber. In furniture, it is often used with more valuable woods. Most flush doors produced in the South have gum veneer faces. Large quantities of gum are processed into plywood and veneers each year.

HACKBERRY

Genus: CELTIS. Principal lumber species: *occidentalis* (hackberry); and *laevigata* (sugarberry). See Fig. 12-17.

Characteristics: Hackberry is a medium density hardwood. It is creamy white with a grayish hue. There is little difference in color between heartwood and sapwood. The annual rings are clearly visible. It is widely used for interior trim and cabinetry.

Hackberry is common, though scattered, throughout the eastern half of the U.S. Sugarberry grows mostly in the southeastern states and is more plentiful. However, the hackberry name is still used for sugarberry lumber.

Hackberry species are members of the elm family. They are gaining popularity as elm substitutes because of similarities to elm. Hackberry is plentiful. Elm is becoming scarce due to Dutch elm disease. Hackberry is resistant to the disease.

Hackberry which is not handled properly will develop sap stain. Sap stain is noted by odd coloring. The wood must be seasoned quickly with caution to prevent this. When care is taken, hackberry is one of the most beautiful American hardwoods.

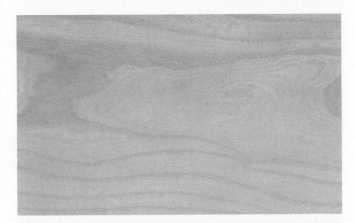

Fig. 12-17. Hackberry, a member of the elm family, is often substituted for American elm. (Fine Hardwood Veneer Assoc.)

HICKORY

Genus: CARYA. Principal lumber species: *ovato* (shagbark hickory); *laciniosa* (big shellbark hickory); *tomentosa* or *alba* (mockernut hickory); and *glabra* (pignut hickory). See Fig. 12-18.

Characteristics: Hickory is a very hard, elastic, and strong hardwood. It is the toughest American

Fig. 12-18. Hickory is strong and elastic. It is valued for bent laminations, such as skis. (Fine Hardwood Veneer Assoc.)

wood and provides the strength for athletic equipment, ladder rungs, etc. It machines, turns, and steam bends well. It has distinct growth rings. The heartwood is light reddish-brown or tan and the sapwood is creamy white.

Hickory and pecan are members of the walnut family. The two are so closely related that individual specimens of hickory and pecan are difficult to identify. An inspector of the National Hardwood Lumber Association will not attempt to separate the two once they are mixed.

Hickory and pecan are slow growing trees. They require 100 years or more to attain timber size. They are scattered across the eastern half of the U.S. and are often found growing with other hardwoods.

Hickory timber is valuable because of its toughness and elasticity. It is used for moulded and bent laminations which require great strength. One example is skis. It is also famous for its use in smoking meats. The "hickory flavor" given smoked food is unique.

LAUAN

Genus: SHOREA (red and tanguile lauans); PENTACME (white lauan). Principal lumber species: *negrosensis* (red lauan); *contorta* (white lauan); *polysperma* (tanguile). See Fig. 12-19.

Characteristics: Lauans are a medium density, coarse textured hardwood with red tint. Tanguile is a dark reddish-brown; red lauan is red to brown; and white lauan is light brown to light reddish-brown. Tanguile has a coarse texture and white lauan has cross grain in it. Red lauan has larger pores, whereas tanguile has smaller pores and finer texture.

Lauan is grown on the Philippine Islands. Red lauan is often called "Philippine mahogany," although not related to the mahogany family.

Lauans are more coarse grained and stringy compared to tropical American and African mahoganies. They require a greater amount of sanding to produce a finished surface. They are also much less stable under moisture changes.

Lauan is very inexpensive and readily available. It is most commonly used as a veneer core for hardwood plywood. Lauans offer an inexpensive alternative to African and American mahoganies for furniture, doors, mouldings, and cabinets.

Fig. 12-19. Red lauan is more commonly known as Philippine mahogany.

LIMBA

Genus: TERMINALIA. Principal lumber species: *superba*. See Fig. 12-20.

Characteristics: Limba has a medium hardness and texture. It machines, glues, and finishes well. It is pale yellow to light brown with large pores. This coloring is often called "natural blonde," a tint which is desired in contemporary furniture. Limba is open grain, but finishes well with the application of filler.

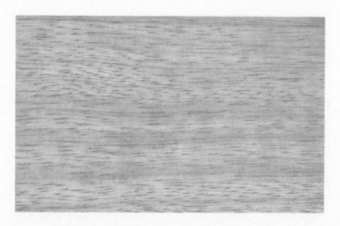

Fig. 12-20. Limba, because of its blonde color, is often selected for contemporary furniture.

Limba comes from West Africa's Belgian Congo. It is currently not produced in volume but has great potential.

GENUINE MAHOGANIES

Genus: SWIETENIA. Principal lumber species: *macrophylla* (tropical American mahogany); *mahagoni* (Cuban mahogany). See Fig. 12-21.

Characteristics: Mahogany is a moderately dense and hard wood with great strength in comparison to its weight. It is stable and durable in situations favoring decay. It has unsurpassed working, bending, and finishing characteristics. It has large open pores which need filler for most finishes. It has an even texture with visible annual growth rings. The color is medium reddish-brown but darkens over time to be a deep, rich, golden brown or reddish brown.

Many woodworkers regard genuine mahoganies as premier cabinet woods. It has all the characteristics for fine furniture, interior trim, and cabinetry. It is a superb carving and turning wood.

Only the genus Swietenia may be sold as "mahogany." Any other genus must have a prefix, such as African mahogany. Philippine mahogany is not a mahogany at all; it is a lauan and should be sold as such.

Both Cuban and tropical American mahoganies have highly figured grain. Cuban mahogany is heavier and harder than similar species. It is extremely durable and wears exceptionally well.

Fig. 12-21. Genuine mahoganies are valued for their appearance, texture, and working qualities.

AFRICAN MAHOGANY

Genus: KHAYA. Principal lumber species: *ivorensis*. See Fig. 12-22.

Characteristics: African mahogany has much the same qualities as genuine mahoganies. All are related botanically, hence, are siimilar in cell structure and appearance. Woodworkers consider American mahogany as superior in working, finishing, and other technical properties. African is more figured with crotch, swirl, and broken stripe grain patterns.

The texture of African mahogany is more coarse than genuine mahogany. It will accept stain better. Be careful when finishing furniture which uses genuine mahogany for structure covered with African mahogany veneer for appearance. Exposed parts of the genuine mahogany will finish differently than the African mahogany veneer.

Fig. 12-22. African mahogany, although coarser and harder to work with, is often selected over genuine mahogany because of its figured grain pattern. (Fine Hardwood Veneer Assoc.)

HARD MAPLE

Genus: ACER. Principal lumber species: *saccharum* (sugar maple); and *nigrum* (black maple). See Fig. 12-23.

Characteristics: Hard maple is a heavy and strong wood. It is famous for resistance to abrasive wear. Hard maple has visible, but not prominent, annual growth rings. The wood has no odor or taste. It does not require filling because the texture and grain are very fine. Heartwood color is very light brown or tan, sometimes with darker mineral streaks. Softwood is white or off-white. The saccharum and nigrum species are so closely related that both are sold as hard maple.

Hard maple is the most valuable and most plentiful member of the maple family. It grows in the eastern U.S. and Canada. The best wood comes from near the Great Lakes, St. Lawrence Valley, and northern New England. The tree is also called sugar maple because of the sweet sap which flows from it during early spring. This sap is the source of maple syrup.

The excellent technical properties of hard maple make it suitable for industrial uses. Its resistance to wear makes it a leader for flooring. Well made hard maple furniture often outlasts the owner. It is suitable for turnery, wooden dishes, and a variety of mill products.

Some trees develop special grain figures such as curly grain, mottle, and bird's eye. Mottled grain is a less distinct grain direction because wood rays cut across the grain. Bird's eye grain has no visible grain direction; dark circles cover the board in a scattered pattern. It was once thought that bird's eye figure was caused by birds pecking at the wood. Although this claim has been disputed, no cause for bird's eye has been found.

SOFT MAPLE

Genus: ACER. Principal lumber species: *rubrum* (red or swamp maple); and *saccharinum* (silver or white maple); *negundo* (box elder). See Fig. 12-24.

Characteristics: Soft maple has medium density and hardness. It is stable and has good machining and finishing properties. The grain is fine textured since the pores are small. Growth rings are not distinct. The color of the heartwood varies from pale

Fig. 12-23. Hard maple has a nondistinct grain pattern. (Fine Hardwood Veneer Assoc.)

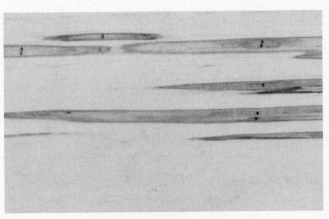

Fig. 12-24. Soft maple is often wormy. (Fine Hardwood Veneer Assoc.)

Cabinet and Furniture Woods   135

tan to reddish-gray, sometimes streaked. Sapwood is off-white to white.

Soft maple is not actually soft compared to most woods. However, it is softer than hard maple. Soft maple trees are found across most of the eastern half of the U.S. Silver maple is less abundant than red maple except in the Mississippi Valley.

Most soft maple is used in the furniture industry. Higher maple grades are used to produce colonial style furniture. Lower grades are used in boxes, crates and other shipping containers. Maple is odorless and tasteless which permits its use for handling food.

Particularly in the South, soft maple contains spot worm holes. Thus, specifications for southern maple include "WHAD" (worm holes a defect) or "WHND" (worm holes no defect). The worm holes in "WHAD" are small and may easily be filled. Worm holes are never so numerous in either grade that they detract from a painted finish.

The box elder is a third soft maple which furnishes limited amounts of lumber. Most box elder trees branch out near the ground. Tall trees are seldom found. Lumber from box elder trees is mixed with other soft maple lumber.

OAK

Genus: QUERCUS. Principal lumber species: *rubra* (red oak); *alba* (white oak); and *robur* (English brown oak). See Fig. 12-25.

Characteristics: Oak is a very heavy, hard, and strong hardwood. It works, turns, carves, and bends well considering its density. Sanding and finishing qualities are excellent. It is also dimensionally stable. Oak has large pores that usually require filler before finishing. The heartwood color of red oak is reddish or light reddish-brown. White oak heartwood is light tan or light brown.

The oaks comprise the most important group of hardwoods in the U.S. None is more widely accepted for contemporary designs. Many different species are included in the oak family. Most are marketed as either red or white oak. Distinctions between the two are as follows.

Red oak
1. The heartwood tends to be a reddish color.
2. Vessels of heartwood have few tyloses (mineral and chemical deposits); thus, the wood is not waterproof.

Fig. 12-25. Oak, especially white oak, is the most chosen wood for contemporary furniture. (Fine Hardwood Veneer Assoc.)

3. Pores in latewood are few.
4. Annual rings are widely separated resulting in a coarser textured wood.
5. Heartwood is not durable when conditions may cause decay.

White oak
1. The heartwood tends to be tan or brownish.
2. Vessels of heartwood contain abundant tyloses which block pore openings and make the wood waterproof.
3. Pores in latewood are small and numerous.
4. Annual rings are compact resulting in a finer textured wood.
5. Heartwood is durable under conditions favoring decay.

Oak is related to beech and chestnut. However, the Quercus family is unique. It is the only genus which bears acorns. It is also one of the few groups which includes both hardwoods (covered here) and softwoods (called "live oak"). The range of growth extends across the U.S. with concentration east of the great plains and on the West Coast.

Oak has been selected for almost every application requiring wood. Oak is a common material for contemporary furniture because of its light color. It is also a standard for hardwood flooring due to durability as well as beauty. In addition to appearance products, oak is a utility wood. It has been used for food crates, bridge timbers, and railway crossties.

Either red or white oak will serve equally well for most purposes. The only exception is to use white oak in areas where decay is likely. White oak pores are filled with mineral and chemical deposits (tyloses). The deposits add to water resistance and durability in moist conditions.

Oak has many wood rays. As discussed in Chapter 11, the method of cutting will either expose the rays, or reduce their appearance. Quarter-sawn oak is cut through the rays. The rays then appear as large flakes. Rift-sawn oak is cut across the rays. The cross-sectioned rays appear very thin. This effect is called comb grain because it looks much like hair.

PALDAO

Genus: DRACONTOMELUM. Principal lumber species: *dao*. See Fig. 12-26.

Characteristics: Paldao is gray to reddish-brown with varied grain effects, usually dark, irregular stripes. Pores are very large and partially plugged. It is a fairly dense hardwood, comparable to walnut.

Paldao is one of the finest Philippine cabinet woods. It is not related to lauan (Philippine mahogany), nor does it resemble that species. It looks much like a striped walnut, although it would

Fig. 12-26. Paldao is comparable to walnut in appearance and working qualities. It is considered an "exotic wood" and used primarily for architectural woodwork.

never be mistaken for walnut. It also has odd finishing qualities. The wood brightens when finishing materials are applied.

Paldao is found in limited quantities. It is considered an "exotic" wood and is used mainly for architectural work.

PECAN

Genus: CARYA. Principal lumber species: *illinoensis*. See Fig. 12-27.

Characterisitics: Pecan is very heavy, hard, and elastic. It machines, turns, and steam bends well. The annual rings are very distinct. The heartwood color is light to dark reddish-brown; the sapwood is white.

Pecan is essentially a southern wood, found in Louisiana, eastern Texas, Mississipi, Arkansas, and the Delta region.

Although pecans and hickories are closely related, there are slight differences. Pecan is not quite as tough as hickory, but is still harder than other species. Generally, the heartwood of pecan is a little

Fig. 12-27. Pecan is related and comparable to hickory. (Fine Hardwood Veneer Assoc.)

darker than hickory and tends to be more red in color.

Pecan has great strength, resistance to abrasive wear, and good finishing qualities. It is an excellent furniture wood.

THE PINES

Pines comprise the most valuable commercial group of timber trees in the world. They supply wood for construction and cabinetmaking and pulp for making paper.

Thirty-five species of pine have been classified. Of these, 28 supply lumber with varying applications. All are softwood, non-porous, and have visible annual rings. Those discussed here have applications in cabinetmaking and millwork.

Ponderosa pine

Genus: PINUS. Principal lumber species: *ponderosa*. See Fig. 12-28.

Characteristics: Even though ponderosa pine is a non-porous softwood, the texture can be coarse or fine. It depends on the region where the tree was harvested. Ponderosa pine has excellent dimensional stability and is easy to work with. It has a low density, however, because of this, it can easily be marred. The heartwood is light tan, sometimes with an orange tint. The sapwood is white.

Ponderosa pine grows in mountainous regions from British Columbia to Mexico and from California to Nebraska. Stands form great forests. A variety of grades are produced by these stands.

Ponderosa pine is our most important mill species. Many large sash and door plants manufacture products entirely from ponderosa pine. Trim, mouldings, and cabinets are also produced from the wood. Large amounts of ponderosa pine plywood are produced.

Most ponderosa pine products are painted. Traditionally stain hasn't been used because the wood

absorbs it in varying amounts. Newer, gel-based stains which control the amount of absorption allow fine finishes to be applied to pine. A lacquer or varnish topcoat is applied over the stained wood for protection.

Ponderosa pine has many knots. It has gained popularity as knotty pine wall in recent years. Common grades of ponderosa pine with mainly knot defects are used for this purpose. Lower grades are cut to common grade dimension lumber and used for light construction and inexpensive shelving.

Sugar white pine

Genus: PINUS. Principal lumber species: *lambertiana*. See Fig. 12-29.

Characteristics: Sugar white pine is easy to work and used to a great extent for mill products. The texture is fine, soft, and uniform. The heartwood is light tan or brown. The sapwood is white. Like any true white pine species, sugar pine offers considerable durability when exposed to decay.

Fig. 12-29. Sugar pine.

Sugar pine is the largest of the pine trees. Older trees have reached 250 ft. (75 m) high and had 12 ft. (3.6 m) diameters. The species is found in Oregon and California, with 80 percent of the stand in California.

The large, coarse knots in sugar pine make it unsuitable for knotty pine wall paneling. Lower grades are used for light construction, boxes, and crates.

Southern yellow pine

Genus: PINUS. Principal lumber species: *palustris* (longleaf pine); *elliottii* (slash pine); *echinata* (shortleaf pine); and *taeda* (loblolly pine). See Fig. 12-30.

Characteristics: Southern yellow pine includes a number of southern pine softwood species. The

Fig. 12-28. Ponderosa pine.

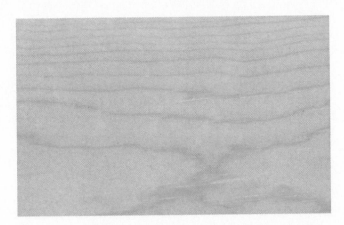

Fig. 12-30. Southern yellow pine.

wood ranges from clear to knotty. It is generally heavy, strong, stiff, and hard. The texture is rather coarse, with clear annual rings. The heartwood is reddish-brown. It is small compared to the large ring of yellowish-white sapwood which surrounds it.

Southern yellow pine species grow in the eastern U.S. Most forest replanting is done with yellow pine so that the species are always abundant. There is no separation of yellow pines by species. Rather, species are grouped into longleaf and shortleaf categories. Longleaf yellow pine includes the palustris and elliottii species. The other species are sold as shortleaf pines.

There are very few differences between the two. Longleaf pines are somewhat harder and stronger than short leaf types. However, single trees can vary in hardness according to the soil, water supply, and climate where they grew.

Yellow pines have great commercial value. They are the source of pulpwood for papermaking and timber for most construction materials. Smaller amounts are fabricated into almost any object which can be made of wood. Often, yellow pine is selected instead of other woods because it is inexpensive and readily available.

PRIMAVERA

Genus: CYBISTAX. Principal lumber species: *donnell-smithii*. See Fig. 12-31.

Characteristics: Primavera is moderately lightweight hardwood. It has medium to coarse texture and straight to slightly wavy grain. It is odorless and tasteless. The wood ranges from yellowish-white to yellowish-brown.

Primavera was formerly marketed as white mahogany. The grain pattern and texture of primavera resemble that of most tropical woods, mahogany in particular. If it were not for the lighter color of primavera, the two could be mistaken.

The wood has excellent finishing properties. It is used much like other fine cabinet woods. Boards with highly figured grain patterns are often used for inlays.

Primavera is found in southern Mexico, Guatemala, Salvador, and Honduras. Most of the wood which reaches the U.S. is grown in Guatemala.

Fig. 12-31. Primavera resembles mahogany in grain pattern. However, it is much lighter in color.

REDWOOD

Genus: SEQUOIA. Principal lumber species: *sempervirens*. See Fig. 12-32.

Characteristics: Redwood is soft and light in weight. The texture and density of redwood varies greatly, but the majority is fine textured. Redwood is seasoned slowly but then is not affected by dimensional change. It is easy to work and one of the most durable of all softwoods. It is free from resin, thus, it takes and holds finish well. The heartwood is cherry-red to reddish-brown and has very low luster. The sapwood is off-white with visible annual growth.

There are two kinds of giant sequoias. One is redwood. The other is the "big tree" *(sequoia gigantea)*. The big tree is no longer cut for lumber. The trees are protected and allowed to reach several hundred feet high. They are found along the western slopes of the Sierra Nevada mountains in central California.

The redwood is found in a narrow strip along the Pacific coast. The redwood may reach heights above the big tree. The diameter of the redwood, however, is less than that of the big tree.

Most sequoias never die of old age. They are felled by storms or destroyed by fire. Their immense trunks may also grow off balance until the tree is overturned by weight.

Redwood is valuable for many purposes. The only limit is weakness across the grain. Its greatest strength is with the grain which is why redwood is often used for columns. Redwood is best suited for areas exposed to decay. It is resistant to

Fig. 12-32. Redwood is very resistant to decay. It is widely used for siding and outdoor furniture.

moisture and can be used for all exterior purposes, including siding, picnic tables, and fences. It is also used in millwork and furniture, but in limited quantities.

Redwood trees sometimes produce large lumps (called burls) on the side of the tree. Sawed burl veneer has beautiful swirling grain patterns.

ROSEWOOD

Genus: DALBERGIA. Principal lumber species: *nigra* (Brazilian rosewood); *latifolio* (East Indian rosewood); *stevensonii* (Honduras rosewood); *greveana* (Madagascar rosewood); and *grenadillo* (San Domingan rosewood). See Fig. 12-33.

Characteristics: Rosewood is a beautiful and valuable hardwood. It is noted by the deep reddish-brown to nearly purple colored heartwood. Small burls, black streaks, or mottlings enhance the appearance. Rosewood is easy to work as it is soft and light, and the grain is closed. Sharp tools must be used during cutting since the wood is splintery. A natural high polish can be obtained because of oils in the wood.

Fig. 12-33. Brazilian rosewood is available in limited amounts for inlaying.

All true rosewoods are members of the Dalbergia genus. They grow in Asia, Madagascar, Brazil, and Central America. The Brazilian rosewood, noted for its dazzling beauty, is becoming scarce. All of the species are rated as valuable and are used in limited amounts. Most are cut as inlay and veneer for fine furniture and cabinet work. Entire boards are rarely available.

SANTOS ROSEWOOD

Genus: MACHAERIUM. Principal lumber species: *spp.* (spp. is the abbreviated plural of species; the machaerium genus includes over 80 trees.) See Fig. 12-34.

Characteristics: Santos rosewood is a heavy, hard, Bolivian and Brazilian hardwood. It is a fine textured wood, having small pores which are barely visible. The heartwood is a lustrous chocolate brown to purple to black color. The sapwood is cream color. Sapwood is sharply, although irregularly, defined from heartwood. The grain pattern is variable. It resembles, and is an excellent substitute for, Brazilian rosewood.

Fig. 12-34. Santos rosewood, also known as Pau Ferro, is similar to Brazilian rosewood, but with a more purplish tint.

SAPELLE

Genus: ENTANDROPHRAGMA. Principal lumber species: *cylindricum.* See Fig. 12-35.

Characteristrics: Sapelle can be used as a substitute for mahogany. It is somewhat tougher, harder, and heavier than African mahogany, but works fairly well. There is considerable variation in grain pattern. Most often, it is straight with light portions jutting out from the stripes. This pattern is called *stripe and bee's wing.*

Sapelle is one of West Africa's most common timbers. It is related to the genuine mahoganies although it is not of the same genus. It has the color,

Fig. 12-35. Sapelle is one of many mahogany substitutes.

grain, and figure of mahogany but is 10 to 15 percent heavier with less dimensional stability.

Sapelle is used mainly in Europe for furniture, cabinets, case goods, and interior decoration. It is readily available as both lumber and veneer.

SASSAFRAS

Genus: SASSAFRAS. Principal lumber species: *albidum*. See Fig. 12-36.

Characteristics: Sassafras is one of the few soft hardwoods with decorative grain character. It is easy to work, but is brittle. Take care not to lift the grain when planing. The pattern is somewhat like ash. The general texture is like ash or hackberry, but much softer. Sassafras also resembles chestnut, except that the lighter color tends to have a yellowish tint instead of grayish.

Sassafras is a beautiful wood for cabinets, rustic wall paneling, and novelty pieces of furniture. It is sometimes used for exterior furniture and siding.

The wood is found in limited amounts over most of the eastern half of the U.S. However, it is so widely scattered that large harvests are not likely.

Fig. 12-36. Sassafras replaces chestnut for many applications. (Fine Hardwood Veneer Assoc.)

In good climates, trees up to 100 ft. (30 m) tall and 3 ft. (3 m) in diameter have been cut. The average tree is much smaller.

SATINWOOD

Genus: CHLOROXYLON. Principal lumber species: *swientenia* (East Indian satinwood); also ZANTHOXYLUM *flavum* (San Domingan or West Indian satinwood). See Fig. 12-37.

Characteristics: Satinwood is a very hard, dense hardwood. It has interlocking grain that tends to check. The pattern is rippled or stripe and bee's wing figure. It is golden yellow in color when cut, but deepens to rich golden brown with age. When freshly cut, it has a strong coconut odor and oily texture and appearance.

San Domingan satinwood is found in Puerto Rico, Honduras, the Bahamas, and in southern Florida. Almost all antique furniture including satinwood is the San Domingan type. East Indian satinwood, grown in Ceylon and southern India has come into some use. However, it is harder, paler in color, and more figured. The cost of satinwood limits its use to fine furniture inlay and banding.

Fig. 12-37. Satinwood has an oily texture and appearance.

SPRUCE

Genus: PICEA. Principal lumber species: *sitchensis* (Sitka spruce); *engelmanni* (Engelmann spruce); the following are marketed as eastern spruce; *canadensis* (white spruce); *rubens* (red spruce); and *mariana* (black spruce). See Fig. 12-38.

Characteristics: Spruce is a non-porous evergreen softwood. It is soft and relatively weak, although Sitka is fairly strong compared to its weight. The machining qualities of eastern and Engelmann spruce are fair, but are poor for Sitka spruce. Dimensional stability of spruce is excellent. The texture is uniform, with visible annual rings. The color of

Fig. 12-38. Only spruce species labeled as Eastern spruce are suitable for cabinet and millwork.

heartwood is light tan or reddish-brown, and the sapwood is off-white.

All spruces are members of the pine family and close relatives of fir trees. Many spruces are trimmed for landscaping because of their beauty.

Sitka spruce grows along the coastal region from Alaska to northern California. It is an important construction material for Alaska. It is also suitable for mill products and, in general, can be used for any purpose requiring a softwood. Poor machining qualities prevent this species from being used in fine cabinet work. The grain is likely to tear unless processed with high speed, sharp machinery.

Engelmann spruce is a highly ornamental tree of little commercial importance. It is relatively weak and used for cabinetwork which requires little durability. The wood grows in the Rocky Mountains from the Yukon to Arizona. Nearly half the stand is in Colorado.

White spruce, red spruce, and black spruce can be found all over the northern U.S. Often these species grow together. They are mixed during harvest and sold simply as eastern spruce. The wood is used for general carpentry, crates, ladder rails, mill products, and light construction.

SYCAMORE

Genus: PLATANUS. Principal lumber species: *occidentalis*. See Fig. 12-39.

Characteristics: Sycamore is one of the softer hardwoods. It has a medium density and average hardness and strength. The grain is closed but the texture is still rather coarse. Its color is flesh pink to brownish-pink with slightly lighter sapwood.

The sycamore is the largest broadleaf tree. Specimens 170 ft. (51 m) tall and 14 ft. (4.2 m) in diameter have been recorded. The average full grown tree is 120 ft. (36 m) high and 2 to 4 ft. (0.6 to 1.2 m) in diameter. Most sycamore grows in the lower Ohio and Mississippi Valleys.

The interwoven fibers of sycamore make it hard to split. It is also hard to work. It is processed best on high speed equipment.

Quarter-sawn lumber displays a very attractive small flake figure. Large quantities of rotary-cut sycamore veneer are used by the packing industry for fruit and vegetable containers. Lumber is fabricated into inexpensive furniture, usually stained to imitate maple. It is a good utility wood for building cabinets, especially hidden parts. One of the principal uses of the wood is for drawer slides.

Fig. 12-39. The interwoven wood fibers of sycamore make it hard to split. (Fine Hardwood Veneer Assoc.)

TEAK

Genus: TECTONA. Principal lumber species: *grandis*. See Fig. 12-40.

Characteristics: Teak is quite hard and strong. It is not difficult to work if you use carbide tools. Ordinary tools dull quickly because of minerals and silicates in the wood. It is usually straight grained, although some lumber is highly figured. Once seasoned, it is dimensionally stable. The color is

Fig. 12-40. Teak is common in Modern Scandinavian and Oriental furniture styles. Lumber supplies are limited, but it is readily available as veneer.

tawny yellow to dark brown, often with light streaks. The wood is similar to fine walnut except that teak feels oily because of the high amount of silicates in the wood.

Teak is imported from Burma, India, and Thailand. It is available as veneer but limited as lumber. Teak is resistant to decay, but because of cost it is not widely used for exterior applications. It is mostly used for interior woodwork and contemporary, Scandinavian, and Oriental furniture styles.

AMERICAN TULIPWOOD

Genus: LIRIODENDRON. Principal lumber species: *tulipifera.* See Fig. 12-41.

Characteristics: American tulip is a moderately soft, low density, open grain hardwood. The texture is fairly fine and uniform because the pores are small. Use of a filler is optional. There is very little difference between earlywood and latewood so annual rings are not distinct. The heartwood is pale olive-brown to yellow-brown; sapwood is off-white to grayish white. American tulip works well with either hand or machine tools and is relatively stable.

Fig. 12-41. American tulipwood has many uses, ranging from plywood veneer, to furniture components and interior trim. (Fine Hardwood Veneer Assoc.)

American tulip is a new name for yellow poplar. The name was recently changed for two reasons. First the tulipifera species is not a poplar; it is a member of the magnolia family. Second, the yellow poplar of other countries is not near the quality of the American species. Thus, foreign countries have refrained from buying the American species. The name change is intended to boost sales.

The American tulip is found throughout most of the eastern U.S. Trees are too widely scattered for mass harvesting in some areas. The best timber growth is in the Ohio Valley region and on mountain slopes in North Carolina and Tennessee. In second growths of Appalachian and eastern stands,

there is a thick band of sapwood which is nearly white. Sapwood lumber is often called "whitewood."

American tulipwood is free from resin. It kiln dries well, glues easily, is stable, and does not split when nailing. It is soft enough to be a favorite wood for working with hand tools. It is easily stained to look like more costly woods.

As veneer, American tulipwood is used for faces, cross-banding, and backs of plywood. As lumber, it is used for furniture component parts, turnery, interior trim and millwork, cabinetry, and exterior trim and siding.

AMERICAN WALNUT

Genus: JUGLANS. Principal lumber species: *nigra.* See Fig. 12-42.

Characteristics: Walnut is moderately dense and hard. It is strong in comparison to its weight. Walnut has excellent machining properties and superb finishing qualities. It has open pores which require filling. The annual growth rings are clearly marked and the texture is fine and even. The grain pattern is highly figured, often with crotch, swirl, stump, and burl wood. The wood polishes to a high luster. The heartwood has varying colors of brown, often with purplish tint.

Walnut is the most valuable furniture and cabinet timber of the U.S. The beauty of walnut is admired by almost everyone. Most homes possess at least one article made of walnut. The principal uses of walnut are furniture, gun stocks, interior trim, cabinets, fixtures, instrument cases, etc. Much is made into veneers for walnut-faced plywood.

Most walnut is plain-sawed or flat-sliced (for veneer). Occasionally, walnut is quarter-sawn or sliced. This method produces "pencil stripe" walnut. Quarter sawing displays the edge of the annual growth rings. They appear like a series of narrow bands or lines. Walnut crotches and stumps are valuable and always cut into veneer. Veneer results in more square footage of wood per log.

Walnut is found as isolated trees as opposed to dense forest stands. Growth is found over the entire U.S. east of the great plains. The best stands are in the middle west, Mississippi and Ohio Valleys, Tennessee, and the lower Appalachian Mountains.

Walnut logs often are hauled over great distances to mills. This raises the cost of the lumber. The walnut log is relatively short, usually sawn into 6 to 10 ft. (2 to 3 m) length. Top grades average about 7 in. (175 mm) in width. Lumber mills which specialize in walnut steam the wood in walnut sawdust to darken the sapwood. The sapwood never quite reaches the color of heartwood. However, a skilled finisher can blend the two perfectly.

Fig. 12-42. Walnut is a popular American hardwood. The grain pattern may be straight (top) or wavy (bottom).

WILLOW

Genus: SALIX. Principal lumber species: *nigra* (black willow). See Fig. 12-43.

Characteristics: Willow is one of the softest American hardwoods, resembling basswood in density. It is very easy to work but is inclined to look and feel "fuzzy" after machining. Willow stains well, especially to resemble walnut. The wood has fairly uniform grain, yet it is somewhat coarse. The color of the heartwood varies from light gray to dark brown or dark reddish-brown. It sometimes has a purplish tint, much like walnut. The sapwood is nearly white, with grayish to light tan cast. Willow is one of the easiest of all woods to glue.

There are many species of willow in the U.S. Only one, black willow, produces trees of saw timber size. It develops best in the rich bottomlands of the lower Ohio and Mississippi Valleys. It is found to some extent all over the eastern half of the country, mostly in areas with much water. Willow grows rapidly, reaching maximum size of 130 ft. (30 m) and diameter of 3 ft. (1 m).

The main use of willow for some time has been plywood core stock, crates, and boxes. It is gaining popularity for inexpensive furniture, mill products, and wall paneling. It is very easy to work and presents a handsome appearance. Careful finishing will make the wood closely resemble walnut.

ZEBRAWOOD

Genus: MICROBERLINIA. Principal lumber species: *brazzavillensis*. See Fig. 12-44.

Characteristics: Zebrawood is noted for its pronounced light gold and dark brown stripes. It is a

Fig. 12-43. Black willow is the only willow specie of saw timber size. It has been mostly used for plywood, but with careful finishing, can resemble walnut. (Fine Hardwood Veneer Assoc.)

Fig. 12-44. Zebrawood is considered an exotic wood, with its light gold and dark brown stripes. It is used sparingly because of its bold appearance.

heavy, hard wood with somewhat coarse texture. The wood finishes to a high luster, but is used sparingly because of its bold appearance. The figure may be straight to wavy, depending on how the wood is cut. Zebrawood grows in African Cameroon, Gaboon, and West Africa.

Zebrawood is considered an exotic wood. It is used mainly for inlays because of its high cost. The bright, bold features of the wood make it an attractive addition to fine furniture.

SUMMARY

Wood is the primary material in shaping our living environment. It is used for tables, chairs, walls, and entire structures. Wood has so many uses because it is both functional and attractive. Functional qualities include hardness, flexibility, and shock resistance. Aesthetic qualities include color, texture, and grain pattern. The chart in Fig. 12-45 summarizes the characteristics of each wood species. Your selection of a wood will be based on those qualities which you feel are most important.

CABINETMAKING TERMS

Hardwood, softwood, open grain, closed grain, cross grain, texture, dimensional stability, density, luster, heartwood, sapwood, machining/working qualities, earlywood, latewood, annual ring.

TEST YOUR KNOWLEDGE

1. Why are common names used to describe most woods rather than the genus/species name?
2. Name two woods which are substituted for mahogany.
3. A very hard, strong wood used for baseball bats, hockey sticks, and tool handles is _____.
4. Any wood which is made into food containers must be _____.
5. Name two woods commonly installed as hardwood floors.
6. One of the best woods for dowels, spools, spindles, and other turnery is _____.
7. Chests and closet liners are often made of _____ because of the wood's unique scent.
8. Considered one of the top furniture hardwoods, _____ can be sanded to a glass-like finish.
9. Lumber from _____ is most wormy.
10. Name two woods especially resistant to moisture and decay.
11. White elm has become scarce because of _____.
12. A wood commonly substituted for elm is _____.
13. A very hard, elastic wood, often used for bent laminations (such as skis), is _____.
14. Lauan, also known as _____, is an inexpensive substitute for mahogany.
15. Name two characteristics which make genuine mahoganies different from African mahogany.
16. "Bird's eye" figuring is common in _____ lumber.
17. Define WHAD and WHND. What wood do these terms refer to?
18. Suppose you were building an outdoor flower box made of oak. Would you choose red oak or white oak?
19. Pecan is closely related to _____.
20. List various applications of the three common pines discussed.
21. Name three decorative woods you might use as inlay.
22. American tulipwood is a new name for _____.
23. List four of the most popular woods for cabinet and furniture making.
24. Select five woods with the best working/machining qualities.

WOOD CHARACTERISTICS Specie	SPECIFIC GRAVITY	WEIGHT (POUNDS PER CUBIC FT. AT 12% MOISTURE CONTENT)	PLANING	DRILLING	SANDING	TURNING	GLUING	NAIL AND SCREW HOLDING (Includes Split Resistance For Nailing)
Alder, red	0.41	28	2					
Ash	0.49	34	3	2	2	2	2	3
Banak	0.44	30	1	3	3	3	3	2
Basswood	0.37	24	2	1	1	4	1	1
Beech	0.64	45	1	1	2	3	1	2
Birch	0.62	43	2	2	2	1	2	2
Butternut	0.38	27	1	2	2	2	2	4
Cedar, arom. red	0.37	26	4	1	1	1	2	4
Cherry	0.50	35	1	3	2	3	2	5
Chestnut	0.43	30	1	1	1	1	2	3
Cottonwood	0.40	28	1	1	3	2	1	2
Cypress, bald	0.46	32	2	1	2	2	1	1
Ebony	1.22	63	4	2	2	2	1	3
Elm, American	0.63	44	3	4	4	3	4	2
Fir, Douglas	0.48	34	3	3	2	3	2	3
Gum, red	0.52	35	3	2	2	4	2	3
Hackberry	0.53	37	2	3	3	2	2	2
Hickory	0.72	50	3	2	2	2	2	3
Lauan (Philippine Mahogany)	0.49	35	2	3	2	3	3	4
Limba	0.49	35	1	2	1	2	2	2
Mahoganies, genuine	0.49	35	2	1	1	2	2	3
Mahogany, African	0.49	35	2	2	1	2	2	2
Maple, hard	0.63	38	3	2	1	2	2	2
Maple, soft	0.54	44	3	2	2	2	4	5
Oak, red or white	0.62	43	3	2	2	2	3	4
Paldao	0.59	44	3	2	2	3	3	3
Pecan	0.66	46	3	3	2	3	3	3
Pine, Ponderosa	0.39	28	1	3	2	3	3	4
Pine, sugar	0.35	26	2	1	2	2	2	2
Pine, yellow	0.40	28	2	1	2	2	2	2
Primavera	0.40	30	2	2	3	2	2	3
Redwood	0.40	28	1	2	1	1	2	2
Rosewood	0.75	50	3	1	1	2	1	3
Santos Rosewood (Pau Ferro)			4	4	4	4	4	3
Sapele	0.54	40	2	2	2	2	2	2
Sassafras	0.46	32	3	2	2	3	2	4
Satinwood	0.83	67	3	4	3	4	3	3
Spruce	0.40	28	2	2	3	3	1	3
Sycamore	0.49	34	3	3	3	3	3	3
Teak	0.62	43	4	4	4	4	4	3
Tulip, American (Yellow Poplar)	0.42	30	2	2	2	2	1	1
Walnut, American	0.55	38	2	2	2	3	3	3
Willow	0.39	26	2	2	3	2	1	1
Zebrawood	0.62	48	3	3	3	4	2	4

1. EXCELLENT
2. GOOD
3. AVERAGE
4. FAIR
5. POOR

Fig. 12-45. Summary of wood characteristics.

BENDING Difficult(1) To Easy (5)	HARDNESS Hard(1) To Soft(5)	COMPRESSION STRENGTH Weak (1) To Strong (5)	SHOCK RESISTANCE Low (1) To High (5)	STIFFNESS Limber (1) To Stiff (5)	AVAILABILITY L (Lumber) V (Veneer)	COST Expensive (1) To Inexpensive (5)
3	2	4	1	3	L	5
4	2	4	4	4	LV	3
4	5	3	2	3	L	3
5	5	2	2	1	L	5
4	2	4	5	4	LV	4
2	2	4	4	4	LV	3
2	4	2	4	2	LV	2
3	3	2	1	1	LV	3
2	3	4	4	4	LV	2
4	4	2	3	2	L	2
2	4	1	2	2	LV	5
2	4	3	4	3	L	3
1	1	4	5	5	L	1
5	2	3	4	4	LV	4
3	4	2	4	4	LV	4
3	2	3	4	4	LV	3
3	2	3	4	3	LV	4
4	4	5	5	4	LV	3
3	3	3	4	3	LV	3
2	3	3	4	3	L	3
3	3	3	4	3	LV	2
3	3	3	4	3	LV	2
2	1	5	5	5	LV	3
4	2	5	4	2	LV	3
1	4	4	4	4	LV	3
2	3	4	4	4	LV	2
4	4	4	4	4	LV	3
3	4	2	2	3	L	4
5	4	2	1	2	L	3
3	3	4	4	4	L	4
3	3	3	4	3	LV	3
3	3	2	4	4	L	3
2	1	5	4	4	V	1
3	3	5	4	4	V	2
2	3	2	4	4	L	3
4	3	4	4	4	V	1
4	4	2	2	3	L	4
3	3	3	4	3	L	3
4	2	4	4	4	LV	1
4	4	3	2	3	LV	5
2	3	4	4	4	LV	2
4	5	1	4	2	L	5
4	1	4	4	4	V	1

Fig. 12-45 continued.

FINISHING SELECTED WOOD SPECIES								
SPECIES	WOOD	TYPE			RECOMMENDED FINISHES			
	Softwood	Hardwood		Filler	Stain	Built-Up Topcoat	Penetrating Oil	Paint
		Open Pores	Closed Pores	(R = Required for Flat Surface)	(O = Optional)			
Alder			●		O	■	■	
Ash		●		R	O	■	■	
Banak	●				O	■	■	
Basswood			●					■
Beech			■		O	■	■	
Birch			●		O	■	■	
Butternut		●		R	O	■	■	
Cedar, Aromatic Red	●					■	■	
Cherry			●		O	■	■	
Chestnut		●		R	O	■	■	
Cottonwood			●					■
Cypress	●					■		■
Ebony			●			■		
Elm		●		R	O	■	■	
Fir, Douglas	●					■	■	■
Gum, red			●		O	■	■	
Hackberry		●		R	O	■	■	
Hickory			●		O	■	■	
Lauan (Philippine Mahogany)		●		R	O	■	■	
Limba		●		R	O	■	■	
Mahoganies, Genuine		●		R	O	■	●	
Mahogany, African		●		R	O	■	●	
Maple, hard			●		O	■	■	
Maple, soft			●		O	■	■	
Oak, red or white		●		R	O	■	■	
Paldao		●		R	O	■	■	
Santos Rosewood (Pau Ferro)			●		O	■	■	
Pecan			●		O	■	■	
Pine, Ponderosa	●				O	■	■	■
Pine, Sugar	●				O	■	■	
Pine, Yellow	●				O	■	■	
Primavera		●		R	O	■	■	
Redwood	●				O	■	■	
Rosewood			●			■		
Sapele		●		R	O	■	■	
Sassafras		●		R	O	■	■	
Satinwood			●		O	■	■	
Spruce	●							■
Sycamore			●		O	■	■	
Teak			●			■		
Tulip, American (Yellow Poplar)			●		O	■		■
Walnut, American		●		R	O	■	■	
Willow			●		O	■	■	
Zebrawood			●			■		

Fig. 12-45 continued.

Chapter 13
MANUFACTURED PANEL PRODUCTS

After studying this chapter, you will be able to:
☐ *Describe the materials found in each category of manufactured panel products.*
☐ *List the methods used to grade panel products.*
☐ *Explain the use of various panel products for cabinets and fine furniture.*

Manufactured panel products are widely used by cabinetmakers to create large surfaces for case goods. They reduce the need for edge gluing lumber to make wide boards. Production time is reduced without sacrificing quality.

Panel products are typically more stable than solid lumber. They warp less because they are constructed with layers of thin wood or wood fibers. There is no continuous grain pattern in a panel. This keeps distortion at a minimum. Some panels are even moisture resistant.

The faces may be rough, textured, smooth, or finished, Fig. 13-1. The appearance of higher grades is suitable for clear finish. Lower grades contain defects. Veneered panels look like solid wood lumber. Those made of wood chips or fibers do not resemble real wood. Selection is based on whether the panel is to be hidden or visible.

The edges of veneered and nonveneered panel products reveal their composition. Edges either are hidden in the joint or covered with wood tape, plastic strips, or edging.

There are three categories of panel products:
1. Structural Wood Panels.
2. Appearance Panels.
3. Engineered Board Products.

STRUCTURAL WOOD PANELS

Structural wood panels are selected when stability and strength are required. Typical uses include roof, wall, and floor sheathing for building construction. Structural panels are used in cabinetmaking when the product requires more stability than beauty. Laminations, such as printed vinyl or high quality veneer, enhance the appearance.

Fig. 13-1. The smooth finish of this walnut paneling blends well with the style of the room. (Georgia-Pacific Corp.)

Structural wood panels are manufactured in various ways. Plywood is made by bonding layers of wood veneer with adhesive. Waferboard, composite board, structural particleboard, and oriented strand board are all made of wood chips or fibers bonded under pressure.

PLYWOOD

Structural plywood is the most common structural panel. It is manufactured with a core material sandwiched between two thin wood sheets, called face veneers.

The veneers are cut on a lathe. This process involves rotating a debarked log, called a peeler block, against a knife. The veneer is sheared from the log in long sheets which are cut to size. The sheets are

A—Bark is removed from the log by knurled wheels.
B—Debarked log is cut into 8 ft. sections, called peeler blocks.
C—Peeler blocks are placed on a lathe. The log is rotated against a stationary knife. Veneer is sheared from the peeler block in long sheets.
D—The clipper cuts veneer sheets into various widths. These sheets are then sent to the dryer.
E—Once dried to a moisture level for gluing, sheets are sorted according to defects.

F—Defects are removed and football-shaped patches are inserted.
G—Glue sheets are placed between layers of veneer. Liquid glue applied by a glue spreader may also be used.
H—The layers of veneer and glue are placed in a hot press. They are bonded into panels under heat and pressure.
I—After bonding, panels are trimmed, sanded, and stacked for inspection. After inspection, they are graded, strapped, and shipped.

Fig. 13-2. The steps taken to manufacture plywood. (American Plywood Assoc.)

sorted according to defects. Defects may be later patched, Fig. 13-2.

Face veneers are sheets applied over the core material. The core may be lumber, particleboard, or veneer plies. Glue is applied to the layers, which are then clamped under heat and pressure until cured. The panel is then trimmed to size and shipped.

Pound for pound, plywood is stronger than steel. Unlike solid wood, which is strong along the grain and weak across the grain, plywood is strong in all directions. The grain direction is altered 90° for each successive layer of wood. This strengthens the panel and equalizes tension of the grain patterns. It also gives plywood its resistance to checks

and splits. Nails and screws can be inserted close to edges without splitting the panel.

Structural plywood is manufactured from softwood. *Hardwood plywood* has hardwood veneer over a hardwood or softwood core. Although structurally sound for cabinetry, hardwood plywood is considered an appearance product.

The core for structural plywood varies according to use. The two most common cores are veneer and lumber.

Veneer-core

Veneer-core plywood is made of 3, 5, 7, or 9 layers of veneer, depending on panel thickness, Fig. 13-3. The veneer thickness may vary from 1/50

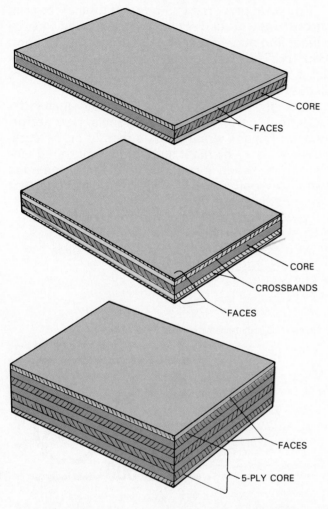

Fig. 13-3. Thickness of veneer-core plywood refers to the number of plies. (Forest Products Laboratory)

in. to 1/4 in. Thinner veneers become face layers while thicker ones make up core plies. Alternating grain direction of successive layers increases strength and reduces warpage.

Panel thickness of veneer-core plywood ranges from 1/8 in. to 1 3/16 in. Common thicknesses range from 1/4 in. to 3/4 in. Three layer, or *ply*, panels usually are 1/4 in. Front and back faces are bonded to a single core. Five plies (two faces and three cores) are used for panels from 5/16 in. to 1/2 in. Seven plies are used for panels up to 3/4 in. and nine plies are used for thicker panels. Standard panel size is 4 ft. by 8 ft. Smaller and larger sizes are available.

Veneer plywood is much less expensive than lumber core. It also has greater structural value. Select veneer plywood when the appearance of the edge is not a concern. Veneer core edges may show core voids and defects.

Lumber core

Lumber core plywood has a solid wood center and thin veneer faces. The core may be thin laminated strips of wood or wider boards. If there are veneer layers between the core and the back and front faces, they are called *crossbands*, Fig. 13-4. The crossband grain is at 90° to the faces. Thicker panels are obtained with two lumber cores separated by a crossband. Standard panel size is 4 ft. by 8 ft. Thickness can range from 5/8 in. to 2 in.

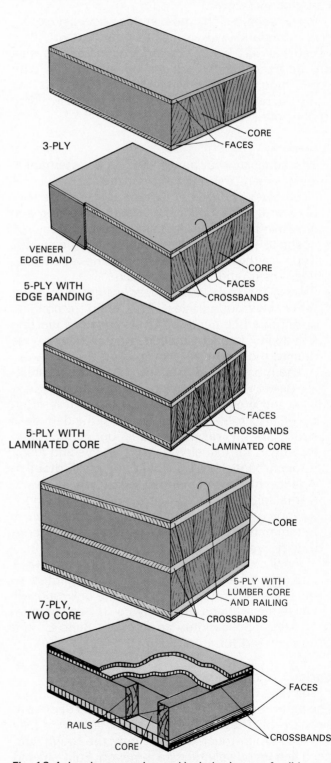

Fig. 13-4. Lumber-core plywood includes layers of solid wood and veneer. Banding may be applied to hide edges. Panels with rails permit machining the edges. (Forest Products Laboratory)

Lumber core plywood is chosen when solid edges are important, such as:
- The edges of the product may be exposed. The cut edges of lumber core plywood are solid.
- Edges will contain jointwork. Machined edges of lumber core plywood are solid wood.
- Hardware will be attached. Lumber core has excellent edge screwholding properties.

Particleboard core

Particleboard is the most stable and least expensive material. However, it has poor screwholding capabilities in edges. Core construction can be seen on the edges, but these are usually hidden with wood tape. It is approximately the same price as veneer-core plywood, but much less expensive than lumber core.

Adhesives

The adhesive that bonds the layers determines, in part, where the plywood is used.
- *Type I fully waterproof adhesives* are for exterior plywood. Type I panels are used for siding and sheathing. They are installed in other areas exposed to excessive moisture and microorganisms. Type I adhesives include melamine-resin, phenolic-resin, and resorcinol-resin.
- *Type II moisture resistant adhesives* are for interior plywood grades. The bond retains its strength when occasionally exposed to wetting and drying. Interior plywood is installed where the moisture content will not exceed 20 percent.

  The most widely used interior plywood adhesive is urea resin. It is inexpensive, extremely flexible, and provides an excellent bond. It is often called urea formaldehyde resin. Formaldehyde is added to the resin to speed up curing time. However, formaldehyde gas is an eye and respiratory irritant. The U.S. Environmental Protection Agency has recommended that lower levels of formaldehyde be used to prevent "outgassing." Interior plywood bonded with exterior glue is recommended. The face veneers are interior quality, yet safer glues are used for bonding.
- *Type III moisture resistant adhesives* retain their strength when only occasionally subjected to moisture. Thorough wetting of the plywood will cause separations of the layers. It has some industrial applications as crating panels, and upholstered furniture blanks.

Surface smoothness

The face veneers of plywood may be smoothed. The panel may be sanded on one side (S1S) or both sides (S2S). They may also be touch sanded or fully sanded. When touch sanded, only the rough sections and wood splinters are removed. Fully sanded panels are ready for finish.

U.S. structural plywood grades

Structural plywood can be performance or non-performance graded. *Performance ratings* classify veneer and non-veneer panels for the construction industry. They are designed to meet requirements for spanning roof or floor joists. These grades are discussed later in the chapter.

Most plywood applications do not require the strength of performance-rated panels. Non-performance plywood grades focus mostly on defects. However, they do meet standard strength requirements. The grade is stamped on the face and edge of the plywood panel, Fig. 13-5. It gives important information about the:
- Type of wood species of the front and back faces.
- Quality of the faces.
- Type of adhesive used to bond the plies.
- Manufacturer of the product.
- Mill number.

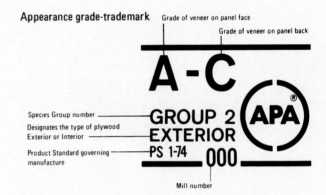

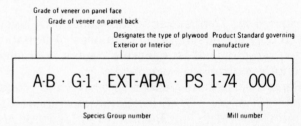

Fig. 13-5. Plywood is stamped with a grade trademark of the APA. The mark provides information on the wood species, quality, and recommended use. (American Plywood Assoc.)

Standards are established by manufacturers' associations such as the American Plywood Association (APA) and the Douglas Fir Plywood Association (DFPA). Governmental specifications are made by the National Bureau of Standards (NBS).

The *group number* in the grade stamp indicates the weakest species used for face veneers. For sanded panels the group number indicates the exact species group. Group 1 contains the strongest and stiffest woods, Fig. 13-6.

SPECIES GROUP CLASSIFICATION

Group 1	Group 2	Group 3	Group 4	Group 5

Apitong
Beech, American
Birch
  Sweet
  Yellow
Douglas Fir 1
Kapur
Keruing
Larch, Western
Maple, Sugar
Pine
  Caribbean
  Ocote
Pine, Southern
  Lablolly
  Longleaf
  Shortleaf
  Slash
Tanoak
	Cedar, Port Orford
	Cypress
	Douglas Fir 2
	Fir
	  California Red
	  Grand
	  Noble
	  Pacific Silver
	  White
	Hemlock, Western
	Lauan
	  Almon
	  Bagtikan
	  Mayapis
	  Red Lauan
	  Tangile
	  White Lauan
	Maple, Black
	Mengkulang
	Meranti, Red
	Mersawa
	Pine
	  Pond
	  Red
	  Virginia
	  Western White
	Spruce
	  Red
	  Sitka
	Sweetgum
	Tamarack
	Yellow-poplar
		Alder, Red
		Birch, Paper
		Cedar, Alaska
		Fir, Subalpine
		Hemlock, Eastern
		Maple, Bigleaf
		Pine
		  Jack
		  Lodgepole
		  Ponderosa
		  Spruce
		Redwood
		Spruce
		  Black
		  Englemann
		  White
			Aspen
			  Bigtooth
			  Quaking
			Cativo
			Cedar
			  Incense
			  Western Red
			Cottonwood
			  Eastern
			  Black (Western
			    Poplar)
			Pine
			  Eastern White
			  Sugar
				Basswood
				Fir, Balsam
				Poplar, Balsam

Fig. 13-6. Species used for face veneers of plywood are grouped according to their strength. Group 5 contains the weakest species. (American Plywood Assoc.)

The quality of the two faces is given by *veneer grades*. Grades refer to the number of defects and the method by which they are patched, Fig. 13-7. They are indicated by letters separated by a hyphen. An example of this is A-C plywood. The grade of the front face veneer is A. The grade of the back face veneer is C.

VENEER GRADES

N	Smooth surface "natural finish" veneer. Select, all heartwood or all sapwood. Free of open defects. Allows not more than 6 repairs, wood only, per 4x8 panel, made parallel to grain and well matched for grain and color.
A	Smooth, paintable. Not more than 18 neatly made repairs, boat, sled, or router type, and parallel to grain, permitted. May be used for natural finish in less demanding applications.
B	Solid surface. Shims, circular repair plugs and tight knots to 1 inch across grain permitted. Some minor splits permitted.
C PLUGGED	Improved C veneer with splits limited to 1/8 inch width and knotholes and borer holes limited to 1/4 x 1/2 inch. Admits some broken grain. Synthetic repairs permitted.
C	Tight knots to 1-1/2 inch. Knotholes to 1 inch across grain and some to 1-1/2 inch if total width of knots and knotholes is within specified limits. Synthetic or wood repairs. Discoloration and sanding defects that do not impair strength permitted. Limited splits allowed.
D	Knots and knotholes to 2-1/2 inch width across grain and 1/2 inch larger within specified limits. Limited splits are permitted. Limited to Interior grades of plywood.

Fig. 13-7. Face veneers are graded by the wood characteristics such as knots and splits. Some defects are patched. (American Plywood Assoc.)

Suppose only the front face side will be seen. You might choose an N grade as the front face and a C or D grade as the back face.

The recommended environment where the panel is used is indicated by either INT (or Interior) and EXT (or Exterior).

Canadian structural plywood grades

Canadian plywood is manufactured according to rules set by the Canadian Standards Association (CSA). Panels must meet CSA standards to be certified by the Council of Forest Industries of British Columbia (COFI).

The CSA has adopted the metric system for sizing panel products. Sizes are comparable to those of U.S. grades, Fig. 13-8. Most existing structures in Canada were constructed with standards similar to those of the U.S. Studs were 16 in. on center. Now they are installed on 400 mm centers. The 1200 by 2400 mm panels fit the new standards. The 1220 mm by 2440 mm panels are made for use in structures based on the old system.

METRIC DIMENSIONS OF COFI EXTERIOR PLYWOOD

THICKNESS	
Sheathing and Select Grades	**Sanded Grades**
7.5 mm replaces 5/16 inch 9.5 mm replaces 3/8 inch 12.5 mm replaces 1/2 inch 15.5 mm replaces 5/8 inch 18.5 mm replaces 3/4 inch	6 mm replaces 1/4 inch 8 mm new thickness 11 mm new thickness 14 mm new thickness 17 mm replaces 11/16 inch
SIZE	
1220 mm x 2440 mm replaces 48 in. x 96 in. 1200 mm x 2400 mm new size	

Fig. 13-8. The Canadian Standards Association has adopted the metric system for plywood dimensions. (Council of Forest Industries of British Columbia)

The COFI certification mark contains information necessary when selecting the panel, Fig. 13-9. The species designation refers to one of two species groups used in COFI plywood. One is Douglas Fir and the other is Canadian Softwood, Fig. 13-10. The COFI mark also indicates mill and CSA standard governing manufacture. The COFI mark does not indicate the veneer ply grade. It is simply an assurance to the buyer that the plywood meets CSA standards. The standards insure that the panel will perform in a satisfactory and predictable manner.

Veneer ply grades designate the face, back, and inner plies. They also note the type of defects in the panel. The face and back veneers may be sanded, unsanded, or covered with resin-fiber overlay, Fig. 13-11.

Face Stamp on COFI EXTERIOR Canadian Softwood Plywood

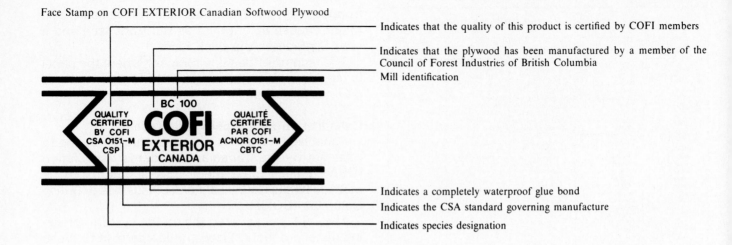

Indicates that the quality of this product is certified by COFI members

Indicates that the plywood has been manufactured by a member of the Council of Forest Industries of British Columbia

Mill identification

Indicates a completely waterproof glue bond

Indicates the CSA standard governing manufacture

Indicates species designation

Edge Stamp on COFI EXTERIOR Canadian Softwood Plywood

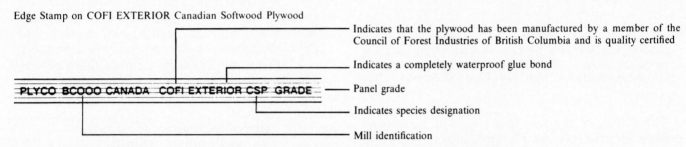

Indicates that the plywood has been manufactured by a member of the Council of Forest Industries of British Columbia and is quality certified

Indicates a completely waterproof glue bond

Panel grade

Indicates species designation

Mill identification

Fig. 13-9. COFI Canadian plywood grade stamp contains information on wood species, glue bond, and CAS standard. (Council of Forest Industries of British Columbia)

SPECIES USED IN COFI PLYWOOD			
DOUGLAS FIR PLYWOOD (DFP)		CANADIAN SOFTWOOD PLYWOOD (CSP)	
Faces and Backs	Inner Plies	Faces and Backs	Inner Plies
Douglas Fir *Backs of 6 mm, 8 mm, 11 mm, and 14 mm good one side grade may be: Western Hemlock True Fir Sitka Spruce Western White Spruce Western Larch Lodgepole Pine	Douglas Fir Western Hemlock True Fir Sitka Spruce Western White Spruce Western Larch Western White Pine Ponderosa Pine Lodgepole Pine	Western Hemlock True Fir Sitka Spruce Western White Spruce Western Larch Lodgepole Pine	Douglas Fir Western Hemlock True Fir Sitka Spruce Western White Spruce Western Larch Western White Pine Ponderosa Pine Lodgepole Pine

Fig. 13-10. Canadian plywood is divided by species into two areas. Inner plies contain the same species for both DFP and CSP. (Council of Forest Industries of British Columbia)

COMPOSITE PANEL

A *composite panel* consists of wood chip or fiber core faced with softwood veneer, Fig. 13-12. In addition to veneer, printed vinyl and paper are used. Composite panels are used in both construction and cabinetmaking. Lower grades serve as floor underlayment as well as roof or wall sheathing. Grades suitable for finishing are installed as wall paneling or frame and panel cabinetry.

WAFERBOARD

Waferboard is made of wood wafers and resin adhesive, refer to Fig. 13-12. Wood wafers are high quality chips of wood approximately 1 in. to 2 in. long of varying widths. The adhesive is generally *phenolic resin* which is waterproof. Panels designed for interior use are fabricated with Type III adhesives. The chips and adhesive are mixed and then formed into panels with heat and pressure.

REGULAR GRADES OF COFI EXTERIOR PLYWOOD					
Grade*	Veneer Grades			Characteristics	Typical Applications
	Face	Inner Plies	Back		
Good Two Sides (G2S)	A	C	A	Sanded. Best appearance both faces. May contain neat wood patches, inlays or synthetic patching material.	Furniture, cabinet doors, partitions, shelving, concrete forms, opaque paint finishes.
Good One Side (G1S)	A	C	C	Sanded. Best appearance one side only. May contain neat wood patches, inlays or synthetic patching material.	Where appearance of one exposed surface is important. Shelving, built-ins, DIY projects. Concrete forms.
Select — Tight Face (SEL TF)	B†	C	C	Unsanded. Permissible face openings filled. May be cleaned and sized.	Underlayment and combined subfloor and underlayment. Hoarding. Construction use where sanded material is not required.
Select (SELECT)	B	C	C	Unsanded. Uniform surface with minor open splits. May be cleaned and sized.	
Sheathing (SHG)	C	C	C	Unsanded. Face may contain limited size knots, knotholes and other minor defects.	Roof, wall, and floor sheathing. Hoarding. Construction and packaging uses where sanded material or uniform surface not required.
High Density Overlaid (HDO − 0/ − 0)	B†	C	B†	Smooth resin-fibre overlaid surface. Further finishing not required.	Bins, tanks, boats, furniture, signs, displays, forms for architectural concrete.
Medium Density Overlaid (Specify one or both sides) (MDO1S, MDO2S)	C†	C	C†	Smooth resin-fibre overlaid surface. Best paint base.	Siding, soffits, paneling, built-in fitments, signs, any use requiring superior paint surface.
COFIFORM COFIFORM SP	A A B C	C C C C	A C C C	Douglas fir panels specially constructed to provide improved and premium strength and stiffness. Available in regular sanded and unsanded grades and specialty grades with resin-fibre overlays or surface coatings of epoxy resin, modified polyurethanes or other proprietary compositions. Also available with factory-applied release agent.	For premium performance applications, particularly in wet service conditions. Concrete formwork and selected structural engineering use and special service industrial applications.
COFIFORM PLUS COFIFORM SP PLUS				Special construction Douglas fir panels with exceptional stiffness and strength. Strength properties exceed those of COFIFORM panels.	

*All grades, including overlays bonded with waterproof phenolic resin glue.
†Permissible openings filled.

Fig. 13-11. Using various veneer grade combinations, Canadian manufacturers produce panels suitable for a variety of uses. (Council of Forest Industries of British Columbia)

Edges are trimmed to square the waferboard.

Waferboard faces often differ. One side might be smooth and slick. The other could have a screen-like texture. The textured side is suitable for veneer or printed plastic laminations.

PARTICLEBOARD

Structural particleboard is composed of small wood flakes, chips, and shavings bonded together with resins or adhesives, refer to Fig. 13-12. It is often called *flakeboard*.

Particleboard is manufactured much like waferboard. However, the wood chips are much smaller. The chips are mixed with glue, then pressed into panels.

Structural particleboard is specially made to withstand the stress and environment required for building materials. A common application is floor underlayment. Higher density layers on the surfaces contain smaller wood chips, extra resin, and wax. The increased density gives the panel greater strength and water repellency.

Particleboard typically is found in 4 ft. by 8 ft. sheets. Thickness may be from 1/4 in. to 1 7/8 in.

ORIENTED STRAND BOARD

Oriented strand board (OSB) is a relatively new product. It is manufactured with strands of wood which are layered perpendicular to each other. OSB is a cross between waferboard and plywood. Like plywood, layers are in alternating directions. However, layers are high quality wood chips, not veneer. OSB is similar to waferboard, except that chips are arranged in a pattern, not at random. Refer to Fig. 13-12. Three layers of chips are bonded with phenolic resin under heat and pressure.

OSB ranges in thickness from 1/4 in. to 23/32 in. Thinner sheets have many applications, such as dividers, shelving, cabinet backs, etc. Sheets from 3/8 in. to 1/2 in. serve as roof deck, wall, and subfloor sheathing. Sheets above 1/2 in. are used for single-layer flooring.

OSB has excellent dimensional stability and stiffness. It is frequently sanded smooth on both sides unless used for roof sheathing. Then, one side is given a textured, skid-resistant surface. When processing OSB, make cuts with carbide tipped blades. The high density of the board will quickly dull normal tools.

PERFORMANCE RATINGS

Performance-rated structural wood panels are designed to span specified distances. Applications include flooring, roof sheathing, and other building construction. Any structural wood panels may be performance rated if they pass test standards. These must meet or exceed U.S. Product Standards.

Standards met by performance panels require rigid control of strength properties, dimensional stability, and bond durability. These are affected by:
1. Wood species used to manufacture the panel.
2. Size, shape, and orientation of wood particles (for non-veneer panels).
3. Board density.
4. Adhesive type.

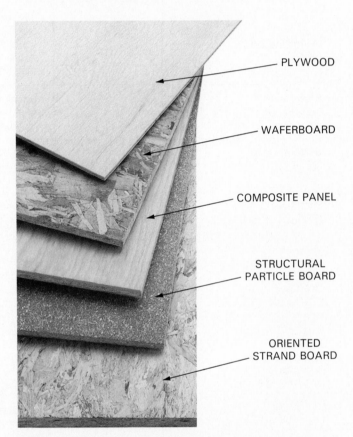

PLYWOOD

WAFERBOARD

COMPOSITE PANEL

STRUCTURAL PARTICLE BOARD

ORIENTED STRAND BOARD

Fig. 13-12. Structural OSB panels are selected for stability and strength. They serve many applications in building construction. (Georgia-Pacific)

The performance rating is stamped on the panel. It indicates certification met through testing done by the American Plywood Association, Fig. 13-13.

APPEARANCE PANELS

Appearance panels may replace lumber in cabinets and fine furniture. They are fabricated to match the grain pattern of a particular wood species. The texture may be smooth or patterned. Most modern cabinet construction is done with unfinished hardwood plywood panels. They provide the appearance and strength of solid hardwood, yet are much less expensive.

Other appearance panels are used primarily as

Grade Designation	Description & Common Uses
APA rated sheathing EXP1 or 2	Specially designed for subflooring and wall and roof sheathing, but can also be used for a broad range of other construction and industrial applications. Can be manufactured as conventional veneered plywood, as a composite, or as a non-veneered panel. For special engineered applications, including high load requirements and certain industrial uses, veneered panels conforming to PS 1 may be required. Specify Exposure 1 when long construction delays are anticipated. Common thicknesses: 5/16, 3/8, 7/16, 1/2 (15/32), 5/8 (19/32), 3/4 (23/32).
APA structural I & II rated sheathing EXP 1	Unsanded panel grades for use where strength properties are of maximum importance: structural diaphragms, box beams, gusset plates, stressed-skin panels, containers, pallet bins. Can be manufactured as conventional veneered plywood, as a composite, or as a non-veneered panel. Made only with exterior glue (Exposure 1). STRUCTURAL I more commonly available. Common thicknesses: 5/16, 3/8, 1/2 (15/32), 5/8 (19/32), 3/4 (23/32).
APA rated Sturd-I-Floor EXP 1 or 2	Specially designed as combination subfloor-underlayment. Provides smooth surface for application of carpet and possesses high concentrated and impact load resistance. Can be manufactured as conventional plywood, as a composite, or as a reconstituted wood panel (waferboard, oriented strand board, structural particleboard). Available square edge or tongue-and-groove. SPAN RATINGS: 16, 20, 24. Specify Exposure 1 when long construction delays are anticipated. Common thicknesses: 19/32, 5/8, 23/32, 3/4.
APA rated Sturd-I-Floor 48 oc (2-4-1) EXP 1	For combination subfloor-underlayment on 32- and 48-inch spans and for heavy timber roof construction. Manufactured only as conventional plywood. Available square edge or tongue-and-groove. SPAN RATING: 48. EXPOSURE DURABILITY CLASSIFICATIONS: Exposure 1. Thickness: 1 1/8.

	EXTERIOR USE
APA rated sheathing EXT	Exterior sheathing panel for subflooring and wall and roof sheathing, siding on service and farm buildings, crating, pallets, pallet bins, cable reels, etc. Can be manufactured as conventional veneered plywood, as a composite, or as a non-veenered panel. Common thicknesses: 5/16, 3/8, 1/2 (15/32), 5/8 (19/32), 3/4 (23/32).
APA Structural I & II rated sheathing EXT	For engineered applications in construction and industry where resistance to permanent exposure to weather or moisture is required. Can be manufactured as conventional veneered plywood, as a composite, or as a non-veenered panel. Unsanded. STRUCTURAL I more commonly available. Common thicknesses: 5/16, 3/8, 1/2, 5/8 (19/32), 3/4 (23/32).
APA rated Sturd-I-Floor EXT	For combination subfloor-underlayment under carpet where severe moisture conditions may be present, as in balcony decks. Possesses high concentrated and impact load resistance. Can be manufactured as conventional veneered plywood, as a composite, or as a non-veenered panel. Available square edge or tongue-and-groove. Common thicknesses: 5/8 (19/32), 3/4 (23/32).

Typical APA Performance-Rated Panel Registered Trademarks

Panel grade — APA RATED SHEATHING — Thickness 15/32 INCH
Span rating — 32/16 SIZED FOR SPACING
EXPOSURE 1 — Exposure durability classification
Mill number — 000
NER-108 — National Research Board report number

Panel grade — APA RATED STURD-I-FLOOR — Thickness 19/32 INCH
Span rating — 20 oc SIZED FOR SPACING
Tongue & groove — T&G NET WIDTH 47-1/2
EXPOSURE 1 — Exposure durability classification
Mill number — 000
NER-108 — National Research Board report number

Typical All-Veneer Products Meeting PS1 Requirements

(Specify when required for engineered applications)

APA RATED SHEATHING 32/16 15/32 INCH SIZED FOR SPACING EXPOSURE 1 000 PS-1-83 C-D INT/EXT GLUE NER-108

APA RATED STURD-I-FLOOR 24 oc 23/32 INCH SIZED FOR SPACING T&G NET WIDTH 47-1/2 EXPOSURE 1 000 INT/EXT GLUE NER-108 PS-1-83

The Exposure 1 rating on a panel means that the panel is intended for protected construction applications where ability to resist moisture during long construction delays or where exposure to conditions of similar severity is required.
The span rating which shows a pair of numbers separated by a slash mark indicates maximum span for roof sheathing (left) and maximum span for subfloor (right). The span rating with O.C. indicates maximum span "on center" of joists.

Fig. 13-13. Any structural panel may be performance rated. The performance-grade trademark is given to panels which meet special strength requirements. (Georgia-Pacific Corp.)

wall covering. They include:
- Prefinished hardwood and softwood veneered plywood.
- Simulated woodgrain finish on plywood.
- Simulated woodgrain finish on wood fiber substrate.
- Prehung wallpaper paneling.

HARDWOOD PLYWOOD

Manufacturers of *hardwood plywood* concentrate on appearance grade plywoods, Fig. 13-14. The panels have hardwood face veneers over lumber, veneer, particleboard, or specialty cores. Hardwood plywood is manufactured much the same as softwood. They both consist of similar cores and adhesives. Hardwood plywood differs in the way face veneers are cut and arranged. The face veneers are matched to create some type of design.

Cabinet manufacturers choose hardwood plywood for many purposes. These include cabinets, fine furniture, and wall paneling. There is a wide selection of thicknesses, veneers, species, and grades.

Face veneer

The *face veneers* of hardwood plywood may be cut from a number of wood species. Ash, birch, cherry, elm, gum, mahogany, maple, oak, pecan, rosewood, teak, and walnut are readily used. The appearance is determined by the:
- Species.
- Portion of the tree where the veneer was cut.
- Method of cut.
- Method of matching.

These topics will be discussed in the next chapter.

Core construction

Hardwood plywood cores may be veneer, lumber, or particleboard. Specialty cores include fiberboard, acoustical, fire-resistant, and lightweight materials.
- *Fiberboard cores* are more dense core than those of particleboard. The edges can be easily machined and closely resemble real wood when left exposed.
- *Acoustical cores* deaden sound transmission. Many acoustical panels are suitable for veneer lamination.
- *Fire-resistant cores* are chemically impregnated or made with mineral materials.
- *Lightweight cores* make use of lightweight materials and the honeycomb structure used by bees. Honeycomb cores have large strength to weight ratios. Typical core materials include kraft paper and aluminum. Other lightweight cores are made of wood coils and grids.

Thickness

The most popular thicknesses in hardwood plywood are 1/4 in. (6 mm) and 3/4 in. (19 mm). Thicker plywood is for casework. Thinner sheets are for backs and drawer bottoms. You can purchase 3/8 in. (9.5 mm) panels. However, these panels are made with top grade veneer and are more expensive.

Hardwood plywood grading

Standards for hardwood plywood are set by the Hardwood Plywood Manufacturers Association (HPMA). The hardwood plywood grade is established by the quality of the two face veneers. Face veneers are graded by the number of defects. No. 1 veneer has few defects. No. 4 contains unlimited defects, Fig. 13-15.
- *Specialty* hardwood plywoods refer to special orders between manufacturers and purchasers. Special cuts of veneer can be ordered. The method of matching the veneer also may be specified. Specialty plywoods are ordered for architectural purposes. The grade is stamped on the face and edge of the panel, Fig. 13-16.
- *Premium A-1* and *Premium A-2* are the finest stock grades of hardwood plywood. Premium grade veneer is applied to the front face. A Premium (or Good) grade veneer is applied to the back face.

Fig. 13-14. Hardwood plywood is fabricated with hardwood face veneers for use where appearance is important. (Georgia-Pacific Corp.)

HARDWOOD PLYWOOD VENEER GRADES

Grade	Face Veneer	Allowable Defects
1	**Premium —** Book matched or slip (repeating grain figure but un-matched joints) matched for pleasing effect.	Burls, pin knots, slight color streaks and inconspicuous small patches in limited amounts.
1	**Good —** Unmatched, but sharp contrasts in color, grain and figure not permitted.	Burls, pin knots, slight color streaks and inconspicuous small patches in limited amounts.
2	**Sound —** Free from open defects.	All appearance defects permitted so long as smooth and sound. Smooth patches permitted.
3	**Utility —** (or Reject)	All natural defects; including open knots, wormholes and splits, maximum size of which are defined.
4	**Backing**	Defects practically unlimited; only strength and serviceability are considered.

Fig. 13-15. The grading system for hardwood plywood face veneers includes five categories. The grade may be given by number or face veneer designation. (Paxton Lumber Co.)

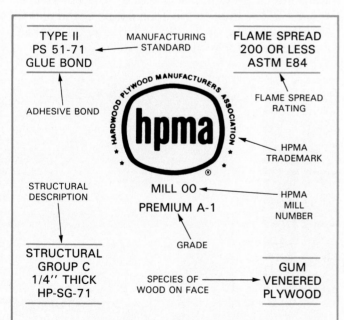

Typical grade marks used on hardwood plywood include: (1) The trademark of the HPMA (Hardwood Plywood Manufacturers Association). (2) The standard governing the manufacture. (3) The HPMA mill number. (4) The type of adhesive bond: Type I (Exterior) or Type II (Interior). (5) The flamespread rating. The lower the number, the slower the flamespread. Asbestos sheet is 0, and red oak is 100. Drapes, rugs, newspapers, clothing, etc., have a flamespread of about 200. (6) Structural description. (7) Species of wood on face. (8) Veneer grade of face. The grade of veneer on back is sometimes shown following grade of face; this is optional.

Fig. 13-16. Hardwood plywood panels are graded using the HPMA grade mark.

- *G1S—So.Bk.* (Good 1 Side—Sound Back is the next grade. The front face veneer of the wood specie you choose has a rating of No. 1 Good. The back veneer is No. 2 Sound. The back veneer is the same wood species as the front, but has some defects. Unless specified, a veneer core of any species of wood will be used. It may not be entirely sound; inner plies frequently have knot holes which show as voids in edges of cut panels. Voids can be filled with wood putty.
- *G1S* (Good 1 Side) front face veneer is No. 1 Good as was the G1S—So.Bk. grade. However, the back is No. 3 Utility (or Reject) of any species the manufacturer selects.
- *Craftsman* or *Shop* grades apply to panels where the front face has unmatching veneer. It may have sharp contrast in color and/or grain pattern.

Any grade combination of face and back veneers can be obtained for hardwood plywood. Dealer stocks are usually limited to those discussed above, but specialty orders can be made.

ORDERING HARDWOOD PLYWOOD

The types of plywood stocked by lumber dealers varies according to region. A variety of cores, veneer species, veneer cut, and veneer match are available. Check with your dealer for the panels they have or can order. When ordering, include the following specifications:

1. Number of panels (not square or board feet).
2. Width, length, and thickness.
3. Number of plies (for veneer core; if choice is given).
4. Core construction (if other than veneer).
5. Species of front face veneer.
6. Method used to cut front face veneer (if choice is given).
7. Method of matching front face veneer (if choice is given).
8. Grade (if grade is G1S—So.Bk., specify wood species of back veneer).
9. Adhesive type.
10. Surfacing (if any).

The following orders are examples which will be understood by any plywood dealer.
- 5 pcs. 3/4 x 48 x 96 in., lumber core, plain sliced Walnut, slip matched, G1S, Ext., S1S
- 3 pcs. 1/4 x 48 x 96 in., 3 ply, half-round sliced Red Oak, G1S—Sound Red Oak Back, Int., S1S

PREFINISHED PLYWOOD PANELING

Prefinished plywood panels are used primarily as wall covering. A variety of styles, colors, and textures are offered, Fig. 13-17. Both hardwood and softwood veneers are used.

Prefinished panels range from 5/32 in. (5 mm) to 7/16 in. (10 mm) thick. They are made of three

Fig. 13-17. Prefinished paneling is used for wall decoration. (Georgia-Pacific Corp.)

Fig. 13-18. Simulated wood grain paneling looks much like real wood. (Georgia-Pacific Corp.)

or five ply construction. Thin panels are usually applied over gypsum board covered walls. Thicker panels are sturdy enough to be attached direcly to wall studs.

Face veneers are either rotary cut or plain sliced. Commonly used species are pine, fir, oak, birch, and walnut. The face veneers are finished with a topcoat for protection against moisture and wear.

Prefinished plywood panels frequently are textured with grooves running the length of the panel. The panel looks like multiple boards of varying widths.

SIMULATED WOODGRAIN FINISH PANELING

Simulated woodgrain panels are plastic laminates over either plywood or a wood fiber substrate. Examples are hardboard or particleboard. The appearance is much the same as prefinished plywood panels, Fig. 13-19. The panel is coated with acrylic finish for moisture protection and wear resistance.

The wood fiber substrate used on some simulated finish panels can be damaged by moisture and heat. Do not install them in hot or moist areas.

PREHUNG WALLPAPER PANELING

Prehung wallpaper paneling combines the ease of panel installation with the design appeal of pat-

terned wallpaper, Fig. 13-19. The paper is laminated onto a plywood or a wood fiber substrate. Grooves add texture to the appearance of the panel. Like other panels, an acrylic finish may be applied to the surface for protection.

Fig. 13-19. Prehung wallpaper paneling can replace wallpaper. Panels are much easier to install. (Georgia-Pacific Corp.)

ENGINEERED BOARD PRODUCTS

Engineered board products are designed and manufactured to meet specific purposes. It may be installed for strength, appearance, or cost criteria not available in other "natural" wood products. Many engineered board products have applications in the furniture industry for strong and durable panels.

Engineered board products are manufactured by various methods. For medium and high density fiberboard, wood fibers are mixed with resin. Then they are bonded by either radio frequency (RF) adhesion or heat. Low density fiberboards and particleboard are fabricated by heat and pressure. The fiber and resin mixture and amount of pressure determine the strength of the board.

CAUTION! Most engineered board products use urea formaldehyde resin as a binder. They may release formaldehyde vapors which can irritate your eyes and upper respiratory system. Use products which are labeled "low formaldehyde" and are HUD (U.S. Department of Housing and Urban Development) approved. Purchase urea formaldehyde-resin products in advance. Allow them to "outgas" in a warm, ventilated space. Applying an approved sealer also will help prevent outgassing.

FIBERBOARD

Fiberboard is a commonly used material for case goods. It is a very dense, strong, and durable material. Fiberboard is manufactured from refined wood fibers separated by either steam or chemicals. The fibers are randomly arranged into a continuous mat which is cut into sheets called wetlaps. The sheets are cured under pressure by heat or radio frequency (RF) bonding. RF bonding performs much like a microwave oven. The panel is "cooked" from the inside out. This provides a continuous density throughout its thickness. The amount of pressure determines panel density. Cured sheets are trimmed to dimension and packaged for shipping.

Fiberboard is classified into three different densities. Each has specific applications in the furniture industry.

HIGH DENSITY FIBERBOARD (HARDBOARD)

High density fiberboard, commonly called *hardboard*, is an extremely rugged material. Advantages over less dense panels include increased durability, strength, and resistance to abrasion. It is widely installed for drawer bottoms, cabinet backs, and paneling.

The strength of hardboard permits thin panels—1/8, 3/16, and 1/4 in. (3 mm to 6 mm)—to be fabricated, Fig. 13-16. Panel measurements are typically 4 ft. wide by 8, 10, 12, or 16 ft. long. Panels can be surfaced on either one side (S1S) or two sides (S2S). The unsurfaced side of S1S has a screen-like texture.

Types of hardboard

Hardboard is classified into three types: standard, tempered, and service.

* *Standard hardboard* is the strongest of the three and has good finishing qualities.
* *Tempered hardboard* is standard hardboard with chemical treatment applied to the surface to increase strength, stiffness, and moisture resistance. This treatment makes it darker in color.
* *Service hardboard* is weaker and lighter than standard hardboard. Use it for lightweight applications. Dimensions of service hardboard may be 4 ft. x 4 ft. in addition to normal 4 ft. x 8 ft. size.

Specialty panels

Hardboard can be purchased in specialty panels. These include:

* *Perforated.* Round, evenly spaced holes are drilled or punched, refer to Fig. 13-20. Perforated hardboard is often called pegboard. Metal hangers

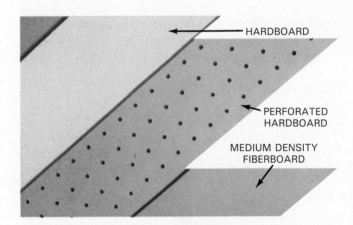

Fig. 13-20. Fiberboards may replace lumber or plywood for many applications. (Georgia-Pacific Corp.)

(pegs) can fit into the holes to support tools, cooking utensils, etc. It then serves as a wall covering and storage panel.

* *Striated.* Closely spaced grooves are applied for texture.
* *Embossed.* Textured patterns, such as basket weave, are pressed into the board.
* *Grooved.* "V" or channel grooves are cut into the board for appearance purposes.

• *Laminated*. Hardboard commonly is used as the wood fiber substrate for simulated wood grain appearance panels.

MEDIUM DENSITY FIBERBOARD

Medium density fiberboard (MDF) is manufactured in much the same way as hardboard, but in greater thickness. It is also formed with less pressure. Refer to Fig. 13-20. The added thickness, lack of grain pattern, and smooth texture of MDF make it ideal for replacing solid lumber. It is the base material for stained, painted, printed, or laminated applications. MDF is commonly used for furniture tops, drawer fronts, mouldings, cabinet construction, shelving, and various millwork.

The random orientation of fibers in MDF means it is equally strong in any direction. There are no problems of grain direction as with solid lumber and plywood. The lack of fiber direction also improves other factors. Warping is almost eliminated. Sawing or machining MDF produces fairly smooth edges. Thus, little or no sanding is necessary.

MDF is available in thicknesses ranging from 3/8 in. (10 mm) to 1 3/4 in. (44 mm). Standard size is 4 ft. or 8 ft. wide by 8 ft. to 16 ft. long in increments of 2 ft.

LOW DENSITY FIBERBOARD

Low density fiberboard (LDF) is a lightweight panel commonly found in the upholstery industry. It provides more bulk than strength. It is approximately half the weight of MDF. Panel sizes typically are 4 ft. by 8 ft. by 1 in.

INDUSTRIAL PARTICLEBOARD

Industrial particleboard is composed of small wood flakes, chips, or shavings. These are bonded together with resins or adhesives, Fig. 13-21. Three layers of wood chips are used. The two surface layers have smaller chips for smooth texture and increased impact resistance. High quality manufacturing insures dimensional stability and machinable edges.

Because of its smooth surface, industrial particleboard is often used as substrate material for laminations. Cabinets, furniture parts, countertops, table tops, and drawer fronts are commonly made of particleboard. It is not as dense as hardboard or MDF. However, it adequately resists denting, cracking, and chipping. It also is less expensive.

Industrial particleboard is fabricated in dimensions suited to cabinetmaking. Besides larger 4 x 8 sheets, countertop and shelving sizes are available. Countertop panels range from 24 in. (600 mm) to 30 in. (750 mm) in width and from 8 ft. (2 400 mm) to 10 ft. (3 000 mm) in length. Shelving panels range from 12 in. (300 mm) to 24 in. (600 mm) in width and from 6 ft. (1 800 mm) to 12 ft. (3 600 mm) in length. Thickness is typically 5/8 in. (16 mm) or 3/4 in. (19 mm). Beware of using particleboard for long span shelving. It has a tendency to sag, especially in areas of high heat or humidity.

MENDE PARTICLEBOARD

Mende particleboard is a low cost alternative to fiberboard. It is less dense than hardboard. It is manufactured in 5/32 in. (4 mm) to 1/4 in. (6 mm) thick sheets. These are suitable for use as drawer bottoms, cabinet backs, picture frame backs, and as substrate for simulated wood grain paneling, Fig. 13-21. It is available in 8 ft. (2 440 mm) sheets which are 4 ft. (1 220 mm) or 5 ft. (1 524 mm) wide.

WORKING WITH PANEL PRODUCTS

Panel products replace solid wood for many cabinets. However, panel products require special considerations.

STORING PANEL PRODUCTS

Panels should be stored flat, never upright. Leaning the panel against a wall causes it to warp. The edges might also be damaged.

Panels are subject to moisture just like solid wood. A dry environment will reduce dimensional changes of the panel which could cause warp.

SAWING

Panels with veneer cores may be sawn using either a hand saw or a power saw. Use a combination saw blade. Always make sure the saw blade is sharp.

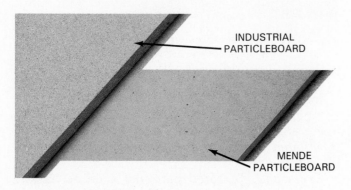

Fig. 13-21. Particleboard is common in cabinets and furniture. It often is covered with a plastic laminate. (Georgia-Pacific Corp.)

Panels which are made of pressed wood chips or fibers should be cut with carbide tipped saw blades. The glue used to bond the chips will quickly dull regular blades.

When using a stationary power saw or hand saw, make sure the good face of the panel is up. The bottom will tend to chip. This will prevent splintering of the face veneer. If you are using a portable circular saw, this rule is reversed. Place the good face down. This is because portable power saw blades turn in the opposite direction. If the panel splinters, it will occur on the top surface.

PLANING

Rarely do panel products need to be planed. Faces are manufactured smooth and the thickness is uniform. If panels are sawn properly, the edges should be straight. If you have to straighten the edges, you may use a hand plane or jointer. Take shallow cuts because the glue bond in the panel is very hard.

MACHINING

Hardboard, medium density fiberboard, and particleboard often are machined for use as countertop or moulding. Shaping these materials is the same as shaping solid wood. The best results are obtained by using sharp carbide-tipped cutters. Since there is no grain in these panels, they will machine very smoothly. They also will not splinter.

When shaping an edge that will be exposed, remember to leave room for edge treatment. Wood tape and most plastic laminates are 1/32 in. to 1/16 in. thick.

SANDING

Most panel products are smooth before they reach you. However, the surface may need minor touch sanding if the panel was dented or scratched. If you machine an edge, this will also require sanding. The same methods of sanding are used on both solid wood and panel products. However, when sanding plywood or other veneer face panels, do not sand heavily. The veneer is very thin. Removing too much wood will expose the core.

USING SCREWS OR NAILS

The nail or screw holding ability a panel has is related to its density. Panels which are light and weak will not hold fasteners as well as heavier and stronger panels. The weakest part of a panel is its edge. There is practically no holding ability in the edges of plywood, waferboard, oriented strand board, or particleboard. Higher density fiberboards have limited edge strength.

The face of a panel has good to excellent screw holding strength. Again, it depends on the density of the panel. For example, mende particleboard is limited in screw holding power. It should be used only when strong joints are not needed. Reinforcement with solid lumber may be required.

The nail or screw you use should be proportional in size to the panel. As a rule of thumb, the length of the fastener should be at least twice as long as the thickness of the panel. For example, when nailing 3/4 in. plywood onto a solid wood frame, use a 1 1/2 in. fastener.

To reduce splitting, predrill a hole. For a nail, use a bit slightly smaller than the nail's diameter. More than one hole size may be needed. Refer to Chapter 16.

Nails and screws should be countersunk into the face material. A plug, button, or wood dough may be put over the fastener to hide it. When using wood dough, apply it higher than the panel surface. Then sand it flush with the panel when it is dry.

APPLYING EDGE TREATMENT

The edges of panel products are usually covered to hide the core composition. Many different edging materials can be used. You can use wood, metal and plastic. The form of the edging and the method of bonding will differ. Common applications are shown in Fig. 13-22.

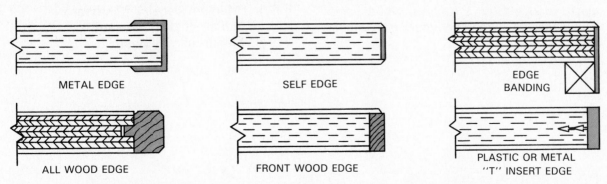

METAL EDGE   SELF EDGE   EDGE BANDING

ALL WOOD EDGE   FRONT WOOD EDGE   PLASTIC OR METAL "T" INSERT EDGE

Fig. 13-22. Plastic, wood, or metal edging is applied to the edges of panel products. It hides the composition of the panel.

SUMMARY

Manufactured panel products are widely applied in case goods and fine furniture. Most consumers seldom know whether the product they are buying is solid lumber or a veneered or laminated panel product. And, for the most part, it doesn't matter. Most manufactured panels are stronger than solid lumber.

The three types of manufactured panel products are structural wood panels, appearance panels, and engineered board products. Most structural wood panels are used in building construction. These are performance-rated panels. Others are used in cabinetmaking. Veneered panels, such as plywood and composite board, can be used in assembling case goods.

Most interior woodwork is made with appearance panels. Hardwood plywood is a common material for modern cabinets and fine furniture. It has the appearance, strength, and durability of solid lumber, yet is much less expensive. Other appearance panels, such as prefinished plywood, simulated wood grain, and prehung wallpaper paneling, make good wall covering.

Engineered board products are fabricated for special purposes. Hardboard and mende particleboard are used as drawer bottoms, cabinet backs, and other applications requiring thin panels. Medium density fiberboard often is used as a substitute for lumber moldings, drawer fronts, and various millwork.

Industrial particleboard is used for countertops and table tops. Its smooth surface permits high quality laminates to be applied.

CABINETMAKING TERMS

Structural wood panels, plywood, structural plywood, hardwood plywood, lumber core plywood, crossbands, veneer core plywood, plies, rotary slicing, peeler block, plywood adhesives, moisture resistant adhesives, performance ratings, group number, veneer grades, composite board, composite panel, waferboard, phenolic resin, particleboard, structural particleboard, oriented strand board, performance-rated structural wood panel, appearance panel, hardwood plywood, face veneer, particleboard core, acoustical core, lightweight core, G1S So. Bk., G1S, Craftsman, Shop, prefinished plywood panel, simulated wood grain finish panel, prehung wallpaper panel, engineered board product, fiberboard, high density fiberboard, hardboard, standard hardboard, tempered hardboard, service hardboard, specialty panels, medium density fiberboard, low density fiberboard, mende particleboard.

TEST YOUR KNOWLEDGE

1. The surface of panel faces may be _____, _____, _____, or _____.
2. Which structural wood panels may be used for cabinetmaking?
3. Explain the manufacture of plywood.
4. Name several plywood cores for structural and hardwood plywood. What are the advantages and disadvantages of each?
5. Waferboard and oriented strand board are bonded by what adhesive?
   a. Melamine resin.
   b. Phenolic resin.
   c. Resorcinol resin.
   d. Urea formaldehyde resin.
6. What is the danger of urea formaldehyde resin?
7. List the information found on a plywood grading stamp.
8. A disadvantage of hardwood plywood compared to solid lumber is that:
   a. Edges must be hidden or taped.
   b. Face veneers do not look like solid lumber.
   c. Hardwood plywood is weaker than lumber.
   d. Screws cannot be used with plywood.
9. Why might exterior adhesive be used on interior grade plywood?
10. Describe how the following products might be used in cabinet construction.
    a. Structural plywood.
    b. Composite panel.
    c. Waferboard.
    d. Oriented strand board.
    e. Hardwood plywood.
    f. Prefinished plywood paneling.
    g. Hardboard.
    h. Medium density fiberboard.
    i. Industrial particleboard.
    j. Mende particleboard.

Chapter 14
VENEERS AND PLASTIC LAMINATES

After studying this chapter, you will be able to:
- □ List the various methods of cutting veneer.
- □ Describe the grain pattern produced by each method of cutting veneer.
- □ Match veneer sheets into pleasing patterns for inlaying or overlaying.
- □ Identify applications of rigid and flexible plastic laminates.

Veneers and plastic laminates are used in most cabinetry and fine furniture manufactured today. They are thin, sheet materials which typically cover a core material, such as plywood or particleboard. The final product looks as if it were constructed with solid lumber.

Plastic laminates have an advantage over wood veneer. Plastics provide a nearly indestructable covering. Plastic laminates are fabricated from layers of synthetic materials. They may be rigid or flexible. Wood grain, solid colors, or decorative designs may be printed in them.

Veneers and plastic laminates are frequently used to create decorative surfaces and edges, Fig. 14-1. The art of veneering (inlaying and overlaying) has existed for centuries. Veneer murals unearthed in Egypt date back to 1500 B.C. During the Dark Ages, veneering was abandoned, but in the 17th and 18th century a revival of veneering was seen in European traditional furniture. Today, most veneer is used as overlay for cabinet surfaces. The "art" of veneering is not so common in modern design. Straight line and plain designs are the preferred style.

Veneer is cut from many wood species. Most softwood veneer is used to make structural plywood for building construction. Hardwood veneer is used for cabinetmaking and architectural purposes, Fig. 14-2. Wood cabinets are seldom

Fig. 14-1. Veneer inlays are placed in diagonal directions to add beauty to this table top.

Fig. 14-2. The walls of this congressional chamber are covered with veneer. (Fine Hardwood Veneer Assoc.)

made from lumber anymore. Plywood and veneer covered particleboard are the primary materials. Hardwood veneer is also laminated to thin plywood or fiberboard to be installed as paneling.

TYPES OF VENEERS

There are two types of veneer: flat and flexible. See Fig. 14-3.

Flat veneer

Flat veneer is sold in thicknesses from 1/28 in. to 1/32 in. The most common is 1/28 in. Despite the name, flat veneer may not always be truly flat. During the drying process, shrinkage of the wood cells causes the veneer to shrivel. The veneer can be straightened by moistening and then pressing it. Lay the damp veneer on a flat surface and cover it with a panel. Additional weight on the panel will help it to dry flat.

Fig. 14-3. Thin, flexible veneer is easily bent around curved surfaces. Flat veneer is less versatile.

Flexible veneer

Flexible veneer is much thinner than flat veneers. Typically it is 1/60 in. thick. Most imported veneers are flexible. Rare woods are cut thin to obtain more square footage from the log.

A plastic backing is usually bonded to flexible veneer to keep it from tearing. A hot-melt glue coating might be applied to the backing. When the veneer is trimmed and ready to be laminated to a wood substrate, it is heated. The glue melts and bonds the veneer. Pressure on the veneer while it

cools assures a good bond. A roller or weight may be used.

CUTTING VENEER

Veneer is cut from select logs which have few defects. The logs are first debarked and cut to length. These are called *peeler blocks*. Peeler blocks may then be halved or quartered depending on the type of cutting method. The sections are called *flitches*. Before cutting, the peeler block or flitch is moistened and heated to insure an easy, smooth cut.

The appearance of veneer depends greatly on the grain pattern. The grain pattern, in turn, is determined by the way the veneer is cut. Certain species, such as oak, are best cut by a particular method to bring out natural beauty of the wood.

There are six methods for shearing veneer. These methods fall into three categories:
1. Rotary cutting—turning the log on a lathe.
2. Slicing—reciprocally moving the flitch against a knife. *Slicing* includes flat slicing and quarter slicing.
3. Stay-log cutting—swinging the flitch against the knife. *Stay-log cutting* includes rift, half-round, and back cutting.

Fig. 14-4 shows each of the six methods of veneer cutting and the resulting grain pattern.

ROTARY CUTTING

Rotary cutting means turning the log against a sharp, stationary knife. Sheets of veneer are peeled off the log like paper towels off a roll. The log is turned either by chucks or by a backup roller.

Chuck turning involves inserting spear-like chucks in the ends of the log. Sometimes, the log binds against the knife but the chucks keep turning. This is called *spinout*. When it occurs, the remainder of the peeler block is waste.

The *backup roller* is a new cutting technology. Instead of using *chucks* in the ends of the log, rollers are placed against the back of the log to push it against the knife, Fig. 14-5. The rollers also rotate the log. Because the chucks are not in the way of the knife, more veneer can be cut from a log. There is also less chance of spinout.

Nearly 90 percent of all veneer is made using the rotary method. Compared to slicing and stay log cutting, the rotary method is much faster. It also produces the most square feet of veneer from a single log.

The grain pattern created by rotary cutting is rippled in birch or maple veneer. Veneer of other species has a marblelike figure. The grain pattern of most rotary cut veneer is spread out. Tighter grain patterns are preferred for furniture. Softwood

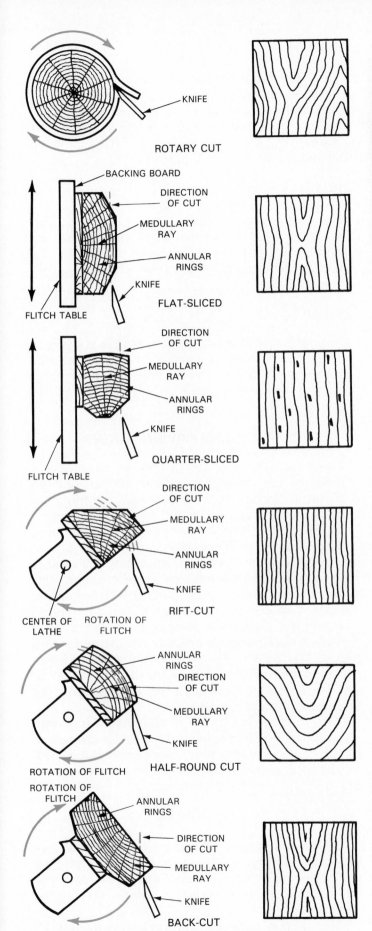

Fig. 14-4. The method of cutting veneer greatly affects the veneer's grain pattern.

ROTARY CUT

BACKING BOARD
DIRECTION OF CUT
MEDULLARY RAY
ANNULAR RINGS
KNIFE
FLAT-SLICED
FLITCH TABLE

DIRECTION OF CUT
MEDULLARY RAY
ANNULAR RINGS
KNIFE
QUARTER-SLICED
FLITCH TABLE

DIRECTION OF CUT
MEDULLARY RAY
ANNULAR RINGS
KNIFE
RIFT-CUT
CENTER OF LATHE
ROTATION OF FLITCH

ANNULAR RINGS
DIRECTION OF CUT
MEDULLARY RAY
KNIFE
HALF-ROUND CUT
ROTATION OF FLITCH

ROTATION OF FLITCH
ANNULAR RINGS
DIRECTION OF CUT
MEDULLARY RAY
KNIFE
BACK-CUT

Fig. 14-5. Backup rollers turn the log as they press it against the knife. Continuous cutting action produces long sheets of veneer.

veneer for plywood may be rotary cut, but little hardwood veneer is cut by this method.

FLAT SLICING

In preparation for *flat slicing* (also called *plain slicing*) the peeler block is cut in half. Each half is called a flitch. The flitch is then secured to a *flitch table.* A knife as long as the flitch table advances under the flitch. The flitch is then moved down against the knife. As the flitch table moves up and down, the knife advances forward peeling off succeeding sheets of veneer. The sheets are log length. The width is as wide as the section of the flitch contacting the knife, Fig. 14-6.

Flat slicing is a popular method for cutting most hardwood species of veneer. The grain figure of veneer from the center of the log has wavy lines surrounding an oval tipped figure. Out from the center, the veneer appears as rippled stripes.

Fig. 14-6. Flat sliced veneer exits the slicer and is stacked. It is later sent to a dryer.

QUARTER SLICING

Logs are sectioned into four flitches for *quarter slicing*. The edges are trimmed so they can be attached to the flitch table. The method of slicing is similar to flat slicing, yet the cuts are made at right angles to the annual rings.

Quarter slicing produces a striped grain figure. The lines may be straight or slightly wavy. *Flakes* can be seen in the veneer where cuts were made through wood rays. Flakes are especially noticeable in oak veneer.

RIFT CUTTING

Rift cutting is used exclusively for species with heavy wood ray growth, such as the oak family. The rift effect is also called *comb grain.* The pattern appears like fine, long, human hair. Comb grain is made by cutting perpendicular to the wood rays. In quality rift cut veneer, no flakes should be seen. They might appear if the knife was not exactly perpendicular to the wood rays.

Flitches for rift cutting are quarter sections of a peeler block. The flitch is attached off center to a *stay-log lathe* which swings the flitch across the knife. The arc on which the veneer is cut is greater than the curve of the annual rings. This produces the extremely thin grain pattern.

Rift oak veneer is very expensive. The time incurred by the sawyer and slicer, and the amount of waste produced, is extensive.

HALF-ROUND CUTTING

Half-round cutting is a method of stay log cutting which produces a large, "U" patterned grain. Flitches are mounted off center in the lathe. The arc of cutting is greater than the annual rings, thus, cuts are made through more of each layer of growth.

BACK CUTTING

Back cutting is a less used method of veneer slicing. Flitches are placed backwards on a stay log lathe. The core of the half log is on the outer diameter and is cut first. The grain pattern resembles that of flat slicing, except that lines are much closer.

SPECIAL VENEERS

Grain pattern is primarily created by the method of cutting. However, the area of the tree from which the veneer is cut also affects the grain pattern. Rotary and half-round cut veneer comes from the lower portion of the trunk. Sliced veneer is taken from the upper portion of the trunk. Decorative veneers are cut from burl, crotch, and stump (butt) wood, Fig. 14-7.

BURL

Burls are lumps formed by new growth on a tree to heal an injury. A branch might have broken off or another injury done which stunted growth. The new thick, twisted, fibrous cells follow the pattern created by the injury. Veneer sliced from burls has a circling, wavy, knotty pattern.

CROTCH

A *crotch* is located where a branch separates from the main trunk. Crotch wood has a very distinct and desirable pattern. Growth rings of the branch and trunk combine in a twisted pattern which is typically a darker color.

STUMP

Stump wood, also called *butt wood*, is at the base of the trunk. The weight of the growing tree compresses the wood cells. Stump veneer has a wrinkled line pattern. There is little difference between layers of a growth.

CLIPPING AND DRYING VENEER

Once the veneer is cut, it may go directly to a clipper or be stored temporarily on reels or on horizontal storage racks. A *green clipper* trims the veneer to various widths and removes defects.

After clipping, the veneer passes through large drying chambers. The veneer moves through the chamber on a conveyer system. Heating elements and fans reduce the moisture content. Some mills have dryers immediately behind rotary cutting lathes. The continuous sheet of veneer passes through the dryer as it comes off the lathe.

Veneers are generally dried to a moisture content below 10 percent. This is close to the recommended equilibrium moisture content for most parts of the country. This moisture level is also suitable for manufacturing plywood.

After drying, the veneer is *dry-clipped* to length in preparation for shipping. It may be spliced or taped together with other sheets to produce hardwood face veneers. Matching may be done during the splicing and taping process.

MATCHING

Veneer matching produces interesting decorative designs. Hardwood face veneers are matched before being bonded as plywood. You may also choose to match veneers when inlaying or overlaying.

Matching is done by splicing veneers together with the grain pattern in specific directions. The veneers you use should be consecutive slices from

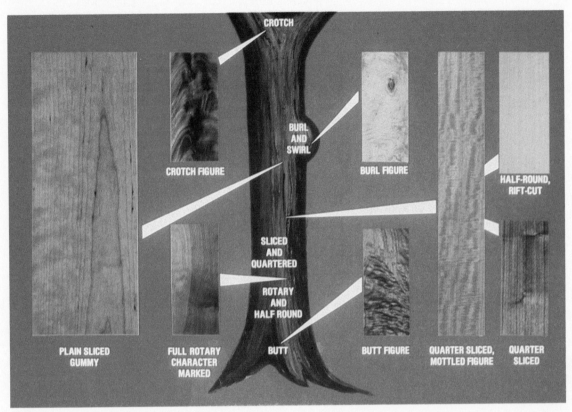

Fig. 14-7. Certain portions of the tree are cut into veneer differently. Highly figured veneers are cut from crotch, burl, and stump wood.

a log. The color and grain pattern of successive slices are the same. There are many established patterns that are used to create veneer designs, Fig. 14-8.

- A *book match* uses successive sheets of veneer. Every other one is turned over. This gives the appearance of an open book.
- In a *slip match*, the veneer is placed side by side. This provides pattern repetition.
- Veneer used to make a *diamond match* is cut at a 45° angle from the original veneer sheet. Four pieces each make 90° angles with the adjacent piece.
- In a *reverse diamond match*, the grain pattern points toward the outer four corners.
- A *four-way center and butt match* uses four pieces of veneer. They are matched with a common center, joined side to side and end to end.
- The *vertical butt and horizontal book leaf match* consists of two book matches butted together end to end.

Other matches include *checkerboard, herringbone, box, reverse box, "V,"* and *random.* You may wish to create your own method of matching.

VENEER INLAYS

Veneer inlays are made by cutting veneer into a pattern and bonding it in a routed wood backing, Fig. 14-9. Using various wood species, colors, and grain patterns produces a pleasing effect. You may make or buy inlays.

Inlays are made by first preparing a pattern. Veneer is then cut according to color and grain which suits the pattern. The cutouts are assembled and paper is glued over the top. The outline of the pattern is routed into a solid wood substrate. The wood side of the assembled cutouts is glued into the routed depression. Pressure with a sandbag insures solid adhesion. After the glue dries, the paper is moistened and removed. Then the surface is ready for sanding and finishing.

VENEER BANDINGS

Veneer bandings are small pieces of veneer assembled into thin strips. The pieces are arranged in a decorative pattern, Fig. 14-10. Bandings are usually 1/20 in. (1.25 mm) thick, 36 in. (900 mm) long, and have varying widths. They may be inserted and bonded into routed grooves or applied to the surface. During the finishing process, wood inlays and bandings must be protected. You may not want stain and filler applied to them. Cover them with masking tape.

VENEER TAPE

Veneer tape is used to cover the edges of veneered panel products. It is usually 1/20 in. (1.25

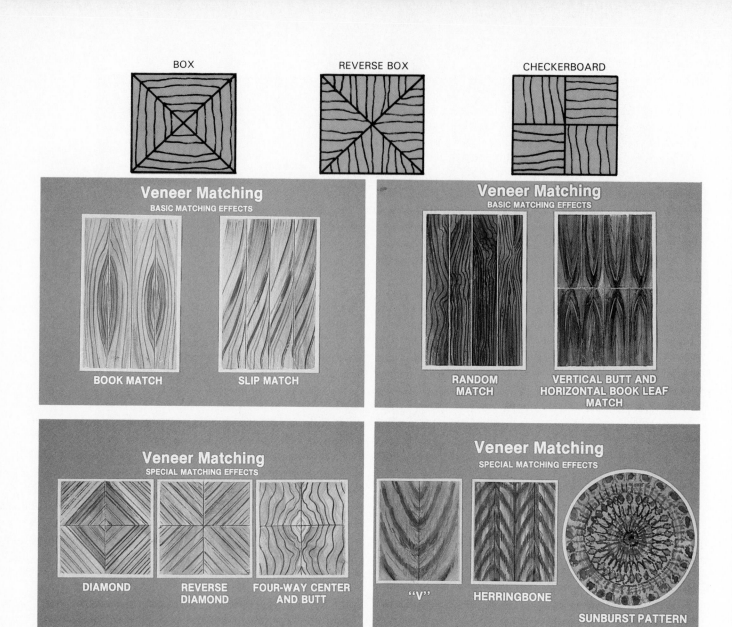

BOX   REVERSE BOX   CHECKERBOARD

Veneer Matching
BASIC MATCHING EFFECTS

BOOK MATCH   SLIP MATCH

Veneer Matching
BASIC MATCHING EFFECTS

RANDOM MATCH   VERTICAL BUTT AND HORIZONTAL BOOK LEAF MATCH

Veneer Matching
SPECIAL MATCHING EFFECTS

DIAMOND   REVERSE DIAMOND   FOUR-WAY CENTER AND BUTT

Veneer Matching
SPECIAL MATCHING EFFECTS

"V"   HERRINGBONE   SUNBURST PATTERN

Fig. 14-8. Veneer sheets are matched to form various decorative patterns.

Fig. 14-9. Veneer inlays outline the drawers of this secretary.

Fig. 14-10. Veneer bandings come in preassembled patterns to be used for inlay. (The Woodworkers' Store)

mm) thick and purchased in rolls, Fig. 14-11. Varying widths are available, but 3/4 in. (19 mm) and 1 1/2 in. (28 mm) are most common. A coating of hot-melt glue is applied to the back. The tape can be applied either by an iron or by a *tape lamination machine*, Fig. 14-12. The machine holds the tape roll, melts the glue backing, and applies it as the panel product is pushed across a pressure roller.

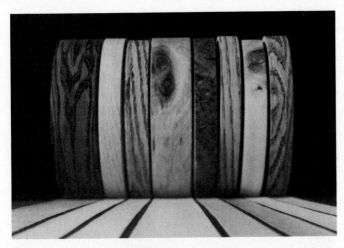

Fig. 14-11. Veneer tape is sold in rolls. It has a hot-melt glue backing. (Woodtape, Inc.)

Fig. 14-13. The surfaces of the cabinets, countertops, and table are covered with plastic laminate. The laminate covers particleboard construction. (Sterling Engineered Products, Inc.)

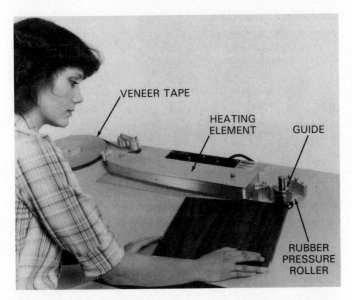

Fig. 14-12. A tape lamination machine applies veneer tape to edges of panel products. (Woodtape, Inc.)

PLASTIC LAMINATES

Plastic laminates are widely used for cabinetmaking. These rigid and flexible laminates cover most kitchen cabinets and built-in case goods, Fig. 14-13. They are also used for counter and table surfaces, wall covering, and trim. Plastic laminates provide a tough, durable surface which resists water, stains, and many household chemicals. Wood grain patterns, geometric shapes, and solid colors are available.

RIGID PLASTIC LAMINATES

Rigid plastic laminates are typically referred to as *high pressure* laminates. They consist of phenolic resin impregnated layers of kraft paper. The layers are bonded under heat and pressure into a plasticlike material, Fig. 14-14. *Kraft paper*, much like brown wrapping paper, gives the panel thickness and rigidity. A *decorative pattern sheet* impregnated with melamine resin is added to provide color and texture. A clear sheet of *melamine treated paper* covers the pattern sheet. A hydraulic press bonds these layers under high pressure and heat to form the rigid laminate. The back of the laminate is made rough. This makes it easier to adhere to a substrate.

Finishes

The type of finish applied to the panel may be gloss, satin, velvet, low glare, oil rub, or a textured

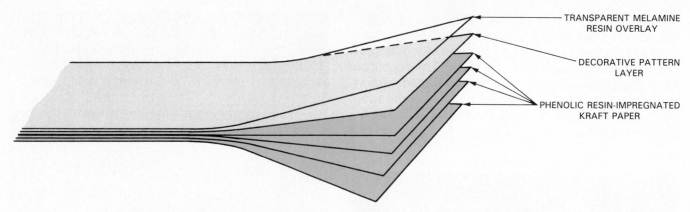

TRANSPARENT MELAMINE
RESIN OVERLAY

DECORATIVE PATTERN
LAYER

PHENOLIC RESIN-IMPREGNATED
KRAFT PAPER

Fig. 14-14. Rigid plastic laminates are composed of layers of resin and kraft paper.

surface, Fig. 14-15. Texture, satin, and low glare laminates are frequently used for wall covering because they do not glare. Wood grain laminates are textured to feel like real wood. Since a number of finishes are unique to specific manufacturers, check their brochures before ordering.

Grades

High pressure (rigid) laminates are divided into four grades.

The *General-Purpose Grade* is the most widely used. The nominal thickness is .050 in. (1.25 mm). It is suitable for both horizontal and vertical surfaces. Also called Standard Grade, it is the most durable of the plastic laminates. It is resistant to impact and stains. The thickness permits a wide variety of patterns and finishes to be included. General-Purpose Grade laminates are used for countertops, residential and commercial furniture, case goods, and wall partitions.

The *Vertical Surface Grade* is designed for use as wall panels and cabinet surfaces. The nominal thickness is .028 in. (.7 mm). It is intended for vertical use where thinner and lighter material is required. It is not as durable as General-Purpose Grade. Strips of this grade are typically cut 1 5/8 in. wide to be used as edge banding.

The *Post Forming Grade* is fabricated so that it can be heated and bent in small curves. It is especially applicable to countertops which include curved corners and edges, Fig. 14-16. Nominal thicknesses are .032 in. (.8 mm) and .042 in. (1.0 mm). Although thinner than General-Purpose Grade, the .042 in. (1.0 mm) Post Forming Grade maintains the same qualities. The .032 in. (0.8 mm) thickness grade is lighter in weight. It is used on light-duty surfaces which are not subject to impact.

Cabinet Liner Grade laminates are made for the interior of cabinets. Thicknesses of 1/16 in., .05 in., 0.3 in., and .02 in. (1.3 mm to 0.5 mm) are sold. Also called a *backer sheet,* it prevents the exposed core material from taking on moisture. Core

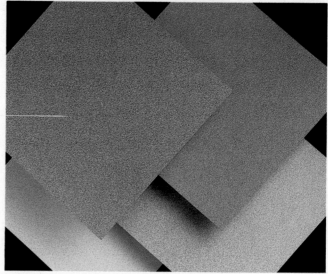

Fig. 14-15. Laminate finishes may have woodgrain or orange peel textures. A variety of colors are available. (Sterling Engineered Products, Inc.)

materials include plywood and particleboard. If plastic laminate is applied to only one side, the panel is likely to warp. Liner grade laminates are much less expensive than the grades used for surfaces. However, they provide minimal wear resistance.

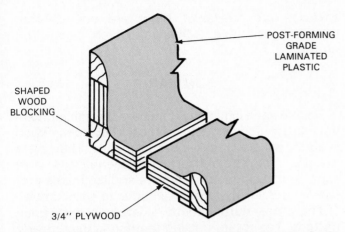

Fig. 14-16. Many cabinet tops are made of Post Forming Grade laminates which are heated and bent around shaped wood.

Special grades

Beyond grading, high-pressure laminates may have special treatments.

Fire-resistant laminates are applied to wall and door covering where building codes specify fire resistant materials. They are designed to resist flamespread for a certain amount of time. Fire resistant laminates are commonly used in public buildings.

Static-free laminates are designed to resist static buildup. Laminates of this special grade are installed on cabinets for computers and other sensitive electronic equipment.

Sheet size

Sheet widths start at 24 in. (600 mm) and increase in increments of 6 in. (150 mm). Many manufacturers add 1/4 in. (6 mm) to sheet width to allow for cutting and trimming edges. Extra width also permits the sheet to be cut into two equal sizes for standard dimensions. For example, 12 in. (300 mm) wide sheets are commonly used for cabinet fronts. Extra width on a 24 in. (600 mm) sheet permits two 12 in. (300 mm) sections to be cut. The extra width allows for trimming the applied laminate.

Sheet lengths will range from 6 ft. (1800 mm) to 12 ft. (3600 mm). It is advised that you order just over the length you need. Rigid plastics are brittle and long sheets are apt to fracture.

Edges

The composition of rigid plastic results in a dark brown line on outside corners where vertical and horizontal panels meet. The edge can appear as part of the design or be covered with edging.

Adhesives

Plastic laminates are always fastened to a core material such as particleboard, Fig. 14-17. They are not rigid enough to provide structure. Various adhesives attach laminate to the core.

Rigid glues, such as urea formaldehyde and resorcinol, need constant pressure over time to insure adhesion. *Contact cements* are called *pressure sensitive.* These require momentary pressure to bond. A roller or mallet may be used. They are made of neoprene and are water emulsion or solvent based. *Hot-melt glue* is a nonsticky solid substance until heated. When melted, hot-melt glue is applied between the laminate and the core material. The layers are pressed together and cooled to insure a secure bond. Hot-melt glue is commonly used for edge banding applications with a tape lamination machine.

FLEXIBLE PLASTIC LAMINATES

Flexible plastic laminates are used for cabinet surfaces and floor coverings. They are made from layers of vinyl, Fig. 14-18. Polystyrene and other plastics are also used in producing flexible laminates. Flexible laminates resist chips, scratches, and most household chemicals. They are easily cut with a mat knife. You can adhere flexible laminates to both flat and curved surfaces using contact cement.

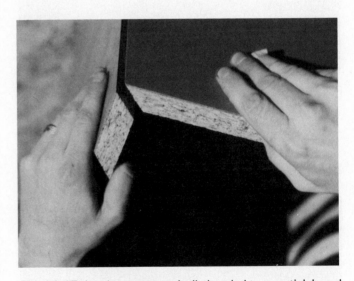

Fig. 14-17. Laminates are typically bonded to a particleboard core. The particleboard supplies strength. The laminate provides the desired appearance. (Columbus Showcase)

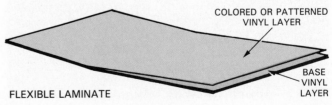

Fig. 14-18. Flexible laminates are composed of layers of vinyl or other flexible plastics.

Various solid color and patterned surfaces are fabricated. Some flexible laminates have reflective surfaces. They may appear to be polished brass, copper, or some other color, Fig. 14-19.

FLEXIBLE PLASTIC BANDING.

Flexible plastic bandings are thin, narrow strips, Fig. 14-20. They are used to decorate edges and corners of cabinetry. Various patterns, shapes, and textures are available. Most are coated with pressure sensitive adhesive which bonds on contact.

Fig. 14-19. These fabricated tables feature suede-finish laminates with glossy edgebanding. (Sterling Engineered Products, Inc.)

Fig. 14-20. Flexible plastic edgebanding may be solid color or wood grain. (Sterling Engineered Products, Inc.)

SUMMARY

Veneers and laminates dominate the cabinetmaking industry for product surfaces. They cover wood product panels, such as particleboard. They are a finished, mar-resistant surface to countertops, table tops, and case goods. Veneers and laminates provide a durable, low cost alternative to solid lumber.

The veneer cutting method determines the grain pattern. The rotary cutting method is used nearly 90 percent of the time. It produces the most square footage of veneer from a log. Other cutting methods may have exclusive applications for a certain wood specie. Once the veneer is cut, it is clipped and dried.

Veneer is often matched to produce pleasing effects. Commonly assembled matches include book, slip, and diamond.

Plastic laminates are almost indestructible. Rigid laminates are manufactured using layers of paper and plastic bonded under heat and pressure with resins. Flexible laminates are made from vinyl. Both provide a durable, stain resistant surface.

Wood veneer and plastic laminates are also used for bandings and trim. Veneer bands are often inlaid into routed grooves in solid wood.

Using veneers and laminates will greatly reduce the cost of your product. When installed carefully, they will provide years of durable service.

CABINETMAKING TERMS

Flat veneer, flexible veneer, peeler block, flitch, slicing, stay-log cutting, rotary cutting, backup roller, chuck, spinout, flat slicing, plain slicing, flitch table, quarter sawing, flakes, rift cutting, comb grain, stay-long lathe, half-round cutting, back cutting, burl, crotch, stump wood, butt wood, green clipper, matching, book match, slip match, diamond match, reverse diamond match, four-way center and butt match, vertical butt and horizontal book leaf match, checkerboard match, herringbone match, box match, reverse box match, "V" match, lot match, center match, balance match, random match, veneer inlay, veneer bandings, veneer tape, tape lamination machine, plastic laminates, rigid plastic laminate, high pressure laminate, kraft paper, phenolic resin, decorative pattern sheet, melamine resin, General-Purpose Grade, Vertical Surface Grade, Post Forming Grade, Cabinet Liner Grade, backer sheet, fire-resistant laminates, rigid glues, contact adhesives, pressure sensitive adhesives, hot-melt glue, flexible plastic laminates, flexible plastic bandings.

TEST YOUR KNOWLEDGE

1. Why might veneer or plastic laminate be used for a cabinet instead of solid wood?
2. Veneer thinner than 1/32 in. is typically referred to as:
   a. Flat veneer.
   b. Flexible veneer.
   c. Stump veneer.
   d. Softwood veneer.
3. What is a flitch?
4. Name the six methods of cutting veneer. Describe the veneer's grain pattern produced by each method.
5. Comb grain refers to _____.
6. Diagram the grain patterns of veneer cut from burl, crotch, and stump wood.
7. Sketch six common methods used for matching veneer. Plan and diagram two additional matches of your own design.
8. Veneer bandings are primarily used for:
   a. Inlay.
   b. Overlay.
   c. Wood edging.
   d. Wood facing.
9. Veneer tape is used to cover _____.
10. Explain the difference between rigid and flexible plastic laminates.
11. What are the four grades for rigid plastic laminates? What applications are each used for?
12. Three adhesives used to apply plastic laminate to a substrate are _____, _____, and _____.

Chapter 15
GLASS, PLASTIC, AND CERAMIC PRODUCTS

After studying this chapter, you will be able to:
□*Describe the various forms of glass, plastics, and ceramics used in cabinetmaking.*
□*Install sheet glass and plastic as panels and windows.*
□*Cut and assemble glass into leaded panels.*
□*List the various plastics and their applications.*
□*Install ceramic tile for counter surfaces, floors, and walls.*

Glass, plastic, and ceramic products are both functional and attractive cabinet components. Glass sheets are used for windows. Plastic may be molded to replace real wood or made in sheets to replace glass. Ceramic tile adds beauty while it protects countertops and other surfaces.

GLASS

Glass is made primarily of silica (sand), soda ash, and limestone. Other ingredients may be added for strength or decoration. The mixture is melted at about 2800°F. It is then made into flat sheets, molded into knobs, pulls and decorations, or spun into thread.

Sheet glass is annealed after it is formed. The glass is reheated, but not melted, to remove internal stress. Annealing helps assure a controlled break when cutting the glass.

Flat glass may be tempered to increase strength. The glass is reheated and quenched (cooled) quickly. Tempered glass will break or crack but does not shatter into tiny pieces. Shower doors, for example, must be tempered.

The use of glass dates back several thousand years. Vases, windows, and mirrors are early products. Glass blowing was the main method for making glass containers. Stained glass was developed almost 1000 years ago. About 300 years ago, glass began to be molded into containers. Today, glass is mounted in cabinet doors and in-

stalled as shelves, Fig. 15-1. It may also serve as a protective surface for wood products.

PLASTIC

Plastics are synthetic compounds also called resins. Two forms of plastic are thermoplastic and thermoset. *Thermoplastic* materials may be reheated and reformed many times. Plastic for win-

Fig. 15-1. Curio cabinets use glass doors and shelves to permit display of china. (Thomasville)

dows is usually thermoplastic. *Thermoset plastics* are formed into products during manufacturing by a chemical reaction. Door and drawer knobs are examples. If they are reheated, they distort beyond use. Early thermoset plastics, made at the turn of the century, were known as *celluloid* and *bakelite.* Since then, plastics have improved and their applications have increased.

Most plastics for cabinetry are available in sheet and molded forms, Fig. 15-2. However, some plastics can be purchased as liquid resin with a separate hardener. You may create a mold, mix the resin and hardener, and cast a plastic product that fits your needs.

Fig. 15-2. Sheet plastics are often used to protect surfaces. The wine rack is formed sheet plastic. (Rohm and Haas)

CERAMICS

Ceramic products are made of pottery clay. Moistened clay may be molded into a shape. The moisture is then allowed to evaporate and the clay object fired (baked) in a kiln. The object becomes very hard and somewhat brittle. Next, a glasslike decorative and protective substance, called *glaze,* is applied to the object. It is again fired to melt and harden the glaze.

The earliest known use for ceramics was pottery. Clay was molded into containers and baked over coals. Nearly 5000 years ago, glazed clay tile were common in Egypt. Thin, flat tile decorated walls and floors.

Ceramic tile is found with many modern cabinets. The tile is typically applied to counter tops, Fig.

15-3. Tile surfaces are hard, smooth, and durable. They resist heat, moisture, stains, and scratches.

Another type of tile is slate. *Slate* is a form of rock. It is mined and later fractured into tile. Then it may be sawed into rectangular shapes. Install it much the same as ceramic tile.

FORMS OF GLASS, PLASTIC, AND CERAMICS

Glass, plastic, and ceramics are available in one or more forms. They may be sheet, molded, or spun-fiber. When combined with wood and hardware, they serve many cabinetmaking needs.

SHEET GLASS AND PLASTIC

Sheet glass and plastic serve as windows, table tops, and shelves. When colored, they can create stained-glass effects. Semitransparent sheets are installed as light-diffusing panels. Mirrored plastic and glass reflect images and provide a sense of depth. A reflective metallic substance is applied to the back of the glass or plastic sheet.

MOLDED GLASS, PLASTIC, AND CERAMIC

Molded forms of glass, plastic, and ceramic create almost unlimited parts for cabinets and furniture. Glass and plastic are formed to make mouldings, legs, spindles, knobs, pulls, and entire pieces of furniture. Ceramics are molded and glazed to

Fig. 15-3. Ceramic tile provides an attractive and durable surface for this kitchen counter. (Mid-West Tile)

become tile, knobs, and pulls. Ceramic tile may also be molded into decorative shapes.

SPUN-GLASS FIBERS

One unique glass material is called *fiberglass.* Clear or colorful glass is spun into thread-like fibers. Fibers can be woven into mats and ''cloth'' rolls. They may also be cut into short pieces called rovings.

Rovings, mats, and cloths are bonded with liquid polyester resin mixed with a hardener. Cloth and mats are coated with layers of resin. Rovings are sprayed over liquid resin. Repeated coatings of fiber and resin are placed in or over a mold. When the resin cures, the very strong and durable fiberglass object can be removed.

SELECTING GLASS SHEETS

Sheets of glass are selected for decorative and/or functional effects. Four kinds of basic glass are manufactured.
1. Flat
2. Decorative
3. Tinted
4. Mirror

FLAT GLASS

Flat glass is the most common glass found in cabinetry. It is used in doors, on tabletops, and as shelves.

The glass-making process has changed. Years ago, flat glass was manufactured by rolling softened glass. If the rollers or rolling tables were dirty or scratched, the glass surface would not be completely flat. Today, flat glass is made through a floating process. Float glass is manufactured by spreading molten glass over molten tin. The tin, as a liquid, is smoother than the rolling tables were. As a result, the process creates a flat, smooth, and polished lower surface. Since the upper surface is untouched by rollers, it is smooth also.

Flat glass is manufactured in different strengths and thicknesses. Two forms are sheet and plate glass. Sheet glass, for the most part, is single or double strength. The thickness of single strength glass is slightly less than 1/8 in. (3 mm). Double strength glass is about 5/32 in. (4 mm). Other thicknesses from 1/16 in. to 7/16 in. (1.5 mm to 11 mm) are available. Install the single strength glass only in frames. Double strength material is appropriate for windows and shelves.

Plate glass is thicker and often stronger than sheet glass. It may also have been tempered. It varies in thickness from 1/4 in. (6 mm) to 1 1/4 in. (30 mm).

The edges of flat glass sheets are either hidden or visible. Visible edges must be ground and polished before you install these components as doors, shelves, etc.

DECORATIVE GLASS

Decorative glass is popular for cabinets. Some is made by altering the normal manufacture of glass. Four types of decorative glass are: patterned, etched, cut, and enameled.

Patterned glass is made by feeding the glass through rough or patterned rollers. The surface of the glass is embossed and becomes translucent. When looking through pattern glass, images are distorted or appear as shadows. Pattern glass is typically 1/8 in. and 7/32 in. thick and may be tempered to increase its strength. It is found in partitions, shower stalls, or wherever privacy is desired without blocking light.

Etched glass is glass treated with acid which removes a thin layer of the surface. The pattern produced can be very decorative.

Cut glass is made by using carbide or diamond sharp cutting tools to score the glass. The cuts reflect light in different angles for a brilliant effect.

Enameled glass has translucent or solid colored surfaces. Special paint is applied to the surface. The colors are more distinct than those in tinted glass.

TINTED GLASS

Tinted glass is made by adding coloring agents to molten glass. It lessens the amount of light which will pass through the glass without distorting the image. Tinted glass is used for table tops, doors, and windows. In architectural design, tinted glass lessens heat from sunlight and prevents glare. The most common tints are bronze or gray.

MIRROR GLASS

Mirror glass is coated on one side with a highly reflective metallic substance, frequently silver. The reflective material is then covered by a protective coating. A backer sheet of glass is often placed over the reflective and protective layers to prevent damage from abrasion. Reflective glass is commonly used in the back of cabinets to give depth. It is also used as wall tile.

INSTALLING GLASS SHEETS

Glass is installed after the cabinet has been assembled and finished. Glass installation includes cutting and mounting. You cut glass by scoring and fracturing. Mounting involves: positioning the glass in sliding and hinged doors, securing it in frames, and installing it as shelves. Edges of unframed glass must be ground and possibly polished. In some cases, drilling might be necessary. Always wear safety glasses and leather gloves when working with glass.

CUTTING GLASS

Glass is not really ''cut.'' It is scored (scratched) and fractured. *Scoring* is done with a carbide steel wheel or diamond-point glass cutter. It may be done with a machine or by hand, Fig. 15-4. Scoring is accomplished by pushing or pulling the wheel across the glass surface with slight pressure. Too little pressure will not score the glass. Too much pressure will chip (flake) the glass around the score line.

Use a lubricant to reduce the amount of flaking of the glass surface. A good fluid lubricant is a mix of 50 percent light oil and 50 percent kerosene. Wipe the surface of the glass before scoring with a rag soaked with lubricant.

Fig. 15-4. Glass is scored with a glass cutter. A straightedge serves as a guide for scoring straight lines. (The Fletcher-Terry Co.)

SCORING

You score lines by hand or with a machine. Straight and curved cuts can be done by each method.

To score a straight line by hand:
1. Place a straightedge about 1/8 in. from where the break is desired.
2. The cutter wheel must be kept perpendicular to the glass panel. Holding it at an angle will cause

an irregular break. Keep the cutter against the straightedge.
3. Push or pull the cutter across the surface of the glass, Fig. 15-5. Use enough pressure to score the glass. Lubricate the cutter wheel to keep it operating freely.

To score a straight line by machine:
1. Clamp the glass in the machine, making sure the desired cut is aligned with the cutter.
2. With firm pressure, pull the cutter downward across the glass, Fig. 15-6.

To score a circle by machine:
1. Set the glass circle cutter to the proper radius.
2. Place the glass on the cutter table.
3. Press down on the swivel knob as you move the cutter, Fig. 15-7A.
4. Make straight line radial scores by hand from the circle to the edge of the glass, Fig. 15-7B. Radial scores permit waste to be removed in order to cleanly fracture the workpiece you need.

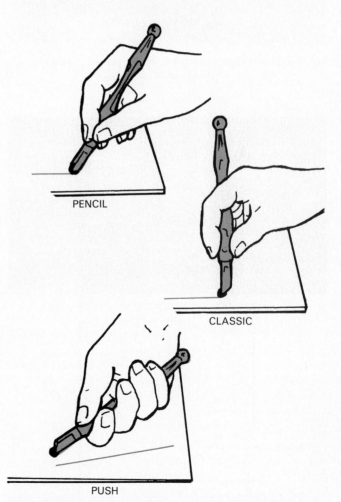

PENCIL

CLASSIC

PUSH

Fig. 15-5. The glass cutter may be pulled or pushed across the glass. Three common ways of holding the cutter are shown. (The Fletcher-Terry Co.)

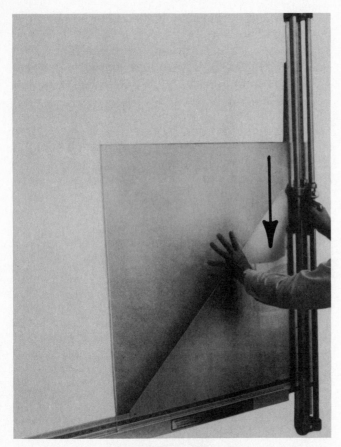

Fig. 15-6. A glass cutting machine assures a straight cut. (Brodhead-Garrett)

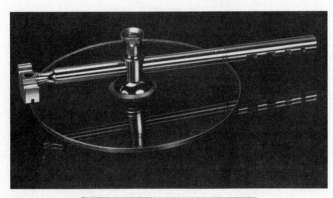

A

B

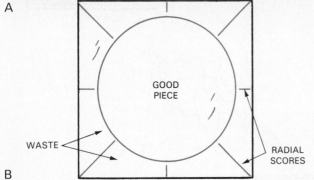

Fig. 15-7. Cutting circles. A—The swivel knob has a rubber bottom which keeps the cutter from moving while you score the glass. (Brookstone Co.) B—Radial scores help separate the waste material, making it easier to remove the glass circle.

To score a curved line by hand:
1. Prepare a paper pattern of the curve you need.
2. Place the glass over the pattern.
3. Trace and score the pattern with the glass cutter, Fig. 15-8.
4. Use radial scores where necessary.

FRACTURING

After scoring, the glass is *fractured.* This is done either by bending or tapping. It is necessary to fracture the glass immediately after scoring it. Glass has a tendency to "heal," making it very difficult to break cleanly. Fracturing by bending is for straight line and some curved line scores. Tapping is done for both curved and straight line scores.

To fracture by bending glass clamped to a scoring machine:
1. Grip the free edge of the glass with your gloved hand.
2. Bend the glass away from you with firm even pressure.
3. If the glass was scored by hand, grip on each side of the score with gloved hands. Bend the outer ends of the glass away from you as in Fig. 15-9.

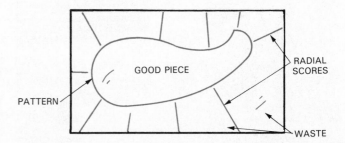

Fig. 15-8. For irregular curves, place the glass over the pattern. Score along the pattern, then make radial scores to remove waste around the workpiece.

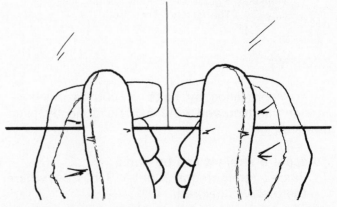

Fig. 15-9. Small straight line fractures are made by bending the piece on both sides of the score line.

To fracture by bending with pliers:

1. Grip the glass with the pliers, making sure the tip of the pliers is right next to the score line.
2. Place the pliers perpendicular to the score mark and squeeze with firm pressure, Fig. 15-10.
3. Bend the glass to fracture it.

Fig. 15-10. Pliers are used to remove small chips which cannot be fractured by hand.

To fracture by tapping:

1. Place the glass on the edge of a table with the score line just overhanging the edge.
2. Grip the unsupported piece of glass with your gloved hand.
3. Tap the underside of the glass with the glass cutter handle.
4. Start at one end of the scored line. The glass should begin to fracture as you tap under the score, Fig. 15-11.

At times the glass needs to be trimmed slightly. Score it along the original score line. Then bend the excess with glass nippers or one of the grooves in the cutter head, Fig. 15-12.

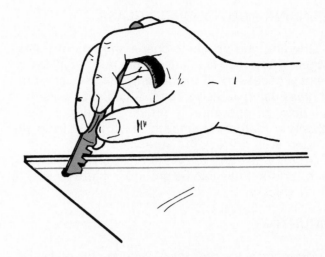

Fig. 15-12. Many glass cutters have grooves for trimming jagged edges.

DRILLING GLASS

Drilling holes for fasteners or hardware is the least desirable mounting process. Drilling creates heat by friction. Heat can cause the glass to fracture. If you must drill holes, use a carbide tipped glass drill, Fig. 15-13. Turn it at a relatively slow speed. Water should be put on the drill and glass to help prevent heat buildup.

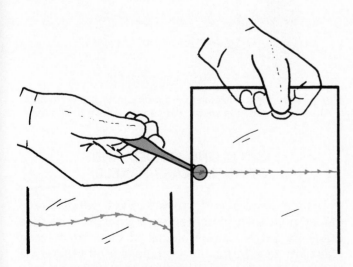

Fig. 15-11. Both straight and curved scores can be fractured by tapping the glass. Use the handle end of the glass cutter.

Fig. 15-13. A glass drill has a spearlike point. It drills by scraping the glass rather than cutting it. (Brookstone Co.)

GRINDING AND POLISHING GLASS

Grinding and polishing shape and smooth glass edges. The processes are simple but much equipment is necessary. *Grinding* removes large amounts of glass using abrasive belts. A coolant flows over the point of operation to prevent buildup of heat. *Polishing* restores a smooth finish by buffing the ground area with a fine abrasive belt.

Grinding is done to create inset pulls for sliding glass doors. Pulls can be ground in plate glass 1/4 in. or thicker.

MOUNTING

Mounting is the process of securing the glass. Different mounts include:
1. Securing glass in a frame.
2. Attaching glass to a cabinet with hardware.
3. Bonding glass (usually a mirror) to surfaces.

Securing glass in a frame

Securing glass in a frame is done with wood or plastic mouldings and button retainers, Fig. 15-14.

When using mouldings, a rabbet joint is cut on the inside of the frame where the glass sits. The moulding is placed over the glass. It is secured to the frame with either finishing nails, brads, or staples.

Flexible plastic mouldings can replace wood mouldings as retainers. A groove is made in the frame just behind where the glass is placed. The plastic moulding is then inserted into the groove.

Plastic button retainers are installed with screws. The glass sits in the rabbet joint and the button pivots over the glass. Tightening the screw holds the glass in place.

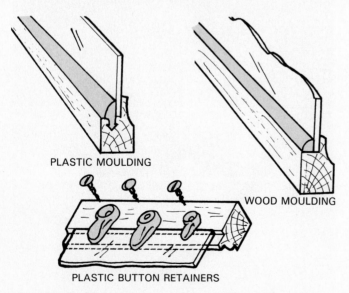

PLASTIC MOULDING

WOOD MOULDING

PLASTIC BUTTON RETAINERS

Fig. 15-14. The glass is placed in a rabbet joint cut in the frame. Mouldings or button retainers secure the glass.

Mounting glass with hardware

Sheet glass, without a frame, is commonly installed as entertainment center doors. The glass is held in place with a glass door hinge. Set screws hold the glass in place. A felt or rubber pad is placed between the metal hinge and the glass. Various types of glass door hinges are available. These are explained in Chapter 17, Hardware.

Bonding mirror glass to surfaces

Mirrors in the shape of 12 in. by 12 in. (300 mm x 300 mm) tiles are common wall decorations. Mirror tile is attached with a special mastic adhesive. Mastic is a very thick paste that dries slowly.

The procedure to follow when installing tile mirrors:
1. Place one to three tablespoons of mastic near each corner of the tile, Fig. 15-15.
2. Press the tile against the wall or other surface.
3. Adjust all tile so the edges are even.

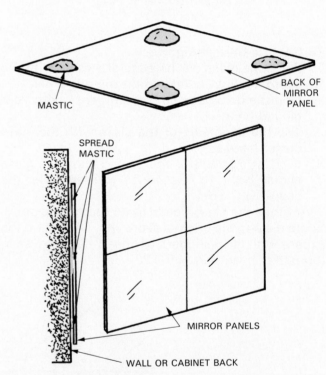

MASTIC

BACK OF MIRROR PANEL

SPREAD MASTIC

MIRROR PANELS

WALL OR CABINET BACK

Fig. 15-15. Mastic is placed in four corners of the tile back. Once mounted, the mirror tile can be adjusted slightly.

INSTALLING LEADED AND STAINED GLASS PANELS

Leaded panels and *stained glass panels* have gained popularity in contemporary design. They are made by setting small pieces of clear or colored glass into lead strips. Leaded glass refers to panels using colorless glass. Stained glass includes colored glass or metal oxides fused to the glass to give color. Leaded and stained glass are most popular in cabinet doors, Fig. 15-16.

The steps included in preparing and installing stained glass panels includes:

1. Laying out a full size pattern.
2. Cutting the glass.
3. Fitting lead came to the glass.
4. Soldering the lead joints.
5. Mounting the glass in the frame.
6. Grouting along the lead seams.

Fig. 15-16. This cabinet contains doors with stained glass panels.

LAYING OUT THE PATTERN

Create a full size pattern from a refined sketch of the finished panel. If the panel will contain several colors of glass, label each section of the pattern according to the color of glass. Separate each section with two lines 1/8 in. (3 mm) apart, Fig. 15-17A. This allows for lead between the glass components.

CUTTING THE GLASS

Cut the glass freehand or with a guide (straightedge, French curve, etc.). You might also use a circle cutter. For irregular curves you will need to trace the pattern. Place the glass over the pattern. Score the curve freehand. Fracture the glass by either bending or tapping methods.

Small, compound curves may be difficult to shape. More than one break may be necessary. For these make the break into sections. Score and fracture each section as you go.

FITTING LEAD CAME

Glass is held together with lead came and solder. *Lead came binder* is ''H''-shaped (to fit between pieces). *Lead came edges* are ''[''-shaped (to fit on the outer edge), Fig. 15-17B.

Caution: when handling lead, keep your hands away from your mouth or food. Lead poisoning can be fatal.

Preparing to fit came

Glass and came are assembled on a flat surface. Use a piece of plywood larger than the pattern. Then proceed as follows:

1. Place the pattern on a plywood base.

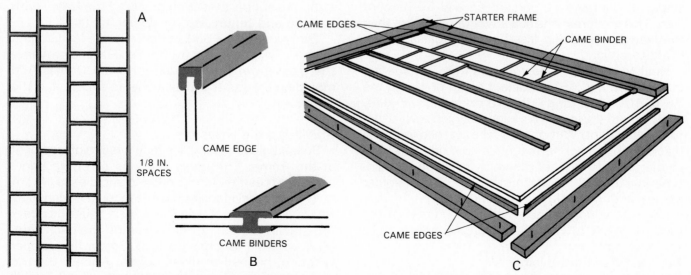

Fig. 15-17. A—The pattern for glass pieces is laid out with space allowance for lead came. B—Lead came fits between glass pieces and on the outer edge of the panel. C—Assemble the panel in a wood frame.

2. Attach two hardboard strips to form a corner. Make sure the corner is square.
3. Cut two pieces of edge came to length. Miter cut the edges of the came.
4. Clean the came with steel wool so it is bright and shiny. This will assure a secure solder bond when assembling the panel.
5. Place the pieces to form the first corner of the panel.

Assembling the panel

Start fitting the panel together in the prepared corner. Set one piece of glass at a time. When you begin:
1. Place the corner section of glass into the corner created by the two pieces of came edge.
2. Bend the came binder to fit where curved pieces of glass meet. Came must be long enough to solder to other lead came strips.
3. Cut each piece of lead with a utility knife. Remember to clean each joint with steel wool.
4. Add glass and surrounding came binder until all pieces are laid in place, Fig. 15-17C.
5. Enclose the glass panel with the other two pieces of came edge. Make sure the ends are mitered so they fit together properly.
6. Clamp or nail two more hardboard strips that hold the entire panel in place.

SOLDERING LEAD JOINTS

Soldering is a simple, but important, operation. Stability of the stained glass panel depends on the quality of the solder joint. Make sure you have a well fit joint, sufficient heat, quality flux, and quality solder.

A joint is bonded by melting the proper solder over the connection. *Solder* contains a mix of lead and tin. For lead came work, use 40/60 wire or bar solder. It contains 40 percent tin and 60 percent lead. This mixture melts at a lower temperature than the lead came. Using less heat, the glass is less likely to crack.

Heat to melt the solder comes from a *soldering gun* or iron, Fig. 15-18. Select a gun or iron in the 75 to 100 watt range. Before soldering the joint, apply *flux* to the joint. This keeps oxygen away from the heated joint. Without flux, the cleaned joint will blacken. The black formation is an oxide (rust-like coating). Solder will not adhere to the oxide. A rosin-type paste flux is recommended. Some solder comes with rosin flux in the core.

Begin soldering at the joints in the center of the pattern. Work toward the sides and corners. To solder a joint:
1. Place flux on the joint.
2. Preheat the joint with the flat tip of the soldering gun.

3. Touch the solder to the lead and soldering gun tip.
4. Melt enough solder to flow across the joint.
5. Remove the solder and tip from the joint.
6. Allow the joint to cool.

Complete the joints on one side of the assembly. Then place a piece of plywood over the glass assembly and turn over the panel, frame, and plywood as one unit. Solder the joints on the panel's other side.

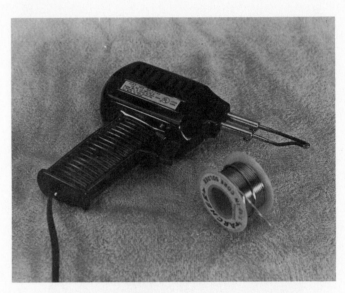

Fig. 15-18. A soldering gun or iron melts the solder to bond the lead came.

MOUNTING THE GLASS ASSEMBLY

You should have a wood frame prepared to receive the glass assembly. Finish should be applied to the wood before mounting the glass. Stained glass panels are very heavy. The frame should be strong to support the weight. Make the frame with mortise and tenon, lap, or dowel joints.

Trim excess lead and solder from the lead edging where it will touch the frame. Excess lead prevents the glass from fitting flush with the frame. Add moulding around the glass panel to secure it in the frame.

Stabilizing the assembly

Stained glass assemblies may need reinforcement in the frame. The glass sections or entire panel might shift as the door is opened and closed. A 1/4 in. (6 mm) steel stabilizing rod is recommended. One rod for each 2 sq. ft. of glass area is helpful. Locate the stabilizer close to the center on the back side. Mark where it touches the lead. Solder fine copper wires to the lead at these points. Anchor the rod under the moulding on the back side. (Notch or drill the moulding as necessary.) Wrap the wires around the rod and twist the ends together. Snip the wires to 1/4 in. (6 mm) long. Solder the wires against the rod, Fig. 15-19.

Grouting

Grout is pressed into the space between lead came and glass to help hold the pieces tight. Grout may be cement-type, resinous, or a combination of both. *Cement grouts* consist of portland cement. *Resinous grouts* are epoxy based and possess high bond strength. However, they are harder to apply.

Mix the grout to a creamy texture with an appropriate thinner. Then press it with a putty knife between the lead and glass on both surfaces, Fig. 15-20. Using a rag soaked with the appropriate thinner, wipe off excess grout before it dries.

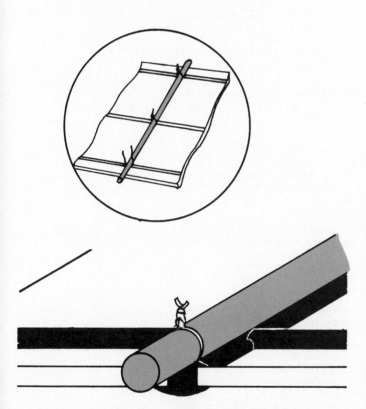

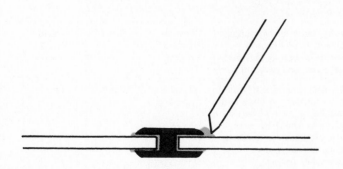

Fig. 15-19. A steel rod stabilizes the leaded panel assembly. Copper wires soldered to the lead came fasten the rod.

Fig. 15-20. Press grout between came and glass pieces.

SELECTING PLASTIC MATERIALS

Plastic is an excellent substitute for wood and glass. It can be molded to look and feel like wood. As a sheet material, it may replace flat glass. Sheets may also be assembled as furniture, Fig. 15-21.

COMMON PLASTICS

There are many different types of plastic materials applied in cabinetmaking. Fig. 15-22 includes the properties and cutting methods for the most popular plastics.

ACRYLIC PLASTIC

Acrylic plastic is a rigid plastic often used for cabinetmaking. The most common form of acrylic is in sheet form. Acrylic sheets replace glass in many applications. Sheets of 1/16 in. (1.5 mm) and 1/4 in. (6 mm) are used most, but thicker materials are available for machining. Acrylic sheets may be clear, tinted, or colored. Other forms of acrylic are squares, round rods, and tubing.

Acrylic is a stong thermoplastic material. It has 6 to 17 times the impact resistance of glass. It can be heated and bent easily. If you make a mistake when bending, reheat the acrylic. It will flatten and can be formed again.

Fig. 15-21. Tinted acrylic plastic is the structure for this furniture. (Rohm and Haas)

THERMOPLASTICS

MAJOR RESIN (PLASTIC)	COMMON NAME	NATURAL COLOR	IMPORTANT PROPERTIES	APPLICATIONS	IMPACT RESISTANCE (Ft./Lb./In. for 1/8 in. sheet)	SCRATCH RESISTANCE	MACHINING PROPERTIES OF THE PLASTIC IN SOLID MOLDED FORM	
Polymethyl Methacrylate	Acrylic	Clear	Weather resistant, colorable, bonds well, transmits light, good surface luster.	Transparent panels for windows, skylights. Containers, rods, tubes, lenses.	Fair	Good	Good	
Acrylonitrile-Butadiene-Styrene	ABS	Light tan opaque	High impact resistance, rigid, tough, tolerates high temperatures, medium chemical resistance, will burn, can be hard or flexible.	Tables, chairs, shower stalls, molded furniture, appliances, plumbing, can be electroplated.	Fair to Excellent	Fair to Good	Good to Excellent	
Polyamides	Nylon	Opaque white	Tough, resists abrasion and chemicals, high surface gloss, colorable, water repellent, fair electrical properties.	Drawer slides, bearings, gears, hinges, rollers, textiles.	Fair to Excellent	Excellent	Excellent	
Polycarbonates	High impact	Clear	Toughest of all plastics, high impact strength, good heat and chemical resistance, weathers well, easily colored.	Window glazing, lighting globes, bottles, coffee pots, sunglass lenses.	Good to Excellent	Good to Excellent	Excellent	
Polyethylene		Translucent Milky white	Flexible, tough, will not tear, resists chemicals, feels waxy, easily colored. Ranges from flexible (low density) to rigid (high density).	Molded furniture, containers, housewares, electrical components.	Fair to Excellent	Fair to Good	Good	
Polypropylene		Translucent Milky white	High impact resistance, lightweight, good flex life, chemical resistance, easily colored, scratch resistant.	Bottles, housewares, appliance housings, hoses, containers with integral hinges (flip top caps), radio and TV cabinets.	Fair to Excellent	Excellent	Good	
Polystyrene		Clear	Water resistant, brittle, yellows with exposure, often used as foam, tasteless and odorless, harmed by cleaning fluid, has a definite metallic ring when tapped.	Tile, sheets for wall coverings, molded furniture parts, plastic plates and cups, packaging containers, insulation, molded imitation wood products.	Fair to Excellent	Fair	Good	
Polyvinyl Chloride	Vinyl PVC	Light blue clear	Good strength and toughness, average chemical resistance, can perform well in low temperatures.	Simulated leather, adhesives, floor tile, outdoor furniture, door and window trim, laminations.	Fair to Excellent	Good	Excellent	

THERMOSETTING PLASTICS

MAJOR RESIN (PLASTIC)	COMMON NAME	NATURAL COLOR	IMPORTANT PROPERTIES	APPLICATIONS	IMPACT RESISTANCE	SCRATCH RESISTANCE	MACHINING PROPERTIES	
Melamine Formaldehyde Urea Formaldehyde (Amino resins)		Pastel, Urea may be white	Durable, hard, abrasion and chemically resistant, easily colored to a glossy finish. Urea may absorb water. Melamine is more water-resistant, but more brittle.	Melamines are used for decorative laminates, countertops, switch plates, dinnerware, doorknobs. Urea is used as a wood adhesive, but also molded into furniture parts.	Fair to Good	Fair to Good	Fair	
Phenol Formaldehyde		Dark gray opaque	Hard, rigid, heat resistant, brittle, low cost, excellent insulating properties, resistant to most chemicals.	Widely used for high impact plastics, bonds panel products, such as plywood, fiberboard, and particleboard.	Good to Excellent	Good	Fair to Good	
Polyesters		Clear	Can be made thin when used with fiberglass, anti-static, stiff and hard, colorable, weather and chemically resistant.	Polyester resin is best known as an adhesive to bond with glass fibers to form fiberglass. Polyester laminated glass mats are used for furniture, boats, airplanes, and automobile panels.	Good	Good	Good	

Fig. 15-22. Characteristics of the most common plastics applied in cabinetmaking.

THERMOPLASTICS

CIRCULAR SAWING MOLDED PLASTIC			BAND SAWING MOLDED PLASTIC			DRILLING		TYPICAL FILLERS USED	COMMON SOLVENT CEMENTS FOR THERMOPLASTICS
BLADE (type)	TEETH (per inch)	SPEED (ft. per min.)	BLADE (type)	TEETH (per inch)	SPEED (ft. per min.)	SPEED	POINT ANGLE		
Hollow Ground	4-6	3000	Metal	5-7	2000-4000	1500-2500	95	None used	Methylene Chloride Ethylene Dichloride Softened by alcohol.
Combination	4-6	4000	Wood (skip tooth)	5-7	1000-3000	500-900	118	Glass fibers	Methyl Ethyl Ketone
Hollow Ground	8-10	5000	Wood (skip tooth)	4-6	1000	900-1500	70-90	Glass fibers	Resists solvents
Hollow Ground	4-6	8000	Metal	10-18	1500	300-800	118	Glass fibers	Methylene Chloride
Hollow Ground	4-6	9000	Wood (skip tooth)	4-6	1200-1500	1000-3000	70-90	Metal powders	Resists solvents
Hollow Ground	8-10	9000	Wood (skip tooth)	4-6	1200-1500	1000-3000	70-90	Glass fibers	Resists solvents
Hollow Ground	4-6	2000	Metal	10-18	3000-4000	1500-2500	95	Glass fibers	Methyl Ethyl Ketone Methylene Chloride
Hollow Ground	4-6	3000	Metal	6-9	2000-3000	900-2000	118	Clay	Methyl Ethyl Ketone

THERMOSETTING PLASTICS

BLADE (type)	TEETH (per inch)	SPEED (ft. per min.)	BLADE (type)	TEETH (per inch)	SPEED (ft. per min.)	SPEED	POINT ANGLE	TYPICAL FILLERS USED	COMMON SOLVENT CEMENTS FOR THERMOPLASTICS
Carbide Tip	8-10	5000	Metal	10-18	2000	600-2000	90	Cellulose pulp, glass fibers	
Carbide Tip	8-10	3000	Metal	10-18	1500	600-2000	90	Wood flour, glass fibers, cotton flock, metal powders.	
Carbide Tip	8-10	5000	Metal	10-18	4000	1000-2000	90	Clay, glass fibers, woven cloth	

Fig. 15-22 cont'd.

Acrylic plastic is sold with a protective paper masking on it because it will scratch. Make all of your layout marks on the paper. Leave the paper on while cutting the sheet. Remove the paper only when you are preparing to heat form or mount the plastic.

POLYESTER RESIN

Polyester resin is a thermoset plastic. It is available as molded parts or liquid ingredients. Molded items include door knobs, pulls, etc. These only have to be installed. Liquid polyester resin is used with fiberglass and as a casting and coating material.

Fiberglass
Fiberglass is a mixture of polyester resin and glass fibers. Fibers are blown over, or layered between, a resin coating. When cure, the mixture is rigid. Fiberglass is molded into furniture, boat hulls, and other structural panels.

Laying up
Laying up polyester with fiberglass requires a sealed mold, glass fibers, liquid resin, hardener, and possibly dye. Layers of fiber and resin are placed on the inside or outside of a sealed mold. The mold may be investment or reusable. An investment mold can become part of the product. It also may be destroyed during component removal. Reusable molds allow you to make duplicate parts. Sides of molds must be tapered to free component after curing. To cast parts with a reusable mold:
1. Measure and cut the fiber mat or cloth slightly larger than the mold.
2. Coat the reusable mold's surface with mold release. (Use silicon or wax.)
3. Coat the mold with resin premixed with hardener.
4. Place the mat or cloth on the wet resin.
5. Smooth the fiber material with a rubber squeegee to remove wrinkles and air bubbles.
6. Immediately apply a coat of resin over the fibers.
7. Allow the assembly to cure completely.
8. Abrade the surface and add more topcoats to achieve the desired total thickness.
9. Remove the finished component after it is totally cured.

Casting
Liquid polyester resin can be cast. Casting resins are mixed with a hardener to cure the plastic. You may include plastic dye or pigments during the mixing process to add color.

Pour the mixture into a prepared mold. Preparing the mold means coating the inside with mold release. Use spray silicone or paste wax as release. Otherwise, the resin will adhere to the mold. The plastic will set in a few hours and cure in a day.

Coating
Liquid polyester resin is also used as a coating. It is extremely durable and resistant to mild acids, alcohol, etc. Mix the resin, color, and hardener as if you were casting. Brush the mixture over a sealed surface. Use a natural hog's hair brush with a wood handle. Synthetic brushes might soften or even melt. Apply polyester resin as you would any other topcoating. Abrade the the cured surface between coats. For further information on topcoating, see the chapters on finishing.

Clean the brush immediately after each coating. Use acetone or lacquer thinner. These solvents will not dissolve natural brushes.

POLYETHYLENE

Polyethylene is a transluscent or opaque thermoplastic material. It resists impact and tears. Polyethylene is available in both rigid and flexible form. Rigid polyethylene is available as sheets, rods, and tubes. Flexible polyethylene sheets are also being used in cabinetry, Fig. 15-23.

Fig. 15-23. These tambour doors are made of flexible polyethylene. (Coroplast, Inc.)

POLYSTYRENE

Polystyrene is a thermoplastic material. It can be molded into components or complete pieces of furniture. With proper mixing, it can resemble wood grain. Polystyrene is generally brittle and has poor resistance to chemicals. Additives blended with the resin during manufacture can increase the plastics flexibility.

POLYURETHANE

Polyurethane is a resin much like vinyl. However, it can be either a thermoplastic or thermoset plastic. It is prepared either as a rigid molding material or flexible material. Polyurethane can be molded and colored to look and feel like real wood. It is an inexpensive way of duplicating carved wood.

Liquid polyurethane is used as a wood finish. When dry, the finish resists impact, scratches, and most chemicals. Flexible foam polyurethane is used as furniture cushioning. Polyurethane components can be assembled with various adhesives.

INSTALLING PLASTIC

Plastic is an easy material to cut, drill, form, and finish. For most operations, you can use common woodworking tools. In sheet form, it can be assembled and mounted much like glass. Before

cutting or drilling, lay out the pattern on the plastic's protective paper cover.

CUTTING PLASTIC

Plastic can be cut two ways. First, it can be fractured like glass. Score the surface with a plastic cutter. Then bend the plastic over a large dowel rod, Fig. 15-24. The plastic should break cleanly along the scored line.

Plastic can also be cut using a circular saw, band saw, or saber saw, Fig. 15-25. It is cut much like manufactured panels or lumber. Refer to Fig. 15-23 for the type of saw blade, number of teeth, and cutting speed. Special saw blades are recommended for cutting certain plastics.

DRILLING PLASTIC

Standard twist drills commonly are used to drill plastic. Special drill bits for plastic reduce the

Fig. 15-24. Steps in fracturing plastic. Left. Score with a plastic cutter. Fracture by bending over a dowel rod. (Rohm and Haas)

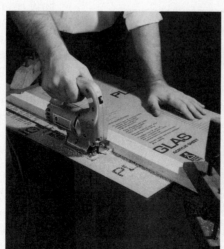

Fig. 15-25. Sawing plastic. Left. Circular sawing with a hollow ground blade for plastics. (The guard has been removed to show the operation). Middle. Sawing straight lines with a saber saw using a clamped straightedge. Right. Saber sawing curves along a layout line. (Rohm and Haas)

amount of cracking. See Fig. 25-55C. A drill press, portable power drill, and hand drill are all satisfactory. While drilling, always place a *backer board* under the plastic, Fig. 15-26. This lessens damage from the drill breaking through the lower surface.

FORMING PLASTIC

Thermoplastic sheets up to 1/4 in. thick can be formed easily.

Plastic can be formed in one or more directions at the same time. Straight line bending is easiest with an *electric strip heater*, Fig. 15-27. Bending in more than one direction requires heating the plastic in an oven. Preheat the oven to the appropriate temperature, Fig. 15-28. Heat the plastic until it is pliable. Remove it from the oven with insulated gloves. Place it in a form or mold. While the plastic cools, it must be held securely in the mold.

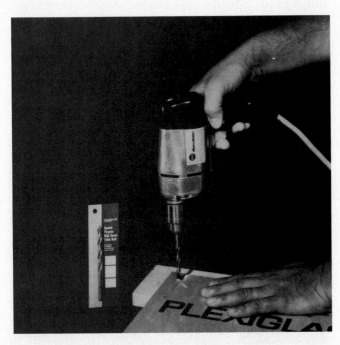

Fig. 15-26. Mark centerlines for drilling on protective paper cover. Place a board under the plastic while drilling. (Rohm and Haas)

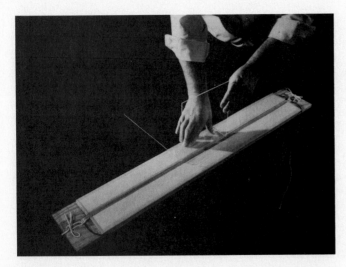

Fig. 15-27. This electric strip heater provides the correct amount of temperature for thermoforming acrylic plastic. (Rohm and Haas)

SHEET PLASTICS FOR THERMOFORMING

	FORMING TEMPERATURE	FORMABILITY
Acrylic	260° to 360°F	Good
ABS	300° to 350°F	Good
Polycarbonates	440° to 475°F	Good
Polystyrene	365° to 385°F	Excellent
Polyvinyl Chloride	225° to 355°F	Excellent

Fig. 15-28. Thermoplastics can be softened by heating them to the proper temperature.

FINISHING

Finishing should be necessary only on the sheet edges. The surface was protected by the paper coating. On the edges, saw or fracture marks might need to be removed. The process involves:

1. Scraping with the back of a hacksaw blade or similar smooth, sharp tool, Fig. 15-29A.
2. Sanding with several grit sizes of wet-or-dry abrasive paper, Fig. 15-29B.
   a. Sand with 360 grit sandpaper to remove saw marks. (Abrade the sheet's surface where solvent will be applied. The rough texture provides for better bonding.)
   b. Finish with 500 to 600 grit paper before polishing.
3. Polishing with a cotton buffing wheel and buffing compound, Fig. 15-29C.
   a. Buff across any surface scratches.
   b. Use light pressure to prevent heat buildup which will melt the plastic.

ASSEMBLING

Assemble plastics by bonding or mechanical fastening. Cements or solvents are applied to bond plastic together. (Use those which are not health hazards.) Machine screws may be used for mechanical fastening. Before assembling, align the workpieces to check their fit.

| A | B | C |

Fig. 15-29. Finishing the edges of sheet plastic. A—Using the back edge of a hacksaw blade. B—Sanding with abrasive paper. (Rohm and Haas) C—Polishing with a buffing wheel. (Rockwell International)

Cement bonding

Cements adhere to the plastic. They will also fill small spaces in the joint. Apply cement to one workpiece, Fig. 15-30. Press both together and maintain pressure until the cement has dried. The cement's container lists drying time. The dried assembly should be clear and free of air bubbles in the joint.

Solvent bonding

Solvents dissolve the plastic. The joint surfaces become softened and the plastic "flows" together. When the solvent evaporates, the joint hardens and the assembly is complete.

A bonding solvent is thin and watery which allows it to spread quickly. It fills only the tiniest of spaces. The components must be matched very accurately. You may tape them together before applying the solvent, Fig. 15-31. Apply the solvent in corners very carefully. Avoid touching the surfaces. The adhesive will soften any plastic it contacts. The adhesive evaporates rapidly. Air pockets are apt to remain. Pressure must be maintained on the joint until the solvent has dried.

MOUNTING PLASTIC

Plastic, like glass, makes good doors and shelves. Both can be mounted with the same hardware. Unlike glass, plastic can be drilled and threaded easily for machine screws.

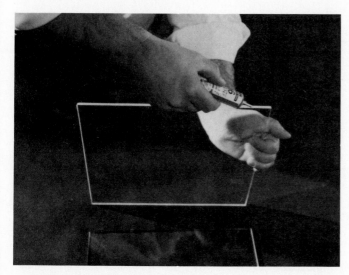

Fig. 15-30. Plastic cement is applied to one surface. Use the proper cement for the type of plastic. (Rohm and Haas)

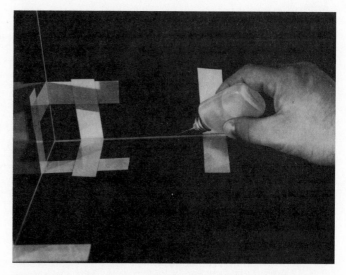

Fig. 15-31. Using a special applicator apply solvents precisely on the joints to be bonded. (Rohm and Hass)

INSTALLING SOLID PLASTIC TOPS

Solid plastic is an alternative to wood, veneer, or laminate countertops. It is tough, simple to install, and needs little care. The surface resists scratches and impact damage. Material is available in 1/4 in. (6 mm), 1/2 in. (12 mm), and 3/4 in. (19 mm) thicknesses. It can be installed on furniture, bathroom vanities, and kitchen cabinets, Fig. 15-32.

Both flat and contoured plastic tops are available. Contoured tops generally have a raised no-drip edge. On furniture you can install flat plastic tops. For kitchens and baths, both flat and contoured material can be used. With either flat or contoured tops you may have to cut out holes for a sink and other plumbing. The edges of flat stock can also be shaped into various contour designs, Fig. 15-33.

Fig. 15-32. Solid plastic often replaces laminates for countertops. The top can be cut, drilled, and shaped with ease. (DuPont)

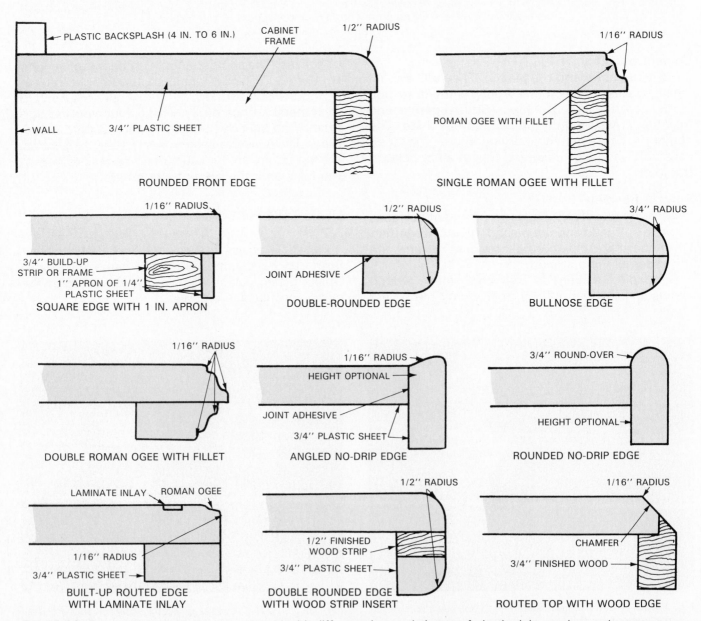

Fig. 15-33. Decorative edge designs are created with different sizes and shapes of plastic. Inlays enhance the appearance.

Solid plastic tops are cut and machined with woodworking tools. However, cutters must be carbide tipped. This includes circular saw blades and router bits. Saber saws, often used on laminates, are not recommended. They tend to chip the plastic.

Two types of adhesives are used with plastic tops: mastic and joint adhesive. *Mastic* is applied to the cabinet frame to bond the plastic top. *Joint adhesive,* supplied by the plastic manufacturer, bonds sheets together at corners.

Plastic tops can be made to look thicker than the sheet material. You can bond two pieces of plastic together. You may also insert wood or contrasting colored plastic between sections of plastic. See Fig. 15-33. The corners may be further shaped using a router.

FITTING AND SETTING PLASTIC TOPS

Measure and lay out the size of the countertop and places where fixtures will be inserted. Cut out openings for fixtures and appliances according to manufacturers' directions. Raise the plastic on wood blocks or saw horses to allow the saw blade to penetrate the plastic. Make sure to support the piece being cut so it will not fall, Fig. 15-34.

Lay out and cut backsplashes and builtup edges. Countertop and backsplash edges may then be shaped with a router. Select a carbide tipped router bit with the shape you wish.

Remove all saw or router marks with 120 to 180 grit silicon carbide wet-or-dry abrasive. An orbital sander is recommended. The surface should be ready for polishing after the plastic is bonded in place.

Fit the top on the cabinet without adhesive. The top of the cabinet or wall mounted frame must be flat. The entire perimeter of the plastic top has to be supported near the edge. It cannot wobble on the frame. If it does, short lengths of masking tape can be applied in low areas.

Inspect the final layout. There should be 1/8 in. of clearance between the edge of the plastic and any wall. Allow 1/16 in. between sheets where a joint is necessary. After positioning the plastic, mark the underside for placement.

Remove the plastic top to clean it. Wipe all of the joints with alcohol and let dry.

To attach the top, first apply small amounts of mastic to the top of the cabinet frame. Do so on the edges and cross supports. Lay the plastic on the frame and position it according to the marks you made earlier. Gently clamp the top to the frame, if necessary, to position the sheet. If two sheets are used, leave 1/16 in. between them.

Now bond the sheets, backsplashes, and edges together. Use a special epoxy joint compound supplied by the plastic manufacturer. Between sheets,

Fig. 15-34. Plastic tops are cut and shaped with conventional woodworking tools. Use carbide tipped saw blades and router bits. (DuPont)

apply enough adhesive to fill the joint half full. Remove any previous clamps. Then push the sheets together until adhesive is squeezed from the joint. Reclamp the sheets to the frame to maintain their positions. Then apply adhesive to the back of the top where the backsplash will set. Also apply mastic to the wall. Clamp the backsplash in place. The edges are bonded with joint adhesive.

Allow the assembly to set for about one hour. Press into a hidden joint with your fingernail. You should not be able to penetrate the adhesive. Now remove all excess adhesive with a block plane or chisel. Follow those with fine abrasives to take off small amounts of adhesive left by the plane or chisel. To finish the top, buff the surface with a polishing pad on an orbital sander.

SELECTING CERAMIC TILE

Ceramic tile is sold in a variety of colors, shapes, and glaze textures. Some tile is smooth and becomes slick when wet. Other types have a textured, non-slip surface. The colors and shapes are selected to suit the design of the cabinet or room.

Tile is available as individual pieces, mats, and mosaics. Individual tiles typically are square, rectangular, or other shapes. A *mat* is a 12 in. by 12 in. square of equally spaced small tiles bonded to a fiber mesh. *Mosaics* are pictures created with tile. These also are bonded to a fiber mesh.

INSTALLING TILE

Tiles are most likely installed after the cabinet is assembled and finished. Tile may be applied on table

tops, counter tops, and as wainscoting (partial wall covering). The process of tiling includes:
1. Preparing the surface.
2. Laying out the pattern.
3. Applying the adhesive.
4. Setting full tile.
5. Cutting and setting partial tile.
6. Grouting.
7. Sealing.
8. Drilling and attaching fixtures.

Preparing the surface

A surface to be tiled should be flat. Sand the surface to remove ragged edges and splinters. These might prevent the tile from lying flush.

Apply a primer or sealer to the surface. A sealer prevents moisture in the tile adhesive from entering the wood or drywall surface. Brush or roll on the primer or sealer recommended by the mastic manufacturer.

Laying out the tile pattern

Pattern layout typically follows one of two methods. One is symmetrical layout. The other is a one edge layout.

Symmetrical layout. A symmetrical layout begins at a center point. Tile is laid from the center outward, Fig. 15-35. Mark the layout with centerlines for the width and length of the area to be tiled. Use a pencil or chalk line.

One edge layout. A one edge layout begins at one edge of the surface. For a countertop, the edge is the front corner of the counter. Tile is laid from the front edge beginning in the center of the counter. Proced toward the counter ends and back, Fig. 15-36.

A one edge layout is also used to install wainscoting. *Wainscoting* is a wall tiled partway from the floor toward the ceiling. The starting edge may be the floor or the top edge of the wainscoting. The height of the wainscoting typically is determined by the number of tile to be laid and the spacing between tile. This avoids having to cut tile at the top or bottom. With an accurate layout, you may need to cut tile only where they meet at an inside corner.

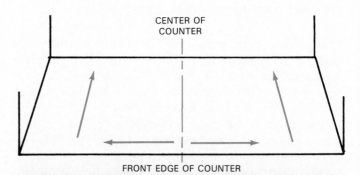

Fig. 15-36. A one edge tile layout begins at the front edge. This type of layout is common for countertops.

Applying the adhesive

Tile mastic is a slow-drying adhesive. It can be applied to a large area without fear of the adhesive setting up too quickly. Spread the mastic at room temperature with a notched trowel, Fig. 15-37.

Setting full tile

Full tiles are easy to set. (Setting is another term for positioning.) Start from the layout lines. The

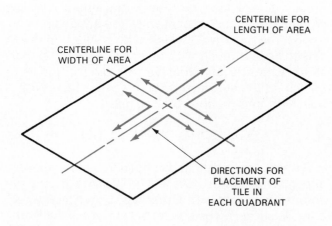

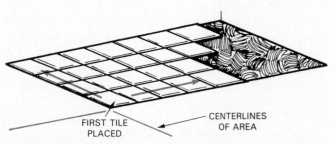

Fig. 15-35. A symmetrical tile layout begins at the center of the area to be tiled. Then lay the tile toward the wall along the centerlines.

lines should be visible through the mastic. Set full tile as follows:

1. Place the first tile against the layout line.
2. Twist it slightly as you align it. This creates a better bond between the tile and mastic. (Do not slide the tile. Sliding removes the mastic.)
3. Remove any adhesive on the tile surface.
4. Space the individual tiles using edge tabs on the tile. (The tabs should touch each other.)

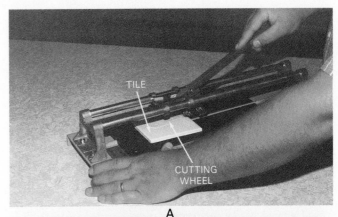

A

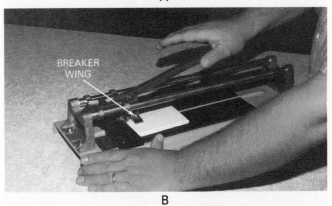

B

Fig. 15-38. A tile cutter scores and breaks tile easily. A—Place marked tile in cutter. Pull the handle toward you to score the tile. B—Locate the breaker wing over the tile and push the handle down to fracture the workpiece.

Fig. 15-37. A notched trowel spreads mastic evenly.

Setting partial tile

Partial tile is cut and set in areas where full tile will no longer fit. There are several methods to cut tile. One is to fracture the tile with a tile cutter or tile nippers. The other is to saw the tile with a carbide blade.

Tile cutter. Use a tile cutter for straight line fracturing. The break may be made parallel or diagonal to the edge depending on your layout. First, score the tile with the cutter wheel, Fig. 15-38A. Then locate the breaking wing over the tile. Press the cutter handle downward. The breaking wing fractures the tile, Fig. 15-38B.

Tile nippers. A tile nippers removes small pieces of tile. It works best for irregular shaped breaks. First, mark the desired shape of the tile with a crayon. Chip away at the tile by squeezing the nippers, then giving a slight downward pressure, Fig. 15-39. Remove small pieces until you reach the crayon line.

Carbide blade. Carbide edged blades are available for saber saws and hacksaws. Mark the tile with a crayon and saw just inside the line. A hacksaw

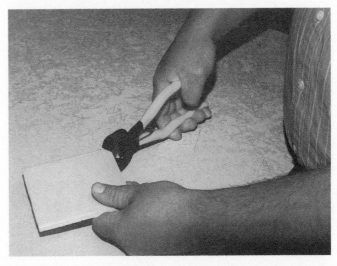

Fig. 15-39. Tile nippers chip off bits of tile for irregular shapes.

works well for irregular shapes, Fig. 15-40A. A saber saw can be used to make holes for pipes or fixtures, Fig. 15-40B.

Set partial tile as you would full tile. Once the partial tile is set, clean all tiles with tile cleaner. Allow the tile mastic to set for 18 to 24 hours. Then apply grout.

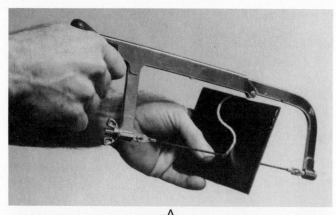

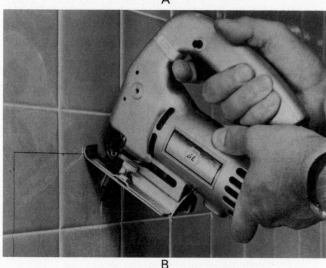

Fig. 15-40. Sawing tile. A—Cut curves with a carbide blade hack saw. B—Cut holes in tile with a saber saw. (Remington Arms Co.)

Grouting

Grout is a form of cement applied in the space between tile. It covers the space between and over the tile tabs. Mix grout by adding water to the dry grout powder. The mixture should be about the consistency of toothpaste. Allow the grout to set for a few minutes. Then mix it again to assure an even texture.

Grout paste has a short pot life. *Pot life* is the time grout or other adhesives can be applied. Mix only the amount which you can spread in 10 minutes.

Apply grout with a *grout float.* This tool is a felt covered block. Use it to press the grout into the space between tiles. Then wipe away excess grout with the float held at a 45° angle to the tile lines.

Allow the grout to set for 15 to 20 minutes. Then clean all residue from the tile faces and grouted spaces with a damp sponge. Rinse the grout out of the sponge frequently. Allow the grout to dry for three to four hours. Then wipe the tile and tile lines lightly with a rough cloth, such as burlap. Remove any remaining dry grout with tile cleaner. Allow the grout to dry for 48 hours before sealing the surface.

Sealing tile

Sealer protects the tiled surface. It is usually a silicone based liquid. Sealer is applied in two ways. If the tile is unglazed, spread sealer over both tile and grout lines. If the tile is glazed, apply sealer only to the grout lines. Use a small artist's paint brush to prevent getting sealer on the tile.

Drilling tile

Tile can be drilled to mount fixtures, such as towel bars or soap dishes. Use a carbide tipped glass drill. Select the bit size for the diameter of anchors used with the mounting screws. Drill slowly to prevent chipping the tile.

SLATE TILE

Slate is an alternative to ceramic tile for floors and counter or table surfaces. *Slate* is a rock that breaks naturally in parallel layers. It may be black, gray, red, or green. It is generally fractured into 1/4 in. and 1/2 in. thicknesses. Sometimes the slabs of slate are irregular shapes. They may be cut into squares or rectangles with an abrasive saw, Fig. 15-41. The shapes may be random or all one size. Sawed slate edges are not often finished (smooth). Plan to cover them with some kind of edging or moulding. Check with your tile distributer for available slate sizes, color, and finishes.

INSTALLING SLATE TILE

Slate tile is installed much like ceramic tile. First, lay out the tile to form a desired pattern. Leave about 3/8 in. between pieces. The pattern may be random or based on colors or sizes. Partial slate tile is cut with a carbide edged blade.

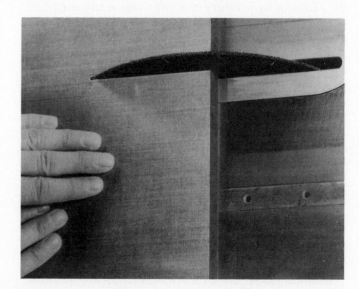

Fig. 15-41. Cut slate with an abrasive blade. Guard is removed to show operation. (Remington Arms Co.)

Lay the pieces aside in the order you want to use them. With a notched trowel, spread mastic on the surface to be slated. Position the pieces as you laid them out originally. Allow the mastic to set at least 24 hours. Press grout into the space between pieces. After the grout has dried, seal the slate surface.

SUMMARY

Glass, plastic, and ceramics are functional and decorative materials. Glass windows and ceramic tile have been used for thousands of years. Molded glass has been formed into knobs and pulls in the past two hundred years. During the past century, plastic has replaced many glass and ceramic products. Plastic typically is stronger, more flexible, and less apt to break. Plastic also can be formed or bonded into complete furniture pieces.

Glass is available in many forms. Flat glass is the most common glass form for cabinetry. Glass may be clear, decorative, tinted, or mirrored. It may also be tempered to increase its strength. Leaded glass panels are made with decorative glass pieces and lead came. The came is soldered around the edges of the glass. Colored glass is used to make stained glass panels.

Plastics may be used to replace other materials. Clear sheet plastic may replace glass. Molded plastic can replace wood components. Plastics are either thermoset or thermoplastics. Thermoset plastic products are permanently shaped during manufacture. Thermoplastics may be heated and reshaped.

Tile may cover floors, cabinet tops, and table surfaces. Ceramic tile is made of baked clay. Tiles are bonded to the surface with mastic. Spaces between tile are filled with grout. Slate, a form of rock, is applied like ceramic tile. Slate size may be random or all one dimension.

Two methods for cutting glass, plastics, and ceramic are fracturing and sawing. Fracturing involves scoring the material and breaking it along the score line. When sawing glass or ceramics, use a carbide tipped blade. Certain plastics also require a carbide blade.

THINK SAFETY—ACT SAFELY

Many health and safety problems are associated with the materials discussed in this chapter. Follow the precautions below.
1. Wear eye protection.
2. Wear leather-palm gloves while working with glass, plastic and ceramic products.
3. Wear a respirator and rubber gloves while working with fiberglass.
4. Work with lead and fiberglass in a well ventilated area.
5. Lead is toxic. Keep your hands away from your face and mouth when handling it.
6. Be aware of allergies to certain substances.

CABINETMAKING TERMS

Glass, plastic, thermoplastic, thermoset plastic, celluloid, bakelite, ceramic, glaze, slate, fiberglass, flat glass, float glass, sheet glass, plate glass, tempered glass, annealing, decorative glass, patterned glass, etched glass, cut glass, enameled glass, tinted glass, mirror glass, scoring, fracturing, grinding, polishing, mounting glass, leaded panels, stained glass panels, lead came binder, lead came edges, solder, flux, grout, cement grout, resinous grout, acrylic plastic, polyester resin, polyethylene, polystyrene, polyurethane, backer board, electric strip heater, cement, solvent, backsplash, ceramic mat, ceramic mosaic, symmetrical tile layout, one edge tile layout, wainscoting, tile mastic, tile cutter, tile nippers, carbide blade, grout float, slate.

TEST YOUR KNOWLEDGE

1. Two forms of glass, plastic, and ceramics are _____ and _____.
2. Mats, rolls, and rovings are forms of _____.
3. During manufacture, glass may be toughened by:
   a. Annealing.
   b. Curing.
   c. Quenching.
   d. Tempering.
4. List the three types of flat glass.
5. What is the difference between ''sheet glass'' and a sheet of glass?
6. The two steps to cut glass are _____ and _____.
7. Describe the four types of decorative glass.
8. List the three methods to fracture glass.
9. Leaded panels are held together with _____ and _____.
10. Explain the steps to assemble leaded glass panels.
11. Describe the two classifications of plastics.
12. Which classification of plastic is suitable for forming? List three formable plastics.
13. Fiberglass is a mixture of glass fibers and _____.
14. Explain the difference between cement and solvent bonding.
15. Ceramic tile can be cut with a hacksaw. True or False?
16. Ceramic tile are spaced by _____.
17. Describe two methods of laying out tile. Which is appropriate for a table top?
18. Sealer should be applied over glazed tile. True or False?

Chapter 16
MECHANICAL FASTENERS

After studying this chapter, you will be able to:
- *Define the purpose for fasteners in cabinetmaking.*
- *List the applications of nails for fastening cabinetry.*
- *Describe the various types of screws and their uses.*
- *Select fasteners to attach cabinets to hollow and solid walls.*
- *Explain the convenience of ready-to-assemble (RTA) cabinets.*
- *Select fasteners for assembling RTA cabinets.*

Cabinets may be assembled and installed with mechanical fasteners. *Fasteners* include nails, staples, screws, anchors, bolts, and RTA (ready to assemble) fasteners. The type of fastener you select depends on the required strength of the joint. Threaded fasteners hold tighter than those without threads. RTA fasteners allow you to disassemble and reassemble cabinets easily. RTA fasteners also work well with manufactured panel products. Other fasteners have limited holding power in these materials.

Fasteners are made of both metal and nonmetal materials. Most are metal such as steel, aluminum, copper, or brass. A few are made of fiber or plastic. Metal fasteners used in cabinets and furniture often are coated with paint or plated with another metal. Platings include brass, copper, chrome, zinc, and nickel. Steel fasteners may be galvanized (plated with zinc) to prevent rust. Others include paint and lacquer which may be sprayed onto fasteners. Brass or copper fasteners may be used. However, these are more expensive than steel fasteners.

UNTHREADED FASTENERS

Unthreaded fasteners, such as nails and staples are selected for less demanding purposes. They have less holding power than screws. As a result, they rarely are used to assemble major parts of the cabinet. Nails are typically used to attach trim to the front of a cabinet. You can set nails below the surface of the trim and cover them with wood putty. Both nails and staples are widely used to attach cabinet backs.

The most common unthreaded fasteners are nails and staples. Corrugated fasteners, chevrons, and Skotch fasteners are also discussed.

NAILS

Nails are made of steel, aluminum, brass, and copper. There are many types of nails. Those used for cabinetmaking are, Fig. 16-1:
1. Common nails.
2. Box nails.
3. Casing nails.
4. Finishing nails.
5. Brads.
6. Wire nails.

Common nails are most often used in carpentry for framing. In cabinetmaking, you might install them where great strength is required. Use common nails where the appearance of the nail does not matter.

Box nails are similar to common nails but are thinner and have smaller heads. They are less likely to split the lumber than common nails. Box nails are used for light construction work. Rarely are they used in assembling cabinetry.

Casing nails have cone shaped heads. They are normally installed where the head is driven below

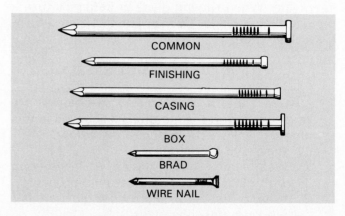

Fig. 16-1. There are many nail sizes and head shapes for you to select. Ringed shanks give extra holding power. (Continental Steel Corp.)

the surface with a nail set. The small hole that remains is covered with wood putty, Fig. 16-2. Casing nails are slightly larger in diameter than finishing nails. Use them to attach trim.

Finishing nails have barrel shaped heads. Like casing nails, they are usually countersunk and covered with wood putty. However, they can be installed flush with the surface of the wood.

Brads look like small finishing nails. They are recommended for light assembly work. They are thinner, shorter, and smaller than finish nails. Brads are often used to attach a back to a cabinet, Fig. 16-3.

Wire nails are sized like brads, except they have flat heads. Like common or box nails, they are not set below the wood surface.

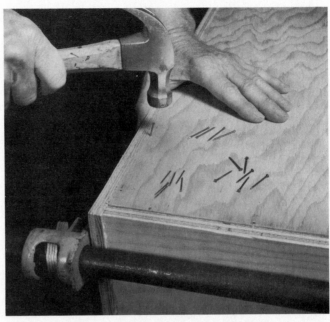

Fig. 16-3. While the glued cabinet assembly is still clamped, the 1/4 in. plywood cabinet back is attached with brads. The back keeps the assembly square. (American Plywood Assoc.)

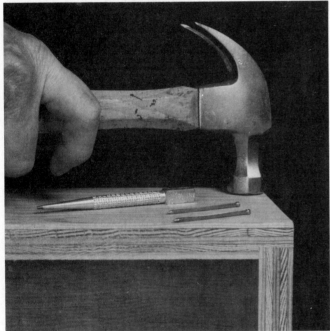

Nail sizes

Nails are measured by two systems: penny size and specific dimension. Common, box, casing, and finishing nails are measured in "penny size." The symbol for penny is "d." The penny size was a standard used in England which meant penny weight per hundred nails. Now the *penny size* refers to nail gauge and length, Fig. 16-4. Brads and wire nails

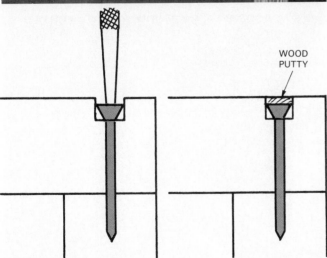

Fig. 16-2. Casing nails have cone-shaped heads so they can be set. Top. The nail is first driven close to surface. (American Plywood Assoc.) Bottom left. Then it is driven below the surface using a nail set. Bottom right. Wood putty covers the nail hole.

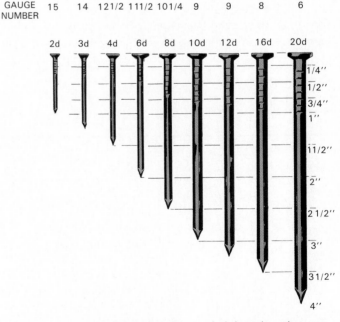

Fig. 16-4. Nails are sized according to their length and gauge thickness of the shank. Size is indicated in pennies (d). (Graves-Humphreys, Inc.)

are measured by gauge and length. The wire gauge numbers range from 12 to 20. The larger the number, the thinner the nail. Lengths range from 3/8 in. to 1 1/2 in., Fig. 16-5.

Nail coatings

Nails may be coated or uncoated. Uncoated steel nails are likely to rust in humid conditions. Rust can stain the wood. *Zinc coated* (galvanized) nails resist rust.

Cement coated nails are covered with an adhesive during manufacture. As the nail is driven, heat from friction softens the adhesive. Later, as the adhesive cools, it hardens creating a bond between the nail and the wood. This increases holding power.

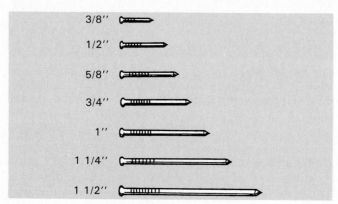

Fig. 16-5. Common brad sizes.
(National Retail Hardware Assoc.)

Fastening with nails

To fasten two workpieces with nails it is important, first of all, to select the correct size and type of nail. For best results, the length of the nail should be three times the thickness of the top workpiece. See the example in Fig. 16-6. Recommended nail types and sizes for plywood are given in Fig. 16-7.

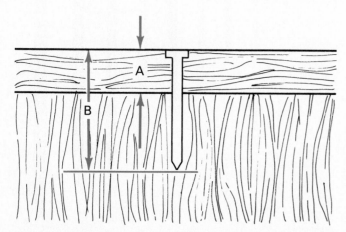

Fig. 16-6. Generally, nails should be three times as long as the top workpiece, A. This assures that 2/3 of the nail is holding the base workpiece, B. (National Retail Hardware Assoc.)

Plywood Thickness	Type of Nail	Size
3/4''	casing	6d
	finishing	6d
5/8''	finishing	6d-8d
1/2''	finishing	4d-6d
3/8''	finishing	3d-4d
1/4''	brads	3/4''-1''
	finishing	3d

Fig. 16-7. Nail types and sizes for plywood.
(National Retail Hardware Assoc., American Plywood Assoc.)

Nails are easy to drive into soft wood. In harder woods, you might apply wax or soap to the nail. For very hard woods, drill a pilot hole slightly smaller than the diameter of the nail, Fig. 16-8.

Fig. 16-8. Drilling a pilot hole will prevent the board from splitting when driving nails.

There are two methods of fastening with nails: straight nailing and toenailing. Straight nailing is driving the nail directly through the top workpiece into the base. Never drive two nails into the same grain line. The wood is likely to split, Fig. 16-9.

Toenailing is used to fasten a T-joint, Fig. 16-10. When toenailing, first start driving the nail perpendicular to the workpiece about 1/8 in. (3 mm) deep. Then push it to a 30° angle and drive it the rest of the way.

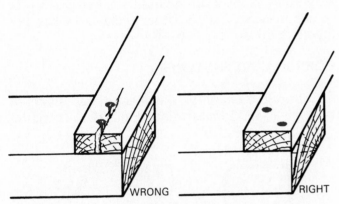

Fig. 16-9. Never drive two nails in the same grain. Stagger them to reduce splitting.

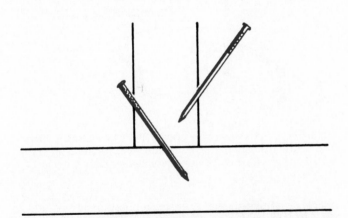

Fig. 16-10. Toenailing is used when straight nailing cannot be done.

Accurately place nails that will support heavy loads. Locate them so that the weight of the load tends to drive them deeper. Nails can also be placed so that the load is supported by the shear angle of the nail. (The shear angle is across the nail.) Avoid driving nails where the load is likely to pull them out, Fig. 16-11.

When attaching wood trim or other visible materials, you may want to hide the nail. Use casing nails, finishing nails, or brads with a nail set for this purpose. A small indent in the head centers the nail set. First, drive nail to within 1/8 in. of the surface. Then place the nail set on the nail head and strike it. Drive

the nail just below the surface. Then fill the hole with wood putty.

Nails also can be concealed in the wood. A splinter of wood is peeled up from the location where the nail is to be driven, Fig. 16-12. Do so with a utility knife. Once the nail is installed, glue the sliver back down.

The force of the load could pull this joint apart.

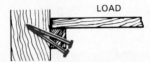

Here, the load drives the nail deeper and also shifts to the two nails placed in shear position.

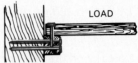

Here's a joint that won't hold!

Nails in shear position support the load better.

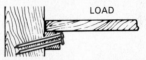

The best nail position for a heavy load uses the load weight to drive the nail deeper.

Nails driven in parallel to each other are easily pulled up. But when they are angled, they reinforce each other.

Fig. 16-11. The angle at which nails are driven partly determines their holding power. (Continental Steel Corp.)

Fig. 16-12. Nails can be concealed under peeled-up shaving of wood. (National Retail Hardware Assoc.)

STAPLES

Staples appear like U-shaped nails. They mostly are installed in hidden areas, such as to attach cabinet backs, Fig. 16-13.

Staples are specified by width and leg length. Width is given by a specificiation number. Legs are 1/4 in. to 9/16 in. long. Cabinetmakers install most staples with spring-action staple guns, Fig. 16-14.

When fastened, the staple should be flush with the surface. Sometimes the staple sticks up after using the staple gun to install it. This means the legs are too long for that material. If it penetrates the surface, the material is too soft or the legs are too short, Fig. 16-15.

Staples with added holding power include outward-flaring, self-crimping, and two-way splay staples. *Outward-flaring* staples have chisel-like points beveled on the inside edges. As the staple is driven, the legs are forced to spread. This staple locks firmly in place so it does not pull out. *Self-crimping* staples work like outward-flaring staples.

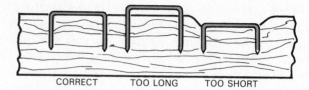

Fig. 16-15. When driven, the staple should be flush with the wood.

However, the staple legs are forced inward. *Two-way splay* staples are pointed so that one leg is forced forward, and the other backward when the staple is driven, Fig. 16-16.

CORRUGATED FASTENERS

Corrugated fasteners are sheet metal fasteners typically used for miter joints, Fig. 16-17. Lengths

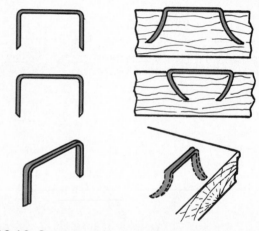

Fig. 16-16. Special staples anchor themselves when driven. Top. Outward-flaring staple. Middle. Inward-crimping staple. Bottom. Two-way splay staple.

Fig. 16-13. Staples can be easily driven to hold cabinet backs. Using this stapler requires a mallet. (American Plywood Assoc.)

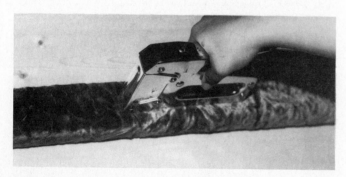

Fig. 16-14. Most staple guns use a spring-action handle for ease of operation.

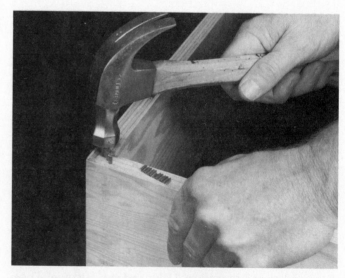

Fig. 16-17. Corrugated fasteners typically fasten miter joints. (American Plywood Assoc.)

range from 3/8 in. to 3/4 in. Width is given in numbers or corrugations. A size may be given as 3/4 in. x 5 corrugations. The fastener is usually hidden, although wood putty may be used to cover it.

CHEVRONS

Chevrons are angled fasteners, Fig. 16-18. They are ideal for picture frames and other products with miter joints. Each side is about 1 in. long. Chevrons penetrate 3/8 in. (9 mm) into the wood.

SKOTCH FASTENERS

Skotch fasteners are eight prong staples which join parts without cutting or splintering wood fibers. There are a variety of sizes, making them more versatile than chevrons. They are numbered from 0 to 3, Fig. 16-19.

CLAMP NAILS

Clamp nails are shaped pieces of steel, Fig. 16-20. They are inserted into kerfs made in both workpieces to be joined. The kerf should be as wide as the thickness of the clamp nail web. Cut the kerfs accurately so that a perfect fit is obtained. As the clamp nail is driven, it aligns the joint. The tapered edges draw the two workpieces of wood together.

Clamp nails are sold in a variety of widths and lengths. Widths are designated by number. The number, placed over 16, tells the width. For example, a No. 6 clamp nail is 6/16 in. (3/8 in.) wide. A No. 14 nail is 14/16 in. (7/8 in.) wide. Lengths range from 1/2 in. to 5 in.

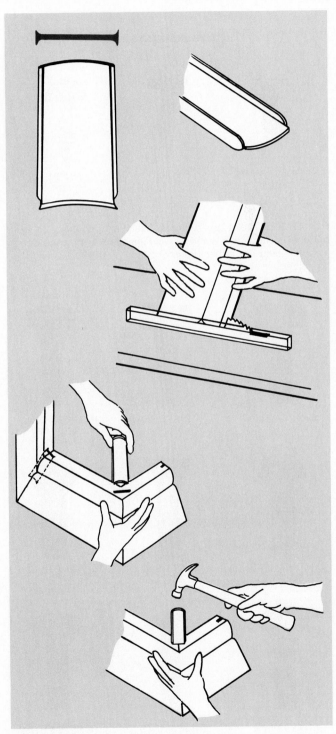

Fig. 16-20. Drive clamp nails into aligned saw kerfs (slots). They are made before the nail is inserted. When driven, a clamp nail aligns the two workpieces as it draws them together. (Wash Co.)

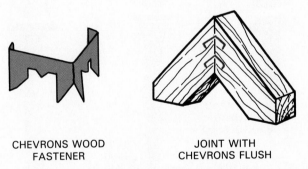

CHEVRONS WOOD FASTENER

JOINT WITH CHEVRONS FLUSH

Fig. 16-18. Chevrons work pieces together to make a tight joint.

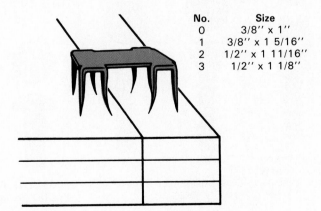

No.	Size
0	3/8'' x 1''
1	3/8'' x 1 5/16''
2	1/2'' x 1 11/16''
3	1/2'' x 1 1/8''

Fig. 16-19. Skotch fasteners have eight staple-like prongs. They are installed with a hammer.

PINS AND TACKS

Smaller nail-like fasteners with special uses include pins and tacks, Fig. 16-21. *Escutcheon pins* are small brass nails with round heads. They are used for decorative purposes. Lengths range from 1/4 in. to 1 1/4 in. (6 mm to 30 mm). Pin diameter is given in wire gauges.

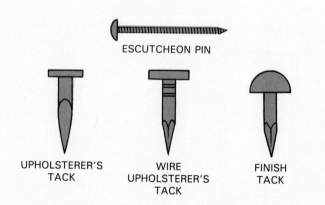

Fig. 16-21. Tacks are typically used in upholstery to hold material or metal to a wood frame. Finish tacks and escutcheon pins are either brass or brass plated steel.

Tacks are used primarily in upholstery. Some are meant to be hidden. These are designed to secure springs, wire, or cloth to a frame. Decorative tacks are those which are visible. Some have rounded heads made of brass or copper.

THREADED FASTENERS

Threaded fasteners, such as screws and bolts have more holding power than nails. They also permit disassembly and reassembly. Some thread directly into lumber, wood products, metal, or plastic. Others pass through the workpiece and are secured with a nut or anchor.

Threaded fasteners are made of steel, brass, aluminum, and copper. They can be electroplated with zinc, chrome, or nickel. Painted finishes are common also. Those made of steel may be blued to prevent rust. Bluing involves heating the fastener to a certain temperature. The fastener is then dipped in oil, turning it dark blue. Unfinished steel screws are referred to as *bright.* When screws will be visible in the cabinet, use those that are finished.

There is a wide variety of head shapes for screws and bolts, Fig. 16-22. The head determines the type

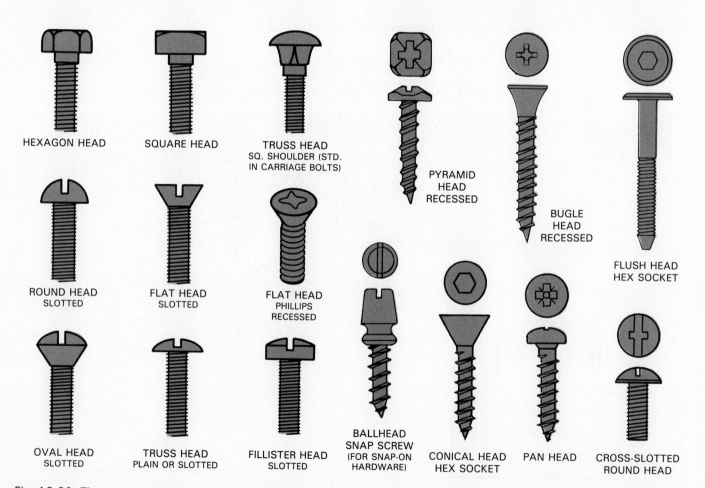

Fig. 16-22. There are many head shapes for screws and bolts. The fastener you wish to use may be available with one or all of these head shapes. (Liberty Hardware)

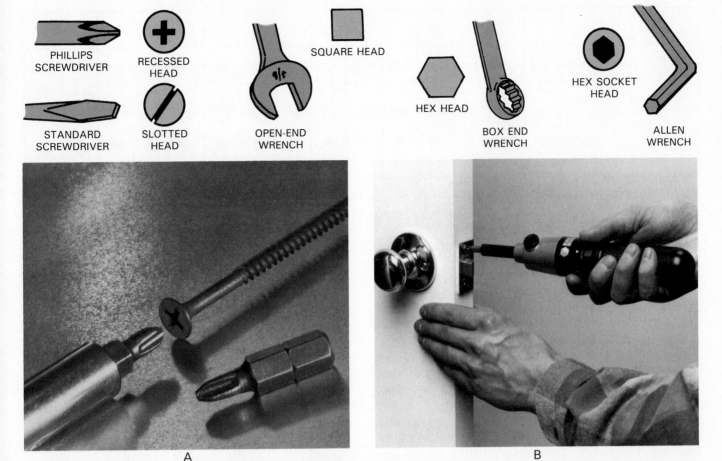

PHILLIPS
SCREWDRIVER

RECESSED
HEAD

STANDARD
SCREWDRIVER

SLOTTED
HEAD

OPEN-END
WRENCH

SQUARE HEAD

HEX HEAD

BOX END
WRENCH

HEX SOCKET
HEAD

ALLEN
WRENCH

A

B

Fig. 16-23. A—Choose an appropriate screwdriver or wrench for the head shape of the fastener. (National Retail Hardware Assoc.) B—Screwbits and a portable drill make driving screws easier. (Black & Decker)

of screwdriver or wrench you should use, Fig. 16-23. Slotted head screws require flat blade screwdrivers. Recessed (Phillips) head screws require a Phillips screwdriver. Hex socket heads require an Allen wrench.

Typical screw products used for cabinetry are:
1. Wood screws.
2. Particleboard screws.
3. One-piece connectors.
4. Sheet metal screws.
5. Lag screws.
6. Cup and shoulder hooks.
7. Machine screws and stove bolts.
8. Cap screws and machine bolts.
9. Carriage bolts
10. Joint connector bolts.

WOOD SCREWS

Wood screws serve a wide range of general assembly purposes. They are the most used fastener in cabinetry.

Wood screws are specified by shank gauge, length, head shape, and finish, Fig. 16-24. Gauge numbers for screws differ from those for nails. As the gauge number increases, the diameter of the

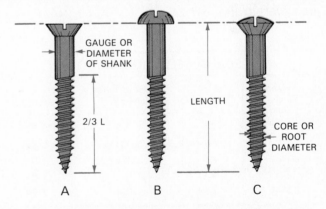

GAUGE OR DIAMETER OF SHANK

2/3 L

LENGTH

CORE OR ROOT DIAMETER

A   B   C

Fig. 16-24. Select wood screws according to head shape, shank gauge, and length. (Forest Products Laboratory)

shank increases .013 in. (0.3 mm), Fig. 16-25. The size of the head also increases accordingly.

The length of screws is measured from the tip of the threads to the top middle, or bottom of the head. See Fig. 16-24. Threads are cut at least 2/3 the length of the shank.

Screws are sold singularly, in plastic packages, or by the box. Boxes may contain 50, 100, or 144 (one gross) screws. To order screws, specify:

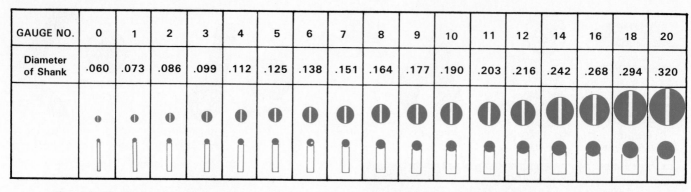

GAUGE NO.	0	1	2	3	4	5	6	7	8	9	10	11	12	14	16	18	20
Diameter of Shank	.060	.073	.086	.099	.112	.125	.138	.151	.164	.177	.190	.203	.216	.242	.268	.294	.320

Fig. 16-25. These are the most common gauge sizes for screws. Head size increases with gauge numbers.

1 box—1 1/2 x No. 8—Flat Head Bright Slotted wood screws.

or

1 box—1 1/4 x No. 8—Round head—Nickel plated Phillips wood screws.

Installing wood screws

Several steps are involved when installing wood screws. They include: selecting screws and screwdrivers, laying out holes, drilling holes, countersinking, counterboring, and driving screws.

Selecting screws and screwdrivers. Select screws at least three times the thickness of the workpiece you are fastening. This assures that all of the threads will enter the base piece. Select the smallest gauge screw which will provide the required holding power. Generally smaller gauge screws are for thinner woods. Recommended screw sizes for plywood are given in Fig. 16-26.

SCREW SELECTION CHART			
Plywood Thickness	screw	Flat-Head Screws length	pilot hole
3/4''	#8	1 1/2''	5/32''
5/8''	#8	1 1/4''	5/32''
1/2''	#6	1 1/4''	1/8''
3/8''	#6	1''	1/8''
1/4''	#4	3/4''	7/64''

Fig. 16-26. Screw sizes for plywood.
(National Retail Hardware Assoc.)

Select the proper screwdriver or wrench for the type of screw. The blade of a standard screwdriver should be as wide as the screw slot, Fig. 16-27. The blade of a Phillips screwdriver should fit snugly in the recessed head.

Laying out holes. Lay out and mark where holes will be located. Then, with a hammer, tap the tip of a nail or scratch awl on the layout mark. This small hole helps guide the drill.

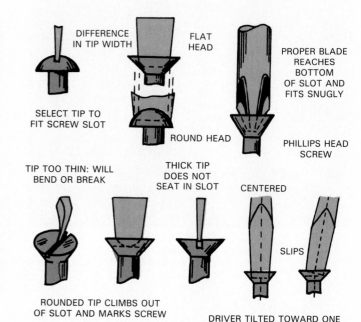

Fig. 16-27. Choose a screwdriver which properly fits the screw head.

Drilling holes. Two or more different holes are drilled when fastening wood with screws, Fig. 16-28. The first is the pilot hole. It is drilled through both workpieces the full length of the screw. Next, bore out the clearance hole in the upper workpiece. The clearance hole provides room for the shank of the screw.

If the holes are not drilled wide or deep enough, the wood is apt to split. The size of the pilot hole is larger for hard, dense woods. This makes inserting the screw easier. Sizes for clearance and pilot holes are given in Fig. 16-29.

Multioperational bits may be used to drill pilot and clearance holes at the same time. They are sized according to the screw gauge and length, Fig. 16-30. Multioperational bits are called Screw-mate drills by one manufacturer. In addition to pilot and clearance holes, they may also drill countersinks and counterbores.

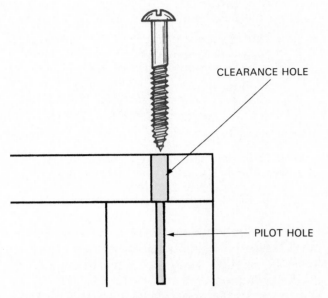

CLEARANCE HOLE

PILOT HOLE

Fig. 16-28. Drill clearance and pilot holes before the screw is inserted.

Countersinking. Flat head screws and others with tapered heads require *countersinking*. A countersink is a drill bit with a cone-shaped tip. Use the countersink to enlarge the top of the clearance hole, Fig. 16-31. This allows the screw to be driven flush with the surface of the wood.

Counterboring. Counterboring allows the screw head to be below the surface of the wood. Drill clearance and pilot holes. Then drill the counterbore just larger than the screw head. Once the screw is inserted, cover the hole with a plug, a button, or wood putty, Fig. 16-32. Select the proper diameter counterbore for plugs and buttons so they will fit.

Driving screws. Drive screws in a clockwise direction by hand or with a screw gun. As the screw turns, the threads dig into the sides of the pilot hole. If the screw holes are drilled properly, you should be able to insert the screw with little effort. Be careful not to apply too much torque or the screw will break. This is especially true with aluminum or

Screw Gauge	0	1	2	3	4	5	6	7	8	9	10	11	12	14	16	18	20
Clearance Hole Hard & Soft Wood	1/16	5/64	3/32	7/64	7/64	1/8	9/64	5/32	11/64	3/16	3/16	13/64	7/32	1/4	17/64	19/64	21/64
Pilot Hole Soft Wood	1/64	1/32	1/32	3/64	3/64	1/16	1/16	1/16	5/64	5/64	3/32	3/32	7/64	7/64	9/64	9/64	11/64
Pilot Hole Hard Wood	1/32	1/32	3/64	1/16	1/16	5/64	5/64	3/32	3/32	7/64	7/64	1/8	1/8	9/64	5/32	3/16	13/64

Fig. 16-29. Clearance and pilot holes are sized according to the screw shank and core diameters.

Fig. 16-30. Multioperational bits replace drilling three separate holes. (Stanley)

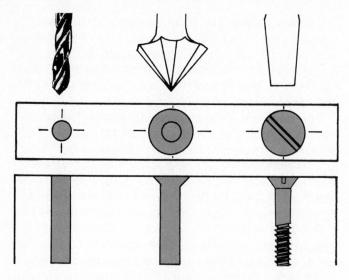

Fig. 16-31. Countersinking permits flat head screws to be flush with the wood.

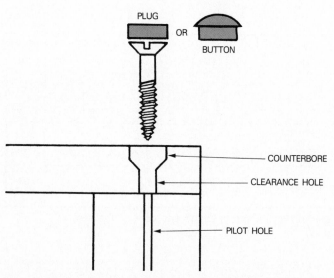

Fig. 16-32. A plug or button covers the screw in a counterbored hole.

brass screws in dense material. Applying wax to the screw threads will make it easier to drive.

PARTICLEBOARD SCREWS

Particleboard screws are designed to hold better in weaker panel products, such as particleboard, composite panels, and waferboard. They have coarser threads than wood screws, Fig. 16-33. This allows for more wood fibers between threads. Particleboard screws may be used with lumber. However, they are more difficult to install in hard, dense woods.

ONE-PIECE CONNECTORS

Screws with cylinder-shaped tips are typically called *one-piece connectors* or *solo connectors.* They resemble particleboard screws because they

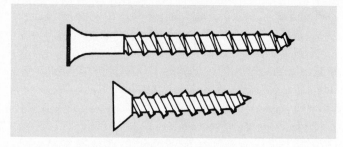

Fig. 16-33. Particleboard screws have coarser threads than wood screws. They hold better in panels made of wood chips. (Liberty Hardware)

have coarse threads, Fig. 16-34A. One-piece connectors have the holding power of particleboard screws. In addition, they also have the ability to align the workpieces.

The screw fits through a clearance hole in the face workpiece. The cylinder-shaped tip then aligns the two workpieces. It centers in a pilot hole, Fig. 16-34B. Both holes must be drilled accurately. When installed, a one-piece connector fits flush with the surface of the wood. A cover cap may be inserted into the socket of the screw head to cover it.

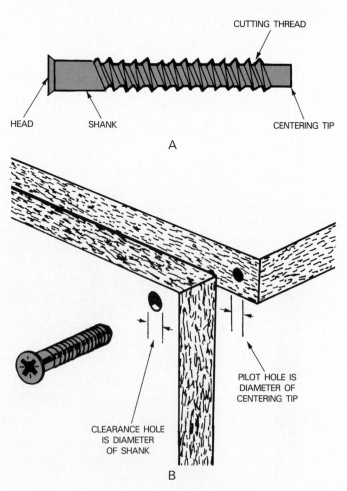

Fig. 16-34. One-piece connectors align the components as they fasten them. (Liberty Hardware)

SHEET METAL SCREWS

Sheet metal screws have threads up to the head, Fig. 16-35. They are ideal for joining metal to wood or wood to metal. Also use them in dense wood because they are made of hardened steel. They are recommended for panel products such as fiberboard.

Sheet metal screws are sized the same as wood screws. Head shapes are either round, flat, pan, oval, truss, or hex. The hex head often has a slot. It can be installed using a wrench or flat blade screwdriver.

Sheet metal screws also attach wood to sheet metal. For example, you might want wood paneling over sheet metal ductwork. Drill a pilot hole through the wood and sheet metal. Then bore the clearance hole in the wood.

LAG SCREWS

Lag screws are installed where the joint requires great holding power. They are commonly used to assemble bunk beds and other large furniture. They are sized by the diameter of the shank and the length. The head may be square or hex shape. Drive the screw with a wrench or socket, Fig. 16-36.

MACHINE SCREWS AND STOVE BOLTS

Machine screws and *stove bolts* have limited use for cabinet work. You usually install handles or pulls with them. They fit through clearance holes in both workpieces and are secured with a nut. Most are threaded the full length, Fig. 16-37. Head shapes and lengths vary like wood screws.

Machine screw and stove bolt threads are measured by two systems: the Unified and American Screw Thread Standard and the ISO Metric Thread Standard. Unified and American Screw Threads include National Coarse (NC) and National Fine (NF) threads. The same diameter NC screw has fewer threads per inch than a NF screw. For example, a 1/4 in. machine screw could have 20 NC threads per inch or 28 NF threads per inch. The specifications will be given as:

1/4—20 NC x 1 1/2 in. (1/4 in. diameter with 20 National Coarse threads per in.)

The diameter may also be given in screw gauge thickness:

#8—32 x 1 1/2 in.

ISO (International Standards Organization) Metric threads are measured by diameter and millimeters per thread. M6 x 2.5 (6 mm shank size and 1.0 mm from thread to thread).

Stove bolts are available in NC threads. They are a poorer quality than machine screws due to their manufacturing process. However, they are less expensive and come with square nuts. Machine screws and nuts are sold separately. Select nuts that match the diameter and thread of the fastener.

CAP SCREWS AND MACHINE BOLTS

Cap screws and *machine bolts* are sized according to the Unified and American Thread Standard

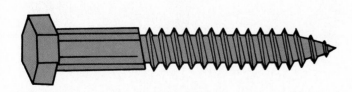

Fig. 16-35. Sheet metal screws have threads their entire length. (Liberty Hardware)

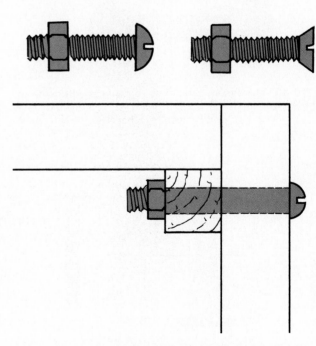

Fig. 16-36. Lag screws may be up to 6 in. long. Use them where strength is essential.

Fig. 16-37. Machine screws and stove bolts may require nuts to fasten workpieces together.
(Liberty Hardware, Graves-Humphreys, Inc.)

and ISO Metric Standard. Those 1 1/2 in. (37 mm) or shorter are fully threaded. Longer fasteners have about 1 1/2 in. of thread plus and unthreaded shank. Cap screws have hex heads. Machine bolts have square heads, Fig. 16-38. They are often electroplated with zinc chromate to prevent rust.

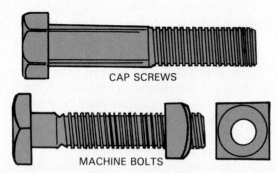

Fig. 16-38. Cap screws and machine bolts are much alike. Cap screws have hex heads. Machine bolts have square heads. (Graves-Humphreys)

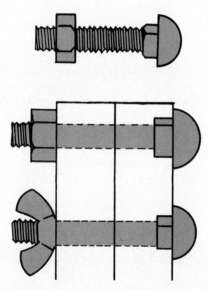

Fig. 16-39. The square shoulder of a carriage bolt holds the bolt from turning in the wood. A wing nut can make installation and removal even easier.

CARRIAGE BOLTS

Carriage bolts have a truss head with a square shoulder, Fig. 16-39. Tightening the nut draws the shoulder into the wood and prevents the bolt from turning in the wood.

Carriage bolts are convenient fasteners for jigs and fixtures. They install and tighten easily. You do not have to hold the bolt with a wrench while tightening the nut. Using a wing nut instead of a hex or square nut simplifies securing the bolt. It can be tightened by hand.

JOINT CONNECTOR BOLTS

Joint connector bolts are made specifically for cabinetmaking. There are different styles of joint connector bolts to fit certain nuts, Fig. 16-40. The head of connector bolts is usually a hex socket. The socket permits the bolt to be fastened tighter than screws with slot or Phillips heads. The socket also allows the flat head to be nearly flush with the surface of the wood. A plastic cap covers the head. Conical head connector bolts are installed when the head must be flush or below the surface of the wood.

The shank of joint connector bolts may be enlarged for use with cap nuts. The clearance hole must be drilled large enough to accept the shank.

CUP HOOKS AND SHOULDER SCREWS

Cup hooks and *shoulder screws* are convenient for storing cups and utensils. Shoulder hooks can be installed in a wall to hang cooking utensils or small tools, Fig. 16-41. Cup hooks can be installed under a shelf.

Cup and shoulder hooks are made out of brass. They often have flanges that reinforce the screw

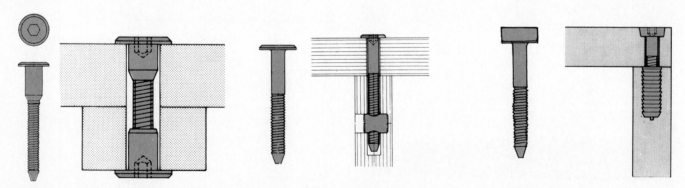

Fig. 16-40. Joint connector bolts are designed specifically for cabinetmaking. Left. Bolt with enlarged shank used with cap nut. Middle. Bolt used with threaded metal cross dowel. Right. Cylindrical head bolt is flush with wood surface. Bolt is threaded into an insert nut. (Liberty Hardware)

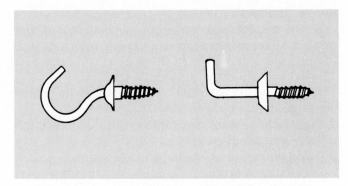

Fig. 16-41. Left. Cup hook. Right. Shoulder hook. (Columbus Hardware)

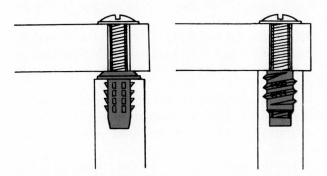

Fig. 16-43. Insert nuts. Left. Knock-in type has teeth. Right. Screw-in type has threads. (Liberty Hardware)

and hide the screw hole. Overall length varies from 7/8 in. to 2 1/8 in. The hook, when installed, may project from 1/2 in. to 1 1/2 in. from the wood.

INSERT NUTS

Install *insert nuts* when frequent assembly and disassembly is desired. Also use them when wood screws lack holding power. The insert nut is installed in the base workpiece. A screw or bolt with NC threads fits into the nut to fasten the assembly, Fig. 16-42.

There are several reasons for using insert nuts and machine screws instead of wood screws. Insert nuts rarely are taken out once driven; thus, they remain secure. Wood screws lose their holding power if the cabinet is taken apart many times. Each time a wood screw is installed, it cuts wood fibers around the pilot hole. If you are repairing furniture which has worn out screw holes, install insert nuts.

You might also select insert nuts if the cabinet is fabricated from weak material, such as particleboard. Insert nuts have teeth for holding power. They may also be glued in place.

Insert nuts may be screw-in or knock-in types, Fig. 16-43. Knock-in insert nuts have teeth or ridges which dig into the wood once they are installed. You

first drill the proper size pilot hole. Then use a hammer to drive in the nut.

Screw-in insert nuts have threads. Again, you must drill a pilot hole. Then use an Allen wrench to screw the nut into the workpiece.

Some knock-in nuts are designed to be inserted with adhesive. They have gaps between ridges to permit glue flow. Apply an adhesive that bonds to both wood and metal.

T-NUTS

T-nuts are similar to insert nuts. They do not have to be held when fastening the bolt. They have prongs which hold in the wood, Fig. 16-44. To insert a T-nut, drill a hole for the barrel. Insert the T-nut barrel into the hole and hammer the nut to a fixed position. Insert the bolt from the opposite side and tighten it.

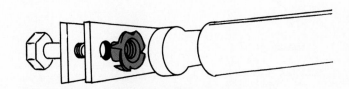

Fig. 16-44. T-nuts hold secure with prongs.

ANCHORS

Anchors are used to attach cabinetry where standard screws and bolts are ineffective. Toggle bolts attach cabinetry to hollow materials, such as gypsum walls and concrete blocks. Screw and bolt anchors attach cabinetry to solid materials, such as brick and concrete.

TOGGLE BOLTS

Toggle bolts include a stove bolt and toggle head. The toggle head spreads open when inserted

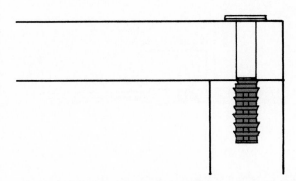

Fig. 16-42. Insert nut with ridges that hold it secure. (Liberty Hardware)

through a clearance hole. Install toggle bolts as follows, Fig. 16-45.

1. Assemble the toggle bolt through the cabinet's mounting holes. The head of the bolt will be on the inside of the cabinet; the toggle head is in back.
2. Drill the appropriate size clearance hole in the wall. The hole must be slightly larger than the diameter of the toggle head wings (when closed).
3. Align the cabinet and bolt assembly over the hole in the wall.
4. Push the toggle bolt through the hole until the wings spring open.
5. Tighten the bolt from the inside of the cabinet to secure the mount.

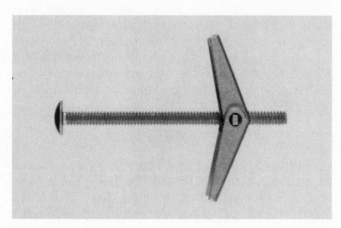

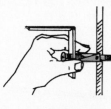

1. Insert bolt through item to be fastened, turn on wings, then fold wings completely back and insert through hole until wings spring open.

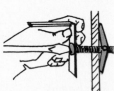

2. Pull back on assembly to hold wings against inside wall—this prevents the wings from spinning while tightening bolt. Turn bolt with screwdriver until firmly tightened.

Fig. 16-45. Toggle bolts attach fixtures to hollow walls. (The Rawlplug Co.)

SCREW AND BOLT ANCHORS

Screw and bolt anchors attach cabinets and other fixtures to solid nonwood materials, such as poured concrete. The anchor is inserted into a hole drilled in the material. A screw or bolt is inserted through the cabinet or fixture, and threads into the anchor. As the screw is tightened the anchor expands. It wedges against the side of the hole to secure the cabinet.

Screw anchors

Screw anchors are used with wood screws, sheet metal screws, or lag screws. Anchors may be made of fiber, metal (typically lead), or plastic (nylon), Fig. 16-46. Install screw anchors as follows:

1. Position the cabinet. Have mounting holes predrilled.
2. Mark the anchor positions on the wall through the mounting holes.
3. Drill holes the diameter of the anchor. For concrete or ceramic tile use a carbide-tipped masonry bit.
4. Slide each anchor into its hole and tap it with a hammer. This will seat it, Fig. 16-47, top.
5. Select the screw. Most anchors have the size of screw you should use marked on them.
6. Position the cabinet over the anchors.
7. Insert the screws through the mounting holes and tighten it, Fig. 16-47, bottom.

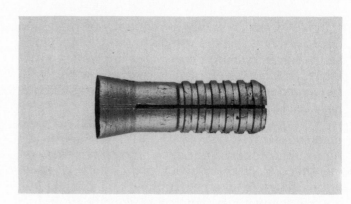

Fig. 16-46. Screw anchors may be made of lead. (The Rawlplug Co.)

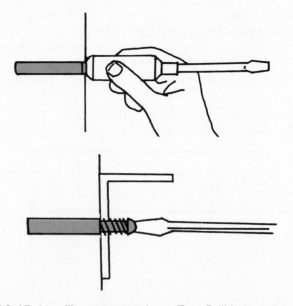

Fig. 16-47. Installing screw anchors. Top. Drill hole and tap in the screw anchor. Bottom. Position fixture and insert screw. (The Rawlplug Co.)

Bolt anchors

Bolt anchors have internal threads to receive a matching machine screw or bolt, Fig. 16-48. Insert the anchor using the procedure for screw anchors. Some bolt anchors must be pre-expanded in the hole with a setting tool.

ONE-PIECE ANCHORS

One-piece anchors combine the anchor and fastener in one assembly, Fig. 16-49. One operation installs the anchor and secures the cabinet or fixture. Install one-piece anchors as follows:
1. Position cabinet against wall or surface. Mounting holes should have been drilled in the cabinet.
2. Drill a hole in the wall through each mount hole. Make holes the same size as the anchor.
3. Set the anchor in the hole and drive it with a hammer. The flange of the anchor will seat against the cabinet.

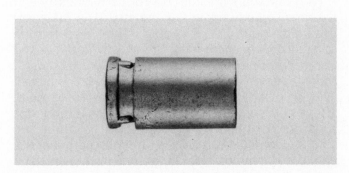

Fig. 16-48. Bolt anchors are prethreaded. (The Rawlplug Co.)

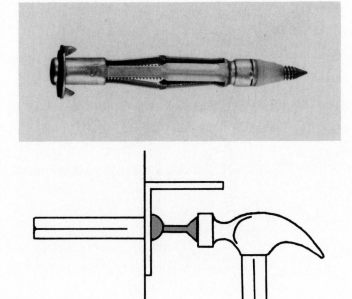

Fig. 16-49. One piece anchors include the anchor and fastener in one assembly. (The Rawlplug Co.)

LIGHT DUTY PLASTIC ANCHORS

Light duty plastic anchors work in any hollow or solid material. Various anchors for drywall, concrete, brick, and thin paneling are available. Fig. 16-50. Install the anchor as follows:
1. Drill a hole in wall the size of a folded anchor, Fig. 16-51A.
2. Fold the anchor and insert it into the hole. Tap it flush with the wall, Fig. 16-51B.
3. For hollow walls, insert a nail to pop the anchor open, Fig. 16-51C.
4. Place the cabinet or fixture over the anchor, Fig. 16-51D.
5. Insert the screw and tighten until the screw head is flush with the cabinet, Fig. 16-51E. Do not overtighten.

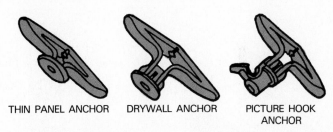

THIN PANEL ANCHOR   DRYWALL ANCHOR   PICTURE HOOK ANCHOR

Fig. 16-50. Plastic anchors are fabricated for various wall thicknesses. (Mechanical Plastics Corp., The Rawlplug Co.)

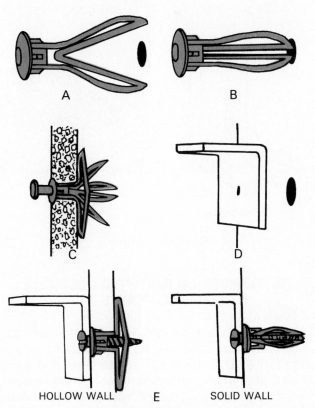

HOLLOW WALL   E   SOLID WALL

Fig. 16-51. Installing plastic anchors. (Mechanical Plastics Corp.)

REPAIR PLATES

Repair plates mend joints where other fasteners have weakened. If appearance is important, do not use them. These plates are made of galvanized steel and are seldom finished to blend with the appearance of the product. Four different types of repair plates are available, Fig. 16-52:

1. Mending plates strengthen butt and lap joints.
2. Flat corner irons strengthen frame corners. Typical uses are for door and window frames.
3. Inside corner braces are installed under chair seats and table tops to support weakening jointwork. They may also support shelves or cabinets.
4. T-plates are attached to frames where rails and stiles meet.

Fig. 16-53. These are ready-to-assemble products. (O'Sullivan Industries)

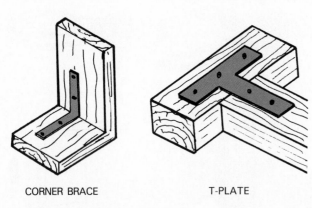

MENDING PLATE   FLAT CORNER IRON

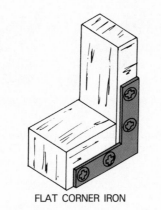

CORNER BRACE   T-PLATE

Fig. 16-52. Repair plates. (Liberty Hardware)

FASTENERS FOR READY-TO-ASSEMBLE (RTA) CABINETS

Ready-To-Assemble (RTA) cabinets are purchased unassembled kits. As a small package or in pieces, the cabinet can fit through small doors and narrow stairways. The consumer then assembles the cabinet with RTA cabinet fasteners. The finished RTA cabinet looks no different than a wood cabinet assembled by a furniture manufacturer, Fig. 16-53.

RTA fasteners are suitable for both industry and the home woodworker. For industry, RTA fasteners eliminate labor for assembly. They also require minimal drilling and boring. Small cabinet shops and home woodworkers often install RTA fasteners. Most fasteners for RTA cabinetry are easy to install. They typically hold as well as screws or glue. However, they permit easy assembly and disassembly of the cabinet.

Many companies manufacture fasteners for RTA cabinetry. Various sizes and styles are available.

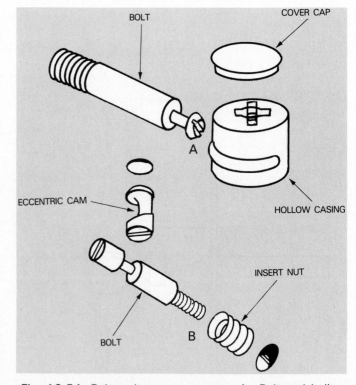

Fig. 16-54. Bolt and cam connectors. A—Bolt and hollow casing. B—Bolt and eccentric cam. (Liberty Hardware)

BOLT AND CAM CONNECTORS

Bolt and cam connecters are common RTA fasteners. They consist of a steel bolt with a special head, a steel or plastic cam, and a cover cap. The cam has a hollow side or interior to receive the bolt. Two types of bolt and cam connectors are available. One has a hollow casing, the other an eccentric cam, Fig. 16-54. Use bolt and cam connectors for cabinet corner and shelf assemblies.

To assemble the cabinet, first insert the bolts. Screw them into the sides of the cabinet at marked locations. Then insert cams in bored holes in components to be fastened, Fig. 16-55. To complete the assembly, fit the shelf (with cam) over the bolt. The hollow opening in the cam should be facing the bolt. Then turn the cam with a screwdriver (or possibly an Allen wrench) to draw the bolt in. When all bolts and cams have been connected and tightened, cover the cams with plastic caps (provided by the manufacturer).

CONCAVE BOLT CONNECTORS

Concave bolt connectors consist of three parts, Fig. 15-56:
1. A steel bolt with a concave hole in the shank.
2. A collar.
3. A set screw.

Concave bolt connectors are assembled in several steps. Insert the bolt into the side of the cabinet. The collar is placed in a predrilled hole in the workpiece to be fastened. To assemble the two components, position the concave bolt into the hole in the collar. A ball end set screw threads into the collar. When tightened, the set screw positions itself in the bolt hole. As the screw positions itself, it draws the bolt toward the collar, Fig. 16-57.

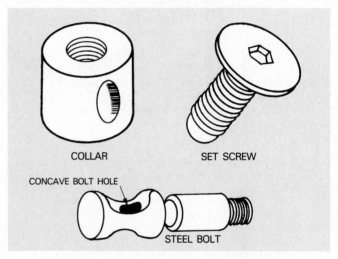

Fig. 16-56. Parts of a concave bolt connector.

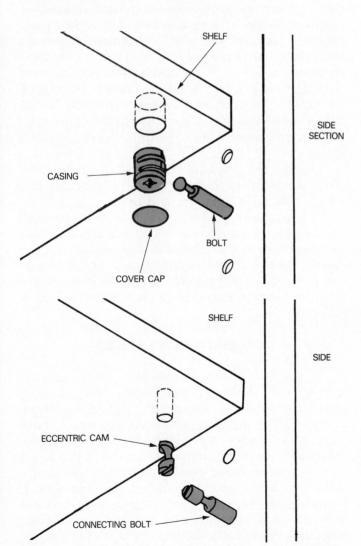

Fig. 16-55. Diagram for assembling cabinets with bolt and cam connectors. Insert bolts into the cabinet sides. Place cams into workpieces to be fastened.

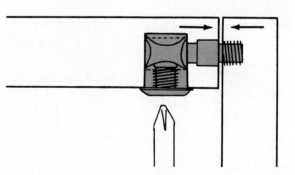

Fig. 16-57. As set screw is tightened, it positions itself in bolt hole. This draws parts together. (Liberty Hardware)

WEDGE PIN CONNECTORS

Wedge pin connectors are more visible than other RTA fasteners. They install quickly and can be used where appearance is not a factor. They consist of three pieces: two plastic mounts and a wedge pin. The mounts are connected to the two pieces of wood to be joined. One mount fits over the other. To fasten the two, a wedge pin is inserted through the fitted mounts, Fig. 16-58.

PLUG AND SOCKET

Plug and socket connectors are designed for joints which require less holding power. The plug is screwed into one workpiece. The socket screws into the other one. The two parts are pressed together to complete the assembly, Fig. 16-59.

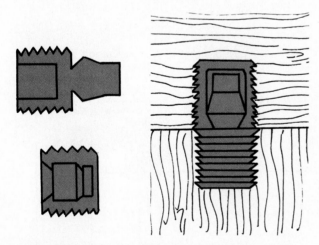

Fig. 16-58. Wedge pin connectors include two plastic parts attached to the wood with screws. A pin is inserted through the two parts to hold the assembly together. (Liberty Hardware)

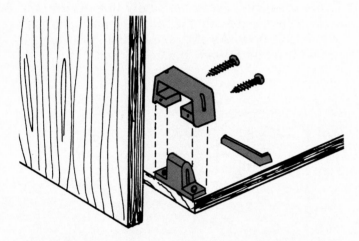

Fig. 16-59. With plug and socket connectors, the two pieces are pressed together to complete the joint. (Liberty Hardware)

SNAP CLIPS

Snap clips are used mostly to attach the toe kick for cabinet bases. Attach clips to the toe kick. Insert bolts inside the base of the cabinet frame. The toe kick is pressed onto the frame, Fig. 16-60. Like plug and socket connectors, snap clips are made for joints requiring little strength.

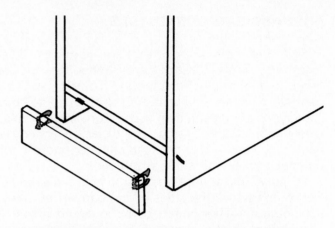

Fig. 16-60. Snap clips are commonly used to attach toe kicks to the bottom of cabinets. (Liberty Hardware)

SUMMARY

Mechanical fasteners include all metal and nonmetal joining devices. Many different styles are available and each may have a general or specific purpose. Wood screws are the most widely used threaded fastener. You will likely assemble cabinets and attach hardware with them. Some unthreaded fasteners are used. Nails and staples are inserted to attach cabinet backs. Casing nails are designed to attach trim; they can be set below the wood. Sheet metal fasteners, such as chevrons and corrugated fasteners, are excellent for fastening miter joints.

Anchors are used to attach cabinets to walls. They are designed for both hollow walls or concrete block, and solid concrete and brick.

RTA fasteners permit cabinets to be assembled and disassembled with ease. The joint strength does not decrease if the cabinet is disassembled many times. Bolt and cam connectors or concave bolt connectors are selected for strength. Snap clips or plug and socket connectors are chosen for quick release.

CABINETMAKING TERMS

Mechanical fastener, common nail, box nail, casing nail, finishing nail, brad, zinc coating, cement-coated nail, escutcheon pin, tack, staple, outward-flaring staple, self-crimping staple, two-way splay staple, corrugated fastener, chevron, Skotch fastener, clamp nail, screw, bolt, wood screw, particleboard screw, one-piece connector, solo connector, sheet metal screw, lag screw, machine screw, stove bolt, cap screw, machine bolt, carriage bolt, joint connector bolt, cup hook, shoulder screw, wire nail, insert nut, T-nut, anchor, toggle bolt, screw anchor, bolt anchor, one-piece anchor, light duty plastic anchor, ready-to-assemble cabinet, knock-down cabinet, bolt and cam connector, concave bolt connector, wedge pin connector, plug and socket connector, snap clip connector.

TEST YOUR KNOWLEDGE

1. The term *penny* and the letter *d* identify sizes for all nails except:
   a. Box nails.
   b. Brads.
   c. Common nails.
   d. Finishing nails.
2. A nail set is placed in the cone-shaped head of a _____ nail to drive it below the surface of the wood.
3. Uncoated steel nails may _____ and cause the wood to stain.
4. Nails are coated with cement to _____.
5. How long should a nail be?
6. Two methods of nailing are _____ and _____.
7. Which of the following sheet metal fasteners can be installed only after making a saw kerf?
   a. Chevron.
   b. Skotch fastener.
   c. Corrugated fastener.
   d. Clamp nail.
8. List three finishes applied to screws.
9. What term indicates that a screw has no finish applied to it?
10. To install wood screws, you must drill _____ and _____ holes.
11. A _____ is drilled in the wood to allow flathead and other tapered head screws to be flush with the wood.
12. Why might machine screws be selected to fasten dense woods?
13. The difference between cap screws and machine bolts is the:
    a. Length of the thread.
    b. Shank diameter.
    c. Shape of the head.
    d. Threads per inch.
14. Describe two features that make joint connector bolts specifically designed for assembling cabinets.
15. List two applications for insert nuts.
16. Anchors are used to attach cabinets to _____ and _____.
17. Explain why a consumer might choose to purchase ready-to-assemble (RTA) cabinets.
18. List two advantages RTA fasteners have over wood screws.

Chapter 17
HARDWARE

After studying this chapter, you will be able to:
☐ *Select knobs and pulls for function and appearance.*
☐ *Install sliding doors.*
☐ *Choose hinges for wood and glass doors according to the style of cabinet.*
☐ *Explain various methods of mounting drawer hardware.*
☐ *Identify special purpose hardware for beds, desks, and folding tables.*

Hardware serves many functions which add convenience to a cabinet. Hinges allow doors to swing open for easy access. Drawer slides provide smooth opening and closing drawers. Shelf rests support adjustable shelving.

Hardware can also enhance the appearance of the cabinet. There are many styles, materials, and finishes, Fig. 17-1. Hidden hinges are typically steel which may be plated with nickel to prevent rust. Decorative hinges are painted or plated with another metal, such as brass. Pulls and knobs may be wood, metal, porcelain, glass, or plastic. Hardware may be brushed (slightly roughened) to reduce gloss, or it may be polished to increase the shine.

Fig. 17-1. The polished brass hardware on this drop lid desk includes bail pulls on the lower drawers, knobs on the small interior drawers, flap hinges for the drop lid, butt hinges for the small interior door, and a lock.
(Fine Hardwood Veneer Assoc.)

PULLS AND KNOBS

Pulls and *knobs* assist you when opening doors and drawers. A variety of styles are available, Fig. 17-2. You should select those which match the cabinet style. Pulls are either flush mount or surface mount. Knobs are mounted on the surface.

Flush mount pulls
Flush mount pulls are level with the face of the door. Install them in sliding doors, Fig. 17-3. The doors pass each other with little clearance.

To install flush mount pulls, make a hole in the door using a router or drill. Press the pull into the

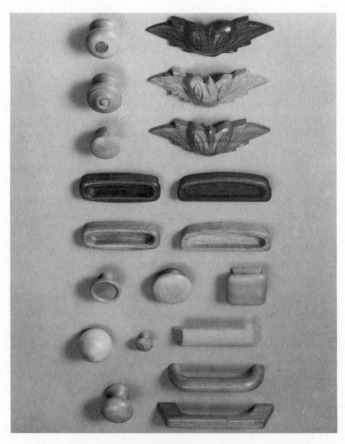

Fig. 17-2. Pulls and knobs may be made of wood.
(The Woodworker's Store).

Fig. 17-3. Flush mount pulls do not interfere with sliding doors. (Brodhead-Garrett)

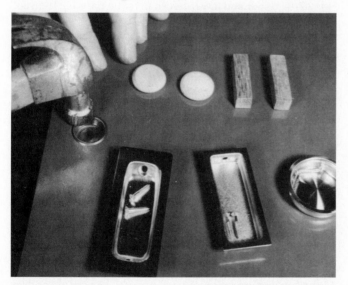

Fig. 17-4. Flush mount pulls are secured by friction, glue, and/or screws. (American Plywood Assoc.)

hole and tap it with a mallet, Fig. 17-4. Most flush mount pulls are friction fit. Some may have screw holes. Others are best installed with adhesive.

Flush mount pulls for sliding glass doors are ground into the glass. These allow your fingers to move the door.

Surface mount pulls and knobs

Surface mount pulls and knobs are attached with screws from the back of the drawer or door. Most wooden hardware is attached with wood screws. Some are fitted with insert nuts to accept machine screws. Metal and plastic hardware is threaded for machine screws.

To install surface mount pulls and knobs, holes must be laid out and drilled accurately. The hardware is then attached, Fig. 17-5. A backplate is often placed between the door or drawer and the hardware. The backplate helps prevent scratches, dirt, and wear when you grasp the pull.

Bail pulls

Bail pulls include a backplate which supports a hinged pull, Fig. 17-6. The pull lays flat against the backplate when not needed. Bail pulls are common on traditional and provincial furniture. Most are made of polished brass and are very decorative.

Fig. 17-5. Surface mount pulls and knobs are attached from the inside of the drawer. (American Plywood Assoc.)

Fig. 17-6. Polished metal bail pulls are decorative. (Thomasville)

Ring pulls.

Ring pulls include a ring which pivots in a backplate, Fig. 17-7. Flush mount ring pulls are chosen when the hardware needs to be below the surface. They are glued in place or attached with screws under the ring. Surface mount ring pulls typically have visible screw holes.

Fig. 17-7. Ring pulls lay flat on the smooth flowing surface of this contemporary furniture. (Bassett)

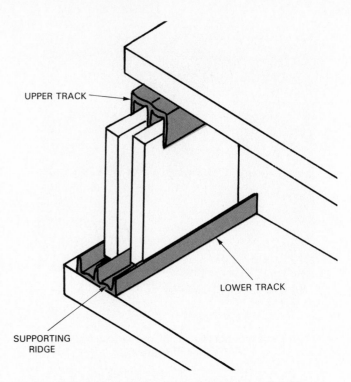

Fig. 17-8. Upper and lower tracks must be parallel. The supporting ridges in the lower track reduce friction.

DOOR HARDWARE

Cabinet doors either slide past each other or swing open on hinges. Sliding doors allow access to only part of the cabinet opening. Hinged doors provide full access to the cabinet opening. However, hinged doors may be a safety hazard when left standing open. To reduce the width and weight of hinged doors, two doors are often used per opening.

Door hardware includes tracks, hinges, and catches.

SLIDING DOOR TRACKS

Sliding doors are supported and guided by metal or plastic *tracks*. The doors slide within about 1/4 in. (6 mm) of each other, making flush mount pulls necessary.

Tracks come in pairs, Fig. 17-8. The upper track is attached to the top of the door opening. The lower track supports the weight of the doors. It contains ridges which prevent the entire edge of the door from seating in the track. This reduces friction which would prevent the door from sliding. Special roller hardware may be installed in tracks to ease movement of the door.

The upper and lower tracks must be parallel. Locate and mark their locations. Attach the tracks with flat head screws.

Door measurements differ according to the style of track. Doors which slide without rollers are measured from the inside of the upper track to the top edge of the lower track. Reduce this measurement by 1/8 in. (3 mm) for clearance.

For doors on rollers, installation may be more involved. The doors typically must be bored or mortised to accept the roller assembly, Fig. 17-9. Follow the manufacturer's instructions for installation.

HINGES FOR WOOD DOORS

Hinges support doors and allow them to swing. Most hinges consist of two pieces of metal, called leaves, held together by a pin. The pins are either tight or loose. *Loose pins* allow you to remove the door quickly.

Other hinge styles include self closing, adjustable, and double action. *Self closing hinges* have a spring which prevents doors from standing open. *Adjustable hinges* have oblate mounting holes. These allow for door adjustment. As the hinge is mounted, it may be moved before the screw is tightly fastened. Another type of adjustable hinge, the concealed or ''European'' hinge, has adjusting screws on the arm. *Double action hinges* permit doors to swing both inward and outward.

Hinge surfaces may be brushed, polished, or textured. Many are plated with chrome, brass, or copper. Some have finish such as enamel, lacquer, or varnish applied to them.

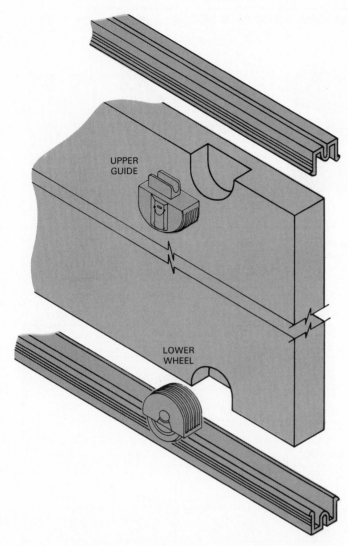

Fig. 17-9. Roller type sliding door hardware may require mortising the doors. (Liberty Hardware)

SELECTING DOOR HINGES

Select hinges to function properly in various cabinet styles. The cabinet front and door design plays a major role in how doors are mounted on the cabinet frame. This, in turn, affects which hinge is appropriate. Common case front styles, Fig. 17-10, include:

• Flush front with face frame.
• Flush front without face frame.
• Flush overlay front.
• Reveal overlay front (with or without face frame).
• Lip edge doors.

You will notice that a face frame is part of several styles. A *face frame* is solid wood border placed on the front of the cabinet assembly. It covers the edges of plywood or particleboard used in constructing the case. Common face frame widths are 1 1/2 in. to 2 in. (37 to 50 mm). With a face frame, the door cannot attach to the side of the cabinet; it must be attached to the side frame.

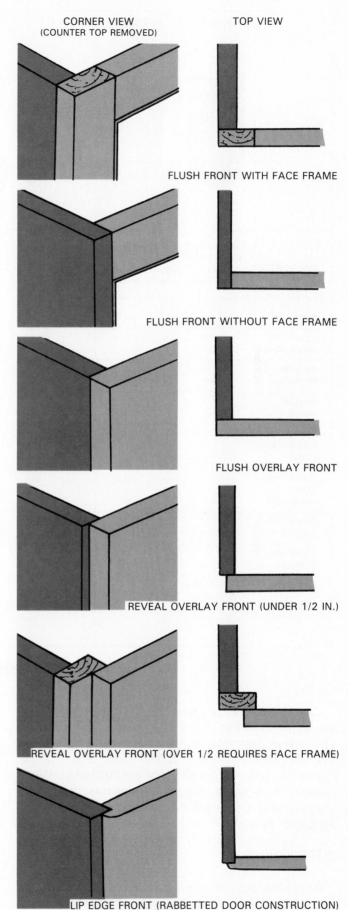

CORNER VIEW (COUNTER TOP REMOVED)   TOP VIEW

FLUSH FRONT WITH FACE FRAME

FLUSH FRONT WITHOUT FACE FRAME

FLUSH OVERLAY FRONT

REVEAL OVERLAY FRONT (UNDER 1/2 IN.)

REVEAL OVERLAY FRONT (OVER 1/2 REQUIRES FACE FRAME)

LIP EDGE FRONT (RABBETTED DOOR CONSTRUCTION)

Fig. 17-10. Flush and overlay doors are common on cabinets with and without face frames.

Hinge Type	BUTT	FORMED	PIVOT	INVISIBLE	EUROPEAN STYLE	PIN	SURFACE
Applications	Conventional Flush Front with Face Frame	Conventional Flush Front Reveal Overlay Flush Overlay	Reveal Overlay Flush Overlay	Conventional Flush with Face Frame	Reveal Overlay Flush Overlay Conventional Flush without Face Frame	Conventional Flush Front	Conventional Flush Front with Face Frame
Strength	High	Very High	Moderate	Low	Moderate	Moderate	High
Concealed when closed	No	No	Semi	Yes	Yes	Yes	No
Requires Mortising	Yes	Occasionally	Usually	Yes	Yes	Yes	No
Cost of Hinge	Low	Moderate	Low	High	High	Low	Low
Ease of Installation (cost)	Moderate	Easy	Moderate	Difficult	Very Easy	Easy	Easy
Adjustment after installation	No	Slight	Slight	No	Yes	Slight	No
Degree of Motion	95°	95°-180°	180°	180°	95°-105°	180°	95°-120°
Automatic Closing	No	Optional	No	Optional	Yes	No	No
Remarks	Door requires hardwood edge			Door requires hardwood edge	1. Specify degree of opening 2. No catch required		

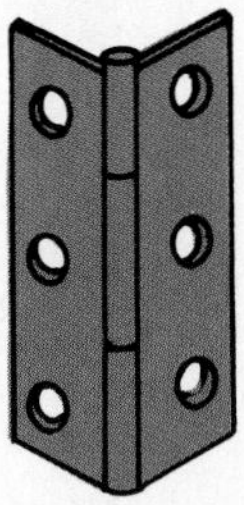

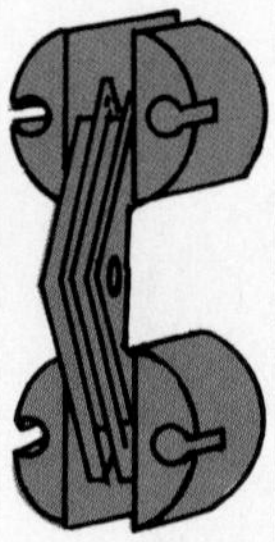

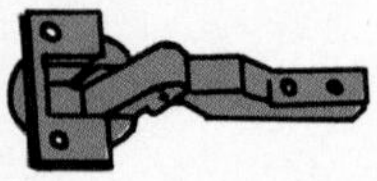

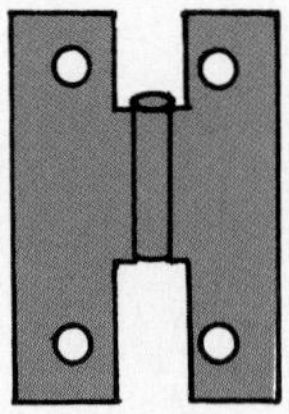

Fig. 17-11. Hinge applications and features.

Examples of hinge types and their appropriate use are is given in Fig. 17-11. The number of hinges you install depends on hinge and type as well as the weight and height of the door, Fig. 17-12. Generally, two hinges per door are sufficient. When using three or more hinges, the pins must be in line. Otherwise the door will not open easily. This is called *hinge bound.*

BUTT HINGES

Butt hinges have two leaves connected by a pin. The leaves fold face to face when installed in the door. There are two types: mortised or non-mortised.

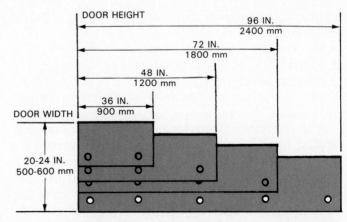

Fig. 17-12. Install hinges according to door height and width. Most cabinet door widths are 24 in. or less.

Mortised butt hinges are placed in routed or chiseled gains in the door and cabinet frame to conceal the hinge, Fig. 17-13. They are designed for flush front cabinetry.

Butt hinges are identified by length and width. Some named by width are *broad, middle,* or *narrow butts.*

Mortised butt hinges may be swaged, non-swaged, or fully swaged. These are classified by how the two leaves form around the pin. The amount of swage determines how close the two leaves fit together, Fig. 17-14. It also determines if the pin is between or to one side of the closed leaves.

Nonmortised butt hinges are designed for flush overlay fronts or reveal overlay fronts with face frames. The outer leaf is attached to the frame. The inner leaf is attached to the back of the door, Fig. 17-15. The metal used in these hinges is thin. Therefore, the hinge is not as strong. However, they are installed quicker.

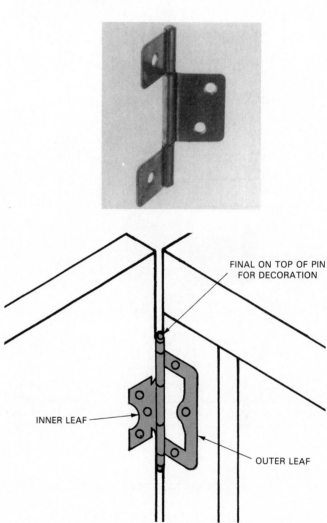

Fig. 17-15. Nonmortised hinges do not require a gain.

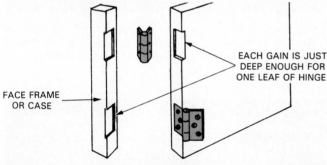

Fig. 17-13. Install mortised butt hinges in gains cut in both the door and cabinet frame.

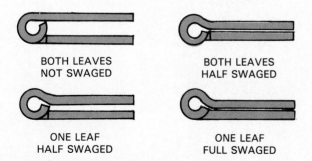

Fig. 17-14. Swage determines pin location and how tightly the two hinge leaves close. No swage leaves a space between the door and frame.

FORMED HINGES

Formed hinges are made for flush overlay, lip edge and reveal overlay doors. One leaf is bent to fit around the frame. The other leaf may be flat or bent and attaches to the back of the door, Fig. 17-16. Some hinge styles have finials attached to the top and bottom of the hinge pins for decoration. Formed hinges are also called *bent hinges* and *wrap-around hinges.*

Formed hinges for lip edge doors

Lip edge doors require specially formed hinges. Each leaf has two bends. The two bends fit in the rabbeted edge of the door. The hinge is attached

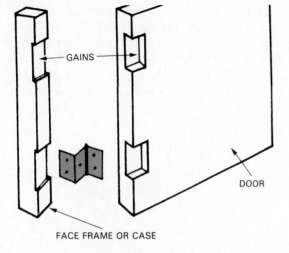

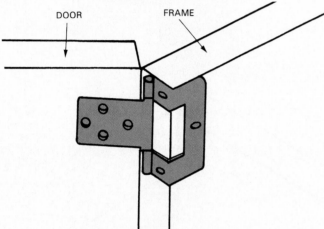

Fig. 17-16. Formed hinges wrap around the frame. Typically they are more secure than a butt hinge. Top. Mortised formed hinges are placed in gains. (The Woodworker's Store) Bottom. Nonmortised formed hinge resembles nonmortised butt hinge. (Liberty Hardware)

to the cabinet side or face frame and door back, Fig. 17-17.

Semiconcealed formed hinges

Semiconcealed hinges are made for reveal overlay doors. The visible part of the hinge is attached to the front of cabinet. It typically is textured and

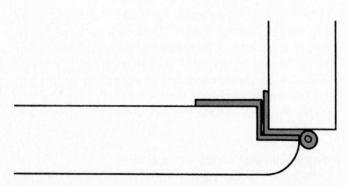

Fig. 17-17. Formed hinges for lip doors have two bends in the door leaf and one in the frame leaf. (Liberty Hardware)

finished in chrome, brass, copper plating, or black paint. The hidden leaf is attached to the back side of the door, Fig. 17-18.

SURFACE HINGES

Surface hinges have ''H'' or ''HL'' shapes and attach directly to the front of the cabinet, Fig. 17-19. They are designed for either conventional flush front or overlay front cabinetry. Overlay surface hinges have a 3/8 in. or 3/4 in. outset. Surface hinges are finished and often textured for decoration. ''HL'' hinges have an extra decorative leg.

Fig. 17-18. One leaf of semiconcealed formed hinges is decorative and installed on the cabinet surface. This one is used with a lip edge door. (American Plywood Assoc.)

Fig. 17-19. ''H'' and ''HL'' surface hinges are used on flush and some lip front cabinets. (American Plywood Assoc.)

PIVOT HINGES

Pivot hinges consist of two plates riveted together. A nylon washer is placed between the two plates to reduce friction when opening the door. Pivot hinges are used for flush overlay and reveal overlay fronts. Some have a wrap-around support which fastens on the inside of the cabinet. When installed, only a narrow edge of the hinge can be seen.

The top and bottom of the door may be mortised when installing pivot hinges, Fig. 17-20. A kerf must be cut in the door if a middle hinge is to be installed.

PIN HINGES

Pin hinges fit into holes drilled in the top and bottom inside surfaces of the cabinet. A nylon washer fits into the holes to prevent the hinge pin from wearing the wood, Fig. 17-21. The door is attached after the hinges have been fitted in the holes. Pin hinges are installed in flush front cabinets.

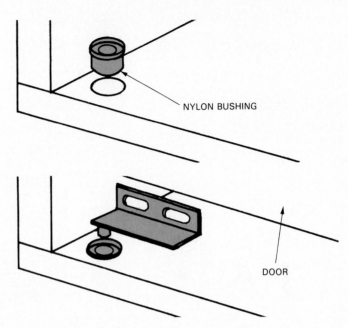

NYLON BUSHING

DOOR

Fig. 17-21. Pin hinges rotate in a nylon bushing. The door is secured from the back of the hinge.

INVISIBLE HINGES

Invisible hinges consist of two metal cylinders with a lever mechanism between them. The two cylinders are inserted into holes bored in the edge of both door and side or frame, Fig. 17-22. To fully fasten the hinge, you must tighten the screws in the end of each cylinder. The screw forces the cylinder to expand. Some invisible hinges have two flanges per cylinder. This hinge can be mounted with wood screws. Once installed, and with the door closed, the hinge is hidden. Only when the door is fully opened can the hinge be seen.

Invisible hinges are used for flush front cabinets, both with and without frames. Sizes begin at 9 mm.

CONCEALED HINGES

Concealed hinges, also called *European hinges,* can be aligned accurately once installed. Set screws move the door up and down, in and out, and side to side. They are installed in reveal overlay, flush overlay, and flush fronts. When the door is closed, the hinge is not visible.

European hinges consist of an arm and a mounting plate. The mounting plate is connected to the cabinet side. The arm is attached to the door. The arm has a "cup" which is inserted into a mounting

Fig. 17-20. These doors are mortised for pivot hinges. (American Plywood Assoc.)

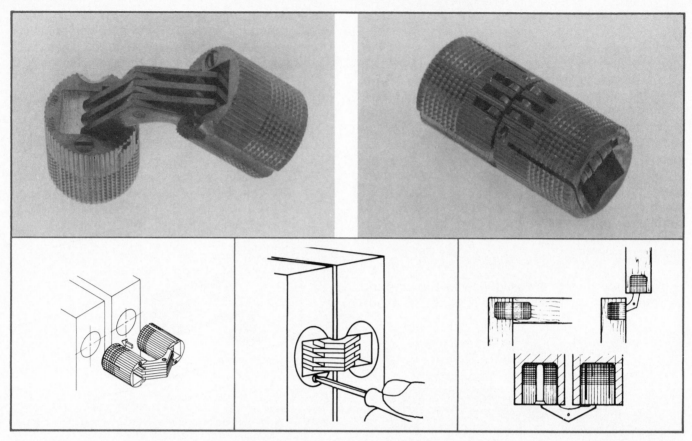

Fig. 17-22. Left. Invisible hinges are inserted into mortised holes. (Liberty Hardware) Middle. Secure the hinges with screws. Right. Invisible hinges allow for 180° of motion. (The Woodworker's Store)

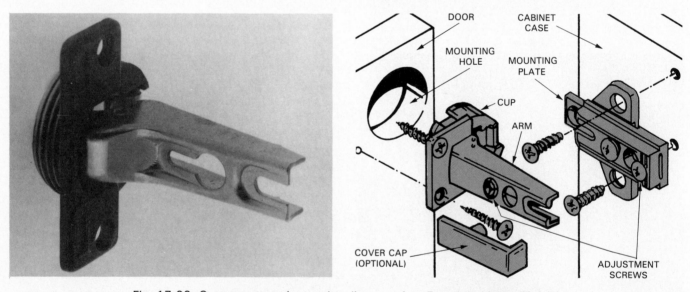

Fig. 17-23. Components and mounting diagram of an European hinge. (Hafele)

hole. The cup is attached to the door with screws, Fig. 17-23. The arm then slides over the mounting plate and is fastened.

Once the arm is attached to the mounting plate, it can be adjusted slightly. Several machine screws allow for up to 4 mm of overlay, depth, and height adjustment, Fig. 17-24.

CONTINUOUS HINGES

Continuous hinges resemble a very long butt hinge. They are described by certain features shown in Fig. 17-25. Hinge lengths are available in 1 ft. (305 mm) to 6 ft. (1 825 mm) lengths. However, continuous hinge is also available in a 50 ft. (15

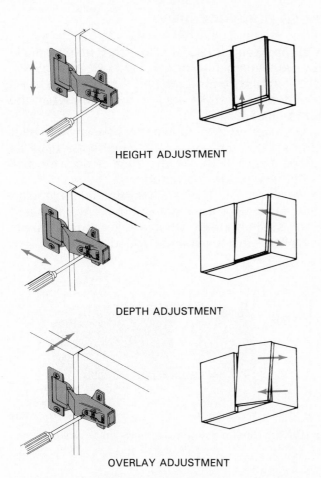

HEIGHT ADJUSTMENT

DEPTH ADJUSTMENT

OVERLAY ADJUSTMENT

Fig. 17-24. Concealed hinges allow for three-way door adjustment.

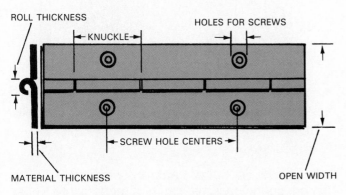

Fig. 17-25. A continuous hinge is specified according to certain standard dimensions. (Hafele)

m) coil. Cut the length you need with a hacksaw. Then file away the sharp edges and saw marks.

HINGES FOR GLASS DOORS

Hinges for glass doors may hold the glass by friction or screws. For some screw mounted hinges, glass drilling may be necessary. Three glass hinge styles are pin, side mount, and European.

Glass door pin hinge

Glass door pin hinges resemble those for wood doors, Fig. 17-26. Drilling the glass is not required. You drill a hole inside the top and bottom surfaces of the cabinet. Then press a nylon bushing in the hole. Hinges are mounted in the bushings first. Then, the glass is inserted into the U-shaped hinge leaf which has one or two set screws on the back. Be sure to locate the rubber and metal pad between the glass and the screws. It prevents the glass from slipping. It also prevents glass breakage when the set screws are tightened. Turn the set screws only snug enough to keep the glass from slipping out of place.

Side mounted glass door hinge

Side mounted glass door hinges are attached on the insides of the cabinet with screws, Fig. 17-27.

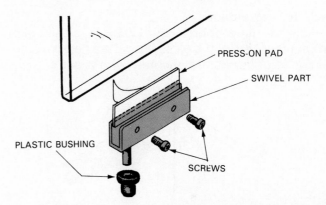

Fig. 17-26. Glass is held in a glass door pin hinge by two set screws. (Hafele)

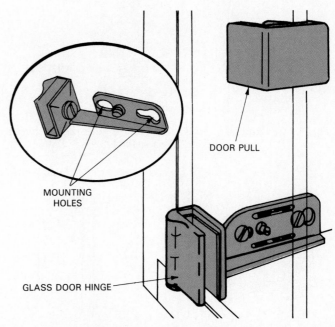

Fig. 17-27. Oblate mounting holes make glass door hinges adjustable. (The Woodworker's Store)

The glass fits into the U-shaped hinge. A set screw and pad holds the glass in place. Side mounted glass hinges may be adjustable. The mounting holes are oblate. This permits the hinge to be moved before the screws are fully tightened.

Concealed glass door hinges

Concealed (or European) glass door hinges resemble those used for wooden doors, Fig. 17-28. 17-28. The mounting plate is screwed into the side of the cabinet. The arm attaches the glass to the mounting plate. A hole must be bored in the glass. The cup part of the arm fits through the glass. The depth of the cup may be 6 mm (1/8 in.) to 8 mm (3/16 in.) depending on the glass thickness. Screws are inserted from the back side of the glass, through the hole, and into a front plate. As the screws are tightened, the front plate draws against the arm, holding the glass between the two.

Pulls for glass doors

Pulls for glass doors, Fig. 17-29, typically slip around the edge of the glass. Some are held in place by friction. Others are secured with a set screw.

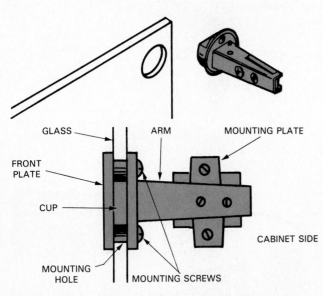

Fig. 17-28. European style glass door hinges require bored mounting holes. (Hafele)

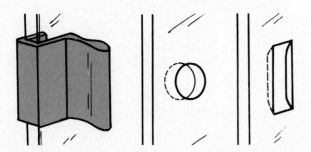

Fig. 17-29. Glass door pulls may slip on. They can also be drilled or ground into the glass.

HINGED DOOR CATCHES

Catches keep doors closed either mechanically or by magnetism. Catches are two-part assemblies. A catch mounts on the cabinet. A strike is fastened to the door. The strike fits into the catch when the door is closed.

Friction catch. A friction catch consists of a bent spring steel catch and a ball head screw used as a strike, Fig. 17-30. As the door closes, the ball head is wedged in the catch.

Roller catches. There are single and double roller catches. Single roller catches have one roller and a hook shaped strike. Double roller catches have two rollers and a spear or round shaped strike. See Fig. 17-31.

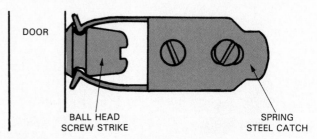

Fig. 17-30. There are no moving parts on a friction catch.

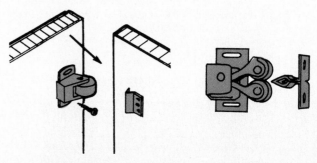

Fig. 17-31. Roller catches. Left. Single roller catch. (Hafele) Right. Double roller catch. (The Woodworker's Store)

Bullet catch. A bullet catch consists of a bullet shaped, spring operated catch. It mounts into a hole drilled in the edge of the cabinet face or in the door. The strike is cup shaped, Fig. 17-32.

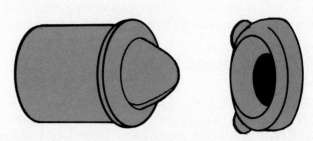

Fig. 17-32. Bullet catch (The Woodworker's Store)

Elbow catch. An elbow catch hooks onto the strike. A spring action lever is pushed to release the catch, Fig. 17-33.

Ball catch. This catch consists of two spring-loaded balls with a strike between them, Fig. 17-34.

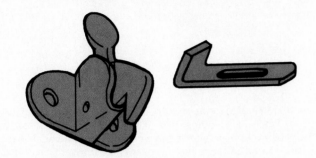

Fig. 17-33. An elbow catch hooks onto a bent strike. (The Woodworker's Store)

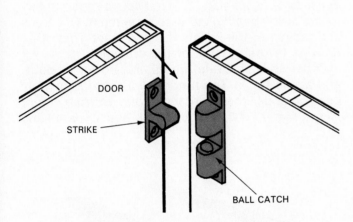

Fig. 17-34. Ball catch. (Hafele)

Magnetic catch. A magnetic catch has a permanent magnet which attracts a flat, plated steel strike, Fig. 17-35.

Spring catch. A spring catch includes a spring arm with a roller. When the door is closed, the roller seats in a concave strike, Fig. 17-36.

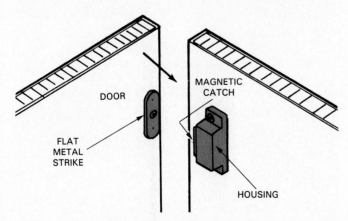

Fig. 17-35. A magnetic catch includes a permanent magnet catch and flat, steel strike. (Hafele)

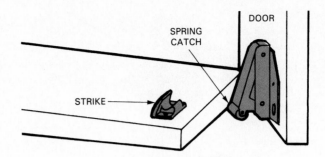

Fig. 17-36. Spring catch.

LATCHES

Latches are slight variations of catches. When the door is closed, the latch works as a catch to hold the door closed. However, if you press on the door face, the latch springs outward to open the door. Doors with latches do not require pulls since the hardware opens the door as well as holds it closed. Two types of latches are push and magnetic.

Push latch. A push latch has a clawlike mechanism which grips the strike as the door is closed, Fig. 17-37. The claws release when you press against the door.

Magnetic touch latches. Magnetic touch latches, Fig. 17-38, hold the door closed with a permanent magnet. The magnet is mounted in a spring mechanism. A slight push on the door trips the mechanism and forces open the door.

DRAWER HARDWARE

Drawer hardware includes pulls, knobs, and slides. Matching pull or knob styles should be installed on the drawer face as was on doors. Drawer slides allow you to pull out a drawer with ease. Most slides move on plastic rollers or ball bearings.

Slide extension

Drawer slides may be standard, full extension, or telescoping. With *standard slides,* all but 4 in. (100 mm) to 6 in. (150 mm) of the drawer body extends out of the cabinet. *Full extension slides* permit the

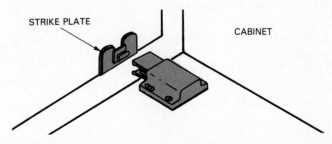

Fig. 17-37. A push latch grips the strike when the door is closed. Pushing the door again releases the latch. (Hafele)

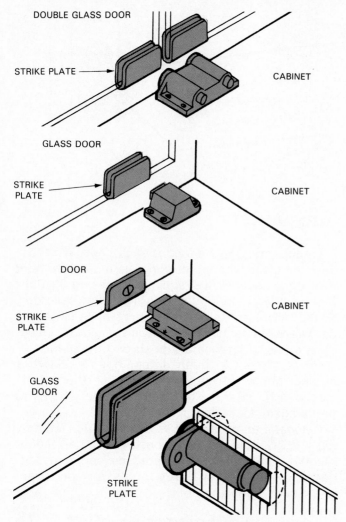

Fig. 17-38. Various types of magnetic touch latches. (Hafele)

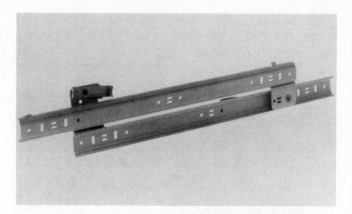

Fig. 17-39. Most side mount drawer slides consist of two tracks, each with a nylon roller. The forward roller, located on the cabinet track, supports the weight of the drawer. The rear roller, located on the drawer, prevents the drawer from tipping forward when it is extended.

consists of two tracks. The tracks are separated by rollers or ball bearings to ease movement. One track is attached to the inside of the cabinet. The other mounts to the outside of the drawer.

Other styles include top mount, bottom mount, and single track. *Top mount slides* are commonly used on under-the-counter drawers. *Bottom mount slides*, Fig. 17-40, are used with both drawers and

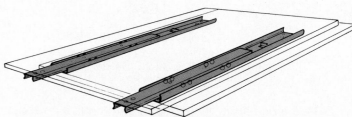

entire drawer body to extend out for easy access. *Telescoping slides*, used for drawers or TV tables, extend beyond the cabinet. Be cautious when selecting full extension and telescoping slides for free standing cabinets. A heavily loaded drawer could easily tip the cabinet over. It is best to use these slides on built-in cabinetry.

Capacity

Load capacity of a drawer slide refers to how much weight it can hold when fully extended. Categories are:
- Light duty (residential slide)—50 pound capacity.
- Medium duty (commercial slide)—75 pound capacity.
- Heavy duty—100 pound capacity.
- Special extra heavy duty—greater than 100 pound capacity.

Mounts

Drawer slides are most often mounted on the side of the drawer, Fig. 17-39. Each *side mount slide*

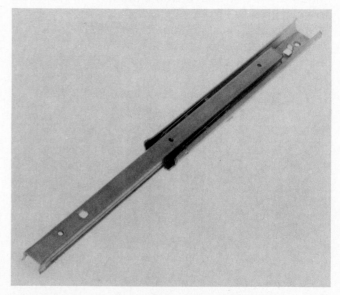

Fig. 17-40. Bottom mount slides are commonly used for pullout shelves. (Liberty Hardware)

pull-out shelves. Bottom mount slides are usually telescoping. One common single track device is the *single track and tri-roller slide*, Fig. 17-41. *Slide guides*, Fig. 17-42, are used with wooden single track slides.

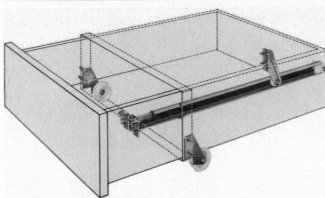

Fig. 17-41. Single track and tri-roller slides are more complicated than standard side mount slides. (National Lock)

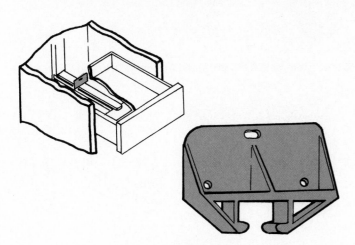

Fig. 17-42. Plastic slide glides prevent wood to wood contact. (The Woodworker's Store)

SHELF SUPPORTS

Shelf supports are small sized rods, brackets, or flat spoons which hold shelves. Supports are inserted into the sides of the cabinet. Different styles are available, Fig. 17-43.

Typically shelf supports are inserted into evenly spaced holes drilled in the cabinet side. The more holes you drill, the greater the possible shelf adjustments, Fig. 17-44.

Shelf supports may also fit a *shelf support strip*, often called a *pilaster*, Fig. 17-45. Two support strips on each side allow for many height locations. Install strips either on the surface or in a routed groove with screws or adhesive. Supports must match the rectangular or round holes.

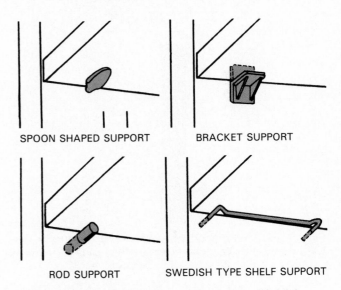

SPOON SHAPED SUPPORT   BRACKET SUPPORT

ROD SUPPORT   SWEDISH TYPE SHELF SUPPORT

Fig. 17-43. Four types of shelf supports. (Hafele)

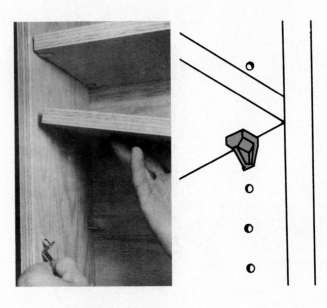

Fig. 17-44. Height adjustments are limited by the number and spacing of holes. (American Plywood Assoc., Liberty Hardware)

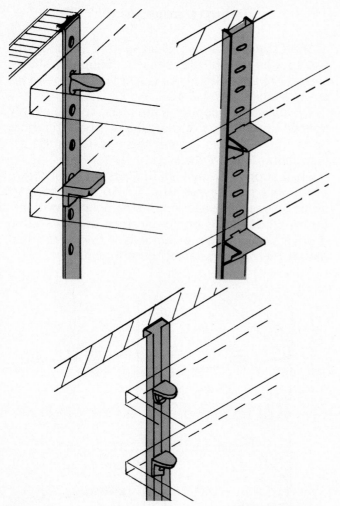

LOCKS

Locks are installed in doors and drawers for protecting contents. Three types are common: bolt action, cam action, and ratchet action, Fig. 17-46. When the key is turned in a *bolt action lock*, the bolt moves in a straight line. A *cam action lock* rotates a flat metal arm into a slot. The body of a cam action lock is flat on one or both sides. This keeps it from rotating in the door or drawer hole. *Ratchet action locks* secure glass sliding doors. No drilling is needed.

Generally lock bodies are a standard diameter (7/8 in. or 21 mm); however, they vary in length. Most are 3/4 in. (19 mm) long. Others are available for thicker doors and drawer fronts.

CASTERS

Casters are mounted on cabinet bottoms for mobility. They may be single or dual wheel, Fig. 17-47. Some have a brake lever to prevent cabinet movement.

Casters may have pin and sleeve or plate mounts. Pin and sleeve casters require a sleeve-sized hole 2 in. (50 mm) deep in the cabinet bottom. Plate mounted casters require screws to attach the mounting plate to a flat surface.

CORNER PROTECTORS

Corner protectors are triangular shaped and fit around cabinet corners. They may be attached with

Fig. 17-45. Shelf support strips may be flush mount or inset, with rectangular or round holes. (Hafele, Liberty Hardware)

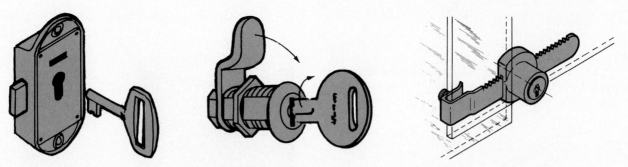

Fig. 17-46. Three types of locks. Left bolt action. Middle. Cam action. Right. Ratchet action. (Hafele)

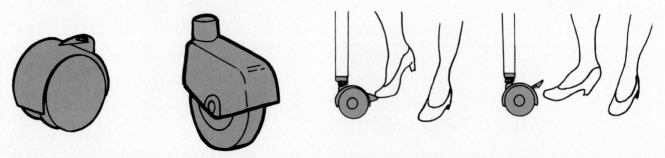

Fig. 17-47. Casters may be dual or single wheel. Locking levers prevent the wheels from moving. (Hafele)

escutcheon pins or screws. Some corners have an adhesive coating on the back. Remove the protective cover and press the corner protector in place. Install protectors after cabinet has been finished.

BED HARDWARE

Bed frames usually are assembled with two-piece *bed rail connectors*, Fig. 17-48. A set of four is required. One part of the connector contains holes. It is mortised into the footboard and headboard. The other part of the connector has hooks. It mounts

on each end of the two bed rails. Bed connectors are designed for quick and easy assembly. Some connectors are surface mounted. They lock together and do not require bedpost or frame mortising.

LID AND DROP LEAF HARDWARE

Lid and drop leaf table hardware includes hinges, lid supports, and lid stays. Hinges allow a table leaf to fold down or a lid or table leaf to fold up, Fig. 17-49. *Lid supports* prevent lids from dropping too far. An adjustable brake may control the speed

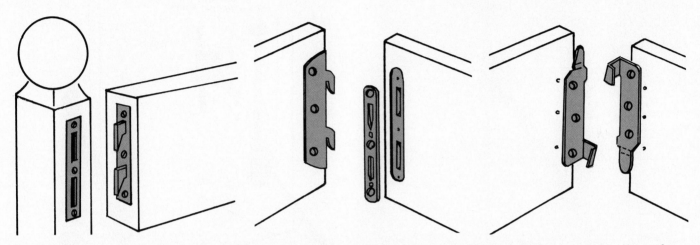

Fig. 17-48. Beds are assembled with hooklike hardware. Connectors may be mortised into the rail or installed on the surface. (Liberty Hardware, Hafele)

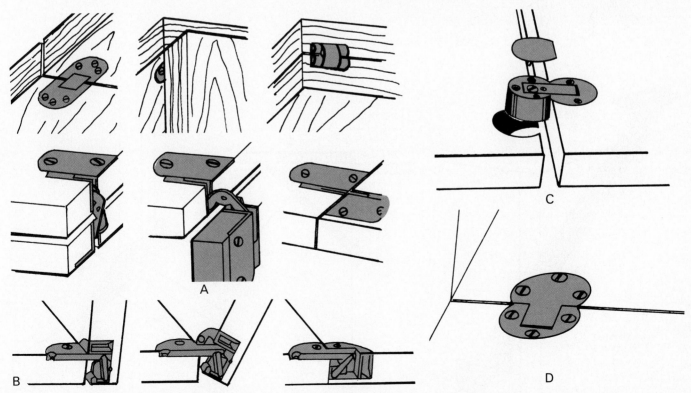

Fig. 17-49. A—Hinges for desk lids and drop leaf tables. B—Hinge folds down and under the table. C—Hinge folds up and over the table. D—Flap hinges are often used for desk lids. (Hafele)

at which the lid may fall. These are common on desk lids, Fig. 17-50. *Lid stays* support lids or table leaves, Fig. 17-51.

FURNITURE GLIDES

Furniture glides protect the bottoms and legs of free standing cabinetry. They raise the cabinet or legs slightly off the floor. This prevents chipping when the item is moved. Since glides reduce surface contact with the floor, moving the cabinet is easier. Glides nail in or are inserted into a drilled hole, Fig. 17-52.

FURNITURE LEVELERS

Furniture levelers, Fig. 17-53, serve two purposes. They allow height adjustment to make the product stable on an uneven surface. They also act as glides. Levelers may screw into an insert nut. They may also attach underneath the cabinet with wood screws.

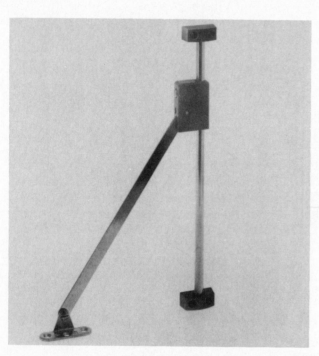

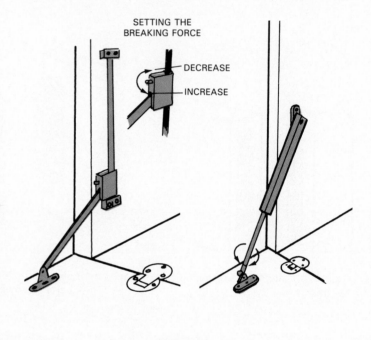

Fig. 17-50. Lid supports have a brake to prevent the lid from dropping too fast. (Hafele)

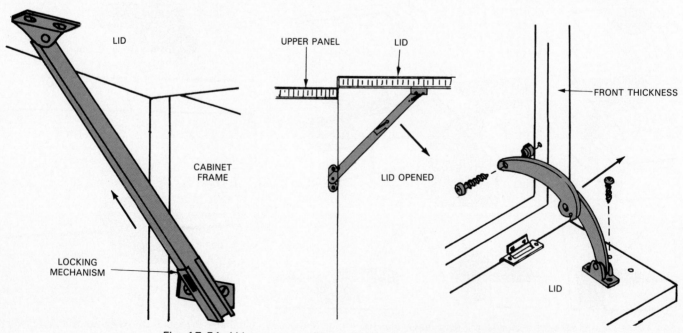

Fig. 17-51. Lid stays may slide or fold to lock into place. (Hafele)

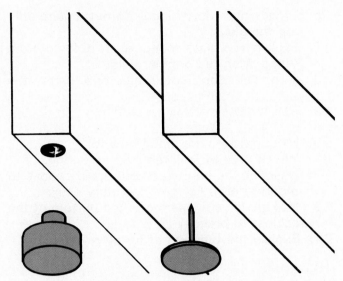

Fig. 17-52. Glides prevent the bottom of the cabinet from chipping or marring the floor.

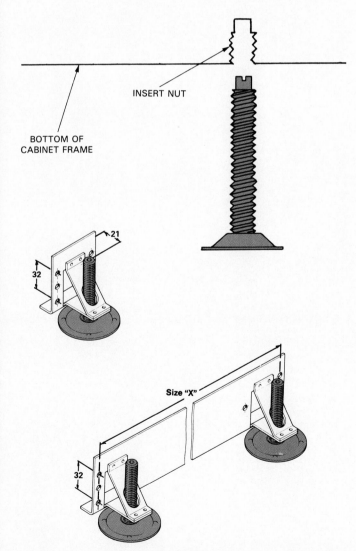

INSERT NUT

BOTTOM OF CABINET FRAME

21

32

Size "X"

32

Fig. 17-53. Levelers can be adjusted to keep the cabinet from wobbling. They may screw into a bracket or into an insert nut in the bottom of the cabinet. (Hafele)

SUMMARY

Hardware adds convenience and beauty to cabinetry. Pulls and knobs assist you when opening doors and drawers. Most are decorative. Door hardware includes hinges and sliding tracks. Many varieties of hinges are available. They may be visible, semiconcealed, or hidden completely. Choose them according to the cabinetry style you intend to build. Catches hold hinged doors closed either mechanically or by magnetism. Latchs both hold the door closed and help to open the door. Drawer slides are selected according to extension, capacity, and type of mount. Shelf supports are small rods or brackets which hold shelves. They may be inserted into a shelf strip or directly into holes in the cabinet sides. Locks are installed to protect contents of the cabinet. Common lock types are cam action, bolt action, and ratchet action. Casters are mounted on cabinet bottoms for mobility. Drop lids and drop leaf tables require hinges as well as lid supports and stays. Furniture glides protect the bottom of the cabinet from chipping. Furniture levelers permit you to stabilize cabinets on an uneven surface.

CABINETMAKING TERMS

Pulls, knobs, flush mount pulls, surface mount pulls, bail pulls, ring pulls, sliding door tracks, loose pin hinge, tight pin hinge, self closing hinge, adjustable hinge, double action hinge, face frame, case front style, butt hinge, mortised butt hinge, nonmortised butt hinge, formed hinge, semi-concealed hinge, surface hinge, pin hinge, pivot hinge, invisible hinge, European hinge, continuous hinge, glass door pin hinge, side mounted glass door hinge, European glass door hinge, door catch, friction catch, roller catch, bullet catch, elbow catch, ball catch, magnetic catch, spring catch, push latch, magnetic touch latch, drawer slides, standard extension slide, full extension slide, telescoping slide, drawer slide load capacity, side mount slide, bottom mount slide, top mount slide, single track and tri-roller slide, slide guide, shelf supports, shelf support strip, bolt action lock, cam action lock, ratchet action lock, caster, corner protector, bed rail, connector, lid support, lid stay, furniture glide, furniture leveler.

TEST YOUR KNOWLEDGE

1. Sliding doors use _____ pulls.
2. Describe the similarities between bail pulls and ring pulls.
3. Why do lower sliding door tracks have a ridge on which the door slides?
4. The height of the sliding door is affected by _____ and _____.
5. Diagram five cabinet front styles. How do they determine the appropriate type of hinge?

MATCHING QUESTIONS: On a separate sheet of paper, match the following hinges to their description.

6. Flaps are bent around the door and/or the frame. Often used for flush overlay doors.
7. Flaps bent around frame and door. Visible part of hinge is finished to enhance cabinet appearance.
8. Fully adjustable hinge. Requires mortising in door.
9. Holes are drilled in the top and bottom inside surfaces of the cabinet. Hinge fits into hole using a nylon bushing.
10. Least visible hinge. Fits into two holes mortised in the edge of the door and inside surface of the cabinet.
11. May be sold in 50 ft. coils.
12. Most visible hinge. May be shaped in "H" or "HL" pattern.
13. Outer flap connected to the frame. Inner flap connected to the door. Designed for flush and reveal overlay fronts with face frame.
14. Two flaps connected by a pin. Must be mortised into the door and frame. Made for conventional flush fronts.
15. Two plates riveted together. Requires mortising the top and bottom, and middle hinge needs a saw kerf to fit properly.

a. Continuous hinge.
b. European hinge.
c. Formed hinge.
d. Invisible hinge.
e. Mortised butt hinge.
f. Non-mortised butt hinge.
g. Pin hinge.
h. Pivot hinge.
i. Semi-concealed formed hinge.
j. Surface hinge.

16. Which glass door hinges do not require drilling the glass.
17. Explain how glass door pulls are different from wood door and drawer pulls.
18. A hinged door catch has two parts: the _____ and _____.
19. Select drawer slides according to _____, _____, and _____.
20. Most drawers are mounted with _____.
21. Which type of lock requires no boring.
22. Describe the hardware you would choose to mount a drop lid for a secretary desk.
23. Nail guides are inserted in the bottom of the cabinet to prevent _____.
24. Explain the function of furniture levelers.

Chapter 18
HEALTH AND SAFETY

After studying this chapter, you will be able to:
☐ *Identify unsafe acts.*
☐ *Reduce or eliminate hazardous conditions around machines and equipment.*
☐ *Handle and store materials properly.*
☐ *Explain procedures to follow if accidents occur.*

No workplace is perfectly safe. All you can do is to make it as risk-free as possible. There are many health and safety concerns for cabinetmakers. They include protecting yourself as well as looking out for others. Always have a well planned, organized, and controlled safety program.

Accidents occur as the result of:
1. Unsafe acts.
2. Hazardous conditions.

These two problems result in accidents and injuries. Data for all kinds of industrial injuries are listed in Fig. 18-1.

You cannot reduce risks simply by ''being more careful so accidents don't happen.'' This is only one part of the approach to safety. You must be aware

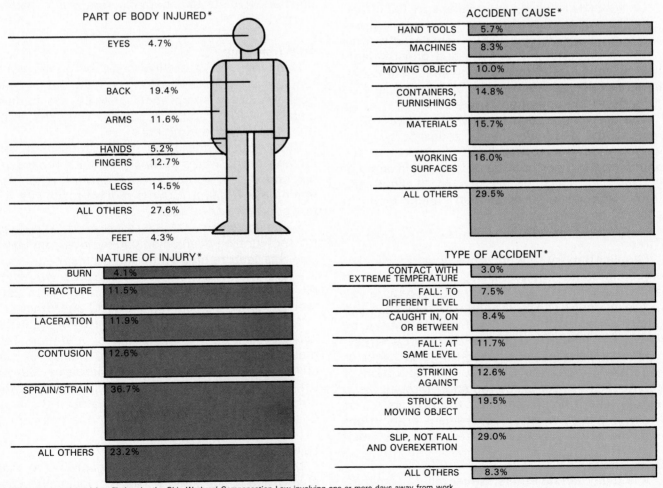

PART OF BODY INJURED*

EYES	4.7%
BACK	19.4%
ARMS	11.6%
HANDS	5.2%
FINGERS	12.7%
LEGS	14.5%
ALL OTHERS	27.6%
FEET	4.3%

ACCIDENT CAUSE*

HAND TOOLS	5.7%
MACHINES	8.3%
MOVING OBJECT	10.0%
CONTAINERS, FURNISHINGS	14.8%
MATERIALS	15.7%
WORKING SURFACES	16.0%
ALL OTHERS	29.5%

NATURE OF INJURY*

BURN	4.1%
FRACTURE	11.5%
LACERATION	11.9%
CONTUSION	12.6%
SPRAIN/STRAIN	36.7%
ALL OTHERS	23.2%

TYPE OF ACCIDENT*

CONTACT WITH EXTREME TEMPERATURE	3.0%
FALL: TO DIFFERENT LEVEL	7.5%
CAUGHT IN, ON OR BETWEEN	8.4%
FALL: AT SAME LEVEL	11.7%
STRIKING AGAINST	12.6%
STRUCK BY MOVING OBJECT	19.5%
SLIP, NOT FALL AND OVEREXERTION	29.0%
ALL OTHERS	8.3%

*Based on lost time claims filed under the Ohio Workers' Compensation Law involving one or more days away from work.

Fig. 18-1. There is a wide range of accident types and their causes. Accidents result in many kinds of injuries.
(Ohio Industrial Commission)

of your surroundings at all times. Machines are only one of the causes for accidents and injuries. You must be alert to all types of hazards. Use common sense when handling materials and operating machines. Always read and follow:

1. Labels on containers.
2. Safety instructions for operating machines.
3. Caution signs posted in the workplace.
4. Written (and verbal) warnings about cabinet-making processes and products.

Instructions and warnings are provided for your benefit. They are there as reminders while you work. Producers of materials and equipment want you to use their products in a risk-free and productive manner.

Most chapters in this book include THINK SAFELY—ACT SAFELY sections. Each points out how you can avoid unsafe acts and hazardous conditions.

UNSAFE ACTS

Unsafe acts are performed by people. Individuals often work carelessly or while under physical or emotional stress.

Carelessness

Carelessness invites injury. People try to perform a machine operation without proper knowledge or thorough planning, Fig. 18-2. These acts often result in personal injury. Cuts and bruises might heal, but the loss of an eye or finger is permanent. In either case, recovery takes longer than it does to perform the operation properly.

The best preparation for any cabinetwork is to *read, watch,* and *understand.* Read all of the information about the process. Then, if possible, watch another person perform the process. And lastly, if you have any questions, ask an expert. Learn to perform tasks skillfully rather than chance injury to yourself or someone else.

Stress

People often try to work while under physical or emotional stress. Physical illness, such as aches and pains, are distracting. Many operations require you to hold materials and tools tightly. Without adequate grip, an accident may occur. Mishaps caused by illness may result from or lead to emotional stress.

Emotional stress, such as feelings of anger or frustration, interferes with your concentration. If you have cut a workpiece too short three times in a row, take a break. Look for the true source of the problem. A wrong measurement or incorrect machine setup may have caused your problem.

Distractions

Avoid distracting others. Never talk to someone who is operating a machine. Wait until they are

Fig. 18-2. This person has thoroughly planned the sawing operation. He has made a jig for stability and has a push stick. Safety glass and the proper stance further reduce the chance of injury. (Shopsmith, Inc.)

finished. To startle someone may be a painful mistake.

Tool handling

Handling and operating hand or power tools requires *common sense.* Keep them out of your pockets. Carry sharp tools only by the handle. Inspect all tool handles regularly. They should be tight and in good condition.

Keep your hands away from blades, bits, and moving parts. Make setups only with the power disconnected. Be even more careful when the machine is running. Guards around machines will not guarantee total safety.

Some portable tools have *trigger locks.* They keep the tool running even when you remove your hand. Use this feature only when the tool is mounted in a stand. An unsupported tool could be wrenched from your hand. This may cause damage to your workpiece as well as injury to you and others.

After you finish using a certain tool or machine, leave it ready for the next person or operation. This means cleaning and storing hand tools. For machines, this includes unplugging them and cleaning off all debris with a cloth or brush. Reinstall the normal blade or bit if you have installed a special one. Put all guards in their protective positions.

Handling materials

Materials should be handled according to size, shape, and weight. Many back injuries occur when people lift heavy or bulky items improperly. Lift with your knees bent, not your back. Keep your back straight and look forward, not down, when you lift.

Moving cabinetmaking materials may require two persons or a cart. Full sheet panel products, such as plywood, are awkward and often heavy. Long lengths of lumber can be difficult to move by yourself. Two people should carry large or heavy materials near machines in operation. A careless move could result in an accident and possible injury.

HAZARDOUS CONDITIONS

Hazardous conditions exist either because people lack the proper safety knowledge or have a poor attitude about safety. Nevertheless, they should be reduced or eliminated. Some conditions will be noticeably dangerous. Others are harder to detect.

WALKING AND WORKING SURFACES

Debris should be cleaned from any surface. Pick up and discard dust, shavings, or wood scraps from floors, tables, and machines. Treat liquid spills with absorbent compounds or dry wood chips. Remove the compound as soon as the spill is absorbed. *Nonskid mats, adhesive strips,* or *coating materials* may be applied to the floor around working areas, Fig. 19-3. These reduce the slippery nature of concrete and wood floors.

Keep walkways clear. This is very important in case of an emergency, such as a fire. Outline aisles and walkways with yellow paint. Keep marked areas totally free of obstruction or materials.

FIRE PROTECTION

Fire protection includes fire alarms, sprinkler systems and fire extinguishers. Check fire alarms regularly. The use of several inexpensive smoke detectors can alert people further to a potentially dangerous fire.

Fig. 18-3. Nonskid mats cover slippery nature of concrete and wood floors. (Brookstone Co.)

A fire requires fuel, heat, and oxygen. Sprinkler systems and fire extinguishers are designed to reduce the heat and/or the supply of oxygen. They activate when heat is present. Sprinkler systems should be checked periodically by a service technician.

Everyone should be able to use fire extinguishers. Locate these devices within 75 ft. of any work area. An extinguisher weighing 40 pounds or more should be mounted within 5 ft. (1500 mm) of the floor. Lighter extinguishers should be located within each reach.

Check the pressure rating on the extinguisher regularly. Most approved types have a pressure dial on them. The needle should be in the green area labeled PROPERLY CHARGED. Also look for inspection tags indicating when the extinguisher was last tested by a technician.

Selecting and using extinguishers

There are three classifications of fires:

1. Class A fires—burning solid waste.
2. Class B fires—flammable and combustible liquids.
3. Class C fire—electrical fire.

NOT ALL FIRE EXTINGUISHERS ARE EFFECTIVE FOR EVERY KIND OF FIRE. The best extinguisher is the ABC multi-purpose dry chemical extinguisher. The chemical removes oxygen and smothers the fire.

The soda acid liquid extinguisher is effective only for Class A fires. A burning liquid (Class B fire) would float on the water. A liquid stream on an electrical fire is a conductor. The person holding the extinguisher could be electrocuted.

The carbon dioxide extinguisher is effective on Class B and C fires. The chemical, if used on specific solid waste fires, could produce toxic fumes. The fumes can make the user ill or unconscious.

Fig. 18-4 shows various extinguishers and their proper uses. Remember that a majority of extinguishers will last for no more than 30 seconds. Some stop working in about 15 seconds. Never try to extinguish a very large fire. Report the fire by dialing the 911 emergency telephone number or the number of your fire department.

To use an extinguisher, first pull out the safety pin. Aim the extinguisher according to the type of fire, see Fig. 18-4. Squeeze the handle to release the contents. Soda acid extinguishers must be held upside down to operate properly. Check the instructions before an emergency arises.

FLAMMABLE LIQUIDS

Flammable liquids ignite easily, burn readily, and are difficult to extinguish. Vapors are apt to explode.

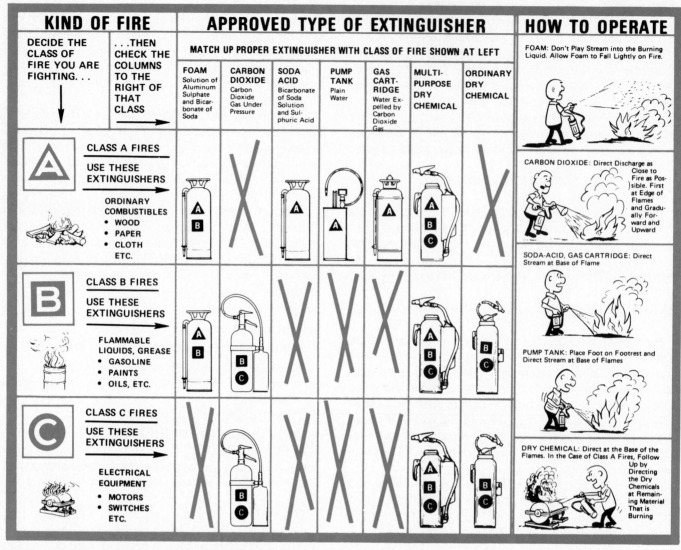

IMPORTANT! USING THE WRONG TYPE EXTINGUISHER FOR THE CLASS OF FIRE MAY BE DANGEROUS!

Fig. 18-4. Not all fire extinguishers will put out every kind of fire. Check the label on the extinguisher. Using the wrong extinguisher may electrocute you or produce toxic fumes. (National Institute for Occupational Safety and Health)

In cabinetmaking finishing materials and adhesives often are flammable. This makes them serious hazards for cabinetmakers.

Flammable liquids are further categorized as shown in Fig. 18-5. The class is determined by the flash point. The *flash point* is the minimum temperature at which the liquid vaporizes enough to ignite. Containers must be labeled according to the class. Class I liquids are the most dangerous because the flash point is within room temperature.

Preventive measures are necessary when using flammable liquids. You might use a lower class (higher flash point) or even a nonflammable liquid.

While filling flammable liquid storage cans, electrically ground them with a copper wire, Fig. 18-6. The wire, attached to a metal object, drains off any static electricity which might spark a fire.

Store flammable liquids only in *approved steel cabinets* and *safety cans.* Cabinets have a certain capacity to resist fire. The walls are thick enough

CLASSIFICATIONS OF HAZARDOUS LIQUIDS			
	LABELING	FLASH POINT	LIQUIDS INCLUDED
Class I	Flammable	Below 100 °F (38 °C)	Acetone Benzene Ethyl alcohol Gasoline Lacquer thinner Mineral spirits Petroleum distillates Turpentine
Class II	Combustible	Between 100 °F (38 °C) and 140 °F (60 °C)	Kerosene
Class III	Combustible	Above 140 °F (60 °C)	Fuel oil

Fig. 18-5. Know the potential hazards before using flammable liquids.

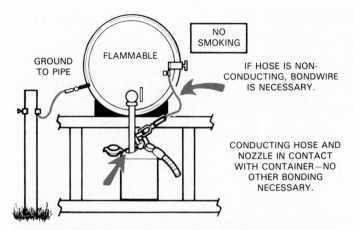

Fig. 18-6. Ground your safety cans when filling from a storage tank. Static electricity could create a spark. (National Institute for Occupational Safety and Health)

Fig. 18-7. An approved safety cabinet will resist fire for a period of time. It also is water tight to retain any leaking fluids. (Eagle Manufacturing Co.)

to contain a fire for more than an hour if the doors remain closed. The bottom of the cabinet is also leakproof up to the doors, Fig. 18-7.

Storage cans, Fig. 18-8, are fitted with flame arrestors. A *flame arrestor* is a wire screen placed in the neck of the can. The wire mesh stops flames from getting inside the can. Further protection is provided by the spring loaded lid. When you release the handle, the lid closes and seals the safety can.

Vapors are the most dangerous aspect of flammable liquids. A ventilation system is necessary for controlling them. It collects and removes vapors from the workplace.

HAZARDOUS SUBSTANCES

Be aware of hazardous substances other than flammable liquids. Most are nuisances and irritants. However, others may be fatal. Read the label of any solid, liquid, or gaseous substance you use, especially if you are unfamiliar with the product. The container's label might recommend wearing a respirator to prevent inhaling dust, fumes, mists, gases, or vapors. Gloves may be recommended to prevent a skin reaction or chemical burn.

EXHAUST AND VENTILATION

Effective workplace exhaust and ventilation systems are essential. *Dust collection systems* remove most small wood chips and dust particles from machines. Others control dust that is in the air, Fig. 18-9. *Exhaust systems* for finishing rooms remove harmful vapors.

FINISHING ROOM HAZARDS

Within finishing areas people breathe toxic fumes and use flammable liquids, often Class I. Respirators should be worn by persons in the finishing room.

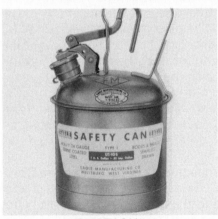

SAFETY CAN

OILY WASTE CAN

SAFETY BENCH CAN

Fig 18-8. Storage cans. Left. Safety can to store new materials. Middle. Safety bench can for disposal of liquid materials. Right. Oily waste can for disposal of rags or other materials saturated with flammable liquids. (Eagle Manfacturing Co.)

Fig. 18-9. Chips and dust should be removed from the work area. Left. Dust collector removes debris from machines. (Donaldson Company, Inc.) Right. Air filtration system removes smaller dust particles from the air. (United Air Specialties)

The potential for igniting a fire is high. Only explosion proof light fixtures and fan motors should be installed in the room. Switches for lights and fans should be either spark proof or located outside of the room. Overspray should be controlled with exhaust filters. Clean and replace filters regularly.

Good housekeeping is essential. Finish and thinner containers should be kept covered and labeled. Place rags, strainers, and other items in approved disposal containers.

PERSONAL PROTECTIVE EQUIPMENT

People must be protected from harmful substances. Hazards include inhalation, absorption, or physical contact with irritants and toxic substances.

Respirators. Respirators, Fig. 18-10, filter out harmful dust and certain gases. Several styles are available. Select a respirator that fits properly and is designed for the type of work you are doing. Thin paper and cloth respirators seldom filter out more than small dust particles.

Gloves. Gloves provide protection from splinters when handling rough lumber. Rubber or vinyl gloves may be required when handling harmful liquids. Wear gloves that cover your hands and forearms up to other clothing. This is particularly important for people who are allergic to certain materials.

REMOVE GLOVES WHILE OPERATING POWER MACHINERY. Gloves can get caught in a machine and draw your hand into the cutting tool or other moving parts. Serious injury could result from failure to remove gloves.

Shoes. Protective footwear prevents injury from sharp or falling objects and solvents. Steel toed shoes reduce injury from falling objects. Some have

Fig. 18-10. Respirators fit tightly over the nose and mouth. The filter, screwed onto the front, can be replaced when dirty. (Willson Safety Products)

solvent-resistant soles. Canvas or vinyl shoe tops with soft rubber soles are not adequate protection.

Eye protection. Eye protection is essential in the shop. *Goggles* and *industrial safety glasses* with side shields are best, Fig. 18-11. You can obtain safety glasses with prescription lenses. Safety lenses are thicker than those people normally wear. Safety glasses are etched with the manufacturer's logo. You can wear approved goggles over prescription glasses. Have an inspection and replacement system to detect and replace pitted or scratched lenses.

Goggles sometimes tend to collect moisture from perspiration. This clouds the user's vision. If this happens wear a face shield instead. It protects you from flying chips and splashing solvents. You are protected best with approved goggles or glasses beneath the shield.

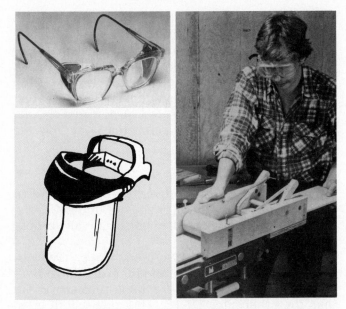

Fig. 18-11. Eye protection. Top. Industrial safety glasses. (MCO) Right. Goggles. (Butler Specialty Company) Bottom. Face shield.

Wearing contact lenses is a poor decision, even when wearing goggles. Dust can get under goggles causing eye irritation and distraction.

Ear protection. Loud noises may cause temporary or permanent hearing impairment. Saws, planers, and jointers create noise when in use. Noise levels increase as cutting tools become dull. Two symptoms of noise overexposure are a feeling of nervousness and a ringing in your ears.

Fig. 18-12. Vinyl ear plugs and ear muffs provide comfortable and effective ear protection. (Henrick)

Ear muffs or fitted *ear plugs* provide approved hearing protection, Fig. 18-12. You should not be exposed to noise over 90 dBA (decibels). Refer to Fig. 18-13.

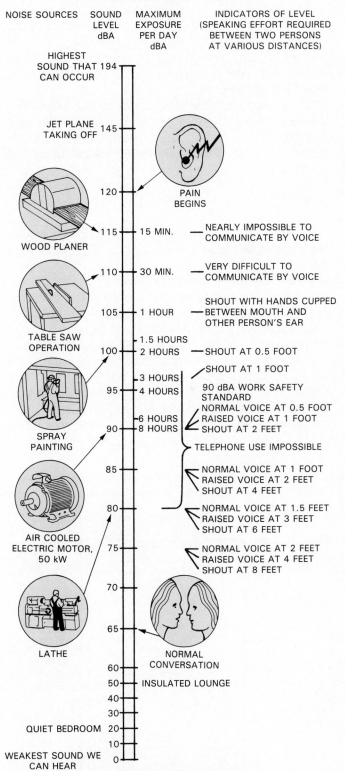

PERMISSIBLE NOISE EXPOSURES

NOISE SOURCES	SOUND LEVEL dBA	MAXIMUM EXPOSURE PER DAY dBA	INDICATORS OF LEVEL (SPEAKING EFFORT REQUIRED BETWEEN TWO PERSONS AT VARIOUS DISTANCES)
HIGHEST SOUND THAT CAN OCCUR	194		
JET PLANE TAKING OFF	145		
	120		PAIN BEGINS
WOOD PLANER	115	15 MIN.	NEARLY IMPOSSIBLE TO COMMUNICATE BY VOICE
	110	30 MIN.	VERY DIFFICULT TO COMMUNICATE BY VOICE
TABLE SAW OPERATION	105	1 HOUR	SHOUT WITH HANDS CUPPED BETWEEN MOUTH AND OTHER PERSON'S EAR
		1.5 HOURS	
	100	2 HOURS	SHOUT AT 0.5 FOOT
			SHOUT AT 1 FOOT
		3 HOURS	90 dBA WORK SAFETY STANDARD
SPRAY PAINTING	95	4 HOURS	NORMAL VOICE AT 0.5 FOOT
	90	6 HOURS 8 HOURS	RAISED VOICE AT 1 FOOT SHOUT AT 2 FEET
			TELEPHONE USE IMPOSSIBLE
	85		NORMAL VOICE AT 1 FOOT RAISED VOICE AT 2 FEET SHOUT AT 4 FEET
AIR COOLED ELECTRIC MOTOR, 50 kW	80		NORMAL VOICE AT 1.5 FEET RAISED VOICE AT 3 FEET SHOUT AT 6 FEET
	75		NORMAL VOICE AT 2 FEET RAISED VOICE AT 4 FEET SHOUT AT 8 FEET
	70		
LATHE	65		
	60		NORMAL CONVERSATION
	50		INSULATED LOUNGE
	40		
	30		
QUIET BEDROOM	20		
	10		
WEAKEST SOUND WE CAN HEAR	0		

Fig. 18-13. Recommended maximum exposure per day to various noise levels. You can quickly determine the noise level according to how loud you have to speak.

Clothes. Wear snug-fitting clothes. Roll up or tightly button long sleeved shirts. Wear a shop apron, otherwise make sure your clothes are tucked in. Remove jewelry such as rings, watches, and especially necklaces.

MATERIAL STORAGE

Many safety problems occur when storing materials. Instead of returning materials to their proper storage place, people tend to leave them elsewhere. Always return tools, equipment, and materials to their proper places.

Store lumber horizontally on sturdy shelves or vertically in racks. Lumber stored horizontally should not extend over aisles. Store wood product panels flat or on an edge. Stack partial pieces flat to reduce warpage.

ELECTRICAL

Nearly all cabinetmakers use electric power equipment. Special precautions must be taken to reduce risks.

Label voltages and intended use for switches, circuit breakers, and other electrical control devices, Fig. 18-14. Apply a label directly on the device. Enclose or guard all switches or other electrical equipment carrying between 50 and 600 volts.

Machines and electrical equipment should be wired in compliance with the National Electrical Code. This includes proper grounding. Stationary machines, rated over 120 V, should have cutoff switches with magnetic controls. New machines

have low voltage transformers on switches to reduce hazards of electrical shock.

Electrical cords can be a source of problems. They must be inspected regularly. With age cords often become brittle. Insulation breaks away exposing bare wires. Tools may also damage cords. A belt sander could cut into the cord. A portable circular saw may sever the cord. Keep cords away from the point-of-operation.

Electrical grounding

Electrical grounding prevents you from being shocked or electrocuted. Inspect electrical tools, especially those that are portable, for proper grounding.

Some tools have only two-prong plugs; however, most have an additional prong for ground. On *two-prong plugs,* one of the prongs is typically wider than the other, Fig. 18-15. This plug will fit in an outlet only *one way.* Notice that outlet slots are of different sizes.

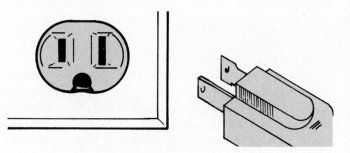

Fig. 18-15. Two-prong plugs can be inserted into the outlet only one way.

Inspect all two-slot outlets for proper grounding. Do so with a continuity tester, Fig. 18-16. The tester lamp will glow when the tester is inserted into both slots. It should also light between the outlet's short slot and the cover screw. The lamp should not glow between the long slot and the screw. If it does, the outlet is wired improperly.

Power tools with a ground wire have *three-prong plugs.* Generally, two prongs are flat and the ground prong is round. THE GROUND PRONG MUST NEVER BE DAMAGED OR REMOVED. The cord for this tool contains three wires. One wire connects the tool's metal housing or case to the ground on the plug. The other wires carry the electrical current.

As a general rule, power tools with metal housings need the ground prong. There is too much danger of electrical shock. Power tools with plastic housings insulate you from electrical power. Those labeled ''double insulated'' further protect you from electrical shock.

Three-prong plugs cannot be connected directly to outlets with just two slots. You must use an

DUST COLLECTOR

START

STOP

220 VOLTS

Fig. 18-14. All switch panels should be clearly marked with intended use and voltage.

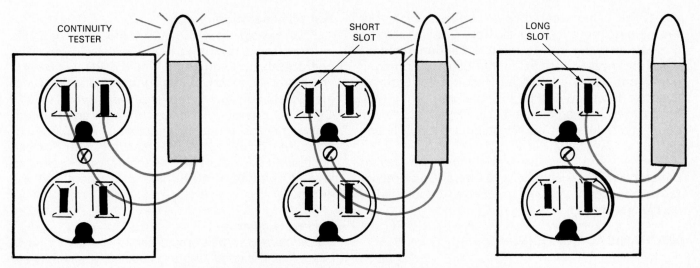

Fig. 18-16. Use a continuity tester to check electrical ground.

adapter. Do so only after you know that the outlet is grounded. Connect the adapter wire to the cover plate screw. The use of the three-prong adapter with its pigtail connected to the center screw which holds the switch plate will provide a ground under certain but not all circumstances. Some wiring systems use nonmetallic cable and provide no grounding system whatever. The test described above will determine if outlets are grounded. That is, if putting one leg of the tester in the hot slot and the other onto the cover screw results in the tester lighting, you can be sure that the outlet has ground, Fig. 18-17.

Some high voltage equipment has a plug with three or four prongs. The receptacle matches the plug. It may be in the wall or hang from an overhead electrical track. Insert the plug in the receptacle, and twist it slightly to lock it in place.

COMPRESSED AIR

Compressed air is used to power air tools and to remove dust, chips, and other debris from machinery. Air hoses for debris removal use a *pressure relief nozzle.* This nozzle has extra holes that lessen the pressure exiting the main nozzle jet. They also allow air to escape if the primary air passage is blocked. Limit air hose pressure to 30 psi if a pressure relief nozzle is not available, Fig. 18-18. Wear safety glasses when using an air noz-

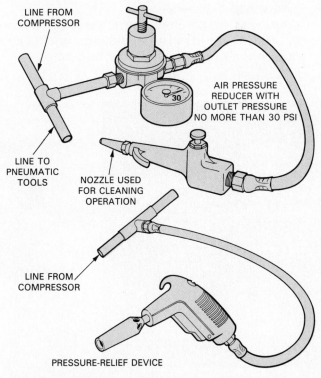

LINE FROM COMPRESSOR

AIR PRESSURE REDUCER WITH OUTLET PRESSURE NO MORE THAN 30 PSI

LINE TO PNEUMATIC TOOLS

NOZZLE USED FOR CLEANING OPERATION

LINE FROM COMPRESSOR

PRESSURE-RELIEF DEVICE

Fig. 18-18. These are two acceptable types of air nozzles to blow debris from surfaces. Each meets the 30 psi requirement. (National Institute for Occupational Safety and Health)

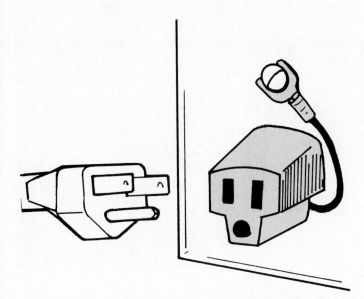

Fig. 18-17. Proper connection for a three-prong adapter plug.

zle. Chips or dust could be blown back into your face. Point the nozzle away from yourself. Using a brush or tack cloth to remove debris is safer.

Air tool hazards are often the result of damaged hoses and worn couplings. Hoses deteriorate or become damaged due to improper use. They may be cracked or severed during use. Inspect hoses and couplings regularly. Couplings should fit tightly and be free of air leaks.

Air lines and pressure tanks should be free of moisture. Air lines should have filters. Compressor tanks have drain valves to remove accumulated condensed water.

MECHANICAL GUARDING

Every moving part of a machine is a potential hazard. You sense that by observing a machine in motion. All belts, pulleys, gears, and cutter edges are dangerous. The operator must be protected. Much of the protection is built in by manufacturers. However, risks are created by operators who do not install or position guards properly.

Proper machine guarding covers all moving parts. The three kinds of motion, shown in Fig. 18-19, can produce a crushing or shearing action:
1. *Rotary motion* includes circular saw blades, pulleys, belts, cutterheads, and spindles.
2. *Reciprocating motion* is back and forth straight line movement. Examples are machines such as jig and saber saws, shears, and presses.
3. *Straight-line motion* occurs with band saw blades and belt sanders.

Guards can be grouped into several classifications. These are point-of-operation, enclosure, interlocking, automatic, and remote control.

Point-of-operation guards

Point-of-operation (PO) guards protect your hands or body from the cutting tool. They also protect the operator from flying chips, Fig. 18-20. PO guards are made of metal or high impact plastic. Clear plastic allows you to observe your work safely. Often PO guarding is moved for tool setup or adjustments and must be reinstalled. A majority of accidents occur when PO guards have not been positioned correctly. New machinery is required to have PO guards. Retrofit older equipment with PO guards.

Enclosure guards

Enclosure guards completely cover moving parts other than the point-of-operation. They generally are removed only for maintenance. They protect you

Fig. 18-20. Clear plastic point-of-operation guards allow you to see your work. (Porter-Cable Corp.)

 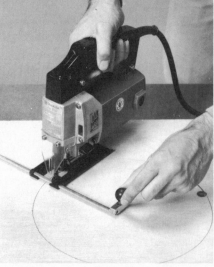 

A   B   C

Fig. 18-19. Beware of motions which can cause injury. A-Rotary. (American Plywood Assoc.) B—Reciprocating. (Makita U.S.A., Inc.) C—Straightline. (Delta International Machinery Corp.)

from motors, shafts, pulleys, belts, Fig. 18-21. Examples are the upper and lower wheel covers on a band saw.

Interlocking guards

Interlocking guards prevent machines from operation while dangerous parts are exposed. An electrical or mechanical device disconnects power while the PO or enclosure guard is off. For example, a microswitch prevents a band saw from being turned on while the wheel enclosure guard is off or not secured.

Automatic guards

Automatic guards act independently of the machine operator. As you push the wood through the point of operation, the guard is raised or pushed aside, Fig. 18-22. It moves only enough to allow the stock to pass. After the material passes the point of operation, the guard returns to its normal position.

Table saws and radial arm have automatic guarding. Sharp toothed antikickback devices lift while stock passes under them. The device prevents the material from being thrown back toward the operator. If the stock attemps to move backwards, the teeth or fingers dig into the wood to stop it.

Jointers also have automatic guards. The guard covers the cutter. As stock is fed through the jointer, the guard moves aside.

Remote control guards

Remote control guards are special purpose guards. They are used primarily in automated cabinetmaking systems. Stock is fed by a chute, hopper, or conveyor. There are no operator access openings on the machine. Automatic feed keeps the operator at a safe distance.

Guards are placed to protect all parts of the body. On foot controlled machines, cover all pedals, treadles, or switches to prevent accidental starting.

Fig. 18-21. Enclosure guards cover mechanical parts. Top. Fixed enclosure guard. (Rockwell International) Bottom. Adjustable enclosure guard also used as PO guard. (Brodhead-Garrett)

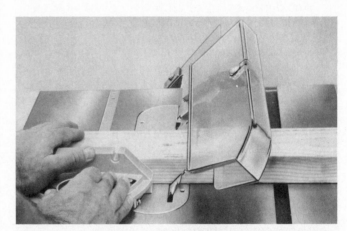

Fig. 18-22. Automatic guards move aside as the stock is cut. (Rockwell International)

On hand controlled machines, move both hands away from the point of operation prior to starting the machine.

FIRST AID

Even the most experienced individuals have accidents. Be able to get the needed assistance in an emergency. Post local numbers or the recently activated 911 emergency number on the telephone.

People who work with tools, materials, and supplies for cabinetmaking should have first aid training. Learn the proper first aid procedures in case of an injury. Read the labeling on hazardous substance containers before using them. Be ready to respond if the need arises.

THINK SAFETY—ACT SAFELY

An accident and injury-free workplace is always a worthy goal. Work carefully, yet also look for hazards that result because of an unsafe environment.

Accidents occur to both the novice and experienced cabinetmaker. Many accidents occur to novice cabinetmakers because they fear the machines. Confidence is very important. It comes from planning your work carefully and gaining experience. Unfortunately, some people become overconfident which leads to carelessness. Be aware of the risks you might take.

People always think about an accident after they are injured. Experienced cabinetmakers say they knew better, but were in a hurry. They took shortcuts and didn't follow all the precautions. The novice cabinetmaker may not know better. This is why novices should try to watch an experienced cabinetmaker in action.

Your shop is only as safe as you make it. Machine guards, eye protection, and other safety items are effective only when used properly. Warnings about unsafe acts and hazardous conditions serve only those who read and heed them.

Having skill and knowledge about machines and processes is not enough to prevent accidents. These are important, but must be accompanied by a positive attitude toward safety. Too often you take risks and your attitude improves only after an injury or a near miss.

Safety tips are given throughout the remaining chapters. They relate to safe practices in each area of cabinetmaking. If you are a novice, read and learn each safety tip. If you are an experienced cabinetmaker, review them as a reminder to you.

CABINETMAKING TERMS

Unsafe acts, trigger lock, hazardous conditions, non-skid mat, fire protection, Class A fire, Class B fire, Class C fire, fire extinguisher, flammable liquid, flash point, safety cabinet, safety can, flame arrestor, dust collection system, exhaust system, respirator, goggles, industrial safety glasses, ear muffs, ear plugs, electrical grounding, two-prong plug, three-prong plug, pressure relief nozzle, rotary motion, reciprocating motion, point-of-operation guard, enclosure guard, interlocking guard.

TEST YOUR KNOWLEDGE

1. Accidents occur as a result of _____ and _____.
2. You can make your workplace perfectly safe. True or False?
3. Explain factors which might lead to an unsafe act.
4. Hazardous conditions exist either because _____ or _____.
5. Describe how you can insure a fast and easy exit in case of emergency.
6. A fire will not burn without _____, _____, and _____.
7. List the three classes of fires and the material which burns in each.
8. The best fire extinguisher to have is the _____.
9. The class of flammable liquid is determined by the _____.
10. Identify storage requirements of flammable liquids.
11. Flame arrestors are placed:
    a. Inside safety cans.
    b. In sprinkler systems.
    c. In the neck of fire extinguishers.
    d. In the wall of safety cabinets.
12. Use explosion proof switches in:
    a. Areas of woodworking machines.
    b. Finishing rooms.
    c. Storage rooms.
    d. Warehouses.
13. Protect your hearing by wearing _____ or _____.
14. List three types of eye protection.
15. How do you detect if a two-prong electrical outlet is properly grounded?
16. The three types of motions which should be guarded are _____, _____, and _____.
17. List the five types of guards and identify two examples of each.

Chapter 19
ORDERING MATERIALS AND SUPPLIES

After studying this chapter, you will be able to:
- Prepare a material order list based on the working drawings and bill of materials.
- Identify and order supplies required to build a product.
- Explain order amounts and packaging by sizes and volumes.

The two most important factors when ordering are to be thorough and economical. Being thorough requires you to know and specify the exact quality and quantity of every material, supply, and tool it will take to complete your product. Being econom-

ical means getting the best quality and quantity of materials for your money.

BE THOROUGH

To be thorough means you must study the working drawings. This includes the product views, bill of materials (BOM), Fig. 19-1, and plan of procedure. Then you must write complete, detailed, and accurate orders for the required materials.

From the bill of materials, make a list of the lumber, manufactured products, mechanical fasteners, and hardware needed. If this information is not

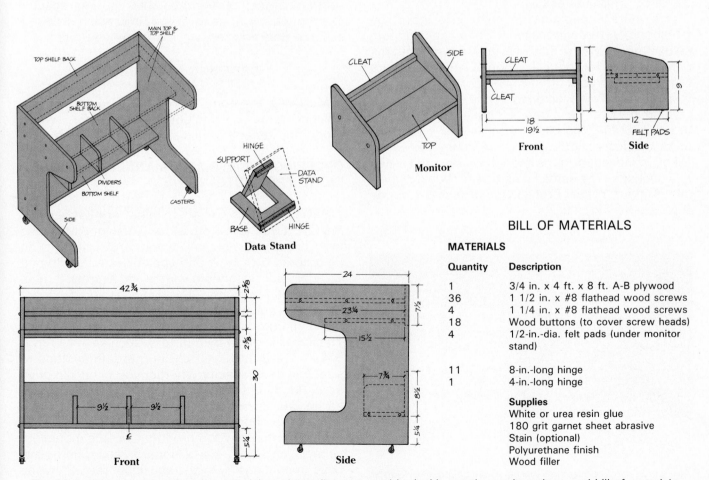

BILL OF MATERIALS

MATERIALS

Quantity	Description
1	3/4 in. x 4 ft. x 8 ft. A-B plywood
36	1 1/2 in. x #8 flathead wood screws
4	1 1/4 in. x #8 flathead wood screws
18	Wood buttons (to cover screw heads)
4	1/2-in.-dia. felt pads (under monitor stand)
11	8-in.-long hinge
1	4-in.-long hinge

Supplies
White or urea resin glue
180 grit garnet sheet abrasive
Stain (optional)
Polyurethane finish
Wood filler

Fig. 19-1. You can determine the materials and supplies you need by looking at the product views and bill of materials. (American Plywood Assoc.)

in the bill of materials, study the detail drawings and notes carefully to find it. Read the steps in the plan of procedure. Itemize supplies, such as adhesives, abrasives, stain, tack cloth, etc. You need to order these if you do not have them on hand. The plan of procedure also may recommend tools, machines, and equipment. Be sure you have similar equipment to perform the work.

BE ECONOMICAL

Economy seems to be the bottom line for making many decisions. Economy of time means: How long must you look for items and how long before you receive them? Economy of money means: What quality and quantity do you get for your money? In time, you will find reliable dealers. In the beginning, make decisions by comparison shopping.

Comparison shopping. Often, time involved in ordering has much to do with comparison shopping. Decide which building supply company, lumber yard, hardware store, or paint dealer has what you need for a reasonable price. This may not mean the lowest cost because quality varies. Remember, the least expensive items may not be the most economical. Low priced boards may contain too many knots, checks, etc. Poor quality tools may dull, bend, or break too easily.

Is it more economical to order in a store, by telephone, or through the mail? Shopping at a store takes time. However, it allows you to inspect items before paying for them. Telephone and mail orders require less of your time. However, the material is inspected and decided upon by the seller, not you.

Price breaks. Be aware of price breaks when ordering. Some products may be cheaper if purchased by the dozen. For example, the money you spend for eight individual items might have bought twelve in a package. The same holds true for liquid materials. A quart of filler probably costs less per ounce than a pint, Fig. 19-2.

Fig. 19-2. Larger containers are generally cheaper per ounce. (Borden, Inc.)

Merchandise returns. Ask dealers about return policies for merchandise. What if you buy too much? Under what conditions will they take it back? If they accept unopened items, is there a restocking charge?

Extra charges. Extra charges often are added when dealers cut lumber and panel products to size for you. For example, suppose you need a half sheet of plywood that is $20.00 per sheet. The dealer quotes you a price of $13.00 per half sheet. You realize you are paying a $3.00 cutting charge. The dealer restocks the other half and waits for someone to buy the remainder for $10.00 or more. In addition, you may not be allowed to return the precut materials.

Reliable dealers. In time, you will come to rely on one or several dealers for your materials. Most of them want to satisfy you to make you a return customer. However, do not overlook sale items which could reduce the cost of your products.

DESCRIBING MATERIALS AND SUPPLIES

In previous chapters on materials, sections on size and quality description were discussed. They covered topics such as grades, sizes, thicknesses, appearance, features, qualities, etc. Review these sections before ordering so that you can specify exactly what you need. Extra time when ordering assures that you receive the items you need.

ORDERING MATERIALS

Materials are items which become part of the finished product. Included are lumber, wood products, fasteners, glass, laminates, finish, etc.

ORDERING LUMBER AND MANUFACTURED WOOD PRODUCTS

Basic materials for any cabinet are lumber and manufactured wood products. Softwood lumber is most available in nominal (dimensioned) sizes. It can be ordered by specie and specific size. Hardwood is usually sold in random widths and lengths. It must be ordered in volume—by thickness and by board footage or cubic meters. Dealer catalogs usually list the minimum and maximum widths and lengths. Thickness is given by quarters, such as 4/4 (1 in.), 5/4 (1 1/4 in.), 6/4 (1 1/2 in.), etc. In addition to size, you must specify whether you want kiln dried or air dried lumber. You might also want it surfaced on one or more sides. Be sure to specify the grade of lumber you need, Fig. 19-3.

Manufactured wood products include moulding, veneer, plywood, particleboard, and fiberboard. Order mouldings by shape and linear feet. Plywood and other panel items normally are 4 ft. by 8 ft.

QUANTITY	MANUFACTURER'S NO.	STOCK NO.	SIZE AND DESCRIPTION	UNIT PRICE	TOTAL
6 PCS.			KD. FIR 1"x10" - 8', NO. I COMMON		
120 BD.FT.			4/4 CHERRY, FAS, RWL, S2S, 6' TO 8' LENGTHS		
60 SQ.FT.			1/2" CHESTNUT, FAS, RWL, ROUGH, 8' TO 10' LENGTHS		
2 PC.			3/4"-12' OAK COVE MOULDING		
1 PC.			48"x 96"- 3/4" OAK PLYWOOD, G2S		

Fig. 19-3. This is a sample order for lumber and wood products. Note the number of specifications required so that you receive the item you need.

(1 200 mm x 2 400 mm). The face quality of plywood panels should be specified (see Chapter 13). Veneer may be sold in random sizes by square footage or in sheets, Fig. 19-4.

Fig. 19-4. Sheet veneer is cut into dimensioned sizes and packaged for easy handling. (Woodtape, Inc.)

Estimating lumber

Plan your lumber order carefully. If you will be using nominal stock, sketch the parts for your product. See how they might be cut from different sizes of stock. Allow extra space (1/4 to 1/2 in. actual size) around each part. From the sketch, you know the size and minimum amount of lumber you must order.

For random widths and lengths of hardwood lumber, determine the board feet needed in your project. Add 15 to 20 percent to that amount. The excess allows for defects and for waste made when cutting out workpieces. After you receive the lumber order, lay out the parts which will come from each board. Avoid defects. You might want to surface the lumber first to see the quality of the wood.

Estimating manufactured panel products

Manufactured products are being used more often than lumber for case construction. Panels are usually 4 ft. (1 200 mm) by 8 ft. (2 400 mm). Sketch a cutout diagram showing how components would be laid out on a panel, Fig. 19-5. Leave space between pieces to allow for a saw kerf. Final cuts can be made later.

When laying out components, be sure that paired doors and drawers are laid out next to each other. This matches the grain pattern, Fig. 19-6.

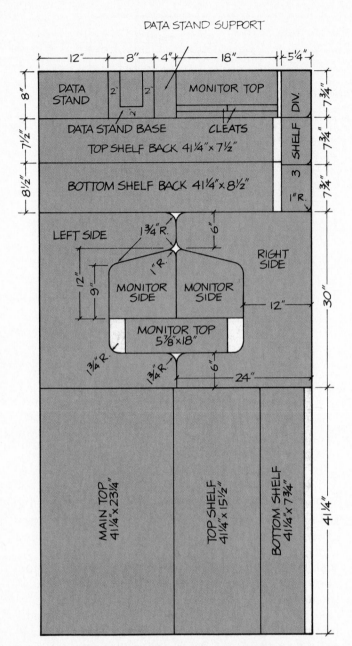

Fig. 19-5. Laying out components on a sheet of plywood. Remember to leave room for saw kerfs when laying out dimensions. (American Plywood Assoc.)

ORDERING GLASS, PLASTICS, CERAMICS, AND LAMINATES

Glass is sized by thickness, dimensions, and special treatment, such as tint. Be sure to specify whether edges are to be ground and/or polished. This is necessary for sliding glass doors.

Solid sheet plastics are generally sold by size. Liquid resins and catalysts for casting are sold by volume.

Ceramic tiles are sold by individual pieces or mesh-backed square foot assemblies. Tiles are packaged anywhere from 1 to 24 in a box. Always specify the tile model number. Make sure you

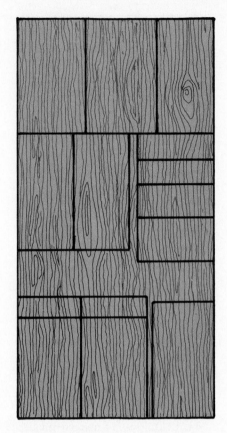

Fig. 19-6. Lay out doors and drawer fronts next to each other so the grain pattern matches.

receive the proper design. Inspect for shipping damage. Also order mastic and grout for laying tile, Fig. 19-7.

Plastic laminates are sold in sheets or rolls. You must specify one of the grades discussed in Chapter 14. Check the sizes offered by the dealer before ordering.

Fig. 19-7. This example shows the range of materials, supplies, and tools you must have to lay tile. (Ceramic Marketing, Inc.)

QUANTITY	MANUFACTURER'S NO.	STOCK NO.	SIZE AND DESCRIPTION	UNIT PRICE	TOTAL
100			#6 × 1¼" F.H. BRIGHT STEEL WOOD SCREWS		
3 LB.			4d CEMENT COATED BOX NAILS		
1 LB.			#16 × 1" BRADS		
10		345	PLASTIC CABINET PULLS, 4", BLACK		
6		A-40	MAGNETIC CABINET CATCHES, TAN PLASTIC		
6 PR.		123	CABINET HINGES FOR LIPDOORS, BRUSH BRONZE		

Fig. 19-8. Sample order for mechanical fasteners and hardware.

ORDERING MECHANICAL FASTENERS

As described in previous chapters, there are many kinds of fasteners. Order them by quantity, model number, manufacturer, finish, and size, Fig. 19-8. Part of the cost for fasteners is packaging. Therefore, ordering larger amounts may reduce the price per item. For example, you can buy fasteners in a plastic bubble from a display, cardboard box, or loose, Fig. 19-9. For the same price, you may get twice as many if you count them from a bin. The cost may be even less if you buy a box of 100. However, can you use the excess fasteners later and is storage space available? Some fasteners, such as nails, are sold by the pound. A chart is usually provided at the store to show you approximately how many nails are in a pound.

Fastener orders may specify the type of finish. Fasteners with a "bright" finish have no coatings. Otherwise, they may be galvanized (zinc coated) or plated with nickel, brass, and other metals. Nails often have cement coatings to increase their holding power.

ORDERING HARDWARE

Hardware items, such as pulls and hinges, may be packaged, boxed, or in bulk forms. Packages of individual pulls, hinges, and catches usually have screws with them. However, box or bulk purchases may not include fasteners. For most orders, you need only specify the stock number or manufacturer's number. See Fig. 19-8. If none is listed, you must specify the type, size, material, surface finish, and other features.

Fig. 19-9. Small quantities of mechanical fasteners are sold in plastic and cardboard packages or loose.

ORDERING FINISHING PRODUCTS

Finishing products include fillers, sealers, stains, and topcoatings. Common quantities are half-pints, pints, quarts, and gallons. The container label should indicate the number of square feet per gallon the finish will cover. The listed figure usually is determined under controlled testing conditions. You will likely cover 10 to 20 percent less surface area with the same amount.

Order solvents for finishing materials in larger sizes, such as one and five gallon containers. You likely will need it for thinning as well as cleanup after the finish is applied. Be sure to order the proper solvent and amount. Most finishes require a compatible type of solvent.

Check the shelf life (storage time) of the product. This is often labeled on the container. Order only the amount you will use within that time. If you will use a gallon, order that amount instead of two quarts now and two later. A gallon is much cheaper per ounce of finish.

ORDERING SUPPLIES

Supplies for cabinetmaking include consumable items which do not become a major part of the cabinet. Examples are abrasives, adhesives, rags, steel wool, and wax.

ORDERING ABRASIVES

You will need an assortment of abrasives (sandpaper). Order by grit, type, and form. Grit size refers to coarseness. Types may be natural (flint, garnet) or synthetic (silicon carbide, aluminum oxide). Forms of abrasives include sheets, belts, disks, sleeves, pads, or powders. The form you choose depends on the tool or sanding machine.

Sheets come in various sizes, but commonly are 9 in. by 11 in. Be sure the size can be cut to fit your hand sander and finishing sander. Sheets are sold as single sheets or in packages, Fig. 19-10.

After purchasing the abrasive, store it in a dry place. Moisture can soften the adhesive holding the grit to the backing. As a result, the abrasive comes off the product. This does not occur with wet-or-dry abrasives designed for use with oil and water.

ORDERING ADHESIVES

Adhesives include cements, glues, and mastics, as discussed in Chapter 32. You can purchase these in various size containers from gallon containers to small squeeze-type plastic bottles and tubes, Fig. 19-11. Construction adhesives often are in tubes for use with a caulking gun.

Check the adhesive's shelf life before buying large quantities. The label may say to store it in a cool place for no longer than six months. In some cases, the expiration date will be listed. Apply the glue before that specific date; otherwise it may not bond properly.

Have the correct solvents on hand to remove excess adhesives. These may be water, mineral spirits, or acetone.

ORDERING TOOLS

Buying tools is most easily done by shopping at the store. You can select the exact model you need.

QUANTITY	MANUFACTURER'S NO.	STOCK NO.	SIZE AND DESCRIPTION	UNIT PRICE	TOTAL
20		P2500	9"x11" SHEET GARNET 280 GRIT	.31	6.20
5		P2530	SILICON CARBIDE PAPER 400 GRIT	.60	3.00
10		P2522	ALUMINUM OXIDE PAPER 120 GRIT	.48	4.80
2		P2574	3"x21" 50X WOOD SANDING BELT	20.95	41.90

A

B

Fig. 19-10. A—Sample order for abrasives. B—Boxed quantities of abrasives can be cheaper than buying individual sheets. (Norton)

Fig. 19-11. Adhesives are sold in various quantities, from 1 oz. to five gallons.

When ordering by mail or phone, specify them by manufacturer and model number. Additional information, such as horsepower for a power saw or teeth per inch for a hand saw may be needed. See Fig. 19-12.

QUANTITY	MANUFACTURER'S NO.	STOCK NO.	SIZE AND DESCRIPTION	UNIT PRICE	TOTAL
1	R-331		2 H.P. RYOBI D-HANDLE ROUTER		
1		#C-8	26" 8-TOOTH CROSSCUT HAND SAW		
1		#CT-2	DOVETAIL ROUTER BIT 1/4" × 7/16" CUTTER 1/4" SHANK		
1			12"-13"GA. CARBIDE TIPPED CIRCULAR SAW BLADE COMBINATION - 20 TEETH 130 KERF		

Fig. 19-12. The router at top is ordered by manufacturer's model number. Other tools might be specified by the store's stock number for that item. (Ryobi America Corp.)

SUMMARY

Be thorough when ordering materials, supplies, and tools. Know exactly your needs when shopping over the counter, by telephone, or through the mail.

Be economical in what you purchase. The least expensive item may well be the most costly if it does not do the job as well. Shopping at a store allows you to inspect items before you pay for them. This is time consuming and may not be economical. Purchases by telephone and mail require less of your time. However, you must be very accurate when preparing your order. Grades, qualities, quantities, model numbers, and other information is essential. Rarely can you include too many specifications. Too little information may prevent filling the order.

You should know your exact needs from the bill of materials. When ordering, look for the highest quality products for the lowest cost. You may wish to buy in quantity to reduce the price. However, if you purchase too much, you have to store it. You also risk the chance of it becoming outdated.

CABINETMAKING TERMS

Thorough, economical, bill of materials, plan of procedure, comparison shopping, price breaks, merchandise returns, extra charges, packaging.

TEST YOUR KNOWLEDGE

1. The two most important factors when ordering are _____ and _____.
2. Where do working drawings provide information about materials, supplies, and tools?
3. The lowest cost item is the one to buy. True or False?
4. You can be sure to receive the item you need when shopping:
   a. In a store.
   b. Through the mail.
   c. Over the telephone.
5. Describe what a cutting charge is.
6. The least expensive way to buy fasteners is in a plastic package. True or False?
7. Describe how you would specify the size of the following items:
   a. Hardwood lumber.
   b. Softwood lumber.
   c. Plywood.
   d. Mouldings.
8. How would you determine the square footage a container of finish will cover?
9. Order abrasives by _____, _____, and _____.
10. The best way to specify tools is by _____ and _____.

Chapter 20
MEASURING AND LAYING OUT MATERIALS

After studying this chapter, you will be able to:
- Select marking, measuring, and layout tools.
- Lay out lines and geometric shapes.
- Maintain measurement and layout tools.

Accurate measurement and layout is essential for high quality cabinetmaking. Your design means very little unless you can transfer the shapes onto your materials. With skillful measuring, you can mark, cut, and assemble parts with precision.

Much of cabinetmaking relies on square edges and joints. *Squareness* simply means that all corners join at a 90° angle, Fig. 20-1. When a piece is not cut square, or two pieces are not assembled square, the entire cabinet is affected.

This chapter describes how to mark accurate geometric shapes on your materials. A number of tools are used by cabinetmakers to complete layouts. These include marking, measuring, and layout tools.

MARKING TOOLS

Most cabinetmakers mark with a pencil. A sharp pencil will make a narrow line. A knife or *scratch awl* (scriber) will also mark the wood, Fig. 20-2. A light cut makes a visible reference line for sawing or other work. A knife is often used when the mark will be used as a locator for a chisel point. A scratch

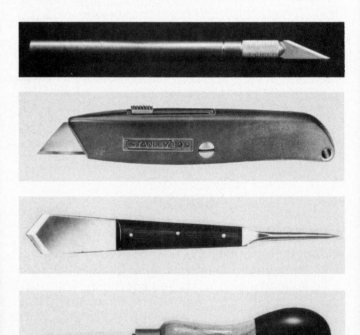

Fig. 20-1. Accurately measured, laid out, and cut material results in high quality products, such as this hutch. (Thomasville)

Fig. 20-2. Knives and scratch awls make precise marks. A variety of styles are used.
(Stanley, Record Ridgway Tools, Brookstone)

awl can indent the wood to center a drill, Fig. 20-3. Avoid ink; it bleeds into wood cells.

MEASURING TOOLS

Measuring tools follow two different systems: customary and metric. Customary rulers and scales measure feet and inches. Smaller units are measured in fractions of an inch, Fig. 20-4A. Find the fractional distance you need by counting spaces across the board. This becomes the numerator (top number). Count the spaces in one inch on the rule. This is the denominator (bottom number). Metric rulers and scales measure in millimeters. They are typically numbered every 10 millimeters, Fig.

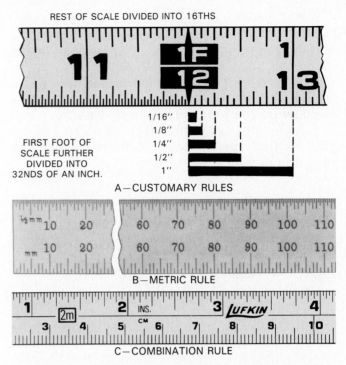

Fig. 20-4. Rule measuring units may be customary, metric, or a combination of both. Use the system designated on the working drawings.
(Lufkin Division—The Cooper Group, The L.S. Starrett Co.)

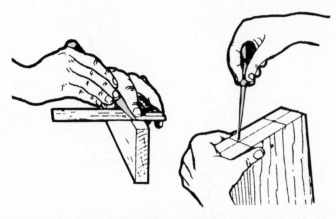

Fig. 20-3. Marking. A—Marking a line with a knife. B—Marking a drill center point with an awl.   (Stanley)

20-4B. The metric rule may be further divided into 0.5 (half) millimeters. Both systems may appear on the same measuring tool.

The measuring system you choose depends on the working drawings. The title block will tell what system is used. It will also provide the scale of the drawing. If the scale reads 1 in. = 1 ft., then each inch on the drawing will be 1 ft. on the layout.

RULE

The rule you select depends mostly on the accuracy you need and which style you prefer. Rules may be flat, flexible, or folding types. They are made of wood, fiberglass, plastic, metal, or cloth.

Often, both customary and metric measurements are found on the rule.

Flat rules are typically wood or plastic. They may be 1 to 4 ft. long. High quality rules have a brass edge. The brass edge is not dented as easily as a wood edge. Rules may also be steel and aluminum.

Rigid *folding rules* are usually 6 ft. long. Metric rules are 2 m long. Some have an extension rule at one end for measuring inside distances, Fig. 20-5.

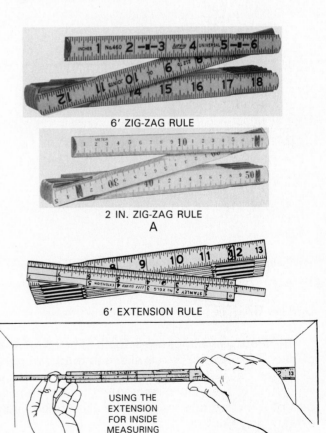

Fig. 20-5. A—Rigid folding rules extend to measure distances. (Lufkin Division—The Cooper Group). B—They also measure inside distances with an extension. (Stanley)

A *flexible rule,* or tape measure, is very convenient, Fig. 20-6. It will measure both straight lengths and curves. Also use it to measure inside distances, such as a doorway. Add 2 in. (51 mm) or 3 in. (75 mm) to the measurement to account for the size of the tape case. Other tapes have a window on the top to read inside distance.

Tape lengths range from 6 ft. (2 m) to 150 ft. (50 m). Both customary and metric measurements may be printed on the tape.

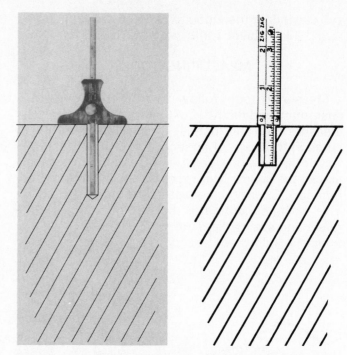

Fig. 20-7. The depth gauge blade or rule extension measures hole depth. Read the dimension at the surface of the hole. (The L.S. Starrett Co.)

index line. Inside dimensions are read at the "in" index line, Fig. 20-8.

SQUARES

There are a number of different kinds of squares. They are used for several purposes, which include:
1. Checking that corners form a 90° angle (squareness).
2. Serving as a straightedge.
3. Measuring distances and angles.

Framing and bench squares

Framing and bench squares are flat steel or aluminum. A *framing square* has a 24 in. (600 mm) body and 16 in. (400 mm) tongue. A *bench square* is smaller, Fig. 20-9. The body and tongue are formed at a 90° angle (right angle). The face of the square is seen when the body is held in the left hand and the tongue in the right hand. The back is the other side of the square. The face and back of the square have scales and tables.

Scales. The scales refer to customary and metric measurements. This makes the scale useful as a rule. Once a measurement is marked, the square can be used to draw a perpendicular line, Fig. 20-10. It can also be used to check the squareness of a constructed joint.

Tables. Tables provide helpful information for commonly used measurements. Two such tables are the brace measure table and the octagon scale, or eight square scale.

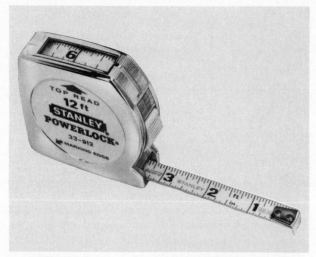

Fig. 20-6. Two types of flexible rules. (Stanley)

DEPTH GAUGE

The *depth gauge* measures depth of holes or other offsets, Fig. 20-7. The rule slides through the body of the gauge. Tighten the adjusting nut before lifting the gauge to read the measurement. The extension part of a folding rule may also be used to measure offsets and depths.

CALIPER RULE

The *caliper rule* measures outside and inside distances. Outside dimensions are read at the "out"

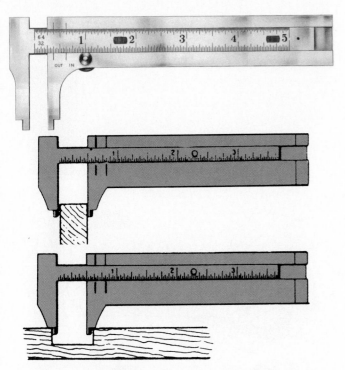

Fig. 20-8. Caliper rules have a head formed to measure outside and inside dimensions. (The L.S. Starrett Co.)

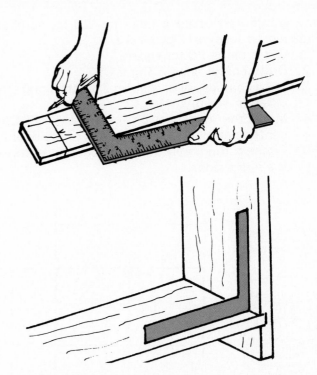

Fig. 20-10. Framing and bench squares are used for measuring and marking, as well as checking squareness.

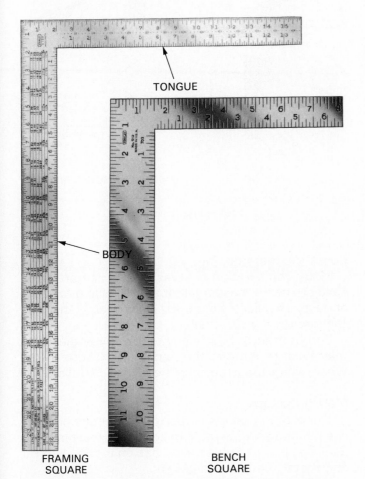

TONGUE

BODY

FRAMING
SQUARE

BENCH
SQUARE

Fig. 20-9. Framing squares are larger than bench squares. The framing square also may have a list of scales and tables printed on it. (Stanley)

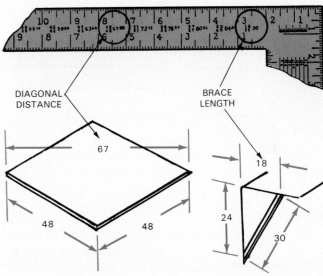

DIAGONAL
DISTANCE

BRACE
LENGTH

67

48   48

18

24   30

Fig. 20-11. The brace measure table shows brace lengths.

The brace *measure table* is on the tongue of most framing squares. It gives diagonal measurements which show the length needed for a diagonal piece, such as a brace to support a shelf, Fig. 20-11. Example: Suppose you have an 18 in. wide shelf and you wish to brace it from 24 in. below the shelf. Find the measurement on the table marked 18/24. You will find the number 30 next to it. This is the proper length of the brace.

The *octagon scale* helps you identify critical measurements for laying out octagons. Suppose you wanted an octagon table top 28 in. across. Proceed as follows, Fig. 20-12:

1. Cut a piece 28 in. square.
2. Draw center lines AB and CD.
3. Set a compass or divider for 28 dots along the octagon scale.
4. Mark the distance on each side of the centerlines along the four edges of the board.
5. Connect the newly marked locations to form the eight sides.

TRY SQUARE

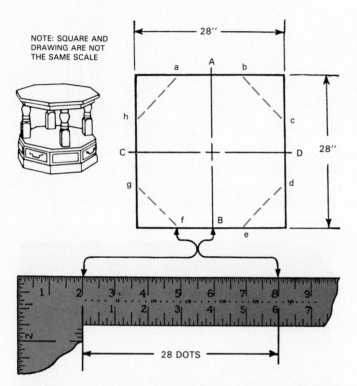

NOTE: SQUARE AND DRAWING ARE NOT THE SAME SCALE

28 DOTS

Fig. 20-12. The octagon scale, found on some framing squares, is a row of numbered dots for laying out octagons. (Stanley)

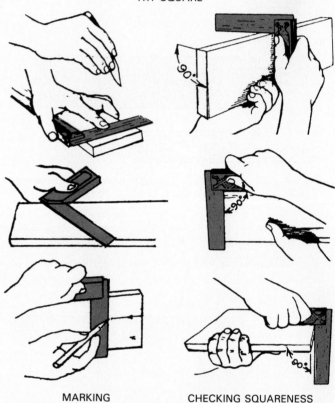

MARKING   CHECKING SQUARENESS

Fig. 20-13. Try squares are for both marking and checking squareness. (Stanley)

Try square

Try squares have a steel blade and a steel or wood handle. Some have a 45° angle cut into the handle. Use them for making layouts or checking squareness, Fig. 20-13.

Combination square

The *combination square* consists of a blade which slides through a handle. It also may have protractor and center heads, Fig. 20-14. You can use a combination square for a number of purposes:

1. Measure distances and depths.
2. Layout 90° angles, 45° diagonal, and parallel lines.
3. Locate centers.

Parallel lines can be laid out easily. Adjust the blade to the intended distance. Place a pencil or knife point against the end of the blade. While holding the pencil against the blade, slide the square

down the material, Fig. 20-15A.

Many combination squares have a center head. Hold the center head against any circular or curved surface. The blade's edge will point directly through the center, Fig. 20-15B.

The protractor head adjusts for any angle. You may wish to remove the handle and center head when using the protractor head, Fig. 20-15C.

Marking gauge

The *marking gauge* is designed to make parallel lines. It has an adjustable head and a steel pin, Fig. 20-16A. It will mark parallel lines on wood, plastic, and metal. To use the gauge:

1. Adjust the head to the appropriate width from the edge of the board to the line, Fig. 20-16B.
2. Place the gauge flat on the material. The steel

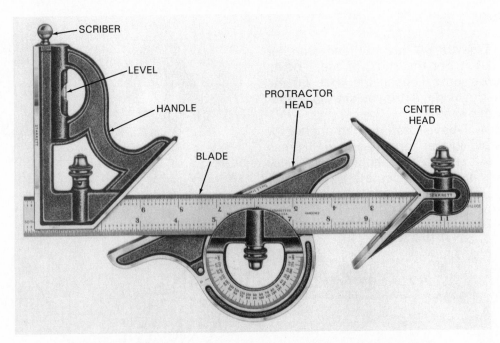

Fig. 20-14. Parts of a combination square. (The L.S. Starrett Co.)

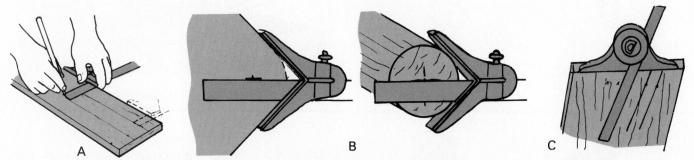

Fig. 20-15. Use the combination square to: A—Mark parallel lines. B—Find centers. C—Mark angles.

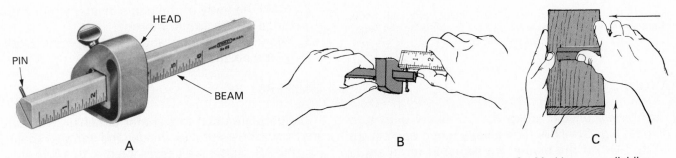

Fig. 20-16. A—Components of a marking gauge. (Stanley) B—Setting the marking gauge. C—Marking a parallel line.

point should point sideways, without touching the wood.

3. Roll the gauge toward you until the awl pin touches the material.

4. Push the gauge away from you. Keep the head against the edge of the work. The point should make a visible score line, Fig. 20-16C.

Also use a marking gauge to transfer dimensions. Set the marking gauge to the size of part you wish to copy. Then mark the new workpiece. This is helpful when duplicating parts.

LAYOUT TOOLS

Layout tools transfer distances, angles, and contours. Most lack scales for measuring distances and angles. They are set with a measuring tool. The following descriptions cover common layout tools.

SLIDING T-BEVEL

The *sliding T-bevel* will lay out and transfer angles, Fig. 20-17. Set the angle of the T-bevel blade with a protractor. Loosen the knob on the handle to move the blade. After you set the proper angle, tighten the knob.

Besides layout, T-bevels can set the angles for table saw blades, jointer fences, and drill press tables. If you are setting 90° angles, use a try square. T-bevels are not as accurate as a square.

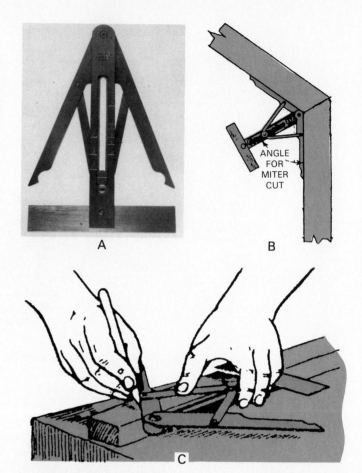

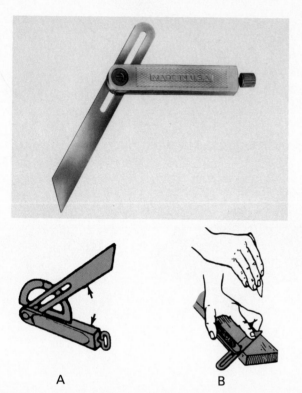

Fig. 20-17. The T-bevel has a body, blade, and lock knob. (Stanley) A— Set it with a protractor. B—Marking the wood with a T-bevel.

ANGLE DIVIDER

An *angle divider* looks like a T-bevel with two blades, Fig. 20-18A. The blades move apart from 0° to 90°. If the blades are adjusted to an angle or a corner, the body bisects the angle. This angle helps when cutting miter joints, Fig. 20-18B.

Angle dividers have numbers on the body and an index mark on the adjusting nut. The numbers on the side of the nut are 30°, 45°, and 60°. Aligning the index mark along these numbers accurately sets the blades to that angle. The numbers on the other side of the nut are 4, 5, 6, 8, 10, and 0. These indicate settings for polygons. Aligning the index nut at 6 will set the angle of the blades for a hexagon (a six sided polygon). The angle between the blades will be 120°. The body will bisect the

Fig. 20-18. Angle dividers are helpful when setting angles for cutting miter joints. (General Hardware)

angle at 60°. When the index mark is set at 0, the blades form a straight line with the body.
Example: To layout an octagon picture frame.
1. Set the index mark even with the 8.
2. Hold the body of the angle divider against the edge of the frame material.
3. Mark the mitering angle and saw the workpiece on that line, Fig. 20-18C.

CALIPERS

Calipers are used to transfer dimensions. There are three kinds: outside, inside, and hermaphrodite, Fig. 20-19. Some are asssembled with a firm (friction) joint. Others have a bow spring with an adjusting screw and nut. Firm joint calipers are quicker to adjust, yet bow spring calipers maintain greater accuracy during use.

Calipers are used most often when wood turning. When the lathe is stopped, you can check or transfer thicknesses and distances.

Outside caliper. An outside caliper checks outside diameters on turnings, Fig. 20-20. Set the caliper with a rule first. Then turn the material until the caliper slips over it. When making duplicate parts, set the caliper by the workpiece being copied.

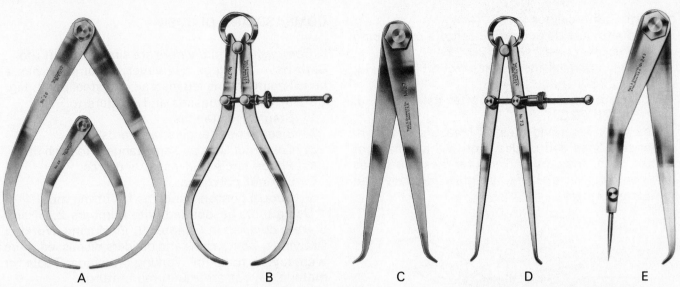

Fig. 20-19. Calipers for transferring outside and inside measurements and parallel lines. A—Firm joint outside calipers. B—Bow spring outside calipers. C—Firm joint inside calipers. D—Bow spring inside calipers. E—Hermaphrodite calipers. (The L.S. Starrett Co.)

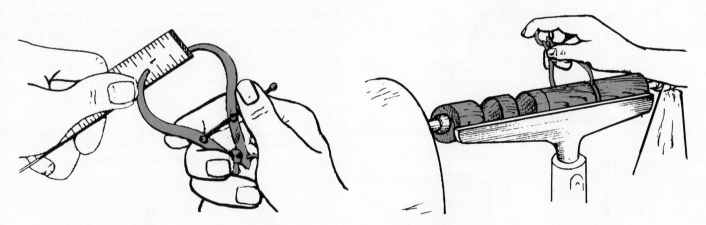

Fig. 20-20. Set and use the outside caliper to check diameter measurements. (The L.S. Starrett Co.)

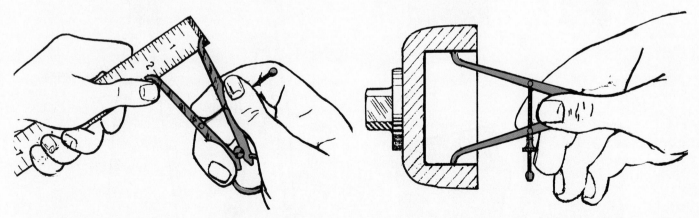

Fig. 20-21. The inside caliper is set and used to check dimensions on the inside of round material. (The L.S. Starrett Co.)

Inside caliper. An inside caliper checks inside diameters. Preset the caliper with a scale. Then turn the work until the diameter is reached, Fig. 20-21.

Hermaphrodite caliper. The hermaphrodite caliper is a firm joint tool. It has one leg like a caliper. The other leg has a needle like point. Use the

hermaphrodite caliper to:
1. Locate outside and inside centers by scribing three or four arcs. Fig. 20-22A.
2. Mark a parallel line on flat or round stock, Fig. 20-22B.
3. Copy a contour, which is often called coping, Fig. 20-22C.

The tools described thus far measure and mark distances, lines and angles. You will also lay out circles, arcs, and curves. Tools for these purposes are compasses, dividers, irregular curves, and template formers.

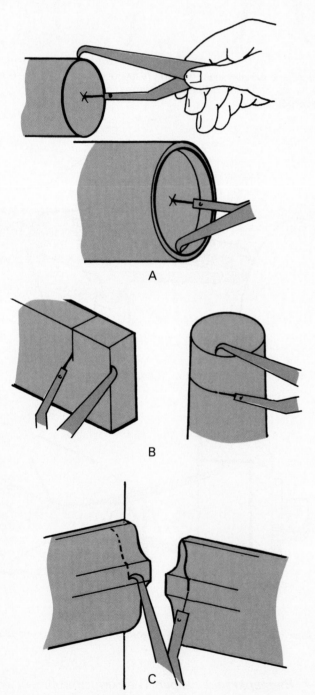

Fig. 20-22. Locate centers and mark parallel lines with the hermaphrodite caliper.

COMPASS AND DIVIDER

Compasses and *dividers* are similar layout tools. Both have two legs. However, a compass has a pencil point on one leg instead of a steel point, Fig. 20-23. Use compasses and dividers to:
1. Step off distances.
2. Bisect lines, angles, and arcs.
3. Construct lines and arcs tangent to each other.
4. Scribe circles, ellipses, and arcs.
5. Lay out polygons.
6. Cope a contour, such as for fitting moulding.

Using tools associated with numbers 2, 3, and 5 were covered in Chapter 9, Producing Working Drawings. Compasses and dividers discussed there were layout tools for working drawings. Tools for material layout are much more sturdy.

Marking with a compass requires some hand coordination. Place one hand on or near the top (joint) of the compass or divider, Fig. 20-24A. The other hand sets the pivot location of the steel point.

Use compasses and dividers as you would when drafting. Adjust the compass or divider to the proper measurement when transferring distances, Fig. 20-24B. Then mark the material. You can also duplicate parts by setting the dividers the size of the original part. Then mark the new material.

TRAMMEL POINTS

Trammel points are used for making large circles and arcs. Two steel points are clamped on a rec-

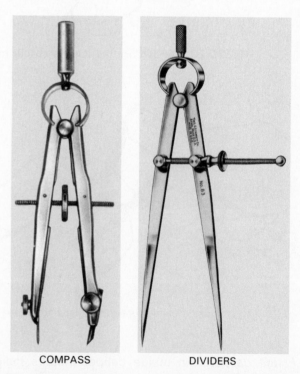

COMPASS   DIVIDERS

Fig. 20-23. Compasses have a pencil and steel point. Dividers have two steel points. (The L.S. Starrett Co.)

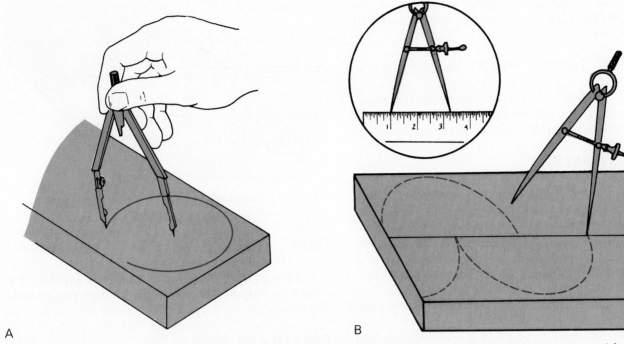

A

B

Fig. 20-24. A—Place and swing the compass on the center point of the circle or arc. B—The divider can be used for stepping off measurements.

tangular piece of lumber, Fig. 20-25A. Some have one point which holds a pencil. This allows either a pencil mark or a scratch for marking the wood.

A

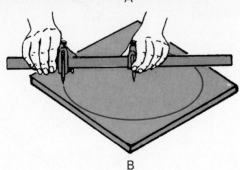

B

Fig. 20-25. A—Clamp trammel points to a piece of lumber. (The Fine Tool Shops) B—They are used to lay out circles larger than are possible with a compass.

The size of the circle is limited only by the length of lumber you choose.

To lay out a circle with trammel points:
1. Adjust the trammel points to the desired radius with a rule.
2. Hold one steel point of the trammel at the center of the circle.
3. Swing the other trammel point in an arc to mark the circle on the material, Fig. 20-25B.

TEMPLATE FORMER

The *template former* is used to copy irregular shapes, Fig. 20-26. Press it against a curved surface. This causes the individual pieces of wire

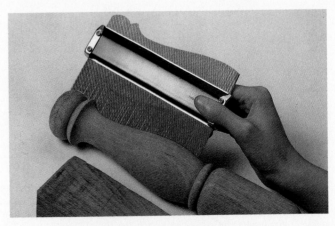

Fig. 20-26. The template former conforms to the shape of the piece to be copied. (The Fine Tool Shops)

to slide. Once shaped, the former's contour can be transferred to a pattern paper or the material to be cut.

LAYOUT PRACTICES

Layout must be done with accuracy. Although layout tools can be used many ways, select the tool which is best suited to your work.

MARKING POINTS

When marking a distance, the best pencil mark to make is an arrow or "V," Fig. 20-27. The point of the arrow shows the proper location. A pencil dot may be lost among the scratches or blemishes in the wood. A short line does not tell which end of the line is the proper measurement. When making the mark, do not press hard. Remember, any pencil marks, dents, or scratches you make during layout must later be removed.

Be sure that the rule you use is undamaged. The end should not have dents. If the corner is damaged, begin measuring from the 1 in. mark. For example, to lay out a distance of 3 in., measure from the rule's 1 in. mark to the 4 in. mark.

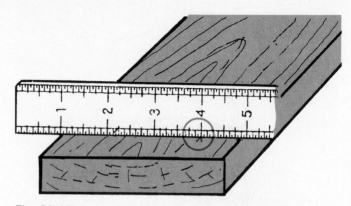

Fig. 20-27. Points are most accurately marked with a "V."

LINES

Most lines are made using a rule or square. For lines which must be parallel to the edge, use a marking gauge or hermaphrodite caliper.

CIRCLES AND ARCS

Compasses, dividers, and trammel points make accurate circles and arcs. To set them, place one leg on the 1 in. (or 10 mm) mark of a rule. Adjust

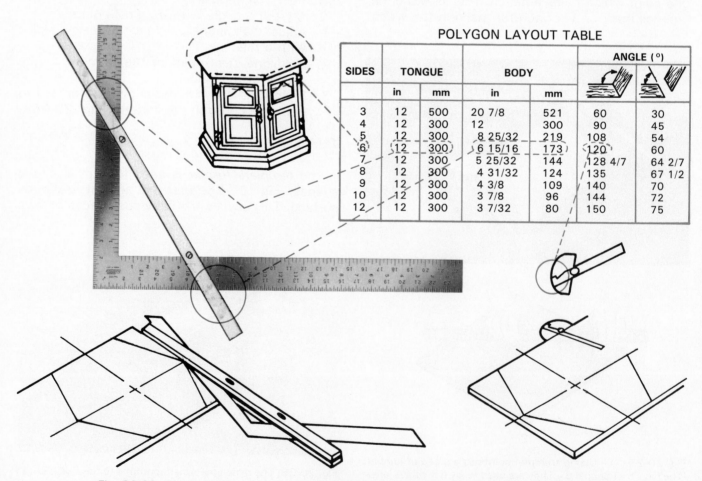

POLYGON LAYOUT TABLE

SIDES	TONGUE		BODY		ANGLE (°)	
	in	mm	in	mm		
3	12	500	20 7/8	521	60	30
4	12	300	12	300	90	45
5	12	300	8 25/32	219	108	54
6	12	300	6 15/16	173	120	60
7	12	300	5 25/32	144	128 4/7	64 2/7
8	12	300	4 31/32	124	135	67 1/2
9	12	300	4 3/8	109	140	70
10	12	300	3 7/8	96	144	72
12	12	300	3 7/32	80	150	75

Fig. 20-28. A protractor or framing square and straightedge may be used for polygon layouts.

the other leg according to the desired measurement. Be sure to account for starting away from the end of the rule.

Arcs are partial circles. The arc has a center point and radius. Set the layout tool for the radius of the arc. Then locate the point of the tool at the arc's center and swing the desired arc.

POLYGONS

Common polygons are triangles, squares, rectangles, hexagons, and octagons. Polygon shapes are used for table tops, mirror and picture frames, clock faces, legs, etc.

Two common tools for laying out polygons are the framing square and protractor. Set angles on the framing square using two pieces of wood and the measurements on the tongue and body, Fig. 20-28.

Certain polygons are often laid out with a compass. Two examples are hexagons (six sides) and octagons (eight sides).

To draw a hexagon, Fig. 20-29:
1. Draw a circle with the radius equal to one side of the hexagon.
2. Keep the same setting of the compass after drawing the circle.
3. Start at any point on the circle and draw an arc which intersects the circle.
4. Move the compass to where the arc intersected the circle and construct another arc. Keep doing so until you divide the circle into six parts.
5. Connect the six intersections to complete the hexagon.

To draw an octagon, Fig. 20-30:
1. Draw a square the size of the octagon.
2. Draw diagonals across the corners of the square.
3. Set the compass to the distance from a corner of the square to the intersection of the diagonals.

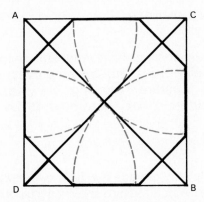

Fig. 20-30. Laying out an octagon with a divider or compass.

4. Place the compass point on each corner of the square and construct arcs.
5. Connect the points where the arcs intersect the edges of the square.

ELLIPSES

An *ellipse* (oval) can be laid out easily with a string. Follow this procedure, Fig. 20-31:
1. Cut out a rectangle the desired size of the ellipse.
2. Make center lines EF and GH.
3. Make an arc using point B as the pivot and line BC as the radius.
4. Measure the length of line AD.
5. Divide that distance by two. (AD/2)
6. Measure this distance on each side of O to locate points I and J.
7. Put thumbtacks or small nails at points E, I, and J.
8. Tie a string tightly around the thumbtacks.
9. Remove the thumbtack at point E.
10. Place a pencil inside the string loop and pull the loop tight. Move the pencil to create the ellipse.

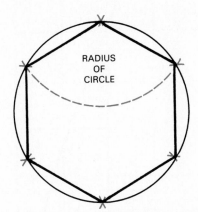

Fig. 20-29. Hexagon layout made by striking arcs with a pair of dividers.

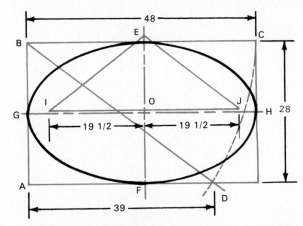

Fig. 20-31. An ellipse for an oval table top can easily be laid out within a rectangle.

IRREGULAR SHAPES

Some cabinet styles have irregularly shaped parts. For example, there are many curves on Early American furniture. Working drawings usually include patterns that show how to lay out the shape.

Patterns

Drawings may provide *full, half,* or *detail patterns,* Fig. 20-32. A half pattern shows detail on one side of a centerline. You mark around the pattern, then turn it over and mark again. A detail pattern may be necessary for more complex shaped parts.

A square grid pattern is a way to transfer complex designs from working drawings to material. Make two square grid patterns: one is traced over the working drawing and the other is a full size pattern. The size of grids should correspond to the scale of the working drawing. If the scale is 1/4 in. equals 1 in., use a 1/4 in. grid sheet. The full size transfer pattern will be 1 in. squares.

Make the grid on tracing paper put over your working drawings. Then, trace the shape from the working drawing, Fig. 20-33A.

Cut a sheet of heavy wrapping paper for the full size pattern. Lay out the proper size squares on the paper. Place a dot on the pattern grid where the design crosses it, Fig. 20-33B. Connect the dots

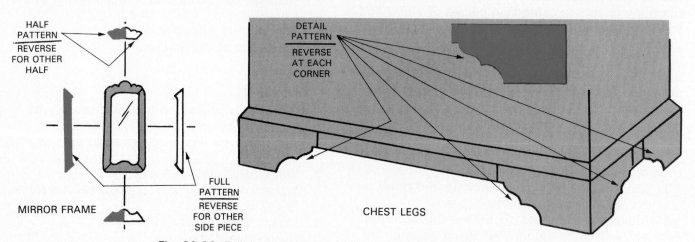

Fig. 20-32. Full, half, and detail patterns are valuable layout devices.

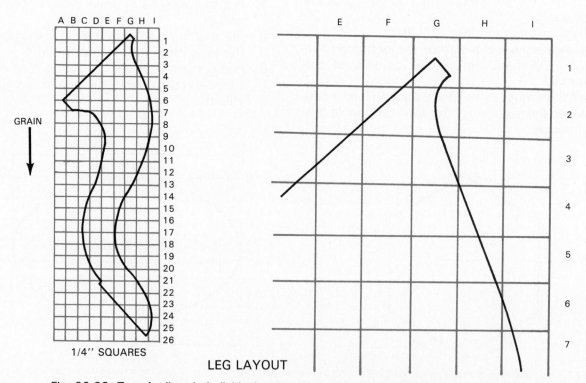

Fig. 20-33. Transfer lines in individual squares from the square grid pattern to the layout.

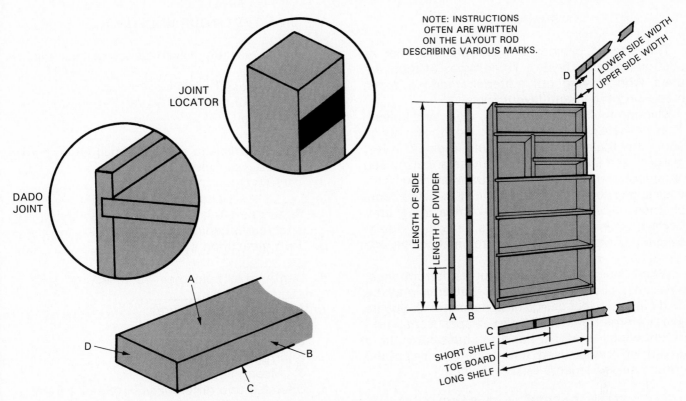

JOINT
LOCATOR

DADO
JOINT

LOWER SIDE WIDTH
UPPER SIDE WIDTH

LENGTH OF SIDE

LENGTH OF DIVIDER

A B

D

A

D

B

C

C

SHORT SHELF
TOE BOARD
LONG SHELF

Fig. 20-34. Layout rods become permanent references for a particular cabinet.

to complete the full size pattern. Cut out the pattern with scissors. Then lay the pattern on the wood and trace around it.

Templates

A *template* is a permanent full size pattern. It may be made of cardboard, hardboard, or thin sheet metal. Make a pattern if you will use the shape several times.

A template is also valuable for guiding a tool. For example, you may lay a template over material to guide a router bit.

Template former

When duplicating irregular curves, use a template former. See Fig. 20-26. It is much simpler than measuring the original part and making a pattern.

LAYOUT ROD

A *layout rod* is a record of often used distances. Plan to make one for standard cabinets you produce. It eliminates repeated measuring with a rule. The rod also helps with machine setups.

The rod is marked with important dimensions of the cabinet, Fig. 20-34. These may be the location of shelves, doors, and joints. Measurements are marked full size. Therefore, make the rod slightly longer than the greatest dimension of the cabinet. The rod is used for height, width, and depth measurements.

A rod is made of 1 x 1 or 1 x 2 lumber. It is surfaced on all four sides. One side may contain width measurements. A second side may contain height measurements. Other sides are used for depth and other needed distances.

MEASURING AND LAYOUT TOOL MAINTENANCE

Measuring and layout tools need very little maintenance. There are few moving parts. However, care is needed during handling and storage of the tool.

Some measuring tools, such as framing and try squares have scales stamped on them. They may become difficult to read. If so, wipe across them with a cloth pad containing white paint. Then remove the excess from the surface of the tool with steel wool. The measurements should be readable again.

Many tools are plated or painted to prevent rust. If rust does occur, possibly on the blade of a try square, remove it with steel wool. Then rub the blade with paste wax. Oil should not be applied to woodworking tools. It will stain your wood.

Moving joints should be rubbed with paste wax for lubrication. However, be careful when lubricating firm joint tools, such as calipers. This might cause the joint to move too freely.

Knives and awls need sharpening. Follow instructions for maintaining hand tools in Chapter 22. The points on dividers, compasses, trammel points, and marking gauges may need sharpening occasionally.

SUMMARY

The size of cabinet components are only as accurate as your layout. Three types of tools are used when laying out material: marking tools, measuring tools, and layout tools.

Marking tools include pencils, awls, and knives. They indicate measurements and location points on your material. Measuring tools include rules, gauges, and squares. Many of these are also used as layout tools. Layout tools transfer distances, angles, and contours. Those without measurements on them must be preset with a measuring tool. Layout tools include T-bevels, angle dividers, calipers, compasses, dividers, trammel points, and template formers.

When laying out material, you construct lines, polygons, circles, and curves. Patterns may be made to trace your design onto the material. Square grid patterns transfer complex shapes from working drawings to stock. For often-built cabinets, a layout rod may be used. It is marked with all of the critical measurements of the cabinet.

THINK SAFETY—ACT SAFELY

When measuring and laying out workpieces:
1. Hold sharp points of tools away from you when carrying them.
2. Cover sharp tool points if you must have them in your pocket.

CABINETMAKING TERMS

Squareness, marking tools, scratch awl, measuring tools, rule, folding rule, flexible rule, tape measure, depth gauge, caliper rule, framing square, bench square, brace measure table, octagon scale, try square, combination square, layout tools, marking gauge, sliding T-bevel, angle divider, outside caliper, inside caliper, hermaphrodite caliper, compass, dividers, trammel points, template former, polygon, half pattern, detail pattern, square grid pattern, template, layout rod.

TEST YOUR KNOWLEDGE

1. Proper measuring and layout result in cabinets that are:
   a. Flawless.
   b. Horizontal.
   c. Plumb.
   d. Square.
2. You do not need a sharp pencil when marking. True or False?
3. Three types of marking tools are _____, _____, and _____.
4. What rule would you select when laying out a tall curio cabinet?
5. Two measuring systems are _____ and _____.
6. Depth of a hole may be measured with a _____ or _____.
7. A caliper rule measures:
   a. Circumference.
   b. Inside and outside distances.
   c. Irregular curves.
   d. Measurements over 1 ft.
8. Describe two differences between a framing square and a bench square.
9. Brace lengths can be found on the framing square _____.
10. The type of square you should use to check small pieces is the:
    a. Bench square.
    b. Combination square.
    c. Framing square.
    d. Try square.
11. Name three components attached to a combination square blade. Explain their use.
12. You set the angle of a sliding T-bevel with a _____.
13. Describe three types of calipers and their use.
14. Circles can be laid out with what tools?
15. The most accurate mark is the:
    a. Arrow.
    b. Dot.
    c. Line.
16. When copying an irregular shape, use a _____.
17. Patterns are permanent templates. True or False?
18. Framing squares should be coated with oil if they rust. True or False?

Chapter 21
SAWING WITH STATIONARY POWER MACHINES

After studying this chapter, you will be able to:
☐ *Select stationary power saws for cutting straight or curved parts:*
☐ *Operate stationary power saws properly.*
☐ *Choose the most appropriate saw blade for a given operation.*
☐ *Maintain stationary power equipment.*

Sawing with stationary power machines is the most fundamental processing operation in cabinetmaking. Cabinetmakers use table saws, radial arm saws, band saws, and scroll saws to cut lumber and composite materials. Although sawing is also an integral part of other cabinetmaking operations, such as joint making, this chapter focuses on the problems of sawing to size and shape.

Stationary sawing equipment is designed for straight-line or curved-line cuts. However, saws for cutting curves will do both with a straightedge or fence. Selecting the proper saw involves several decisions.

1. Select the safest saw for the cut you want to make.
2. Choose an appropriate saw for the cut.
3. Make sure the saw is available.
4. Have prior instruction and experience with the machine.
5. If more than one saw is appropriate, choose the one you most prefer.

Once you have chosen the machine, consider the following suggestions for safe and efficient operation of the saw:

1. Be sure the saw blade is clean and sharp.
2. Perform major set-up steps, such as changing blades and setting the fence, with the power turned off.
3. Measure accurately. "Measure twice, cut once."
4. Have adjusted point-of-operation guards in place.
5. Feed material into the saw properly.
6. Support material before and after the cut.

HANDEDNESS

Problems with machine operations can be caused by *handedness.* This refers to whether the user is left or right handed. In this book, right-handed setups and operations are illustrated. The left-handed person may follow them as shown, or reverse the setups. However, some sawing operations should be set up one way. One example is beveling with the table saw, described later in the chapter.

SAWING STRAIGHT LINES

Sawing straight lines is a standard operation for reducing stock to workpiece dimensions. Sawing stock square—all corners are 90°—is essential to producing high quality products. Blade selection is also important. You may be sawing lumber or composite materials, such as plywood or MDF panels. The proper blade often depends upon whether the material has grain or not.

The most accurate straight-line sawing is done on equipment having a circular saw blade. The diameter of the blade keeps the cut straight. Stationary power saws which use a circular blade include: the tilting arbor table saw, tilting table saw, and radial arm saw. The maximum recommended blade diameter that can be installed determines machine size. Blades vary from 8 to 16 in., with 10 in. being most common.

Material is guided past the blade on tilting arbor saws or tilting table saws. You must support the material before and after the cut. The saw table may be large enough to do so. However, for long lumber or full sheets of manufactured panels, obtain additional supports, such as table extensions, rollers, or another person. The radial arm saw has an advantage over table saws for supporting lumber. The lumber is laid stationary on the table and the saw is pulled across. This makes cutting long lumber into shorter lengths very easy.

Material may be too long or heavy to control on some stationary saws. You could cut it to rough size first with a portable circular saw. Full size sheets of plywood, particleboard, or other composite materials are best cut on a panel saw. (See Chapter 28.)

TILTING ARBOR TABLE SAW

A *tilting arbor table saw,* Fig. 21-1, also is known as a table saw, circular saw, and variety saw. It has the following major components:
1. Horizontal table on a machine frame.
2. Circular blade that extends up through a table insert.
3. Tilting arbor that adjusts the blade angle from 0° to 45°.
4. Motor.

There are a number of table saw features. The *blade-raising handwheel* changes the blade height. The *tilt handwheel* changes the blade angle. A *tilt scale* displays approximate blade angle. All blade control handwheels have lock knobs to prevent them from moving once set.

An ON/OFF switch is within easy reach under the table. On newer machines, the switch is recessed into the switch plate. This prevents the machine from being turned on if you bump the switch plate.

GUIDING MATERIAL

Material is guided past the blade with one of several attachments: rip fence, miter gauge, or jig.

Rip fence

A *rip fence* guides material parallel to the blade. It typically is in place when ripping stock to width. The fence, on a guide bar or tubes, is locked in place by a fence clamp. Make minor adjustments for the blade-to-fence distance by turning the micro-set knob before unclamping the fence. A rip scale may be printed on the guide bar to help you set the fence, Fig. 21-2.

Miter gauge

A *miter gauge* controls cutting at angles other than parallel to the blade. It usually is adjustable 180°. A 0° setting positions the gauge perpendicular to the blade for squaring material to length. The miter gauge slides in table slots found on each side of the blade. On some machines, these are T-slots. The miter gauge slide has a matching "T" shape. It can be inserted only at the edge of the table. The T-slot is better than a rectangular one. The miter gauge cannot tip or be raised out of the slot.

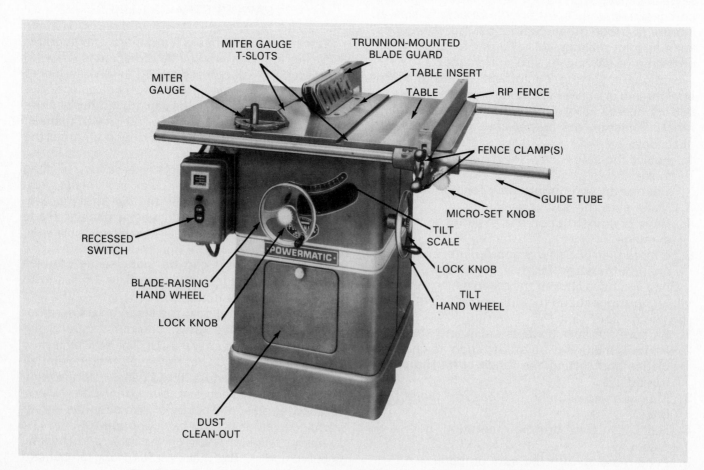

Fig. 21-1. The table saw has a number of features and adjustments. (Powermatic)

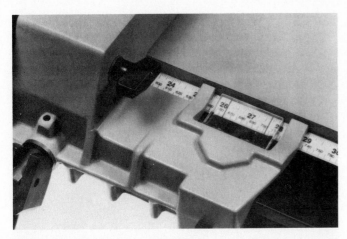

Fig. 21-2. A rip scale may be printed on the table saw's guide bar. (Delta)

Jig

If neither the fence nor miter gauge is adequate, purchase or build a jig. User-made jigs must be sturdy and hold the workpiece firmly. Make the jig of lumber, plywood, or fiberboard. It might clamp to the rip fence or miter gauge. You could also attach wood strips to the jig bottom so it slides in both table slots.

BLADE GUARDS

A blade guard is essential. It helps keep your hands away from the blade and helps control sawdust. It may mount on the saw trunnion or attach to the table edge.

A *trunnion-mounted guard,* Fig. 21-3, bolts to the saw trunnion. This is the main machine part that supports the motor and blade. When you change the blade angle the guard also tilts. The assembly consists of the blade guard, splitter, and pawls. The

guard rests over the blade and is hinged to the splitter. The *splitter* keeps the saw kerf open as the cut is made. Without a splitter, lumber which warps during the cut could squeeze against the blade and bind the saw. The lumber might be thrown back toward you. With a splitter-type guard, you must saw completely through the material.

If material binds, *anti-kickback pawls,* attached to the splitter should prevent the material from being thrown. The pawls ride on top of the material after it passes the blade. Then, if the material kicks back, the pawls dig in to stop it.

If it becomes difficult to feed the material, press it against the table with a push stick or by hand. With the other hand, reach down and turn off the power. Remove the material after the saw stops.

A *table-mounted guard,* Fig. 21-4, attaches to the edge of the saw table. Each side of the guard may move separately. This type of guard has no splitter. Some table-mounted guards have a spring-loaded, anti-kickback pawl with teethlike sharp points. A knob on the top of the guard adjusts the pawl downward to prevent kickback. Adjust a table-mounted guard independently of the blade.

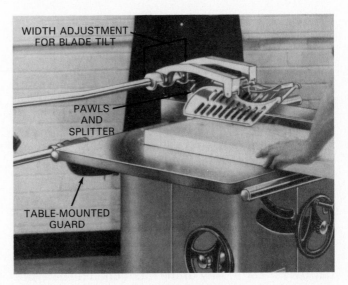

Fig. 21-4. Blade guards may be mounted to the table edge. (Delta)

SELECTING AND INSTALLING SAW BLADES

Circular saw blades are categorized by tooth style, set, kerf, blade body thickness, and other features. You can often tell the blade type by looking at its shape, Fig. 21-5. The blade may also be labeled according to the grain direction or material it cuts. For example, a *rip blade* saws along the grain. A *crosscut blade* saws across the grain. *Combination blades* do both. A *planer blade* produces a very smooth cut edge. *Plywood blades*

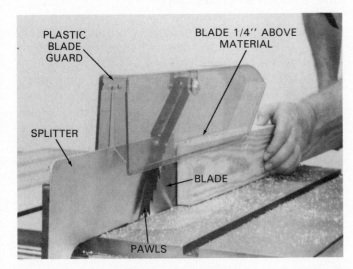

Fig. 21-3. This blade guard is mounted to the saw trunnion under the table. (Delta)

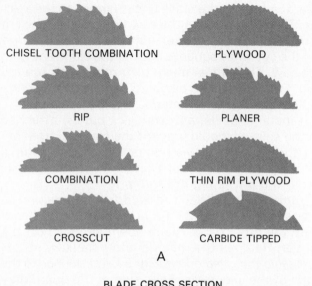

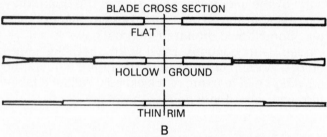

Fig. 21-5. A—Learn to recognize saw blades by their shapes. B—Cross-sections of three circular blade thicknesses.

Fig. 21-6. To remove the blade, pull the wrench from in front of the machine.

resemble crosscut blades, but with smaller teeth that reduce chipping.

There are several other blade features, Fig. 21-5. First, blades may be flat, hollow ground, or thin rim. This pertains to the blade thickness. *Flat blades* have *set* in them. The teeth are bent slightly outward. This creates a kerf wider than the blade. The saw is less likely to bind. *Hollow ground blade* teeth have no set. To prevent binding, the blade body is made thinner near the arbor hole. (Planer blades and some plywood blades are hollow ground.) *Thin rim blades* have thinner teeth and bodies to produce the narrowest kerfs. Any of the mentioned blade types may be carbide tipped for increased durability. A more detailed discussion of blade design is given later in the chapter.

Install saw blades as follows:
1. Disconnect electrical power to the machine.
2. Remove the table insert (and blade guard, if necessary).
3. Raise the blade so the nut on the arbor can be reached easily.
4. Place a wrench on the nut and wedge a piece of softwood lumber against the teeth.
5. Pull the wrench toward the front of the saw to loosen the nut, Fig. 21-6.
6. Remove the nut, collar, and blade.
7. Remove pitch, gum, or rust from the arbor,

flange, collar, and nut with mineral spirits and fine steel wool.
8. Install the replacement blade with teeth pointing toward the front of the table (in the direction of blade rotation).
9. Install the collar and thread the nut on finger-tight.
10. Tighten the nut. While standing behind the machine, pull the wrench toward you. Wedge a piece of softwood lumber in the teeth to keep the blade stationary.
11. Replace the table insert and guard.

SETTING UP A TABLE SAW

Saw setup includes deciding whether to use a rip fence or miter gauge, setting blade height, and squaring the blade.

The following guidelines should help you make decisions when to use a rip fence or miter gauge.

As shown in Fig. 21-7, use the rip fence when:
1. The saw cut will be longer than the distance from the blade to the fence.
2. The workpiece will pass between the fence and the blade. Hold and feed stock with push sticks when the blade-to-fence distance is less than 4 in. (100 mm).

As shown in Fig. 21-8, use the miter gauge when:
1. The saw cut is shorter than the length of the material, and;
2. The saw cut will be shorter than the distance from the blade to the front edge of the table.

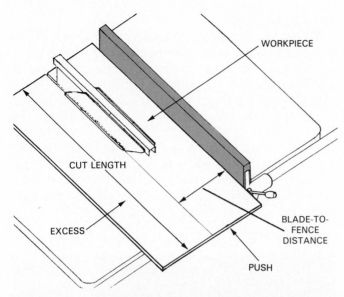

Fig. 21-7. A rip fence is used when the blade-to-fence distance is less than the cut length.

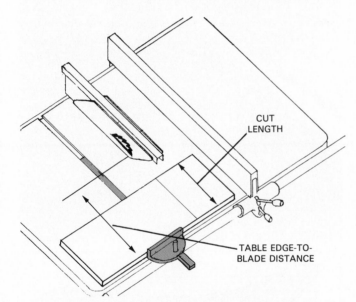

Fig. 21-8. Use a miter gauge when the material width is less than the distance from the blade to the table edge.

Use the rip fence *and* miter gauge only when:
1. The blade height is less than the material thickness. The material is not cut off. This might occur when making certain joints, Fig. 21-9. (See Chapter 29.)
2. The rip fence supports a stop block for sawing duplicate parts of equal length. The stop block provides clearance between the workpiece and the fence.

Setting blade height
Set blade height as follows:
1. Disconnect power to the saw.
2. Loosen the blade-raising handwheel's lock knob.

Fig. 21-9. Both the rip fence and miter gauge are used for cuts not completely through the material. A dado cut is shown. The guard has been removed to show the operation.

3. Rotate the blade by hand so a tooth is pointing vertically.
4. Hold a ruler near the blade and adjust the height. You could also use a blade height gauge, Fig. 21-10.
5. Tighten the lock knob.

Squaring the blade
For cuts other than bevels, the blade must be at 90° to the table. Check the blade angle between saw setups and after blade changes. Place a square on the table and against the blade, Fig. 21-11. The square should rest between two blade teeth. Loosen the arbor tilt lock and adjust the angle until the square rests flush against the blade body. Tighten the arbor tilt lock.

Fig. 21-10. Blade height is set easily with this gauge. (The Fine Tool Shops)

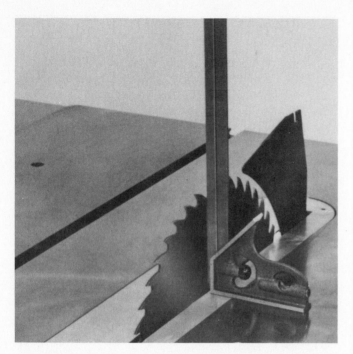

Fig. 21-11. Squaring the blade 90° to the table. (Delta)

OPERATING THE TABLE SAW

The table saw performs many different operations. Those discussed here are ripping, crosscutting, beveling, mitering, and resawing. Other operations include compound mitering, shaping, tapering, and joint making. These applications are found in other chapters.

Ripping lumber

Ripping is cutting lumber along the grain, Fig. 21-12. Install a standard or carbide tipped rip blade. Set the blade height 1/4 in. (6 mm) above the material thickness. Unlock and move the rip fence to the desired width. Measure from the fence to a tooth set toward the fence. It is better to measure twice and saw once than to measure once wrong and need to saw twice. Finally, make sure the blade guard's antikickback pawls contact the workpiece.

Stock to be ripped must have one face and one edge surfaced. The face rests on the table and the edge rides along the rip fence. Turn on the saw and feed the wood past the blade. Hold it firmly on the table and against the fence. Have another person support long lengths of material. Stand to one side of the cutting line. Keep your hands at least 4 in. (100 mm) from the blade by using a push stick.

Remember that lumber may tend to warp while being ripped. This is because you are relieving internal stresses. The splitter should prevent sawn lumber from pinching the blade. However, have a firm hold and be prepared for kickback should feeding the material become difficult.

Ripping plywood

Plywood, a stable manufactured product, is ripped along the face grain like lumber, Fig. 21-13. Install and use a standard or carbide-tipped rip or panel blade. Set the blade height 1/4 in. (6 mm) above the panel thickness. If using a hollow ground panel blade (to produce a smoother cut edge), set the blade height 1 to 2 in. (25 to 50 mm) above the workpiece. Hollow ground blades are thinner near the arbor than flat blades. With 1/4 in. clearance, the rim tends to overheat as it rubs against the workpiece. Adjust the rip fence and saw plywood as if you were ripping lumber.

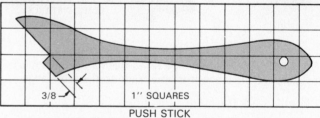

Fig. 21-12. Top. For ripping narrow widths, use push sticks to hold and feed the material. The guard was removed to show the operation. Bottom. Dimensions for a typical push stick.

Crosscutting lumber and plywood

Crosscutting is sawing through lumber and plywood across the face grain, Fig. 21-14. Install a standard or carbide-tipped crosscut blade. For an unsplintered cut on plywood, use a hollow ground panel blade. Set blade height at 1/4 in. (6 mm) above the workpiece thickness for flat blades and 1 in. (25 mm) above for hollow ground blades.

Typically, you guide the material with a miter gauge positioned in the left table slot. This is the

Fig. 21-13. Ripping plywood. (Delta)

Fig. 21-14. Crosscutting with the miter gauge. The guard was removed to show the operation.

normal cutting position of a right-handed person. Mark the cut to be made. Hold the workpiece firmly against the gauge with the left hand while feeding with the right hand. With the saw off, align your cutting line with the blade. Make sure the width of the blade is on the waste side of the cutting line. Pull the workpiece back so it does not touch the blade. Start saw and feed stock through cut.

The face of most miter gauges is about 6 in. (150 mm) wide and 2 or 3 in. (50 to 75 mm) from the blade. Many times, this is not close enough to the blade to support short parts. Fasten an auxiliary wood face to the miter gauge which extends to the blade. Bond abrasive paper to the wood face to help grip your work. Short workpieces can then be easily crosscut.

It is sometimes difficult to use a miter gauge for crosscutting to length. Suppose the workpiece width is larger than the distance from the blade to the table edge. If so, use a radial arm saw, portable circular saw, or panel saw.

Crosscutting duplicate parts to length
There are two methods to cut a number of workpieces to equal lengths: stop rod or stop block.

Stop rod
A *stop rod* is attached to the miter gauge, Fig. 21-15. To adjust the stop rod, mark the desired length on your first part to be cut. Align the mark with the saw blade, then butt the rod to the workpiece. Make a test cut and adjust the rod position if necessary.

Fig. 21-15. Use a stop rod for cutting duplicate parts to length. The guard was taken off to show the operation.

Stop block
A *stop block* is clamped to the fence, Fig. 21-16A. A miter gauge and fence cannot be used together for cutting parts to length. The workpiece would bind between the blade and fence and could possibly be thrown. A stop block provides clearance. The cutting length is the distance from the block to a tooth on the blade set toward the fence. Measure and set the cutting length with the stop clamped beside the blade, Fig. 21-16B. Then reclamp the stop several inches in front of the blade. Guide your work with a miter gauge.

Sawing non-grain manufactured products
More applications are being found for particleboard, fiberboard, and similar materials. These lack grain pattern. Generally, you will install a carbide-tipped combination, crosscut, or panel blade. Again, set the blade height 1/4 in. above the material

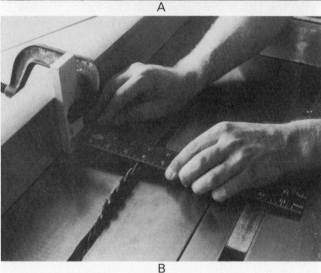

Fig. 21-16. A—Stop block clamped to the rip fence determines the length of parts cut to duplicate lengths. B—Set the blade-to-stop block distance with the block clamped to the fence near the blade. Guards are removed to show these procedures.

thickness. Use the rip fence or miter gauge as for sawing lumber.

Beveling

Beveling is sawing with the blade tilted. This typically is done as a joint making or shaping operation. On most table saws, the blade tilts 45° in one direction only. The blade angle can be set with a T-bevel (see Fig. 21-17), protractor, or triangle. Plan beveling operations so the blade tilts away from the fence or miter gauge. You want the waste to remain on the table below the blade. If the table tilts toward the miter gauge or fence, the excess falls onto the moving blade and could kick back.

With a bevel cut edge, the workpiece dimensions differ on the top and bottom faces. Usually, the longer of the two faces is dimensioned on the drawing. It is difficult to set the rip fence or position the workpiece accurately against the miter gauge for a bevel. You should estimate the dimension, make a test cut, and then make the final cut.

Fig. 21-17. Set blade tilt with a T-bevel. First set the T-bevel angle with a protractor. Remove the guard for this set up.

For rip beveling, Fig. 21-18A, estimate the distance from the blade to the fence. Start a saw kerf 2 in. (50 mm) into a test piece which has been surfaced and squared. Measure the width and make adjustments so the workpiece will be the desired width.

For crosscut beveling, Fig. 21-18B, it is best to make test kerfs on the waste side of your cutting

A

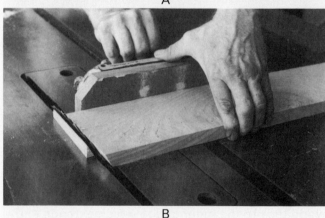

B

Fig. 21-18. When beveling, feed stock so the excess falls off below the blade. Guards have been removed to show the operation. A—Ripping. B—Crosscutting.

line. Reposition your work against the miter gauge after each kerf until the cutting line aligns with the blade.

Mitering

Make *miter cuts,* Fig. 21-19, with the miter gauge. Set the blade square to the table. Adjust the gauge to the required angle. For sawing lumber at angles up to 45°, install a crosscut blade. Above 45°, a rip blade may be more effective.

Your workpiece may tend to "creep" along the face of the gauge when sawing. To prevent this, fasten an abrasive covered auxiliary wood face to the gauge.

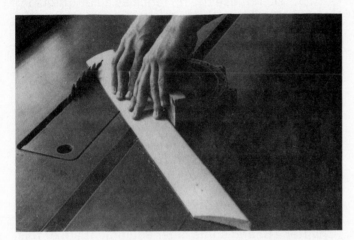

Fig. 21-19. Sawing a miter. The guard has been removed to show the operation.

Resawing

Resawing creates two or more thin pieces from thicker lumber on edge. This helps conserve wood. For example, you can get two 1/4 in. (6 mm)thick boards from 3/4 in. (19 mm) lumber. One or two passes are required to resaw with the table saw. If the stock width is less than the maximum blade height, resawing can be done with one pass, Fig. 21-20. If the stock width is greater than the maximum blade height, two passes are required. Cut just over half way through on the first pass, Fig. 21-21A. Turn the material over with the same face against the fence. Separate the two pieces with a second pass.

A blade guard cannot be used during the first pass of a two-pass resawing operation. A trunnion guard will not allow the lumber to feed past the splitter. A table-mount guard would also interfere. You must be very cautious when no guard is installed. Keep your hands away from the area around the blade by using one or two push sticks, Fig. 21-21B.

The two-pass resawing procedure is as follows:
1. Disconnect power to the saw.
2. Remove the guard for two-pass cuts only.

Fig. 21-20. A one-pass resawing operation. This split guard has one side raised. (Delta)

3. Adjust the blade to 1/4 in. (6 mm) higher than half the height of the stock. Lock the blade height and tilt adjustments.
4. Position the fence so that the blade will separate pieces of equal thickness.
5. Plan to have help or lumber supports if the material is more than 3 ft. long.
6. Make the first pass. Use pushsticks when the end of the material comes within 12 in. (300 mm) of the blade.

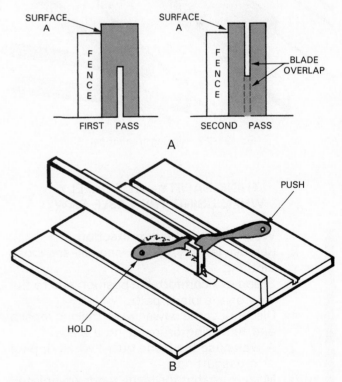

Fig. 21-21. A two-pass resawing operation. A—Set the blade height just over half the material width. Keep the same surface against the fence for both passes. B—Use push sticks to feed the material as it nears the blade.

7. Be cautious when the material clears the blade. Have a firm footing and stand to one side of the cutting line. Keep your eye on the blade as you withdraw your hands and push sticks.
8. Turn the material over and feed it through with the same face against the fence.

Ripping thin strips

Thin strips of wood are often needed for inlay work. When ripping 1 to 2 in. wide strips, feed the material with push sticks. When ripping strips less than 1 in., a different sawing method is used. This is because the fence would have to be positioned too close to the blade. Rip strips less than 1 in. on the opposite edge of the board. This set up is shown in Fig. 21-22. The blade guard is not used because it will interfere with the operation. Make sure the edges of your board are parallel. You must reset the fence after each cut. Joint the board's edge before you cut off the strip. This produces a surfaced strip, ready for veneering or inlay. Use push sticks when feeding the material. The strip can kick back if it gets caught between the blade and table insert opening.

Fig. 21-22. Ripping thin strips.

THINK SAFETY—ACT SAFELY WHEN USING THE TABLE SAW

1. Wear approved eye protection.
2. Remove jewelry; secure long hair and loose clothing.
3. Stand in a comfortable position and to the side of the blade path.
4. Disconnect the power when making repairs and removing or installing a blade.
5. Always use the blade guard when ripping or crosscutting.
6. Make sure that the blade teeth are pointed forward and the nut is tight.
7. Tighten the fence clamp or miter gauge adjusting knob.

8. Blade should be sharp, properly set, and free of resin.
9. Always think through an operation before performing it.
10. Hold the stock firmly against the fence or miter gauge.
11. Use a push stick for ripping material narrower than 4 in. (100 mm).
12. Never operate a saw without the miter gauge, rip fence, or other guide.
13. Adjust the saw blade to 1/4 in. (6 mm) above the workpiece thickness. Position hollow ground blades 1 in. above.
14. Never reach across, over, or behind the blade.
15. Do not use the rip fence as a cut-off guide. Clamp a clearance block to it.
16. Remove the rip fence when crosscutting.
17. Do not attempt to free work that is caught in the machine; stop the machine first.
18. Provide support for along or wide workpieces before and after the cut.
19. Do not look around when making a cut. Concentrate on the point of operation. Keep your fingers away from the blade.

TILTING TABLE SAW

On some circular saws, the table tilts instead of the saw arbor. Multipurpose woodworking machines (Chapter 28) and some older equipment are of this type. Operations, except beveling, are the same as the tilting arbor table saw. When tilting the table for beveling, follow these guidelines:
1. Have the workpiece below the blade when using the rip fence, Fig. 21-23A. Prevent cut-off waste material from sliding into the blade. Another person may need to help you with long stock.
2. Have the workpiece above the blade when using the miter gauge, Fig. 21-23B. The excess will slide away from the blade after the cut is complete.

RADIAL ARM SAW

A *radial arm saw,* Fig. 21-24, is a versatile machine in the cabinetmaking shop. In addition to sawing, operations may include surfacing, drilling, shaping, and sanding. The radial arm saw is most noted for sawing stock to length. Imagine trying to crosscut a 12 ft. long piece of lumber with a table saw. This task is made easy with the radial arm saw.

The radial arm saw blade, blade guard, and motor are above the table. All of these are mounted on a *yoke* which moves toward and away from you on the *arm.* The arm and/or motor assembly turns in several different directions. The entire frame can be on legs or mounted on a bench. Radial arm saws

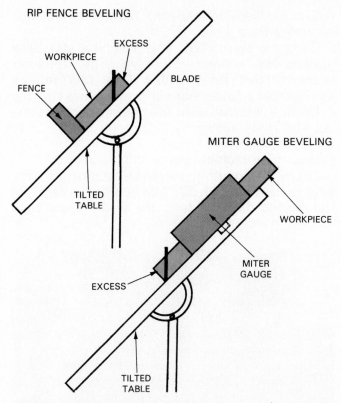

RIP FENCE BEVELING

EXCESS

WORKPIECE

FENCE

BLADE

TILTED TABLE

MITER GAUGE BEVELING

WORKPIECE

MITER GAUGE

EXCESS

TILTED TABLE

Fig. 21-23. Beveling on tilting table saw. Guard not shown.

are sized according to blade diameter, from 8 to 16 in., with 10 in. being the most common.

CHANGING THE BLADE

Blade changing is required when the blade is dull or when setting up for a different sawing operation. Radial arm and table saws use the same blades. To change the blade, first remove the guard. Secure the motor arbor so you can loosen the arbor nut. There may be a hex hole in the end of the shaft for an Allen wrench. There could be two flat surfaces behind the blade for an open-end wrench. If no method of holding the arbor is seen, clamp a hand-screw to the blade above the teeth. Remove the old blade and place the new blade with the teeth pointed toward the fence, Fig. 21-25.

For most operations, especially ripping, install a blade with set. Most sawing is done near the rim. Ripping with a hollow ground blade would burn and dull the rim of the blade. This may not be true with crosscutting, since this is a quick operation. The blade would not likely overheat.

Once the blade is installed, tighten the arbor nut securely. Do not overtorque the nut. This could strip the threads.

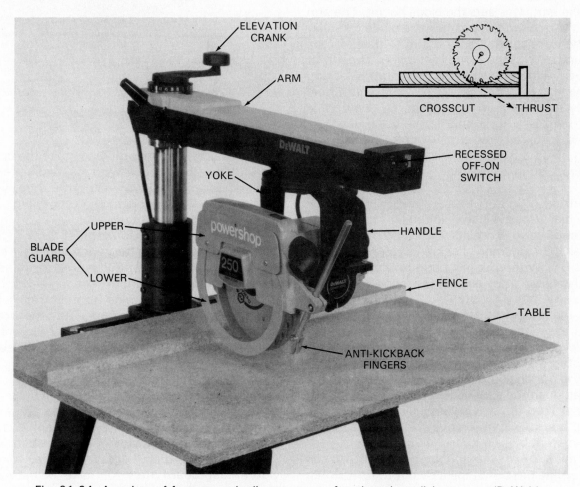

ELEVATION CRANK

ARM

CROSSCUT   THRUST

RECESSED OFF-ON SWITCH

YOKE

HANDLE

UPPER

BLADE GUARD

LOWER

FENCE

TABLE

ANTI-KICKBACK FINGERS

Fig. 21-24. A variety of features and adjustments are found on the radial arm saw. (DeWalt)

Fig. 21-25. Changing a radial arm saw blade.

SAW SETUP

The versatility of the radial arm saw comes from its wide range of adjustments. The *elevation crank,* found on the *column* or machine frame, raises and lowers the arm. This sets the blade height. The arm pivots at the column to position the blade for miter cuts. The yoke rotates on the arm to position the blade parallel with the fence for ripping. The motor pivots 90° within the yoke for beveling. A locking mechanism is provided for each of these settings. The only machine part which can be allowed to move during saw operation is the yoke. It slides back and forth on the arm for crosscutting and mitering. This setting, too, is locked for certain procedures, such as ripping.

Crosscutting

The radial arm saw is well suited for crosscutting lumber and wood products, Fig. 21-26. Lock the arm in the 0° position. Lock the yoke pivot and bevel at 0°. With your left hand or a clamp, hold the material stationary against the fence away from the cut.

With the machine off, pull the blade until it touches the workpiece. Align the blade to the excess side of the cutting mark. Then, back the blade off and start the motor. Grip the handle. Pull the saw across the material just far enough to complete the cut. Then push the saw back through the kerf past the fence. Turn the saw off and allow the blade to coast to a stop. Then remove the workpiece and excess material.

Determine the maximum material width you can cut in a single pass. Pull the saw out to its farthest travel and measure from the fence to the point where the blade touches the table. This distance may vary from 12 in. to 24 in.

On some equipment, you push the saw back against the column. More recently, retractor systems have been added. The saw returns automatically to its normal position next to the column. It returns when the operator finishes the cut and stops pulling.

Crosscutting multiple parts

Cut multiple parts to length by attaching a *stop,* as shown in Fig. 21-27. Clamp it to the fence at the desired distance from the blade. Place each

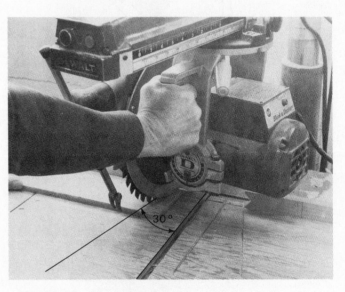

Fig. 21-26. Crosscutting at 30° with a radial arm saw.

workpiece against the stop and make the cut. Turn the stop's adjusting screw to make minor changes in distance to the blade. Without a stop, you can clamp a block of wood to the fence, Fig. 21-28.

Crosscutting extra wide material

Material widths up to twice the saw's travel distance can be cut. Attach a stop to the fence at the desired length. Support the panel if it can tip. Cut across the material as far as possible. Return the blade to its column position. Turn the workpiece over and finish the cut. Saws with 24 in. travel will cut 4 ft. wide sheet material in two passes.

Mitering

Make miter cuts with the saw's arm swung to the right or left, Fig. 21-29. Most saws pivot to 45° both ways. Right-hand miters (arm angled to right) are preferred. The motor does not obstruct your view of the cut. Install crosscut blades for miters. Cut a test board first to make adjustments to measurements and stops.

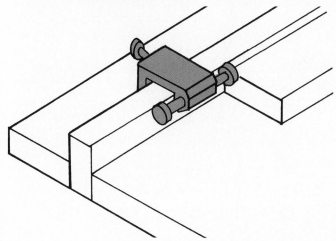

Fig. 21-27. Top. A stop positions stock for sawing multiple parts to length. (Black & Decker) Bottom. Make minor changes by turning the adjusting screw.

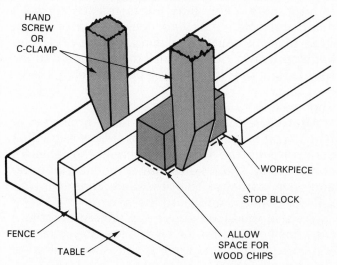

Fig. 21-28. If a stop is not available, clamp a block of wood to the fence. Raise it slightly to allow dust and chips to pass under.

Ripping material

Ripping is done with the blade parallel to the fence. The yoke pivots left or right 90° and locks in place. Tighten the rip lock so the blade is the proper distance from the fence. The rip lock prevents the yoke from moving along the arm.

Fig. 21-29. Compound mitering with the radial arm saw.

There are two ripping modes: in-rip and out-rip. The *in-rip mode,* where the blade is between the motor and fence, is the most common setup, Fig. 21-30A. The *out-rip mode* allows wider parts to be cut, Fig. 21-30B. Notice that the direction of feed is opposite. Place the workpiece, not the excess, between the fence and the blade.

Fig. 21-30. Feed material against the rotation of the blade when ripping. (DeWalt)

When a workpiece is 3 in. or narrower, use a special pusherboard, Fig. 21-31A. Dimension "A" must be such that the workpiece is fed completely past the blade, but short enough to prevent the pusherboard from passing under the anti-kickback device, Fig. 21-31B.

The ripping procedure is as follows:

1. Install a rip blade. The teeth should be about 1/4 in. (6 mm) above the table.
2. Pivot the motor and blade assembly into the in-rip or out-rip mode.
3. Measure and lock the desired blade distance to the fence. Measure from a saw blade tooth set toward the fence.
4. Tilt the blade guard forward to protect you from flying wood chips.
5. Adjust the anti-kickback pawls 1/8 in. (3 mm) below the top surface of the material being cut.
6. Start the motor and let it reach full speed.
7. Lower the overarm until the teeth touch the table protector.
8. Feed the material against the blade rotation and along the fence until it is beyond the blade and antikickback device. Use a pushboard if the workpiece will be less than 3 in. wide.
9. Push the STOP button and allow the blade to stop before removing your work.

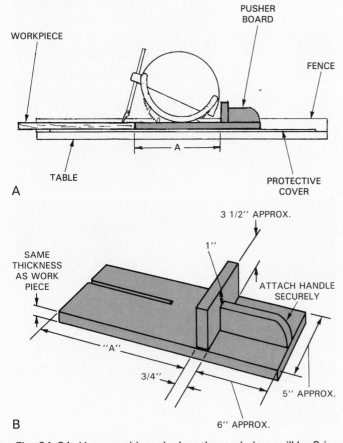

Fig. 21-31. Use a pushboard when the workpiece will be 3 in. or narrower in width. (DeWalt)

Beveling

The radial arm saw motor and blade assembly tilts 45° left and right for beveling. Beveling can be done in the crosscutting or ripping mode, Fig. 21-32. Select the proper blade for the operation you intend to perform. Feed against the blade rotation as you would for crosscutting or ripping operations.

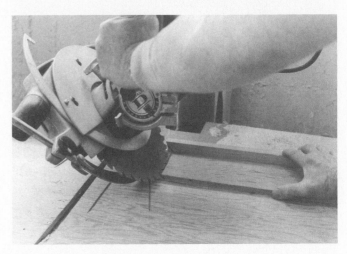

Fig. 21-32. Beveling with a radial arm saw.

Protecting the table

Every different saw setting makes another kerf mark in the saw table. This is because the saw blade is positioned 1/16 in. below the table surface for through cuts. Over time, kerfs resulting from a number of different settings make the table rough. Resurface the table by placing a piece of 1/4 in. hardboard on it. Screw or nail the hardboard to the saw table away from the blade's travel.

Kerf making

After replacing a damaged table protector or fence, you must recut saw kerfs. This should be done through the fence and across the table for crosscutting. Later, kerfs may be needed for miter and bevel settings. The procedure is as follows:

1. Disconnect power to the saw.
2. Raise the blade above the table protector.
3. Position the motor/blade assembly over the center of the table for the crosscut, miter, or bevel setting.
4. Tighten the rip and yoke locks.
5. Lower the blade until it touches the table protector. Then raise it 1/16 in. Note how far you turn the lever while raising the blade.
6. Tighten arm adjustments.
7. Connect power and start the saw. Allow it to reach full speed.
8. Lower the blade twice as far as you raised it. The cut will be 1/16 in. into the table protector.

9. Hold the handle securely and loosen the rip lock.
10. With a tight grip on the handle, push the blade slowly toward the column and cut through the fence.

A kerf mark is also necessary for ripping. Raise the blade above the table. Pivot the yoke into the ripping position. Set the miter scale at 0°. Move the yoke to the width of cut and tighten the rip lock. Turn the machine on and lower the blade 1/16 in. into the table.

THINK SAFETY—ACT SAFELY
WHEN USING THE RADIAL ARM SAW

1. Wear eye protection; remove jewelry; secure long hair and loose clothing.
2. Hold stock firmly on the table and against the fence for all crosscutting operations. Support long boards and wide panels.
3. Be certain that all clamps and locking devices are tight and the depth of cut is correct before starting the motor.
4. Always return the saw to the rear of the table after completing a crosscut or miter cut. Do not remove stock from the table until the saw has returned and the blade has stopped.
5. Maintain a 4 in. margin of safety.
6. Shut off the motor, wait for the blade to stop, and disconnect power before making any adjustments.
7. Clean the table of scraps or sawdust before and after using the machine.
8. When ripping stock it must be flat and have one straight edge to move along the fence.
9. When ripping, always feed stock into the blade so that the bottom teeth are turning toward you.

SAWING CURVED LINES

Stationary machines which cut curved parts include the band saw and scroll saw. Both machines saw with narrow blades which control the radius of the curve, Fig. 21-33. Choose a band saw for cutting large radius curves and large cabinet components. A scroll saw, with its smaller blade, is best for small radii, and intricate curves.

RELIEF CUTS

Relief cuts allow waste material to break loose as you saw your workpiece. Each cut is made through excess material almost to the cutting line. Both band saw and scroll saw operations require relief cuts, Fig. 21-34, for making curves when:
1. There is a sharp inside or outside curve.

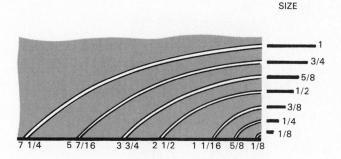

BLADE SIZE

1
3/4
5/8
1/2
3/8
1/4
1/8

7 1/4   5 7/16   3 3/4   2 1/2   1 1/16   5/8   1/8

MINIMUM RECOMMENDED KERF RADIUS

Fig. 21-33. There is a minimum cutting radius for each band or scroll saw blade width.

2. The curve changes direction: left to right or right to left.
3. Your cabinet part will be cut from a large piece of stock. The excess material may be difficult to control. Make relief cuts at least every 4 to 6 in.

When excess material is removed with relief cuts, there is less chance to twist or break the blade. With relief cuts, you do not need to withdraw the workpiece back through a long, irregular kerf.

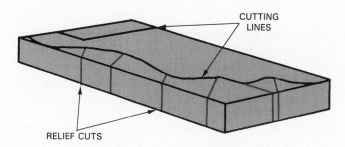

CUTTING LINES

RELIEF CUTS

Fig. 21-34. Relief cuts are made to irregular curves.

BAND SAW

A *band saw,* Fig. 21-35, is a very versatile machine. Besides making irregular curves and arcs, it can rip, bevel, and resaw. Install a rip fence or use a miter gauge for these operations. With the appropriate jig, the band saw can cut complete circles.

The band saw consists of a continuous, thin steel blade that travels on two wheels. The blade is exposed where it passes through the table (the point of operation). The table tilts for beveling. *Blade guides* position and control the blade at the table. The upper set of guides are on the *guide post* above your work. The post is set 1/4 in. (6 mm) above the material and held by a lock knob. The other set of blade guides is below the table.

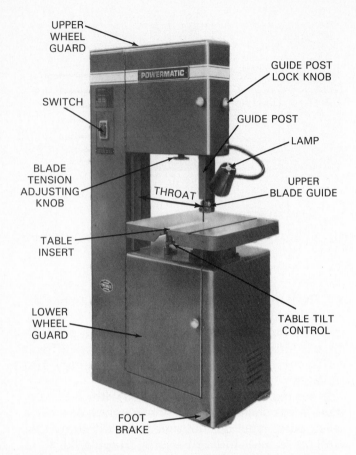

Fig. 21-35. Features of the band saw. (Powermatic)

Most band saws have two wheels. The bottom wheel drives the blade. The top wheel turns freely and is adjustable to control blade tension and alignment. Proper tension insures the blade does not stray from the line of cut. With correct alignment, the blade tracks in the center of the wheels. The wheels have rubber tires to prevent damage to the set of the blade teeth.

The throat is the distance from the blade to the side frame. See Fig. 21-35. This depth determines the widest cut which can be made. The throat depth is usually determined by the diameter of the wheels. See Fig. 21-36A. However, there are band saws which have three wheels. They maintain a large throat depth, but use smaller wheels. These machines are noted by their frame shape. See Fig. 21-39.

SELECTING AND INSTALLING BLADES

Review your product plans when selecting blades. Knowing the material and radii of curves being sawn helps you choose the proper blade. Select blades according to: width, length, tooth shape, blade set, teeth per inch (or points per inch), and blade gauge (thickness). These terms are discussed later in the chapter.

The procedure for changing blades is as follows:
1. Disconnect power to the machine.

2. Remove or swing aside the upper and lower wheel guards, Fig. 21-36A.
3. Release the blade tension by turning the tension control knob, Fig. 21-36B.
4. Remove the table insert if necessary.
5. Remove the old blade from the wheels and guides, then slip it through the slot in the table.
6. Hold the replacement blade up in front of the machine. Be sure the teeth are pointed downward and toward you over the table.
7. Slide the replacement blade through the table slot, between the guides, and onto the wheels.

A

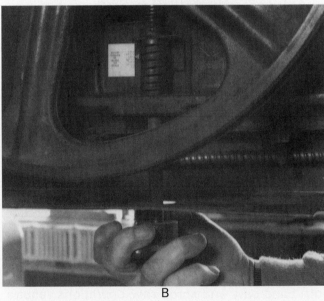

B

Fig. 21-36. A—Remove or swing aside guards to gain access to the blade. (Delta) B—Loosening blade tension.

8. Reset the blade tension. Most machines have a scale to show the correct tension for various blade widths. (See Fig. 21-71B.)

9. Adjust the blade guides, Fig. 21-37, if the replacement blade is a different width. The front edge of the side guides should be even or slightly in back of the tooth gullets. THEY SHOULD NEVER TOUCH THE TEETH. The rear guide (blade support wheel) shoud be 1/64 in. away from the blade.

10. Turn the upper wheel, by hand, three or four turns to see that the blade is tracking in the center of the wheels.

11. Replace the wheel guards and throat plate.

12. Reconnect power to the machine.

13. Start the machine. Allow it to reach full speed, then turn it off. Stop the machine with the foot brake if there is one.

14. Check that the blade location is in the center of the wheel tire. If not, adjust the tracking control knob which tilts the upper wheel slightly to bring the blade back into alignment, Fig. 21-38.

BAND SAW OPERATION

Plan your sawing sequence before starting the band saw. Short and/or relief cuts are made first. Then determine whether the workpiece will be to the right or left of the saw blade. Saw on the waste side of the cutting line to allow for sanding.

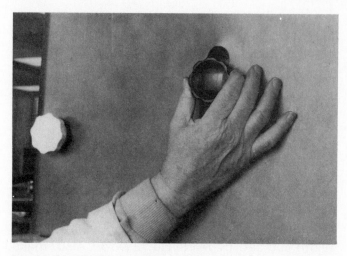

Fig. 21-38. Tracking adjustment is found on the back of the machine behind the upper wheel.

Before making the cut, check your setup. Were all adjustments made? Is the guard 1/4 in. (6 mm) above the workpiece? Are all locking devices secure? How will you control your workpiece and waste before and after the cut? Are you standing comfortably in place? Is there a foot brake within reach that stops the machine from coasting after it is turned off?

Large components, such as those shown in Fig. 21-39, are often difficult to cut. The stock could

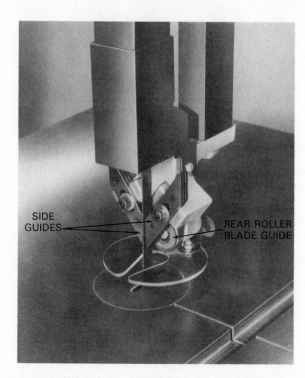

Fig. 21-37. Side guides, behind the saw teeth, keep the blade from twisting or turning. The rear guide is 1/64 in. behind the blade. (Rockwell)

Fig. 21-39. With large, curved workpieces, first cut away as much waste as possible to prevent it from hitting the machine frame. (Delta)

strike the machine frame as you move the work-piece from side to side to follow the curve. If the frame interferes, slowly withdraw the material through the kerf. Be careful not to pull the blade forward from between the blade guides. It could bind, come off of the wheels, and even break. More waste material may need to be cut off to feed the workpiece without hitting the frame. If the workpiece is just too large for the band saw, use a saber saw.

Curved-line sawing

The primary purpose of the band saw is to cut curved parts. The cutting radius depends on blade width and set. (Refer to Fig. 21-33.) Also, make relief cuts where the curve changes direction, Fig. 21-40.

When changing direction during a cut, do not push the workpiece against the side of the blade. Anticipate turning your work before you need to change the curve direction.

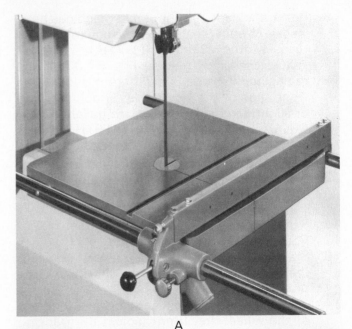

A

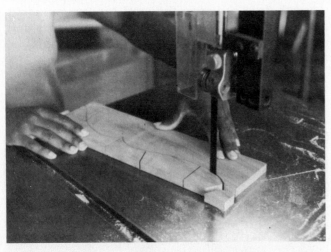

Fig. 21-40. Guide the workpiece with both hands when sawing curves. Blade guide and guard raised for photo.

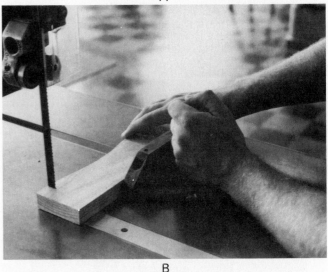

B

Fig. 21-41. Accessories are needed to saw straight lines. A—Rip fence. (Rockwell) B—Miter gauge. Blade guard and guide raised for photo.

Straight line sawing

Ripping and crosscutting a straight line requires that you use some device to guide your work. Attach a rip fence or clamp a straightedge to the table, Fig. 21-41A. Install a miter gauge for short cuts, Fig. 21-41B. For sawing multiple parts to length, attach a miter gauge stop rod or clamp a stop block near the front of the table as you would with a table saw.

Ripping thin strips

Thin strips, 1/8 to 1/2 in. (3 to 12 mm) wide, are often ripped for bent wood products and inlaying. Measure the desired dimension from the fence to the blade. It is better to cut strips with the band saw than with the table or other saw. Joint the edge

before cutting. Usually the cut edge will be smooth enough for gluing.

Pocket cutting

A *pocket cut* is one where three sides of an opening are sawn. The edges of the pocket may be straight or curved. There may not be room enough for relief cuts. Several alternatives include:

1. Saw straight into the pocket on each side. Withdraw the workpiece carefully after each pass. Then cut a curve as small as your blade size allows. Complete the pocket by sawing away any remaining waste. See Fig. 21-42A.
2. Drill two turn-around holes. These provide room in the corners for you to change the workpiece direction without twisting the blade. Clean up

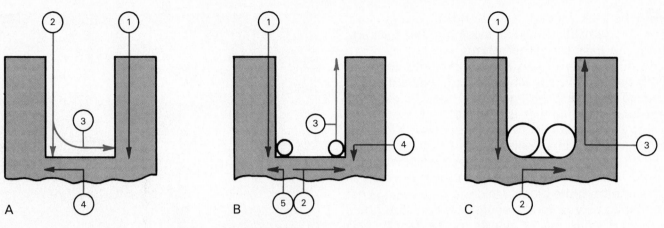

Fig. 21-42. Series of drilled holes and kerfs for pocket cutting.

the corners with an extra cut or a file. See Fig. 21-42B.

3. It is possible that the inside corners of the pocket are curved as part of the cabinet design. In this situation, bore the holes with the proper radius bit. Then saw the waste material away. See Fig. 21-42C.

Beveling

Band saw tables tilt for bevel sawing. Loosen the table tilt lock knob and adjust the angle according to the tilt scale, Fig. 21-43. If no tilt scale is offered, set and measure with a T-bevel.

For straight bevels, you need a rip fence or miter gauge. Feed workpieces for curved cuts as you would if the table was flat, Fig. 21-44. Once you begin the cut, continue only in one direction. Otherwise you would cut a reverse bevel. Remember, the

kerf made on the other face differs from the cutting line you follow.

Sawing multiple parts to size

Multiple parts can be cut to size in a single operation. Stack and fasten workpieces together with nails located away from the cutting line, Fig. 21-45. Make relief cuts on each side of the nails and

Fig. 21-44. Beveling on the band saw.

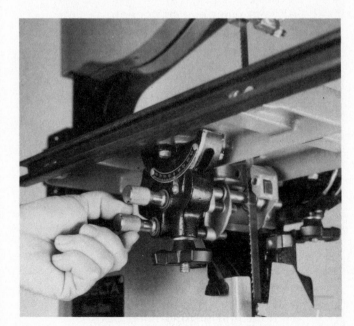

Fig. 21-43. Adjust the table angle according to the tilt scale. (Delta)

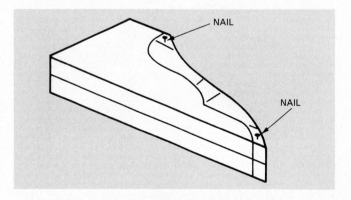

Fig. 21-45. Stack material when sawing duplicate workpieces.

elsewhere as needed. Saw along the cutting line. The last two cuts should be those that free the parts from the nailed-together waste.

In addition, you can hold workpieces together with two-sided tape. This prevents blade damage caused by sawing through nails. However, tape will not hold if the lumber is warped.

For sawing duplicate workpieces with parallel edges, such as chair rails, attach a ''round fence,'' Fig. 21-46. Saw the first workpiece to establish the shape. Then secure the fence to the table a given distance from the blade. Hold the material against the fence as you feed through the cut. You could attach a small caster wheel to the fence. This prevents uneven motion caused by the sawn edge.

Resawing

Resawing can be done with a table saw and fence as discussed earlier. Another method is to use a band saw and round fence. The width of material that can be resawed depends on how high the upper guide post rises. The blade becomes more flexible at the point of operation when the guide post is raised high.

Resawing on the band saw is a one-pass process, Fig. 21-47. Clamp the round fence away from the blade at a distance equal to the desired material

Fig. 21-47. Resawing on the band saw is a one-pass operation. Hold material firmly against a rounded auxiliary fence.

thickness. Also mark the resaw line on the material. You may have to adjust your feed left or right during the cut. This is necessary if the blade has more set on one side. Also, hard growth rings, knots, and soft wood between rings affects blade travel. Use a push stick as you near the last 2 or 3 in. of the workpiece. Support stock behind the table.

THINK SAFETY—ACT SAFELY WHEN USING THE BAND SAW

1. Fasten loose clothing, secure long hair, and remove jewelry.
2. Always wear eye protection.
3. If you hear a rhythmic click as the wood is being cut, there may be a cracked blade. Stop and inspect the machine.
4. If the blade breaks, shut off the power. Remove it after the machine comes to a complete stop.
5. Make sure you adjust the proper tension.
6. Make sure the teeth are pointing down, toward the table.
7. Lock the upper guide, about 1/4 in. above the work.
8. Hold the stock firmly on the table as you cut.
9. Maintain your balance as you cut.
10. Make relief cuts as necesssary.
11. Keep your fingers away from the point of operation while the blade is moving.
12. Do not cut a small radius with a wide blade without first making relief cuts.
13. Minimize backing out of a kerf. This could pull the blade off the wheels.

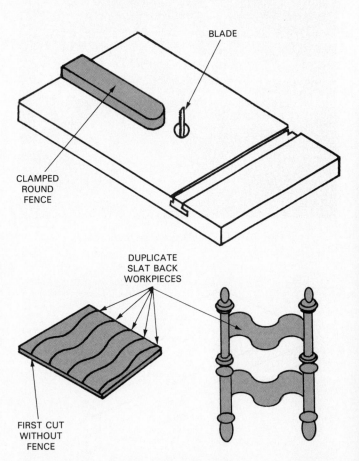

Fig. 21-46. A round fence helps saw duplicate workpieces having gentle curves.

SCROLL SAW

The *scroll saw* cuts small radius curves. Its thin, narrow blade saws intricate work, such as marquetry and inlay. The scroll saw operates much like the band saw. However, unlike the band saw, the scroll saw will cut out interior openings.

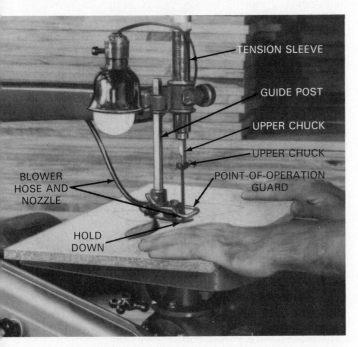

TENSION SLEEVE

GUIDE POST

UPPER CHUCK

UPPER CHUCK

POINT-OF-OPERATION GUARD

BLOWER HOSE AND NOZZLE

HOLD DOWN

Fig. 21-48. Features and adjustments of a scroll saw. (Delta)

SCROLL SAW FEATURES

Scroll saw features include a table, *hold-down, blade guide, blade chucks, blower nozzle,* and guard, Fig. 21-48. The table tilts for making bevel cuts. A hold-down keeps material from vibrating on the table. It is attached to the machine frame or to a guide post. The blade, held by two chucks, cuts reciprocally on the downward stroke. The lower chuck drives the reciprocal motion of the blade. The upper chuck is spring-loaded and retains blade tension. The blade guides support the blade so it does not break due to excess feed pressure. The blower nozzle is attached to an air supply line. It blows away chips so the cutting line remains visible.

There are two types of scroll saws. They differ in how they apply tension to the blade. The tension prevents the blade from bending on the return stroke. Tension in a sleeve design scroll saw, Fig. 21-48, is supplied by a spring-loaded sleeve in the upper chuck. Tension is adjusted with a knob on the overarm beside the sleeve. With rear tension scroll saws, the entire overarm pivots with the blade motion. (See Fig. 21-49.) Blade tension is adjusted at the rear of the machine. The advantage of rear tension saws is that the blade moves slightly back from the workpiece. This helps prevent the workpiece from "jumping" up and down. The hold-down serves as a guard for rear tension scroll saws.

Scroll saw size is based on the distance from the blade to the back of the overarm. This is called the

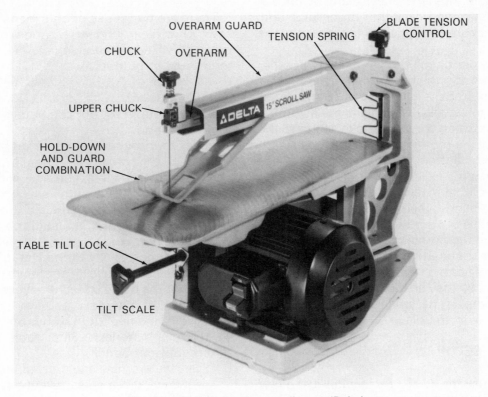

OVERARM GUARD

CHUCK

OVERARM

TENSION SPRING

BLADE TENSION CONTROL

UPPER CHUCK

HOLD-DOWN AND GUARD COMBINATION

TABLE TILT LOCK

TILT SCALE

Fig. 21-49. Rear tension scroll saw. (Delta)

throat depth and may vary from 12 to 24 in. The throat depth limits the length of material that can be cut.

SELECTING AND INSTALLING SCROLL SAW BLADES

Blades for scroll saws are very narrow and thus, are capable of sawing a small radius. The number of teeth per inch varies. A rule of thumb is to select blades which will have three or more teeth in contact with the wood at all times. The edge next to the kerf will not splinter as much.

The procedure to change a blade is as follows:
1. Disconnect power to the saw.
2. Remove the table insert.
3. Move the lower chuck to the top of its stroke by turning the motor shaft knob.
4. Loosen the thumb screws or set screws on upper and lower chucks.
5. Remove the old blade.
6. Slip the replacement blade into the lower chuck. Point the teeth downward and toward the front of the machine.
7. Align the blade with the slot in the blade guide, Fig. 21-50.
8. Tighten the lower chuck to secure the blade. NOTE: If the blade extends above the upper chuck at this point, you must adjust the tension device. For sleeve-type saws, loosen the knob. Then raise the sleeve until the upper chuck is about 1/2 in. (13 mm) above the blade end. Tighten the sleeve clamp knob. For rear tension saws, adjust the tension knob until the upper chuck is positioned 1/2 in. above the blade end.
9. Pull the upper chuck down, insert the blade, and tighten the thumb screw.
10. Turn the motor shaft knob to raise and lower the blade one cycle. If the blade bends during either the cutting or return stroke, increase the tension. If the motor shaft knob is very hard to turn at the bottom of the saw stoke, release some tension.
11. Install the table insert.

On many machines, the blade guide is circular. It contains a series of variable size slots and a roller. The slots accommodate blades of different thicknesses. Rotate the guide to the proper slot for a given blade. The teeth on the blade must be in front of the guide slot so they are not damaged when the blade reciprocates. The small roller, behind the blade, rotates with the blade.

SCROLL SAW SETUP

Preparing to use the scroll saw requires just a few simple steps. For saws having a guide post, lower

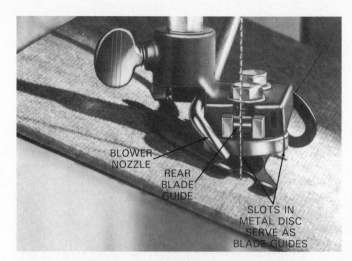

Fig. 21-50. The scroll saw blade is controlled by blade guide slots in a metal disk and a rear guide. (Delta)

or raise the post so material can pass under the hold-down.

The scroll saw may have one of three speed adjustments.
1. Electronic. A speed knob adjusts the speed, which is displayed in a digital readout.
2. Variable. A variable speed scroll saw adjusts while the machine is running.
3. Pulleys. A belt is tracked over opposing step pulleys. Make sure that the power is disconnected while you move the belt.

SCROLL SAW OPERATION

There are two types of cuts made with the scroll saw. One is around or through the workpiece, typically called an outside cut. The other is an interior cut for cutouts.

Outside cuts

The procedure for outside cuts is very similar to the band saw:
1. Plan your sequence for making relief cuts. Even though the scroll saw has a narrow blade, relief cuts may help when cutting small radius curves.
2. On tension sleeve scroll saws, lower the hold-down until it rests on the material. Press lightly on the blade guard, then tighten the guide post. The hold down on some rear tension saws adjusts automatically to the workpiece thickness.
3. Aim the air nozzle at the point of operation.
4. Adjust the blade speed if necessary. Saw thick and hard materials at slow speeds. Faster speeds and fine tooth blades are appropriate for thinner materials. Fine tooth blades leave smooth cut edges.
5. Start the machine and procede with your cutting sequence. Relief cuts prevent having to back the blade out of a long saw kerf.

Beveling

Beveling on the scroll saw is much like the band-saw operation. Tilt the table, then adjust the hold down to the tilt angle. (Refer to Fig. 21-49.) Keep the workpiece on the same side of the blade until the cut is complete.

Interior cuts

The scroll saw cuts interior openings easily. Since the blade is not a continuous loop, it can be threaded through a hole in the workpiece, Fig. 21-51. After you drill holes in the waste section, proceed as follows:

1. Disconnect power to the scroll saw.
2. Raise the chuck to the top of the stroke by turning the motor shaft.
3. Loosen the upper chuck clamp to free the blade.
4. Bend the blade slightly to slide it through the hole drilled in your workpiece.
5. Place the material on the table and rechuck the blade.
6. Make sure the hold-down presses lightly on the material.
7. Holding the material down with one hand, press the START button.
8. Proceed with the inside cut. If there are sharp curves and inside corners, relief cuts may be needed, Fig. 21-52.
9. When finished with the cutout, stop the machine, disconnect power, and loosen the top chuck to free the blade. Repeat the procedure for additional cutouts.

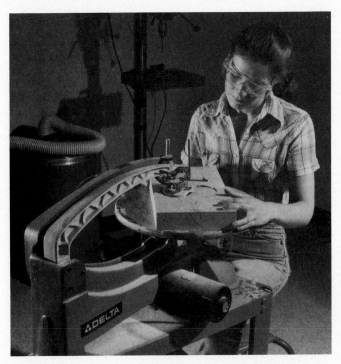

Fig. 21-52. Completing an interior cut. (Delta)

USING SABER SAW BLADES

A saber saw blade may be installed in the scroll saw's lower chuck, Fig. 21-53. It is especially helpful for making cutouts. You do not have to unchuck the top part of the blade to move from one cutout section to the hole drilled in the next section. A blade guide is still attached on tension sleeve scroll saws. Select the proper blade guide slot, attach it to the guide post, and lower the assembly next to the blade. Feed material as you would when using the scroll saw blade. Since the saber saw blade is thicker and wider, the minimum cutting radius will be increased.

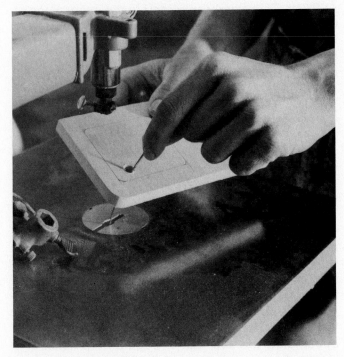

Fig. 21-51. When cutting interior curves, unchuck the blade and thread it through a predrilled hole.

Fig. 21-53. A saber saw blade can be installed in the bottom chuck of most scroll saws.

THINK SAFETY—ACT SAFELY WHEN USING THE SCROLL SAW

1. Fasten loose clothing, secure long hair, and remove jewelry.
2. Wear safety glasses, goggles, or a face shield.
3. Make sure the saw blade's teeth point down.
4. Make sure the proper blade size and type is installed.
5. Keep the floor around work area clean and free from sawdust and scraps.
6. Change blades (and speed on machines having step pulleys) with the power disconnected.
7. Check all adjustments by rotating the motor by hand before turning power on.
8. The hold-down must press lightly on the material being cut.
9. Stop the machine before removing excess stock from the table.
10. Do not attempt to saw large stock without means of support.
11. Hold material firmly and feed it into the blade at a moderate speed.
12. Make relief cuts before cutting curves.
13. Shut off the power and let the machine come to a complete stop before leaving it.

SELECTING BLADES

Blades, regardless of the machine they are on, are designed to cut efficiently and effectively. Selecting the proper blade is an important part of sawing. Using the wrong blade may ruin the workpiece and/or dull the blade. For example, crosscutting with a rip blade creates a problem. Rip teeth are larger and have a different cutting angle which will splinter the wood. The edge is left rough and makes the wood look splintered.

The blade you choose depends on the sawing operation. You may be sawing lumber or plywood across or along the grain. You could also be cutting non-grain composites such as hardboard, particleboard, and even plastic.

After making a cut, inspect the cut edges of the workpiece. Look to see how rough or smooth they are. There could be burn marks from either using a dull blade or advancing the blade too slowly. Inspection helps determine how well the blade is performing.

Saw blade performance is based on tooth design and chip load. Chip loading is the amount of material in the gullet of each tooth. Chip load depends on the:
1. Number of teeth per inch.
2. Speed of the blade.
3. Rate of feed.

Chip load is a factor for all types and styles of blade. If wood chips totally fill the gullet, the blade cuts poorly. This is because there is no more room in the blade to hold sawn chips. You can feed faster with large tooth blades, yet the sawn edge will be rougher. However, too much pressure causes the blade to heat up due to increased friction. Excess heat can remove temper from a blade.

Blade quality relates mostly to the life of any blade used properly. Select blades which are stainless steel, alloy steel, or high carbon steel.

CIRCULAR BLADE

Circular blades are used on the table saw and radial arm saw. Blade specifications include diameter, number of teeth, shape of the teeth, cross-sectional shape, as well as size of the arbor hole.

Blade diameter usually describes the capacity of the machine (10 in. table saw, 7 1/4 in. portable circular saw, for example). Smaller diameter blades reduce the maximum depth of cut. Most 10 in. blades will saw through 2 in. material.

The number of teeth is important for blade selection. The number does not distinguish a rip blade from a crosscut or combination blade. Rather, it suggests the relative cut-edge quality among the same blade type. Fewer teeth could suggest a rip saw that leaves a rough edge. However, there are combination blades of the same diameter with fewer teeth which leave a much smoother edge.

Blades for thin plywood, veneer, and plastic always have a greater total number of teeth (150 to 300). This clearly emphasizes the importance of chip loading. Using a plywood blade for 5/4 in. lumber would be disastrous. Therefore, you must be able to "read the blade."

To identify specific blades, you must know several terms, Fig. 21-54. They include:
1. Chisel, bevel, and raker teeth.
2. Hook angle.
3. Gullet.

Teeth may be *raker (square), chisel-like,* or *bevel* shaped. Some combination blades may have teeth shaped several ways. One tooth is square followed by several that are beveled.

Hook angle determines the angle at which the front edge of the tooth contacts the material. This angle is created between the tooth edge and a line that extends from the tooth point to the arbor hole. Rip blades have a large hook angle. Other blades have less hook and some even have 0° or a negative hook angle.

Between each tooth is a *gullet.* It is where chips accumulate as teeth cut through the material. The chips absorb heat from the blade and are then thrown out when the tooth exits the stock.

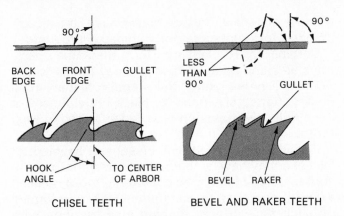

CHISEL TEETH   BEVEL AND RAKER TEETH

Fig. 21-54. The type of material and grain direction through which a blade will cut is based on tooth shape.

Circular blades are either flat, hollow ground, or thin rim, Fig. 21-5B. *Flat Blades* have set to create a wider saw kerf. The kerf prevents the blade body from binding. A *hollow ground blade* has no set. It leaves a smoother cut edge on the workpiece. The thinner cross section of the blade reduces binding. However, binding and heating will occur if the blade is not raised 1 in. (25 mm) above the table, Fig. 21-55A. A *thin rim* (thin kerf) *blade* creates the narrowest kerf and thus, conserves material. However, heat buildup is a problem unless you are sawing veneer.

Sawing efficiency is affected by water and resin in lumber. Recall that nominal size softwood generally is sold at a higher moisture content than hardwood. Moisture and resin can accumulate like glue on the blade, Fig. 21-55B. This increases friction, which causes the blade to become warm and possibly bind. Blades for sawing moist wood need more set than those for dry wood. They will also require cleaning more often.

Part of identifying blades involves inspecting the blade teeth. There are several styles of blades identified by tooth shapes. They are rip, crosscut, combination, planer, plywood, and plastic blades, Fig. 52-56.

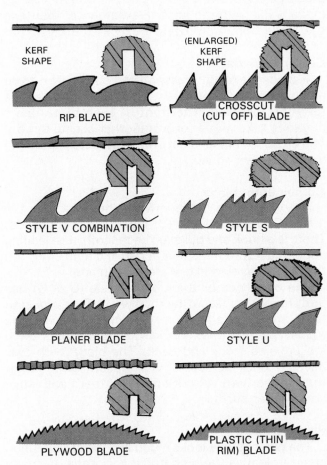

Fig. 21-56. You should be able to "read the blade" and identify its use.

Fig. 21-55. A—Set hollow ground blades high. The guard has been removed to show the operation. B—Resin buildup (dark material) results from sawing only on the rim of a hollow ground blade.

Rip blade

Blades for ripping typically have flat-top teeth sharpened to a chisel point. Teeth have a positive hook angle, sometimes called rake angle. The front edge of the tooth may be straight or curved from the gullet to the point. The back of each tooth is a curved arc from the point to the gullet. The rip blade is flat with the teeth alternately set (bent) so the blade body can rotate freely in the kerf.

Crosscut blade

A crosscut blade is recognized easily. The front and back of each tooth is straight. Both sides of the teeth are beveled. The front of each tooth has a negative rake angle for a smoother slicing action. The crosscut blade is flat with teeth alternately set for blade clearance.

Combination blade

A combination blade saws along or across the grain. One blade style (V) looks like a rip blade. There is a hook and gullet on each tooth. The leading edge of each tooth is sharpened like a rip saw, but the tip is beveled like a crosscut blade.

The other combination blade style (U or S) has both rip and crosscut teeth. Two or four crosscut teeth are followed by a raker tooth. The raker has a chisel point plus hook and a gullet. The other teeth are beveled front and back. The blade with two beveled teeth per section will cut somewhat faster than those with four. More bevel teeth will leave a smoother surface.

Planer blade

The planer blade looks much like the combination blade. It leaves the smoothest kerf edge. In many instances it can almost eliminate sanding. This is because the blade is hollow ground. Although teeth have both bevel and chisel shapes, they are not set (bent outward). This results in a narrower kerf.

Plywood blade

A plywood blade has many fine crosscut-type teeth. The blade may be flat with set teeth. It can also be hollow ground without set.

Plastics blade

Plastic blades, similar to those used for plywood, saw sheet plastics such as acrylic, polyethylene, and styrene. Blades may be flat, hollow ground, or thin rim.

Carbide tipped blade

Thus far, blade selection has focused on sawing lumber and some plastics. However, composition materials such as fiberboard, waferboard, and particleboard (tempered and untempered) are used more and more. Plastic laminates often are applied to these materials. *Carbide tipped blades* are recommended for composite and laminated products.

Carbide tipped blades perform the same operations as standard steel blades. They remain sharp 10 to 20 times longer than regular blades. High quality, flat steel is used for blade body. Pieces of extremely hard tungsten carbide are brazed to each tooth.

Carbide tipped teeth will be square, beveled, or look like they have a chamfer on one or both of the corners, Fig. 21-57. The *chamfered tooth* is called a *double-chip* or *triple-chip* tooth. One chip is formed by each flat surface. Ripping may be done with square top or alternating square and triple-chip blades. Crosscutting most likely is done with beveled teeth. There are two styles of combination blades. They have one square (raker tooth) and two or four beveled teeth per set. Finer cutting blades for plywood, plastics, and particleboard may have: alternating bevel teeth, alternating double- or triple-chip and beveled teeth, or alternating double- or triple-chip and square teeth.

Tooth shapes identify sawing direction. Square teeth generally are for ripping. Beveled teeth score the kerf for crosscutting. You will find plywood, plastic, and particleboard saw blades with bevel-

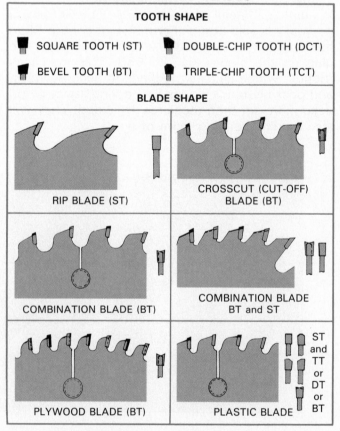

Fig. 21-57. Tough, long lasting tungsten carbide tipped blade out-perform standard blades. (Peerless)

tooth designs. The triple-chip tooth is recommended for cuts on hardwood or when there is no concern for grain direction. Multiple-chip teeth leave fewer splinters or nicks.

Another form of carbide blade can be used on plywood, fiberboard, plastic laminate, fiberglass, and composition board. Rather than brazed teeth, this blade has hundreds of carbide chips bonded to the blade edge, Fig. 21-58. The chips are cut with an abrasive action rather than the typical chip removal process associated with toothed blades. These blades are reversible which can increase their usable life up to 25 percent. Set up this blade as you would one that is hollow ground.

Some blades (standard and carbide tipped) may be designed with an expansion slot (see Fig. 21-57). It relieves heat stress in the blade. A warm blade could warp and affect the smoothness and width of the kerf. On carbide blades over 12'' in diameter, holes at the bottom of the expansion slots are fitted with aluminum plugs. These help reduce noise and vibration, resulting in a smoother cut.

As you can see, proper blade selection is important. For moist wood, flat blades with plenty of set are best. For dry wood, hollow ground or thin rim blades leave smoother edges. Combination blades reduce the number of blade changes you have to make. Blades with positive hook angles (such as rip blades) cut faster. However, splintering is likely to occur. Beveled teeth with 0° or negative rake angle reduce splintering. Using fine tooth blades reduces splintering and chipping.

BAND SAW BLADE

A band saw blade is an endless bonded loop of thin narrow steel with teeth on one edge. Select band saw blades according to various specifications. The length of the loop is critical. You may purchase a blade of a given length, such as 12 ft. You could also buy a 100 ft. to 500 ft. coil and then cut and weld together your own blades.

Blade width is important. It may vary from 1/8 in. to 1 in. or wider. Blades 1/8 in. to 1/2 in. are used most often for sawing irregular kerfs. Wider blades are more appropriate for resawing.

Blades vary in hardness. Some inexpensive blades are made of untempered steel. Others may have a flame hardened cutting edge and possibly a hard tempered back.

There are several alternative tooth shapes and blade sets available, Fig. 21-59. The regular blade

STRAIGHT BLADES

SETS			SHAPES		
RAKER	WAVY	ALTERNATE	REGULAR	HOOK	SKIP

Fig. 21-59. Band saw blades shapes and sets.

Fig. 21-58. A carbide grit edge blade saws composite products as well as ceramics. The guard has been removed to show the operation. (Remington Arms Co.)

has a 0° hook angle and a straight front and back on each tooth. The hook tooth blade has about a 10° positive hook angle. The skip-tooth blade has a straight tooth front, 0° hook, and a long gullet. Regular and hook tooth blades have teeth set alternately left and right. The skip-tooth blade may have a raker tooth set. Rakers are chisel teeth placed between sets of beveled teeth. A third set type is the wavy tooth blade. Several teeth are set right and then left. They are separated by a raker tooth. A regular blade works best for wood only. The hook tooth cuts well on most wood, fiberglass, and plastic laminate. The skip tooth blade is better for soft woods and plastics. These may overload and clog other blades' gullets.

A carbide chip blade is also available. This blade will saw fiberglass, plastic laminate, particleboard, and ceramic tile, Fig. 21-60. It can be reversed to extend the life of the blade.

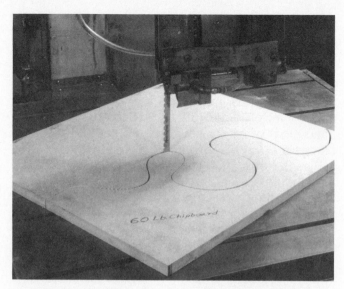

Fig. 21-60. Carbide chip band saw blades are available for cutting composite materials and ceramics. Guard raised to show operation. (Remington Arms Co.)

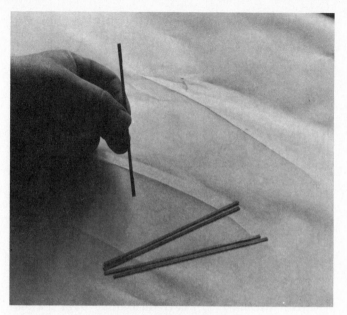

Fig. 21-61. Scroll saw blades.

SCROLL SAW BLADE

The scroll saw uses several different blades also, Fig. 21-61. Standard blades cut in only one direction. They vary in width and number of teeth per inch (tpi). Common widths are 1/8 to 1/4 in. (3 to 6 mm).

Scroll saw blades typically have 7 to 20 teeth-per-inch (tpi). They have beveled teeth that are alternately set. Normally, at least three teeth should contact the material at all times. A 7 tpi blade would be best for soft lumber with high moisture content. A 20 tpi blade, about 1/32 in. wide, is proper for veneer and other very thin material. The standard blade length is 5 in. In addition, a round blade with spiral teeth is available. You can move the material in any direction while cutting.

MAINTAINING SAW BLADES

Saw blades should be sharp to the touch, have adequate set, and be free of rust or resin. Inspect them frequently for cracks (especially in the gullets), warpage, bluish color (sign of overheating), and missing or damaged carbide teeth. Proper maintenance may include cleaning and sharpening or discarding.

Clean blades with paint thinner. Oven cleaner may be used on more stubborn resins. Be sure to protect your hands with rubber gloves. Rust can be removed with oil and fine steel wool. Remove the oil and coat the blade with paste wax or silicone spray before storing it.

Blade sharpening is a time-consuming operation. You must decide whether to have blades machine sharpened accurately or try to do it less accurately by hand. Blade sharpening machines will joint, set, and file or grind the blades precisely. Machine grinding is the only method to sharpen a carbide tip blade. Hand sharpening is limited to jointing, setting, and filing. A small hand stone could be used to touch up a standard blade. However, hand sharpening is not recommended.

To determine if you can sharpen a given standard blade by hand, push a file across a tooth. If file marks appear, the blade may be sharpened. If not, the blade is too hard. Carbide tip and hardened steel blades cannot be hand sharpened.

SHARPENING CIRCULAR BLADES

Circular saw blade sharpening involves jointing, gumming, setting, and filing. Jointing makes all teeth edges the same distance to the center of the arbor. Gumming returns blade gullets to the size they were when the blade was new. After being jointed, set, and filed several times, gullets become shallow and cannot operate with an efficient chip load. Therefore, gullets should be reshaped periodically.

Setting is the process of bending the teeth outward. By hand, it requires the use of a stake and setting hammer. Blade thickness is measured by sheet metal thickness gauge sizes. Set teeth one and one-half to two gauge thicknesses per side for dry hardwood and softwood, Fig. 21-62. For example, if the saw is 14 gauge (.083), 2 gauges set per side would make saw kerf 10 gauge (.134) or .0255'' per side. More set is needed for sawing green lumber.

File only the back surfaces on chisel and raker teeth. File both sides of the bevel teeth for crosscut,

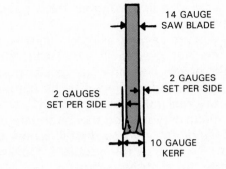

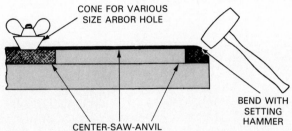

Thickness of Saw	With 2 Gauges Set Per Side of Saw Kerf Will Be	Set Per Side	With 2½ Gauges Set Per Side of Saw Kerf Will Be	Set Per Side
14 ga.	10 ga. (.134)	.0255	9 ga. (.148)	.032
16 ga.	12 ga. (.109)	.0220	11 ga. (.120)	.027
17 ga.	13 ga. (.095)	.0185	12 ga. (.109)	.0255
18 ga.	14 ga. (.083)	.0170	13 ga. (.095)	.023
19 ga.	15 ga. (.072)	.0150		
20 ga.	16 ga. (.065)	.0150		

Fig. 21-62. Circular saw blades can be set properly by hand. (Peerless)

combination, planer, plywood, and plastic blades.

Sharpen the blade when the teeth leave burn marks after sawing a workpiece. Machine sharpening will result in more consistent set, gullet sizes and hook angles.

Hand sharpening is time consuming and less accurate. Tools you will need include:
1. Setting stake. (Do not set a hollow ground blade).
2. Clamp.
3. Flat file.
4. Triangular file.
5. Jig for jointing and filing (if available).

The procedure to set teeth is as follows:
1. Place the blade on a stake and bend only the outer 1/4th of alternate teeth to the anvil of the stake. Refer to Fig. 21-62.
   NOTE: Use a lead, brass, or other soft-faced hammer. You might use a short piece of brass or aluminum rod and strike that with a steel hammer. A regular hammer will dent the tooth.
2. Turn the blade over and set the remaining alternate teeth the other way.

The procedure to joint teeth is as follows:
1. Rotate the secure blade against the file in a hand jointer, Fig. 21-63.

Fig. 21-63. This Style V combination blade is being jointed by hand. (Brookstone)

2. Rotate the blade by hand while it is on the setting stake. Use a file or hand stone on high teeth as they pass.
   NOTE: End this procedure when each tooth point reflects a small, shiny, flat spot.

File chisel, bevel, and raker teeth separately. A filing jig, Fig. 21-64, is helpful. Try to maintain the original tooth angle (square or beveled). Stop when the shiny flat spot (caused by jointing) disappears and the tooth is sharp. File ONLY the backs of raker and chisel teeth. Filing the fronts will change the hook angle.

Restore chisel teeth with a flat file by:
1. Filing only the back surface of each tooth.
2. Making the same number of strokes on each tooth.
3. Filing as few strokes as possible.

Fig. 21-64. This saw filer is adjustable for various tooth angles. (Brookstone)

Restore bevel teeth with a triangular file:
1. File two surfaces on each stroke: the front of one tooth and the back of the next tooth.
2. Make as few strokes as possible.
3. File only until the shiny jointed flats disappear.

Restore raker teeth with a flat file. They are found on combination and planer blades between sets of bevel teeth. They are shorter than the bevel teeth, Fig. 21-65A. The difference in height is 1/64 in. on a 12 in. or smaller blade. On larger blades, it is 1/32 in.

Using a raker gauge, Fig. 21-65B, is helpful. It has an anvil that is set to the height difference. Hold it against the blade and joint raker tooth tips even with the gauge anvil, Fig. 21-65C.

Restore the raker sharpness as follows:
1. File the entire back surface ONLY with a flat file.
2. Remove the shiny spot made while jointing.

MAINTAINING POWER SAWS

Maintaining stationary power saws properly will increase their usable life. Inspect, clean, adjust, and lubricate saws periodically. The machine MUST be disconnected from electrical power before service. For complex repairs, refer to the owner's manual.

TABLE SAW

Table saws should cut material accurately. Suppose you check a workpiece and find it out of square. This could indicate a table, miter gauge, or fence problem.

Suppose you are sawing using the miter gauge. You notice the workpiece pulls away from or feeds in toward the blade. The miter gauge slot may not be parallel to the blade. Check this by comparing readings with a dial indicator, Fig. 21-66. The dial should not move as you slide the miter gauge. (Be sure the blade is not warped. Install a new blade for the test.) To correct this problem, loosen and turn the table top slightly.

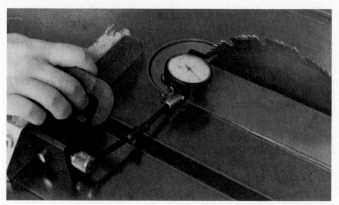

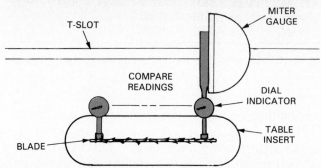

Fig. 21-66. Check distance readings from the blade to the table to determine whether the arbor and table are aligned.

Suppose you are sawing using the rip fence. The workpiece pulls away from or rubs tightly against the fence. This indicates the fence is out of alignment. If the fence has been dropped at some time, one or more locking mechanism bolts or nuts may have slipped. Loosen them, move the fence to align it, and then retighten the bolts or nuts.

Make accurate adjustments with a dial indicator, Fig. 21-67. Without the indicator, make the same comparisons with a wood block. However, this method is less accurate.

At times, handwheels become hard to turn. First check to see that the lock knobs are loose. If they are, lubricate screw threads with silicone spray or powdered graphite. Saw dust will stick to oil and may create a gummy condition worse than before.

Your sense of smell is valuable around a table saw. The smell of rubber or varnish may be present.

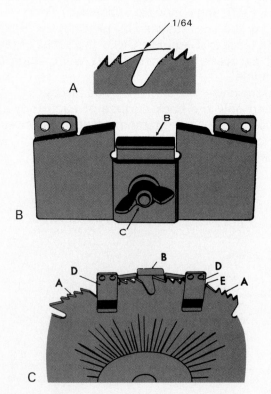

Fig. 21-65. Sharpening a Style S or V combination blade requires a raker gauge. (Peerless)

A rubber scent likely will occur when the belt is not tracking properly. The belt overheats, gets hot, and may harden. Then it can crack and probably break. An overheated motor has a definite varnish-like smell. Motors often have a built-in circulating fan. It can attract sawdust. Sawdust accumulation can slow the motor and cause overheating and possible burn out.

Rust appears on unpainted steel parts. Remove the rust with oil and steel wool or fine emery cloth. Wipe the oil away because it will stain your wood. Then coat the table and other parts with paste wax. Wax is less likely to be absorbed into the wood being sawed.

RADIAL ARM SAW

The radial arm saw has many movable parts. Rust, lack of lubrication, and excessive torque on levers are sources of maintenance problems. Check table and fence alignments before making cuts. Do so with a square, protractor, T-bevel, or other device. Machine scales may not be accurate.

The table may have to be leveled so the blade will be square. Do so by removing the table protector and wood top. Adjust the leveling bolts as necessary and reset the locknuts, Fig. 21-68.

Sometimes the saw kerf is not straight. The saw assembly movement bearings inside the overarm could be out of adjustment and allowing side play. Adjustment may or may not be possible. If not, the bearings will need to be replaced.

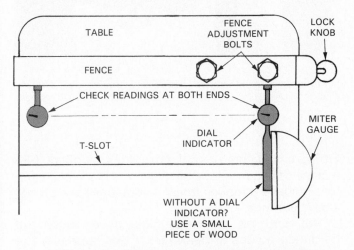

Fig. 21-67. With the fence clamped, check the distance from the fence to a table slot at both the front and back.

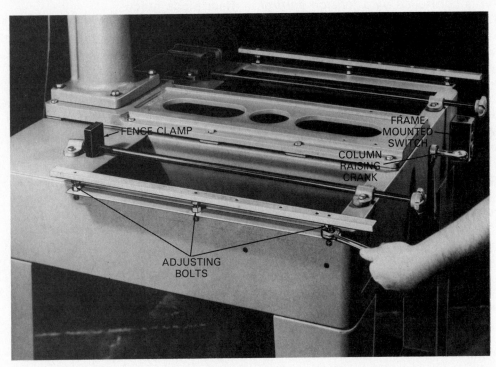

Fig. 21-68. A radial arm saw table should be flat and level. Remove the table and adjust the bolts under the platform. (Delta)

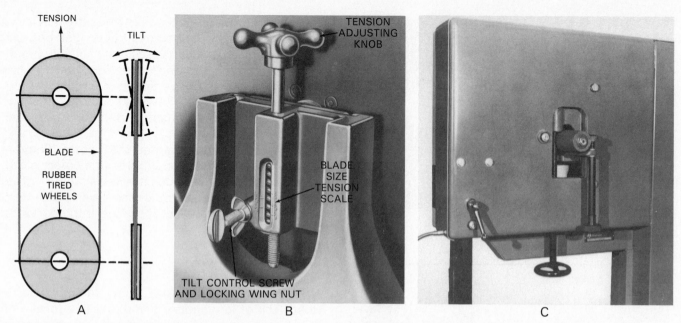

Fig. 21-69. A—The upper wheel on a band saw blade raises and lowers for tension adjustment and tilts for tracking adjustment. B—The tension control has a scale to indicate proper tension for various width blades. C—Tracking adjustment. (Rockwell)

BAND SAW

With band saws, you must be able to apply the proper blade tension, adjust the tilt on the upper wheel, Fig. 21-69A, align the upper and lower blade guides, and set the rear blade guide for different blade widths.

Blade tension

Blade tension is controlled by a *tension control knob,* Fig. 21-69B. It moves the upper wheel toward or away from the lower wheel. Most machines have a scale and marker to note proper tension for a given blade width. Proper tension is reached when the marker is aligned with the scale. When there is no scale, estimate the tension. Snap the back edge of the blade with your finger- or thumbnail as you would a guitar string. A medium pitch ringing sound indicates approximate tension.

Blade tracking

The *tracking adjustment* moves the upper wheel toward or away from the operator. The adjusting mechanism generally is located on the back of the upper wheel housing, Fig. 21-69C. When a blade is installed with the proper tension, turn the upper wheel slowly. See that the blade remains centered on the tire. Turn the wheel at least three or four revolutions. Adjust the tracking knob or screw as necessary.

Side blade guides

Guides may be hardened pieces of steel, Fig. 21-70, or ball bearings on each side of the blade.

Fitting a blade between these guides is critical. Slip a piece of paper or tape between the blade and each side guide. If it moves freely, the guides have proper side clearance.

The teeth on the blade must never touch the hardened guides or bearings. If this happens, the blade loses its set. It may pinch in the kerf, heat up, and burn the material being cut.

Rear blade guide

A rear guide is behind the blade. There should be 1/64" between it and the back of the blade. This adjustment may be made by moving the guide.

Blade repairing

Broken band saw blades are repaired by welding the ends together. Some saws have welders

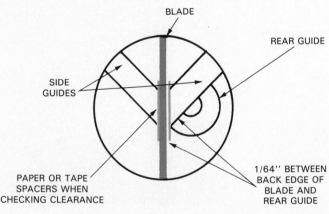

Fig. 21-70. Set steel and ball bearing guides so that the blade travels freely.

attached. Otherwise, use a separate blade welding unit. These tools come with instructions on how to weld blades, Fig. 21-71.

You can make a jig and braze blades, Fig. 21-72. Obtain the following supplies and equipment.
1. Grinder.
2. Hard solder.
3. Hard soldering flux.
4. A small propane torch or other fuel source.
5. Two small c-clamps.
6. A flat file.

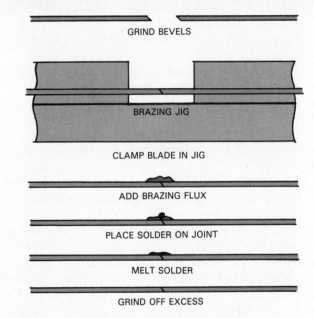

GRIND BEVELS

BRAZING JIG

CLAMP BLADE IN JIG

ADD BRAZING FLUX

PLACE SOLDER ON JOINT

MELT SOLDER

GRIND OFF EXCESS

Fig. 21-72. Top. Repairing a band saw blade clamped in a jig. Bottom. Steps to repair the blade.

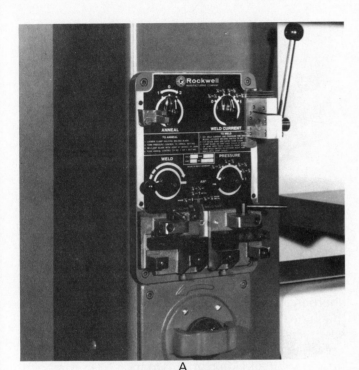

Fig. 21-71. A—Blade welder attached to the band saw. (Rockwell) B—Separate blade welding unit. (Oliver Machinery Co.)

To repair a blade by hand:
1. Grind the broken ends square with a 45° bevel to the face.
2. Clamp the blade ends together over the open part off the jig. The bevels must touch each other.
3. Apply a small amount of brazing flux across the joint.
4. Apply heat under the blade until the flux melts. It will look like liquid glass.
5. Place a pin-head size piece of hard solder on the flux. With a pair of tweezers, locate it exactly over the joint before the flux hardens.
6. Reheat the joint, flux, and solder. The solder will melt suddenly and flow throughout the beveled joint.
7. Chip off excess flux after the blade cools.
8. File away any solder that remains on the blade surface. The blade must fit between the blade guides. Therefore, this step is important.

Storing a band saw blade

Band saw blades can be coiled for storage. They may be hung or boxed easily when coiled into a triple loop. To coil the blade, Fig. 21-73, you must:

1. Hold the blade vertically in front of you with both hands. One hand is in the center of each side of the loop. Thumbs are up and on the outside of the blade. Fingers are curled toward you on the inside gripping the blade.
2. Turn both wrists so you can see your thumbnails. The blade begins to twist.
3. While turning, bend your wrists downward. The top of the loop moves away from you and drops toward the floor.
4. Bring your wrists together and cross them without changing your grip.
5. As you cross your wrists push them toward the floor.
6. The top of the loop in Step 1 will curl back toward you and the three-loop coil will form.

SCROLL SAW

Scroll saws are maintained like other machines. Be sure to:

1. Select the proper blade guide slot for the blade being used. It guides the blade and prevents tooth damage.
2. Set the tension sleeve or rear tension device as described earlier.
3. Check the oil level periodically in the housing under the saw table. Oil prevents wear and heat build-up.
4. Add a small amount of oil or graphite in the tension sleeve or rocker pins. This will prevent excessive wear.

Some scroll saws have an air pump, hose, and nozzle. This assembly blows off chips to keep the cutting line visible while sawing. Check the air flow periodically because the pump could get damaged or the hose could be loose or broken.

SUMMARY

Sawing is a fundamental process in cabinetmaking. Stationary power saws cut lumber and composite materials to component sizes. Choose a saw and proper blade according to the material and direction of cut. For sawing straight parts, choose a table saw or radial arm saw. For cutting curved components, select a band saw or scroll saw.

The saw blade makes a big difference in the edge. The proper saw blade makes the operation efficient. Selecting the wrong blade may result in a splintered surface or burnt edge.

To saw efficiently, blades must be sharp. Jointing, setting, gumming, and filing (grinding) are all steps in sharpening. Some blades can be hand

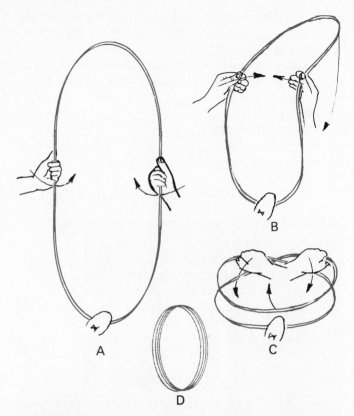

Fig. 21-73. With practice, you can coil a band saw blade into three equal loops.

sharpened. However, it is best to have blades sharpened by a professional with the appropriate machines. Also maintain machines properly. Inspect, clean, adjust, and lubricate them periodically.

Follow all safety guidelines as you work. Have a firm footing and keep your distance from the point of operation. Use your senses of sight, sound, touch, and smell to detect potential problems. Think safety and act safely.

CABINETMAKING TERMS

Handedness, table saw, blade-raising handwheel, tilt handwheel, tilt scale, rip fence, miter gauge, table insert, trunnion-mounted guard, splitter, anti-kickback pawls, table-mounted guard, rip blade, crosscut blade, combination blade, planer blade, plywood blade, flat blade, set, hollow ground blade, thin rim blade, ripping, crosscutting, stop rod, stop block, beveling, miter cut, resawing, tilting table saw, radial arm saw, yoke, track, arm, elevation crank, column, radial arm saw stop, in-rip mode, out-rip mode, relief cut, band saw, blade guides, guide post, pocket cut, scroll saw, blade chucks, blower nozzle, sleeve design scroll saw, rear tension scroll saw, hook angle, gullet, chip loading, carbide tipped blade, chamfered tooth, double-chip tooth, triple-chip tooth, tension control knob, tracking adjustment.

TEST YOUR KNOWLEDGE

1. List two saws you might choose for straight-line cutting.
2. Describe how you adapt a saw designed for cutting curved lines to cut straight.
3. The slot made as a saw blade cuts through the material is called a _____.
4. List three methods of guiding material past the blade on a table saw.
5. What table saw safety feature helps prevent material from being thrown back toward the operator?
6. List three blades you might select for cutting 1/2 in. lumber across the grain.
7. Which direction do you turn the table saw arbor nut to loosen it?
8. The miter gauge and rip fence must not be used together when cutting completely through material. True or False?
9. Describe two setup procedures for positioning the table saw blade.
10. To keep your hands from coming within 4 in. of a table saw blade when ripping stock, use _____ _____ to hold and feed the material.
11. A hollow ground blade is generally set _____ higher above the material than a flat blade.
12. Name two methods of controlling part length when cutting duplicate parts on a table saw.
13. On a table saw, the _____ is tilted for beveling.
14. When is resawing on the table saw a one-pass operation?
15. What radial arm saw adjustment does the elevation crank perform?
    a. Raise or lower the blade.
    b. Position the blade for a miter cut.
    c. Position the blade for ripping in the in-rip mode.
    d. Position the blade for beveling.
16. Describe the procedure for crosscutting a 4x8 ft. sheet of plywood on the radial arm saw.
17. The _____ _____ controls the curve radius which can be cut on a band saw or scroll saw.
18. To saw a component with sharp inside or outside curves that change direction, _____ _____ are necessary.
19. To control a band saw properly, blade guides should touch the teeth. True or False?
20. What adjustment is made when the band saw blade travels to one side of the wheels?
21. To cut a bevel with a band saw, you must tilt the blade. True or False?
22. Describe how a scroll saw can cut interior holes and cutouts.
23. Explain the difference between sleeve tension and rear tension scroll saws.
24. What characteristics would you look for to select the following circular blades?
    a. Rip.
    b. Crosscut.
    c. Combination.
    d. Planer.
    e. Plywood.
    f. Triple-chip carbide tipped.
25. List three common shapes of band saw blades and the materials they cut.

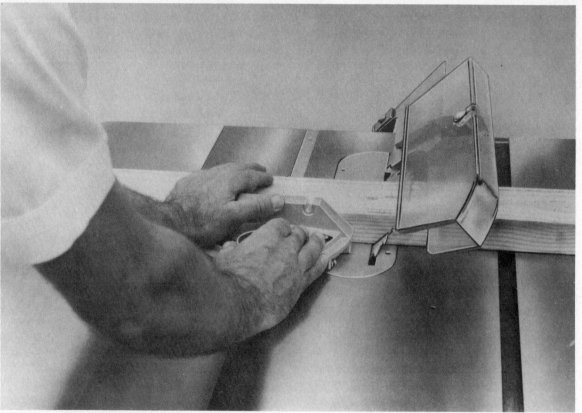

SAFETY REMINDER: Saws are versatile tools that work best when proper attention is given to safety. In all cases, proper clothing is important. Wear a short sleeved shirt or roll the sleeves above the elbow. Remove rings. Top left. Proper use of a saw for cutting a dado. Operator is using a feather board, push stick, and pusher block to control the workpiece. Top right. Proper technique for ripping keeps hands away from the blade. Guard, splitter, and anti-kickback device are in place. Bottom. Proper cross cutting procedure. Operator keeps hands well away. He uses miter gauge to push workpiece, has guard in place, and stands well away from the path of any flying wood chips. (Shopsmith, Inc. and Delta)

Chapter 22
SAWING WITH HAND AND PORTABLE POWER TOOLS

After studying this chapter, you will be able to:
☐*Select and use handsaws.*
☐*Select and use portable power saws.*
☐*Follow the maintenance requirements for hand and portable power saws.*
☐*Sharpen handsaws.*

Stationary power saws are used by most cabinetmakers. However, there are many situations when you will select a handsaw or portable power saw instead of a stationary machine, Fig. 22-1. For some cuts, stationary saw setup time may take too long. Other times, you may be installing on-site architectural base, trim, and other woodwork where stationary machines are not available. The sawing characteristics of various wood species are given in Fig. 12-45.

HANDSAWS

Handsaws fit in one of two groups: narrow or wide blade. Those with wide blades are designed to cut straight. These include rip, crosscut, com-

bination, backsaw, dovetail, and offset dovetail saws. Those with narrow blades are best for sawing curved workpieces. These include compass, keyhole, and coping saws. However, with skill and a straightedge, these saws cut straight.

Handsaws should be limited to cutting lumber and low density manufactured wood products, such as plywood. Resins in high density fiberboard or particleboard dull the blade quickly. Sawing these materials also takes much time and effort. Instead, use a portable power saw with a carbide blade.

SAWING STRAIGHT LINES

Rip and crosscut saws are the most used handsaws. They look very similar, but are different in tooth shape, *teeth per inch* (TPI), and handle design. Fig. 22-2 shows a rip saw. Fig. 22-3 shows a

Fig. 22-1. Portable power tools, such as this saber saw, are often an excellent alternative to stationary power tools. (Robert Bosch Power Tool Corp.)

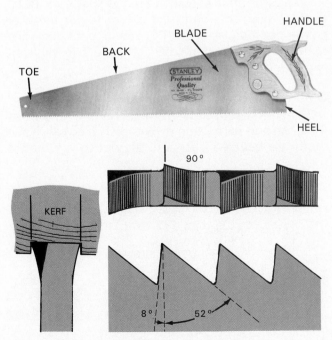

Fig. 22-2. Top. Parts of a standard rip saw. Bottom. Rip saws have chisel-shaped teeth. (Stanley, Porter)

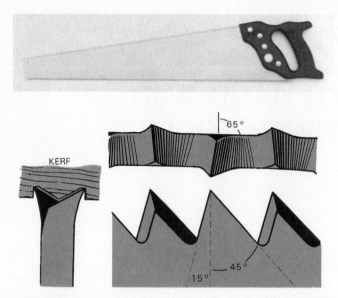

Fig. 22-3. Top. Crosscut saw. (Vermont American Tool Co.) Bottom. Bevel teeth have knifelike points which score the crossgrain before removing material from the kerf. (Porter)

crosscut saw. Some handsaw manufacturers use TPI to specify saws. Others use *points per inch* (PPI), Fig. 22-4. The number used to identify the TPI or PPI is imprinted on the blade.

Rip saw

Rip saws are designed to cut lumber along the grain. The teeth are shaped like chisels and set (spread) outward 1/3 the thickness of the blade. This makes the saw kerf wider than the blade thickness. This keeps the blade from binding in the kerf.

Standard rip saw blades are 24 to 28 in. (610 to 711 mm) long and have six or fewer teeth or points per inch. A 5 1/2 PPI saw is common. The teeth are sharpened at a 60° angle (8° on the front angle and 52° on the back).

Crosscut saw

Select *crosscut saws* for cutting lumber across the grain and for cutting plywood. The edges of the teeth are beveled outward, almost to a knifelike

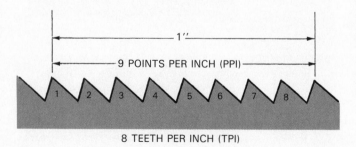

Fig. 22-4. Blades may be labeled by number of teeth or points in one inch.

point. The points score the wood fibers before the teeth actually remove material from the kerf. This reduces chipping and tearing the grain.

Standard saw size is 20 to 28 in. (508 to 711 mm) long. The 26 in. (660 mm) crosscut saw is the most popular. There will be from 7 to 12 PPI. Those with fewer points per inch will cut faster. However, saws with more teeth leave a smoother kerf edge. The teeth are sharpened at 60° angles (15° on the front side and 45° on the back).

Combination saw

The *combination saw* rips on one edge and crosscuts on the other, Fig. 22-5. A unique feature of this saw is that it cuts on the pull stroke. Most saws cut on the push stroke.

Backsaw

A *backsaw,* Fig. 22-6A, makes smooth and accurate straight cuts. The saw may be 10 to 30

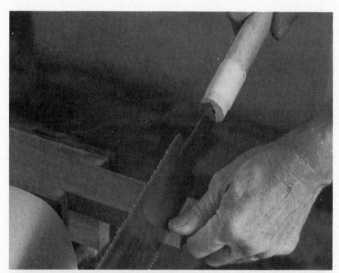

Fig. 22-5. The pull-stroke combination saw can be used for both crosscutting and ripping.

in. (254 to 762 mm) long with 10 to 15 PPI. There is a rigid rib on the back edge to keep the blade straight. Because of its accuracy, the backsaw is often used for joint making.

To use it, clamp workpieces horizontally and saw at a low angle, almost horizontal. A block of wood clamped parallel to the saw mark on the workpiece provides a guide, Fig. 22-6B. Keep the saw snug against the block to assure a straight cut.

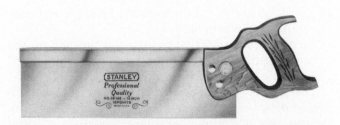

A

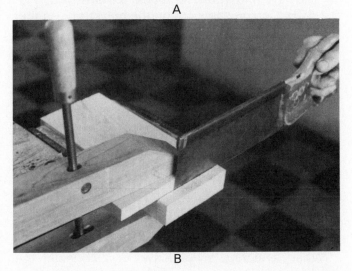

B

Fig. 22-6. A—The backsaw has a rib which keeps the blade rigid. (Stanley) B—A block of wood clamped to the workpiece can be used as a guide.

Dovetail saw

The *dovetail saw* looks much like a narrow backsaw, Fig. 22-7A. Typically it is 10 in. (254 mm) long with 15 to 21 PPI. The name comes from the dovetail joint, which the saw was originally made to cut, Fig. 22-7B.

Offset dovetail saw

The *offset dovetail saw* is designed to cut flush with a surface, Fig. 22-8. The handle is offset from the saw blade. A reversible handle permits sawing flush on either the left or right side.

SAWING CURVED LINES

Handsaws for curved lines have narrower blades than those for cutting straight. This allows the blade

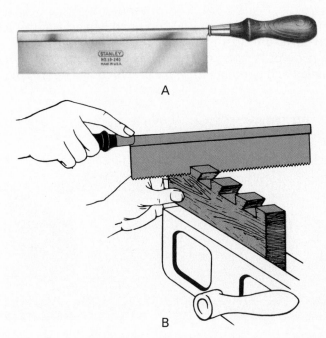

A

B

Fig. 22-7. A—Dovetail saw. (Stanley). B—The saw is named after the dovetail joint which it was designed to cut. (Porter)

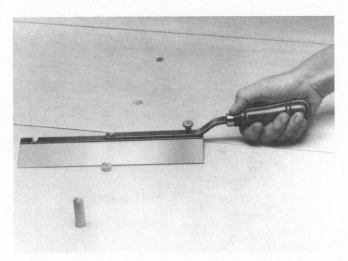

Fig. 22-8. The offset dovetail saw can cut flush with the surface. (Brookstone)

to change direction as it cuts through the workpiece. There are three saw styles: compass, keyhole, and coping.

Compass saw

Compass and *keyhole saws* look very similar. They both cut curves, Fig. 22-9A. Most people consider compass and keyhole saws the same tool. However, the compass saw has 8 or 10 PPI. The keyhole saw is finer, with 12 or 14 PPI. Kerf edges will be smoother if a keyhole saw is used.

The blade is tapered. Long saw strokes allow you to cut larger curves. You can cut a smaller radius curve using the narrower end of the blade with short strokes, Fig. 22-9B. Some manufacturers produce nested saws. These have one handle and a number of different size blades.

Compass and keyhole saws will cut out interior holes and curves, Fig. 22-9C. First drill a hole in the area to be removed. Make the hole larger than the narrow end of the blade. Then insert the blade and saw the contour.

Coping saw

The *coping saw* is a versatile curve cutting tool. It consists of a handle, frame, and removable blade, Fig. 22-10A. Blades may vary from 5 to 32 teeth per inch. A slotted *pawl* at each end of the frame holds the blade. Frame *throat depth, the distance from the blade to the frame,* is either 4 5/8 or 6 in. (117 or 152 mm). It determines how far you can saw into the workpiece.

To install a blade, first loosen the threads on the handle. Fit the blade with the teeth pointed toward the handle and retighten.

The pawls turn and allow the blade to cut in different directions. The saw can cut away from you, to the left and right, or back toward you, Fig. 22-10B. Coping saws cut on the pull stroke so that less pressure is applied to the blade. Otherwise, the blade is likely to break.

Coping saws are often used for cutting out small internal areas. First drill a small hole in the cutout space. Slip the blade through the hole and secure it in the frame. Then saw the contour.

SAWING BY HAND

To saw accurately by hand, first select the proper saw. Then use the proper procedure for that saw.

SELECTING HANDSAWS

When selecting a handsaw, first consider the workpiece you are making. Select a wide blade saw for straight workpieces and a narrow blade saw for curved workpieces. Also decide on the teeth per inch needed. More teeth produce a smoother edge.

Another consideration is the thickness of the material you are cutting. Try to have three or more teeth in contact with the material at all times. For example, a 5 1/2 points per inch saw should not be used with 1/4 in. wood. Only two teeth would touch the material at one time. This can cause chipping.

Other factors which affect saw selection are blade thickness and coating. The blade thickness determines how rigid the saw will be. This is a personal choice. Some cabinetmakers prefer a stiffer blade. Handsaws may have a teflon coating to reduce friction. This coating also prevents rust. A stainless steel blade will not rust.

SAWING PROPERLY

Use reciprocal (back and forth) motion when sawing by hand. Move the saw in a straight line,

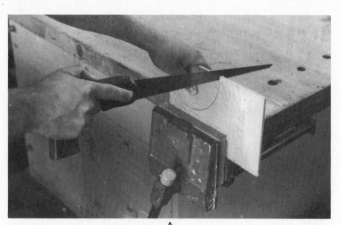

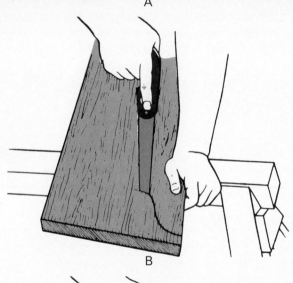

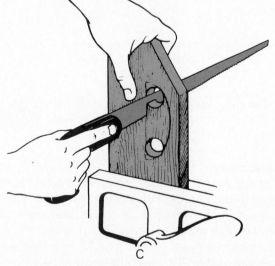

Fig. 22-9. A—Compass and keyhole saws are used for large radius curves. B—The narrow end of the blade will cut a smaller radius curve. C—Holes must first be drilled before cutting internal curves. (Porter)

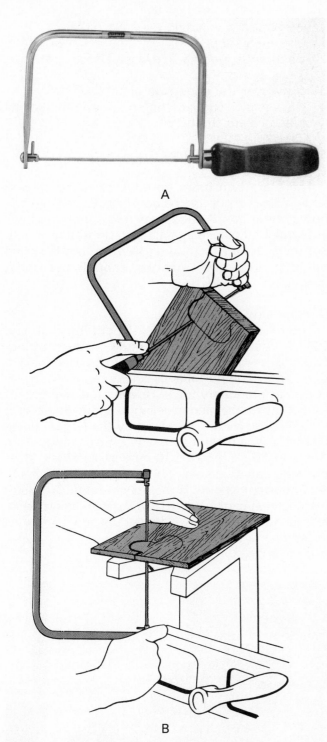

Fig. 22-10. A—The coping saw has a narrow blade held by a frame. (Stanley) B—This saw is excellent for small radius curves and internal cutting. (Porter)

holding it at the proper angle. The angle will vary with the saw used. Keep the rip saw at a 60° angle. Hold the crosscut saw at a 45° angle, Fig. 22-11. Other saws are held at 90° to or parallel with the workpiece. Saw with a full stroke as much as possible. Your stroke may be limited on curved cuts. If the saw teeth are sharp, only slight pressure should be necessary.

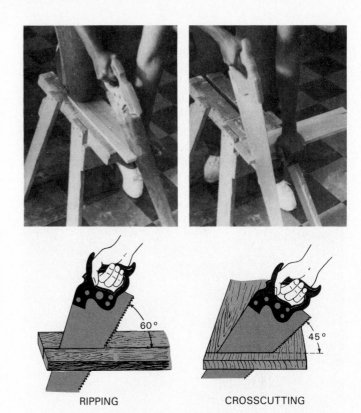

Fig. 22-11. Ripping should be done at a 60° angle, while crosscutting is at a 45° angle. (Porter)

The steps in sawing apply generally to most or all handsaw operations. Follow the procedure listed below.

1. Select the correct saw according to the grain direction and type of cut.
2. Align the blade beside your thumb at the saw mark. For precision cuts, clamp a straight board along the mark.
3. Start the kerf by pulling the blade on the return stroke across a corner, Fig. 22-12A.
4. Gradually increase to a full stroke, Fig. 22-12B.

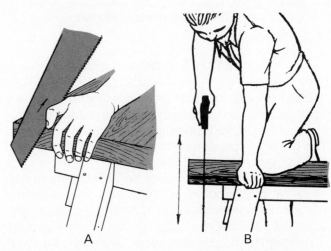

Fig. 22-12. A—Start a cut using your thumb as a guide. B—Then proceed with long strokes. (Porter)

5. Apply slight downward pressure to keep the blade from jumping out of the kerf.
6. Relax the pressure on the back stroke. No cutting is being done.
7. Use a guide if possible to maintain alignment. A miter box or jig could be helpful, Fig. 22-13.
8. Shorten the stroke and reduce pressure as you near the end of the cut. Also support the part being cut. This prevents the workpiece from falling or splintering.

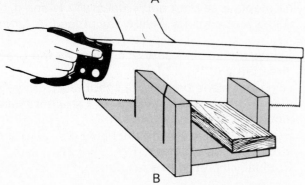

Fig. 22-13. A—Miter box with blade guides and angle lock. B—Homemade miter box. (Porter)

PORTABLE POWER SAWS

Power tools are preferred over hand tools for sawing. They are lightweight and easily guided over the material. Like stationary power and handsaws, the blade shape determines whether the tool will cut straight or curved lines.

Plan your sawing sequence before starting to cut. Mark all cuts, including relief cuts when sawing curves. Plan how you will control the saw, workpiece, and the excess being removed. This can pose a problem with portable tools because you must hold the saw, workpiece, and excess. Decide how to support the material before and after it is cut.

Several options include:
1. Use a sawhorse.
2. Secure the material in a vise. Also consider using a clamp.
3. Saw over the edge of a bench.
4. Raise the workpiece on scrap material so the blade clears the bench.

SAWING STRAIGHT LINES

There are two basic portable tools for sawing straight lines. They are the portable circular saw and power miter box. A saber saw (reciprocal saw) will cut straight if placed against a straightedge. These are more suited for curved sawing, but a skilled operator can saw straight enough for most purposes.

Circular saw

The *circular saw* is a versatile cutting tool, Fig. 22-14. It can be set up for ripping, crosscutting, mitering, and beveling. It may even be used for cutting joints. The portable circular saw is not as accurate as stationary tools. However, it is excellent for cutting lumber and paneling to approximate size.

Circular saws are classified by the largest blade diameter which can be installed. Sizes range from 3 3/4 to 16 in. (95 to 406 mm) in diameter. Most portable saws use a 7 1/4 in. blade, Fig. 22-15. An important feature is the maximum thickness of material that can be sawed. This specification usually is listed for both 90° square cuts and 45° bevel cuts.

Fig. 22-14. A portable power saw is a handy tool for rough-cutting lumber. (Milwaukee Electric Tool Corp.)

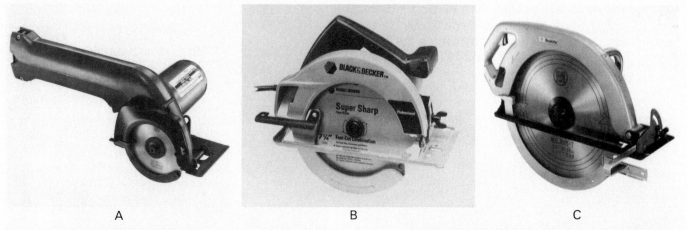

Fig. 22-15. Several circular saw sizes. A—3 3/8 in. B—7 1/4 in. is most common. (Black and Decker) C—16 3/8 in. (Makita)

A wide range of blades are available, including rip, crosscut, combination, paneling, and others. The number and style of teeth determine what material the blade is suited to cut.

Another saw feature is a clutch that stops the blade under a number of conditions. These include dull teeth, inadequate set, resin buildup, high moisture content in lumber, unsupported workpiece, and trying to turn the saw while cutting. These conditions all could result in the blade burning the wood or binding in the saw kerf.

Saw setup. There are two adjustments on the portable circular saw. One tilts the blade from 0° to 45°. The other moves the base to expose more or less of the blade. This allows you to set the recommended blade depth 1/8 in. greater than the material thickness, the safest depth setting. Unfortunately, this setting makes the saw work harder because more teeth contact the workpiece at the same time. A blade set for a deeper cut can reduce loading and lets the saw work easier. However, when fewer teeth contact the workpiece, there is a greater chance of splintering.

Inspect the blade before you begin the operation. Be sure the correct blade is installed and it is sharp.

Blade changing. To install a different blade, you must:
1. Disconnect power to the saw.
2. Lay the saw on its side. (Notice the direction the teeth are pointing.)
3. Secure the blade so it cannot turn. Some saws have an arbor lock. This prevents the motor shaft from turning. For those with no lock, insert a block of softwood between the teeth and base. You might also clamp a C-clamp or handscrew to the blade.
4. Remove the retaining screw or nut. It may have right or left hand threads.
5. Swing the retractable guard around from beneath the saw base.
6. Slide the blade out through the slot in the base.

7. Wipe chips from the arbor where the replacement blade will sit.
8. Install the replacement blade. The teeth should point upward toward the front. Make sure the blade seats properly and the arbor hole matches the arbor, Fig. 22-16. Instructions are printed on some blades for matching the blade hole.
9. Replace and tighten the retaining screw or nut. Secure the arbor or blade as you did when loosening the nut.
10. Allow the guard to swing back into position and reconnect electrical power.

Saw operation. Circular saws cut lumber, paneling, and manufactured composite products. The direction of the grain in lumber and plywood usually determines which blade you use. Carbide tipped blades work best when sawing composite material.

Circular saws cut in an upward direction. Splintering occurs on the top surface, especially when crosscutting. Mark the cutting line to be sawed on the poor side of your work. If cutting paneling or plywood, have the prefinished or decorative face down.

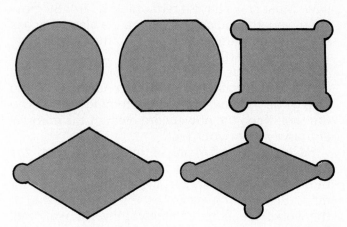

Fig. 22-16. Saw manufacturers often use exclusive arbor shapes.

Once the material has been marked, select depth, Fig. 22-17, and bevel angle as necessary. Loosen and tighten the knob for each and position the blade. Most saws provide a scale showing approximate depth and angle.

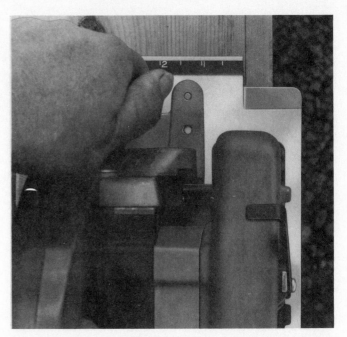

Fig. 22-18. Align the saw notch with the line marked on the material. (Milwaukee Electric Tool Corp.)

Fig. 22-17. Set the blade 1/8 in. deeper than the material thickness. (Milwaukee Electric Tool Corp.)

When ready to saw, align the indent or mark on the saw base, Fig. 22-18, with the marked line on the workpiece. The greatest amount of material should be under the base. If you are making a bevel cut, the 90° base mark cannot be used because the saw will not enter the material on the line, Fig. 22-19. Some manufacturers provide two marks: one marks alignment when making a square (90°) cut; the other is used for 45° beveling.

Check the blade alignment before starting the saw. Most saws have a retractable guard. By moving the guard, you can see where the blade touches the material. Return the guard to its normal position before starting the saw.

Circular saws contain a trigger switch in the handle. Most have a knob or secondary handle to help guide the saw. Have a firm footing when using the tool. Keep the power cord clear of the material and away from your feet.

Back the saw 1/4 in. (6 mm) away from the material and turn it on. Move the saw forward through the material, keeping it aligned with your mark. Support the excess as you reach the end of the workpiece. After completing the cut, wait until the blade stops before putting the saw down. Check to see that the guard has returned to its proper

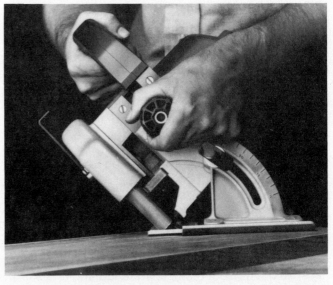

Fig. 22-19. It is difficult to align with a marked line when beveling. (Milwaukee Electric Tool Corp.)

position. A splinter or loose knot could wedge the guard open.

Ripping lumber presents several problems for the operator. For a long workpiece, you must move along beside the saw. Using a rip fence or straightedge will help your accuracy. If no device is available, use the measurement marks on the saw base, Fig. 22-20.

On long lengths of lumber, the saw kerf may tend to close. This can cause the saw blade to bind. To prevent this, use one or more kerf spreaders, Fig. 22-21. They work much like the splitter on a table

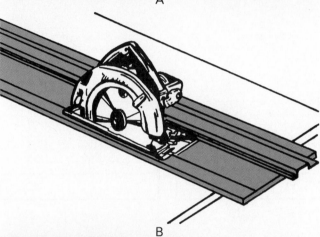

Fig. 22-20. Three methods of guiding a circular saw. A—Using a saw guide. B—Clamping a straightedge. (Makita). C—Guiding with your fingers and the measurement marks on the saw. (Milwaukee Electric Tool Corp.)

Fig. 22-21. Kerf spreaders decrease the chance of the saw blade binding in the kerf. (Adjustable Clamp Co.)

saw. You might use wooden wedges or screwdrivers as kerf spreaders.

Angled (miter) cuts may be sawed freehand or with an accessory. The one shown in Fig. 22-22 aligns and guides the saw.

Plunge cuts. *Plunge cuts* are made to cut slots or pockets in the material. The saw blade touches the surface first. The procedure, Fig. 22-23, is as follows:

1. Preset the saw blade at 90° and at the proper depth.
2. Place the front edge of the saw base on the material over the cut out section. The saw

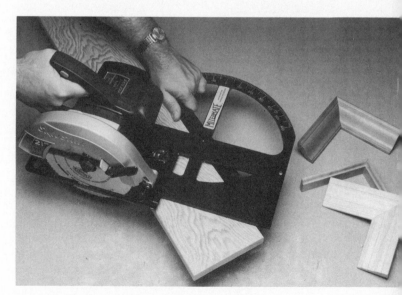

Fig. 22-22. This circular saw accessory allows you to cut angles. (Matrix Enterprises)

blade should enter at about the middle of the line to be cut.

3. Rotate the retractable blade away from the blade. This can be hazardous. Keep your fingers above the saw base and away from the blade.
4. Start the saw with the teeth slightly above the material.
5. Lower the saw slowly until the base is flat on the material.
6. Release the guard and complete one-half of the cut.
7. Release the trigger switch and allow the saw blade to come to a complete stop.
8. Lift the saw out of the kerf and turn the saw around.
9. Insert the blade and saw to the other end of the line.

Fig. 22-24. Power miter box set to cut moulding. (Makita)

Fig. 22-23. Plunge cutting.

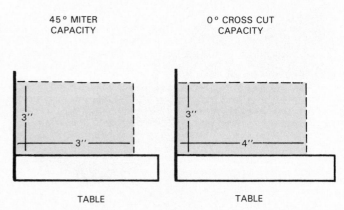

Fig. 22-25. Most power miter boxes have limited material capacity.

Power miter box

The *power miter box,* Fig. 22-24, is a precision crosscutting tool. It operates similar to portable and stationary circular saws. However, it has a limited capacity in width of cut and depth of travel. For example, the capacity of a saw at a 0° cutting angle may be 3 in. high and 4 in. wide. At a 45° angle, it might handle material only 3 in. high and 3 in. wide, Fig. 22-25.

The saw cuts in a downward direction. The operator is protected by a plastic shield. While sawing, keep hands 4 in. (100 mm) away from the point of operation. Clamp short workpieces.

Operate the power miter box as follows:

1. Be sure the material dimensions are within the saw's capacity.
2. Set the pivot handle to the desired angle.
3. Release the lock button if the saw is in a down position.
4. Place marked material on the saw table against the fence.
5. Align the cut by lowering the blade next to the cutting mark. Make sure the blade is on the excess side of the cutting mark.
6. Allow the blade to return to its normal position.
7. Hold the material against the fence with your left hand or a clamp.
8. Grip the saw handle firmly.
9. Turn the saw on. Allow the saw to reach full speed before cutting.
10. Push handle downward gently to make the cut.
11. When the cut is complete, release pressure. The saw will return to its normal position.
12. Release the trigger and allow the blade to stop completely. Some saws have an automatic brake that stops the blade quickly.
13. Remove the workpiece and excess.

SAWING CURVED LINES

Two basic portable tools, the saber saw and reciprocal saw, are best suited for curved sawing. But a skilled operator can also make accurate straight cuts using a straightedge.

Saber saw

The *saber saw,* Fig. 22-26, also called a bayonet saw, has many uses in the cabinetmaking shop. It can cut outside curves and internal holes. With the proper blade, you can cut wood, metal, ceramics, and plastics. With the proper jig, you can cut circles and arcs.

Saber saws offer many styles and features. Included are saws which:
1. Are operated with one or two hands.
2. Have single or variable speed.
3. Saw in one or two directions.
4. Cut only at 90° or bevel to 45°.
5. Have blade shafts which swivel in any direction.

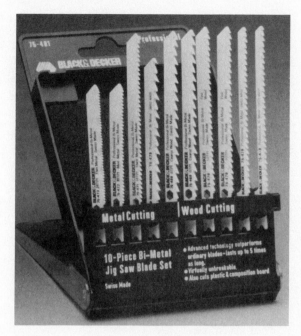

Fig. 22-27. Saber saw blades for wood and metal. (Black and Decker)

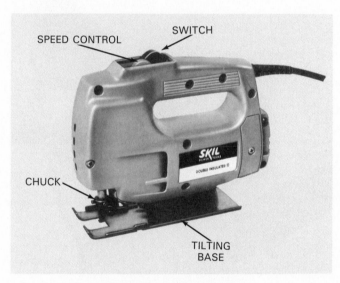

Fig. 22-26. Saber saw. (Skil)

Saw setup. Know the capabilities of your saber saw. Be familiar with its settings and the type of blade it requires. Change blades when sawing different materials or when the blade becomes dull. Most blades for wood cutting have 6 to 12 teeth per inch, Fig. 22-27. A 10 TPI blade is adequate for most sawing. Select a finer tooth blade for thin material. Remember, at least three teeth should contact the material at all times. Not all blades will fit in every saw chuck. Different tool manufacturers may have different style blades and chucks.

To change a blade, you must:
1. Disconnect power to the saber saw.
2. Loosen the setscrew(s) in the side of the chuck and remove the blade.

3. Install the new blade with the teeth pointed forward.
4. Tighten the setscrews.
5. Reconnect electricity.

Saw operation. Saber saws cut on the upward stroke. Have the better surface of the material facing downward. For sawing curved lines, you should make relief cuts in the excess along the curve, Fig. 22-28. Straight cuts can be made by guiding the saw base along a straightedge. Bevel cuts can be made by tilting the saw on its base. Circles are best cut with a guide and pivot, Fig. 22-29.

Fig. 22-28. Saw curved lines after making relief cuts.

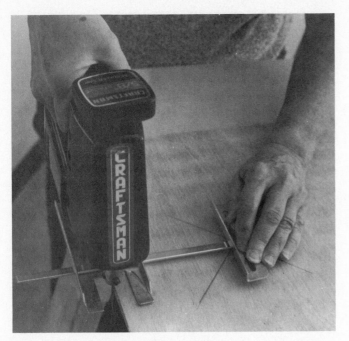

Fig. 22-29. Saw accurate circles with a guide and pivot accessory.

Reciprocal saw

Rarely is the *reciprocal saw* used in cabinetmaking. It might come in handy for rough cutting in plumbing or electrical work when installing cabinets. The saw resembles a heavy duty saber saw, Fig. 22-31. It typically has a wider and thicker blade, but can perform the same functions. There are one speed, two speed, and variable speed models. Saw dense materials at a slow speed and soft materials at a high speed.

The tool has a trigger, handle, and lock. A second handle is used for added control. The shoe rests on the material. It is comparable to the base on a saber saw. However, the shoe is always movable.

Saw setup. There are only two setup steps for the reciprocal saw: shoe positioning and blade changing. Although the shoe is movable, it can be secured in two positions for different amounts of

You can plunge cut with a saber saw. However, you must be careful because the blade can be broken easily. The procedure for a plunge cut, Fig. 22-30, is as follows:

1. Make sure the base is at 90° angle.
2. Rest the saw on the front edge of the base.
3. Align the blade with the marked line. Make sure the blade is on the waste side of your workpiece.
4. Tilt the blade to about a 60° to 80° angle.
5. Hold the machine firmly against the material and start the saw.
6. Slowly pivot the blade downward into the material. After the blade cuts through the lower surface, place the base flat and proceed.
7. When the cut is complete, turn off the saw.
8. Allow the blade to stop before removing it from the kerf.

Fig. 22-31. Reciprocal saw.   (Milwaukee)

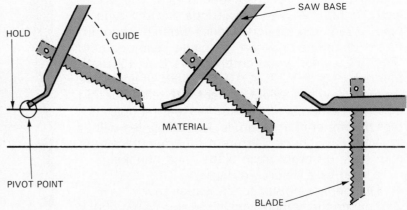

Fig. 22-30. Plunge cutting with a saber saw. The tip of the blade must not "bounce" on the material.

blade exposure. To change the blade, loosen the chuck set screw, replace the blade, and retighten the screw(s).

Saw operation. Place the saw's shoe firmly against the material while cutting. Large radius, irregular or curved cuts can be sawn without relief cuts.

There is one major difference between saber and reciprocating saw blades. On the saber saw, the teeth are in line with the shaft. On the reciprocating saw, the blade follows a different path. It is angled forward. This angle is called cant. Cant allows the blade to be free of the saw kerf on the back stroke. The teeth do not rub the material, thus the blade stays sharp longer.

MAINTAINING HAND AND PORTABLE POWER SAWS

Little maintenance is needed for most hand and portable power saws. Handsaws should be kept free of rust by rubbing the blade with steel wool. A coat of wax or silicone will protect the blade from moisture and reduce friction while sawing. Inspect the handle screws periodically to see that they are tight.

Portable saws may or may not need lubrication. Some saws have ''sealed'' bearings and self-lubricating mechanical parts. These should not need lubrication for the life of the saw. Those which do, will have a maintenance label. Generally, you need to put heavy grease in gear drive mechanisms. There will be a removable plate or screw on the saw housing. Apply silicone to adjusting knobs, screws, and movable parts outside the motor and drive.

Keep all saws clean and free from moisture or resin buildup. Periodically check all power cords for deterioration and damage. Replace any defective parts.

MAINTAINING SAW BLADES

Saw blades should have adequate set and be sharp to the touch. Keep them free of rust and resin. Inspect blades frequently for cracks (especially in the gullets), warpage, bluish color from overheating, and missing or damaged teeth.

Proper maintenance may include cleaning, sharpening, or discarding the blade. Clean resin from the blade with paint thinner or oven cleaner. Wear rubber gloves when working with hazardous materials. Remove rust with oil and fine steel wool. Then wipe away the oil and coat the blade with paste wax or silicone spray.

Blade sharpening is a time consuming process. You should decide whether to have the blades machine-sharpened accurately or do it by hand. Blade sharpening machines will joint, set, and file

or grind the blade very accurately. This is the only method for sharpening a carbide tip blade. Hand sharpening generally is limited to jointing, setting, and filing standard rip and crosscut blades.

Jointing assures that the teeth are all the same height. Setting staggers the teeth outward. This allows room for the blade to pass through the saw kerf without binding. Filing the teeth is the last step.

To determine if you can sharpen a given blade by hand, push a file across one tooth near the handle. Use only one stroke. If file marks are made, the blade can be sharpened by hand. If no file marks are made, the blade is too hard. Carbide tip and hardened steel blades cannot be hand-sharpened.

SHARPENING HANDSAW BLADES

You can sharpen chisel-tooth and bevel-tooth handsaw blades. To do so, you need several tools. They are a saw clamp, saw set, and several files. The saw clamp holds the blade securely. A saw set bends the teeth outward. Setting the blade may not be required each time a blade is sharpened. Both flat and small triangular files are needed. The flat file joints the blade. The triangular files sharpen the teeth.

Chisel-tooth handsaw blades

Chisel-like teeth are found on rip, compass, and keyhole handsaws.

The procedure for sharpening chisel-tooth blades involves:

1. Securing the saw in the vise. The bottom of the teeth should be about 1/4 in. (6 mm) above the vise. This reduces chatter while filing. (Chatter is a screeching noise made when the blade vibrates.)
2. Jointing the teeth. Lay the flat file squarely on the teeth. Push it forward to make the teeth all the same height, Fig. 22-32. A shiny flat spot will appear when each tooth has been touched by the file.
3. Setting the teeth. Adjust the saw set to the proper teeth per inch setting for the saw, Fig. 22-33A. Place the saw set over teeth that point

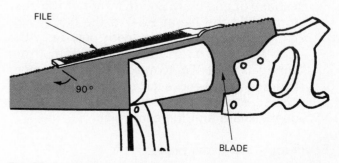

Fig. 22-32. Teeth on handsaw blades must first be jointed flat. (Stanley)

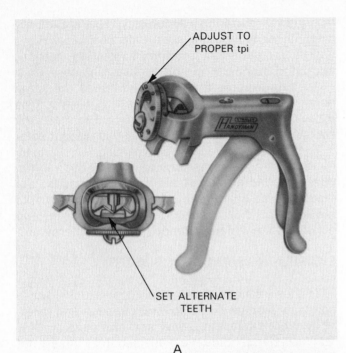

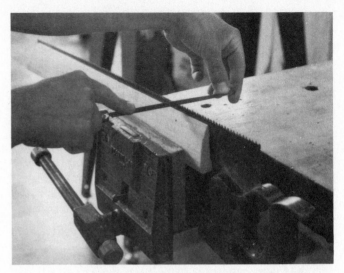

Fig. 22-34. File all teeth to the proper angle. Hold the file at 90° to the saw.

blades. Filing is done differently. The procedure for filing is as follows:
1. Clamp the saw with the handle to the right.
2. Locate a tooth which points toward you.
3. Place the triangular file in the space to the left of that tooth.
4. Turn the file about 25° left and about 10° down, Fig. 22-35.

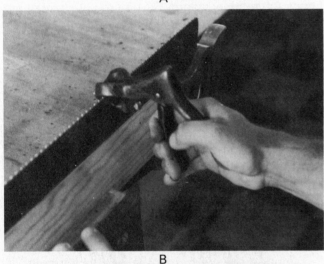

Fig. 22-33. A—Adjust the TPI on the setter. (Stanley) B— Place the saw set over the teeth and squeeze the handle.

away from you and squeeze the handle, Fig. 22-33B. When these teeth are set, reverse the blade and set the remaining ones.
4. Filing the teeth. Place a file horizontally against the back of one tooth and the front of the next tooth. Hold the file at 90° to the blade, Fig. 22-34. File between the teeth only until the shiny flat spot on the tip of the tooth (from jointing) is gone. Try to make the same number of strokes between each of the teeth. When finished, inspect the blade. All teeth should be equally sharp and the same size.

Bevel-tooth handsaw blades

The procedures for jointing and setting bevel-tooth blades is the same as that for chisel-tooth

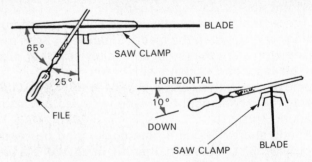

Fig. 22-35. On a crosscut saw, file every other tooth at angles shown. Then turn blade around and complete job.

5. File two or three strokes on the front of that tooth. At the same time, the file should touch the back of the next tooth.
6. File the same number of strokes between every other tooth.
7. Reverse the blade and file alternate teeth not already sharpened. Hold the blade 25° to the right and 10° down for these.

SHARPENING POWER SAW BLADES

Sharpen portable circular saw blades as described in Chapter 21. Saber and reciprocal saw blades are tempered (hardened) steel, and are not sharpened.

SUMMARY

Hand and portable power saws are used when a stationary power saw is not appropriate or unavailable. Handsaws are best suited for cutting lumber and low density manufactured wood products. Power saws equipped with carbide tipped blades will cut through most any material.

Handsaws for straight cutting include the rip and crosscut saws. When a smoother edge is needed, select a saw with more teeth or points per inch. These include backsaws and dovetail saws for accurate cuts and jointmaking.

Portable power saws for cutting straight lines include the circular saw and power miter box. These are used on construction sites for cutting, framing, lumber, and paneling. The power miter box cuts trim and base. In cabinetmaking, you can saw standard stock and paneling to approximate sizes. Some jointwork can even be done with the power miter box. It is accurate, but has limitations on the size of material it can cut.

Portable power saws for cutting curved lines include the saber saw and reciprocal saw. These two are somewhat similar. They both use a straight, flat, blade and cut with short reciprocating strokes. The saber saw is more accurate, because you can control it better. The reciprocal saw is harder to handle, but is excellent for rough cuts.   Most saws need relatively little maintenance. Hand saws should be rubbed with steel wool to remove rust. The blade should be periodically checked and sharpened if

necessary. Portable power saws may or may not need lubrication. Check the maintenance manual or look for lubrication instructions on the saw housing.

CABINETMAKING TERMS

Teeth per inch, points per inch, rip saw, crosscut saw, combination saw, backsaw, dovetail saw, offset dovetail saw, compass saw, keyhole saw, coping saw, circular saw, clutch, plunge cut, saber saw, reciprocal saw.

TEST YOUR KNOWLEDGE

1. Why are wide blade saws more suited for straight line cutting than are narrow blade saws?
2. List the two methods for specifying the teeth on a saw blade.
3. Rip saws are designed to cut _____ the grain.
4. Crosscut saws are designed to cut _____ the grain.
5. Which two handsaws are often used for joint making?
6. Would a coping saw or keyhole saw be the more appropriate tool for cutting a small radius curve?
7. How many saw teeth should be in contact with the workpiece at all times?
8. A handsaw will not cut without moderate downward pressure. True or False?
9. Circular saws are classified by _____ size.
10. What two adjustments to a circular saw might you make when preparing to cut a bevel?
11. When using a circular saw, should the decorative face of the material be facing up or down?
12. List three methods of guiding a circular saw when ripping a large sheet of plywood.
13. A power miter box can be used for ripping stock. True or False?
14. Saber saw blades for cutting wood have _____ to _____ TPI.
15. List the procedure for sharpening bevel-tooth handsaw blades.

Chapter 23

SURFACING WITH THE JOINTER AND PLANER

After studying this chapter, you will be able to:
☐ Read wood grain to prevent chipping workpieces while surfacing.
☐ Set up and operate the jointer.
☐ Set up and operate the planer.
☐ Explain the sequence of steps to square workpieces.
☐ Maintain the jointer and planer.
☐ Sharpen jointer and planer knives.

Lumber faces, edges, and end grain are surfaced to produce flat and smooth cabinet parts. A high quality surface is obtained through the proper setup, operation, and maintenance of surfacing machinery. Practicing these skills lessens the time you spend sanding the product. The surfacing characteristics of various wood species are given in Fig. 12-45.

Jointers and planers are the principle machines for surfacing, Fig. 23-1. Suppose you begin with rough-sawn stock. One face is surfaced with a jointer. The other face is surfaced with the planer.

Jointing, followed by planing, brings stock to an even thickness. The amount of surfacing needed depends on the lumber. Rough lumber obviously will require much work. Lumber purchased as quarter-sawn and S2S (surfaced two sides) may not need surfacing. Flat-sawn S2S lumber may need some surfacing if the lumber is warped.

Surfacing usually corrects lumber warpage. However, to eliminate warp, extra stock must be removed. Removing a cup or bow lessens thickness. Eliminating crook reduces the board's width. The degree of twist limits both thickness and width.

Fig. 23-1. Surface lumber square on jointers and planers. (Delta)

READING WOOD GRAIN

The results of surfacing can be disastrous unless you can "read the grain." The grain pattern is the figure formed by cutting across the annual rings of a tree. This pattern will be different for flat-sawn, quarter-sawn, and other sawing procedures. Basically, these sawing processes produce lumber with either straight grain or crossgrain.

In lumber with straight grain, the lines formed by the annual rings run parallel to each other the full length of the board. In lumber with crossgrain, the grain angles or forms "V" shapes. problems arise when surfacing crossgrain lumber. Feeding the wrong direction can result in the cutter chipping, tearing, or splitting the wood.

Proper feed directions are shown in Fig. 23-2. Straight grain lumber can be fed in either direction, for faces and edges, on both the planer or jointer. Crossgrain lumber is fed so the cutter doesn't chip up the layers of wood growth. When surfacing faces, feed so the grain pattern "V" shape points away from the cutter. For edges, feed so the "V" shape points toward the jointer cutter.

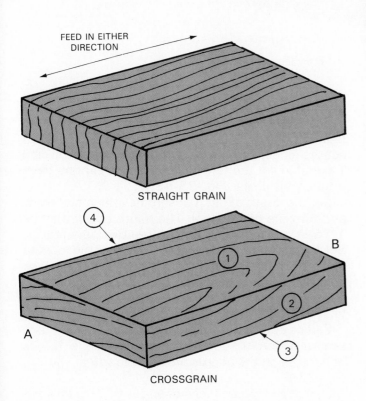

Surface	Machine	End to Feed First
1	Jointer	A
2	Jointer	B
3	Planer	B
4	Saw/Jointer	B

Fig. 23-2. Plane and joint surfaces so the grain doesn't tear.

THINK SAFETY—ACT SAFELY

Operating jointers, planers, and other power equipment for surfacing requires concentration and planning. Be attentive to your own actions. Plan your material handling steps thoroughly, both before and after processing the material. Always stay a reasonably safe distance from the point-of-operation. Other safety tips are:

1. Wear eye protection.
2. Remove jewelry and secure loose clothing.
3. Have a solid footing.
4. Use pushing devices for safer control of small workpieces.
5. Know that 3 in. by 12 in. is the minimum dimensions any workpiece should be for jointer, planer, or radial arm saw surfacing.
6. Keep point-of-operation and other safety devices in place.
7. Use fences on jointers and radial arm saws to guide your work.
8. Know where to reach the STOP switch. In an emergency, you need it immediately without having to look for it.
9. Stand slightly to the side of the workpiece being processed.
10. Have someone help you handle long stock.
11. Wait for the planer to coast to a complete stop before removing a wedged workpiece.
12. Inspect your work regularly for defects indicating inaccurate machine adjustments.
13. Maintain equipment properly for efficient surfacing.
14. Control wood chips and shavings with an exhaust system.

JOINTER

The *jointer* is a multipurpose tool for surfacing face, edge, and end grain. When squaring lumber, a face and edge are first jointed. The board is then cut to width and the edge jointed to remove saw marks. End grain may be surfaced after cutting workpieces to length.

JOINTER COMPONENTS

The jointer consists of four major components: cutterhead, infeed table, fence, and outfeed table, Fig. 23-3. Machine size is based on the maximum width of lumber that can be surfaced.

Cutterhead. The *cutterhead* has three or four *knives* which rotate at about 4000 to 5000 rpm. The length of the cutterhead, which varies from 4 to 12 in., limits the maximum width of lumber that can be surfaced. A movable *cutterhead guard* covers the point-of-operation.

Infeed table. Material is fed into the cutterhead by sliding it along the *infeed table*. The depth of cut

Fig. 23-3. Components of a jointer. (Powermatic)

is set by raising or lowering the infeed table below the top of the cutterhead. This is done by loosening the *infeed table lock* and turning the *infeed table adjusting handwheel.* Look at the depth-of-cut scale for the amount of material to be removed. After setting the infeed table, retighten the table lock.

Fence. The *fence* guides the workpiece into the cutterhead. It can be angled to bevel edges. However, most often it is set square to joint at 90°. To tilt the fence, loosen the *fence tilt lock* and set the fence angle. You can also slide the fence across the cutterhead. This determines what portion the cutterhead does the surfacing. Move the fence from time to time. Using the same part of the cutter dulls the knives quickly. Loosen the *fence lock knob,* slide the fence, and retighten the knob.

Outfeed table. The *outfeed table* supports the workpiece after it passes the cutterhead. The outfeed table should be set at exactly the same height as the cutterhead knives. Adjust the table by loosening the *outfeed table lock* and turning the *table adjusting knob.*

PREPARING FOR JOINTER SURFACING

There are several important decisions to make before operating a jointer. First, check the setup.

Then decide how to feed the lumber.

Set the fence position to vertical for a 90° (square) corner. Use a try or combination square to set the fence, Fig. 23-4A. For beveling, use a sliding T-bevel to set the fence angle. Some jointers have a fence tilt scale, Fig. 23-4B.

Set the depth of cut. Loosen the infeed table lock and turn the handwheel. The depth of cut may be 1/16 in. (1.6 mm) or less to remove saw marks. Set the depth according to the depth scale located under the infeed table. If there is no depth scale, look at the difference between the infeed and outfeed fence heights. (The outfeed table should be even with the cutterhead.) This is the actual depth of cut.

Select appropriate push boards or sticks. Have several different sizes and shapes available. Knobs or handles on the boards provide the safest control, Fig. 23-5.

Determine which faces or edges of the stock are to be jointed. Read the grain of the stock. Remember, you feed in different directions for edge and face jointing. Also inspect for warp. If the workpiece is warped, always place the concave side down.

Check the workpiece length. It should be at least 12 in. (305 mm) long for jointing. Use a hand or portable power plane for shorter workpieces. The material should be at least 3 in. (76 mm) wide to

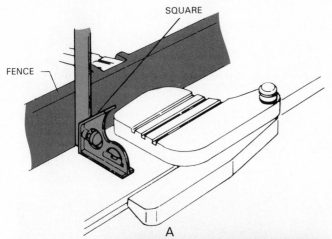

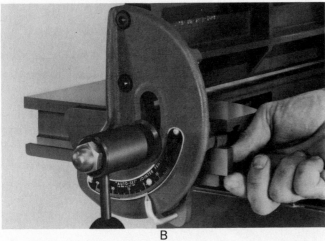

Fig. 23-4. A—Set the jointer fence at 90° using a square. (Powermatic) B—Some jointers have a fence tilt scale located at one end. (Delta International Machinery Corp.)

hold it down with push boards when face-surfacing. Otherwise, use a push stick. The material should also be at least 1/2 in. (13 mm) thick. Thinner material could splinter.

Reposition the fence periodically when jointing narrow material. Slide and lock the fence over a different section of the cutterhead. This assures the entire knife width is used so dulling will occur more evenly and knives require sharpening less often.

OPERATING THE JOINTER

Jointers are used first when squaring lumber. Normally, you will joint one face of a board, then one edge. Next, you surface the other face to final thickness with the planer. Then, you rip the board to width. You may wish to rip the board slightly oversize. Then return to the jointer and remove the saw marks. Once all faces and edges are flat and corners are square, cut one end square. Then cut the workpiece to length. You may cut the workpiece 1/16 in. (1.6 mm) over the length to allow for jointing end grain.

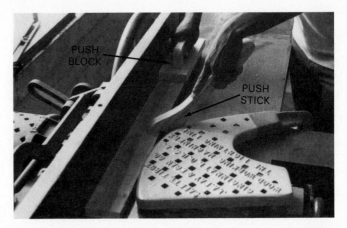

Fig. 23-5. Use push sticks and push boards when jointing.

Jointing a face

To joint a face, Fig. 23-6, proceed as follows:
1. Set the depth of cut at 1/16 in. (1.6 mm).
2. Set the fence to accommodate the workpiece width.
3. Be sure the guard will move freely when you push the lumber past the cutterhead.
4. Turn on the jointer.
5. Determine which direction to feed the workpiece. (See Fig. 23-2.)
6. Hold the front of the pushboard down with your left hand. Guide the workpiece forward with your right hand on the pusher handle. Press down lightly with both hands. When the pusher or workpiece reaches the cutter guard, it will push the guard aside. Keep both hands on the pushboard.
7. Feed the workpiece at a moderate rate. Rapid movement will tear or splinter the wood. If moved too slowly, black burn marks will appear.
8. You may need to support the material beyond the outfeed table. Use a roller accessory at the outfeed table height, or have another person support the lumber.

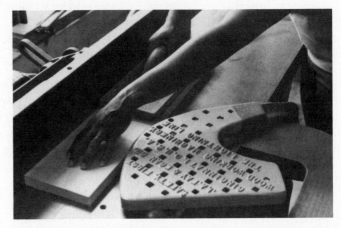

Fig. 23-6. Hold the board firmly against the table when face jointing. (Delta International Machinery Corp.)

If the workpiece is cupped, place the concave side down to prevent the material from rocking, Fig. 23-7. If the material is cupped excessively, rip it in half, joint the faces and edges, then reglue it. Otherwise, you reduce the thickness of the stock too much when removing the cup.

Twisted stock will rock diagonally when placed on the infeed table. Hold the lumber with a pushboard. Keep the two rocking corners equal distance from the infeed table as you joint the workpiece. You may wish to hand plane the two high corners some before jointing.

Fig. 23-7. The concave side of a cupped face should be placed down.

Jointing an edge

There are two methods for jointing an edge. One is done with the fence perpendicular to the cutterhead. The other is with the fence skewed at an angle. Skewing can reduce chipping and washboard effects.

The procedure for jointing an edge, Fig. 23-8, is as follows:

1. Set the depth of cut 1/16 in.
2. Check to see that the fence is at a 90° angle to the table.
3. Set fence to accommodate stock width. Some jointer fences can be angled (skewed) to cutter head, Fig. 23-9. This reduces chipping or tearing crossgrain wood.
4. Check that the guard will move freely when you push the workpiece past the cutter head.
5. Turn on the jointer.
6. Determine direction to feed workpiece.
7. Hold down workpiece with your left hand. Guide it forward with slight downward pressure of right hand. Use push sticks to keep hands over 4 in. (100 mm) from the cutter head.
8. Feed the workpiece at a moderate rate.

For a bow or crook, first make sure you have just enough stock length needed for the cabinet part. Then place the concave side down, this prevents the material from rocking from end to end.

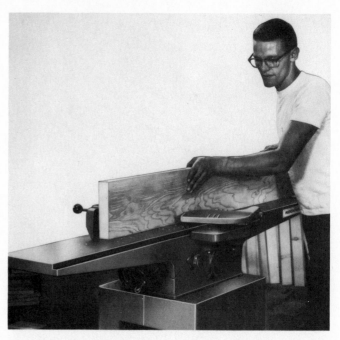

Fig. 23-8. Edge-jointing. Your left hand holds the workpiece against the fence. Your right hand does the feeding. (Delta)

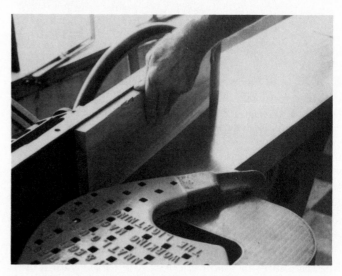

Fig. 23-9. Skewing the fence lessens chipping.

Jointing end grain

End grain may be surfaced on the jointer using a special procedure. Jointing the board's entire length will chip out the trailing edge. Again, the minimum length of cut should be 12 in. (300 mm). The procedure shown in Fig. 23-10 is as follows:

1. Set the depth of cut to 1/32 in. (1 mm).
2. Hold the workpiece face against the fence.
3. Advance the end about 1 in. (25 mm) into the cutterhead, Fig. 23-10A.
4. Lift and turn the workpiece around.
5. Joint the end, Fig. 23-10B. Apply pressure to the outfeed table as you near the 1 in. portion you previously jointed.

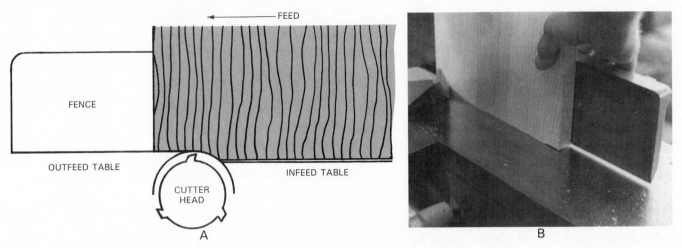

Fig. 23-10. Jointing an end. A—Joint about 1 in. of an end. B—Turn the board around and finish surfacing.

BEVELING

To bevel on the jointer, tilt the fence to the required angle. Then follow the edge-jointing procedure, Fig. 23-11A. For narrow strips, clamp a feather board to the fence, Fig. 23-11B, or use push sticks.

It is more efficient to rip the bevel slightly oversize on the table saw. Then one or two thin cuts on the jointer will remove any saw marks.

OTHER JOINTER OPERATIONS

Several other operations can be performed on the jointer. Cutting rabbet joints is one example. These are more specialized and are discussed in Chapter 29, Joint Making.

PLANER

The second face of a board is usually surfaced using a *planer,* Fig. 23-12. The planer has a wider

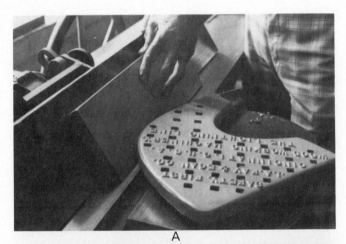

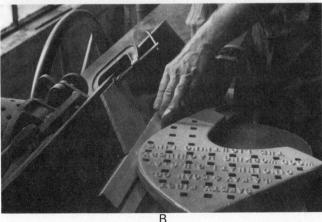

Fig. 23-11. A—Jointing a bevel. B—Use a feather board when jointing narrow materials.

Fig. 23-12. Planers surface material to thickness after jointing the first face. (Delta)

cutting head than does the jointer. Like the jointer, the cutting head determines the maximum workpiece width and the size of the machine. Planer sizes range from 12 to 48 in.

A planer should NOT be used to surface both faces of stock because it presses material against the table as it cuts. If there is a cup, bow, or twist in the lumber, it will be pressed down while surfacing. The warp will then spring back when material leaves the planer. This is why both jointer and planer are needed for proper squaring operations.

PLANER COMPONENTS

A planer is one of the larger, more automated woodworking machines. The interior components are shown in Fig. 23-13. Lumber is fed into the planer between the *infeed roller* and a *table roller.* The infeed roller is corrugated to grab onto the wood and pull it through. The lumber passes under the rotating cutterhead. The cutterhead knives remove wood from the upper surface. The *chip breaker* holds the workpiece down and reduces splintering. The *pressure bar* holds the workpiece against the table after the cut is made. The *outfeed roller* and second *table roller* grab stock to pull it out.

Some infeed rollers and chip breakers are in sections. This feature allows workpieces of different thicknesses to be surfaced side-by-side on the first pass. Without section rollers, stock must be fed one piece at a time until all pieces reach a uniform thickness. Then they can be fed side-by-side.

The exterior components of the planer are shown in Fig. 23-14. The *table adjusting handwheel* raises and lowers the table. The approximate planed thickness of stock is shown on the *thickness scale.* A *feed rate handwheel* may be present on variable feed speed machines. An indicator tells the feed rate

(feet per minute) of material being planed. There may be one or two switches. With two-switch planers, one controls the cutterhead motor, the other controls the motor for the feed rollers. The last adjustment is the *table roller adjusting lever.* It raises and lowers the table rollers. Not all planes have this feature.

PLANER SETUP

Follow these steps to prepare the planer for surfacing:
1. Measure the lumber thickness. One face should have already been jointed.
2. Turn the table adjusting handwheel to raise or lower the table. Watch the index mark on the scale. Set the table-to-cutter thickness 1/16 to 1/8 in. less than the lumber thickness.
3. Adjust the feed rate. If the feed rate is changed by a shift mechanism, the planer must be off. If it is changed by a variable speed handwheel, the planer must be turned on first.

The feed rate is chosen according to the width and density of the material. Slow the feed rate for hardwoods, such as oak. Increase the feed for soft woods, such as pine.

PLANER OPERATION

Planer operation is relatively simple. Follow these steps:
1. Inspect the surface to be planed. Loose knots or bark should first be removed.
2. Read the grain to determine which end of the stock will be fed first.
3. Start the machine and allow it to reach operating speed. Turn on the feed rollers if there is a separate switch.

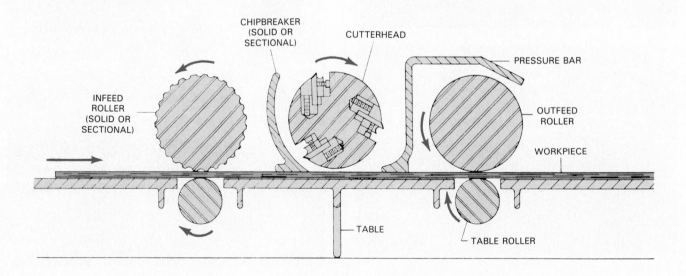

Fig. 23-13. Internal components of a planer. (Powermatic)

Fig. 23-14. External features of a planer. (Powermatic)

4. Feed the lumber straight into the planer. The infeed roller will take hold and control the feed. If it does not, remove the stock and raise the table.
5. Support the lumber as it exits the planer.
6. Raise the table and repeat the above steps until the lumber reaches the final thickness. Do not use the planer's thickness gauge if the dimension must be accurate. For the final pass, measure each piece with a ruler or vernier caliper for a more exact thickness.

If the stock sticks during the pass, first try pushing on the infeed end of the lumber. If this fails to feed the stock, move the table roller lever to a higher setting. Otherwise, turn off the planer, wait until the cutter stops, lower the table, and remove the workpiece.

Workpieces must be at least as long as the distance between the table rollers (generally 12 to 15 in.). Shorter workpieces can become wedged under the chip breaker or pressure bar. If wedging occurs for any reason, you should:
1. Step to the switch side of the infeed opening.
2. Turn off the planer.
3. Lower the table after the cutterhead stops.
4. Push the workpiece out with a push stick or other excess material. Never use your hand.

Planing glued stock

A wide board composed of several narrow workpieces glued together generally warps less than solid lumber. Each piece should have one face and both edges jointed. Glue them together with the jointed faces toward the clamps. Remove excess dry glue with a scraper. Then plane the entire panel to thickness. Use a feed rate slower than normal.

Planing thin stock

The minimum thickness for stock should be 3/8 in. However, you can plane thinner material using a backing board. It should be longer and wider than the workpiece, and at least 3/4 in. (19 mm) thick. Set the planer cutting depth to 1/16 in. smaller than the combined workpiece and backing board thickness. Feed the workpiece and backing board into the planer together, Fig. 23-15.

Fig. 23-15. Surfacing thin material requires a backing board.

COMBINATION JOINTER/PLANER

The planer and jointer are considered companion machines. They often are placed beside each other. To save space, a single tool, the combination *jointer/planer* is available, Fig. 23-16.

STATIONARY CUTTERHEAD PLANER

The *stationary cutterhead planer* has a fixed head with a knife, Fig. 23-17A. A conveyor draws stock against the cutterhead which slices off material. The cutting angle can be changed to reduce tearing by rotating the cutterhead assembly, Fig. 23-17B. Workpieces smaller than 12 in. can be planed with this machine.

RADIAL ARM SAW SURFACING

The versatile radial arm saw has surfacing abilities if you have the proper accessories. They include a surfacing cutterhead and a guard, Fig. 23-18. With these attachments, you can surface one face. The other face must have already been jointed so it can slide along the table easily. One edge must also have been jointed so it can slide along the fence.

MAINTAINING SURFACING MACHINES

Surfacing machines must be kept clean, properly adjusted, and lubricated. The cutter should be kept sharp. Machine maintenance and sharpening are critical to producing flat, unblemished surfaces.

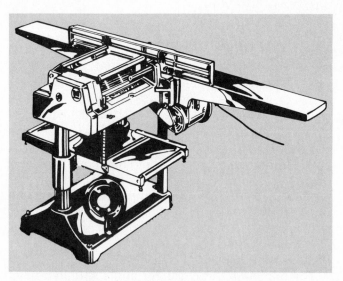

Fig. 23-16. For surfacing operations in a small shop, the jointer/planer is a compact alternative.

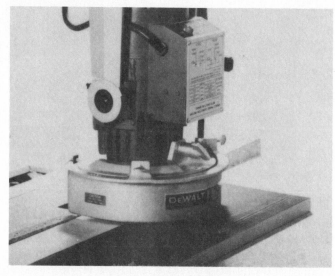

Fig. 23-18. The radial arm saw can be converted to a surfacer with a cutter and guard. The arbor is placed down. (DeWalt)

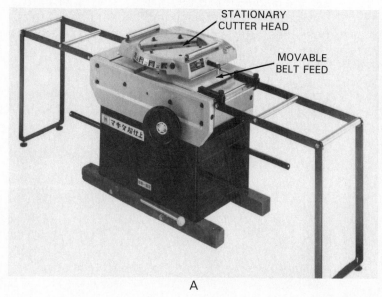

STATIONARY CUTTER HEAD

MOVABLE BELT FEED

A

B

Fig. 23-17. A—Stationary cutterhead planer. B—Material is removed in long continuous chips. (Makita)

LUBRICATION

Lubrication is necessary preventive maintenance. Moving machine parts have to be protected from excessive wear. The maintenance manual for a surfacing machine should list lubrication procedures. It will show a diagram of lubrication points as well as provide a time schedule. Generally, you should:
1. Lubricate rotating shafts and enclosed gear housings. Putting oil on other mechanisms attracts dust, making adjustment difficult.
2. Use paste wax, powdered graphite, talcum powder, or spray silicone for lubricating machine slides, adjusting screw threads, and similar mechanisms.

Partial disassembly may be necessary to locate some lubrication points. Look for grease fittings, oil holes, spring-top oil cups, and screw-type grease cups. Fill these, then make sure the tops are closed. Sealed bearings cannot be lubricated and must be replaced if worn.

RUST PREVENTION

Unpainted and unplated surfaces may rust over time. Rust can cause excessive friction between the table and the workpiece. Use fine steel wool to remove the rust. Then apply paste wax or spray silicone to the metal. This will lessen friction without staining the wood.

RESIN BUILDUP PREVENTION

Wood resins can build up on machine surfaces and cause many problems. Buildup on threads, slides, and gears can interfere with adjustments. Buildup on the cutterhead, feed rollers, and table rollers can leave dents and grooves in the planed surface.

Remove resin with turpentine, paint thinner, or kerosene. You may have to disassemble parts of the planer to access resin buildup areas. Apply a protective coating of paste wax or silicone to the cleaned parts.

SHARPENING STATIONARY SURFACING MACHINES

Keeping tools sharp is a constant concern. Taking the time to sharpen machine knives and cutters increases surfacing quality and reduces machining time.

Sharpening includes grinding and honing. *Grinding* is done to remove nicks and excessive wear from knives. *Honing* puts a slight bevel on the ground edge to increase tool life.

Sharpening is an involved process. When surfac-

ing, prevent damage to cutting edges by checking for:
1. Nails or other metal fasteners in the wood.
2. Excess glue. Remove all surface glue.
3. Any finishing materials. Some pigments are rock-hard and can dull a cutting edge quickly.

INSPECTING THE MACHINE

You can tell the sharpness of knives by both looking at and listening to the machine. Restrain from touching knives since even a dull edge can cut you.

Partial disassembly may be needed to look at the cutter knives. Observe the cutting edge in good light. If the tip has a rounded, shiny spot, the knife edge is dull. If the edge is nicked or uneven, it needs grinding, Fig. 23-19.

Also listen to the machine while it is operating. A low pitch, low volume sound usually indicates sharpness because the knives are removing material with ease. A high pitch, high volume sound, and vibration, can indicate dullness. The knives are forcing their way into the material.

GRIND AND/OR HONE?

After looking at the cutter, you must make a decision. Should you grind and hone or only hone the edge? Grinding is necessary if there are nicks in the edge or if the knife has been honed a number of times. Honing restores the slight bevel edge on the knife tip.

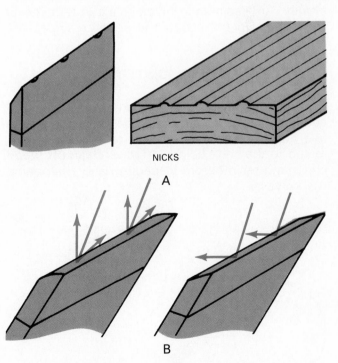

NICKS

A

B

Fig. 23-19. A—Nicks in a planer or jointer blade leave ridges on surfaced material. B—A sharp edge and a dull, rounded edge reflect light differently.

Surfacing with the Jointer and Planer 331

Grinding

Grinding restores a cutting edge which has been nicked or rounded by wear. The tool may be hand-held or secured in a fixture. In some cases the grinder is attached to the machine. Bench grinders may be adapted with special holding fixtures to secure the knife at the proper angle.

Carbide-tipped jointer and planer knives present a special problem because carbide is very hard. Grinding must be done under special conditions with a carbide-grinding wheel and coolant. These cutters should be ground by a professional.

Excessive pressure during grinding can cause overheating. This can be seen if the knife begins to turn blue. The temper (hardening) is reduced, the knife becomes soft, and it dulls faster. The knife can still be used, but will need sharpening more frequently. When grinding by hand, dip the knife in water often.

Be very observant while grinding. Sparks which fly around the wheel indicate the edge is dull. The sparks created will fly over the cutting edge when it is sharp, Fig. 23-20.

Honing

Honing restores the sharp bevel edge and removes grinding burrs. The edge is hand-rubbed at a 5° angle over a fine abrasive stone. Some grinders are equipped with very fine circular honing stones. Honing is done on both cutting edge surfaces. This bends any burrs back and forth until they break off. To check the sharpness, slide a piece of paper across the edge. The paper should slice readily. Any resistance indicates a burr remains on the edge. Do not touch the edge to check the sharpness.

SHARPENING JOINTER KNIVES

Sharpening jointer knives involves two procedures. First, each knife must be honed, or ground and honed. Then, the outfeed table must be adjusted to the knife height. Always clean off wood chips and resin before inspecting and sharpening the knives.

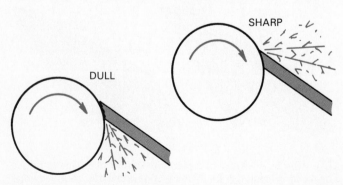

Fig. 23-20. Sparks fly over the tool when it is ground sharp.

KNIFE HONING

Hand-honing cutter knives is the easiest of sharpening methods. The process, as shown in Fig. 23-21 and 23-22, is as follows:

1. Disconnect the electrical power.
2. Move the guard aside or remove it.
3. Remove the fence.
4. Lower the infeed table to its greatest depth of cut.
5. Protect the infeed table with paper and masking tape.
6. Wedge a thin piece of hardboard or plastic laminate between the cutterhead and blade, Fig. 23-21. This holds the cutterhead and further protects the table from damage.
7. Place the stone on the beveled edge of the knife. Rest it on the hardboard or laminate.
8. Slide the stone across each knife the same number of strokes. This should create a very small bevel on the tip of the blade.
9. Move the hardboard behind the knife, as shown in Fig. 23-22. Slide the stone across the flat (unground) face of the knives.
10. Raise the table.
11. Replace the guard and fence.
12. Reconnect electrical power to the machine.

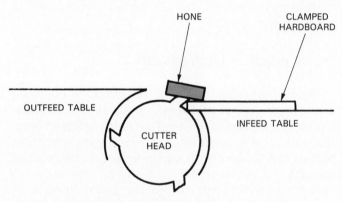

Fig. 23-21. Honing the backs of the jointer knives.

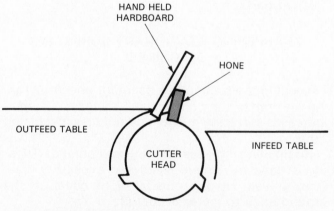

Fig. 23-22. Honing the fronts of the jointer knives.

JOINTER TROUBLESHOOTING HINTS

Clues to jointer operation problems come from workpiece inspection after making a cut. Refer to the illustrations for each type of problem:

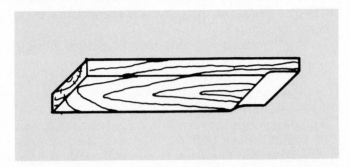

Snipe. Outfeed table is lower than the arc of the knives. Raise the table until snipe disappears.

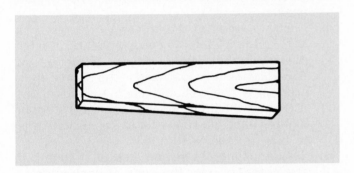

Unwanted taper. Outfeed table is too high. Lower it until the knife arc is even with table surface.

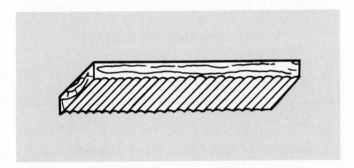

Washboarding. Workpiece pushed through the jointer too quickly (or jointer knives uneven).

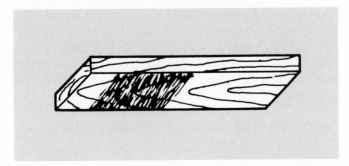

Knife burns on surface. Knives are dull or feed is too slow.

KNIFE GRINDING

Jointer knives may be ground while installed in or removed from the machine. An accessory is needed when grinding is done on the machine. It mounts on the outfeed table.

The attachment to grind knives on the machine is shown in Fig. 23-23. The procedure is as follows:
1. Disconnect power to the jointer.
2. Remove the guard and fence.
3. Mount the knife grinder.
4. Lock the cutterhead in the proper position using the indexer.
5. Hold a piece of paper between the knife edge and the grinding wheel.
6. Lower the grinding wheel to contact the paper, then remove the paper.
7. Move the grinder to one end of the slide.
8. Start the grinder.
9. Move the grinder from side to side. Lower it slightly each time until small sparks are created.
10. Grind each knife at this setting.
11. Lower the grinder and repeat Step 9.
12. Remove the grinding accessory and indexer.
13. Hone the knives if a thin, wiry edge remains.
14. Replace the fence and guard.
15. Reconnect electrical power to the jointer.

REMOVING JOINTER KNIVES

If jointer knives need to be removed, there are special alignment problems when the knives are replaced. They must each extend an equal distance

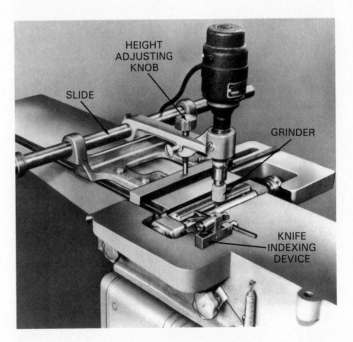

Fig. 23-23. Attachment for grinding knives on the jointer. (Delta)

from the cutterhead. Otherwise, all edges will not contact the workpiece. This can cause ripple in the jointed surface.

The procedure to remove jointer knives, shown in Fig. 23-26, is as follows:
1. Disconnect electrical power to the jointer.
2. Remove the guard and fence.
3. Loosen all *gib retainer screws* 1/8 to 1/4 turn. Consider using a fixture to hold the cutterhead and knife steady, Fig. 23-24A. Otherwise, place hardboard over the knife. Pull up and away from the cutting edge to loosen the screws, Fig. 23-24B. Use the proper wrench, start from one end, and proceed across the knife. Apply a penetrating solvent if the screws will not turn.
4. Further loosen the screws until the gib can be lifted out.
5. Remove the jointer knife.

After removing knives, clean the gibs, gib screws, and cutterhead with mineral spirits or other solvent.

Knives should be ground on proper equipment by experienced technicians. A standard bench grinder and fixture should not be used. It is not accurate enough for the precision required of the jointer.

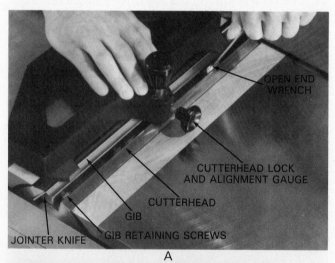

CUTTERHEAD LOCK
AND ALIGNMENT GAUGE

OPEN END WRENCH

CUTTERHEAD

GIB

GIB RETAINING SCREWS

JOINTER KNIFE

A

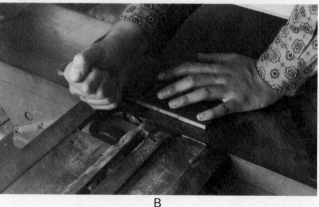

B

Fig. 23-24. A—Loosen the gib retaining screws to remove knives. A fixture holds the cutterhead in place. (Delta) B—Without a fixture, use hardboard to protect your hands.

Professionals will also hone the knives for you after grinding them.

INSTALLING JOINTER KNIVES

Installing the sharpened knives requires accurate setting so all knives extend the same amount from the cutterhead. You may use:
1. A gauge especially designed for setting knives, Fig. 23-25A.
2. A magnet. The magnet should be perfectly flat. A horseshoe magnet is best, Fig. 23-25B.
3. A straightedge, Fig. 23-25C.

The procedure for installing knives is as follows:
1. Check to see that the *lifter adjusting screws* turn easily. There are two or three *lifters* in the bottom of each knife slot. Both the gib and knife sit on the lifters.
2. Place the knife in the slot properly with the gib against it.
3. Align the ends of the knives.
   NOTE: Some jointers have a rabbeting arm for making rabbet joints. If your jointer is so equipped, you must align the knife ends precisely. They should each extend about .005 in. (0.15 mm) beyond the table's edge.
4. Tighten each gib screw for all knives with one to two pounds of torque.
5. Set the alignment device (gauge, magnet, or straightedge) near the ends of each knife.
6. Adjust the height of every knife by turning the lifter screws. Manufacturers provide specifications for the amount the knife protrudes from the cutterhead. Many recommend a maximum .125 in. (3 mm) from the knife edge to the cutterhead.
7. Recheck the knife height using the gauge, magnet, or straightedge.
8. Torque each retainer screw to about 40 to 50 ft. lbs.
9. Replace the fence and guard.
10. Reconnect electrical power to the jointer.
11. Stand aside and turn the machine on and off once. Listen for any unusual sounds.

After the jointer is reassembled, check the outfeed table adjustment. It should be perfectly even with the edge of the knives. If not, there will be a snipe (gouge) in the surface. Loosen the outfeed table lock. Change the outfeed table setting. Place a straightedge from the outfeed table over the knives, Fig. 23-26. When the table and knives align, tighten the table lock.

CHECKING FOR UNPARALLEL INFEED AND OUTFEED TABLES

The last periodic adjustment concerns whether the infeed and outfeed table are parallel. Suppose

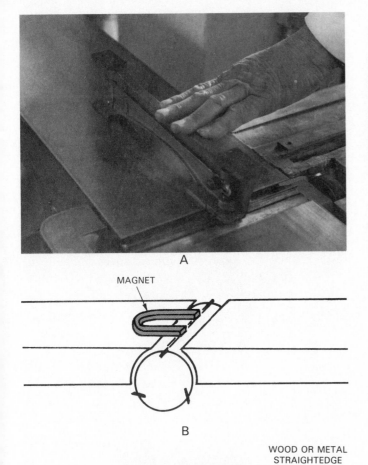

A

MAGNET

B

WOOD OR METAL
STRAIGHTEDGE

OUTFEED
TABLE

INFEED
TABLE

C

Fig. 23-25. Setting the height of jointer knives. A—Gauge.
B—Magnet. C—Straightedge.

Fig. 23-26. The outfeed table should be the same height as
the tip of the jointer knives. (Rockwell International)

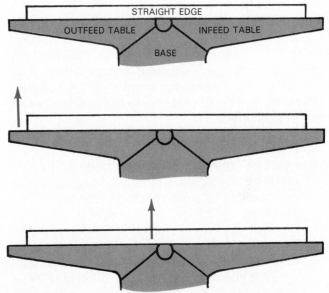

STRAIGHT EDGE

OUTFEED TABLE   INFEED TABLE

BASE

Fig. 23-27. Inspect whether infeed and outfeed tables are
parallel. Adjust the outfeed table as necessary.

you have made several passes with the jointer.
When you check the workpiece, you find the jointer
is cutting a taper. More material is being removed
at one end than the other. To correct this problem,
you should:
1. Set the infeed table to zero cut.
2. Place a long straightedge across both tables.
3. Look between the straightedge and the tables,
   Fig. 23-27. There should be no light passing
   through.
4. If the tables are not parallel, adjust the outfeed
   table as instructed in the manufacturer's
   maintenance manual. For example, there may
   be an adjustable cam for this purpose. When
   there are no adjustments provided, place metal
   shims where the outfeed table and machine
   base castings join.

MAINTAINING THE PLANER

Planer maintenance includes sharpening the
planer knives and adjusting the tables, rollers, and
other components of the machine. If the planer is
not properly adjusted, serious defects will result in
surfaced lumber, Fig. 23-28.

SHARPENING PLANER KNIVES

Planer knives can be jointed or ground. These
processes can be done with the knives in the
machine using special attachments.

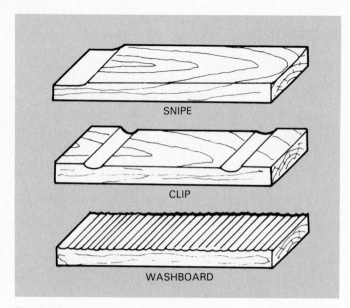

Fig. 23-28. Snipe, clip, and washboard result from inaccurate planer settings.

Jointing planer knives

Jointing restores the cutting edge to planer knives. The jointing procedure may vary slightly among planers. Each machine manufacturer may have different sharpening attachment setup procedure. However, the process is basically the same and is as follows:

1. Disconnect electrical power to the machine.
2. Remove the top cover.
3. Position the jointing attachment on the machine, Fig. 23-29. On some machines, this attachment is permanently mounted in the machine.
4. Secure the jointing bracket in the attachment. The bracket holds the jointing stone.
5. Lower the stone. It should touch a high spot on the knife very lightly. This is likely to be at one end of the knife. This is where the cutting edges have been used the least.
6. Move the jointing assembly to the left or right on each knife. Raise the stone if it drags on any of the knives.
7. Position the jointing bracket to the side of the machine next to the handwheel.
8. .Reconnect electrical power.
9. Stand to the side of the machine on the side of the jointing attachment handwheel. Be out of line with the table. Turn on the machine.
10. Turn the handwheel so the jointing stone traverses the full lenth of the knives. Light sparks will fly as the stone makes its pass. Sparks will not be seen where the knives are worn.
11. Lower the stone very slightly. STOP WHEN YOU SEE THE FIRST SPARKS.

12. Turn the handwheel and move the stone back across the knives. Watch the sparks. If you see light sparks throughout the travel, then stop the machine.
13. Inspect the knives. You should see a secondary surface on the knife edge. This is called the *land* and should be .01 in. (0.25 mm) or less in width.
14. Remove the jointing attachment and replace the top cover.

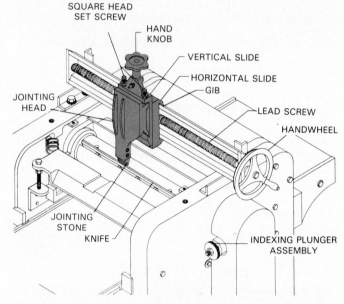

Fig. 23-29. Jointing restores sharpness to dull planer knives. This attachment is bolted to the machine. (Powermatic)

Grinding planer knives

You may joint the knives several times before the bevel, or land, on the edge of the knife exceeds 1/64 (.016) in. (0.4 mm). Then grinding is necessary. Grinding may be done while knives are installed or after they are removed.

The method for grinding knives while they are installed in the machine is:

1. Disconnect electrical power to the machine.
2. Remove the top cover.
3. Install the grinding assembly, Fig. 23-30.
4. Lock the cutterhead in postion with the indexing plunger assembly. A knife must be directly under the grinding wheel.
5. Lower the grinding wheel until it touches the knife. Do this at the highest point on the knife's length. UNDER NO CONDITION SHOULD THE GRINDING WHEEL TOUCH THE CUTTERHEAD.
6. Turn the grinding wheel by hand. It should produce a few very light scratches on the knife. These will show if the wheel is touching the knife properly.

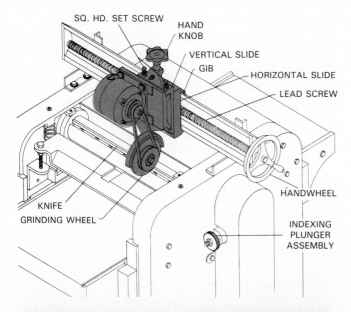

SQ. HD. SET SCREW
HAND KNOB
VERTICAL SLIDE
GIB
HORIZONTAL SLIDE
LEAD SCREW
HANDWHEEL
KNIFE
GRINDING WHEEL
INDEXING PLUNGER ASSEMBLY

Fig. 23-30. Grinding attachments. (Powermatic, Rockwell International)

7. Move the grinding wheel off the end of the knife by turning the handwheel.
8. Connect the grinder to electrical power.
9. Turn the handwheel while the grinder is operating. Traverse the entire length of the cutterhead. Do not let the grinding wheel sit at one spot on a knife.
10. Lower the grinding wheel slightly. Again, move the wheel the entire length of the knife. Do this until the knife edge is about .003 in. (0.08 mm) wide. (This is approximately the thickness of a piece of paper. There is no need to remove all of the surface. This results in a thin, wiry edge, which can easily break off.
11. Note the setting on the grinding wheel. Then raise it just more than the total distance you lowered it. (This is done so the wheel clears the next knife.)

12. Unlock the indexing plunger and rotate the cutterhead so another knife is facing up. Relock it.
13. Continue to grind knives and rotate the cutterhead. Grind until you reach the depth noted on the first knife.
14. Remove the grinding attachment.
15. Secure the top cover.
16. Reconnect electrical power.

If you do not have a grinding attachment, remove the knives and have them ground by a technician. To remove the knives, you must:

1. Disconnect electrical power and remove the planer's top cover.
2. Loosen the gib retaining screws, Fig. 23-31. They hold the gibs against the knives. Pull up and away from the cutting edge to prevent cutting yourself. Accumulated resins might make the screws difficult to loosen. Use mineral spirits or paint thinner to dissolve resin.
3. Lift the knives out by the ends.
4. Remove the gibs.

Fig. 23-31. Loosen gib retaining screws to remove planer knives. (Delta)

Once removed, the knives should be ground by a technician. Then the knives must be reinstalled and precisely adjusted. This process is:

1. Turn the lifter screws so the knife lifter sits at the bottom of the knife slot.
2. Place the knives and gibs in the cutterhead slots.
3. Tighten the end screws on each gib with about one to two ft.lbs. of torque. This is snug enough so they will stay in place. Always tighten screws by pulling the wrench. Do not push it toward the cutting edge.

Surfacing with the Jointer and Planer 337

4. Adjust each knife with a template or dial indicator, Fig. 23-32. Place the template or indicator over the sharp edge. Turn the adjusting screws as necessary. Raise the knife by turning the adjusting screws clockwise. When lowering the knife, turn adjusting screws counter-clockwise. Then tap on the knife with a piece of wood to lower it.
5. Tighten each gib screw with 30 to 50 ft. lbs. of torque. This is about as tight as you can turn.
6. Inspect each knife setting when the gibs are secure. Use the template or dial indicator.

Some machines have very long knives which tend to warp. The center of the installed knife may be low or high. Check both ends and the center when the gib screws are lightly torqued. If the center is high, set the center lifter first. Moderately torque one or two of the center gib screws. Then turn the lifter adjusting screws on each end. This will raise the knife ends to the same setting as the center.

If the center is low, set both end adjusters first. Next torque several end gib screws. Then turn the center knife lifter screws to raise the center. Finally, fully torque all of the gibs.

ALIGNING THE PLANER

Adjustments should be checked after the knives are sharpened. You need a dial indicator on a flat

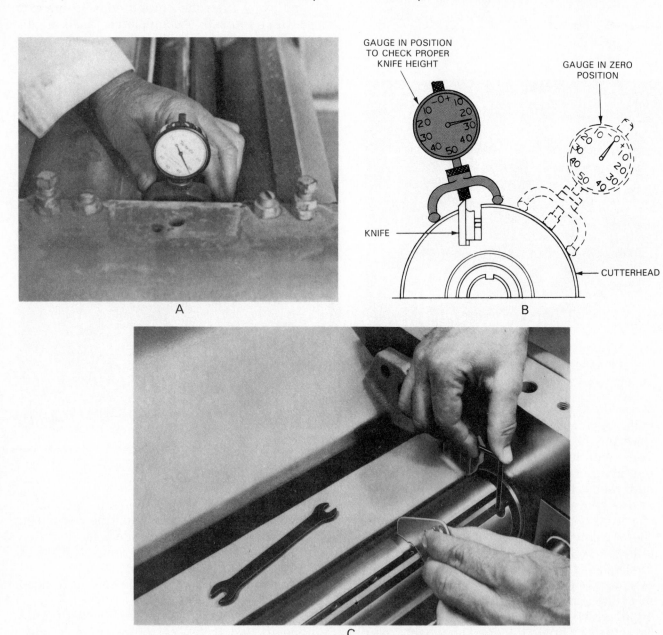

Fig. 23-32. Setting planer knife height. A—A dial indicator is very accurate. B—The indicator should read zero over the cutterhead. (Powermatic) C—A template can also be used to set knife height. (Rockwell International)

base, Fig. 23-33. Settings to be checked include:
1. Planer table.
2. Infeed roller.
3. Chip breaker.
4. Outfeed roller.
5. Pressure bar.
6. Table rollers.

Table setting

The planer table generally is set first. The table-to-knife distance must be the same on the left and right sides. Rarely do you need to adjust the table. However, periodically check it as follows:
1. Place the dial indicator directly under the cutterhead. Set it to the left or right side of the table. The knife edge must be at its lowest point.
2. Raise the table until you get a reading.
3. Move the indicator to the other side. Compare the dial readings. They should be within .001 in. (0.03 mm) of each other.
4. If adjustments are necessary, look for an adjusting nut and set screw where the table raising screw and table meet. Loosen the set screw. Turn the adjusting nut to correct the difference. Retighten the set screw.

Infeed roller adjustment

The infeed roller may be solid or in sections. It is mounted on a spring which allows the roller to raise when lumber is fed into the machine. The roller must be set lower than the table-to-knife setting. On a solid roller, it should be 1/32 in. (0.8 mm) lower. On a sectional roller, it should be 1/16 in. (1.6 mm) lower.

Compare dial readings under the knife and under the roller. They should differ by .06 in. (1.6 mm) for solid rollers or .03 in. (0.8 mm) for sectional rollers.

Fig. 23-33. Table and all roller adjustments are made using a dial indicator on a flat base.

Chip breaker adjustment

The chip breaker is also spring loaded like the infeed roller. You will find a set screw and lock nut at each end of the breaker. Using a dial indicator, adjust these so the breaker is 1/32 in. (0.8 mm) below the knife edge. A chip breaker set too low will prevent the workpiece from feeding. A high setting may allow wood to tear and split. The same setting is used for solid and sectional breakers. If you adjust the infeed roller, you must adjust the chip breaker.

Pressure bar adjustment

Many planer-caused defects are the result of an improperly set pressure bar. Its function is to hold material down after passing under the cutterhead. The bar should be in line with the arc of the cutterhead knives. If it is too high, a shallow clip will occur about 6 in. (152 mm) from each end of the board. (See Fig. 23-28.) If it is set too low, stock will not feed through.

To set the pressure bar, first place a dial indicator on the table bed under the cutterhead. Adjust the table so the bottom arc of the cutter just touches the indicator. Then move the block under the pressure bar. Adjust the bar so it is .000 to .001 in. (0.02 mm) above the arc of the cutterhead. Fine adjustments may still have to be made after a test cut.

Outfeed roller adjustment

Behind the pressure bar is the outfeed roller. It is spring loaded also. Its setting is identical to the chip breaker adjustment. Set screws and lock nuts at the ends control the setting.

Table roller adjustment

Table rollers raise the workpiece of the planer table as it passes through. This reduces friction so the infeed and outfeed rollers can move the stock easier. On most planers, table rollers are set .008 in. (0.3 mm) above the table with the table roller adjustment lever set at zero. (Some smaller planers do not have table roller adjustments.)

Some dial indicators can be set up to check the roller adjustment. Preset the dial at "0" against the table. Then move the indicator over the roller. Set screws and lock nuts hold the rollers at the proper setting.

TESTING THE PLANER

After all adjustments have been made, plane a length of excess lumber. There may be some visible planer defects. The most common are clip, snipe, and washboard. (See Fig. 23-28.) These and other problems can be troubleshot and eliminated, Fig. 23-24. This may require resetting some of the planer adjustments.

TROUBLE-SHOOTING HINTS

PROBLEM	CAUSE	SOLUTION
Board will not feed through.	1. Pressure bar too low. (most common cause) 2. Table rollers too low. 3. Insufficient pressure on infeed roller or outfeed roller. 4. Cut too deep.	1. Readjust pressure bar. 2. Raise roller with quick-set handle. 3. Increase pressure equally on both sides. 4. Reduce cut to capacity of machine.
Snipe appears at beginning of board only.	1. Front table roller set too high.	1. Readjust front table roller.
Snipe appears at end of board only.	1. Read table roller set too high.	1. Readjust rear table roller.
Clip appears 3-6'' (7.6-15.2 cm) from both ends of the board.	1. Pressure bar set too high. 2. Table roller set too high.	1. Readjust pressure bar. 2. Check position of quick-set handle and if at zero, readjust table rollers.
Board appears to splinter out.	1. Excessive feed. 2. Cutting against grain. 3. Chipbreaker too high. 4. Green lumber.	1. Reduce feed. 2. Reverse starting end of workpiece. 3. Lower chipbreaker. 4. Accept surface as is or change stock.
Knives raise grain.	1. Dull knives. 2. Green lumber.	1. Sharpen knives. 2. Accept surface as is or change stock.
Chip marks appear on stock.	1. Exhaust system not working properly. 2. Loose connection in exhaust system. 3. Chips stuck on outfeed roller.	1. Repair or replace. Check for proper duct sizing. 2. Repair. 3. Clean roller.
Taper across width.	1. Table not parallel with cutterhead.	True table to cutterhead.
Glossy or glazed surface appearance on stock.	1. Dull knives. 2. Too slow a feed.	1. Resharpen knives. 2. Increase feed.
Washboard surface finish.	1. Knives not set at the same height. 2. Too fast a feed rate. 3. Table gibs loose.	1. Reset knives. 2. Reduce feed rate. 3. Readjust gibs.
Chatter marks across width of board. (Small washboard.)	1. Table rollers too high (particularly noticeable on thin material).	1. Use backing board.
Line on workpiece parallel to feed direction.	1. Nick in knives. 2. Scratch in pressure bar.	1. (a) Resharpen knives, to remove nick. (b) Offset nick mark if possible. (c) Replace knives if nick too wide or deep. 2. Hone pressure bar smooth.
Excessive noise.	1. Dull knives. 2. Joint on knives too wide. 3. Table roller too high for workpiece thickness.	1. Resharpen knives. 2. Regrind knives. 3. Lower table rollers.
Excessive vibration.	1. Knives not sharpened evenly such that they are different heights.	1. (a) Measure knives, set for even overall height and resharpen. (b) Replace knives.
Workpiece twists while feeding.	1. Pressure bar not parallel. 2. Table rollers not parallel with table. 3. Uneven pressure on infeed or outfeed roller. 4. Chipbreaker not parallel. 5. Resin build-up on table.	1. Readjust pressure bar. 2. Reset table rollers. 3. Readjust for even pressure. 4. Readjust chipbreaker. 5. Clean table.
Main drive motor kicks out.	1. Excessive cut. 2. Bad motor. 3. Dull knives.	1. (a) Reduce depth of cut. (b) Reduce feed rate. 2. Replace motor. 3. Resharpen knives.
Feed motor stalls.	1. Bad motor. 2. Lack of lubrication on idlers.	1. Replace motor. 2. Lubricate idlers.

Fig. 23-34. Learn to troubleshoot and correct planer problems. (Powermatic)

SUMMARY

Surfacing is a fundamental process in cabinetmaking. Creating flat and square cabinet parts is essential for producing high quality products. The jointer and planer are part of this process. One surface and both edges are jointed. The second surface is planed. The radial arm saw can also be used for surfacing.

Machines will work best when properly maintained. You should periodically inspect, clean, lubricate, and adjust machine parts. Knowing the function of machine parts will help you when maintaining and adjusting them for proper function.

All processing must be done safely. Many operations, in both processing and maintenance, expose you to sharp, rotating cutters. Keep a safe distance between you and any cutter, moving or stationary. You can replace push blocks and sticks, but you cannot replace fingers.

CABINETMAKING TERMS

Surfacing, jointing, planing, reading the grain, jointer, cutterhead, knives, cutterhead guard, infeed table, infeed table lock, infeed table adjusting handwheel, fence, fence tilt lock, fence lock knob, outfeed table, outfeed table lock, table adjusting knob, planer, infeed roller, table roller, chip breaker, pressure bar, outfeed roller, table adjusting handwheel, thickness scale, feed rate handwheel, table roller adjusting lever, jointer/planer, stationary cutterhead planer, grinding, honing, jointing, gib, gib retainer screws, lifters, lifter adjusting screws, knife land.

TEST YOUR KNOWLEDGE

1. Surfacing produces _____ and _____ workpieces.
2. When surfacing faces, the crossgrain should point up and back toward you. True or False?
3. When jointing an edge, the crossgrain should point up and back toward you. True or False?
4. List the four major components of a jointer.
5. For a jointer, set the depth of cut by raising or lowering the _____ _____ _____ _____.
6. The outfeed table should be 1/16 in. (1.5 mm) lower than the cutterhead. True or False?
7. The depth of cut for most jointing should be _____.
8. List the steps taken when squaring a board.
9. When jointing a face or planing, should the concave side of a cupped board be placed up or down?
10. A bevel is best jointed by first _____, then jointing.
11. Describe why the planer infeed roller is corrugated, but the outfeed roller is not?
12. During planer setup, raise or lower the planer table so it is _____ in. less than the stock thickness.
13. Stock less than 3/8 in. should be fed on top of a _____ _____.
14. The stationary cutterhead planer has a pivoting, two-knife cutterhead. True or False?
15. Lubricate slides and screw threads with _____.
16. You can tell the sharpness of knives by both _____ and _____ the machine.
17. Grinding is necessary each time jointer knives are sharpened. True or False?
18. When removing both jointer and planer knives, you must loosen the _____ _____ _____ which hold the knives in the slots.
19. List the tools used to set knife height for both jointers and planers.
20. List the acceptable tolerances when checking the planer table, infeed roller, chip breaker, outfeed roller, pressure bar, and table roller.

Chapter 24
SURFACING WITH PLANES AND SCRAPERS

After studying this chapter, you will be able to:
☐ *List the various hand planes for surfacing face, edge, and end grain.*
☐ *Describe the use of hand and cabinet scrapers.*
☐ *Explain the operation of a portable power plane.*
☐ *Follow procedures to sharpen plane irons and scraper blades.*
☐ *Remove the cutterhead from a power plane for sharpening.*

Though most surfacing is done with jointers and planers, hand and portable power planes remain valuable to the cabinetmaker. Hand planes are needed for very small cabinet parts which cannot be machine surfaced. Portable power planes are used for on-site architectural woodwork. Scrapers are used for removing dried glue from joints and smoothing large surfaces. These tools, used properly, will reduce the time you spend sanding. Fig. 12-45 gives the planing characteristics for various wood species.

You must read the wood grain before planing, just as you did before using the planer or jointer. Hand and portable power planes also chip and tear the surface when the cutter moves against the grain.

HAND PLANE SURFACING

Various hand planes will surface lumber faces as well as plywood edges. You can also plane composition materials, such as fiberboard and particleboard. However, the adhesives which bond these materials can dull cutting edges rapidly. With low density composites, planing may make the surface even rougher.

Always scrape away excess adhesive from joints before planing. Use a chisel or scraper. The cutting edge on a chisel or scraper can be restored quicker than the edge on a plane iron.

Face and edge grain are surfaced with bench planes. Use a block plane to surface end grain. There are additional hand planes, such as the router

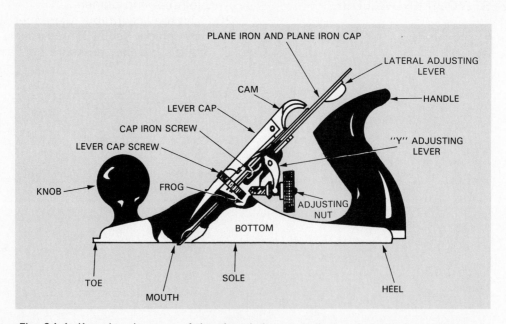

Fig. 24-1. Knowing the parts of the plane helps you adjust and use the tool. (Stanley)

plane and rabbet plane. These are used when making joints to smooth the bottoms of grooves and rabbet edges. They are covered in Chapter 29, Joint Making.

BENCH PLANES

Bench planes include the jack, fore, jointer, and smooth planes. The standard parts of bench planes are shown in Fig. 24-1.

The most universally used bench plane is the *jack plane.* It is 12 to 14 in. (300 to 350 mm) long with a 2 to 2 3/8 in. (50 to 60 mm) wide plane iron.

The *fore plane,* 18 in. (450 mm) long, is slightly larger and heavier than the jack plane, Fig. 24-2. The longer sole helps the plane straighten longer workpieces. It has less tendency to follow contours of warped lumber.

The largest plane is the *jointer plane.* It has a 20 to 24 in. (500 to 600 mm) sole with a 2 5/8 in. (65 mm) iron width. This plane might be used to smooth large surface areas as well as door and plywood edges.

The *smooth plane* is the shortest of the bench planes, Fig. 24-3. It is 6 to 10 in. (150 mm to 250

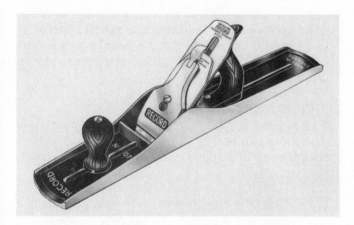

Fig. 24-2. Fore plane. (Record Ridgeway)

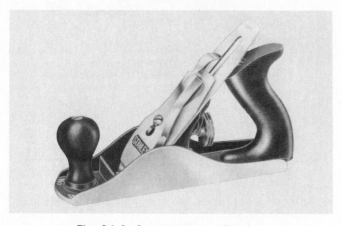

Fig. 24-3. Smooth plane. (Stanley)

mm) long. Generally, the cutting edge is 2 in. (50 mm) wide or less. Some of these planes have a series of grooves in the sole.

Adjusting the bench plane

Bench plane adjustments control the *plane iron,* which is the cutter. The iron moves in and out through a hole in the sole, called the *mouth.* This controls the depth of cut, Fig. 24-4A. The *frog* holds the iron at a 45° angle. The *adjusting nut* moves the ''Y'' lever. As a result, the plane iron slides across the frog to adjust the depth of cut. The *lateral adjusting lever* moves the plane iron left and right, Fig. 24-4B. It keeps an even amount of cutting edge extended through the mouth. The *plane*

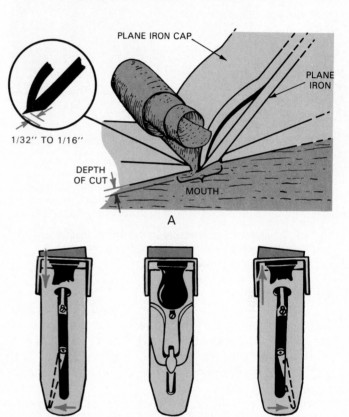

Fig. 24-4. A—The plane iron extends 1/32 to 1/16 in. beyond the cap for smooth cutting action. B—Moving the lateral adjusting lever changes the lateral angle of the plane iron. (Stanley)

iron cap is placed on top of the plane iron. The cap has a slot for the Y-lever and a threaded hole for the cap screw. The *cap screw* secures the plane cap to the plane iron. They must be held tightly enough to prevent slippage. Tension to hold the entire assembly in place is provided by the *lever cap.*

Before planing, check the plane iron sharpness and the plane cap to iron spacing. To do so, lift up the lever cap and remove the plane iron and cap assembly. Adjust the plane iron cap to within 1/32 to 1/16 in. (0.5 to 1.5 mm) of the plane iron edge. (Refer to Fig. 24-4.) Place the iron and cap assembly on the frog and resecure it with the lever cap. Turn the plane upside down and sight down the sole, Fig. 24-5. The iron should protrude from the mouth an even amount on each end. If it is uneven, move the lateral adjusting lever.

Fig. 24-6. Turn the plane at an angle for easier cutting. The shavings should be thin.

Planing an edge

The procedure for planing an edge is much the same as for planing a surface. However, there are some special cautions.
1. Mark a line to which you will cut. This shows if you are removing even amounts at the center and ends.
2. Crossgrain lines angle down and toward you.
3. Be especially careful to hold the plane square. On narrow material, the plane tends to rock. It is sometimes helpful to hold your fingers under the toe of the plane and against the stock to keep the tool square.

BLOCK PLANE SURFACING

The *block plane,* Fig. 23-7A, is designed to surface end grain. Compared to bench planes, the block

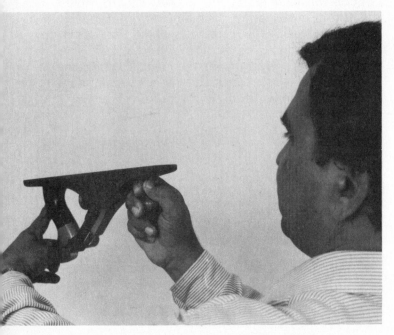

Fig. 24-5. Sight down the sole to check whether the plane iron extends equally through the mouth.

Surface planing

When planing a surface, you should get thin and feathery shavings. Taking deep cuts will result in grooves. Use long strokes with the grain. Short strokes cause small ridges to appear across the grain. Turning the plane 10° to 20° makes it easier to push, Fig. 24-6.

The basic procedure to follow when planing a surface is:
1. Clamp the workpiece in a vise or between a vise and bench stop.
2. Have a firm footing.
3. Start with the toe of the plane at one end. Push downward on the knob as you start.
4. Push downward on both the knob and handle for most of the distance.
5. At the end of the pass, push downward only on the handle.
6. Continue passes along the surface until it is flat.
7. When finished, place the plane on its side to prevent damage to the cutting edge.

Fore planes work well for removing a cup. Push the plane diagonally across the surface to remove the warp. Then plane with the grain to remove any diagonal marks or rough grain.

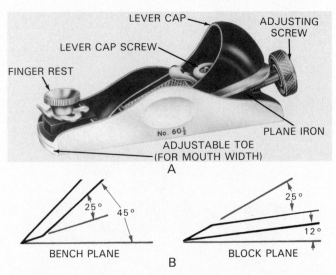

Fig. 24-7. A—The block plane is effective on end grain. (Stanley) B—Bench and block plane irons are installed differently.

plane is smaller, lighter, and has fewer moving parts. The plane iron is set at a different angle, Fig. 24-7B. The block plane is held in the palm of your hand, Fig. 24-8. An adjusting screw changes the depth of cut. The lever cap screw secures the iron once it is set. The plane iron is set at a lower angle than bench planes. The bevel on the iron faces up, instead of down.

To prepare a block plane, first unlock the lever cap and remove the iron. Check the sharpness of the cutting edge. Reposition the iron in the plane with the bevel up. Align the notches on the iron with the adjusting screw nut. Replace the lever cap and tighten the screw. Sight down the sole of the plane bottom and adjust the depth of cut. Also check lateral adjustment so the iron protrudes an even amount from the mouth. Tighten the lever cap screw once the iron is set.

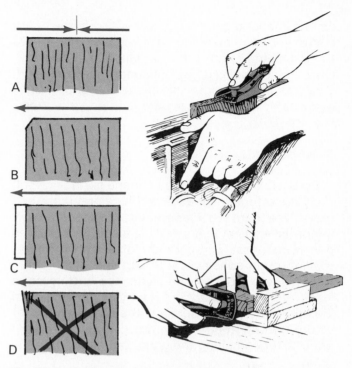

Fig. 24-9. A—Plane from both sides. B—Plane to a bevel. C—Plane over a piece of excess. D—Planing off the end will damage the edge.

Fig. 24-8. Hold a block plane in the palm of your hand.

There are several ways to plane end grain properly, Fig. 24-9. You can work both ways from the edges to the center, Fig. 24-9A. If you wish to plane in one direction, you should:

1. Plane a 45° bevel on one corner. Then plane from the opposite corner, Fig. 24-9B.
2. Clamp a piece of scrap material to the workpiece. Then plane across both the workpiece and excess, Fig. 24-9C.

Fig. 24-9D shows how a workpiece can splinter if you plane over the opposite edge.

SQUARING A BOARD WITH HAND PLANES

To square a board, you must first surface one face flat. Then check the flatness using the blade of a try square, Fig. 24-10A. Turn the board over and plane the other face. Again, check the flatness with a straightedge. Next, clamp the board in a vise and plane one edge. Check the squareness of your work with a try square, Fig. 24-10B. Then mark the width

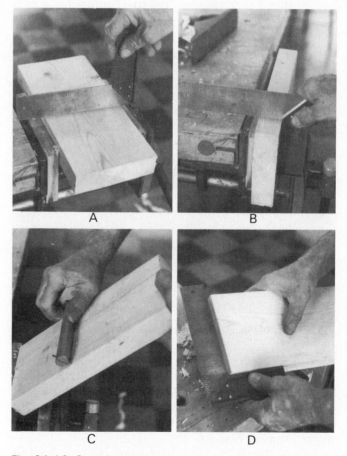

Fig. 24-10. Squaring a board by hand. A—Plane the face and make sure it is flat. B—Plane and edge and check for squareness. C—Mark the width of the workpiece and plane to it. D—Plane the end grain and check squareness.

using a marking gauge, Fig. 24-10C. Rip the board just beyond the marked width and plane the board to size, being careful not to plane past the mark. Once the faces and edges are done, square one end. Saw the board length and plane the end grain if necessary. Check the squareness of your work, Fig. 24-10D.

SCRAPERS

Scrapers are another type of hand surfacing tool. They are effective on edge and face grain, not end grain. Use them when another cutting tool has left minor defects in the surface. The scraper removes this roughness. Scrapers are also useful for removing dried adhesive from surfaces.

When you work with a plane, the cutting edge leads into the material. This is why reading the grain is important. With a scraper, the blade is in front of the cutting edge. Therefore you can scrape in either direction along the grain, but not across the grain.

Hand scraper

A *hand scraper* may be rectangular or contoured, Fig. 24-11. A rectangular scraper is best for flat surfaces. It is 2 1/2 to 3 in. (64 to 76 mm) wide and

Fig. 24-11. Hand scrapers may be rectangular or contoured. (The Fine Tool Shop)

5 to 6 in. (127 to 152 mm) long. The scraper's cutting edge appears to be square, but actually has a small, sharp burr. It is held in both hands at about a 75° angle, Fig. 24-12.

As you push or pull the scraper, a thin shaving should be cut from the surface. If you are removing only dust or chips, the tool is dull. Sharpening a scraper is discussed later in the chapter.

A

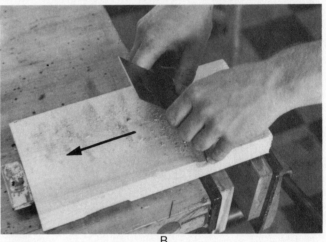
B

Fig. 24-12. A—Cabinet scrapers are an excellent tool for smoothing the surface of parquet surfaces. (Butler Specialty Co.) B—Scrape with blade leaning toward the direction of cut.

Cabinet scraper

A *cabinet scraper* looks like a hand scraper blade mounted rigidly in a handled body, Fig. 24-13. The *clamp screws* secure the blade at a 75° angle. The adjusting thumb screw changes the depth of cut. The edge itself is at a 45° angle, Fig. 24-14.

Scraping the surface is the final step before using abrasives. The cabinet scraper will remove chips, especially around knots. It also removes ridges made by a plane iron or surfacer knives.

To install the blade, turn the thumb screw back even with the body casting. Be sure that the clamp screws are loose. Hold the blade near the sharpened end. Slide the unsharpened end through the mouth from the bottom. The bevel on the cutting edge must face the adjusting thumb screw. Place the cabinet scraper on a flat wooden surface, Fig. 24-15. Press lightly against the top edge of the blade. Tighten the clamping thumb screws. Pick up the scraper and turn it over to inspect that neither blade corner extends out of the body. If one does, loosen the screws and correct the problem. While looking at the bottom of the body, turn the adjusting screw clockwise. The blade will bend slightly at the

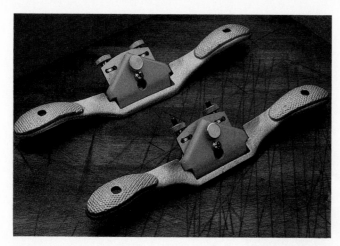

Fig. 24-13. Cabinet scrapers have a handle, clamp, blade, and adjusting screw. (The Fine Tool Shops)

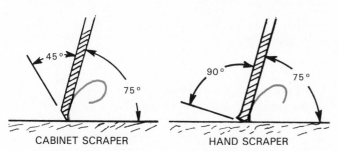

Fig. 24-14. Cabinet and hand scraper edges are shaped differently.

Fig. 24-15. Change depth of cut with the adjusting screw. (Stanley)

Fig. 24-16. Cabinet scrapers are easier to hold and use than hand scrapers.

75° mounting angle. This forces a center portion of the blade out of the body to set the depth of cut.

When using the cabinet scraper, place your thumbs on each side of the adjusting screw. Turn the tool slightly to one side or the other. Then the blade will be at an angle, making the scraper easier to push, Fig. 24-16.

THINK SAFETY—ACT SAFELY
WHEN SURFACING WITH HAND TOOLS

Surfacing with hand tools is a relatively safe operation. However, to reduce the chance of accidental injury, you should:
1. Wear eye protection.
2. Remove jewelry and secure loose clothing.
3. Have a safe, solid footing.
4. Clamp the material securely.
5. Keep both hands behind the cutting edge.
6. Remove shavings and chips that accumulate on the floor.

PORTABLE POWER PLANE SURFACING

Surfacing with portable power tools is quicker and easier than using hand tools. They can be moved from one work station to another.

The *portable power plane,* Fig. 24-17, serves the same purpose as the bench plane. You hold it by a knob at front and handle at the rear. The handle contains a trigger switch. The bottom of the plane is in two parts. The *front shoe* is adjustable up to a 3/32 in. (2.4 mm) depth of cut, much like the infeed table on a jointer. A *chip deflector* directs the chips away from the operator. A fence controls squaring and beveling. Use a T-bevel or square to position the fence.

Two styles of cutterheads are available. One is straight and one is helical, Fig. 24-18. The straight cutterhead works like the knives on a jointer or planer. The *helical cutterhead* cuts at a slight angle which reduces waviness and other planer marks.

Plane setup

Plane setup includes two adjustments: setting the depth of cut and positioning the fence. The procedure is as follows:
1. Disconnect power.
2. Move the depth adjusting lever to 0.
3. Turn the plane upside down.

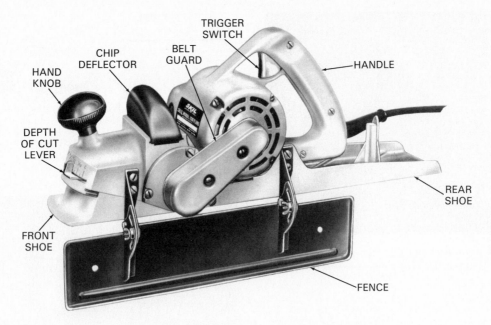

Fig. 24-17. Portable power plane.   (Skil)

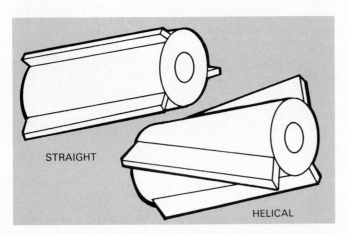

Fig. 24-18. Cutterheads for power planes are straight or helical.

4. Inspect the alignment of the front and rear shoes. A straightedge should remain flat across both. Check the service manual for proper adjustment procedures.
5. With the cutter depth at zero, the cutter should just touch the straightedge.
6. Adjust the fence, if it is to be used. Use a T-bevel or try square. Wing nuts usually hold the fence in place.

Planer operation

The procedure for using the portable power plane is as follows:
1. Adjust the depth of cut. The last cut made on a surface should be 1/32 in. or less. This will provide the smoothest surface.
2. Remove the fence if you will be planing a surface. Install and set the fence before planing an edge.

3. Place the front shoe of the plane on the workpiece. Make sure the cord is out of the way.
4. Start the motor and let it reach full speed.
5. Slowly slide the plane onto the surface. For edge planing and beveling, keep the fence snug against the face, Fig. 24-19.
6. Reduce pressure on the toe of the planer as you reach the end of the cut.
7. When finished, let the planer come to a stop. Then set the planer on its side to prevent damage to the blade.

Fig. 24-19. Portable power plane are useful for on-site architectural woodwork.   (Rockwell)

THINK SAFETY—ACT SAFELY
WHEN SURFACING WITH PORTABLE PLANES

Operating a power plane requires planning and concentration. You must determine your direction of cut. Also decide on a safe place to put the machine when you are finished. Follow these safety precautions.
1. Wear eye protection.
2. Remove jewelry and secure loose clothing.
3. Have a safe, clean, and solid footing.
4. Adjust fences and secure them properly.
5. Keep the cord away from the point of operation.
6. Be sure the cord is long enough for the length of cut.
7. Connect power to the machine only after the adjustments are made. Be sure the switch is in the off position when reconnecting power.
8. Operate the tool with your right hand on the handle. The chip chute will throw chips away from you.
9. Let the motor reach full speed before cutting.
10. Move the tool with constant pressure against the workpiece.
11. Set the machine out of your way when you are finished.

SHARPENING SURFACING TOOLS

The quality of any surfacing operation relies on the cabinetmaker's skill. It also depends on how the tools are maintained. Scrapers and planer blades must be sharpened regularly to cut properly.

SHARPENING PLANE IRONS

Plane irons can be honed or ground and honed. Honing restores the edge. Grinding puts a new bevel on the plane iron.

Honing
Plane irons can be honed several times before grinding is needed. Apply a small amount of oil to a medium grade oilstone. Place the bevel of the plane iron on the stone, then raise the back end up about 5° so just the cutting edge rests on the stone, Fig. 24-20A. (The plane iron will be about 30° to 35° from horizontal.) Move it in a small figure eight motion until you achieve a fine, wiry cutting edge. Then turn the plane iron over, lay it flat on the oilstone, and stroke several times, Fig. 24-20B. A wiry burr may remain on the honed cutting edge. This is removed by repeating the honing procedure on a fine hone.

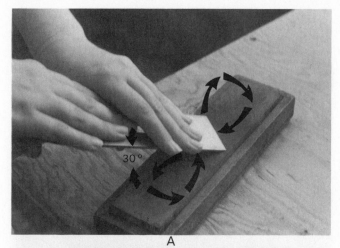

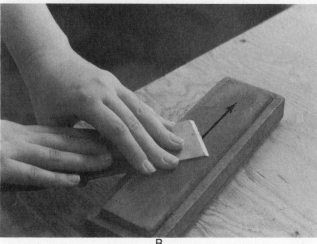

Fig. 24-20. A—Hone the cutting edge at an angle just greater than the bevel. B—Then hone several strokes on the flat side of the iron.

Grinding
After the plane iron bevel has been honed several times, the hollow grind becomes flattened. Grinding is then needed. A bench grinder and sharpening fixture is used to grind plane irons, Fig. 24-21. Holding the knife by hand is not recommended. Clamp the plane iron in the fixture so that the bevel you grind will be two and one-half times the thickness of the plane iron. For example, a standard 1/8 in. plane iron will have a 5/16 in. bevel. The final bevel angle should be about 25°. See Fig. 24-22.

Make a light cut across the grinding wheel and check the angle. If it is correct, continue grinding with light pressure. Move the plane iron back and forth across the wheel. The cutting edge should not turn blue. This indicates overheating. Dip the plane iron frequently in water to cool it.

Grind the outside corners so they will be slightly rounded (about 1/64 in. less than the center). This prevents gouge marks when using the plane. Continue grinding until the edge is thin and a slight burr forms.

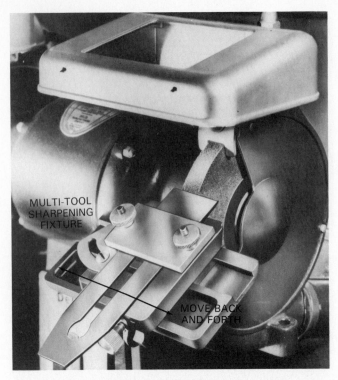

Fig. 24-21. Place the iron in the grinding fixture at the proper angle. (Rockwell International)

SHARPENING HAND SCRAPERS

Scrapers are sharpened differently than most hand tools. The scraper is first filed square. Then a burnisher is used to bend the edge into cutting position.

The procedure to sharpen a hand scraper, Fig. 24-23, is:

1. Clamp the blade in a vise with the cutting edge up.

2. File the edge straight and square.
3. Burnish both edges. Bend the metal with a series of burnisher strokes. Place the burnisher flat on the edge for one or two strokes. Then tilt the handle down about 5° each way with several strokes to bend the corners.
4. Test the scraper on a surface.

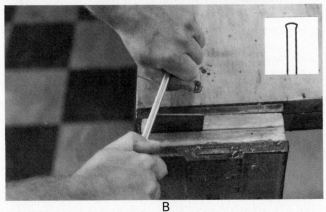

Fig. 24-23. A—File a hand scraper blade square. B—Then burnish the edge.

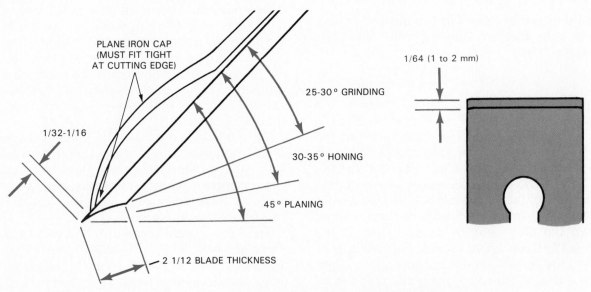

Fig. 24-22. Honing, grinding, and planing angles of the plane iron.

PLANE IRON CAP (MUST FIT TIGHT AT CUTTING EDGE)

25-30° GRINDING

30-35° HONING

45° PLANING

1/32-1/16

2 1/12 BLADE THICKNESS

1/64 (1 to 2 mm)

SHARPENING CABINET SCRAPER BLADES

Cabinet scraper blades differ from hand scrapers. The blade is narrower and the edge is filed to a 45° angle. The procedure to sharpen the cabinet scraper blade, as shown in Fig. 24-24, is as follows:

1. Clamp the blade in a vise with the cutting edge up.
2. File the edge straight, at a 45° angle, Fig. 24-24A.
3. Remove the blade from the vise and hone the 45° bevel and flat face, Fig. 24-24B. First use a medium grit stone, then a fine one.
4. Replace the blade in the vise.
5. Burnish the edge several strokes. Start at a 45° angle. Change the angle on successive strokes until you reach about 75°, Fig. 24-24C.
6. Remove the blade from the vise, inspect, and install it in the handle.

MAINTAINING PORTABLE POWER PLANES

Portable power tools operate much like stationary surfacing machinery. Therefore, you must check lubricants, motor brushes, and belts regularly. Tools with sealed bearings require little, if any, lubrication. Carbon brushes on the motor should be inspected for wear at regular intervals. Check drive belts for wear, cracks, and other damage.

Power plane cutters are helical or straight. Most are hardened steel and can be sharpened. Carbide tipped cutters must be sharpened by a technician.

Some portable power planes with helical cutters have a grinding attachment on one side, Fig. 24-25. A small grinding wheel fits in the chuck on the motor shaft. The cutter is placed in the side accessory when the machine is off. Then, with the machine on, rotate the cutter by hand against the grinding wheel.

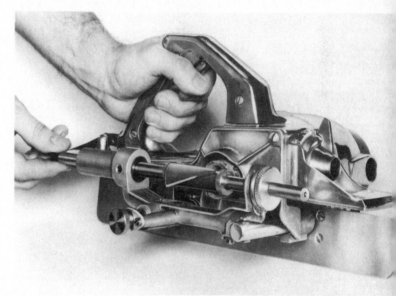

Fig. 24-25. Some portable power planes have a grinding attachment. The stone is attached to the motor. The cutter is held in a fixture on the side of the plane.
(Delta International Machinery Corp.)

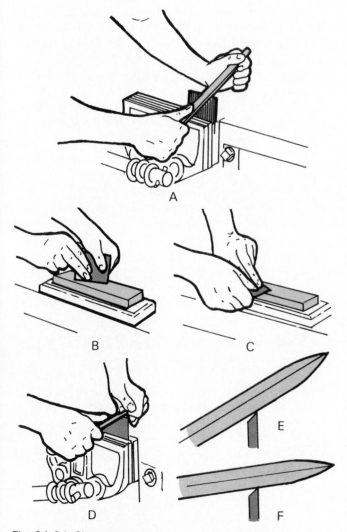

Fig. 24-24. Sharpening a cabinet scraper blade. A—File a 45° bevel. B—Hone the bevel. C—Hone the flat side to remove the wiry edge. D—Burnish with a few firm strokes. E—The first stroke should be at a 45° angle. F—The last stroke should be at a 75° angle. (Stanley)

To remove the cutter for sharpening, you will have to disassemble part of the power plate. First disconnect power to the tool. Then remove any covers or guards over the cutterhead. To remove the cutter, you must hold the shaft stationary and remove the nut holding the cutter. Some planes have a shaft lock. On others, you must use two wrenches.

After reassembling the plane, inspect the angle on the rear shoe. Both front and rear shoes should be parallel when the depth of cut is at zero. If not, follow the manufacturer's procedure for adjusting them.

SUMMARY

Although most surfacing is done with jointers and planers, hand tools are useful for small cabinet parts and on-site architectural woodwork. Jack, fore, jointer, and smooth planes surface edges and faces. Block planes are used to surface end grain. Scrapers will remove excess glue and minor surface defects often caused by surfacing machines. Portable power planes make the work much easier. They can be used for face, edge, and end grain.

Surfacing tools and machines will serve you best when they are properly maintained. Periodically check for blade sharpness, rust, needed lubrication, and other items recommended in the manufacturer's operation and maintenance manuals.

CABINETMAKING TERMS

Bench planes, jack plane, fore plane, jointer plane, smooth plane, plane iron, mouth, frog, adjusting nut, Y lever, lateral adjusting lever, plane iron cap, cap screw, lever cap, block plane, hand scraper, cabinet scraper, adjusting thumb screw, portable power plane, helical cutterhead, power block plane.

TEST YOUR KNOWLEDGE

1. Describe two situations in which you would choose a hand plane over a stationary surfacing machine.
2. Of bench planes, the _____ plane is the longest and the _____ plane is the shortest.
3. The most used bench plane is the _____ plane.
4. Name the adjustment which determines how much of the plane iron protrudes out of the mouth.
5. The plane iron cap should be within _____ in. of the cutting edge of the plane iron.
6. When surfacing a face, should you stroke with or against the grain?
7. Explain how you can use a plane to remove a cup in the face of a board.
8. List three methods of planing end grain without splintering the edge.
9. File the edge of cabinet scraper blades at a _____ ° angle before burnishing.
10. The two types of cutterheads available on power planes are _____ and _____.
11. Plane irons are ground at a _____ ° angle.
12. Plane irons are honed at a _____ ° angle.
13. The process of pulling the plane iron across a strip of leather to remove the burr is called _____.
14. List the steps taken to square a board using hand planes.
15. The front and rear shoes of a power plane should be _____ when the depth adjustment is set at zero.

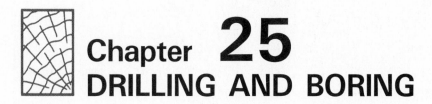

Chapter 25
DRILLING AND BORING

After studying this chapter, you will be able to:
☐ Select drills and bits based on the hole to be made.
☐ Operate hand, portable, and stationary drilling equipment.
☐ Follow procedures for drilling through and blind holes, holes at an angle, and flat or cylindrical workpieces.
☐ Sharpen drills, bits, and cutters.
☐ Maintain hand and power drilling equipment.

Drilling and boring are holemaking processes as basic to cabinetmaking as sawing and surfacing. Holes are necessary for installing hardware, making joints, and producing various cabinet design features.

As a rule, drilling refers to making holes smaller than 1/4 in. with twist drills and drill points. Boring describes making larger holes with different types of boring bits. The type of drill or bit you choose depends on the hole to be made, Fig. 25-1. What diameter and how accurate must the hole be? Will it be a flat bottom hole bored part way into the workpiece? How smooth should the hole surface be? In addition, bit type, wood species, or manufactured panel composition also will affect the hole's surface. (See Fig. 12-45.) These are all important considerations when you select a drilling tool.

Drills and bits may be made of carbon steel, high speed steel, or be carbide tipped. Carbon steel bits are the least expensive. They are weaker than other bits, and should be limited to drilling wood, plastic and aluminum. Bits marked HS (High Speed) or HSS (High Speed Steel) are more durable than carbon bits and will cut through most materials. (However, the design of some HS bits limits them to boring wood only.) Carbide-tipped bits drill through hard materials, such as ceramic tile and concrete. High speed drills and bits are the most cost-effective for cabinetmaking.

Drilling is done with hand tools, portable power drills, and stationary machines. The end shape of the bit determines whether it can be used in a particular tool. Bits with round shanks are inserted into drilling tools that have three-jaw chucks. Three

or six flat surfaces ground into the shank hold a bit more securely. Square, tapered ends of auger bits limit their use to a hand brace.

Certain operating speeds are recommended for drills and bits, Fig. 25-2. Drilling at the correct speed, with the proper feed, will produce the best results. A high speed or an incorrect feed rate will cause the bit to heat up, which can damage the tool permanently.

AUGER BIT

Auger bits, Fig. 25-3, produce holes in face and edge grain, but are not effective in end grain. Auger bits have two sharpened cutting lips and spurs. The spurs score the wood before the cutting lips remove chips. A threaded feed screw pulls the bit into the workpiece. The twist carries chips out of the hole. The tapered square tang is secured in a brace chuck. The combined length of the twist and the shank determines the maximum hole depth. That may be 7 in. to 10 in. (175 mm to 250 mm).

Fig. 25-1. Select the correct bit and drilling tool for making precise holes. (Rockwell)

H = HAND TOOL   S = STATIONARY POWER   P = PORTABLE POWER

TOOL NAME	DRILLING PRACTICE	MAX. NO-LOAD MACHINE SPEEDS (R.P.M.)	
		Stationary	Portable
AUGER BIT	H,S,P	1000	1000
EXPANSIVE BIT	H,S	300 to 150*	
TWIST DRILL — WOOD 1/16'' TO 1/2'' HS	H,S,P	6000 TO 2000*	2800 TO 1000*
TWIST DRILL — WOOD 1/16'' TO 1/2'' CARBON	H,S,P	3000 TO 1000*	2000 TO 600*
TWIST DRILL — STEEL 1/16'' TO 1/2'' HS	H,S,P	3000 TO 600*	2000 TO 600*
TWIST DRILL — STEEL 1/16'' TO 1/2'' CARBON	H,S,P	1500 TO 300*	1000 TO 450*
SPADE BIT 1/4'' TO 1 1/2''	S,P	3000	2000
SPUR BIT	S,P	3000	2000
MULTISPUR BIT 1'' TO 5''	S	600 TO 200	
FORSTNER BIT 1/4'' TO 4''	H,S	2000 TO 150	
POWER BORE BIT®	S,P	2000	2000
DRILL POINT	H		
CIRCLE CUTTER	S	250	
ADJUSTABLE DIAL SAW	S	250	
HOLE SAW 1'' TO 5''	S,P	600 TO 150*	600 TO 150*
COUNTERSINK	H,S,P	3000	2000
SCREW MATE®	H,S,P	3000	2000
PLUG CUTTER	S	3000	
COUNTERSINK	S,P	SEE TWIST DRILL SPEEDS	
COUNTERBORE			
MASONRY AND GLASS DRILL	S,P	600	600

A

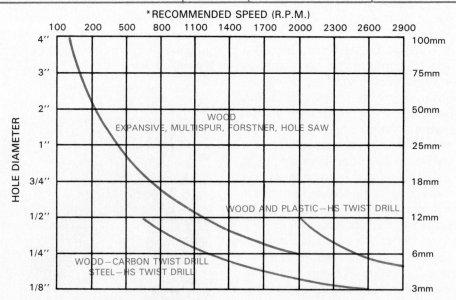

Fig. 25-2. A—Use proper speeds when drilling. B—Safe drilling speeds vary by bit size.

When using an auger bit, you must drill the proper size hole the first time. You cannot enlarge it with another auger bit. To counterbore a hole with an auger bit, drill the larger hole first. Then continue with a smaller bit.

Auger bits are sized by two systems: U.S. customary and SI (System International) metric. Auger bits come in sets of 13. Customary sizes are numbered 4 to 16. Metric sets are sized from 6 mm to 25 mm. The size is stamped on the tang or shank.

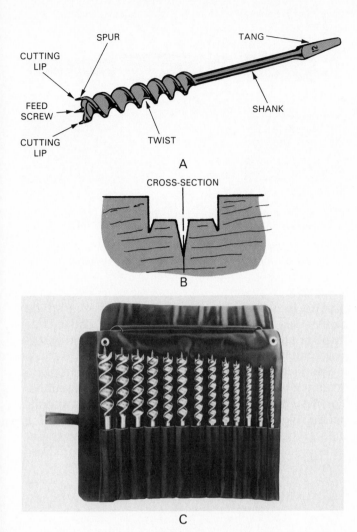

Fig. 25-3. A—Parts of an auger bit. B—Section view of hole created by auger bit. C—Bits come in sets of 13. (Stanley Tools)

Only a single number appears. The number is the increments in 16ths of an inch. Thus a 4 indicates 4/16 in., or 1/4 in. A number 16 would label a 16/16 in., or 1 in. bit.

The tapered square tang limits the use of auger bits. They can only be held in a brace. However, some auger bits can be modified to work in three jaw chucks found on hand drills as well as portable and stationary power drills. If the shank has three or six flat surfaces, you can saw off the tang, Fig. 25-4.

Auger bits are slow speed bits. Most often they are used in a hand brace. When used in power equipment, drilling speeds must be kept between 300 to 800 rpm.

A dowel bit looks much like a short auger bit. It is about 5 in. long. There are three diameter sizes: 1/4 in., 3/8 in., and 1/2 in. The dowel bit diameter is .003 in. (.08 mm) over the marked size. Auger bits are about .015 in. (.4 mm) oversize. The close tolerance of dowel bits makes them more suitable for drilling holes for dowel joints.

Fig. 25-4. Auger bit shanks have a tang fit in a brace. The tang can be sawed off so the bit can be used in power drills. (Irwin)

EXPANSIVE BIT

An *expansive bit,* Fig. 25-5, is an adjustable auger bit. The feed screw helps pull the bit into the workpiece. One cutting lip is located on the body just above the feed screw. The other is on the adjustable cutter. The cutter also has spurs to score the wood before removing material.

Expansive bits adjust from 5/8 in. to 3 in. Metric sizes are also available. Adjust the hole diameter according to the index mark and scale printed on the adjustable cutter.

Some expansive bits may have a round shank instead of a tang. These may be used in drill presses at a very slow speed, about 300 rpm.

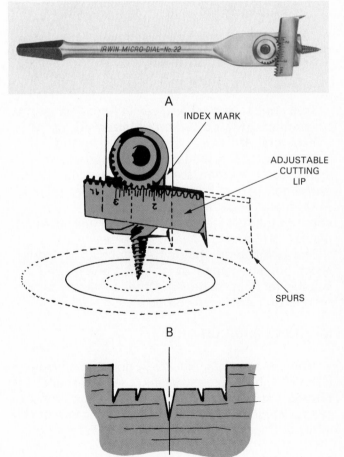

Fig. 25-5. A—Expansive bit. B—Adjust the bit's lip and spur to vary hole sizes. (Irwin) C—Section view of hole created by an expansive bit.

TWIST DRILL

The *twist drill,* also sometimes called a *twist drill bit,* is shown in Fig. 25-6. It has a round, straight shank. At the end of the bit are two sharp cutting lips. Flutes carry wood chips away from the point of operation.

The shank may or may not be the same size as the flutes. If not, common shank sizes will likely be 1/4 in., 3/8 in., or 1/2 in. Large bits with small shanks can fit into portable power drills.

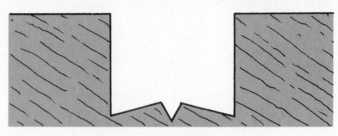

Fig. 25-7. Machine spur bit with a reduced shank to fit in smaller portable drill chucks. (Brookstone)

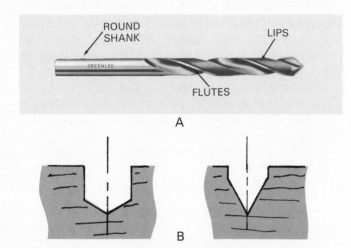

Fig. 25-6. A—Twist drills have round shanks, flutes, and two cutting lips. (Greenlee) B—Section view of holes created by twist drills.

Twist drill sizes may be given in fractions, letters, or numbers. Metric twist drill sizes are noted in millimeters.

Twist drills are made of either carbon or high speed steel. Carbon steel drills are adequate for wood and soft metals. High speed twist drills remain sharp longer and are less likely to bend. You can turn them at faster speeds when drilling wood, plastic, and steel.

The point angle may differ among twist drills. Most are sharpened at a 118° angle, and are suitable for many materials. Other angles are recommended for drilling wood or plastic.

MACHINE SPUR BIT

Machine spur bits, Fig. 25-7, drill a flat bottomed hole. They have a round shank, two flutes, and two cutting lips. Spurs at the end score the wood to reduce chipping. A short brad point centers the bit while drilling. Bit sizes range from 3/16 to 1 1/4 in.

SPADE BIT

A spade bit is flat with a fairly long brad point to center it, Fig. 25-8A. The spade has cutting lips

ground into the bottom. The width of the spade determines the hole diameter. The shank usually has three or six flat surfaces which hold better in three-jaw chucks.

Spade bits do not produce the most accurate holes. However they are inexpensive and adaptable. You may grind the sides or cutting edges for special needs, Fig. 25-8B. For example, you could drill a tapered hole by grinding the edges of the spade at an angle. You can also create a round bottom hole

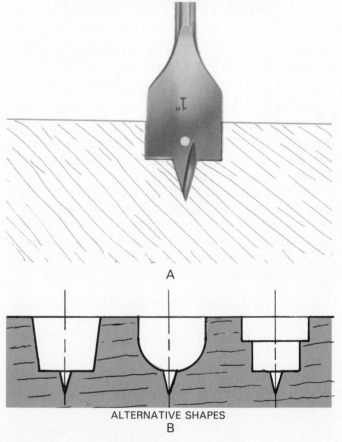

ALTERNATIVE SHAPES
B

Fig. 25-8. A—Spade bit. (Irwin) B—The spade can be ground to create different hole shapes.

by grinding a curved cutting edge. By grinding the spade at two different widths, you can counterbore a hole.

MULTISPUR BIT

The *multispur bit*, Fig. 25-9, looks somewhat like a saw. A series of sawtooth spurs surround a brad point. There is one cutting lip between the point and spurs. This serves as a chip breaker. The tool has a standard 1/2 in. shank. This style of bit drills flat bottomed holes from 1/2 to 4 in. (13 to 100 mm) in diameter. There are 37 different sizes available.

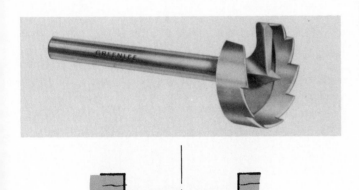

Fig. 25-9. Multispur bit. (Greenlee)

FORSTNER BIT

The *Forstner bit* is a high quality tool used to drill flat bottomed holes, Fig. 25-10A. The circumference of a Forstner bit is smooth, but very sharp. One or two cutting lips are located at the bottom. A small brad point helps center the bit before boring. Once the hole is started, the sharp circumference guides the tool.

A Forstner bit creates a very smooth hole surface. It is especially effective when drilling blind holes. (They do not go all the way through the workpiece.) Forstner bits are also very sturdy. The brad does not have to be used to center the bit. Fig. 25-10B shows angled holes and holes in an edge of the workpiece.

Bit sizes range from 3/8 in. to 3 in. (10 to 75 mm). Shank sizes are usually 1/2 in. because the bit is used in a drill press. However, 3/8 in. shanks are also available.

POWER BORE BIT

The *power bore bit,* Fig. 25-11, functions much like spade and multispur bits. It has a 1/4 in. shank,

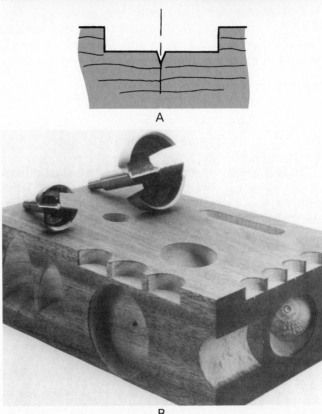

Fig. 25-10. A—Forstner bits drill flat bottomed holes. (Connecticut Valley Manufacturing) B—Because its circumference guides the bit, you can bore at any angle. (The Fine Tool Shops)

one brad point, one spur, and one cutting lip. Bit diameters range from 3/8 in. to 1 in. (10 to 25 mm).

The design of the power bore bit is to lessen friction between the bit and the wood. Forstner and multispur bits have smooth sides which slightly rub the wood. The power bore bit has little surface contact with the wood.

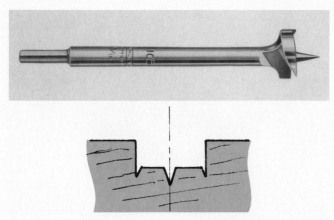

Fig. 25-11. A power bore bit is easier to control than a spade bit. (Stanley)

DRILL POINTS

Drill points are used with the push drill, Fig. 25-12. They have straight flutes with two cutting lips sharpened like a twist drill. Drill points are effective for drilling pilot holes for screws or nails.

CIRCLE CUTTER

A *circle cutter,* Fig. 25-13, can create large holes through a workpiece. The material removed is wheel-shaped.

To drill, set the desired radius. It is adjustable from 1 3/4 to 8 in. (44 to 200 mm) diameter. Then tighten the cutter with a screwdriver or Allen wrench. Use this bit only in a drill press at a maximum speed of 250 rpm.

Adjustable dial saw

The *adjustable dial saw,* Fig. 25-14, is like the circle cutter. It has a center guide drill with three

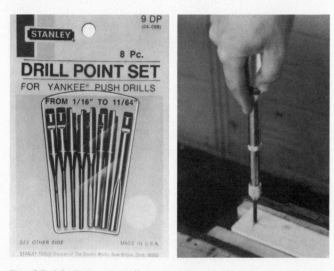

Fig. 25-12. Drill points fit in a push drill. They make holes for screws, brads, and other purposes. (Stanley)

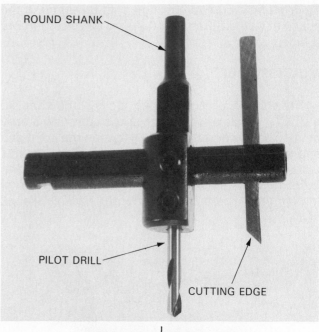

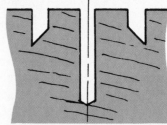

Fig. 25-13. Circle cutters produce holes up to 8 in. in diameter. Use them in a drill press. (General Manufacturing)

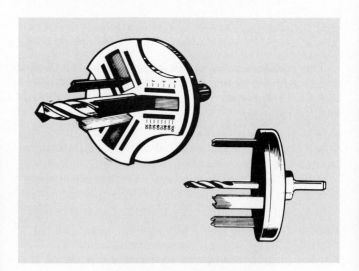

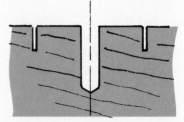

Fig. 25-14. The adjustable dial saw has a center drill and three cutter arms. Use them in a drill press. (Brodhead-Garrett)

surrounding arms. Each arm has two saw teeth. Set the diameter according to the dial index. Then tighten the hex nut on the top. The dial saw is a slow speed tool. Use it in a drill press at 250 rpm.

HOLE SAW

A sturdier tool than the dial saw is the *hole saw,* Fig. 25-15. It has a guide drill. The circumference is a series of saw teeth. A different saw tooth insert is necessary for each diameter. These are attached to a common size shank.

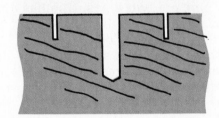

Fig. 25-15. Hole saws. (The L.S. Starrett Co.)

COUNTERSINK BIT

The *countersink bit* angles hole tops which allows flat head screws to set flush. One end is an 82° V-shaped point with several cutting lips. The other end is a square tang or round shank, Fig. 25-16. Even though metric screw heads are formed at a 90° angle, the 82° countersink works equally well.

MULTIOPERATIONAL BITS

Multioperational bits include *screw-mate drills* (see Fig. 16-30) and *countersink/counterbore cutters,* Fig. 25-17. Screw-mates drill pilot holes and clearance holes for wood screws. Countersink/

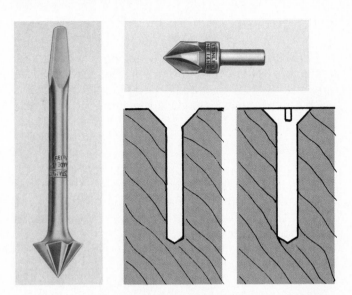

Fig. 25-16. Countersinks angle the end of a hole to accept flat head screws. (Stanley)

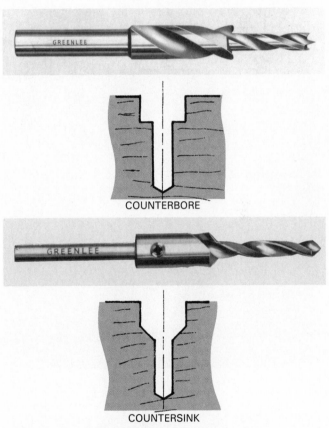

Fig. 25-17. Counterbore bits drill two size holes at one time. Multioperation countersinks drill clearance, countersink, and possibly counterbore holes. (Greenlee)

counterbore cutters drill, countersink, and/or counterbore at the same time. Countersinks leave the bottom of the hole at 82°. Counterbore cutters leave a square (90°) shoulder. Use this if you want a nut and washer or round head screw below the surface.

PLUG CUTTER

Plug cutters make plugs to cover mechanic fasteners in counterbored holes, Fig. 25-18. Sizes are 3/8 in., 1/2 in., and 5/8 in. Counterbore holes with one of these sizes. Use the same wood specie as your cabinet for the plug.

STAR DRILL

A *star drill* makes holes in concrete for cabinet installations, Fig. 25-19A. Typical diameters are 1/4 in. to 1 in. Tool lengths vary. Power star drills fit in hammer drills.

MASONRY DRILL

Masonry drills have carbide tips. They drill holes in concrete and ceramic materials, Fig. 25-19B. Use a masonry drill to make holes for screw anchors to install cabinetry to concrete walls. Also drill ceramic tile surfaces with masonry drills. Diameters range from 1/4 in. to 3/4 in.

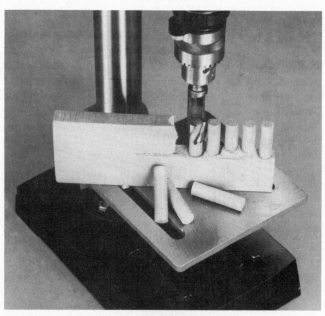

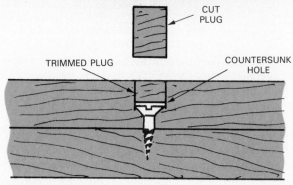

Fig. 25-18. Make plugs to cover counterbores. Make sure to match workpiece grain. (Delta)

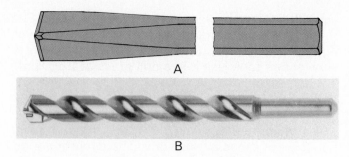

Fig. 25-19. A—Star drill. B—Masonry drill.
(Vermont American Tool Co.)

GLASS DRILL

Glass can be drilled with a spear-shaped, carbide-tipped *glass drill,* Fig. 25-20. Various sizes are available for drilling holes to mount hardware.

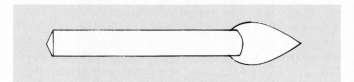

Fig. 25-20. Glass drill.

BELL HANGER'S DRILL

Drill extra long holes with a *bell hanger's drill,* Fig. 25-21. There are two types. One has a tang and is used in a brace. The other has a round shank for a drill press or portable drill.

Bell hanger's drills are sized from 1/4 in. to 3/4 in. in diameter. Shank sizes vary from 1/4 in. to 3/8 in. Lengths are 12 in., 18 in., 24 in., and 30 in. Some are available with carbide tips to drill in concrete.

DRILL EXTENSIONS

Drill extensions allow you to make long holes with standard drills and bits, Fig. 25-22. These extensions are 18 in. long. The shank may be round or six-sided for a portable power drill. Do not use drill extensions in a drill press.

HAND TOOLS FOR DRILLING

Drilling by hand is done with braces, hand drills, and push drills.

BRACE

A *brace,* Fig. 25-23, holds only square tang bits. Turning the chuck tightens two angled jaws which

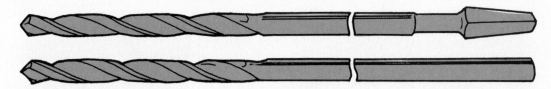

Fig. 25-21. Bell hanger's drills are 18 in. long. Some have a straight shank and others have a tang.

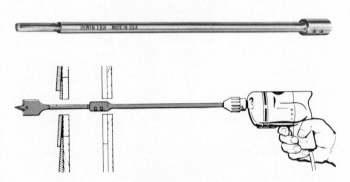

Fig. 25-22. Portable power drill extensions lengthen your drill bits reach. (Irwin)

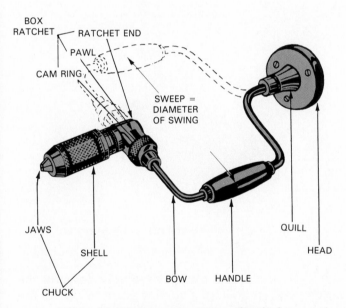

Fig. 25-23. Parts of a brace. (Stanley)

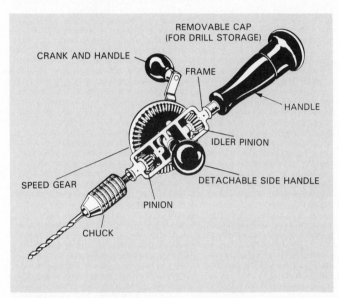

Fig. 25-24. A hand drill is satifactory for making holes up to 3/8 in. (10 mm). (Stanley)

grasp the tang. The sweep of the brace's bow determines the size of the brace. Sweep is the diameter of the circle made as you rotate the handle. A box ratchet on the chuck allows you to drill next to a wall or corner without a full circle swing.

HAND DRILL

A *hand drill,* Fig. 25-24, holds round shank twist drills in a three-jaw chuck. A crank and handle rotate the chuck while the top handle is held securely to steady the tool. Some have storage for drill bits inside the handle.

PUSH DRILL

A *push drill,* Fig. 25-25, is operated with one hand. A spring mechanism turns the chuck as you push on the drill. Drill points are used with the push drill for making small holes, such as pilot holes for screws. To change points, press the locking ring so the knurled chuck slides down. The point can then be inserted. Some models store points in the handle.

STATIONARY POWER MACHINES FOR DRILLING

Nearly all production and custom cabinetmaking shops use stationary power drills. Even the home woodworker is likely to have a floor or bench model drill press. It is more accurate than hand and portable drills.

DRILL PRESS

The *drill press* is the most common vertical stationary power drill used by cabinetmakers, Fig. 25-26. The *table* clamps to the *column* and slides up or down as needed. It can also tilt for drilling at an angle. The motor drives the spindle and chuck. Change drilling speed by moving belts on motor and spindle step pulleys or turn a *variable rate handwheel.*

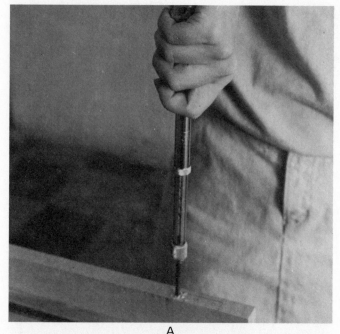

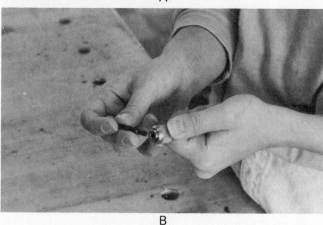

Fig. 25-25. A—Push drills are very efficient for drilling small holes. B—Insert bits in the push drill by pushing the knurled chuck forward.

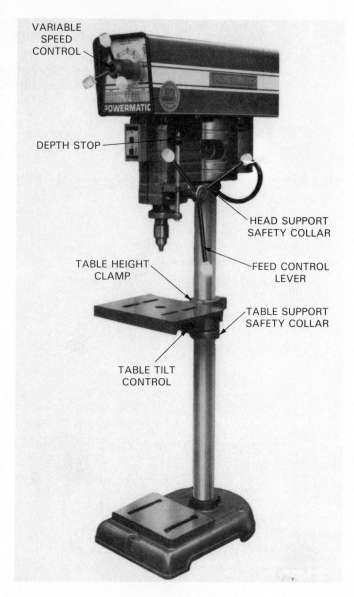

VARIABLE
SPEED
CONTROL

DEPTH STOP

HEAD SUPPORT
SAFETY COLLAR

FEED CONTROL
LEVER

TABLE HEIGHT
CLAMP

TABLE SUPPORT
SAFETY COLLAR

TABLE TILT
CONTROL

Fig. 25-26. Vertical drill press. (Powermatic)

Drill presses are specified by the distance between the chuck and the column, multiplied by two. For example, a 20 in. drill press has a distance of 10 in. between the chuck and column. It can drill a hole in the center of a 20 in. diameter circular workpiece.

Bits are clamped in the chuck and fed into the workpiece with the feed control lever. Most drill presses have a 1/2 in. shank capacity chuck. The spindle's depth of travel can be limited using the depth stop.

RADIAL ARM SAW

The versatility of the radial arm saw makes it a drilling machine, Fig. 25-27. Thread a chuck on the motor arbor and place the workpiece against the fence. The yoke clamping levers and scales align

the drill. Push the motor assembly toward the column when drilling. You may want to clamp the workpiece to the fence when drilling at angles other than 90° to the fence.

PORTABLE POWER TOOLS FOR DRILLING

Portable power tools are the quickest way to make holes. Although not as accurate as stationary drills, they take little setup time and are flexible. A portable drill can often fit in enclosed spaces and tight corners.

PORTABLE POWER DRILL

The *portable power drill* is the most used portable drilling tool. There are many types and shapes, Fig. 25-28. Some are light and require only one hand

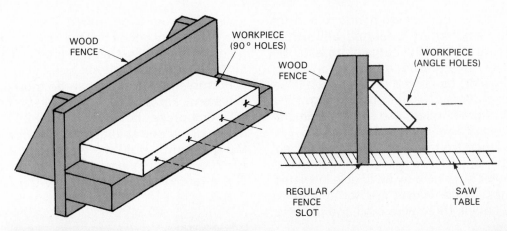

Fig. 25-27. The versatile radial arm saw can be used as a horizontal boring machine. Make attachments which clamp to the table. These hold the workpiece at the proper angle. (DeWalt)

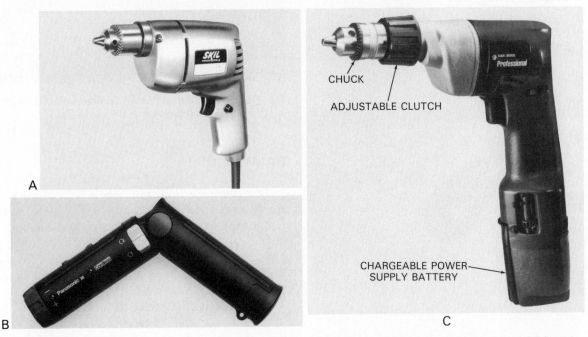

Fig. 25-28. A—Portable power drill. (Skil) B—Cordless drill and power screwdriver. It can bend to 90° angles. (Panasonic) C—This battery operated drill has an adjustable, five position clutch for matching drill torque to workpiece. This prevents it from stripping screws when using a screw bit. (Black & Decker)

for operation. Others require two hands to control the drill. A cordless battery operated drill offers added flexibility. An overnight charge often lasts the entire work day. Have a second battery charging just in case. Smaller, hand-held drills are available for power screwdrivers and light duty drilling. (See Fig. 16-23.) For tight corners, use a *right angle drill* or a *right angle head* on a standard drill, Fig. 25-29.

Motor sizes range from 1/7 to 2/5 horsepower. Using a light duty drill for heavy work may burn out the motor. The drill housing may be double insulated to prevent shock. Those which are not double insulated should have a three wire cord and grounded plug.

Drills are one, dual, or variable speed. Variable speeds allow you to start holes at a slow speed and then drill through at a high speed. Some are reversible so you can back out the bit or unscrew fasteners. A trigger switch lock maintains the speed when you remove your finger. However, this can be dangerous if the bit binds. The bit stops, but the drill will still try to turn.

Chuck sizes range from 1/4 to 1/2 in. (6 to 12 mm). You may need to use a large diameter bit with a power drill having a small chuck. Then choose a bit with a reduced shank size.

Portable power drills can be mounted vertically in a stand, Fig. 25-30. This setup is not as accurate as a drill press; however, it is reliable and convenient. Use a portable drill with a trigger lock. Lock the drill "on." Hold the workpiece with one hand and operate the feed lever with the other. After drilling, a return spring helps raise the drill.

Fig. 25-30. A drill press stand converts a portable drill into a drill press. (Makita, U.S.A.)

HAMMER DRILL

The *hammer drill,* Fig. 25-31, hammers on and turns masonry bits to make holes in concrete. Cabinetmakers use this tool when setting screw anchors for hanging cabinets on concrete walls. Masonry bits will also work with standard portable drills, but using the hammer drill is quicker.

DRILLING AND BORING HOLES WITH HAND TOOLS

Select the proper drilling tool for the bit you wish to use. For inserting bits in a brace, unscrew the

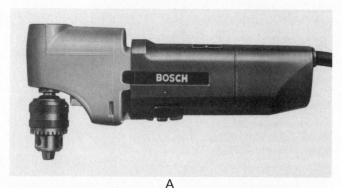

A

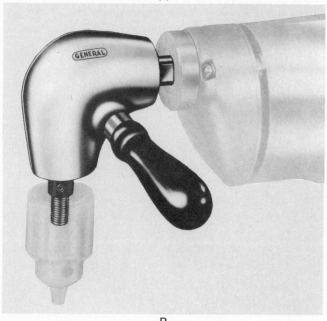

B

Fig. 25-29. A—Right angle drill. (Bosch) B—Right angle drive for power drill. (General Manufacturing)

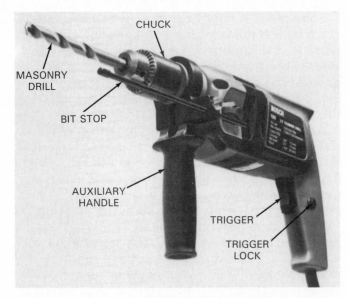

Fig. 25-31. Hammer drills create holes in concrete for basement cabinet installations. (Bosch)

Secure workpieces in a vise or with clamps when drilling large holes or holes at angles. Vise jaws covered with wood blocks are recommended, Fig. 25-33A. This reduces damage to the workpiece when tightening the vise. Flat workpieces can be held between the vise and a bench stop. Hold or clamp cylindrical workpieces in a V-block or V-shaped grooves in the vise, Fig. 25-33B.

Keep the tool at the proper angle when boring. Use both hands, Fig. 25-34.

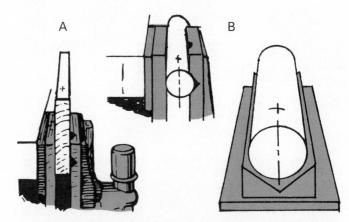

Fig. 25-33. Clamp or hold the workpiece securely when preparing to drill. (Stanley)

chuck shell and insert a bit with a tang. Turn the shell clockwise until the bit is snug, Fig. 25-32.

For a hand drill, select a straight shank drill or bit. One with three flats formed into the shank is less likely to turn in the chuck.

Fig. 25-32. For both a brace and hand drill, install the bit and tighten the chuck by hand.

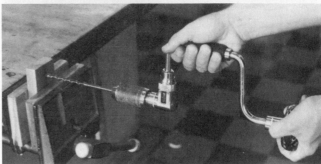

Fig. 25-34. Vertical and horizontal drilling with hand tools.

Before boring, use a scratch awl to make a small dent at the hole layout mark. This helps center the bit point. A try square or T-bevel can help keep the bit aligned.

If the hole will be drilled through the material, clamp a backing board under the workpiece. This prevents splintering when the bit cuts through the opposite face, Fig. 25-35.

Fig. 25-35. Back up your workpiece when drilling a through hole. Failure to do so may tear the wood.

A

B

Fig. 25-36. Boring a through hole by drilling from both sides. A—Bore until the feed screw breaks through the other side. B—Turn the workpiece around and bore the hole through.

Sometimes it is not convenient to place waste stock behind the workpiece when boring a through hole. In this situation, you must bore from both sides. Bore from one face until the feed screw or point of the bit breaks through the opposite face, Fig. 25-36A. Then complete the hole, boring from the other side, Fig. 25-36B.

A blind hole does not go through the workpiece. Use a *depth gauge, drill stop,* or tape to limit how far the bit enters the workpiece, Fig. 25-37. A depth gauge clamps onto the bit. A drill stop slips over the bit and is secured with a set screw. For less precise depth, wrap a few turns of masking or electrical tape around the bit.

To bore holes at an angle, first start the bit vertical. Once it penetrates the surface, tilt it to the required angle. Check your angle using a T-bevel. When multiple holes need to be drilled at an angle, make a boring jig. A simple jig is a block of wood with an angled hole. Clamp the jig to the workpiece and drill through the jig, Fig. 25-38.

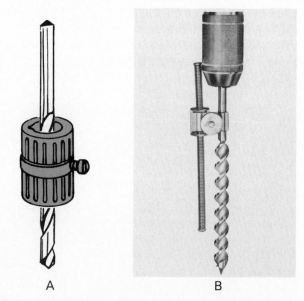

A   B

Fig. 25-37. Two attachments for determining depth. A—Depth gauge. (Stanley) B—Drill stop. (General Hardware)

Fig. 25-38. Angled holes can be accurately drilled with a jig.

DRILLING AND BORING WITH THE DRILL PRESS

The general procedure for drilling and boring with the drill press is as follows:

1. Set the drill press speed. A chart on the machine shows you how to move the belt on the pulleys to change speed. Drill speeds for certain bits and sizes are shown in Fig. 25-2A and 2B.
2. Insert the bit in the chuck. A chuck key is used to tighten the chuck. Remember to remove the chuck key before using the drill.

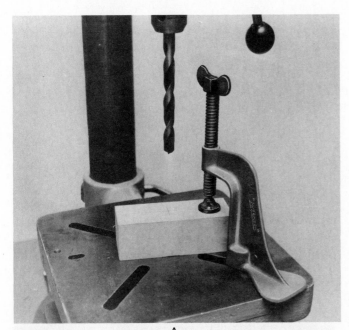

A

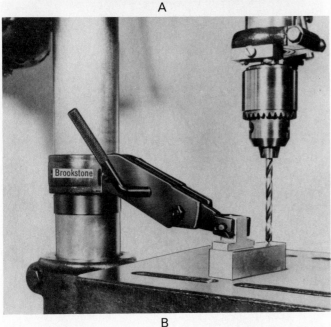

B

Fig. 25-39. Clamp the workpiece securely. A—Hold down clamp. (Adjustable Clamp Company) B—Quick clamp. (Brookstone Co.)

3. Clamp your workpiece to the table when drilling large holes, holes at an angle, or when using saw tooth and adjustable bits, Fig. 25-39. Lower the bit with the feed lever and align the tip with hole layout marks. Back workpieces if the hole is to be bored through.
4. Adjust the table. Move the table so the bit is 1/2 in. above your work. Support the table as you loosen the column clamp. The table is heavy and can injure you if it falls. When the table is positioned, retighten the clamp.
5. Turn on the motor.
6. Hold the workpiece tightly if it has not been clamped.
7. Turn the feed lever to lower the bit into the workpiece. Feed the bit in at a moderate rate. If you see dust instead of wood chips, you are feeding too slow or the bit is dull. In either case, heat is created which can dull the bit and/or burn the wood.
8. When the hole is through, raise the bit.

DRILLING DEEP HOLES

Often, deep holes are required. Bore first with a standard twist drill. Then use a bell hanger's drill of the same size. The length of spindle travel on the drill press is only about 6 in. You will need to raise the table after each feed.

Another method to bore deep holes is to bore from both ends. This can present problems when aligning the second hole. The first hole bored must be directly under the drill. To do this, you make a jig. The following procedure, as shown in Fig. 25-40, illustrates drilling a 3/8 in. (10 mm) hole through a lamp stand.

1. Cut a board the size of the drill press table. Drill a 1/4 in. hole in the center.
2. Insert a 3/8 in. dowel in the drill press chuck. It should be a few inches longer than the workpiece.
3. Put a 3/8 in. plug cutter with a 1/4 in. shank in the 1/4 in. jig hole.
4. Place the jig on the table just beneath the dowel.
5. Lower the dowel onto the plug cutter. Align the jig with the drill press chuck, Fig. 25-40A.
6. Remove the dowel and replace with a 3/8 in. twist drill.
7. Replace the plug cutter with a countersink.
8. Layout the centers of the workpiece ends and mark them with a scratch awl.
9. Position the lower end of the workpiece on the countersink, Fig. 25-40B.
10. Hold the workpiece firmly and turn on the machine. Lower the drill to align with the center of the upper end of the workpiece. Then drill as deep as possible.

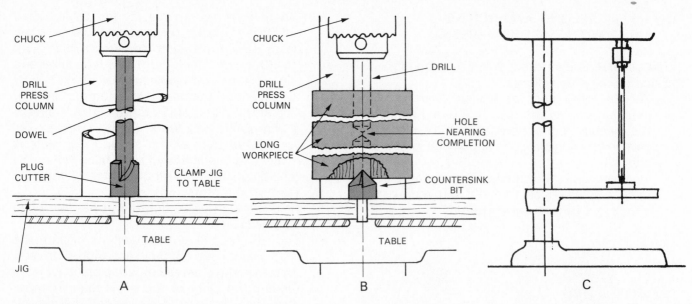

Fig. 25-40. Dowel and drill alignment are critical when drilling from both ends. A—Align a dowel in the chuck with a plug cutter in the jig. B—Insert the workpiece between the bit and a countersink bit inserted in the jig. C—As the hole nears completion, it should align precisely.

11. Raise the bit, turn the workpiece over, and drill from the other end, Fig. 25-40C.
12. For very long parts, insert a bell hanger's drill in the chuck after drilling from both ends to complete the hole.

DRILLING AT AN ANGLE

Drill holes at an angle by tilting the machine table or using a fixture. To tilt the table, loosen the tilt control and set the table using a T-bevel or protractor with a level, Fig. 25-41. Then tighten the tilt control. Clamp the workpiece with the hole mark centered under the bit. Then turn on the machine and make the hole, Fig. 25-42.

Fig. 25-41. Use a protractor with level to set the table angle.

Fig. 25-42. Drilling at an angle with a spade bit.

A tilt fixture has two boards, hinged at one side, with slides clamped to hold the top boards at an angle, Fig. 25-43. Clamp the bottom board to the table, Fig. 25-44. Set angles for both the fixtures using a protractor with level.

Installing the secondary table fixture on a tilted table is an added convenience. You are able to drill compound angles, Fig. 25-45.

Bits with long centerpoints and Forstner bits will enter the workpiece at an angle rather easily. Simply mark the hole using a scratch awl and bore the hole. Twist drills lack a long centerpoint. Therefore, they may tend to bend out of position when you start to drill. Small diameter drills can be damaged or broken. Feed carefully, or use another type of bit if you have a choice.

Fig. 25-45. Both the jig and table are tilted for compound angles.

Fig. 25-43. Fixture for drilling at an angle.

DRILLING BLIND HOLES

A blind hole does not go through the workpiece. Drill presses have an *adjustable scale* and *stop* to limit bit travel, Fig. 25-46. A *depth scale* shows how far you lower the spindle. However, it is best

Fig. 25-44. Raise the jig and tighten the slides.

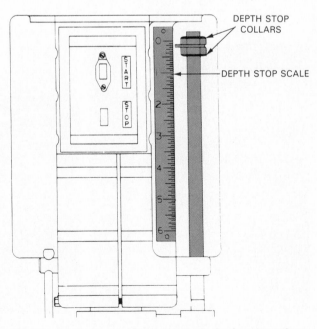

Fig. 25-46. Depth stop on drill press stops the feed lever from turning at preset depth. (Powermatic)

to not use the scale because of different bit lengths and table heights. The scale reading can be inaccurate. Instead, mark the depth on the edge of the workpiece. Then lower the bit beside the workpiece until the cutting lips are in line with the mark, Fig. 25-47. Turn the two threaded depth collars until they stop. While drilling, the feed lever will not move past the preset depth.

You can also use a depth gauge, bit stop, or tape to mark how far the bit should enter the workpiece. A depth gauge clamps onto the bit. A bit stop slips over the bit and is secured with a set screw. (See Fig. 25-37.)

DRILLING ROUND WORKPIECES

Round workpieces should be held in a *V-block*. The V must be centered under the drill. If drilling at an angle, clamp the workpiece to the block. See Fig. 25-48.

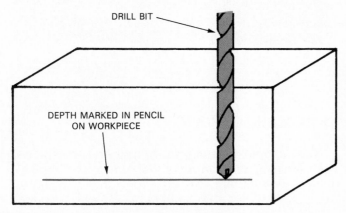

Fig. 25-47. Set depth by lowering the bit next to the workpiece, then adjust depth collars.

DRILLING EQUALLY SPACED HOLES

Drilling equally spaced holes can be done either of two ways. You could lay out all of the hole locations. However, this is time consuming. A more efficient method is to make a jig.

One useful jig for equally spaced through holes has a stop block, Fig. 25-49. After drilling the first

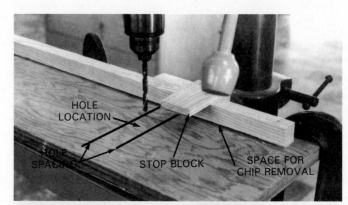

Fig. 25-49. Use a jig for drilling equally spaced holes. Insert a dowel in the previously drilled hole. Move workpiece until dowel hits stop block to measure off distance between holes.

A   B   C

Fig. 25-48. Drilling cylindrical workpieces. A—Horizontal. B—Vertical. C—Angled.

hole in the workpiece, insert a dowel rod in the hole. Then move the workpiece until the dowel hits the stop block. This works for both blind holes and through holes. The distance between the drill bit and the top block determines the distance between holes.

For small holes, replace the dowel rod with a nail or bolt the same size as the drill bit. For example, when drilling evenly spaced 5 mm holes for 32 mm cabinetry, use a 5 mm diameter bolt.

Wood chips can interfere with accuracy when positioning the workpiece against a solid fence. Consider using three or more dowel rods as a fence, Fig. 25-50. Accumulated chips are pushed aside easily.

When counterboring, you only enlarge one end of a hole. This is done so that the screw or bolt head sits below the wood's surface. You can hide the hole with a plug or button. The best method to counterbore is to drill the large-diameter counterbore hole first. Then drill the smaller clearance hole.

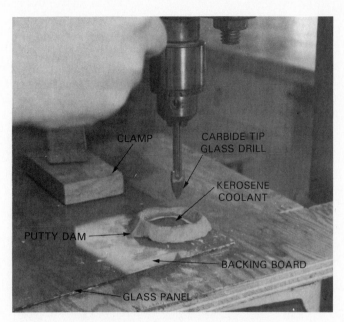

Fig. 25-51. Setup for drilling glass.

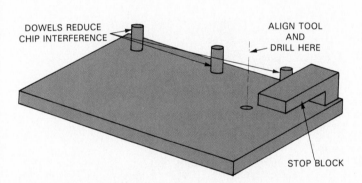

Fig. 25-50. A dowel fence on a jig lessens the interference caused by accumulated wood chips.

DRILLING GLASS

Glass is a difficult material to drill. However, you may need holes for mounting glass door hinges and pulls. One method of drilling glass is shown in Fig. 25-51. Mark the hole location with crayon or a glass marker. You could also attach masking tape and mark on it. Next, clamp the glass panel on the drill press table with the mark directly under the drill. You must have a special carbide glass drill. The glass needs to remain cool while drilling to prevent cracking. Do so by putting kerosene within a putty dam. The backing board keeps you from losing kerosene until the hole is finished. Drill at a slow speed (500 to 800 rpm).

DRILLING WITH PORTABLE DRILLS

Portable drills are popular for cabinetmaking. Many of the procedures for hand and stationary drilling machines hold true for portable tools. With portable drills, disconnect power before installing bits. Mark the holes using a scratch awl to center the bit. Use a vise or clamp to secure the workpiece. Use a V-block for cylindrical work. When drilling angles, use an angle jig, like the one for hand drills, to guide the bit. Drill larger holes at a slower speed and use two hands to hold the drill.

Drilling holes in line is more difficult with portable tools. With a drill press, you can set up a fence. With a portable drill, use a jig. Mark lines on the jig which help center it on the workpiece. (See Fig. 25-38.) Hold the workpiece and jig securely when drilling.

MAINTENANCE

Maintenance involves keeping drill bits sharp, plus keeping hand and power tools lubricated and clean. Most drilling tools can be sharpened by the cabinetmaker using the proper file, stone, or grinding wheel. Lubrication is needed on all moving parts of equipment.

SHARPENING BITS, DRILLS, AND CUTTERS

Bits, cutters, and drills are sharpened with files or abrasives. Those made of high speed steel marked (HS or HSS) cannot be sharpened with a file. They would ruin the file teeth. If the bit is not marked, perform a simple test. Push the corner of the file lightly across the shank. If an obvious nick is made, the bit can be file-sharpened. If no mark is made, or a high pitch screeching is heard, the bit is hardened. It cannot be sharpened with a file.

High speed steel bits are sharpened on the grinder. However, carbide-tipped bits cannot be sharpened on a standard wheel. In many cases, it may be less expensive to discard and replace the bit than to have it sharpened.

Before sharpening, check to see that the bit is straight. Sometimes drills and bits can be straightened. Support the ends and hold it firmly with the curve up. Then strike it with a mallet or hammer, Fig. 25-52. Tools marked HS or HSS may be straightened a few thousandths of an inch. Carbon steel drills and bits bend easier. However, if you cannot correctly shape the drill or bit, discard it. A bent bit will wobble, creating oversized holes.

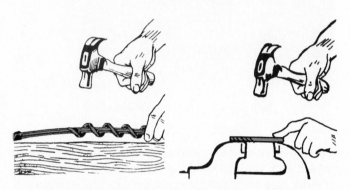

Fig. 25-52. Often you are able to straighten drills with light mallet or hammer blows.

Sharpening an auger bit

An auger bit can be sharpened with a file or small stone. An auger bit file is preferred, Fig. 25-53A. Only two surfaces at the end of the file have teeth. This prevents damage to adjacent surfaces.

File only four surfaces on the bit: both inside spur surfaces, Fig. 25-53B, and the two cutting lips, Fig. 25-53C. Keep the spurs and cutting lips even. Use the same number of strokes on both lips and spurs.

Sharpening expansive and power bore bits

Use the auger bit procedure on expansive bits. File the adjustable cutting lip and spur while in a vise. A power bore bit is sharpened like the auger or expansive bit. Only the front edge of the cutting lip and spur is filed.

Sharpening twist drills

Twist drills are probably the most difficult bit to sharpen by hand. Therefore jigs and machines are provided for this purpose, Fig. 25-54.

A

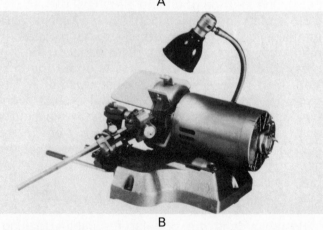

B

Fig. 25-54. A—Jig for sharpening twist drills. (General Hardware) B—Jig installed on bench grinder. (Brodhead-Garrett)

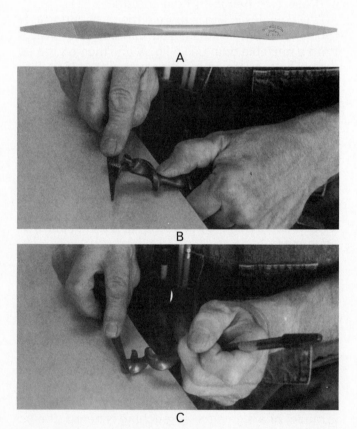

A

B

C

Fig. 25-53. A—Auger bit file. (The Cooper Group). B—Sharpen only the insides of the spurs. C—Sharpen cutting lips from the top.

You can sharpen twist drills by hand with practice. Note the proper terms and angles shown in Fig. 25-55. First practice the procedure below with the grinder off. Hold the drill between the thumb and first finger of your left hand. Have the drill shank in your right hand. Place your hand on the bench grinders tool rest. Point the drill toward the wheel arbor, not above or below it. Have the cutting lip horizontal, Fig. 25-56A.

Touch the drill against the wheel at the desired lip angle. As you grind, turn your right wrist about 30° clockwise. Also lower it to the left about 20°, Fig. 25-56B. Maintain grinder contact across the entire cutting edge. When finished, rotate the drill 180° and grind the other cutting lip. The cutting lips, point angles, and clearances must be the same, Fig. 25-56C.

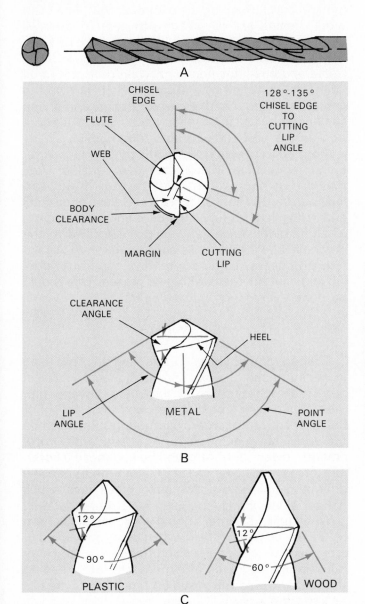

Fig. 25-55. A—Side and end views of twist drills. B—Critical twist drill angles. C—The point angle differs for metal, plastic, and wood.

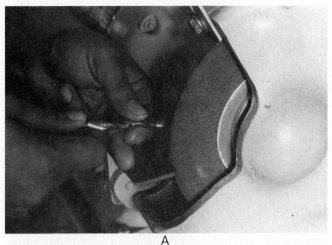

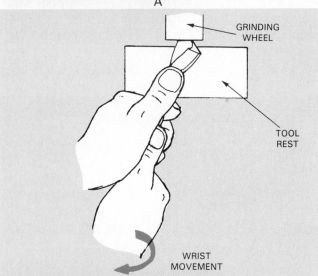

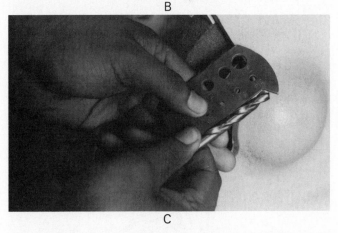

Fig. 25-56. Grinding a twist drill. A—Align bit with center of wheel. Have the cutting lip horizontal. B—Place hand on rest and turn your wrist while grinding the clearance angle. C—Check the sharpened cutting lip angle with a gauge.

Sharpening spade bits

Spade bits can be sharpened by grinding, honing, or filing. The two cutting lips must be even. There must be about a 10° clearance angle (angle back from cutting edge to other side of spade) on the lips and brad point, Fig. 25-57.

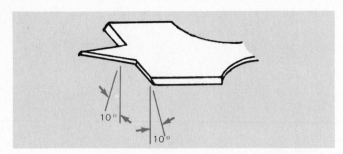

Fig. 25-57. Critical cutting angles for a spade bit.

Sharpening the spur bit

A spur bit is sharpened by filing or honing the spurs and cutting lips. The spurs are sharpened like the auger bit. Both cutting lips are filed or honed evenly at the end of the bit. This maintains the 10° clearance angle, Fig. 25-58.

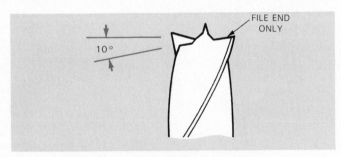

Fig. 25-58. Sharpening a multispur bit.

Sharpening a Forstner bit

Use an auger bit file and a hone, Fig. 25-59. File only the leading edges of the cutting lips. Hone only the inside surface on the sharpened rim. The surface is very narrow so about all you can do is remove burrs.

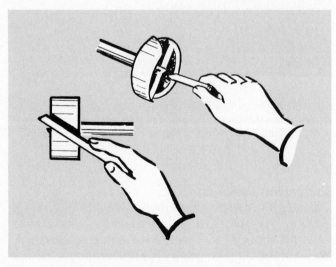

Fig. 25-59. Sharpening a Forstner bit.

Sharpening the multispur bit and hole saw

These drilling tools are sharpened similarly. The teeth are sharpened like a rip saw blade. The cutting lip is filed like the Forstner bit. The center drill is sharpened like a twist drill.

Sharpening other bits

Sharpening drill points, countersinks, plug cutters, and countersink/counterbore bits may not be worthwhile. Drill points are inexpensive and best replaced. The cutting angles for other bits may be too complicated and are best replaced.

CLEANING AND LUBRICATION

All tools need periodic cleaning and lubrication. Rust and wood resins cling to tools and hamper moving parts. Rust can be wiped off with fine steel wool. Resins are removed with paint thinner. A coating of paste wax should then be applied.

Hand tools need lubrication on moving parts. Gears and bushings need lightweight oil. Often oil holes are identified by a stamp saying OIL. On the brace, the head, handkey, box ratchet, and chuck shell need oiling. Push drills need internal lubrication on the pawl that rotates the chuck.

Most power tools have relatively few places requiring lubrication. Many bearings are sealed. They may or may not last the life of the tool. If the bearing goes bad, it must be replaced. Grease or oil cups and fittings are found on spindles and moving parts of some older machines. Keep these filled to the proper level. Portable drills need grease in the speed reducing gears. To do so, remove the front housing and coat the teeth with gear grease. This should be done every two or three years.

SUMMARY

A broad range of bits, cutters, and drills are used in cabinetmaking. Some are designed for use in hand tools while others are limited to power equipment. For drilling smaller holes, use twist drills. For holes 1/4 in. and larger, use boring bits, such as the auger bit, machine spur, and spade bit. For a smooth, clean, flat-bottomed hole, choose a Forstner bit. Larger holes can be made with expansive drills and hole saws. For deep holes, use a bell hanger's drill or drill extension with your twist drill.

When drilling, clamp or hold your workpiece firmly. Select the proper speed when using power equipment. Too much speed will burn the wood and may ruin the bit. Also feed at a moderate rate. Feeding too fast will chip the wood and may break the bit. Feeding too slow will cause excess heat and will burn the wood.

Proper maintenance of drills, bits, and equipment is necessary. Most drills and bits can be sharpened by the cabinetmaker. Decide whether it is more efficient for you to sharpen the bit or have it professionally sharpened. In some instances, it may be more cost-effective to discard the old bit and buy a new one. Maintain hand and power machinery by removing rust and lubricating moving points. Parts of the machine which contact wood should be lubricated with silicone or paste wax. Gear housings and other internal parts are lubricated with oil or grease.

CABINETMAKING TERMS

Drilling, boring, auger bit, cutting lips, spurs, feed screw, twist, expansive bit, twist drill, machine spur bit, spade bit, multispur bit, Forstner bit, power bore bit, drill points, circle cutter, adjustable dial saw, hole saw, countersink bit, screw-mate, countersink/counterbore cutters, plug cutter, start drill, masonry drill, glass drill, bell hanger's drill, drill extension, screw bit, brace, hand drill, push drill, drill press, vertical boring machine, horizontal boring machine, portable power drill, right angle drill, right angle head, hammer drill, depth gauge, drill stop, adjustable depth stop, depth scale, V-block.

TEST YOUR KNOWLEDGE

1. Drills and bits may be made of _____, _____, or be _____.
2. What purpose does an auger bit feed screw serve?
3. Describe how auger bit size is marked.
4. What does the HS stamped on a drills shank mean?
5. When you counterbore with an auger bit, drill the small hole first. True or False?
6. You can drill holes of various shapes by grinding a _____ bit.

7. Auger bits will not drill effectively:
   a. At an angle.
   b. In face grain.
   c. In edge grain.
   d. In end grain.
8. List the bits which look like circular saws.
9. The Forstner bit does not have a long center point. What guides it through the hole?
10. For enlarging a hole to accept flat head screws, use a:
    a. Countersink bit.
    b. Twist drill.
    c. Drill point.
    d. Power bore bit.
11. Diagram a section through a piece of wood which shows both a countersunk hole and counterbored hole.
12. Drill extensions are not used with stationary power tools. True or False?
13. The chuck size of a portable or stationary power drill determines the size of _____ which can be used.
14. Explain when you might use a V-block.
15. Name two methods for drilling through holes in a workpiece without splintering the wood on the back side.
16. A drill used with the drill press to make deep holes is _____ _____ _____.
17. Describe two methods of drilling holes at an angle on the drill press.
18. When sharpening an auger bit, file only the _____ and _____.
19. Explain why you might use dowels for a fence on a drilling jig instead of attaching a solid fence.
20. Rust can be removed from tools with _____ _____.
21. Moving drill parts which may contact the wood are lubricated with _____ or _____.

Chapter 26
SHAPING

After studying this chapter, you will be able to:
□ Choose the proper shaper cutter.
□ Set up and operate the spindle shaper.
□ Choose the proper router bit.
□ Set up and operate the overarm router.
□ Set up and operate the portable router.
□ Adapt the table saw, radial arm saw, and drill press for shaping.
□ Select and use hand tools for shaping contours and decorative surfaces.

Shaping is the process of making contoured surfaces and edges for decorative purposes or joinery. Cabinet cases, doors, and drawers may have shaped edges. Moulding and trim are some examples of decorative products made by shaping.

Shaping equipment includes stationary power machines, portable power tools, and hand tools. Most shaping is done with stationary and portable power equipment because of accuracy, speed, and quality, Fig. 26-1. Power tools rotate a cutter at high speeds to produce very smooth surfaces which require little sanding. Note that the high speed of the cutter can make power shaping equipment dangerous if misused.

SHAPING WITH STATIONARY POWER MACHINES

Equipment strictly for shaping includes shapers and routers. The table saw, drill press, and radial arm saw can be adapted for shaping.

SPINDLE SHAPER

The spindle shaper consists of four basic components: spindle, table, and two fences, Fig. 26-2. The cutter is mounted on the spindle of a high speed shaper motor. Spindle sizes vary from 1/2 to 1 in.

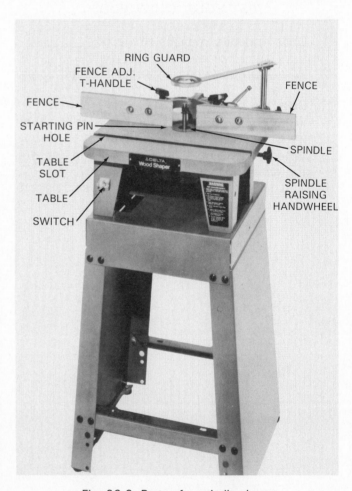

Fig. 26-2. Parts of a spindle shaper.
(Delta International Machinery Corp.)

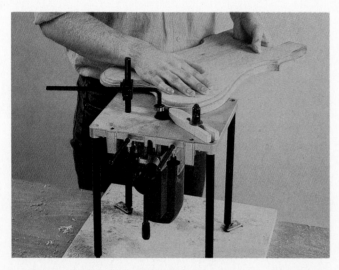

Fig. 26-1. Shaping is the process of making contoured surfaces. (Black & Decker)

Spindle height is set by turning a handwheel. Spindle speeds range from 4000 to 10,000 rpm. Some machines have more than one speed. Turning a speed control switch or moving belts on the motor and spindle pulleys changes the rpm.

Guide workpieces into the cutter using a fence, Fig. 26-3, miter gauge, Fig. 26-4, or starting pin and collar, Fig. 26-5. The fences are held in place

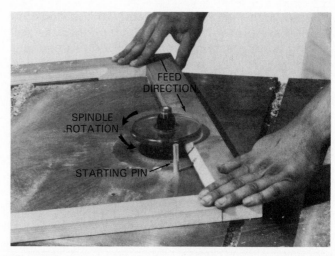

Fig. 26-5. With a collar and starting pin, neither a fence nor miter gauge is needed. (Delta)

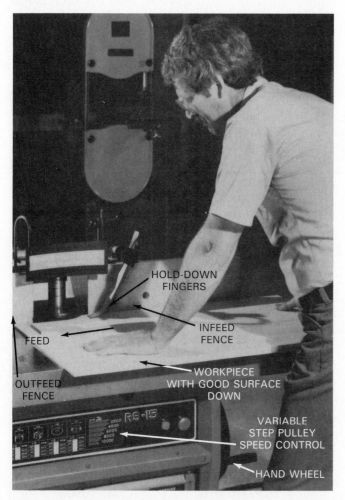

Fig. 26-3. Guide straight edges along the fence. (Delta)

with two T—handle bolts. A table slot guides the miter gauge. Remove fences and install a starting pin to do freehand cutting. A collar installed with the cutter limits the depth of cut.

Stock may be fed from left to right or right to left. A reversing switch changes the spindle direction from counterclockwise to clockwise, Fig. 26-6. Note that material must always feed against the cutter rotation.

A point-of-operation guard protects you from the cutter. A vacuum dust collecter installed behind the guard collects wood chips. Set the collecter as close to the spindle as possible. Holding devices may be installed to guide the workpiece against the table and fence. (See Fig. 26-3.)

SPINDLE SHAPER CUTTERS

Shaper cutters, Fig. 26-7, come in a variety of sizes and shapes. Numerous contours can be

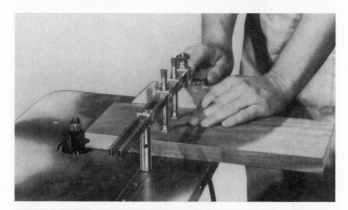

Fig. 26-4. Narrow workpieces are held in a miter gauge. The guard has been removed to show the operation. (Delta)

Fig. 26-6. Spindle rotation controls feed direction.

created with just a few cutters. This is done by varying the cutter height and using either the full cutting lip or just a portion of it. Before choosing a cutter, carefully analyze the shape you want to make. The cutter shape is just the opposite.

An additional cutter specification is *lips,* or *cutting flutes.* This refers to the number of cutting edges. Cutters may have from two to four lips. Those with more lips cut the smoothest contours. You can also feed the workpiece faster.

Shaper cutters may be solid or sectional. Solid cutters are one piece steel with a 1/2, 3/4, or 1 in. arbor hole. Sectional cutters have two or three separate solid cutters which are mounted together. By altering the position of these cutters, several shapes can be created. Most shaper cutters produced today are carbide tipped. They are more durable and cost-effective compared to high speed steel cutters.

You may find that a single cutter does not meet your needs. More than one setup of a given cutter may be required or more than one cutter could be used. You might also have to feed the workpiece vertically or at some other angle. Setups required for some shaped table edges are shown in Fig. 26-8.

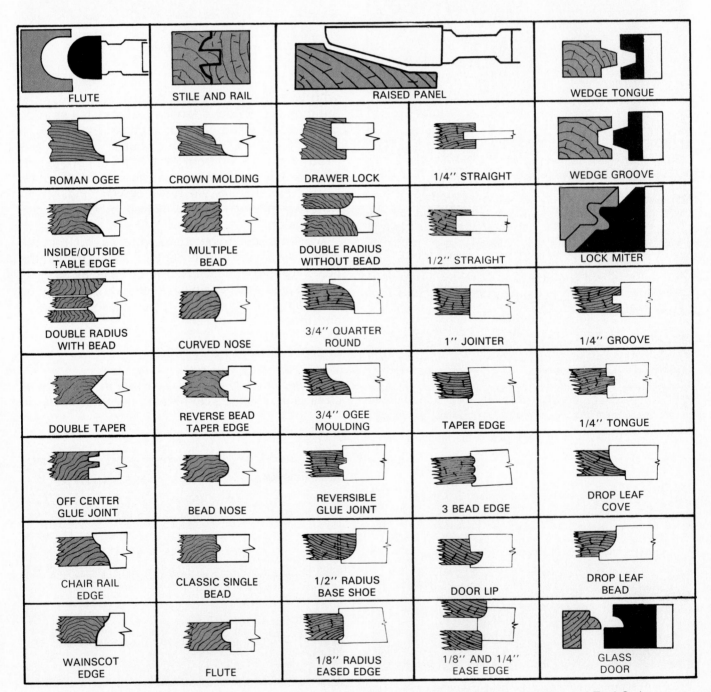

Fig. 26-7. Typical cutter shapes and the workpiece edge they create. (American Machine and Tool Co.)

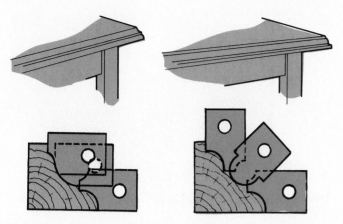

Fig. 26-8. Several passes may be necessary to create the designed shape. (Delta)

Installing the cutter

Cutters are installed on the spindle and held by a *lock nut* and *keyed washer,* Fig. 26-9. *Collars* may be placed under or over the cutter. These help to set the cutter height and depth of cut. Place the cutter so the spindle rotation causes the cutting edge to lead into the workpiece.

Install the cutter so that the heaviest amount of cut (largest diameter of the cutter) is nearest the table. If a workpiece should tip while being shaped, the depth of cut is reduced but the workpiece is not damaged. Simply feed the part through again. However, by positioning the cutter with heaviest amount of cut on top, a workpiece will be damaged if it tips. As the edge rises, it moves further into the cutter and increases the depth of cut. This can ruin the workpiece.

A special keyed washer must always be placed under the lock nut. The washer key fits in the spindle keyway. The key prevents the cutter from loosening the nut. This feature makes both clockwise and counterclockwise rotation safe. Be extremely cautious about securing the cutter on the spindle. The nut must remain tight. When installing the nut, first check whether the threads are left or right hand. Hold the spindle with one wrench while you tighten the lock nut with another wrench.

Install the guard

Install a point-of-operation guard. One is the *clear plastic spindle guard,* Fig. 26-10A. It fits on the spindle under the washer and rotates with the cutter. Another is the *ring guard* which is clamped to the table and positioned just above the cutter and spindle, Fig. 26-10B.

A

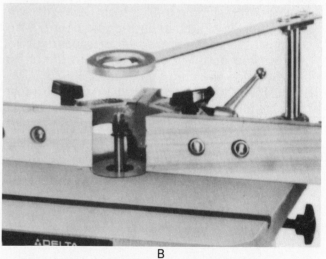

B

Fig. 26-10. Shaper guards. A—Clear plastic spindle-mounted guard. (Delta) B—Table-mounted ring guard is adjusted over the spindle. (Delta)

SPINDLE PARTS

LOCK NUT

KEYED WASHER— ALWAYS USED UNDER NUT

KEY GROOVE IN SPINDLE

SPINDLE

COLLARS—VARIOUS HEIGHTS— USED UNDER OR OVER CUTTERS OR BOTH WAYS—HELP TO SET HEIGHT OF CUTTER ON SPINDLE—ALSO USED WHEN FREEHAND SHAPING

Fig. 26-9. Order of items installed on a shaper spindle.

SHAPER SETUP AND OPERATION

There are a number of options for operating a spindle shaper. These include using:
1. Fences.
2. A collar and starting pin.
3. A collar, starting pin, and template.
4. Various jigs.

Shaping with fences

Install infeed and outfeed fences when cutting straight edges. Workpieces can be guided quickly and easily along the fence across the cutter. Each fence is adjusted independently. Locate them about 1/4 in. (6 mm) beyond the arc of the cutter.

The fences will be aligned or offset. When you are shaping only a portion of the edge, they are aligned, Fig. 26-11A. If the entire edge will be shaped, the fences can be offset, Fig. 26-11B. The infeed fence is offset for the depth of cut. The outfeed fence is aligned with the shaped workpiece edge, not with the infeed fence. The outfeed fence supports the workpiece as it exits the cutterhead. cutterhead.

The procedure for setting up and operating the spindle shaper is as follows:

1. Disconnect electrical power to the machine.
2. Obtain a squared piece of scrap stock which is the same thickness as your workpiece. This test board is used to make adjustments.
3. Place the cutter edge against the end grain of the test board. Trace the design to be shaped, Fig. 26-12A.
4. Install the cutter and collars. Be sure to determine the spindle rotation first. Place collars under the cutter if it needs to be higher than the handwheel can raise the spindle.
5. Place the test board on the table. Raise or lower the spindle until the cutter aligns with the design sketched on the test board. Also, move the infeed fence to the proper depth of cut. The cutter should align with the shape traced on the end grain, Fig. 26-12B.
6. Position the outfeed table even with the infeed table for aligned cuts. Offset the outfeed fence when shaping the full edge.

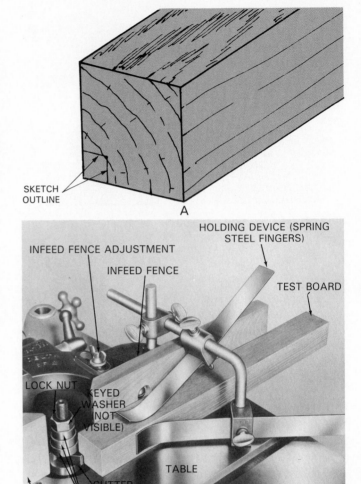

Fig. 26-12. A—Trace the design on the test board. B—Spring steel fingers steady the workpiece as you push it across the cutter. The ring guard has been removed to show the operation. (Delta)

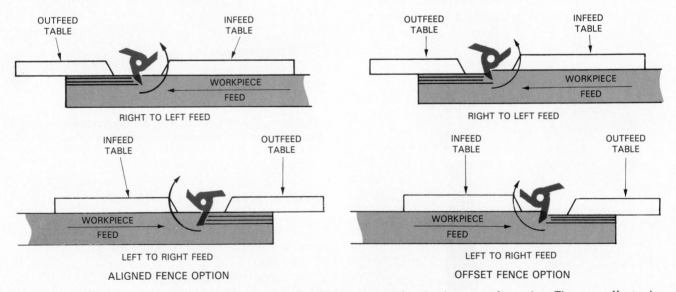

Fig. 26-11. Feed direction varies with cutter rotation. Fences are aligned for shaping part of an edge. They are offset when shaping the entire edge.

7. Position and secure the point-of-operation guard. If it is a spindle mounted guard, install it under the washer and lock nut.
8. Turn the spindle by hand to be sure it spins freely. There should be some clearance between the cutter, table insert, guard, and fences.
9. Turn the machine on and off quickly. Check for any loose settings or unusual noises. Verify the direction of spindle rotation.
10. Turn on the machine and feed the test board about 2 in. into the cutter. Pull the board from the cutter and turn off the machine.
11. Check the contour created. Readjust the fences and cutter height if necessary.
12. Install holding devices, depending on the cut to be made. Spring steel fingers press the workpiece against the table and fence, Fig. 26-12. A featherboard clamped to the fence may be sufficient, Fig. 26-13.
13. Now you are prepared to shape a straight edge. Hold the workpiece against the table and fence. Turn on the shaper. Feed at a moderate rate past the cutter.

There is an order for shaping edge and end grain, Fig. 26-14A. End grain should be done first. This is because the shaper has a tendency to chip out the trailing edge, Fig. 26-14B. Reduce the chance of chipping by slowing the feed rate at the end of the cut. A miter gauge clamp holds the workpiece when shaping the ends of narrow workpieces, Fig. 26-14C. Shape edge grain after shaping the end grain. Shaping the edge usually removes material which was chipped when shaping ends.

Workpieces must be at least 12 in. long to shape using only the fences. Narrower or shorter workpieces may be shaped using the miter gauge and fences. Hold gauge as if you were sawing.

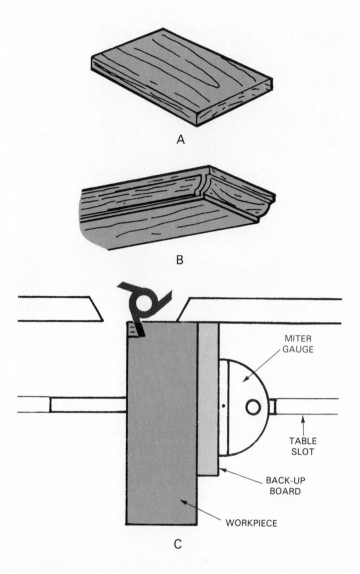

Fig. 26-14. A—End grain is shaped before edge grain. B—The edges often tear out when end grain is shaped. C—A back-up board supports the trailing edge of the workpiece to prevent chipping.

Fig. 26-13. Featherboard hold down jig. (Delta)

If you are shaping on end grain, reduce splintering by using a back-up board. Place it between the workpiece and the miter gauge. Feed both past the cutter. The back-up board will support the trailing edge of the workpiece.

Shaping with a collar and starting pin

A collar and *starting pin* are used when the fence is not appropriate. This may be for shaping irregular curves, Fig. 26-15. Collars come in sets of different diameters. Install the collar with the cutter to limit the depth of cut. You hold the workpiece against the starting pin before guiding it into the cutter.

Collars may be solid or ball bearing. Ball bearing cutters rotate independent of the spindle. The solid collar rotates with the spindle and may burn the wood. The workpiece rubbing the collar must be smooth. The collar rides on and will follow any im-

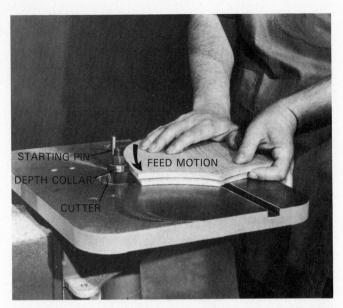

Fig. 26-15. A collar and starting pin are installed for shaping irregular surfaces. The guard has been removed to show the operation. (Delta)

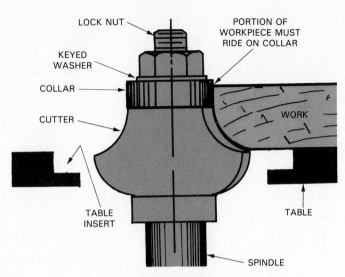

Fig. 26-16. Shaping with a collar. A portion of the workpiece must ride on the collar.

perfections in the workpiece. When using a collar, only part of the edge can be shaped. There must be enough unshaped edge against the collar to guide the work, Fig. 26-16.

A ring guard or plastic spindle mounted guard must be attached. Keep the workpiece between you and the guarded cutter. Feed against the direction of cutter rotation. Feeding with the cutter rotation may throw the workpiece from the table or draw your hand into the cutter.

To begin a cut, first hold the workpiece against the starting pin. Then guide an edge into the cutter. With no starting pin, you would plunge the workpiece into the cutter. This would cause kickback.

The procedure for setting up and using a collar and starting pin is as follows:

1. Disconnect power to the machine.
2. Install the diameter collar which will give you the depth of cut desired. The collar should be above the cutter. This is generally safer.
3. Raise or lower the spindle to position the cutter height.
4. Thread a starting pin into a hole on the shaper table on the infeed side of the cutter.
5. Make a trial pass without the shaper running. Decide on the feed direction and how you will start the cut.
6. Decide where to begin and end the pass. Consider cutting end grain first. Avoid beginning at a corner. The cutter can catch the corner and throw the workpiece. Begin along a side or a relatively gentle curve.
7. Install the ring guard within 1/4 in. (6 mm) of the upper workpiece surface.

8. Turn the spindle by hand to be sure it spins freely. It must not touch the guard or table insert.
9. Reconnect power to the machine. Turn the machine on and off quickly to verify direction of the cutter.
10. Turn the shaper on.
11. Position the workpiece against the starting pin, but not the cutter.
12. Ease the workpiece into the cutter.
13. Start feeding after the workpiece touches the collar. You do not need to use the pin from this point until the end of the cut.
14. Go slowly when shaping a corner. Keep the workpiece in contact with the collar at all times.
15. When finished with the cut, pull the workpiece away from the cutter and turn off the machine.

Shaping with a starting pin, collar, and template

Templates are patterns used to duplicate workpieces. With a template, the entire workpiece edge can be shaped. The template rides on the collar, Fig. 26-17. The template can be made of fiberboard or plywood. It must be smooth and accurate.

Stock is first band-sawed to approximate workpiece size. Attach the template above the workpiece with mechanical fasteners. The same feeding procedure is used for template shaping as for using a collar and starting pin.

Shaping with jigs

Cabinetmakers can produce jigs for various operations. The jig should be adaptable; otherwise, the time spent making it is not worthwhile. One jig is the angle jig. It supports the workpiece at an angle

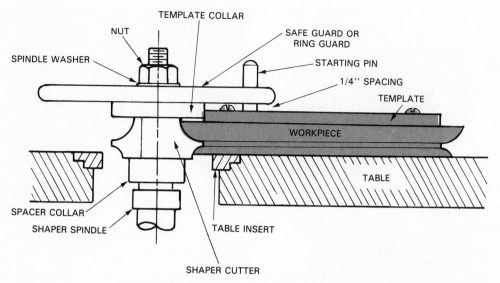

Fig. 26-17. Guiding the workpiece with a template.

for shaping bevels and miters, Fig. 26-18. It can be clamped in position or bolted into two of the threaded table holes. You might also make a jig that slides in the table slot.

Just about any jig can be made or adapted for the shaper. However, they must be safe. Include a point-of-operation guard.

THINK SAFETY—ACT SAFELY WHEN USING THE SPINDLE SHAPER

Follow these precautions when using the shaper.
1. Wear eye protection, remove jewelry, and tie up loose hair and clothing.
2. Install the cutter with the greatest depth of cut on the bottom.
3. Make sure the lock nut is tightened securely.
4. The outfeed fence should be set to guide the work after it has passed the cutter.
5. Always feed against the rotation of the cutter. Keep hands 4 in. (100 mm) away.
6. Never shape pieces smaller than 12 in. without a jig or other means of support.
7. Use a depth collar and starting pin when shaping irregular work.
8. Examine wood for knots, grain direction, and defects.

OVERARM ROUTER

Overarm routers are very practical shaping devices. They are much like the shaper, except that the cutter, a router bit, is located above the workpiece. Both floor and bench models are available, Fig. 26-19.

Overarm routers use shank mounted bits. The bit is held in a collet on the overarm. The table is rais-

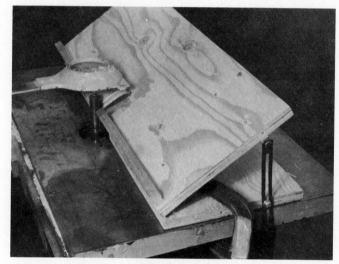

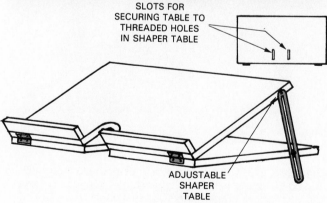

Fig. 26-18. An angle jig allows you to shape edges at an angle other than 90°.

ed and lowered with a handwheel. The workpiece is positioned on the table just under the bit. A foot control or feed lever lowers the bit into the workpiece. The depth the bit enters the workpiece is set with a depth stop. The table contains a

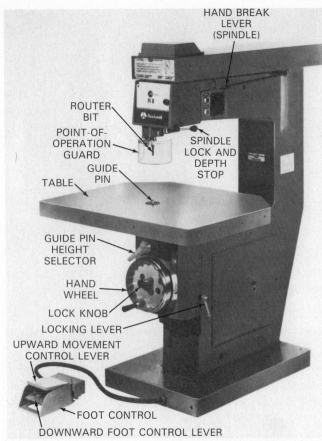

HAND BREAK
LEVER
(SPINDLE)

ROUTER
BIT

POINT-OF-
OPERATION
GUARD

SPINDLE
LOCK AND
DEPTH
STOP

GUIDE
PIN

TABLE

GUIDE PIN
HEIGHT
SELECTOR

HAND
WHEEL

LOCK KNOB

LOCKING LEVER

UPWARD MOVEMENT
CONTROL LEVER

FOOT CONTROL

DOWNWARD FOOT CONTROL LEVER

A

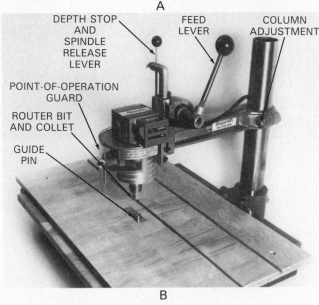

DEPTH STOP
AND
SPINDLE
RELEASE
LEVER

FEED
LEVER

COLUMN
ADJUSTMENT

POINT-OF-OPERATION
GUARD

ROUTER BIT
AND COLLET

GUIDE
PIN

B

Fig. 26-19. A—Components of a floor mounted router. (Delta)
B—Where space is limited, a bench model overarm router is
appropriate. (Shopsmith)

removable guide pin for "pin routing." The pin
height is altered using a height selector.

ROUTER BITS

Overarm routers and portable routers use round
shank *router bits,* Fig. 26-20. Shanks are 1/4 in.,

Fig. 26-20. Router bits. Notice that some are assembled, while
others are one piece. (Bosch)

3/8 in., and 1/2 in. in diameter. The bit fits into a
collet on the motor. Turning a nut tightens the collet
to hold the bit. Some bits are assembled shank and
cutters, Fig. 26-21. The cutters are mounted on the
arbor and held by a nut.

Router bits are available at three quality levels:
high speed steel, carbide tipped, and solid carbide.
Most bits are carbide tipped because solid carbide
is too expensive. Bits have two, three, or four cutting lips. Three-lipped cutters are the most common.

Router bits may have a pilot at the end. A *pilot*
is a round guide which limits the depth of cut by
riding along the edge of the workpiece, Fig. 26-22.
Bits with pilots are typically installed in portable
routers for edge-shaping.

The pilot may be part of the bit or an attached
ball bearing. Solid pilots rub the surface and may
burn the wood. Ball bearing pilots roll instead of
rubbing the workpiece.

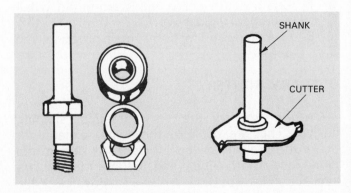

SHANK

CUTTER

Fig. 26-21. Some router bits are an assembled shank and
cutters.

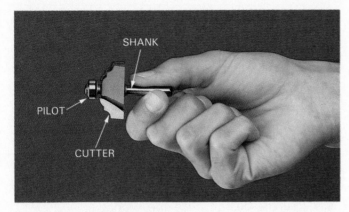

Fig. 26-22. This ball bearing pilot is screwed onto the end of the shank. (Bosch)

Overarm routers are capable of lowering the bit into the workpiece. This process is called *plunging.* For any plunging operation, you must choose a plunge-type router bit. The end has cutting edges much like a drill bit and cannot have a pilot.

There are many shapes and sizes of router bits. Some are shown in Fig. 26-23. Several are designed simply to create a decorative edge. Others have special purposes. For example, the dovetail and rabbeting bits are for making joints. Trimmer bits are used to trim laminate and veneer flush with an edge. Slotting bits make slots for T-moulding in table edges. The stile and rail bit is an example of a shank with removable cutters. By rearranging cutters, you can cut both the stile and rail joint for frame and panel construction. The panel bit cuts the raised panel.

Installing bits in the overarm router

Router bits are installed in a collet. The procedure is as follows:
1. Disconnect power to the router.
2. Engage the spindle lock. This prevents the router shaft from turning.
3. Remove the guard.
4. Loosen the collet nut with an open-end wrench.
5. Insert the bit and tighten the collet nut.
6. Replace the guard.
7. Disengage the arbor lock.

OVERARM ROUTER OPERATION

There are several options for using the overarm router. These include:
1. Routing with a fence.
2. Freehand shaping.
3. Pin routing.

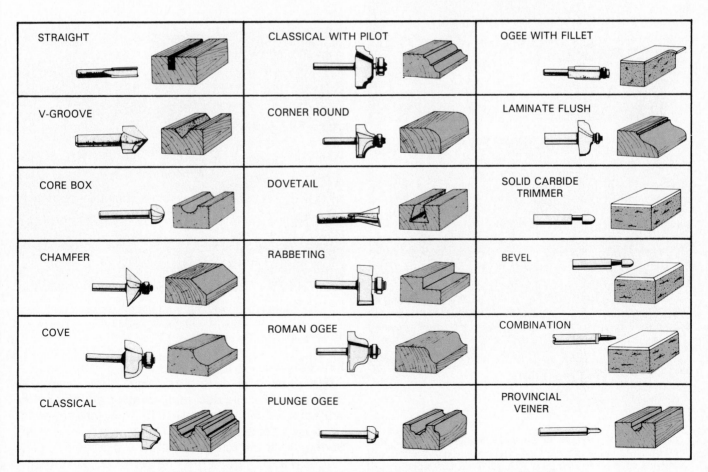

Fig. 26-23. Typical router bit shapes and the shapes they create. (Bosch)

Using a fence

The fence is installed for shaping edges or cutting grooves, Fig. 26-24. Align both fences if only a portion of the edge will be shaped. Offset the infeed and outfeed fences if the entire edge will be shaped. The infeed fence generally is located on the left because the cutter spins clockwise. Set the cutter height by raising or lowering the table and/or bit. Bench top models do not have a movable table. Bit height is set by adjusting the column clamp or feed lever. Mark the end grain of the workpiece to set the depth as you did when adjusting the spindle shaper. Feed workpieces from left to right.

You may need to make a fence for a bench-mounted overarm router. Install T-nuts on the underside of the table. Make two slots in the fence arms. Insert bolts through the fence arms into the T-nuts. Then depth-of-cut adjustments can be made easily. The fence must be in two sections for shaping an entire workpiece edge. The infeed fence is adjusted separately.

Freehand routing

Freehand shaping with an overarm router should be done only by experienced cabinetmakers. Since no fence or guide is used, you must hold the workpiece firmly, Fig. 26-25. Otherwise, it could be thrown from the table.

The procedure for freehand routing is as follows:
1. Copy the design onto the wood.
2. Install a small diameter plunge-type router bit.
3. Raise the table so the workpiece is just under the bit.
4. Set the depth stops which determine how far the bit enters the workpiece.
5. Turn on the router.
6. Press the foot pedal to gently lower the bit into the workpiece. For bench models, lower the bit with the feed lever.
7. While shaping, keep your hands 4 in. (100 mm) away from the cutter.
8. Raise the bit.
9. Turn off the machine and remove the completed component.

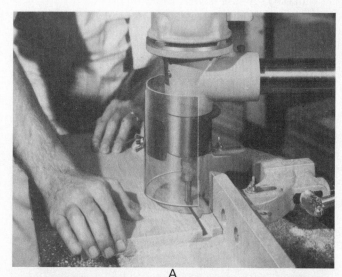

A

Fig. 26-25. Freehand routing. The guard has been removed to show the operation. (Delta)

Pin routing

Pin routing is a rather unique way to make duplicate parts or a design. It involves attaching the workpiece over a template. The template shape is the design to be duplicated. Holes or grooves in the underside of the template follow the guide pin, Fig. 26-26. At the same time, the cutter above is shaping the workpiece.

B

Fig. 26-24. Overarm routing with a fence. A—Notice the point-of-operation guard is set very close to the workpiece. This fence is a solid piece of lumber. (Delta) B—A U-shaped guard is fastened around the bit. (Craft Products)

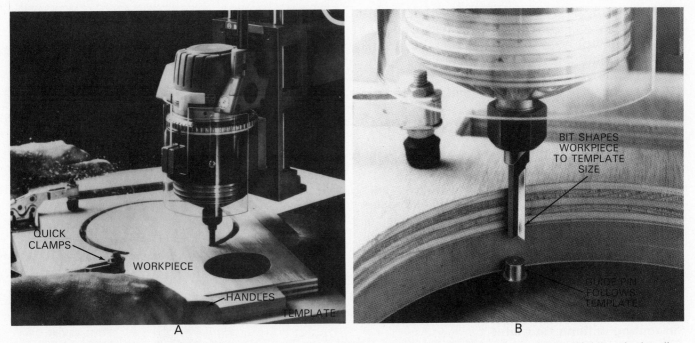

Fig. 26-26. Overarm pin routing with a template. A—The workpiece is held to the template with clamps. Holding the handles assures your fingers are away from the point of operation. B—Close-up of the pin function. The pin rides in the template while the cutter above shapes the workpiece.

The procedure for pin routing is as follows:

1. Install a plunge-type router bit in the collet.
2. Install the guide pin in the table. The pin you use should be the same diameter or smaller than the slot in the prepared template. If slot is wider, make a pass against each side.
3. Lower the bit using the lower foot pedal.
4. Attach the workpiece to the template with clamps or fasteners. Place the workpiece and template assembly next to the bit.
5. Adjust the table height to set the approximate depth of cut. You cannot move the table on bench-top routers.
6. Adjust the depth stop on the overarm. This determines the exact depth of cut. A shallow cut would provide a decorative surface. A deep cut could cut completely through the workpiece. This is done to cut parts which are duplicates of the template.
7. Raise the bit with the foot pedal.
8. Set the point-of-operation guard 1/4 in. above the workpiece.
9. Lower the template over the guide pin. This also locates the workpiece properly under the cutter, Fig. 26-27.
10. Start the machine.

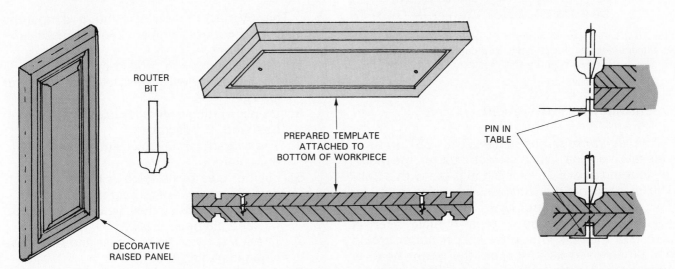

Fig. 26-27. The prepared template for making the raised panel has a groove cut in the bottom. Right—The pin follows along the edge, then in the groove, to complete the panel.

11. Lower the bit by pressing the foot pedal. The bench model overarm router usually does not have a foot lever. A feed lever on the head is used. Hold the workpiece securely with one hand as you turn the lever.
12. Advance the workpiece as guided by the pin and template.
13. When the cut is finished, raise the bit and turn off the machine.

Template making

Accurate template making is essential to high quality pin routing. The product is only as precise as the template. Use 3/4 in. (19 mm) lumber or fiberboard. Particleboard and plywood could serve short production runs or designs requiring less precision. The grooves or openings in the template must be smooth. They should be at least 3/8 in. (10 mm) deep and as wide as the pin diameter.

Pin routing without templates

It is not necessary to use a template when pin routing. You can shape edges by guiding the workpiece against the pin, Fig. 26-28. The router bit you choose should be larger in diameter than the pin. You cannot shape the entire edge of the workpiece. Some portion must ride on the guide pin.

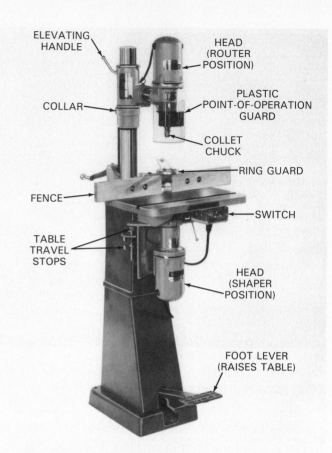

Fig. 26-29. An overarm router/shaper combines the function of two machines into one compact, floor-standing model. (Delta)

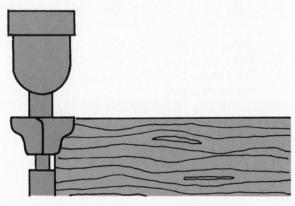

Fig. 26-28. Pin routing without a template. A portion of the workpiece rides against the pin. You cannot shape the entire edge by this method.

OVERARM ROUTER/SHAPER

The *overarm router/shaper,* Fig. 26-29, is a versatile machine. When used as a router, the motor is mounted above. It is locked in place with a bolt. The bit is fed into the workpiece by raising the table. This is done with a foot lever. The exact height is adjusted with two depth stops. A table insert is placed in the hole where the shaper cutter would be. When used as a shaper, the motor head is clamped under the table. Cutter height is set with a fine thread adjustment feature.

Operation of the overarm router/shaper is the same as that for each individual machine. Router feed is from left to right. Shaper feed is from right to left. Align or offset the infeed and outfeed fences as required.

THINK SAFETY—ACT SAFELY WHEN USING THE OVERARM ROUTER

The overarm router can be a dangerous machine if not used properly. Follow these safety precautions.
1. Always wear eye protection.
2. Do not work with loose clothing, hair, or jewelry.
3. Do pin routing with a template, rather than freehand, if possible.
4. The overarm should be clamped securely to the column.
5. Lock or clamp the table in place after setting the approximate height.
6. Install all guards so they clear the work, cutter, and clamps.
7. Check bits twice for tightness and sharpness when installing them.
8. Feed the work in the correct direction.
9. Keep hands clear of the cutter.

INVERTED ROUTER

The *inverted router* is much like an overarm router, except that the bit is located below the workpiece, Fig. 26-30. This machine is designed primarily for pin routing. It boasts some advantages above overarm routers, including: quick setup, fast plunge cuts, and better depth control since the part faces down. It also holds a safety advantage in that the operator has less exposure to the cutting tool.

A unique spiral bit is installed in the inverted router. It helps hold the workpiece to the table as the cut is made. Several depth stops determine how far the bit extends out of the table. Pressing a foot pedal raises the bit. A pedal lock holds the spindle in an UP position for shaping work. A 1/4, 3/8, or 1/2 in. guide pin is installed in the retractable pin assembly. The guide pin is lowered by pneumatic controls.

Several applications of the inverted pin router are shown in Fig. 26-31.

TABLE SAW

The table saw is adaptable for shaping using a *moulding cutterhead* and special table insert. The cutterhead functions well on straight surfaces for

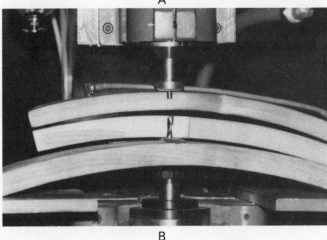

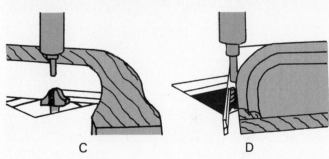

Fig. 26-31. Typical inverted router operations. A—Guiding the workpiece with a template. B—Duplicating a curved component. C—Shaping a portion of an edge. D—Trimming an edge flush to the moulding. (C.R. Onsrud)

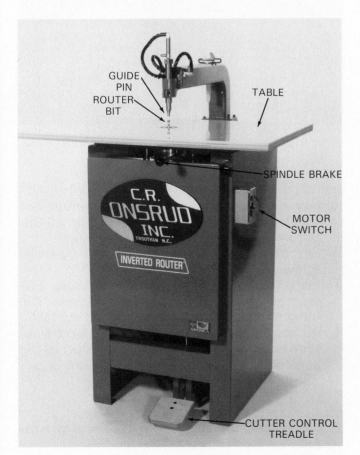

Fig. 26-30. The inverted router has the guide pin above the bit. (C.R. Onsrud)

shaping part of the edge. A portion of the edge must remain since the table supports it.

Three matching knives are inserted in a cutterhead and secured by set screws, Fig. 26-32. Install the cutterhead using the blade installation procedure discussed in Chapter 21. Replace the normal table insert with the large opening insert.

Attach a wood auxiliary fence to the table saw fence when edge shaping, Fig. 26-33. Make a cutout in the wood fence so the fence can be positioned over the cutterhead. Lower the moulding head below the table surface. Move the fence slightly over the cutter. Turn on the saw and raise the cutter just over the height at which you will be shaping. This procedure allows you to set the fence for the proper cutterhead height and depth of cut.

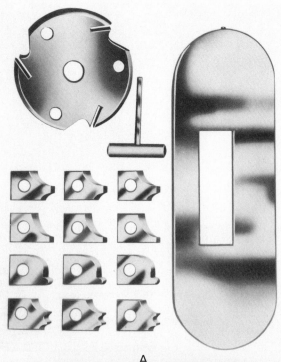

A

Fig. 26-33. Shaping an edge on the table saw.

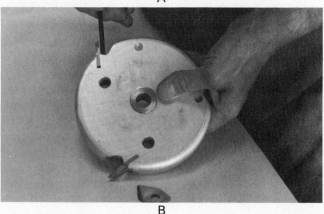

B

Fig. 26-32. A—Attachments needed to convert a table saw into a shaper. (Delta) B—Tighten three matching knives in the cutterhead.

Fig. 26-34. Shaping a face on the table saw.

Clamp featherboards to the fence and table to help guide the workpiece. Use a push stick when working within 4 in. (100 mm) of the point of operation. The cutterhead can be tilted for shaping at an angle. If tilted too far, the knives could damage the table insert. With the power disconnected, always rotate the cutterhead by hand once to make sure it does not contact the table insert or fence.

The table saw is also used for shaping faces. Use the miter gauge or fence, Fig. 26-34. Be sure the cutterhead height does not exceed the workpiece thickness. Hold the workpiece firmly since the cutter has a tendency to raise it.

Ploughing

Ploughing is a shaping operation done with a table saw blade. You make a concave cut diagonally across the table. Often you cut the workpiece in half for two pieces of cove moulding. To perform the ploughing operation, follow these steps, Fig. 26-35:

1. Set the saw blade to the desired height.
2. Set the width of the desired cut with a parallel frame.
3. Place the frame over the saw blade. One side touches the blade where it enters the table. The other touches where it comes out of the table.
4. Position a framing square against the frame. With chalk, mark where the square touches the miter gauge slot. This gives the angle and position for the secondary fence.
5. Lower the blade completely.
6. Clamp the secondary fence in place.
7. Raise the blade about 1/16 in. (1.5 mm) for each pass.
8. You can cut the workpiece in half for cove moulding.

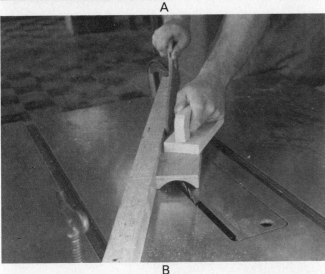

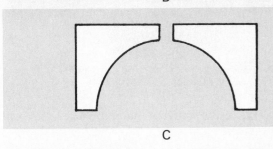

Fig. 26-35. A—Setting the angle of the auxiliary fence for plough cutting. B—Making the cut. C—Saw the shaped piece in half for two cove mouldings.

When using the moulding head in the crosscut position, make a cutout in the saw fence. This allows the cutterhead to pass through from the retracted position.

Use standard radial arm saw techniques when shaping. Remember to always feed AGAINST the rotation of the cutterhead.

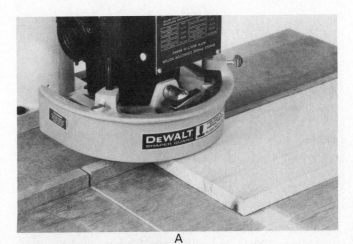

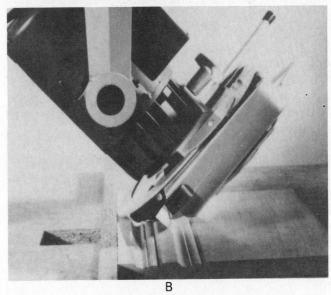

Fig. 26-36. A—A cutterhead guard is necessary when the cutterhead is set in the horizontal shaping position. B—Shaping at an angle. (DeWalt)

RADIAL ARM SAW

A radial arm adapts to shaping. Fit it with the table saw cutter head assembly and guard or drill press spindle adaptor. Saw can shape in rip or crosscut mode, and at an angle, Fig. 26-36.

Each radial arm saw manufacturer produces adaptors so router bits and shaper cutters can be installed. The adaptor threads onto the saw arbor and has a bolt to accept cutters. The router bit adaptor has a collet to accept round shank router bits.

DRILL PRESS

A drill press is adaptable to shaping and routing, Fig. 26-37. Tighten router bits in the chuck. For a threaded spindle, unscrew the drill press chuck and screw on the proper shaping adaptor. A shaper adaptor accepts 1/2 in. bore shaper cutters. For a router bit, there is a collet adaptor.

The hole in the drill press table must be large enough to allow the cutter to pass through. If it is not, bolt a secondary wood table to the drill press

Fig. 26-37. Convert the drill press to a shaper by replacing the chuck with a spindle adaptor. (Shopsmith, Inc.)

table. Use 3/4 in. plywood, fiberboard, or particleboard with a plastic laminate face. Attach fences or a starting pin as needed, Fig. 26-38. Install a guard around the cutterhead. You might also place featherboards or another type of holder to guide the workpiece.

SHAPING WITH PORTABLE POWER TOOLS

Several portable power tools are available for shaping. These include the portable router, laminate trimmer, and Moto-Tool® .

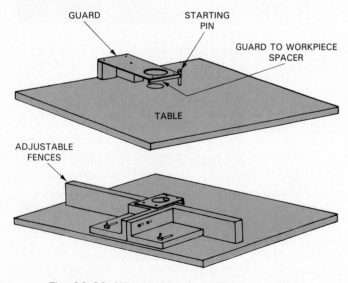

Fig. 26-38. Wood tables for drill press routing.

SHAPING WITH THE PORTABLE ROUTER

One of the cabinetmaker's most preferred shaping tools is the *portable router.* The router's versatility and ease of use make it appropriate for almost any shaping operation.

The parts of a router are shown in Fig. 26-39. A router consists of a motor clamped in a *base.* Motors vary from 1/2 horsepower (hp) in light duty models to 3 hp for heavy duty models. A 1 1/2 or 2 hp router is adequate for most operations. On the end of the motor arbor is a collet to hold the bit. Collet sizes are 1/4, 3/8, and 1/2 in. Depth of cut is set by changing the motor position in the base using a *depth adjusting ring.* A plastic *sub-base* may be attached to the base.

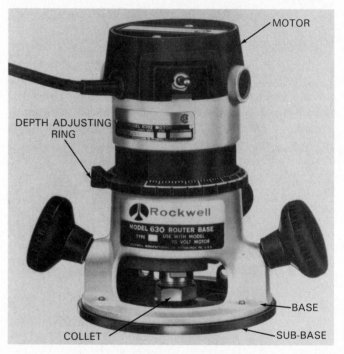

Fig. 26-39. Portable router. (Delta)

CONVENTIONAL AND PLUNGE ROUTERS

Many router operations call for you to insert the rotating bit into the face of a workpiece. This process is called plunging. Router names are based on the router's ability to plunge cut. *Conventional routers* are preset to a fixed depth of cut. To plunge the bit into the face of a workpiece, you have to balance the router on the edge of the base, start the motor, and carefully tilt the bit into the wood. This often results in less accurate cuts.

With *plunge routers,* the entire motor and bit assembly slides up and down (against spring tension) on two posts connected to the base, Fig. 26-40. To plunge the bit into the workpiece, simply

Fig. 26-40. Plunge router motor moves up and down on spring loaded posts. (Ryobi)

set the base on the wood, start the motor, and press down. A locking mechanism holds the depth of cut.

Plunge routers have their drawbacks. The depth adjustment mechanism on plunge routers is harder to set accurately. This is because of play in the up/down movement of the motor and in the locking mechanism. Also, most models have a large hole in the base. A large hole size can be remedied by installing a sub-base with a smaller hole.

METHODS OF GUIDING THE ROUTER

A router, without any accessory, is guided freehand across the workpiece. However, most cuts must conform to a straight or circular shape.

A good straightedge is the metal type used for circular saws. A squared piece of lumber of suitable length will also do. The base of the router rides along the straightedge, Fig. 26-41. The straightedge is clamped a certain distance from the cut to be made.

This distance to the cut is the radius of the base, minus the radius of the cutter, Fig. 26-42.

Router guides are provided by the manufacturer. They include fences, circle guides, and other accessories for producing straight or curved cuts, Fig. 26-43. Most are attached to the router base. The distance is adjusted with wing nuts.

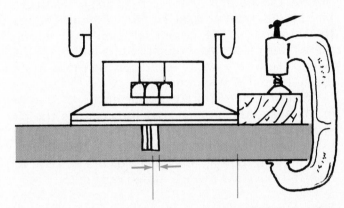

Fig. 26-42. Calculate the distance the straightedge must be from the cut to be made.

A

Fig. 26-41. The router base rides along the straight edge for grooving this door panel. (Black & Decker)

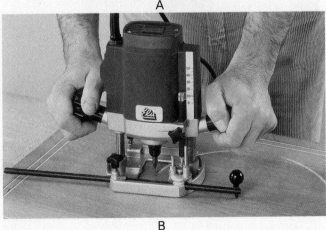

B

Fig. 26-43. Router guides provided by the manufacturer. A—Fence. (Makita) B—Circle guide. (Black & Decker)

Other methods of guiding the cut include pilots and templates. Pilots are used for shaping edges. Templates are used for producing multiple products.

INSTALLING BITS AND SETTING DEPTH

Select the proper router bit to create the shape or joint. Insert it into the collet. You may have to remove the motor from the base to do so. Insert the bit into the collet at least 1/2 in. (13 mm). Engage the *arbor lock* so the motor shaft won't turn as you tighten the collet. Most routers come with a special wrench to fit the collet nut. Place the motor back in the base if it was removed.

To set the depth of cut, lightly clamp the motor in the base. Measure and set the distance the bit protrudes from the base. Fine adjustments are made by turning a depth ring. Have the base clamp loose. Markings on the ring and base indicate how far to turn for a certain change in depth of cut.

Edge shaping

Edge shaping can be done with a fence or with bits having a pilot. With a fence, edge shaping is limited to the distance the fence can extend, Fig. 26-44. However, most edge shaping is done with bits having a pilot. A pilot rides along the edge of the workpiece, Fig. 26-45. The edge must be smooth; otherwise, the pilot follows the defects. Preset the depth of cut. For a plunge router, lock the depth before turning on the router. The rotation of the cutter is clockwise; therefore, feed the router from left to right along an edge facing you. Use slight pressure to keep the pilot against the workpiece. Feed at a moderate rate. If the motor slows considerably, you are feeding too fast or taking too deep of cut. Feeding too slowly causes the bit to heat and burn the wood.

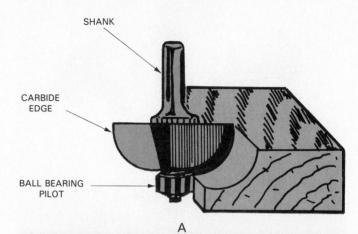

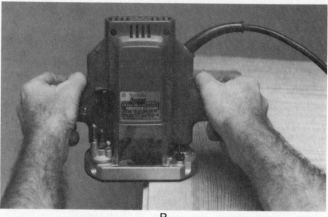

Fig. 26-45. A—Shaping an edge with a pilot to guide the bit. (Makita) B—The pilot rides along the edge of the workpiece.

Routing a dado

Dados are slots across the grain pattern. To rout a dado, clamp a straightedge to the workpiece. Choose a straight bit. Set the depth of cut. Hold the router against the straightedge. Turn on the machine and proceed across the workpiece, Fig. 26-46. Slow the rate of speed as the bit exits the workpiece. This prevents chipping. You might also back up the edge with another board.

Some dados are wider than the largest diameter straight bit. You might use straightedges on both sides of the router. One straightedge determines the location of the first cut. The second one controls the width of the dado.

Routing a groove or flute

Grooves and flutes run with the grain of the wood. Generally, you can attach a fence to the router. The flutes being cut in Fig. 26-43A show a fence and jig setup to guide the router. Notice that the depth of cut is changed for each flute on the moulding.

Freehand routing

Routers come in handy for removing excess material in preparation for a wood carving, Fig.

Fig. 26-44. Shaping an edge using a router fence to guide the bit. (Black & Decker)

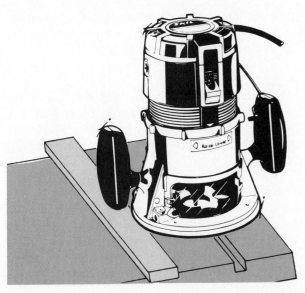

Fig. 26-46. Guide the router with a straightedge to cut a dado.

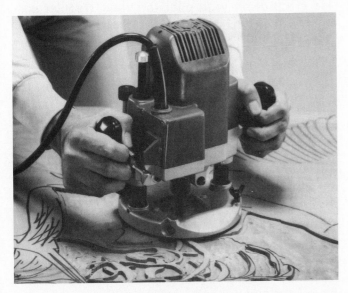

Fig. 26-47. Work on carving may begin with routing out excess material. (Makita)

26-47. The design is copied on the surface and then cut with a router. This must be done freehand since no attachment would follow the intricate shape. To route some of the interior detail, the bit must be plunged into the workpiece. A plunge router is better for this purpose as discussed earlier. Finally, the woodworker uses hand tools to finish the carving.

Routing joints

With the proper setup or jig, the portable router can cut a number of cabinet joints. In fact, some joints, such as a dovetail joint, are cut most accurately with a portable router and jig. Cabinet joints are discussed in Chapter 29.

Routing using templates

Templates are often used to guide the portable router. On a portable router, you have two choices for guiding the router with a template. You can use the outer edge of the sub-base; or, you may attach a template guide to the router base. It serves much like a collar.

When guiding the router along the sub-base, the template must be larger than the design. For example, to route the holes for a speaker mounting panel, Fig. 26-48, you would:
1. Determine the hole size.
2. Select a straight router bit.
3. Subtract the cutter radius from the sub-base radius. This measurement then is the amount the template should be oversize. For example, suppose you are using a 1/2 in. (13 mm) bit in a 6 in. (152 mm) router base. The template must be 2 3/4 in. (70 mm) larger than the design at any point.
4. Cut the template.
5. Align and clamp the template over the workpiece.
6. Plunge the router bit into the workpiece to cut out the hole.

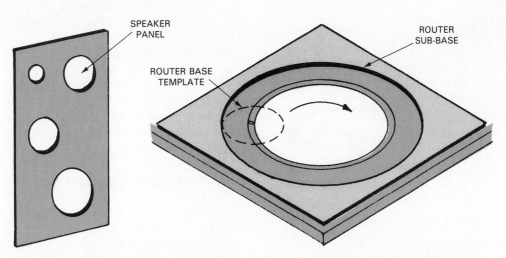

Fig. 26-48. The router sub-base may ride along the template to guide the bit.

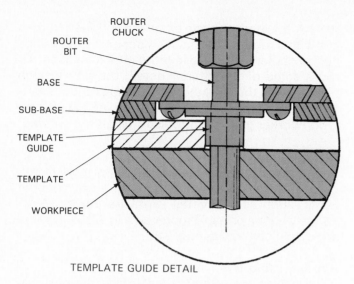

TEMPLATE GUIDE DETAIL

Fig. 26-49. A template guide, attached to the base, may ride along the template to guide the bit.

A template guide is a router accessory. It fits inside the center of the sub-base. Screws attach it to the router base, Fig. 26-49. As you guide the router, the template guide rubs on the template and follows the contour, Fig. 26-50. The template can

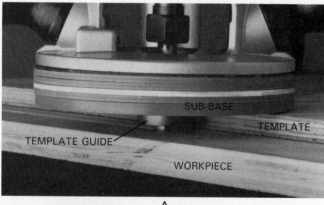

A

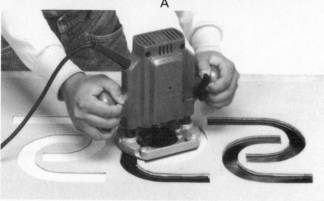

B

Fig. 26-50. Routing with a template guide. A—The template is placed over the workpiece. The plunge router shown here plunges the bit into the workpiece to start the cut. (Makita) B—The template guide then rides along the template. (Bosch)

be made smaller than that where the sub-base guides the router. Few guides are interchangable among manufacturers' routers.

Router jigs

There are a number of jigs available which make the router an even more versatile tool. The one shown in Fig. 26-51 produces carved cabinet door fronts. Other jigs make the router applicable for cutting joints.

Table mounted portable router

The portable router can be mounted under a table for use as a shaper, Fig. 26-52. Router tables are commercially available or you can make your own. The base is attached to the table with screws or bolts. The router motor moves in the base to determine the depth of cut.

Setup and operating procedures are much like the shaper. Use a fence for straightedge routing. Use a router bit with pilot to shape irregular surfaces. A ring-type point-of-operation guard must be in place. Feed from left to right.

THINK SAFETY—ACT SAFELY
WHEN USING PORTABLE ROUTERS

The portable router can be one of the cabinetmaker's favorite tools, if used properly. Follow these safety precautions.
1. Wear eye protection, remove jewelry, and tie up loose hair and clothing.
2. Insert bits into the collet at least 1/2 in.
3. Tighten the base fence, or other attachments before turning on the machine.
4. Feed the router at a moderate rate. Slow feeding results in burned wood. Fast feeding causes a rippled, washboard effect on the surface.
5. Always let the router come to a complete stop before setting it down.
6. Disconnect power to the router before making adjustments or installing bits.

LAMINATE TRIMMER

The laminate trimmer is a smaller version of a router. It is specially designed to trim excess plastic laminate from a core material. The laminate trimmer is discussed in detail in Chapter 36, Installing Plastic Laminates.

SHAPING WITH THE MOTO-TOOL

The *Moto-Tool*® will shape intricate areas. Straight shank cutters with spiral cutting lips remove excess material quickly. The tool will also hold twist drills, abrasive disks and drums, and

Fig. 26-51. This jig reproduces cabinet door designs. (Bosch)

A

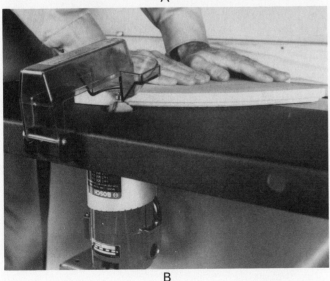

B

Fig. 26-52. A—Mounting a router under a commercial router table. B—The router is then used like a shaper. (Bosch)

miniature grinding wheels, Fig. 26-53.

With a shaping bit, set the Moto-Tool® at the highest speed. For larger areas, install a spherical or cylindrical bit. For small areas, install a small radius, straight bit. While shaping, guide the tool carefully. It will chew away wood from any surface it touches.

Fig. 26-53. A Moto-Tool® comes with various bits. Shaping bits remove material quickly from small areas. (Dremel)

SHAPING WITH HAND TOOLS

Hand tools for shaping include spokeshaves, specialty planes, Surform® tools, and contour scrapers. The spokeshave and curved plane create smooth contours. The Surform tool shapes irregular contours. Contour scrapers remove small defects left by other tools.

SPOKESHAVE

There are two types of *spokeshaves.* One is for convex surfaces. It has a flat bottom about 3/4 in. (19 mm) wide, Fig. 26-54. The other is for concave surfaces. It has a convex (curved) base. When sharpened and adjusted properly, the spokeshave is an effective tool. Originally, the tool was designed to shape wagon wheel spokes.

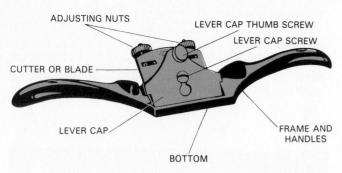

Fig. 26-54. Spokeshave. (Stanley)

A spokeshave works like a plane. Push or pull the tool along the workpiece in a planing motion, Fig. 26-55. Work along the grain to avoid splintering the wood. Wood chips are removed with a blade about 2 in. (50 mm) long. The blade is installed similar to a bench plane iron. It is held by a lever cap. A thumb screw tightens the cap against the blade. Two adjusting nuts align the blade parallel to the bottom of the spokeshave.

Turn the spokeshave at a slight angle on large radius curves. Less forward pressure will be required. Watch for grain direction changes. Otherwise, the tool may skip and/or gouge the workpiece.

CIRCULAR PLANE

The *circular plane* has a flexible sole which adjusts to match the intended contour, Fig. 26-56. Depth of cut is adjusted like a bench plane. Turn the adjusting nut to flex the sole.

COMBINATION PLANE

A *combination plane* allows you to do contouring. A set of changeable tool bits are shaped for ploughing, tonguing, beading, reeding, fluting, and sash shaping, Fig. 26-57. An adjustable fence helps position the plane.

Set up and use a combination plane like a regular plane. However, hold it at 90° to the work. Setup includes installing and adjusting the cutter. A notch on each cutter fits over the depth adjusting screw.

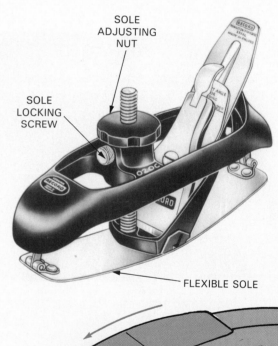

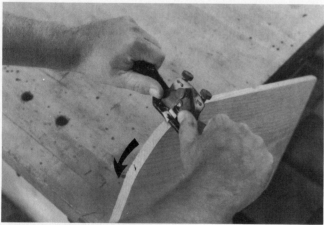

Fig. 26-55. Push or pull the spokeshave around contours with the blade leaning away from the direction of cut.

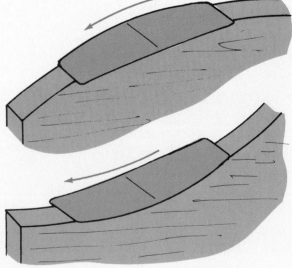

Fig. 26-56. A circular plane smooths convex and concave curves. (Record-Ridgeway)

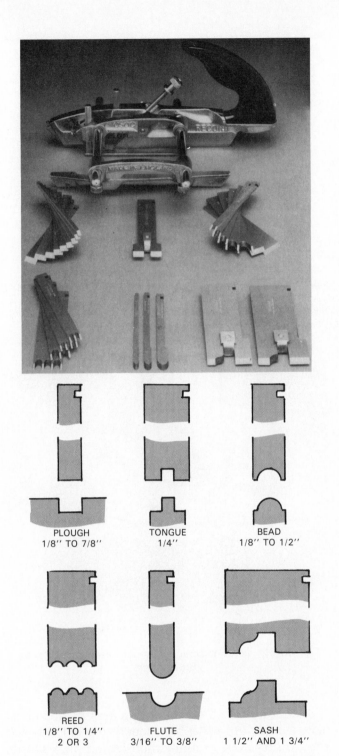

Fig. 26-58. The hardened steel teeth of a Surform tool remove material without clogging. (Stanley)

Fig. 26-59. Surform tool designed for use in a portable drill. (Stanley)

PLOUGH
1/8'' TO 7/8''

TONGUE
1/4''

BEAD
1/8'' TO 1/2''

REED
1/8'' TO 1/4''
2 OR 3

FLUTE
3/16'' TO 3/8''

SASH
1 1/2'' AND 1 3/4''

Fig. 26-57. Shape lumber by hand with a combination plane. (Record-Ridgeway)

SURFORM TOOLS

Surform tools have perforated metal blades with many individual cutting edges, Fig. 26-58. You can use Surform tools on many materials, such as lumber, plywood, fiberboard, plastics, fiberglass, and some aluminums. Surform tool shapes include flat, half round, round, and curved. You can also purchase a circular Surform with a shaft to fit in portable power tools, Fig. 26-59.

Using the Surform at different angles results in different amounts of wood removed, Fig. 26-60. When pushed at an angle to the right, the Surform removes the maximum material. With the Surform body parallel to the workpiece, produced chips are smaller and the surface is smoother. With the Surform handle to the left, a smooth surface which will require very little sanding results.

DRAW KNIFE

A *draw knife,* Fig. 26-61, is appropriate for creating chamfers and for curved contours. It has an open-beveled blade with handles on both ends.

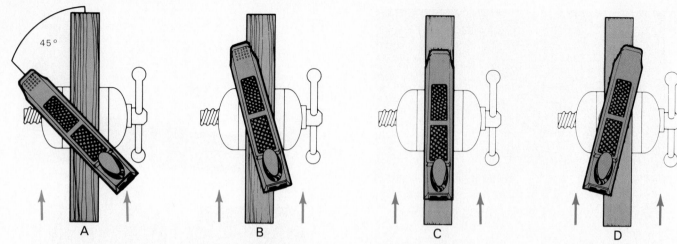

Fig. 26-60. Surface quality is controlled by the Surform tool's position. A—To remove a maximum amount of material, simply hold the tool at 45° to the direction of the stroke. B—To remove less material and obtain a smoother surface, reduce angle. C—To finely smooth the work surface, simply direct the tool parallel to it. D—And you can achieve an almost polishing effect by directing the tool at a slightly reversed angle. (Stanley)

Fig. 26-61. A draw knife shapes table legs quickly. (American Machine and Tool Co.)

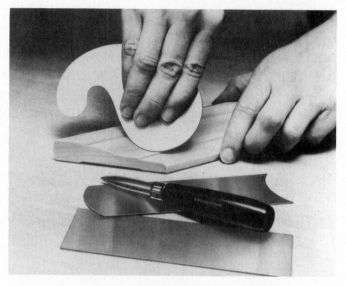

Fig. 26-62. Contour scrapers smooth irregular surfaces. (Brookstone)

CONTOUR SCRAPERS

A *contour scraper* is actually a curved hand scraper, Fig. 26-62. It smooths shaped surfaces. Using and maintaining scrapers was discussed in Chapter 24.

MAINTAINING SHAPING TOOLS

High quality shaping depends on sharp tools and well maintained machines and equipment. Hand tool sharpening techniques for the spokeshave and contour scraper are the same as those discussed in Chapter 24 for bench planes and hand scrapers. However, sharpening shaper cutters and router bits requires special procedures.

Shaper cutters and router bits may be solid carbide, carbide tipped, or high speed steel. High speed steel cutters are ground, then honed on a stone. Carbide cutters and bits can be sharpened only with silicon carbide wheels and hones on special machines by grinding technicians. The cost of carbide cutters may seem high. However, they perform 10 to 20 times longer between grindings than high speed steel cutters.

Preventive maintenance is very important. Removing built-up resins on cutters with paint thinner will prolong the life of the cutting edge.

Generally, you can tell when a cutter is getting dull. It creates a loud high-pitched noise. The workpiece becomes more difficult to feed. The chips are smaller and more dust is created. There is greater heat buildup. Heat can cause bits to lose their hardness (temper). The bit then requires more frequent sharpening.

SHARPENING SHAPER CUTTERS

Grind cutters only when the cutting lip is chipped. Grind only the flat front surface of the cutting lip. Grinding the bevel edge will change the shape. Hold the bit against the side of the wheel. Take very light cuts, just enough to regain the cutting edge.

Grinding should rarely be necessary. Most often, the cutter can be sharpened by honing. Place the cutter's face on the stone's surface. Move it back and forth over the corner of the stone as shown in Fig. 26-63. Lightly touch the bevel of the cutter with a slip stone to remove burrs.

Fig. 26-63. Hone only the leading surface on shaper cutters and router bits.

Fig. 26-64. This grinding jig allows you to sharpen router bits. (Stanley)

SHARPENING ROUTER BITS

Router bits can be ground using the attachment shown in Fig. 26-64. The procedure is as follows:
1. Disconnect your router and turn it upside down.
2. Secure a small cup grinding wheel in the router collet as if installing a bit.
3. Secure the router bit in the grinding jig. Adjust the jig so the cutter is at its highest position.
4. Align the router's depth of cut mechanism. The grinding surface of the wheel must be just below the bit.
5. Connect power to and turn on the router.
6. Lower the bit just until a few sparks fly.
7. Grind the full length of the cutting lip. Reduce the bevel on the cutting edge to .003 in.
8. Rotate the router bit 180° in the jig. Repeat Step 7.
9. Strop the cutting edge to remove burrs.

You can sharpen the bit by honing many times between grindings. Use the honing procedure for shaper cutters.

CLEANING AND LUBRICATING MACHINERY

Shaping machines operate at high speeds. To maintain those speeds, bearings must be friction free. Most bearings are sealed.

Various slide and screw mechanisms on machinery should be lubricated. Use lubricating oil in areas where there is no dust. (Dust will adhere to oil. An accumulation will prevent free movement of slides and screws.) Use silicone spray or paraffin wax where dust is present. Also, wood will not absorb these lubricants, so use them on table surfaces.

Inspect machine belts regularly. Proper tension maintains spindle and collet speeds. The belt should not move side-to-side more than 1 in.

Maintaining portable tools is relatively simple. Keep them clean and free of rust. Apply silicone or wax to slides and locking mechanisms. Router bases and motor housings are often aluminum.

Fig. 26-65. Always remember to charge cordless tools overnight. (Makita)

Handle them with care. Use the proper wrenches, packaged with new machines, when making adjustments. Adjustable jaw wrenches tend to strip the corners on lock nuts and collets.

RECHARGING CORDLESS TOOLS

Battery-operated, cordless routers allow free movement around the workpiece. There is no power cord to interfere. Many routers will run for approximately an hour on a full charge. However, you must remember to charge the battery overnight. Release the clip and remove the battery from the router, Fig. 26-65. Then insert the battery in the charger.

SUMMARY

Shaping meets many functional and design needs in cabinetmaking. Smooth contours and decorative effects are achieved by using the right tool, machine, and cutter.

Stationary shaping machines include the spindle shaper, overarm router, inverted router, and overarm router/shaper. You can also adapt the table saw, radial arm saw, and drill press for shaping. Portable shaping tools include the portable router, plunge router, laminate trimmer, and Moto-tool. Hand tools include the spokeshave, circular plane, combination plane, Surform tools, draw knife, and contour scrapers.

Take extra caution when setting up power equipment, install point-of-operation guards. Select the proper bit or cutter for the job. Check the tightness of the bit twice. If possible, avoid freehand shaping by using fences, starting pins, jigs, or other means of guiding the tool or workpiece.

CABINETMAKING TERMS

Shaping, spindle shaper, spindle, shaper cutter, cutting lips, spindle guard, ring guard, collar, starting pin, template, overarm router, router bit, pilot, collet, plunging, pin routing, overarm router/shaper, inverted router, spiral bit, moulding cutterhead, portable router, base, depth adjusting ring, subbase, conventional router, plunge router, arbor lock, Moto-tool, spokeshave, circular plane, combination plane, Surform tool, draw knife, contour scraper.

TEST YOUR KNOWLEDGE

1. Why is it essential that you use a *keyed* washer when installing a shaper cutter?
2. Describe two types of spindle shaper guards.
3. The spindle shaper uses a _____ cutter while routers use _____ bits.
4. More than one pass or cutter may be necessary to make the desired shape. True or False?
5. List, in order, the items placed on the spindle when installing a shaper cutter.
6. Describe four options for guiding the workpiece when using a spindle shaper.
7. Explain when a shaper's infeed and outfeed fences are aligned, and when they are not.
8. List the order for shaping four sides of a board.
9. Describe how a router bit pilot and shaper collar function similarly.
10. Explain how to set bit depth for both floor standing and bench model overarm routers.
11. Router bits with cutting lips on the ends are for _____.
12. Why must you feed against the rotation of the cutter for any power shaping machine?

13. For pin routing, the guide pin is:
    a. Directly under the router bit.
    b. Directly under the shaper cutter.
    c. Offset to the infeed side.
    d. Offset to the outfeed side.
14. Is it necessary to have a template when pin routing?
15. Identify the method for setting bit depth on the overarm router/shaper.
16. What safety advantage is gained by using an inverted router rather then an overarm router?
17. The table saw is adaptable for shaping by installing a _____.
18. To use a shaper cutter or router bit on the radial arm saw, you must install a _____ or _____.
19. A drill press adaptable for shaping or routing:
    a. Must be variable speed.
    b. Should be a 20 in. model.
    c. Turns both clockwise and counterclockwise.
    d. Has a chuck threaded to the spindle.
20. Depth of cut for a portable router is set by changing the_____position in the_____.
21. Describe the primary differences between conventional and plunge routers.
22. Name two methods used to guide the portable router.
23. For which portable router operations do you use a bit with pilot?
24. Explain why a spokeshave is more appropriate for curves than is a smooth plane.
25. The angle at which the Surform tool is pushed determines the _____.
26. A combination plane is a hand tool which allows you to shape multiple contours in a single pass. True or False?
27. Shaper cutters and router bits are ground and honed on:
    a. All surfaces.
    b. The front surface of each cutting lip.
    c. On the back side of each cutting lip.
    d. The edge of the lip.

Chapter 27
TURNING

After studying this chapter, you will be able to:
- *Identify components made by spindle and faceplate turning.*
- *Select lumber for turning.*
- *Mount stock between centers or on a faceplate.*
- *Work with turning tools to create desired shapes.*
- *Follow steps to turn cylinders, beads, coves, and grooves.*

Turning processes produce round parts on a lathe. Stock is mounted between centers or on a faceplate. A turning tool is held against and moved along the rotating workpiece to remove material. *Spindle turning,* or between-center turning, Fig. 27-1, creates cylindrical, tapered, or countoured parts. These include table and chair legs, stair banisters, and bed posts, Fig. 27-2. When the workpiece is mounted on a faceplate, you can turn the face as well as the edges, Fig. 27-3. This produces products such as bowls, knobs, pulls, stool seats, and table tops. Stock can be held by other methods as discussed later in the chapter.

LATHES

There are lathes for production turning and for small cabinet shop or home use. Production lathes turn numerous parts automatically. The turning tool, or bit, is guided by electrical mechanical controls. Discussed in this chapter are the standard and bowl lathes. Suitable for small cabinet shop and home use, these turn one part at a time. They make custom products or duplicate damaged parts when

Fig. 27-2. These bedposts were turned between centers. (Trendwest)

Fig. 27-1. Between-center turning for making spindle products. The guard was removed to show the operation.

Fig. 27-3. Faceplate turning. (Delta)

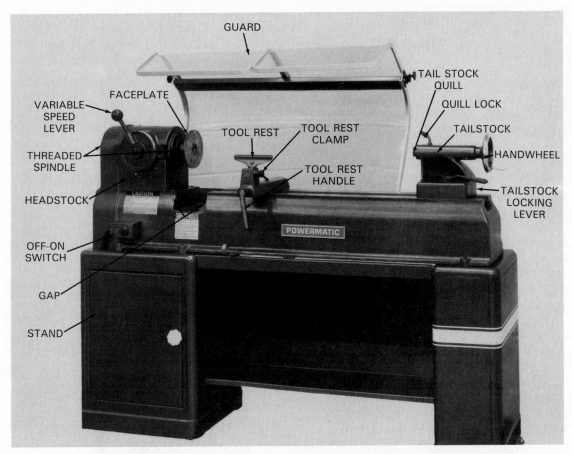

Fig. 27-4. The standard woodturning lathe. (Powermatic)

restoring furniture. A duplicator accessory allows you to turn multiple parts.

STANDARD LATHE

Most wood turning operations are performed on the *standard lathe,* Fig. 27-4. The machine consists of the headstock, bed, tailstock, tool rest, and guard. The *headstock* houses the spindle which drives the workpiece. There are threads at both ends of the spindle on which a faceplate can be mounted. The spindle is hollow and tapered to accept a center. The tapered center and spindle form a friction fit to hold the center in place. To the right of the headstock is the *bed.* It consists of two flat rails on which the tool rest and tailstock are mounted. The tool rest and tailstock move along the bed to accommodate any workpiece length. The bed aligns the tailstock quill with the center of the spindle. The hollow, tapered *tailstock quill* holds the second center between which stock may be mounted. The bed also supports an adjustable tool rest. On some lathes, there is a gap between the headstock and bed. A *gap bed lathe* allows larger diameter parts to be faceplate turned.

Standard lathe sizes are measured by swing, overall bed length, and distance between centers.

The *swing* is the largest diameter workpiece that can be turned. The *overall bed length* is the distance between the headstock and the end of the bed. The *distance between centers* determines the maximum length of stock that can be turned.

Lathe speed is set with a variable speed lever or with step pulleys. An OFF-ON switch will be near the headstock. Sometimes, the switch and speed control are on one lever.

The user is protected from flying chips by a clear plastic or wire mesh *guard.* It mounts on the back of the lathe. Lift the guard and rest it in an upward position when mounting stock. When the spindle is turning, lower the guard into place.

BOWL LATHE

The *bowl lathe* is a special machine for faceplate turning only, Fig. 27-5. Many of its parts are the same as the standard lathe.

TURNING TOOLS

Turning tools include a number of chisel-like cutters. There are five tools in a standard set: gouge, skew, parting tool, round-nose tool, and spear-point tool. All are about 17 in. long, Fig. 27-6. Carbide

Fig. 27-5. The bowl lathe is for faceplate turning only.
(Brodhead-Garrett)

27-8. A scraping action enhances this roughness because chips can be torn, especially from open grain wood. Careful turning with sharp tools, especially a cutting action with the skew, reduces the need for abrasives. This is important since abrasives can leave crossgrain scratches.

The gouge rough-cuts stock to near workpiece diameter. It can be used for either cutting or scrap-

tipped cutting edges are more durable, but are not necessary for most operations.

Turning is either a cutting or scraping action, depending on how the tool is held, Fig. 27-7. For cutting, hold the tool on the rest at a slightly upward angle. A scraping action occurs when the tool is held at about 90° to the workpiece center.

The sharpness and angle of the cutting tool control the smoothness of the cut. However, grain direction and pattern are also factors. Certain portions of the circumference remain rough, Fig.

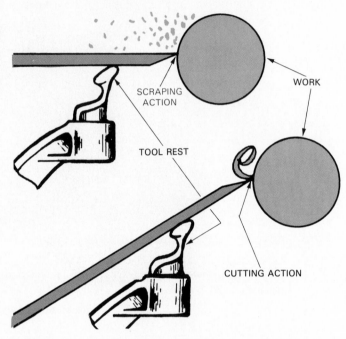

Fig. 27-7. Turning can be a cutting or scraping action.

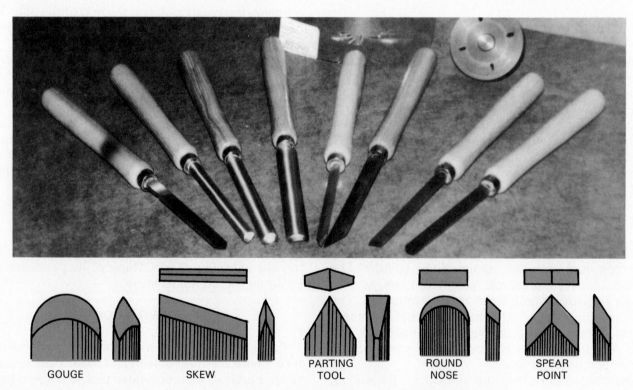

Fig. 27-6. Turning tools, shapes, and angles. (Brodhead-Garrett)

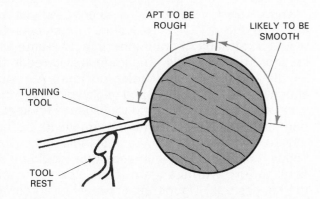

Fig. 27-8. Grain direction affects the smoothness of the surface.

ing, Fig. 27-9. The parting tool is held in the scraping or cutting position to produce square shoulders, inside corners, and grooves, Fig. 27-10. Select the round-nose tool, held in the scraping position, for concave curves, Fig. 27-11. The spear-point tool scrapes ''V'' grooves, beads, chamfers, inside corners, and square shoulders, Fig. 27-12.

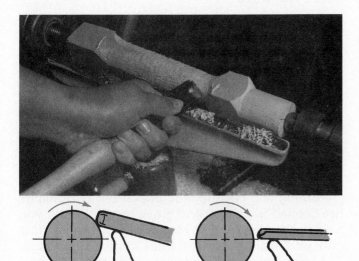

CUTTING   SCRAPING

Fig. 27-9. Cutting and scraping with gouge. The guard was removed to show the operation.

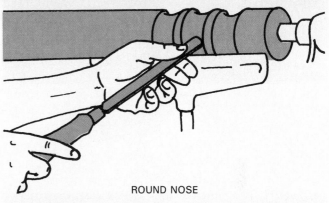

ROUND NOSE

Fig. 27-11. Scraping a cove with the round-nose tool. The guard was removed to show the operation.

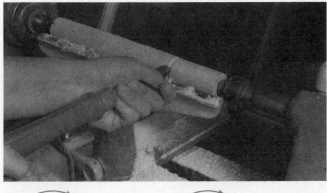

CUTTING   SCRAPING

Fig. 27-10. Cutting and scraping with the parting tool. The guard was removed to show the operation.

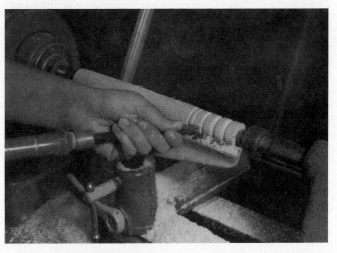

Fig. 27-12. Scraping V-grooves with the spear-point tool. The guard was removed to show the operation.

The skew cuts or scrapes "V" grooves, beads, cylinders, tapers, and other shapes. The tool is made so versatile simply by holding it at different angles, Fig. 27-13. Skew cutting, done carefully, greatly reduces the need for sanding when spindle turning. This is why the skew is generally used last for detail work. With faceplate turning, it is difficult to control the skew. The point tends to catch in end grain and gouge the wood.

The cabinetmaker often finds that special shaped tools are valuable. For example, a square-end tool, which looks like a long chisel, performs similar to the spear-point tool. Some suppliers sell this and other tool shapes in add-on sets.

Knife inserts made for a special handle are available, Fig. 27-14. The knives turn shapes that would be difficult, if not impossible, to create with standard turning tools. The knife is secured in the handle and used in a scraping position. A cutting action would lift up chips and might ruin fine detail.

Another option is to grind tool shapes for special purposes. Suppose a number of duplicate decorative spindles are needed. Each spindle has several beads, coves, and ogee shapes that would be difficult to turn with standard tools. You can create the shapes out of good quality steel or an old flat file. Grind and hone the cutting edge, then attach a handle.

TOOL HOLDING

A *tool rest* supports the turning tool during your operation. It adjusts vertically and laterally, and it pivots. Position the rest 1/8 in. away from the workpiece and about 1/8 in. above the work center line, Fig. 27-15.

Tool rests come in different widths. A short width tool rest might be mounted when turning a knob. Install a longer rest when turning table legs, chair rungs, and long spindles. A 90° tool rest can be positioned over the bed for turning the face and edge of a product.

Turning is a two-handed operation; both hands are needed to control and move the tool. How you hold the turning tool is a matter of preference. Most cabinetmakers hold the handle in their right hand. The left hand thumb is placed on the top of the tool and your fingers are under it. The tool's depth of cut is guided by your index finger against the tool

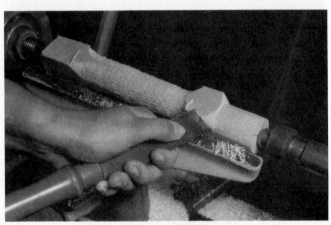

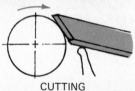

CUTTING

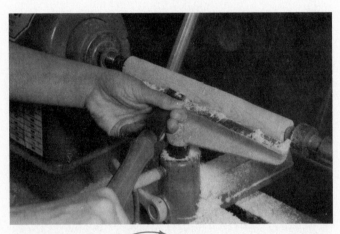

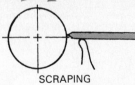

SCRAPING

Fig. 27-13. Scraping and cutting with the skew. The guard was removed to show the operation.

Fig. 27-14. Interchangeable cutters allow you to create additional contours. (Shopsmith)

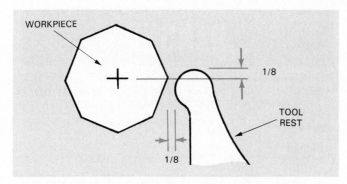

Fig. 27-15. Position of the tool rest.

rest. Another hold has the hand over the blade and thumb underneath. The user's little finger rubs against the tool rest to control depth of cut.

Feed the chisel with moderate pressure. Forcing it into your work will result in a rough surface and may gouge the wood. Apply just enough force to maintain a cutting or scraping action. Otherwise, the tool simply rubs against the wood.

MOUNTING STOCK

As stated earlier, stock can be mounted one of several ways: between centers, faceplate, screw-thread faceplate, or lathe chuck, Fig. 27-16.

When spindle turning, stock is mounted between a spur (drive) center and a live or dead center. The *spur center* has a cone point and four sharp spurs which drive the workpiece. Its Morse taper shank fits snugly into the spindle. Inserted into the tailstock quill, another center supports the workpiece. The *dead center* has a cup with a sharp

circular rim and center point. A dead center remains stationary while the workpiece turns against it. To reduce heat buildup, oil or wax is applied. The *live center* has a ball bearing and cupped point. The workpiece does not rotate against the point. Rather, the ball bearing allows the center to turn with the workpiece. This prevents the workpiece from burning or becoming loose. These problems occur with dead centers.

When faceplate turning, secure stock with several screws to a faceplate. *Faceplates,* ranging in diameter from 2 to 6 in., thread onto either the inboard or outboard side of the headstock. *Inboard turning* is done with the faceplate mounted on the bed side of the headstock. *Outboard turning* is done with the faceplate mounted on the spindle side opposite the bed. You need a separate *tripod stand* for the tool rest when outboard turning. The advantage of outboard turning is that part diameter up to 16 in. can be created. Workpiece weight should control the turning speed.

A handwheel is threaded onto the outboard end of the spindle. It may serve as a faceplate if there are holes for screws drilled in it. However, it also lets you turn the spindle by hand when checking tool rest and workpiece clearance. Place your hand against it to stop a coasting lathe. Never grab the rotating workpiece to stop it. You may wind up having a hand full of splinters.

For turning small parts, such as knobs and pulls, use a *screw-thread faceplate,* also called a screw center. The faceplate, usually 1 1/2 in. in diameter, has a 3/4 to 1 in. threaded screw-like center. To mount stock, first drill a pilot hole, then thread the stock onto the screw, Fig. 27-17.

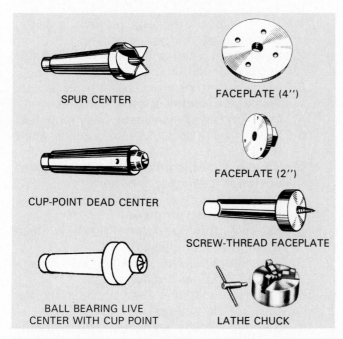

Fig. 27-16. Stock is mounted with various accessories. (Delta)

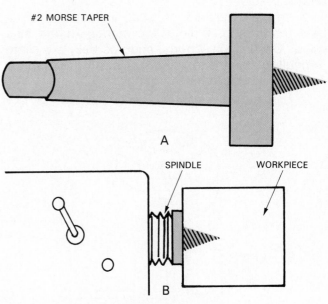

Fig. 27-17. Mounting a workpiece on a screw-thread faceplate. A—Insert the faceplate into the spindle. B—Thread on the workpiece.

When you need to turn without centers, but do not want screws in your workpiece, choose a *lathe chuck.* The chuck mounts on the spindle and can hold round stock from 1/8 in. up to 4 or 6 in. in diameter, Fig. 27-18. The chuck can also be inserted in the tailstock for drilling operations. The workpiece is mounted on a faceplate. Insert a drill bit in the chuck and move the tailstock close to your work. Turn the tailstock handwheel to feed the bit into the rotating wood.

LATHE SPEEDS

Lathe speeds are controlled by one of two methods. Some machines have step pulleys on both the motor and spindle. Speed is determined by the size relationship between pulleys. Mount the belt on a small motor and large spindle pulleys for slow speeds. Using a large motor pulley results in higher speeds. Most lathes are variable speed and adjusted while the machine is running. Lathe speeds are usually printed on the stand or near the speed lever. Otherwise, use a tachometer or calculate the speed mathematically based on the pulley sizes and motor rpm. You must know the speed range settings for turning, Fig. 27-19. A rule of thumb is to use slow speeds for large work and fast speeds for small work. Established maximum speeds have been set for various turning operations. These are for the protection of the machine and operator.

LUMBER

Carefully select clear lumber for turning. Some species turn better than others. (See Fig. 12-45.) Stock with defects, such as knots and cracks, is unacceptable.

Close grain hardwoods, such as maple, are the best for turning. Walnut and mahogany are also good. Open grain woods, such as oak, are more difficult to turn and require a cutting action. A scraping action tears the grain.

DANGER

DO NOT EXCEED THESE RECOMMENDED SPEEDS. SERIOUS INJURY CAN RESULT IF PARTS BEING TURNED ARE THROWN FROM THE LATHE.

DIA. OF WORK	ROUGHING R.P.M.	GEN CUTTING R.P.M.	FINISHING R.P.M.
UNDER 2	1520	3000	3000
2 TO 4	760	1600	2480
4 TO 6	510	1080	1650
6 TO 8	380	810	1240
8 TO 10	300	650	1000
10 TO 12	255	540	830
12 TO 14	220	460	710
14 TO 16	190	400	620

Fig. 27-19. Always refer to speed instructions. (Powermatic)

Softwoods are difficult to turn. They tend to split and tear. Like open grain hardwoods, softwoods are best turned with a cutting action. If scraped, a fuzzy, rough surface results. Extra sanding is necessary.

It is advisable to purchase turning squares for spindle turning. *Turning squares* are square lumber samples of varying sizes and lengths, selected for their straight grain and few defects.

Select quarter sawn lumber for faceplate turning. It tends not to tear, splinter, or warp. When you glue layers together to increase thickness, alternate each layer 90°.

THINK SAFETY—ACT SAFELY WHEN USING THE WOOD LATHE

1. Wear eye protection, remove jewelry, secure loose hair and clothing.
2. Keep tools clean and sharp with handles in good condition.
3. Never turn stock which has checks, knots, weak glue joints, or other defects.
4. Make certain all stock is properly mounted.
5. Always have safety shield in place while turning.
6. Rotate stock by hand after mounting it to ensure it clears the tool rest.
7. Lock the tail stock and tool rest securely before turning on power.
8. Never lay turning tools on the lathe. Place them in a nearby rack.
9. Turn rough square stock or large dimensioned stock at a slow speed.
10. Stop the machine before adjusting the tailstock or tool rest.
11. Remove excess shavings only with the machine stopped.

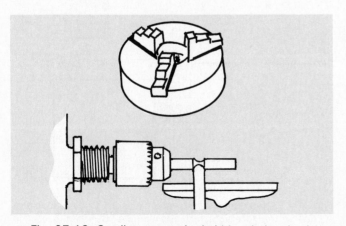

Fig. 27-18. Small parts can be held in a lathe chuck.

BETWEEN-CENTER TURNING

Between-center turning, or spindle turning as it is often called, involves several steps. You must prepare and mount the material, select spindle speeds, and then proceed through a series of turning operations.

PREPARING MATERIAL FOR TURNING BETWEEN CENTERS

Turning generally begins with a length of square stock that is 2 to 4 in. longer than the designed component. It might be solid wood or several layers laminated together. Begin with stock having the ends cut square.

Locate centers
Locate the center of each end by drawing diagonal lines. Then use a scratch awl or drill to make a hole in both ends where the diagonals meet, Fig. 27-20A. Next, saw a kerf along the diagonal lines on the spur center end of the stock, Fig. 27-20B. This further ensures a solid hold when the stock is turned.

If you choose to begin turning with round stock, a *center finder* is useful, Fig. 27-21. Hold it against the edge and end of the stock and draw one diagonal. Then turn it 90° and draw another diagonal. Their intersection marks the center.

Bevel corners
Once the you locate centers, bevel the corners of the workpiece. Do this only to sections which will be turned. Beveling reduces tearing or splintering on corners where the material is weakest. Some turnings have both square and round sections along

Fig. 27-21. Center finder for round stock. (American Machine and Tool Co.)

their length. With a pencil, mark those portions that are to be beveled. The corners can be taken off with a plane, jointer, band saw, or table saw, Fig. 27-22. Do not bevel corners within 1 in. of sections that are to be left square. For example, the portion of a table leg which meets the table top and apron often is not turned.

Setting speed
Adjust the spindle speed on step pulley lathes to the roughing rpm before mounting the stock. This allows you to check the speed without the hazard of rotating mounted stock too fast. Refer to the speed table on the lathe.

Set the speed on variable speed lathes while the lathe is running. Refer to the speed table or digital speed readout every time you turn the machine on.

Mounting stock for between-center turning
Mounting involves inserting the spur center into the stock and securing the stock between the

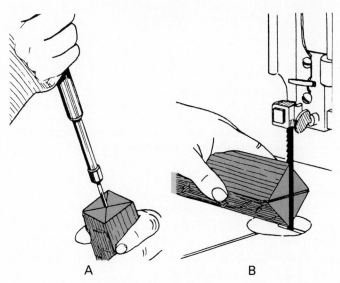
Fig. 27-20. Mark the center and make kerfs in the drive end of the workpiece.

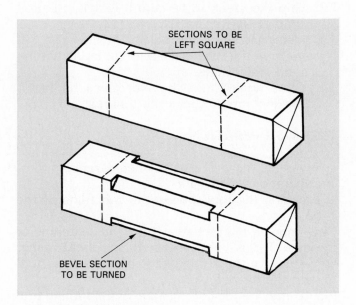
Fig. 27-22. Bevel the edges of sections to be turned.

headstock and tailstock. The step-by-step procedure is as follows:

1. Place the workpiece on the bed of the lathe touching the headstock.
2. Secure the tailstock about 4 in. (100 mm) beyond the workpiece length.
3. If the spur center is still in the spindle, remove it with a knockout rod. Insert the rod through the hollow spindle from the outboard end. Hold the center with your hand so it cannot fall out and be damaged. Be careful not to hold the center directly in line with the spurs. Rap the center free with the knockout rod.
4. Align the spur center in kerfed end of the stock. With a soft-face hammer or mallet, strike the center to seat it, Fig. 27-23A.
5. Insert a dead or live center into the tailstock quill, Fig. 27-23B.
6. Slide the spur center into the spindle without letting the workpiece pull free.
7. Turn the tailstock handwheel to insert the center 1/32 to 1/16 in. into the other end of the workpiece. The distance marks on the quill should show 1 to 2 in. (25 to 50 mm). If you see all the marks on the quill, move the tailstock closer. Then reset the quill.
8. Tighten the quill lock.
9. With the guard in place, turn the workpiece by hand. It should move freely and clear the tool rest support.
10. If a dead center is used, lubricate it. Release the quill lock and back off the center. Rub candle wax or place two drops of oil on the center. Repeat this procedure several times while turning. Reset the center and tighten the quill lock.
11. Turn the machine on and off quickly. Let the workpiece coast to a stop.
12. Grip the stock to be sure it is still mounted tightly.
13. Install and adjust the tool rest. It should be 1/8 in. from the workpiece and 1/8 in. above the work center line.
14. Once again, turn the workpiece by hand, making sure it clears the tool rest.

TURNING OPERATIONS

Several terms will be used when describing turning operations. They are:

In—feeding the tool toward the centerline of the lathe.

Out—moving the tool away from the centerline of the lathe. This is limited mostly to faceplate turning.

Left—moving the cutting edge of the turning tool toward the headstock.

Right—moving the cutting edge of the turning tool toward the tailstock.

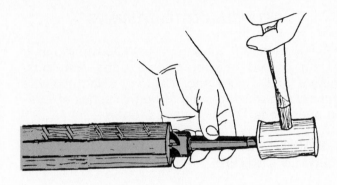

A

B

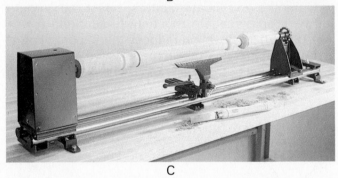

C

Fig. 27-23. Mounting stock between centers. A—Drive the spur center into the workpiece. B—Insert the live (or dead) center into the tailstock quill. C—Insert the spur center into the spindle and press the cup into the other end of the workpiece. (American Machine and Tool Co.)

Rough turning

Rough turning balances, or centers, the workpiece. With the gouge, begin turning those sections to be round. Avoid touching portions marked to be left square. Use the gouge for rough turning, Fig. 27-24, as follows:

1. Lower the guard and turn on the lathe at rough cutting speed.

Fig. 27-24. Rough-turn 3 to 4 in. sections to bring the stock to a constant diameter. The guard was removed to show the operation.

2. Hold the gouge handle about 15° down from horizontal and 15° to the left. You may have to alter these angles as the workpiece becomes smaller.
3. Roll the gouge clockwise about 30° to 45°. The right side of the cutting edge will contact the wood first. This will throw chips to the side so they do not block your vision.
4. Turn 3 or 4 in. sections at a time. Cut to the right, starting about 3 in. from tailstock end.
5. Turn only until the stock is round. Do not turn to the final diameter at this point.
6. Turn off the machine and move the tool rest when necessary.

To rough turn areas where square and round sections meet, use the method shown in Fig. 27-25.

Turning to approximate diameter

The desired contour of the part may contain a number of different diameters, curves, and square shoulders. You first need to lay out the location of these diameters on the rough-turned stock. With a pencil, mark lines every 2 in. or when the diameters change size, as shown on the drawing, Fig. 27-26A. On a piece of paper, mark the diameter each line denotes.

Next, adjust the speed for general turning. Set it according to the current diameter of your workpiece. Reduce the speed 10 to 15 percent if square sections remain.

Use the parting tool to locate diameters. At each of your layout lines, turn diameters 1/8 in. (3 mm) greater than the dimensions indicate, Fig. 27-26B. Check the diameter several times as you turn to prevent undercutting the dimension. You can check by several methods. One is to use outside calipers preset to 1/8 in. greater than the finished diameter, Fig. 27-26C. Periodically, turn the lathe off. Place

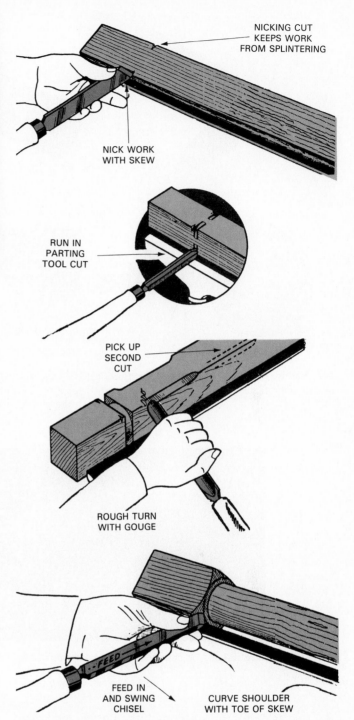

Fig. 27-25. Use the skew, parting tool, and gouge where square and round sections meet. (Delta)

the caliper in the groove. Stop turning when the caliper slips over the workpiece. Two other methods are a sizing tool, Fig. 27-26D, and template, Fig. 27-26E.

Cut with the parting tool as follows:
1. Set the tool rest about 1/4 in. below center. Lower the guard. Rotate the workpiece twice by hand, then turn on the machine.
2. Point the tool straight into the workpiece, with the handle down about 15°.

Turning 413

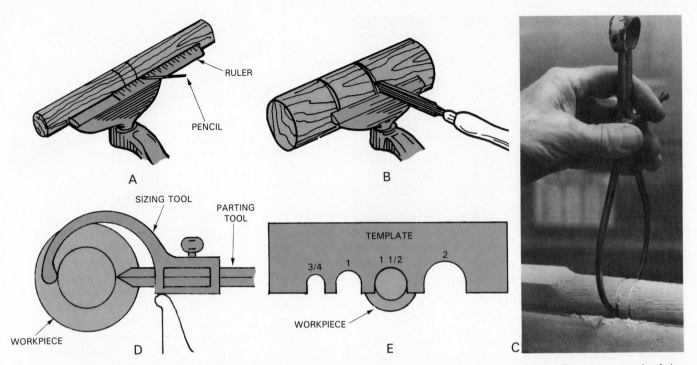

Fig. 27-26. A—Lay out locations of different diameters. B—With the parting tool, turn to approximate diameter at each of the layout lines. (Delta) C—Checking diameter with calipers. D—Turning the diameter with parting tool and sizing tool. E—Checking diameter with a template.

Fig. 27-27. A steadyrest increases stability and reduces chatter. The guard was removed to show the operation. (Shopsmith)

3. As the diameter is reduced, the handle may need to be raised horizontal.
4. Remember to stop the lathe and check each diameter you turn.

Planning is essential to successful turning. Turn and smooth all contours greater than 3/4 in. (19 mm) first. Then contour small diameters. Leaving small diameter sections for last reduces chatter. *Chatter* is a noisy vibration caused by a flexing workpiece. It often increases while scraping with dull turning tools. A series of rough surface rings are produced as the workpiece vibrates against the turning tool. If this occurs, first reduce pressure on the tool. Then check the sharpness of your tool. If neither helps, turn the machine off. Check that the

workpiece is secure between the centers.

Another remedy for chatter is to use a steadyrest, Fig. 27-27. The *steadyrest* rollers contact the workpiece on the side opposite the tool. This prevents flexing of long, small diameter spindles. Position the steadyrest against a short center section turned to the approximate diameter. Select a location where details are minimal. Turn and smooth the workpiece except for the supported section. Then remove the steadyrest and complete the workpiece.

Once grooves have been made with the parting tool to locate diameters, continue turning with the gouge. Use the grooves as a guide to rough turn the contours. Stop turning when you near the approximate diameters. The final details are made with other turning tools.

Turning cylinders and tapers

Cylinders are the same diameter from one end to the other. Tapers are cone-shaped. These are first turned with a gouge. Then use a skew or block plane to smooth them, Fig. 27-28. To scrape with a skew, place the skew flat on the tool rest. Have the cutting edge even with the workpiece center. For a cutting action, tip the point of the skew slightly up as you feed the tool along the tool rest. The cutting action should be performed by more experienced wood turners. A novice tends to let the point of the skew touch the workpiece. It catches and gouges the wood. Make contact with the workpiece in the middle of the cutting edge only. Start about 3 in. from the tailstock end and cut or scrape in either direction.

Use a block plane to smooth a cylinder or taper after turning to approximate diameter. Place the sole of the plane on the tool rest. Turn the plane about 15° to the spindle. Move the plane left or right and maintain a cutting action. The block plane will straighten variations in diameters from one end to the other.

Turning V-grooves

V-grooves can be scraped with the spear-point tool or cut with a skew, Fig. 27-29. Place the spear-point tool flat on the rest. Feed it into the wood to the desired depth. With a skew, only the corner touches the tool rest. Hold the skew on edge and feed it to the desired depth. Angle the tool left or right to widen and deepen the groove.

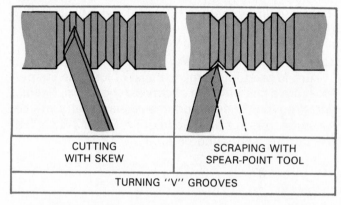

Fig. 27-29. Turning V-grooves by cutting and scraping.

Turning beads

Beads are turned with a spear-point tool or skew, Fig. 27-30. First use a parting tool (if beads are separated) and reach the proper diameter. To scrape a bead, hold the spear-point tool horizontal. Feed the cutting edge into the groove, while moving the handle left or right according to the curve. Keep the point from cutting into the next bead by slightly rotating the tool.

With the skew, cut with the heel end half of the blade's edge. The handle should be down about 15° to 25°. Start near the center of the bead. As you cut, roll the tool into the groove twice to form each half of the bead.

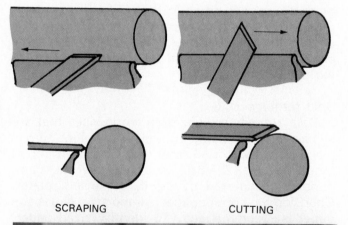

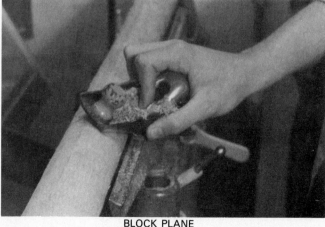

Fig. 27-28. Turning a cylinder by scraping, cutting, or planing. The guard was removed to show the operation.

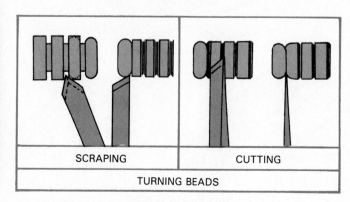

Fig. 27-30. Turning beads by scraping with a spear-point tool or cutting with a skew. (Delta)

Turning coves

Coves, or concave curves, are made with the round-nose tool in the scraping position, Fig. 27-31. Rough-cut the cove with a gouge. Then, adjust a caliper to the smallest diameter of the cove. Feed the round-nose tool into the center of the cove. Pivot the tool to form a smooth contour.

Turning shoulders

Shoulders are turned with the parting tool, gouge, and skew, Fig. 27-32. Feed the parting tool in to the approximate diameter. Then turn down the shoulder with a gouge and finish with a skew. True the shoulder by feeding the tip of a skew along the shoulder's face.

Turning complex shapes

Turned products rarely consist of just one shape. Most are a combination of curves, shoulders, beads, and grooves. These products require that you use a number of tools and techniques, Fig. 27-33. Plan the cutting sequence carefully.

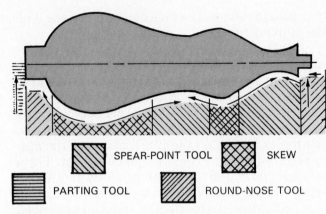

SPEAR-POINT TOOL   SKEW

PARTING TOOL   ROUND-NOSE TOOL

Fig. 27-33. Complex shapes require a number of turning operations.

Turning glued-up stock

Turnings are not always made of solid lumber. Several layers of stock may be glued together. With different species of wood, you get interesting color combinations.

Stock may also be glued together for special purposes. For example, suppose you are turning a spindle for a lamp stand. You need a hole through the center for the electrical cord. The length of the spindle could prevent drilling a straight hole through it. One remedy is to use two pieces of stock. Saw or rout a groove through both. Then, glue them together with the grooves aligned, and a square plug about 1 in. long in each end, Fig. 27-34. The plugs provide a firm contact for the centers while turning. Drill them out later.

Split turnings

Split turnings are glued-up workpieces that are separated after being turned. You might turn a piece of stock round, then split it for half-round moulding, Fig. 27-35. Glue together the components, separated by sized, or sealed, paper. Choosing the correct paper is important. Notebook paper is recommended. To identify sized paper, write on it with a ball point pen. If the inked line

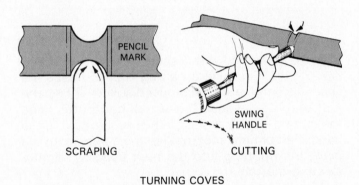

PENCIL MARK

SCRAPING

SWING HANDLE

CUTTING

TURNING COVES

Fig. 27-31. Turning coves with the round-nose tool.

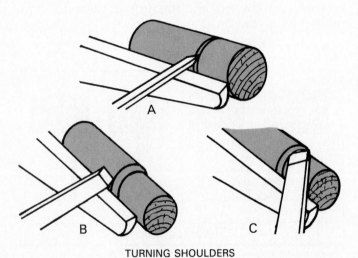

A

B   C

TURNING SHOULDERS

Fig. 27-32. Turning shoulders. (Delta)

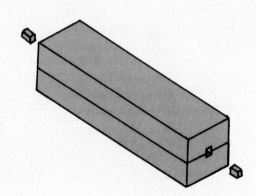

Fig. 27-34. Groove, glue, and plug a workpiece which needs a hole through it.

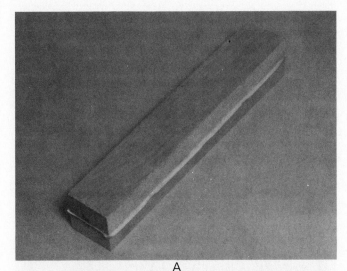

A

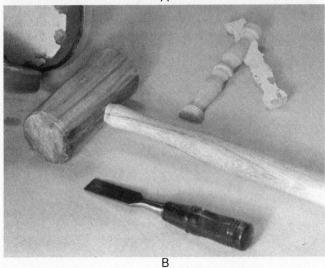

B

Fig. 27-35. Split turning. A—Glue two pieces of stock together, separated by sized paper. B—Turn the desired shape, then split the parts with a mallet and chisel.

bleeds (spreads), the paper is not sized. After turning, split the pieces with a chisel and mallet.

Turning duplicate workpieces

Cabinets and furniture often make use of several identical turned parts. For example, spindles in a chair back should look alike. Duplicating parts may be done in several ways. The most difficult practice is to measure each detail independently. A better method is to use a template. The best practice is to mount a duplicating accessory to the lathe.

Using a template. Make a template of heavy paper or sheet metal. Linear dimensions can be placed on the template's straight edge. The other edge is cut to the shape of the desired contour, Fig. 27-36. First rough turn the workpiece round. Then mark the linear distances and cut depths with a parting tool. As you continue turning the workpiece, stop the lathe periodically to compare your turning with

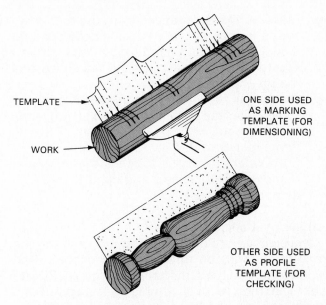

Fig. 27-36. Duplicate parts are sized with a template. (Shopsmith)

the template. When the turned contour matches the template, remove tool marks with abrasive paper.

Using a duplicator. A *duplicator* is the best tool for creating many similar parts. The procedure to use this accessory, as shown in Fig. 27-37, is as follows.

1. Rough-turn all workpieces to a diameter that is 1/4 in. larger than the largest diameter of the finished part.
2. Prepare and attach a contoured hardboard template to the duplicator.
3. Mount the duplicator parallel to the center line of the lathe.
4. Set the tool guide stylus against the hardboard template.
5. Determine the tool offset (workpiece radius) at both ends of the spindle.

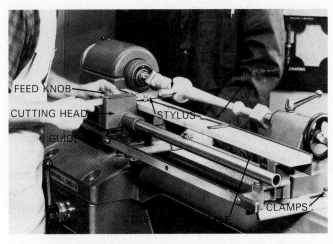

Fig. 27-37. Duplicator attachment. The guard was removed to show the operation. (Rockwell International)

6. Measure these distances from the tool bit to the centerpoints of the live and dead centers. Add 1/16 in. for smoothing.
7. Tighten the duplicator to the lathe bed and mount the workpiece.
8. Contour all sections. Move the tool laterally by turning the feed knob with one hand. Move the tool in or out with the other hand.
9. Remove 1/8 to 1/4 in. (3 to 6 mm) layers.
10. Stop when the stylus touches the template.
11. Remove the duplicator and sand the spindle as necessary.

Turning oval spindles

Oval spindles are made by mounting and turning stock three times on three different centers. The spindles that support the table in Fig. 2-32D are oval. The trick to oval turning is laying out the centers. Follow this procedure:

1. Lay out oval shape on paper, Fig. 27-38A.
2. Draw a circle slightly larger than the oval. Mark the circle's center as A, Fig. 27-38B.
3. Without changing your compass, draw a circle tangent to one arc (lower portion) of your oval shape. Mark that circle's center as B, Fig. 27-38C.
4. Draw a third circle tangent to the other arc (upper portion) of your oval shape. Mark that circle's center as C, Fig. 27-38D.
5. Measure the distance between centers.
6. Lay out the three centers on each end of the stock, Fig. 27-38E. Make saw kerfs for the drive center spurs.
7. Mount the workpiece on center A and turn the diameter. Operate the lathe at roughing rpm.
8. Reduce the lathe speed 25 to 35 percent for turning on centers B and C because these are out-of-balance turning operations.
9. Remount the workpiece on center B and turn the second diameter. The turning tool touches only a portion of the circumference.
10. Remount the workpiece on center C and repeat the operation.
11. Remove the workpiece from the lathe and smooth it with abrasive paper to remove any ridge lines.

FACEPLATE TURNING

Faceplate turning may be done on a bowl lathe and the inboard or outboard side of a standard lathe. Bowls, trays, stool seats, and small round table tops are turned while attached to a faceplate.

PREPARING MATERIAL FOR FACEPLATE TURNING

Determine from the product design (working drawings) whether you must laminate several layers

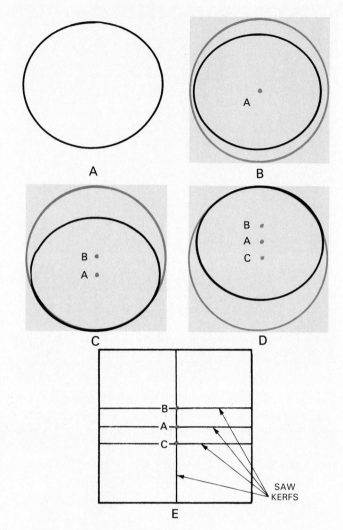

Fig. 27-38. Procedure for laying out an oval turning.

of stock together, Fig. 27-39. Some products are designed thicker than standard lumber thicknesses.

Mount material for faceplate turning one of two ways: attach the faceplate directly into workpiece or to a backup board, Fig. 27-40. Screws can extend through the faceplate directly into the workpiece. However, with this method, you wind up with holes in the bottom of your product. An alternative method is to attach the faceplate to a backup board. Here, the workpiece is glued to the backup block separated with sized paper, Fig. 27-41. This practice is the same as that for split turning between centers. Once the product is turned, the backup board and product are separated by a chisel.

To attach the faceplate, first draw two diagonals on the workpiece. From their intersection, lay out two concentric circles. The inner circle locates the faceplate; the outer circle locates the size of the workpiece. With a band saw, cut the workpiece 1/4 in. to 1/2 in. (6 to 13 mm) greater than the outer circle.

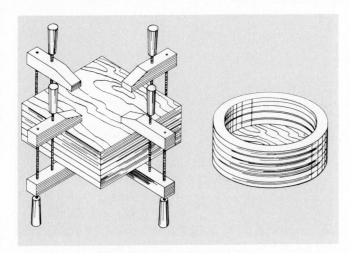

Fig. 27-39. Some turnings, such as this deep bowl, may require gluing layers together. (Shopsmith, Inc.)

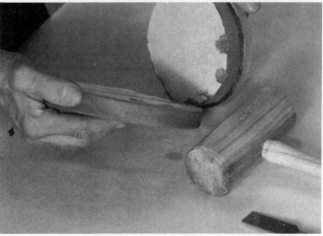

Fig. 27-41. Top. Screws enter the backup board but not the workpiece. Bottom. The backup board is separated from the workpiece with a mallet and chisel.

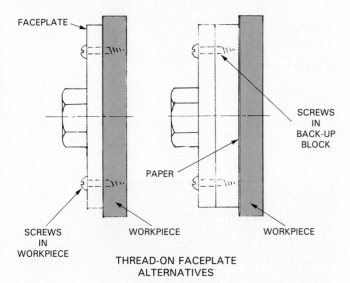

FACEPLATE

SCREWS IN BACK-UP BLOCK

PAPER

SCREWS IN WORKPIECE

WORKPIECE

WORKPIECE

THREAD-ON FACEPLATE ALTERNATIVES

Fig. 27-40. Workpieces can be attached to a faceplate with, or without, a backup board.

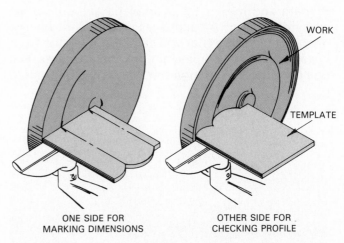

WORK

TEMPLATE

ONE SIDE FOR MARKING DIMENSIONS

OTHER SIDE FOR CHECKING PROFILE

Fig. 27-42. Templates help you to turn shapes precisely. (Shopsmith, Inc.)

Next, draw layout lines on the face of the workpiece. These mark where the contours will be located. Also consider using a template. Leave one side of the template straight, and mark linear distances from the center. Cut the other side to the shape of half the finished contour, Fig. 27-42.

Position and secure the faceplate on the back of the workpiece within circle drawn earlier. Use screws long enough to hold the material securely, but short enough that they do not interfere with the turning tool. If a backup board is used, cut it the size of the faceplate. Align it within the circle drawn on the workpiece for the faceplate.

Once the faceplate is attached, thread it (and the attached workpiece) onto the spindle. Depending on the size of the workpiece, you will mount the faceplate on either the inboard or outboard side of the headstock.

INBOARD FACEPLATE TURNING

The size of a workpiece mounted on the spindle side of the bed is limited by the lathe's swing. Lathes with a gap bed increase the maximum swing by about 25 percent. The steps for inboard turning are as follows.

1. Prepare the workpiece as described above.
2. Remove the spur center, clean off the threads, and thread on the faceplate.

3. To prevent the faceplate from being wedged against the spindle shoulder, install a heavy leather washer on the spindle first.
4. Mount the workpiece on the lathe.
5. Adjust the tool rest near to the edge of the workpiece. Set the speed according to the workpiece diameter.
6. Lower the guard into position.
7. Use a gouge, then spear point tool to smooth the outside edge of the disk, Fig. 27-43. This balances the stock.
8. Adjust the tool rest parallel to the face of the workpiece.
9. Use the appropriate tools to create the contour, Fig. 27-44. Begin the cut in the center and move the tool outward.
10. Place the template against your work. Check your progress at regular intervals.
11. Stop turning when you come within 1/16 in. of the desired size.

Some lathe models have a right angle tool rest, Fig. 27-45. It prevents your having to reposition the tool rest from edge to face turning.

OUTBOARD FACEPLATE TURNING

Stock too large for inboard turning is mounted on the outboard side of the lathe, Fig. 27-46. A tripod supports the tool rest. Set the lathe accordingly. Prepare and mount the workpiece as you did for inboard turning. Attach a large faceplate on the inboard spindle so that you can stop the lathe from coasting. Use a scraping action when turning. The size of outboard turnings should be only 25 percent

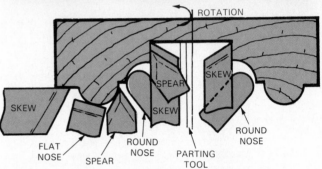

Fig. 27-44. Several turning tools are needed to turn the desired contour. The guard was removed to show the operation.

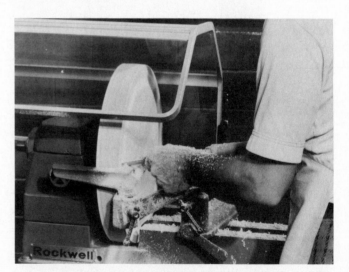

Fig. 27-45. Both the face and edge can be turned without having to reposition a right angle tool rest. (Delta)

more than that allowed by the inboard swing. Circular workpieces larger than this should be made by sawing and shaping practices.

SCREW-THREAD FACEPLATE

The screw-thread faceplate is appropriate for small turned parts. Prepare the stock as described earlier. Drill a pilot hole in the wood for the screw

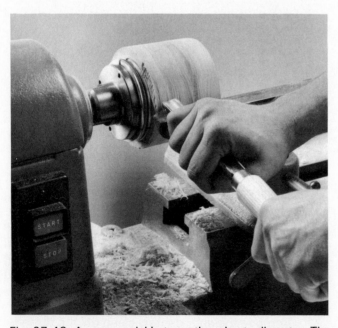

Fig. 27-43. A gouge quickly turns the edge to diameter. The guard was removed to show the operation. (Delta)

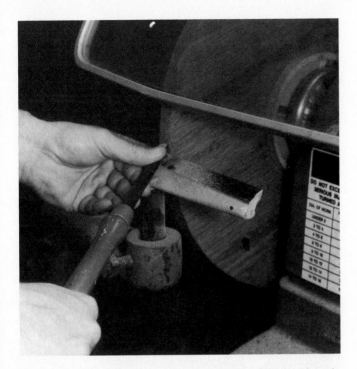

Fig. 27-46. Guard slides to the outboard side of the headstock.

thread center. Remove any chips from the spindle hole. Press the tapered shaft of the faceplate into the spindle by hand. Hold the handwheel and screw the workpiece onto the threaded center. Turn the workpiece as though faceplate mounted. Cabinetmakers likely will find limited use for the screw-thread faceplate, except for custom knobs and pulls which generally are purchased.

CHUCK TURNING

Dowels and round workpieces are held easily in a lathe chuck. Use care when tightening the chuck as excessive torque could dent the workpiece.

SMOOTHING TURNED PRODUCTS

A sharp tool, used properly, greatly reduces the need for smoothing the turned part. Yet, there are times when filing or sanding is needed. If the product is made from open grain hardwood or softwood, turning tools may leave the surface rough.

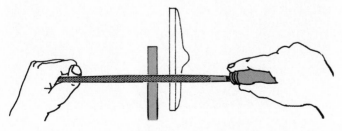

Fig. 27-47. A file is handy to smooth the turned part.

You can use a file instead of turning tools to reach the final diameter. Set the machine at roughing speed. Grip the file at each end and hold it at a 90° angle to your work, Fig. 27-47. Apply light pressure and move the file with a slow forward motion. A small flat or triangular file will smooth fine detail.

If abrasives are needed, remember that they will create cross grain scratches that are difficult to remove. Select the finest abrasive that will do the job. You can use an abrasive pad or cord, Fig. 27-48. Remove the tool rest. Hold an abrasive pad beneath the workpiece while it turns. Keep the lathe speed slow to reduce heat buildup. You are not as likely to burn your fingers while holding the pad. You

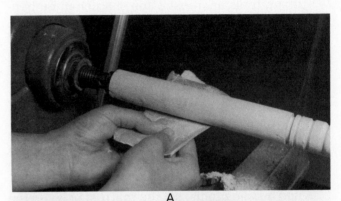

A

B

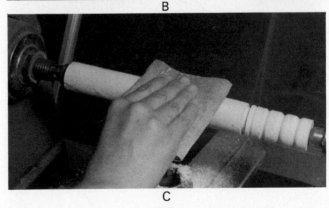

C

Fig. 27-48. A—Apply abrasive paper under the rotating workpiece to remove tool marks. The guard was removed to show the operation. B—Abrasive cord for sanding detail. (Woodworker's Supply) C—Remove circular scratches by sanding the workpiece along the grain. Do not have the lathe on for this operation.

might loop an abrasive cord or strip of paper around the workpiece to smooth grooves and beads. When only fine scratches left by the abrasive are visible, stop the lathe. Sand with the grain to remove any circular scratches.

MAINTAINING LATHES AND TOOLS

The condition of tools and equipment directly affects the quality of your work and safety of the operation. Tools must be kept sharp. The lathe needs to be cleaned and lubricated periodically.

SHARPENING LATHE TOOLS

Turning tools are most often sharpened by honing. Grinding is done only when the edge has been damaged. Frequent honing keeps edges in good condition. In fact, some lathe operators will hone a tool several times during each hour of use.

Tool angles when grinding and honing are important. Angles for the five common turning tools were shown in Fig. 27-6.

Honing is done with an oil stone. Lightly touch both sides of the cutting edge to remove dull edges or grinding burrs. A flat stone and slip stone will hone the shapes of most turning tools, Fig. 27-49.

When grinding tools, set the tool rest or jig on the grinder to position the tool, Fig. 27-50. Use only the wheel surface directly in front of the tool rest. This will hollow grind the tool slightly.

Flat ground tools can be sharpened on a power sander having an aluminum oxide or emery abrasive. Be sure to maintain the proper tool angle. A jig for sharpening lathe chisels on the disk sander is shown in Fig. 27-51.

When ground, the tool should have a narrow, reflective, sharpened edge. Do not hone the tool to a thin wire edge because it becomes weaker.

MAINTAINING THE LATHE

A wood turning lathe is relatively maintenance free. Prevent an accumulation of wood chips and rust. A limited number of lubricating points exist. Service might be needed for the variable speed mechanism, spindle bearings, or quill threads.

Be sure the centers and chucks fit properly. All have a Morse taper shank. Always use a mallet to set a spur center firmly in the workpiece. A steel

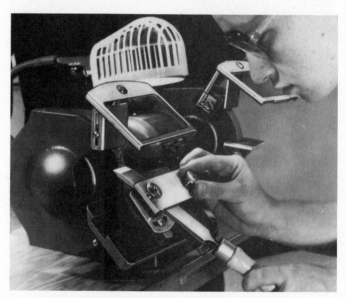

Fig. 27-50. A jig allows you to precisely set the tool angle. (Rockwell International)

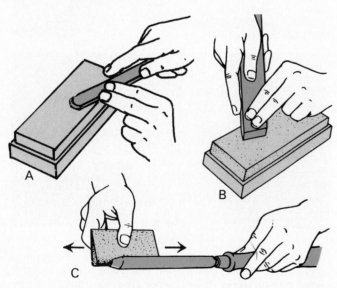

Fig. 27-49 Honing turning tools. A—Honing the ground edge of a gouge. B—Honing the inner edge of the gouge. C—Honing flat-ground tools on a stone. (Disston)

Fig. 27-51. Jig designed for sharpening the skew on a disk sander. (Shopsmith)

hammer can damage the shank. This could prevent an adequate friction fit. Keep the spur center lips from being damaged. File away any burrs.

At the tailstock end of the lathe, centers should be easy to remove when you retract the quill. The center should slip out into your hand. If it does not, the quill will have to be removed and checked. Turn the handwheel the opposite direction until the quill is free. You will then need a knockout rod. Insert it through the quill and tap the center until it slips out.

Some clamping levers can cause problems. For example, suppose the tool holder cannot be secured with the handle. This indicates that the nut under the bed needs to be tightened slightly.

SUMMARY

Turning is the process of producing round products, such as table legs, bed posts, bowls, and knobs. There are two basic operations used to create turned products: between-center turning and faceplate turning.

Between-center turning is done on a standard lathe. Stock is held between a spur, or drive, center and live or dead tailstock center. The tool rest is positioned within 1/8 in. of your work. An assortment of turning tools are used to shape the wood. These include the gouge, skew, spear-point tool, parting tool, and round-nose tool. Each is appropriate for creating unique shapes.

Faceplate turning is done on a bowl lathe or on either the inboard or outboard side of a standard lathe. Stock is attached to a faceplate which is then threaded on to the lathe spindle. A backup board may be glued to the workpiece before the faceplate is attached. It prevents the screws from entering the workpiece.

High quality turning is done with properly sharpened tools on a well-maintained lathe. Tools should be honed often and ground rarely. Maintain the lathe by removing wood chips and rust. Check belt-driven lathes for belt wear. Make sure that all tool rest and tailstock clamps tighten properly.

CABINETMAKING TERMS

Turning, between-center turning, standard lathe, headstock, bed, tailstock, tailstock quill, gap bed lathe, swing, overall bed length, distance between centers, lathe guard, bowl lathe, turning tools, cutting action, scraping action, gouge, skew, parting tool, round-nose tool, spear-point tool, tool rest, spur center, dead center, live center, faceplate, inboard turning, outboard turning, tripod stand, screw-thread faceplate, lathe chuck, turning squares, center finder, chatter, steadyrest, split turnings, duplicator.

TEST YOUR KNOWLEDGE

1. Two common types of lathes for small shop and home use are the _____ and _____.
2. List the standard lathe specifications which determine the largest diameter and longest workpiece you can turn.
3. How would you mount the following products to be turned?
   a. Chair leg.
   b. 6 in. diameter bowl.
   c. 15 in. diameter stool seat.
   d. 5 ft. bed post.
   e. Drawer knob.
   f. 3 in. long finial.
4. Explain why you might you choose a scraping action over a cutting action.
5. List the five turning tools found in a standard set.
6. The best position for the tool rest is _____ in. away from your work and _____ in. above the work center line.
7. Describe why you would choose a ball bearing live center over a dead center for supporting the tailstock end of your work.
8. Lumber should be free of defects, especially _____ and _____.
9. List the steps taken to prepare material for between-center turning.
10. After rough turning, you turn to approximate diameter. How do you know when you have reached the approximate diameter?
11. Chatter is usually the result of:
    a. Using sharp turning tools.
    b. Using dull turning tools.
    c. Turning a long, small diameter workpiece.
    d. Faceplate turning a thin disk.
12. List the tools which can be used to turn the following features:
    a. Cylinder.
    b. V-groove.
    c. Bead.
    d. Cove.
    e. Shoulder.
13. Select _____ paper for split turnings.
14. How many times must you mount the workpiece when turning oval spindles?
15. Give steps for mounting a workpiece, including a backup board, for faceplate turning.
16. What additional accessory is needed for outboard turning?
17. Explain two methods to turn duplicate parts.
18. Chatter can be reduced by mounting a _____.
19. Tools must be ground each time they are sharpened. True or False?
20. List several lathe maintenance checks you should make.

Chapter 28
ACCESSORIES, JIGS, AND SPECIAL MACHINES

After studying this chapter, you will be able to:
☐ *Identify accessories which increase the convenience of a machine.*
☐ *Describe several applications of jigs and fixtures.*
☐ *Select equipment to cut large or bulky panel products.*
☐ *Explain the advantages and disadvantages of multi-purpose machinery.*

Standard machines discussed in previous chapters will produce most every product you design. Yet, there are times when add-on equipment makes a standard machine more efficient, and often safer. On some occasions a special machine may be even more appropriate. This chapter covers accessories, jigs, and special machines. The list is by no means complete. Hundreds of vendors manufacture gadgets, attachments, and accessories that make your work easier. The tools presented in this chapter indicate the wide range of equipment you might choose.

ACCESSORIES

Accessories increase the convenience or use of a machine. A number of devices have been described in past chapters. For example, with a moulding cutterhead, you can convert a table saw into a shaper.

Accessories, often called attachments, connect to a basic machine. Some make major changes to machines and tools. Those designed to be permanent usually fit only one model.

TABLE EXTENSIONS

Table extensions help you support awkward stock. The table saw extensions shown in Fig. 28-1 allow wider and longer material to be cut. A special fence and fence guide was added to make use of the full table size. The power miter saw table extension shown in Fig. 28-2 extends the available workpiece support to 8 ft. (2400 mm).

Fig. 28-1. Table attachments make saw operations easier, safer, and more accurate. (Biesemeyer)

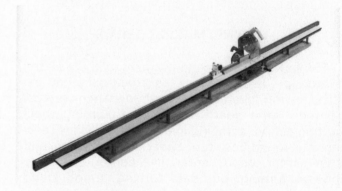

Fig. 28-2. Longer stock can be cut on the radial arm saw with table attachments. (Biesemeyer)

GLIDING TABLE

The *gliding table* is a movable saw table and miter gauge, Fig. 28-3. With a standard miter gauge, the workpiece size is limited without support for the weight. The table glides along with the material. Holding the workpiece and maintaining the cutting angle is easy.

Fig. 28-3. A gliding table supports longer and heavier stock for cross grain and miter cuts. (Delta)

RIPPING GUIDES

A *ripping guide* holds stock against the saw table and fence as you feed it past the blade, Fig. 28-4. A locking device to hinder kickback prevents the wheels from rotating backwards. The device is attached to the fence by screws or clamps. The wheels are spring loaded to adjust to any stock thickness. A similar device, Fig. 28-5, is much like the ripping guide. However, it fits the shaper and other equipment with fences.

Fig. 28-4. Ripping guides keep material against the table and fence, and prevent kickback. The guard was removed to show the operation. (Fisher Hill Products)

A

B

Fig. 28-5. Guides hold material against the table and fence and prevent kickback. A—Mounted on the table saw. B—Mounted on the shaper. (Western Commercial Products)

POWER FEED

Power feed attachments, Fig. 28-6, allow automatic feed control. They keep the user's hands away from the point of operation. A power feed attachment can be installed on table saws and shapers. A column crank adjusts the height according to the workpiece thickness. Power rollers move the workpiece at a set feed rate past the blade or cutter. Start the material under the rollers just as you would material into a planer. Move to the outfeed side of the machine to receive and support the material.

ROLLER TABLES

Roller tables make feeding long or bulky stock much easier. They are used for both infeed and outfeed sides of the machine, Fig. 28-7A. When not in use, the table can be stored upright by folding the legs. A stand with one roller, Fig. 28-7B, often is adequate. Locate it on the infeed or outfeed side of saws, shapers, planers, and jointers.

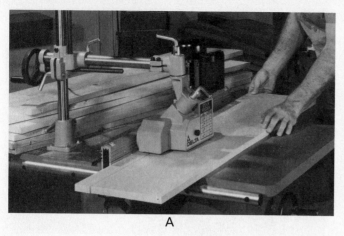

A

B

Fig. 28-6. Power feed attachments help one operator control long stock. A—Mounted on table saw. B—Mounted on shaper. (Delta)

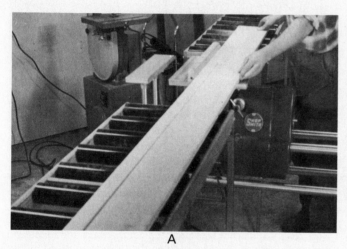

A

B

Fig. 28-7. Roller tables help one person support and feed stock. The guard was removed to show the operation. (Turning Point)

PORTABLE DRILL ATTACHMENT

Attachments are not limited to stationary machines. The flexibility of a portable electric drill can be increased greatly. A typical *portable drill attachment* consists of a spindle adaptor, two guides, and a ring base. Some applications of this accessory are shown in Fig. 28-8.

PORTABLE TOOL FRAME

Frames expand the applications of portable tools. The tool glides on tubes or rails. The frame shown in Fig. 28-9 increases the accuracy of square and miter cuts. It also positions a router for making dados or grooves. The frame shown in Fig. 28-10 allows you to rout letters.

FOLDING TABLE

Folding tables are appropriate when space in the shop is limited. The table shown in Fig. 28-11

consists of metal folding legs attached to a 7/8 in. (22 mm) sheet of particle board. A guide placed on top of the table allows paneling to be cut with a circular saw.

PORTABLE TOOL TABLES

Tables can convert a portable tool into a stationary machine. The table in Fig. 28-12A, for example, converts a router into a shaper. You can also attach a saber saw for scroll saw operations.

JIGS AND FIXTURES

Jigs and fixtures increase the accuracy of a machine or stability of a workpiece. They may be purchased or designed and built. *Jigs* hold a workpiece in position and also guide the tool or workpiece. Jigs are a great asset to cabinetmakers. Some jigs, such as the dovetail jig, allow you to perform cuts which are difficult to do freehand. *Fixtures* are holding devices that do not guide the

Fig. 28-8. A drilling attachment increases the use and accuracy of a portable drill. A—90° drilling on a flat surface. B—Centering on round stock. C—Centering on a narrow edge. D—Accurate 90° hole sawing. E—Routing. F—Attached under a table as a drum sander. (Portalign Tool Corp.)

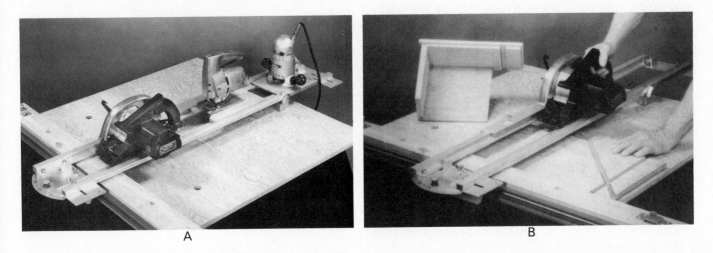

Fig. 28-9. A—Frames make portable tools more accurate. B—Crosscutting with a portable saw. (Brett-Hauer Co.)

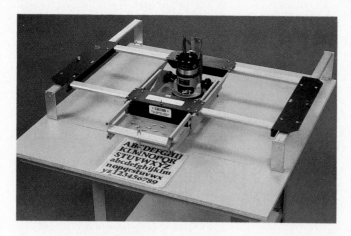

Fig. 28-10. Frame guide to rout letters. (Woodworker's Supply of New Mexico)

Fig. 28-11. Folding tables support bulky material and can be stored easily. (Saw-Mate Corp.)

tool. Clamps, as discussed in Chapter 33, are one type of fixture.

A jig or fixture is recommended when making a number of duplicate parts. When it aligns the stock and guides the tool, there is less chance for error. Most often you will set up or build jigs and fixtures for mass-producing products. For the most part, purchased devices are safe and self explanatory. Those you create must be safe. You must account for the tool, workpiece, and chips created by the operation. The failure of a jig or fixture typically is not its ability to hold the workpiece or guide the tool. The failure occurs when the designer forgets that chips will accumulate in the device. This prevents the device from performing properly.

DOWELING JIG

The *doweling jig*, Fig. 28-13, allows you to drill holes precisely in the center of an edge or end of a board. As you turn the clamp handle, both jaws

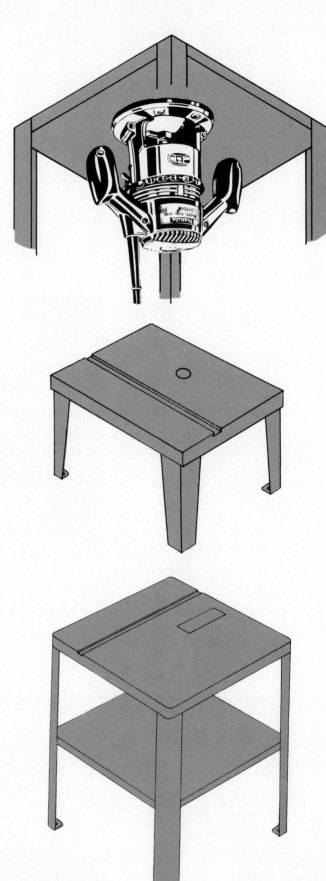

Fig. 28-12. Tables convert portable tools into stationary equipment. (Makita)

Fig. 28-13. Doweling jig centers the drill bit on the edge of material. (The Fine Tool Shops)

move equally toward the center. Holes and hole inserts in the jig permit several drill bit sizes. This jig is discussed further in Chapter 29.

DOVETAIL JIG

The *dovetail jig* guides a portable router for making dovetail joints, Fig. 28-14. It is one of the most valuable joint making jigs. Dovetailing by hand is a very tedious process. This jig, discussed further in Chapter 29, is widely used when constructing drawers.

TAPER JIGS

Jigs for sawing tapers may be a one-piece or adjustable two-piece device. A one-piece *taper jig* is cut from one piece of material. Lay out the taper and cut a wedge or notches, Fig. 28-15. A handle can be added to the jig for safe operation. To use the jig, set the rip fence, allowing for the jig width and desired taper. Then complete the cut.

Fig. 28-14. A dovetail jig allows you to cut dovetail joints with a portable router. (American Machine and Tool)

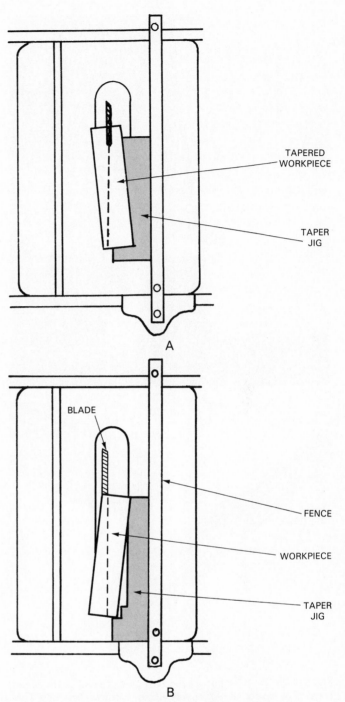

Fig. 28-15. One-piece taper jigs align stock at the proper angle. A—Single taper. B—Adjustable taper.

Adjustable taper jigs, Fig. 28-16, can meet many needs. Tapers may be cut on one or more surfaces. The adjustable taper jig and other taper cut operations are discussed in Chapter 40 since most tapers are cut for making tapered square legs and bases.

CIRCLE CUTTING JIG

Sawing an accurate circle on the band saw is best done with a *circle jig.* The jig may be purchased or

A

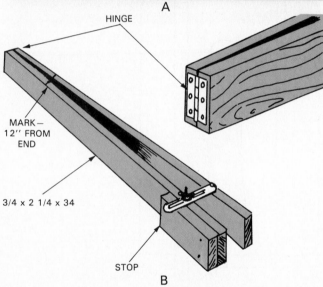

HINGE

MARK—
12'' FROM
END

3/4 x 2 1/4 x 34

STOP

B

Fig. 28-16. A—This purchased two-piece taper jig can be set for angles up to 15° or tapers up to 1 in./ft. (The Fine Tool Shops) B—Jig you might build.

custom made and can be located above or below the saw table. One type is clamped to the guide post above the table, Fig. 28-17. The one you might make slides in the saw table slot, Fig. 28-18. Follow the steps shown in Fig. 28-19 to set up and use this jig.

1. Position the jig on the table with the jig guide.
2. Push it forward until the pivot pin is even with the blade's teeth. Remember, the blade width determines the minimum radius for the circle.
3. Secure the jig stop against the machine table edge.

4. Measure the circle radius from the pivot to the blade.
5. Drill a pivot size hole in the workpiece.
6. Place the workpiece on the pivot. Slide the jig forward making a straight cut until the jig stop touches the table.
7. Turn the workpiece and cut the circle.
8. When the circle is cut, pull the jig toward you. The blade should pull from the kerf.

Fig. 28-17. Circle cutting jig attached to the guide post of the band saw. (Delta)

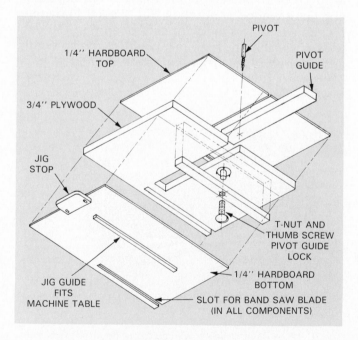

PIVOT

1/4'' HARDBOARD
TOP

PIVOT
GUIDE

3/4'' PLYWOOD

JIG
STOP

T-NUT AND
THUMB SCREW
PIVOT GUIDE
LOCK

JIG GUIDE
FITS
MACHINE TABLE

1/4'' HARDBOARD
BOTTOM

SLOT FOR BAND SAW BLADE
(IN ALL COMPONENTS)

Fig. 28-18. Circle cutting jig construction.

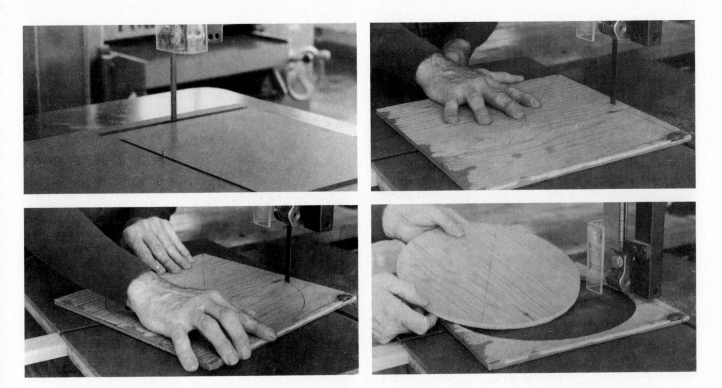

Fig. 28-19. Procedure for using a shop-made circle cutting jig. The guard was raised to show the operation.

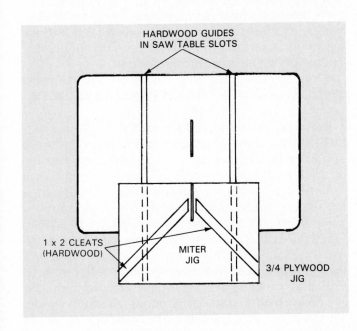

Fig. 28-20. A miter jig is an alternative to a miter gauge.

MITER JIG

A *miter jig* can be used instead of a miter gauge for 45° cuts. The jig slides in the table slots found on each side of the blade, Fig. 28-20. The two angle fences provide for left- and right-hand miters. This jig holds and guides moulding or framing strips of various shapes.

DRILLING FIXTURES

Hole drilling fixtures position a workpiece on the drill press. Clamped to the drill table, most fixtures are very simple. Typically, they include an auxiliary table, two fences, or a fence and stop block. A solid fence, Fig. 28-21A, is not recommended because chips accumulate. Chips prevent the stock from seating properly unless they are brushed away after each cut. A better fence is to use three dowels, Fig. 28-21B. When you load new stock, the chips are pushed aside. The locating hole in the center of the fixture allows you to align the jig on the drill press table. Insert a bit the same diameter as the hole. Lower the bit and move the jig until the bit enters the locating hole. Then clamp the fixture.

Modern cabinets typically have a number of holes drilled on the inside. This permits flexibility when positioning shelves. The holes are also used to mount hardware in the 32 mm system of cabinet construction. Discussed in Chapter 38, the 32 mm system has 5 mm holes that are equally spaced 32 mm. Fig. 28-22 shows a fixture you can make for this purpose.

VISE INSERT

A *vise insert* helps you clamp odd-shaped parts in a woodworking vise. This fixture consists of a wedge and pivot dowel, Fig. 28-21. Blocks attached to the vise jaws have half-round grooves cut

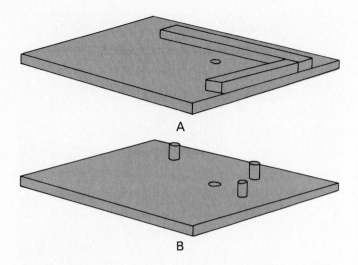

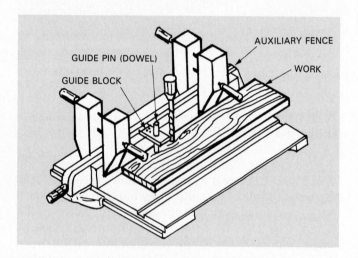

Fig. 28-21. A—Chips accumulate against a solid fence. B—Chips can be pushed past a dowel fence.

Fig. 28-22. This jig ensures equally spaced holes. (Shopsmith)

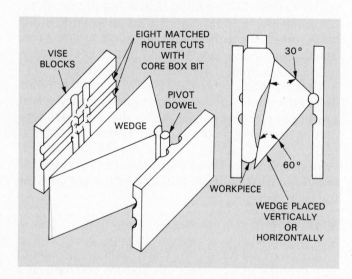

Fig. 28-23. Routed vise blocks with a wedge and dowel hold irregular workpieces.

in them. The wedge pivots to conform to the workpiece being held.

FRAMING CLAMP

As you will learn in Chapter 33, there are many types of clamps for holding glued and assembled components. Frame assembly poses a special problem. Clamping a miter joint frame could involve four clamps. With the *framing fixture,* Fig. 28-24, one handscrew meets all needs. Clamping pressure is equal at all joints. Make sure the handscrew jaws are kept parallel when applying pressure.

VERTICAL CLAMP

A special clamp holds stock vertical, Fig. 28-25. Stock clamped vertically in a woodworking vise may not be secure enough. Clamps which rotate to almost any position are also available.

SPECIAL MACHINERY

Standard stationary and portable equipment has been discussed in previous chapters. Many of the machines were described as being adaptable to meet special needs. In addition, there are special machines designed for one purpose and those designed to perform most all processing operations. These are discussed in this section.

SAWING MANUFACTURED PANEL PRODUCTS

Handling large and bulky materials is often a problem in the cabinetmaking shop. Panel products are one example. They may be large, thin, and flexible or thick and heavy. Handling these materials may require two people. To cut full size sheets of paneling, use a *panel saw* rather than a table saw.

Horizontal and vertical panel saws are available, Fig. 28-26. The horizontal machine functions much like the radial arm saw. The panel is well supported on the table. The saw moves completely across it. This may be controlled manually or automatically.

The horizontal panel saw occupies much space. You may not saw paneling often enough to justify space for this machine. A vertical panel saw may be a better use of space. Place the panel on the frame. Most machines saw in both a vertical and horizontal direction.

Several panel saws can be fitted with a router. This allows you to groove paneling as well as cut it. Select a ''V'' shaped or straight bit.

You can saw paneling and conserve space using a folding table like that shown in Fig. 28-11. When not in use, it is folded and stored conveniently. An added advantage is that you can take the machine and table on location.

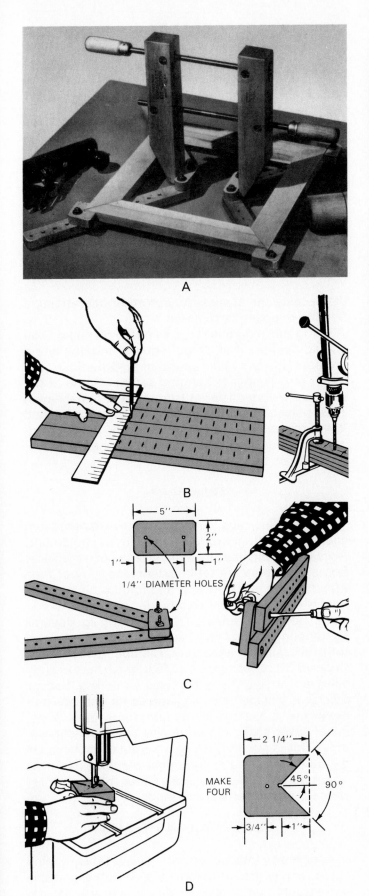

Fig. 28-25. This vise holds stock in a vertical position.
(The Fine Tool Shops)

Fig. 28-24. A—Frame clamping fixture applies equal pressure to all four miter joints. B—Instructions for building the framing fixture. (Adjustable Clamp Co.)

MITER TRIMMER

The *miter trimmer,* Fig. 28-27, trims and fits precise 45° miter joints for moulding. Some trimmers cut other angles also. To use the tool, first saw the material 1/8 to 1/4 in. longer than needed. You can use a less precise portable saw for this cut. Then position the material against the fence of the trimmer and pull back on the handle. This tool is excellent for on-site architectural woodwork where a stationary saw might not be available.

MULTIPURPOSE MACHINE

Up to now you have studied machines that have a single purpose but can be adapted for other operations. You can retrofit a table saw for shaping. A radial arm saw can be set up for shaping, sanding, and drilling. In addition, there are machines designed to perform many operations.

The *multipurpose machine,* Fig. 28-28, is a versatile machine for small workspaces. The machine consists of a motor, frame, table, fence, and accessories. It performs a number of operations: circular sawing, band sawing, scroll sawing, jointing, planing, drilling, mortising, shaping, pin routing, faceplate or between-center turning, as well as belt sanding, disk sanding, and drum sanding. The motor and frame can be positioned horizontally and vertically. Some tooling connected directly to the spin-

A

B

C

Fig. 28-26. Panel saws. A—Manual horizontal. (Henrick) B—Automatic horizontal. (Parks) C—Vertical. (Safety Speed Cut)

Fig. 28-27. The miter trimmer shears perfect miters on moulding. (The Fine Tool Shops)

dle operate the accessory. For other operations, a flexible coupling is required.

Using this machine requires much planning. You should decide on all steps required to complete a project. Group similar operations. Otherwise, too much time is spent changing setups. Some of the setups are very different from standard machines. To set blade height for sawing, you must raise and lower the table rather than the arbor. When turning, the dead center is attached to the rip fence, rather than to a tailstock.

SUMMARY

Accessories, jigs, and special machines often accompany standard cabinetmaking equipment. Accessories increase the convenience of a machine. Some examples are table extensions, power feed attachments, roller tables, and folding tables. Jigs hold a workpiece and also guide the tool or workpiece. Some examples are the doweling jig, dovetail jig, tapering jig, and miter jig. Fixtures secure a part for processing or assembly. Clamps, discussed in Chapter 33, are one type of fixture. Others include vises and shop designed fixtures for drilling. Special machines include those engineered for only one purpose and those made for numerous operations. Panel saws easily cut large and bulky panel products. This is primarily a single purpose machine. On the other hand, the multipurpose machine performs a number of tasks. It saws, joints, planes, drills, shapes, routs, turns, and sands.

CABINETMAKING TERMS

Accessory, table extension, gliding table, ripping guide, power feed attachment, roller table, portable drill attachment, frame, folding table, jig, fixture, doweling jig, tapering jig, circle jig, miter jig, vise insert, framing clamp, panel saw, miter trimmer, multipurpose machine.

Fig. 28-28. A multipurpose machine performs numerous operations. (Shopsmith, Inc.)

TEST YOUR KNOWLEDGE

1. An accessory which supports wide or long stock when sawing is a(n) _____ _____.
2. A movable saw table and miter gauge accessory is the _____ _____.
3. List the three functions of a ripping guide.
4. Identify two accessories which make feeding long or bulky stock much easier.
5. Describe the difference between a jig and a fixture.
6. The failure of a fixture to align a workpiece accurately is often due to _____.
7. Name three jigs you might purchase.
8. What accessory can you name that is needed to convert a portable router, drill, or saw into a stationary tool?
9. A woodworking vise can be adapted to hold irregular shape workpieces. True or False?
10. Since supporting bulky panel products can cause injury, what machine might you choose to cut these?

Chapter 29
JOINT MAKING

After studying this chapter, you will be able to:
☐ *Select appropriate joints based on the product and material.*
☐ *Select hand tools, power equipment, and special jigs or accessories for joinery.*
☐ *Create and assemble nonpositioned, positioned, and reinforced joints.*

One of the most important elements affecting the durability of a product is joinery. This chapter covers typical joints for assembling furniture and cabinets. Looking at a finished joint reveals little about its structure. The components you see are combined, Fig. 29-1. It is the internal structure of the joint, either simple or complex, that affects the strength and stability of the product.

JOINTS AND GRAIN DIRECTION

The direction of grain in a solid wood joint affects the joint's strength. The parts which meet will have end grain, radial (edge) grain, or tangential (face) grain. The holding power, or strength, of radial and tangential grain is equal since the joint meets "along the grain." The abbreviation "AG" is used to describe a joint which involves radial or tangential grain. A joint where mating components meet along the grain (abbreviated as AG/AG) is the strongest. When end grain (EG) is involved, such as an AG/EG or EG/EG joint, the strength is only 10 to 25 percent that of an AG/AG joint. Fig. 29-2 clarifies AG/AG, AG/EG, and EG/EG joinery.

Although radial and tangential grain have the same holding power, they shrink at different rates.

Fig. 29-1. It is difficult to determine what types of joints were used to assemble these products. (Spartus, Ethan Allen)

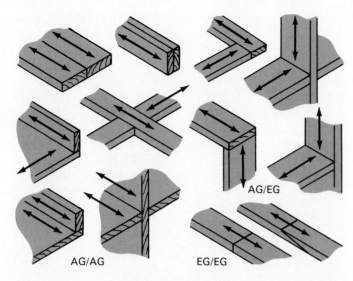

Fig. 29-2. Grain direction of the joining components can affect the joint's strength.

Radial grain bonded to radial grain offers maximum strength. Tangential grain surfaces glued together are equally as strong. This is because they have consistent shrinkage rates. However, a joint where radial grain meets tangential grain is not quite as strong. These joints may possibly crack and separate as each component shrinks a different amount. You can reduce shrinkage by using wood that has a low moisture content. In addition, adhesives that remain flexible when cured are recommended.

JOINTS IN MANUFACTURED PANEL PRODUCTS

A majority of cabinets made today consist of particle board, fiberboard, or other manufactured panel products. These materials present an entirely new set of considerations. Solid wood joints rely on the grain direction and strength of the wood for structure. Products made of fiberboard, plywood, or particle board cannot. There are only a few joints that are suitable for panel products. These include butt, rabbet, dado, and miter joints. Even then, a method of reinforcement is added. Plate joinery is gaining popularity as a reinforcing joint. Staples and nails driven with a pneumatic gun are often used in production. Panels are first glued so that the joint does not rely entirely on the fastener. Particle board screws, one-piece connectors, and ready-to-assemble fasteners are also becoming popular. Still, the cabinetmaker must be careful. Both threaded and nonthreaded fasteners driven into the edge of a panel product tend to split the material.

JOINT TYPES

When designing a product, choose joints according to the estimated stress that the product will receive. Although there are hundreds of joints, all fall into one of these three categories:
1. Nonpositioned.
2. Positioned.
3. Reinforced.

A *nonpositioned joint* is one where two components simply meet without any position or locking effect. Only the adhesive or fasteners holds the joint permanently. A nonpositioned joint has little surface area for the adhesive to contact. Some examples are butt and plain miter joints. joints.

In a *positioned joint,* one or both components have a machined contour which holds the assembly in place. Adhesives solidify the joint. The mortise and tenon, dovetail, and locked miter joints are examples. Although more time consuming to create, positioned joints are stronger than nonpositioned joints. There is more surface area between the mating parts for the adhesive bond.

Reinforced joints have some element in addition to adhesive that helps hold the joint. For extra support, butt and miter joints are often reinforced with dowels, splines, and plates. Glue blocks are bonded into hidden corners to help strengthen the joint. Mechanical fasteners also reinforce joints. Clamp nails, corrugated fasteners, nails, and staples may provide permanent or temporary position to the joint while the adhesive dries. Fasteners for ready-to-assemble furniture, such as the bolt and cam connector, do not require adhesive.

JOINERY DECISIONS

While designing a product, the cabinetmaker decides which joints will be used to hold a cabinet, piece of furniture, or other wood product together. It is best to choose the simplest joint that meets the strength requirements of the product. In the furniture industry, two parts in a hidden area typically are joined with a butt joint reinforced with dowels, glue blocks, or mechanical fasteners. This is nearly as strong as a mortise and tenon or other positioned joint, but costs much less to produce.

Joinery begins once material has been surfaced and cut to size. Some parts must be cut oversize to allow for machined features of the joint. Remember, the internal structure of a joint may be much different than what you see in the finished product. Consult the working drawings before you cut material to size. Usually, a cutting list is provided. These measurements should allow for joinery.

The machines covered in Chapters 21 through 28 will produce most of the joints discussed in this chapter. However, special jigs, machinery, or attachments may be more effective for making some positioned joints with intricate contours. These are discussed in this chapter.

During layout, make all measurements from a common starting point. Use the appropriate layout tools. Lay out joints so that the components fit together freely. Leave room for the adhesive and expansion or contraction due to moisture changes.

Plan your sequence of operations carefully. Decide which processes should be done first, second, and so on. For example, when making a mortise and tenon joint, cut the mortise (recess) first. Then cut the tenon to fit. Sometimes the order is not important. On a shaper, either the tongue or groove of a tongue and groove joint can be made first. The accuracy of your machine setup ensures a snug fit.

Regardless of the joint being made, an accurate setup is essential. Make practice passes on scrap material to position the blade, bit, or cutting tool. Jigs, fixtures, or other setup steps may be helpful or even required.

BUTT JOINT

A *butt joint* is a nonpositioned joint where the square surface of one piece meets the face, edge, or end of another, Fig. 29-3. The edge-to-edge butt joint is used without reinforcement to form wider material. (This process is discussed in Chapter 33.) Butt joints, other than edge-to-edge or edge-to-face, are very weak. They must be reinforced with glue and mechanical fasteners, such as corrugated fasteners, screws, staples, brads, or insert nuts and bolts, Fig. 29-4. Doweled butt joints, discussed later in the chapter, are very strong.

Glue blocks add even more strength to a butt joint. Glue and nail them to one piece of material. Then drill clearance and pilot holes for screws to attach the block to the other piece of material, Fig. 29-5. Clamps are not necessary while the glue dries.

Fig. 29-4. One-piece connecters are used to reinforce the butt joints used to assemble this computer desk. (O'Sullivan)

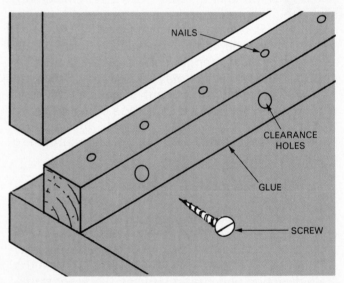
Fig. 29-5. The glue block is bonded and nailed to one component. The second part is attached with screws through the glue block.

DADO AND GROOVE JOINTS

A *dado joint* is a slot cut across the grain. A *groove* is a slot cut with the grain. Dado typically are positioned EG/AG assemblies. You often find them used to mount shelves for cabinets and bookcases, Fig. 29-6. There are several types of dados, Fig. 29-7. In a *through dado,* the joint is exposed. If you choose not to see the joint, make it blind. This dado is cut partway and the joining component is notched to fit. A *half dado* is a combination dado and rabbet joint. It helps keep components square and is often found as a back corner (back-to-side) drawer joint. A dado and rabbet, discussed later, is used in drawer construction.

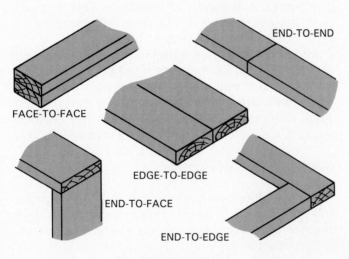
Fig. 29-3. Butt joints.

Fig. 29-6. Dado joint to support a shelf. (American Plywood Assoc.)

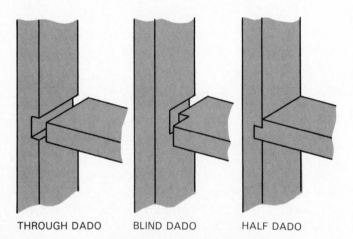

THROUGH DADO   BLIND DADO   HALF DADO

Fig. 29-7. Dado joint variations.

Dados and grooves are most often cut on the table saw or radial arm saw using a dado cutterhead. Two types of dado heads are available, Fig. 29-8. The *adjustable dado cutter* (sometimes called a wobble dado) rotates with a controlled side-to-side motion. The dado width is set by rotating the blade within its guide according to the scale. Another dado head consists of two blades and assorted chippers. Each blade makes a 1/8 in. (3 mm) kerf. The width of the dado is set by adding chippers between the blades, Fig. 29-9.

Most dados require only one pass of the cutter blade, Fig. 29-10. If the joint must be wider than the maximum width of the cutter, make more passes. Since the cut does not pass through the workpiece, you can use a fence and miter gauge together for the setup. There is always a hazard of kickback. Clamp a featherboard to the fence to hold the material down. When within 4 in. (100 mm) of the blade, feed stock with pushsticks.

Dados and grooves can also be cut with the router and straight bit. Usually, two passes are necessary to rout the full width because router bit diameters are limited. To rout accurate dados, use a fence or guide, Fig. 29-11. See Chapter 26 for further discussion of the router.

A difference between sawing or routing operations can be seen in the blind dado. Plan a method to stop the blade or bit. Clamp a stop block to the table saw or to the workpiece when routing. After the dado is cut on the table saw, use a chisel to square the curved inside corner left by the blade. The router will square this corner, but leave a radius at the corners of the dado. Square those with a chisel. The corner of the joining component must be removed to fit the blind dado. Use the table saw

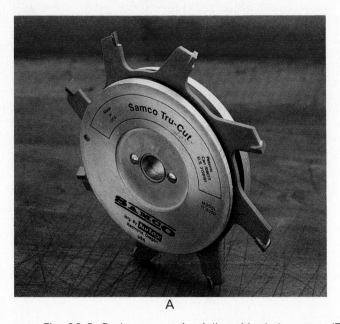

A

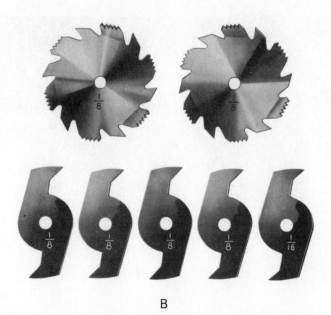

B

Fig. 29-8. Dado cutters. A—Adjustable dado cutter. (The Fine Tool Shops) B—Dado blades and chippers. (Delta)

Fig. 29-9. Chippers between the blades make this dado a one-pass operation. Guard removed to show operation.   (Delta)

Fig. 29-11. Routing a dado using a guide. (Delta)

A

B

Fig. 29-10. A—Crosscutting a dado. B—Ripping a groove. Guard was removed to show operation.   (Delta)

with the workpiece on edge. Leave the blade height unchanged from cutting the dado. This assures an exact fit.

RABBET JOINT

Rabbet joints, often used for simple case construction, are similar to dados, except for the joint's location. Rabbets are cut on the end or edge of the workpiece. A typical full rabbet joint has one part on edge at a width equal to the thickness of the adjoining part. The depth should be one-half to two-thirds the thickness, Fig. 29-12.

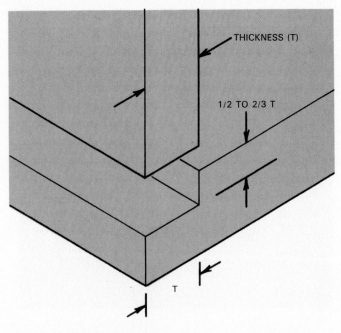

Fig. 29-12. Critical dimensions of a full rabbet joint.

The rabbet joint is commonly used to attach back panels to cabinets, bookcases, and other casework. The joint conceals end grain of the back panel so that it is not visible from the side of the product, Fig. 29-13.

There are several variations of the rabbet joint. With the *half rabbet,* both components are cut the same way. Sometimes, a rabbet and dado are combined, which makes positioning easier. These include the *dado and rabbet,* and *dado tongue and rabbet,* Fig. 29-14.

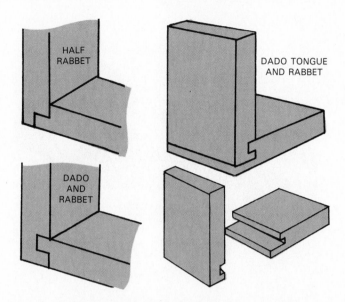

Fig. 29-14. Types of rabbet joints other than the full rabbet.

Rabbet joints can be made using the dado head, Fig. 29-15, or router bit as are dado joints. You may use the router with a square-end cutter and a pilot to control the depth of cut. Without these tools, take multiple passes on the saw to create the full width of the rabbet. Two passes with a standard blade on the table saw will produce the joint. Make one pass with the workpiece surface on the table. Make a second pass with the same surface against the fence.

Rabbet joints can also be made with two specialized hand planes: the rabbet and bull-nose planes. The *rabbet plane* cuts accurate, long rabbets. A fence helps guide the tool, Fig. 29-16. In a *bull-nose plane,* the plane iron is up front. This allows you to plane into corners, Fig. 29-17. The irons in both rabbet and bull-nose planes are set like a block plane. Several passes are necessary to attain the depth of cut needed.

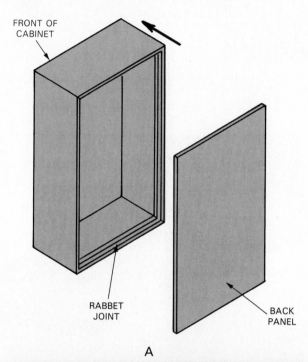

A

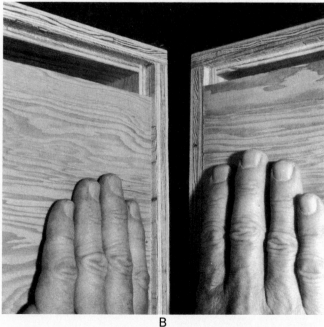

B

Fig. 29-13. Rabbet joints are often used to hide the edge and end grain of a back panel. (American Plywood Association.)

Fig. 29-15. Ripping a rabbet with a dado blade. (Delta)

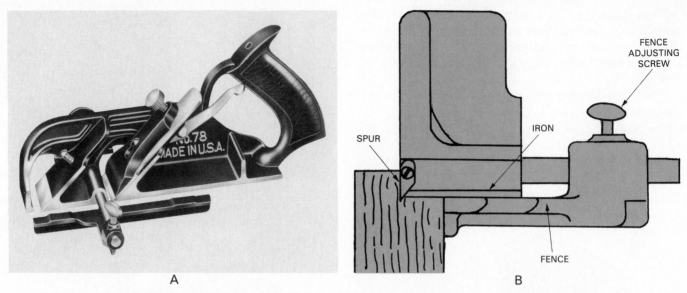

Fig. 29-16. A—Rabbet plane. (Stanley) B—Position of the plane when cutting a rabbet joint.

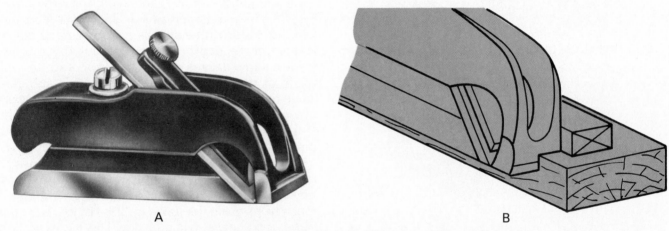

Fig. 29-17. A—Bull-nose plane. (Stanley) B—This plane rabbets into a corner.

Some rabbet planes are fitted with a *spur*. This is an attachment which scores the wood at the edge of the cut. This prevents the wood fibers from tearing as the plane iron cuts. If your plane has no spur, it is a good idea to score the surface of the wood with a knife, Fig. 29-18.

LAP JOINT

Lap joints are positioned joints in which one component laps over the other. The parts, which can meet at any angle, join with rabbets or dados cut equal to the workpiece width. Lap joints are given different names according to where the components meet, Fig. 29-19. Lap joints are often called half laps because equal parts of each component are removed at the lap. Lap joints that meet at an angle other than 90° are called the *oblique lap* and *three-way lap* joints. Oblique laps are often found where

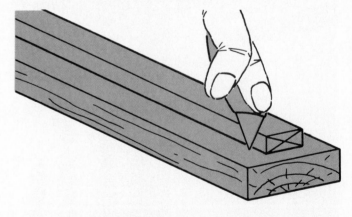

Fig. 29-18. Score the wood along the layout line to prevent tearing the grain when cutting the rabbet with hand tools.

diagonal stretchers meet, such as in the table shown in Fig. 29-20.

Lap joints may be sawn or routed. Sawing is done with a dado head or multiple-passes with a stan-

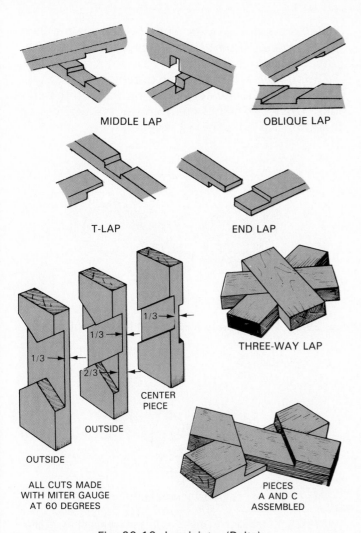

MIDDLE LAP

OBLIQUE LAP

T-LAP

END LAP

THREE-WAY LAP

1/3

1/3

1/3

1/3

2/3

CENTER
PIECE

OUTSIDE

OUTSIDE

ALL CUTS MADE
WITH MITER GAUGE
AT 60 DEGREES

PIECES
A AND C
ASSEMBLED

Fig. 29-19. Lap joints. (Delta)

OBLIQUE LAP

Fig. 29-20. The oblique lap connects stretchers at their intersection. (Thomasville)

dard blade. Both the radial arm saw and table saw are appropriate. Routing makes use of the square-end bit and guide.

MITER JOINT

Miter joints are much like butt joints, but conceal all or part of the end grain because they are cut at a 45° angle. This makes the joint much more attractive. The two most common joints are the flat and plain miters. All that is visible is a 45° line, Fig. 29-21. The *flat miter* is also called a *frame miter* since it is widely used for frame and panel construction. The *plain miter* is also called the *carcase miter* because it joins the edges of panels in case construction.

In its simplest form, the miter joint is a weak, non-positioned, end grain-to-end grain assembly. However, it can be made stronger when positioned. Most miters can be reinforced with dowels, splines, or plate joinery. Positioned miters include the rabbet miter, lock miter, half-lap miter, or lap and tenon miter joints.

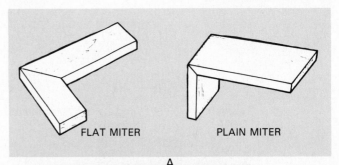

FLAT MITER

PLAIN MITER

A

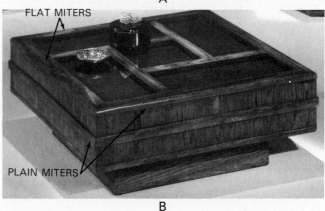

FLAT MITERS

PLAIN MITERS

B

Fig. 29-21. A—Simple miter joints. (Delta) B—Flat and plain miters on a square cocktail table. (Bassett)

Miter joints typically are sawn using a power miter box. On a table saw, tilt the blade to bevel a plain miter. To cut a flat miter, place the blade at 90° and rotate the miter gauge 45°. For some positioned miters, such as the *rabbeted miter,* a sequence of cuts are necessary, Fig. 29-22.

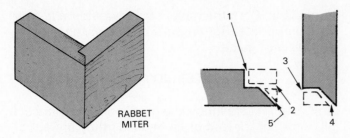

Fig. 29-22. Making a rabbet miter. (Delta)

The *lock miter* is an even more intricate joint. It could be described as a rabbeted miter with an extra locking tab, Fig. 29-23. There are two methods to cut the components. If made by sawing, a sequence of six passes are needed. You could also make a lock with a shaper and a special cutter. Place the first component flat on the machine table as you feed it past the cutter. Stand the second up against the fence.

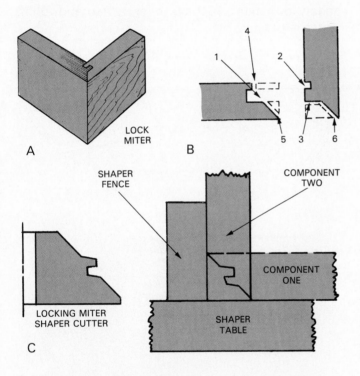

Fig. 29-23. A—Lock miter. (Delta) B—Series of cuts taken on the table saw to create the joint. C—The lock miter can also be cut on the shaper with a single cutter.

A *half-lap miter* combines a miter and lap joint, Fig. 29-24. Cut the half lap in the first component; then cut the miter. On the second component, cut a miter half the workpiece thickness.

A *lap and tenon miter* has different features at each one-third of the workpiece thickness, Fig. 29-25. First cut an open mortise in the end of part one. This can be done with a dado blade and tenon-

ing jig, or several rip cuts. Then cut the lap one-third the thickness of part two. Finally, make the miter cuts.

Clamp-nails reinforce plain miter joints. (See Fig. 16-20.) A thin saw kerf is cut on the mitered surface. Drive the clamp nail to draw the two pieces together. No adhesive is required.

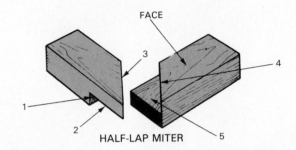

Fig. 29-24. Cuts taken to make a half-lap miter. (Delta)

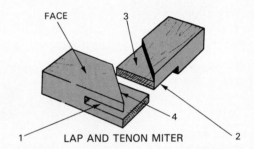

Fig. 29-25. Cuts taken to make a lap and tenon miter. (Delta)

TONGUE AND GROOVE JOINT

The *tongue and groove joint* is a positioned version of the butt joint. The tongue is made on one component and the groove on the other, each cut one-third the workpiece thickness, Fig. 29-26. As an edge-to-edge joint, it can replace the butt joint when gluing stock to make a wider workpiece, such as a table top. With more surface contact than a butt joint, the tongue and groove increases the bonding surface.

A tongue and groove joint can be cut with a dado head on the table saw or radial arm saw, Fig. 29-27. With a standard blade, make two passes on each side to create the tongue. Make several passes through the joining component to create the groove.

In a production milling setting, the tongues and grooves are shaped by a matched pair of shaper cutters. One cutter shapes the tongue while the other shapes the grooves. Install the first cutter, set the height and depth, and machine the first half of the joint. Then exchange the cutter and machine the other components. Do not alter the spindle height or fence setting when installing the matching cutter.

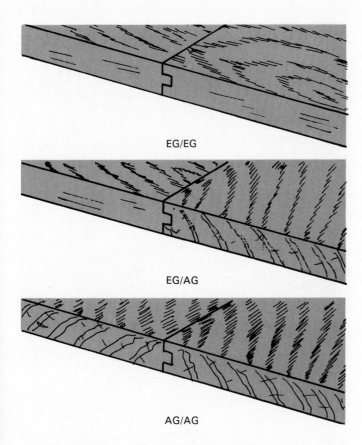

EG/EG

EG/AG

AG/AG

Fig. 29-26. The tongue and groove position the joint and strengthen it by increasing the glue surface.

Fig. 29-27. Cutting the groove with a radial arm saw and dado blade. (DeWalt)

MORTISE AND TENON JOINT

The *mortise and tenon joint* has long been a sign of quality furniture construction. It is typically found connecting rails and aprons to table and chair legs. The joint consists of a *tenon,* or projecting tab on one member, and a *mortise,* or cavity, into which the tenon fits. In looking at a mortise and tenon

joint, the joining components appear to butt together. Yet, the fit of the tenon and mortise is actually an extremely strong AG/AG assembly, Fig. 29-28.

There are many variations of the mortise and tenon. Some shown in Fig. 29-29 include:

1. *Through mortise and tenon.* End grain is visible.
2. *Blind mortise and tenon.* Most common mortise and tenon joint. End grain is not visible.
3. *Open mortise and through tenon.* Eye appealing joint at the expense of reduced strength.
4. *Blind mortise and bare-face tenon.* Often used when the tenoned piece is thinner than the one that is mortised.
5. *Blind mortise and haunched tenon.* Used in frame construction for added strength.
6. *Blind mortise and blind haunched tenon.* Similar to haunched tenon, except that the groove is cut at an angle so that it does not appear in the final joint.
7. *Through mortise and wedged tenon.* Useful where added strength is required.
8. *Blind mortise and wedged tenon.* Added strength where a through tenon cannot be used.
9. *Open or blind mortise and mitered tenon.*
10. *Open or blind mortise and bare-face tenon.*

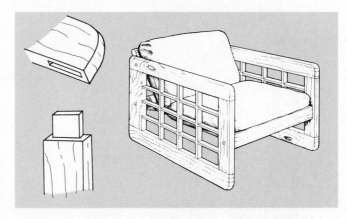

Fig. 29-28. Components of the most common mortise and tenon joint, the blind mortise and tenon. (Unfinished Furniture Store)

MORTISING AND TENONING EQUIPMENT

Special equipment is available for making mortise and tenon joints. A drill press equipped with the mortising attachment makes square holes to create the mortise, Fig. 29-30. A *mortising chisel* fits into the attachment. The chisel, which does not rotate, lowers into the workpiece to square the hole as the drill bit turns inside it. The workpiece is held against the fence and table with guides. A drill press having

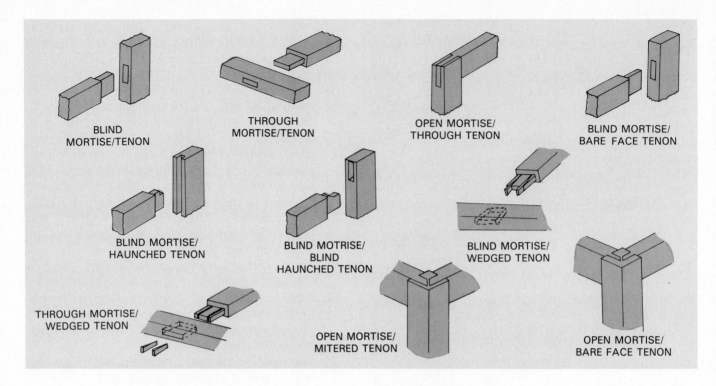

Fig. 29-29. Mortise and tenon variations. (Delta, Stanley)

BLIND MORTISE/TENON

THROUGH MORTISE/TENON

OPEN MORTISE/ THROUGH TENON

BLIND MORTISE/ BARE FACE TENON

BLIND MORTISE/ HAUNCHED TENON

BLIND MORTISE/ BLIND HAUNCHED TENON

BLIND MORTISE/ WEDGED TENON

THROUGH MORTISE/ WEDGED TENON

OPEN MORTISE/ MITERED TENON

OPEN MORTISE/ BARE FACE TENON

foot feed works best for this operation. It leaves your hands free to position the workpiece.

The mortise can also be made with a router, preferably a plunge router. Insert a square-end bit having a diameter the width of the mortise. Set the depth of cut for the mortise. Align the bit with one end of the mortise. Turn on the router, plunge the bit into the wood, and feed it the mortise length. A router guide or fence accessory helps keep the mortise straight.

The *tenoning jig,* Fig. 29-31, slides in the table slots like a miter gauge and supports the component at 90° to the table. It usually is manufactured for a specific saw model. To protect yourself since

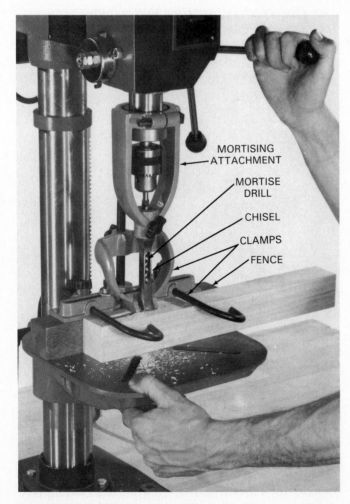

MORTISING ATTACHMENT

MORTISE DRILL

CHISEL

CLAMPS

FENCE

Fig. 29-30. Mortising attachment on the drill press. (Delta)

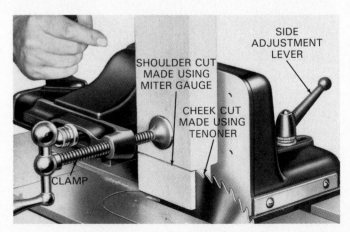

SIDE ADJUSTMENT LEVER

SHOULDER CUT MADE USING MITER GAUGE

CHEEK CUT MADE USING TENONER

CLAMP

Fig. 29-31. Tenoning accessory for cutting tenons on the table saw. (Delta)

the tenoner cannot be used with a guard, place the jig in the left table slot. Then stand to the left of the machine setup. This keeps the accessory between you and the blade.

You can also make tenoning jigs for the table saw, Fig. 29-32. They straddle the fence instead of sliding in the table slots. A guide or quick clamp holds the workpiece vertical. Hold onto the jig well above the blade.

In a mass production setting, there are two machines for producing this joint: the mortising machine and tenoner. The *mortising machine* appears much like a drill press retrofitted for mortising, Fig. 29-33. However, there are some additional features that make it more efficient. First, an automatic feed moves the table the width of the mortising chisel after each plunge. Stops limit the table travel for a given mortise length. A cross feed handwheel controls table movement to position the workpiece under the chisel. The height adjusting handwheel raises or lowers the table. A foot pedal feeds the tool into the work.

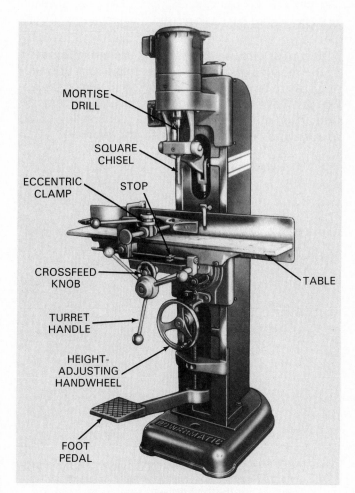

Fig. 29-33. Mortising machine. (Powermatic)

There are two types of production tenoners: single-end and double-end. The machine shown in Fig. 29-34 is a *single-end tenoner.* The workpiece is placed on the table which moves it toward two sets of cutterheads. One cycle of the machine makes all necessary cuts to produce the tenon. A *double-end tenoner* produces tenons on both ends of a workpiece with each cycle.

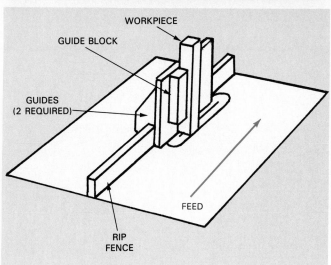

Fig. 29-32. User-made jigs for cutting tenons on the table saw.

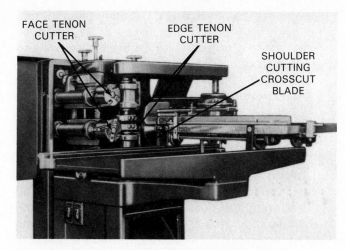

Fig. 29-34. Single-end tenoner. (Powermatic)

Joint Making 447

MAKING A BLIND MORTISE AND TENON JOINT

The *blind mortise and tenon* is the most common of the mortise and tenon joints. It is found connecting rails to legs in chairs and apron to legs in tables, Fig. 29-35. Create this joint by cutting the mortise first. Then cut the tenon. This sequence allows you to trim and fit the tenon to fit the mortise.

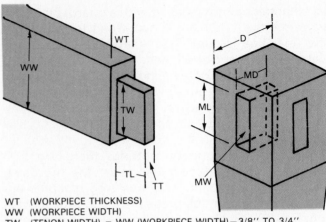

WT (WORKPIECE THICKNESS)
WW (WORKPIECE WIDTH)
TW (TENON WIDTH) = WW (WORKPIECE WIDTH) — 3/8'' TO 3/4''
TL (TENON LENGTH) = ⟨ 2/3 D (DEPTH OF MORTISED COMPONENT)
TT (TENON THICKNESS) = 1/2 WW (WORKPIECE THICKNESS)
MD (MORTISE DEPTH) = TL + 1/8''
MW (MORTISE WIDTH)

Fig. 29-36. Standard dimensions of a blind mortise and tenon.

Fig. 29-35. The apron under the table top of this curio table is connected to the legs with mortise and tenon joints. (Butler Specialty Co.)

There are several factors to consider before making the joint. First, the tenon thickness should be about one-half the stock thickness. The tenon width should be 3/8 to 3/4 in. (about 10 to 19 mm) narrower than the stock width. This allows for a 3/16 to 3/8 in. (5 to 10 mm) shoulder. See Fig. 29-36. The tenon length should be no longer than two-thirds the width of the thicker piece. The mortise should be 1/8 in. (3 mm) deeper than the tenon. If the mortise is routed, round the tenon corners or chisel square the mortise so the mating parts match.

Follow this procedure to make a 3/8 in. blind mortise using a tenoning jig on the table saw and mortising attachment on the drill press.

1. Lay out the mortise width one-half the thickness of the tenon. The mortise length should be 3/8 in. (10 mm) less than the tenon width to create a 3/16 in. (5 mm) shoulder on each end.
2. Secure a 3/8 in. mortising chisel in the mortising adaptor of the drill press. Insert and tighten the drill in the chuck. Start and stop the machine quickly. A high pitch squealing noise indicates the bit is touching the inside of the chisel. If this occurs, loosen the drill only and lower it about 1/32 in. (1 mm). Some-

times the chisel and drill bit are a combined assembly, Fig. 29-37. Make sure the chisel is square to the fence, Fig. 29-38A.
3. Clamp the workpiece to the table. It should already have been cut to size.
4. Align one end of the laid-out mortise with the chisel.
5. Adjust the depth stop so that the mortise is 1/8 in. (3 mm) deeper than the tenon length, Fig. 29-38B.
6. Drill the first square hole. Then move the workpiece about three-fourths the width of the chisel and drill another square hole, Fig. 29-39. Repeat this process until the mortise is complete.
7. Lay out and mark the measurements on the tenon.

Fig. 29-37. One-piece drill bit and mortising chisel assembly. (American Machine & Tool Co.)

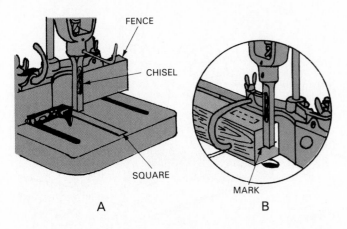

Fig. 29-38. A—Square the chisel to the fence. B—A mortise depth mark on the end of the stock helps set the chisel height. (Delta)

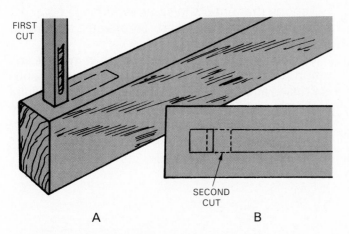

Fig. 29-39. Successive mortising cuts. A—First cut. B—Lap slightly over the previous cut. (Delta)

8. Set the blade height at 3/16 in. (one-fourth the workpiece thickness). See Fig. 29-40.
9. Cut shoulders on all four sides of the workpiece. Use the miter gauge.
10. Set the blade height 1/16 in. less than the tenon length so that you do not cut beyond the shoulder into the part. See Fig. 29-41.
11. Make cheek cuts on all four sides with the workpiece positioned in the tenoning jig.

MORTISE AND TENON VARIATIONS

The layout and procedure for making the blind mortise and tenon apply to many other variations of the mortise and tenon joint. However, some of the methods may differ according to the joint.

An *open mortise and tenon joint* can be made on the table saw with a tenoner jig. Make several passes to cut the open slot mortise. Then make two *shoulder cuts* on the tenon. Finally clamp the tenon part in the tenoner to make *cheek cuts.* Then turn

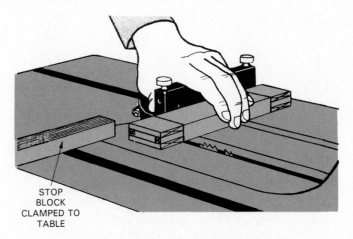

Fig. 29-40. Making shoulders cuts.

Fig. 29-41. Making cheek cuts with the stock poisitioned vertical by a user-made tenoning jig.

the workpiece around to complete the second cheek cut. See Fig. 29-42.

The router also is suited for making open or blind mortises. First lay out the mortise. Then install a square-end bit in the router. Set the depth according to the layout. Lower the bit into a blind mortise. (A plunge router works best for this operation.) For the open slot mortise, simply enter the end of the

Fig. 29-42. Making cheek cuts with the tenoning jig. (Delta)

workpiece. Square the corners of the mortise or round the corners of the tenon so that the two match.

Tenons can also be cut in a horizontal position with a dado head or several passes on the table saw. See Fig. 29-43. Raise the blade to the width of the shoulder. Position a stop to the length of the tenon. Use the miter gauge and make the necessary passes to cut on two or four sides, depending on the type of mortise and tenon.

Tenons that enter the same workpiece could hit each other in the mortises. To prevent this, miter the tenons, Fig. 29-44.

Wedges can be added for strength in mortise and tenon joints. When this is specified, mortise ends are drilled at 5° to 8°. The blind wedged tenon joint presents special problems. Check the length and spreading capacity of the wedges. You might not be able to fit the tenon into the mortise. This occurs if the wedges are too long or too wide.

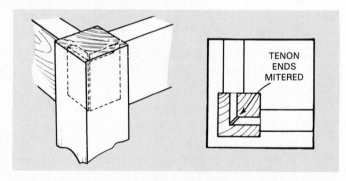

Fig. 29-44. Miter tenons if they meet in the component. (Delta)

MAKING MORTISE AND TENON JOINTS WITH HAND TOOLS

If you desire a challenge, make the mortise and tenon joint with hand tools, Fig. 29-45. Lay out the mortise and drill a series of holes to the proper depth. Then clean out the mortise with a chisel. Cut the shoulders of the tenon with a backsaw. Have a square piece of stock clamped next to the layout line to keep the saw square. When sawing the cheeks, create a jig or guide to keep the saw straight. After making all the cuts, fit and trim the tenon with a chisel. Each joint must be individually fit, then marked for assembly.

Fig. 29-43. Sawing tenons by making a series of crosscut passes.

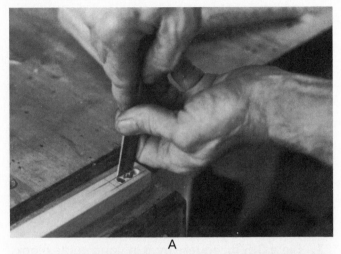

A

B

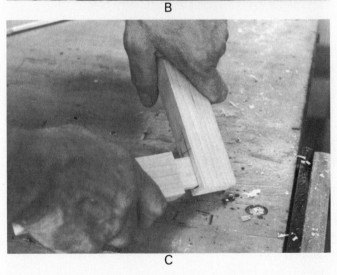

C

Fig. 29-45. Hand mortising. A—After drilling several holes, chisel out the mortise. B—After making shoulder and cheek cuts with a backsaw or dovetail saw, chisel the tenon square. C—Assembling the joint.

DECORATIVE MORTISE AND TENON JOINTS

Several of the standard mortise and tenon joints can be modified to be more decorative, Fig. 29-46. An example of the *tusk tenon* on Early American furniture is shown in Fig. 29-47.

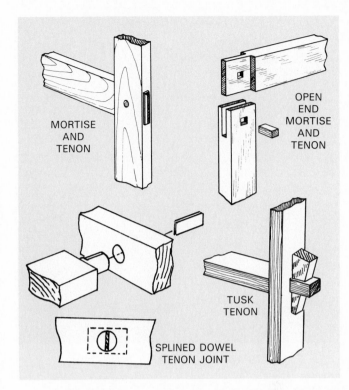

Fig. 29-46. Decorative mortise and tenon joints. (Delta)

Fig. 29-47. Tusk tenon on an Early American coffee table. (Craft Products)

BOX JOINT

The *box joint,* sometimes called a *finger-lap joint,* consists of alternating squares of end and surface grain, Fig. 29-48. It is both a strong and decorative joint, often used to assemble drawers. Box joints generally are made using a dado head on the table saw. You must have an adjustable jig attached to the miter gauge. The jig's stop positions each cut for the joint.

Fig. 29-48. Box joints on a jewelry box.

Fig. 29-49 and the steps that follow show how to process a box joint having 3/8 in. fingers. It is very important that you set up the jig and saw accurately. Also, mark the pieces so that you process them in the same direction.

1. Create an adjustable jig for the miter gauge.

The dimensions for one to make 3/8 in. box joints is shown in Fig. 29-49A.

2. Install a dado cutter 3/8 in. wide.
3. Adjust the blade height to the thickness of the stock.
4. Attach the box joint jig to the miter gauge and adjust it so that the guide stop is 3/8 in. from the blade.
5. Place board one (side component of box or drawer) against the stop. The edge to face up should rest against the guide stop. Make the first pass, Fig. 29-49B.
6. Reposition the board with the kerf over the stop and make pass two, Fig. 29-49C. Continue to do this until all cuts have been made.
7. Rip a 3/8 in. square by 6 in. long guide block. This is needed to offset the fingers of the joining component.
8. Place the guide block against the stop. Place board number two (box or drawer front) against the guide block. Then make the first pass, Fig. 29-49D.
9. Reposition the board so that the kerf made rests against the stop. Make pass two, Fig. 29-49E.
10. Continue relocating board two against the stop until all of the cuts have been made.

Carefully choose which parts to process with and without initially using the guide block. The fingers of mating parts must mesh, Fig. 29-49F.

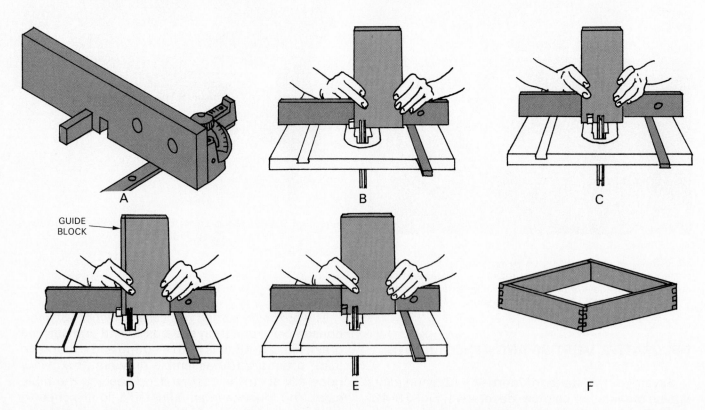

Fig. 29-49. Cutting a box joint. A—Jig. B—First pass of first component. C—Second and successive cuts. D—First pass on second component. E—Second and successive cuts. F—An assembled product.

DOVETAIL JOINT

A *dovetail joint* is much like a box joint, except that the fingers are replaced by tails. Each tail and socket is cut at an angle to provide a locking effect that strengthens the joint. The angle of the individual fingers also makes the joint quite attractive, Fig. 29-50. Several different dovetail styles, shown in Fig. 29-51, include:

1. *Multiple dovetail (through multiple dovetail).*
2. *Half-blind multiple dovetail.*
3. *Blind multiple dovetail.*
4. *Blind miter dovetail.*
5. *Through and blind single dovetail.*
6. *Lap dovetail.*
7. *Half-lap dovetail.*
8. *Half-dovetail and half-lap dovetail.*
9. *Dovetail dado and half-dovetail dado.*

Dovetail joints have two parts: the *tail,* which fits into the *socket.* These parts may be produced by hand or machine. Through and lap dovetails can be cut by hand. Blind dovetails should be done by machine. The procedures for cutting popular dovetails are discussed in this section.

ROUTING A HALF-BLIND DOVETAIL JOINT

The *half-blind dovetail* is the most popular dovetail, widely used in quality drawer construction. This joint is cut with a router, template guide, dovetail bit, and *dovetail jig.* Fig. 29-52 and the procedure to follow show how to cut the half-blind dovetail.

Fig. 29-50. Dovetails are an intricate, but attractive joint.

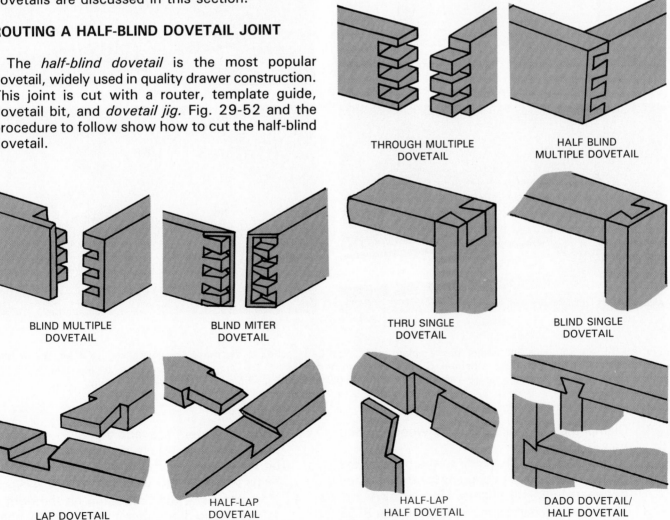

THROUGH MULTIPLE DOVETAIL

HALF BLIND MULTIPLE DOVETAIL

BLIND MULTIPLE DOVETAIL

BLIND MITER DOVETAIL

THRU SINGLE DOVETAIL

BLIND SINGLE DOVETAIL

LAP DOVETAIL

HALF-LAP DOVETAIL

HALF-LAP HALF DOVETAIL

DADO DOVETAIL/ HALF DOVETAIL

Fig. 29-51. Dovetail variations. (Stanley)

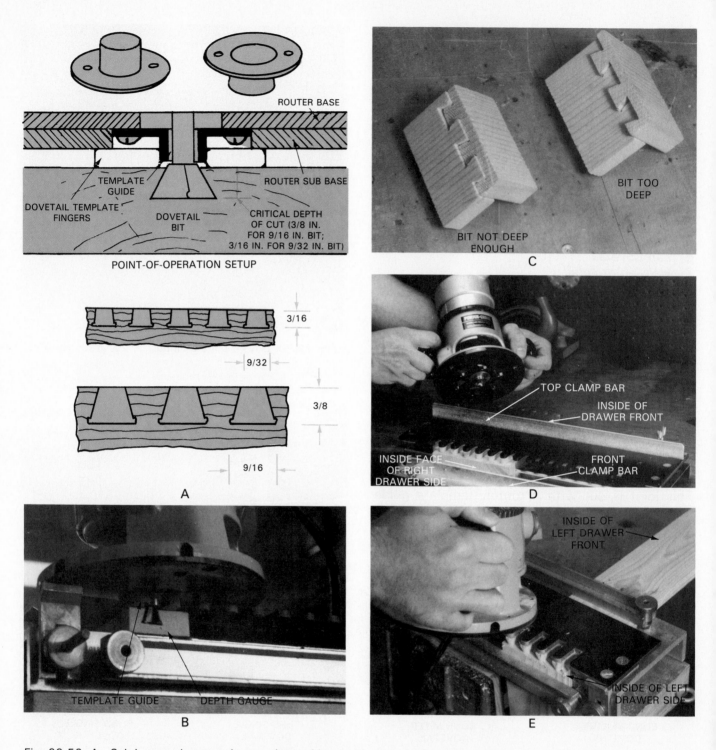

Fig. 29-52. A—Sub-base and proper size template guide must be attached to the router for dovetailing. (Klockit) B—Setting the dovetail bit depth. A gauge is helpful. C—Improperly fit dovetail joint. D—Material positioned on the left side of the jig. (Shopsmith, Inc.) E—Material positioned against locating pins on the right side of the jig.

1. Clamp the dovetail jig to the woodworking bench.
2. Attach the template guide to the base of the router. Insert the proper guide for the distance between template fingers, Fig. 29-52A.
3. There are two basic sizes of dovetail bits: 9/32 and 9/16 in. wide. Depth of cut is critical. Set this distance, Fig. 29-52B. If you measure

from the router base, add the thickness of the finger template. Make a gauge block for the bit you use regularly for quicker set up. This helps prevent inaccuracies, Fig. 29-52C.
4. You can make the first setup on the right or left of the jig. For either a small jewelry chest or drawer, this description begins on the left, Fig. 29-52D.

5. Make a scrap test joint first. When the cut is complete, let the router come to a complete stop before removing it from the jig.

   NEVER RAISE THE ROUTER OUT OF THE WORKPIECE OR JIG WHILE THE MOTOR IS RUNNING.

   Remove the two components and check the fit. (See Fig. 29-52C.) If the joint is too loose, the bit was too deep. Raise it 1/64 in. If the joint is too tight, the bit was not deep enough. Lower the bit 1/64 in. In addition, if the joint is too shallow or deep, adjust the template position in or out accordingly.

6. Place the right side of the drawer or chest vertically. Its edge must be against a locating pin on the left (behind the front clamp bar). The surface that will be inside must face out (touch the front clamp bar). Clamp it lightly.

7. Position the chest or drawer front in the horizontal position against the locating pin on top. The horizontal piece should be the same height and must touch the vertical piece.

8. Tighten both the top and front clamp bars.

9. Attach the template to rest evenly on the material.

10. Hold the router on the template with the bit clear of the work. Turn on the motor and feed the bit slowly into the wood at the locating pin end. Continue to follow the template, cutting the socket and tails at the same time.

11. Position the left side of the drawer or chest vertically on the right, Fig. 29-52E. Have the inside out as before. Put it against a locating pin to the right. Hold it there with the front clamp.

12. Position the other end of the chest or drawer front against another locating pin on the right. Again, the front and side should be the same height and must touch.

13. Tighten both the top and front clamp bars.

14. Start on the right and complete the cut as on the left. The back and sides can be joined in a similar manner. Be sure to mark the matching corners. Always keep the bottom or top edges against locating pins.

It is best to make several trial cuts in scrap stock first. These test boards should be the same size as the stock to be joined.

To cut the blind dovetail joint in lip front drawers, the front or back and sides must be cut searately. See Chapter 42, Drawers, for details.

ROUTING A THROUGH MULTIPLE DOVETAIL

The procedure for routing a *through multiple dovetail joint* is almost the same as that for a blind dovetail. However, the workpiece thickness is limited to 3/8 in. Plus you must place a shim under the horizontal component, Fig. 29-53. This pre-

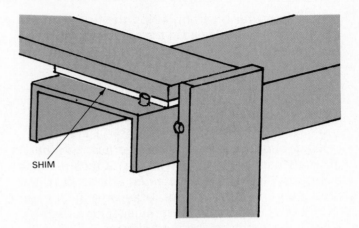

Fig. 29-53. Add a shim to protect the jig when making through multiple dovetails.

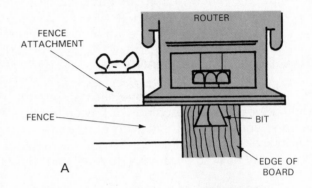

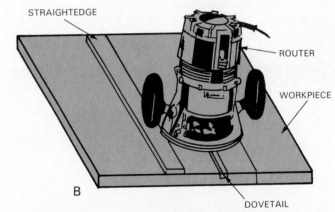

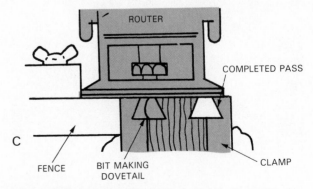

Fig. 29-54. Making blind and through single dovetails. A—Routing the socket in an edge. B—Routing a socket in a surface. C—Routing the tail is two-pass process.

vents the router bit from hitting the jig. Align the components as explained in the previous procedure. Set the depth of cut to the thickness of the two parts.

ROUTING BLIND AND THROUGH SINGLE DOVETAILS

Blind and through *single dovetails* and *dado dovetails* can be cut easily with the router and fence accessory. Insert the dovetail bit and set it to the proper depth. To cut the socket on an edge, center the bit on the edge of the workpiece, Fig. 29-54A. Adjust the fence to the workpiece.

To cut the socket in a face, clamp a straightedge to the workpiece for the router to ride against, Fig. 29-54B. To cut the tail, keep the depth setting the same. Adjust the fence so that one cut is made on each side to form the tail. Refer to Fig. 29-54C.

CUTTING DOVETAILS BY HAND

The through single and lap dovetails can be cut by hand. Lay out each matching workpiece with a T-bevel and square. Cut them with a backsaw or dovetail saw and a chisel. Fig. 29-55 and the steps to follow show how to produce a dovetail joint by hand.
1. Lay out 80° angles on the socket piece end grain.

2. Square the depth of the socket (tail piece thickness).
3. Saw and/or chisel the excess within the sockets.
4. Lay out the tail piece using the socket for a template.
5. Saw and/or chisel away the excess from the tail.

DOWEL JOINT

Dowels are wood or plastic pins that position and reinforce several other joints. Wood dowels are made of hardwood, such as maple or hickory, with diameters from 1/8 to 1 in. *Dowel rod* comes in 3 ft. standard lengths. Some are precut and may have grooves (flutes). Spiral cuts in the dowels allow adhesive to spread and air to rise from the dowel hole. They also retain adhesive, adding to a dowel's holding ability. Plastic right-angle dowels are available for using in mitered corners. See Fig. 29-56.

Fig. 29-55. Dovetailing by hand.

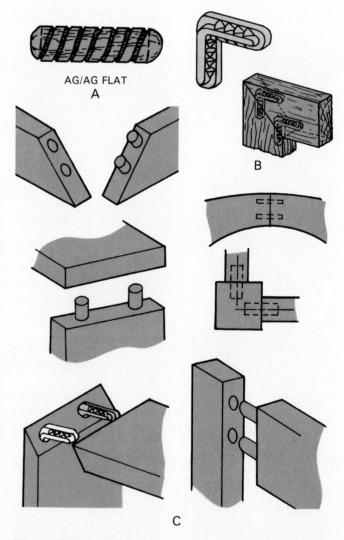

Fig. 29-56. A—Spiral groove dowel. B—Plastic right-angle dowel for reinforcing miter joints. C—Various uses of dowels.

Wood dowels are best kept in a dry environment. When later inserted into a joint, they expand a little and add strength to the joint.

Some considerations to make when reinforcing a joint with dowels:
1. Choose a dowel diameter not less than one-fourth nor more than one-half the thickness of the wood to be joined.
2. Dowel length depends on the two workpieces being joined. A dowel should extend into each workpiece to a depth approximately 2 1/2 times its diameter. For example, a 3/8 in. diameter dowel should extend into each workpiece about 15/16 in.
3. Drill holes in each workpiece to a depth 1/8 greater than half the dowel length.
4. In any joint, use at least two dowels.

Dowel holes must be drilled accurately for the two parts to align. Therefore, make an accurate layout. Multiple parts to be drilled are aligned with a fixture or jig. This ensures that matching dowel holes are properly aligned.

When only a few dowel joints are being made, the best method to locate and drill dowel holes is with a *doweling jig.* The jig drills accurately centered holes for joining two parts end-to-end or edge-to-edge.
1. Square a line across both workpieces where the dowel will be located, Fig. 29-57A.
2. For each component, place the jig and align the jig's index mark on the layout line. There is a different mark for each guide hole, Fig. 29-57B.
3. Insert an auger bit or twist drill in the drill chuck.
4. Drill the holes at each line to the proper depth. Use a depth stop or other method to control hole depth.

On occasions, paired holes cannot be drilled with the jig. For example, suppose you are joining a table apron to a leg with dowels. A doweling jig cannot be clamped to the thick leg. To accurately match these components, use *dowel centers.* See Fig. 29-58. First drill the holes in one part. Insert dowel centers in the holes. Press the two parts together. Then drill the other set of dowel holes at the indentations made by the center points.

PLATE JOINERY

Plate joinery is a strong, fast, and accurate method to join practically any woodworking material together. The joint is made with *joining plates,* also called *biscuits* and *wafers,* inserted into slots cut by a plate joining machine, Fig. 29-59. The process is used primarily in a production setting to join panel products, such as plywood or particle board, to assemble frameless cabinets. In addition, plate joinery is excellent for connecting plastic-laminated materials which will not accept a glue bond.

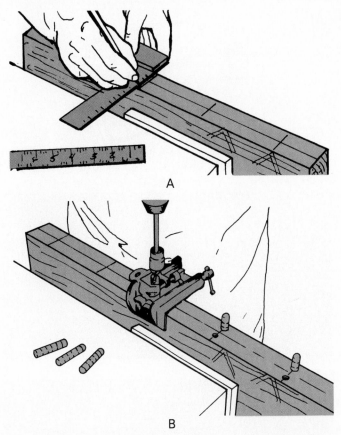

Fig. 29-57. A—When marking locations for dowels in edge-to-edge joints, clamp the two parts and mark both at the same time. B—Placing the self-centering doweling jig over the edge. (Brookstone)

PLATE JOINING MACHINE

The *plate joining machine* is a portable power tool which looks much like a miniature power saw. It consists of a base, fence, handle, and circular blade or cutter. The base and adjustable fence align the machine. The blade remains hidden in the base until you push the machine down on a workpiece. This causes the base to retract, expose the cutter, and make a plunge cut. The cut is slightly deeper and wider than a plate, leaving room for glue and movement of the two components when aligning the joint.

PLATES

Plates, made of compressed beechwood, come in three sizes, all 5/32 in. thick: 5/8 x 1 3/4 in., 3/4 x 2 1/8 in., and 1 x 2 3/8 in. They are labeled by numbers: #0, #10, and #20 respectively. Use adhesives thinned or mixed with water, such as PVA and hide glue. These cause inserted plates to expand, producing a tight fit. Several plates are used per joint. Glue is necessary only in the slots and the assembly needs to be clamped for only 10 minutes.

Fig. 29-58. A—Dowel centers. B—Drilling holes in apron end for dowel joint to leg. C—Place dowel centers in the apron to mark hole locations. D—Keep the parts square while pressing the apron to the leg. E—Drill dowel holes in the leg at locations marked by the centers. F—Assembling the leg and apron.

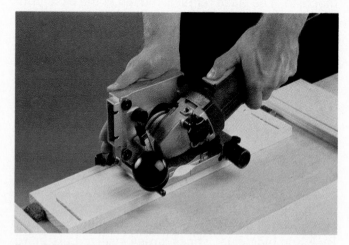

Fig. 29-59. Using plate joinery to assemble a drawer. Recognize the joining plates, or biscuits. Also notice the semicircular slot made in the wood by the plate joining machine. (Black & Decker)

MAKING A PLATE JOINT

The steps taken to make a plate joint are as follows:

1. Set the depth of cut for the size plate being used. This is done with a locking nut or sliding scale and wing nut.
2. Lay out the positions of the joints. Hold the components together and mark the slot locations freehand. The number of plates needed depends on the size, strength, and weight of the material being joined. Consider the stress the assembly will receive. Always try to use at least two plates, even on frame assemblies.
3. Set the machine fence depth and angle for the joint being cut. Some typical setups are shown in Fig. 29-60. In a center butt joint (edge-to-surface joint), the joining workpiece is used to

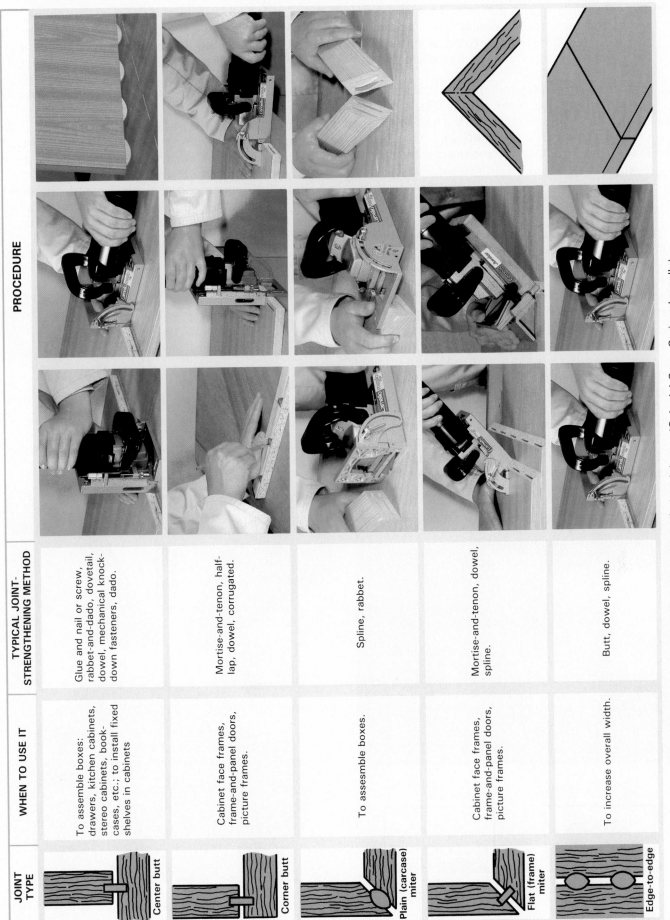

JOINT TYPE	WHEN TO USE IT	TYPICAL JOINT-STRENGTHENING METHOD	PROCEDURE
Center butt	To assemble boxes: drawers, kitchen cabinets, stereo cabinets, book-cases, etc.; to install fixed shelves in cabinets	Glue and nail or screw, rabbet-and-dado, dovetail, dowel, mechanical knock-down fasteners, dado.	
Corner butt	Cabinet face frames, frame-and-panel doors, picture frames.	Mortise-and-tenon, half-lap, dowel, corrugated.	
Plain (carcase) miter	To assemble boxes.	Spline, rabbet.	
Flat (frame) miter	Cabinet face frames, frame-and-panel doors, picture frames.	Mortise-and-tenon, dowel, spline.	
Edge-to-edge	To increase overall width.	Butt, dowel, spline.	

Fig. 29-60. Applications of plate joinery. (Colonial Saw, Steiner-Lamello)

align the slots in the surface. To make edge slots, the fence must be positioned according to the joint: 90° for edge-to-edge joints; 45° for carcase (plain) miter or frame (flat) miter joints.

4. Hold the machine against the material and align the index mark with the layout line.
5. Switch on the motor and push the handle to feed the cutter fully into the material.
6. Release the handle and move the machine to the next joint location.

SPLINE JOINT

A *spline* can be used to position and reinforce most joint assemblies. It is a thin piece of hardboard, plywood, or lumber inserted into grooves cut in the joining components. The spline functions much like a tongue in a tongue and groove joint. The groove can be cut through the edge to make the spline visible or not to make the spline hidden (blind). When using lumber for the spline, the spline grain must be perpendicular to the grain of the wood it joins. Otherwise the strength of the spline will be lost. See Fig. 29-61 and Fig. 29-62.

A *keyed spline* is a short triangular spline. It fits into a slot cut in the corner of a flat miter joint.

The table saw cuts grooves into which the spline fits. Install a standard blade to cut 1/8 in. slots. Install a dado head to make cuts for thicker splines.

Set the blade height at half the width of spline. To cut grooves for an edge-to-edge joint, use the rip fence. For a splined flat miter or keyed spline, use the jig shown in Fig. 29-62. For splined plain miters, use the jig shown in Fig. 29-63. Always have matching surfaces of the two workpieces against the fence or jig.

Splines are not necessarily attractive. You may want them blind. Place stop blocks in front of workpiece or jig. Then make the necessary pass until you reach the stop block.

Slots for splines can also be cut with the plate joining machine. After plunging the cutter into the material, feed the machine along the edge or face.

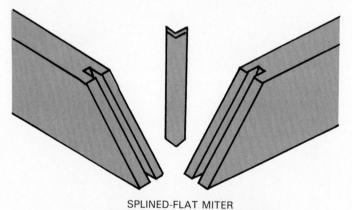

EDGE TO EDGE SPLINED   JOINT WITH BLIND GROOVE

SPLINED-FLAT MITER

SPLINED MITER (WORK ON EDGE)

WEAK

SPLINES FOR EDGE MITERS SHOULD BE ABOUT 3/4 THE THICKNESS OF STOCK

PLENTY OF WOOD HERE

SAME JOINT WITH BLIND GROOVE

SPLINED PLAIN MITER

Fig. 29-62. Use of splines in various joints. (Delta)

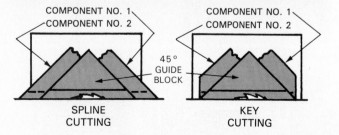

COMPONENT NO. 1
COMPONENT NO. 2

COMPONENT NO. 1
COMPONENT NO. 2

45° GUIDE BLOCK

SPLINE CUTTING

KEY CUTTING

Fig. 29-61. Jig for making splined flat miters and keyed splines.

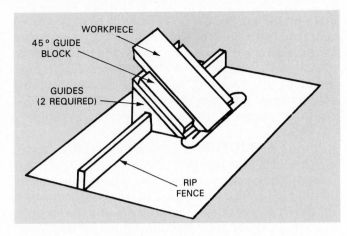

Fig. 29-63. Jig for making splined plain miters.

BUTTERFLY JOINT

The *butterfly joint* is a combination of the dovetail and spline joints. In addition to reinforcement, it gives a decorative effect to any surface, Fig. 29-64. The butterfly's grain lies across the assembly it reinforces. The butterfly itself may be a decorative inlay or solid wood extending totally through the workpiece. See Fig. 29-65.

Produce this joint by making the butterfly first. Then prepare the socket. For sawing the butterfy, set the table saw blade at 10° at a height half the stock thickness. Bevel the stock four times as shown in Fig. 29-66. Then cut the stock into individual butterflies.

To make the socket, first prepare a template of the butterfly. Use the template and knife edge to score the shape. Cut the recess with square-end bit and router, then chisel out the corners. You can also chisel out the entire recess by hand.

For a butterfly passing through the components, saw inside the template shape with a band saw or scroll saw. Finally, fit the butterflies in place. Use a knife or file to make minor adjustments to the shape of the butterfly and socket.

Fig. 29-64. Butterfly joints in a sofa table. (Mersman Tables)

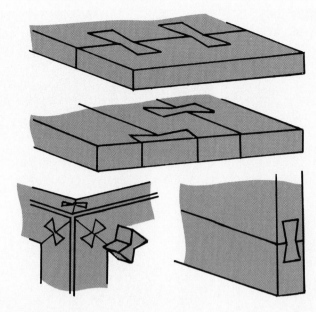

Fig. 29-65. Various uses of butterfly joints. (Shopsmith)

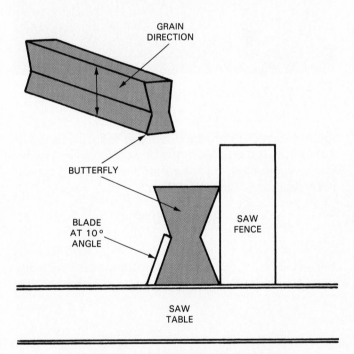

Fig. 29-66. Cutting butterfly stock.

POCKET JOINT

The *pocket joint* allows the cabinetmaker to use screws to connect components end-to-end or edge-to-edge. A pocket cutting accessory and bit creates clearance and pilot holes at an angle, Fig. 29-67. Screws are driven through the pocket into the joining component.

The pocket is cut into the component which joins at end grain. In this manner, the screw is driven into the part having edge grain. Since pockets are unsightly, they are usually hidden. Suppose you are

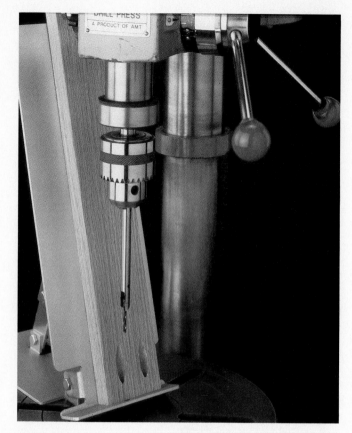

Fig. 29-67. Jig for making pocket joints. (Portalign Tool Corp.)

joining parts which make up the face frame for a cabinet. Cut the holes in the back side of the frame. Once assembled, turn the frame around and attach it to the case, Fig. 29-68.

SCARF JOINT

A *scarf joint* connects components end-to-end, Fig. 29-69. It can be a decorative joint or simply used to join boards to increase the length of stock.

Long lengths of moulding consist of several pieces scarf jointed together. Decreasing the scarf angle increases the surface contact between joining parts. This, in turn, increases the strength of the joint. Saw the scarf at about a 6° to 10° angle on the table saw or radial arm saw in a miter position. By aligning grain patterns, the joint is almost invisible.

STRUCTURAL FINGER JOINTS

Structural finger joints look like multiple scarf joints, Fig. 29-70. They position and add strength to the material being jointed. Some dimension lumber you buy may include finger joints. Short pieces of lumber are joined together rather than wasted. A production shaper cutter is used to make the joint.

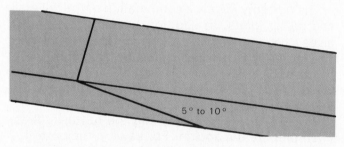

Fig. 29-69. Scarf joint.

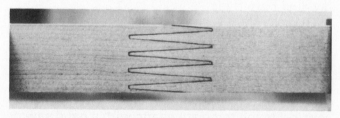

Fig. 29-70. Structural finger joint. (Forest Products Laboratory)

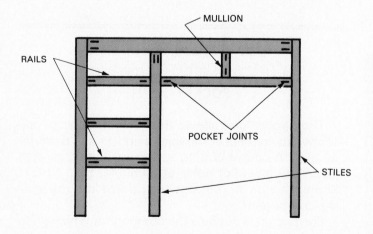

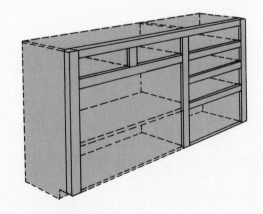

Fig. 29-68. A—Pocket joint placement for assembling a face frame. B—When the frame is turned around and attached, the pockets are not visible.

THREADS

Like metal, wood can also be threaded. Notice that broom handles often thread into the bristle holder. You might also thread chair and table rails into the legs. To make a threaded joint, you need a wood *tap* and *die,* Fig. 29-71. The standard size thread is 3/4 in. Drill a hole 5/8 in. in diameter. Then insert and turn the tap to create the internal threads. Select a 3/4 in. hardwood dowel for the joining component. Place the die over the dowel and rotate it one-half turn clockwise, then one-quarter turn counterclockwise. Continue this routine for the length of the thread.

Fig. 29-71. Making threaded joints. The die produces external threads and the tap produces internal threads. (American Machine & Tool Co.)

THINK SAFETY—ACT SAFELY

In making joints, various woodworking machines are used. You should review safety procedures for these machines. In addition, always observe these general rules:
1. Never operate a machine when tired or ill.
2. Think through the operation before starting. Be certain of what to do and what the machine can do.
3. Make all the needed adjustments to the machine before turning it on.
4. Feed the work carefully and not too fast for the machine.

SUMMARY

Joint making is a critical step of the furniture and cabinetmaking process. The type and quality of joint you choose greatly affects the stability and durability of a product. You have a choice of nonpositioned, positioned, and reinforced joints. Also important is the material. The grain direction of solid wood affects the strength of some joint types.

Throughout the design stages, there are many joinery decisions. It is best to choose the simplest joint that meets the strength requirements of the product. Equally important is the appearance of the joint. In some assemblies, the joint is visible. In others, it is hidden. Visible joints add a decorative effect to the product.

Butt joints are the simplest of all joints. The squared surface of one piece meets the face, edge, or end of another. In a dado joint, one component fits into a slot. The slot, or dado, provides a supporting ledge. The rabbet joint is much like the dado, except it is cut along the edge or end of the workpiece. With the lap joint, components fit into dados or rabbets cut in each. This forms a flush fit. To form a miter joint, the edges or ends of both components are cut at an angle. There are many variations of the miter joint to make it more secure. The mortise and tenon joint is a popular furniture construction technique. A tenon, or tab, fits into a mortise which provides a strong assembly. The box joint consists of interlocking fingers. The dovetail is like a box joint, except that the fingers are cut at an angle, forming tails and sockets. This gives a strong locking effect.

A number of joints consist of some standard joint with additional reinforcement. In a dowel joint, a wood or plastic dowel is used to provide a strong connection. Plate joinery connects parts with plates inserted into slots cut by a plate joining machine. This is a strong, fast, safe, and accurate method to join almost any material. The spline joint involves reinforcement by adding a spline into grooves cut in both components. A butterfly joint is a combination dovetail and spline which provides both reinforcement and decoration. A pocket joint consists of a butt joint reinforced with screws driven at an angle.

The primary purpose for the scarf and structural finger joints is to create usable stock from shorter material. A scarf joins several pieces of stock end-to-end to make longer material. Long lengths of moulding usually consists of shorter lengths scarf jointed together. A structural finger joint is a multiple scarf joint, often found in dimensioned lumber.

CABINETMAKING TERMS

Nonpositioned joint, positioned joint, reinforced joint, butt joint, dado joint, groove joint, adjustable dado cutter, dado blades and chippers, rabbet joint, rabbet plane, bull-nose plane, spur, lap joint, oblique lap, three-way lap, miter joint, flat miter, plain miter, tongue and groove joint, mortise and tenon joint, half-blind mortise and tenon joint, mortiser, mortising chisel, tenoning jig, mortising machine, single-end tenoner, double-end tenoner, shoulder cut, cheek cut, tusk tenon, box joint, dovetail joint, half-blind multiple dovetail, tail, socket, dovetail jig, dovetail router bit, dowel, dowel rod, doweling jig, dowel centers, plate joinery, spline joint, keyed spline, butterfly joint, pocket joint, scarf joint, structural finger joint, threaded joint, tap, die.

TEST YOUR KNOWLEDGE

1. List three factors affecting joint strength.
2. Explain why there is a limited number of joints you can choose for joining panel products.
3. The three general categories of joints are _____, _____, and _____.
4. Cabinetmakers choose the type of joint to assemble a product once the working drawings have been forwarded to production. True or False?
5. Joinery begins once the components have been squared to size. True or False?
6. During layout, make all joint measurements from:
   a. One face of the material.
   b. A common starting point.
   c. The edge of the material.
   d. The end of the material.
7. A butt joint is a positioned joint when screws are used to hold the two components together. True or False?
8. When might you choose to use a blind dado to mount a shelf rather than a through dado?
9. List three ways to cut a dado.
10. Describe how a rabbet joint is similar to and different from a dado joint.
11. A lap joint where the two components meet at an angle other than 90° is called an _____ lap.
12. List alternate names for and give one application of the flat miter and plain miter joints.
13. Identify two uses of the tongue and groove joint.
14. List three ways to create the mortise of a mortise and tenon joint.
15. List two methods to create the tenon of a mortise and tenon joint.
16. A drill press can be converted to a mortiser by adding a _____ _____ and inserting a _____ _____.
17. The most popular of the mortise and tenon joint variations is the:
   a. Blind mortise and haunched tenon.
   b. Open-slot mortise and tenon.
   c. Blind mortise and tenon.
   d. Through mortise and tenon.

18. What must you do to a routed mortise to insert a sawn tenon?
19. The mortise generally is made before the tenon. True or False?
20. To accurately cut a box joint on the table saw, you must obtain or make a _____ _____ _____.
21. Why do you place a guide block between the jig stop and workpiece when cutting one component of a box joint?
22. The tail and socket of a dovetail joint are cut at an angle to provide a _____ _____.
23. The most popular dovetail is the _____ _____ _____.
24. The two basic sizes of dovetail bits are _____ and _____. Depth of cut with the smaller bit is _____. With the larger bit, it is _____ deep.
25. To rout a through multiple dovetail, a _____ is placed under the component clamped horizontal in the dovetail jig.
26. Explain how you would calculate the diameter and length of dowel to use based on the thickness of the joining parts.
27. Dowel holes can be accurately drilled in edge and end grain using a _____ _____.
28. Identify how you would accurately locate dowel holes in material too thick for the doweling jig.
29. Joining plates come in what three sizes? How are these sizes labeled?
30. Explain why you are able to lay out location marks for joining plates freehand, rather than using layout tools.
31. One jig can be made for cutting both splined flat miters and keyed splines. True or False?
32. A pocket joint consists of a butt joint reinforced with _____.
33. The primary purpose of a scarf joint is to:
   a. Join stock to make wider workpieces.
   b. Join stock to make longer workpieces.
   c. Join stock to make thicker workpieces.
   d. Reinforce butt joints.

Chapter 30
ABRASIVES

After studying this chapter, you will be able to:
- Select abrasive materials for smoothing surfaces.
- Identify the major natural and synthetic abrasive materials.
- Choose abrasive grain type and grit size.
- Recognize the adhesives and backings for various coated abrasives.
- Describe the use of abrasives in solid and loose form.

Abrasives are used by cabinetmakers to smooth surfaces in preparation for assembly or finishing, Fig. 30-1. Various types and forms of abrasives are used during the cabinetmaking process.

Coated abrasives. Coated abrasives are grains of a natural mineral or synthetic substance bonded to a cloth or paper backing. They are manufactured into sheets, disks, and many other forms. When the abrasive is rubbed against a surface, each grain acts as a miniature cutting tool. Coated abrasives are often misnamed sandpaper; the grains are not sand.

Solid abrasives. Solid abrasives are grains bonded into stones and grinding wheels. These are used to sharpen planer knives, chisels, and other cutters.

Loose abrasives. Loose abrasives, such as pumice and rottenstone are finely crushed abrasives. These are mixed in water or oil solvent and applied when rubbing a built-up finish.

Abrasive tools. Besides grains, there are abrasive tools. Files, rasps, surforms, textured metal sheet abrasive, and metal screens are examples. In some instances, a file may be more appropriate than a coated abrasive.

Steel wool, a fiber steel mesh, is another abrasive material. It is rubbed over a dried built-up finish to remove brush marks and dust particles.

ABRASIVE GRAINS

Abrasive grains, Fig. 30-2, may be of natural or synthetic origin. Natural abrasives are crushed minerals. Synthetic abrasives are manufactured and are generally harder and more durable than natural minerals. However, they often are more expensive.

Fig. 30-1. Abrasives are used to smooth workpieces before finishing. Here, drawer assemblies are being smoothed. (Rockwell International)

Fig. 30-2. Abrasive grains are the essential ingredient for making solid and coated abrasives. (Norton)

NATURAL ABRASIVES

Cabinetmakers use several natural mineral abrasives. These are flint, garnet, emery, pumice, rottenstone, and tripoli.

Flint is crushed quartz (silicon oxide) and is off-white in color. It is manufactured into coated abrasive sheets used mostly for hand sanding. It is inexpensive and the least durable abrasive. Flint dulls quickly and coated flint abrasive sheets clog often.

Garnet is a hard glasslike material. It is made by crushing semiprecious garnet jewel stone. The grains produced are narrow wedge shapes. Garnet is slightly more expensive than flint. However, it lasts four to five times as long. Garnet is mostly found as a coated abrasive for hand and light machine operations, usually as a preparation for finish. It has a distinct red color.

Emery is a black mineral that is very effective on metals. It is limited mostly to tool sharpening and cleaning rust-coated machine surfaces. Do not use it on wood because it clogs easily.

Pumice is a white, porous, volcanic rock. It is ground into flour and mixed with water or oil. Rubbing the mixture on built-up finishes produces a high luster.

Rottenstone is a flour form of limestone. It is brown or tan and is finer than pumice. Mix it with rubbing oil for the same use as pumice.

Tripoli is finely ground limestone. It typically contains some impurities which give it a white, gray, pink, or yellow color. It is formed into solid cakes and used for polishing plastics.

SYNTHETIC ABRASIVES

Synthetic abrasives are manufactured from natural materials. They undergo a process which melts the minerals in an electric furnace. After they cool, they are crushed. The result is a more effective and durable abrasive. Synthetic abrasives used by cabinetmakers include aluminum oxide, silicon carbide, and industrial diamond.

Aluminum oxide is a very efficient abrasive for sanding woods. It is brown or gray in color and crushed into wide wedge grains. Aluminum oxide lasts several times longer than garnet. It is used as a coated abrasive and as a bonded solid for grinding wheels, stones, and hones.

Silicon carbide is the hardest and most expensive synthetic abrasive. It is black and ground finer than other abrasives. You use it mostly as coated wet-or-dry sheets for smoothing finish coats or plastics. Silicon carbide is also made into honing stones for sharpening tools.

Industrial diamond materials are manufactured to grind and sharpen carbide cutters. They are bonded onto grinding wheels made of metal or another stable core. Synthetic diamond chips are pressed into the cutting surface. While grinding, coolant flows over the point of operation to prevent overheating. Another use for industrial diamond wheels is cutting ceramic materials. Chips are pressed into the edge of a metal disk, much like teeth on a circular saw blade. Again using coolant, you can cut ceramic tile and glass.

ABRASIVE GRAIN SIZES

Abrasives are crushed into grit, powder, and flour sizes. A series of procedures are used to reduce minerals into small grains. Raw material is broken into 6 in. or smaller chunks by jaw crushers. Chunks are then grated to about 2 in. in diameter or smaller. Next they are crushed by rollers or presses to usable grain sizes.

The grains are sifted through a set of shaking screens to separate grain sizes. Screens are made of woven wire or silk. Grit size refers to the screen holes per linear inch. (Window screen has about 16 openings per inch, or 256 holes per square inch.) Grains stop falling when they can no longer go through the screen's openings. The range of abrasive sizes is created using a series of screens, each with a different opening size. This method is used for sizes from 16 to 220 grit.

Smaller grit sizes are called powder or flour grades. These are separated by floating. The tiniest particles float higher in water or air than heavier

GRIT NO.	SYMBOL NO.	COMMON NAME	APPLICATION
600	—		
500	—		
400	(10/0)		
360	—	Very Fine	Polishing After Finish Has Been Applied
320	(9/0)		
280	(8/0)		
240	(7/0)		
220	(6/0)		
180	(5/0)		
150	(4/0)	Fine	Smoothing Before Applying Finish
120	(3/0)		
100	(2/0)		
80	(0)	Medium	Removing Small Marks and Scratches
60	(½)		
50	(1)		
40	(1½)	Coarse	Removing Saw Marks
36	(2)		
30	(2½)		
24	(3)	Very Coarse	For Very Rough Surfaces
20	(3½)		
16	(4)		

Fig. 30-3. Abrasive grains are sized by two systems, grid number and symbol number. The symbol numbers are being phased out because grit numbers are more meaningful.

particles. Powdered grades are 240 to 600 grit sizes. Silicon carbide is powdered into these sizes. Flour grades are F, FF, FFF, and FFFF, with FFFF being the smallest. Pumice is graded by this system.

An older system of grading coated abrasives is still found. It is an arbitrary symbol system that compares to grit sizes shown in Fig. 30-3.

COATED ABRASIVES

Coated abrasives are the most widely used for hand and machine sanding. Grains are bonded with adhesive to a backing material. The coated material is then cut as a sheet, Fig. 30-4, or formed into belts, disks, sleeves, and other shapes.

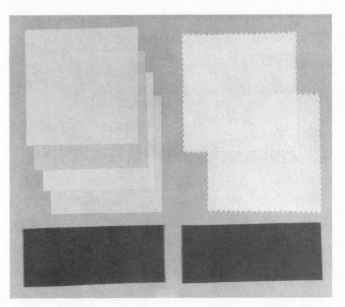

Fig. 30-5. Backing materials. Top-left. Paper. Top-right. Cloth. Bottom. Fiber composition. (Norton)

PAPER PRODUCT IDENTIFICATION

LETTER	WEIGHT (lb.)	DUTY	USE
A	40	Light	Hand
C	70	Light to medium	Hand and light, portable electric pad sanders
D	90 to 100	Medium to heavy	Portable and stationary belt and disk sanders
E	130	Heavy	Drum, stroke and wide belt machines

Fig. 30-6. Letters specify paper product backing weight.

Fig. 30-4. Sheets of coated abrasives. (Norton)

Backing

Backing materials include paper, cloth, and fiber, Fig. 30-5. They have weight and strength differences.

Paper backing is identified by letters A through E, with E being the heaviest. The weights for paper backing shown in Fig. 30-6 refer to 480 26 x 48 in. sheets. Lighter backings are coated with finer abrasives. Heavy backings are coated with coarse or fine abrasives for machine sanding.

Cloth backings include J, or jeans cloth, and X, or drill cloth. J grade cloth backings are light and flexible. They are for belt and hand sanding machines. The X grade is heavier, stronger, and treated for durability. It is used for flat sanding belts on large production machinery.

Fiber backings are made of a chemically treated, laminated paper and cotton rag base. They are able to withstand the heat from prolonged sanding. Heavy-duty disk and drum abrasives are made with fiber backing.

Combination backings are two layers, paper and cloth, Fig. 30-7. Abrasives are bonded to the cloth side. These are used for extra heavy duty disk sanding.

Adhesive

Abrasive grains are attached to the backing by a two-step process. One layer of adhesive is coated to the backing. This is the make coat. The abrasive grains are bonded to this coat. A second coat of adhesive called the size coat anchors the abrasive firmly, Fig. 30-8. There are five basic adhesive combinations for the make and size coats.
1. Glue over glue. Traditionally, hide glue has been used for both the make and size coats with

Fig. 30-7. Combination backings consist of paper and cloth layers. (Norton)

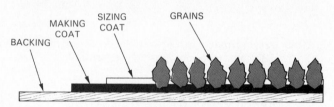

Fig. 30-8. Abrasive grains are attached to the backing between two separate coatings of adhesive. (Norton)

paper-backed coated abrasives. Glue-bonded products have low resistance to sanding heat and moisture. Prolonged storage of this type permits moisture to separate the grit and backing.

2. Glue and filler. Filler material is added to the glue in both layers. It produces a more durable bond.

3. Resin over glue. The hide glue make coat and adhered grains are covered with a synthetic resin. This combination has greater resistance to heat than glue over glue.

4. Resin over Resin. Both make and size coats are synthetic resins. This is the toughest, most durable, heat resistant bond.

5. Waterproof. This is a special make and size coating of synthetic resins. It is used on waterproof paper backing. The coated abrasive then can be used with water or oil.

COATING PRACTICES

Coated abrasives are made with one of two types of abrasive coatings. These are open coat and close coat.

An open coat refers to space between the grains. Only 50 to 70 percent of the backing is covered with abrasive grains. Although it leaves a somewhat rough surface, this type cuts faster and clogs less. A special coating of zinc stearate may be sprayed to open coat abrasives to further resist clogging.

A close coat means that grains cover the entire surface. This type can be found for the full range of abrasive grades. Use finer grit, close coat abrasives where loading (wood chips becoming stuck between abrasive grains) is not a problem and where a smoother finish is desired.

MANUFACTURING COATED ABRASIVES

Abrasive products are manufactured in a continuous process. Backing material is fed from large

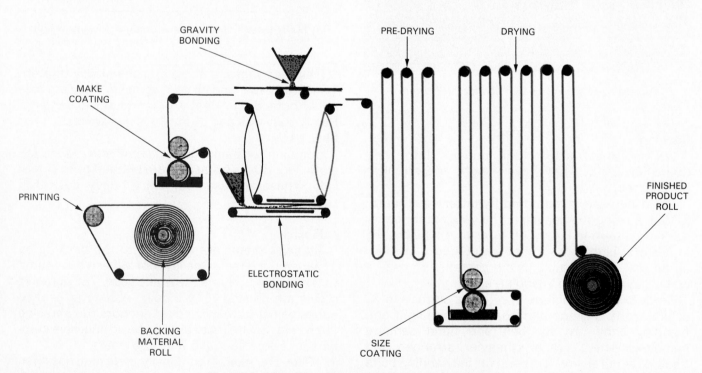

Fig. 30-9. Manufacturing process for coated abrasives.

rolls through coating, bonding, drying, flexing, cutting, and forming processes.

BONDING GRAINS

Grains are deposited in one of two ways, Fig. 30-9, depending on grain size:
1. By gravity. Grains of 150 grit or coarser are dropped directly on the wet make coating.
2. Electrostatically. Finer grits are dropped onto a conveyor belt. They then move through an electromatic field and are magnetically attracted upward to the make coat. The electrostatic process actually aligns grains better for more efficient cutting. Once the grains are bonded, the size coat is applied.

FLEXING

Once the grains, backing, and adhesive cure, the coated abrasive is *flexed.* The adhesives are not especially flexible. Thus, the coated paper or cloth is bent at 90° and/or 45° angles. The direction and spacing of the breaks are important for abrasive contouring. Fig. 30-10 shows the four different flexing practices.

 SINGLEFLEX. The bond is broken at a 90° angle to the width. The abrasive product is stiff in one direction, flexible in the other. This prevents ruptures from occurring when the abrasive is in use over a drum, pulley or curved surface. Singleflex is standard for most cloth sheets.

 DOUBLEFLEX has the bond broken at two 45° angles to the width. This flex is desirable for sanding contours, such as mouldings.

 TRIPLEFLEX is a combination of single and double flexing. It is specified for sanding sharp or irregular contours.

 Q-FLEX provides a uniform flex over the entire surface in all directions. Its excellent self-cleaning property makes it ideal for edge-sanding applications.

Fig. 30-10. Coated abrasives are flexed in one or more directions to give flexibility. (Norton)

CUTTING AND FORMING

After flexing, the abrasive coated backing is cut into sheets or formed.

Sheets are cut into 9 x 11, 9 x 12, and 9 x 13 3/4 in. sheet sizes. These fit popular makes of portable power sanders, Fig. 30-11. The sheets can be torn into halves, thirds, or quarters to fit smaller sanding equipment.

Fig. 30-11. Sheet abrasive is commonly used with portable orbital sanders. (Black and Decker)

Forms include belts, disks, blocks, sleeves, flap-wheels, rolls, spirals, and pencils. These fit a number of sanding machines.

Belts range from less than 1 in. to 52 in. wide with lengths of 12 in. or longer. They are used on portable equipment such as the belt sander, Fig. 30-12, to large stroke sanders and abrasive planers.

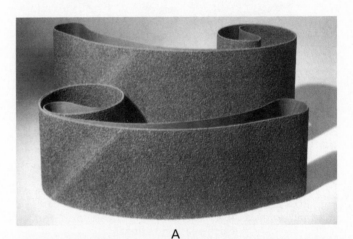

A

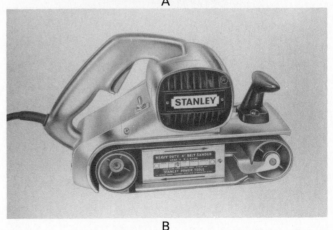

B

Fig. 30-12. A—Abrasive belts. (Norton) B—Belts are used on portable belt sanders. (Stanley)

Disks are found in diameters of 5 through 9 in. Smaller diameters are used for portable disk sanders, Fig. 30-13. Some have a hole punched to attach the disk to the sander. Larger diameters have no hole. They are bonded to stationary disk sanders.

Sanding blocks are coated abrasives bonded to a flexible sponge, Fig. 30-14. They can be used on flat or contoured surfaces. The adhesive used is waterproof so the block can be used for wet or dry sanding.

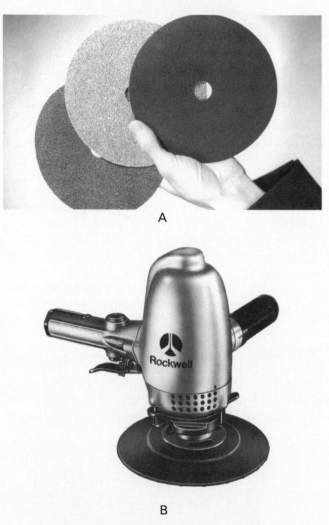

Fig. 30-13. A—Disks for portable power disk sanders are punched with a hole. (Norton) B—Portable disk sander. (Rockwell International)

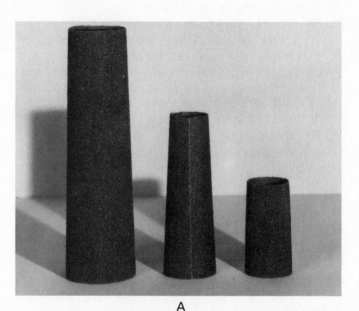

Fig. 30-15. A—Coated abrasive in sleeve form. B—Sleeves are used on drum sanders and spindle sanders.

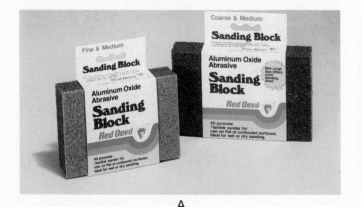
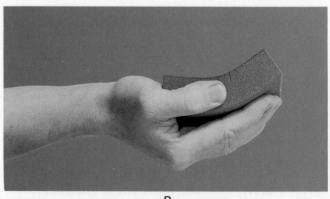

Fig. 30-14. A—One relatively new form of coated abrasive is the sanding block. B—The block is flexible to fit contours. (Red Devil)

Sleeves are made for drum and spindle sanders, Fig. 30-15. Various diameters and lengths are available. You slide the abrasive sleeve over a drum or spindle which is then expanded to secure it.

Flap wheels are scored sheets of abrasive bound to a center core with a shaft. The flap wheel is inserted into a drill, Fig. 30-16. The many narrow pieces of abrasive smooth contoured surfaces.

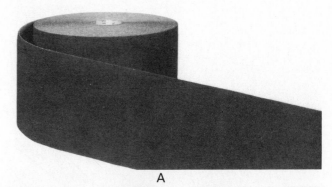
A

B

Fig. 30-16. Flap wheels mounted on a drill will smooth in tight corners and around contours. (Norton)

Other forms include rolls, spirals, and pencils, Fig. 30-17. Rolls are available in various widths up to 48 in. Widths narrower than 1/16 in. are called cords. These can be threaded through hard-to-reach areas. Spirals are used for sanding fillets, recesses, and small contours. They are used with metal mandrels. Pencils are used for sanding channels, recesses and bottoms of blind holes. They are attached to a metal mandrel.

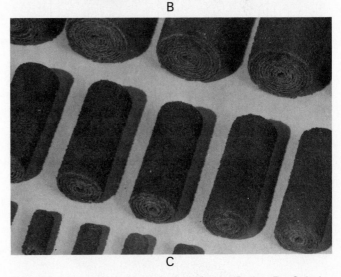
C

Fig. 30-17. Other abrasive forms. A—Rolls. B—Spirals. C—Pencils. (Norton)

SOLID ABRASIVES

Solid abrasives are a combination of abrasives and bonding agent. This mix is formed into grinding wheels, Fig. 30-18, and stones to sharpen tools.

The process for manufacturing solid abrasives is complex. The abrasive grains and bonding agent are first mixed. Then they are pressed into molds. Next, they are heated slowly in an oven. Here the product is fused together. After heating, the solid abrasive is left to cool slowly.

The most common bonding process is called "vitrified bond." A silica agent, when heated, liquifies into glass. This permanently bonds the material in the shape of the mold.

Fig. 30-18. Grinding wheels are solid bonded abrasive wheels. (American Machine and Tool Co.)

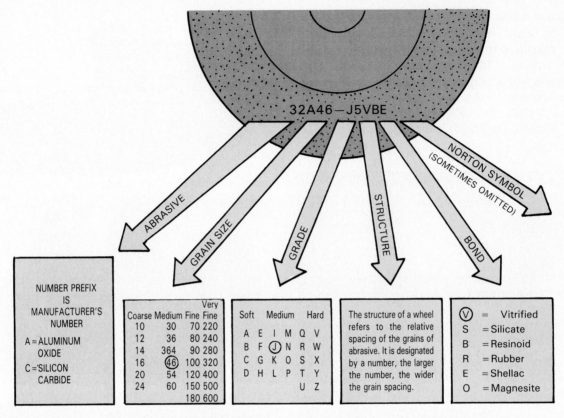

32A46—J5VBE

ABRASIVE

GRAIN SIZE

GRADE

STRUCTURE

BOND

NORTON SYMBOL
(SOMETIMES OMITTED)

NUMBER PREFIX
IS
MANUFACTURER'S
NUMBER

A = ALUMINUM
OXIDE

C = SILICON
CARBIDE

Coarse	Medium	Fine	Very Fine
10	30	70	220
12	36	80	240
14	364	90	280
16	(46)	100	320
20	54	120	400
24	60	150	500
		180	600

Soft	Medium	Hard
A	E	I	M	Q	V
B	F	(J)	N	R	W
C	G	K	O	S	X
D	H	L	P	T	Y
				U	Z

The structure of a wheel refers to the relative spacing of the grains of abrasive. It is designated by a number, the larger the number, the wider the grain spacing.

V	= Vitrified
S	= Silicate
B	= Resinoid
R	= Rubber
E	= Shellac
O	= Magnesite

Fig. 30-19. Grinding wheels are classified by a number of factors.

GRINDING WHEELS

Grinding wheels are most commonly a vitrified bond of aluminum oxide grains. There is a broad range of grits and sizes. For most purposes, 46 and 60 grit are suitable for grinding tools and blades. As the chart for Fig. 30-19 (above) shows, grinding wheels are labled to reflect the qualities in six

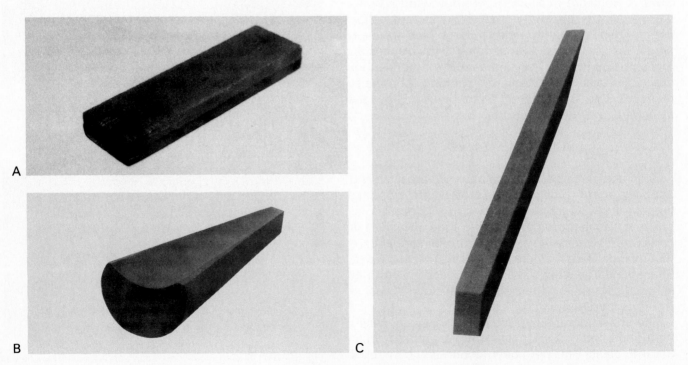

A

B

C

Fig. 30-20. Stones. A—Bench, combination grit. B—Slip. C—File.   (Woodcraft Supply Co.)

specifications. These specifications are:

1. Abrasive type. It may be aluminum oxide or silicon carbide.
2. Grain size. This will usually be 46 to 60, but grain sizes from 10 to 600 are available.
3. Grade. Grade refers to the hardness of the wheel. Grades A through H are soft. Grades I through P are medium-hard. Grades Q through Z are hard. Tool sharpening is done with medium-hard wheels.
4. Structure. Structure is the spacing between abrasive grains. Grains which are more dense are called close. A less dense structure is called open. Structure is rated from 1 (dense) to 15 (open). A smoother finish is achieved with a dense structure.
5. Bond. Usually vitrified bond is preferred over other agents, such as silicate, rubber, shellac, and resinoid.
6. Dimensions. This is the outside diameter and width. Wheels generally come with sleeves to adapt to fit machine shafts.

STONES

Sharpening and honing tools often is done with natural and synthetic abrasive *stones.* Natural stones are called Arkansas (pronounced Ar-kan-sas) stones. These are rated by either a hard or soft bond. A natural stone with coarse grains is named a Washita (wash'-ih-tah) stone.

Synthetic stones are silicon carbide (black) or aluminum oxide (gray or brown). Grit sizes are coarse or fine. Coarse stones cut faster and wear quicker. Fine stones (both hard and soft grades) cut slower and wear longer.

Stones come in a variety of shapes and sizes. Cabinetmakers use bench, slip, and file stones, Fig. 30-20. Rectangular bench stones may be single or combination grit. Combination stones are made of coarse and fine synthetic grains or synthetic and natural grains. Slips are identified by their round edges. File stones are flat, round, and half round, as are steel files.

Cake abrasives (made of tripoli) are for polishing with a buffer. They are a mixture of abrasive and a soft bonding agent. The raw mixture, similar to cake batter, is poured into cake molds. The liquid evaporates and the cakes are removed for use.

SUMMARY

Abrasives include tools and materials to smooth surfaces. Abrasive tools include files, steel wool, rasps, and screens. Products using abrasive grains include coated, solid, and loose abrasives. Abrasive grains may be natural or synthetic. Natural grains include flint, garnet, emery, pumice, rottenstone,

and tripoli. Synthetic abrasives include aluminum oxide, silicon carbide, and industrial diamond.

Abrasive grains are sized by grit, powder, and flour sizes. Sizes from 16 to 220 are sifted through screens with varying hole sizes. Smaller sizes are floated in air or water to separate them.

Coated abrasives consist of a backing, two layers of adhesive, and the grains. Backings include paper, cloth, fiber, and a combination of paper and cloth. Adhesives include glues and resins, in varying combinations for make and size coats. Coated abrasives may be cut into sheets or formed into belts, disks, sleeves, blocks, and flap wheels.

Solid abrasives include grinding wheels and stones. Both are made by mixing abrasive grains in a bonding agent. The mixture may then be left to cure or heated in an oven for greater durability.

CABINETMAKING TERMS

Abrasives, coated abrasives, solid abrasives, loose abrasives, abrasive tools, abrasive grains, flint, garnet, emery, pumice, rottenstone, tripoli, synthetic abrasives, aluminum oxide, silicon carbide, industrial diamond, abrasive grain sizes, backing, flexing, grinding wheel, stone.

TEST YOUR KNOWLEDGE

1. List six natural abrasives and a typical application for each.
2. List three synthetic abrasives and a typical application for each.
3. How do abrasive manufacturers separate the different size grains?
4. Smaller grain sizes are called _____ and _____ grades.
5. Name four types of abrasive backings.
6. The two coatings of adhesive when making coated abrasives are _____ and _____ coats.
7. Which of the following adhesive combinations is the most durable?
   a. Glue over glue.
   b. Glue and filler.
   c. Resin over resin.
   d. Resin over glue.
8. How might you identify an open coat abrasive as compared to a close coat abrasive?
9. Gravity and electrostatic coating are two methods of _____ _____.
10. Why are coated abrasives flexed?
11. List the four methods of flexing coated abrasives.
12. Identify three common forms of coated abrasives.
13. Name five features by which you would select a grinding wheel.
14. List the three stone shapes.

Chapter 31
USING ABRASIVES AND SANDING MACHINES

After studying this chapter, you will be able to:
☐ *Inspect material surfaces to decide if abrading is necessary.*
☐ *Select abrasives by type and grit size.*
☐ *Use abrasives by hand.*
☐ *Operate various portable and stationary power sanding equipment.*
☐ *Inspect surfaces ready for product assembly or finishing.*
☐ *Maintain electrical and air-operated power tools.*

Smoothing with abrasives is the process of removing surface wood cells to achieve a smooth, blemish-free surface, Fig. 31-1. The terms "abrading" and "sanding" are used interchangeably to describe the smoothing process. There are abrasive planers and sanding machines, such as the disk sander and belt sander. However, the term "abrading" is most proper because coated abrasives are not actually covered with sand.

Fig. 31-1. This assembled product is abraded with an in-line sander before applying finish. (Porter-Cable Corp.)

products other than coated abrasives will smooth a surface by abrading. A file is an example.

Abrading leaves scratches in the surface. The depth of the scratch is determined by the abrasive grit size or file's cutting edge. Abrading is done along the grain; thus scratches follow the grain and are less noticeable than those across the grain. By using successively smaller grit sizes, the scratches become even shallower. Eventually, you cannot detect grit marks in the wood. The surface is then ready to finish. Face and edge grain should need the least amount of abrading. End grain will require more effort.

INSPECTING THE WOOD SURFACE

Abrading usually follows sawing, surfacing, shaping, and turning. These processes should bring workpieces to their final size. However, they usually leave marks that need abrading. If sharp tools are used for processing, this task is minimized.

You should inspect all surfaces before using abrasives. Look for any cuts, marks, or other wood defects, especially:
1. Saw tooth marks.
2. Rippled (washboard) effects from using jointers, shapers, and planers.
3. Grooves caused by planing or scraping.
4. Dents from dropping a tool or other object on the wood surface.

Small marks may not be detected at first. Hold the wood toward a light source and look across the surface. You will likely see scratches and dents you could not find before.

SELECTING ABRASIVES

Select abrasives by grain type, form, and grit size. Flint is rarely used because it lacks toughness and durability. Garnet, the most widely used natural abrasive, is for abrading softwoods and for finish sanding all wood types. Aluminum oxide is harder, tougher, cuts faster, and lasts longer than natural abrasives. It is excellent for smoothing hardwoods and for production sanding.

Although not as hard as aluminum oxide, silicon carbide is used widely for portable belt sanders. Wet-or-dry, fine silicon carbide is used with water or oil to flatten dry, finished surfaces.

Abrasives come in several forms. When hand sanding use sheets. For production sanding select the form (disk, belt, sheet, sleeve, etc.) that fits the sanding machine.

ABRADING PROCESS

Selecting the proper grit size is important. The correct grit will make considerable difference in the speed and quality of your work. For heavily marked surfaces, it is easier to use a sequence of abrasives from No. 80 to No. 120 to No. 180. For a planed surface, you might start with No. 150 paper, then use No. 180. Use a very fine (No. 220) paper last. Each finer grit size removes the marks of the abrasive before it.

Before using abrasive paper, you should have raised dents and removed saw marks. Dents are simply crushed wood cells. First, open the cells by wetting the dented area with water. Then, place a wet cloth over the dent. Heat the cloth with a warm iron to increase the swelling of wood cells, Fig. 31-2. Pencil marks should be removed with an eraser.

For saw kerf marks, a file is quicker. Then choose the first grit size abrasive. After smoothing the surfaces as much as possible with it, proceed to a finer abrasive.

Increase grit size by no more than two grade numbers at a time. After each change of abrasive,

remove dust with a tack cloth or air pressure. As you continue, using finer abrasives will polish the grain making it more visible.

The entire surface must be abraded equally. Often the sections near corners receive less attention. This causes grain cloudiness; you cannot see the grain near the edges as clearly. A poor quality finish will result.

HAND SANDING

You can make or buy tools for sanding by hand. Most manufactured *hand sanders* have a rubber or padded rectangular flat surface, Fig. 31-3. You might also cut sanding blocks from a 3 in. by 4 in. (75 mm to 100 mm) block of wood. Avoid holding the abrasive with only your hand. This causes more sanding to be done under the fingertips. However, you can use just your hand for contoured surfaces or in areas difficult to reach.

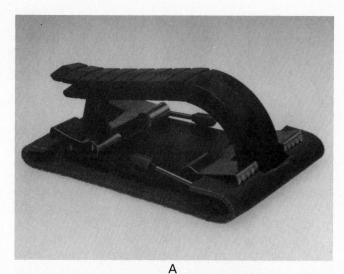

A

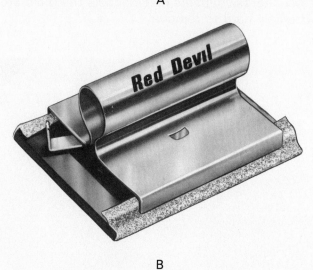

B

Fig. 31-3. Hand sanders. A—This sander holds 1/3 of an abrasive sheet over a felt pad. B—One-quarter sheet hand sanders are more common. (Red Devil)

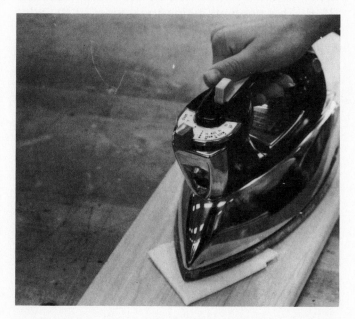

Fig. 31-2. Raise dents with water or a wet pad and an iron before abrading. (Glit, Inc.)

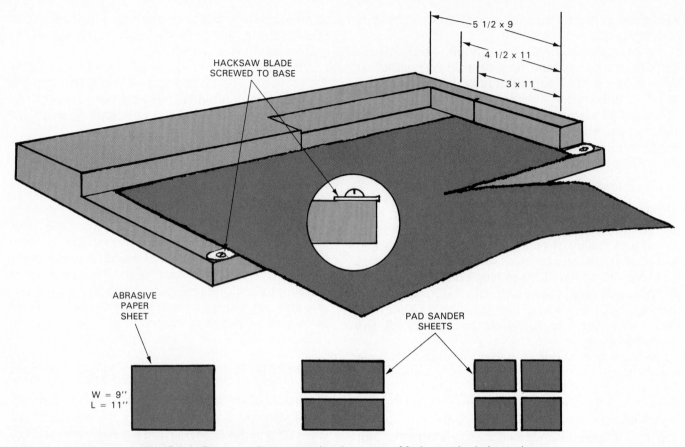

HACKSAW BLADE
SCREWED TO BASE

5 1/2 x 9

4 1/2 x 11

3 x 11

ABRASIVE
PAPER
SHEET

PAD SANDER
SHEETS

W = 9"
L = 11"

Fig. 31-4. Prepare a jig to tear abrasive paper. Mark standard sheet sizes.

Tear a 9 in. by 11 in. sheet into fourths, thirds, or halves to fit the portable sander or wood block. Use a steel bench rule or hacksaw blade jig, Fig. 31-4. Insert the paper into the hand sander clamps or fold it over the edges of the sanding block.

Sanding should be done ALONG THE GRAIN, Fig. 31-5, even though working across the grain seems faster. Abrasive marks made across the grain are extremely hard to remove.

CAUTION: Be careful when abrading plywood and other veneered surfaces. It takes little effort to go through the thin veneer.

When sanding end grain, it is a good idea to place scrap wood on each side of the workpiece, Fig. 31-6. This prevents tilting the sander at the edge of the lumber, causing chamfers. Contours can be sanded by using a contoured sanding block or strips of abrasive, Fig. 31-7.

Fig. 31-5. Sanding along the wood grain makes abrasive scratch marks less visible. (Norton Co.)

Fig. 31-6. Use C clamps to secure scrap wood when sanding end grain. (Norton Co.)

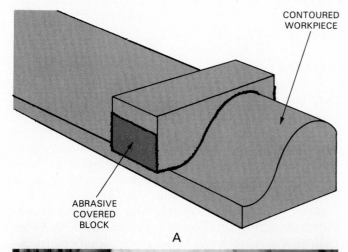

Fig. 31-7. A—Make a contour block to sand mouldings, trim, and other curved surfaces. B—Strips of abrasive used by hand or in a bow sander work well with turned pieces. (Glit, Inc.)

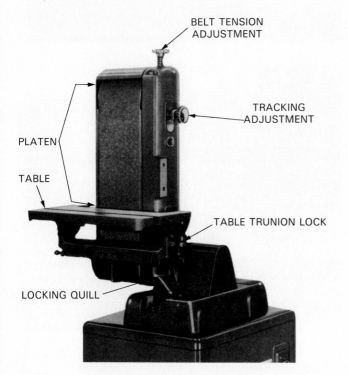

Fig. 31-8. Locate adjustment levers and knobs on your belt sander. (Powermatic Houdaille)

STATIONARY POWER SANDING MACHINES

There are many types and sizes of stationary sanding machines. Some are designed for mass production of furniture parts. Others have applications for small cabinet shops and the home cabinetmaker. The most common are belt sanders, disk sanders, spindle sanders, drum sanders, and abrasive planers. Each requires a different form of coated abrasive.

BELT SANDER

The *belt sander,* Fig. 31-8, consists of a 6 in. abrasive belt which travels over two drums. A flat 6 in. by 15 in. steel platen is behind the belt to assure a flat sanding surface. The belt can be tilted from vertical to horizontal, Fig. 31-9. End cap can be removed for special operations, Fig. 31-10. Some machines have fences along or across the belt.

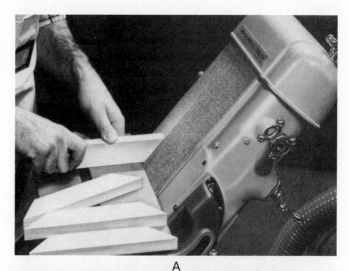

Fig. 31-9. Tilt the belt sander table for convenience. A—Smoothing miter cuts. B—Smoothing surfaces. The table keeps your work positioned on the abrasive. (Delta International Machinery Corp.)

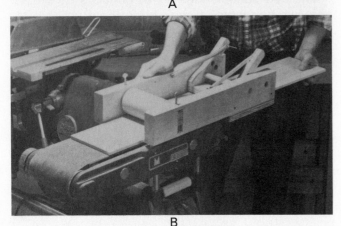

A

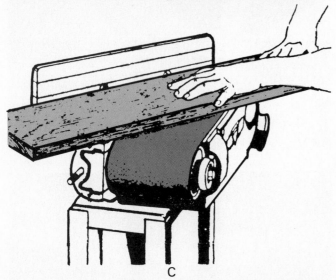

B

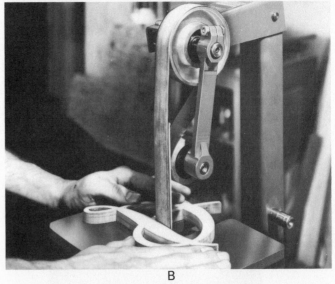

C

Fig. 31-10. The belt sander table and end cap can be removed.
A—Using the top drum to smooth contours. (Delta International
Machinery Corp.) B—Both the end cap and table are removed
to use the abrasive planer jig. (Shopsmith) C—Smooth wide
boards by tilting the table angle while the belt is horizontal.
Scratches made across the grain can later be removed with
a finishing sander.

Adjusting table and belt angles

Changing the position of the abrasive belt requires
loosening the *locking quill.* Adjust the angle of the
belt and tighten the quill. To adjust the table, loosen
the *table trunnion lock* and tilt the table to the

desired angle. Tighten the trunnion lock firmly. Set
table and belt angles using a T-bevel.

Installing belts

Disconnect electrical power before servicing any
machine. Remove the end cap guard and side panel.
Loosen idler drum adjusting screw to release belt
tension. Slide belt over drums. Be sure belt is
mounted properly—arrow printed on belt indicates
direction of motion. Tighten drum adjusting screw
to increase belt tension. Rotate belt with your hand
to check tracking. Belt should stay centered on the
drums. If not, turn the tracking adjusting screw
either direction until tracking is correct. Reinstall
guards and restore electrical power. Recheck tracking when you first turn on the machine. If the belt
moves off-center, reset the drum adjusting screw.

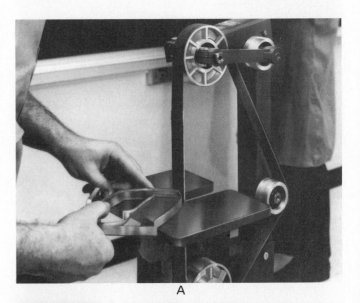

A

B

Fig. 31-11. A—The 1 in. belt sander is useful for small
workpieces. B—By adjusting the idler wheel, the sander can
be used for inside surfaces.
(Delta International Machinery Corp.)

One inch belt sander

The 1 in. belt sander, also called a *sander/grinder,* is for sanding small workpieces. The table will tilt to sand bevels. You can use it on outside as well as inside surfaces, Fig. 31-11. You must alter belt roller positions when you make this change. Belts from 1/8 in. to 1 in. (3 mm to 25 mm) will fit.

DISK SANDER

The *disk sander,* Fig. 31-12, is used for smoothing edge and end grain. The table can be adjusted for bevels. A miter gauge fits in the table slot to guide workpieces with angled surfaces.

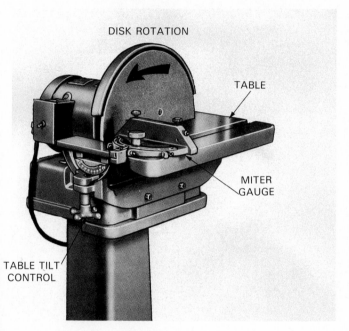

Fig. 31-12. Locate table adjustment controls and rotation of the disk before using the disk sander. (Powermatic Houdaille)

Installing abrasive disks

The abrasive disk bonds to a metal disk with pressure sensitive, nondrying adhesive. Worn abrasive disks can be peeled off. Clean off any dirt or old adhesive from the metal disk. New disks often come with an adhesive backing. Remove the protective plastic cover and press the disk in place. If the disk does not have a coating, then stick or liquid adhesive must be applied to the metal before mounting the abrasive disk.

Using the disk sander

ONLY USE THE HALF OF THE DISK THAT ROTATES DOWNWARD. The other half throws chips and dust upward. Keep the workpiece moving along the disk to prevent heat buildup. Heat reduces disk life and causes the wood to burn. Set table angles with a square or T-bevel as needed. A

miter gauge guides workpieces at the proper angle to the disk. A clamp assists working with larger components. See Fig. 31-13.

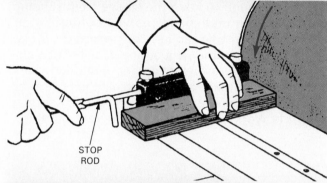

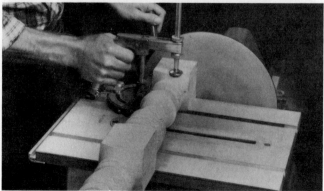

Fig. 31-13. By using a miter gauge or tilting the table, many different workpieces can be abraded.
(Shopsmith, Delta International Machinery Corp.)

SPINDLE SANDER

Spindle sanders, Fig. 31-14, have a rotating and oscillating spindle. (The spindle turns and moves up and down.) This allows more of the abrasive sleeve to be used.

This machine primarily is used to sand the edges of irregular curves. Different diameter spindles accommodate small and large curved workpieces. Change table inserts when a different size spindle is installed. The insert supports workpieces near the spindle. The insert opening is oval so that the table can be titled without rubbing against the abrasive.

Abrasive paper for spindle sanders may be sheet or sleeve form. Sheet abrasive is attached in a spindle slot and held by turning a key. For abrasive sleeves, first loosen the nut on the top of the spindle. Slide the sleeve on the spindle. Tighten the nut only enough to keep the sleeve from slipping. (The rubber drum expands as you tighten.)

To use the spindle sander, first choose the proper size spindle. Use the largest one possible because you get more abrasive action per revolution. Hand tighten it in the machine. Then adjust the table angle and place the proper table insert. While sanding, keep the workpiece moving to prevent burning.

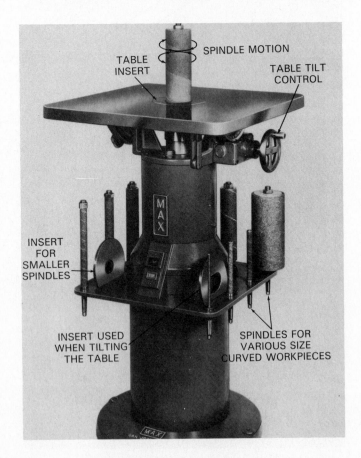

Fig. 31-14. The spindle sander smoothes irregular curves. Install the largest spindle size and table insert to fit the workpiece. (Brodhead-Garrett)

DRUM SANDER

Drum sanders work similar to spindle sanders. However, drum sanders do not have an oscillating motion. Workpieces are held by hand and moved back and forth across the abrasive. Drums are of different diameters and lengths, Fig. 31-15.

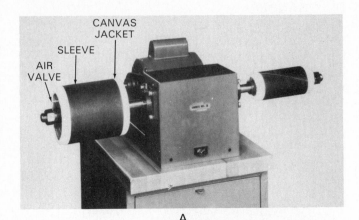

A

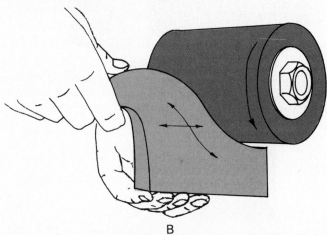

B

Fig. 31-15. A—This drum sander has two different size inflatable drums. (Brodhead-Garrett) B—Move workpieces across the drum to obtain good abrasive action and prevent clogging (loading) the abrasive.

Some drums are inflated. These consist of a metal housing with a rubber tube and canvas jacket. The sleeve abrasive slips over the jacket. Then the tube is filled with air. Varing the air pressure allows the drum to conform more to the workpiece contour.

Moving the workpiece continually reduces chip loading. *Loading* occurs when chips adhere to the abrasive because of moisture and resin in the lumber. Loaded abrasives are less efficient and more likely to burn the wood.

ABRASIVE PLANERS AND WIDEBELT SANDERS

Abrasive planers and widebelt sanders are production equipment. Both use wide abrasive belts for smoothing and surfacing stock.

Abrasive planers

Abrasive planers are gaining use as an alternative to knife-type planing machines. They use wide abrasive belts on rollers, Fig. 31-16. The abrasive does not tear grain around knots. It also eliminates planer skip, chatter, grain tear out, and wavy dressing. Fig. 31-17 shows the resulting difference between knife planing and abrasive planing.

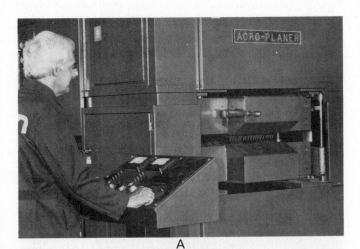

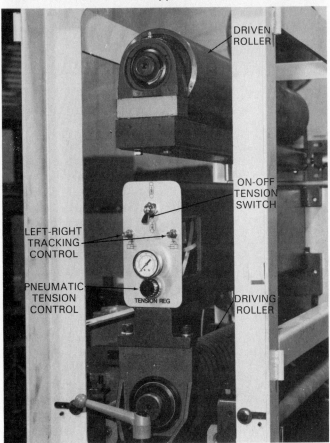

A

B

Fig. 31-16. A—The abrasive planer heads are enclosed in a large guarding and dust collection enclosure. B—The planer head has tension and tracking controls. The abrasive belt is placed over the two rollers.
(Abrasive Engineering and Manufacturing Inc.)

Fig. 31-17. The left board was planed with abrasive. The right board was knife planed. Notice the amount of torn grain from knives. (Abrasive Engineering and Manufacturing Inc.)

Some abrasive planers surface both sides of the stock in a single pass. A self-centering feature assures that equal amounts are removed from both sides, Fig. 31-18.

Machine capacity may vary from 13 in. to 64 in. Thicknesses from near 0 in. to 5 1/2 in. can be planed. Abrasive planers use 20, 24, or 36 grit sizes. This coarse grit will not produce a finished surface. Secondary sanding is required, usually done with a widebelt sander.

Widebelt sanders

Widebelt sanders are very similar to abrasive planers. Both feed stock automatically into abrasive belts for stock removal. However, widebelt sanders

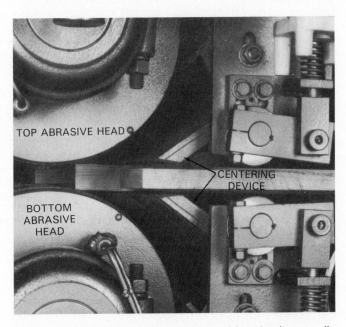

Fig. 31-18. The self-centering device positions lumber equally between abrasive heads. (Timesavers, Inc.)

produce a finished surface only on one side, Fig. 31-19. The stock must then be turned over.

Widebelt sander heads use contact rollers and/or platens to hold the belt against the stock. Contact rollers are used for aggressive sanding with coarser abrasives. The platen is for flat polishing and holds a thickness tolerance within 0.007 in. Typically, a contact roll is used on the first head. It has a grit size from 50 to 120. A platen is used on the second head with 120 to 220 grit abrasive, Fig. 31-20. Three- and four-head sanders are available. These surface rough lumber to finished size in one pass.

Fig. 31-19. Widebelt sanders typically smooth only one surface at a time. (Timesavers, Inc.)

Setting up abrasive planers and widebelt sanders

Before servicing machinery, disconnect electrical power. Then remove guards covering the abrading heads. To remove an abrasive belt, first release the belt tension. Tension may be set mechanically (a screw mechanism) or with air pressure. Remove the old belt. Slip the new belt over the contact rollers or platen and reset the tension. Reinstall guards and connect electrical service. Tracking then may have to be set. Tracking assures that the belt stays centered on the rollers. A belt which travels to one side can be ruined. Tracking must be set manually while the machine is running. Some machines automatically set tracking by sensing the position of the belt.

Operating abrasive planers and widebelt sanders

The depth of cut you set depends on the type of machine and number of heads. The maximum cut for most abrasive planers and single head sanders is 1/4 in. (6 mm). However, check the machine operating manual for accurate cut depths according to abrasive grit size. Three and four head machines can surface and smooth rough lumber. These single pass machines are set according to the desired final thickness.

A feed belt draws stock into the abrasive heads. The operator should support the workpiece as it exits the outfeed side of the table.

STROKE SANDER

The *stroke sander* is an abrasive belt sander for smoothing large surfaces, Fig. 31-21. It has a movable table under a long belt suspended between two pulleys. With one hand, you hold a pad over the belt and against the workpiece surface. The other hand controls table movement.

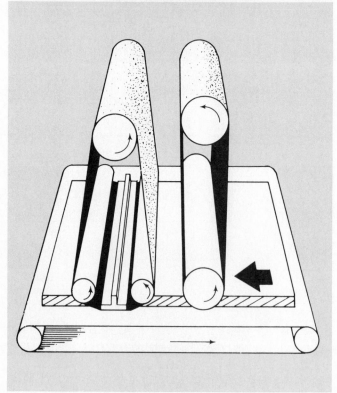

Fig. 31-20. Double head sanders generally have both a platen and contact roller. The roller does the initial smoothing while the platen completes the surface. (Timesavers, Inc.)

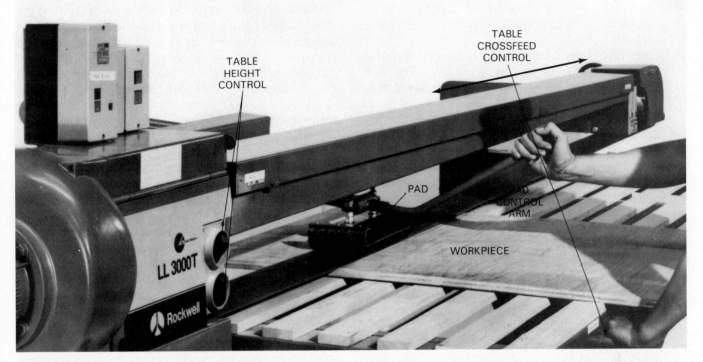

Fig. 31-21. Large, flat surfaces can be smoothed with the stroke sander. (Delta International Machinery Corp.)

To use the stroke sander, first place the workpiece on the table with the grain direction in line with the belt. You can smooth the surface by moving the table slowly toward or away from you with the pad in one place. Moving the table too fast will produce cross grain scratches. A second method is to move the pad along the length of the workpiece without moving the table. Then position the table to the next section to be smoothed.

PORTABLE SANDING TOOLS

Portable sanding tools are commonly used when stationary equipment is not available. They are also used for small workpieces. Portable machines may be powered by electricity or compressed air. They are handy to use when preparing for the assembly finish. Portable sanding tools include the portable belt sander, finishing sander, portable disk sander, and portable drum sander.

BELT SANDER

Portable belt sanders are very similar to stationary belt sanders. They are sized according to belt width and length. Belt sizes range from 2 in. to 4 in. wide and 21 in. to 27 in. long. A dust collection bag is attached to the machine, Fig. 31-22.

Install or replace belts as follows.
1. Disconnect power to the machine.
2. Place the movable pulley in the locked position

Fig. 31-22. Portable belt sanders are commonly used abrading tools. (Delta International Machinery Corp.)

to relieve belt tension. This is typically done with a lever on the side or inside the belt loop.
3. Remove the worn belt and slide the new belt over the pulleys. Look for the arrow printed on the belt. It must be pointed in the direction the belt will move.
4. Align the belt even with the end of the pulley.
5. Release the locking mechanism to restore belt tension.

6. Reconnect electrical service after making sure the trigger switch is in the off position.
7. Hold the sander so the belt is not against any surface.
8. Turn the machine on with the trigger switch. (Do not engage the trigger lock button.) The belt should remain aligned with the pulleys. If it moves off center, adjust the tracking knob located on the side of the sander. Turn it until the belt remains centered.
9. Release the switch and place the machine down after the belt stops coasting.

When using the belt sander, never engage the trigger lock mechanism. If you lost grip of the sander, it would move by itself across the workpiece and might be damaged after falling from the workbench. The lock may be used when the machine is mounted under a stand. In this manner, you can use it as a stationary machine.

Operate the sander as follows:
1. Lift the sander above the workpiece.
2. Start the machine.
3. Lower the machine on the workpiece. Place it carefully and evenly onto the surface. The belt should run in the direction of the grain.
4. Keep the sander moving in overlapping strokes as shown in Fig. 31-23.
5. To smooth the outer edges, allow the belt to extend beyond the edge slightly. Make sure the sander doesn't tilt.
6. After smoothing the entire surface, lift the sander off the surface; then turn it off.

Fig. 31-23. Move the belt sander in short overlapping strokes. Check the tracking for proper adjustment before and while using the tool. (Makita U.S.A., Inc.)

7. Change to finer abrasive belts as necessary.
Belt sander manufacturers know the weight of the machines. That weight is sufficient pressure for the sander to operate efficiently. All the user should do is guide the machine. Downward pressure can slow belt movement, overheat the machine, and possibly cause damage. It can also gouge the wood.

FINISHING SANDER

Finishing sanders are used with fine abrasives to prepare workpieces for finish or to smooth between finish coats. They are not designed for removing saw marks. Using them with coarse abrasives or excessive pressure may ruin the motor. The sander is held by hand. The abrasive is attached to a pad. The pad moves in either an in-line or orbital motion.

In-line finishing sanders move the abrasive back and forth in a straight line, Fig. 31-24. Scratches blend with the direction of the grain. These sanders are used just before finish is applied.

A

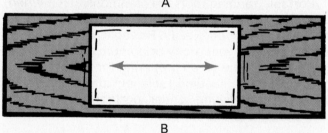

B

Fig. 31-24. A—In-line finishing sanders prepare surfaces for finish. B—The in-line motion abrades along the grain pattern. (Makita U.S.A., Inc.)

Orbital action finishing sanders move the abrasive in a 3/16 in. circular motion, Fig. 31-25. This action removes wood quicker, but leaves circular scratches across the grain. They must be removed by hand sanding or by using an in-line finishing sander. Orbital action is practical where grain direction is not

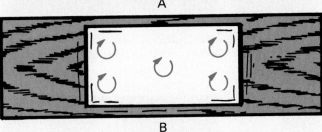

Fig. 31-25. A—Orbital sanders may leave swirl marks. B—Marks are less noticeable if the orbital action of the machine is greater than 10,000 rpm.

a factor. One example is abrading successive coats of built-up finish. Orbital action tends to smooth brush marks and spray overlap.

Finishing sanders use sheet or disk forms of coated abrasives. Those which use sheets may require 1/4, 1/3, or 1/2 of a regular 9 in. by 11 in. sheet. The abrasive is held against the sanding pad by two clamps or two screws. Disks for finishing sanders, Fig. 31-26, are generally applied with adhesive. Most abrasive disks already have pre-applied adhesive. Just remove the protective cover and press the abrasive in place. Some sanders now have Velcro pads which accept Velcro-backed abrasives.

Fig. 31-26. Abrasive disks are used on some orbital and in-line finishing sanders. (Makita U.S.A., Inc.)

DISK SANDER

Portable disk sanders typically are used when the grain will be hidden or appearance does not matter. The circular motion of the disk leaves swirling scratches which are difficult to remove, Fig. 31-27. Scratch size is determined by the disk radius where contact occurs. Usually, you use this machine on surfaces to be painted. When clear finish is to be applied, use belt and in-line finishing sanders.

Fig. 31-27. Use disk sanders when the surface will be hidden. (Norton Co.)

DRUM SANDER

Portable drum sanders compare with stationary horizontal drum sanders. However, portable units are more versatile. They may be powered by electricity or compressed air. Drums are either solid rubber or inflated to hold the abrasive in place. They may be hand held or inserted into portable power drills, Fig. 31-28.

ADAPTING MACHINES FOR ABRADING

Certain power equipment can be fitted to become an abrading tool. Three of these are the radial arm saw, drill press, and lathe.

You can purchase disk and drum attachments to fit in a radial arm saw. To use the drum, you should raise the table surface around it, Fig. 31-29A. This permits use of the full length of abrasive. You could also clamp a board next to the drum, Fig. 31-29B. The radial arm saw disk is excellent for smoothing at various angles, Fig. 31-29C. Make sure you have a fence behind the workpiece. Otherwise, the wood might be thrown.

The drill press is often used for drum sanding. You can insert a piece of abrasive paper attached to a wood dowel in the chuck, Fig. 31-30. Like the radial

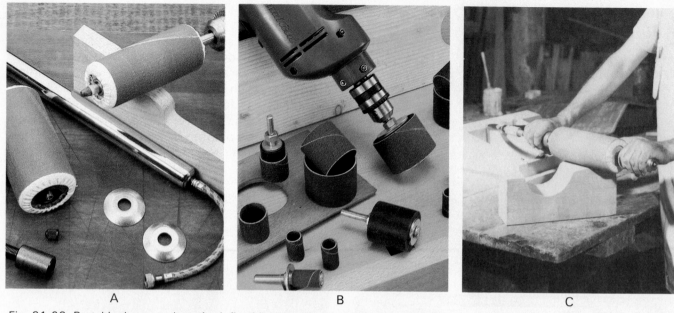

Fig. 31-28. Portable drum sanders. A—Inflatable drums used with a portable drill. B—Hard rubber drums used with a portable drill. (The Fine Tool Shops) C—Air-operated inflatable portable drum sander. (Elstrom, Carlson)

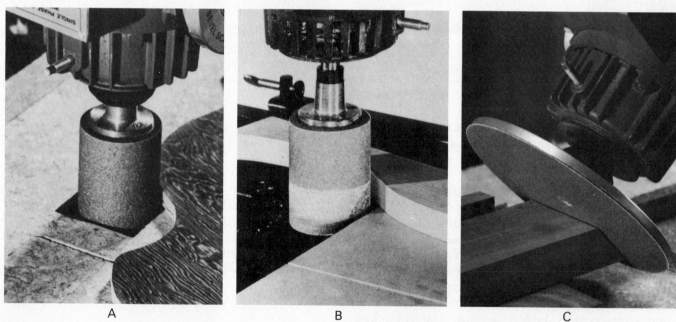

Fig. 31-29. A—Two pieces of particleboard raise the table surface when using a radial arm saw as a vertical drum sander. B—The raised table surface allows the drum to pass below, allowing more usable abrasive surface. C—A disk accessory changes the radial arm saw into a disk sander. (DeWalt)

arm saw, you should clamp a scrap piece of wood to the table. Cut a hole in it just larger than the dowel. Raise the table so the dowel fits in the hole. Flap wheels are also used with a lathe or drill press, Fig. 31-31A. The wheel is made of many thin strips of abrasive, Fig. 31-31B. It is used to smooth contours.

The lathe can be used as a horizontal drum sander. Turn a hardwood cylinder and attach an abrasive sheet to it as shown in Fig. 31-32. Make sure to secure the wedge tightly.

ABRASIVE TOOL MAINTENANCE

General

1. Check dust collection hoses and bags for tears and loose connections.
2. Empty dust from collection storage and make sure exhaust system is operating properly.
3. Check electrical cords and air hoses for damage and wear. Keep cords and hoses away from the abrasive.
4. Replace those which have cracked, deteri-

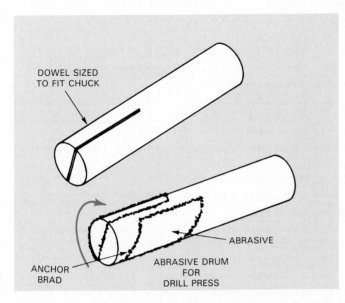

Fig. 31-30. Slit a dowel with a band saw to make an abrasive drum for the drill press.

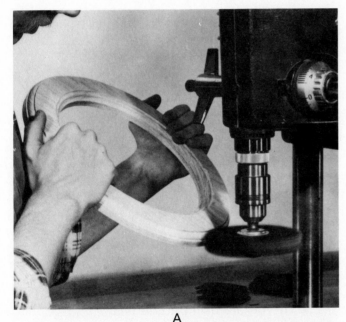

A

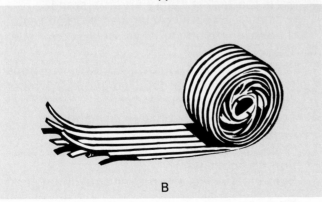

B

Fig. 31-31. A—Flap wheels can smooth contoured surfaces. B—The flap wheel is made of scored abrasive strips. (Shopsmith)

orated, or have been damaged by the machine.

5. With an air hose, blow dust from all moving parts, electrical boxes and motor vents.
6. Remove rust from machine tables and metal surfaces with fine steel wool. Wipe them with paraffin wax.
7. Check abrasives for excessive wear or chip loading (clogging). Replace if necessary.
8. Secure tables by tightening clamps, trunnion locks, and quill pins.
9. Check motor belt tension.
10. Check all adjustments, bolts and fittings for wear. Lubricate if specified by manufacturer.

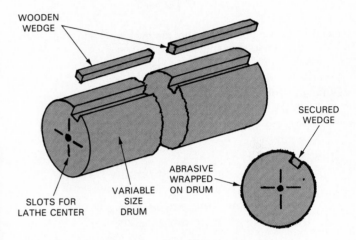

ABRASIVE DRUM FOR LATHE

Fig. 31-32. You can make an abrasive drum for the lathe from a hardwood cylinder and a wooden wedge.

11. Follow the machine maintenance schedule included with the machine. It may be necessary to oil the bearings, lubricate parts, clean the brushes, or check other important features.
12. Secure and tighten all safety guards properly.
13. Remove resin and chips from loaded and clogged abrasives with a rubber cleaning block, Fig. 31-33. Some soft shoe soles can be substituted for the blocks. Rub the cleaning block against the moving abrasive. This extends the effective life of the abrasive.
14. Some air-operated machines have oil added in the air line to lubricate bearings. Check the oil level periodically. Use separate hoses for abrading and spray finishing operations.

Belt sander

1. Inspect the abrasive belt for loose, torn, or raveled conditions.
2. Check tracking and tension adjustments.
3. Check the platen position. It should extend 1/32 in. (0.8 mm) beyond the front of the drum surface.

Fig. 31-33. A rubberlike cleaner removes resin and chips from abrasive sheets. (Brookstone Co.)

Disk sander
1. Check abrasive disk for proper adhesion.
2. Square table to disk.

Spindle sander
1. Check the spindle fit. It should be snug, but not too tight.
2. Adjust table trunnions properly.
3. Install the correct table insert.

SUMMARY

Smoothing with abrasives is the process of abrading workpieces in preparation for assembly or finishing. Abrasives are chosen according to the workpiece surface. Coarse abrasives remove saw or other machine marks. Medium abrasives remove coarse abrasive marks. Continue with finer abrasives until a quality surface is achieved. Minimum use of abrasives is recommended, so stop when the surface quality is acceptable.

Abrading may be done by hand or machine. By hand, the process is slow. Do so only when a sanding machine is not available or in hard-to-reach places. Electric or air-powered sanding machines reduce abrading time. With stationary machines, you hold and move the workpiece. With portable machines, you move the tool over the workpieces.

CABINETMAKING TERMS

Abrading, hand sander, belt sander, platen, locking quill, table trunnion lock, sander/grinder, disk sander, spindle sander, drum sander, abrasive planer, loading, widebelt sander, stroke sander, portable belt sander, finishing sander, ortibal action, in-line action, portable disk sander, portable drum sander.

TEST YOUR KNOWLEDGE

1. The purpose for abrading is to obtain _____.
2. List four items you should check on the workpiece before abrading.
3. Why should you use a series of coarse to fine abrasives, rather than starting with a fine abrasive?
4. Each finer abrasive grit size removes the _____ of the abrasive before it.
5. Explain how you would position the belt sander and miter gauge to smooth the following surfaces.
   a. Square edge of a flat-sawed board.
   b. Flat face of a board, 4 in. across the grain and 6 in. with the grain.
   c. Bevel across the end.
   d. Bevel across the edge.
   e. Face of a board, 7 in. across the grain and 48 in. with the grain.
   f. Square end of a quarter-sawed board.
6. A disk sander is primarily for _____ and _____.
7. Two stationary power sanders for smoothing contours are the _____ and _____.
8. The main advantage of an abrasive planer over a knife planer is _____.
9. Describe the differences between abrasive planers and widebelt sanders.
10. Large, flat workpieces can be abraded easiest on a:
    a. Sander/grinder.
    b. Disk sander.
    c. Belt sander.
    d. Stroke sander.
11. End grain is the most difficult to get smooth. True or False?
12. Describe why an in-line finishing sander better prepares a workpiece for finish than an orbital sander.
13. Use a trigger lock on a portable sander only:
    a. If you are using a fine belt.
    b. If the tool is stationary in a stand.
    c. When smoothing clamped workpieces.
    d. While smoothing large workpieces.
14. Tracking means _____.
15. Finishing sanders can be used for heavy stock removal if a coarse abrasive is used. True or False?
16. To clean a coated abrasive, use a(n) _____ or possibly a(n) _____.
17. How is an abrasive belt marked to show direction for movement?
18. Before servicing any power equipment, first _____.
19. List six general maintenance items you should check both before and after using a sanding machine.

Chapter 32
ADHESIVES

After studying this chapter, you will be able to:
- ☐ Select the proper adhesive for assembling your product.
- ☐ Identify adhesive characterisitcs which affect the assembly time and strength of your product.
- ☐ Describe the proper application of adhesives.

Cabinetmakers bond many kinds of workpieces together with adhesives. In the early stages of production, you might bond lumber together to make wider components. Later you may assemble the cabinet with adhesives, then apply veneer and plastic laminates.

Today, you can find an adhesive to bond almost any two materials. The adhesive may have single (join similar materials) or multiple uses (join dissimilar materials). Included are lumber, paneling, paper, cloth, leather, ceramics, rubber, vinyl, and numerous other materials, Fig. 32-1.

SELECTING ADHESIVES

The term adhesive can be confusing. It may or may not be printed on the container label. Instead, the words cement, glue, mastic, or resin could appear. Each of these are adhesives that will bond similar and/or dissimilar materials.

Adhesion occurs by adding some substance, liquid or solid, which "sticks" two objects together, Fig. 32-2A. Do not confuse adhesion with cohesion, discussed in Chapter 15 when bonding plastics together. Cohesion is different from adhesion. Cohesion occurs when a solvent is applied to plastic which dissolves the surfaces, Fig. 32-2B. Material flows together, the solvent evaporates, and the bond is complete.

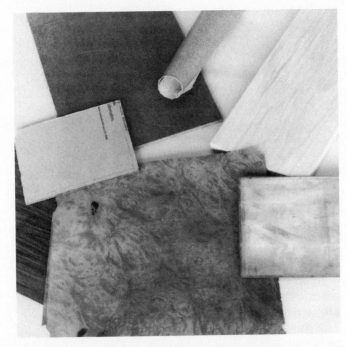

Fig. 32-1. By selecting the proper adhesive, you can bond plastic, veneer, metal, lumber, vinyl, hardboard, and plastic laminate.

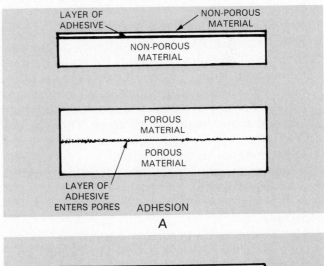

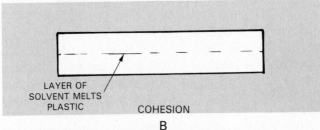

Fig. 32-2. Materials may be bonded two ways. A—Adhesion results when a thin layer of adhesive "sticks" two components together. B—Cohesion results when cement solvents dissolve and blend the surface of two workpieces.

ADHESIVE TERMS

Select adhesives according to the materials they will bond. Also consider shelf life, pot life, setting time, drying time, and curing time.

Shelf life

Shelf life, or *storage time,* refers to how long the adhesive is effective. A date may appear on the container. Suppose the shelf life of a glue is one year and you use one quart a year. Do not buy five gallons. Over time, heat, moisture, and chemical reaction will cause the adhesive not to bond. Most containers read "Store in a cool, dry place."

Pot life

Pot life describes the time you have for applying the material. This may be ten seconds, ten minutes, or longer. Then the adhesive begins to set.

Setting time

When an adhesive sets, the solvents, such as water or thinner, evaporate, leaving only a solid bonding substance. Then, the adhesive will hold the components together. This may take seconds, minutes, or hours. Once the adhesive is set you can remove any clamps which held the workpieces together. However, the bond does not reach full strength until the assembly dries, or cures.

Curing time

Curing time refers to the time before the joint reaches full strength. The water or solvent must fully evaporate. Then the resins bond to each other and the material. For most adhesives, curing time is more than an hour. However, for some contact cements and "super" glues, it occurs in seconds.

Read the adhesive manufacturers' instructions carefully. For any material or condition, you must select and apply the proper adhesive. The type you choose depends on two important factors:
1. The material to be fastened.
2. The conditions to which the assembled product will be exposed.

Materials

Materials may be porous or nonporous. *Porous* woods allow the adhesive to flow into nearby wood cells to hold tightly. Metal and plastics are *nonporous.* A thin layer of adhesive must be able to bond to the surface of these materials. Carefully select an adhesive to bond porous to nonporous materials. Check the container label which lists materials it will bond.

The nature of wood affects the strength of a bonded joint. The best bonds result when wood is glued face to face, face to edge, or edge to edge. Poor bonds result when end grain is bonded. Wood glues, when dry, tend to pull out of end grain pores.

Jointwork quality, in any grain direction, affects the strength of the glue bond. The more surface contact between workpieces, the better the joint. Poorly made joints have less surface contact, thus are weak. For example, a dado is better than a butt joint due to added surface contact.

Joints should slip together easily when assembled. Overly tight fits may cause too much adhesive to squeeze out. The result can be a weak, "glue starved" joint.

Exposure

The environment where products are bonded with adhesives is very important. Temperature, moisture, and stress affect the joint's durability. Use waterproof glue on outdoor furniture, for example. If the product will be exposed to stress, such as chair legs are, the joint should be strong, but flexible.

Certain adhesives leave a colored "glue line" when dry. It will be wider on a poorly fit joint. If the glue line might be visible in the finished product, apply an adhesive that dries clear.

Also consider whether the adhesive is toxic. Is it hazardous to people when applying it or using the product? Be especially concerned about ventilation when using toxic materials.

Many "brand name" products are available. However, there are relatively few types. You must determine which one or several meet your needs. The types discussed in this chapter are:
1. Wood adhesives.
2. Contact cements.
3. Construction adhesives.
4. Specialty adhesives.

SELECTING WOOD ADHESIVES

Wood adhesives are available in three forms:
1. *Ready-to-use.* Mixing is not required.
2. *Water-mixed.* A powdered resin is mixed with water.
3. *Two-part.* Two substances must be mixed together. They are a liquid resin and powdered catalyst.

Each of these adhesives achieve a strong, permanent bond when applied properly. It should be stronger than the wood itself, Fig. 32-3.

READY-TO-USE ADHESIVES

Ready-to-use adhesives are the most popular among commercial and home woodworkers. They are widely used for joints, veneers, and laminates. The most common of these are glues, such as liquid hide, aliphatic, and polyvinyl acetate, Fig. 32-4. Apply them directly from the container by brushing, dipping, rolling, or spraying.

Fig. 32-3. Shear test on wood glue bonds show that glue can be stronger than the wood itself.

Liquid hide glue is ready to use, Fig. 32-5. The solid type must be placed in lukewarm water overnight or prepared to manufacturer's instructions. The glue is then heated temporarily to about 150°F in an electric glue pot. A double boiler can also be used for heat. Hide glue, reheated several times, will lose its strength.

Setting time is two to three hours, slow compared to that of other ready-to-use adhesives. Drying time is eight hours or more, depending on humidity, which increases drying time.

Unlike most wood adhesives, hide glues do not clog abrasives during sanding.

Fig. 32-4. Ready-to-use adhesives: hide glue, polyvinyl acetate "white glue," and aliphatic resin. (Franklin International)

Ready-to-use adhesives have different characteristics. They are spreadability, wet tack, and temperature range.

Spreadability is the ease of application. *Wet tack* is how well the adhesive initially sticks to the workpiece. Wet tack reduces spreadability by brushing, but does not affect it when glue is forced to spread. For example, tack prevents glue from being scraped off a tight dowel inserted into a dowel hole. However, when the dowel is forced in by clamping, the glue still spreads. *Temperature* affects adhesives differently. Cooling causes them to thicken. This lessens spreadability. Exposure to heat has the opposite effect; it causes the adhesive to thin. Prolonged heating of hide glue (about 140°F) causes it to lose strength. Heating aliphatic resins and polyvinyl acetates to 120°F has the same weakening effect.

Humidity also affects drying time. Very humid air may increase drying time up to 30 percent.

Hide glue

Hide glue is a clear, amber, multipurpose adhesive. It is among the oldest types available. You can buy it as a liquid or a solid. Both are manufactured from animal hides, bones, and tendons.

Fig. 32-5. Liquid hide glue being applied directly from the plastic container. (Franklin International)

Polyvinyl acetate glue

Polyvinyl acetate glue (PVA) is one of the most common ready-to-use adhesives. It is known as "white glue," and should be used for porous applications. It is not waterproof, so it is limited to interior applications.

PVA is nontoxic, nonflammable, and odorless. It spreads smoothly without running. Clamping is necessary during the one hour setting time. Surplus glue should be cleaned with a damp cloth while the adhesive is wet. Drying requires about 24 hours. When dry, PVA is clear. However, it may be softened by some solvents in finishing materials.

Aliphatic resin glue

Aliphatic resin glue is a cream colored, multipurpose product. Most of its characteristics are similar to PVA. However, it is stronger, and set time is only 20 to 30 minutes. It can be applied at lower temperatures, but the setting and curing times increase.

Aliphatic glues resist solvents in varnish, lacquer, or paint. Therefore, they are more suitable to these finishes than is PVA. Aliphatic glue can also be colored with water soluble dyes to match the finish. Use dyes if a light glue line would be very obvious.

A list of characteristics for aliphatic glue and other ready-to-use adhesives is given in Fig. 32-6.

COMPARISON OF TYPICAL READY-USE ADHESIVES			
	Aliphatic Resin Glue	Polyvinyl Acetate Glue	Liquid Hide Glue
Appearance Spreadability Acidity (pH level*)	Cream Good 4.5-5.0	Clear white Good 4.5-5.0	Clear amber Fair 7.0
Speed of Set Stress Resistance†	Very fast Good	Fast Fair	Slow Good
Moisture Resistance	Fair	Fair	Poor
Heat Resistance	Good	Poor	Excellent
Solvent Resistance‡	Good	Poor	Good
Gap Filling	Fair	Fair	Fair
Wet Tack	High	None	High
Working Temperature	45°-110°F	60°-90°F	70°-90°F
Film Clarity	Translucent	Very clear	Clear but amber
Film Flexibility	Moderate	Flexible	Brittle
Sandability	Good	FAir (will soften)	Excellent
Storage (shelf life)	Excellent	Excellent	Good

*pH—glues with a pH of less than 6 are considered acidic and thus could stain acid woods such as cedar, walnut, oak, cherry, and mahogany.
†Stress resistance—refers to the tendency of a product to give way under constant pressure.
‡Solvent resistance—ability of finishing materials such as varnishes, lacquers, and stains to take over a glued joint.

Fig. 32-6. Ready-to-use adhesives differ in application, appearance, and durability. (Franklin International)

WATER-MIXED ADHESIVES

As the name implies, *water-mixed adhesives* are dry powder resins mixed in water. Powders must be kept covered tightly except while mixing. Air moisture let into the container can shorten the adhesive's shelf life.

There are two basic types of water-mixed adhesives. They are casein and plastic resin. Each has a relatively short pot life.

Casein glue

Casein glue is made from nontoxic milk protein and has a light beige color. You mix the protein powder with cold water. Once mixed, it has about an eight hour pot life. Clamp casein glue bonds two to three hours and let dry at least 24 hours.

Casein glue is moisture resistant but not waterproof. It has many exterior product applications, especially if the wood is later painted.

The glue has some special applications and cautions. It will bond wood species that feel oily, such as teak. Other glues are not effective. You should not apply casein on dark or acid woods. It tends to stain them.

Plastic resin glue

Plastic resin glue, also called *urea formaldehyde,* is a light tan color. It is made from urea resins that are highly water resistant and very strong, but brittle. If applied to poorly fit joints, it will be weak.

Plastic resin has a short, 30 minute pot life. You must mix small amounts and spread it quickly. Use cold water for mixing, then allow the mixture to set for several minutes. Then restir it. This should produce a smooth, creamy texture. If lumps remain after mixing, the resin is too old. Plastic resins require clamps during the 12 hour set time. Curing takes another 12 hours. Plastic resins leave little or no glue line.

TWO-PART ADHESIVES

A *two-part adhesive* is packaged in two containers. One holds the resin liquid and the other a powder catalyst. The *catalyst* hardens the resin once the two are mixed. Two-part adhesives include resorcinol and acrylic resin.

Combine two part adhesives in measured amounts specified by the manufacturer. Prepare small amounts because the adhesive has a short pot life.

Resorcinol

Resorcinol is a high strength, waterproof adhesive for wood. One part is a light tan powdered hardener (catalyst). The other is a cherry-red resin, Fig. 32-7.

Fig. 32-7. Measure proportions of resin and catalyst in two part adhesives accurately. (Franklin International)

The resulting mixture is dark brown with a two to three hour pot life. Changes in the mixture and/or room temperature shorten or lengthen that time. The adhesive sets faster than others and cures in 10 to 12 hours. At a temperature higher than 70 °F, resorcinol begins to cure quicker. At 90 °F it will cure in about five hours.

Excess resorcinol, while wet, can be wiped away with a rag and warm water. Dry adhesive is removed with a scraper.

Acrylic resin glue

Like resorcinols, *acrylic resins* are waterproof and strong. In addition to wood, this glue bonds metal, glass, concrete, but not plastic. Setting time, normally about 5 minutes, is adjusted by the mix of powder and liquid. Acetone is used to remove excess adhesive. Clamping is needed only to position the joint.

Fig. 32-8 lists the characteristics of typical water-mixed and two part adhesives.

COMPARISON OF TYPICAL WATER-MIXED AND TWO-PART ADHESIVES			
	Casein	**Plastic Resin**	**Resorcinol**
Appearance	Cream	Tan	Dark reddish brown
Spreadability	Fair	Excellent	Good
Speed of Set	Slow	Slow	Medium
Stress Resistance	Good	Good	Good
Moisture Resistance	Good	Good	Waterproof
Heat Resistance	Good	Good	Good
Solvent Resistance	Good	Good	Good
Gap Filling Ability	Fair to Good	Fair	Fair
Wet Tack	Poor	Poor	Poor
Working Temperature	32°-110 °F	70°-100 °F	70°-120 °F
Film Clarity	Opaque	Opaque	Opaque
Film Flexibility	Tough	Brittle	Brittle
Sandability	Good	Good	Good
Storage (shelf life)	1 year	1 year	1 year

Fig. 32-8. Water-mixed and two-part adhesives have similar characteristics. (Franklin International)

SELECTING CONTACT CEMENTS

Contact cements are liquid, multipurpose adhesives. They bond similar and dissimilar porous and nonporous materials. Contact cement is used to bond wood, cloth, leather, plastic, rubber, metal, and ceramic products. It has high heat and moisture resistance. It fills gaps well and does not require clamping.

The application of contact cement is unique. Adhesive is applied to both surfaces of the work-

pieces to be joined. However the parts are not joined. The adhesive first must set and lose its tack (stickiness to the touch). The film should be clear and glossy. If it is dull, apply another coat.

When the adhesive on both surfaces has set, press the components together. The bond is instantaneous and once joined the pieces cannot be moved. No clamping is necessary.

Contact cement bonds many materials, however there are some surfaces to which it will not bond. One example is the decorative face of plastic laminate. Contact cement adheres to the laminate back but not to the face. To test whether contact cement will bond to a surface, apply a small amount to a test piece of material. When the cement sets, rub the coated surface with your hand. If the cement rolls up, it did not adhere to that surface.

Cement can be applied by brushing, dipping, spraying, and troweling. A notched trowel is the preferred applicator, Fig. 32-9. Otherwise use a discarded natural bristle paint brush with a wood handle. Keep applicators for cement spreading separate from thos for applying finishes. Cleaning cement applicators is difficult. Some solvents may dissolve the bristles or brush. Tool cleaning must be done while the cement is wet.

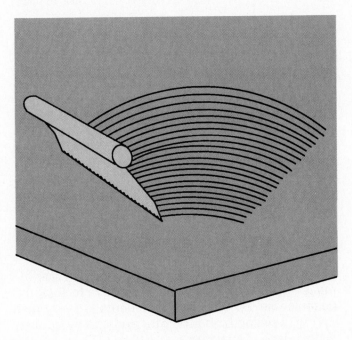

Fig. 32-9. Apply contact cement with a notched spreader.

Control the spread of contact cement carefully. Apply a thin even layer only to the surfaces you want bonded. If some is spilled, wipe it up according to the instructions on the container label.

There are three types of contact cement. They are: solvent-, chlorinated-, and water-based. The characteristics of each are given in Fig. 32-10.

	COLOR	SPEED OF SET	GRADES	FLAMMABLE	TOXIC
	Tan	5-10 Minutes	Two	Yes	Very
Solvent					
	Green	5-10 Minutes	One	No	Slightly
Chlorinated					
	Milky White	Up to One Hour	One	No	No
Water					

Fig. 32-10. Three available contact cements. (Bordon, Inc.; Franklin International)

SOLVENT-BASE CONTACT CEMENT

Solvent-base cements are quick drying, high strength adhesives used primarily for bonding a plastic laminate to a particleboard or hardboard core. They come in two grades: spray and brush. Spray grades are thinned with solvents. Brush grades are thicker and can be applied by dipping, rolling or troweling. Apply solvent-base cements in a well ventilated area. They are both toxic and flammable.

CHLORINATED-BASE CONTACT CEMENT

Chlorinated-base cements provide the cabinetmaker with a nonflammable alternative to solvent-based cements. Chlorinated cements are very fast drying, develop high strength, and can be applied in a variety of manners.

The chlorine odor of this cement can be irritating. It may produce a burning sensation in the eyes. Apply it only in well ventilated areas.

Solvents for cleanup include xylene, toluene, and other products recommended by the manufacturer. Clean tools while the cement is still wet. If the cement has dried, soak the tools in solvent for a few minutes. Then scrape and wipe away the softened cement.

WATER-BASE CONTACT CEMENT

Water-base cements are nontoxic and nonflammable. They are commonly used where other cements could be a health hazard. They also are well suited to foam plastics which would melt if a solvent-base cement was applied.

Water-base cements will not damage lacquered, painted, or varnished surfaces. Wipe up spills and clean tools with water while the cement is wet. Chlorinated solvents will remove dried cement.

Some water-base cements contain alkaline solutions which are eye irritants. Check the label before applying the cement.

Water-base cements should not be used with metal or wood veneer. The adhesive may cause metal to rust. It can also soak through wood veneer, leaving a stain. Another disadvantage for this product is the long setting time. It will also not adhere properly if the temperature is below 40°F.

SELECTING CONSTRUCTION ADHESIVES

Construction adhesives bond a variety of materials such as paneling, vinyl trim, tile, and brick veneer. Adhesives are available in cans and cartridges, Fig. 32-11. One product, grout, is a powder and mixes with water or a solvent.

Fig. 32-11. Some popular construction adhesives are applied by cabinetmakers. (Franklin International)

PANEL ADHESIVE

Wall paneling adhesives may be multipurpose or single purpose. They bond unfinished and prefinished plywood, hardboard, and similar panels to wood, metal and concrete, Fig. 32-12. Most panel adhesives have good wet tack, meaning long term pressure or clamping is not necessary. The caulking gun cartridge form of adhesive is most common.

Fig. 32-12. Prefinished plywood panels are attached with panel adhesive which has been applied to wall studs. (Franklin International)

VINYL BASE ADHESIVE

Vinyl base can be installed where paneling, tile, or some other material meets the floor. It typically replaces wood trim. *Vinyl adhesives* are designed to attach vinyl trim, Fig. 32-13. They are applied with a putty knife, trowel, or caulking gun and have good wet tack. Some are waterproof and others are moisture resistant.

Fig. 32-13. Install vinyl trim, base, and mouldings with a vinyl adhesive. (Franklin International)

TILE ADHESIVES

Various kinds of tile require different adhesives. Tile materials include slate, ceramic, metal, and plastic. The tile manufacturer will recommend a tile adhesive to suit their products. They will be moisture resistant or waterproof. Apply tile adhesives with a trowel, Fig. 32-14, as discussed in Chapter 15.

GROUT

Grout is a cement or resin based powder which is mixed with water or solvents. Press grout into the joints between ceramic and slate tile, Fig. 32-15. It is also applied between the glass and came of leaded glass panels. Grout is sealed to protect it from wear and moisture absorbtion. Use an appropriate grout sealer.

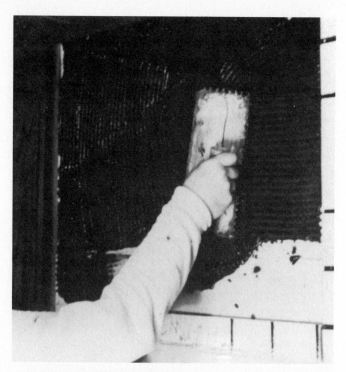

Fig. 32-14. Apply tile adhesives with a notched trowel. (Franklin International)

SELECTING SPECIALTY ADHESIVES

Specialty adhesives include a wide range of cements, glues, adhesives, and mastics. Most are made for specific purposes such as bonding different plastics. When the product fails to make a permanent bond, it is often due to two factors: improper material or applications. Read and follow the manufacturers' instructions carefully. Two of the more commonly used specialty adhesives are cyanoacrylate and epoxy.

CYANOACRYLATE ADHESIVES

Cyanoacrylate adhesives are known as "super," "instant," and "miracle" glues. They bond only nonporous materials in as little as 10 seconds. Cyanoacrylate adhesives dry even without oxygen to evaporate solvents. While setting time is only 10 to 30 seconds, the glued assembly should be left to cure for three to six hours. Acetone (fingernail polish remover) is used for cleanup.

These adhesives bond similar and dissimilar materials, such as ceramics, metal, rubber, and plastic. Almost a 100 percent joint surface contact is necessary however. Also, cyanocrylics do not withstand heat over 160 °F, continuous immersion in water, and many chemicals.

CAUTION: Cyanoacrylate will bond skin to skin almost immediately. Seek medical assistance if you experience this problem. There have been cases where surgical separation was necessary. Acetone (fingernail polish remover) will separate some cyanoacrylic bonds. However, follow the manufacturers' instructions on the packaging.

EPOXY ADHESIVES

Epoxies are used for both porous and nonporous materials. Like cyanoacrylics, they dry chemically. They are available in liquid or stick putty form.

Liquid epoxy

Liquid epoxy is a two-part adhesive. A resin and hardener are mixed in a 50:50 or 60:40 ratio, Fig. 32-16. A 60 percent hardener mix adds flexibility to the bond. This increases resistance to impact. A 60 percent resin mix is stronger, but more brittle.

A

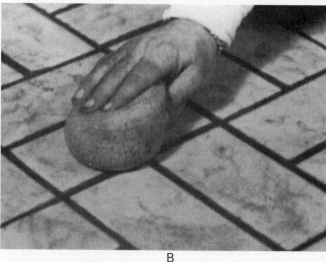

B

Fig. 32-15. Steps in applying grout. A—Spread grout into spaces between tiles with a grout float. B—Wiping off excess grout with a wet sponge. (Franklin International)

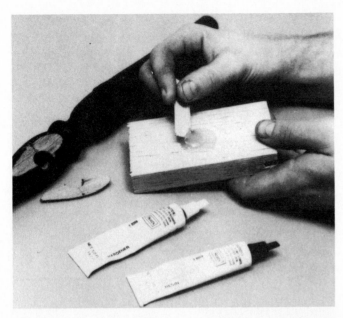

Fig. 32-16. Mix resin and hardener thoroughly with a small stick. (Franklin International)

Mix liquid epoxies in small amounts due to the short pot life. Once the resin and hardener are combined, they cannot be stored.

Stick epoxy

Stick epoxy will fill gaps in materials. Apply it as you would putty. You cut off and knead together equal parts of a stick of resin and stick of hardener. Knead them with a putty knife or place them in a plastic bag and knead with your fingers. Spread the mixture with a putty knife or stick. Seal unused epoxy sticks in separate, air-tight containers.

CAUTION: Epoxy adhesives, like cyanoacrylates, may cause irritations if they contact the skin. Follow the manufacturers' instructions on the packaging if problems occur.

APPLYING ADHESIVES

There are several procedures for applying adhesives. Glues which have a creamy consistency at room temperature can be brushed or rolled. Many can also be sprayed if thinned with solvent or water. Some are applied with heat.

Before gluing workpieces together, make sure they are at the equilibrium moisture content. This will range from 6 to 10 percent. If the wood is too moist or too dry, the glue joint will be weak.

TRADITIONAL GLUING

Traditional gluing refers to applying liquid adhesive and clamping the assembly while the adhesive dries or cures at room temperature. Fit

your assembly together before applying glue. This is referred to as a dry run. Clamp the entire assembly. Check to see that all the workpieces fit properly. Then wipe any dust or debris off of each workpiece.

Glue is spread on surfaces by a number of means, Fig. 32-17. It is recommended that you cover the entire surface to be joined. You cannot be sure that a thin line of glue will spread to fill the joint when the assembly is clamped.

A

B

Fig. 32-17. A—Apply adhesive with a stick. (Franklin International) B—In holes, use a glue syringe. (Shopsmith, Inc.)

Once you have applied glue, clamp the assembly, Fig. 32-18. Small beads should ooze from the joint. This tells the cabinetmaker that sufficient glue was used. If no glue oozes, take the assembly apart immediately and reglue. If there are drips or runs, too much glue was used. In this case, wipe off the excess glue with a wet cloth. Adjust the amount you apply next time.

Fig. 32-18. Clamps hold the assembly together while the glue sets. (Adjustable Clamp Co.)

HOT MELT GLUING

Hot melt gluing is an efficient method of bonding many materials. It is done with an *electric glue gun*, Fig. 32-19. You place a small cylinder of solid adhesive in the gun. As you pull the trigger (electric switch) the adhesive warms and liquifies. It then flows onto the workpiece surfaces being bonded. With larger guns, pulling the trigger feeds the adhesive automatically. On small guns, feeding the adhesive stick is done by hand.

Workpieces must be assembled quickly after the melted glue is applied. The glue cools and sets in approximately 15 seconds. Coat only an area which can be covered in about 10 seconds. Then hold the components together for 10 seconds. In 60 seconds the bond is at 90 percent of its strength.

Hot melt glue has many uses. Select the proper type of adhesive for wood, wood products, plastic, fabric, paper, and some rubber products.

RADIO FREQUENCY GLUING

Radio Frequency gluing (RF) is a method of using high frequency radio waves to heat and cure the glue joint. RF gluing is also called *High Frequency Heating* and *Dielectric Heating.* It is similar to microwave cooking.

RF gluing equipment consists of a generator and pair of electrodes. The generator creates radio

waves and sends them to electrodes placed on each side of the glue joint, Fig. 32-20. The radio waves cycle through the wood and glue causing molecular friction. This generates heat. However, the heat is concentrated on the glue joint. This causes the glue joint to set and dry much quicker. You are able to remove the clamps in a few minutes, rather than wait hours.

An RF glue gun has both electrodes mounted on the bottom. The electrodes are shaped for flat surfaces and corner joints, Fig. 32-21.

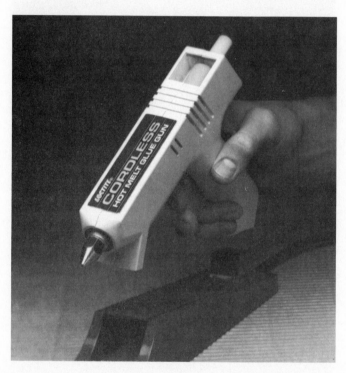

Fig. 32-19. This cordless electric glue gun ejects hot melt adhesive through the small nozzle tip. (Locktite Corp.)

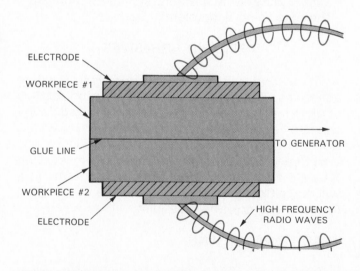

Fig. 32-20. RF gluing sends high frequency waves through the glue and workpieces. The glue heats and sets quickly. The wood stays relatively cool.

Larger RF gluing systems have electrode plates, one is positioned on top of the assembly. Another is positioned on the bottom. Clamping is generally done automatically by the RF machine, Fig. 32-22.

Adhesive selection

Adhesives which cure chemically, not by a loss of water, are the best for RF gluing. Examples are:

1. *Urea formaldehyde resin.* This is one of the least expensive and best suited adhesives for RF.
2. *Cross-linking polyvinyl acetate resin.* This is the most widely used adhesive for RF gluing. It differs from polyvinyl acetate (white glue) in that it is set by an acidic salt chemical reaction, not by water loss.
3. *Resorcinal.* This is a less used adhesive because it can become too hot during the RF cycle. Excess heat produces burnt glue lines.
4. *Aliphatic resin.* These resins cure slower because they are set by water evaporation.

Other readily available adhesives are not adaptable to RF gluing. Polyvinyl acetate (PVA), "white glue," is not used because it is apt to melt uncontrollably during RF curing. Hide glues and caseins cannot by used for RF gluing. Hide glues are softened and weaked by heat. Caseins cannot be set or cured by this process. The adhesive will foam and leave a weak joint.

Setup

To prepare to use the RF gluing equipment, first read the manufacturer's manual. It contains information on what material types and thicknesses you can bond.

Fig. 32-21. The electrodes on RF gluing guns are shaped according to the joint you are bonding. (Workrite)

Fig. 32-22. Large scale RF gluing machines clamp the stock. Here, a 15 piece face-to-face lamination is being RF glued. (Mann-Russell Electronics)

Clamp your assembly together as described in Chapter 33. Be sure that the metal clamps do not interfere with moving the RF gun across the glue line. Touching the electrodes of the gun to the clamps could cause permanent damage to the RF equipment. After clamping, wipe off any excess adhesive.

System operation

Always follow the manufacturer's procedure when operating the RF equipment. Each machine has specific features that affect its use. If recommended cure times (cycles) are not given, you can determine them for the piece you are gluing.

RF gluing gun procedure

Most RF gluing guns work as follows:
1. Glue and clamp your assembly.
2. Turn on the welder switch.
3. Keep your free hand at least 12 in. (300 mm) from the gun electrodes.
4. Position the gun over the joint, one electrode on each side the glue line.
5. Squeeze the trigger on the gun handle to begin the frequency curing.
6. The glue should heat and bubble from the glue line. You should not hold the trigger for more than 15 seconds per position. Longer time can damage the equipment.
7. Move to another position over the joint.
8. Repeat steps 5 through 7 at about 4 in. (100 mm) intervals.
9. Remove clamps.

SUMMARY

Adhesives serve the cabinetmaker in many ways. Choosing the right adhesive affects the strength, durability, and appearance of your product. When selecting the adhesive, carefully consider the following questions:
1. What is the adhesive's shelf life?
2. How quickly will the adhesive begin to set? This determines the time you have to clamp.
3. What joint strength and durability is required?
4. Must the adhesive resist heat and/or moisture?
5. Must the adhesive resist solvents (paint or lacquer thinner)?
6. Will the adhesive have to fill gaps of poorly fit joints?
7. Should the adhesive have a good wet tack?
8. Within what temperatures should the adhesive be applied?
9. Once the adhesive dries, is the glue line visible?
10. Can excess adhesive be removed with water or solvent; or must you remove it with a scraper or abrasive after it dries?
11. Will you use RF, hot melt, or traditional means of gluing?

THINK SAFETY—ACT SAFELY

A number of safety concerns are associated with adhesives. These are identified on container label. They inform you of toxic, skin irritating, and flammable ingredients. When using adhesives, follow these precautions:
1. Wear safety eyewear to protect yourself from splashing adhesives and solvents.
2. Read all adhesive container lables and product instruction sheets, Fig. 32-23.

Fig. 32-23. Read the adhesive container label for important information, such as flammability and toxicity. (Franklin International)

3. Apply toxic adhesives in a well ventilated area. Forced air exhaust systems are best.
4. Extinguish all flames while using flammable adhesives and solvents.
5. Protect sensitive skin with rubber or plastic gloves.
6. If you experience any adverse symptoms while applying adhesive, contact you physician immediately.
7. Touch only the handles of hot glue or RF guns during use.
8. Keep your free hand at least one foot from the RF gun while using it. Your moist skin near the gun could attract an arc from the gun similar to lightning. A serious third degree burn could result.

CABINETMAKING TERMS

Adhesive, cohesion, adhesion, shelf life, pot life, setting time, drying time, curing time, porous materials, nonporous materials, ready-to-use adhesive, spreadability, wet tack, temperature, hide glue, polyvinyl acetate glue, aliphatic resin glue, water-mixed adhesive, casein glue, plastic resin glue, urea formaldehyde glue, two-part adhesive, catalyst, resorcinol, acrylic resin, contact cement, solvent-base contact cement, chlorinated-base contact cement, water-base contact cement, panel adhesive, vinyl adhesive, tile adhesive, grout, cyanoacrylate adhesive, epoxy adhesive, electric glue gun, radio frequency gluing, generator, electrode, RF cure cycle.

TEST YOUR KNOWLEDGE

1. Explain the difference between adhesion and cohesion.
MATCHING TEST: On a separate sheet of paper, match the terms with the appropriate definition.
2. Shelf life.
3. Pot life.
4. Drying time.
5. Setting time.
6. Curing time.
7. Wet tack.
   a. Time for glue joint to reach full strength.
   b. Length of time the adhesive is spreadable.
   c. Describes how well the adhesive sticks on the surface where it is applied.
   d. Length of time the adhesive can be stored before it is unusable.
   e. Chemical reaction time for the adhesive to reach full strength.
   f. Length of time from spreading the adhesive to the time when clamps can be removed.

8. All adhesives are applied at room temperature. True or False?
MATCHING TEST: On a separate sheet of paper, match the adhesive with the appropriate category.
9. Casein.
10. Hide.
11. Plastic resin.
12. Acrylic resin.
13. Aliphatic resin.
14. Resorcinol.
15. Hide.
   a. Ready-to-use liquid.
   b. Powder mixed with water.
   c. Liquid mixed with a powdered catalyst.
16. Bond components together with contact cement:
   a. Immediately after spreading the cement.
   b. Immediately after the cement sets.
   c. Immediately after the cement cures.
   d. Any time.
17. The contact cement that is safest to use is _____.
18. Three construction adhesives are _____, _____, and _____.
19. Where is grout used?
20. "Super glue" refers to:
   a. Contact cement.
   b. Epoxy adhesives.
   c. Cyanoacrylate adhesives.
21. An adhesive in both liquid and solid stick forms is _____.
22. Adhesives can be applied by _____, _____, and _____.
23. The hot melt glue system will bond many different materials. True or False?
24. Name three adhesives adaptable to radio frequency gluing.

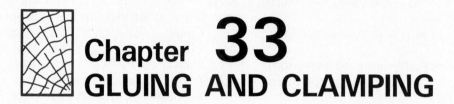

Chapter 33
GLUING AND CLAMPING

After studying this chapter, you will be able to:
☐*Identify types of clamping devices.*
☐*Select clamps to assemble various joints.*
☐*Describe how to protect workpieces from clamp damage.*
☐*Explain the procedure for assembling your product with clamps.*

Clamps have many applications for the cabinet-maker. Clamps are like another pair of hands. They may hold a workpiece while you are processing it. They can secure a jig in place. They might also hold featherboards or stop blocks so your hands stay away from the point of operation. Use clamps to reduce accident risks when you work with tools and machinery.

Clamping is most often associated with adhesive bonding when assembling a product. Here, clamping is a two-step procedure. First, you position and secure workpieces without adhesive. This is called a trial assembly, or dry run. Then you spread the adhesive and clamp the assembly.

Clamps come in many shapes and sizes. Some are designed for one specific joint. Others hold glue joints as well as attach jigs and fixtures. With most, you can control the amount of clamp pressure. However, spring clamp pressure depends on the strength of the spring. The clamps discussed in this chapter are positioned and tightened by hand. Clamping machines are discussed in Chapter 52, Industrial Production Cabinetmaking. These use hydraulic or pneumatic pressure.

SPRING CLAMPS

Spring clamps, Fig. 33-1, range in size from 4 in. to 12 in. They may have vinyl coated jaws and handles to prevent marring the material. Dip clamp jaws in liquid plastic. The plastic, which cures to be a soft protective covering, is available in most hardware stores. The coated handles also improve your grip.

Spring clamps are easy to use. Pressure is constant depending on spring tension. However, you

Fig. 33-1. Spring clamps work much like clothespins. (Franklin International)

cannot control the pressure as with screw thread clamps. You might attach trim or inlays with spring clamps.

You can improvise a spring clamp with a pair of pliers and a rubber band, Fig. 33-2A. You might also use vise grips, Fig. 33-2B. Place a protective piece of material between your workpiece and the jaws.

SCREW CLAMPS

Screw clamps allow you to vary the amount of pressure. This is both an advantage and disadvantage. While screw clamps allow you to properly tighten the joint, you can also overtighten them. When bonding an assembly, too much pressure both crushes the wood cells and causes a starved joint. A *starved joint* is one which does not have enough adhesive. The adhesive squeezes out or too little was applied in the first place. Another disadvantage of screw clamps is you can fail to give enough pressure to glue joints.

Hand screws

Hand screws are one of the oldest woodworking clamps known. They range in size from a 4 in. (100

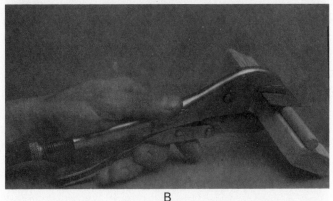

Fig. 33-2. Improvising a spring clamp. A—Using pliers and a rubber band. B—Using vise grips. (Franklin International)

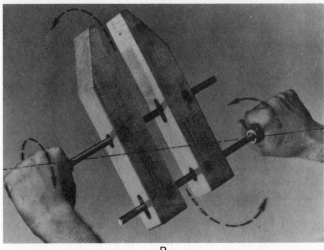

Fig. 33-3. A—Hand screw jaws set parallel apply pressure evenly along the entire length. The jaws of the right clamp are not parallel. B—Swing clamp on centerline shown to keep jaws parallel as the clamp opens or closes. (Franklin International)

mm) jaw length and maximum opening of 2 in. (50 mm) to a 24 in. (600 mm) jaw length and a 17 in. (430 mm) opening, Fig. 33-3A.

People assume that screw clamps will not mar a workpiece because they are made of wood. This is not true. It will happen if the clamp is made of a harder wood than the material being held. Also, dried adhesive on the jaws is apt to dent the material.

You can adjust the jaw opening one handle at a time or by rotating both handles. For quick changes, swing the hand screw with both handles. This keeps the jaws parallel as the clamp opens, Fig. 33-3B.

When applying pressure, use the full surface of the jaws. Also make sure that the jaws are parallel. Otherwise, unqeual pressure is applied and the workpieces are apt to separate.

Bar clamps

Bar clamps can be used for short and long spans. They range from 6 in. (150 mm) to 8 ft. (2 400 mm), depending on the style, Fig. 33-4. They consist of a steel bar or pipe, fixed jaw (or head), movable jaw (or head), and screw handle.

To use a bar clamp, first turn the screw handle counterclockwise as far as it will go. Slide the movable jaw to the jaw's maximum opening. You may have to press a lever on the movable jaw or

lift it from a notch in the bar. Place the fixed jaw against one side of the assembly. Place backing blocks (scrap wood) between the workpiece and the jaws. Then slide the movable jaw against the other side. Finally, tighten the screw handle to exert the correct amount of pressure on the assembly. For a glue joint, adhesive should ooze from the joint.

Edge clamp fixture

An *edge clamp fixture* is a bar clamp accessory. It is often used to attach edging or trim, Fig. 33-5, or hold some types of joints. Slip the edge clamp between the bar clamp and the workpiece before tightening the bar clamp.

C clamps

C clamps, often called *carriage clamps,* are used quite often in the shop, Fig. 33-6. They can secure

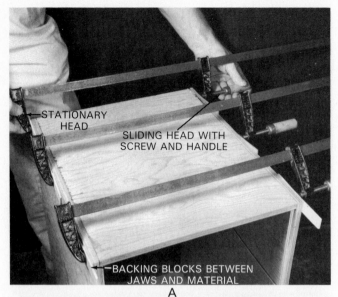

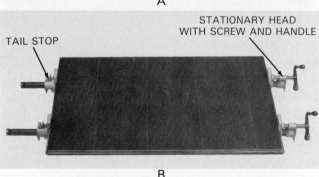

Fig. 33-4. A—These sliding head bar clamps range in size from 42 in. to 30 in. B—Rubber clamp pads are placed on the jaws of this fixed head clamp. (Adjustable Clamp Co.)

Fig. 33-5. Use edge clamp fixtures to apply bond around the edge of table tops. (Franklin International)

jigs to table tops and machines as well as bond some types of joints.

The maximum opening (frame size) may range from 1 in. (25 mm) to 18 in. (460 mm). The throat depth from screw to frame can be 1 in. (25 mm)

to 4 in. (100 mm). C clamps may be further classified as light or industrial duty, depending on their strength. At the end of the screw jaw is a "foot" which swivels to prevent the screw from digging into the material. Again, it is best to place backing blocks between the jaws and the material.

Fig. 33-6. C clamps can secure mitered corners. (Franklin International)

3-way edging clamp

The *3-way edging clamp* is a combined C clamp and an edge clamp fixture, Fig. 33-7. However, unlike the C clamp, two screws hold the clamp.

Web and band clamps

Web and *band clamps* apply pressure in one direction—toward the center of the assembly. They are essential for irregular shapes. A cloth webbing, rubber strap, or steel band is pulled tight around the assembly, Fig. 33-8. A friction lock prevents the belt from loosening. A screw handle or steel hook allows you to apply the final pressure.

Light duty clamps are called *web clamps.* They have a 1 in. (25 mm) nylon web or belt about 12 ft. (3 660 mm) to 15 ft. (4 570 mm) long. Heavy duty clamps, called *band clamps,* have a 2 in. (50 mm) fabric or steel band.

One type of band clamp uses stretchable rubber straps and steel hooks. Place hooks on the strap at a distance slightly less than the perimeter of the

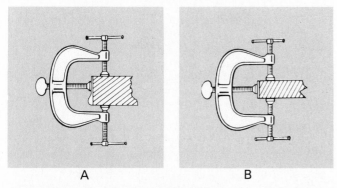

Fig. 33-7. A—3-way edging clamps may be applied with the right angle screw off center. B—Right angle screw is centered. (Shopsmith)

Fig. 33-8. A web clamp holds this chair frame until the adhesive sets. (Adjustable Clamp Co.)

A

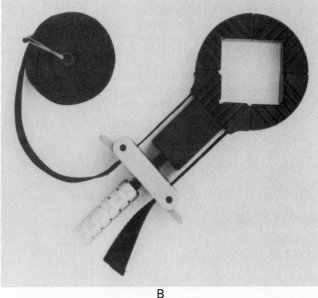

B

Fig. 33-9. A—The rubber cord is looped through the metal hook to adjust the length of the band clamp. (Brookstone Co.) B—This clamp has 90° corner blocks for frames and other rectangular assemblies. (Vermont American Tool Co.)

assembly. Stretch the strap and slip the two hooks together, Fig. 33-9A.

Another band clamp includes 90° corner blocks. They can be moved to fit around frames. The band slides through them while tightening, Fig. 33-9B. These clamps can increase efficiency. One band may replace four or more bar clamps, for example. Test the use of this clamp during your dry run.

Miter clamps

Miter clamps are designed specifically for miter joints. Two screws hold the workpieces at the proper 90° angle, Fig. 33-10A. There is no direct pressure on the joint so it is important that you position and hold the workpieces while tightening.

Another miter clamp style can be used for workpieces which joint at angles other than 90°. However, you must drill holes in the workpieces, Fig. 33-10B. Holes can later be hidden.

Maxi-clamp system

The *maxi-clamp system* is a set of screws and fixtures which can be fastened many ways, Fig. 33-11. Arrange the clamp to fit your needs. Pressure can be applied in one, two, or three directions. Arrange the clamp setup during your trial assembly.

Workbench vises

Many cabinetmakers find that workbench vises often meet their clamping needs. The vise may be built in or attached to the bench, Fig. 33-12.

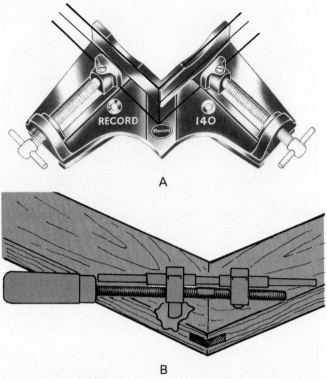

A

B

Fig. 33-10. A—Miter clamps can apply pressure across corners. (Record Ridgway Tools) B—This clamp pulls workpieces together using holes drilled in the back of the frame. (Shopsmith)

A

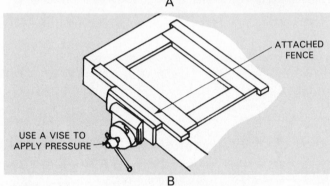

ATTACHED FENCE

USE A VISE TO APPLY PRESSURE

B

Fig. 33-12. A—Vises may be built into the workbench. B—Using a fence and vise you can apply pressure to a frame.

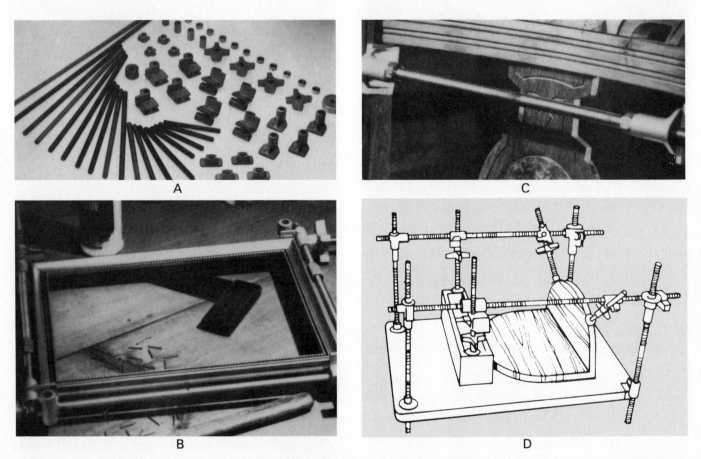

A

B

C

D

Fig. 33-11. A—Maxi-clamp system parts. B—Clamping a frame. C—Attaching a chair back. D—Clamping in three directions. (Shopsmith, Leichtung, Inc.)

Hold-down clamps

Hold-down clamps temporarily secure an assembly to the table or bench top. This keeps the components in the same plane. They may be used to clamp lap, miter, and other joints when installing fasteners. The clamp attaches through the bench stop hole with a bolt, Fig. 33-13. It may also fasten to the slot of a machine table.

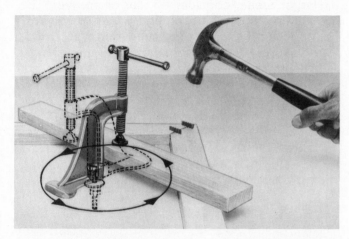

Fig. 33-13. Position hold down clamps where needed. (Adjustable Clamp Co.)

Veneer press

Veneer presses are used to hold veneer to a wood substrate when gluing. This process is called veneering or overlaying. The practice has decreased since cabinetmakers can purchase hardwood veneer plywood. However, many woodworkers still overlay rare and expensive hardwood veneers to low priced materials such as particleboard.

A veneer press has one or several rows of bolts mounted in a *bed frame,* Fig. 33-14. The bolts apply pressure on an *upper caul.* Sandwiched between the upper and *lower cauls* is your work.

Fig. 33-14. Parts of a veneer press. (Franklin International)

OTHER CLAMPS

Several other common hand clamps are quick release clamps, cam clamps, and wedge clamps. These use neither screws nor springs to apply pressure.

Quick-release clamps

Quick-release clamps can be used to quickly apply a preset, uniform pressure on an assembly. They may be lever or air pressure operated. You will often use use them with a jig or fixture, Fig. 33-15, to assemble multiple products. The clamp is attached to the jig with screws or bolts. You might also attach them to a drill press table.

Cam clamps

Cam clamps consist of a fence, locating pins, and cams. These are placed on a drilled hardwood *locator board,* Fig. 33-16. The board's holes are spaced for standard sizes.

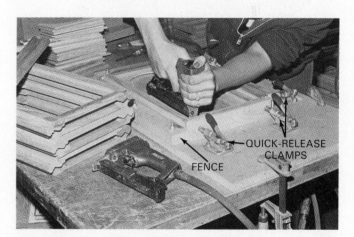

Fig. 33-15. Quick-release clamps are often bolted to a jig. This jig, made of plywood with a fence and clamps, is for assembling picture frames. It is clamped to the workbench with a bar clamp. (Craft Products)

Fig. 33-16. Cam clamps, positioned on the locator board, adjust to frame sizes. (Meyer Vise Co.)

Cam clamps are versatile. Many sizes of frames can be clamped quickly. Position a trial asssembly to accurately arrange the pins and fences, then cams. Turn the hex head of the cam with a wrench to apply pressure. The simple action of the cam permits quick assembly.

Wedge clamps

You can make *wedge clamps* to suit a variety of frame clamping purposes. The clamp consists of four fences attached to a metal covered bottom board, Fig. 33-17. The metal prevents excess adhesive from bonding the frame to the clamp. Pairs of wooden wedges slide past each other to apply pressure. Tap the wedges with a mallet to fully hold the assembly.

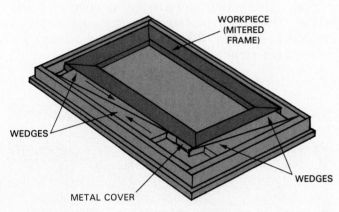

Fig. 33-17. Make a simple wedge clamp to assemble small frames quickly.

CLAMPING GLUE JOINTS

The quality of your product depends greatly on the care you take to process and assemble it. Clamps provide help for these purposes. Clamping helps you saw, drill, and process workpieces accurately. When you are ready to assemble the product, clamps provide the necessary pressure for good glue joints. Before clamping glue joints, make sure all workpieces are smooth and that the proper tools are available.

GATHERING TOOLS AND SUPPLIES

The following tools and supplies must be readily available when preparing to assemble a product:
1. Select the proper adhesive. For water-base and two-part adhesives, have measuring devices handy. Mix the adhesive only when you are ready to spread it. Squeeze bottles, with nozzles, are best for ready-to-use adhesives. If you will be RF gluing the product, check that all equipment is present and in good working condition.

2. Lay out the correct number and type of clamps preset to the approximate opening. Select clamps which will provide adequate pressure and clamp to workpiece contact.
3. Make *backing blocks* or buy clamp pads to place between the clamp and wood to prevent marring the surface, Fig. 33-18.
4. Acquire the proper adhesive applicator. For small areas, use a bottle, brush, or stick. For larger areas, consider a roller or sprayer.
5. Obtain a sponge or rag and water or solvent to wipe off excess adhesive when wet. Dried adhesive will not absorb stain during finishing. Therefore, that area will retain its natural color.
6. Cut and place wax paper between clamps or backer blocks and the workpiece at a glue joint. This prevents clamps from being bonded to the assembly. It also retards stain marks caused by glue contact with metal clamps, Fig. 33-19. For wood handscrews, consider coating them with paste wax or silicone spray.

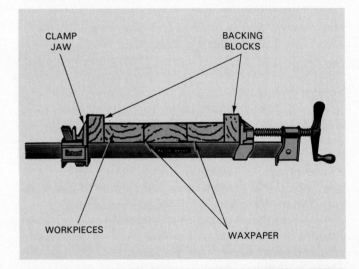

Fig. 33-18. Backing blocks and clamp pads protect your product from damage caused by clamp jaws. (Adjustable Clamp Co.)

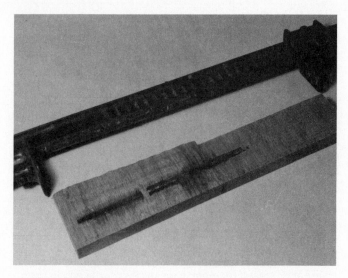

Fig. 33-19. Typical wood stain caused by bar clamp.

Fig. 33-20. The same number of clamps have been placed on each side of this case assembly. Doing so balances clamp pressure. (Franklin International)

7. Have mallet handy to tap joints into alignment once the assembly is glued and clamped.
8. Select a framing and/or try square to check squareness of the assembly. When necessary, have a sliding T-bevel preset to check angles of your product.
9. Use a straightedge to check the flatness of glued panels. For case assemblies, use it to see if excess pressure was applied which would cause cupping.

CLAMPING PROCEDURE

The procedure for clamping includes making a trial assembly (also called a dry run), applying adhesive, and clamping the assembly.

Trial assembly

First, secure the components without adhesive. Use pads or backing blocks to protect the wood. Position clamps so that joints are given the necessary pressure. Have as much clamp surface in contact with the workpiece as possible. Place bar clamps alternately over and under the workpiece where possible. This evens out pressure and prevents cupping the wood. Also clamp workpieces with hand screws against bar clamps to prevent cupping. Whenever feasible, use clamps in pairs on both sides of the assembly, Fig. 33-20. This prevents one end from being separated while the other is being joined.

Inspect all joints, dimensions, and angles of the clamped assembly. The joints should fit well without excessive pressure. See that all dimensions are correct. Be sure that corners are square or at the angle shown on your shop drawings.

If the assembly fits properly, loosen the clamps just enough to remove them. Lay them aside in an orderly manner. You will want to reuse them after

the adhesive is spread. They should not need to be adjusted again.

As you disassemble the workpieces, you may wish to mark them. With a pencil, lightly write letters or numbers on adjoining workpieces. These help identify mating parts during reassembly.

Applying adhesive

Your next step will be to apply the adhesive. Lay all workpieces out in an orderly manner. This will make clamping more efficient. If you are using a two-part adhesive, mix the proper amount. Then spread the adhesive to all surfaces being bonded. Applying adhesive to both parts of a glue joint is better than a single spread. However, with hot melt glue, one surface is sufficient.

For glues with a short pot life, layout and glue subassemblies first. Then glue these together later to complete the product assembly.

For liquid adhesives, once you have spread the glue, let it set for about a minute. This increases the wet tack. Then it is necessary to fit workpieces together quickly and accurately.

Clamping the wet glue assembly

After the glue is spread, reassemble the components. Insert wax paper between joints and clamps.

At first, lightly tighten all of the clamps. Use a square and T-bevel to check squareness frequently. Have a rubber mallet handy to tap joints into alignment. Then tighten clamps evenly. Again check the squareness and alignment of components. If necessary, use a block of softwood and a mallet or hammer to move misaligned joints. Place a straightedge over flat surfaces to check whether components have bowed under pressure. If so, relieve pressure slightly.

Properly fit glue joints require little pressure. Over-tightening the clamps will result in a starved joint. Properly clamped joints will have small beads of glue at intervals along the joint, Fig. 33-21.

As soon as the assembly is securely clamped, wipe off all excess adhesive. Throw sawdust over the oozing glue beads to make the adhesive easier to remove. Dried adhesive can later be removed with a sharp chisel or cabinet scraper. Do not wash the product surface with water or solvent. This only spreads the glue. The glue film would have to later be removed by sanding.

Allow the glue to reach its set time before removing clamps. When possible, it is advised to leave clamps on during the curing time also. This is because materials and environments affect the adhesive set time.

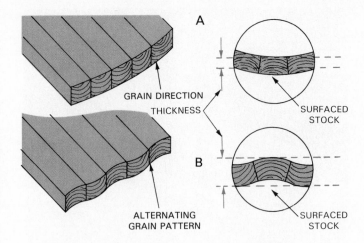

Fig. 33-22. A—Edge-gluing workpieces without alternating grain pattern results in more warp and less surfaced thickness. B—Properly positioned workpieces results in less warp and greater surfaced thickness.

Fig. 33-21. A properly clamped glue joint should have glue beads, but not runs. The absence of beads indicates a "starved joint."

EDGE-TO-EDGE BONDING

Frequently, a cabinetmaker needs boards wider than can be purchased. Make them by edge-gluing narrower stock. The component arrangement is most important when edge gluing. Alternate the end grain (curve of the annual rings) with each piece, Fig. 33-22. This lessens the amount of cup in the assembled board.

Some lumber will be wide enough, but cupped. Removing the cup by planing the surfaces will likely reduce the thickness too much. You can rip the board into narrow pieces and edge-glue them back together as shown in Fig. 33-22B.

The procedure for edge-gluing stock to make wider boards is:
1. Rip and joint narrow stock.
2. Cut all workpieces 1/2 in. longer than the final length of the component.
3. Arrange the end grain pattern and mark mating joints, Fig. 33-23.
4. Place bar clamps on a flat surface and place the workpieces on it. Position bar clamps every 10 to 20 in. (250 to 500 mm). Two clamps should be located near the ends.
5. Place wax paper over the clamps to prevent discoloring the wood.
6. Arrange workpieces on the clamps as marked.
7. Apply adhesive to the workpiece edges and press them together.
8. Lay wax paper over the glued joints.

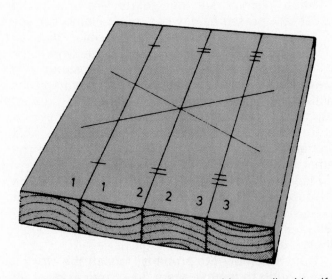

Fig. 33-23. Lightly mark workpieces with a pencil to identify mating joints.

9. Place bar clamps over the assembled, spaced between the bottom clamps, Fig. 33-24.
10. Tighten the bar clamps, making sure the workpieces lie flat on the bottom clamps. Also check that joints remain aligned; if not, strike them with a mallet.
11. If one or several pieces are cupped, clamp them to the bottom bars with hand screws, Fig. 33-25.

If you are edge-gluing boards of the same thickness, double clamps work well for alignment, Fig. 33-26. First, slide the lumber between the bars. Then set the clamps to the approximate width. Twist the double bar clamps as you tighten the screw. One bar will be flush above and the other will align the boards below.

Fig. 33-24. Alternate bar clamps on top and bottom of assembly. Use a mallet to position boards which slip out of place. (Franklin International)

Fig. 33-26. Double bar clamps align the boards while clamping.

FACE-TO-FACE BONDING

For thicker components, bond workpieces face-to-face. By reversing the end grain pattern, a component made of two pieces is less apt to warp than solid lumber. Match grain patterns if possible. Straight grain patterns are less likely to warp than figured grain.

Use handscrews when clamping workpieces face-to-face, Fig. 33-27. This puts pressure in the center and at the edges. The procedure is as follows:
1. Preset the clamp jaws parallel and to the approximate opening of the assembly.
2. Apply a double spread of adhesive.
3. Place the workpieces together with the end grain (annual rings) opposite each other.
4. Position and tighten the first handscrew at one end of the assembly.
5. Set additional clamps working toward the other end. Space them about 10 to 20 in. apart. If the glue doesn't ooze from the joint, add more clamps.

CLAMPING FRAMES

When clamping frames, it is important that you work on a flat surface. This helps align the frame. Fig. 33-28 shows a typical frame clamping arrangement. If the frame becomes out of square, shift one or two bar clamps at a slight angle. This diagonal force pulls the frame into alignment. Then look across the frame to be sure it is not twisted.

Fig. 33-25. Handscrews hold boards against bar clamp for alignment.

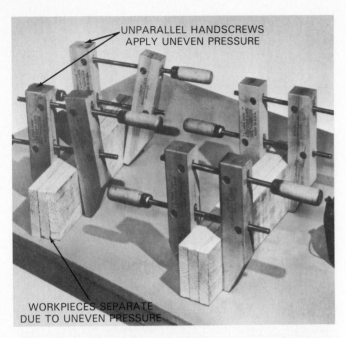

Fig. 33-27. Hand screw jaws should be adjusted parallel with the surfaces. Notice how clamped assembly at left has separated because of uneven pressure. (Adjustable Clamp Co.)

UNPARALLEL HANDSCREWS APPLY UNEVEN PRESSURE

WORKPIECES SEPARATE DUE TO UNEVEN PRESSURE

Fig. 33-28. Clamping a frame with 8 ft. and 3 ft. bar clamps. (Adjustable Clamp Co.)

SUMMARY

Clamps are used to position and hold assemblies. They also serve as extra hands while you are processing materials. They can hold jigs and fixtures in place during production.

Clamp pressure is achieved with springs, screw threads, levers, cams, and wedges. Hand clamp pressure is adequate for most cabinetmaking purposes. Hand clamps include spring clamps, hand screws, bar clamps, edging clamps, band clamps, and miter clamps. Quick-release, cam, and wedge clamps are also common. Machine clamps are used for high production operations. Clamp pressure is supplied by pneumatic or hydraulic rams.

The bonding procedure involves a trial assembly, spreading the adhesive, and clamping the glued assembly. The trial assembly is made to check the fit of joints. It also lets you experiment with positioning clamps for proper pressure. Then adhesive is spread on the components, after which they are reassembled and clamped.

CABINETMAKING TERMS

Spring clamp, screw clamps, starved joint, hand screws, bar clamps, sliding head bar clamp, fixed head clamp, edge clamp fixture, C clamp, 3-way edging clamp, web clamp, band clamp, miter clamp, maxi-clamp system, hold-down clamp, veneer press, bed frame, upper caul, lower caul, quick-release clamp, cam clamp, locator board, wedge clamp, backing blocks.

TEST YOUR KNOWLEDGE

1. Clamps are used for both _____ and _____.
2. With a spring clamp you cannot adjust the _____.
3. List an advantage and a disadvantage of using screw clamps.
4. The position of hand screw jaws when clamped should apply pressure:
   a. At the tip of the jaws.
   b. At the back end of the jaws.
   c. The entire length of the jaws.
   d. Only with the top jaw to prevent workpiece damage.
5. Two styles of bar clamps are _____ and _____.
6. An edge clamp fixture is used with a _____ clamp.
7. A light duty band clamp is called a _____.
8. Quick-release clamps are often part of a _____ or _____.
9. Cam clamps are most used to assemble _____.
10. List eight tools or supplies you should have on hand before clamping.
11. You assemble your product without adhesive during a _____.
12. Explain four considerations when positioning clamps.
13. Diagram the direction of the annual rings when gluing stock edge-to-edge.
14. Stock glued face-to-face is weaker than solid lumber. True or False?

Chapter 34
BENDING AND LAMINATING WOOD

After studying this chapter, you will be able to:
□ Identify methods of dry bending wood.
□ Describe the procedures for wet bending wood.
□ Follow the procedures for laminating flat and curved components.

Many furniture designs require processes beyond cutting and assembling solid wood components. Thicker and stronger cabinet parts are made by bonding two or more pieces of wood together. This is laminating. Curved pieces, such as drawer fronts, chair backs, and table aprons are made by bending and/or laminating the wood.

WOOD BENDING

Wood bending is the process of forming a piece of solid lumber into a curve, Fig. 34-1. Under pressure, wood fibers compress on the inside of the curve and stretch those on the outside.

Fig. 34-1. These chair backs and arms were steam bent to form gentle curves. (Thomasville)

All wood species bend to some radius, Fig. 34-2. This is called *elasticity*. However, the grain pattern and the amount of defects in the wood is more important than the species. Select straight grain wood for bending. Samples with figured grain are more likely to split. There should be few defects in wood. Use wood free of knots, checks, splits, and other separations of the grain. Blue stain or other surface blemishes do not affect bendability.

SPECIE	MINIMUM BEND RADIUS					
	Dry 1/8″ (3 mm)		Steam 1″ (25 mm)			
			w/mold		wo/mold	
	(inch)	(mm)	(inch)	(mm)	(inch)	(mm)
Ash	4.8	122	4.5	110	13	330
Beech	4.5	114	1.5	38	13	330
Birch	*	*	3	76	17	430
Cherry	5.9	150	2	51	17	430
Chestnut	7.5	191	18	460	33	840
Douglas Fir	7.8	198	14	360	27	690
Elm	4.6	117	1.7	43	12.5	320
Hemlock	8.8	223	19	480	36	910
Hickory	5.8	147	1.8	46	15	380
Mahogany	8.5	216	36	910	32	810
Maple	6.4	163	*	*	*	*
Oak	5.4	137	1	25	11.5	290
Pine	5.9	150	34	860	29	740
Poplar	6.3	160	32	810	26	660
Sitka Spruce	5.4	137	36	910	32	810
Sycamore	4.0	102	1.5	38	14.5	370
Walnut	6.0	152	1	25	11	280
Western Red Cedar	8.0	203	35	390	37	940

*Data not available

Fig. 34-2. This table shows the approximate radius for bending selected wood samples. Numbers indicate the smallest radius that should be attempted. This may vary according to what type of machines or pressure are used. Dry bending samples were tested at 12% moisture content. Steam bends were tested at 25% M.C. (Forest Products Laboratory)

Moisture content in the wood also affects the radius of the bend. Moistening increases bendability. This is why most lumber is steamed before being bent.

Plywood and fiberboard also can be bent. However, the bending radius is limited, Fig. 34-3. This is due to cross grain fibers and adhesive.

Bending requires pressure. The sharper the curve's radius, the greater the required pressure. The pressure is usually supplied by a mold and clamps. The mold is the shape of the desired curve. Clamps or a press hold the wood to the mold. Gentle curves form with the aid of clamps or wedges. Sharp bends may require a hydraulic press and several tons of pressure.

Listen to and watch the material during the bending process. If a cracking noise can be heard, the bend radius is too sharp. You may have to plane the lumber thinner.

Wood bent dry must be held in place permanently by glue, joints, or mechanical fasteners. This method of holding the wood should be designed into the product. Stress is produced when wood is bent without moisture.

Moisture, heat, and chemicals make wood easier to bend. This is called *plasticizing.* Heat speeds up absorption of moisture by the wood fibers. After the wood is formed and left to cool and dry, it will closely hold the formed shape. Some *spring-back* is likely to occur. This is the wood's attempt to return to its orginal straight shape.

DRY BENDING

There are two ways to bend lumber dry. One is to bend the workpiece by hand and hold it in place with fasteners. The other is a process called kerfing.

Plain bending

Workpieces to be bent dry should pass a stress test. A sample is bent to the desired shape. If it cracks or splinters, plane the workpiece thinner and try again. Secure the bent wood with adhesive, trim, screws, or other fasteners.

Kerf bending

In *kerf bending,* you cut saw kerfs in one face of the wood. This allows sharper and easier bends than solid dry lumber. However, a kerf-bent curve is weak. It should be attached to another component, much as an apron is attached to a table top.

Three measurements control the bending radius. One is the width of the kerfs. This is determined by the saw blade. The second is the depth of the kerfs. Generally, these are cut to about 1/16 in. (1.5 mm) from the opposite surface. The third is the distance between kerfs. Making the kerfs too deep or too far apart is seen as a fold when the piece is bent. Cut kerfs in a scrap piece to test the bending characteristics of the wood you are using.

You can kerf bend convex as well as concave curves, Fig. 34-4. In both cases, cut kerfs in back (hidden side) of the workpiece. If both sides are visible, kerf the concave side. Bend the workpiece to the desired shape (when the kerfs close). Then overlay the kerf side with veneer.

When kerf bending, you must find three distances.
1. The circumference of the desired curve.
2. The length of lumber needed.
3. The distance between kerfs.

To demonstrate the kerfing procedure, let's make an apron for a round table. The table is 25 in. (635 mm) in diameter and has a 23'' (585 mm) apron. First calculate the circumference of the apron:

PLYWOOD BENDING		
PLYWOOD THICKNESS	**Parallel to Face Grain**	**Perpendicular Face Grain**
(in) (mm)	(in) (mm)	(in) (mm)
1/4 6.0	64 1626	20 508
3/8 9.5	88 2235	40 1016
1/2 12.5	112 2845	80 2032
5/8 16.0	152 3860	100 2540
3/4 19.0	216 5486	164 4166

A

MINIMUM BENDING RADIUS												
Thickness		Cold Wet Bends				Cold Dry Bends				Heated Bends		
		Out#		In#		Out#		In#		Out#		In#	
(in)	(mm)	(in)	(mm)	(in)	(mm)	(in)	(mm)	(in)	(mm)	(in)	(mm)	(in)	(mm)
1/8	3.0	7	175	5	125	12	300	10	250	2.5	62.5	2	50
3/16	4.5	10	250	8	200	18	450	16	400	3.5	87.5	3	75
1/4	6.0	15	375	12	300	27	675	24	600	5	125	4	100
5/16	7.5	22	550	18	450	35	875	30	750	7	175	6	150

B

Fig. 34-3. A—This table shows the dry bending radius for plywood. Wet bending could soften the adhesive and separate the layers. B—Both untempered and tempered high density fiberboard (hardboard) can be bent. The radius varies on whether the smooth side of the board is outside or inside the bend. Heat bending was done between 300 and 400 °F.
(Forest Products Laboratory)

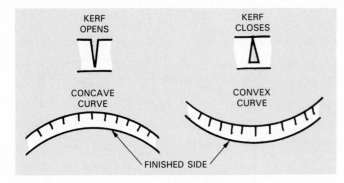

Fig. 34-4. Kerfs can be made for both concave and convex curves.

Circumference = Pi × diameter
                = 3.14 × 22 in.
                = 69 in.

You need to bend four individual pieces to make the entire curve. This means that each one will be 1/4 of the circumference, or 18 in. (457 mm). However, 3/4 in. tenons will be cut in the apron pieces to insert into the table leg mortises. Subtract the width of the table legs to determine how much of the apron piece is to be kerfed for bending. Each table leg is 2 in. (51 mm), making the bend length 16 in. (406 mm). See Fig. 34-5. Add on two 3/4 in. tenons and each piece is 17 1/2 in. long.

To determine the spacing between saw kerfs, proceed as follows. See Fig. 34-6.
1. Cut a test board the exact width and thickness, but longer, than the apron pieces.
2. From one end of the board, mark the distance of the radius of the curve (11 in. [279 mm] in this example).
3. Make a saw kerf at this point to a depth of 1/16 in. (1.5 mm) from the other face of the board. A radial arm saw works best.
4. Securely clamp the board with the kerf up. Place the end of the board with the table edge.
5. Lift the board until the kerf closes.
6. Measure the distance between the end of the board and the table. (Suppose it is 1 in.) This is the distance between kerfs.

Kerfs are easily cut using a radial arm saw. Set the saw blade 1/16 in. above the table. Cut the workpieces as follows:
1. Evenly space kerfs along the bent length. For our example of 16 in. bending length, the distance will be 1 in. from the end of the tenons and 1 in. between kerfs centers, Fig. 34-7. Mark kerf centers.
2. Set the saw 1/16 in. (1.6 mm) above the saw table.
3. Cut the kerfs.

Once the cuts are made, bend the workpiece to the proper radius and hold it in place with glue or fasteners.

A

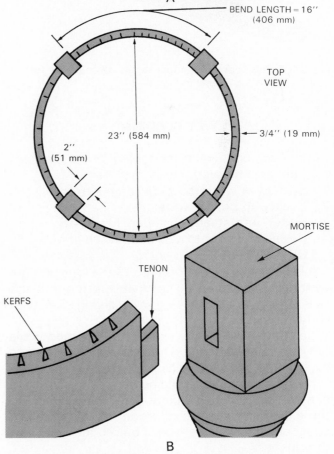

B

Fig. 34-5. A—This round lamp table has an apron attached underneath. (Bassett) B—The apron is made of four kerf bent pieces attached to the legs with mortise and tenon joints.

Bending and Laminating Wood 515

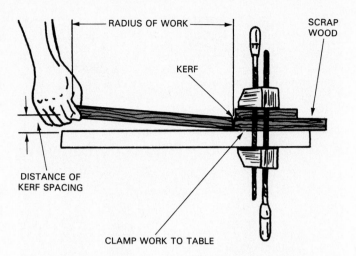

Fig. 34-6. The distance between kerfs is found by bending a sample piece of material.

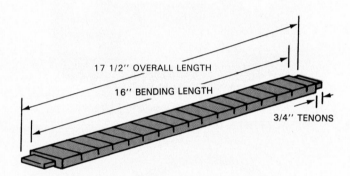

Fig. 34-7. This is one of the four kerfed apron pieces for the table in Fig. 34-5A.

WET BENDING

Wet bending involves softening, or *plasticizing,* the lumber. The workpieces may be:
1. Soaked in water at room temperature.
2. Soaked in boiling water.
3. Placed in a steam chamber, Fig. 34-8.
4. Wrapped in wet towels and placed in a 200 °F (98 °C) oven.

It is advisable to seal the ends of the wood before wetting. This limits moisture absorption into the cells and prevents checking while drying. Seal with varnish.

Separate workpieces with strips of wood while they are being softened. This lets moisture surround each piece of wood. The final moisture content (M.C.) of the wood should be between 20 and 30 percent for good bendability. The higher the M.C., the easier any species of wood will bend. Allow about one hour of steaming or boiling for every inch of thickness.

Several kinds of molds (forms) can be used to shape the moistened wood. Molds can be one-piece or two-piece. Wood is clamped to one-piece molds

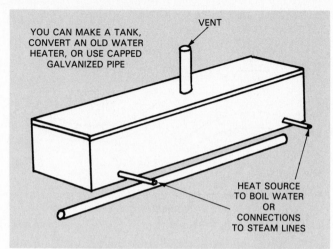

Fig. 34-8. For soaking or steaming wood, use a nonrusting container that holds water. If you will be using a direct heat source, make sure the container is nonflammable.

with clamps, blocks, or wedges, Fig. 34-9. The curve can also be maintained with a form and a band clamp to hold the wood to the form, Fig. 34-10. In a two-piece mold, the wood is held between male and female forms. See Fig. 34-14. Mold surfaces that will touch the workpiece should be covered, generally with plastic or sheet rubber. No nails or screws should penetrate the mold surfaces. They could rust and stain the wood.

Pressure should be kept on bent wood until it dries. This may take several days. Removing the pressure too soon results in spring-back. Drying time will vary for each kind of wood and the thickness of the workpiece.

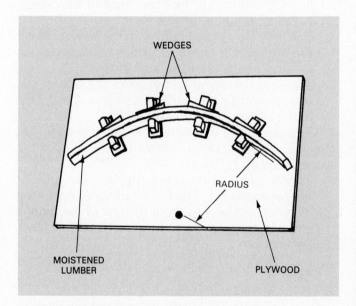

Fig. 34-9. The wood must be held in place until it is thoroughly dry. Here, wedge clamps and blocks are attached in a curve on a plywood base.

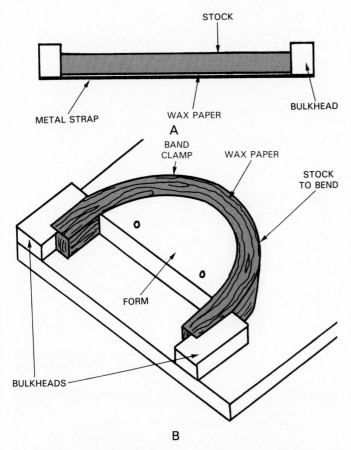

Fig. 34-10. A—When free bending, the ends are not contained. This allows the back of the wood to stretch. B—With end pressure supplied by bulkheads, the wood cannot stretch, only compress. The metal strap withstands the tensile force.

LAMINATING

Wood laminating is the process of bonding two or more layers of lumber or veneer. The layers may be clamped flat or molded into contours.

Laminating is done for several reasons.

1. A laminated component is typically stronger than the same size piece of solid lumber.
2. By alternating grain patterns, laminating helps stabilize dimensional changes. Solid wood has a tendency to warp.
3. Layers of wood can be bonded into curved shapes. These are stronger than the same shape cut from lumber.

Some of the more common laminations are tennis rackets, skis, and chair backs or seats. Most of these products could be cut from solid wood. However, because they must endure stress, bonded layers of wood are used. A wood beam is another example of a lamination, Fig. 34-11. A laminated wood beam may be stronger than the same size steel beam.

Most laminating of curved products is done with successive layers having the same grain direction. Thinner layers allow the wood to bend easier. Some

Fig. 34-11. This lamination will be an arch for a cathedral ceiling. (Forest Products Laboratory)

products, such as molded plywood, are two dimensional laminations. Here, each layer of wood is turned 90° from the previous layer. Although more difficult to form, two dimensional laminations are exceptionally strong.

SELECTING WOOD

Both softwoods and hardwoods can be laminated. Hardwoods have somewhat better bending characteristics. Softwoods are used primarily for structural laminations, such as beams and plywood.

For curved laminations, the amount of bend is affected by the defects and elasticity of the wood specie. This was discussed earlier in the chapter. Rigid woods tend to split, and would be poor choices for curved laminations.

Try to select straight-grained lumber without structural defects (knots, splits, and checks). These may split under pressure and weaken the strength of the lamination. If possible, identify the radial and tangential faces of the lumber, Fig. 34-12. It is better to use tangential faces for straight laminations because of wood's tendency to cup across that face. You will encourage the wood to warp when making curved laminations. For curves use either radial or tangential faces.

SELECTING ADHESIVES

Adhesives for laminating should have a long set time. Resin-type adhesives, such as urea resin glue, are the best. They have a lengthy set time, which gives you more time to position the wood layers. Casein glues are often used in industry for beams and other structural laminations. However, casein has a tendency to stain the wood.

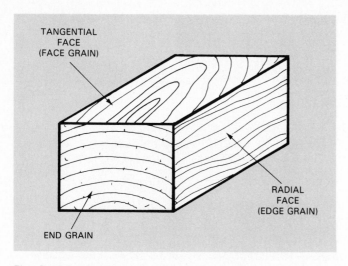

Fig. 34-12. It is important that you identify the three grain directions for proper laminating.

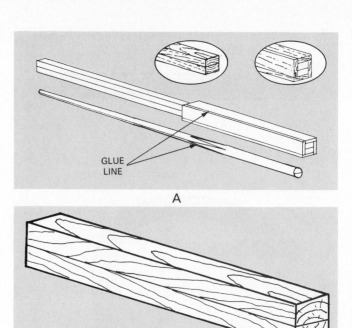

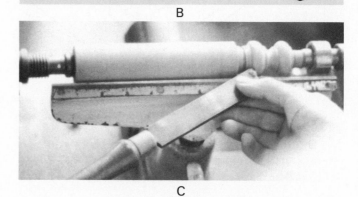

Fig. 34-13. A—A billiards cue is a lamination of several pieces of wood. The proper direction of the wood grain limits the amount the cue will warp. B—Two pieces to be turned into a spindle. Notice how the annual rings of the end grain oppose each other. This balances the warp of each piece of wood. C—Turning the laminated part. The guard has been removed to show the operation.

LAMINATING STRAIGHT COMPONENTS

With straight laminations, you increase strength and/or increase thickness. The more layers used, the less the lamination will warp. A common straight lamination is to make thick workpieces for turning spindles, Fig. 34-13. You might use two or more layers to build up the thickness. Follow this procedure:
1. Resaw or rip the material across the tangential face.
2. Cut workpieces slightly oversize, then plane them to size.
3. Reverse the direction of the annual rings (seen in the end grain) as shown in Fig. 34-13B.
4. Select the proper size and type of clamps.
5. Double spread the adhesive.
6. Follow the proper clamping procedure found in Chapter 33.

LAMINATING CURVED COMPONENTS

Curved workpieces can be made by sawing. This is adequate for slight curves. However, with sharper curves, there is more crossgrain material, resulting in a weaker product. As a result, it will break more easily. Laminating several layers of wood to obtain the curve will result in a much stronger product. Curved laminations are made one of three ways: full surface, partial surface, or segment.

Full surface, one direction curved laminations

When straight laminating, you alternated the grain pattern to prevent warpage. With *full surface, one direction laminations* you do just the opposite. Grain direction is not reversed so that curving of the wood is encouraged.

Cutting veneer. Curved laminations are made with veneer or thin strips. Most bending can be done with 1/8 in. thick layers. Generally, for one direction laminations, you cut material so it will be bent along its length. Flexible veneer can be cut with a scissors. (Before cutting, wet the veneer to prevent splitting.) Flat veneer is cut with a jig saw or band saw. Thin stock can be ripped or resawed with a table saw. Check the minimum bending radius, Fig. 34-2, to determine how thin the stock can be and still bend properly.

Sawed stock can be used but must be surfaced. This is a time-consuming task and wastes a great deal of wood. It may be more economical of both time and money to use veneer.

Preparing the mold. A mold is used to control the contour. It must keep pressure on the laminates until the adhesive cures. A one-piece mold with a web clamp may be adequate. You might also make an adjustable form out of plywood and wedge clamps. A two-piece mold works well for thin and thick laminations. See Fig. 34-14.

Molds should have rubber or plastic faces. This prevents damage to the wood and evens pressure across the surface. Lining the mold with wax paper or silicone spray prevents the adhesive from sticking.

Stacking layers. The method of stacking the layers is very important. For across-the-grain bending, look at the end grain. Stack layers with the growth rings parallel, Fig. 34-15. The curve of the rings should be opposite the curve of the mold. This is the natural cupping direction for lumber. To bend along the grain, look at the edge (radial) grain. Stack all layers with parallel radial grain.

Laminating procedure. The steps to follow when making curved, one direction laminations are:

1. Cut material oversize. Allow 1/2 in. (12 mm) extra across the curve and 2 in. (51 mm) or more extra with the curve. This allows material to form the curve and compensates for slippage when clamping.
2. Stack the components, without adhesive, and properly align the grain of each layer.
3. Clamp and bend the laminates against the mold without an adhesive. Release the clamps.

If the wood cracks or splinters when bent, you must either reduce the thickness of each layer, or preform the components by wet bending.

4. Line the mold with wax paper or mold release.
5. Apply a thin, even layer of glue to each matched surface.
6. Reassemble the layers.
7. Slowly tighten the clamps. Begin at the middle of the mold, then tighten outer clamps.
8. Allow the assembly to cure for at least 24 hours or the time given on the adhesive container.
9. Remove the lamination and scrape excess paper and glue from the surface.
10. Mark and cut the final shape using a band saw. Then sand and finish.

Full surface, two direction curved laminations

You can laminate gentle, two-directional curves using layers of veneer, Fig. 34-16. Each layer is turned 90° to the previous one. The two halves of the mold should be well matched. Otherwise, air pockets may remain between layers after the adhesive dries. A veneer press or hydraulic press will provide ample clamping power.

Partial surface laminations

A *partial surface lamination* is done when you want to curve only the ends or edges of a work-

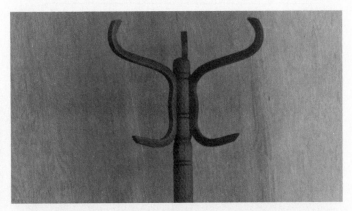

Fig. 34-14. Three two-piece molds were required to make the bent parts of the hall tree.

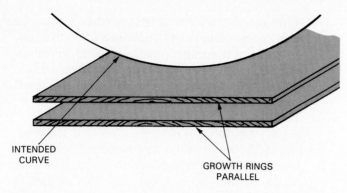

Fig. 34-15. Make sure the growth rings are parallel for curved laminations of veneer. The direction of the rings should be opposite the intended curve.

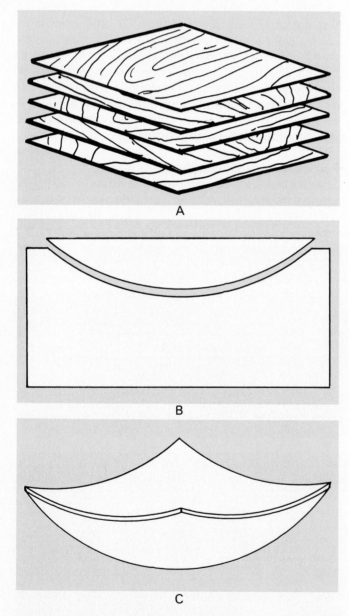

Fig. 34-16. Molded plywood. A—Successive layers of veneer should alternate grain pattern 90°. B—The two mold halves should match perfectly. C—The molded plywood will retain its shape without spring-back.

piece. An example is the tips of water skis. The procedure is as follows:

1. Make a series of resawing kerfs parallel with the face surface, Fig. 34-17A. At least two are needed, depending on the wood thickness.
2. Clamp the workpiece, without adhesive, in a mold. It should bend without excessive stress or splintering. Remove the clamps.
3. Fit pieces of veneer into the saw kerfs, Fig. 34-17B. They can fit snugly but not tight.
4. Remove the veneer and apply adhesive to all surfaces being bonded. Wet a cloth with adhesive. Pull it through the saw kerfs to coat them.
5. Slide the veneer into the kerfs.
6. Reset the clamps and tighten, Fig. 34-17C.
7. Allow the assembly to cure, Fig. 34-17D.

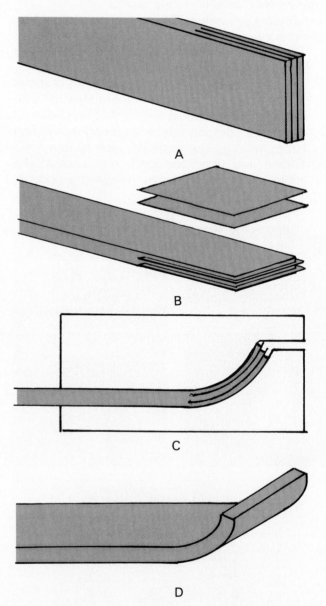

Fig. 34-17. Partial curved laminations. A—Kerfing. B—Inserting veneer in the kerfs. C—Gluing and clamping the lamination. D—Finished product.

Segment laminations

Segment laminations are curves built of rows of solid wood pieces. Each layer is staggered, much like brick laying, with a minimum of three layers, Fig. 34-18A. This way, there is no continuous joint from layer to layer. The procedure is:
1. Lay out a full-size pattern of the curve.
2. Establish the length of each segment. Select a length that covers both inside and outside layout lines.
3. Determine the angle for segment ends.
4. Saw all of the segments. Use a miter saw or table saw with a miter gauge.
5. Apply adhesive and assemble the segments on the layout.
6. Apply pressure until the adhesive dries. (Use hold-down clamps or place weight on the top layer.)
7. Saw the outer and/or inner segment curves on the band saw. You may not wish to saw a hidden side.

Another method is to curve the edge of each segment before assembling them. First make a template of one segment. Then saw all segments using a scroll or saber saw and the template. Assemble the components as you did in steps 5 and 6 above.

After the segment curve has dried, you should smooth it with a plane, scraper, and/or abrasives. Veneer may be applied to hide the segment joints.

THINK SAFETY—ACT SAFELY WHEN BENDING WOOD

Wood is bent using pressures which vary according to wood specie. Machine pressure may exceed 100,000 pounds. There is always a danger of the wood snapping or your becoming caught in a press. When bending wood:
1. Wear eye and face protection.
2. Wear heavy gloves.
3. Use care around heat and steam sources to avoid burns.
4. Stay clear of presses in operation.

SUMMARY

Bending and laminating are processes used to make curved components and thicker or stronger straight workpieces. These are involved processes and require skill in many areas of woodworking.

Bends can be made dry or with moisture and heat. Gentle curves can be made with relative ease. Sharp bends likely will require molds or forms and a source of pressure.

Bends made by laminating are much easier than bending solid wood. Layers of veneer can be coted with adhesive and held in a form until dry. Straight laminations are made to increase the size and/or thickness of a part.

CABINETMAKING TERMS

Wood bending, elasticity, plasticizing, springback, kerf bending, wet bending, free bending, wood laminating, full surface one direction lamination, partial surface lamination, segment lamination.

TEST YOUR KNOWLEDGE

1. When bending wood, fibers on the inside of the curve are _____.
2. Wet lumber is more elastic than dry lumber. True or False?
3. Bending wood dry is done by _____ or _____.
4. When kerfing, you must know the _____, _____, and _____.
5. Name three ways to plasticize wood.

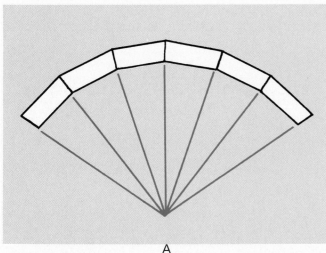

A

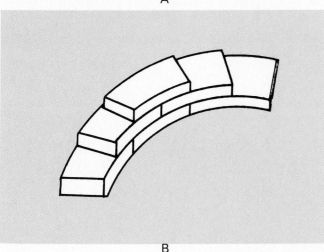

B

Fig. 34-18. A—Segment laminations made of bonded short wood pieces. B—The assembly is band sawed to the final curve.

6. Wet bending is done at moisture contents around:
   a. 50%.
   b. 25%.
   c. 15%.
   d. 10%.
7. To reach the proper moisture content for wet bending, you should steam or boil 2'' lumber about:
   a. 4 hours.
   b. 3 hours.
   c. 2 hours.
   d. 1 hour.
8. Resin-type adhesives are used for wood laminating because they:
   a. Set slowly.
   b. Contain solvents.
   c. Are brittle.
   d. Cure very rapidly.
9. Sketch the end grain patterns for laminating two pieces of wood when (a) you want the lamination to bend and (b) you want the lamination not to warp.
10. Segment laminating involves the use of:
    a. Long narrow strips of lumber.
    b. Rigid lengths of particleboard.
    c. Short lengths of lumber.
    d. Veneer.

Chapter 35
OVERLAYING AND INLAYING VENEER

After studying this chapter, you will be able to:
☐ Overlay surfaces with veneer.
☐ Edgeband panels with veneer or wood tape.
☐ Assemble decorative surfaces using parquetry.
☐ Inlay designs using marquetry and intarsia.
☐ Inlay bandings to create borders and geometric shapes.
☐ Prevent inlays from being discolored during finishing.

Overlaying and *inlaying* are methods of applying veneer or thin wood to enhance the appearance of a wood product, Fig. 35-1. The veneer or wood may be cut into decorative patterns, shapes, picture mosaics, and strips.

Fig. 35-1. Mahogany and prima vera veneers make these doors very attractive. (Lane Accents)

Overlaying includes veneering and parquetry. When *veneering,* you bond flat or flexible veneer to a core material. *Parquetry* is the art of arranging a geometric pattern of thin wood blocks, then bonding them to a core.

Inlaying involves making a recess in a wood surface and bonding veneer or thin wood in the recess. Like overlaying, there are two practices, marquetry and intarsia. *Marquetry* is inlaying veneer patterns. *Intarsia* is inlaying thin wood patterns, Fig. 35-2.

Bandings are strips of veneer on thin wood inlayed in the surface. They may be very decorative or simply a different wood specie.

The surface to be decorated is called a *core.* For overlaying, the material may be lumber, fiberboard, particleboard, or plywood. You cover the core completely. For inlaying, the core is surfaced, solid lumber, which will be visible around the inlay. Later, you will be applying finish to the inlay decoration and core.

MATERIALS, TOOLS, AND SUPPLIES

Overlaying or inlaying a surface involves cutting, assembling, bonding, and pressing the veneer or wood to the core. Select the proper cutting tools, adhesives, and clamps.

MATERIALS

The materials you need for inlaying and overlaying include a core and veneer (for marquetry and veneering) or thin wood strips (for parquetry and intarsia). The core material is usually cut to size before being decorated. It may be a single board or, in some cases, a completely assembled cabinet.

Veneer types were discussed in Chapter 14. For a quick review, there are two types of veneer. Flat veneer is usually 1/28 in. thick. Flexible veneer is typically 1/60 in. Veneer may be bought as dimensioned sheets or random sizes (you must splice these together). How the veneer was cut determines the grain pattern. Generally, rotary and flat slicing methods produce figured grain. Quartered and rift cut veneer have straight grain.

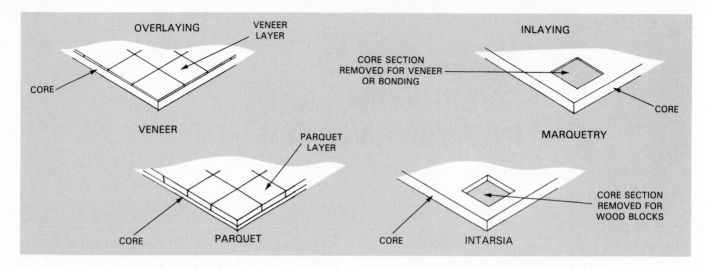

Fig. 35-2. Overlaying or inlaying processes vary according to the thickness of the material.

Veneer warps and distorts during storage due to moisture changes. To correct this, prepare a glycerine solution. Mix 2 oz. of glycerine to 1 qt. water. Apply the solution with a damp sponge. Immediately place the veneer between a sandwich of kraft paper (brown wrapping paper) and plywood. Clamp this setup for a few days. Change the paper daily. The glycerine makes the veneer flat, stronger, and more flexible. It does not affect the finishing characteristics.

CUTTING TOOLS

Veneer may be sheared or sawed. Shearing means to cut the veneer with a single-edge razor, scissors, or knife. Specialty veneer strippers and trimmers also are available. Sawing is done with a *veneer saw* or coping saw, Fig. 35-3. Veneer saws cut on both the push and pull strokes. For coping saws, use a fine-tooth blade and a pull stroke.

Fig. 35-3. A veneer saw is used for thick veneers. (Woodcraft Supply Corp.)

ASSEMBLING SUPPLIES

A few supplies will be needed when assembling veneers. *Gummed veneer tape* or masking tape will hold veneer pieces together. *Veneer pins* help align and hold materials in place. They are much like plastic head push tacks; however, they have very sharp points.

ADHESIVES

Choose adhesives depending on the needed set time. Resin-based, water solvent adhesives have a long tack time. They are used when you will need time to align the veneer. They also contain a slight amount of moisture which flattens wavy, dry veneer. Contact adhesives provide an instant bond. No clamps are necessary. Adjustments cannot be made after the decorative surface touches the core.

Contact cement tends to lose its bond when oil finish is applied to the veneer. To avoid this problem, coat the veneer with a glue size. This is a mixture of one part aliphatic resin or PVA glue to three parts water. Place the coated veneer between wax paper and plywood. Let the veneer dry a couple of days. The glue size strengthens the veneer, but does not affect the finish.

Hot melt glue is an alternative to liquid adhesives. Some dimensioned veneer has the glue already applied to the back. Glue sheets with glue on one side of a peel-off paper is also available. The veneer is aligned, then heated to melt the glue.

As a general rule, when applying veneer, use only a thin coat of adhesive. It may be applied by brush or roller. A thin adhesive coat should not penetrate the veneer's wood cells. If it fills cells, it reduces stain and filler penetration. Hide glue does this and is, thus, not appropriate for veneering.

PRESSING TOOLS

Pressure must be applied to the adhesive coated veneer to create a permanent bond. The pressure may be short term for contact cement or long term for other adhesives. Light, even pressure is all that is required. It must be maintained until the adhesive sets.

For contact cements, a *veneer roller,* or rolling pin works well to bond the veneer. For contours, place a sand bag over the veneer and strike it with a mallet, Fig. 35-4.

Resin adhesives require clamping or pressure until the adhesive cures. Hand screws, "C," and bar clamps are used for small areas. Use a veneer press for clamping large areas. For decorative overlays (parquetry), sand bags are sufficient. Place wax paper between clamps, core, and veneer. Otherwise, you might bond your work to the clamps.

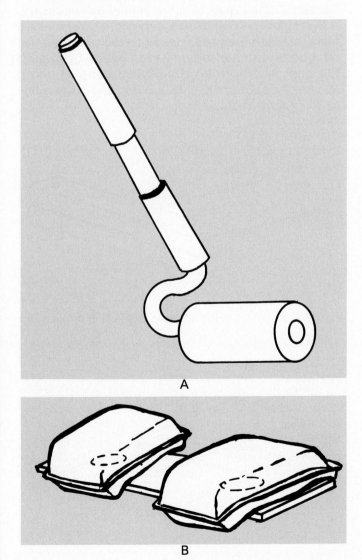

A

B

Fig. 35-4. A—This "J" roller works well for pressing veneers bonded with contact cement. B—Sandbags apply continuous pressure when resin-base adhesives are used.

OVERLAYING

Overlaying, including veneering and parquetry, adds thickness to the core material. By fitting pieces of veneer or wood together, you can create decorative patterns. Adding moulding or trim to the veneered product gives contour and protects the edges of the overlay.

VENEERING

Veneering is the process of covering a core with wood veneer. The finished core looks like solid lumber. Typically, the veneer is standard 1/28 in. (0.9 mm) flat veneer or 1/64 in. (0.4 mm) flexible veneer. Mostly, you will use hardwood species for veneering.

Veneering typically involves covering the entire surface. Groups of flitches (veneer pieces) may be fitted together to form matches. Various matches were shown in Chapter 14. You can also create geometric shapes or designs. Preassembled veneer pictures or designs are available from many woodworking suppliers.

Producing a veneered surface requires artistic ability, patience, and skill. Your artistic talents show when selecting flitches and laying out patterns. Patience and skill are necessary when cutting, trimming, and assembling the veneers.

Selecting flitches

Select flitches on the basis of grain pattern, defects, and overall appearance. For some surfaces, you will want matched grain forms. Try to obtain flitches in the order they were sliced from the log. The grain pattern will almost be identical. Sometimes, you might choose veneers of contrasting colors. They may be heart and sapwood of the same wood specie or flitches from different species.

Laying out patterns

Pattern layout depends on whether you will be using one or several flitches of veneer. If you are using one dimensioned sheet, there is little to lay out. Only mark the size to fit over the core. If you will be matching several flitches, lay out grain direction. You must determine the angle and size to cut the veneer, Fig. 35-5.

Cutting veneer

Always use a sharp tool and some kind of guide to cut veneer. Freehand cutting is discouraged. With a saw, use a wood straightedge as you do when back sawing. With a knife, use a metal straightedge, square, or metal template (for curves). Tape or pin the veneer to the table while cutting. Always cut veneers oversize to allow trimming.

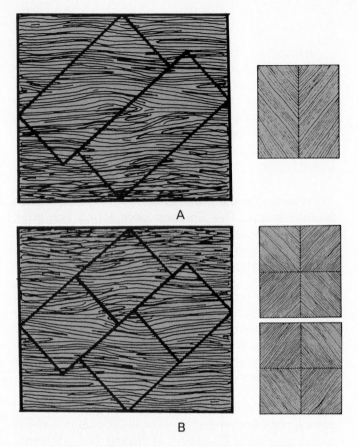

Fig. 35-5. A—Layout for "V" match. B—Layout for reverse diamond and diamond matches.

Cutting should not be done in one pass. This tends to split or splinter the veneer. It also crushes the wood cells. Light pressure on a knife or forward and backward saw motion is best. Several passes with the knife are necessary.

When cutting veneers which will be laid side by side, cut both at one time. Overlap them slightly and cut on the overlap, Fig. 35-6. This assures that adjacent pieces will match. Cutting them separately means you will have to trim and fit each of them.

Trimming

Place the veneers on a contrasting color surface. Surface color will show through where the veneers do not fit properly and need trimming.

Trimming straight edges is done with a sharp, small plane. The veneer is placed in a clamping jig to prevent it from bending, Fig. 35-7. First mark the section where the fit is poor, then clamp the material. Trim the flitch edge to the correct shape.

Curves can be trimmed with a sharp knife. Lay out the pieces as they will be assembled. Then trim them as necessary.

Assembling

Once the pieces are trimmed, place them together. Make sure all the joints fit. Now cover the joints (on the visible side) with masking or gummed veneer tape, Fig. 35-8. Press the tape firmly in place. Turn the panel over. Hold the assembled panel to a light and check for gaps between the flitches. Adjust or re-trim the veneer as necessary.

If you will be using resin-type adhesive, make a trial run. Place the veneer panel on the core material. (The core material should have already been cut.) Position clamps to be used when bonding. Then release the pressure evenly and lay the clamps aside in an orderly fashion.

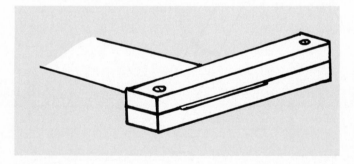

Fig. 35-7. Place veneer in a clamping jig before trimming it with a plane.

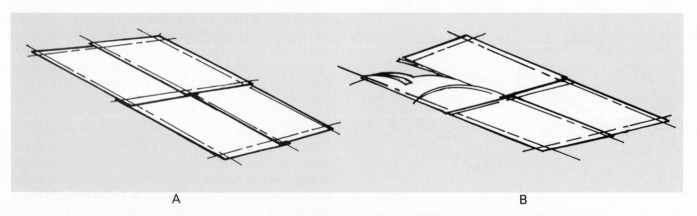

Fig. 35-6. The overlapping method of fitting veneers. A—The four flitches are overlapped slightly at the ends and edges. B—Cuts are made on the overlap to assure a perfect fit.

Fig. 35-8. Press the veneers together and apply masking or gummed veneer tape. The first pieces should pull the flitches together. A longer piece covers the joint.

Bonding

The bonding process involves first gluing the veneer edges, then applying the veneer to the core. Bonding to the core differs slightly for resin-type adhesives, contact cements, and hot glue.

Before bonding the veneer to the core, you should edgeglue the veneer sections together. Lift the assembly at each taped joint. Apply a small amount of adhesive to the edges, Fig. 35-9. Lay the assembly flat on its good face and wipe off the excess glue. Then proceed to bond the veneer to the core.

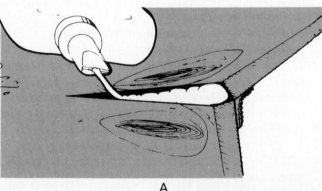

A

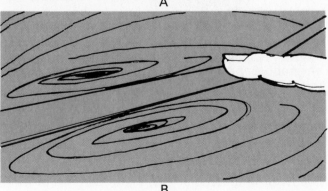

B

Fig. 35-9. Bonding flitches together. A—Bend the joint and apply glue. B— Lay the veneer flat on its face, wipe off excess glue, and apply tape.

Contact cement. Before applying contact cement, it is advisable to glue size the sheet as discussed earlier. Then apply a layer of contact cement to both the core and the back of the veneer. Let it set until a piece of paper will not adhere to the surface (approximately 10 to 15 minutes). The cement coating should be glossy. Dull spots require an additional application of cement.

Place dowel rods or a sheet of kraft paper over the core. Then lay the veneer panel, cement side down, on the paper. Position the veneer carefully, Fig. 35-10. Then, still holding the veneer, pull out the paper about 1 in. With a roller, press down on the exposed section of veneer to adhere it. Keep pulling out paper (or additional dowels) and rolling the veneer down until the entire surface is bonded. Then use extra pressure on the roller.

Resin glue. Coat both the core and the veneer panel back with adhesive. Place the panel on the core. Then clamp the assembly. Your assembly should be sandwiched between plywood to prevent damaging it.

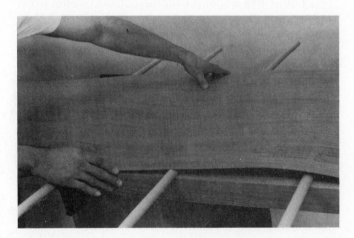

Fig. 35-10. Using dowels to separate veneer from the core. (Franklin International)

If you are using a veneer press, place the assembly, veneer side down, at the bottom of the press. Put wax paper between the press and the veneer. Clamp the panel snugly. Remove any excess glue. Let the panel cure for at least 24 hours.

Hot melt glue. Hot melt glue comes in sheet form or may already be applied to the veneer back. The sheet has one side of glue and the other is a release paper. Place the sheet, glue side down on the core, and heat it with an iron. Then pull off the release paper and place the veneer on the glue coating. Heat the veneer with an iron and apply pressure. For preglued veneer, simply place the veneer and heat it with an iron. Apply pressure to the heated areas while the glue cools. Otherwise bubbles may form preventing good adhesion.

Overlaying and Inlaying Veneer 527

Repairing

After removing any clamps, inspect the surface. You may see an obvious *bubble* or raised edge. Then tap on the surface with a fingernail. If you hear a dead or hollow sound, that area of veneer is loose. These locations need repairing.

There are two approaches to making repairs. First, try pressing a 300° to 350° iron on a piece of cloth over the loose area. Then apply pressure without the iron. This should correct veneers bonded with contact cement or hot melt glue. For resin-glued veneers, raise the edge or corner with a knife point. Apply more glue with a scrap of paper or sliver of wood. For regluing bubbles, make a knife cut on each side of the loose area. Cuts should be along the grain. Insert adhesive with a glue injector or paper scrap. A small cut on each side of the bubble prevents air from being trapped behind the glue. Reclamp the loose area.

EDGEBANDING

Edgebanding is an overlaying process in which you cover the edges of manufactured panel products. The panel faces typically have already been veneered. Panel edges should be relatively smooth. Generally, cutting the material with a sharp power saw blade will produce an acceptable edge.

You can either cut veneer for edgebanding or use manufactured *veneer tape.* Strips of cut veneer are bonded to the edge with adhesive and an edge clamp. The process is similar to veneering. Using veneer tape is easier. The tape is typically 3/4 or 1 1/2 in. wide. Some have a hot melt glue coating on the back. It is applied to the edges of the panel with an iron or with a tape lamination machine. Contact cement is used to apply veneer having no preapplied adhesive.

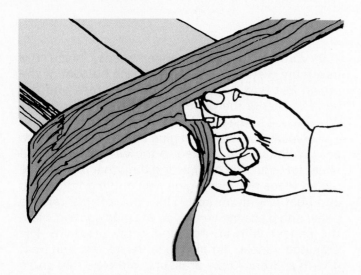

Fig. 35-11. Trim veneer tape with a single edge razor. Hold the razor against the surface.

To apply tape with an iron, clamp the panel with the edge facing up. Cut a strip of veneer tape about 2 in. longer than the edge. Use an iron set at the "wool" heat setting. Start at one edge, holding the iron on the tape. Then lift the iron and hold the tape down with a rag. This attaches one edge. Proceed toward the other edge, moving the iron along. Follow with a rag to apply pressure while the glue cools. Trim the excess tape from the edges and ends with a single edge razor blade, Fig. 35-11.

You can apply tape with a *tape lamination machine,* Fig. 35-12. First turn the machine on and let it warm for about 15 minutes. Thread the tape over the tension wheel and around to the front. Wrap the end around the leading edge of the panel to be edgebanded. Hold the leading edge against the heating element. Then slowly move the panel along the heating element and across the pressure roller. The tape should bubble as it leaves the heating element. Once the panel has passed the roller, snip the tape. It may be necessary to press down loose edges with an iron.

PARQUETRY

Parquetry is the process of bonding geometric wood blocks to a core. The blocks are attached to each other and to the core. They may be assembled independently or preassembled into components, Fig. 35-13. Parquetry differs from veneering because the material is thicker. Wood about 1/8 in. (3 mm) thick is recommended. (Parquet flooring will be even thicker.)

Decorative designs can be made two ways. One is by assembling wood blocks in different grain directions. The other is using contrasting colors of wood.

Parqueting involves several steps. They include:
1. Preparing a pattern.
2. Cutting the pieces.
3. Assembling the shaped pieces.
4. Bonding the wood pieces to each other and to the core.

Preparing a pattern

Most often, parquetry involves straight line geometric shapes. These are fairly easy to lay out on graph paper. Add lines or shading on the pattern to designate contrasting grain pattern or color in the wood.

Cutting

Saw blocks according to the pattern. They must be cut very accurately with a fine tooth blade. A hollow ground circular saw blade with 40 or more teeth is recommended. Cut about 25 percent more pieces than you require. Use only those with the most accurate dimensions and fewest defects.

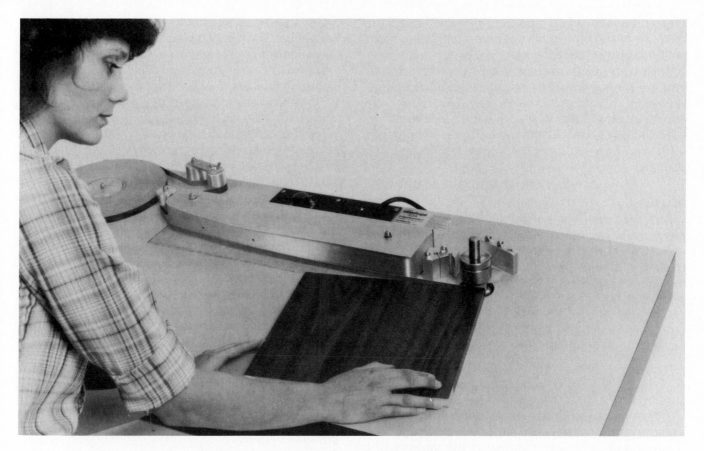

Fig. 35-12. Important components of a tape lamination machine. Note direction of feed. (Wood Tape, Inc.)

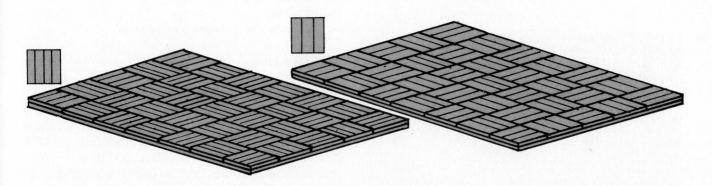

Fig. 35-13. Components consist of preassembled wood blocks. The components are then laid as a parquetry design.

Assembling

Small blocks, difficult to assemble separately, may be preassembled. Then bond the individual pieces or components to the core. First fit them without adhesive. Be sure even the smallest splinters are removed. Start at or near the center. Guidelines on the core are helpful for alignment. Clamp the assembly together. Band clamps may be selected because they exert pressure toward the center. You might also use bar clamps, but first place pieces of softwood around the assembly. This prevents the clamp from marring the sides and also evens out pressure along the assembly. Once the clamps are preset, release and set them aside. You will also need sandbags, a veneer press, or other pressure to bond the blocks to the core.

Bonding

Much time is required to apply adhesive to each joining surface. Therefore, coat only part of the core at a time. Then glue and fit that section of the blocks together. Remove excess adhesive from the section after the adhesive has set. Allow 10 to 15 minutes to assemble each section. Use slow setting adhesives when parqueting larger surfaces. Because of the time involved, preassembled parquet sections are recommended.

Select clamps for the surface, large or small, that you are parqueting. You might use a band clamp. However, it may need to be removed when the adhesive sets. Otherwise, the band could interfere with the block-to-core pressure. Cover the parquet with wax paper to prevent it from bonding to the clamps.

Mouldings

Most parqueted surfaces have a protective moulding surrounding the edge. This covers the end and edge grain of the parquet material. It also covers the edge of the core. (Styles of moulding were discussed in Chapter 11.) Miter cut the moulding and place it in position around the parqueted core. Check the fit at corners where two pieces meet. Apply adhesive on both the moulding and the parquet design, then apply clamp pressure.

ATTACHING CARVINGS

Carvings are precut, decorative overlays. They can provide an acccent to surfaces. You might put a carving on a cabinet door, or in the corners of a dresser. Many of the traditional styles use carvings on the cabinet surface. Queen Anne furniture is an example.

Fig. 35-14. The center shapes of this design show intarsia. The outer design consists of inlaid bandings. (The Woodworker's Store)

Carvings may be sculptured wood or molded wood fiber. Both may have the same shape and take stain and finish. However, sculptured wood carvings also have a grain pattern. This may be desirable to match the grain of the wood core.

To attach carvings, you must make a *stencil.* This allows adhesive to be applied only where the carving will be located. Trace around the overlay on a piece of thin posterboard or heavy paper. Then cut out the interior slightly smaller than the overlay itself. Tape the stencil where the carving will be located. Apply a thin coat of adhesive on the core through the stencil. Then lightly coat the back of the carving. Remove the stencil and attach the carving. Apply pressure with a sandbag or clamp. If contact cement was applied, you need only to press the carving in place.

INLAYING PRACTICES

Inlaying is a method of decorating a surface without adding thickness. The inlayed veneer or wood is placed in a routed recess (or inlet) in the core material. When veneer is used, this process is called marquetry. Setting thicker materials into the surface is called intarsia, Fig. 35-14. The inlaying process includes:
1. Selecting designs and veneers.
2. Laying out the pattern.
3. Cutting the wood.
4. Assembling the design.
5. Inletting
6. Bonding the design to the core.

MARQUETRY

Marquetry is the art of fitting together pieces of veneer to make a design. You can make marquetry patterns or buy the veneer pieces precut. Designs can be created by changing the grain directions of different veneer sections. Also, you may produce contrasting color designs by using several species of veneer, Fig. 35-15A. First prepare a sketch that shows grain direction and/or colors, Fig. 35-15B. Make as many copies of the sketch as you will use veneer types.

Marquetry pieces can be cut one of two ways: cutting each piece separately or by *overlapping.* The overlapping method is the easiest. One full size sheet of veneer is needed for each different grain pattern or color used in the design. You cut all the different pieces at one time. This assures that they will fit together. For example, suppose you wish to inlay three different veneers in a jewelry box lid.

Cut each veneer sheet 1 in. larger in each direction than the design. The excess holds the material together until cutting is complete. Flatten the veneer if it is wrinkled. (Use water or the glycerin solution

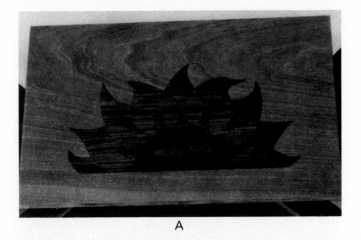

A

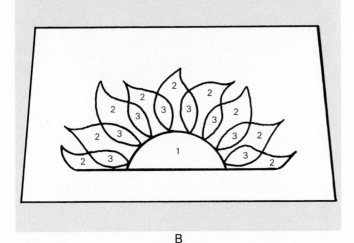

B

Fig. 35-15. A—This design was made by using different species of veneer. (Shopsmith) B—Pattern made to produce the design.

Fig. 35-16. Place the veneer between the pattern and a poster-board base. Tape the edges.

discussed earlier.) Stack the three sheets and tape them to a bottom layer of posterboard the same size. Tape your sketch on the top layer of veneer. See Fig. 35-16.

Make cuts using several passes with a sharp knife. Do not try to cut the entire stack with one pass. It may split or rip the veneer. Hold the knife vertical at all times. Cutting at an angle will make the pieces different sizes. Begin with the center piece. As you cut out the first shape, remove the three layers of veneer. Place them on the copied sketches. Continue to cut components from the center outward.

After cutting through the veneers, you will have enough components for as many designs as you have layers of veneer. (Three in this example.) To assemble the shapes, fit them together and place masking tape over the joints. Inspect the back side to see if components fit.

Place the inlay in an inlet in the core, Fig. 35-17. The inlet (or recess) will be as deep as the veneer. To cut the inlet, first position one piece of the excess (outer part of cut veneer sheet) on the core. Secure the edges with tape. Make knife cuts around the inside of the excess to the needed depth. Lift off the excess and router or chisel away the space the inlay will occupy.

Place the inlay in position. Be sure it is flat and even with the core surface. If it is above the surface, you must remove more material from the inlet. If it is below the surface, you must build up the low area. Spread wood putty or a white glue and sanding dust mix in the low area. Let this set before proceeding.

To bond the inlay in place, coat the inlay's back and edges and the inlet of the core with adhesive. Press the inlay in place and remove excess adhesive.

Fig. 35-17. Carve or rout an inlet to accept the inlay.

Put a sheet of wax paper over the inlay and apply pressure with clamps or sand bags. When the adhesive dries, remove the masking tape. Smooth and finish the surface.

INTARSIA

Intarsia is much like inlaying a parquet pattern. Thin blocks of wood are preassembled and placed in routed or chiseled inlet in a core material. Like marquetry, you can cut stacked wood layers. However, because of the thickness, you must use a band, saber, or scroll saw. Use the thinnest blade possible. The thickness of the blade determines how much space will be left between pieces. You might lay out and cut them slightly larger to compensate for the kerf. This means you must leave about 1/16 in. between the shapes on the design.

When cutting, start from one corner, not the center as you did with marquetry. Make cuts through all layers. As each shape is cut, place the layers on separate design sketches. Remember, you will have as many designs as you have layers of wood.

To assemble, hold all the components together on a contrasting color surface. Inspect them to see if trimming can reduce any spaces between workpieces. (You might spread filler in the spaces when finishing the product.) Tape the tops of each assembly. As you tape shapes together, brush adhesive on the edges. When finished, apply pressure to hold the assembled design together. (Consider using a band clamp, rubber band, or tied string.) After the assembly cures, trim and shape the outer edges.

Position the inlay on the core material and mark around it. Rout or chisel away the space the inlay will occupy. All sides of the inlet should be vertical or undercut.

To adhere the inlay, coat the inlay's bottom surface, edges, and the core inlet with adhesive. Position the inlay and apply pressure for the adhesive's set time.

INLAYING BANDINGS

Bandings are narrow strips of wood or asssembled veneer pieces. They may be overlaid or inlaid into an inlet to form borders or geometric designs, Fig. 35-18. Some contain metal and plastic for added color. Most are 1/28 in. thick and come in strips 36 in. long.

Applying bandings is a simple operation. First, rout out an inlet to the desired width and slightly shallower than the banding, Fig. 35-19. Position the bandings without adhesive. Overlap the bandings at corners and miter cut them with a knife. Glue the bandings in place. When the adhesive sets, lightly

Fig. 35-18. Bandings are inlaid around the outside of the game case. (The Woodworker's Store)

sand them until they are flush with the surface. Try not to make heavy cross grain scratches as you sand the inlay. Finish abrading with a very fine grit.

SPECIAL PRACTICES FOR FINISHING OVERLAID AND INLAID SURFACES

Finishing a decorated surface may be a special problem. Grain may run in several directions. There will likely be contrasting colors. For example, suppose you have a maple veneer banding to be inlaid in a walnut surface. The walnut will be stained and filled. However, you do not want the maple discolored. There are several approaches to solving this problem:

1. You can stain and fill the walnut surface without the banding. However, be sure not to get stain or filler in the banding's inlet. Stain and filler can fill the pores and add oil to the wood. Adhesive might not bond to such a surface.
2. You can seal the banding with shellac to prevent it from absorbing the color of the stain. Tape outside the banding to keep shellac off the walnut.
3. A third approach is to tape the banding when applying filler and stain to the walnut surface.

Another point to consider is sanding the surface before applying finish. Bandings and inlays often have grain running opposite to that of the core material. How do you keep from scratching the inlay? The easiest solution is to use a very fine grit (220 to 360) abrasive with a finishing sander. The scratches

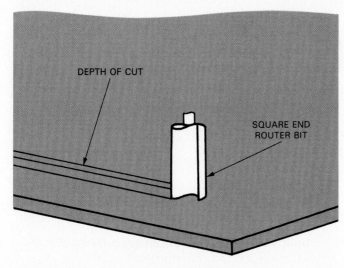

Fig. 35-19. Use a router bit the width of the banding to create a groove.

made are so small that they are hardly visible. However, you could also tape the inlay to prevent sanding it. Or, you could sand the pieces before adhering the banding. Simply hold the banding in its groove and sand it flush with the core. Then remove the banding and finish it and the core material separately.

SUMMARY

Overlaying and inlaying are surface decorating processes. For full surface veneering and marquetry use 1/28 in. veneer. Thicker material of up to 1/4 in. is used for parquetry and intarsia. Veneer tape covers the edges of panel products. Bandings provide decorative borders.

A few special tools and supplies are needed. They include a veneer saw, sharp knife, and possibly an iron or tape lamination machine. Supplies include veneer pins, masking tape, and adhesives.

Applying an overlay involves selecting the veneer, laying out the pattern, cutting, assembling, bonding, and pressing. Using this procedure, you can apply a decorative surface to an inexpensive core material. Applying an inlay requires many of the same processes, but includes inletting. Inletting is routing or chiseling a recess or groove in a solid hardwood core. Then, the assembled design is bonded into the recess.

Maintaining the color contrast from core to inlay can be a special problem. Some open grain woods may need staining and filling, while the inlay needs none. Where you do not want discoloration, apply shellac or tape to the surface.

CABINETMAKING TERMS

Overlaying, inlaying, veneering, parquetry, marquetry, intarsia, core, veneer saw, gummed veneer tape, veneer pins, veneer roller, flitch, edgebanding, veneer tape, tape lamination machine, carvings, stencil, overlapping method, bandings.

TEST YOUR KNOWLEDGE

1. Parquetry and intarsia are similar in that they both use _____.
2. When overlaying, you should select a solid hardwood core because it will be seen in the finished product. True or False?
3. Veneer flitches are held together during assembly with _____.
4. Why is hide glue not suitable for veneering?
5. Before bonding veneer with contact cement, you might apply a _____ to prevent the veneer from separating when oil-based finishes are applied.
6. List several uses for sandbags when overlaying and inlaying veneer.
7. How do you hold veneer when trimming it with a plane?
8. Tape on the back side of the veneer assembly should be removed before applying the veneer to the core. True or False?
9. Even though you may not see a raised edge or bubble, you can check for loose bonds by:
   a. Peeling off the veneer.
   b. Slipping a knife under the edge of the veneer.
   c. Tapping the veneer with your fingernail.
   d. Cutting through the veneer surface.
10. Describe two procedures to repair loose veneer bonds.
11. Edgebanding is most commonly applied to _____.
12. Patterns for parquetry can be preassembled. True or False?
13. Why must you make a stencil when attaching carvings with contact cement?
14. When using the overlapping method of cutting marquetry patterns, you will have as many complete designs as you have _____.
15. Two methods making an inlet (recess) in a core material are _____ and _____.
16. Bandings are the same thickness as veneer. True or False?
17. List several considerations you must make when sanding and finishing bandings, overlays, and inlays.

Chapter 36
INSTALLING PLASTIC LAMINATES

After studying this chapter, you will be able to:
☐ *Describe steps taken to prepare the surface for plastic laminate.*
☐ *Identify tools to cut rigid and flexible laminates.*
☐ *Select appropriate adhesives for applying plastic laminates.*
☐ *Follow the appropriate procedure to bond laminate to edges and surfaces.*
☐ *List the steps used to form materials around curves.*

Plastic laminates cover many modern cabinets. They provide a colorful, decorative surface resistant to water, chemicals, abrasion, impact, and normal household wear and tear, Fig. 36-1. These features make plastic laminates a desirable alternative to solid wood or veneer for countertops, tables, and cabinetry.

Fig. 36-1. Plastic laminates provide a clean, contemporary atmosphere to this kitchen. (Formica Corp.)

Plastic laminates are either rigid (phenolic resin and kraft paper composition) or flexible (vinyl composition). Both must be bonded to a *core material,* such as plywood, fiberboard, or particleboard. A solid lumber core is not recommended because it expands and contracts with changes in humidity. Plywood is the most sturdy. Install at least 3/4 in. thick exterior grade for horizontal surfaces and 1/2 in. (3/4 in. is recommended) for vertical surfaces. The sides to be laminated should be A or B grade with no surface voids. Particleboard cores should be at least 3/4 in. thick for both vertical and horizontal surfaces.

Most cabinet and countertop laminations are done with rigid laminates because of their wear resistance. The types of rigid laminates used for cabinet, countertop, and tabletop surfaces are:
1. *General Purpose Grade,* 1/16 in. (1.6 mm) thick, is for horizontal surfaces subject to wear.
2. *Vertical Grade,* 1/32 in. (0.8 mm) thick, is for vertical surfaces.
3. *Post Forming Grade,* 1/20 in. (1.3 mm) thick, can be heat-formed around curves.
These and other grades are discussed in detail in Chapter 14.

PREPARING THE SURFACE FOR LAMINATES

For a laminate to stay bonded, the core material must be stable. It cannot expand or contract. Likewise, the surface must be smooth, sealed, and joints must be secure.

Most surfaces consist of two or more joined components. If these shift, the plastic might delaminate. Secure core materials using one of the joints discussed in Chapter 29. An edge rabbet or tongue and groove is recommended; however, a butt joint is often used. It is also a good idea to attach a 4 in. wide wood *cleat.* Place the cleat over the joint underneath the core, Fig. 36-2. The core's surface should remain smooth across the joint.

The surface to be covered with laminate must be clean. Adhesives used for laminating, usually contact cements, will not bond to oily, moist, or dirty

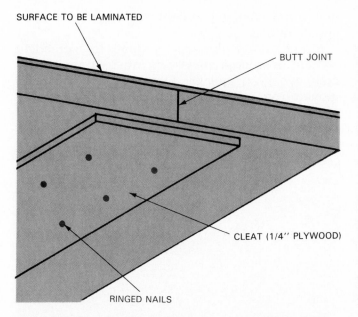

SURFACE TO BE LAMINATED

BUTT JOINT

CLEAT (1/4'' PLYWOOD)

RINGED NAILS

Fig. 36-2. If the back side of the core joints will be hidden, fasten a cleat for extra strength. Laminate joints must not align with core joints.

surfaces. When in doubt, wipe the surface with cement solvent. You may have to sand the surface if the dirty area will not come clean.

CUTTING LAMINATES

Laminates are cut to approximate sizes before being adhered to the core. Both hand and power tools will cut rigid and flexible laminate. Tools that are commonly used are hacksaws, compass saws, saber saws, table saws, shears, and routers, Fig. 36-3. You can also score and fracture rigid laminates as you would glass.

CUTTING RIGID LAMINATES

Power equipment should be fitted with carbide edge blades and cutters. The denstiy of laminate will quickly dull ordinary steel cutting edges. For table saws, use hollow ground circular saw blades. Raise the blade as high as it will go. The saw teeth should enter the laminate at as close to a 90° angle as possible. Be aware of the hazards a raised blade can cause. Always use a guard.

Make sure the cutting edge of the tool enters the decorative side of the laminate. For most saws, the decorative side should be up. For a saber saw, the back side is up. When the cutting edge exits, it has a tendency to chip the material. Chips on the back side of the laminate are not visible.

Select a sheet size that will more than cover the entire surface. Laminates are cut 1/4 (6 mm) to 1/2 in. (12 mm) or more oversize. The excess is later trimmed off with a router or *laminate trimmer*

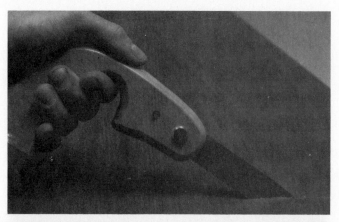

Fig. 36-3. Laminate can be cut with a number of tools. The saw teeth must enter the decorative side of the laminate on the cutting stroke. Guard was removed to show operation. (Franklin International)

to produce a smooth edge. However, when two pieces will be butted against each other, an accurate cut is necessary. This is done with a router. The adjacent laminates are overlapped and clamped. Make the cut through the overlap using one of the clamp boards as a guide, Fig. 36-4.

CUTTING FLEXIBLE LAMINATES

Flexible vinyl laminate is easier to cut than rigid laminates. Use scissors, shears, or a utility knife. Leave excess as you do with rigid laminate.

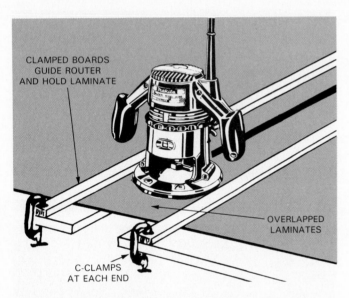

Fig. 36-4. Laminate butt joints are made by overlapping the laminates. Cut through the overlap with a straight router bit.

APPLYING ADHESIVE

Contact cement is the primary adhesive for laminating. It bonds quickly, and if the laminate and core are clean, will last many years without delamination.

Before using any cement, read the label. It may contain safety information and application instructions. Chlorinated and water-base cement can be brushed, sprayed, and troweled on with a fine notch spreader. Solvent-type cements can be applied the same way but spraying requires that you purchase spray grade cement.

The temperature and humidity of the room can affect bonding. The temperature should be no lower than 65 °F. The relative humidity should be between 35 and 80 percent.

Stir the cement thoroughly, then apply an even double spread to the core surface and laminate back. If you apply too little cement, or if a porous core material absorbs it, the adhesive film will appear dull. In this case, apply a second coat to the

dull spots. When the cement sets, the surface should appear glossy.

A fine notch spreader is good for spreading cement over large areas, Fig. 36-5. It applies cement evenly and quickly. Excess cement can be removed from surfaces and tools with solvent.

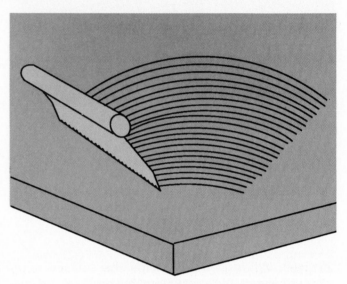

Fig. 36-5. Spread cement evenly across core and laminate back. (Franklin International)

Flexible plastic laminates may have a hot-melt glue or *pressure sensitive backing.* Those with hot-melt glue are applied by warming them with an iron. Those with pressure sensitive adhesive are installed by removing a plastic backing. Then the laminate is pressed in place. This is similar to using contact cement. The core material must be sealed with a shellac, varnish, or lacquer sealer coat before applying these two adhesives.

INSTALLING LAMINATES ON FLAT SURFACES

The order in which you apply laminate to surfaces and edges depends on which face receives the most wear. Generally, you apply a laminate edge before applying a surface, Fig. 36-6. This is done because the top surface receives the most wear. You can purchase precut edge strips, called edgebanding, which are 13/16 in. wide for 3/4 in. thick cores and 1 9/16 in. wide for 1 1/2 in. cores. The edgebandings are 1/16 in. wider so you can trim them.

The edges of doors and drawers are also laminated before the surface. The front surface covers all of the edges. When the door or drawer is closed, seams are not visible.

Edges. Follow this procedure to apply edges:
1. Cut the edge piece slightly oversize so it can be trimmed later. Purchased edgebandings are

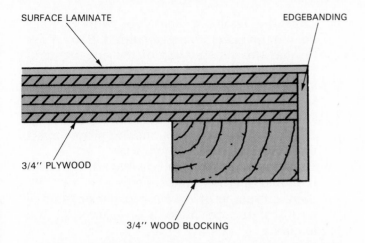

Fig. 36-6. Surface laminate overlaps the edgebanding. The 3/4 in. wood blocking is for appearance. It makes the table top look thicker.

already oversize. Butt joints between two strips can be made by overlapping them. Then cut through the overlap with a thin blade hacksaw. The ends should match well. If not, file them.

2. Coat both the laminate back and the core edge with cement. Keep them separated.
3. Allow the cement to set. Test with a piece of kraft (brown wrapping) paper. The paper should not stick to the dry adhesive.
4. Position the laminate over the core. Make sure the laminate hangs over the core edges, Fig. 36-7A.
5. Press the laminate against the edge.
6. Apply pressure by rapping a hardwood block with a mallet or hammer, Fig. 36-7B.

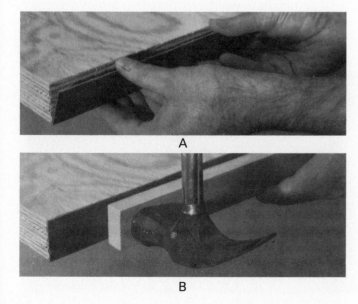

Fig. 36-7. A—Position the edge carefully. Make sure it covers the core thickness. B—Once positioned, rap the laminate to assure a good bond. (Franklin International)

7. Trim the excess laminate with a laminate trimmer, router, or mill file. The edge should be trimmed flush with the surface, Fig. 36-8.

There are times when you do not apply edges before surfaces. This is when a solid wood, metal, or plastic edge will be installed. In this case, the top (and possibly a bottom) surface is applied. Then the edge is placed over or flush with the laminate, Fig. 36-9.

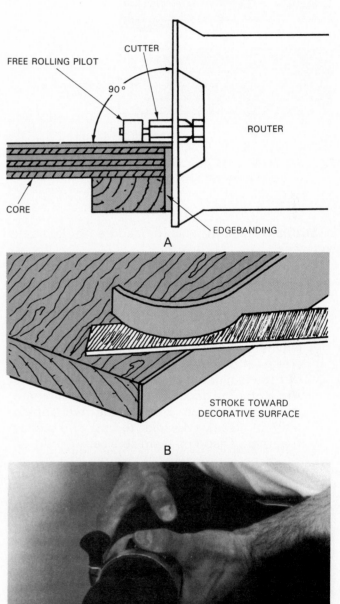

Fig. 36-8. A—The pilot keeps the cutter flush with the surface as you move the router along the edge. B—Excess material can also be removed with a mill file. C—Using the router.

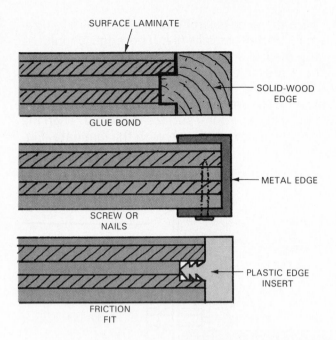

SURFACE LAMINATE

SOLID-WOOD EDGE

GLUE BOND

METAL EDGE

SCREW OR NAILS

PLASTIC EDGE INSERT

FRICTION FIT

Fig. 36-9. Surface laminates are bonded before applying wood, metal, or plastic insert edges.

Surfaces. Follow this procedure to laminate surfaces:

1. Measure the surface to be covered. Purchase a single sheet of laminate larger than the surface. Cut it 1/2 in. (12 mm) wider and longer than the surface.
2. For irregularly shaped surfaces, lay the laminate on the surface. Mark it 1/2 in. oversize with a grease pencil.
3. Cut the laminate. Make sure the teeth of the saw enter the decorative side of the laminate on the cutting stroke. Use the overlapping method discussed earlier to butt two pieces together. Then cut them to size.

4. Coat the laminate and core with contact cement and keep them separated. Remember to coat the visible edge of the edgebanding applied earlier. Let the cement set.
5. Place dowel rods or a layer of newspaper on the core.
6. Position the laminate on the rods or paper, Fig. 36-10A. This keeps the mating pieces apart until you are ready to join them.
7. Place the laminate over one edge of the core. It should overhang the edge by about 1/2 in. Slide out some of the newspaper or remove a dowel rod to bond one section of the laminate.
8. Continue to slide out the paper or remove dowels until the entire laminate is bonded, Fig. 36-10B. At this stage, the laminate can no longer be adjusted.
9. Apply pressure with a J-roller or rolling pin to remove air pockets and fully bond the laminate, Fig. 36-11. Roll from the center to the edges. The more pressure you apply, the better the bond.
10. Trim the laminate overhang with a router (or laminate trimmer) and flush cutter, Fig. 36-12A. Rub petroleum jelly on the edge. This protects it from burning when the cutter's pilot is held against the edge. You can also trim with several hand tools that score and fracture the laminate, Fig. 36-12B.
11. Bevel the corner about 20°. This can be done with a router or file, Fig. 36-13. Beveling removes the sharp corner and extends the wear life of the laminate edge.
12. If necessary, sand the bevel with 180 grit abrasive wrapped around a wood block.

After laminate has been installed, remove excess adhesive. Either rub it off with your fingers or wipe it off with a rag soaked in solvent. (Be careful not

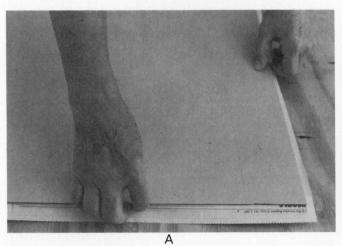

A

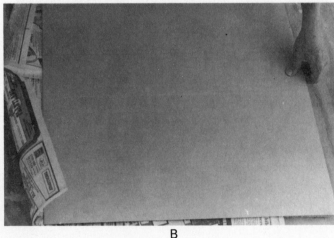

B

Fig. 36-10. A—Position the laminate on the core and separate them with paper. B—Proceed to bond the laminate by sliding out the paper.

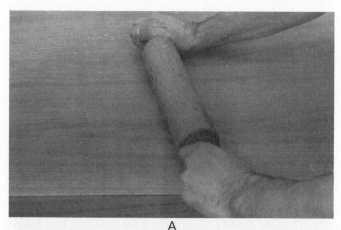

A

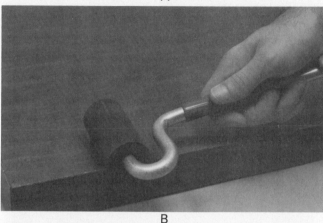

B

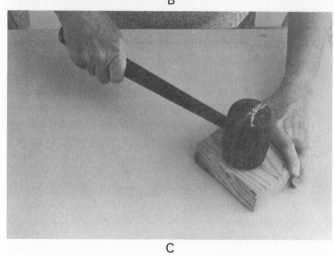

C

Fig. 36-11. A—With a rolling pin, roll outward from the center to remove air bubbles. B—You can apply more pressure to the ends with a J-roller. C—Rap the surface with a wood block and hammer. (Franklin International)

to let solvent enter joints between laminate pieces.) Then use soap and water or alcohol to restore the original finish.

If a bubble forms in the laminate, place newspaper over it and press with an iron set at "silk." Press until heat penetrates the entire area. Lower the heat setting if the newspaper scorches. Remove the iron and apply pressure with a J-roller until the area cools.

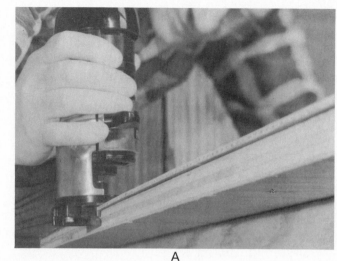

A

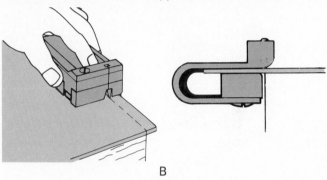

B

Fig. 36-12. A—A hand held laminate trimmer is efficient for trimming the surface flush with the edge. (Delta International Machinery Corp.) B—Hand trimmers score the surface. The waste is broken up and off, leaving an unchipped edge which may need filing. (The Woodworker's Store)

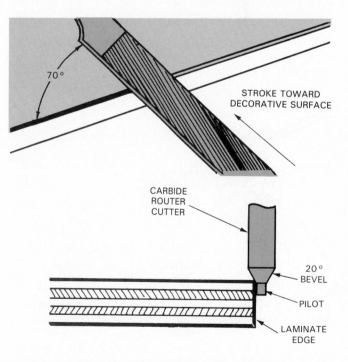

Fig. 36-13. Bevel the surface laminate 20° with a bevel cutter or mill file. (Franklin International)

FORMING CURVES

Cabinet surfaces and edges are not always flat. You may have to apply laminate to a curved table or countertop edge, Fig. 36-14. The procedure is as follows:

1. Select post forming grade laminate.
2. Cut the laminate oversize to allow material for the curve.
3. Coat the core and laminate with contact cement. Place newspaper over the core.
4. Position and bond one end of the laminate.
5. In one hand, hold a warm (300°F.) iron to the laminate. (A heat lamp can also be used.) With the other hand, pull the laminate around the curve, Fig. 36-15.

6. When a section of the laminate has formed around the curve, remove paper under that section and bond the plastic. Apply pressure with a roller.
7. Continue to heat, form, bond, and roll the laminate until the entire curved surface is complete.
8. Trim as necessary.

SUMMARY

Plastic laminates are an alternative to solid wood or veneer surfaces. They are durable, decorative, and relatively easy to apply. You can cut laminate with hand and power saws, or you can score and fracture it much like glass. The tool you select depends on whether the laminate is rigid or flexible. To bond the plastic, coat it and the core material with contact cement. Apply a generous, but even, layer and allow it to dry to the touch. Once the laminate contacts the core, it cannot be adjusted. Place newspaper or dowel rods between them while you position the sheet. Excess laminate can be trimmed with a laminate trimmer, router, hand trimmer, or mill file.

CABINETMAKING TERMS

Core material, wood cleat, laminate trimmer, pressure sensitive backing.

TEST YOUR KNOWLEDGE

1. A solid lumber core is recommended in environments with high humidity. True or False?
2. A loose joint between two core pieces could cause the laminate to _____.
3. The cutting edge of a saw should enter the decorative side of the laminate. True or False?
4. The most appropriate adhesive for applying plastic laminate is:
   a. Polyvinyl.
   b. Contact cement.
   c. Resorcinol.
   d. Aliphatic resin.
5. Applying an uneven layer of adhesive could cause _____ and _____.
6. In general, should the edge or surface laminate be applied first?
7. After applying edgebanding, trim it at a 20° angle. True or False?
8. Why should you place dowels or newspaper between the core and laminate after they have been coated with contact cement?
9. What grade of laminate should you choose when planning to heat-form it around a curve?

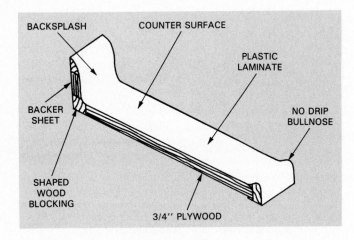

Fig. 36-14. Many modern counter surfaces consist of a single sheet of laminate. It must be formed around the backsplash and no drip bullnose. Purchased countertops are factory formed.

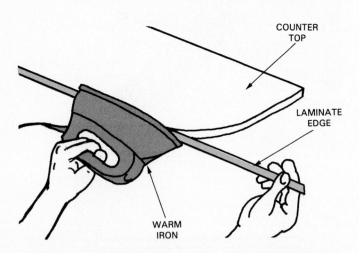

Fig. 36-15. Heating a post forming grade laminate makes it flexible. Pull the laminate around the curve and press it against the core.

Plastic laminate is available in a variety of colors and finishes. (VT Industries, Inc.)

Chapter 37
CANING AND BASIC UPHOLSTERING

After studying this chapter, you will be able to:
- Select caning materials, tools, and supplies.
- Install cane webbing in a chair frame.
- Identify conventional, basket, open, and closed weaves.
- Weave cane in a frame.
- Weave a conventional rush design.
- Upholster a slip seat.

Caning and upholstering are methods of creating a soft covering on furniture. Caning consists of weaving a design using cane, reed, or rush. Upholstering refers to completely covering a surface with fabric, leather, or vinyl.

CANING

Caning is the process of weaving a fibrous bark material into decorative patterns. Cane is woven for chair seats, backs, and decorative covering on doors and panels, Fig. 37-1.

For centuries, cane, rush, and reed have been used in furniture making. These materials were first introduced to reduce the weight of furniture. Instead of installing a panel inside a frame, cane was woven through the frame. Cane is widely used today because its natural blond color blends with many contemporary furniture styles.

Fig. 37-1. The color of these caned chair backs blends with the light oak color of modern furniture. (Thomasville)

MATERIALS

Caning is done with cane, reed, and rush. *Cane* comes from the rattan palm, which has long, slender stems. This palm is also the source of rattan furniture. The outer bark of the stem is stripped off and dried. The outer surface of the bark is hard, smooth and shiny. *Reed* comes from another specie of palm which grows in warm moist climates. The plants are stripped of their leaves and bark. Then they are split, shaped, and dried. Reed has a softer, duller, and more porous surface than cane. *Rush* is the name given to many stemlike plants of the sedge family. (Cattail is a member.) When the plant leaves dry, they are cut off and twisted together. Cords of rush are sold as "twisted fiber rush."

Cane is cut into several widths for different purposes. *Chair cane,* used for most weaving, is 1/16 in. (2 mm) to 9/64 in. (3.5 mm) wide. These sizes are named as shown in Fig. 37-2A. It is sold in 1000 ft. hanks. Chair cane is woven through holes drilled in the frame around an opening. *Binding cane* is 5/32 in. (4 mm) to 1/4 in. (6 mm) wide, Fig. 37-2B, and sold in 500 ft. hanks. It is installed over the edges of woven chair cane to hide the holes in the frame.

Reed is cut into several shapes and sizes. *Flat reed, flat oval reed,* and *round reed* are used for weaving, Fig. 37-2C. They are 3/16 in. (5 mm) to 5/8 in. (16 mm) wide and sold in 1 lb. hanks or 55 lb. bales. Round reed is 3/64 in. (1.25 mm) to 3/16 in. (5 mm) and is sold in 1 lb. coils. Reed is woven around the frame.

Rush, or *twisted fiber rush,* is made into 5/32 in. (4 mm) and 3/16 in. (5 mm) cords, Fig. 37-2D. It is wound around spools and sold by weight. Usually, 2 lbs. of rush are needed for an average chair seat. Rush, like reed, is woven around the frame, not through holes drilled in the frame.

Most of today's caning is done with *webbing,* which is prewoven cane and/or reed. Weaving single strands of cane and reed is simply too time consuming. Webbing is machine woven into many designs, Fig. 37-3. It is made into 14 in. (350 mm)

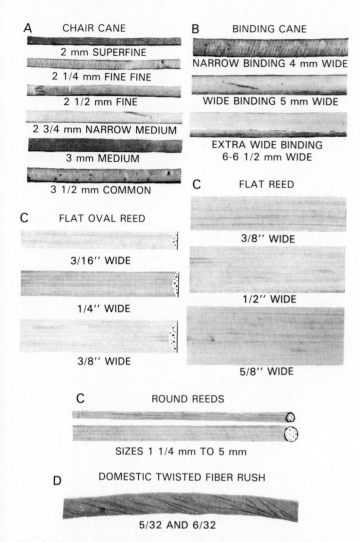

A CHAIR CANE

2 mm SUPERFINE

2 1/4 mm FINE FINE

2 1/2 mm FINE

2 3/4 mm NARROW MEDIUM

3 mm MEDIUM

3 1/2 mm COMMON

C FLAT OVAL REED

3/16'' WIDE

1/4'' WIDE

3/8'' WIDE

C ROUND REEDS

SIZES 1 1/4 mm TO 5 mm

D DOMESTIC TWISTED FIBER RUSH

5/32 AND 6/32

B BINDING CANE

NARROW BINDING 4 mm WIDE

WIDE BINDING 5 mm WIDE

EXTRA WIDE BINDING
6-6 1/2 mm WIDE

C FLAT REED

3/8'' WIDE

1/2'' WIDE

5/8'' WIDE

Fig. 37-2. A—Chair cane is identified by name and size. B—Binding cane comes in three widths. C—Three styles of weaving reed. D—Twisted fiber rush is made into cords. (The Otto Gerdau Co.)

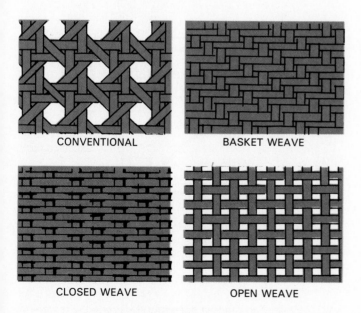

CONVENTIONAL   BASKET WEAVE

CLOSED WEAVE   OPEN WEAVE

Fig. 37-3. These are the four most common designs for webbing and for weaving loose cane.

to 24 in. (500 mm) wide sheets and sold by the square foot. *Spline reed,* another reed shape, holds webbing in a groove. The groove is made in the frame around the opening to be caned. Spline reed is a wedge shape, Fig. 37-4. It is specified by three dimensions: height, width across the top, and width across the bottom. The most commonly used spline reed is 3/16 in. (4.75 mm) x 5/32 in. (4 mm) x 3/32 in. (3.25 mm).

The biggest concern you have when caning is moisture control. Cane, reed, and rush strands must be woven, or installed, while wet. Moisture makes fibrous materials more flexible. If they are not damp enough, pulling a strand around a sharp curve might crack it. However, leaving these materials in water too long will discolor them.

Moisture serves another purpose. It expands the material. When the woven strands or webbing are dry, they shrink and tighten the weave. This is why you do not have to pull the strands as tight as you want the completed seat.

The dry cane, reed, and rush can be finished like wood. However, apply stain to the wood frame first. Stain the cane after it is installed. Then, a suitable topcoating can be applied to both the wood and cane. You may prefer to leave the cane unfinished.

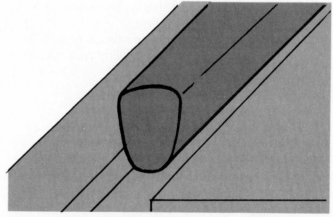

Fig. 37-4. Spline reed is shaped so it wedges into a groove made in the frame. (The Otto Gerdau Co.)

TOOLS AND SUPPLIES FOR CANING

Few tools are necessary to install cane, reed, and rush. For webbing, you need scissors or tin snips, a mallet, and a small chisel. Supplies include *caning wedges* and hide or aliphatic resin (yellow) glue. For weaving loose cane, you also need a scratch awl and *caning pegs.* The wedges and pegs, Fig. 37-5, hold stretched cane during installation. A sponge or cloth and water should be handy for keeping the cane moist.

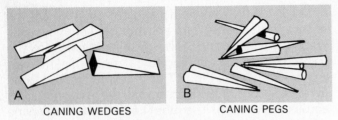

CANING WEDGES   CANING PEGS

Fig. 37-5. A—Caning wedges hold webbing in place. B—Caning pegs hold single strands of cane during weaving. (The Woodworker's Store)

INSTALLING CANE WEBBING

Webbing is installed in a groove in the frame. A spline reed holds the webbing in the groove, Fig. 37-6. Cut the groove before measuring the webbing. It should be about 3/16 in. (4.5 mm) wide and 3/8 in. (9 mm) deep. These dimensions accommodate the most common size spline reed. If you are using a different size spline, cut the groove so the spline fits loosely in the groove. Rout the groove about 5/8 to 3/4 in. (16 to 19 mm) from the inside edge of the frame. An easy way to do so is first make a hardboard template. Rout around the template with a straight shank router bit and template guide. You could also use a chisel.

Draw a pattern of the groove on heavy paper (or use the template if you made one). Place the pattern on the cane and cut the webbing about 1 in. (25 mm) larger in all directions.

Soak the cane in warm water about two to four hours. It will absorb water, expand slightly, and become pliable. An alternative method is to soak the cane in a *glycerin solution* for about 20 minutes. Make the solution 1 1/2 tablespoons (20 mL) glycerin to 1 cup (250 mL) water. Soaking the cane too long will cause it to darken.

Prepare caning wedges while soaking the cane. You will need one for every 3 in. (75 mm) of the groove. Make them about 1 in. long with the narrow end of the wedge slightly smaller than the width of the groove.

Cut spline reeds. Prepare enough reed to fill the total length of the groove. Spline reed will bend around circular frames or curves on irregularly shaped frames. For rectangular frames, cut one reed for each side 1 in. longer than the groove lengths.

Remove the cane panel from the water. Place it between layers of paper or a towel to absorb excess water. Then center the cane panel over the opening. Make sure you align the strands with the edges of the opening.

Next, install wedges in the groove to hold the webbing. Wet the end of a wedge. Position it in the groove at the back of the frame. Tap the wedge against the cane and into the groove, Fig. 37-7A. The wedge should be snug and about half way in-

Fig. 37-6. Spline reeds should fit loosely in the groove. Later, they will be pressed over cane into the groove to bond the webbing.

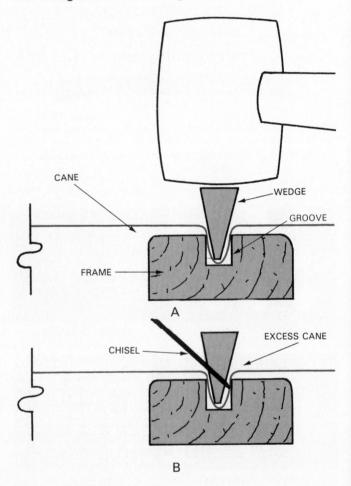

Fig. 37-7. A—Tap the wet cane into the groove with caning wedges. B—Remove wedges when cutting off excess cane with a chisel.

to the groove. Insert additional wedges in the center of the front, then the sides. Proceed to install more wedges at 3 in. (75 mm) intervals, working from the center toward the corners.

Excess cane will be left around the outside of the groove. Remove loose strands from the panel which are outside the wedges. Then cut the remaining loose strands with a chisel and mallet. Cut them 1/8 in. below the top of the groove, Fig. 37-7B. At this point, check the dampness of the webbing. If it feels dry, wipe it with a wet sponge.

Now install the spline reed. For circular frames, begin in the least visible place. For rectangular frames, begin at one corner. First miter one end of each length of reed. Soak them in water for a few minutes. Then wipe them to remove excess water. Remove a corner wedge and spread glue in the open groove. Position the mitered end of the spline reed in the corner. The narrow edge goes in first. With a mallet, tap the side of a wedge on top of the spline to position it. Remove more wedges one at a time, add glue to the groove, and tap in more length of spline. When you reach the end of a groove, miter and bond that end of the spline. Wipe away excess glue. Follow the same procedure on all grooves.

As you install splines, make sure that they do not slip out. When all splines are inserted, again dampen the webbing. If it dries and contracts before the glue sets, the splines may pull out. Allow the assembly to dry for 24 to 48 hours. The webbing will become taut.

WEAVING CANE IN A CONVENTIONAL DESIGN

Weaving cane is a tedious process. Single strands of cane are woven through a series of holes drilled in the frame. Three layers are woven. Then binding cane is placed to cover the holes. This lengthy process may be the reason why most caning today is done with webbing.

As with webbing, keep all cane moist until the job is complete. In addition, always install cane with the shiny side up.

Fig. 37-8 shows the size and spacing of the frame holes for various widths of cane. Most weaving is done with medium size chair cane.

First layer

Weave the first layer back to front and front to back. Begin from the second hole from the corner on the back of frame (away from you), Fig. 37-9. Put about 3 in. of cane into the hole. Secure it with a caning peg. Feed the other end of the strand down through the hole directly across on the front (nearest you). Pull the cane snug and twist it toward the next hole on the front. Then insert a peg to hold the tension.

Bring the strand up through the next hole on the front. Pull it snug and twist it so the slick, shiny side is up. Insert a caning peg in this hole. Feed the cane down through the next hole from where you started on the back part of the frame. Then pull it up through the next hole (third on the back). Repeat this sequence—two holes in front and two holes in back—until the cane is installed in one direction.

Eventually you will need another strand. As you near a strand's end, rewet the cane. Pull it down through the last hole it will reach. All ends are tied on the underside. To do so, loop the end twice around a nearby stretched strand. Slip the end back under the second loop and pull it tight. Cut the end about 1/4 in. long. Be sure no nearby hole is covered. Also use this procedure to tie the first end of the woven cane. Tie it before removing the peg.

REMEMBER: The shiny side of the cane should always face up.

Second layer

The second layer is installed side to side. Start in the hole across the corner from where you started

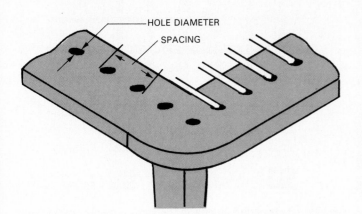

CHAIR CANE SIZE	HOLE	SPACING
Common (9/64'', 3.5 mm)	5/16'', 8 mm	7/8'', 22 mm
Medium (1/8'', 3 mm)	1/4'', 6.4 mm	3/4'', 19 mm
Fine (3/32'', 2.5 mm)	3/16'', 4.8 mm	5/8'', 16 mm
Fine Fine (5/64'', 2.25 mm)	3/16'', 4.8 mm	1/2'', 12.7 mm
Superfine (1/16'', 2 mm)	3/16'', 4.8 mm	3/8'', 9.5 mm

Fig. 37-8. Hole size and spacing varies according to the chair cane size.

the first layer. See Fig. 37-9. Use the same procedure as the first layer. No weaving should be done at this time. All of the second layer strands lie over the first layer.

Third layer

The third layer is basically a repeat of the first layer procedure. Start in the beginning hole of the first layer. Secure the end with a peg as before. Position strands beside those of the first layer. Push strands together with an extra caning peg. Install the strands over the second layer.

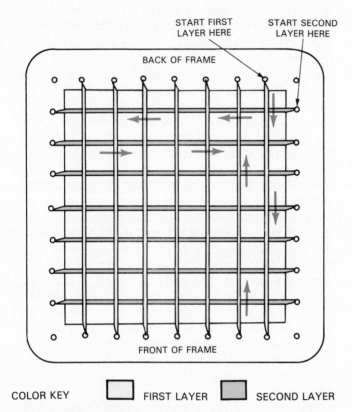

COLOR KEY ▢ FIRST LAYER ▢ SECOND LAYER

Fig. 37-9. The first layer is a front to back weave. The second layer, placed over the first layer, goes from side to side.

Fourth layer

The fourth layer is true weaving. The strands lie parallel to those from the second layer and in the same holes. However, you will weave over the strands of the third layer and under the strands of the first layer. Begin in the same hole as you did the second layer. Weave a few strands, then go back and pull the cane snug and peg it. After weaving all of the fourth layer, tie the ends. Now your woven frame should look like the one in Fig. 37-10.

Diagonal layer

The diagonal layer creates the six-sided effect of a conventional design. Start in the right front corner (the chair frame should be facing you) and weave toward the back left corner. Weave over layers two and four and under layers one and three. Work with one hand over and one under the frame. Tighten and peg the strand after each direction. Repeat another diagonal layer in the other direction. The result is seen in Fig. 37-11.

Binding

Binder cane covers all holes and gives a finished appearance. The conventional woven frame in Fig. 37-11 has binding cane attached. Be sure all strand ends of the previous five layers are knotted securely before attaching binder.

First cut the binding cane. You need four pieces. Make them about 12 in. longer than the row of holes on each side. Cut 8 in. lengths of chair cane for every hole in the frame. These become loops to hold the binding. Soak them in water for a few minutes.

Push one end of the binding cane down into a corner hole and secure the end underneath the frame. Lay the loose length of binding cane over the holes on one side. Push the loose end down into the corner hole at the other end. The length will be secured with the 8 in. (200 mm) strips of chair cane.

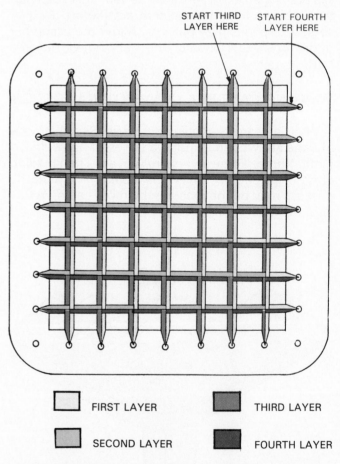

▢ FIRST LAYER ▢ THIRD LAYER

▢ SECOND LAYER ▢ FOURTH LAYER

Fig. 37-10. The third layer is in the same direction as the first and lies over the first and second layers. The fourth layer weaves over the third layer and under the first.

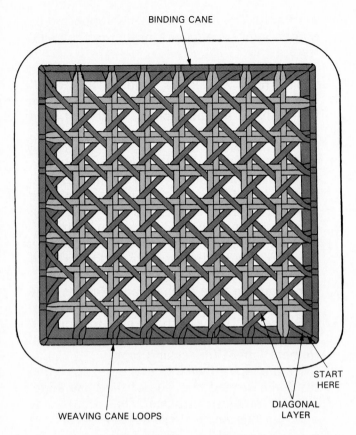

Fig. 37-11. The diagonal layers complete the conventional design. Binding cane has already been placed over the frame holes.

Push one end of an 8 in. length of weaving cane into each hole beside the binder. Loop and secure it around the weaving cane under the frame. Make a loop over the binding cane and push the loose end down through the same hole, Fig. 37-12. Pull the binding cane tight and draw the loops against it. Secure the ends underneath the frame.

Install all binding cane and loops one side at a time. Then add the four corner loops to tie together all four pieces of binding cane. Keep the cane wet until you are finished. Finally, trim all cane ends about 1/4 in. (6 mm) from the loops and knots.

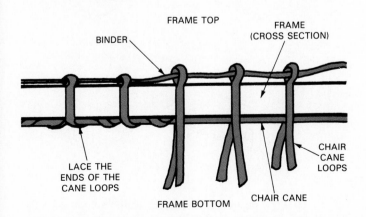

Fig. 37-12. Binding cane is held down by loops of chair cane.

Finishing

Caned surfaces may be finished like any other wood or be left natural. If stained, there will be heavy concentrations of coloring where several layers of weave intersect. This irregular distribution of stain is generally considered a pleasing effect.

WEAVING RUSH

Rush is woven *around* the frame, not through holes. Materials and supplies for rush weaving include rush, bits of rush or cloth padding, and tacks.

Before weaving, the rush fiber should be soaked for about 10 minutes. This makes it flexible. It will become rigid when it dries and shrinks.

Start at one corner, laying the end of a strand of rush over the first rail. Draw the strand over the rail, under, and back over the adjacent rail. Pull this loop tight to secure the loose end. Then draw the strand to the opposite rail and loop it around as shown in Fig. 37-13. Continue this weaving procedure until the entire seat is 2/3 complete. Then stuff the area between the two layers of rush with bits of rush or cloth padding. After stuffing, continue with the weave until the surface is finished. Tap a softwood block against strands to keep them close together. Tack the final strand to the frame. A completed seat is shown in Fig. 37-14.

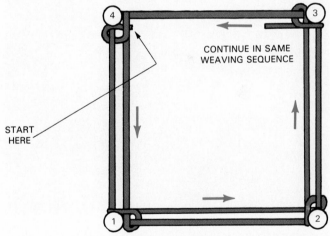

Fig. 37-13. Weave rush using the same sequence until the surface is finished.

UPHOLSTERING SLIP SEATS

Slip seats, Fig. 37-15, are padded seats commonly found on dining room chairs, kitchen chairs, stools, occasional chairs, and vanity benches. They consist of a foam pad covered with fabric, leather, or vinyl. The pad, attached to a 1/4 or 1/2 in. (6 or 13 mm) plywood base, is fastened to the chair frame.

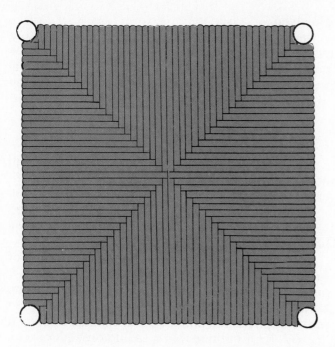

Fig. 37-14. A completed rush woven seat.

Fig. 37-15. Dining room chairs usually have padded slip seats.

Slip seat upholstery requires only a small amount of materials, supplies, and tools. Materials you will need to complete the project include plywood, padding material (foam rubber, cotton, or animal hair), and the covering. Supplies include tacking tape or muslin and rubber cement, upholsterer's tacks, and staples. Tools include a tack hammer, staple gun, scissors, and a 1/4 in. drill.

The procedure for making a slip seat is as follows:

1. Cut the plywood base to size. It should be 1/4 in. smaller in all directions from the inside of the frame. The plywood base is supported by corner brackets or cleats inside the chair seat frame.
2. Drill 1/4 in. holes, spaced 3 in. apart in the base. These will let the padding "breathe."
3. Determine the edge design for the seat. Three basic styles are cushioned, feathered, and squared, Fig. 37-16.
4. Lay the plywood base on 2 in. of padding material. Trace around the base with a marker. For a cushioned edge, A, add 3/4 in. (19 mm) to all sides of the padding. For feathered and squared edges, B and C, add 1/4 in. (6 mm).
5. Cut the padding with scissors. For foam rubber, dip the scissors in water. This acts as a lubricant. Undercut the feathered edges 3/4 in. See Fig. 37-16B.
6. Bond tacking tape to the foam. Put the tape on the top surface around cushioned and feathered edges. Place it on the side for squared edges. You can substitute muslin bonded with rubber cement for tacking tape.
7. Once the tape adheres to the foam, pull it and the foam around one side of the base edge. Tack or staple it in place. Then secure the opposite side. Next, staple the other two. Start

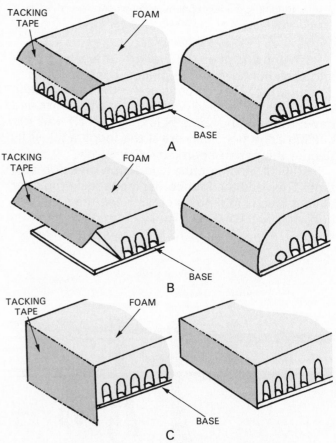

Fig. 37-16. Edge designs for slip seats. Note how the material is cut and fastened to the base with tacking tape. A—Cushioned edge. B—Feathered edge. C—Squared edge.

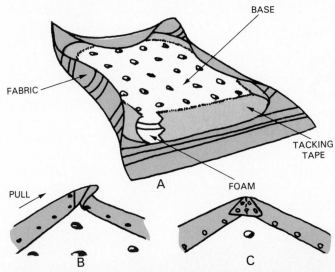

Fig. 37-17. Procedure to fasten covering to the padded base. A—Lay the seat, base up, on the back of the covering. Pull the sides onto the base and tack in the center. B—Pull the fabric from the center toward the corner as you tack. C—Fold down the excess loop of material and tack that also.

tacking or stapling in the center and work toward the corners. The amount you pull the tape under varies with the type of edge. You may want to rubber cement the foam to the plywood. This prevents it from shifting.

8. Place the covering, face down, on a clean surface. Then center the seat, plywood base up, on it, Fig. 37-17a. Cut a covering large enough to wrap around the seat with about 2 in. extra per side. Secure the center of the first side. Pull the covering and staple it toward each corner. Make sure the covering is tight but not stretched. If it wrinkles, remove the necessary tacks or staples. Take out the wrinkles and retack the fabric.
9. Secure the covering from the center toward the corners on the opposite side. Pull the fabric gently toward the corner to remove wrinkles. When four sides are done, you will have a small loop of fabric at each corner, Fig. 37-17B.
10. Press the excess fabric on the corners flat against the plywood. Tack them so they look alike, Fig. 37-17C.
11. Attach the seat in the chair frame with wood screws from underneath. Be sure there are clearance holes through the cleats or corner brackets. Four screws will hold the seat firmly. Screw length should be 1/4 to 3/8 in. longer than the cleat or bracket thickness.

SUMMARY

Caning and upholstery provide a decorative, often textured, surface to furniture. Caning has a long

history of applications. First it was used to reduce furniture weight. Now it is done for appearance reasons. Most cane installed today is purchased as webbing. You cut and install panels of webbing. However, you might also choose to weave loose strands of cane, reed, or rush.

Slip seats are upholstered surfaces commonly found on various chairs, stools, or benches. As shown in Fig. 37-1, you might find both caned and upholstered surfaces on a piece of furniture.

CABINETMAKING TERMS

Caning, cane, reed, rush, chair cane, binding cane, flat reed, flat oval reed, round reed, twisted fiber rush, webbing, spline reed, caning wedges, caning pegs, glycerin solution.

TEST YOUR KNOWLEDGE

1. Explain the difference between cane, reed, and rush.
2. Weaving is done with what type of cane?
3. Most caning today is done with _____.
4. Hold webbing in place with _____ _____.
5. Caning wedges are inserted to hold cane after the spline reed is removed. True or False?
6. Caning pegs are used to hold webbing in place. True or False?
7. List two reasons for soaking cane before installing it.
8. Cane is finished with the same supplies as wood. True or False?
9. List the steps to install cane webbing.
10. When weaving strands of cane, how do you hold stretched strands in place while you continue to weave through another hole?
11. Cane ends, when weaving, are secured with:
    a. Glue and nails.
    b. Nails only.
    c. Loops and knots.
    d. Glue only.
12. Which of the four layers of woven cane is threaded above and below previous layers?
13. The side of cane that should always face up is _____.
14. Binding cane is secured with:
    a. Spline reeds.
    b. Caning pegs.
    c. Glue.
    d. Chair cane.
15. When weaving rush, you must stop after each layer to change direction of the weave. True or False?
16. A rush seat is stuffed with _____ or _____ when it is 2/3 done to soften the seat.
17. Describe the construction of a normal slip seat.

Chapter 38
CASE CONSTRUCTION

After studying this chapter, you will be able to:
- ☐ Explain the purpose of cases.
- ☐ Identify the types of case construction.
- ☐ Select materials used in case construction.
- ☐ List the components of a typical case.
- ☐ Recognize assembly steps for casework.
- ☐ Describe the advantages offered by using the 32 mm system of case construction.

Cases are storage units that hold or display items. They basically consist of a box, open to the top or front. Shelves and dividers may be added to create compartments. Some typical cases are: jewelry boxes, chests of drawers, gun cabinets, desks, microwave carts, china hutches, bookcases, storage chests, and kitchen cabinets. The case can be open or fitted with doors.

TYPES OF CASE CONSTRUCTION

Three types of case construction are common: face frame, frameless, and frame and panel. A fourth, less used method, is V-groove design. Each have unique advantages and disadvantages.

A *face frame case* begins with a case made of solid wood, plywood, or particleboard. You do not have to edgeband the visible cut edges of plywood or particleboard. A frame is then attached to the front, Fig. 38-1. It can be made of solid wood, edgebanded plywood, or laminated particleboard. The frame adds stability to keep the case square. It also supports the door hinges. Face frame construction remains popular, despite the growth of frameless casework.

A *frameless case* has no face frame; the edges of top, bottom, and side members are exposed, Fig. 38-2. If the case is made of plywood, particleboard or MDF, the edges are banded with laminate or veneer. The back provides most of the structure to keep the case from racking. Door hinges attach directly to the side. The doors are usually full overlay. The most popular variation of frameless construction is the 32 mm system. It sets size standards for components, hardware, and fasteners.

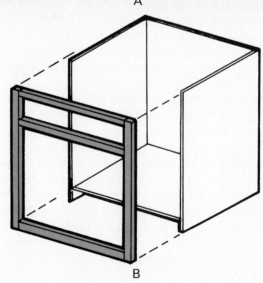

A

B

Fig. 38-1. A—Face frame casework. B—The frame is attached with glue and/or mechanical fasteners. (Kemper)

Fig. 38-2. With frameless cabinets, the doors attach directly to the case side. (Quaker Maid)

This allows for interchangeable parts. The 32 mm system is covered in detail later in this chapter.

A *frame and panel case* surface is not flat. Surfaces are made with thinner panels mounted to or within a frame. This decreases the weight of the product. You often see finished frame and panel construction for desk sides and cabinet doors, Fig. 38-3. Web frame cases are a form of frame and panel construction. They have surface panels attached to an internal frame. This technique, widely used for high quality casework, is covered in Chapter 39.

Regardless of which method you choose, any assembled case should be perfectly square. This requires matching components and joints accurately. An out-of-square product might lean away from a wall or leave gaps between adjacent cabinets.

CASE MATERIALS

Consider these factors when choosing materials for casework:
1. Uses for the case? Kitchen cabinets are made to be rugged. A bookcase, on the other hand, may receive little wear.

2. Will the case be lifted or moved often? There are both movable and built-in cases. Movable cases generally sit on casters or glides so that the wood does not chip or mar the floor. In addition, a large case should be made as light as possible.
3. What surfaces will be visible when the case is in use? Exposed parts include the exterior and the front-facing edges of shelves and dividers. Undersides of cases less than two feet from the floor are considered hidden and generally are not finished.
4. How will surfaces be coated or covered? The finish or laminate must protect the case from daily wear.
5. Will wood products be better, both in structure and cost, than lumber?

Answers to these and other questions affect decisions about materials.

LUMBER OR MANUFACTURED WOOD PANELS?

Solid lumber is costly to buy and process. To form large panels, it must be surfaced, glued, resurfaced, and smoothed. As much as 20 percent could be wasted. In addition, lumber comes in random sizes

Fig. 38-3. With frame and panel doors, a glass or wood panel is held within a solid wood frame. (Thomasville)

and requires more storage space than manufactured panel products. Lumber can also change in dimension plus or minus 1/8 in. (3 mm) for each 12 in. (305 mm) of width. The expansion or contraction, caused by moisture content changes, often results in joint failure. Waterproof finishes slow the effects somewhat, but cannot stop them entirely. Do not use construction grade lumber. It has a high moisture content and is likely to warp.

Plywood, MDF, and particleboard are wise alternatives to lumber. They are more stable and less expensive. Veneer or laminate surfaces, on one or both sides, vary by specie and grade. They can match solid lumber parts used in the case. Bond edgebanding to the edges of frameless products.

Hardboard might be used for case backs, drawer bottoms, and dust panels. Install tempered hardboard where more strength is needed, such as in the bottoms of wide drawers.

Manufactured panel products (other than plywood) contain much resin. This dulls standard steel tools. Select carbide or carbide-tipped tools— saw blades, jointer knives, router bits, etc.—when processing composite wood products.

CASE COMPONENTS

A typical case has many components. Included are the front, top, bottom, sides, shelves, and dividers. Doors and drawers may be installed on or in the basic case. A separate base (plinth) might be placed under the case. This discussion focuses on traditional methods of case construction, including the face frame. The section on 32 mm construction details the use of special mechanical fasteners, hardware, and methods for frameless cases.

CASE BODY

The *case body* refers to the top, bottom, and sides. The body opens either to the top or front, Fig. 38-4. Examples of cases that open to the top include toy boxes and cedar chests. Those that open to the front include dressers, bookcases, and kitchen cabinets.

The corners of wood cases can be joined with many joints, Fig. 38-5. Joints should be cut so that a minimal amount of end grain is visible. Install glue blocks where they will be hidden. (Make sure that

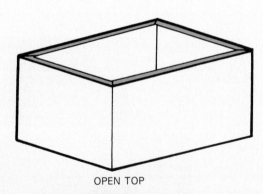

OPEN TOP

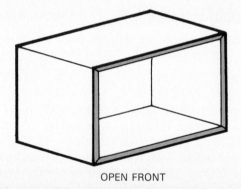

OPEN FRONT

Fig. 38-4. Cases may open to the top or front. (Southern Mobile, Bernhardt)

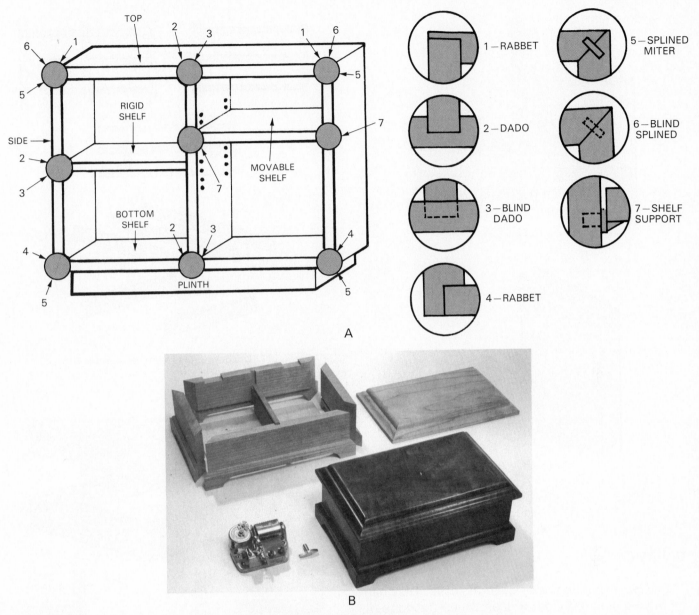

Fig. 38-5. A—Several alternative joints can be used on case goods. B—The corners of this jewelry case are mitered and the bottom is dadoed. (Craft Products)

they will not interfere with shelves or drawers.) Most manufactured panel products should be reinforced with glue blocks or mechanical fasteners. Edgeband plywood or particleboard if a face frame is not attached.

SHELVES

Shelves divide a case into levels for storage. Plywood or particleboard shelving is less likely to warp than solid lumber. Shelves may be fixed or adjustable.

Fixed shelving can be installed several ways. You can use dado joints or cleats. Create the joints or glue the cleats to the case sides before assembly.

Be certain they are aligned so the shelves are level. Like glue blocks, cleats are unattractive. Use them where they will be hidden, such as behind a door.

The type of dado—through or blind—depends on the application. For cases with face frames, it is easier to cut a through dado. The frame will cover the exposed joint. You can also use a through dado with frameless cases that are edgebanded. When using solid wood sides, cut a blind, or stop dado. See Fig. 38-6.

It is wise to install adjustable shelves. Several styles of shelf supports were described in Chapter 17. Standard 3/4 in. (19 mm) thick shelving should not be placed on supports spaced more than 42 in. (1 067 mm) apart.

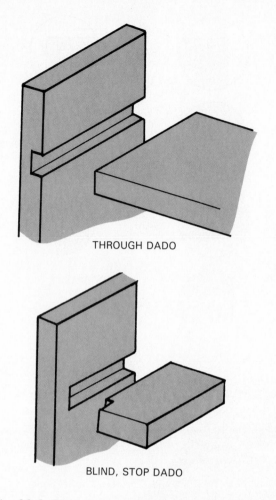

THROUGH DADO

BLIND, STOP DADO

Fig. 38-6. Blind or through dados hold fixed shelves.

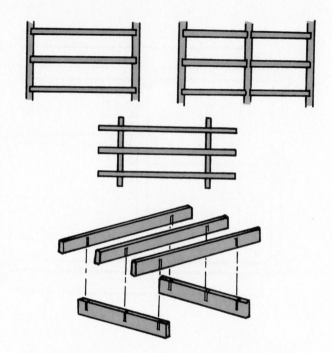

Fig. 38-7. Dividers create individual storage areas.

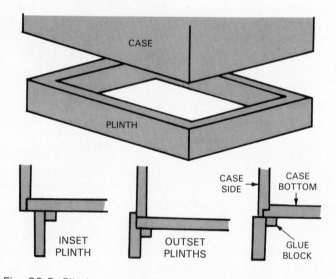

Fig. 38-8. Plinths, or base frames, may be inset or outset.

DIVIDERS

Dividers separate the inside of the case. They can be placed horizontal or vertical. When the edge of a divider is visible on the finished case (frameless construction), cover it with veneer or laminate edgebanding.

Dividers can be positioned easily with dado joints. Dados usually are cut halfway through the supporting components. At times, dividers are on each side of a support. In this situation, cut the dado only 1/3 the thickness. Cut half-lap joints when dividers cross. Saw all cross-lap joints at the same distance setting—one-half the width. See Fig. 38-7.

PLINTH

Cases may set directly on floors, legs, shaped frames, or plinths. A *plinth,* or base, provides toe clearance on one or more sides, Fig. 38-8. (The term *kick plate* is given to the plinth under kitchen cabinets.) The frame usually is 4 in. (100 mm) high and inset 3 in. (75 mm). It can be made of lumber, plywood, or laminated (or veneered) particleboard.

The plinth is fastened to the case with glue blocks, cleats, pocket joints, corner brace plates, or other fasteners. Install glides on movable cases to prevent them from chipping when moved. Install casters on frequently moved cases.

The plinth can be recessed under or outset from the case. Sometimes the top edge of outside plinths is shaped. Mouldings may be attached as an alternative to shaping. The corners can be rabbeted or mitered, often with a spline. Plinths usually are added after the case body is assembled and the glue joints have cured.

BACK

For face frame casework, the *case back* usually is 1/10 to 1/4 in. (3 to 6 mm) thick hardboard, plywood, or particleboard set in a rabbet joint. The rabbet, formed around the inside of the back edges, should be slightly deeper than the thickness of the back. For frameless case, a 1/4 to 3/8 in. (6 to 10 mm) back is placed in a dado joint cut in the sides. It makes up for most of the strength lost by not having a face frame.

CASE TOP

The *case top* may be fixed, removable, or hinged. Those which open to the front are usually fixed. Tops on cases which open up are generally hinged.

Fixed tops

On tall cases with doors, a fixed top is not seen. Therefore, it can be rabbeted and glued, dadoed, or otherwise fastened. The top can be made of plywood, particleboard, or solid wood. Cover exposed surfaces of manufactured panel products with veneer or plastic laminate.

A visible top, such as a dresser, should be made of solid wood, plywood, veneered particleboard, or MDF. Most often, the top is a separate component attached to the case with corner blocks. The edges may be contoured.

Hinged tops

Case goods which open upward usually have lid-type hinged tops. Smaller case tops may include part of the front, sides, and back. Examples are recipe boxes and cedar chests. For these, you rabbet, glue, and assemble the entire case, including the top. The box is completely sealed. After the glue cures, cut the case open on a table saw or band saw, Fig. 38-9. Thus the figure in the grain continues all across the surface. This method also helps prevent warpage.

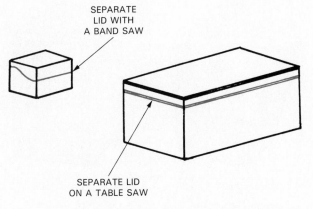

SEPARATE LID WITH A BAND SAW

SEPARATE LID ON A TABLE SAW

Fig. 38-9. You can saw cases to separate the lid.

Air-cushioned tops

An *air-cushioned top* slows the fall of a hinged lid or top. Wood strips inside or decorative moulding outside restricts airflow as the top lowers.

For an inside air cushion, Fig. 38-10A, fit strips on the front and 2 sides of the case lid. Use the same material as the case if you wish. However, 1/4 in. (6 mm) hardboard is sufficient on small boxes.

To make an outside air cushion, Fig. 38-10B, glue flat or shaped moulding to the outside of the lid front and ends. Use the same specie of lumber as the case. Miter the moulding at the corners. The overlap should be 3/4 in. (19 mm) or more.

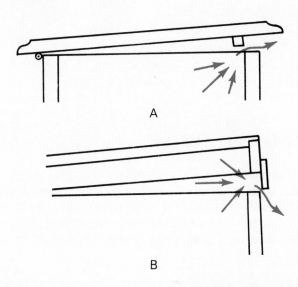

A

B

Fig. 38-10. Air-cushion strips trap air and lower lids slowly.

FACE FRAME

A *face frame* attached to the front of the case provides strength and style. The frame can be made of solid wood, edgebanded plywood, or laminated particleboard. It keeps the case from racking (becoming out-of-square). The frame typically covers the exposed edges of the top, bottom, sides, and dividers. Doors or drawers usually fit within the frame openings. Horizontal parts of the frame are called rails. Vertical parts of the frame are called stiles. They vary in size from 1 to 2 1/2 in. (25 to 64 mm) depending on the particular design. They can be assembled with mortise and tenon joints, dowels, plate joinery, or pocket joints, Fig. 38-11. Butt and miter joints do not provide the needed strength.

Most often, the face frame is glued and clamped to the body. It can also be secured with clips. Nails, set below the surface and then filled, also help position the frame.

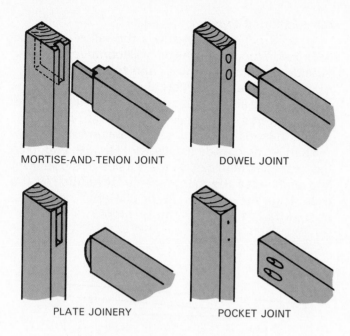

MORTISE-AND-TENON JOINT   DOWEL JOINT

PLATE JOINERY   POCKET JOINT

Fig. 38-11. Joinery for face frames.

DOORS AND DRAWERS

The proper space—width, height, and depth—must be left for doors and drawers. For drawers, also take into account the dimensions of the slides. Refer to the plans to determine whether doors are flush, overlay, or lip edge. Each requires different hardware.

CASE ASSEMBLY

Successful case assembly requires planning and preparation. All components must be sized accurately and sanded smooth. All joints have to fit exactly. Preset clamps to their approximate openings. Use small blocks or bar clamp pads to prevent clamp damage. Select the proper adhesive based on set and clamp time. A quick- setting adhesive may not allow enough time for assembly.

In a production setting, cases may be assembled with nails and staples driven with a pneumatic gun. Staples have better holding power, but are more difficult to cover. They are mostly used to assemble parts that will not be seen on the finished product. High quality casework should not have any visible fasteners.

Assemble the case without adhesive first (a dry run). This is necessary to preset clamps and be sure all corners are at 90 degrees. It also helps determine the steps in assembly. Check all of the joints to make sure they fit properly. You do not need to position hardboard backs that will be reinforced with nails or staples. Glue blocks can be left off unless they position some components. Those needed

should be secured to one side of the joint. Plan to apply the glue to parts in the order that you put the unit together dry.

Once you verify the dry run, disassemble the case. Lay the clamps, protective blocks, and components aside in an orderly manner.

Begin the final assembly. (Follow the assembly and clamping procedure presented in Chapters 32 and 33.) Spread the adhesive evenly, according to your plan. Fit the pieces together. Position the protective blocks and clamps. Tighten the clamps only enough to hold them in place. When all components are assembled, increase the clamping pressure as you check for squareness. Excessive pressure can damage soft surfaces and break weak components.

Inspect all joints immediately after assembly. They should be closed and square. Wipe away all excess adhesive with a damp sponge or cloth. This is easier than scraping or sanding off excess dry adhesive. Keep water away from places where steel clamps touch the case. Moistened metal can stain the wood black.

V-GROOVE ASSEMBLY

V-groove assembly, also known as miter folding, involves folding a grooved panel to create the case, Fig. 38-12. The case begins with a sheet of particleboard covered with flexible laminate. Cuts for each corner are made at a 90 degree included angle to a precise depth equal to the particleboard thickness. This forms two 45 degree miter cuts. Do not cut through the laminate.

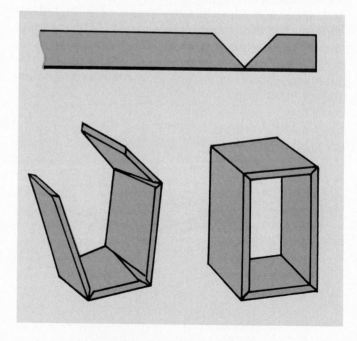

Fig. 38-12. V-groove assembly.

The V-grooves can be cut on a table saw or panel saw. Production firms have special computer-controlled routers that accurately cut "V" grooves.

When designing cases for V-groove assembly, carefully consider how the different surfaces will fold together. It may be simple to create a box with three cuts. However, adding cross grooves for folded edges can make the layout quite complex.

32 MILLIMETER CONSTRUCTION

The *32 mm (1.25 in.) system* is a standard form of frameless case construction. It provides a modular system of case assembly and hardware installation. Furniture makers can quickly tailor a cabinet to meet a customer's needs, yet still produce it with interchangeable parts. Individual wood panels make up the building blocks for any case.

The 32 mm system, illustrated in Fig. 38-13, is based on the following set of standard dimensions.

1. Side panels feature two vertical rows of holes on 32 mm centers.
2. The distance from front or rear edge to hole centerline is 37 mm (1.50 in.).
3. System hole diameter is 5 mm. For assembly purposes, 8, 15, and 35 mm holes may be bored.
4. Accurate hole location automatically ensures precise fit and smooth operation of installed hardware.

The 32 mm dimension is not random. It is governed by the minimum spacing of spindles on a multiple-spindle boring machine. Any further reduction in the spindle spacing could shorten the service life of spindle bearings and gears.

BENEFITS OF THE 32 MILLIMETER SYSTEM

The beauty of the 32 mm system is that it standardizes case construction and hardware mounting. It allows you to do all the work—from cutting panels to installing hinges and drawer glides—*before* the case is assembled. To keep the case square and assure stiffness, place a plywood panel back in slots cut in the case sides or staple it to the back.

From a manufacturing standpoint, fewer people can complete more frameless cases than face frame cases in a single shift. However, hole size, location, and spacing must be precise to guarantee interchangeable parts. Each component must fit together perfectly during assembly.

Once the 32 mm system is in place, a furniture manufacturer can expect the following benefits:

1. Increased productivity.
2. Simple and automated machines provide high precision and high quality.
3. The furniture manufacturer is less dependent on skilled labor.
4. Material costs are reduced due to standard component sizes that make efficient use of manufactured wood panels. Accurate cutting lists also reduce waste.
5. Errors show up immediately because there is a minimum number of features and dimensions.
6. The furniture manufacturer can avoid the dimensional instability of solid lumber by using veneered or plastic-laminated particleboard.
7. Components can be produced at different locations, stored for any length of time, and assembled later with accurate fit.

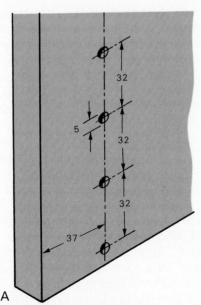 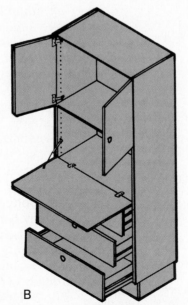 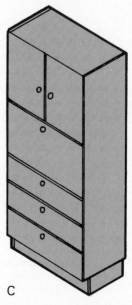

Fig. 38-13. A—Spacing for 5 mm "system" holes. B—Completed case showing hardware and horizontal members attached. C—Closed case looks no different from one assembled with traditional joints and hardware. (Hafele)

HOLE SIZES AND SPACING

The 5 mm *system holes* are spaced 32 mm apart and 37 mm from the front and rear edge of the panel. They are used for mounting drawer slides, hinges, shelf pins, and other accessories. The 37 mm corresponds to the mounting depth needed by drawer slides and concealed door hinges. Remember, the hardware purchased is made for use with the system.

Ideally, the height of case side panels should be a multiple of 32 mm, plus the material thickness, Fig. 38-14. This allows the spaced holes to be drilled one-half the material thickness from the top or bottom of the case. A connector bolt is inserted in the final hole to attach the top or bottom member flush. However, this is not necessary. A customer might want the top offset from the side. If so, change the end hole location on side panels accordingly, Fig. 38-15.

The case is held together with dowels in 8 mm or RTA fasteners in 15 mm *construction holes.* For *dowel construction,* the 8 mm holes may be spaced horizontally along the top, bottom, and midsection of the sides. They typically are placed in pairs 22 mm from the edges and 64 mm apart, Fig. 38-16A.

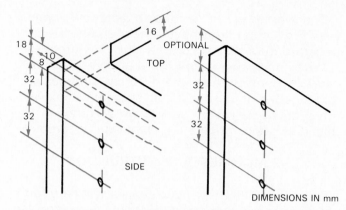

Fig. 38-15. Top and bottom horizontal members do not have to fit flush.

For *RTA fastener construction,* 15 mm holes are drilled in the top, bottom, and other horizontal components, in place of the 8 mm holes, to accept RTA connectors for easy assembly. The bolt of a bolt-and-cam or casing connector is threaded into one of the 5 mm holes, Fig. 38-16B. The bolt head fits into the cam through a hole drilled in the end of the horizontal member. (See Chapter 17.) A turn of the cam or casing draws in the bolt and tightens the joint.

In doors, 35 mm holes are drilled for the cup of concealed hinges, Fig. 38-16C. The hinge arm fastens into two 5 mm holes. (See Fig. 17-23.) As illustrated in Fig. 17-24, the door hinge is fully adjustable.

Other 32 mm details for base and wall kitchen cabinets are given in Fig. 38-16D.

DESIGN ADVANTAGES

Products manufactured using 32 mm features have several advantages. One primary purpose is because the products assemble easily, they are shipped disassembled to save space during transportation.

If made with RTA fasteners, assembled products can be disassembled to move through doorways or up stairs. Then simply reassemble the parts.

Flexibility in production is a trademark of the 32 mm system. The standardized hole distance presents a wide range of options. Refer to Fig. 38-17 for three options available from the same case body.

Many persons associate the 32 mm system with plastic laminates and particleboard. This is not necessarily correct. Some companies use plywood with wood veneer edges. A few even use solid lumber. In fact, the overall appearance of the case is no different than one made of lumber. In the past, laminates have had dark "laminate lines" (beveled edges of the laminate). This is not necessarily true

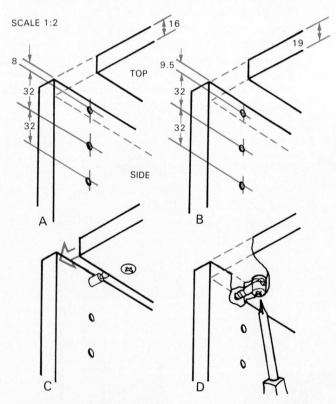

Fig. 38-14. A—Hole spacing from the top so that a 16 mm (5/8 in.) thick horizontal member fits flush. B—Hole spacing from the top so that a 19 mm (3/4 in.) thick horizontal member fits flush. C—A bolt is threaded into a 5 mm hole. D—Turn the cam or casing to draw the horizontal and vertical members together. (Hafele)

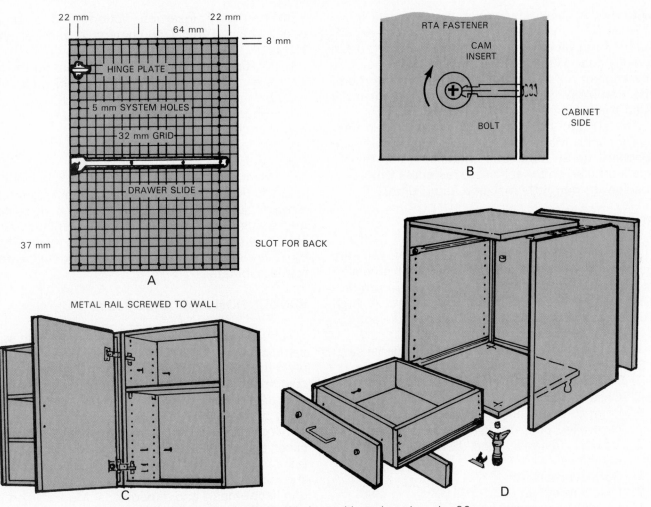

Fig. 38-16. Production details for kitchen cabinets based on the 32 mm system.

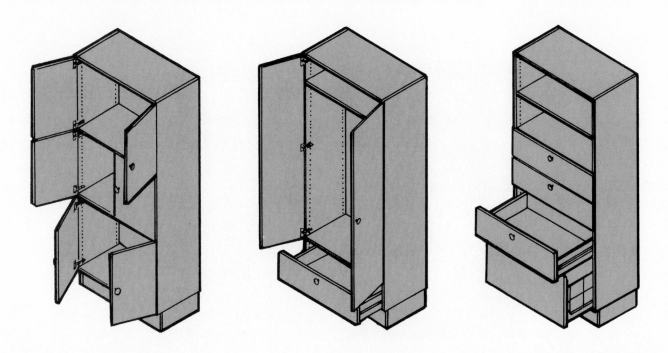

Fig. 38-17. Three different cabinet designs are made easily using the same case sides, top, and bottom. (Hafele)

with modern laminates which have no dark lines.

Most 32 mm constructed products look no different from face frame construction having a full overlay door. Plus, you save time and money on raw material for the face frame and labor. Furthermore, the frameless cabinet is laid out more efficiently than that of face frame cabinetry.

The simple, yet sturdy, 32 mm design is very economical. Many traditional joints require long machine setup time and multiple cuts. Evenly spaced holes and mechanical fasteners provide a precise fit, and little machine setup time.

EQUIPMENT

To run the 32 mm construction system, you may use simple traditional machines, but high precision is required. To fully implement a 32 mm production system requires much equipment. A high volume cabinetmaking firm will spend thousands of dollars to purchase:

1. Computer numerical control (CNC) panel saw.
2. Automated double-sided edgebander.
3. Two or more multiple-spindle boring machines.
4. Case clamp.
5. Point-to-point boring machine. (Computer-controlled point-to-point router.)
7. Dowel, fastener, and hardware insertion machines.
8. Conveyor system.
9. Finishing system.

The small shop can produce equal quality cabinets with less equipment. The drawback is reduced production. It is necessary to have a panel saw, multispindle vertical and horizontal boring machines

with hardware insertion option, and a simple edgebander. Typical equipment in a small shop includes:

1. Multiple-spindle boring attachment for the drill press. (Drilling equally spaced holes can also be done with a jig, Fig. 38-18.)
2. Hinge-boring and setting machine.
3. Laminate trimmer or router.
4. Panel saw.
5. Table saw.
6. Manually operated, single-sided edgebander.

In addition, either large or small firms might have a planer, jointer, and shaper for producing custom doors. Also, frameless construction still accounts for only a small portion of the cabinets made. Thus, most firms are fully equipped for producing face frame cabinets.

PRODUCTION AND ASSEMBLY

Firms establishing a 32 mm system first set standard part sizes. They then set the machinery to comply with those dimensions. Trying to manufacture custom products defeats the purpose of the system. The 32 mm system is flexible enough to satisfy most designs.

Planning is the key. Take into account all of the case parts, doors, drawers, kick plates, and fasteners, Fig. 38-19A. Create a bill of materials and cutting list. Mark parts with a part number, cutting list number, and dimensions. Mark this on the edges when edgebanding will cover the area later. Otherwise, mark the information on tape.

Almost all assembly steps are done with the prefinished panels lying flat on the workbench. In-

Fig. 38-18. You can drill individual 5 mm holes for the 32 mm system using a jig.

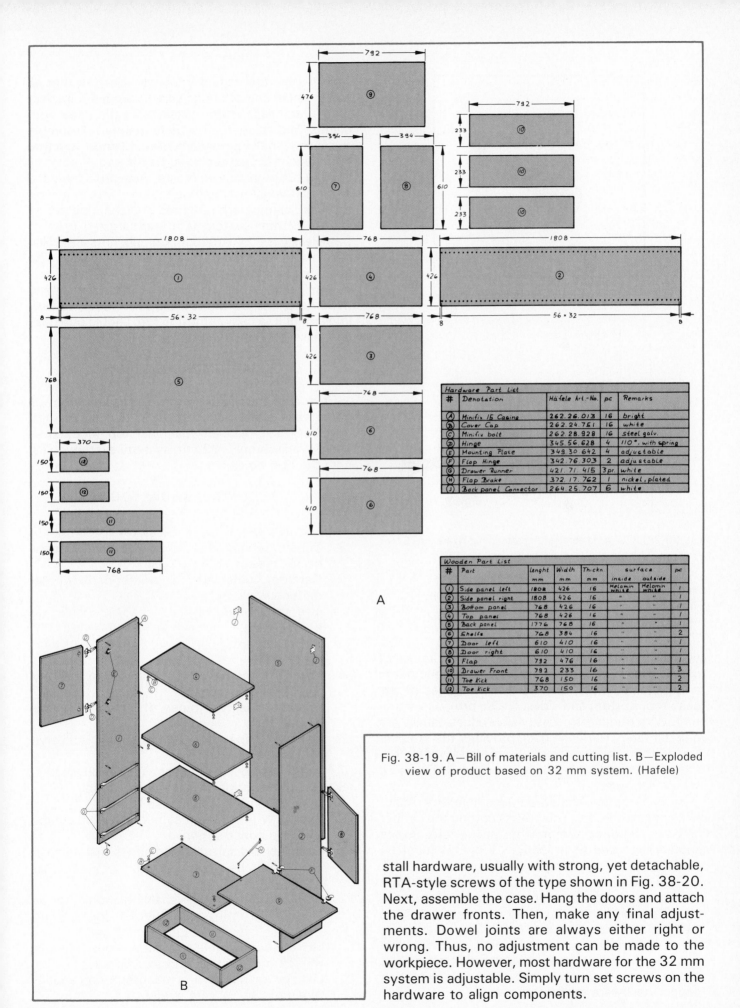

A

Hardware Part List			
#	Denotation	Häfele Art.-No.	pc	Remarks
A	Minifix 15 Casing	262.26.013	16	bright
B	Cover Cap	262.24.751	16	white
C	Minifix bolt	262.28.928	16	steel galv.
D	Hinge	345.56.628	4	110°, with spring
E	Mounting Plate	349.30.642	4	adjustable
F	Flap Hinge	342.76.303	2	adjustable
G	Drawer Runner	421.71.415	3pr.	white
H	Flap Brake	372.17.762	1	nickel, plated
J	Back panel Connector	264.25.707	6	white

Wooden Part List						
#	Part	lenght mm	Width mm	Thickn mm	surface inside	surface outside	pc
1	Side panel left	1808	426	16	Melamin white	Melamin white	1
2	Side panel right	1808	426	16	"	"	1
3	Bottom panel	768	426	16	"	"	1
4	Top panel	768	426	16	"	"	1
5	Back panel	1776	768	16	"	"	1
6	Shelfs	768	384	16	"	"	2
7	Door left	610	410	16	"	"	1
8	Door right	610	410	16	"	"	1
9	Flap	792	476	16	"	"	1
10	Drawer Front	792	233	16	"	"	3
11	Toe Kick	768	150	16	"	"	2
12	Toe Kick	370	150	16	"	"	2

B

Fig. 38-19. A—Bill of materials and cutting list. B—Exploded view of product based on 32 mm system. (Hafele)

stall hardware, usually with strong, yet detachable, RTA-style screws of the type shown in Fig. 38-20. Next, assemble the case. Hang the doors and attach the drawer fronts. Then, make any final adjustments. Dowel joints are always either right or wrong. Thus, no adjustment can be made to the workpiece. However, most hardware for the 32 mm system is adjustable. Simply turn set screws on the hardware to align components.

Fig. 38-20. RTA-style screws that attach hardware into 5 mm holes.

Assemble the case dry initially. Be sure that all surfaces are smooth and joints fit properly. Inspect for squareness. Then disassemble the case with clamps laid aside in an orderly manner. Assemble the case with the proper adhesive. Clamp it together and inspect for squareness. Be sure to remove all excess adhesive before it sets. Assemble the base or plinth and allow the glue to cure. Attach it after the case clamps are removed and the glue cures.

The 32 mm system is a standardized form of frameless case construction. Components are drilled with accurately located, standard size drills. The holes accommodate special mechanical fasteners, hinges, and other hardware. There are many benefits to the 32 mm system. However, to fully implement it, a cabinetmaking firm should purchase specialized machinery.

CABINETMAKING TERMS

Case, face frame case, frameless case, frame and panel case, case body, shelves, dividers, plinth, case back, case top, air-cushioned top, face frame, V-groove assembly, 32 mm system, system holes, construction holes.

TEST YOUR KNOWLEDGE

1. List five examples of casework.
2. Construction grade lumber is not recommended for cases. True or False?
3. Carbide tools are recommended for all materials, except:
   a. Particleboard.
   b. Plywood.
   c. Hardboard.
   d. MDF.
4. When are dado joints cut only 1/3 of the way through a component?
5. Describe the two types of air cushions for hinged tops.
6. List two steps taken before adding adhesive to assemble a cabinet.
7. Plinths are cabinet bases. True or False?
8. List three forms of case construction.
9. A face frame keeps a case from _____.
10. Explain why lumber may not be a wise choice for case construction.
11. Particleboard surfaces and edges that are visible should be covered with _____ or _____.
12. Standard 3/4 in. thick shelving should not be placed on supports spaced more than _____ in. (_____ mm) apart.
13. List the critical hole size dimensions found in the 32 mm system and explain each.
14. List several design and manufacturing advantages of the 32 mm system.

SUMMARY

Cases are storage units designed to hold or display items. There are three common types of case construction: face frame, frameless, and frame and panel. A face frame covers the edges of the case top, bottom and sides. It also provides structure. With frameless cases, visible edges usually are edgebanded. The case back provides the stability lost without a face frame. Frame and panel construction consists of thinner wood panels mounted within a frame.

All case goods should be assembled carefully, with square corners. This means cutting the lumber or wood product components accurately. Joints should align and fit properly. All of this must be assured before applying the adhesive.

Case lids are of two types. Some may be lids that are added. Others are rabbeted and glued to the case sides and ends. Then the top is cut off. Tops may make noise when they close. To prevent this, consider installing an air cushion.

Cases may have shelves and/or dividers inside. These typically involve accurately placed shelf hanger hardware or dado joints.

Casework construction techniques can be used for a variety of applications. (Formica Corp.)

Fig. 39-1. Frame and panel products. A—Frame and panel doors. (Kemper) B—Frames with glass panels. (Bassett) C—Frame with metal grille panel. (Bassett) D—The dresser has frame and panel sides. The mirror is framed. (Thomasville)

Chapter 39
FRAME AND PANEL COMPONENTS

After studying this chapter, you will be able to:
☐ *Identify the applications of frame and panel components.*
☐ *Create square- or profiled-edge frames.*
☐ *Saw or shape raised panels.*
☐ *Select joints for frame assembly.*
☐ *Describe web frame case construction.*

Frame and panel assemblies are an alternative to solid wood or wood product surfaces. They consist of a flat or contoured panel held in a grooved or rabbeted wood frame. You will find frame and panel parts used for cabinet sides, fronts, doors, and partitions between drawers, Fig. 39-1.

A frame and panel component serves both design and engineering purposes. As a design factor, it:
1. Gives contour to otherwise plain, flat surfaces.
2. Allows you to use glass, plastic, cane, fabric, ornamental metal, and veneer for appearance.

As an engineering factor, a frame and panel assembly:
1. Provides a stable surface. You might choose plywood for the panel since solid wood tends to warp as a result of moisture changes. The distortion is greatest when only one face is finished.
2. Reduces the weight of the product. A thin panel set in a wood frame weighs much less than an equal size solid component.
3. Allows a large panel surface to expand or contract within a narrow frame.
4. Can use precoated or covered panels, which cost less than lumber of a comparable size. This bypasses surfacing, gluing, smoothing, and some finishing operations.
5. Can be sized rather quickly when the frames are precut.

You can also use a frame without a panel. This is done for a face frame, Fig. 39-2, or for drawer supports in web frame construction.

FRAME COMPONENTS

Frames and panels are typically sawn to size and shaped separately. Work from your drawings and

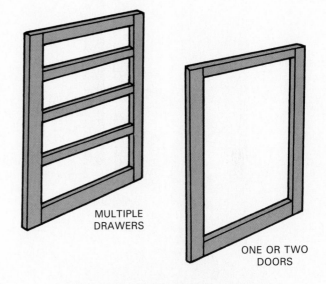

MULTIPLE DRAWERS

ONE OR TWO DOORS

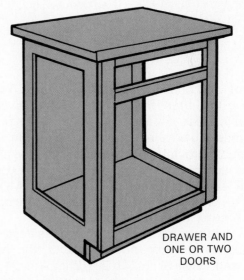

DRAWER AND ONE OR TWO DOORS

Fig. 39-2. Face frame is a frame and panel assembly, without the panel.

specifications to be sure that the two parts fit when assembled.

Several terms are associated with frames, Fig. 39-3. Vertical frame side members are called *stiles.* They are the full height of the frame. Horizontal frame members are called *rails.* There will be top,

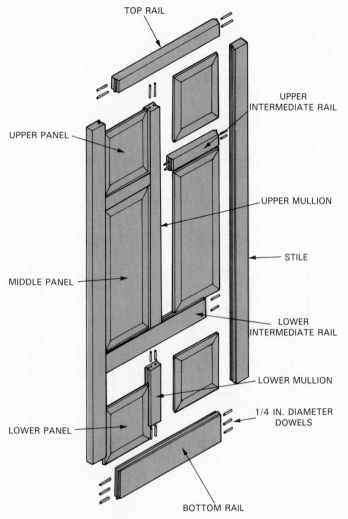

Fig. 39-3. Learn the individual part names of a frame and panel assembly. (Shopsmith, Inc.)

TOP RAIL

UPPER INTERMEDIATE RAIL

UPPER PANEL

UPPER MULLION

STILE

MIDDLE PANEL

LOWER INTERMEDIATE RAIL

LOWER MULLION

1/4 IN. DIAMETER DOWELS

LOWER PANEL

BOTTOM RAIL

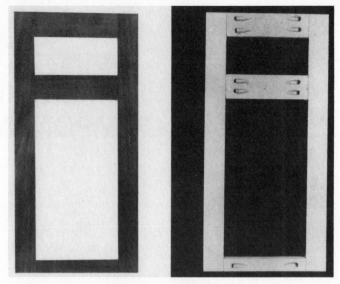

Fig. 39-4. This is a laminated particleboard frame assembled with pocket joints. (Evans Rotork)

bottom, and possibly *intermediate rails.* A vertical piece other than the outside frame is called a *mullion.* These separate glass panels or drawers.

Frames usually are made of 5/8 or 3/4 in. lumber. Plywood, particleboard, and MDF are also common materials. You must edge band plywood. Cover all visible surfaces of particleboard and MDF with laminate or veneer, Fig. 39-4. Composite products offer greater dimensional stability.

The width of frame members varies according to the application. For most products, the width of stiles and rails is 1 1/2 to 2 1/2 in. A large, paneled door or table top might require a larger frame.

Shaping the inside edge of frame members is known as profiling. This process changes the appearance of the frame. The most common profiles are square, bead, bead and cove, and ogee. The shape of the panel set in the frame can also vary. See Fig. 39-5.

A groove is cut around the inside edge of the frame for the panel. It must hold the panel securely without adhesive. Usually, the groove is 1/4 in.

wide and 3/8 to 1/2 in. deep. However, if a solid wood panel is used, make the groove deeper in the stiles to allow cross-grain expansion. When framing glass panels, a rabbet and stop are used instead of the groove. This allows you to insert the glass

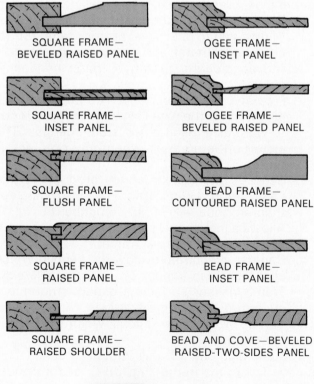

SQUARE FRAME—
BEVELED RAISED PANEL

OGEE FRAME—
INSET PANEL

SQUARE FRAME—
INSET PANEL

OGEE FRAME—
BEVELED RAISED PANEL

SQUARE FRAME—
FLUSH PANEL

BEAD FRAME—
CONTOURED RAISED PANEL

SQUARE FRAME—
RAISED PANEL

BEAD FRAME—
INSET PANEL

SQUARE FRAME—
RAISED SHOULDER

BEAD AND COVE—BEVELED
RAISED-TWO-SIDES PANEL

BEAD AND COVE FRAME—
INSET PANEL

Fig. 39-5. Frame and panel profiles.

into the finished frame. You can also replace the glass if it is broken.

The type of frame you make depends on answers to several questions:

1. What tools, machines, and accessories are available?
2. Will the frame be open or paneled?
3. Will the frame edges be visible after the product is assembled?
4. Will you install the panel while assembling the frame or add it later?

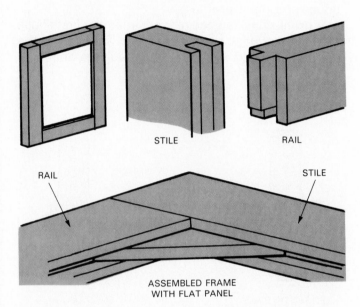

ASSEMBLED FRAME
WITH FLAT PANEL

Fig. 39-6. A stub mortise and tenon is a popular frame joint because the panel groove also serves as the mortise.

SQUARE-EDGE FRAME

The square-edge frame is one of the easiest to make. You typically use the same type of joint at each corner. These include mortise and tenon, lap, dowel, plate, and pocket joints. Simplify the frame joints as much as possible.

A stub mortise and tenon can be made quickly. See Fig. 39-6. Add the stub lengths to the total rail length. Then cut the groove around the inside edge of all members. The groove also serves as the mortise. Finally, cut shoulders to form the stub tenon. Reinforce the corners with gussets (mending plates) or add dowels to strengthen the joint further, Fig. 39-7. A haunched mortise and tenon does not require dowels, Fig. 39-8.

Select dowel, plate, or pocket joints for open frames (no panel). A doweled butt joint is adequate. Drill two holes in each rail. Use dowel centers to align and mark hole locations on the stile edges. Then drill the stiles using a doweling jig. Insert dowels and assemble the frame dry. Inspect for

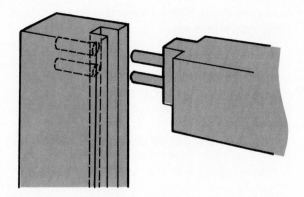

Fig. 39-7. Dowels reinforce a stub mortise and tenon.

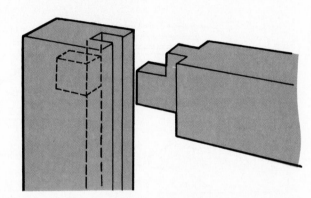

Fig. 39-8. A haunched tenon adds strength to the joint.

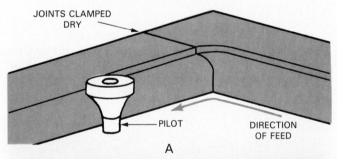

Fig. 39-9. A—Contour the edges of assembled frames with a router bit and pilot. B—The doors on this desk show a routed profile. (Thomasville)

squareness. Disassemble the frame, add glue, reclamp, and square it.

Occasionally, edges on an open frame can be inset or hidden. This occurs if the frame is between two other cabinet sections. Another option is to cover visible edges with moulding. Since the edge and end grain are hidden, most any joint is appropriate.

You may choose to shape or route frame edges after assembly. Before doing so, make sure the glue is dry. If you shape the inside edge, remember that

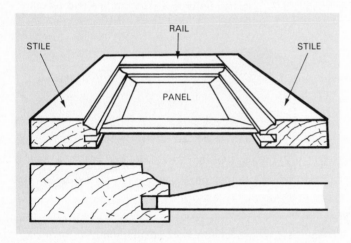

Fig. 39-10. A profiled-edge frame. The contoured edge also serves as the joint. (MCS)

you will round the corners. Use a router bit with a pilot. See Fig. 39-9. Contour the edges on one or both sides as desired. However, to have square in-

side corners, shape the profile before assembly using a matched pair of router or shaper cutters.

PROFILED-EDGE FRAME

A contoured inside edge is made by routing or shaping the rails and stiles before assembly. Then, the inside corners are square, not rounded. The contour also serves as a joint, Fig. 39-10. This cut requires special two-piece router bits or a matched set of shaper cutters. There are bead, bead and cove, and ogee profiles.

A profiled inside edge requires that you first shape the inside edges of stiles and rails. Then shape the ends of rails and mullions. Matched sets of shaper cutters are shown in Fig. 39-11.

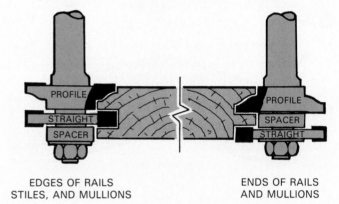

EDGES OF RAILS STILES, AND MULLIONS

ENDS OF RAILS AND MULLIONS

Fig. 39-12. Two-piece router bit for profiling. Note how the position of the cutters is changed. (MCS)

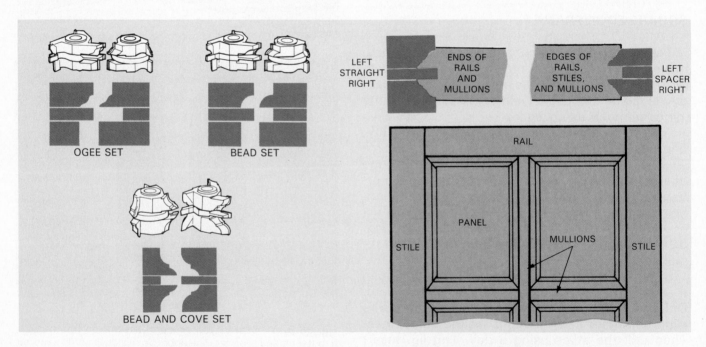

Fig. 39-11. Profile one or two sides of a panel frame with one-pass matched shaper cutters. (Delta)

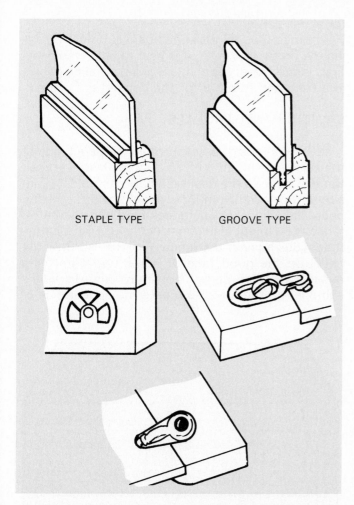

STAPLE TYPE   GROOVE TYPE

Fig. 39-13. Wood or vinyl stops and plastic retainers hold panels in rabbeted frames. (The Woodworker's Store)

A two-piece router bit is shown in Fig. 39-12. One bit shapes and grooves the stile edges. To cope the rail edges, reverse the position of cutters on the bit.

Try to change cutters without adjusting the bit height. Matched cutters usually are the same thickness. Shape a rail end on scrap material and compare it with a stile just cut. Then, shape the ends of the rails. Use a miter gauge with clamp on the shaper to hold the part.

ADDING PANELS AFTER FRAME ASSEMBLY

To install a panel after the frame is assembled, you must cut a rabbet, rather than a groove. Cut the joint along the inside edge of the back of the frame. Fit the panel inside the rabbet and secure it with stops made of plain or decorative lengths of wood or vinyl, Fig. 39-13. Miter or cope the corners as you cut the stops to length. Secure the wood stops with brads or staples. Some vinyl stops are pressed into a groove in the frame.

PANEL COMPONENTS

Panels may be inset, raised, or flush with the frame. Refer to Fig. 39-5. *Raised* or *beveled and raised panels* provide decoration or the look of depth. The raised, beveled one-side panel is the most common, especially on furniture doors. The inside is flat, while the outside is shaped. The *beveled-two-sides panel* often is found on doors visible from both sides.

A *flush* panel is made when the surfaces of a product should be flat. Be extremely accurate when measuring and cutting the frame and panel. Gaps can occur if either component is out-of-square.

An *inset panel* lies below the surface of the frame. It may be flat or have a shoulder cut.

Panels can be made of plywood, particleboard, or glued-up stock. Standard plywood is not recom-

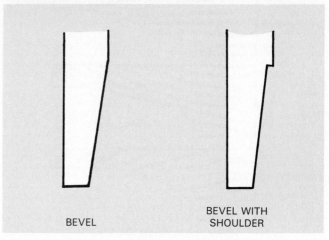

BEVEL   BEVEL WITH SHOULDER

Fig. 39-14. Beveling the panel on the table saw.

mended for raised paneling because there may be voids in the crossbands. Also, because crossbands are rotary cut, they are likely to split and tear when sawn or shaped. Smoothing them may not be worth the time or effort. Furniture manufacturers often select custom-made plywood with extra thick veneer faces or special crossbands.

Particleboard is not often used for raised panels. It is difficult to cover the shaped edges with plastic laminate. However, you could select particleboard for a flat panel.

At times, you might install panels before applying the finish. However, it is best to finish the panel first. Install glass, cane, metal grille, or fabric panels in a rabbeted frame after the cabinet is finished.

SAWING PANEL PROFILES

To saw a raised, beveled-one-side panel, adjust the table saw blade 5 to 15 degrees from vertical. Set the blade to the desired height, about 1 1/2 in. above the table. Stand the panel against a facing board (auxiliary wood fence) fastened to the rip fence. You might also construct a jig, with clamps, that slides against the fence, Fig. 39-14. Saw the bevel on the good face or make two cuts for a raised-two-sides panel. You may wish to add a shoulder on the bevel to create the appearance of

VERTICAL PANEL RAISING

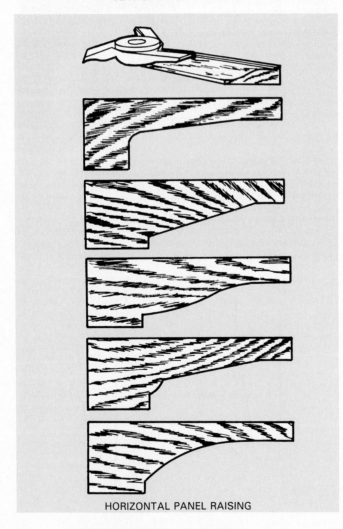

HORIZONTAL PANEL RAISING

Fig. 39-15. Shaping raised panels. (Delta)

Fig. 39-16. Web frame construction with internal frame and solid sides.

depth. To do so, move the fence closer to the blade. Remove saw marks with abrasives before assembling the panel and frame.

SHAPING PANEL PROFILES

Before using the router or shaper, review setup, operation, and safety topics covered in Chapter 26. With some cutters, you hold the material vertical-

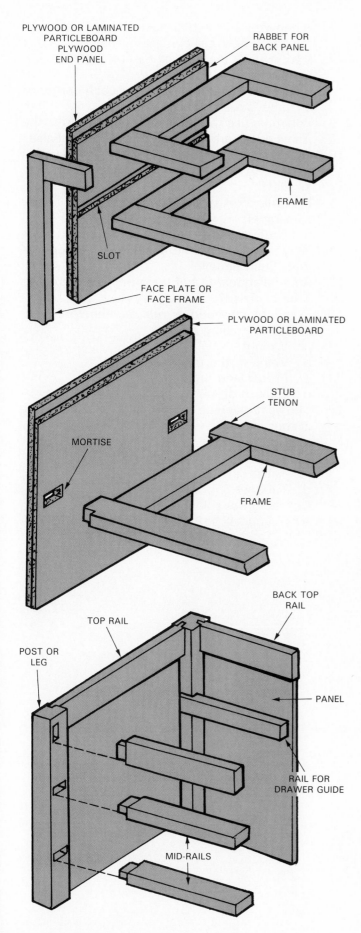

PLYWOOD OR LAMINATED PARTICLEBOARD
PLYWOOD END PANEL

RABBET FOR BACK PANEL

FRAME

SLOT

FACE PLATE OR FACE FRAME

PLYWOOD OR LAMINATED PARTICLEBOARD

STUB TENON

MORTISE

FRAME

BACK TOP RAIL

TOP RAIL

POST OR LEG

PANEL

RAIL FOR DRAWER GUIDE

MID-RAILS

Fig. 39-17. Joinery in web frame construction.

ly. With others, you feed the panel horizontally with the best surface against the shaper table, Fig. 39-15. Adjust the height so that the edge of the panel will slide into the frame groove. Make a test cut to check your setup. Shape the end grain of solid wood panels first.

FITTING PANELS

Solid wood and wood product panels are installed in frames differently. Any panel should slide snugly into the frame. However, since lumber tends to expand and contract with moisture changes, the panel should not fill the groove completely, and should not be glued in place.

WEB FRAME CASE CONSTRUCTION

Web frame case construction represents high-quality cabinetry. The web is an internal frame that adds stability and provides support for drawers. Solid outer surfaces or frame and panel assemblies are added to the frame, Fig. 39-16. While open frames are acceptable, a thin hardboard panel usually is placed within the frame to form a dust panel. It prevents dust from falling from one drawer into the next. It also divides chests with locked drawers to prevent access to the drawer below simply by pulling out the drawer above.

There are several methods used to assemble the case, Fig. 39-17. When the frames fit into side panels, cut dados or stub mortise and tenon joints. If the frame fits into legs or corner posts, cut mortise and tenon joints. Cut a groove along the inside edge of the frame to support a drawer guide and dust panels. Normally, the groove is cut just deep enough to hold the tenon. After assembly, trim the frame to size as needed.

In some quality furniture construction, you see framed panels used for the entire case. The legs become the stiles. Rails are attached directly to the legs. Grooves cut in the rails and legs hold the panels. To mount flush panels, rabbet the legs and rails.

SUMMARY

Frame and panel assemblies serve many purposes in cabinetmaking. From a design standpoint, they add contour to otherwise flat, unattractive surfaces. In addition to wood, panels can be made of glass, cane, fabric, or other materials. From an engineering standpoint, frame and panel components are stable, weigh less, and can reduce the cost of a product.

The product design, available tools, materials, and experience all affect your decision for using frames and panels. In some situations, special equipment is needed. For example, a matched pair of shaper cutters is needed to shape a profiled-edge frame.

Panels may be flush, raised, or inset. They can be flat or profiled to give the appearance of depth. In most cases, the panels are installed in grooves cut along the inside edge of the frame. Glass, metal grille, and other special panels are held in a rabbet joint by stops.

CABINETMAKING TERMS

Frame and panel assembly, stile, rail, intermediate rail, mullion, sticking, raised panel, beveled panel, inset panel, flush panel, web frame case construction.

TEST YOUR KNOWLEDGE

1. Frame and panel assemblies are not intended to replace:
   a. Partitions.
   b. Cabinet sides.
   c. Drawers.
   d. Doors.
2. Name four materials used for panels.
3. Vertical members of a frame are called _____ and _____.
4. Horizontal members of a frame are called _____.
5. The shaped inside edge of frame members is called _____.
6. When you shape the inside edge of a frame after assembly, the corners will be _____.
7. Both frames and panels can be made of particleboard. True or False?
8. Select the same joint type for each corner of a frame. True or False?
9. You must use the same joint type whether the frame edges are seen or hidden. True or False?
10. The easiest square-edge frame joint to use is the:
    a. Butt.
    b. Stub mortise and tenon.
    c. Dowel.
    d. Tongue and groove.
11. Why might you avoid designing components with flush panels?
12. A panel should fit tightly in the frame groove. True or False?
13. Standard plywood is not recommended for profiled paneling due to:
    a. Weight.
    b. Voids in the crossbands.
    c. Processing time.
    d. Lack of stability.
14. The best machine for profiling the frame edge is the:
    a. Router.
    b. Shaper.
    c. Table saw.
    d. Tenoner.
15. Cut the groove deeper in the _____ _____ when you will be installing a solid wood panel.

Chapter 40
CABINET SUPPORTS

After studying this chapter, you will be able to:
☐ Identify the types of cabinet supports.
☐ Prepare feet, legs, plinths, and sides as supports.
☐ Assemble legs to aprons and stretchers.
☐ Install glides and levelers to protect cabinet supports.

Cabinet supports raise cases or furniture above the floor. They include feet, legs, posts, and plinths. On a perfectly flat floor, any support system is stable. On a slightly uneven floor, lumber and wood products may be flexible enough to make the furniture stable. However, when the floor is quite uneven, you will need to install adjustable glides and levelers. These are covered later in the chapter.

FEET

Feet are short supports, in a variety of shapes and sizes, under casework. Those made from short lengths of square or round stock are the easiest to create. You could also produce bracket feet. These consist of two parts joined at 90 degrees with a miter, usually splined.

There are two types of bracket feet: flat and ogee. *Flat bracket feet* are quite simple to make since no shaping is needed, Fig. 40-1. On the other hand, each side of an *ogee bracket foot* is S-shaped, Fig. 40-2. The concave curve is made on the table saw using a plough cut. The convex curve is made on the shaper using a large-radius cutter. It is better to shape one long piece of stock, then cut it into eight individual pieces. Make sure the grain will be parallel to the floor. Miter and assemble the parts in pairs and add glue blocks or mechanical fasteners to strengthen the foot and attach it to the case.

LEGS

Legs are longer supports for tables, chairs, and some casework. They may be round, square, tapered, turned, shaped, or fluted. They could be

Fig. 40-1. Each flat bracket foot consists of two parts joined with a reinforced miter joint. Here the edges are shaped for appearance. (Mersman Tables)

Fig. 40-2. An ogee bracket foot is shaped. (Thomasville)

Cabinet Supports 573

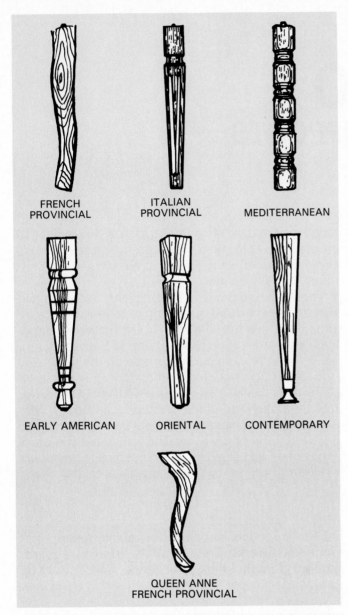

Fig. 40-3. Match leg styles with the cabinet. (Gerber)

Fig. 40-4. Assembled legs often are easier than the one-piece legs to create. (Mersman Tables)

lumber or laminated materials, and are usually shaped to match a particular cabinet style, Fig. 40-3.

Leg selection is a make-buy decision. Some manufactured shapes and lengths come already smooth, with mounting hardware, ready to install and finish. However, you may not be able to find legs made of the same wood specie as your product. Stain the manufactured legs to match the cabinet or design and produce custom legs.

Most straight or tapered one-piece legs follow Early American, contemporary, and similar cabinet styles. They can be square, round, or a combination of both. Shaped legs, such as the cabriole leg, are commonly found on Queen Ann, French Provincial, and Chippendale furniture.

Legs can also be assembled, Fig. 40-4. Made of

several pieces glued together, they are sturdy, but weigh less than solid wood legs.

MOUNTING LEGS

You can mount legs vertical or at an angle, Fig. 40-5. Tall cabinets with vertical legs often look top-heavy, Fig. 40-6. Legs at a slight angle appear to add stability; however, no part of the leg should extend beyond the top surface. Someone could trip over it. A common angle is 5 to 12 degrees. Too large an angle makes the legs look weak.

You can bond legs permanently to the product or attach them with fasteners. With fasteners, the legs can fold or disassemble for easy storage.

Mounting four legs vertical

There are four basic methods to mount legs vertical:

1. Direct assembly with wood joinery.
2. Direct assembly with clinch nut plates.
3. Leg-and-apron construction with wood joinery.
4. Leg-and-apron construction with steel corner braces.

Remember that wood joinery makes the support permanent. Select mechanical fasteners if you might need to disassemble the product in the future.

Direct assembly. You can attach legs directly to most cabinetry with dowels, glue blocks, clinch nut

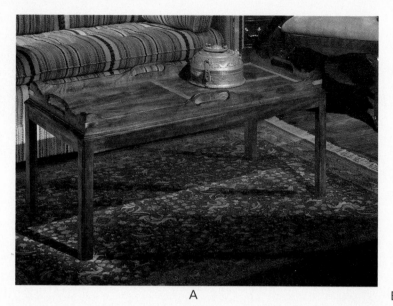

Fig. 40-5. A—Vertical legs. (Thomasville) B—Legs at an angle. (Butler)

Fig. 40-6. Tall cabinets with vertical legs may appear top-heavy, but this often is a design feature. (Thomasville)

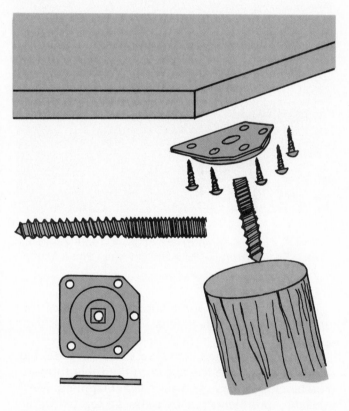

Fig. 40-7. A hanger bolt, screwed into the leg, threads into a clinch nut plate under the chair seat or table top to attach the leg.

plates and hanger bolts. A *clinch nut plate,* Fig. 40-7, fastens to the underside of the cabinetry or chair seat. Screw a hanger bolt into the leg and thread it into the clinch plate.

Leg-and-apron construction. A more sturdy support than direct assembly is *leg-and-apron construction,* Fig. 40-8. The legs and apron assemble with corner braces or joinery. The apron attaches to the underside of the table top. Stretchers, discussed later in the chapter, further strengthen the legs.

A

B

Fig. 40-8. Leg-and-apron construction. A—With contoured legs. (Thomasville) B—With straight legs. (Ethan Allen)

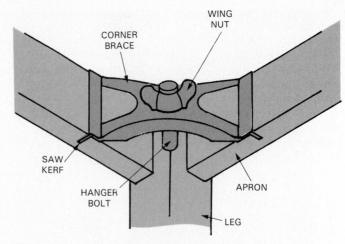

Fig. 40-9. Use a corner brace, hanger bolt, and wing nut to secure removable legs to the apron.

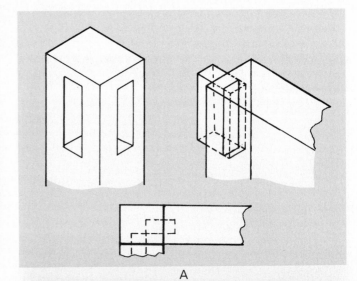

A

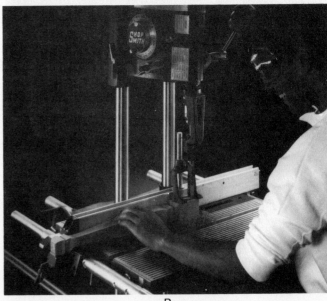

B

Fig. 40-10. A—Miter apron tenons so that they fit in the mortises. B—Mortising the legs on the drill press. (Shopsmith)

The basic leg-and-apron support consists of four legs and four apron pieces. The legs should be square where they attach to the apron.

For removable legs, use steel corner braces, Fig. 40-9. First, attach the apron to the table top with glue blocks, joinery, or mechanical fasteners. Make sure the apron length allows the leg to fit squarely in the corner. Cut saw kerfs in the apron ends to match the size of the corner brace. Then install a hanger bolt in the inside corner of each leg. Tighten the leg in place with a wing nut.

For a permanent support, attach the legs to the apron using wood joinery. A mortise and tenon traditionally has been the joint of choice. You should miter the tenons as shown in Fig. 40-10. Dowels are now used more often than mortise and tenon to reduce costs and processing time.

Another solid bond for leg-and-apron components

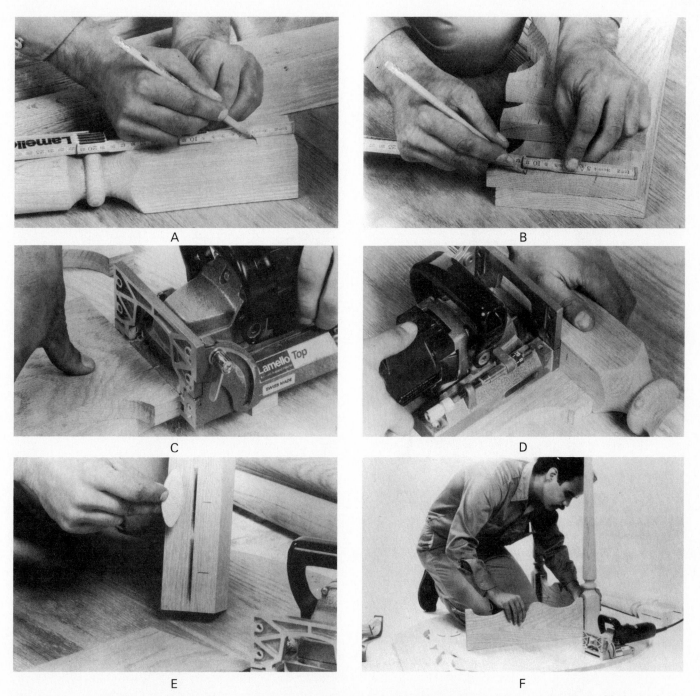

Fig. 40-11. Assembling the legs and apron pieces using plate joinery. A—Mark slot locations on the legs. B—Mark slot locations on the apron pieces. C—Cut the apron slots. D—Align the apron and leg to cut the leg slots. E—Put glue and a plate (biscuit) in both slots on one leg. F—Assemble the legs and apron on a flat surface. (Steiner-Lamello)

is plate joinery. Fig. 40-11 shows slotting and assembling workpieces by this method.

Mounting legs at an angle

Slanted legs can mount at equal or unequal work angles. In addition, two legs might mount at an angle while the other two are vertical. This is quite common in chairs. Always lay out and drill screw holes or make socket joints while the seat or table top is square. By shaping the seat first, you lose reference corners from which to mark hole locations.

Equal work angles. You can mount removable or permanent legs at equal work angles. Suppose you were making a valet chair, such as that shown in Fig. 40-12. Using clinch nut plates to attach removable legs, select a plate type that will provide slanted legs. The shape of the clinch plate sets the angle, usually eight degrees. Screw a hanger bolt into a pilot hole drilled in the leg. Thread a cap nut on the machine screw end. Screw the hanger bolt into the leg with a socket wrench. Then thread the leg into the clinch nut plate.

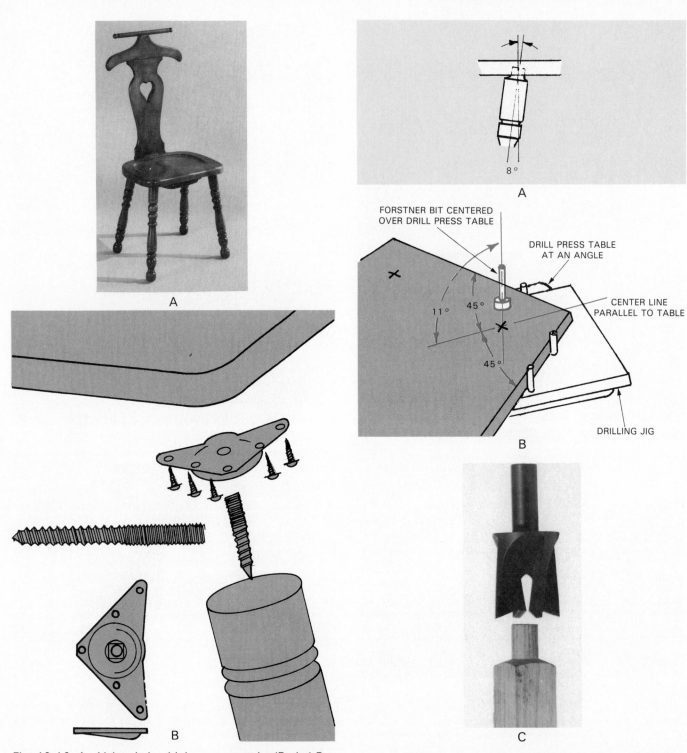

Fig. 40-12. A—Valet chair with legs at an angle. (Butler) B—Select the proper shape clinch nut plate to attach the legs.

Fig. 40-13. A—Typical angle for chair legs. B—Jig for drilling the chair seat. C—Making the tenon for socket joints requires a tool similar to a plug cutter. (Woodcraft)

Permanent legs at an angle are more difficult to make. Although dowel and mortise and tenon joints are common, you might choose a socket joint. This joint is made by shaping a round tenon on the leg using a tool similar to a plug cutter, Fig. 40-13. Drill the holes in the chair seat or table top at an angle, called the work angle. Use a T-bevel or protractor to set the angle of the drill press table. Make a fixture to hold the seat or top at the proper angles.

Select a Forstner bit for drilling the socket and drill the hole just smaller than the tenon. Then squeeze the tenon with pliers to help remove excess glue from the joint. Moisture in the adhesive expands the tenon during assembly creating a strong joint.

Unequal work angles. For some furniture styles, the front and back legs mount at different angles. This is typical with chairs, Fig. 40-14. Usually, the

Fig. 40-14. Example of a chair which has vertical front legs and angled back legs. (Thomasville)

back legs are one piece that is curved slightly for stability.

Mounting tripod legs

Tripod legs, Fig. 40-15, join a central pedestal with dowels, dovetail joints, or mechanical fasteners. Refer to the assembly details in Chapter 29 to

Fig. 40-15. Tripod legs for a clothes tree.

attach legs with joinery, Fig. 40-16. Select mechanical fasteners to make the legs removable.

Removable tripod legs can be fastened with screws and insert nuts, Fig. 40-17. Align and drill two holes through the pedestal. The top hole should be a dowel size, such as 3/8 in. (10 mm). The lower hole should be a screw size, typically 1/4 in. (6 mm). Then, align and mark the hole locations on each leg using dowel centers. Drill a blind hole in upper part of the leg for the dowel. Drill another blind hole large and deep enough to install an insert nut. Glue a dowel in the upper hole on the leg. Insert the machine screw through the pedestal and tighten it into the insert nut. Bond a plug over the screw head.

Make the surfaces match where the leg and pedestal meet. For a round pedestal, flatten the sec-

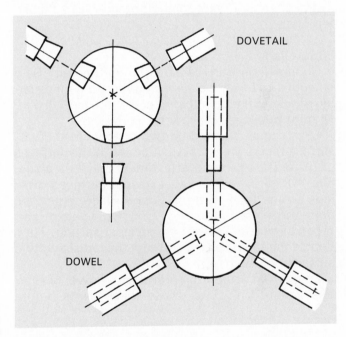

Fig. 40-16. Typical wood joints for fastening tripod legs to a pedestal.

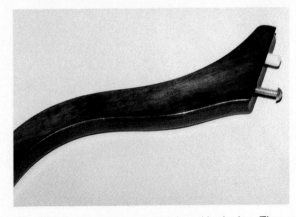

Fig. 40-17. Place an insert nut and dowel in the leg. The screw travels through the pedestal and threads into the insert nut.

tion where the leg attaches or contour the mating surface of the leg.

MAKING LEGS

As mentioned before, selecting legs is a make-buy decision. Although it is easier to purchase premade legs, you may find that some furniture styles require custom parts. Legs can be square, round, or shaped as well as straight or tapered.

Round legs

Round legs are turned between centers on a lathe. Mount the top end of the leg at the headstock. When possible, select a long tool rest so that you do not have to reset it while turning. When making a number of matching legs, use the duplicator. Check your work on tapered or straight legs with a straightedge. Check contoured legs with a shaped template.

Square legs

Square legs can be straight or tapered. Saw straight legs using the standard procedure for squaring stock. Make sure that you saw the leg 1/16 in. (2 mm) oversize to allow for surfacing.

Legs can be tapered on two or four sides. Two-surface tapers are usually cut on the inside surfaces of the leg. Use a taper attachment and a rip blade, Fig. 40-18. Saw the two adjacent surfaces of all legs at one taper setting. Four-surface tapers are done much the same way. Cut two adjacent surfaces of all legs using the first taper setting. Then double the taper setting and saw the remaining two surfaces of each leg.

Legs often attach to aprons with dowel or mortise and tenon joints. Make these joints before

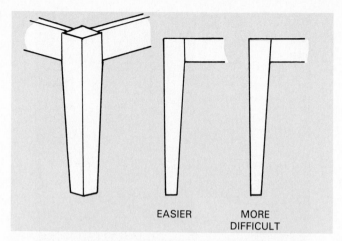

Fig. 40-19. It is easier to join the apron to a square section of the leg rather than a tapered section.

tapering the legs. Start the taper below where the apron meets the leg. You can angle the apron end, Fig. 40-19, but flat surfaces are easier to align and clamp for mortising and drilling.

Assembled legs

Assembled legs can be straight or tapered on two sides. They may be sawn to size before or after assembly. Install corner blocks for reinforcement when necessary, Fig. 40-20.

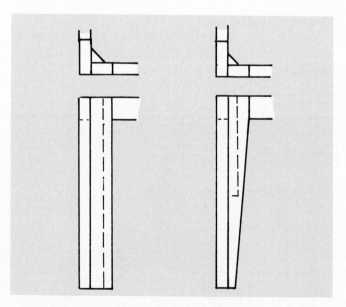

Fig. 40-20. Assembled legs appear strong and are not as heavy as solid wood legs.

Fluted or reeded legs

Fluting and reeding decorate legs and often make them match a particular cabinet style. *Fluting* is a series of equally-spaced parallel grooves around the leg. *Reeding* is a series of narrow, equally spaced convex mouldings. See Fig. 40-21.

Fig. 40-18. Make a taper jig to cut tapered legs. The guard was removed to show the operation.

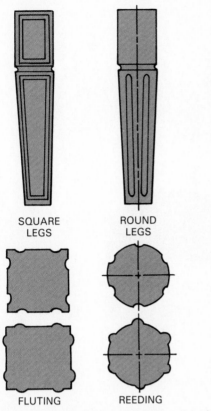

SQUARE LEGS   ROUND LEGS

FLUTING   REEDING

Fig. 40-21. Elevation and section views of fluted and reeded legs.

On round legs, fluting is done with a router or shaper accessory, Fig. 40-22. With a router accessory, the leg is held between centers and the router slides over it. A shaper accessory slides in the table slot to move the leg past the cutter. For square legs, fluting is done on the shaper or table saw with a moulding cutter.

To make reeds, shape a piece of excess material with a bead cutter. Then saw off and glue the reeds in place like moulding.

Cabriole legs

The *cabriole leg* is a distinguishing feature of Queen Anne, French Provincial, and other 18th century furniture. The shape varies according to the period style. In French Provincial furniture, the leg is slender, with more emphasis on the foot, Fig. 40-23. In Queen Anne furniture, the knee is bulky and the leg typically has additions called *ears* extending from each side, Fig. 40-24.

Legs that attach to rectangular tables have a square top. Those that attach to round tables have rabbets or mortises cut so that the leg fits flush with the apron. Prepare dowel holes or mortises before contouring the leg. Also, drill pilot holes for screws before shaping the leg, if possible.

Contouring cabriole legs is a challenging task.

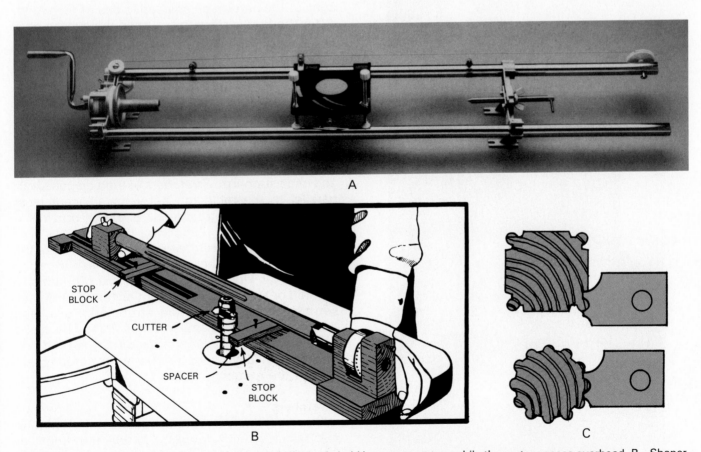

A

STOP BLOCK

CUTTER

SPACER

STOP BLOCK

B   C

Fig. 40-22. A—Router accessory for fluting legs. The leg is held between centers while the router passes overhead. B—Shaper accessory for fluting legs. The guard has been removed to show the operation. C—Details of cutting reeds on square and round legs. (Woodcraft Supply Corp.)

Fig. 40-23. French Provincial cabriole legs. (Bassett)

Fig. 40-24. Queen Anne cabriole legs.

Refer to Fig. 40-25 as you follow these steps. Begin with square stock and a template. Trace mirror images of the pattern on adjacent sides of the wood. After the first surface is cut, tape the excess back to the leg for support. Then saw the second surface. Curve the surface further by hand with Surform tools, rasps, and files. Smooth the leg by hand or with an inflatable drum sander to avoid changing the shape.

STRETCHERS, RUNGS, AND SHELVES

Stretchers, rungs, and shelves strengthen table and chair supports. *Stretchers* extend diagonally or parallel to the table top between adjacent legs. *Rungs* connect stretchers. *Shelves* provide a storage area while reinforcing the legs.

Before cutting stretchers or rungs, assemble the legs and apron without adhesive. Check the rung or stretcher length, especially if the product has tapered or angled legs. Without accurate drill press setups, angled and turned stretchers, legs, and rungs can be a problem. At times, it may be easier to drill assembly holes before turning stretchers. Turn a small diameter stretcher with a steady rest behind the material.

Stretchers

Stretchers may be round, square, or rectangular and fastened with dowels, mortise and tenon, or socket joints, Fig. 40-26. On tapered square legs, bevel the stretcher ends slightly to match the taper.

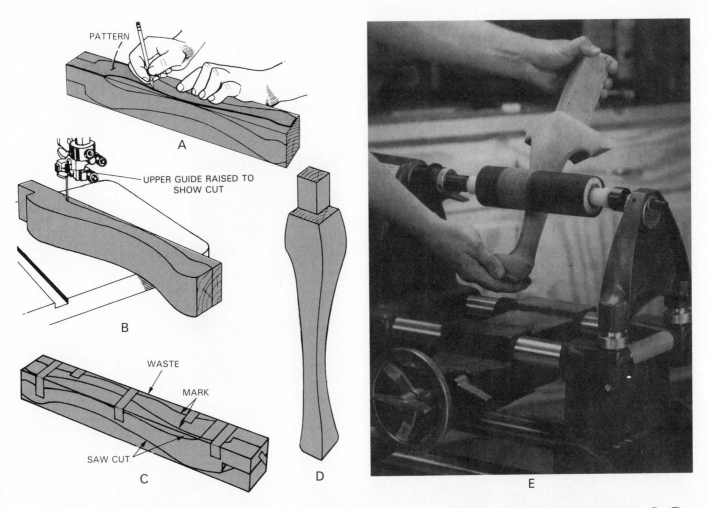

Fig. 40-25. A—Marking stock using the pattern. B—Cut the first profile shape. C—Tape the waste back to the leg. D—The leg after cutting the second profile and removing the waste. E—Smoothing the final leg shape. (Shopsmith)

PATTERN

UPPER GUIDE RAISED TO SHOW CUT

WASTE

MARK

SAW CUT

A

B

C

D

E

Fig. 40-26. Stretchers. A—Between adjacent legs, with shelving. (Mersman Tables) B—On the upper portion of the legs. C—Diagonal, joined with a lap joint. (Thomasville)

A

B

C

On round legs, flatten the area around the joint or contour the stretcher end for a good fit.

Diagonal stretchers are more difficult to fit. Refer to Fig. 40-26C. Cut an oblique lap joint where the stretchers cross. Round stretchers will likely fit into a center hub. Carefully measure the angles to drill holes for assembling the stretcher and legs.

Rungs

Rungs, either round, square, or rectangular, fit between stretchers. They usually fasten with a dowel-like socket joint. For greater strength, drive a brad in the underside of each joint to prevent twisting. A square tenon on the rung also prevents twisting.

Shelves

Shelves, installed instead of stretchers and rungs, provide storage area and strength, Fig. 40-27. The shelf can be made of solid wood, a wood product, or a frame and panel assembly. In addition, you might groove or rabbet the stretchers to accept a lumber or wood product panel. Grooves control warpage better than rabbet joints. Cover particleboard and other wood product shelves with veneer or plastic laminate before inserting them in the frame. Cane also creates an attractive shelf.

Spindles can also support shelves for bookcases. A series of shelves and spindles are layered and assembled with dowel screws, Fig. 40-28.

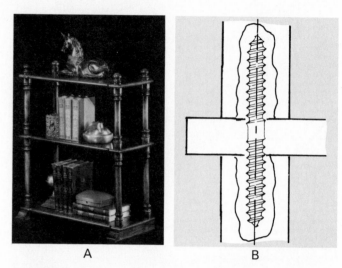

Fig. 40-28. A—Bookcase made by assembling shelves and spindles. (Butler) B—Select dowel screws to connect the spindles.

POSTS

Posts are similar to legs in shape and design, but longer. You usually see posts supporting beds, Fig. 40-29. A round post usually has a section left square where the rails connect. Some cabinetmakers refer to the two vertical supports for chair backs as posts.

A

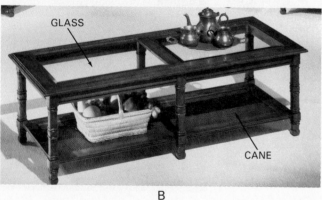

B

Fig. 40-27. A—Install a shelf rather than stretchers when you want extra storage space. (Bassett) B—Cane creates an attractive shelf surface.

Fig. 40-29. Posts are frequently used instead of legs for bed assemblies. (Thomasville)

PLINTHS

Cases can rest directly on floors, legs, feet, or on plinths, Fig. 40-30. A lumber or manufactured wood product, *plinth* provides toe clearance on one or more sides. Fasten it to the case with glue blocks, cleats, pocket joints, corner brace plates, or other fasteners.

A plinth can be either vertical or tapered. Vertical plinths use the same corner joinery, fasteners, and assembly procedures as frames and bracket feet. Tapered plinths are much more complex.

Tapered plinths have corners that are cut at compound angles. This simply means that there are two angle settings to make before sawing the parts. The cuts can be made on either the radial arm saw or table saw.

TABLE SAW

There are few adjustments to make after the initial setup when tapering with the table saw. Three examples are shown for four and six side pyramid-like tapered plinths. See the shaded areas in Fig. 40-31 for the angle settings used in these examples.

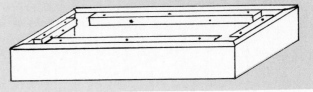

Fig. 40-30. Plinths are common supports for contemporary furniture. (Dyrlund-Smith)

WORKPIECE	4 SIDE BUTT		4 SIDE MITER		6 SIDE MITER		8 SIDE MITER	
Tilt Angle	Blade Angle	Overarm, Taper Guide, or Miter Gauge	Blade Angle	Overarm or Miter Gauge Left and Right	Blade Angle	Overarm or Miter Gauge Left and Right	Blade Angle	Overarm or Miter Gauge Left and Right
5	1/2	5	44 3/4	5	29 3/4	2 1/2	22 1/4	2
10	1 1/2	9 3/4	44 1/4	9 3/4	29 1/2	5 1/2	22	4
15	3 3/4	14 1/2	43 1/4	14 1/2	29	8 1/4	21 1/2	6
20	6 1/4	18 3/4	41 3/4	18 3/4	28 1/4	11	21	8
25	10	23	40	23	27 1/4	13 1/2	20 1/4	10
30	14 1/2	26 1/2	37 3/4	26 1/2	26	16	19 1/2	11 3/4
35	19 1/2	29 3/4	35 1/4	29 3/4	24 1/2	18 1/4	18 1/4	13 1/4
40	24 1/2	32 3/4	32 1/2	32 3/4	22 3/4	20 1/4	17	15
45	30	35 1/4	30	35 1/4	21	22 1/4	15 3/4	16 1/4
50	36	37 1/2	27	37 1/2	19	23 3/4	14 1/4	17 1/2
55	42	39 1/4	24	39 1/4	16 3/4	25 1/4	12 1/2	18 3/4
60	48	41	21	41	14 1/2	26 1/2	11	19 3/4

Fig. 40-31. Compound settings for sawing tapered plinths. Numbers represent degrees.

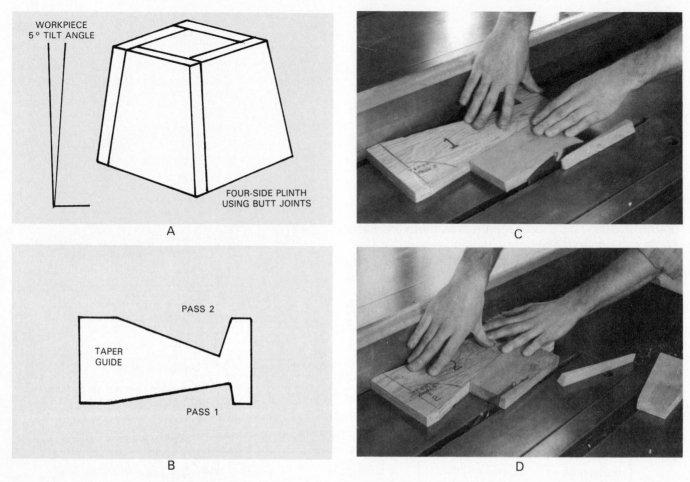

Fig. 40-32. A—Four-sided plinth assembled with butt joints. B—The taper guide has 5 and 10 degree settings. C—Saw the first taper with the five degree guide. D—Saw the second taper with the 10 degree guide. The guard was removed to show the operation.

The first example is a four-sided plinth assembled with butt joints at five degree angles, Fig. 40-32. Make a taper guide with one cutout (pass one) equal to the tilt angle and the second cutout (pass two) equal to double the tilt angle. Cut the components as shown. Compound settings are not required for butt joints.

The second example is a four-sided plinth assembled with compound miter joints, Fig. 40-33. To make the plinth sides at five degree angles,

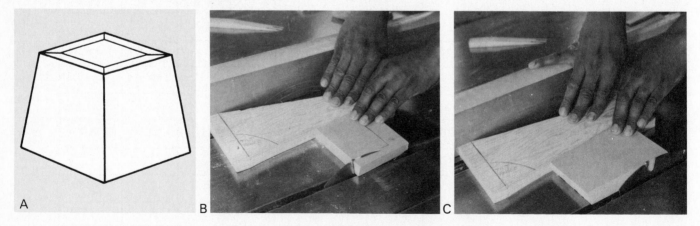

Fig. 40-33. A—Four-sided plinth assembled with compound miter joints. B—Sawing pass one with the five degree taper guide, and with the blade at 44.75 degrees. C—Sawing pass two using the 10 degree taper guide. The guard was removed to show the operation.

select the same taper guide used for the previous example. Also tilt the blade to a 44.75 degree angle.

The third example is a six-sided plinth assembled with compound miter joints, Fig. 40-34. To make the plinth sides with 10 degree angles requires the use of a miter gauge. First position the blade and miter gauge at the proper angles. Have a backup board clamped in position on the gauge. It should extend 4 to 6 in. (100 to 150 mm) beyond either end. First position the miter gauge in the right table slot. Make the first pass with the good face of the workpiece up and with the bottom of the base next to your fingers. For the next pass, move the miter gauge to the left table slot. Position each workpiece with the good face down and have the bottom of the base against the gauge.

RADIAL ARM SAW

With the radial arm saw, adjust the motor and overarm for every cut. Use setup steps shown in Fig. 40-31. You must fit the motor and blade to the right for one pass and to the left for the other. You must also set the overarm at the required angle. For the first pass, tilt the saw to the left. For the second cut, tilt the saw to the right. Saw the parts with the good side up.

SIDES

Having the case sides on the floor is the simplest method of support, Fig. 40-35. This design also makes the product look stable. Occasionally, the sides are contoured to look like feet or legs.

A

B

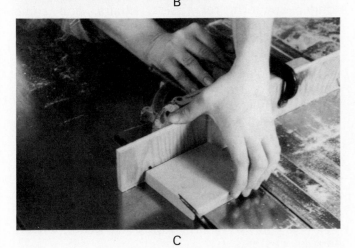

C

Fig. 40-34. A—Six sided plinth assembled with compound miter joints. B—Sawing pass one with the blade angle at 29.5 degrees and the miter gauge at 5.5 degrees in the right table slot. C—Sawing pass two with the miter gauge at 5.5 degrees in the left table slot. The guard was removed to show the operation.

Fig. 40-35. The simplest form of support is the cabinet sides. Note that glides were inserted between the floor and cabinet. (O'Sullivan)

Cabinet Supports 587

GLIDES, LEVELERS, AND CASTERS

Any part of a cabinet that contacts the floor should be protected. Otherwise, when you move the cabinet, the bottom wood surface can chip or splinter. To prevent this, install glides, levelers, ferrules, or casters.

Glides look like large round thumb tacks, Fig. 40-36. Insert glides having a nail point with a hammer. Glue those with a round tab into holes drilled in the bottom of the cabinet.

Adjustable levelers, Fig. 40-37, serve a dual function. They protect the bottom of the cabinet and floor as well as level the cabinet. The leveler consist of a socket or plate and a bolt. The socket has internal threads and fits into a hole drilled in the cabinet bottom. The plate also has internal threads but fastens to the surface of the cabinet. The bolt, which has a swivel glide at the end, threads into the socket or plate. Make adjustments to the cabinet by turning the bolt.

Ferrules slip onto the ends of tapered round legs, Fig. 40-38. They usually have a swivel glide tip. The ferrule may fit friction tight or need a nail driven through it into the end of the leg.

Casters, Fig. 40-39, make moving furniture easier. There are two ways to attach the caster. Some you screw onto the support through a flange. Others need a socket sleeve inserted into a hole drilled in the bottom of the support. Then insert the stem of the caster into the sleeve.

Fig. 40-36. Glides.

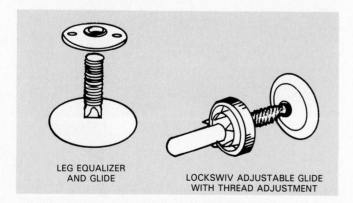

LEG EQUALIZER
AND GLIDE

LOCKSWIV ADJUSTABLE GLIDE
WITH THREAD ADJUSTMENT

Fig. 40-37. Levelers.

Fig. 40-38. Ferrule.

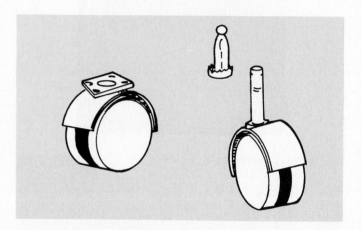

Fig. 40-39. Casters.

SUMMARY

Cabinet supports—feet, legs, posts, and plinths—raise casework and furniture above the floor. Feet are short supports under casework. You can use simple round and square lumber or create more complex assembled and shaped feet. Legs are longer supports for tables, chairs, and some casework. They can be round, square, straight, tapered, contoured, or a combination of shapes. Stretchers or shelves, fastened between legs, add strength and stability. Posts resemble legs, but are longer, and typically used as decorative bed rail supports. Plinths, or frames, provide toe clearance under cases.

CABINETMAKING TERMS

Cabinet supports, feet, flat bracket foot, ogee bracket foot, legs, clinch nut plate, plinth, leg-and-apron construction, tripod legs, fluting, reeding, cabriole leg, stretcher, rung, post, glide, leveler, ferrule, caster.

TEST YOUR KNOWLEDGE

1. To make a concave curve of an ogee bracket foot on the table saw involves a _____ cut.

2. When might you choose to make custom legs rather than buying manufactured legs?
3. Explain the purpose of ferrules and glides.
4. The standard range of leg angles is _____ to _____ degrees.
5. Tall cabinets with vertical legs often look _____.
6. List the four basic methods to mount legs vertical.
7. Clinch nut plates can be used to fasten both vertical and angled legs. True or False?
8. With leg-and-apron construction, the legs are attached directly to the table in addition to the apron. True or False?
9. Why should you drill holes for angled legs before shaping the edges of chair seats?
10. Tripod legs can be jointed to a central pedestal with butt joints. True or False?
11. Explain why two taper angles are needed to cut four-sided tapered legs.
12. How do socket and dowel joints differ? How are they alike?
13. Diagonal stretchers are more difficult to install than parallel stretchers. True or False?
14. Explain why the waste of the first pass is taped back on when making a cabriole leg.
15. What type of cutter should be used to cut flutes and reeds?

Chapter 41
DOORS

After studying this chapter, you will be able to:
- *Identify the appropriate hinge types for mounting different doors.*
- *List the steps for making a sliding door.*
- *Cut and assemble a tambour door.*
- *Install hinged, sliding, and tambour doors.*

Doors add function and beauty to cabinets. Wood doors, such as those on kitchen cabinets and toy chests, conceal the contents. Glass doors, such as those found on china cabinets, are meant to display the contents, Fig. 41-1. Both wood and glass doors may have locks. *Doors* may be mounted in vertical, horizontal, and slanted positions. (Some people refer to horizontal and slanted doors as *lids*.) There are three basic types of doors: hinged, sliding, and tambour.

The number of doors needed depends on the cabinet design, door type, and size of the opening. Hinged doors can be solid lumber, plywood, plastic, particleboard, or glass. Solid lumber doors usually consist of several pieces glued edge to edge. You can also make frame and panel and louvered door assemblies. Sliding doors have two or three panels that glide in upper and lower tracks. Tambour doors consist of wood slats bonded to a heavy cloth backing. The flexible door moves inside tracks or slots in the cabinet sides or top and bottom.

A

B

Fig. 41-1. A—This sectional cabinet contains framed glass and framed wood door styles. (Dyrlund-Smith) B—Some louvered doors allow ventilation.

HINGED WOOD DOORS

The most prominent door style is hinge mounted. Doors can be solid wood, a manufactured panel product, or frame and panel assembly. All are treated alike during installation. Large openings, wider than 24 in., usually require two doors. A single door would be heavy and might swing too far into the traffic path. Openings less than 24 in. could have only one door mounted with heavy-duty hinges. However, two doors could be used for design reasons. On face frame cases, a mullion may separate one large opening into two smaller entrances.

SURFACE DECORATION

You can enhance the appearance of solid wood doors by shaping the surface with a router. The routed design might even simulate the raised panel of a frame and panel assembly. Route the design with the aid of a special router attachment, Fig. 41-2. Clamp the template frame to the face of the door. Attach the template for the desired shape. Install a router bit that creates the desired groove shape. To cut arcs, use the arc attachment that pivots on template frame.

HINGED DOOR MOUNTS

As shown in Fig. 41-3, there are four basic ways that hinged vertical doors mount to the cabinet:
1. *Flush front* (face frame of frameless). Door faces are flush inside the face frame or case edges.
2. *Flush overlay* (face frame or frameless). The door hides the entire face frame or case edges.
3. *Reveal overlay* (face frame or frameless). The face frame or case edges are partially visible around and between doors.
4. *Lip-edge.* A rabbet is cut in the door edge.

Overlay and lip-edge doors stop against the cabinet side or face frame. Flush front doors bump against a stop or catch. Otherwise, the door would try to swing inside the cabinet. In addition, you might bevel the striker edge of flush doors at a three-degree clearance angle. This prevents a tight-fitting door from rubbing against the cabinet side or frame.

Hinged doors have a *hinged side* and *striker side.* When installing hinges, make sure the pins of the hinges align perfectly. Otherwise, the door will not swing freely, a condition called *hinge bound.*

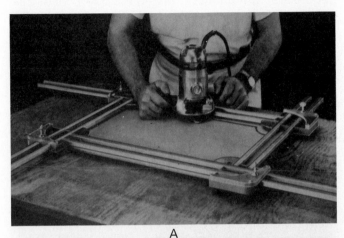

Fig. 41-2. A—Routing a groove in a door front. B—Arc attachment. (Wing)

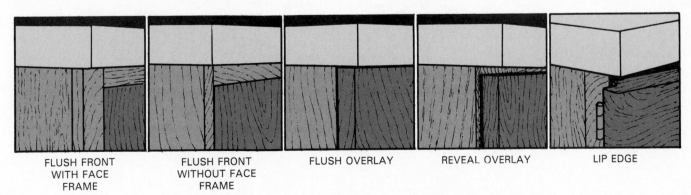

FLUSH FRONT WITH FACE FRAME   FLUSH FRONT WITHOUT FACE FRAME   FLUSH OVERLAY   REVEAL OVERLAY   LIP EDGE

Fig. 41-3. There are different way to mount doors to a cabinet. (Architectural Woodwork Institute)

Door hinges do not have to be equally spaced. Some designs have the hinges slightly higher from the bottom than they are from the top. For example, you might set the top hinge 1 1/2 in. (38 mm) away from the top, but locate the lower hinge 2 to 2 1/2 in. (50 to 63 mm) up from the bottom.

Doors over 3 ft. long should have more hinges to help maintain door alignment. See Fig. 17-12.

When selecting fasteners to mount doors, make sure that the screws are 1/8 in. (3 mm) shorter than the door or case thickness. Always drill pilot holes so that screws do not split the wood.

When mounting plywood or particleboard doors, select hinges that mount to the case and door faces. Screws will not hold in the edges of these products.

MOUNTING HINGED WOOD DOORS

The various types of door hinges were discussed in Chapter 17. The one you choose depends on the cabinet style and door mount. Fig. 17-11 charts the application of hinges to specific door mounts.

When installing double doors, grain pattern is a concern. Measure the opening as if you were installing one door. Saw a single door to this size. If the design calls for contoured edges, shape them as if making one door. Then cut the panel in half to separate the two doors. The grain pattern should match perfectly.

You can treat the striker edges on double door installations one of several ways, Fig. 41-4. First, they can be butted with a slight space between them. Bevel the edges three degrees so that they do not rub when closing. A second method is to attach a cap strip on the outside of one door. This gives the appearance that there is a mullion behind the doors. A third method is to add a backing strip to the inside. This works if the door edges are square, not shaped. A fourth method is to rabbet the doors. This requires that you cut the doors different widths, one about 1/4 in. (6 mm) wider than the other.

If you mount the double doors using one of the last three methods, one door must be opened before the other. This usually is the right door since most people are right handed. Having the doors meet this way is also recommended when you plan to install locks. A catch usually fastens inside the left door. Install mortised or nonmortised locks in right door.

Flush mount

A flush mount door is difficult to fit accurately. Gaps can occur if the door or opening is even slightly out-of-square. The misalignment gives the appearance of poor quality cabinetry. To help prevent this, inset or outset the door 1/16 to 1/8 in. (2 to 3 mm). Any sizing errors will become less noticeable.

Door sizing. Size the width and length of a single flush mount door 1/8 to 3/16 in. (3 to 5 mm) less than the opening. Do the same for a double flush mount door with mullion. For two doors without a mullion, cut each door 3/32 in. (2 mm) narrower than half the opening. Bevel the striker edges of both doors at 3 degrees.

Door installation. There are several ways to hang flush doors. You might choose butt, formed, invisible, concealed (European), pin, or surface hinges, Fig. 41-5. For plywood or particleboard doors, use concealed or surface hinges. The halves of the hinge mount on the faces, rather than edges, of the door and cabinet.

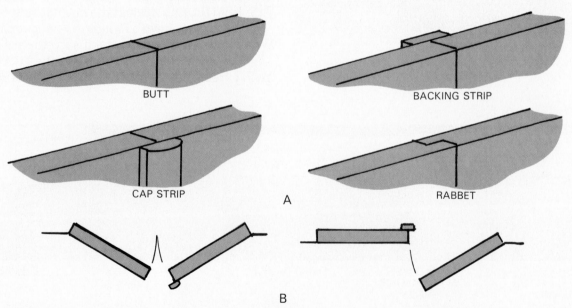

Fig. 41-4. The striker edges of double doors can meet several ways.

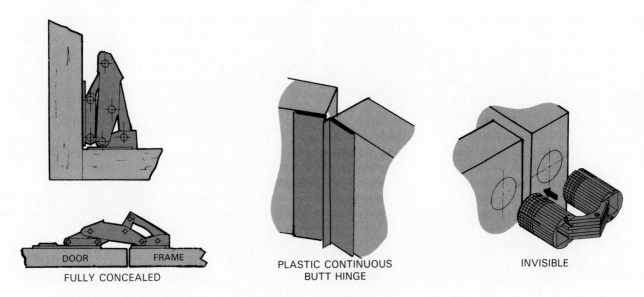

FULLY CONCEALED

PLASTIC CONTINUOUS
BUTT HINGE

INVISIBLE

Fig. 41-5. These are special hinge types for mounting flush doors. (Liberty Hardware)

Butt hinges, found in quality cabinetry, are one of the few hinge types still recessed into the door and/or frame. For a very tight fit, make sure that both leaves are half swaged or one leaf is full swaged. See Fig. 41-6 and refer to Fig. 17-14. You can recess butt hinges one of three ways. For one with both leaves half swaged, cut gains equal to one hinge leaf thickness in both the frame and door edge. Butt hinges with one full swaged leaf are set in a full thickness gain cut in *either* the frame or door. The procedure for cutting gains for mortised butt hinges is shown in Fig. 47-7.

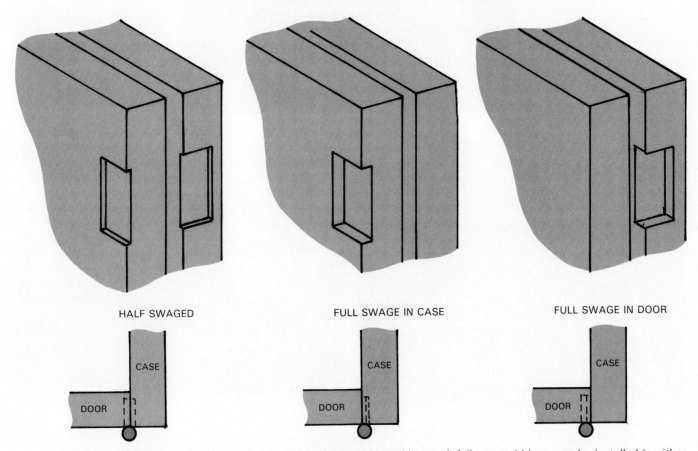

HALF SWAGED

FULL SWAGE IN CASE

FULL SWAGE IN DOOR

Fig. 41-6. Mortise the grains differently for full- and half-swaged butt hinges. A full-swaged hinge can be installed in either the door or case.

Fig. 41-7. Fastening a butt hinge. A—Cut around the hinge leaf with a knife. B—Cut on the line with a chisel. C—Chisel out the pocket. D—Check the hinge fit. E—Drill the pilot holes and install the hinge.

Fasten a stop or catch in the cabinet on the striker side of the door. Stops made of 1/4 x 1/2 in. (6 x 13 mm) wood strips are recommended. Several types of catches were described in Chapter 17.

Overlay mount

Overlay doors cover some or all of the face frame, or case edges in frameless cabinetry. Errors in sizing the door or opening are not as obvious as they are for flush doors.

Door sizing. Plan for doors to cover as much of the face frame or case side as desired. Reveal and full overlay doors are both popular.

Door installation. You can hang overlay doors with formed, pivot, concealed (European), and non-mortised butt hinges, Fig. 41-8. They fasten to the back of the door and to the face frame or inside surface of the cabinet.

Lip-edge mount

Lip-edge doors have a 3/8 in. (10 mm) rabbet cut in the edges and ends. When mounted and closed, part of the door thickness is outside the cabinet. The remainder is inside, Fig. 41-9.

Door sizing. For a single door, measure the inside of the opening. Add 1/2 in. (13 mm) to the length and width to calculate the door size. The 3/8 in. (10 mm) rabbet leaves an added 1/8 in. (3 mm) of space for clearance and door alignment. Usually, the rabbet is half the door thickness.

Door installation. Mount doors with concealed or 3/8 in. (10 mm) formed hinges. Position and align formed hinge barrels with the rabbet. Anchor the hinges on the door. Then center, square, and install the door over the opening. You can make adjustments to concealed hinges after attaching the hinge cup and mounting plate.

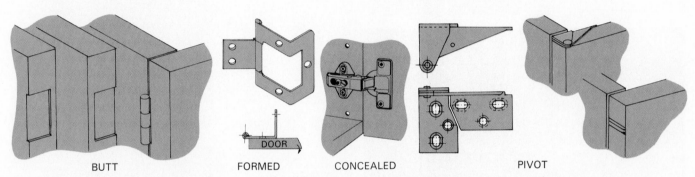

BUTT   FORMED   CONCEALED   PIVOT

Fig. 41-8. Hinge types to mount overlay doors.

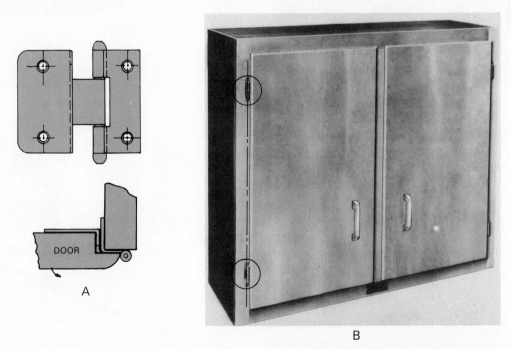

DOOR

A

B

Fig. 41-9. A—Install lip-edge doors with nonmortised hinges. (Liberty Hardware) B—Make sure the barrels are aligned so that the door does not become hinge bound. (Brodhead-Garrett)

HINGED WOOD LIDS

Wooden lids can attach with mortised or nonmortised hinges. Mortised flap hinges are specially designed for lids and fold-up table top sections, Fig. 41-10. On desktops which have large lids, it is wise to install a lid support to prevent the lid from dropping too far or too fast, Fig. 41-11.

When a lid folds upward, you could install a counterbalance hinge. It adjusts for the lid weight, Fig. 41-12. Thus, the lid stays where positioned.

Heavy lids usually require stays to help the hinges support the weight, Fig. 41-13. In addition, you might install a stay on a fold-up table top. The stay locks the lid in position so that it cannot fall. It would help support books, possibly a typewriter, or other objects. You must manually release the stay to let the lid down.

Fig. 41-12. A—Counterbalance hinges keep a raised lid in place. (National Lock) B—Typical application of counterbalance hinges on a stereo cabinet. (Sauder)

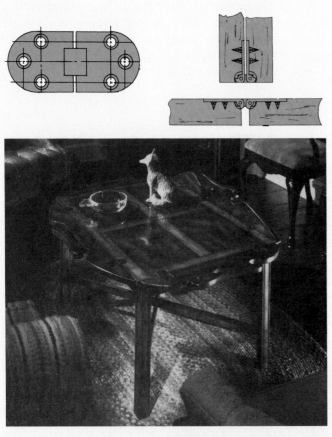

Fig. 41-10. Flap hinges are common on lids and hinged-leaf tables. (Thomasville)

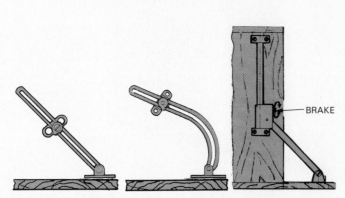

Fig. 41-11. Types of lid supports. The left two prevent the lid from falling too far. The far right support also slows the fall of the lid with an adjustable brake. (Liberty Hardware)

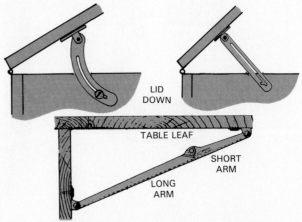

Fig. 41-13. Lid stays keep a lid raised. They lock on a screw or fold into place. (Liberty Hardware)

GLASS AND PLASTIC DOORS OR LIDS

Plastic and glass are attractive materials for doors and lids. See Figs. 41-1 and 41-11. You can install flush and overlay glass and plastic doors with or without a frame. Use hinges for wood doors when the glass is framed.

Select tempered glass or acrylic plastic with polished edges for unframed doors. Purchase sized sheet glass with ground and polished edges. You can smooth and polish the edges of plastic. Refer to Chapter 15.

Chapter 17 covers hinges for vertical glass and plastic doors in detail. Normally, unframed glass doors rest in a U-shaped hinge leaf and are held there by set screws, Fig. 41-14. A metal pad between the glass and screws prevents the glass from breaking when you tighten the screws. Other hinge styles require drilled holes.

Unframed glass lids, such as those covering a stereo stand, mount with counterbalance hinges. They stay in any position without the help of a lid support.

SLIDING DOORS

Sliding doors have two or three panels that glide past each other. They are held in upper and lower tracks, Fig. 41-15. The panels may be plywood, glass, or plastic. With two doors, only half of the cabinet opening is accessible at any one time. Three sliding doors can be fitted in two or three tracks.

With three, you have access to two-thirds of the cabinet opening. When placed in two tracks, three doors give you access to only one-third of the opening. The advantage of sliding doors is that they do not swing into and obstruct the traffic path. You will not bump against them as you would a hinged door left standing open.

VERTICAL DOOR TRACKS

Sliding doors are supported and guided by a pair of metal or plastic tracks, Fig. 41-16. The doors slide within about 1/4 in. (6 mm) of each other. Both upper and lower tracks have two grooves. The lower track supports the weight of the doors. To reduce friction, it contains ridges. These prevent the entire edge of the door from rubbing. Special roller

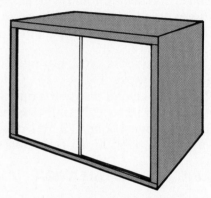

Fig. 41-15. Double sliding doors.

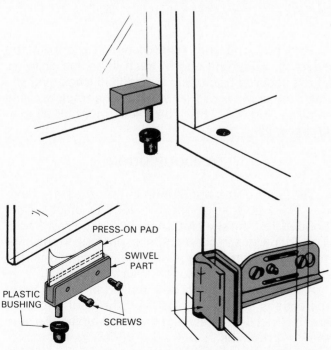

Fig. 41-14. Glass door pin hinges and side-mounted hinges. Both hold the glass in a U-shaped hinge leaf.

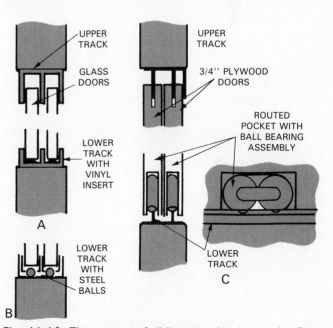

Fig. 41-16. Three types of sliding door hardware. A—Glass doors rest on a vinyl insert in the lower track. B—Glass and wood doors can ride on ball bearings. C—Heavy doors usually need rollers.

hardware mounted on the door bottom allows the door to slide and move more freely. The upper track guides the door. Its grooves, about 1/2 in. (13 mm), are deeper than those in the lower track, about 1/4 in. (6 mm). Upper and lower tracks must be parallel and aligned.

Purchase tracks according to the number of doors, door thickness, and width of the opening. Two doors require two-groove tracks. Three doors require only two grooves, but three-groove tracks allow greater access. Typical door thicknesses are: 1/8 in. (3 mm) hardboard, 1/4 in. (6 mm) glass, and 3/4 in. (19 mm) plywood. Each groove will be just wider than the intended door thickness. The length of the tracks depends on the width of the opening.

Doors weighing more than three pounds should ride on roller hardware. To install the rollers, you must mortise two pockets in the bottom end of the door about 1 in. (25 mm) from each edge. Insert the assemblies and secure them with screws. Note that the lower track is different because the ball bearings ride on the track's edge centered under the door.

For small sliding doors, you can make grooves rather than install tracks, Fig. 41-17. Cut grooves in the surfaces above and below the opening. Saw the lower groove 3/16 to 1/4 in. (5 to 6 mm) deep. Saw the upper groove 1/2 in. (13 mm) deep. Space the grooves about 3/16 in. (5 mm) apart.

DOOR SIZING AND INSTALLATION

The height of a sliding door is critical. It must measure 1/16 in. (2 mm) less than the distance between the inside of the top track and the top edge of the bottom track. To install the door, lift and insert it into the top groove. Swing the lower end over the bottom track or groove and then set the door down.

Door widths are less critical, but doors should overlap. Make them wider than half the opening. For double doors, make each about 1/4 to 1/2 in. (6 to 13 mm) wider than half the opening. For triple doors, make each about 1/4 to 1/2 in. (6 to 13 mm) wider than one-third the opening.

HORIZONTAL SLIDING LIDS

Sliding lids mount with tracks in much the same way as vertical sliding doors. However, both tracks are the same depth.

Horizontal sliding lids may be a wood panel, hardboard, glass, plastic, or plywood. Size the panels with the tracks installed. Measure across the opening between the bottoms of the track grooves. Subtract 1/8 in. (3 mm) for clearance to obtain the lid height, Fig. 41-18A. Lid widths should result in a 1/4 to 1/2 in. (6 to 13 mm) overlap.

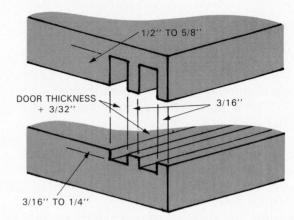

Fig. 41-17. You can saw or rout your own sliding door tracks for lightweight doors.

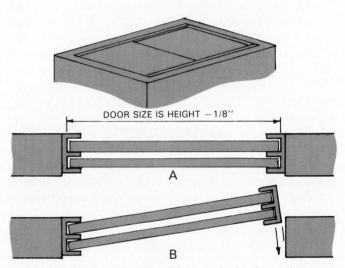

Fig. 41-18. Horizontal sliding lids must be in place when you fasten the second track.

To install the lids, remove one track from the opening. Slide one end of each lid in the grooves of the secured track. Slip the second track over the lids' free ends. Lower and fasten the track and lids in place, Fig. 41-18B. The tracks must be aligned and parallel.

TAMBOUR DOOR

Tambour doors are unique in that they are flexible. They consist of narrow wood or plastic slats bonded to a heavy cloth backing, usually canvas. The door slides in curved tracks, or slots, in the case top and bottom or sides. In most installations, the door is hidden when open. See Fig. 41-19.

A tambour door can be installed before or after the case is assembled. Usually, the door and case are finished separately and then assembled. Be sure the door remains in its track through its full movement. This is necessary whether the door is visible or hidden. You might need a pin, or other mechani-

A

B

Fig. 41-19. A—Rolltop desk. (Unfinished Furniture Stores.) B—When open, the doors are usually hidden. (Dyrlund-Smith)

cal fastener, installed at the end of one track prevents the door from sliding out of the case.

SLAT MAKING

Tambour door slats are usually trapezoid or half-round shapes. Two factors determine slat size and shape: track radius and span.

The track radius is the size of the curve. Most doors follow one or more curves. The smaller the curve radius, the narrower the slats. For example, slats for a jewelry box tambour door would be thinner and narrower than those for a rolltop desk.

Span is the distance across the opening. The slats must be strong enough to resist sagging when horizontal.

Determine the length of the slats by measuring across the opening, including the depth of both tracks. Saw the stock to length 1/8 in. (3 mm) less than that distance.

You can make half-round or trapezoid-shaped slats, Fig. 41-20. To saw trapezoid slats, rip them to width on the table saw. Install a hollow ground planer blade. It will leave fewer saw marks. Set the blade to the required angle, most likely 5 to 15 degrees. Position the rip fence for the proper slat width. Rip the first slat. Turn the stock over to rip the second slat. Reverse the stock for each pass. This method produces no waste. You also help prevent the assembled door from warping by alternating the grain pattern. Smooth the slats, and cut them to length.

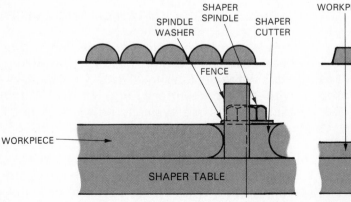

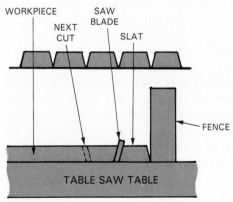

Fig. 41-20. Tambour door slats can be shaped round or sawed trapezoidal.

To make half-round slats, shape an edge on the stock. Set the table saw fence to the slat thickness. Then saw off the rounded edge to separate individual slats. This is a slower procedure and it creates more waste than making trapezoid slats.

The first slat, called the *lifter bar,* usually is wider and possibly thicker than the others. When opening the door, you grab the bar itself or a pull. Insert two flush- or surface-mount pulls in doors over 2 ft. wide.

To add a lock, the lifter bar must be thick. However, a thick bar will not fit in the tracks. Thus, you must cut tenons or rabbets in the ends. The lifter bar can also be made of two slats: one on each side of the canvas and fastened with screws. The outer slat fits in the grooves. The inner slat, cut shorter to not interfere with door movement, adds strength.

The length of visible track determines the number of slats needed. Measure this distance and divide by the size of each slat. Add the lifter bar width and the opening should be fully covered. Track length, visible and hidden, should be nearly twice the length of the assembled door, Fig. 41-21.

DOOR ASSEMBLY

Bonding the slats to cloth is the key to tambour door assembly. Begin by washing, drying, and pressing the cloth. This will shrink the material. It also removes any resin that makes textiles stiff.

Cut the cloth greater than the door width but 1/4'' (6 mm) narrower than the distance between tracks. Lay the cloth on a metal or plastic laminate surface. Make a jig with two clamps that keeps the cloth taut. See Fig. 41-22. Clamp another straightedge along one side of the cloth. The slats align against it.

Mix an estimated amount of thinned aliphatic resin or PVA adhesive. It should have a brushing or spraying consistency. Coat the cloth and the back of the first slat. Position the first slat against the end and side straightedges. Position remaining slats against the side straightedge and previous slat. You may not be able to add the lifter bar at this time. Cover the door assembly with sandbags or other weight and allow the glue to cure.

TRACK MAKING

Tambour door tracks should be about 1/16 to 1/8 in. (2 to 3 mm) wider than the tambour strip thickness. There are two methods to make door tracks. You can saw the contour in a piece of lumber, and then attach it to the case. You can also rout the tracks directly into opposing surfaces of the case.

To saw the tracks, begin with a piece of stock the same wood specie as the cabinet. Saw the track

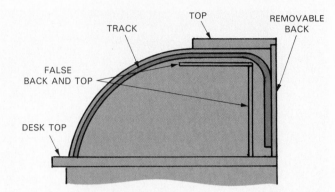

Fig. 41-21. The tracks should be nearly twice as long as the opening. A false back and top hide the door.

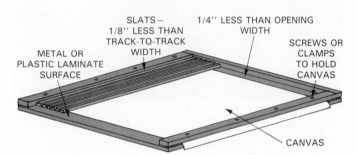

Fig. 41-22. Keep the canvas taut while you bond the slats. Position the slats against the straightedge and against each other.

contour with a band saw or saber saw. Make two cuts to remove excess equal to the track width. Smooth any saw marks and attach the two pieces to the cabinet surface with adhesive or screws. If you use glue, leave one end of the track open. Otherwise, you cannot install the tambour door.

Routing grooves for the tracks is much easier. Cut a template to match the track curve you wish to make. Insert a template and straight bit, the size of the track width, in the router. Set the bit depth at about half the material thickness. After routing one side, turn the template over to rout the second side. Be sure one end of the track opens to an edge so that you can install the door.

PULLS, KNOBS, CATCHES, AND LATCHES

Pulls and *knobs* help you open doors. Most are decorative and many are manufactured to replicate a cabinet style. Pulls for sliding doors must be flush with the door surface, Fig. 41-23. Remember, sliding doors are typically no more than 1/4 in. apart. Catches hold hinged doors closed either mechanically or by magnetism. Latches hold the door closed and help open it. Pushing in a latch activates a release mechanism which forces the door open. Doors with latches normally do not require pulls since the hardware opens the door for you.

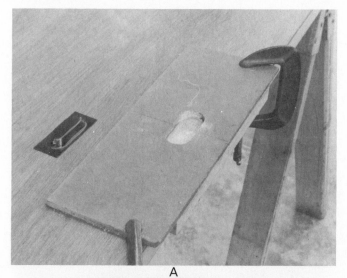

A

B

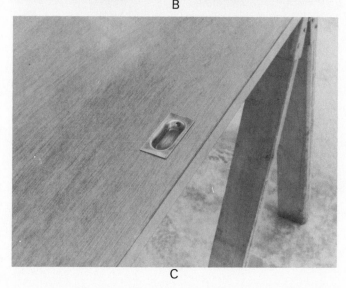

C

Fig. 41-23. Routing a mortise for a flush pull in a sliding door. A—Clamp the template over the door. B—Rout the template opening to the proper depth. C—Install the pull.

Chapter 17 discusses pulls, knobs, catches, and latches in more detail. Many contemporary styles have no visible hardware. To open the door, you push it to release the latch or grasp a finger grip shaped in the door edge.

SUMMARY

Doors and lids are valuable parts of cabinetry. They add function by concealing contents and, when locked, add security to the cabinet. Doors also add beauty. Glass doors allow you to display the contents. A routed or shaped wood door can be very attractive.

Frame and panels, plywood, and laminated wood products all make attractive doors. Glass and plastic work well for display cases.

Doors pivot on hinges or slide in tracks. The type of hinge you select depends on the door mount which could be flush, full overlay, reveal overlay, or lip-edge. Tracks are needed for sliding and tambour doors. A tambour door track may be a slot routed in the case sides.

CABINETMAKING TERMS

Lid, flush front, flush overlay, reveal overlay, hinge side, striker side, hinge bound, sliding doors, tambour door, lifter bar.

TEST YOUR KNOWLEDGE

1. The most prominent door style is the _____ _____.
2. When a door will not swing freely because the hinges are not aligned the condition is called _____ _____.
3. List the four basic ways to mount hinged vertical doors.
4. The edges of unframed glass doors should be _____ and _____.
5. The striker side of the door supports the hinges. True or False?
6. Why would you bevel the edges of a double door?
7. How do you determine the size of sliding lid panels?
8. How do you measure for sliding door height?
9. Slats for tambour doors must be beveled on the back. True or False?
10. Identify four ways to fit the striker side edges of double doors if no mullion is installed.
11. A lifter bar is not thick enough to contain a lock. True or False?

Drawers may be used for concealment as well as storage. (Quaker Maid)

Chapter 42 DRAWERS

After studying this chapter, you will be able to:
- □ Describe design and engineering factors that influence drawer construction.
- □ Design and process drawer components.
- □ Assemble drawers using various joints.
- □ Mount drawers with conventional and commercial glides, slides, and tracks.
- □ Install drawer pulls and knobs.

Drawers are handy compartments for organizing and storing objects, Fig. 42-1. Items in drawers are more accessible than those on shelves. Opening a drawer brings its contents close to you; you often have to reach for items on a shelf. Two factors affect drawer construction: design and engineering.

Another design factor is the way that the drawer fronts fit in or against the cabinet. They correspond to the four standard styles for hinged doors. The drawer type and door mount should be the same. Look at Fig. 42-2.

1. *Flush front* (face frame or frameless). Drawer fronts are flush inside the face frame or with the case edges.
2. *Flush overlay front* (face frame or frameless). The drawer front covers the entire face frame or case edges.
3. *Reveal overlay front* (face frame or frameless). Part of the face frame or case edges are visible around and between drawers and doors.

Fig. 42-1. This kitchen drawer stores spices efficiently. (Quaker Maid)

DESIGN FACTORS

The principles of design influence drawer placement. Drawers in a chest generally are deeper near the floor than they are at the top. They store bulky, seasonal, and less used items. Items used more frequently are stored above.

Fig. 42-2. Having the same drawer and door styles ties the design together. (Quaker Maid)

4. *Lip-edge front.* Rabbet cut in drawer edge.

Overlay and lip-edge drawers stop against the cabinet side or face frame. Flush front drawers rest against the case back or a stop in the drawer slides.

Shallow drawers, or trays, often slide into the cabinet and hide behind the doors. The tray can rest on shelves, in a drawer, or be mounted with slides. The slides usually run the full depth of the cabinet and allow the tray to extend its full length.

ENGINEERING FACTORS

Engineer drawers to serve a purpose. Those that store cooking utensils usually have partitions to prevent items from moving when the drawer is opened and closed, Fig. 42-3. Drawers in an entertainment center might have slots for cassettes and video tapes. Desk drawers might have dividers to separate envelopes, stationary, paper clips, and rubber bands.

Despite their advantages over shelves, drawers are an expensive way to organize and store items. You will need extra wood, wood products, veneer, plastic laminate, drawer guide hardware, and pulls or knobs. Production time includes machine setup, processing, assembling, and finishing. You can recognize fine cabinetry by the materials, joinery, and time spent making the drawers.

You may need jigs and attachments to machine the drawer joints. For example, to make a dovetail joint efficiently requires a dovetail jig and router. This is high-quality drawer joinery. You can also assemble drawers with dado, rabbet, and miter joints.

Fig. 42-3. Partitions help you organize drawer contents. (Quaker Maid)

One last factor is that you must plan in advance how to install the drawer. Some commercial slides need extra clearance between the drawer sides and cabinet.

DRAWER COMPONENTS

A drawer consists of five parts: front, back, bottom, and two sides. One extra component, a false front, may also be attached. See Fig. 42-4.

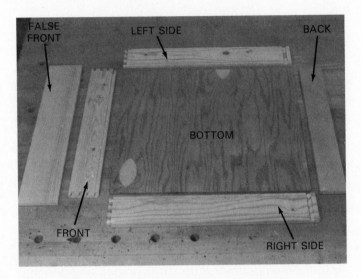

Fig. 42-4. Typical drawer components.

DRAWER FRONT

Drawer fronts are usually made of the same lumber specie as the cabinet. You can also cover particleboard or a less expensive hardwood core with veneer or plastic laminate. Although you can use plywood, the edges should be banded to cover voids in the crossbands. Fronts vary in thickness from 3/4 to over 1 in. (19 to 25 mm).

False fronts can be fastened over a less expensive drawer front. For example, you might make the front, sides, and back with particleboard. Then attach a solid wood, veneered, or laminated front to match the cabinet. This method saves production time. The false front might be flush, full overlay, reveal overlay, or look like a lip edge.

Veneer bands, mouldings, and wood carvings can accent drawer fronts. Moreover, the fronts may be curved or the edges shaped for design effects. The front may be routed to match a design in the doors. See Chapter 41.

DRAWER SIDES

Drawer sides are typically made of inexpensive, close-grain hardwood lumber, such as chestnut.

Although particleboard and plywood are suitable, you must select the corner joints carefully. Most drawer sides are 1/2 in. (13 mm) thick. This provides adequate strength, yet keeps the drawer light. The top corners of drawer sides are usually rounded slightly.

The length of the drawer sides varies according to cabinet depth. The sides often act as a stop on a flush drawer. Otherwise, length is controlled by the hardware selected for the particular cabinet under construction.

DRAWER BACK

Drawer backs are usually made of the same material as the sides. Most often, the back is 1/4 to 1/2 in. (9 to 13 mm) thick. Thinner material reduces costs.

DRAWER BOTTOM

Drawer bottoms can be made of 1/4 in. plywood or 1/8 to 1/4 in. hardboard. These materials are very stable and strong. The bottom fits into grooves cut in the front and sides. A fitted bottom also rests in a groove cut in the back. A slide-in bottom is cut so that the back sits on the bottom; thus, the back is not grooved. See Fig. 42-5. A slide-in bottom fastens from underneath into the back with screws.

DRAWER ASSEMBLIES

Drawers receive use and abuse. This is especially true when they are filled to capacity with heavy items. The front corners must withstand pulling and pushing forces. Thus, a good sign of quality drawer construction is the type of corner joint chosen. The front and sides usually are joined with locking joints, such as multiple dovetails, locking miters, or box joints. The sides and back are dadoed or rabbeted together.

Sand all drawer parts before you cut the joints. Smoothing the parts afterwards could make the joints loose. Plus, it is difficult to smooth the inside corners of an assembled drawer.

To assemble a drawer, apply glue to the front-side and side-back joints. Do not put glue in the drawer bottom groove. See that the drawer is square after you tighten the clamps. This is essential to a good fit and smooth drawer operation.

FRONT-SIDE JOINTS

Joints that assemble the drawer front and sides should be locked. This adds strength. Of those men-

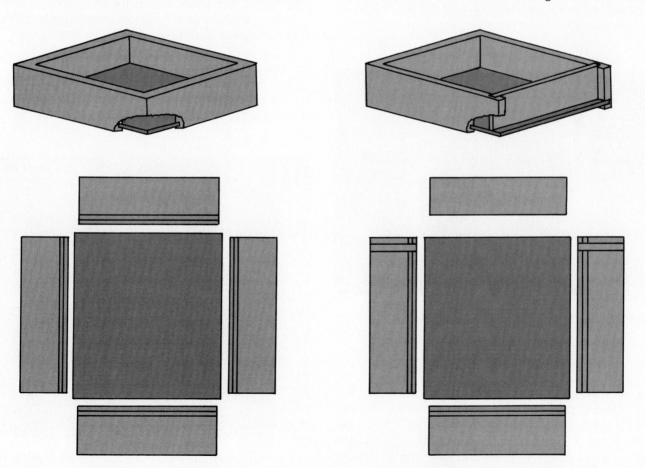

Fig. 42-5. Drawers have fitted or slide-in bottoms.

tioned earlier, the half-blind multiple dovetail is the most common, Fig. 42-6.

Fig. 42-6. Half-blind dovetails used for the front-side and side-back joints.

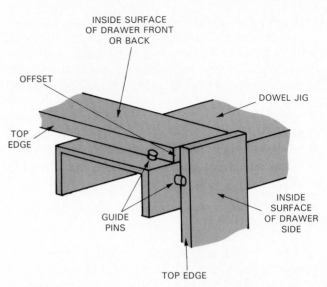

Fig. 42-8. Use guide pins to align the drawer front and side when making a half-blind dovetail.

Half-blind dovetail

For accuracy, you should make a half-blind dovetail joint using a dovetail jig, template, and router with the appropriate bit, Fig. 42-7. Secure the template to the router base. The template glides against the jig fingers to guide the cutter. Insert the cutter in the router collet. Set the depth according to manufacturers instructions and guidelines given in Chapter 29.

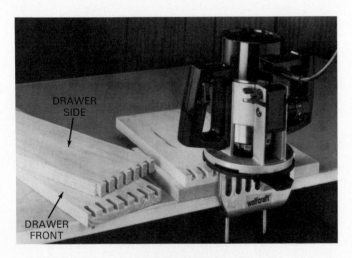

Fig. 42-7. This dovetail jig setup will make a half-blind dovetail joint. (Wolcraft)

Clamp the right drawer side vertically under the jig fingers and against the left locating pin. The end should be flush with the edge of the jig. Clamp the drawer front in the horizontal position against the top locating pin. The front and side should touch; however, they will be offset. See Fig. 42-8.

Rout the dovetail by cutting into the drawer side and front. Repeat the cut in each finger. This will complete the front-right corner drawer joint.

Now rout the front-left corner. Do so with the same general setup and bit depth. However, align the drawer side and front on the right end of the jig against the other set of locating pins.

Refer to Chapter 29 for specific details on cutting half-blind dovetails.

Lip-edge dovetail

The lip-edge dovetail poses a special problem. Unlike a normal front, the end of a lip-edge front is not flush with the side, Fig. 42-9. This occurs

Fig. 42-9. Lip-edge dovetail. The drawer front end and drawer side are not flush.

because a lip-edge front has an overhang that butts against the face frame or case edge. Therefore, each front corner joint must be cut in two operations.

To make a lip-edge dovetail, first cut a dado larger than the lip in a piece of scrap material. Use this dado to position the drawer front, Fig. 42-10A. The inside end of the lip is now flush with the jig front. Set the dovetail bit at the standard depth. Now shape the dovetail portion of the drawer front.

To shape the drawer side, Fig. 42-10B, replace the front with a piece of scrap the same thickness. Insert a spacer the same size as the door lip between the drawer side and locating pin. Then cut a normal half-blind dovetail. The excess protects the drawer side from splintering.

Making lip-edge dovetails is time consuming. Consider attaching a false front. First, create a normal flush front drawer with dovetailed corners. Then glue a finished panel of the desired thickness to the drawer front.

Single dovetail

The single or dado dovetail is another common side-to-front joint, Fig. 42-11. To rout the dovetail sockets in the drawer front accurately, make a jig,

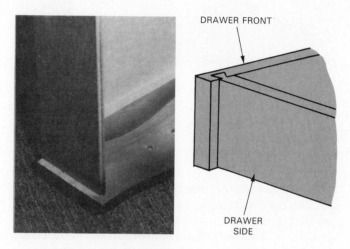

Fig. 42-11. Single dovetail joins the front and side.

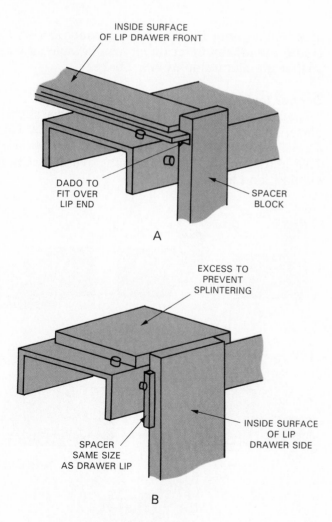

Fig. 42-10. Dovetails on lip drawers are shaped independently. A—Aligning the lip edge with the dovetail jig. Once aligned, remove the spacer block. B—The spacer accounts for the side of the lip in the drawer front. The excess prevents splintering.

Fig. 42-12. To the router base, attach the proper diameter template to match the jig. Clamp the jig over the drawer front and to the workbench. Rout the first socket. Then mount the jig on the other end and rout the second socket.

You can also make the sockets on the shaper. Set the miter gauge at 90 degrees and adjust the cutter depth. Set the fence-to-cutter measurement at the distance the sockets should be from the drawer front ends, Fig. 42-13. On flush drawers, feed the front, with the good face up, through the cutter. On overlay drawers, start the cut at the bottom edge, but stop before you reach the top. This will create a blind dovetail. Feed the workpiece from the left for the first socket. Feed from the right for the second socket.

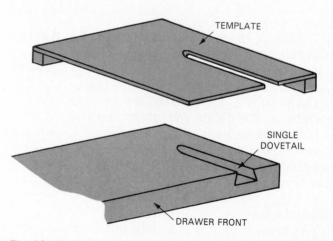

Fig. 42-12. Make a template to rout single dovetails accurately.

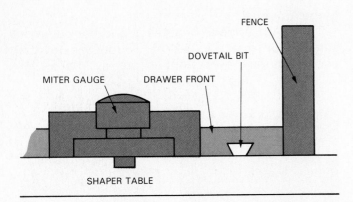

Fig. 42-13. You can shape a single dovetail socket using a miter gauge on the shaper. Make sure the fence-to-cutter distance is set properly. Guard is not shown.

Cut the tails on each drawer side using two passes on the shaper, Fig. 42-14. Secure the cutter in the shaper collet according to the depth of cut. Align the fences over the cutter. They could touch. Make practice cuts on a board the same thickness as the drawer side. Make cuts on both sides with drawer side vertical against the fence.

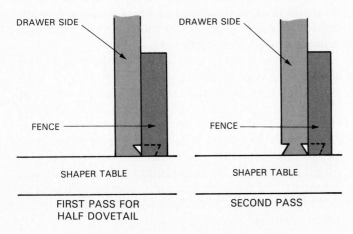

Fig. 42-14. Shaping the tail on the sides.

Dado, tongue, and rabbet

The dado, tongue, and rabbet joint, Fig. 42-15, is both strong and easy to make. With a series of passes on the table saw, each feature of the drawer front portion is cut one-third the thickness. The features in the drawer side are cut one-half the thickness. The dados and rabbets can be cut with a 1/4 in. dado blade or two passes of a standard combination blade. Make the same pass on every drawer front before resetting the saw blade or the fence.

Locked miter

The locked miter is a strong, but intricate joint. Its advantage is that no end grain shows in the

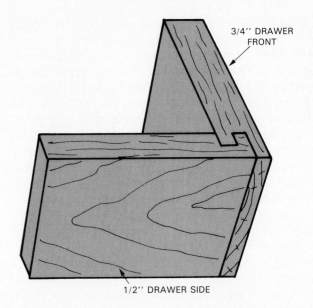

Fig. 42-15. The dado, tongue, and rabbet joint is easy to make, yet quite strong.

assembled joint. The series of passes needed to create the locked miter on either the table saw or shaper are illustrated in Fig. 29-23.

Drawer lock

Drawer lock joints are made using a special shaper cutter. There are two types, as shown in Fig. 42-16. The only difference is the number of tabs. This joint can be used for flush, overlay, reveal overlay, and lip-edge drawers.

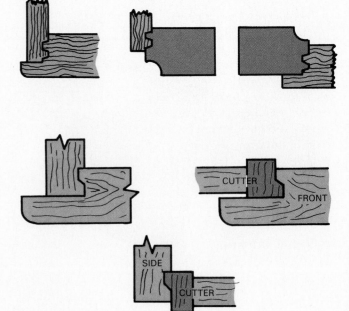

Fig. 42-16. Two types of drawer lock joints. Their only difference is the number of tabs shaped.

SIDE-BACK JOINTS

Although you can join the back and sides with the same joint chosen for the front, most cabinetmakers prefer simpler ones. Most select a dado or dado and rabbet, Fig. 42-17.

A dado is cut in the drawer sides. It should be located at least 1/2 in. from the back end of the sides. A dado and rabbet joint requires that you dado the side and rabbet the back. This joint is somewhat stronger and tends to keep the drawer square.

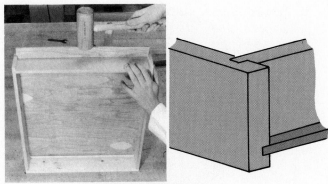

A—SLIDE-IN BOTTOM

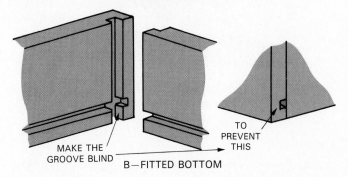

MAKE THE GROOVE BLIND

B—FITTED BOTTOM

TO PREVENT THIS

Fig. 42-18. A—Slide-in bottoms are inserted after the drawer has been assembled. B—A fitted bottom is inserted during assembly. Make the groove blind to prevent its showing in the finished drawer.

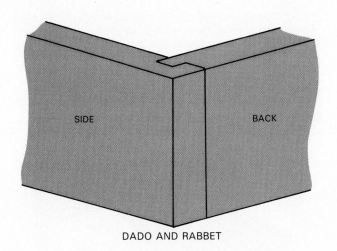

SIDE

BACK

DADO AND RABBET

Fig. 42-17. Typical side-back joints.

DRAWER BOTTOMS

The drawer bottom fits into grooves cut in the drawer front, sides, and possibly the back. High-quality cabinetry has a *fitted bottom* set in a groove cut in all pieces. An alternative is to have a *slide-in bottom* where the drawer back rests on the bottom. See Fig. 42-18. The bottom may then be fastened to the edge of the back with screws or nails.

The distance from the bottom edge of the drawer to the bottom depends on the type of slide. If you mount the drawer with side-mount slides, the drawer bottom can be quite low. However, if you use a center-mount plastic guide, more clearance may be needed. Always select the drawer support before you construct the drawer.

The groove should be cut 1/32 in. (1 mm) wider and deeper than the drawer bottom. This allows for slight squaring adjustments during assembly.

TRAYS

The term "tray" could refer to two different items. A *roll-out tray* is a combination drawer and shelf. If it does have sides and a back, they are

usually very shallow. Another type of tray fits inside a drawer, such as those that organize silverware. See Fig. 42-3. They can be made of wood or plastic.

DRAWER AND TRAY PARTITIONS

Partitions, or *dividers,* prevent the contents from sliding around when the drawer is opened and closed. They can be dadoed into the sides, fronts, and backs. Cross lap joints are cut where the partitions intersect. Be sure that the sections are shallow or large enough for easy access. Plastic divider guides, Fig. 42-19, eliminate the need for cutting joints.

INSTALLING DRAWERS

Drawer installation is a "make/buy" decision. You can make and install wood drawer supports, or you can buy one of the many commercial slides, guides, and tracks. Remember that while designing the drawer you must allow clearance for hardware.

WOOD DRAWER GUIDES

Most producers of high-quality, solid wood cabinetry use web frame construction. Frames, assembled with thin hardboard dust panels,

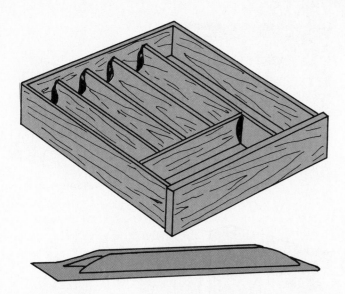

Fig. 42-19. Partition guides do not require sawing or routing the dividers or drawer components. (Shopsmith)

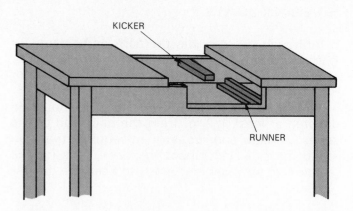

Fig. 42-21. Attach runners and a kicker where there is no frame to support the drawer. Runners support and guide the drawer. A kicker above prevents the drawer from tipping.

separate drawer compartments, Fig. 42-20. The panels prevent dust from falling from one drawer into the next. They also divide chests with lockable drawers to prevent access from one drawer to another. The drawer rides on the frame and is guided by the case sides.

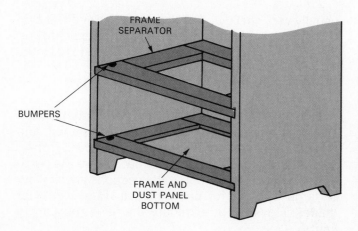

Fig. 42-20. Web frame construction provides drawer support.

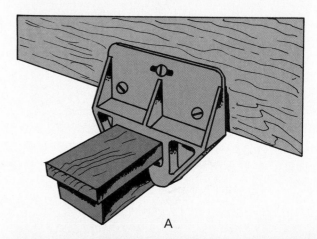

A

B

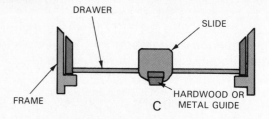

Where there is no web frame, install *hardwood runners,* Fig. 42-21. These require a *kicker block,* placed above the center of the drawer, that keeps the drawer from tipping.

Another method to keep the drawer from tipping is a plastic or metal *slide guide.* It holds the drawer down and rides on a hardwood center guide. The guide can attach to the drawer back, Fig. 42-22A. You can also have a full length metal guide on the drawer bottom, Fig. 42-22B. Both ride on a center guide, and runners hold drawers level, Fig. 42-22C.

Fig. 42-22. Two types of slide guides. A—This type attaches to the drawer back. B—A full-length guide provides additional support. C—Even with a guide, the drawer still must rest on runners at each side.

An excess amount of friction occurs when wood slides on wood. *Bumpers,* similar to nylon-head thumb tacks, are placed near the front edge of the frame to reduce friction. Some you drive into the frame and others are friction-fit in a predrilled hole. See Fig. 42-23.

Drawers in less expensive casework may be fitted with a runner or the bottom may provide adequate support, Fig. 42-24.

Fig. 42-23. Slick nylon bumpers make it easier to open and close drawers. (The Woodworker's Store)

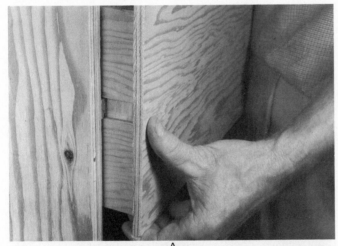

A

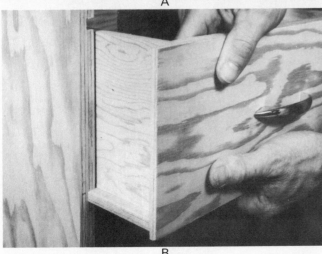

B

Fig. 42-24. Drawer support in inexpensive cabinet construction. A—Side runner. B—Bottom used as a runner. (American Plywood Association)

COMMERCIAL DRAWER SLIDES

Commercial drawer slide hardware comes in many shapes and sizes. The most common, and simplest, is the side-mount runner, Fig. 42-25. There are other styles to suit every situation, Fig. 42-26. Decide on the type during the design stage since most slides require extra clearance between the drawer and case. Most are made of metal with nylon rollers or metal ball bearings.

Slides may mount on the sides, near the corners, above, or under the drawer. *Side-mount slides* are most common. *Top-mount slides* work well for under-the-counter drawers. *Bottom-mount slides* are made for drawers and pull-out shelves. The *single track and tri-roller slide* is quite common in kitchen cabinets.

Drawer slides are classified as standard, full extension, or telescoping. *Standard slides* allow all but 4 to 6 in. (100 to 150 mm) of the drawer body to extend out of the cabinet. *Full extension slides* permit the entire drawer to pull out for easy

SIDE-MOUNT RUNNER

Fig. 42-25. The side-mount runner is the most common commercial drawer slide. (The Woodworker's Store)

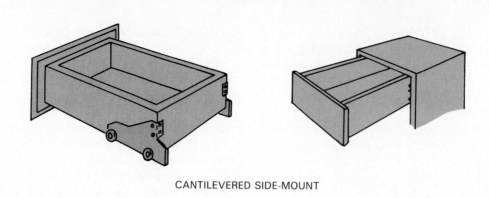

CANTILEVERED SIDE-MOUNT

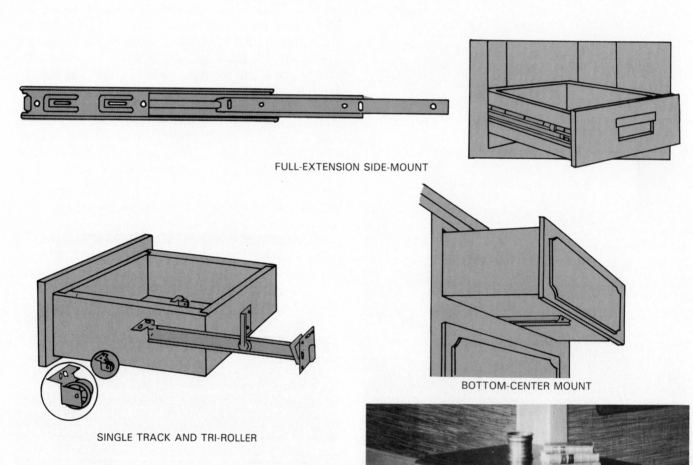

FULL-EXTENSION SIDE-MOUNT

BOTTOM-CENTER MOUNT

SINGLE TRACK AND TRI-ROLLER

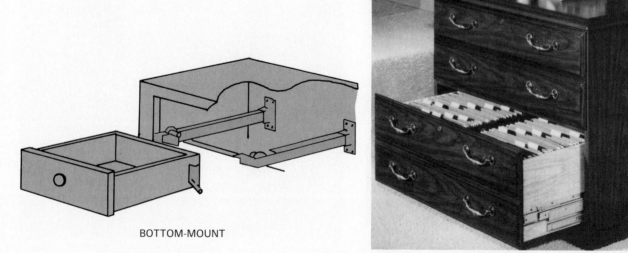

BOTTOM-MOUNT

Fig. 42-26. Commercial drawer slides come in all shapes and sizes. (The Woodworker's Store)

access. *Telescoping slides,* used for slide-out trays or heavy-duty TV supports, can extend beyond the cabinet. Be cautious when selecting full extension and telescoping slides for free-standing cabinets. A heavily loaded drawer could tip the cabinet.

Slides are also rated by load capacity. This is how much weight the slide can support when the drawer is fully extended. *Light-duty slides* (residential quality) will support 50 pounds. *Medium-duty slides* (commercial quality) will support 75 pounds. Heavy-duty slides hold up to 100 pounds.

PLASTIC DRAWER COMPONENTS

Plastic has become a common material in the cabinetmaking industry. Now you can purchase preformed plastic drawer sides and backs. They snap together and then fit on mounting brackets fastened to the wood drawer front with screws, Fig. 42-27. A slot formed around the inside bottom of the back and sides accepts a 1/8 in. hardboard bottom. You must cut a groove in the drawer front. The drawer sides include a formed channel that fits special roller slides.

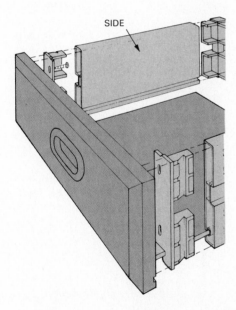

SIDE

Fig. 42-27. Plastic drawer components make assembly much quicker. (Shopsmith, Inc.)

INSTALLING DRAWER PULLS AND KNOBS

How you open a drawer depends on the product's design. On some furniture, the design specifies that no hardware should be seen. For these, you must shape hidden finger pulls in door and drawer edges. Other cabinet styles call for pulls and knobs that stand out from the surface, swivel, or hang. Still other designs call for recessed pulls.

Several factors help determine the number and placement of pulls.
1. The weight of the drawer and its contents.
2. Friction when opening and closing the drawer.
3. Width of the drawer.
4. Distance from the drawer front to back.
Drawers up to 18 in. (460 mm) wide can usually be controlled with a single pull if they ride on good-quality slides. On the other hand, a poorly fit or mounted drawer even 12 in. (305 mm) wide may need two pulls to guide the drawer. This is likely to occur when you mount the drawer only on a wood frame. Drawers wider than 18 in. should have two pulls.

SUMMARY

Well-constructed drawers are a sign of high-quality cabinetry. A basic drawer consists of a front, two sides, a back, and bottom. They must be measured, cut, and assembled accurately.

Drawer fronts usually follow the same style as doors on the product. They may be flush, overlay, or lip-edge. In addition, the front may be curved (bent), shaped, or routed for added design features.

Drawers may have fitted or slide-in bottoms. Fitted bottoms indicate a better quality drawer, but take longer to make. A 1/8 or 1/4 in. plywood or hardboard bottom fits in grooves cut in the front, sides, and back. On drawers with slide-in bottoms, only the front and sides are grooved. The back is narrower and not grooved. After assembling the drawer, slide the bottom in place and secure it with screws.

A number of joints are used for drawer assembly. The front-side corners should be assembled with locking joints due to the force required to open a drawer. The side-back joints should be positioned, but do not have to lock. A dado or dado and rabbet joint is best. Joints that rely only on the adhesive for strength, such as butt joints, are poor choices.

Drawers and trays may contain partitions. They help organize the contents. Make them shallow or large enough for easy access.

You can make or buy drawer support systems. Wood drawer supports can be quite simple to create. However, they may not work as smoothly as commercial slides, guides, and tracks. Remember that when designing the drawer, you must allow clearance for drawer hardware.

A cabinet's style will help determine which drawer pulls or knobs to use. For some designs, drawer fronts have finger grips shaped in the bottom edge instead of pulls.

CABINETMAKING TERMS

Drawer, flush front, flush overlay front, reveal overlay front, lip-edge front, drawer front, false front, drawer side, drawer back, drawer bottom, fitted bottom, slide-in bottom, roll-out tray, partitions, hardwood runners, kicker block, slide guide, bumper, side-mount slide, top-mount slide, bottom-mount slide, single track and tri-roller slide, standard slide, full-extension slide, telescoping slide, light-duty slide, medium-duty slide, heavy-duty slide.

TEST YOUR KNOWLEDGE

1. Drawers are one of the least-expensive forms of storage. True or False?
2. You can recognize high-quality cabinetry:
   a. Drawer size.
   b. Length of the sides.
   c. Depth.
   d. Drawer joinery.
3. List the five components of a typical drawer.
4. What methods are available to decorate and accent drawer fronts?
5. The drawer sides are longer than the inside dimensions of the cabinet when:
   a. Dovetail joints are used to connect the front and sides.
   b. Particleboard is used for the drawer sides.
   c. Hardware holds the drawer.
   d. The sides act as a stop.
6. Why would you not use particleboard for the drawer bottom?
7. The drawer front and sides are usually joined with single or multiple _____ _____.
8. Name the two joints typically chosen to assemble the back and sides.
9. The same terms are used to describe ways to install drawers as to hang doors. True or False?
10. Describe two ways to cut a single dovetail socket in the drawer front.
11. Drawer lock joints are made with a _____ _____.
12. Why might a fitted bottom be more secure than a slide-in bottom?
13. A plastic or metal slide guide rides on a hardwood _____ _____.
14. To reduce friction, _____ are placed under drawers that ride on a web frame.
15. The most common drawer support is a:
    a. Bottom-mount slide.
    b. Side-mount slide.
    c. Top-mount slide.

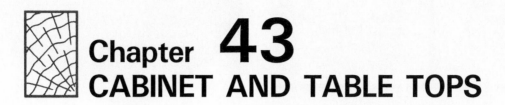

Chapter 43
CABINET AND TABLE TOPS

After studying this chapter, you will be able to:
- Identify materials used to make cabinet and table tops.
- Select edge shapes according to material and style.
- Attach one-piece tops with glue blocks, joinery, and mechanical fasteners.
- Describe design options for building a drop-leaf table.
- Explain the features of extension tops and trestle tables.
- Describe the installation of glass and ceramics on countertops and tabletops.

The top of a cabinet or table is usually the most visible surface. In addition to being attractive, it must be wear resistant, Fig. 43-1. Tops are one-piece or assembled components. Typically, the cabinet or table top is the last part to be assembled.

MATERIALS

Tops can be made of lumber or wood products covered with veneer or plastic laminate. There are also solid plastic tops, possibly with wood edging, Fig. 43-2. These are mostly for kitchen countertops. This chapter focuses on lumber and wood products.

Solid wood tops tend to expand and contract. This can weaken the joints unless you allow for it when attaching the top. You can significantly reduce the amount of expansion and contraction by sealing ALL surfaces, top and bottom.

Solid tops made from a single board tend to warp with moisture changes. To prevent warpage, do not make the top from a single board. Instead, glue a series of 4 to 6 in. (100 to 150 mm) wide strips together, alternating the faces.

Manufactured panel products, such as plywood and particleboard, are more stable. In addition, you can laminate hardwood veneer or plastic laminate over particleboard or a less-expensive wood core. Plastic laminates are more resistant to damage than hardwood veneer and come in a variety of wood grain patterns.

Wood products, though more stable and less expensive, have some drawbacks. Because plywood often contains voids in the core, you must cover the edges. Wood chips in particleboard also make a poor appearance, so you should cover the edges and surfaces.

A

B

Fig. 43-1. Furniture tops are typically the most visible, and used, surface of the product. A—Solid wood top. B—Glass top. (Mersman Tables)

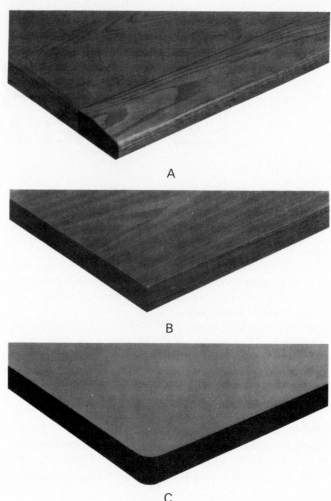

Fig. 43-3. Three edge treatments. A—Wood band. B—Edge banding with veneer or plastic laminate. C—Manufactured plastic edge. (Roth)

Fig. 43-2. Solid plastic tops have found wide acceptance in contemporary kitchens. (Formica)

EDGE TREATMENT

The shape of the edge depends on two factors, style and material. Some styles, such as Early American and French Provincial, have rounded edges. Contemporary styles often dictate a square edge. Still other styles emphasize shaped edges.

The material chosen also affects how you shape the edge, Fig. 43-3. The primary methods are:

1. Lumber. Lumber tops can have almost any edge shape. Common shapes include: chamfer, rounded, moulded, and square.
2. Wood product (plywood, particleboard, MDF) with a wood band, or frame. Because the edge is lumber, this top can also be shaped or routed. This is usually done after the band has been glued to the core.
3. Wood product having edges covered with veneer tape or plastic laminate edge banding. Leave a square edge on wood products with no wood band. It is hard to cover the curved edge of shaped plywood and particleboard with veneer or edge banding.
4. Wood or wood product with a manufactured edge. To install a manufactured edge, you must cut the top's edges square.

WOOD BANDS

Wood strips, called *wood bands* or frames, can be attached to plywood and particleboard panels using a process much like frame and panel construction. The bands are mitered at the corners and attached to the top with a positioning joint, such as the tongue and groove or spline joint. Manufactured wood bands are usually sold as *T-moulding* with a precut T-shaped tongue, Fig. 43-4. A dado and rabbet joint serves well when wide bands are attached to make the top look thicker and heavier. See Fig. 43-5.

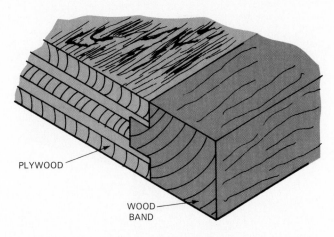

Fig. 43-4. This wood band is manufactured T-moulding.

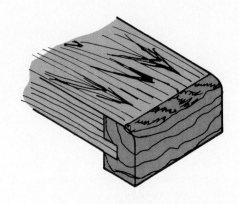

Fig. 43-5. A dado and rabbet joint used with thick banding to make the top look thicker and heavier.

Most bands are flush with the top surface. If you use particleboard as the core material, cover the surfaces with veneer or plastic laminate before applying the bands. You can shape the bands before or after assembly.

EDGE BANDING

Edge banding is the process of covering the edges of manufactured panel products with lumber bandings, veneer tape, or plastic laminate edge banding. Most edge banding materials will bend around corners. Some bond with contact cement while others have a pre-applied coating of hot-melt glue. Make sure the panel edges are relatively smooth. Generally, cutting the material with a sharp, fine tooth power saw blade will produce an acceptable edge.

Veneer bandings

Veneer bandings are small pieces of veneer arranged in a decorative pattern and assembled into thin strips. They are usually 1/20 in. (1.25 mm) thick, 36 in. (900 mm) long, and come in various widths. You apply veneer bandings with contact cement or white glue. See Chapter 14.

Veneer tape

Veneer tape is a continuous strip of narrow veneer purchased in rolls. The tape is 13/16 in. (21 mm) wide for 3/4 in. panels and 1 9/16 in. wide for 1 1/2 in. panels. The extra 1/16 in. allows for trimming. Veneer tape, precoated with hot-melt glue, is applied with an iron or tape lamination machine. See Chapters 14 and 35.

Plastic edge banding

Plastic edge banding is thin, narrow strips of flexible plastic laminate. Various patterns, shapes, and textures are available. Most are coated with pressure-sensitive adhesive which bonds on contact. Precut edge banding is 13/16 in. wide for 3/4 in. cores and 1 9/16 in. wide for 1 1/2 in. cores.

When laminating all surfaces of particleboard, you usually glue on the plastic laminate edge before applying the surfaces. You may want the top surface to overlap the edge to reduce wear. Follow the procedure given in Chapter 36 to apply laminate edge banding.

MANUFACTURED METAL AND PLASTIC EDGING

There are situations when you may want a more durable edge on your cabinet or table top. This is done with solid plastic or metal edging.

When you place a manufactured edging over a particleboard core, laminate the surfaces first. Then the edging is placed over or flush with the laminate.

Plastic edging

Flexible *plastic edging* is soft and can serve as a bumper. Usually sold as *plastic T-moulding*, plastic edging is preshaped with a T-shaped tongue which fits in a groove sawed in the edge, Fig. 43-6. Sawtooth tabs hold it in place.

Metal edging

Metal edging is U-shaped stainless steel or aluminum that slips over the panel edge. Although once very popular for kitchen countertop edges, metal edging has largely been replaced by durable plastic laminates.

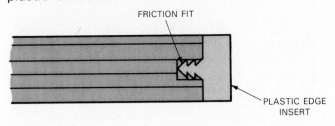

Fig. 43-6. Plastic T-moulding is plastic edging preshaped with a T-shaped tongue.

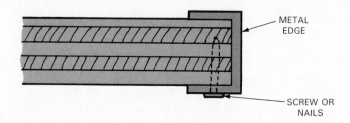

Fig. 43-7. Metal edging attached with a nail installed from underneath the top.

Metal edging is best attached with a nail or screw installed from underneath the top, Fig. 43-7. However, you can hold it in place with screws through the front. Cover the screw heads with plastic strip inserts to prevent the screws from snagging a person's clothing.

Make the edging in one piece if possible. Miter the sides, but not the face, to bend the metal around corners. A joint at the corner is sharp and could cause an injury. Butt the metal ends together in the center of one edge.

SECURING ONE-PIECE TOPS

Secure one-piece cabinet tops with adhesives and/or mechanical fasteners. Select a procedure that will not interfere with the drawers. Remember that humidity affects solid lumber tops. Allow them to expand and contract with the type of mount you choose.

HARDWARE

Hardware for attaching tops typically includes braces, desktop fasteners, and clips. *Corner braces,* shown in Fig. 43-8, add rigidity to the case and allow for easy attachment of the top. Install them to the case sides with screws. Some braces, being plastic, are intended to be fastened with staples.

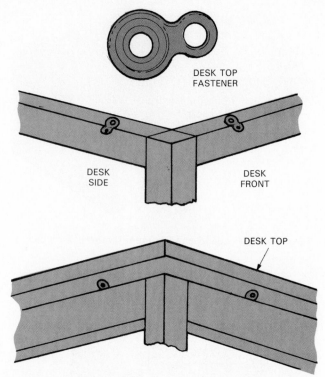

Fig. 43-9. Desktop fasteners screw into the top and table apron or case side.

A coating of adhesive helps secure the brace when you attach it with staples.

Desktop fasteners are recessed into either the case side or the top, Fig. 43-9. First, attach the fasteners to the table apron or case with screws. Place them about every 6 in. Then position the top and fasten it with screws.

Tabletop clips fit into a slot in the apron or case side and a screw secures them to the top, Fig. 43-10. A common technique is to place a glue block

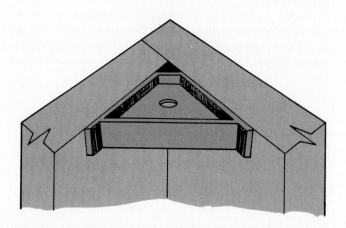

Fig. 43-8. Plastic corner brace attached with staples and glue.

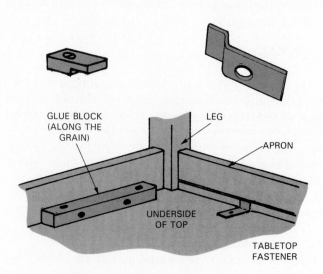

Fig. 43-10. Table clips fit into a slot and screw to the top. You can have one side secured with a glue block to help keep the top square.

that runs along the grain on one side. The other three sides contain grooves for clips. This insures squareness yet allows for expansion and contraction.

Tops 3/4 in. or thinner do not hold screws well because there is minimum thread contact. Unfortunately, people tend to lift tables and cabinets by the top. The screws could easily pull out of a heavy table or cabinet.

GLUE BLOCKS

Probably the simplest and least expensive method to attach a top is with glue blocks. For tabletops made of lumber, use 18 in. (450 mm) blocks placed inside the table apron or case sides, Fig. 43-11. Predrill 1/16 in. oversize clearance holes for attaching the top. Plan to install round head screws and washer.

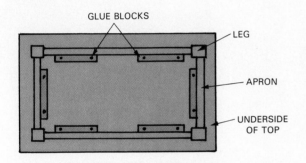

Fig. 43-11. Top attached with glue blocks.

Attach the blocks with glue to the table apron or case sides first. Then position the top and mark hole locations through the clearance holes in the glue blocks. Turn the top over and drill pilot holes. Make sure you do not drill through the top. It is best to measure the depth and wrap tape around the drill bit. Then position the top and drive the screws and washers snug; this allows for lumber expansion.

If the top is quite heavy, you may want to drill pilot holes with the top in place. Again, mark the depth with tape on your drill bit. Drill the pilot holes through the clearance holes in the glue blocks.

JOINERY

For small tables and cabinets, several joints can be used to permanently attach the top. Dowels placed 4 to 6 in. apart provide adequate strength. Pocket joints are another acceptable method, Fig. 43-12. For products that have been assembled with plate joinery, it may be convenient to attach the top in the same manner, Fig. 43-13. (See Chapter 40 for a discussion of assembling legs and aprons with plate joinery.)

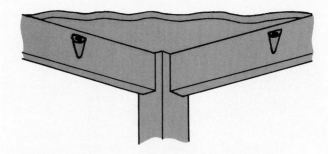

Fig. 43-12. Top attached with pocket joints.

Remember that you must seal lumber tops to reduce expansion and contraction. This is especially important if you choose joinery to attach the top.

ADJUSTABLE TABLETOPS

Tables, especially those for dining, often have adjustable tops. Drop-leaf and extension tabletops provide added surface area when needed, but then fold to conserve space when not in use.

DROP-LEAF TABLES

Drop-leaf tables have one or two sections (leaves) that hang when the table is not in use, Fig. 43-14. Raise one or both for added surface area. The stationary section of the tabletop attaches to the apron and legs like any other one-piece top. The leaves are hinged, usually with flap, butt, or special hinges for shaped leaves. The hinge you choose should have screw holes 1/4 in. (6 mm) or more away from the joint.

Drop-leaf joints

The joint where the leaf meets the tabletop can be square, beveled, or shaped. The shaped joint, called a *rule joint,* is a feature of most Traditional furniture.

In a rule joint, the leaf has a cove-shaped edge that slides over a bead-shaped edge on the tabletop, Fig. 43-15. Most manufacturers sell a matched pair of cutters for rule joints. Shape the cove radius on the leaves 1/32 in. larger than the bead radius for clearance.

You should purchase special drop-leaf table hinges for rule joints. One hinge flap is longer than the other to reach across the joint and fasten to the table leaf. The knuckle of the hinge fits into a shallow slot cut in the tabletop. The hinge pin must be in line with the bead edge.

Drop-leaf supports

When raised, the leaves require some form of support. You can buy hardware or make supports out of hardwood.

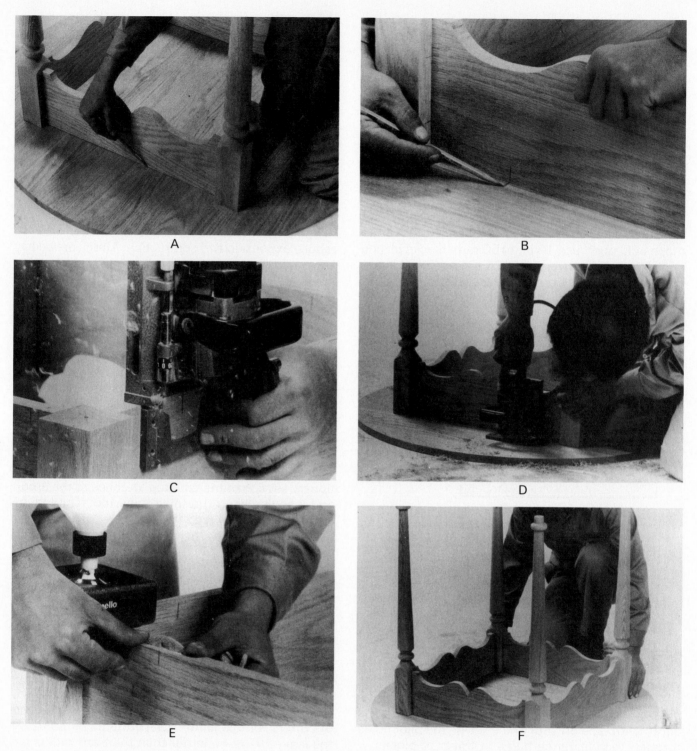

Fig. 43-13. Attaching a tabletop with plate joinery. A—Mark the apron location on the top. B—Mark position of biscuits (plates). C—Cut slots in apron. D—Cut slots in top. E—Insert biscuits with glue. F—Put glue in table slots and position apron. (Colonial Saw)

Pull-out support. A *pull-out support* consists of a hardwood shaft and metal bracket. The support mounts underneath the table, Fig. 43-16. The shaft, usually 3/4 by 1 1/2 in., pulls out to support the leaf. One support is sufficient for small leaves. Wider leaves require two supports per leaf. The metal bracket is usually 12 to 18 in. long. The

length of the shaft depends on the table size, but must be long enough to adequately support the leaf.

Pivot support. A *pivot support* is a movable section of the table apron, Fig. 43-17. Once you lift the leaf, rotate the support 90 degrees into position. About half of the support is behind the apron while supporting the top. Use a sturdy hardwood

Fig. 43-14. Drop-leaf table in Hepplewhite style. (Thomasville)

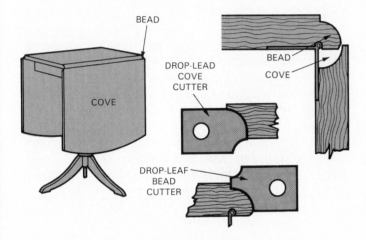

Fig. 43-15. Shaping and assembling a rule joint for drop-leaves.

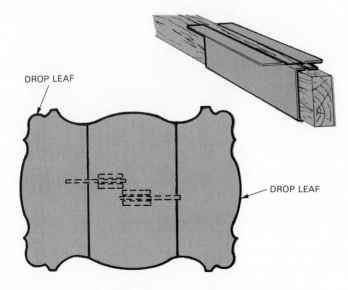

Fig. 43-16. Pull-out support for drop-leaf table.
(The Woodworker's Store)

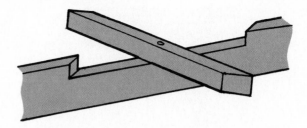

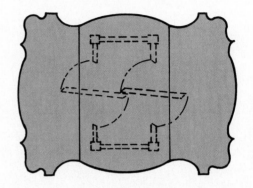

Fig. 43-17. Pivot support.

specie for this support. The pivot pin should be a hardwood or metal dowel.

Butterfly and gateleg table supports. Pull-out and pivot supports provide fair support for most leaves. However, leaves that support heavier objects— potted plants or appliances, for example—must be stronger. Use a butterfly- or gateleg-style table.

The *butterfly table* is named after its butterfly wing-shaped support. A wood wing is installed vertically between the stretcher and a block placed under the table top, Fig. 43-18. It pivots on wood or metal dowels at both ends. After lifting the top, turn the wing outward. It will contact a stop fastened under the leaf to position the wing.

You can also use a long wood screw rather than a dowel for the pivot. Drill holes through the block and the stretcher. Place screws through the block (on top) and stretcher (on bottom) to secure the wing. The smooth shank portion of the screws *must* be within the block and apron. Otherwise, the screw threads would rub and begin to cut away the wood around them.

A *gateleg table* has an extra leg attached to a *fly rail* with stretchers. The fly rail pivots between the table stretcher and apron, Fig. 43-19. The gateleg support offers greater strength.

Drop-leaf support hardware. There are several hardware supports you can purchase. Most have an armlike action that locks into place when the leaf is horizontal, Fig. 43-20.

There is also a spring loaded hinge requiring no other support. More than two may be necessary to prevent the leaves from sagging.

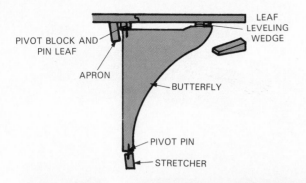

PIVOT BLOCK AND
PIN LEAF

APRON

BUTTERFLY

PIVOT PIN

STRETCHER

LEAF
LEVELING
WEDGE

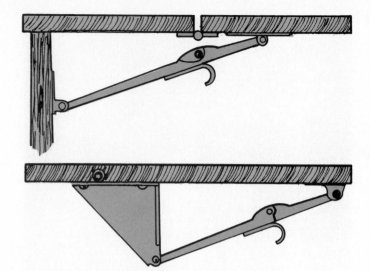

Fig. 43-20. Hardware supports pivot and lock into position to support the leaf.

Fig. 43-18. Butterfly tables have a wood wing to support the leaf. (Ethan Allen)

EXTENSION TOPS

An *extension top* with removable leaves is popular for dining tables, Fig. 43-21. The top is actually two sections held together by hardwood or metal slides installed under the tabletop. You pull the sections apart and insert leaves for extra table surface.

The two most popular extension table styles are *dividing four leg* and *nondividing pedestal,* Fig. 43-22. Selecting table extension slides is a make-

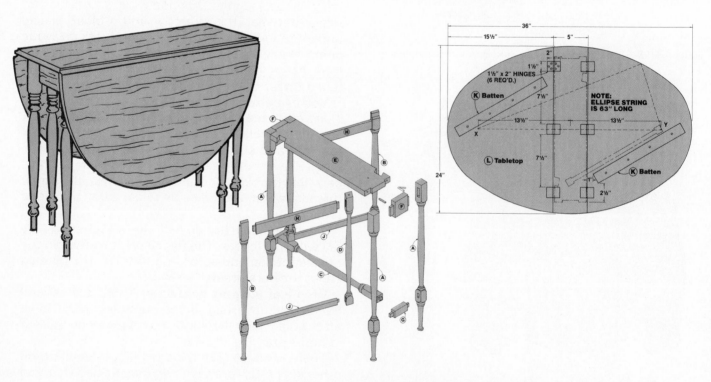

Fig. 43-19. Many components are needed for a gateleg table. (Unfinished Furniture, Shopsmith, Inc.)

Fig. 43-21. Note the extra leaf added in the middle of this dining table. (Thomasville)

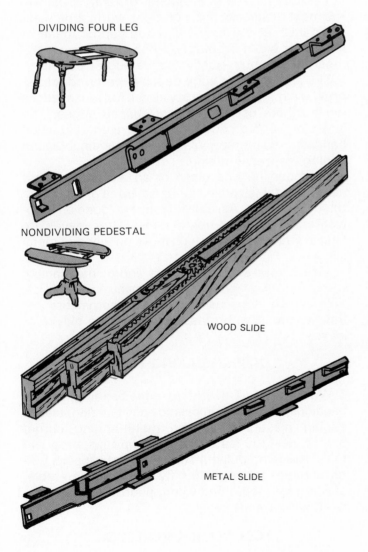

DIVIDING FOUR LEG

NONDIVIDING PEDESTAL

WOOD SLIDE

METAL SLIDE

Fig. 43-22. The two most popular extension table styles. Each requires a different type of slide. (The Woodworker's Store)

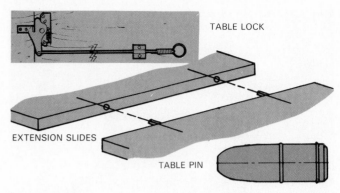

TABLE LOCK

EXTENSION SLIDES

TABLE PIN

Fig. 43-23. Leaves of an extension table are aligned with table pins. When no leaves are installed, the table is secured with a lock. (The Woodworker's Store)

buy decision. Most hardwood slides are dovetail or T-shaped and made of three or more pieces. Metal slides consist of three ball bearing rails. The slides must support the two halves and added leaves.

Two wood or metal *table pins* keep the top and leaves aligned. The pins are found in the edge of one tabletop section and each extra leaf. Sometimes a *table lock* keeps the top locked together when no leaves are installed. See Fig. 43-23.

Install extensions parallel and spaced across the tabletop dividing the width in thirds. Between the extensions, you might add two or three leaf supports for self-contained leaf storage.

Extension tables often have a fifth leg. It provides added support when multiple leaves are added. It attaches to the center extension slide under the tabletop. Some legs have a threaded leveler on the bottom for stability.

TRESTLE TABLE

A *trestle table* is much like an extension table, except that leaves are added on the ends rather than in the middle, Fig 43-24. Most trestle tables follow the Early American style. First you pull the slides out. Then you can place a leaf on them. The leaves are stored under the tabletop.

GLASS AND CERAMIC TOPS

No discussion of cabinet and table tops would be complete without mentioning glass and ceramics. Modern dining and occasional tables often have heavy tempered glass tops that simply rest on a wood or metal support, Fig. 43-25. The edges of the glass are polished smooth. The support consists of legs connected to an apron and stretchers.

Glass can also be framed. Wood frames are usually made up from 5/8 to 3/4 in. stock. Width will vary from one application to another. Normally, stile width will be from 1 1/2 to 2 1/2 in. wide.

A

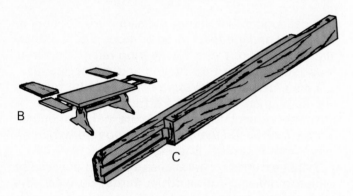

Fig. 43-24. A—Trestle table. (Ethan Allen) B—The leaves install at the ends. C—A special trestle table slide. (The Woodworker's Store)

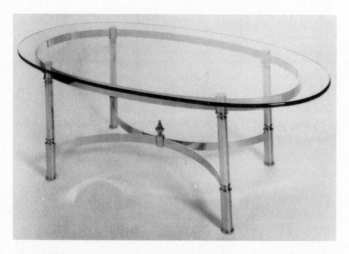

Fig. 43-25. Heavy glass tops are common in contemporary furniture.

Follow the techniques for frame and panel construction in Chapter 39.

Ceramic tile is another option for countertops and tabletops. The tile is bonded to a plywood or particleboard core. Refer to ceramics in Chapter 15.

HINGED TOPS

Case goods which open upward usually have lid-type hinged tops. The lid can be fastened with many different styles of hinges. For a more detailed discussion of hinged tops, and coverage of air-cushioned tops, see Chapter 38.

HIDDEN TOPS

On tall cases with doors, the top is visible only from the inside of the case. Thus, it is often rabbeted and glued, dadoed, or otherwise fastened. The top can be made of plywood, particleboard, or lumber. Cover visible surfaces of manufactured panel products with veneer or plastic laminate. It is wise to coat hidden surfaces with sealer to prevent warpage and moisture damage.

SUMMARY

The top surface of a cabinet or table is usually the most visible part of a product. It must be wear resistant, yet attractive. The top can be made of lumber or wood products. Wood products are the most stable, but usually require edge treatment.

The shape of the edge depends on two factors, style and material. Some styles call for square edges while others use rounded or shaped edges. The edges of wood products can be covered with wood banding, veneer tape, plastic edge banding, plastic edging, or metal edging.

Tops can be one piece or an assembly. Most cases and tables have one-piece wood or manufactured panel tops. Assembled tops are found on drop-leaf, extension, and trestle tables. Drop leaves are hinged while extension tops move on wood or metal slides.

Attach tops with adhesives and/or mechanical fasteners. Allow wood tops to expand and contract. This can be done using clips and corner braces. Smaller tops can be fastened with glue blocks or joinery.

CABINETMAKING TERMS

Wood bands, T-moulding, edge banding, veneer bandings, veneer tape, plastic edge banding, plastic edging, plastic T-moulding, metal edging, corner braces, desktop fasteners, tabletop clips, drop-leaf table, rule joint, pull-out support, pivot support, butterfly table, gateleg table, fly rail, extension table, dividing four leg, nondividing pedestal, table pins, table lock, trestle table.

TEST YOUR KNOWLEDGE

1. Cabinet and table tops are visible, and should be _____ and _____ _____.

2. Name two materials used to make tabletops.
3. The shape of the edge depends on two factors, _____ and _____.
4. List three types of wood product edge treatment.
5. Name the two edge treatments that can be shaped with a router.
6. Edge banding is the process of covering edges with _____ _____, _____ _____, or _____ _____.
7. Always install plastic or metal edging before laminating the top surfaces. True or False?
8. Explain the most important consideration when installing lumber one-piece tops.
9. Hardware for installing cabinet and tabletops includes _____ _____, _____ _____, and _____ _____.
10. Identify the steps taken to attach a tabletop with plate joinery.
11. Hinges chosen for drop-leaf tables should have screw holes no closer than _____ away from the joint.
12. The shaped drop-leaf joint that is a feature of most Traditional furniture is the _____ _____.
13. List four drop-leaf supports.
14. Name two popular extension table styles.
15. What aligns the table leaves with the top in an extension top?

The beauty of fine furniture and cabinetry is enhanced by properly applied stains and finishes.

Chapter 44
FINISHING DECISIONS

After studying this chapter, you will be able to:
☐ *Make decisions for finishing wood and wood products.*
☐ *Identify coatings for finishing wood and metal surfaces.*
☐ *Select methods for applying coating materials.*

Finishing involves applying the proper coating materials to assembled products. The finish, which can be clear, colored, or opaque, protects wood, wood products, and metal from moisture, harmful substances, and wear, Fig. 44-1. A number of decisions surround the process of finishing.

WOOD FINISHING DECISIONS

Finishing decisions apply to selecting finishing materials and application methods. Various wood species and wood products require unique finishing techniques, Fig. 41-2. Understanding the entire system for finishing is important. Become familiar with each of these steps:
1. Preparing surfaces for finish.
2. Choosing materials and application methods.
3. Preparing surfaces for topcoating.
4. Applying topcoating to surfaces.
5. Creating decorative effects.

Making the right decision at each stage is essential. Applying a finish improperly results in a low-quality cabinet. This chapter provides a preview of finishing techniques, which are covered in detail in the chapters to follow.

PREPARING SURFACES FOR FINISH

Preparing the surface begins with an inspection. Areas to be finished should be free of blemishes and

A

B

Fig. 44-1. A—These shelf units are finished with stain and a clear topcoat. (Bernhardt) B—This dresser is finished with an opaque topcoat. (The Lane Co.)

This chart recommends finishing practices for popular softwoods and hardwoods. The table suggests procedures for finishing these woods with opaque or clear coatings. Stains may be optional (O). Filler may be required (R) to produce a flat surface on some open grain species.

SPECIES	WOOD TYPE			FINISH				Filler
	Softwood	Open	Closed	Penetrating	Opaque	Built-Up	Stain	
Alder			●	■		■	O	
Ash		●		■		■	O	R
Banak	●			■		■	O	
Basswood			●		■			
Beech			●	■		■	O	
Birch			●	■		■	O	
Butternut		●		■		■	O	R
Cedar	●			■		■		
Cherry			●	■		■	O	
Chestnut		●		■		■	O	R
Cottonwood			●		■			
Cypress, bald	●				■	■		
Ebony			●			■		
Elm, American		●		■		■	O	R
Fir, Douglas	●			■	■	■		
Gum, red			●	■		■	O	
Hackberry		●		■		■	O	R
Hickory		●		■		■	O	
Lauan (Philippine Mahogany)		●		■		■	O	R
Limba		●		■		■	O	R
Mahoganies, Genuine		●		●		■	O	R
Mahogany, African		●		●		■	O	R
Maple, hard			●	■		■	O	
Maple, soft			●	■		■	O	
Oak, red or white		●		■		■	O	R
Paldao		●		■		■	O	R
Santo Rosewood (Pau Ferro)			●			■	O	
Pecan			●	■		■	O	
Pine, Ponderosa	●			■	■	■	O	
Pine, Sugar (white)	●			■		■	O	
Pine, Yellow	●			■		■	O	
Primavera		●		■		■	O	R
Redwood	●			■		■	O	
Rosewood			●			■		
Sapele		●		■		■	O	R
Sassafras		●		■		■	O	R
Satinwood			●	■		■	O	
Spruce	●				■			
Sycamore			●	■		■	O	
Teak			●	■				
Tulip, American (Yellow Poplar)			●		■	■	O	
Walnut, American		●		■		■	O	R
Willow			●	■		■	O	
Zebrawood			●			■		

Fig. 44-2. The finishing procedure differs according to the wood species.

stains. Unwanted natural coloring (mineral deposits, blue stain, etc.) can be removed by *bleaching*, Fig. 44-3. Dried adhesives should be scraped off. Dents, open joints, chips, and scratches also need attention. Once these are fixed, the surfaces are sanded.

At times, defects are desirable to make a surface look worn, or even abused. *Scorching* a surface with a torch blackens the wood so it appears old and worn. *Distressing* a surface involves marring the wood with a hammer, length of chain, or other blunt object. This creates the effect of longtime use and wear. *Imitation distressing* does not mar the wood. Simply spatter the surface with black enamel before applying the final topcoat. This creates the same effect as distressing, but you can remove the imitation distressing with paint remover if

Fig. 44-3. Bleaching removes natural color and stains from the wood.

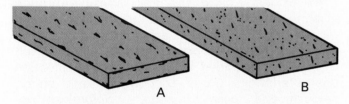

Fig. 44-4. Distressing causes a surface to look worn. A—Distressing done with a chain. B—Imitation distressing applied by splattering stain on the surface.

necessary. See Fig. 44-4.

Preparation steps are discussed in detail in Chapter 45.

APPLYING COATING MATERIALS

The most effective application procedure varies for different finishes. Application methods include brushing, dipping, spraying, rolling, and wiping. Some materials, such as stain, can be applied by any of these methods. Other coatings, such as spray lacquer, are best applied by a single method. Be sure that you have enough finish on hand before starting the job, Fig. 44-5.

Environmental factors also affect application. Maintain a moderate temperature and humidity; these affect drying time. Also provide ventilation for fumes and dust.

PREPARING SURFACES FOR TOPCOATING

Preparing to apply the topcoating involves several steps. They include staining, filling, sealing, and ap-

plying decorative finishes. Filling and sealing are done primarily for built-up topcoats.

Stain changes the color of the wood. There are two kinds of stains: penetrating and pigment. Penetrating stains contain dyes and resins that are almost totally absorbed into the wood. Spirit stain, one type of penetrating stain, darkens sapwood to look like heartwood. Pigment stains differ because they contain insoluble powdered colors which bond to the wood surface with resins.

A *washcoat* is a thinned coat of sealer that often is applied before stain. It reduces the amount of dye absorbed, especially in end grain. If the entire surface is washcoated, the stain colors more evenly. Otherwise, end grain, some sapwood, and other areas will absorb more stain and be much darker.

Open grain hardwoods have a rough texture when finished unless they are filled. *Filler* is a liquid or paste material that contains finely powdered silica (sand) and a resin. The silica fills the open pores. The resin, sometimes called a binder, is an adhesive to hold the silica in place. Filler may be applied before staining. However, stain can be added to the filler and applied in one operation.

Once the surface is stained and filled, it is either sealed or primed in preparation for topcoating. A *sealer* is a thin clear coat that fills wood pores and serves as a barrier coating. Sealing the pores is important, especially if the wood was not filled. The sealer film reduces the amount of topcoating absorbed into the wood. Sealer also serves as a barrier between the stain and topcoating. This prevents dye stains from bleeding into the topcoat. You can determine, years after a product is finished, whether

MATERIAL	COVERAGE sq.ft./gal.
Finish Preparation	
Bleach solution	250-300
Water stain	350-400
Non-grain-raising stain	275-325
Penetrating oil stain	300-350
Pigment oil stain	350-400
Spirit stain	250-300
Alkyd and latex stain	350-400
Thick filler	50-150
Medium filler	150-250
Thin filler	250-350
Sanding sealer	500-600
Lacquer sealer	350-400
Topcoatings	
Varnish (gloss)	500-600
Varnish (semigloss)	450-500
Varnish (satin)	350-450
Lacquer (spray)	200-300
Lacquer (brush)	150-200
Enamel	350-600
Shellac (3 lb. cut)	300-350

Fig. 44-5. Approximate coverage for common finishing materials.

sealer was applied. Buff the wood with furniture wax using a polishing cloth. Stain on the cloth indicates a sealer was not used.

Primer prepares surfaces for opaque coatings (enamels). These materials become base coats for decorative finishes. Alkyd, latex, and oil-based enamels are best applied over a coat of primer.

TOPCOATING

Topcoating is the final protective film that resists moisture, dirt, chemicals, and other harmful substances. Some topcoats totally penetrate the wood. Others bond to the surface and build up as a thick film.

Penetrating finishes

Penetrating finishes, typically called oil finishes, soak into the wood. Natural penetrating finishes include linseed oil, tung oil, and wax. Synthetic materials include alkyd and phenolic resin-oil coatings. See Fig. 44-6. Both natural and synthetic products may contain dyes so that staining and topcoating is a one-step process. After application, you can still feel the wood texture. Nevertheless, the wood surface is protected.

One advantage of penetrating finishes over built-up topcoats is that scratches or stains are easy to fix. Simply apply another coat of penetrating finish. Remove mars, ring marks, and stains by rubbing with fine steel wool dipped in finish. If necessary, lightly sand the wood first. A disadvantage of penetrating finishes is that they are not resistant to everyday wear and tear.

Built-up finishes

Built-up finishes do not penetrate the wood; they form a film on the surface. Skillfully applied and polished built-up topcoatings are very durable. Select and apply them on furniture and cabinets that will be used regularly.

Built-up topcoating materials are either natural or synthetic. Natural coatings include shellac, lacquer, varnish, and enamel. Synthetic products include synthetic varnish, synthetic lacquer, and enamel. Synthetic materials generally are more durable and resistant to moisture and chemicals. See Fig. 44-7.

A built-up finish requires little maintenance unless it is damaged extensively. Then you may have to remove the old finish and apply a new coat.

Built-up coatings can be classified as either high-build or low-build. High-build coatings—varnish, enamel, and polyurethane—create a thicker protective film quicker. Low-build coatings—shellac and spray lacquer—require more coats to achieve the same thickness.

All, or nearly all, of the grain is visible through clear coatings. Shellac, polyurethane, lacquer, and most penetrating finishes are clear. Some built-up finishes can cloud the grain. This is usually the result of ingredients added to change image reflection characteristics. *Gloss* topcoatings are shiny, smooth, and nearly transparent. *Semigloss* topcoatings are not quite as shiny, and the film may

Topcoating	Solvents or Thinners	Applications	Advantages	Disadvantages
NATURAL				
Linseed oil	Mineral spirits or Turpentine	Table legs Lamps Picture frames Boxes	Resists moderate heat Soft Dull finish	Slow drying Yellows with age Requires frequent rubbing with oil
Tung oil		Small cabinets	Resists moderate heat Hard Glossy or satin Stable color Durable Easy to apply	Recoat as needed if surface is marred
Wax	None needed	Any	Extra protection from moisture	
SYNTHETIC				
Alkyd	Mineral spirits	Paneling	Glossy Inexpensive Easy to apply	Damaged by alcohol, solvents, and food acids
Phenolic-resin oil	Turpentine	Tabletops	Glossy More expensive than alkyds Easy to apply	Highly resistant to common household chemicals

Fig. 44-6. Comparing clear penetrating coatings.

Topcoating	Solvents	Applications	Advantages	Disadvantages
NATURAL				
Shellac	Alcohol	Cabinets Furniture Tables	Durable Scratches easy to hide	Surface should be kept dry Not resistant to water

**Lacquer, clear and
  opaque (rarely
  applied)**
	Lacquer thinner	Cabinets
		Furniture
		Tables
			Hard
			Glossy
			Scratches hide easily
			Resists chemicals
				Toxic during application

Varnish	Turpentine
	  or
	Mineral spirits
		Cabinets
		Furniture
		Tables
			Durable
			Various gloss levels
			May contain stain for
			  coloring and protecting
				Yellows over time

Enamel	Turpentine
	  or
	Mineral spirits
		Cabinets
		Furniture
		Tables
			Durable
			Various gloss levels
				Bright colors
				  may fade

SYNTHETIC				

**Varnish
  Acrylic
  Alkyd
  Polyurethane
  Urethane**
	Mineral spirits	Same as natural
		finishes
			Chemical curing for
			  toughness
			Some clean up with
			  soap and water
			Less yellowing than
			  natural finishes
			Various gloss levels	

Lacquer, clear and opaque	Lacquer thinner	Same as natural finishes	Improved over natural Various gloss levels	Same as natural
Enamel	Read container label.	Toe boards Inside cabinets	Durable Stable colors Various gloss levels	May lose gloss over time

Fig. 44-7. Comparing built-up topcoatings.

be somewhat cloudy. *Satin* topcoatings have a distinct amount of surface texture which diffuses light reflection. These characteristics are controlled by the amounts of silica and binder that are present in the material. Binder settles around the powdered silica, leaving a somewhat uneven surface, Fig. 44-8. Although colorless, silica tends to cloud the grain. Only use semigloss and satin finishes as the final coat. If you want a satin finish, apply several base coats of gloss finish. Then add a layer of satin finish.

Drying time

The *drying time* of a topcoating consists of two stages: setting and curing. When *setting*, the volatile liquid (water or solvent) in the finish evaporates, leaving the nonvolatile materials (pigments, resins, silica, and dye). At this point, the surface is dry to touch. Further drying occurs through *curing*, a chemical change where the oils and resins become hard. Coatings with fast setting and curing times dry relatively dust free, but are more likely to chip or crack. Lacquer is one example. A retarder

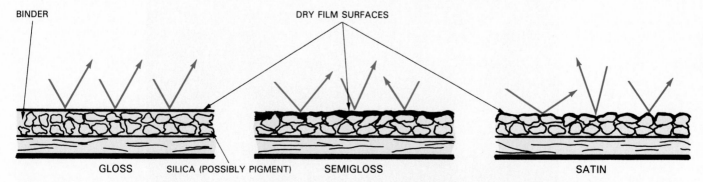

Fig. 44-8. Topcoatings consist of silica (and possibly pigment) suspended in binder and solvent. When the solvent evaporates, only the binder and silica remain. The proportion of these materials determines the reflection of the film.

can be added to lacquer to slow the drying process. Slow drying materials, such as varnish and polyurethane, are more likely to have dust settle on them. Yet, the finish is more flexible, and less likely to crack or chip.

SURFACE ACCENTS

Surface accents—decals, stencils, and stripes—are added to enhance the product or make it conform to a particular style. Decals are ink transfers bonded to the surface. Stencils are open patterns where you can brush or spray on the design. Paper, plastic, and metal plate stencils are available, or you can make your own. Stripes can be applied in several ways: as vinyl tape, sprayed on between masking tape guides or freehand, or by rolling.

POLISHING

Polishing involves buffing the surface with wax. This generally is the last step in the finishing process. Before polishing, you can rub the surface with a fine abrasive to create a soft luster called *sheen*. Use pumice stone, rottenstone, or polishing compound to rub the surface to remove the glare. Most high-quality cabinets and furniture are hand rubbed to achieve sheen.

DECORATIVE EFFECTS

Decorative coatings are an alternative to clear topcoatings. *Antiquing* is a process which ages the cabinet. The surface is treated to appear worn. *Gilding* is the addition of gold accents, especially on edges. *Graining* makes an opaque surface resemble wood grain. *Marbleizing* gives wood the appearance of marble. *Mottling* provides a visual effect of texturing; yet, the surface remains smooth.

METAL FINISHING DECISIONS

Hardware and other metal products may be finished. Usually, clear lacquer is applied to a clean polished surface to prevent tarnishing. Sometimes metal surfaces are covered with an opaque enamel coating. This protects the surface and hides the metal. Lacquers and acrylic enamels are applied over a primer coat.

For either coating procedure, the surface must be clean. Remove any rust with steel wool. If the metal was buffed, wipe it with a tack cloth to remove leftover polishing compound.

Finishes have trouble adhering to galvanized metals because the oxidized zinc oxide coating causes a weak bond. To remedy this, rub the surface with steel wool to remove any oxidation. Then wash the metal with vinegar. A white powdery coating will form as the solution dries. Remove this

Fig. 44-9. Applying paint remover softens the finish. (Klean-Strip)

with steel wool and begin applying the finish immediately.

FINISH REMOVAL

There are instances when you need to remove either an old finish or a poorly applied built-up finish. Shellac can be taken off with alcohol. Lacquer thinner will remove lacquer. Enamel, polyurethane, and varnish are softened and removed with liquid or gel-type paint remover, Fig. 44-9.

One recommended procedure is:

1. Apply remover and allow it to remain on the surface several minutes.
2. Remove the softened finish with a scraper, steel wool, and a soft wire brush. The scraper does well on flat surfaces. Steel wool works best on curved surfaces. The brush fits into tight corners and intricate detail.
3. Check the container label for application and safety instructions. Wash the surface according to directions on the container. Removing the excess softened finish with water or mineral spirits (see manufacturer's recommendation) will later reduce clogging of the abrasive.
4. Allow the surface to dry thoroughly.
5. Smooth the dried surface with steel wool or abrasives.

PLANNING A FINISHING PROCEDURE

Before applying any finish, make sure you can answer the following questions.

1. Are any of the finishing materials toxic, flammable, or hazardous?
2. Is the finishing room or area properly ventilated?
3. Have you covered, taped, or otherwise protected areas which should not be finished?
4. What surfaces will be coated first, second, third, etc.?
5. Should knobs, pulls, hinges, and other hardware be removed or covered?
6. Where will removed parts be stored while coatings are drying?
7. What is the drying time for the chosen finish?
8. What solvents will you need?
9. Are tools, supplies, and equipment ready for use?
10. Have unwanted stains and blemishes been removed?
11. Do you have the proper solvent to thin coating materials and clean equipment?

Include clean-up procedures in your plans. Allow brushes and spray equipment to dry before storing them. Discard waste materials properly.

An example finishing sequence follows. Suppose you want a stained, clear satin finish on an attractive open grain hardwood cabinet. The proper steps to apply this finish are:

1. Gather the necessary tools and supplies.
2. Prepare the surface. Remove defects, bleach if necessary, and sand the wood with increasingly finer grades of abrasive paper.
3. Wash coat the wood with shellac.
4. Spread and rub in prestained filler.
5. Remove any excess filler with mineral spirits. Rub across the grain with steel wool if necessary.
6. Brush on gloss polyurethane.
7. Sand with a fine abrasive. Use wet or dry paper and water after the last coat.
8. Repeat Steps 6 and 7 until the desired film thickness and smooth texture are reached.
9. Apply one coat of satin polyurethane.
10. Clean tools and discard cleaning solvents.
11. Discard dirty and solvent-soaked cloths.
12. Spread and buff a wax coat.

These steps represent one strategy for finishing. As you can see, there are many alternatives and many decisions to make.

THINK SAFETY—ACT SAFELY

A number of health and safety factors are associated with finishing materials. Read the container label before opening any can of finish. Look for warnings that the material is toxic, an irritant, or flammable. When applying finishing materials:

1. Wear eye and face protection to guard against splattered or sprayed materials.
2. Wear protective clothing and respirator if solvents are toxic.
3. Wear rubber or plastic gloves to protect sensitive skin. Some solvents may melt plastic.
4. Read the contents to make sure you are not allergic to any of the ingredients.
5. Have a fire blanket available.
6. Have the proper fire extinguisher and know its location.
7. Extinguish all flames and provide ventilation before using finishing materials.
8. If you experience any discomfort associated with using a finish, contact a physician.

SUMMARY

Finishing is the final step in manufacturing cabinets and furniture. The steps include preparing the surface, applying a washcoat, staining, filling, sealing, and topcoating. In addition, you may choose to add surface accents or even apply a novelty finish. The many decisions which concern finishing techniques are covered in the chapters to follow. Study these carefully because even a perfectly-constructed cabinet can be ruined by a poorly-applied finish.

CABINETMAKING TERMS

Finishing, bleaching, scorching, distressing, stain, washcoat, filler, sealer, topcoat, penetrating finish, built-up finish, gloss, semigloss, satin, drying time, setting, curing, surface accents, polishing, antiquing, gilding, graining, mottling, marbelizing.

TEST YOUR KNOWLEDGE

1. Distressing causes a wood surface to look _____.
2. Before applying any finish, you should _____.
3. List four techniques to apply finish.
4. Why would a pigment stain not be compatible with a penetrating topcoat?
5. How are the sealer and washcoat similar? How are they different?
6. When the topcoat sets, the:
   a. Volatile materials evaporate.
   b. Nonvolatile materials evaporate.
   c. Volatile materials cure.
   d. Nonvolatile materials cure.
7. Close grain hardwoods do not require:
   a. Bleaching.
   b. Grain raising.
   c. Staining.
   d. Filling.
   e. Varnishing.
8. Fast-drying topcoatings are more likely to chip than slow-drying topcoatings. True or False?
9. A synthetic penetrating finish is:
   a. Tung oil.
   b. Alkyd oil.
   c. Linseed oil.
   d. Wax.
10. Sealers may be applied before and after stain. True or False?
11. Sheen results from:
    a. Rubbing.
    b. Applying wax.
    c. Colorless pigments.
    d. Silica.
12. Clean wood surfaces with alcohol after using paint remover. True or False?
13. Finishing materials applied to metals penetrate the surface. True or False?
14. Galvanized metal must be washed with _____ before it can be primed.
15. List equipment that can make your finishing area safe.

Chapter 45
PREPARING SURFACES FOR FINISH

After studying this chapter, you will be able to:
☐ *Correct surface defects such as dents, cracks, and voids.*
☐ *Remove natural color or stains by bleaching.*
☐ *Create an aged effect by distressing or scorching the wood.*
☐ *Follow the proper sequence for raising the grain.*

After assembly, most all cabinets require a certain amount of preparation before finish is applied. This includes correcting defects, removing color (bleaching), adding color (staining), smoothing, and creating special effects. The method used to prepare the surface depends on the final finish. For example, when you apply opaque finish (enamel), you could leave a film of dried glue on the wood surface. In fact, the glue would serve as a sealer. However, when applying stain under a clear finish, you must remove any dried glue. Glue will not absorb stain, leaving a spot of natural wood color.

THINK SAFETY—ACT SAFELY
WHEN PREPARING SURFACES FOR FINISH

Pay close attention to health and safety guidelines when working with finishing materials. Check the container labels for warnings to see if the finish is toxic, an irritant, or flammable. When preparing to apply finish:
1. Have adequate ventilation.
2. Wear a face shield, especially when bleaching.
3. Wear leather gloves when scorching the wood.
4. Wear plastic or rubber gloves and protective clothing.
5. Store bleaching chemicals in glass, earthenware, or stainless steel containers.
6. Contact a physician if you experience any discomfort.
7. Choose the proper solvent as a finish thinner or cleaning solution.

REPAIRING SURFACE DEFECTS

To prepare a smooth surface, begin with a visual inspection, Fig. 45-1. Look for dents, chips, open joints, excess dried adhesive, dirt, oil spots, and scratches. Also check for pencil marks left from layout. If not corrected, these defects detract from the finished cabinet's appearance, Fig. 45-2.

REPAIRING DENTS

Dents, which are simply crushed wood cells, can often be raised with a drop of water. Press a pin

Fig. 45-1. Inspect surfaces and remove defects before applying finish. (Columbus Showcase)

Fig. 45-2. Correct minor scratches with abrasives. (Carver-Tripp)

Fig. 45-4. Common repair materials include wood putty, wood dough, stick shellac, and wax stick putty.

point into deep, dampened dents several times to help open the wood cells. Wait for the water to evaporate. Then inspect the surface to see if the wood cells have expanded to raise the dent. If not, try once again. If the dent remains, place a wet cloth, folded several times, over it. Apply a medium-hot clothes iron or soldering iron to the surface, Fig. 45-3. This should raise all but the worst dents.

REPAIRING CHIPS, SCRATCHES, AND VOIDS

There are many ways to repair chips, scratches, and voids. Various putties and fillers are available, Fig. 45-4. To repair surfaces for clear coats, apply a precolored filler or one that accepts stain. Patching a surface for an opaque finish is easier since you do not have to match colors. The finish hides both the patch and any discoloration in the wood.

Chips, dents, and abrasive scratches absorb extra stain. In fact, the stain will make them more ob-

vious. Fig. 45-5 shows a test panel with defects that were overlooked. Stain was rubbed from the high spots left by the planer. Extra stain collected in coarse abrasive marks. An excess amount of stain soaked into raised dents that were not sanded enough.

Your goal should be to remove all defects. This is nearly impossible since even fine abrasives leave shallow scratches. Those which run along the grain are not noticeable in the finished product. However, you must remove scratches made across the grain because stain highlights these flaws.

Defects under clear coatings

Before using any patching mixture under a clear coating, read the manufacturers' instructions. Plastic-based materials may not accept stain when dry. Some types already have stain added to them.

Fig. 45-3. Apply a damp cloth pad and warm iron to raise stubborn dents.

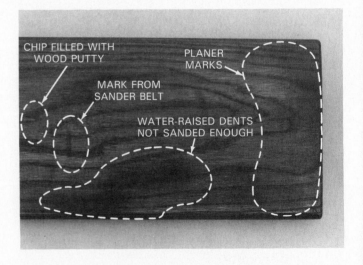

Fig. 45-5. Defects may become noticeable if not repaired before finish is applied.

Be wary of products where you do not have control over the color. They may not match the stain you choose for the product. Testing the color may be necessary.

There are two basic techniques used to control the color of your repairs. If the repair material (when dry) accepts stain, there should be little color variation between the stained wood and the patch. With some products, you may notice slight color variations. With others, you should add stain to the repair material before making the patch. First stain a test board (same wood specie as the product) to determine the final color. Then mix stain into a small amount of patching compound. Press the mixture into a defect in an unstained portion of your test board. When choosing a stain, note that a pigment stain covers quite well, but will also partially hide the grain.

Wood putty. Wood putty, or wood dough, consists of real wood flour in a resin (glue) and works well for small defects. It is sold as a paste or a powder ready to be mixed with water. A common mixture ratio is four to five parts of powder to one part of water. Prepare only as much as you can apply in about five minutes. Then, the mixture starts to set. You can extend the pot life of water-mixed wood putty by adding two or three drops of vinegar or milk per teaspoon of water.

Dried wood putty accepts most oil, water, and alcohol stains. Yet, it is best to color the putty before application to match the natural wood color or desired stained color. Select a water-soluble or aniline dye stain. Let the patch dry for one hour before smoothing it with abrasives.

Wood plastics. Wood plastics are cellulose fiber fillers typically found under the names Plastic Wood, Wood Plastic, and Wood Forming Plastic. Most wood plastics are very hard and nonabsorbent when cured. They are often found in manufactured colors. In addition, a neutral color product can be colored with pigment or penetrating dye stains before application. Some products will accept an alcohol-thinned dye stain when dry.

Wood plastic dries hard. Large fibers in the mixture make shallow or narrow defects hard to fill. Spread the paste with a putty knife. At times, the material is difficult to apply. On deep defects, apply several layers, each about 1/16 in. (1.5 mm) thick. Allow each layer to set. Fill the defect and leave a slight crown of excess patch. Wait several days for it to dry. During this time, the cellulose shrinks. Then sand the surface using a sanding block to make the patch flush. Do not be surprised if a slight dent appears in a large patch several months later. Cellulose tends to continue to shrink.

Glue and wood dust. White or yellow liquid adhesive can be pressed into nail holes and small cracks. Then sand over the area while the glue is wet so that wood dust adheres. You can also mix glue and dust together to make the patch. However, this repair will not accept stain, and is hard to stain before making the patch.

Stick putty. Precolored stick putty, made of wax, fills small holes or cracks. There is a wide range of colors available for various wood species. If necessary, blend two colors together to match the stained wood. Rub the stick on the defect to make the repair before staining the cabinet. Stick putty typically will not adhere to a stained product. Make sure you have stained a test board to match colors.

Stick shellac. Stick shellac, made in colors, is melted to fill the defect. There are two ways to apply shellac. A burn-in knife, looks like a soldering iron with a spatula tip, Fig. 45-6. It heats and spreads the shellac in one pass. You can also melt the shellac with a flame to drip onto the defect. Press the droplet flat with a heated putty knife, Fig. 45-7.

A wide range of stick shellac colors are made to match most any fine cabinet wood. Apply shellac before stain. Stick shellac will not accept stain; thus, choose a color to match the stained wood.

Defects under opaque coatings

The surface under an opaque finish can be repaired with most any patch material. Since the patch will not be seen, choose an inexpensive compound. Knife-grade *spackling compound*, probably the most economical, is easy to apply. It is available

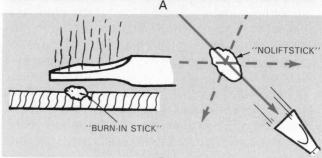

Fig. 45-6. A—Burn-in knife for melting and spreading stick shellac. (Woodcraft) B—Rub over the shellac droplet different ways to flatten it. (Mohawk Finishing Products)

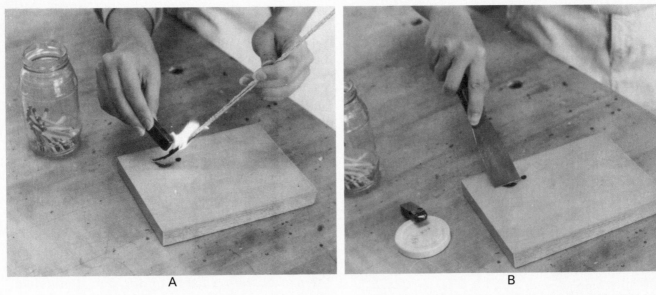

Fig. 45-7. A—Melting a drop of stick shellac over the defect. B—Spread the shellac with a warm putty knife.

in paste or powder forms. Mix powdered spackling with water and allow the compound to set for a few minutes. Mix only the amount usable within an hour since spackling sets quickly. Apply paste compound straight from the container.

Fill the defect using a putty knife and leave a slight amount of excess. Cover cracks by applying the compound across the opening. Moving a knife along the opening may lift out the spackling material. Allow the patch to dry about one hour. After that, the surface will need smoothing. Sand it with the same grit abrasive used just before filling the defect.

Some cabinetmakers recommend filling defects for opaque finishes after the first coat. The coat fills smaller defects, leaving only larger ones to be fixed.

REMOVING DRIED ADHESIVE

Excess dried adhesive is a typical problem with many finishes. Cured adhesive will not absorb stain. Because most glues dry clear, the excess is overlooked. This leaves unsightly light spots in corners and along glue joints. With careless handling, you can leave fingerprints of glue on the surface. Even without stain, adhesive left on the wood is a problem. Varnished wood yellows as it ages, but does not do so where glue is present. The more the natural wood yellows, the more noticeable the glue becomes.

To help locate dry glue, wet the wood, Fig. 45-8. Dampen one surface at a time with a wet cloth or sponge. The wood darkens slightly when moist unless the area is coated with glue. There, the area remains light-colored. Lightly circle the glue area with a pencil.

Remove excess dry glue with a hand or cabinet scraper, followed by abrasive paper. Be careful not

to create a dent or scrape away the wood. Work along the grain to prevent making scratches across the grain. You can wet the wood again to see if the glue spot is gone. Avoid using a chisel because it has a tendency to gouge the wood.

REMOVING OIL SPOTS

Since many woodworking machines are lubricated, oil spots may appear on the wood. These areas will not accept stain. Try to dissolve and remove oil with mineral spirits or lacquer thinner. Oil-based products, such as crayon and ink pen, should also be dissolved because these can bleed through the finish.

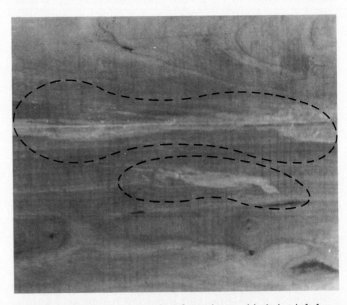

Fig. 45-8. Wetting the wood surface shows dried glue left from assembly (light-colored areas).

BLEACHING THE SURFACE

Bleaching removes natural coloring and stains. Contemporary furniture is often bleached to create the pale blond effect desired by many consumers. Natural stains include mineral dyes and blue stain. These are especially visible in sapwood. Several defects occur from improper storage. Water stains materials if it is allowed to sit on the wood during storage. Mildew, a dark fungus, will grow on wood that remains moist. Stains also may result from clamping. During assembly, you should wipe away excess liquid adhesive with water. Water left to dry where metal bar or C-clamps touch the wood results in black stains.

Bleaching chemicals remove color to an effective depth of 1/1000 to 1/32 in. Bleaching is not equally effective on all wood species, Fig. 45-9. It works well to remove stains, but does not always take out natural coloring.

Bleaching can lighten a finished product. However, since most bleaches are water soluble, they may not be effective on penetrating oil stains. Water usually does not penetrate and dissolve the dye and oil; instead, it floats on top. Use mineral spirits to dissolve penetrating oil stains before bleaching the wood. Trying to bleach out a pigment stain may be even less effective. You likely will need to dissolve the stain with paint remover first.

You can buy or prepare chemicals for bleaching. There may be one or more steps for application. Mild bleaches are a one-step process. Stronger acid bleaches are applied in one step and neutralized in another. Follow the manufacturer's instructions very closely when preparing and using strong bleaches.

Bleaching chemicals should be stored in, and used from, specified containers. Sealable glass, earthenware, or stainless steel containers are acceptable. Galvanized containers discolor the solution and reduce its effectiveness.

Allow the wood to dry thoroughly after bleaching. Some of the color removed may be mildew. If the wood retains any moisture, the fungus typically begins to grow again. Wait at least 24 hours before applying any other coating material. In humid weather, even more drying time may be necessary.

APPLYING COMMERCIALLY PREPARED BLEACHES

Most wood bleaches you buy are two-step applications efficient on stubborn stains and deep natural color. The strong chemical solutions are referred to as "A" and "B" or "1" and "2." The bleaching process involves applying the first solution and then neutralizing it with the second solution. The container label recommends chemical proportions that obtain the best results.

Place adequate amounts of the solutions in two well-marked separate containers. Apply a liberal amount of the solution marked "1" or "A" with a cloth, sponge, or worn nylon brush, Fig. 45-10. Wear protective gloves, clothing, and a face shield. At the specified time, while the surface is still damp, apply a liberal amount of the solution marked "2" or "B." Use a different applicator. Let the surface dry thoroughly. Then rinse the surface with clear water or a two percent solution of white vinegar

Wood	Bleaching
Ash	Fairly easy
Basswood	Difficult
Beech	Fairly easy
Birch	Easy
Cedar	No effect
Cherry	Difficult
Chestnut	Difficult
Cypress	Difficult
Ebony	Difficult
Douglas fir	No effect
Gum	Fairly easy
Hemlock	No effect
Holly	Easy
Lauan (Phillippine mahogany)	Fairly easy
Maple	Fairly easy
Oak	Easy
Pine (white)	No effect
Pine (yellow)	No effect
Poplar	Difficult
Redwood	No effect
Rosewood	Difficult
Spruce	No effect
Sycamore	Easy
Teakwood	Fairly easy
Walnut	Fairly easy

Fig. 45-9. Bleaching affects wood species differently.

Fig. 45-10. One method to apply bleach is with a sponge attached to a length of dowel.

in water to remove any remaining chemicals. Finally, let the wood dry entirely.

APPLYING USER-PREPARED BLEACHES

You can prepare bleaches with laundry bleach or oxalic acid. Both are mixed with water. There may be two to four steps involved in applying the solutions, Fig. 45-11.

Chlorine laundry bleach (weak hypochloride) is readily available in liquid form. The strength varies among manufacturers. Mix two to four ounces in a quart of water at room temperature. Apply a liberal, even coat of bleach with a cloth, sponge, or worn nylon brush. As each application begins to dry, repeat coats at five minute intervals until you reach the desired color. Then let the bleached surface dry thoroughly. Rinse the surface with water to remove any remaining chemicals. Let the surface dry before smoothing any raised grain with fine abrasives.

Oxalic acid, available in crystal and powder forms, is used frequently in bleaching solutions. You can dissolve three or four ounces of the acid in a quart of hot water. The solution works best when applied hot, but you can apply it at room temperatures. Wait several minutes after application before rinsing the surface with water. You might neutralize the acid with one ounce of borax in a quart of water before rinsing the wood with plain water.

A still stronger oxalic acid bleaching method involves applying a second, intermediate solution. Prepare the oxalic acid mixture just described. Also mix 3 ounces of *sodium hyposulphite* (photographer's HYPO solution) in a quart of water. Apply this to the damp, not wet, oxalic-acid-soaked wood surface. Follow this with a hot water rinse after the surface dries. You could also apply a borax solution neutralizer before the water rinse.

RAISING THE GRAIN

After sanding the wood smooth with fine abrasive paper (180 or 220 grit), and before applying finish, it is wise to raise the wood grain. *Grain raising* is the process of swelling wood fibers and any last dents, dimples, or other pressure marks. Dampen the wood with a sponge soaked in water. Allow the surface to dry, then sand it once again. After raising the grain, you might apply a washcoat of shellac, a commercial sanding sealer, or nonsealing glue size. After this, lightly sand the surface with the same abrasive grade last used.

FINAL INSPECTION

Before finishing a product, reinspect it, especially the repairs. Then dust all surfaces with a fine mesh cloth. Nylon hose is ideal. It will snag on any defects or rough spots, indicating that additional sanding is needed.

DISTRESSING THE SURFACE

Occasionally, you may notice that a new cabinet's surface is damaged, worn, or looks aged, Fig. 45-12. This is the result of *distressing* and is done as a design feature. It is not an alternative to quality cabinetmaking.

SURFACE DAMAGE

True distressing involves striking the surface repeatedly with a chain or other hard object, Fig. 45-13. This gives the appearance of years of use. Strike the cabinet only enough to achieve the desired wear.

STEP	LAUNDRY CHEMICALS	OXALIC ACID	OXALIC ACID AND HYPO
1	3-4 oz. (90-120 mL) Clorox bleach in 1 qt. (950 mL) water	3-4 oz. (84-112 g) Oxalic acid crystals or powder in 1 qt. (950 mL) water	3-4 oz. (84-112 g) Oxalic acid crystals or powder in 1 qt. (950 mL) water
2	Water	1 oz. (28 g) Borax powder in 1 qt. water	3 oz. (84 g) Sodium photographer's HYPO (hyposulphite)
3		Water	1 oz. (28 g) Borax powder in 1 qt. water
4			Water or 2% vinegar and water solution

Fig. 45-11. Contents and applications of homemade bleaching solutions.

Fig. 45-12. Distressed surfaces give an aged appearance.
(Thomasville)

Fig. 45-14. Simulated distressing caused by tapping a brush dipped in enamel against a scrap board, splattering finish onto the surface.

opaque finishes. This less damaging method is preferred, although not as realistic as actual surface marks. This practice is used often by commercial furniture manufacturers.

SCORCHING

Scorching is done to highlight areas of a product, Fig. 45-15. Choose a strong heat source, such as a propane torch. A heavy duty soldering iron (over 1000 watts) could be used. These tools provide

Fig. 45-13. Actual surface distressing with a length of chain. Notice the distressed effect once stain is added.

SIMULATED DISTRESSING

Simulated distressing, often called imitation distressing, involves splattering the surface with black or brown enamel, Fig. 45-14. Simulated distressing can be done under clear or over

Fig. 45-15. Scorched areas highlight a breakfast table.

surface color contrast to light colored wood.

To create the scorched effect:

1. Decide what areas you want to highlight.
2. Wet a cloth with water to have ready in case the wood catches fire.
3. Wear leather gloves while using a torch or soldering iron.
4. Move the flame or heating element over the surface to be discolored, Fig. 45-16. If using a torch, do not touch the wood. Start with the flame 2 to 3 in. from the surface. Adjust this distance according to how fast the wood changes color. Rub the soldering iron on the surface.
5. When finished, set the torch or soldering iron in a safe place to cool.
6. Lightly sand any unevenly colored areas.

Scorching must be done with care. Have plenty of ventilation because some wood species give off toxic fumes when burnt. Work well away from any flammable materials.

Fig. 45-16. Scorching the surface with a propane torch. Notice the water-soaked rag ready in case the wood catches fire.

SUMMARY

Preparing a surface for finish requires skill and patience. Begin with a careful inspection of the assembled product. Identify any natural defects or flaws caused during production by carelessness.

A variety of materials fill cracks, chips, dents, voids. Wood putty is a real wood material for fixing smaller defects. Wood plastics dry hard, but shrink. Stick putty is excellent for holes and cracks. Stick shellac is melted into defects with a burn-in knife or putty knife. Under opaque coatings, spackling compound is more economical.

Bleaching is a color-removal process to take out natural coloring, natural stains, and user-made stains. You can use household chemicals or purchase bleaching solutions. Many of these products are toxic and must be spread with extreme caution.

To achieve an aged effect, products may be distressed. This involves either physically damaging the product or splattering brown or black enamel on the surface. Imitation distressing is less damaging and can be removed with paint stripper, if necessary. Scorching, another special effect, highlights portions of the product.

CABINETMAKING TERMS

Dent, wood putty, wood plastic, stick putty, stick shellac, spackling compound, bleaching, chlorine laundry bleach, oxalic acid, sodium hyposulphite, grain raising, distressing, simulated distressing, scorching.

TEST YOUR KNOWLEDGE

1. List four defects likely to be found when preparing surfaces for finish.
2. If you cannot raise a dent with water alone, apply:
   a. Spackling compound.
   b. Wood plastic.
   c. A wet rag and warm iron.
   d. Contact cement or epoxy adhesive.
3. Identify the difference between wood putty and wood plastic patching compounds.
4. Explain why it is better to add stain to a patching compound before fixing a defect.
5. The pot life of water-mixed wood putty can be extended with:
   a. Paint thinner.
   b. Water.
   c. Mineral spirits.
   d. Vinegar.
6. Oil spots can be bleached. True or False?
7. Describe how dried adhesives affect the wood's ability to accept stain.
8. What method can be used to locate dried adhesive?
9. An aged effect can be achieved by what two distressing techniques?
10. After bleaching, rinse the surface with _____ before applying finish.

Three-step process for applying stain—sanding, applying stain with a brush, and rubbing the stain with a soft cloth to obtain penetration.   (Parks Corp.)

Chapter 46
APPLYING FINISHING MATERIALS

After studying this chapter, you will be able to:
☐ *Select tools and equipment to apply finishing materials.*
☐ *Apply finish by brushing, spraying, wiping, dipping, or rolling.*
☐ *Clean and maintain tools and equipment.*

Finishing a product involves applying a protective coating that either penetrates or builds up on a wood or metal surface. Application practices which produce a quality finish include: brushing, spraying, wiping, dipping, and rolling. Select the method based on the following guidelines:
1. Manufacturers' recommendations. Instructions on the container label suggest effective application methods. The label also may contain cautions, warnings, suggested solvents, thinning techniques, and cleanup routines.
2. Availability of tools and equipment. Application techniques other than spraying involve hand tools. Spraying requires either compressed air and a spray gun or airless spray equipment.
3. Personal preference. Over time, cabinetmakers begin to favor some application techniques over others.

Before applying any finish, plan a step-by-step procedure. Creating a high-quality finish involves more than just selecting the material and application technique. Do not overlook decisions on how to store wet assemblies. Dust settling on the product can spoil a good finish.

BRUSHING

Brushing is a common method to apply coating materials. Although slow compared to spraying, applying finishes with brushes involves a limited amount of equipment by comparison. Producing a quality finish with a brush involves selecting the proper brush, using it correctly, and following good maintenance procedures.

SELECTING BRUSHES

Be concerned when selecting brushes. A good brush has the following features:
1. Spreads coatings smoothly and evenly with minimum effort.
2. Is balanced so it can be handled easily.
3. Can be cleaned readily.
4. Will last for a long time.

Not all brushes are equal. There are two basic kinds: natural and synthetic. Each has unique purposes.

Natural bristle brushes
Natural bristles, made of hog's hair, are suitable for applying oil-base stain, filler, sealer, and most topcoating materials, including lacquer and shellac. They do not work well with latex or other water-base finishes. Water soaks into natural bristles and weakens them. Soft bristles will not control an even spread of finish.

Natural brushes are typically more expensive than synthetic brushes. They also wear faster. Nevertheless, many cabinetmakers still prefer them.

Synthetic bristle brushes
Synthetic bristles are made of nylon or polyester, or a blend of both. Nylon bristles perform well with both water-base and oil-base finishes other than shellac and lacquer. These weaken the nylon. Polyester bristles are the newest type on the market. They are suited best for water-base finishes, but will work with oil-base materials. Synthetic-blend brushes have universal applications.

Determining brush quality
High quality brushes have the features shown in Fig. 46-1. A good brush has more bristles than one that is less expensive. The bristles on the sides are shorter to permit an even flow of material through the brush. The ends of the bristles are split so that each tip becomes a tiny brush. A good brush holds

finish better. Once dipped, it should spread the film with fewer strokes.

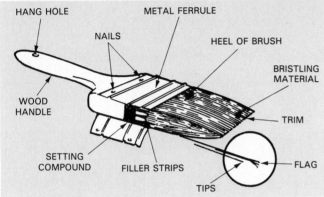

Fig. 46-1. Parts of a quality paint brush.

USING BRUSHES

Choose a brush size according to the product. Wide brushes cover a surface quicker. Narrow brushes coat edges and reach into corners easily. Artist's brushes are good for touch-up work.

There are two concerns when using a brush: loading and spreading.

Loading

Loading a brush means to dip it in finish. Cover no more than 50 percent of the bristle length. Then tap the brush on the inside edge of the container, Fig. 46-2. This removes excess finish to prevent

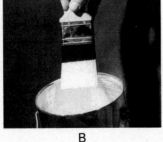

Fig. 46-2. A—Dip brush bristles only halfway into the finish. B—Tap, do not rub, the brush on the container.

dripping. Do not wipe the brush against the container. This causes excessive wear and makes the brush release finish unevenly.

Spreading

Spreading refers to applying an even film of finish. This takes practice. The steps illustrated in Fig. 46-3 are as follows

1. Touch the loaded brush to the surface. Liquid begins flowing from the bristles, Fig. 46-3A.
2. Keep the brush at a 15 degree angle while moving it along the grain.
3. Work toward the wet edges of a coated area.
4. Apply light pressure.
5. Overlap passes about 10 percent or less when staining, Fig. 46-3B. Overlap 50 percent when spreading filler, and 25 percent when applying a topcoating, Fig. 46-3C.
6. Avoid repeated brush strokes over any area. This thins the coating and may make the film uneven.
7. When brushing vertical surfaces, curl your hand around the handle with the thumb resting against the handle, Fig. 46-3D.
8. Remove runs, sags, air bubbles, and dust by holding the brush perpendicular. Touch only the split ends of the bristles to the surface.

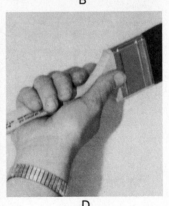

Fig. 46-3. Brushing on a finish. A—Touch the brush to the surface at a 15 degree angle. B—Overlap 50 percent when spreading filler. C—Overlap 25 percent when applying topcoating. (Carver-Tripp) D—Brushing vertical surfaces.

Fig. 46-4. A—There are a number of commercially available solvents. (Klean-Strip) B—Choose the proper solvent for thinning finish and cleaning tools. (Parks Corp.)

	Thinning Uses	Oil Based Enamels or Stains	Latex Enamels or Stains	Varnishes	Lacquers	Shellac	Polyurethanes	Epoxies 2-Part Coatings	Oil Finishes	Cleaning Uses	Oil Based Enamel, Varnish, or Polyurethane Application Tools	Latex Enamel or Stain Appl. Tools	Lacquer Application Tools	Shellac Application Tools	Epoxy Application Tools	Enameling Tools with Dried Hardened Coatings	Clean New Wood Before Finishing	Clean Oil Coatings Before Refinishing	Degrease Painted Metal Parts	Degrease Bare Metal
Paint Thinner		■					■		■		■						■	■	■	■
Mineral Spirits		■							■		■							■	■	■
Alcohol						■								■						
Lacquer Thinner					■								■		■	■			■	■
Turpentines		■		■					■		■							■		
Acetone								■					■		■	■			■	■
VM&P Naphtha		■		■					■		■						■	■	■	■
Toluol					■								■						■	■
Xylol					■								■						■	■
MEK					■			■					■		■	■			■	■
Kerosene		■									■							■	■	■
Raw Linseed Oil									■											
Boiled Linseed Oil									■											

MAINTAINING BRUSHES

Good brushes, maintained correctly, will offer years of continuous service. Follow this procedure to clean and store a brush.

1. Wash the brush in the proper solvent. Assorted solvents for thinning finishes and cleaning tools are shown in Fig. 46-4.
2. Remove set finish from the ferrule and bristles, Fig. 46-5. Use a putty knife, coarse comb, and/or wire brush.
3. Rinse away any loose, set finish.
4. Squeeze, do not wring, the bristles to remove excess solvent.
5. Spin the brush between your hands inside a container. This further removes solvents and debris from the brush.

Fig. 46-5. Be sure brushes are completely clean. Comb through them.

Brushes can be stored wet or dry. Hang brushes that are used regularly with the bristles covered in clean solvent, Fig. 46-6. Choose a container so the bristles do not touch the bottom. Close the container tightly to prevent the solvent from evaporating. When storing brushes dry, wrap the bristles in paper and store the brush flat.

SPRAYING

Spraying is the fastest way to apply natural and synthetic coatings. Finish is *atomized* (broken up) into tiny droplets which flow from the gun nozzle in a spray pattern. Spraying equipment is efficient and capable of producing a flat, nearly flawless film. Handling and using spraying equipment requires skills gained through experience.

There are three distinct categories of spraying: air, airless, and aerosol. Each method requires different equipment.

AIR SPRAYING

Air spraying provides a high-quality finish. Compressed air and finish are mixed by the gun and expelled as a fine mist from the nozzle in a spray pattern, Fig. 46-7. Most any finish, including stain, sealer, and topcoating, can be air sprayed.

Spraying with air requires several pieces of equipment, including:

1. A compressor to supply an adequate amount of pressurized air.
2. Valves to control air pressure. Tank pressure is controlled by a regulator, usually built into the compressor. An air transformer regulates the amount of pressure delivered to the gun.
3. A hose of the right size, usually 3/8 in. (10 mm), with quick disconnect couplings. A small hose can restrict the air flow rate.
4. A spray gun to atomize the coating material.
5. Container to hold the liquid finish. This may be a cup that screws onto the gun or a pot connected to the gun by a hose.

Air compressors

Air compressors supply pressurized air to operate the spray gun. They are rated by maximum pressure and air volume capacity. Air pressure is given in

Fig. 46-6. This container allows you to hang brushes in solvent.

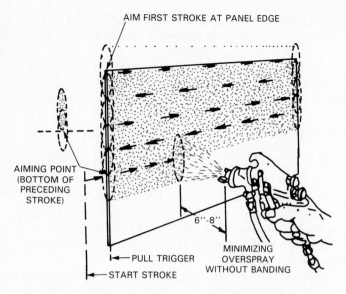

Fig. 46-7. Spraying is a quick, effective way to apply finish.

pounds per square inch (psi). The volume of air delivered is given in cubic feet per minute (cfm). Metric capacities are kilopascals (kPa) of air pressure and liters per minute (lpm) of volume. Typical specifications vary from 30 to 80 psi (207 to 552 kPa) and 5 to 15 cfm (142 to 425 lpm).

The most important unit of all compressors is the *air pump*. On most compressors, the pump pressurizes an attached storage tank, Fig. 46-8. It cycles on and off automatically to maintain near constant pressure in the tank.

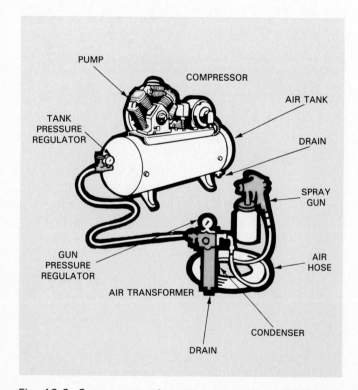

Fig. 46-8. Components of an air spray system. (DeVilbiss)

A *regulator* on the compressor limits the air pressure by shutting off the pump once a preset pressure is reached. This safety feature prevents an explosion of the compressor or air line. A tank gauge, if present, indicates the current pressure.

Small, portable compressors without a tank run continuously to deliver steady air pressure. They are lightweight and transportable, but often deliver less air pressure and flow. The safe maximum pressure for portable units typically is 30 psi (207 kPa).

Stationary compressors are designed for heavy shop use. They can quickly supply hundreds of psi. In larger cabinet shops, the unit is located at a remote site. Air is delivered to the finishing room by an air line. Between the compressor and the gun is an air transformer. It usually is located at the gun connection where you are spraying. The *air transformer* reduces air line pressure to the necessary gun pressure. It also filters out moisture and compressor oil.

The size of the hose controls air flow. Spray operations normally require 5 to 15 cfm (142 to 425 lpm). An undersize hose could resist the flow rate and cause a poor spray pattern. Use the gun manufacturer's recommended hose size and air pressure. Most hoses connect with a *quick-disconnect coupling*. Slide the knurled sleeve back and the hoses separate. To connect the hose, slide the sleeve back, push the coupling into place, and let the sleeve spring back. Some hoses have threaded connectors and are tightened with a wrench.

Spray gun manufacturers specify maximum pressures for their equipment. Learn what this pressure is before using any gun. For example, the maximum pressure on one model is 40 psi (275 kPa). If a coating material does not spray properly, you cannot increase the pressure above 40 psi. Rather, you must thin the liquid so it will flow through the nozzle more easily.

Air spray guns

Air spray equipment includes bleeder and nonbleeder guns. They can be further defined as either suction or pressure feed.

Bleeder gun. *Bleeder guns* do not have a valve to shut off air flow. Even when not spraying, you can feel and hear the air coming through the gun's nozzle, Fig. 46-9. Pulling the trigger controls only the flow of liquid. The gun normally is attached to a tankless air compressor (one where the pump runs continuously). The compressor has a safety valve to closely regulate air pressure.

Nonbleeder gun. *Nonbleeder guns* allow the user to control the air and liquid flow rates, Fig 46-10. The trigger opens both valves together. However, each valve is adjusted independently. This type of gun operates best from a tank-type air compressor.

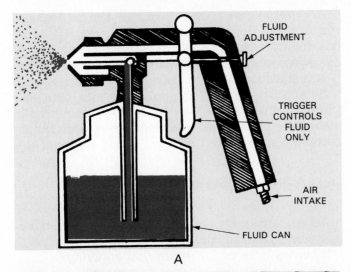

FLUID
ADJUSTMENT

TRIGGER
CONTROLS
FLUID
ONLY

AIR
INTAKE

FLUID CAN

A

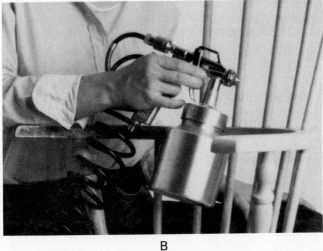

B

Fig. 46-9. A bleeder gun lets air through the nozzle constantly. A—Parts. B—External appearance. (Ingersoll-Rand)

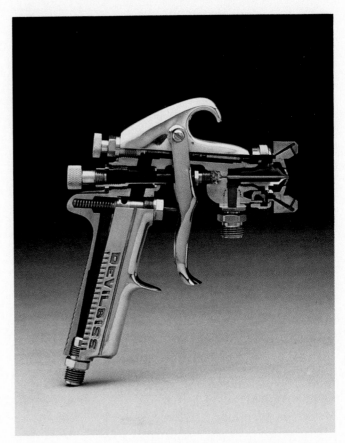

Fig. 46-10. A nonbleeder gun has separate fluid and air (pattern spreader) controls. (DeVilbiss)

Nonbleeder guns feed liquid to the nozzle by one
of two methods: suction or pressure.

A *suction-feed gun* has a fluid cup with a small
air hole in the top. When you press the trigger, the

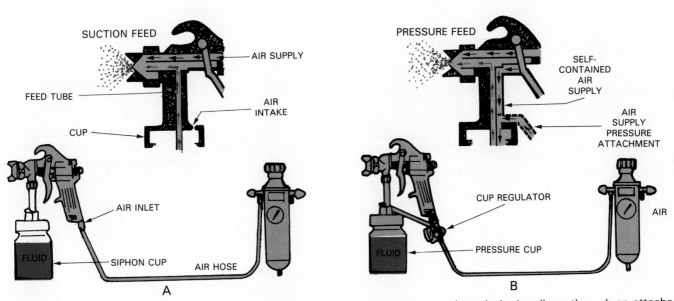

SUCTION FEED

AIR SUPPLY

FEED TUBE

AIR
INTAKE

CUP

AIR INLET

FLUID

SIPHON CUP   AIR HOSE

A

PRESSURE FEED

SELF-
CONTAINED
AIR
SUPPLY

AIR
SUPPLY
PRESSURE
ATTACHMENT

CUP REGULATOR

AIR

FLUID

PRESSURE CUP

B

Fig. 46-11. A—Suction-feed gun. B—Pressure-feed gun. Air pressure may come through the handle or through an attached
air supply hose. (Binks)

flow of air draws finish through the feed tube to be atomized with air in the nozzle, Fig. 46-11A. Select suction-feed guns for spraying lacquer, shellac, stain, and similar thin materials. Varnish, polyurethane, enamel, and latex finishes usually can be thinned enough for suction spraying. The gun manufacturer recommends finish/solvent ratios. The hole on top of the cup allows air to replace drawn liquid. Covering this hole will cause the gun to operate improperly.

A *pressure-feed* system forces finish up into the nozzle, Fig. 46-11B. Thicker liquids can be sprayed with this equipment. The finish is forced into the gun from a cup or from a pressurized tank. When a cup is attached, compressed air enters both the cup and the nozzle. Air pressure enters the cup through either a self-contained air supply within the handle or an air supply attachment to the cup. Remember that the connection between gun and cup must be air tight. When a pressure tank is used, fluid is forced through another hose into the gun.

A *combination gun* is available. It has a valve that you can open for suction feed or close for pressure feed. A lever on the gun allows liquid to be drawn or forced. This allows the gun to apply both thin and thick finishes.

Air spray gun nozzles

A spray gun's *nozzle* is responsible for mixing air and fluid. It contains a fluid nozzle and air cap; both are critical parts of all air spray guns. Nozzles are either external or internal mix.

An *external-mix nozzle* atomizes air and fluid outside the air cap, Fig. 46-12A. Although it can be used for all finishes, it is best installed for spraying lacquer, stain, sealer, and other thin fluids. The external-mix nozzle can be installed on all suction-feed guns and some pressure-feed guns.

An *internal-mix nozzle* mixes air and fluid inside the air cap before discharging them, Fig. 46-12B. It is appropriate for heavy, slow drying fluids, such as varnish, polyurethane, enamel, and latex finishes. It is installed only on a pressure-feed gun.

Be sure the proper size fluid nozzle is installed. Various finishes require different nozzle hole diameters, fluid feed methods, and application techniques, Fig. 46-13.

OPERATING AIR SPRAY EQUIPMENT

As you assemble equipment and supplies, have answers to the following questions first.
1. What type of finish are you spraying?
2. Do you have a bleeder or nonbleeder gun?
3. Is the gun a suction or pressure-feed system?
4. Is the proper size and type fluid nozzle in place?
5. Is there proper ventilation? If using a dust and vapor removal system, are the proper filters in place?

Using air spray equipment involves these steps: preparing the material, filling the cup, adjusting the gun, and spraying.

Preparing the coating material

Finish must be able to flow through the gun easily. Most purchased finishes are at a brushing viscosity (thickness). Some products may be sold as "spray" finish. These can be used straight from the can. Otherwise, you must thin the finish. Usually, the container label specifies the proper finish/solvent ratio to spray the product. If no mixture ratios are given on the label, test different proportions by spraying each on a test board. Record the ratios you are mixing. You may need to spray the same mix in the future.

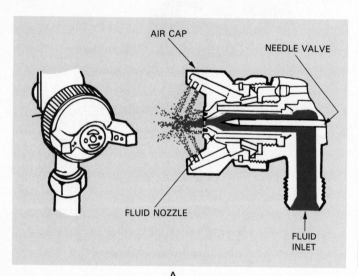

A

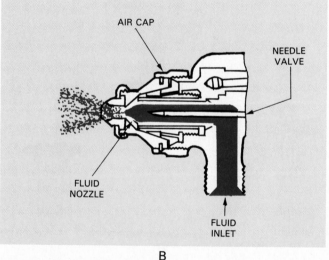

B

Fig. 46-12. A—External-mix nozzle. B—Internal-mix nozzle. (Binks)

MATERIAL	PRESSURES		NOZZLE HOLE		PROCESS
	psi	(kPa)	in.	(mm)	
Stain (NGR preferred)	25	(175)	.040	(1.0)	Best with suction gun and external-mix nozzle. Good with any other combination.
Enamel (oil-base)	40	(275)	.060	(1.5)	Pressure feed. Apply enamels specified for spraying, if available. Avoid thinning unless directed otherwise.
Enamel (latex-base)	40	(275)	.060	(1.5)	Pressure feed only. Spray as thick as possible. Adjust gun to maximum flow rate. Flush gun with mineral spirits after cleaning with water to prevent rust. Pattern size at 8 to 12 in. (200 to 300 mm). Distance from surface at 6 to 8 in. (150 to 200 mm).
Lacquer	30-40	(210-275)	.060	(1.5)	Reduce clear lacquer 25 percent. Reduce opaque lacquer up to 100 percent. Use a suction gun with external mix nozzle. Wet film must strike surface. Pattern size at 5 to 6 in. (125 to 150 mm). Distance from surface at 6 in. (150 mm).
Shellac 1 1/2 lb. cut	30	(210)	.040	(1.0)	Pressure or suction feed.
3 lb. cut	40	(275)	.060	(1.5)	Spray during low humidity conditions.
Varnishes (natural and synthetic)	40	(275)	.040	(1.0)	Suction or pressure feed. Temperature above 70°F. Spray gloss at can consistency. Thin semigloss and satin about 25 percent. Distance from surface at 6 in. (150 mm).

Fig. 46-13. Pressures and nozzle hole sizes for specific finish materials.

Another alternative is to use a *viscosity cup* to test the consistency of the thinned finish. Dip the cup into the finish until it is full. Then lift it above the container and time the number of seconds it takes for the cup to empty. Compare the time against a viscosity chart.

Filling the cup

Stir the finish thoroughly before using it. Wipe out the cup with a compatible solvent. Strain finish into the clean cup, Fig. 46-14. This removes any dust particles or other debris. Carefully fill the gun's cup. Avoid spilling any finish on the outside. Finally, position and lock the cup on the gun handle.

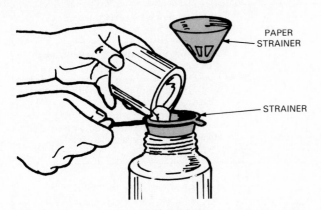

PAPER STRAINER

STRAINER

Fig. 46-14. Strain out debris before filling the finish cup. (DeVilbiss)

Adjusting the gun

Adjustments are much the same for bleeder and nonbleeder suction-feed guns. Pressure-feed systems require some unique adjustments. If you have a combination gun, set the control valve for pressure or suction feed and follow the proper steps outlined here.

Suction feed: Follow these steps to set up a suction-feed gun:

1. Connect the air line from the compressor outlet to the air transformer.
2. Connect the air hose leading from the transformer to the air inlet on the gun.
3. Turn the nozzle to create either a horizontal or vertical spray pattern, Fig. 46-15.
4. Fill the cup and attach it to the gun.
5. Set the air pressure to the gun at the proper psi. Typically, set the pressure at the air transformer to obtain 40 psi at the gun.
6. Turn the fluid needle valve adjusting screw to stop all fluid flow.
7. Pull the trigger while opening the fluid needle valve gradually. This controls the spray pattern.
8. Spray across a test panel with the gun about 6 to 8 in. (150 to 200 mm) from the surface.
9. Inspect the spray pattern. There should be an even distribution of finish across the full width of the pattern. If not, refer to the troubleshooting guide in Fig. 46-16.

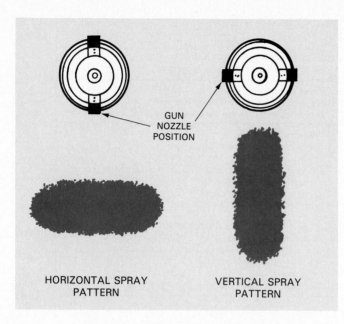

Fig. 46-15. Adjust the nozzle to attain the desired spray pattern. (DeVilbiss)

HORIZONTAL SPRAY PATTERN

VERTICAL SPRAY PATTERN

GUN NOZZLE POSITION

Pressure feed. Follow these steps to set up a pressure-feed gun:

1. Connect the air line from the compressor outlet to the air transformer.
2. Connect the air hose leading from the transformer to the air inlet on the gun.
3. Fill the cup or tank with finish.
4. Pressurize the fluid one of three ways, depending on the gun.
   a. Attach and lock the cup. Connect the air hose to the gun handle. Air pressure is delivered to the cup through a built-in air supply in the handle.
   b. Connect the air supply directly to an attachment on the cup.
   c. Connect the fluid hose from the outlet on the fluid tank to inlet on gun.
5. Turn on air pressure to the fluid cup or tank. If the cup pressure is self-contained, close the inlet valve to the air cap. Set gauge pressure to the fluid cup according to the equipment.

SPRAY PATTERN TROUBLE	PROBABLE CAUSE	REMEDY
Bottom or top heavy pattern.	Debris in gun nozzle.	Remove and clean air cap and fluid tip.
Pattern heavy on side.	One hole in external-mix air cap is clogged.	Remove cap and clean air holes.
Pattern heavy in center.	Material too thick. Too little air pressure. Fluid tip too large for film being sprayed.	Increase air volume and pressure. Thin the coating fluid. Change fluid tip.
Split pattern.	Partially clogged fluid tip.	Remove and clean tip and cap.

GUN PERFORMANCE TROUBLE	PROBABLE CAUSE	REMEDY
Constant fluttering spray.	Loose fluid tip. Low on fluid in cup. Gun and cup tipped too much. Clogged fluid tube.	Tighten tip. Refill cup. Hold gun upright. Disassemble and clean gun.
(suction gun)	Fluid too thick. Clogged cup lid vent. Leaky fluid tube or needle packing. Leaky nut or seal around fluid cup top.	Thin fluid. Open vent hole. Tighten leaky connection. Tighten leaky connection.
Fluid leaks at packing nut.	Loose packing nut and hard or defective packing.	Tighten or remove packing and soften with oil or replace.
Fluid leaks at nozzle.	Needle not seating.	Remove tip and clean or replace needle if defective.
No fluid flow.	Out of material. Clogged spray system.	Clean system and refill cup with strained material.
No fluid flow from pressure gun.	Lack of air pressure in cup or pot. Leaky gasket on cup/gun connection or pot. Clogged internal air hole in cup or pot.	Remove cup or pot lid; clean air hole and inspect gasket; replace if defective.
No fluid flow from suction gun.	Dirty air cap and fluid tip. Clogged air vent. Leaky gun connections.	Clean gun and tighten connections.

Fig. 46-16. Air spray system troubleshooting guide.

WORK APPEARANCE TROUBLE	PROBABLE CAUSE	REMEDY
Sags and runs.	Dirty gun nozzle. High fluid pressure. Fluid too thick or thin. Gun too close or at wrong angle to work. Slow gun movement. Improper triggering by starting or stopping over work.	Clean and adjust system. Correct viscosity. Improve gun control.
Streaks	Dirty gun nozzle. Air pressure too high. Gun too far from or at wrong angle to work. Gun moved too rapidly.	Clean and adjust nozzle. Lower air pressure. Improve gun control.
Excessive fog (overspray)	Air pressure too high. Fluid pressure too low. Material too thin. Gun too far from work. Spray beyond work at end of pass.	Make adjustments in air and fluid pressures. Remix material. Improve gun control.
Rough surface (orange peel)	Low air pressure. Material too thick. Poor quality thinner or poorly mixed and strained. Gun too close, too far, or moved too rapidly. Overspray strikes tacky surface.	Make change in pressure and material. Improve gun control.

Fig. 46-16 continued.

6. Turn the fluid needle adjusting screw so that just a thin thread of finish is discharged when the trigger is pulled.
7. Set the air pressure to the gun at the proper psi, usually 40 to begin.
8. Pull the trigger while opening the fluid needle valve gradually. This controls the proper spray pattern.
9. Spray across a test panel with the gun about 6 to 8 in. (150 to 200 mm) from the surface.
10. Inspect the spray pattern. There should be an even distribution of finish across the full width of the pattern. If not, refer to the troubleshooting guide in Fig. 46-16.

Spraying with the gun

Proper setup and adjustment of the equipment makes spraying easy. Hold the gun 6 to 8 in. from the surface, Fig. 46-17. Aim the gun off to the side of the product. Move the gun in a straight motion and squeeze the trigger just before reaching the product. Spray an even film across the surface with every pass, Fig. 46-18. Release the trigger after you pass the product's edge and before stopping the gun's motion. Spray the entire surface lapping the wet edges about 50 percent. Move the gun in only one direction during each pass. Changing the gun's direction over the surface results in a concentration of finish which likely will cause runs. Spray the entire surface. Then spray the second coat at 90 degrees to the first series of passes.

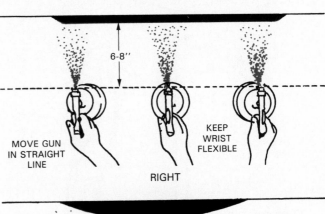

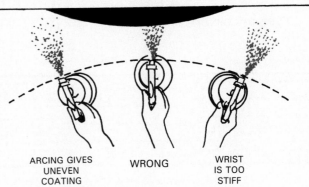

Fig. 46-17. Holding the gun too close or too far causes problems. (DeVilbiss)

Fig. 46-18. Hold the gun level and move it in a straight line. (DeVilbiss)

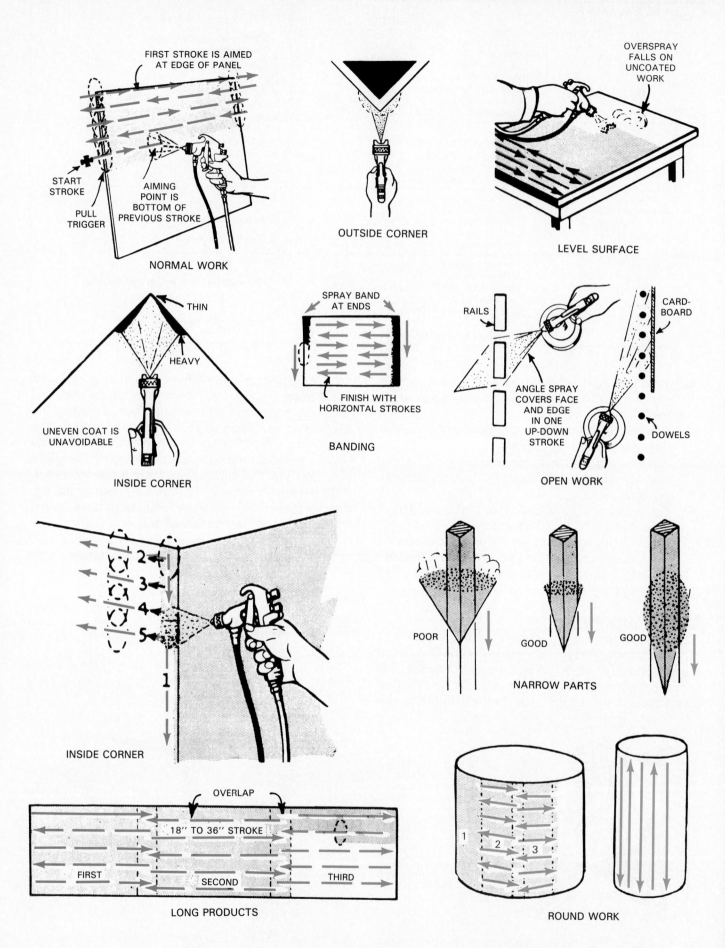

FIRST STROKE IS AIMED AT EDGE OF PANEL

START STROKE

PULL TRIGGER

AIMING POINT IS BOTTOM OF PREVIOUS STROKE

NORMAL WORK

OUTSIDE CORNER

OVERSPRAY FALLS ON UNCOATED WORK

LEVEL SURFACE

THIN

HEAVY

UNEVEN COAT IS UNAVOIDABLE

INSIDE CORNER

SPRAY BAND AT ENDS

FINISH WITH HORIZONTAL STROKES

BANDING

RAILS

CARD-BOARD

ANGLE SPRAY COVERS FACE AND EDGE IN ONE UP-DOWN STROKE

DOWELS

OPEN WORK

INSIDE CORNER

POOR

GOOD

GOOD

NARROW PARTS

OVERLAP

18" TO 36" STROKE

FIRST

SECOND

THIRD

LONG PRODUCTS

ROUND WORK

Fig. 46-19. Spray motions for some common situations. (DeVilbiss)

Fig. 46-19 shows the pattern of passes for various spraying tasks. Problem areas, such as edges and corners, should be sprayed first. Hold the gun slightly closer than normal to reduce the pattern size. Move the stroke faster to avoid applying too much finish. A vertical oval spray pattern works well for inside corners. When spraying curved surfaces, keep the gun perpendicular to the surface at all times. Spray flat surfaces after completing edges and corners.

Troubleshooting air spray problems

Problems may occur with the spray pattern, gun performance, and work appearance. The spray pattern may have a heavy end or center. It might be curved, peanut shape, or split. Adjusting the air and fluid flow rates and/or pressure, in addition to cleaning gun parts should correct these problems. If the gun leaks air or fluid, tighten or make adjustments to valves, nuts, screws, and other gun components. If this does not help, look for and replace damaged gun parts. A bent needle valve rod or worn needle valve tip are common problems.

Cleaning spray equipment

Clean the gun after every spraying task. Refer to Fig. 46-20 as you follow these steps:

1. Remove the cup and pour leftover finish into a separate sealable container.
2. Loosen the air cap one full turn.
3. Hold a rag over the air cap.
4. With air pressure still attached and the cup under the fluid tube, pull the trigger for a couple of seconds. This forces the coating material back through the fluid tube and into the cup.
5. Empty the discharged fluid from the cup.
6. Wipe off the fluid tube.
7. Dry out the inside of the cup.
8. Place a small amount of solvent in the cup.
9. Tighten the air cap and cup. Spray a scrap panel until the mist is only clear solvent.
10. Loosen the air cap. Hold a rag over the air cap and pull the trigger to force solvent from the fluid tube.
11. Remove and soak the air cap and fluid nozzle in solvent.
12. Clean the air cap and fluid nozzle holes with a small wire if necessary.
13. Blow away solvent remaining on the clean air cap and fluid tip with compressed air.
14. Wipe the gun clean with solvent. Guns which sprayed latex or water-base materials may rust. Wipe them dry. Then run some mineral spirits through the gun. This removes any leftover moisture.

The gun does not need to be disassembled further for cleaning after each use. However, every few months it should be disassembled completely and cleaned carefully.

Maintaining air spray equipment

Air spray systems need maintenance for the compressor, regulator, transformer, and gun. Lubricate compressors and compressor motors periodically with the specified oil. Compressors with tanks usually contain compressor oil. The level of fluid should be checked occasionally. Follow the manufacturer's recommendations for oil types and maintenance procedures.

Compressor tanks accumulate moisture from the air they store. Condensation must be removed regularly. To do so, turn off the electrical supply to the compressor. You may have to bleed all air pressure first by pushing (opening) the pressure release valve located on the compressor tank. Position a container under the drain and then, open the valve. Close the valve tightly once the water is removed.

Air transformers need occasional maintenance. They contain a filter to remove dust and moisture from the air. Some have a drain to remove air line condensation. Replace the filter periodically. With

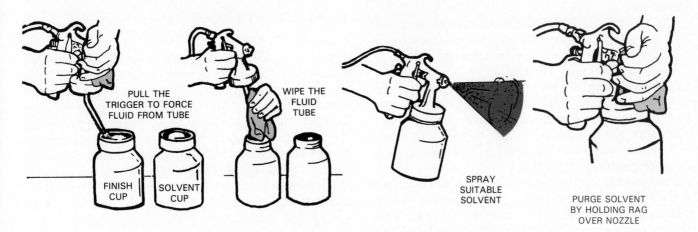

PULL THE TRIGGER TO FORCE FLUID FROM TUBE

FINISH CUP

SOLVENT CUP

WIPE THE FLUID TUBE

SPRAY SUITABLE SOLVENT

PURGE SOLVENT BY HOLDING RAG OVER NOZZLE

Fig. 46-20. Follow these steps when cleaning the air spray gun. (DeVilbiss)

a bad filter, moisture could mix with the spray fluid causing water bubbles on the wet finished surface.

Guns occasionally need to have moving parts oiled to prevent wear, Fig. 46-21. Put a drop of lubricating oil on packing nuts to prevent leaks at the fittings. Many times, tightening the nut will stop the leak. If neither of these is effective, replace the packing or fitting.

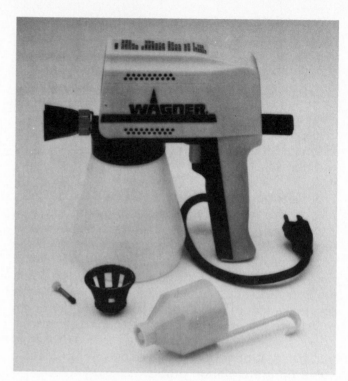

Fig. 46-22. Home-use airless spray guns have the motor and pump self-contained. (Wagner)

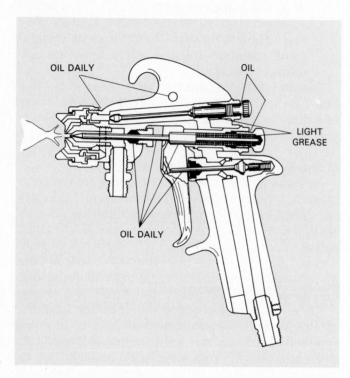

Fig. 46-21. Lubricate the gun regularly. (DeVilbiss)

AIRLESS SPRAYING

Airless spraying does not require air pressure to atomize finish into a fine mist. Instead, a *fluid pump* forces finish up into the gun nozzle where high pressure causes atomization. Airless equipment has several important advantages over air-spray equipment.

1. Convenience. Airless spray systems are driven by electric or gasoline motors and do not require a compressor. Some units are even self-contained, Fig. 46-22.
2. Faster, thicker spreading. Because of the high rate of material flow, airless systems can deliver heavy coats of liquid.
3. Less overspray, Fig. 46-23. Because the finish is not mixed with air, there is less misting, fogging, and overspray.

The one significant drawback to airless systems is that they often produce a poorer quality finish. It is generally difficult to fine-tune the spray pattern. The gun delivers a somewhat coarse mist which produces a slightly textured film.

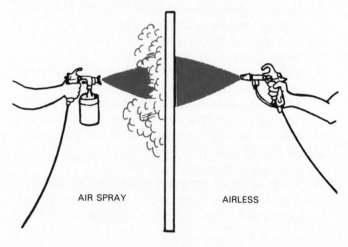

Fig. 46-23. Less misting occurs with airless spraying. (Binks)

Selecting and adjusting airless spray equipment

Airless equipment consists of a pump, gun, and fluid container, Fig. 46-24. Between the fluid and gun is a filter and pressure relief valve. Setting up airless equipment is fairly easy. There are few parts to connect and adjustments to make. The pressure pump pressurizes and moves the coating material. On home-use equipment, it is built into the gun. On commercial equipment, it is separate. The airless spray gun, Fig. 46-25, consists of a fluid inlet, trigger, valve, and nozzle or tip. Guns may have safety locks on the trigger to prevent accidental spraying.

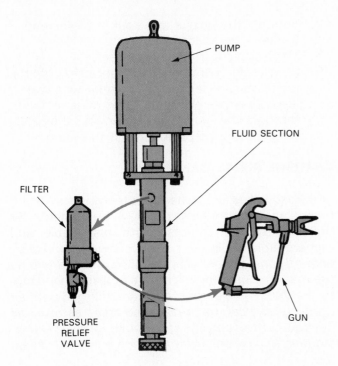

Fig. 46-24. Components of a commercial airless spray system. (Binks)

Nozzle tips, often simply called tips, come in the three basic sizes shown in Fig. 46-26. For example, the enamel spray tip with a 0.06 mm hole will apply enamel, varnish, and other thick finishes. The fine top has a 0.02 mm hole and will spray thin coating materials. The stain tip has a 0.04 mm hole and will apply stain or other material with pigment too coarse to pass through the fine tip.

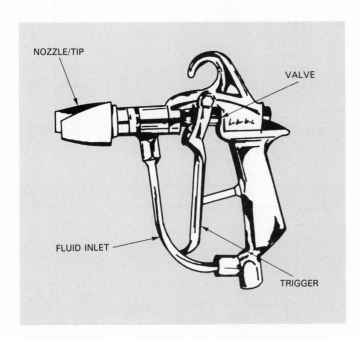

Fig. 46-25. Parts of a commercial airless spray system gun. (Binks)

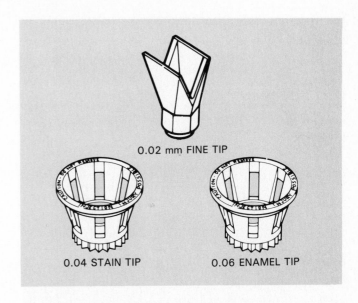

Fig. 46-26. Tips are categorized by their hole size. (Wagner)

You may wish to test the viscosity of the coating material you plan to spray. To do so, fill the viscosity cup with finish. Determine how long it takes the fluid to drain through the hole in the cup. If this is 25 seconds or less, install a fine tip. If it takes longer than 50 seconds, install an enamel tip.

Setting up airless equipment

To set up airless equipment, first be sure that the components are connected properly. Strain the finish into the container. Thinning is usually unnecessary. Be sure the finish is well mixed. Select and install the proper nozzle. Then adjust the pressure control knob to the midpoint of its movement.

Operating airless equipment

To operate airless equipment, first plug in the unit. Squeeze the trigger to start the fluid flow. Spray a test pattern. Adjust the pattern by turning the pressure control knob one way or the other. Hold the gun about 12 in. (300 mm) from the surface, Fig. 46-27. Move it in the same manner as the air spray gun.

Troubleshooting airless equipment

Be alert to possible problems as you spray. Blemishes that occur in the spray pattern or gun performance may indicate a worn tip or improper pressure adjustment. Refer to the troubleshooting guide in Fig. 46-28.

Cleaning airless equipment

Airless equipment is simple to clean. To do so:
1. Disconnect the electrical service.
2. Trigger the gun to see if any pressure remains.

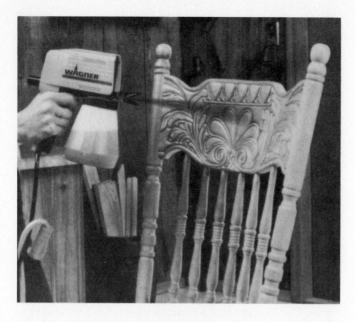

Fig. 46-27. Hold airless spray guns about 12 in. from the surface. (Wagner)

3. Remove the nozzle and soak it in solvent.
4. Connect the electrical service.
5. Place solvent in the container.
6. Spray solvent into a waste container until the mist appears clean. If the solvent was water, also spray a small amount of mineral spirits through the gun. This removes chemicals which could corrode parts in the gun.

AEROSOL SPRAY CANS

Aerosol cans are a handy alternative to using bulky and inconvenient spray equipment for finishing small products. Both disposable and rechargeable equipment are available. *Disposable aerosol cans*, Fig. 46-29, are filled and charged by the manufacturer and cannot be refilled when empty. *Rechargeable aerosol cans* are charged with air pressure and can be pressurized again as often as needed. Both types will spray stain, primer, sealer, lacquer, epoxy, polyurethane, and enamel finishes.

SPRAY PATTERN TROUBLE	CAUSE	REMEDY
Excessive fogging.	Sprayer too far from surface. Material too thin. Pressure too high. Worn spray tip.	Hold sprayer at 12 in. (300 mm). Check viscosity. Install smaller tip. Turn control knob to lower pressure. Replace tip.
Material splitting or globbing.	Cup empty. Sprayer at angle. Material too thick. Intake tube drawing in air. Control knob set improperly. Debris in nozzle. Oversize or worn tip. Worn valve.	Refill. Hold sprayer upright. Thin and check viscosity. Inspect for leak in siphon hose or tube. Reset knob accordingly. Clean nozzle tip. Change or replace tip. Replace valve.
No material flow.	Pump motor not running. Pump not operating. Loose or damaged intake tube. Liquid too thick. Filter screen clogged. Pressure control knob closed. Valve not opening. Clogged tip.	Turn on pump. Replace defective motor. Check. Replace defective pump. Tighten or replace tube. Thin liquid. Clean screen and strain material. Open pressure control knob. Replace fluid valve. Clean tip.
Tails in spray pattern.	Inadequate fluid delivery. Fluid not atomizing.	Increase fluid pressure. Change to larger tip size. Reduce fluid viscosity. Clean gun and tip. Increase fluid pressure.
Hour glass pattern.	Inadequate fluid delivery. Plugged or worn tip.	Increase fluid pressure. Change to larger tip size. Reduce fluid viscosity. Clean or replace nozzle tip.
Pattern surging.	Pulsating fluid delivery.	Change to smaller tip size. Check pump operation. Clean nozzle tip.
Runs and sags.	Sprayer movement too slow. Spray too close to product. Excess material flow. Liquid too thin.	Quicken stroke. Maintain 12 in. (300 mm) distance. Reduce fluid pressure. Remix finish.

Fig. 46-28. Airless spray system troubleshooting guide.

Fig. 46-29. Disposable aerosol cans work successfully for coating smaller products. (Minwax)

To mix the contents, shake disposable cans. Some contain a steel ball that settles into the finishing material. Once you hear the steel ball rattle, continue shaking for one minute. With reusable cans, mix the finish in the container. Then close and lock the lid. Finally, pressurize the canister to the manufacturer's recommended maximum pressure.

Once the finish is mixed, hold the can 12 in. (300 mm) from the surface in an upright position. Use the same movement as applied for spray equipment.

After the surface is coated, clean the aerosol can. Turn disposable cans upside down and press the valve until you see only air vapor spray. This means the nozzle is clean. After using the rechargeable can, turn it upside down also. Press the nozzle until the pressure is released. Open the container and empty the contents. Clean it as you would a spray gun.

WIPING

Wiping is a simple coating practice used to apply stain and penetrating finishes. The only tool you need is a clean, lint-free cloth pad or sponge. Cotton ear swabs work well in small areas. You can also buy foam pads that are used much like a paint brush. Any material you choose must be lint-free. See Fig. 46-30.

To wipe the finish on a product, first pour a small amount of finish into a clean container. Then touch the pad to the finish. Do not immerse it. Spread finish, working from dry to wet areas. Wear rubber gloves because some finishes are irritants.

Discard applicators other than foam pads. Foam pads usually can be rinsed in solvent. If you need to store a pad only for a short time, place it in a tightly closed container with a small amount of solvent. Squeeze out the excess solvent every time you use the pad.

A

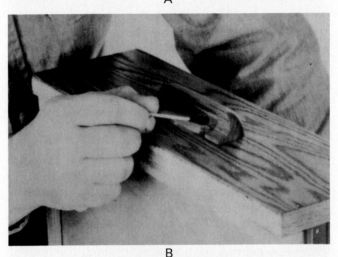

B

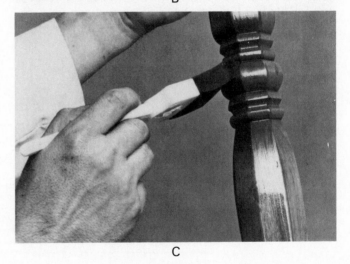

C

Fig. 46-30. Wiping on a finish. A—Cloth pad. B—Using an ear swab. (Minwax) C—Foam brush. (Carver-Tripp)

DIPPING

Dipping is done to apply an even layer of finish to small components quickly, Fig. 46-31. Stains, sealers, and topcoats can be applied by this method. A dip tank is necessary. Avoid dipping parts into the original can of finish. Any dust left on the product can contaminate the liquid. Rather, select

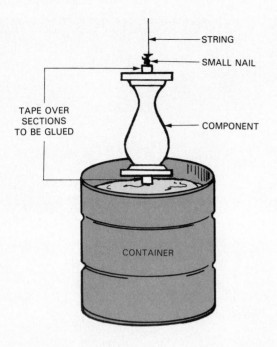

STRING

SMALL NAIL

TAPE OVER
SECTIONS
TO BE GLUED

COMPONENT

CONTAINER

Fig. 46-31. Dipping is a quick application method.

a 5 lb. coffee can or similar container. A capped piece of pipe could be used for dipping spindles and other long objects. Once coated, the product must be hung to dry. Protect the area below the parts with a drip pan to catch excess finish. Brush or wipe away any excess coating that forms at the lowest point. This is where drops of finish will accumulate. Prevent the wet component from touching anything as it dries.

Some coating materials fill wood pores and prevent glue joints from bonding well. It is wise to apply masking tape over areas where adhesives will be used. For example, cover the bottom of finials or the ends of spindles.

ROLLING

Rolling may be done to apply stain, sealer, and topcoating. When choosing rollers, carefully consider the roller cover. They are available in several sizes, shapes, and materials.

SELECTING ROLLER COVERS

Roller covers consist of a core and nap. The *core*, which can be made of plastic, fiber, or cardboard, gives rigidity to the cover. Covers with plastic and fiber cores can be cleaned and used repeatedly. Those made of cardboard are disposable. They cannot be cleaned satisfactorily because solvent softens the core adhesive.

The *nap* is a layer of natural or synthetic fibers which holds and spreads the finish, Fig. 46-32. For cabinetmaking, use 1/8 to 1/4 in. (3 to 6 mm) thick nap. Short nap rollers apply a smoother film than long nap rollers, which create a stippled (slightly textured) surface. Nap is not a factor on foam rollers.

USING ROLLERS

Place finish to be rolled in a special pan designed to help load the roller evenly. Prepare the roller cover by rubbing it briskly with your hand to remove any loose fiber, lint, or dry particles left from the last time it was used. Then mount the roller on the han-

MATERIAL	SOLVENT BASE	APPLICATION
Natural		
Mohair	Water/oil	Produces the smoothest surface. Holds large amounts of material. Use primarily with enamels.
Lamb's wool	Oil	Produces a slightly stippled surface. Holds large amounts of material. Wears well.
Synthetic		
Nylon	Water/oil	Produces a slightly stippled surface. Usually combined with polyester. Wears well.
Polyester	Water/oil	Produces smooth to slightly stippled surface. Most common cover available. Holds large amounts of material. Wears well.
Foam	Water/oil	Produces a smooth surface. Holds medium amount of material. Low cost. Does not wear well.

Fig. 46-32. Select roller covers according to the finish and desired surface texture.

dle. Follow these steps to roll on a finish properly:
1. Place finish in the pan to a depth of approximately 1 in. (25 mm).
2. Roll the finish up the slanted pan surface several times to coat the nap.
3. Spread the first roller of material on a sheet of white paper. This helps remove any remaining lint, dirt, or dust from the cover.
4. Spread the finish from a dry area to a wet surface area or to the edge. Overlap about 75 percent, more than if you were working with a brush.
5. Continue to spread to a wet edge until the surface is coated.

MAINTAINING ROLLER COVERS AND PANS

Plastic and fiber core rollers are reusable. Clean and store them immediately after use. Follow this procedure:
1. Scrape excess material from the wet roller cover. Use a straightedge, putty knife, or roller scraper.
2. Empty and clean the pan.
3. Immerse the cover in solvent placed in the clean pan.
4. Scrape the excess thinned material from the roller cover.
5. Repeat Steps 2 through 4 until all finish has been removed from the nap.
6. Spin the roller inside a large container to remove excess material and solvent.
7. Stand roller covers on end or hang them to dry. Laying rollers flat will mat the nap.
8. Place covers over the rollers to prevent dust from settling on them.

WHEN APPLYING COATING MATERIALS

A number of health and safety factors are associated with finishing practices. Those identified on finish container labels warn the user if the finish is toxic, a skin irritant, or that it contains flammable ingredients. When applying finishing materials:
1. Wear eye and face protection to guard against splashed liquids.
2. Wear protective clothing.
3. Wear rubber or plastic gloves to protect sensitive skin.
4. Read container labels to make sure you are not allergic to any of the chemicals.
5. Have a fire blanket available.
6. Have the proper fire extinguisher and know its location.
7. Extinguish all flames and provide ventilation before using finishing materials.

8. If you experience any discomfort, contact a physician.

SUMMARY

There are five basic methods to apply a finish: brushing, spraying, wiping, dipping, and rolling. Most of the materials you apply may be spread more than one way. Usually you select the method unless the manufacturer makes a strong recommendation. If more than one method is given, choose the application technique you feel will give the best results. For example, stain can be applied by most any technique. Wiping would work best for small areas and spraying would be the quickest for large areas. Lacquer can be brushed or sprayed. Usually, lacquer comes in a brushing viscosity, but can be thinned to be sprayed.

Consider the size of the product and setup time when choosing an application method. Dipping is quickest and most effective for small objects. Spraying is effective for coating large surfaces. However, spray equipment is costly and requires extensive setup time. If you do not need a perfect finish, consider rolling the surface.

The bottom line on choosing among the techniques is quality. Never sacrifice quality for the sake of speed. Doing so may result in an unacceptable product, wasting the many hours spent processing materials and assembling the product.

CABINETMAKING TERMS

Brushing, natural bristles, synthetic bristles, loading, spreading, spraying, atomized, air spraying, air compressor, regulator, air transformer, bleeder gun, nonbleeder gun, suction-feed gun, pressure-feed system, combination gun, external-mix nozzle, internal-mix nozzle, viscosity cup, airless spraying, fluid pump, nozzle tip, aerosol can, wiping, dipping, rolling, roller cover, core, nap.

TEST YOUR KNOWLEDGE

1. Natural bristle brushes should not be used with:
   a. Varnish.
   b. Shellac.
   c. Latex.
   d. Enamel.
2. Nylon bristle brushes should not be used with:
   a. Varnish.
   b. Shellac.
   c. Latex.
   d. Enamel.
3. When loading a brush, cover three-fourths of the bristles. True or False?

4. When loading a brush, wipe the bristles against the side of the container to remove excess finish. True or False?
5. When spreading finish, hold a brush at about a _____ degree angle.
6. Identify the primary difference between a bleeder gun and nonbleeder gun.
7. Would you choose a suction-feed gun or pressure-feed gun for applying lacquer?
8. Changing from an internal- to external-mix nozzle is made by:
   a. Using a different gun.
   b. Increasing the air pressure.
   c. Replacing the air cap.
   d. Reducing the air pressure.
9. List the components of an airless spray system.
10. Describe how to clean fluid from a disposable aerosol can nozzle.
11. The nap length on rollers for applying a smooth finish should be _____ in.
12. Name the two ways to store roller covers.
13. List the various applicators you might choose when wiping on a finish.
14. Identify two health factors associated with applying finish.
15. Why would you protect areas so that they do not receive finish?

Chapter 47
PREPARING THE SURFACE FOR TOPCOATING

After studying this chapter, you will be able to:
☐ *Select and apply various types of stain.*
☐ *Fill pores of open grain hardwoods.*
☐ *Seal or prime lumber, manufactured wood products, and metal.*
☐ *Create decorative effects on wood surfaces.*

Preparing the surface for topcoating involves adding color (staining), filling open grain hardwoods, sealing or priming wood surfaces, and applying decorative coatings. This phase of the cabinetmaking process changes the wood's appearance most.

There is no clear-cut order of events for applying stain, filler, and sealer. Stain most often is applied by itself. Yet, it can also be mixed with filler or with the topcoating material. (Combination stain and topcoat finishes are discussed in Chapter 48.) Filler can be applied before stain, with stain, or after stain for different effects. Sealing may be done at several times. A thinned coat of sealer applied before stain (called a washcoat) helps even out stain penetration in springwood, summerwood, and end grain. Sealer applied after stain or filler provides a barrier coat under the topcoat. Primer, an opaque sealer, prepares wood and metal surfaces for enamel.

Decorative finishes include antiquing, gilding, graining, marbleizing, mottling, stippling, and splattering. Most are opaque, and consist of a glaze coat applied over a base coat. These treatments are typical on poorer quality lumber and manufactured wood products to provide an attractive appearance.

Before working with any finishing material, read the container label. Identify the recommended applications and note any cautions or warnings, Fig. 47-1. Also refer to the table, Finishing Selected Wood Species, in Chapter 44 to determine suggested finishes for the wood specie you have chosen.

WASHCOATING

A *washcoat* is a coat of thinned sealer or special material that helps control stain penetration. It also holds wood fibers in place during finishing. A wash-

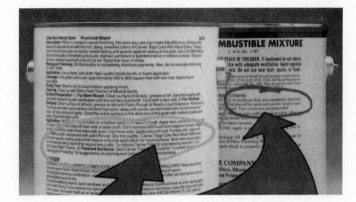

Fig. 47-1. Always check the container label before using any finish. (Carver-Tripp)

coat promotes consistent stain absorption of springwood and summerwood, Fig. 47-2. The wood density between these two areas varies considerably. Apply a washcoat to end grain for the same purposes.

You can thin shellac and lacquer sealer or purchase a specific washcoat product. A shellac washcoat consists of one part 3-lb. shellac in five to seven parts alcohol. This becomes less than a half-pound cut of shellac. A lacquer washcoat may consist of one part spray-grade lacquer thinned in four parts of thinner. Commercially available sealers are sold under the names "prestain wood sealant," "stain controller," and "wood conditioner," Fig. 47-3. Some "sanding sealers," if thinned, can be used before stain. (Read the container label.) Another formula is a solution of 1 part white glue mixed with 20 parts water.

Apply the washcoat to a prepared test panel first. Let it dry thoroughly and then apply stain. Compare the coloring between springwood and summerwood. Do likewise for face, edge, and end grain on lumber.

Control the spread of the washcoat carefully. Be sure to remove all runs, drips, and thick areas. These might act as sealer and prevent even stain penetration. If coating only the end grain on lumber, pro-

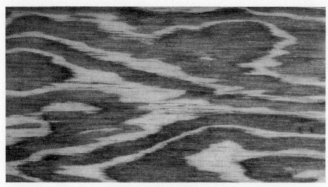

STAIN AND WASHCOAT

WASHCOAT AND STAIN

Fig. 47-2. A washcoating prevents the "wild grain" that occurs with wood having great density changes between springwood and summerwood.

tect nearby face and edge grain with masking tape. After several hours, lightly sand the surface with very fine abrasive.

STAINING

Staining alters a wood's color, accents grain patterns, or hides unattractive grain. Stain may be applied to make a low-cost wood look like a more expensive specie. It can also even out natural color

Fig. 47-3. "Wood conditioner" is just one name given to washcoating products. (Minwax)

shades, such as the difference between heartwood and sapwood. Stains which both color and mask the surface might be used to cover particleboard or other manufactured wood products.

There is a broad range of stain colors available. Although each is designed to be equally effective, the results will vary among wood species. Do not expect to apply mahogany stain to pine and have the wood look like mahogany. The stain only has a mahogany (reddish-brown) tint, and the effect is not the same on each specie. Likewise, pine and gum both coated with walnut stain still look different. To make these species look alike, you would need to choose a darker stain for pine.

TYPES OF STAIN

Stain is a combination of dyes and/or pigments suspended in a solvent. Soluble *dyes* dissolve in compatible solvents and provide greater grain clarity. Insoluble *pigments* are finely ground coloring materials which disperse, but do not dissolve in solvent. Pigments tend to cloud the grain. In fact, they tend to settle to the bottom of the can. Frequent stirring is needed. Both ingredients may be either natural or synthetic. Natural coloring comes from organic matter (plant, animal, earth) or from a chemical reaction of the finish with the wood. Synthetic dyes are manufactured chemicals. Synthetic stains, often identified with the word "synthetic," will likely furnish the most consistent coloring.

Select stains according to the characteristics given in Fig. 47-4. The information about advantages and disadvantages is important. Yet other factors must be taken into account. How should the stain be applied? What solvent is needed for thinning and cleanup? Does the solvent raise the grain? How much drying time is needed before the surface can be restained or topcoated? Will the stain hide the grain once the solvent evaporates? If so, is this acceptable? Will the coloring fade or bleed?

There are many types and colors of stain on the market. It is wise to stain a prepared test board or hidden area on the cabinet first, Fig. 47-5. The results may not be exactly what you expected.

Water stain

Water stains are transparent and fast drying. They accent the beauty of the grain and penetrate the wood deeply and evenly. Water stains are *water-soluble aniline dyes* that resist both fading and bleeding. Since dyes offer excellent clarity, you can apply several coats to darken the surface.

Water stain comes as a powdered dye or pre-mixed liquid. The dry powder stain takes a little time to prepare. Dissolve the aniline dye in very warm (180°F) water. A common proportion is one to two ounces of dye per quart of water (30 to 60 grams

	NATURAL				SYNTHETIC		
	Water	Non-Grain-Raising	Penetrating Oil	Pigment Oil	Spirit	Latex	Alkyd Oil
Purpose	Small, quickly-covered lumber.	Open grain hardwood.	All lumber and veneer.	Lumber, plywood, wood products. Some not for use under lacquer.	Darken sap streaks and hiding scratches.	Lumber and manufactured wood panels, not plywood.	Lumber and manufactured wood panels, not plywood.
Advantages	Excellent color that is permanent. Low cost, nonfading. Clean with soap and water.	Quick drying. Penetrates deeply.	Penetrates evenly and deeply. Excellent color. Convenient to apply.	Penetrates evenly. Good color that is nonfading.	Very fast drying. Shallow penetration. Excellent for sapwood and shading.	Colors well, especially on rough wall panels.	Colors well, especially on rough wall panels.
Disadvantages	Raises grain. Could soften water-base adhesives. Penetrates quickly, thus shows overlap marks.	Dries too fast to brush.	Fades in sunlight. Tends to bleed unless sealed with shellac.	Fades in sunlight. Shallow penetration. Slow drying. Difficult to touch up. Overlap shows.	Tends to fade and bleed. Difficult to apply evenly.	Bleeds with some natural wood resins. Visible nails will rust.	Bleeds with some natural wood resins. Visible nails will rust.
Application	Spray Brush	Spray	Brush Spray Wipe	Brush Spray Wipe	Brush on sap wood. Spray for shading.	Brush Roll Spray Wipe	Brush Roll Spray Wipe
Solvent	Water	Alcohol Glycol	Mineral spirits Turpentine Naptha	Mineral spirits Turpentine	Denatured alcohol Acetone	Water	Mineral spirits
Relative cost	Low	High	Medium	Medium	High	Low	Medium
Grain raising	Bad	Very little to none	None	None	Very little	Bad	None
Grain clarity	Excellent	Excellent	Excellent	Good	Good	Some	Some
Bleeding	None	Very little to none	Bad	None	Bad	Little	Little
Fading	None	None	Some	None	Some	Some	Some
Drying time to recoat	12 hours	10 minutes to 3 hours	24 hours	3 to 12 hours	10 to 15 minutes	2 to 4 hours	2 to 4 hours
Color source	Water soluble aniline dyes	Alcohol soluble aniline dyes	Oil soluble aniline dyes	Pigments and sometime dyes	Alcohol soluble aniline dyes	Pigment	Pigment

Fig. 47-4. Characteristics of various stains.

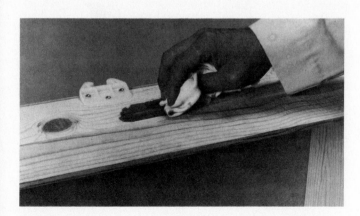

Fig. 47-5. Test stain on a hidden surface before applying it elsewhere.

per liter). The premixed stain can be thinned somewhat or applied straight from the can.

Water stain tends to raise the grain. You may want to raise the grain and smooth the surface several times before applying it. Additional sanding may be necessary after staining. Areas where stain is removed by sanding will require touch-up. Apply a washcoat of shellac or water to end grain to help the stain penetrate more evenly.

Apply water stain by spraying or brushing. Spraying is preferred because brushing tends to leave overlap marks. If you use a brush, select one as large as practical. Load the brush with the same amount of stain each time. Excessive brushing results in uneven penetration. Wipe the surface with a damp tack cloth immediately after stain is applied to hide overlap marks and remove runs.

Non-grain-raising stain

Non-grain-raising (NGR) stain is so named because it raises the grain little, if at all. In addition, it has several advantages over other products. NGR stains penetrate like water stain, and resist fading and bleeding. The stain consists of *alcohol-soluble aniline dyes.* Most products contain glycol, an alcohol derivative, to help the stain spread evenly. A small amount of pigment may also be added.

One major disadvantage is that NGR stains dry rapidly since the alcohol solvent evaporates quickly. This leaves spraying as the only acceptable application method. You might touch up a small area by brushing or wiping. However, overlap marks are likely to show. NGR stain is not recommended for pine, spruce, fir, and other woods having great variations in density between springwood and summerwood.

Oil stain

Oil stains consist of dyes and/or pigments dissolved in light oil or a solvent gel. They are divided into two major categories: penetrating and pigment. Neither penetrates as deeply as water stain. However, they are slow drying. This gives you more time to spread and even out overlap marks. First apply the stain. Then leave it on for a short time to penetrate. Finally, remove excess stain with a tack cloth, Fig. 47-6.

Penetrating oil stain. *Penetrating oil stain* is a mixture of oil-soluble dyes in a vehicle of mineral spirits, naptha, or a similar solvent. The vehicle may contain small amounts of resins.

Penetrating stain is convenient. It is easy to apply and penetrates deeply and evenly. It is equally effective with open and close grain wood. It mixes readily with wood filler to create a one-step stain and filler application.

There are two disadvantages related to penetrating oil stain. It tends to bleed and fade. Fading is controlled by keeping the cabinet or piece of furniture out of direct sunlight. You can prevent the stain from bleeding into varnish and lacquer topcoats by sealing it with shellac or a commercial sanding sealer.

Although penetrating oil stains do not dry quickly, they do penetrate fast. It is best to apply the finish by spraying. On larger areas, the stain will most likely soak into the wood before you can wipe off excess. However, you can remove small amounts of stain immediately after application by wiping with a solvent-soaked tack cloth.

Pigment oil stain. *Pigment oil stain* contains both insoluble pigments and soluble dyes in a vehicle of resin, oil, drier, and mineral spirits. Because of the high pigment content, these stains are least likely to fade. Pigment stains are preferred for closed grain wood and manufactured paneling. They do not raise the grain.

Added coats of pigment oil stain change the color or tone of the surface very little. Pigments in the stain remain bonded by resins on the wood surface. This prevents a second coat from adding very much color. In fact, applying a second coat only clouds the grain more.

To change the stain color, add ''colors-in-oil'' or ''universal colorant'' to the liquid stain. These products are available as concentrated pigments and dyes the consistency of toothpaste. If you add colorant, or the ingredients mention dye, apply a shellac sealer before the topcoat.

There are disadvantages with pigment stains. They take from several hours to a day to dry enough for topcoating. In addition, smoothing rough spots (raised grain or other defects) with fine abrasives after the coating dries will rub off pigments. The sanded area may require touch-up.

Pigment stains can be applied by any technique. Apply a washcoat or mineral spirits to end grain.

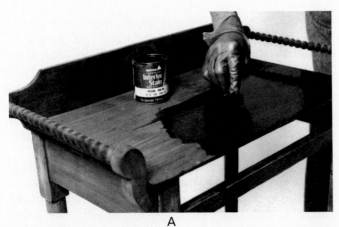
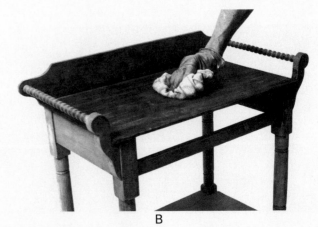

Fig. 47-6. Applying oil stains. A—Apply the stain with a small pad or brush. B—Wipe off the excess after the stain has had a chance to soak in. (Benjamin Moore)

Stir the container of stain about every ten minutes because pigments tend to settle to the bottom. Refer to directions on the can for the set time. This determines how long you must wait before wiping off excess stain. Wipe off any excess stain with a dry, clean cloth using strokes parallel to the grain. Wiping too soon leaves a light color. Stain left to dry too long becomes gummy and is difficult to remove. To wipe off thickened stain, dampen your tack cloth with mineral spirits. This technique also blends overlap marks and runs. For wood species having contrasting grain colors, wipe stain off dark areas first to even the tone.

Gel stain. *Gel stains* are pigmented stains in a thickened vehicle. Pigments stay mixed evenly. Upon application, the thick nature prevents drips and splatters. Gels can be spread by brushing or wiping. They are excellent for shading and antiquing, two of the decorative coatings discussed in this chapter.

Spirit stain

Spirit stains are used in furniture restoration and for evening the tone between sapwood and heartwood. The stain consists of aniline dyes dissolved in alcohol or acetone. The most popular application for spirit stain is to darken sap streaks. For example, you might apply spirit stain to the light sapwood in walnut beneath another stain. Spirit stain is also used for refinishing since it penetrates old varnish finishes. One drawback is that there is a slight tendency for spirit stain to fade and bleed.

Apply the stain by brushing or wiping with an artist's brush or ear swab, Fig. 47-7. Touch only those areas to be darkened. Spirit stain dries very rapidly, especially when acetone is the solvent. You can increase the drying time by adding a small amount of shellac. Then apply a prestain washcoat of shellac.

Latex stain

Latex stain consists of pigments in a vehicle of latex emulsion and water. Although it darkens the wood color with each additional coat, the stain tends to hide the grain as would a thinned paint. Therefore, do not choose this product for high quality cabinetmaking. It is used primarily to coat manufactured wood panels and exterior woodwork.

The water solvent makes latex stain nonflammable, easy to apply, quick drying. A second coat can be applied in 2 to 4 hours. Clean tools with soap and water. On the other hand, there are some problems with latex other than hiding the grain. The emulsion bonds to the surface and does not penetrate deeply into the wood fibers. Springwood will absorb more stain than summerwood. This allows color variations. A washcoat of shellac should be applied first.

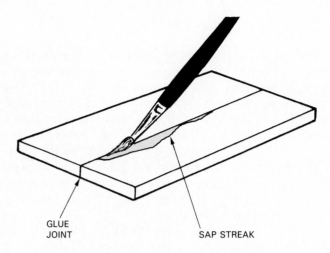

GLUE JOINT

SAP STREAK

Fig. 47-7. Darken sap streaks with spirit stain.

Latex stain can be brushed, sprayed, or wiped. Remove all runs and drips before the coating begins to set. Avoid using abrasives to smooth the surface once stain is applied. Otherwise, touch-up work will be needed.

Alkyd stain

Alkyd stain is similar to latex or pigment oil stains in that it hides the surface. Unlike latex stain, it is less inclined to raise the grain. With the pigment, resin, and solvent, it covers like an oil base stain, but it is not necessary to wipe off excess finish. Emulsified alkyd oils (specified on the container label) will clean up with soap and water.

STAINING TIPS

The best directions to follow when staining are those printed on the container label. Each manufacturer may recommend a slightly different application method. In addition, consider these tips as you prepare to alter the color of your cabinet.

1. Begin with a light, rather than dark, stain. It is much easier to add color with a second coat than it is to remove color.
2. Two light coats are better than one heavy coat. Thick coats are likely to brush on unevenly.
3. Apply the stain with the surface horizontal to minimize drips, runs, and overlap marks.
4. Work stain into pores of open grain woods to prevent color lapses.
5. If the stain appears to soak in more than you want, wipe the surface with a rag saturated in solvent.
6. Consider mixing stains of the same type to create unique colors.
7. Apply stain in strong natural daylight. Colors do not appear true in artificial light.
8. Apply stain at normal room temperature, in an environment free from dust, heat, and drafts.

FILLING

Filling is the process of packing a paste material into the large pores of open grain woods such as oak, mahogany, hickory, and ash, Fig. 47-8. The filler levels the surface in preparation for topcoating. If this step is omitted, the topcoating will have a textured, rippled effect. This is desirable for penetrating topcoatings, but may not be for built-up topcoatings. Without filler, achieving a smooth built-up finish requires numerous coats, each rubbed smooth. In time, the pores fill with topcoat and the surface becomes level.

Suppose you choose not to apply filler initially, and then change your mind. You should be able to coat a penetrating oil finish with filler. Rub the surface first with a burlap pad soaked in solvent. Once the solvent evaporates, spread the filler. You cannot apply filler to a surface already coated with a built-up finish without first removing the topcoat.

Fig. 47-8. Note the large, open pores of this sample of oak.

FILLER MATERIAL

The most common filler is *paste filler* made of a variety of ingredients. Oil-base fillers contain silica, linseed oil, drier, and mineral spirits. Water-base fillers contain a latex formula. Paste filler must be thinned before it will work effectively. Some manufacturers produce a prethinned *liquid filler*.

Paste filler typically is sold by the pound, which measures to be about one cup. At a spreadable consistency, a pound of filler covers approximately 40 square ft.

Filler can be applied before, after, or along with stain. The natural color of filler is either gray or tan. This may result in a "two-tone" effect if applied after stain, Fig. 47-9. Some synthetic fillers are semitransparent and do not hide the stain. You can buy precolored filler or color the filler yourself.

Fig. 47-9. Applying a different color shade of filler gives a "two-tone" effect. A—Natural lauan. B—Stained lauan. C—Light stain with a darker filler.

Choose a stain which is compatible. For example, select a water-base stain for latex fillers. Adding stain to filler does not give the same quality results as does staining, then filling.

APPLYING FILLER

Inspect the wood grain (lumber or veneer surface) before mixing filler. Pore sizes vary between species and even within a single specie. The size determines the consistency of the filler. Most products must be thinned. Follow directions on the container. As a general formula, mix equal parts of paste and the recommended solvent. Large pores require a thicker mix than do small pores. A slightly thinner mixture should be spread on butternut, limba, and walnut. Remember, less thinner is needed if you add liquid stain. Start with about equal portions of stain and thinner. The final consistency for most applications should be that of paint. Proportions of filler and thinner for various consistencies are shown in Fig. 47-10.

Mix only what is needed. Filler begins to set after a few hours and becomes useless. Calculate the area to be filled. For example, note the four-shelf bookcase in Fig. 47-11. It is 3 ft. wide, 5 ft. high, and 1 ft. deep. You want to fill both surfaces of the sides, shelves, and top. The back and bottom need only one surface filled. The total area is about 65 sq. ft. Thus, mix about 1 1/3 lbs. of filler.

HEAVY MIX (16-LB. BASE)		
Approx. Amount Needed	Paste	Thinner
2 gal.	16 lb.	1 gal.
5 pt.	5 lb.	2 1/2 pt.
2 qt.	4 lb.	1 qt.
2 pt.	2 lb.	1 pt.
1 pt.	1 lb.	1/2 pt.
1/2 pt.	1/2 lb.	4 oz.
MEDIUM MIX (12-LB. BASE)		
Approx. Amount Needed	Paste	Thinner
1 gal. 3 qt.	12 lb.	1 gal.
3 qt.	5 lb.	3 pt. 5 oz.
2 qt. 10 oz.	4 lb.	2 pt. 10 oz.
1 qt. 5 oz.	2 lb.	1 pt. 5 oz.
1 pt. 20 oz.	1 lb.	10 1/2 oz.
9 oz.	1/2 lb.	5 1/4 oz.
THIN MIX (8-LB. BASE)		
Approx. Amount Needed	Paste	Thinner
1 1/2 gal.	8 lb.	1 gal.
1 gal.	5 lb.	5 pt.
3 qt.	4 lb.	2 qt.
3 pt.	2 lb.	2 pt.
1 1/2 pt.	1 lb.	1 pt.
12 oz.	1/2 lb.	1/2 pt.

Fig. 47-10. A heavy mix works best with woods having large open pores, such as oak. A medium mix is adequate for most woods. A thin mix might be made to smooth woods having small pores.

The most common method for filling involves applying filler with a brush and wiping off the excess with burlap or a coarse cloth. Prepare a separate brush for filler applications. Cut the bristles about half their normal length. You can also wipe on filler with a pad of burlap or coarse cloth. You can discard the pad afterwards or save it with a bit of solvent in a sealed glass container. Have a different wiping pad jar for each color of filler applied regularly.

The steps to apply filler are as follows:

1. Dust the surface with tack cloth or vacuum cleaner.
2. Spread and rub in a proper mix of filler along and across the grain.
3. Leave a wet, even film of excess paste on the surface.
4. Allow the filler to set until the solvent evaporates (the surface becomes dull). This takes 15 to 30 minutes.
5. Rub a burlap pad across the grain to remove excess filler. This also packs filler into the pores.
6. Wipe lightly along the grain with a soft tack cloth. Any streaks across the grain should disappear, Fig. 47-12.
7. Remove filler from inside corners with rag over stick.
8. Areas where the filler has dried too much can be wiped clean using a rag moistened with solvent. Filler left on the surface will feel rough and cloud the grain.
9. Inspect the surface. Be sure excess filler is removed. Make sure all pores are filled level.
10. Let the surface dry at least overnight, preferably one to two days.

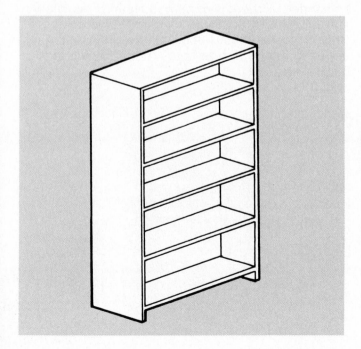

Fig. 47-11. Consider all exposed surfaces when estimating quantities of filler.

Fig. 47-12. The last step in filling is to wipe lightly along the grain to remove any leftover filler and smooth out streaks. (Carver-Tripp)

Filler contains drier. If you fail to remove unwanted filler before it cures, solvent may not remove it later. Abrasives are then needed. You may have to restain the sanded area.

When using a stain/filler mixture, achieve the desired color the first time. If the surface appears too dark, you can lighten it somewhat by rubbing with a tack cloth saturated with solvent before the filler and stain dry. To darken a surface before the filler dries, lightly wipe on another coat of stain. Use penetrating stain for oil-base fillers. If the coating has dried, a pigment stain may be needed to darken the surface.

Once the filler has dried, topcoat the surface with a penetrating finish or seal it for a built-up finish.

SEALING

Sealing means to apply a barrier coat between the stain or filler and the topcoating. A coat of sealer is needed for built-up topcoatings on lumber and wood products for two reasons:

1. Prevent stain or filler dyes from bleeding into the topcoat. Without sealer, dyes can work their way to the surface for years after the finish is applied. This is evident when you see stain on a dusting cloth, especially when cleaning with furniture polish. Bleeding is more likely to happen when natural, rather than synthetic, materials are applied.
2. Prevent the topcoat from being absorbed into the wood. Wood fibers are like a sponge. Sealers reduce or prevent future coatings from being absorbed, allowing the topcoat to dry more evenly. You should not be able to see contrasting dull and shiny areas after applying a topcoat.

TYPES OF SEALERS

It is important that you select the right sealer. Over water soluble dye stains, apply a sealer with an alcohol or mineral spirits solvent. For alcohol soluble stains, apply a sealer that thins with mineral spirits. Over oil stains and other stains thinned with mineral spirits, shellac makes a good barrier. Many synthetic topcoatings provide their own barrier to dye penetration. Read the container label if there is a question.

Sealers generally are identified by the compatible topcoating they protect. The three basic types are shellac, varnish, and lacquer. Some have limited applications. They can be used only on one type of topcoating. For example, lacquer applied over a varnish sealer likely would react as paint remover. Check the manufacturer's instructions on the container of topcoating before making a selection. They might tell you not to use a sealer.

Shellac sealer

A *shellac sealer* provides an excellent barrier under most topcoatings thinned with alcohol and mineral spirits. Apply white or orange shellac thinned to about a 1 1/2 lb. cut. This prepares the surface for thicker shellac, varnish, and enamel. However, remember that shellac is not resistant to water. Therefore, do not allow the surface to accidentally become wet before the topcoating is applied. Also consult the container label before applying a shellac sealer. Some new synthetic finishes will not adhere well to shellac.

Varnish sealer

Products labeled as *varnish sealer* for natural resin varnish may consist of shellac, thinned varnish, or a synthetic material. Varnish thinned 50 percent with mineral spirits makes an adequate sealer.

Lacquer sealer

A thinned coat of lacquer may not be adequate under a lacquer topcoat. Unlike other finishes, a new coating of lacquer dissolves the previous layer somewhat. Select products specifically advertised as "lacquer sealer" or "lacquer sanding sealer." *Lacquer sealer* contains added ingredients which prevent it from dissolving under a fresh lacquer topcoat.

Sanding sealer

Sanding sealer is a multipurpose material generally compatible with varnish, lacquer, and synthetic varnishes, Fig. 47-13. Except for spraying, it likely will not need to be thinned. Sanding sealer can be sanded without a gummy buildup. This allows you to smooth dust particles and minor defects. Check the container label for the drying time. It varies from one to two hours, but each product is a little different.

Fig. 47-13. This sanding sealer is especially formulated for lacquer. (Parks)

SEALING WOOD

Apply sealers by any method; spraying provides the best results. Be aware that topcoatings are too thick to be used as a sealer and must be thinned first. Thinning increases the penetration of sealer resins into the wood fibers. A good rule of thumb is to mix equal amounts of sealer and solvent. However, some manufacturers recommend 20 percent thinner and 80 percent sealer. Check the label of the topcoating container.

SEALING METAL

Sealing metal does not serve the same purpose as it does for wood. The sealing coat on metal usually is thinned clear lacquer used to help the topcoat adhere better. This technique would be used on a decorative polished metal surface, such as a brass nameplate.

Metal polishes contain very fine abrasives and wax. They must be removed with a solvent, such as acetone or lacquer reducer. Do not touch the metal surface after cleaning it. Oil in your skin can tarnish the metal and prevent good adhesion of the sealer coat.

PRIMING

Priming prepares the surface for an opaque coating. Primer seals wood pores and hides the grain in preparation for opaque built-up topcoatings, Fig. 47-14. It also is applied to metal to help the topcoating adhere. It might also form the base coat for a decorative glaze or finish.

Good quality primers are highly pigmented and resinous. They hide all grain, water marks, and stains. Using a color of primer different than the topcoating helps you detect thin areas in the topcoating. Sealers also can be applied beneath opaque finishes. However, an extra application of topcoat may be necessary.

Priming materials must be compatible with the topcoatings. Manufacturers often suggest primers, such as:

1. Oil-base primers for oil-base or alkyd enamels.
2. Latex primers for water-base or alkyd enamels.
3. Lacquer-base primers for opaque lacquer.

In addition, spot priming, or sealing, is recommended on construction grade lumber. You can apply aluminum paint or shellac to knots and end grain. This prevents natural resins from bleeding into the topcoat.

APPLYING PRIMER COATINGS

Most any application method is suitable for primer. Coat all surfaces evenly and wait for the film to dry completely. Inspect for any rough areas, as well as thick or thin areas. Sand rough places and apply more primer if necessary.

PRIMING WOOD PRODUCTS

Manufactured wood products are gaining popularity as cabinetmaking materials. Fiberboard and particleboard are treated differently from plywood which is sealed and primed like lumber. Composite products are manufactured in wax-coated molds. The wax helps release the bonded

A   B

Fig. 47-14. A—Prime wood surfaces which will receive an enamel topcoat. (Carver-Tripp) B—The even tone of an opaque topcoat is found in contemporary furniture. (Lane)

material from the mold. Wax can interfere with the adhesion of a finish. Therefore, wipe the surface using a cloth wet with mineral spirits or lacquer thinner. Then apply sealer or primer as on other wood surfaces.

PRIMING METAL

Metal products often need priming, especially as a preparation for an enamel topcoat. White, gray, red, or black primers are available. Apply a colored primer that will contrast with the topcoat color. It helps show where topcoatings are thin.

Before applying a primer, rub the surface with fine grit silicon carbide paper or steel wool. A wire brush may be necessary to remove any rust or roughness. Finally, clean the surface with acetone or lacquer thinner.

Spraying is the best method for priming metal. Coat small areas using an aerosol can.

DECORATIVE FINISHES

Several kinds of decorative surfaces appear in cabinetry and furniture. Most of these are made by applying a contrasting color glaze over a base coat. The exception is shading, in which a dark stain is applied over a light stain or sealed natural surfaces. Once the two coats are applied, the surface is scraped, wiped, or otherwise treated to create the novelty effect. A protective clear topcoating may be applied last if the glaze is not durable enough. The various decorative finishes covered in this section include:
1. Antiquing.
2. Shading.
3. Gilding.
4. Graining.
5. Marbleizing.
6. Mottling.
7. Spattering.
8. Stippling.

The *base coat* is an opaque finish needed to give the surface a consistent solid color. This allows you to use hardboard, particleboard, or other panel product materials. The *glaze coat* provides the decorative finish. Special glazing compounds are available. You can also use oil or latex enamel. The glaze coat is treated while wet. Work on limited areas, especially with latex materials. They begin to set sooner than oil base glazes.

Decorative finishes require practice to perfect. Consider making test panels before applying finish to any product.

Antiquing

Antiquing highlights a surface and makes it look worn, Fig. 47-15. This is done by wiping portions

Fig. 47-15. Antiquing makes a surface look worn.

of a glaze coat so that the base coat shows through. This effect is similar to shading, where stain is wiped for highlighting.

Begin by studying the shape of the product. Decide where it might receive the most wear. These are the areas where the glaze will be wiped away. Then apply a base coat of the desired color. Prime first or apply two base coats to unfinished wood. Next, apply an even coat of commercial glazing liquid. You might also purchase an "antiquing kit" which includes glaze. Let the glaze coat set until it is tacky. Then, rub the surface with a cloth. (Dampen the cloth with solvent if the glaze does not wipe up easily.) Rub those areas where wear is most likely to occur—edges of tables, around drawers and door pulls, and along smooth leg surfaces. Once the glaze coat dries, apply a clear built-up finish, such as polyurethane.

Shading

Shading is much like antiquing, but highlights stained surfaces so that the grain is still visible, Fig. 47-16. The final effect looks similar to scorching, explained in Chapter 45. The base coat is either sealer over unfinished wood or a light stain and then sealer. You need to prevent the "glaze" coat from bleeding into the base coat. Then spread on a thin coat of darker stain. Wipe away the stain where wear would occur, allowing the original stain to show through. Apply another sealer coat to prevent the stain from bleeding into the topcoat.

Gilding

Gilding involves outlining and highlighting edges and other areas with gold paint, Fig. 47-17. Finish the product first. Usually, gilding is done over opaque finishes. Then add the gold enamel or paint

Fig. 47-16. Shading is much like antiquing, except that the grain shows through.

Fig. 47-17. Gilding over an opaque lacquer topcoat.

with an artist's paint brush. You might want to use masking tape to guide your work. Otherwise, have a cloth wet with solvent to remove any unwanted gilding.

Graining

Graining gives the appearance of wood grain over poorer quality woods and manufactured panel products, Fig. 47-18. Begin with a tan or light brown base coat. The color depends on the wood you want to imitate. For example, imitating mahogany would require a little red coloring in the base coat. The graining or glazing color should be similar to the base coat, but provide enough con-

trast to give the grained effect. The grain lines are made with a brush or coarse comblike applicator. The procedure is as follows:

1. Spread a thin layer of the grain, or glaze, coat. Allow it to just begin to set. This prevents the glaze from flowing once you comb it.
2. Rake the applicator over the surface lightly.
3. Allow the glazing to set several minutes more.
4. Brush lightly over the grained area with a clean, dry paint brush. Make short brush strokes to blend the glazing and base coat somewhat.

You can add imitation knots with a fingerprint. Then curve nearby grain around the fingerprint with an artist's paint brush.

A

B

Fig. 47-18. A—Graining with a brush. B—Graining with a comblike applicator.

Marbleizing

Marbleizing creates a simulated marble surface. It produces a vivid effect and is most often applied to the top surface. The steps illustrated in Fig. 47-19 are as follows:

1. Spread the wet glaze over a dry base coat. You can coat a light glaze coat over dark base coat

or just the opposite. Select colors that imitate marble.

2. Press crumpled wax paper or plastic wrap lightly against the glaze.
3. Lift the plastic or paper straight up from the surface.
4. Add to the decorative streaks by going over some of the lines with a stiff plastic edge.

Another technique is to create additional contrasting streaks and/or color spot effects. Do so by dripping glaze on a wet base coat. No brushing or rubbing should be done. Allowing the glaze to set a few minutes before applying it will lessen the amount it spreads over the base coat.

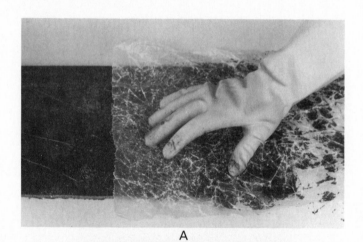

A

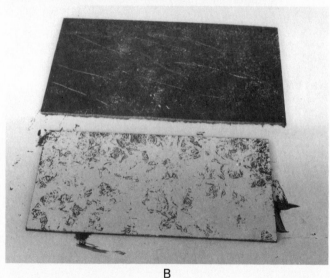

B

Fig. 47-19. A—Marbleizing being done with a black glaze coat over a white base coat. B—The color effects can also be reversed.

Mottling

Mottling provides overall color and pattern variations, Fig. 47-20. This can be achieved by adding or removing glaze from a base coat. For this effect, you need to make a mottling applicator. It can be a small piece of sponge, textured carpet, or pad of burlap. Shape it into the pattern you wish to create.

Fig. 47-20. Mottling provides blotches of different shades.

To give a mottled effect by adding glaze to the base coat:
1. Dip the applicator into the glaze.
2. Press it against the dry base coat.
3. Add to the effect by twisting the applicator.

To create the mottled effect by removing glaze:
1. Spread a smooth glaze coat.
2. Press a solvent-dampened mottling applicator against the wet surface. Twist it if you wish.

Spattering

Spattering involves applying a simulated distressing to an opaque base coat. Dip a paint brush in dark enamel and tap the handle against a dowel or wood scrap to create random dots on the surface.

Stippling

Stippling creates an even textured pattern on the surface with a series of dots, Fig. 47-21. Apply a base coat and let it dry. Pour a small amount of glaze coat into a flat container. A paint can lid works well.

Fig. 47-21. Stippling gives a textured appearance. It can be done with a sponge or nylon scrubbing net.

Select a stiff stippling brush, plastic netting, or other coarse material to create the effect. Touch the bristle tips or netting to the glaze. Then transfer the colored dots to the base coat.

THINK SAFETY—ACT SAFELY WHEN PREPARING SURFACES FOR TOPCOATING

Note any health and safety cautions printed on the label of the finish container. They may identify that the product is toxic, a skin irritant, or flammable. Follow these guidelines when working with finishes and solvents.
1. Wear eye and face protection.
2. Wear protective clothing.
3. Wear rubber or plastic gloves to protect sensitive skin.
4. Check whether you are allergic to any of the ingredients.
5. Have a fire blanket handy.
6. Have the proper fire extinguisher and know its location.
7. Extinguish all flames and provide ventilation.
8. If you experience any discomfort, contact a physician.

SUMMARY

This chapter has covered a number of steps in the finishing process. The most common order of events to prepare for topcoating includes washcoating, staining, filling, and sealing. The sealer is omitted if you plan to apply a penetrating topcoating. Each step plays an important role in the attractiveness of the completed product. The washcoating evens stain penetration, especially in species having great variations in density between springwood and summerwood. Staining alters the color of the wood. This may be done to enhance the grain, conceal the grain, or make a low-cost wood look like a more expensive species. Filling may be done before or after staining. Packing filler into the large pores of open grain wood levels the surface. Sealing follows filling when a built-up topcoating will be applied. Sealer prevents stain from bleeding into the topcoat. It also prevents the topcoat from soaking into the wood.

CABINETMAKING TERMS

Washcoat, stain, dye, pigment, water stain, water-soluble aniline dyes, non-grain-raising stain, alcohol-soluble aniline dyes, oil stain, penetrating oil stain, pigment oil stain, gel stain, spirit stain, latex stain, alkyd stain, filling, paste filler, liquid filler, shellac sealer, varnish sealer, lacquer sealer, sanding sealer, priming, base coat, glaze coat, antiquing, shading, gilding, graining, marbleizing, mottling, spattering, stippling.

TEST YOUR KNOWLEDGE

1. Describe the effect different densities of springwood and summerwood have on staining.
2. Coating a prepared wood surface with thinned sealer or "stain controller" is known as _____.
3. When might you choose a pigment oil stain over a penetrating stain?
4. Identify the advantage NGR stains have over water stains. Are there any disadvantages?
5. What is the primary purpose of spirit stain?
6. A water stain can give you the proper color with one coat. True or False?
7. When might you choose not to use filler on an open grain wood?
8. List the steps taken to apply a paste filler.
9. What type of built-up topcoating materials may not require a sealer?
10. Sanding sealers generally are compatible with all topcoatings. True or False?
11. Sealing metal means to close the open pores of brass and steel.
12. Primer is applied to metal to help the topcoating _____.
13. Why would you select a primer color that contrasts with your enamel topcoating?
14. Two decorative finishes that make the product look worn are _____ and _____.
15. A decorative finish that gives the appearance of wood over an opaque base coat is _____.

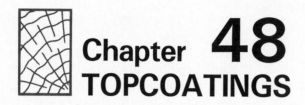

Chapter 48
TOPCOATINGS

After studying this chapter, you will be able to:
- Select and apply penetrating or built-up topcoatings.
- Degloss the surface between coats of finish.
- Polish a dry film.
- Apply decals, stencils, stripes, and other surface accents.
- Remove old or unsatisfactory coatings.

Topcoating is the final protective film on an assembled product. It is a penetrating or built-up layer of finish that resists moisture, dirt, chemicals, stains, and daily wear. Traditionally, natural materials have been used for the topcoating. However, synthetic products offer improved characteristics such as hardness, fade resistance, durability, and elasticity.

The topcoating may be clear or opaque. Clear coatings are applied over fine woods so that you see the beauty of the grain. Opaque coatings hide the surface and are applied to manufactured wood products and poor quality lumber.

Ingredients in a topcoating are either volatile or nonvolatile. The *volatile liquid* evaporates as the finish dries. It includes the solvent or water that helps you spread the finish. The *nonvolatile materials* form the protective coating and do not evaporate. They may include resins, silica, oil, driers, and possible pigments or dyes.

Always consider the environment when applying any topcoating. Dust in the air may settle on a wet coating and create a rough surface. High humidity can slow the setting and curing time for finishing materials. Ventilation is necessary where toxic solvents and resins are present. Also, prepare a nearby place to store newly coated, wet products. Make it easy to transfer a product to drying area.

Topcoatings, skillfully applied, help create high quality products. The topics described in this chapter include selecting and applying penetrating and built-up topcoatings, deglossing, polishing, and applying surface accents.

PENETRATING TOPCOATINGS

Penetrating finishes soak into the wood, leaving the grain texture as they protect the surface. The primary advantage of penetrating finishes over built-up films is that scratches or stains are easy to fix. Most often, you simply apply another coat. Rubbing scratches, ring marks, and stains with fine steel wool dipped in finish covers these defects.

Remember that these products need to penetrate. Therefore, do not apply a sealer or pigment stain. There are natural oil and synthetic resin penetrating finishes. Each are applied by wiping, Fig. 48-1.

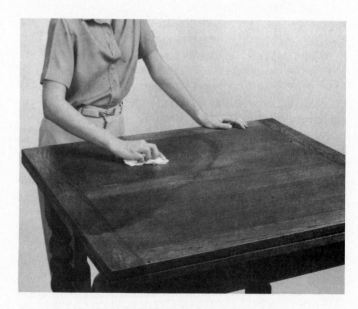

Fig. 48-1. Penetrating finishes are wiped onto the surface. (Klean-Strip)

NATURAL FINISHES

Natural penetrating finishes are organic materials. They include linseed oil, tung oil, and penetrating wax. Natural oil finishes take time, patience, and much rubbing. Multiple coats are required. Each may take several days to dry.

Linseed oil

Linseed oil is extracted from the seed of the flax plant. It is available in a raw or boiled form, Fig. 48-2. Raw linseed oil is a greenish-brown, slow drying liquid. It is water repellent and helps restore natural oils to unfinished wood. Boiled linseed oil is processed to reduce drying time. Yet, it retains the same water repellent properties of raw oil. With either product, you must apply multiple coats, waiting a day or more between applications. A properly applied linseed oil finish can take several months to achieve. As many as 10 or more applications may be needed to bring out a beautiful soft luster. Yet, the coating resists water, heat, and most stains.

Linseed oil is best applied while warm. When heated, it is thinner and penetrates better. The steps to apply a linseed oil finish are:

1. Thin two parts of linseed oil with one part of turpentine or mineral spirits.
2. Heat the mixture so that it is warm, but not hot, to the touch. Use a double boiler to prevent the danger of fire.
3. Wipe on a generous amount of oil, spreading the film over small areas at a time.
4. Rub each section until the linseed oil is absorbed. This takes from 5 to 30 minutes, depending on the condition of the wood and the temperature of the oil.
5. Wipe the surface with a tack cloth containing mineral spirits to remove excess oil.
6. Wait one to three days and repeat the procedure. Wait longer between later coats, up to a week after 10 coats.

Fig. 48-2. Two forms of linseed oil. (Klean-Strip)

Tung oil

Tung oil comes from the seeds in the fruit of the tung tree. You can find pure tung oil, but it dries much too slowly. It is best to use polymerized tung oil, the equivalent of boiled linseed oil, Fig. 48-3. You can, however, speed up the drying time of pure tung oil by adding a drier. Typically, this product is sold as "Japan drier."

When applied, tung oil has a slightly amber color. It dries rapidly to a hard, durable glossy film resistant to water, heat, and most stains. Once applied, the color and gloss level remain fairly stable.

Tung oil is easier to apply than linseed oil. Fewer coats and less rubbing is needed to create the desired luster. The steps are:

1. Cover small areas (one to two square feet) at a time.
2. Rub the oil into the surface.
3. Continue to work to a dry edge in small areas until the entire surface is coated.
4. Recoat areas where you see that the gloss is uneven.
5. Allow the coat to dry overnight or as directed on the container.
6. Apply two or more coats.
7. Reapply a coat as needed to maintain the luster of the finish.

Fig. 48-3. Tung oil. (Minwax)

Penetrating wax

Penetrating wax is a combination of oil and wax, and possibly stain. Typically, a penetrating wax requires only one or two wiped coats. After 10 to 15 minutes, buff away the excess to bring out the luster.

SYNTHETIC PENETRATING FINISHES

Synthetic penetrating finishes contain either alkyd or phenolic resins. They are the easiest coatings to apply and among the most durable. Unlike oils, they typically require only one coat. Additional coats build up on the surface, hide surface damage, and offer more protection.

Alkyd resins

Alkyd resin coatings are relatively inexpensive and provide a glossy finish. Since they are not water-proof, limit their use to wall paneling and other surfaces which do not receive daily wear. Alkyd resins lack resistance to solvents, such as alcohol, and some acidic foods.

Phenolic resin

Phenolic resin finish, Fig. 48-4, is more durable. The dried film has the glossiness of an alkyd, but resists moisture, household chemicals, and food stains. The resin seals wood pores, leaving a hard film. Two phenolic resin finishes you might encounter are sold as "Danish oil" and "antique oil finish."

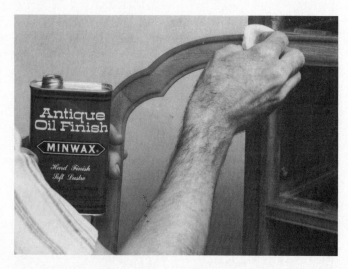

Fig. 48-4. Phenolic resin finish offers excellent protection. (Minwax)

Applying synthetic resinous coatings

Penetrating synthetic resins are easy to apply. They dry in less than 24 hours. The finish can be brushed or wiped on. Coat the surface evenly. Softer portions of the wood or veneer absorb more liquid than dense areas. Continue to apply coatings until no dull spots are seen and the gloss level is even. Allow the film to dry. This could take from 8 to 24 hours. Hand rub the dry surface with steel wool or other fine abrasive. A second coat may be applied. However, always check the directions given on the container label.

BUILT-UP TOPCOATINGS

Built-up topcoatings, Fig. 48-5, consist of one or more layers of finish built up on the wood's surface. A skillfully-applied built-up finish is beautiful and requires little maintenance unless damaged. At times, you may have to remove an old finish and replace it.

Like penetrating finishes, built-up topcoating materials can be either natural or synthetic. Natural coatings include shellac, lacquer, varnish, and enamel. Synthetic products generally are more durable and resistant to moisture and chemicals. They include synthetic varnish, synthetic lacquer, epoxy, and enamel. Some synthetic finishes come in two parts, a resin and a catalyst. These are mixed together at the time of application.

Fig. 48-5. Built-up topcoats form a smooth, wear-resistant film. (Thomasville)

Built-up topcoatings contain various amounts of resins, oils, silica, driers, and possibly pigments. Resins, oils, and driers dissolve in the solvent. Pigments and silica are insoluble. They are held on the surface by dried resins. *Pigment* is finely powdered coloring added to primers, enamels, and sometimes clear coatings with stain. *Silica* is clear, powdered sand that adds thickness and controls surface reflection. Finish may be labeled as gloss, semigloss, satin, or possibly flat.

Drier is an additive that causes chemical changes in the coating material. Once dry, the film is not affected by the solvent used to thin the finish. For example, you can clean a dry varnish or latex finish with minerals spirits or water. By contrast, there is no drier in shellac and lacquer. Rubbing these films with alcohol or lacquer thinner softens the coating.

The oils in a built-up finish help spread the wet film. For many years, linseed oil was the accepted oil additive. A recent advancement in technology is emulsified oil. It mixes with a mineral spirits solvent finish and allows you to cleanup with soap and warm water. Always read the instructions on the container label for application and cleanup.

The viscosity of a finish also affects how well it spreads. Not all built-up finishes are ''liquids.'' The words ''dripless'' or ''gel'' may appear on the container label. These materials are thicker than normal and leave fewer runs or sags. You might perform a viscosity test when preparing to spray a finish. (See Chapter 46.)

Finishes are also classified as low-build and high-build. *High-build coatings*—varnish, enamel, and polyurethane—create a thick protective film quicker. *Low-build coatings*—shellac and spray lacquer— require more coats to achieve the same thickness.

SHELLAC

Shellac is a natural resin used for washcoating, sealer, and topcoating. A dried shellac film is hard, but can be softened by water and heat. The resin is sap taken from trees in southeast Asia. It is extracted and converted by a small lac bug to a honey-like substance deposited on tree trunks. The dark brown, gummy material is harvested, refined, and sold as *orange shellac*, Fig. 48-6. However, most shellac is bleached and sold as the more popular *white shellac*. Orange shellac is applied to dark woods or to darken lighter wood surfaces. White shellac has little effect on surface color. Mixing orange and white shellac for color effects is not recommended. Deeper colors can be obtained by mixing alcohol-soluble aniline stain with alcohol, and adding it to the prepared shellac liquid.

Fig. 48-6. Shellac is a nontoxic, natural finish. (Parks)

Shellac has a given shelf life. Check the expiration date on the container label. As it ages, shellac becomes gummy and will not dry properly.

Shellac is sold as a liquid, or as flakes ready to be dissolved in denatured alcohol or shellac solvent (synthetic alcohol). The consistency of shellac is rated by *cut*, Fig. 48-7. For example, a 3-lb. cut is the consistency of 3 lb. of shellac mixed in a gallon of solvent. Thinner cuts spread easier. Brush or spray the first and second coats with 1/2- to 1 1/2-lb. cut. For the final film, mix a 2- or 3-lb. cut. When brushing, keep your strokes to a minimum. Apply the liquid quickly with one or two strokes. Go over the area just enough to remove bubbles or blemishes. The same cut is used for spraying. Allow two to four hours between the first and second coats. Wait eight hours between successive coats and before buffing the final coat. Sand surface between coats with 150 to 180 grit paper.

SHELLAC CUTS		MIX RATIO	
Original Cut	Desired Cut	Parts Alcohol	Parts Shellac
4 lb.	3 lb.	1	4
4	2	3	4
4	1 1/2	3	2
4	1	3	1
4	1/2	5	1
3	2	2	5
3	1 1/2	1	1
3	1	4	3
3	1/2	4	1

Fig. 48-7. Thin shellac so that it spreads easier.

FRENCH POLISH

French polish creates a beautiful luster and has been used for generations on quality furniture. The process consists of applying a combination of shellac and boiled linseed oil. Mix a 3-lb. cut of shellac. Then add an equal amount of oil.

Applying a French polish requires heat. On a flat surface, the heat is generated by rubbing a cloth dipped in the mixture with rapid, straight strokes. After several applications, rub with a circular motion. Allow each coat to dry completely. As you can see, a French polish requires strenuous work. This is why it is mostly applied on the lathe, where the turning part creates friction heat, Fig. 48-8.

LACQUER

Lacquer is a hard, durable, and water resistant finish most noted by its fast drying time. Until the early part of the 20th century, lacquer was a refined form of resin produced by the lac bug. Today, most lacquer is synthetic, Fig. 48-9. The fast dry-

Fig. 48-8. French polish applied on a turned part. Guard removed to show operation.

ing time of lacquer deters the problem of dust settling on the newly-coated product. Like shellac, natural lacquer does not repel direct exposure to water, which can turn the finish a milky color.

Synthetic lacquer typically includes one or more clear resins, a plasticizer, and solvent. Resins which provide body for the film include nitrocellulose, acrylic, and vinyl. The plasticizer gives the dried film added flexibility, especially needed on woods with poor dimensional stability. Lacquer is thinned only in a special solvent that contains acetates, alcohols, and hydrocarbons. It is wise to purchase thinner and lacquer from the same manufacturer.

Silica may be added to change the reflective nature of the dried film. You can buy gloss, satin, and flat lacquer. However, the final sheen can be changed by polishing. Several brands of lacquer can be purchased with pigments added for color.

Lacquer is applied by brushing or spraying. For quality work, spraying is recommended. You must purchase lacquer based on the application methods. Lacquer is sold in one of two forms: brushing or

Fig. 48-9. Clear gloss synthetic lacquer is best applied by spraying. (Parks)

spray-grade. Brushing lacquer contains a retarder that increases tack time by slowing evaporation. This type can be thinned for spraying. Spray-grade lacquer is thin and fast drying. Brushing a spray lacquer leaves the surface rough with brush marks.

Apply lacquer products over water and NGR stains. Penetrating stains bleed into the topcoat. A lacquer sealer coat between stain or filler and the topcoat is best. Also apply a sealer over mahogany and rosewood; their natural dyes bleed into lacquer solvent.

Lacquer vapors are extremely flammable. Extinguish all nearby flames, such as pilot lights. Be sure that the finishing room is well ventilated. Wear a respirator to prevent you from inhaling toxic fumes.

Thin four parts lacquer with one or two parts solvent for all but the final coat. This ratio will spread easier and there will be fewer blemishes.

Spraying is done following the guidelines given in Chapter 46 and the directions on the lacquer container label. Two or three coats usually are sufficient. Beware of a heavy-center spray pattern. This indicates that the mixture is atomizing poorly and should be thinned. Increasing the air pressure or lowering the fluid feed pressure also may solve this problem. Except for blemishes, it is not necessary to sand each dried coat. Lacquer softens the previous coat somewhat, thus promoting good adhesion. However, you might sand the surface with 180 to 220 grit abrasive paper to remove dust.

VARNISH

Varnish is an excellent topcoat for wood and manufactured wood products. It consists of resins (natural or synthetic) in a vehicle of solvent and drier. When the solvent and drier evaporate, a durable, thick film of resin remains. This film resists heat, impact, abrasion, alcohol, water, and most chemicals. Varnish is sold in aerosol cans and various size containers, Fig. 48-10.

Varnish for cabinetmaking generally is clear, with gloss, semigloss, or satin shine. Stain may be added to make the topcoat a one-step process, Fig. 48-11. This can be done because the thick film of varnish usually does not require a sealer over bare wood. Colorants make varnish a suitable glaze coating for an opaque coating on manufactured wood products.

The properties of a varnish depend on the resin. Products with natural resins are not as tough as synthetics. They also tend to yellow. Except for some rubbing types, natural resin varnish is no longer used. Synthetic varnishes are sold under the name of a number of manufactured resins, such as acrylic, polyurethane, and urethane.

Varnishes sold under the name "spar" or "marine" are extra tough products. The ingredients

Fig. 48-10. Varnish comes under different names in various forms. (Carver-Tripp)

Fig. 48-11. Varnish with stain added is a one-step finishing process. (Benjamin Moore)

vary among manufacturers, but all dry hard and resist heat, acid, moisture, and chemicals. They are good for wooden boats, patio furniture, doors, and other exterior applications.

Natural varnish

In *natural varnish*, the resin is rosin. Linseed oil is the drier. Turpentine or mineral spirits is the solvent. These varnishes are slightly yellow in color and continue to yellow over time. The film is formed by evaporation of the solvent, leaving the resin deposited as a decorative and protective coating.

Oleoresinous varnish

Oleoresinous varnish (oil and resin combination) is a modified natural resin topcoating. The resin may be ester gum or rosin, and synthetic resins may be mixed in for special applications. Drying oils likely

will be synthetic. Mineral spirits or turpentine is the solvent. Unlike natural varnishes, oleoresins cure by a chemical reaction, not by evaporation. This coating is moisture-resistant, and tends to darken with age.

Synthetic varnish

Synthetic varnishes are similar to natural products. They too contain a mixture of resin, drying oil, and solvent. Most set by solvent evaporation and cure by a chemical reaction, either with air or with another chemical. Some contain emulsified oils, which allow you to clean up equipment with soap and warm water. A powdered silica "flattener" may be added to create a satin, rather than glossy, luster.

Most synthetic varnishes can be used without any special preparation. Two-part catalyst varnishes have to be mixed according to directions when you are ready to apply them. They cure by chemical reaction and must be spread within a short period of time. Mixed finish cannot be stored.

Each type of resin offers unique physical properties. Some companies mix several resins to produce special products. A container of varnish may not even say "varnish." Instead, the product is simply labeled by the resin.

Acrylic varnish. Acrylic is a tough, very clear protective film. Some acrylics use emulsified oils.

Alkyd varnish. Alkyd resin varnish varies from clear to somewhat yellow, depending on the manufacturer. It does not yellow further over time. The dried film is tough, hard, and durable, but can be brittle. The alkyd-base spar varnish contains an ultraviolet inhibitor to make it less susceptible to fading caused by sunlight.

Epoxy varnish. Epoxy varnish is extremely tough, elastic, and durable. It comes as a two-part product. Proportions of resin and catalyst are mixed at the time of application.

Phenolic varnish. Phenolic resin varnish has very high resistance to water, alcohol, and other corrosive materials. It is excellent for marine use as well as for bars and table tops. The finish comes as either a one-part or two-part coating. Like natural varnish, phenolic resin varnish can yellow over time.

Polyurethane varnish. Polyurethane is the most wear-resistant of synthetic varnishes, Fig. 48-12. It can be applied, without thinner, straight to unsealed wood. No separate sealer is needed. It is elastic and will withstand impact well. Polyurethane also resists abrasion better than other synthetic resins. It holds up well against commonly-used chemicals (alcohol, food acids, household cleaners). Polyurethane is available as a gloss, semigloss, satin, and flat finish. You can also buy it with stain already added. Clear polyurethane may yellow slightly.

Fig. 48-12. Polyurethane forms a hard, durable surface for floors, furniture, and paneling. (Parks)

Urethane varnish. Urethane and polyurethane have the same film characteristics and durability. The difference is that urethanes are more moisture resistant. They come as either one- or two-part coatings. Single mixtures dry by evaporation or moisture curing. Moisture-curing urethane absorbs moisture from the air to shorten the curing time.

Two-component urethanes are similar to epoxy coatings. They have high resistance to many liquids. The film is flexible and durable, but tends to yellow. Bowling lanes and gym floors often receive this treatment.

Applying varnish

Varnish, because it is a thick liquid, can trap air bubbles. Stir, never shake, varnish to mix the ingredients. Then let it sit for several minutes to allow air bubbles to rise to the top. Otherwise, the bubbles are transferred to the surface.

Varnish, at the proper viscosity, spreads easily by brushing. Keep brush strokes to a minimum, one or two strokes. Excessive brushing will produce an uneven film layer.

Small objects can be dipped. However, you must watch closely for runs and sags.

Most varnishes cannot be sprayed at can consistency. It is best to thin three parts liquid with one part thinner to prevent a heavy-center spray pattern. Applying varnish by rolling and wiping is not recommended. Rolling tends to create air bubbles in the film. Wiping results in an uneven layer of finish.

The final layer of varnish can be polished after it is dry. This produces sheen with a gloss varnish. A less reflective surface can be achieved by applying a final coat of semigloss or satin finish. Only use semigloss and satin finishes as a final coat. Silica in these products tends to cloud the grain slightly.

ENAMEL

Enamel contains many of the same resins, drying oils, and solvents as varnish. To this is added color pigments which make the coating opaque. Like varnish, enamels may be natural or synthetic, water or oil base, and may come in gloss, semigloss, satin, and flat grades.

Today, natural oil-base enamel is rarely used. It is not very hard, nor resistant to abrasion, chemicals, or solvents. It usually contains linseed oil. Tung, caster, fish, soya, and other oils might be found also. Most enamels today are synthetic. There are both oil-base and water-base products. There also may be emulsified oils which clean up in soap and warm water.

Alkyd oil enamel

Alkyd oil enamel is by far the most used oil-base wood coating, fig. 48-13. There are both interior and exterior grades, and finishes from flat to gloss. The exterior grade has additives that resist ultraviolet light, mildew, and fading. Apply an exterior grade on interior cabinets if the humidity is high (such as in basements). The solvent for alkyd enamels is mineral spirits.

Fig. 48-13. Alkyd oil enamel is the most popular opaque finish for interior and exterior applications. (Carver-Tripp)

Polyurethane enamel

Polyurethane enamel begins with clear polyurethane finish. To this, pigments are added to make it opaque, Fig. 48-14. The dried film has all of the same characteristics as polyurethane varnish.

Fig. 48-14. Polyurethane works well on interior and exterior wood and metal furniture. (Plasti-kote)

Synthetic water-base enamel

In recent years, *synthetic water-base enamels* have become very popular. They have many desirable characteristics, including:

1. Ease of application.
2. Ease of cleanup with water and soap.
3. Color retention.
4. Durability.
5. Elasticity.
6. Low toxicity.
7. Low odor.
8. Low cost.

The resin in the finish makes a big difference. Acrylic, alkyd, epoxy, latex, and urethane are used alone and in combinations. Acrylic latex coatings are adaptable to interior or exterior use. They provide satin to gloss surfaces. Acrylic makes the film durable, fade resistant, and elastic. Latex makes it easy to apply and clean up, Fig. 48-15. Acrylic epoxy is a two-part coating that is an extremely hard and durable semigloss or gloss film. It resists chemicals and abrasion. Alkyd enamel has good color retention, hiding qualities, and resistance to stains and abrasion. There is little odor from this material. Urethane-latex enamels are extremely tough and abrasion resistant. They are very practical for use on floors. Other tough and durable combinations include urethane-alkyd and vinyl-acrylic.

Applying enamel

Apply enamel as you would varnish. Stir, never shake, enamel to mix the ingredients. Let custom-colored enamel sit for a while after mixing to allow air bubbles to rise. At the proper viscosity, enamel spreads easily by brushing. However, excessive brushing will produce an uneven film layer. Allow the liquid to flow at its own rate.

BETWEEN-COAT DEGLOSSING

Most built-up finishes require two or more coats of finish. The dried surface usually needs some preparation for the next wet film. This is called deglossing. Without abrasive or liquid deglossing, successive films may not bond well. The process is necessary only for varnish and enamel topcoatings, which contain drier. Others, such as shellac and lacquer, soften themselves when the wet coat is applied to form a good bond. These are abraded only to remove dust particles.

Fig. 48-15. Latex enamel is fast drying, has several gloss levels, and cleans up with water. (Carver-Tripp)

ABRASIVE DEGLOSSING

Between coats, the surface should be rubbed with a 180 grit or finer abrasive, Fig. 48-16. Orbital sanders do the task very effectively. Otherwise, use a sanding block to maintain a flat surface. On curved surfaces, hold the abrasive sheet or steel wool pad by hand.

Abrasives serve two purposes. First, they remove coating blemishes. Sand these with silicon carbide paper after all of the coating film is dry. If runs, sags, or other film defects are not thoroughly dry, the uncured film will roll off when sanded. Second,

Fig. 48-1. Between-coat deglossing with 180 grit abrasive paper. (Carver-Tripp)

Fig. 48-17. This one-step multipurpose finish combines stain and polyurethane. (Minwax)

sanding creates scratches on purpose. They provide ''tooth'' to which the next film adheres.

LIQUID DEGLOSSER

Liquid deglosser is similar to diluted paint and varnish remover. It roughens the dry film slightly through chemical reaction. Choose a liquid deglosser rather than abrasive when you do not need to remove blemishes.

SELECTING MULTIPURPOSE FINISHES

Some finishing product manufacturers market ''finishing systems.'' These products originated with Seal-A-Cell, a three step process. Most of today's finishing systems consist of two products. The first is a sealer that is a mixture of waxes, oils, and alkyd resins. This blend seals wood cells against moisture. The second is a penetrating wood finish, satin or gloss, that forms a lasting topcoat. These finishes are applied by wiping.

There also are one-step seal, stain, and topcoat finishes. These were developed in response to strong consumer demand for one-step wood finishing products that can deliver top quality results for inexperienced do-it-yourself wood refinisher. Most often, they consist of polyurethane with a stain added, Fig. 48-17. You coat unsealed wood directly by brushing or spraying from an aerosol can.

RUBBING AND POLISHING BUILT-UP TOPCOATINGS

After the final film has dried, inspect the surface. It may need further treatment to remove dust particles, create the desired sheen, or smooth an uneven film. This is done by rubbing the surface with fine powdered or sheet abrasives. Then comes the last step in the finishing process, *polishing*. A coat of paste wax is buffed on as a final protective

treatment. This is generally not done to penetrating finishes because wax clogs wood pores and remains in small crevices. Liquid wax is preferred.

The gloss of shellac, lacquer, and varnish can be changed by *rubbing* the surface with sheet or powdered abrasives. A film with some waviness may first be smoothed with dampened 240 to 600 grit wet-or-dry silicon carbide paper. Then the sheen is brought out with finely powdered *pumice stone*. Follow this with *rottenstone* and *polishing compound,* which are finer yet and increase the sheen. Rubbing can reduce the shininess of a gloss film or increase the luster of semigloss films.

Pumice and rottenstone are spread with water or rubbing oil using a felt or heavy cloth pad as an applicator. Water allows for faster cutting. It is also cleaner and leaves a brighter gloss surface. Oil reduces the cutting action of the abrasive. It also leaves a film which is hard to remove, even with mineral spirits. Paraffin oil is used most often, although a thin mineral oil may be used as a substitute.

Fig. 48-18. After the final film of built-up lacquer or enamel topcoating, smooth the surface with 400 grit wet-or-dry silicon carbide abrasive and water. (Norton)

Follow this procedure:

1. Rub the surface with wet abrasive paper and water. Select a wet-or-dry silicon carbide abrasive. Start with 240 grit if the film is wavy or dusty. Otherwise select 400 or more grit wet-or-dry abrasive paper with water, Fig. 48-18. For turnings and curves, hold the damp folded abrasive sheet in your hand while rubbing.
2. Wipe away the white liquid created by rubbing with a clean, dry cloth. This is topcoating mixed with water.
3. Obtain a felt applicator, free from grit, dust, bits of steel wool, or other debris which might mar a rubbed surface.
4. Spread a film of water or rubbing oil on small areas at a time. (Do not use water on shellac.) Sprinkle pumice stone on the wet surface. Use grade F for coarse rubbing and either grade FF or FFF for fine rubbing.
5. Rub the surface along the grain, Fig. 48-19. Pumice breaks down as you rub, providing an even finer abrasive. Add more water as needed, but no more pumice. Fresh pumice will scratch and damage the work already done.
6. Wipe away the pumice and water or oil with a clean water- or solvent-soaked cloth.
7. Allow the surface to dry. Wipe off any remaining pumice powder.
8. Inspect the surface. Both water- and oil-rubbed surfaces will be a satiny to flat sheen. If this is acceptable, apply paste or liquid wax and buff with a soft, dry cloth.
9. To create a higher sheen, rub the surface with rottenstone and oil using a different felt-covered block. A still higher gloss can be achieved with rottenstone and water, followed by polishing oil.

10. Wipe off any remaining water, oil, and abrasive.
11. Finally, apply a coat of wax and buff the surface.

APPLYING DECALS, STENCILS, AND STRIPES

Decals, stencils, and stripes accent cabinet surfaces and make them conform to style. *Decals* are manufactured transfer films. *Stencils* are open patterns through which you can produce a design. Paper, plastic, and metal plate stencils are available, or you can make your own. *Stripes* can be applied as vinyl tape, brushed on between masking tape guides, or applied with a roller.

Surface accents may be applied at two different times. The easiest is when the topcoating is complete. Add them just before applying the final coat of wax. Accents can also be sandwiched between topcoating films. With a protective layer over them, they are less likely to be rubbed away. However, be cautious about sandwiching decals or stencils. Make sure the topcoating will not soften them. Decals or stencil inks could be destroyed by lacquer.

Fig. 48-20. Decals applied to an opaque, lacquered chest.

APPLYING DECALS

Decals, Fig. 48-20, are bonded to an adhesive backing. The adhesive is loosened by water or heat. To attach a water-separated decal:

1. Align the dry film on the surface.
2. Place masking tape against two sides of the decal. This helps position it later.
3. Moisten the decal and backing as instructed.
4. Position the film.
5. Press lightly on the backing. Push air bubbles from the center toward the edges.

Fig. 48-19. Rubbing the surface with pumice stone creates sheen.

6. Slide away the backing as instructed.
7. Remove excess backing adhesive with a wet sponge.

To apply a heat-bonded decal:
1. Align the film on the surface.
2. Press the decal backing with a warm iron.
3. Peel away the backing material.

APPLYING STENCILS

Stencils may be single or multiple color designs. The patterns are made of oil-treated paper, plastic, or metal. See Fig. 48-21. For multicolored stencils, each color has its own pattern and the stencil ink is applied separately. There will be registration marks for every color to align each stencil. Each color must dry before adding the next.

The procedure to apply a single color stencil is:
1. Align the stencil on the surface.
2. Hold it in position with masking tape.
3. Touch the stencil brush in the colored ink or enamel.
4. Tap on the pattern openings with the brush.
5. Begin in the center and work toward the edges of each section. This reduces the changes for the coating to run under the stencil.

The procedure to apply a multicolor stencil is:
1. Align one of the stencils on the surface. You might begin with a light color area first. Then proceed to darker colors.
2. Register the stencil with two pieces of masking tape next to it.
3. Spread the finish for that color as you would a single color stencil.
4. Wait until the coating dries.
5. Repeat the steps for each color, using the appropriate stencil.

When spraying a stencil, follow the steps as directed. Be sure to mask the surface around the stencil pattern. Also make sure the stencil pattern lies perfectly flat. These cautions prevent overspray

around and under the pattern. An aerosol can works best. Spray as you would any other surface.

APPLYING STRIPES

Striping may be accomplished in three ways. The first, and easiest, is to purchase and apply adhesive-backed vinyl striping, Fig. 48-22. It is available in colors. The type with the color strip fixed to a clear vinyl covering is recommended. They adhere better and the clear portion protects the stripe from damage. Simply align the vinyl with a masking tape guide and press it to the surface. Try not to stretch the strip. It might pull away later.

The second method involves rolling on stripes using an opaque finish and a narrow roller. This practice requires much more skill. Striping tools have a narrow roller attached to a tube of finish.

The third method involves painting on the stripe between two strips of masking tape. Apply masking tape on each side of the area to be striped. Then spray or brush on the coating.

Fig. 48-22. Adding stripes to raised panel door between topcoats.

NONSCRATCH SURFACES

Nonscratch surfaces are made with felt or flocking. For example, the insides of jewelry boxes or silverware chests are lined with felt to prevent the contents from being scratched. The bottoms of lamps have a nonscratch coating to prevent them from marring furniture.

FELT

Felt is the quickest way to apply a nonscratch surface. You can purchase pressure-sensitive-adhesive-backed felt in squares. Cut it to size while

Fig. 48-21. Stencils, stencil brush, and created patterns. (Brookstone)

the paper backing is still on. Then peel off a section of the paper and begin pressing the felt in place. Pull away more of the paper back as you proceed.

FLOCKING

Flocking involves applying nylon fibers over a colored enamel base coat. It is a two step coating process. You need the following materials shown in Fig. 48-23.
1. Colored nylon fibers.
2. Colored base coat enamel adhesive.
3. A paint brush.
4. A flocking gun.

Fig. 48-23. Flocking supplies. (Donjer)

The procedure is relatively simple. Start with a finished surface roughened slightly with abrasives to provide tooth. Fill the flocking gun with the desired color of fibers. Coat areas to be flocked with the colored undercoat enamel adhesive. It should be close to the same color as the fibers. While the adhesive is wet, spray on the fibers. Allow the surface to dry. Then lightly brush away excess fibers.

REMOVING TOPCOATINGS

A topcoating might be removed for one of two reasons. Most often, you are removing an old finish. For example, you might remove an opaque finish from an antique table to apply a stain and varnish finish. A second reason for removing the topcoating is to take off an unsatisfactory finish. Some problems are given in Fig. 48-24. It is important that you inspect the product at each stage of the finishing process. Poor results are disastrous and can require that you remove the finish and repeat the process.

Shellac can be taken off with alcohol. Lacquer thinner will remove lacquer. Before chemicals were readily available, old or poor varnish finishes had to be removed with abrasives, Fig. 48-25. Now, liquid and paste paint removers take off these topcoatings easily, Fig. 48-26. These are strong chemicals. Be sure to wear rubber gloves to pro-

SURFACE DEFECT	PROBABLE CAUSE	REMEDY
Bleeding (stain color works to surface)	Improper sealer applied.	Refinish.
Blistering (bubbling of dry film)	Exposure to excessive heat. Excessive moisture content in wood.	Refinish.
Bloom (clear film cloudiness)	High humidity during application.	Refinish under better conditions.
Cratering (lacelike pattern on wet film)	Slick or oily surface.	Remove wet film with solvent. Degloss dry film. Reapply coating.
Crawling (wet film gathers in globules)	Slick or wet surface. Glossy dry film beneath. Temperature of air and/or finish too cold. Build up finish material too thick. Thinned with improper solvent.	Same as for cratering. Apply film at higher temperature— see can label. Stir in proper thinner.
Crazing (fine cracks in dry film)	Rapid temperature change during curing.	Refinish.
Flat Spots (dry film areas without gloss)	Uneven sealer coat.	Refinish.
Orange Peel (wrinkles in dry film when spraying)	Topcoat material too thick.	Refinish with properly thinned topcoating.

Fig. 48-24. Inspect surfaces and remedy defects before considering a cabinet complete.

Pinholing (small holes in dry film)	Shaking finish can—especially varnish. Surface not dry.	Stir, do not shake container. Refinish.
Runs and Sags (irregular wet or dry film thickness)	Excessive material applied to surface. Too much solvent in material.	Better control of application method. Correct mixture. Wet films might be removed with cloth. Refinish when thick areas are completely cured.
Specks or Nibs (small, hard rough spots in wet or dry film)	Dirty equipment—brush, roller, spray gun, wiping cloth. Dust in air when applying film.	Remove wet film with solvent and recoat. Refinish. Improve maintenance procedures.
Spotty Setting (uneven evaporation of solvent in wet film)	Poor surface preparation.	Remove wet film with solvent, if possible, then degloss and recoat. Refinish otherwise.
Sweating (change in gloss level of dry film)	Topcoating applied over uncured sealer.	Allow more curing time, otherwise refinish.
Tackiness (slow setting)	No barrier coat. Filler, stain, or sealer not dry before coating. Poor ventilation.	Allow more time for setting and curing. Increase ventilation. Otherwise refinish.
Withering (loss of dry film gloss)	Surface not sealed or not sealed evenly. Sealer not dry before topcoating.	Degloss and apply another topcoat film.
Wrinkling (uneven surface on dry brush-applied film)	Topcoating too thick. Excessive brushing after setting begins.	Refinish with thinner and use less brushing.

Fig. 48-24 continued.

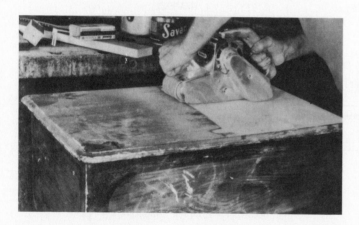

Fig. 48-25. Removing a finish with abrasives leaves unwanted marks. It is also time consuming, especially when removing finish from intricate details. (Norton)

Fig. 48-26. Paint remover comes in a variety of forms. (Klean-Strip)

tect your skin against accidental contact. Furthermore, most removers are flammable and toxic. Work only in ventilated areas.

Liquid remover

Liquid removers are the least expensive and most appropriate for horizontal surfaces. They are thin and tend to run or drip. Suppose you wanted to

remove only the top surface of a table. Remover that contacts another portion of the table would destroy that surface also.

Paste remover

Thicker bodied paste, semipaste, and gel removers are easier to control. *Paste removers* tend not to run or drip, unlike liquid removers, and can be applied to vertical as well as horizontal surfaces. They take longer to work, but are effective on tough, synthetic coatings.

Apply remover with a brush. Stroke the brush only in one direction. Reverse strokes roll away softened coatings and reduce the remover's effectiveness. The best procedure is as follows:

1. Coat areas about 2 sq. ft. (186 000 mm²) in size.
2. Allow the remove to wrinkle and loosen the films. This may take 10 to 30 minutes, depending on the chemical. Do not be fooled into thinking the remover has lost effectiveness when on layer peels. The chemical keeps working on deeper layers. Consult the label for when to begin removing softened finish.
3. Carefully remove the coating with a scraper or wire brush, Fig. 48-27. The scraper does well on flat surfaces. A wire brush works best on curved surfaces. If the coating dries before you scrape it off, work in smaller areas.

Fig. 48-27. After the remover has been absorbed, take off peeled coatings with a putty knife or wire brush. (Carver-Tripp)

4. Wash the surface according to directions on the container. Some remover instructions require that you use mineral spirits. Others recommend water. Washing takes off leftover waxes and reduces clogging of the abrasive. This step is essential before refinishing can begin. Use a minimum amount of water if a water-soluble adhesive was used for product assembly. In addition, some manufacturers make a special wash solution for their remover.
5. Allow the surface to dry thoroughly.
6. Smooth the dried surface with coarse steel wool, Fig. 48-28, or abrasives.

Fig. 48-28. After washing the surfaces, rub with steel wool. (Benjamin Moore)

THINK SAFETY—ACT SAFELY WHEN PREPARING SURFACES FOR TOPCOATING

Note any health and safety cautions printed on the label of the finish container. They may identify the product as toxic, a skin irritant, or flammable. Follow these guidelines when working with finishes and solvents.

1. Wear eye and face protection.
2. Wear protective clothing.
3. Wear a respirator when using toxic solvents.
4. Have plenty of cross ventilation while applying or removing topcoatings.
5. Wear rubber gloves while handling paint removers and other strong chemicals.
6. Acetone and paint removers will dissolve plastic eyeglass lenses and face shields.
7. Learn whether you are allergic to any of the finishing ingredients.
8. Have a fire blanket handy.
9. Have the proper fire extinguisher and know its location.
10. Extinguish all nearby flames.
11. If you experience any discomfort, contact a physician.

SUMMARY

Topcoating is the final protective film on a cabinet or piece of furniture. There are two types of topcoatings: penetrating and built-up. Penetrating finishes soak into the wood, leaving the grain texture. Natural penetrating finishes include linseed oil, tung oil, and penetrating wax. Synthetic penetrating finishes include alkyd and phenolic resins. Built-up topcoatings form a film on the wood surface. Natural products include shellac, French polish, lacquer, and varnish. Synthetic products include lacquer, as well as varnishes and enamels.

Repeated coats of shellac and lacquer soften the previous film to improve adhesion. This does not happen with varnish and other finishes containing drier. Deglossing is needed between coats to provide ''tooth'' for the next film. This can be done with sheet abrasives or a liquid deglosser.

Built-up topcoatings can be rubbed and polished to increase or decrease sheen. Rubbing is done first with dampened fine grit wet-or-dry sheet abrasives. Follow that with even finer powdered abrasives. Polishing involves buffing the surface with liquid or paste wax.

Surface accents can be applied between coats or on the final topcoat. Accents include decals, stencils, and stripes. Be cautious when placing accents between layers of finish. Some solvents can damage them.

Unwanted films can be removed with liquid or paste removers. You might remove old finish from an antique or a newly applied, but unsatisfactory finish. Removers soften and peel the topcoating, allowing you to brush or scrape it away.

CABINETMAKING TERMS

Topcoating, volatile liquid, nonvolatile materials, penetrating finish, natural oil penetrating finish, linseed oil, tung oil, penetrating wax, resinous penetrating finish, alkyd resin penetrating finish, phenolic resin penetrating finish, built-up topcoating, pigment, silica, drier, emulsified oil, high-build coating, low-build coating, shellac, orange shellac, white shellac, cut, French polish, lacquer, synthetic lacquer, varnish, natural varnish, oleoresinous varnish, synthetic varnish, acrylic varnish, alkyd varnish, epoxy varnish, phenolic varnish, polyurethane varnish, urethane varnish, enamel, alkyd enamel polyurethane enamel, synthetic water-base enamel, liquid deglosser, polishing, rubbing, pumice stone, rottenstone, polishing compound, decal, stencil, stripe, flocking, liquid remover, paste remover.

TEST YOUR KNOWLEDGE

1. Topcoatings are divided into what two categories?
2. The purpose for deglossing is to:
   a. Provide a sheen.
   b. Give tooth to the dry coating.
   c. Dull the surface.
   d. Make flat enamel from gloss enamel.
3. Two built-up topcoating materials which must be removed with liquid or paste remover are _____ and _____.
4. Coatings which contain _____ oils can be cleaned up with soap and water.
5. List two resin-based and two oil-based penetrating coatings.
6. Name two high-build and two low-build top coatings.
7. Varnish may contain _____ that gives it color.
8. Two forms of shellac are _____ and _____.
9. Which synthetic varnish is the most durable?
10. Place numbers where these steps would occur when applying a built-up varnish topcoat on open grain wood.
    a. Apply simulated distressing.
    b. Rub the surface with pumice stone and water.
    c. Apply an NGR stain.
    d. Rub the surface with rottenstone and water.
    e. Coat the surface with a washcoat of stain controller.
    f. Apply a coat of sanding sealer.
    g. Apply paste wax and buff the finished surface.
    h. Raise the grain.
11. How do you align the different patterns of a multicolor stencil?
12. Commercial finish removers are available in _____ and _____ forms.
13. What advantage do boiled linseed oil and polymerized tung oil have over raw linseed and tung oils?
14. What is the most time consuming part of applying a linseed oil finish?
15. The most durable penetrating finish is _____.
16. Penetrating finishes are applied by _____.
17. Two finishes which require heat during application are _____ and _____.
18. Why is spray-grade lacquer not suitable for brushing?
19. What slows the evaporation rate of brushing lacquer?
20. Apply lacquer over only _____ and _____ stains.
21. Explain why you should never shake varnish just before application to mix it.
22. Why should you not add fresh pumice stone once you begin rubbing?
23. Nonscratch surfaces include _____ and _____.
24. What materials remove shellac and lacquer finishes?
25. Mineral spirits or turpentine will remove a varnish finish. True or False?

Chapter 49
KITCHEN CABINETS

After studying this chapter, you will be able to:
☐ *Lay out traffic patterns.*
☐ *Identify work centers and appliance areas.*
☐ *Recognize various kitchen designs and arrangements.*
☐ *Select cabinet types that maximize storage.*
☐ *Explain how to lay out a kitchen.*
☐ *Install base and wall cabinets.*
☐ *Produce base and wall cabinets.*
☐ *Install manufactured and on-site constructed cabinets.*
☐ *Identify metric measurements for kitchen cabinets.*

Kitchens are an integral part of the home and offer one of the most prominent markets for cabinetmaking. *Kitchen cabinets* provide practical storage and convenient work areas for numerous food preparation tasks. In addition, kitchens are used for dining, study, office space, laundry, and watching television, Fig. 49-1.

Designing kitchen cabinets to suit a home is a challenge for the cabinetmaker. Some cabinets are built to architectural standard sizes. Custom units must take into account the human factors discussed in Chapter 5. Kitchen cabinets must be well made, durable, and attractive. Surfaces should be wear-resistant since they generally receive more use than do other cabinets in the home. In addition, the appearance must blend with surrounding furniture and the style of the home.

In the body of this chapter, all measurements are given in inches. At the end of the chapter, metric measurements are given. The two are separated because standard metric cabinet dimensions are not always exact conversions from inches. If no metric standard is given, multiply the inch measurement by 25.4 to obtain the equivalent in millimeters.

KITCHEN REQUIREMENTS

To meet kitchen needs, you must consider storage, work centers, appliance areas, and utilities. Also remember that appliances and materials in the kitchen can be harmful to children and adults.

Fig. 49-2. Storage space is one purpose of a kitchen.

Try to decide what items will be stored where. Size, weight, and frequency of use will be factors, Fig. 49-2. While planning, you could number the cabinet doors and drawers. Then list their contents.

Fig. 49-1. Plan kitchens for convenience and efficiency. (Quaker Maid)

STORAGE

The primary purpose of any cabinet is storage. Examples of items to be stored include:
1. Small appliances (blenders, can openers, mixers, toasters).
2. Metal and glass bakeware (cookie sheets, pie pans, cake pans, casseroles).
3. Cooking utensils (knives, spoons, measuring cups, thermometers, spatulas, graters, tongs, etc.).
4. Dinnerware (plates, bowls, cups, saucers, glasses).
5. Flatware (forks, knives, spoons).
6. Boxed, canned, and bottled goods.
7. Fresh fruit and vegetables.
8. Cookware (saucepans, pots, skillets, bowls).
9. Instruction materials (cookbooks, recipe files, appliance manuals).
10. Cooking and cleaning supplies (dishwashing powders and liquids, scrub pads, towels, pot holders, cleaning supplies).

WORK CENTERS

Work centers refer to counter or table top areas where certain tasks are performed. Appliances, cookware, foods, and recipes are set there when in use. These areas also may be used for storing canisters of flour or sugar, a toaster, microwave oven, or television. In a small kitchen, a table top could double as an eating area and workspace. The major work centers are:
1. *Food preparation center.* This area includes the refrigerator-freezer, nearby countertop, and surrounding cabinets. Have at least 18 in. of countertop available on the side(s) to which the door opens. Plan for the door to swing away from an adjoining work surface. This area also contains countertop space for mixing appliances as well as storage for utensils and bowls.
2. *Cooking and serving center.* This area includes the cooktop and oven or range-oven and surrounding counter space. The cabinets hold cookware and cooking utensils. Provide ample counter top space, 36 in. on one side or 18 to 24 in. on either side.
3. *Cleanup center.* This area contains the sink, dishwasher, garbage disposal, trash compactor, and surrounding counter top. Cleanup includes cleaning vegetables, fruits, and other food as well as cleaning dishes. Provide 18 to 36 in. on the left side and 24 to 36 in. on the right side.
4. *Eating center.* An eating center might be a small breakfast table, pullout counter, snack counter on a peninsula, or table, Fig. 49-3.

Fig. 49-3. One section of the kitchen may serve as an eating center. (Quaker Maid)

5. *Planning center.* This area could be used for meal planning or as office space for the homemaker. A phone jack might be located nearby. Desktop space would hold cookbooks, recipe files, and notepads. See Fig. 49-4.

Fig. 49-4. A planning center provides work space for meal planning and other activities. (Quaker Maid)

7. *Laundry center.* A washer and dryer might be part of the kitchen away from the food preparation area. These appliances are often placed in a closet behind bifold doors. Already having water and sewer hookups handy may make this a good idea.

APPLIANCE AREAS

Appliances require large amounts of space. Every kitchen needs at least two major appliances, the range-oven and refrigerator. Nice-to-have appliances include a dishwasher, garbage disposal, trash compactor, microwave oven, and cooktops with a separate oven. General width requirements are: 20 to 40 in. for a freestanding range-oven; 22 to 30 in. for a drop-in range; 12 to 48 in. for a cooktop; 21 to 24 1/4 in. for built-in wall ovens; 24 to 36 in. for the refrigerator; 23 to 27 in. for the dishwasher; 28 to 46 in. for a double sink; 11 1/2 to 33 in. for a single sink; and 11 to 18 for a trash compactor. The microwave oven may be built-in or a countertop model. Have the appliance measurements before designing a kitchen.

Portable appliances also need storage or counter top space. Plan for a mixer, blender, food processor, electric skillet, toaster, toaster-oven, coffee maker, waffle iron, slow cooker, electric wok, and can opener.

Under-the-cabinet appliances are the latest trend. These mount beneath wall cabinets to increase counter space. Make sure enough room is left between the countertop and appliance.

If you will be responsible for purchasing electrical appliances, they should have the (UL) Underwriters Laboratories seal. Gas appliances should have the blue star certification of the American Gas Association.

UTILITIES

Every kitchen is served by utilities. You must have electricity, water, and sewer connections. You might also need a gas connection for the range and oven. Most of these are designed into the kitchen by the architect. They are installed by contractors and must meet local building codes.

Consider wiring GFCI (ground fault circuit interrupter) into any grounded 110 volt receptacle outlet. The National Electrical Code recommends at least one GFCI per branch circuit have countertop outlets on one or more circuits. Ranges, ovens, and other cooking units usually require 240 volt service.

Electricity is also needed for the garbage disposal, dishwasher, and trash compactor. Electrical service for these appliances runs through the cabinet and must be "roughed in" before cabinet installation.

A range hood that removes heat and cooking odors requires electrical service through the wall cabinets above the stove. Some vent to the inside and others require a wall or ceiling duct to the outside.

Electrical service is also needed for lighting. A lack of natural or artificial light may result in eye strain and accidents. The amount of lighting needed depends on the number of windows in the room, size of the room, and the appliance arrangement. Lighting can come from three sources: natural, artificial from the ceiling, and artificial directly over the work surface. Plan for fixtures above the sink and under wall cabinets.

Gas service is needed for gas ranges and ovens. Have a qualified technician run piping into the kitchen. Make sure there is a shutoff valve as required by the local building code.

Water is necessary for sinks, dishwashers, and refrigerators with ice makers. Make sure that the proper piping and connections are in place before cabinets are installed.

Plan for sewer drains from the sink, dishwasher, and garbage disposal. Locate the dishwasher near the sink to shorten hot water and sewer piping. The sink usually is a double bowl unit. The garbage disposal is placed under one side.

KITCHEN PLANNING

Begin kitchen planning by identifying major household tasks to be performed. Consider the work centers just discussed. Then decide on the layout of major appliances and cabinets.

KITCHEN DESIGNS

A kitchen should provide practical storage and convenient work areas for numerous tasks. To be

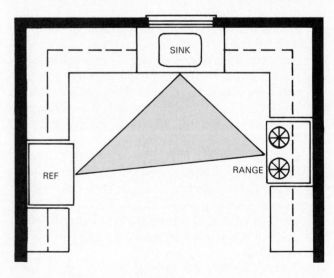

Fig. 49-5. An efficient kitchen has a triangle measuring less than 21 ft.

convenient, the design must minimize walking between the range-oven, refrigerator, and sink. This is called the *kitchen triangle,* Fig. 49-5. The smaller the triangle, the less walking you must do. The optimum design is seven feet between appliances. The total distance around the kitchen triangle should not exceed 21 ft.

Kitchens follow one of six basic designs, Fig. 49-6. Determine which works best for the space you have.

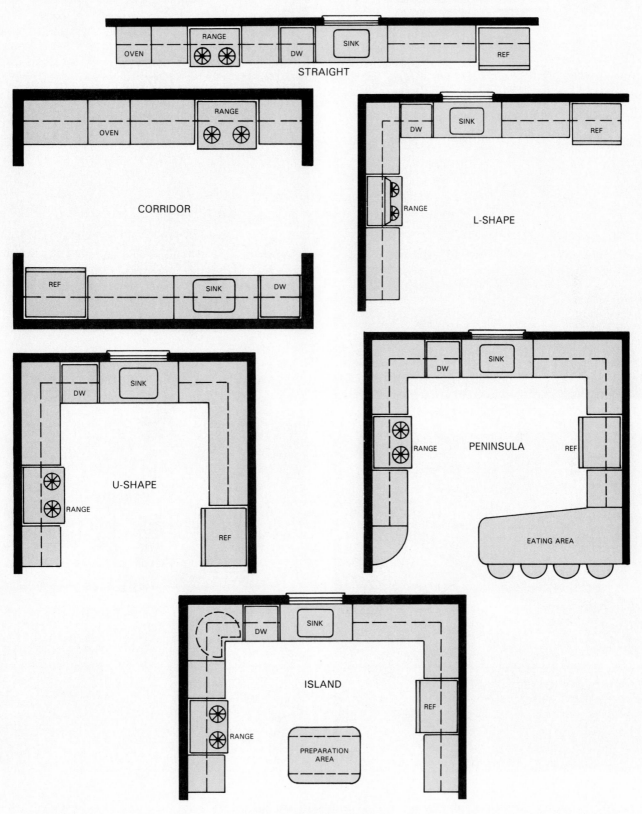

Fig. 49-6. Kitchen designs.

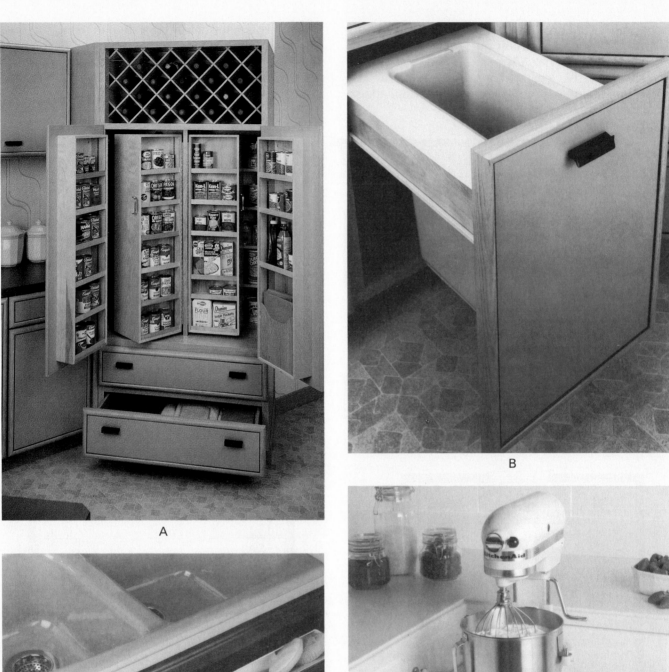

A

C

D

Fig. 49-7. Cabinet accessories. A—Swing-out shelves. B—Dry storage bin. C—False-front trays. D—Swing-up shelf. (Quaker Maid)

A straight or *one-wall kitchen* has all cabinets and appliances lined up along a single wall. It is not efficient because there is too much distance between appliances. Most often, this style is found in apartments.

A *corridor kitchen* has cabinets and appliances on two opposite walls. The layout is very efficient and has no "dead" storage corner areas. It does have one drawback. The kitchen becomes a traffic pattern problem if both ends lead to other rooms. If possible, close one end.

The *L-shaped kitchen* accommodates a dining area or breakfast nook in the opposite corner. This layout is efficient, because the traffic pattern is open to more than one person.

A *U-shaped kitchen* is compact and efficient for one person. The two corners often waste space. You can install corner units with rotating shelves (Lazy Susan).

A *peninsula kitchen* is U-shaped with a counter extending from one end. This style is often used to separate the kitchen from an adjoining family or dining room. It could be the range-oven or sink corner of the triangle as well as for an eating space. These are as high as the counter top. Therefore, stools are used while eating instead of chairs.

To one of the above designs, an *island kitchen* adds a work area of cabinets in the middle of the room. In addition, the range or sink may be located on the island.

SAFETY

Planning for safety, especially in the cooking area, includes several factors:
1. Properly ground electrical equipment and outlets.
2. Install smoke detectors.
3. Mount ABC-type fire extinguishers within reach. (Refer to Chapter 18).
4. Have adequate exhaust systems.
5. Place safety locks or catches on all base cabinet doors, especially those where chemicals are stored.

CONVENIENT WORK CENTERS

A convenient work center has countertop space around appliances. You need space on each side of the sink, one or two sides of the cooking unit, and the opening side of the refrigerator. Minimum distances for work centers were given earlier in the chapter. The same area can serve more than one purpose. For example, space between the refrigerator and sink could serve cleanup and food preparation tasks.

Allow space for clearance as well as for appliances. For example, you need ample space (at least 42 in.) in front of the oven and dishwasher. This measurement is taken with a person kneeling in front of the open door.

MAXIMIZE STORAGE

Kitchen cabinets must be adaptable to a wide range of storage requirements. Adjustable shelves accommodate most kitchen equipment. Drawers store utensils and cookbooks. You would like to have everything close at hand. However, this is not possible. Store items that are used less often, such as popcorn poppers or waffle irons, near the floor or ceiling.

A typical base cabinet has a drawer on top and one shelf in the lower part. This may not be the best arrangement, depending on items stored. It may be better to install cabinet accessories, Fig. 49-7. For example, *roll-out trays* and *vertical dividers* easily store cookie sheets and other flat items. *False-front trays* in the sink base unit store sponges and cleaning items. *Dry storage bins* store flour, sugar, and fresh vegetables. A *slide-out towel rack* might be installed under the sink. *Swing-out shelves* help you access food or cookware. A *swing-up shelf* might hold a mixer. A wide range of cabinet accessories are available.

KINDS OF KITCHEN CABINETS

There are three types of kitchen cabinets: base, wall, and tall, Fig. 49-8. Manufactured kitchen cabinets and most custom-built units follow standard sizes. This is a *modular system* based on 3 in. width increments and several standard heights and depths. Built-in appliances usually conform to modular dimensions. Specialty units may be installed for handicapped individuals. Standard cabinets may be sold assembled or as unfinished ready-to-assemble kits.

BASE CABINETS

Base cabinets are floor units 34 1/2 in. high and 24 in. deep with widths from 9 to 48 in. in 3 in. increments. The unit may have only drawers, only doors, or a combination of both, Fig. 49-9. A typical base unit has one or two drawers arranged horizontally and one or two doors covering the lower portion. The base cabinet may have adjustable or fixed shelves and possibly roll-out trays.

A *sink/cooktop base cabinet* is used under the sink and drop-in cooktops, Fig. 49-10. It has no drawers, but may have false drawer fronts. You can order false front trays for the sink base. These pivot out for storing dish rags, sponges, or other cleaning supplies. A sink base should be at least 3 in. wider than the sink length.

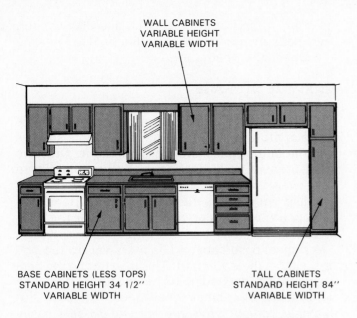

Fig. 49-8. Kitchens contain base, wall, and tall cabinets. (National Kitchen and Bathroom Association)

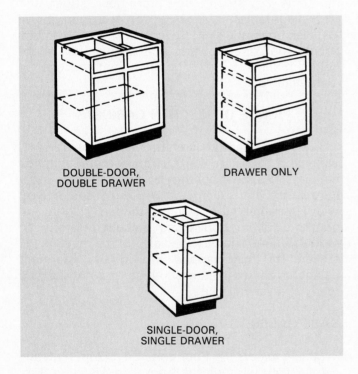

Fig. 49-9. Typical base cabinets. (American Woodmark Corp.)

A *sink/cooktop front* has no sides. It consists of a frame with doors attached, Fig. 49-11. A front is placed between two base cabinets that have finished sides. It serves the same purpose as a sink/cooktop base, but costs less.

Countertops are made to order in sections generally 25 in. deep and 1 1/2 in. thick. The surface may be ceramic, metal, wood, or laminated plastic. This is adhered over a reinforced particleboard or plywood core.

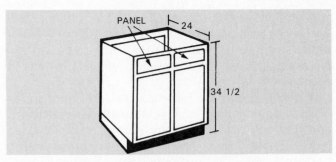

Fig. 49-10. Sink/cooktop base cabinet. (American Woodmark Corp.)

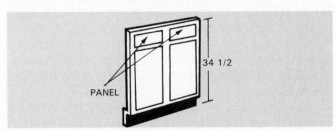

Fig. 49-11. Sink/cooktop front. (American Woodmark Corp.)

Floor space between base cabinets may be necessary for appliances. Built-in dishwashers and trash compactors fit under the countertop.

WALL CABINETS

Wall cabinets are hanging units 15 to 30 in. high and 12 or 13 in. deep. They range in width from 12 to 48 in. in 3 in. increments. They can have one or two doors, and fixed or adjustable shelves, Fig. 49-12. Wall cabinets extend out less to allow you to work over the counter area. Most wall cabinets above countertop workspaces are 30 in. high. This allows the minimum 18 in. between the countertop and wall cabinet. Over ranges, sinks, and refrigerators, install cabinets less than 30 in. As a rule, select 18 in. high wall units over sinks, where there is no window to interfere. Install 12 in. or 15 in. high units over refrigerators and eye-level ovens over ranges. Install 18 or 24 in. units for a range cover. The tops of wall cabinets are set at 84 in.

Usually, wall cabinets contain shelves. Consider having adjustable shelves for the greatest flexibility in storage. Several adjustable hardware styles were shown in Chapter 17. You can also purchase or design units with racks, swing-out shelves, and roll-out trays.

TALL CABINETS

Tall cabinets are 84 in. high units that extend from the floor to the soffit, Fig. 49-13. With shelves, they serve as a pantry. Without shelves,

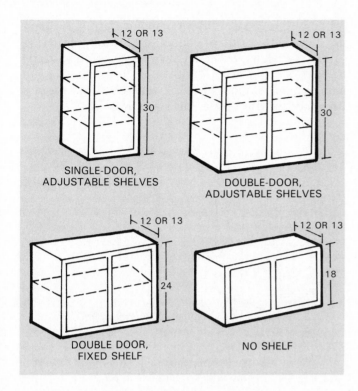

Fig. 49-12. Typical wall cabinets. (American Woodmark Corp.)

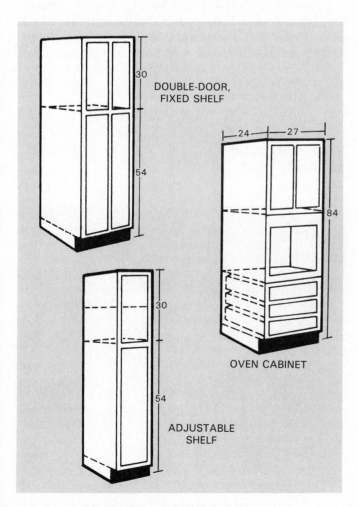

Fig. 49-13. Tall and oven cabinets. (American Woodmark Corp.)

tall units are used for storing brooms, mops, and sweeper accessories. *Oven cabinets* are 84 in. high cabinets with an opening for a built-in oven. Tall and oven cabinets should be placed at the end of a row of lower cabinets. This gives you unbroken counter space and unblocked light.

SPECIALTY CABINETS

Specialty cabinets include a wide range of units to suit everyone's needs. Some of the more common products are corner cabinets, suspended units, hutches, bottle racks, and appliance garages.

Corner cabinets are designed to maximize storage space in a corner. There are three types: blind corner, base carousel, and diagonal wall cabinets.

A *blind corner cabinet* has one half without doors or drawers. You butt an adjoining cabinet, Fig. 49-14. The size follows standard modular unit sizes. A blind peninsula has double doors on one side, but only a single door on the other, Fig. 49-15.

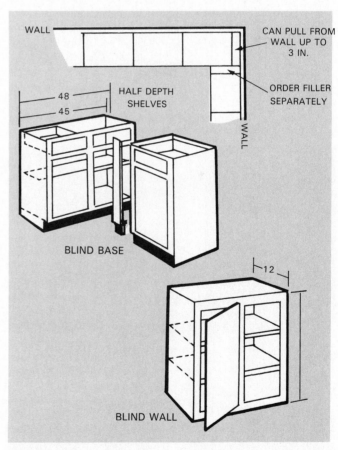

Fig. 49-14. Blind corner cabinets. (American Woodmark Corp.)

A *corner base carousel* is a single round rotating unit. It does not have sides or a back. The front is attached to adjoining cabinets, Fig. 49-16.

A *diagonal wall cabinet,* is a single corner unit.

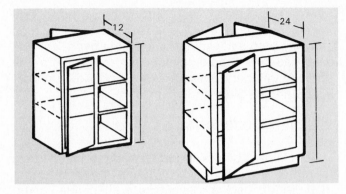

Fig. 49-15. Blind corner cabinets for peninsulas with doors on both sides. (American Woodmark Corp.)

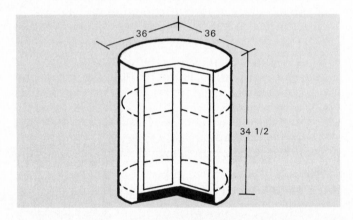

Fig. 49-16. Corner base carousel. (American Woodmark Corp.)

It has a beveled or curved back so that items cannot be pushed out of reach. It typically contains rotating shelves, called a Lazy Susan, to bring items to the front, Fig. 49-17. However, fixed shelves are also available, Fig. 49-18. These cabinets require 24 in. from the corner on each wall.

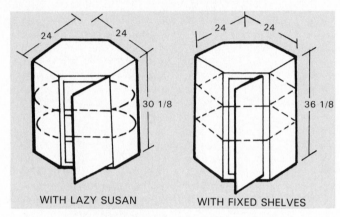

WITH LAZY SUSAN   WITH FIXED SHELVES

Fig. 49-18. Diagonal wall cabinets. (American Woodmark Corp.)

Suspended cabinets can be found over islands and peninsulas. They are fastened to the ceiling joists. Refer to the manufacturer's directions. When positioned over a cooktop, the unit usually contains an exhaust hood, fan, and lighting. The fan may exhaust outside through a duct or through a filter back into the kitchen.

Hutches are open wall units for storing china, crystal, and other display items. Those with an open bottom sit on top of a base cabinet. Others are designed to hang on the wall.

Fig. 49-17. Maximize corner space with corner base carousel and diagonal wall cabinets. (Quaker Maid)

Fig. 49-19. Bottles may be stored vertically in a drawer with a bottle rack. (Quaker Maid)

Bottle racks have holes cut in them for storing long-neck bottles horizontally or vertically. They may sit on the countertop or be an integral part of a cabinet, Fig. 49-19.

An *appliance garage* fits between the countertop and wall cabinet. Refer to Fig. 49-17. It hides appliances and other kitchen tools. They come in various heights and widths. Most have a decorative tambour door.

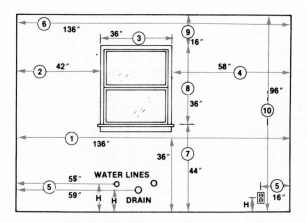

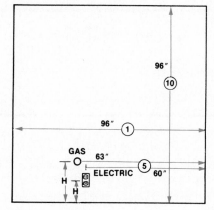

Fig. 49-20. Mark the height and width locations of windows, doors, and utilities on elevation sketches. (Jae Company)

KITCHEN LAYOUT

Before a house is built, a kitchen designer decides on the location of cabinets and appliances. This establishes the placement of utilities. Once in place, a kitchen layout rarely changes where water and sewer services exist. Electrical utilities can be changed rather easily.

MEASURE THE KITCHEN AREA

To lay out a kitchen, first measure and record the total area, wall lengths, along with window and door placements. Also consider home heating and air conditioning registers and air returns. Electrical service outlets, and possibly piping for gas, should

be noted. Draw a rough sketch of the kitchen on graph paper. Draw both plan and elevation views. Now look at Fig. 49-20 carefully as you follow these steps:

1. Measure all walls at 36 in. height. Write the measurements in inches and fractions within 1/4 in.
2. Measure from the corners of the room to window and door trim.
3. Measure across door and window openings, including the trim.
4. Measure from the trim edge to the next corner. Total your individual measurements from Steps 2, 3, and 4. They should agree with the total wall length found in Step 1.
5. Mark the exact location of water, drain, gas lines, and electrical outlets and switches on your drawing.
6. Measure from wall to wall at 84 in. and compare the figure to Step 1 to see if your walls are parallel.
7. Measure from the floor to window sills.
8. Measure from the window sills to the top of the windows.
9. Measure from the top of the windows to the ceiling.
10. Measure from the floor to the ceiling. This figure should agree with that found in Steps 7, 8, and 9.
11. Draw accurate scaled sketches of the kitchen plan and elevations. Add all of the features you have measured. Use graph paper and make each square a 3 in. module, Fig. 49-21.

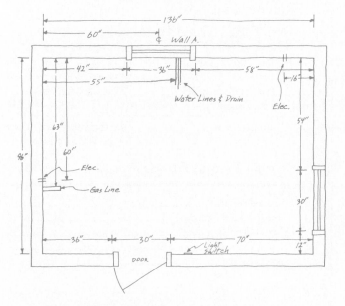

Fig. 49-21. Using graph paper, sketch the plan view of the measured kitchen. (Jae Company)

Checklist

Before you visit your kitchen specialist, fill out this handy checklist designed to help you determine your own personal kitchen requirements.

Cabinetry

Cabinet Style _____ Color _____
Wood Type (or Laminate) _____

Appliances

Electric or Gas Range _____   Built-in Oven _____
Electric or Gas Cooktop _____ Built-in Double Oven _____
Downdraft Cooktop _____   Microwave Oven _____
Grill _____   Built-in Oven/Microwave Combination _____
Electric or Gas Burner/Grill Combination _____   Ventilation System _____
Refrigerator _____   Trash Compactor _____
Freezer _____   Waste Disposer _____
Dishwasher _____   Other _____

Special Options

☐ Butler's Pantry   ☐ Bake Center   ☐ Special Sink   ☐ Plate Rail
☐ Snack Bar   ☐ Center Work Island   ☐ Second Sink   ☐ Other _____
☐ Appliance Garage   ☐ Range Hood   ☐ Custom Beam
☐ Planning Desk   ☐ Decorative Glass Door Inserts ☐ Custom Appliance Panels

Accessories

(See our Accessories Guide
for the complete selection of kitchen accessories.)

Wall Cabinets

☐ Microwave Cabinet   ☐ Spice Rack   ☐ Corner Tambour Cabinet   ☐ Hinged Glass Doors
☐ Open Shelf Cabinet   ☐ Corner Lazy Susan   ☐ Wall Quarter Circle Cabinet ☐ Other _____
☐ Wall Wine Rack   ☐ Tambour Cabinet   ☐ Pigeon Hole

Base Cabinets

☐ Cutlery Divider   ☐ Pull-Out Table   ☐ Base Hamper   ☐ Visible Storage Rack
☐ Tray Divider   ☐ Tote Trays   ☐ Tilt-Out Soap Tray   Baskets
☐ Bread Box   ☐ Waste Basket   ☐ Corner Lazy Susan   ☐ Other _____
☐ Pull-Out Chopping Block   ☐ Pull-Up Mixer Shelf ☐ Adjustable Roll-Out Shelves

Tall Cabinets

☐ Tray Divider   ☐ Visible Storage Rack/Baskets ☐ Multi-Storage Cabinet   ☐ Other _____
☐ Base Hamper   ☐ Built-in Oven Cabinet   ☐ Adjustable Roll-Out Shelves

Other Design Considerations

Sink and Fixtures _____   Type of Wall Covering _____
Special Window Treatment _____ Space Arrangement Changes _____
Type of Flooring _____
Type of Counter Top _____   Special Design Needs _____
Type of Lighting _____

Fig. 49-22. Complete a checklist to help you determine the kitchen requirements. (Quaker Maid)

Appliance	Brand/Make	Model Number	Width Left to Right	Depth Front to Back	Height
Free Standing Range					
Drop-In Range					
Countertop Cooktop					
Built-in Wall Oven					
Microwave					
Built-In Dishwasher					
Built-In Trash Compactor					
Refrigerator					
Sink					
Other					
Other					

Fig. 49-23. List the measurements of appliances in a chart. (American Woodmark Corp.)

DETERMINE APPLIANCES AND KITCHEN FEATURES

List required and nice-to-have appliances and kitchen features. Most cabinet companies provide a checklist to help you determine your own personal kitchen requirements, Fig. 49-22. Place model numbers and measurements in a chart, Fig. 49-23.

ARRANGE APPLIANCES AND SELECT CABINETS

Before you begin to arrange appliances and cabinets, consider duplicating the present kitchen layout. Moving plumbing, windows, and electrical outlets can be costly.

Begin with the floor sketch. Mark the sink placement first. Normally it is located below the window because of available natural light and head room. However, sinks are also placed in corners, peninsulas, or islands. Now complete the kitchen triangle by adding the refrigerator and range. It is best to leave 36 in. for the refrigerator, even if you plan to purchase a smaller unit. This allows you to install 36 in. unit later, if necessary. Allow 1/4 to 1/2 in. clearance for dishwashers, ranges, and trash compactors. At this point, your sketch might appear similar to that in Fig. 49-24. Of course, your kitchen may be U-shape, corridor, one-wall, or straight.

Next, create the elevation sketch(es), Fig. 49-25. Position the sink, range and refrigerator according to your floor plan. Now add cabinet unit locations. It is best to conform to standard 3 in. modular sizes. Manufactured cabinets conform to this standard. If there is an odd measurement, the cabinets may not completely fill the wall space. You can pull the cabinets up to 3 in. from the adjacent wall. The space is covered by an adjoining cabinet or a filler strip at one or both ends.

In corners, remember the possible dead space problem. Do not put a door there. Note the cabinet

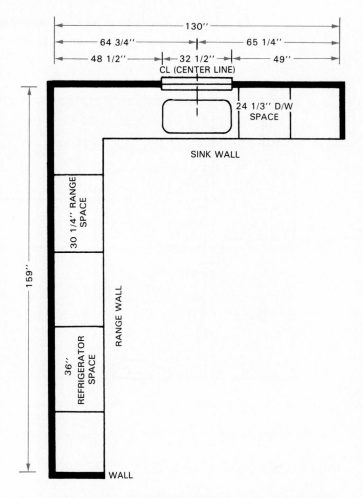

Fig. 49-24. Lay out the position of major appliances to scale. (American Woodmark Corp.)

doors according to the swing (hinge location). You may have double door and single door cabinets. Single doors can swing either left or right. Many times both face frame stiles are drilled so that you can change the hinge side. Ordinarily, upper cabinets open away from the sink, for example. This makes access easier when storing dishes.

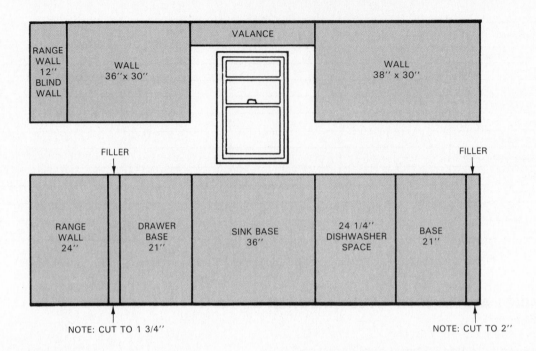

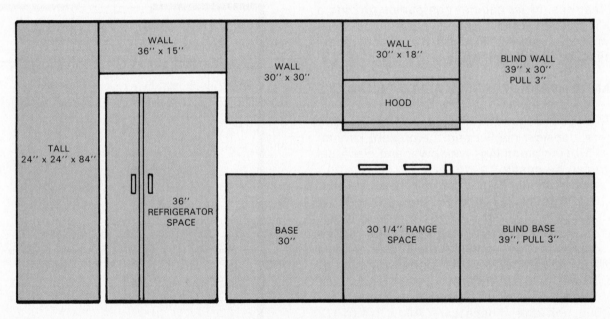

Fig. 49-25. On elevations sketch, mark the position of each cabinet. Include the cabinet name, model number, and dimensions. (American Woodmark Corp.)

INSTALLING MODULAR KITCHEN CABINETS

Kitchen cabinets are easy to install. First collect the needed tools and equipment. Then accurately lay out measurements and mark the walls. Install wall cabinets first, then base and tall cabinets.

ORGANIZE TOOLS

Cabinet installation is easy only if you have the right tools and equipment:

1. Chalk line. A chalk line lays out lengthy straight reference lines. You stretch the chalk-coated line between two points and snap it.
2. Level. Select a 4 ft. level.
3. Plumb bob. A plumb bob helps lay out vertical lines. Hang it on a plumb line or chalk line.
4. Portable electric drill with clearance and pilot bits, and a countersink.
5. Tape measure.
6. Framing square.
7. Step ladder.
8. Screwdriver (regular and Phillips). Using a portable electrical drill and screw bits, makes installation easier.
9. Flat and round head wood screws, and

washers. A supply of 2 1/2 X No. 8 and 2 1/2 X No. 6 wood screws is recommended.
10. Two 4 in. C-clamps.
11. Hammer and finishing nails.
12. Extension cord.

LAYING OUT THE WALLS

It is important to mount cabinets plumb and square. This affects both function and appearance. Make sure the walls and floors are clear except for roughed-in utilities. Remove moulding and baseboard. If the floor is warped, find the highest point on the floor using a level and mark it. Measure all wall heights from this location.

Next, locate wall studs, Fig. 49-26. You must attach cabinets to wall studs for firm support. You can use a magnetic stud finder to locate nail heads holding the plaster lath and gypsum board. You could also drive nails to locate studs. Once you find one stud on each wall, locate the others by measuring 16 in. left and right.

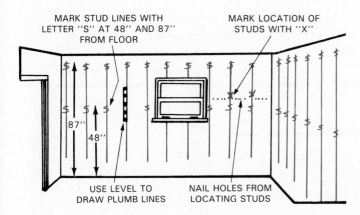

MARK STUD LINES WITH LETTER "S" AT 48" AND 87" FROM FLOOR

MARK LOCATION OF STUDS WITH "X"

87"

48"

USE LEVEL TO DRAW PLUMB LINES

NAIL HOLES FROM LOCATING STUDS

Fig. 49-26. Mark the location of studs. After you find one stud, measure 16 in. on center to locate the others. (Jae Company)

Next mark the horizontal references. Measure 34 1/2 in. up the wall and draw a horizontal line using a level. This is the top height of the base cabinets. The countertop thickness is not included. Then measure 54 in. up from the high point on the floor and mark the bottom line of 30 in. cabinets. Then measure 84 in. up the wall and draw another horizontal line. This will be the top height of your wall cabinets. See Fig. 49-27. These measurements leave 12 in. for a soffit with standard 8 ft. high ceilings. The wall cabinets may be placed lower. However, make sure there is at least 18 in. between base and wall cabinets.

Now mark the specific positions for wall and base cabinets, and appliances drawn on your floor plan. Identify each cabinet by name, dimensions, and product number, Fig. 49-28.

Now that you have all details laid out, prime and paint or finish the walls and floor as desired. This includes the soffit. Some lines may be covered by paint or vinyl floor covering. However, you still should have enough reference marks.

INSTALLING A SOFFIT

A soffit encloses the space between the ceiling and wall cabinets. Usually, it is installed before the wall cabinets, and extends 14 in. out from the wall. This allows you to place moulding to cover any space between the soffit and the cabinet. The steps shown in Fig. 49-29 are as follows:
1. Assemble a 2 X 4 in. soffit frame with vertical supports every 16 in.
2. Position the lowest part of the frame 84 1/2 in. above the floor. This allows you to cover the lower soffit surface with 1/2 in. drywall.
3. Nail the soffit frame into the ceiling joists. Many times the soffit is parallel to the ceiling joists. In new construction, 2 X 4 in. supports should have been placed between joists about every 2 ft. Otherwise, attach the frame with toggle bolts.
4. Install and finish drywall or paneling on the soffit frame.
5. To attach the lower part of the frame, drive screws through the cabinet into the soffit frame about every 4 ft.
6. Install mouldings over the soffit/cabinet joint if desired.

INSTALLING WALL CABINETS

Wall cabinets are hung by fastening them to the wall through the hanging rails. These are horizontal rails along the top and bottom edges inside the cabinet.

Cabinets can be heavy and bulky. To hold them in place against the soffit, assemble a T-shaped padded support, Fig. 49-30. Without a soffit, make a two-legged support. This will position the cabinet while you drive the screws.

The cabinet to hang first will be one in a corner. It might be a regular wall unit. It could be a diagonal wall cabinet in L- and U-shaped kitchens.

Follow these steps to install the wall cabinets:
1. Predrill clearance holes through the cabinet back and hanging rails. Make sure the holes will align with the studs.
2. Position and level the first cabinet. Be sure the cabinet front and side are vertical. Other cabinets depend on the first unit being aligned.
3. Support the cabinet in position with the padded post. The top should touch the soffit or align with the 84 in. mark.
4. Drill pilot holes 1 3/4 in. into studs, Fig. 49-31.

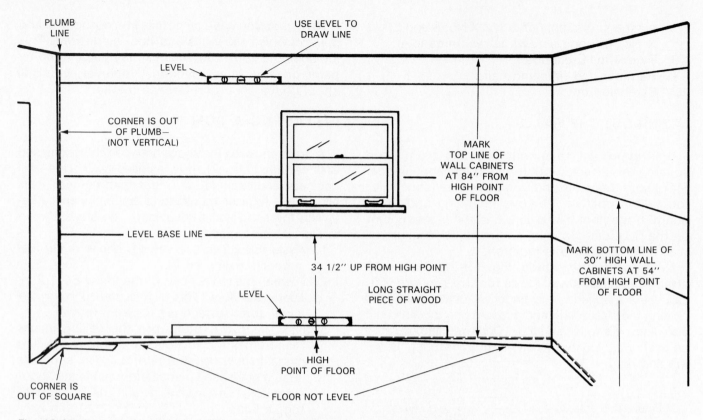

Fig. 49-27. Lay out the cabinets heights from the highest point on the floor. Mark the measurements across the wall using a chalk line. (Jae Company)

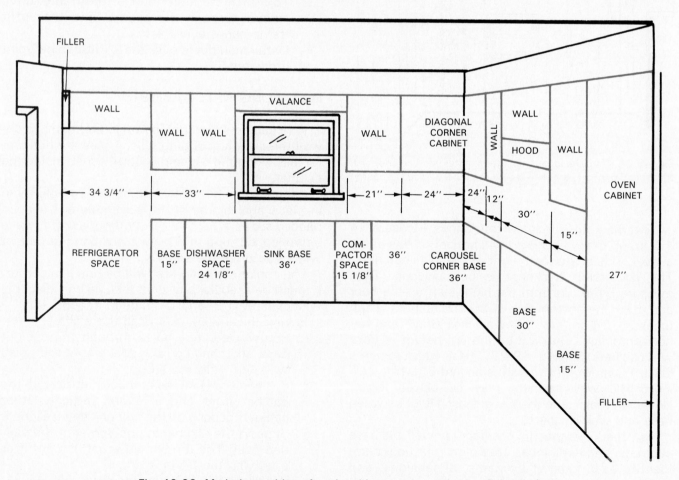

Fig. 49-28. Mark the position of each cabinet on the wall. (Jae Company)

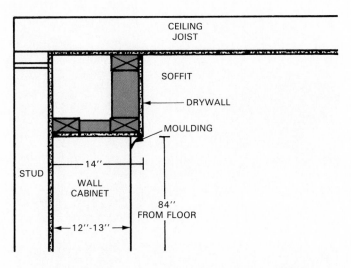

Fig. 49-29. Soffit installation details. (Jae Company)

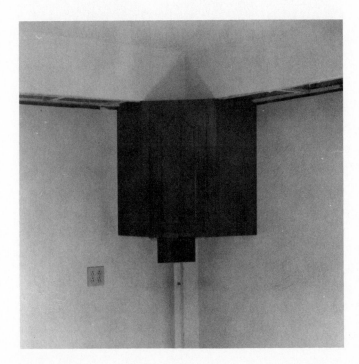

Fig. 49-30. Install cabinets beginning in the corner with the first wall cabinet. Note that a padded post is used to support the cabinet.

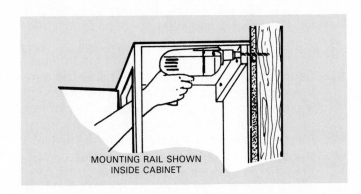

Fig. 49-31. After you drill clearance holes in the cabinet, drill pilot holes into the stud. (Jae Company)

5. Fasten the cabinet with No. 8 X 2 1/2 in. round head wood screws and washers. Installation is easier when you choose a screw gun or variable speed drill and screwdriver bit. Leave the screws a half-turn loose.

6. Support and fasten the next cabinet.

7. Make final leveling and ''shim'' adjustments for the first two cabinets. Tightening a cabinet against a crooked wall without shims can damage the hanging rail.

8. Place C-clamps to hold the cabinets securely at the top and bottom while fastening them together, Fig. 49-32. For frame cabinets, drill pilot and clearance holes in the adjoining stiles. Countersink the clearance hole. Fasten the cabinets together with two 2 1/2 X No. 6 flat head wood screws. To hide these connecting screws, remove the door and hinge; then drill and fasten cabinets under the hinge plate. When you replace the doors, the screws will be hidden.

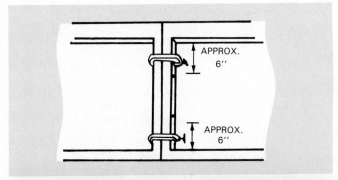

Fig. 49-32. Hang the cabinets, then fasten them to each other. (Jae Company).

9. Hang and secure two cabinets at a time across the wall. There may be cabinets along the wall and more around a corner. If so, you likely will need a filler strip cut to size, Fig. 49-33.

10. You usually install the valance above the window last. Trim it to fit between the wall cabinets on each side of the sink.

11. Saw the range hood vent pipe opening, if necessary, before hanging the cabinet.

12. Trim away any excess shim material that remains after all cabinets are aligned, Fig. 49-34. You can hide shim ends or uneven wall openings with moulding.

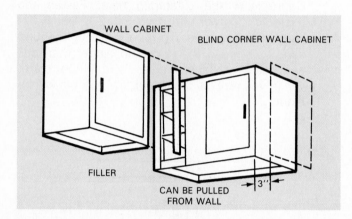

Fig. 49-33. Blind corner cabinets can be pulled from the wall to accommodate a nonmodular wall length. (American Woodmark Corp.)

INSTALLING BASE CABINETS

Base cabinets are installed much like wall cabinets. They are attached to the wall through the hanging rail. Follow these steps to install base cabinets.

1. Begin by installing a cabinet in a corner. If the kitchen is U- or L-shape, the corner may be void, have a blind corner cabinet, or house a Lazy Susan. Install furring strips behind a Lazy Susan or void corner to support the countertop. See Fig. 49-35.

2. Level the cabinet. Have the front and sides vertical.

3. Slip shims behind cabinets to correct for an uneven wall. Place shims under the cabinets to level them. See Fig. 49-36.

4. Drill through the cabinet back and hanging rail making a clearance hole. The holes should align with wall studs.

5. Drill pilot holes 1 3/4 in. into wall studs.

6. Fasten the cabinet loosely with No. 8 x 2 1/2 in. flat head wood screws.

7. Level and attach the next cabinet to the wall.

8. Fasten the cabinets together. Make sure frames (or fronts for frameless cabinets) are

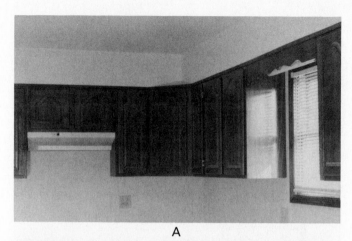

A

B

Fig. 49-34. A—Installed wall cabinets, range hood, and valance. B—Installed short cabinet over refrigerator and tall utility cabinet.

flush at the top and bottom. Refer to Step 8 for installing wall cabinets.

9. Tighten the first cabinet to the wall.

10. Attach, level, and connect cabinets in pairs.

11. Set the sink cabinet or front. A filler strip may be needed on each side. Drill or saw openings for the water supply and drain. This is not necessary if you are using only a sink front.

12. As you continue to position cabinets, measure the spaces for appliances accurately.

13. Tall utility cabinets slip under the soffit. You may need a filler strip on the side, if there is extra space. If so, install it before setting this unit.

14. Trim away any excess shim material.

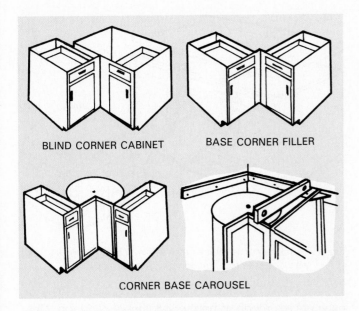

BLIND CORNER CABINET   BASE CORNER FILLER

CORNER BASE CAROUSEL

Fig. 49-35. Start installing base cabinets in the corner. U- or L-shape kitchens have special treatment, such as blind corner cabinets, base corner fillers, or a corner base carousel. Note that support strips are needed to support the counter top. (American Woodmark Corp.)

INSTALLING THE COUNTERTOP

Countertops are available several ways. You can order them to exact sizes with capped ends. You can buy nominal lengths to trim and cap yourself. You might want to install a plywood or particleboard type and laminate it. For L- and U-shaped tops, buy tops with mitered corners.

Purchase end caps with or without adhesive. Usually, the preapplied adhesive is a hot-melt glue You apply the cap with a warm iron. Otherwise, use contact cement. Follow the procedure described in Chapter 36.

The countertop is installed once the base cabinets are fully secure. If you purchased precut lengths, proceed to fasten the top with screws 1/4 in. (6 mm) shorter than the combined corner block and countertop thickness. For nominal lengths, proceed as follows:

1. Cut the countertop to length. Leave 1/2 to 1 in. (13 to 25 mm) of overhang.
2. Bond miter or butt joints with water resistant adhesive. Install clamping hardware while the glue is wet, Fig. 49-37A. Draw the pieces snug, but not tight.
3. Align the joint with a mallet as needed, Fig. 49-37B. Tighten the hardware.
4. Trim the backsplash, as needed. Allow for irregular walls, Fig. 49-37C.
5. Attach the countertop, Fig. 49-38. Drive the proper length screws through corner blocks into the top.
6. Bond laminate caps to visible cut edges, Fig. 49-39A. Trim the excess with a laminate trimmer or file, Fig. 49-39B.
7. Add special precolored joint filler in visible cracks, as necessary, Fig. 49-39C.
8. Make cutouts, as necessary, for sink and cooking units. Follow the directions in Chapter 21 for using a saber saw. Use a fine-tooth carbide blade. Special clips are provided with the installation rims to mount these units.

PRODUCING CABINETS

Most commercial and custom cabinets built today are made of manufactured panel products, such as structural particleboard and MDF. For appearance, these products are covered with melamine laminate and edgebanding. A variety of colors and wood grain patterns are available. Most look like real wood. A few

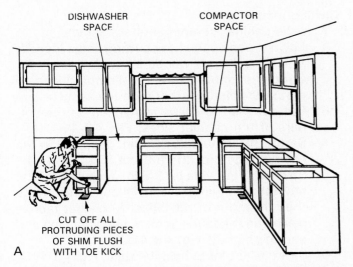

DISHWASHER SPACE   COMPACTOR SPACE

CUT OFF ALL PROTRUDING PIECES OF SHIM FLUSH WITH TOE KICK

A

B

Fig. 49-36. A—Shim behind and under cabinets to account for irregular walls and floors. (Jae Company) B—Finished installation before the countertop.

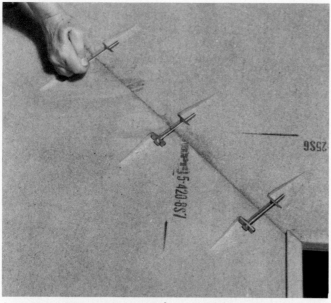

A

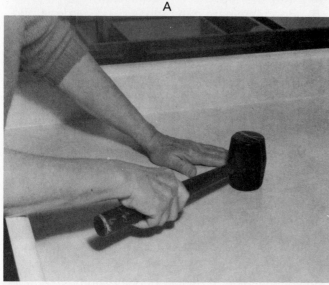

B

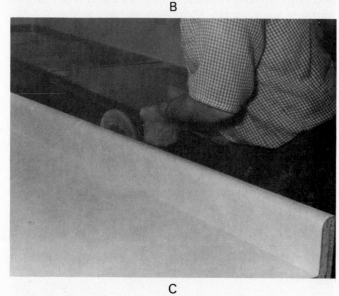

C

Fig. 49-37. A—Assemble the counter top and miter corner with glue and fasteners. B—Align the miter joint with a mallet. C—Trim the backsplash if walls are irregular.

Fig. 49-38. Use corner blocks through which screws will attach the counter top. (American Woodmark Corp.)

cabinets are made of hardwood veneer plywood. Only the highest quality (and most expensive) cabinets are constructed of lumber.

Begin with sketches or drawings that include dimensions. It is wise to follow the modular unit 3 in. width increment. Conform to standard depth and height. From the drawings, create a cutting list and bill of materials. The cutting list should show what components are to be cut from a standard size sheet of material.

MAKING A BASE CABINET

The base cabinet for this example is 24 in. wide. The sides, bottom, and shelf are made of 3/4 in. structural particleboard. The back is 1/4 in. plywood. From this information, create a bill of materials and cutting list. The construction details are shown in Fig. 49-40. The sides are to be covered with a wood grain laminate or by graining (a special finishing procedure).

Cutting joints

Cut the cabinet components as follows:
1. Lay out panels to show cutting lines. Identify where each part will be located.
2. Cut components to size. When possible, saw matched pairs together with the same setup.
3. Cut out the toe space allowance on the corners of the cabinet sides, Fig. 49-41A.
4. Saw a 3/4 in. wide by 3/8 in. deep slot in the cabinet sides for the bottom, Fig. 49-41B.
5. Saw a 3/8 in. wide by 3/8 in. deep slot for the rabbeted hanging rails. This cut is not made the full length of the sides. Note that tape is placed on the fence to mark the beginning and end of the cut, Fig. 49-41C.
6. Saw a blind slot to hold the shelf, Fig. 49-41D.
7. Saw 3/8 in. by 3/8 in. rabbets between the hanger rail slots on each side for the back.

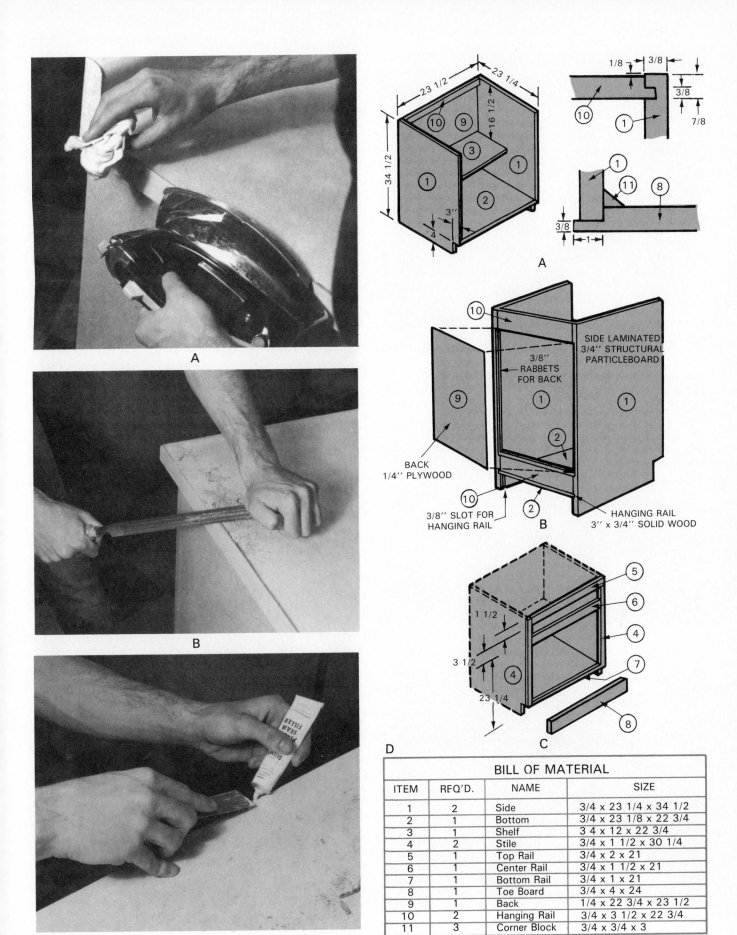

Fig. 49-39. A—Bond the end caps. B—Trim excess laminate. C—Apply seam filler as needed.

Fig. 49-40. Construction details for a base cabinet. A—Front view. B—Back view. C—With face frame. D—Bill of materials.

A

B

SIDE LAMINATED 3/4'' STRUCTURAL PARTICLEBOARD

3/8'' RABBETS FOR BACK

BACK 1/4'' PLYWOOD

3/8'' SLOT FOR HANGING RAIL

HANGING RAIL 3'' x 3/4'' SOLID WOOD

C

D

BILL OF MATERIAL			
ITEM	REQ'D.	NAME	SIZE
1	2	Side	3/4 x 23 1/4 x 34 1/2
2	1	Bottom	3/4 x 23 1/8 x 22 3/4
3	1	Shelf	3 4 x 12 x 22 3/4
4	2	Stile	3/4 x 1 1/2 x 30 1/4
5	1	Top Rail	3/4 x 2 x 21
6	1	Center Rail	3/4 x 1 1/2 x 21
7	1	Bottom Rail	3/4 x 1 x 21
8	1	Toe Board	3/4 x 4 x 24
9	1	Back	1/4 x 22 3/4 x 23 1/2
10	2	Hanging Rail	3/4 x 3 1/2 x 22 3/4
11	3	Corner Block	3/4 x 3/4 x 3

Fig. 49-41. Constructing a base cabinet. A—Saw sides for toe space. B—Saw the slots for the bottom. C—Tape marks where the saw kerf for the hanging rails begins and ends. D—Saw only one side to pencil mark for blind slot to hold shelf. E—Make a rabbet for the back. Note start and stop marks.

Again, use pencil marks on the component and tape on the fence to mark the beginning and end of the cut. See Fig. 49-41E.

8. Saw a 3/8 by 3/8 in. rabbet in each of the hanging rails to accept the cabinet back.

Assembly

The components are now ready for assembly, Fig. 49-42. Make a dry run (clamp without adhesive) to check for joint fits and overall squareness. Then glue and clamp the cabinet case, Fig. 49-43. Again check the squareness and adjust the clamps as necessary. Note that hanging rails and rabbets for the back are inset slightly. This allows for flush mounting the cabinet if walls are slightly irregular. Once the assembly is dry, you should apply laminate or graining to the sides.

Attaching the face frame

The width of the stiles and rails can vary. The face frame for this particular cabinet style has 1 1/2 in. stiles and 1 1/2 in. rails, except for a 1 in. bottom rail, Fig. 49-44. If two drawers were to be placed on top, a 1 1/2 in. wide mullion would separate them. If two doors are placed on bottom, no mullion is needed. (Install mullions only if each door is 18 in. or wider.) The frame is made slightly wider than the cabinet to allow adjacent cabinets to fit flush. Usually, the case width is 1/2 in. narrower than the face frame.

Fig. 49-44. Case, frame, and back ready for assembly.

Fig. 49-42. Cabinet components ready for assembly.

A   B

Fig. 49-43. A—Assemble the cabinet with glue and bar clamps. B—Check the squareness.

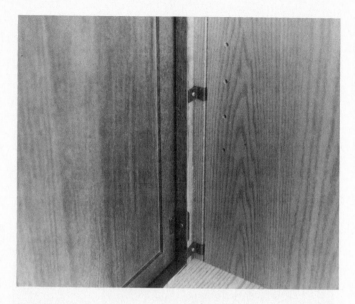

Fig. 49-45. The face frame may be attached to clips set in a groove in the cabinet side.

Face frame parts can be joined with dowels, mortise and tenon joints, or pocket joints. The frame is attached to the case by glue and nails or metal clips. Clips are fitted into a slot in the cabinet side and screwed to the frame, Fig 49-45. Plate joinery is also becoming popular for attaching the face frame to the case.

Attaching the toe board, corner blocks, and back

Next attach the toe board. It is as long as the cabinet frame is wide. It fits across the cabinet next to the floor. Glue and nail it in place with blocks, Fig. 49-46. Add corner blocks for the top, Fig. 49-47. They are glued in place and reinforced with screws. Install the back with brads or staples.

Fig. 49-46. Toe board glued with blocks and fastened with brads.

Fig. 49-47. Corner blocks position and secure the cabinet top.

Installing drawers

With the drawer assembled (see Chapter 42), add the drawer slides. One track attaches to the case and the other to the drawer side, Fig. 49-48. A spacer glued to the cabinet side may be needed to bring the drawer slide flush with the inside edge of the face frame. Once you install the slides, attach the finished front and fasten the drawer pulls.

Installing doors and pulls

Place the cabinet with its back on the floor. Mount the hinges on the door back. Position the doors to cover the opening evenly. Leave 1/16 in. between them. Drill plot holes in the frame and secure the hinges. Install magnetic or friction catches unless self-closing hinges are installed. Mark door handle locations on masking tape. Drill clearance holes for screws and install the pulls.

MAKING A WALL CABINET

Wall cabinet construction details are shown in Fig. 49-49. Wall and base units are constructed very much alike. However, the wall cabinet top is dadoed into the sides. Like base cabinets, the hanging rails are rabbeted and inserted into slots cut in the cabinet sides. This provides enough support for the cabinet and contents.

INSTALLING SITE-BUILT CABINETS

Site-built cabinets refer to custom units constructed on location. The installation varies slightly from the modular units. You install and level plinths first. This is the framework that supports the cabinets and provides toe space. They should be 21 in. from the wall. Then build the base cabinet cases in long sections. Attach face frames. Screw the cases to the plinth and to the wall. Then install built-in appliances and countertops.

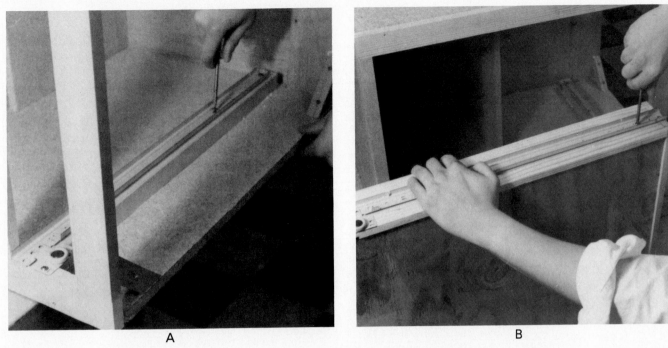

Fig. 49-48. Attaching the drawer slides. A—To the cabinet side. B—To the drawer. Make sure you align the two tracks accurately.

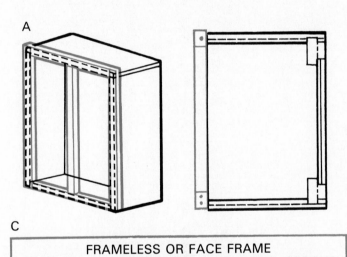

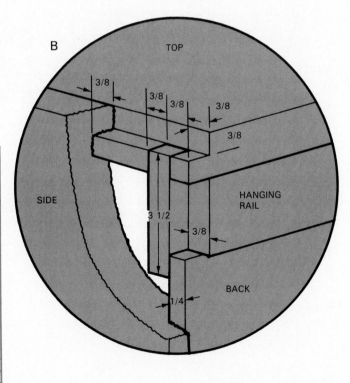

C

FRAMELESS OR FACE FRAME 24W x 30H x 12 DEEP TWO DOOR WALL CABINET WITH TWO SHELVES, FIXED OR ADJUSTABLE		
COMPONENT	FRAMELESS	FACE FRAME
Top	3/4 x 12 x 23 1/4	3/4 x 11 1/4 x 22 3/4
Side (2)	3/4 x 12 x 30	3/4 x 11 1/4 x 29 3/4
Bottom	3/4 x 12 x 23 1/4	3/4 x 11 1/4 x 22 3/4
Hanging Rail (2)	3/4 x 3 1/2 x 23 1/4	3/4 x 3 1/2 x 22 3/4
Back	1/4 x 23 1/4 x 23 3/4	1/4 x 22 3/4 x 23 1/2
Fixed Shelf (2)	3/4 x 11 5/8 x 23 1/4	3/4 x 10 7/8 x 22 3/4
OR Adjustable Shelf (2)	3/4 x 11 5/8 x 22 1/4	3/4 x 10 7/8 x 21 3/4
Top Rail		3/4 x 1 1/2 x 21
Bottom Rail		3/4 x 1 x 21
Stile (2)		3/4 x 1 1/2 x 30
Mullion		3/4 x 1 1/2 x 27
Dowels		1/4 D x 1 1/2

Fig. 49-49. A—Wall cabinet construction details with and without face frame. B—Hanging rail joinery details. C—Bill of materials.

Hole line on side panel

Standard heights of cabinets	Dimensions in inch.	mm	Number of holes	Distance
Tall cabinet (and higher)	89.449	2,272	71	32
	88.189	2,240	70	32
	86.929	2,208	69	32
	85.512	2,172	68	32
	84.409	2,144	67	32
	83.150	2,112	66	32
	81.890	2,080	65	32
	80.630	2,048	64	32
	79.370	2,016	63	32
	78.110	1,984	62	32
	76.850	1,952	61	32
	75.591	1,920	60	32
	74.331	1,888	59	32
	73.071	1,856	58	32
	71.811	1,824	57	32
	70.551	1,792	56	32
	69.291	1,760	55	32
	68.031	1,728	54	32
	66.772	1,696	53	32
	65.512	1,664	52	32
Wall cabinet	64.252	1,632	51	32
	62.992	1,600	50	32
	61.732	1,568	49	32
	60.472	1,536	48	32
	59.213	1,504	47	32
	57.953	1,472	46	32
	56.693	1,440	45	32
	55.433	1,408	44	32
	54.173	1,376	43	32
High board	52.913	1,344	42	32
	51.654	1,312	41	32
	50.394	1,280	40	32
	49.134	1,248	39	32
	47.874	1,216	38	32
	46.614	1,184	37	32
	45.354	1,152	36	32
	44.094	1,120	35	32
	42.835	1,088	34	32
	41.575	1,056	33	32
Base cabinet counter top	40.315	1,024	32	32
	39.055	992	31	32
	37.795	960	30	32
	36.535	928	29	32
	35.276	896	28	32
	34.016	864	27	32
	32.756	832	26	32
	31.496	800	25	32
Side board	30.236	768	24	32
	28.976	736	23	32
	27.717	704	22	32
	26.457	672	21	32
	25.197	640	20	32
	23.937	608	19	32
	22.677	576	18	32
	21.417	544	17	32
	20.157	512	16	32
	18.898	480	15	32
	17.638	448	14	32
	16.378	416	13	32
	15.118	384	12	32
	13.858	352	11	32
	12.598	320	10	32
	11.339	288	9	32
	10.079	256	8	32
	8.819	224	7	32
	7.559	192	6	32
	6.299	160	5	32
Toekick area	5.039	128	4	32
	3.780	96	3	32
	2.520	64	2	32
	1.259	32	1	32
	0	0	0	32

add wood thickness for top and bottom shelves. **See on page 4.3**

32 mm grid · hole line

Inches into mm

inches	mm
1	**25.40**
2	50.80
3	76.20
4	101.60
5	127.00
6	152.40
7	177.80
8	203.20
9	228.60
10	254.00
11	279.40
12	304.80
13	330.20
14	355.60
15	381.00
16	406.40
17	431.80
18	457.20
19	482.60
20	508.00
21	533.40
22	558.80
23	584.20
24	609.60
25	635.00
26	660.40
27	685.80
28	711.20
29	736.60
30	762.00
31	787.40
32	812.80
33	838.20
34	863.60
35	889.00
36	914.40
37	939.80
38	965.20
39	990.60
40	1,016.00
41	1,041.40
42	1,066.80
43	1,092.20
44	1,117.60
45	1,143.00
46	1,168.40
47	1,193.80
48	1,219.20
49	1,244.60
50	1,270.00
100	2,540.00
200	5,080.00
300	7,620.00
400	10,160.00
500	12,700.00
1000	25,400.00

Fractions into mm

inches	mm
1/16	1.59
1/8	3.18
3/16	4.76
1/4	6.35
5/16	7.94
3/8	9.53
7/16	11.11
1/2	12.70
9/16	14.29
5/8	15.88
11/16	17.46
3/4	19.05
13/16	20.64
7/8	22.23
15/16	23.81
1	**25.40**

Millimeter into inches

mm	inches
1	.039
2	.078
3	.118
4	.157
5	.197
6	.236
7	.276
8	.315
9	.354
10	.394
20	.787
30	1.181
40	1.575
50	1.968
60	2.362
70	2.756
80	3.150
90	3.543
100	**3.937**

1 Meter = 1000 mm

An example:

70.551 inch. × 25.4 mm =
1,791.99 ≈ 1,792 mm = 1.79 meter

66,772 mm ∕ 3,937 = 16.96 inch. ≈ 17 inch.

Fig. 49-50. Conversion chart to help you lay out height and hole spacing for side panels of the 32 mm system. (Hafele)

METRIC KITCHEN CABINET MEASUREMENTS

All industrialized countries, except the United States, use metric measurements. Many metric standards for kitchen cabinets are not exact conversions. Be aware of these and other measurements:

- Base cabinet height with toe space: 884 mm.
- Base cabinet height (without toe space): 784 mm.
- Base cabinet depth: 570 mm.
- Toe space height: 100 mm.
- Toe space depth: 75 mm.
- Countertop thickness: 40 mm.
- Countertop depth: 600 mm.
- Wall unit depth: 280 to 300 mm.
- Wall unit heights: 752, 560, 464, 368 mm.
- Tall cabinet height: 2 132 mm.
- Modular widths (coordinate with inch-standard cabinets): 1 220, 1 070, 920, 610, 533, 457, 381, 305 mm.
- Modular widths (metric only): 300, 400, 450, 600, 900, 1 0000, 1 2000 mm.
- Material thickness: 13, 16, 19 mm.
- Lowest edge of range hood: 650 mm.
- Height of pull-out surfaces to allow a knee space: 650 to 700 mm.

The chart given in Fig. 49-50 provides inch-to-metric conversions for typical cabinet heights. The format allows you to lay out the 32 mm holes. As noted, remember to add the wood thickness to the side panel height. This allows the cabinet bottom and top to fasten flush with the sides.

SUMMARY

The kitchen is one of the most functional rooms of a home. It must be designed to be convenient and efficient. Planning begins with determining the tasks to be performed. Many activities are related to the preparation and consumption of food.

To support kitchen activities, you must consider storage, work centers, appliance areas, utilities, and other potential uses of the room. One measure of function is the kitchen triangle. Short paths between the sink, range-oven, and refrigerator are part of an efficient kitchen. Designs you might choose include one-wall, corridor, L-shape, U-shape, peninsula, and island layouts.

The four basic types of cabinets are wall, base, tall, and specialty units. Manufactured base cabinets come as standard height and depth, in 3 in. width increments. Wall units can vary in height, as well as width. Tall units are 84 in. high with varying widths. Specialty cabinets include corner units, sink/cooktop fronts, suspended units, hutches, bottle racks, and appliance garages.

When planning a kitchen, first measure the available area and make a rough sketch. Then determine kitchen appliances and features. Arrange the appliances and cabinets in an attractive and efficient manner. Work carefully. Once installed, utilities are expensive to relocate.

Installation follows. Lay out the walls by locating studs and measuring cabinet heights and position. Have the kitchen walls and soffit finished. Finally, install wall, then base units. It is best to connect the range hood and vent before the base units. Otherwise, you must reach over the base cabinets. Cabinets are attached to the wall and to each other. The final steps are to mount the countertop and make any necessary cutouts for the sink or cooktop.

CABINETMAKING TERMS

Kitchen cabinets, work center, kitchen triangle, one-wall kitchen, corridor kitchen, L-shaped kitchen, U-shaped kitchen, peninsula kitchen, island kitchen, roll-out tray, vertical dividers, false-front tray, dry-storage bin, slide-out towel rack, swing-out shelves, swing-up shelf, base cabinet, sink/cooktop base, wall cabinet, tall cabinet, oven cabinet, corner cabinet, blind corner cabinet, corner base carousel, diagonal wall cabinet, sink/cooktop front, suspended cabinet, hutch, appliance garage, countertop.

TEST YOUR KNOWLEDGE

1. The primary purpose of any cabinet is _____.
2. List five work centers.
3. Name three essential large kitchen appliances.
4. Find the height and width measurements of the three appliances listed in Question 3. in Question 3.
5. A utility not needed for a sink with a disposal is:
   a. Electricity.
   b. Water.
   c. Sewer.
   d. Gas.
6. A kitchen should provide _____ and _____.
7. The kitchen triangle is the path between the _____, _____, and _____.
8. List six kitchen designs, or layouts.
9. Name a cabinet accessory that helps store cookie sheets.
10. On what cabinet accessory might a mixer be mounted?
11. The four categories of kitchen cabinet types are:
12. Manufactured kitchen cabinet sizes are based on a _____ _____.
13. Why must you use a sink/cooktop base or false front under a sink?
14. Countertops are made to order in sections

generally _____ in. deep and _____ in. thick.

15. Sketch two specialty cabinet arrangements that maximize storage space in a corner.
16. Lazy Susans improve access in:
    a. Wall cabinets.
    b. Corner cabinets.
    c. Tall cabinets.
    d. Base cabinets.
17. Kitchen cabinets are manufactured in modular width increments of:
    a. 3 in.
    b. 4 in.
    c. 6 in.
    d. 12 in.

18. Most often, the sink is centered under a _____.
19. List the three steps of kitchen layout.
20. When laying out a kitchen, you need only elevation sketches. True or False?
21. You can locate studs without driving nails into the walls. True or False?
22. Explain why you clamp face frames together when fastening adjoining cabinets.
23. Generally, the soffit is installed after the wall cabinets are hung. True or False?
24. All kitchen range hood vents exhaust air to the outside. True or False?
25. Counter top cutouts are needed for _____ and _____.

Chapter 50
FURNITURE

After studying this chapter, you will be able to:
☐*Describe several types of desks.*
☐*Identify the details involved in making a clock.*
☐*Construct bed frames for standard and water-filled mattresses.*
☐*Recognize the purposes of a canopy bed.*
☐*Identify a cheval mirror.*
☐*Design flat and case-type room dividers.*
☐*Explain the advantages of dual purpose furniture.*

Many cabinetmaking procedures and products have been described in this text. You have learned about case goods, kitchens, frame and panel construction, and many other cabinetmaking techniques. Actually, there is no end to the number of creative products you might build.

This chapter samples the wide range of furniture and cabinet products you might encounter. Exploded views are used to show the design information needed to thoroughly plan a product.

DESKS

There are many styles of desks. They may have drawers on one or both sides. Rolltop desks include a top section and tambour door. Fig. 50-1 shows several styles of executive desks. Fig. 50-2 shows a set of plans for a pedestal desk.

Desks often have multiple parts that are the same size—the sides, drawer parts, frames, etc. Always process duplicate parts at the same time. You set up the machine only once to insure that all components are the same size.

CLOCKS

Clocks hang, sit on mantels and tables, or stand on the floor. Fig. 50-3 shows the working drawings for several clocks. One is a mantel clock and the other a Shaker style clock to hang on the wall. Study them carefully and note the components and subassemblies. This detailed work is part of planning a product.

A

B

C

Fig. 50-1. A—Solid cherry seven-drawer desk. (Miller Desk) B—Scandinavian style desk. (Dyrlund-Smith) C—Laminated particleboard desk made with RTA fasteners. (O'Sullivan)

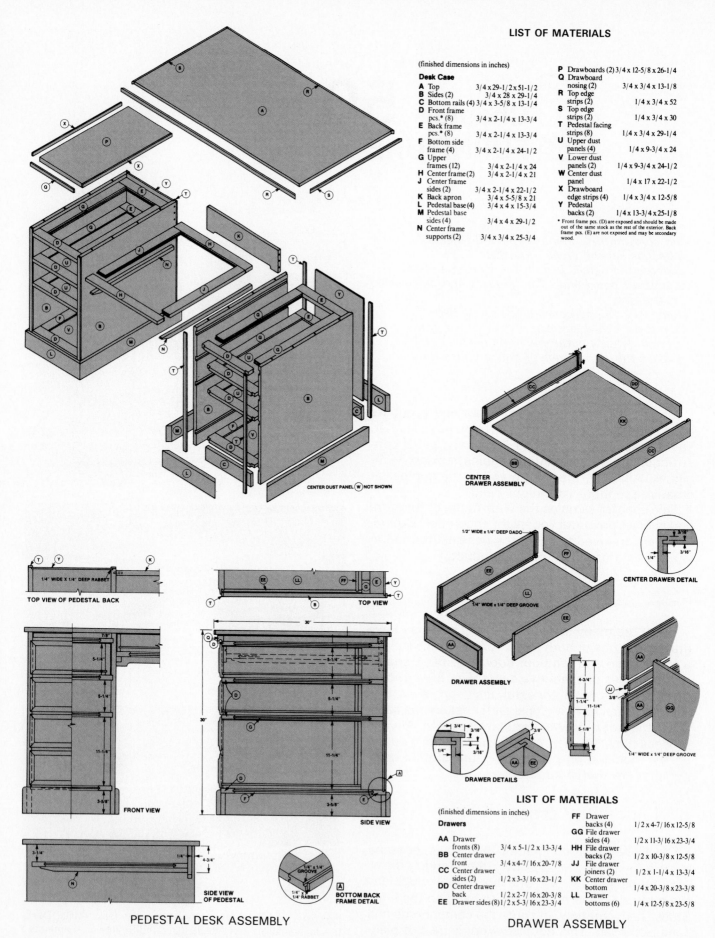

LIST OF MATERIALS

(finished dimensions in inches)

Desk Case

A	Top	3/4 x 29-1/2 x 51-1/2
B	Sides (2)	3/4 x 28 x 29-1/4
C	Bottom rails (4)	3/4 x 3-5/8 x 13-1/4
D	Front frame pcs.* (8)	3/4 x 2-1/4 x 13-3/4
E	Back frame pcs.* (8)	3/4 x 2-1/4 x 13-3/4
F	Bottom side frame (4)	3/4 x 2-1/4 x 24-1/2
G	Upper frames (12)	3/4 x 2-1/4 x 24
H	Center frame (2)	3/4 x 2-1/4 x 21
J	Center frame sides (2)	3/4 x 2-1/4 x 22-1/2
K	Back apron	3/4 x 5-5/8 x 21
L	Pedestal base (4)	3/4 x 4 x 15-3/4
M	Pedestal base sides (4)	3/4 x 4 x 29-1/2
N	Center frame supports (2)	3/4 x 3/4 x 25-3/4

P	Drawboards (2)	3/4 x 12-5/8 x 26-1/4
Q	Drawboard nosing (2)	3/4 x 3/4 x 13-1/8
R	Top edge strips (2)	1/4 x 3/4 x 52
S	Top edge strips (2)	1/4 x 3/4 x 30
T	Pedestal facing strips (8)	1/4 x 3/4 x 29-1/4
U	Upper dust panels (4)	1/4 x 9-3/4 x 24
V	Lower dust panels (2)	1/4 x 9-3/4 x 24-1/2
W	Center dust panel	1/4 x 17 x 22-1/2
X	Drawboard edge strips (4)	1/4 x 3/4 x 12-5/8
Y	Pedestal backs (2)	1/4 x 13-3/4 x 25-1/8

* Front frame pcs. (D) are exposed and should be made out of the same stock as the rest of the exterior. Back frame pcs. (E) are not exposed and may be secondary wood.

CENTER DUST PANEL (W) NOT SHOWN

CENTER DRAWER ASSEMBLY

1/2" WIDE x 1/4" DEEP DADO

CENTER DRAWER DETAIL

DRAWER ASSEMBLY

1/4" WIDE x 1/4" DEEP GROOVE

DRAWER DETAILS

1/4" WIDE x 1/4" DEEP GROOVE

TOP VIEW OF PEDESTAL BACK

1/4" WIDE x 1/4" DEEP RABBET

TOP VIEW

FRONT VIEW

SIDE VIEW

SIDE VIEW OF PEDESTAL

BOTTOM BACK FRAME DETAIL

1/4" x 1/4" GROOVE

1/4" RABBET

PEDESTAL DESK ASSEMBLY

DRAWER ASSEMBLY

LIST OF MATERIALS

(finished dimensions in inches)

Drawers

AA	Drawer fronts (8)	3/4 x 5-1/2 x 13-3/4
BB	Center drawer front	3/4 x 4-7/16 x 20-7/8
CC	Center drawer sides (2)	1/2 x 3-3/16 x 23-1/2
DD	Center drawer back	1/2 x 2-7/16 x 20-3/8
EE	Drawer sides (8)	1/2 x 5-3/16 x 23-3/4

FF	Drawer backs (4)	1/2 x 4-7/16 x 12-5/8
GG	File drawer sides (4)	1/2 x 11-3/16 x 23-3/4
HH	File drawer backs (2)	1/2 x 10-3/8 x 12-5/8
JJ	File drawer joiners (2)	1/2 x 1-1/4 x 13-3/4
KK	Center drawer bottom	1/4 x 20-3/8 x 23-3/8
LL	Drawer bottoms (6)	1/4 x 12-5/8 x 23-5/8

Fig. 50-2. Plans for a desk with a pedestal base. (Shopsmith, Inc.)

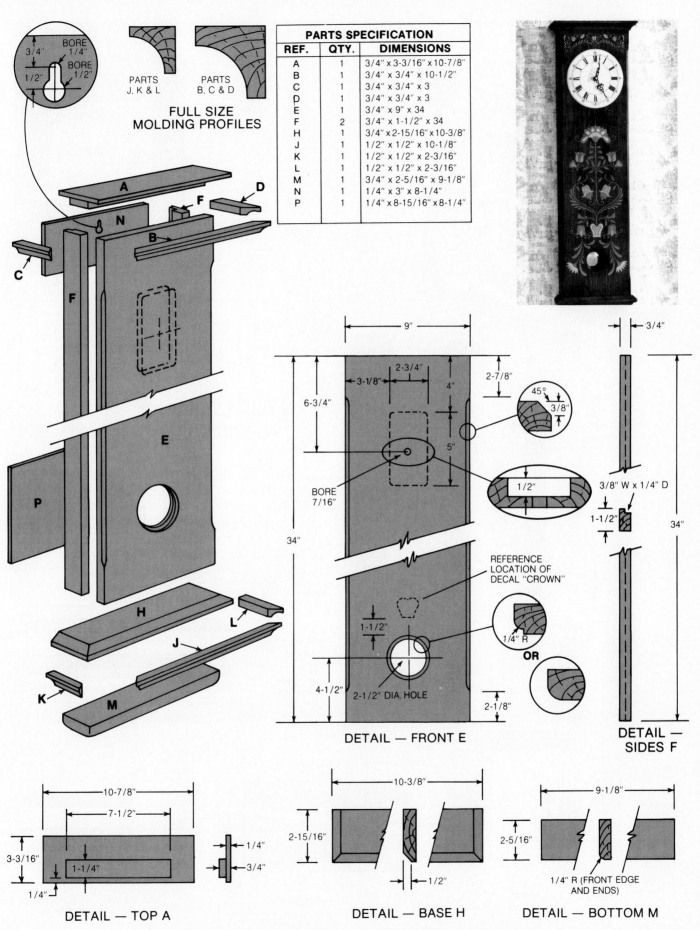

BORE 1/4"
3/4"
BORE 1/2"
1/2"   1/2"

PARTS J, K & L   PARTS B, C & D

FULL SIZE MOLDING PROFILES

PARTS SPECIFICATION		
REF.	**QTY.**	**DIMENSIONS**
A	1	3/4" x 3-3/16" x 10-7/8"
B	1	3/4" x 3/4" x 10-1/2"
C	1	3/4" x 3/4" x 3
D	1	3/4" x 3/4" x 3
E	1	3/4" x 9" x 34
F	2	3/4" x 1-1/2" x 34
H	1	3/4" x 2-15/16" x 10-3/8"
J	1	1/2" x 1/2" x 10-1/8"
K	1	1/2" x 1/2" x 2-3/16"
L	1	1/2" x 1/2" x 2-3/16"
M	1	3/4" x 2-5/16" x 9-1/8"
N	1	1/4" x 3" x 8-1/4"
P	1	1/4" x 8-15/16" x 8-1/4"

A
D
F
N
B
C
F
P
E
H
L
J
K
M

9"
2-3/4"
3-1/8"
4"
2-7/8"
6-3/4"
45°
3/8"
5"
BORE 7/16"
1/2"
34"
1-1/2"
REFERENCE LOCATION OF DECAL "CROWN"
1-1/2"
1/4" R
OR
4-1/2"
2-1/2" DIA. HOLE
2-1/8"

DETAIL — FRONT E

3/4"
3/8" W x 1/4" D
1-1/2"
34"

DETAIL — SIDES F

10-7/8"
7-1/2"
3-3/16"
1-1/4"
1/4"
1/4"
3/4"

DETAIL — TOP A

10-3/8"
2-15/16"
1/2"

DETAIL — BASE H

9-1/8"
2-5/16"
1/4" R (FRONT EDGE AND ENDS)

DETAIL — BOTTOM M

Fig. 50-3. A—Shaker style clock and working drawings. (Craft Products)   Fig. 50-3 continued.

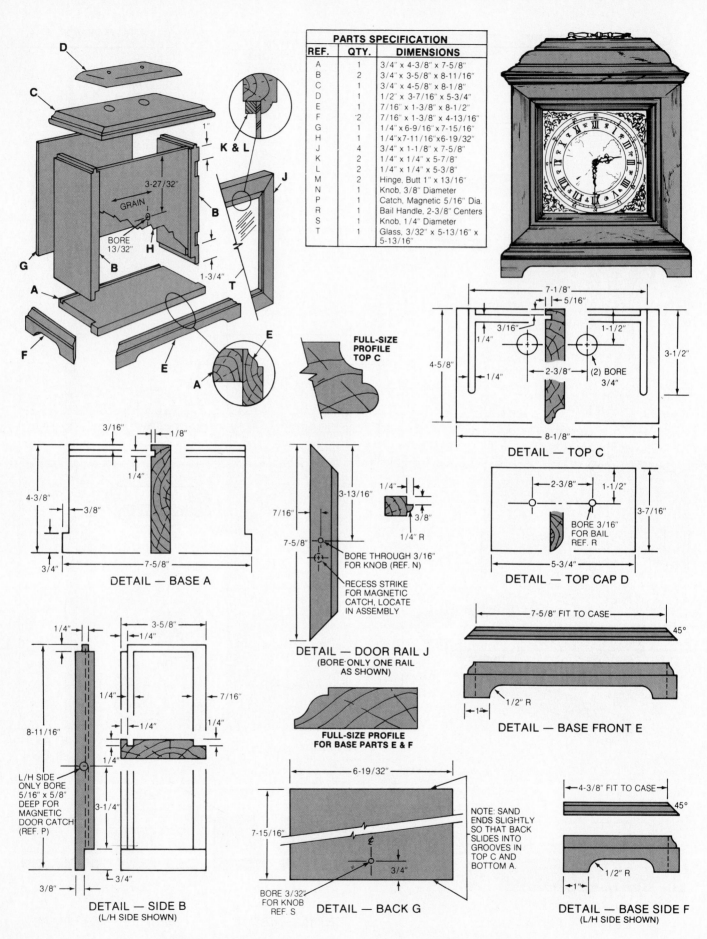

PARTS SPECIFICATION

REF.	QTY.	DIMENSIONS
A	1	3/4" x 4-3/8" x 7-5/8"
B	2	3/4" x 3-5/8" x 8-11/16"
C	1	3/4" x 4-5/8" x 8-1/8"
D	1	1/2" x 3-7/16" x 5-3/4"
E	1	7/16" x 1-3/8" x 8-1/2"
F	2	7/16" x 1-3/8" x 4-13/16"
G	1	1/4" x 6-9/16" x 7-15/16"
H	1	1/4"x 7-11/16"x 6-19/32"
J	4	3/4" x 1-1/8" x 7-5/8"
K	2	1/4" x 1/4" x 5-7/8"
L	2	1/4" x 1/4" x 5-3/8"
M	2	Hinge, Butt 1" x 13/16"
N	1	Knob, 3/8" Diameter
P	1	Catch, Magnetic 5/16" Dia.
R	1	Bail Handle, 2-3/8" Centers
S	1	Knob, 1/4" Diameter
T	1	Glass, 3/32" x 5-13/16" x 5-13/16"

DETAIL — TOP C

DETAIL — TOP CAP D

DETAIL — BASE A

DETAIL — BASE FRONT E

DETAIL — DOOR RAIL J
(BORE ONLY ONE RAIL AS SHOWN)

FULL-SIZE PROFILE FOR BASE PARTS E & F

FULL-SIZE PROFILE TOP C

DETAIL — SIDE B
(L/H SIDE SHOWN)

DETAIL — BACK G

DETAIL — BASE SIDE F
(L/H SIDE SHOWN)

Fig. 50-3. B—Mantel clock and working drawings. (Craft Products)

Clocks have always been a favorite product of amateur and experienced cabinetmakers alike. Early cabinetmakers made clocks with hand-carved wooden movements. The *movement* is the mechanism that keeps time. Today, clocks are mechanically wound, use electric motors, or have battery-driven quartz movements. Choose the desired movement during the design stage since it often affects the clock size, Fig. 50-4.

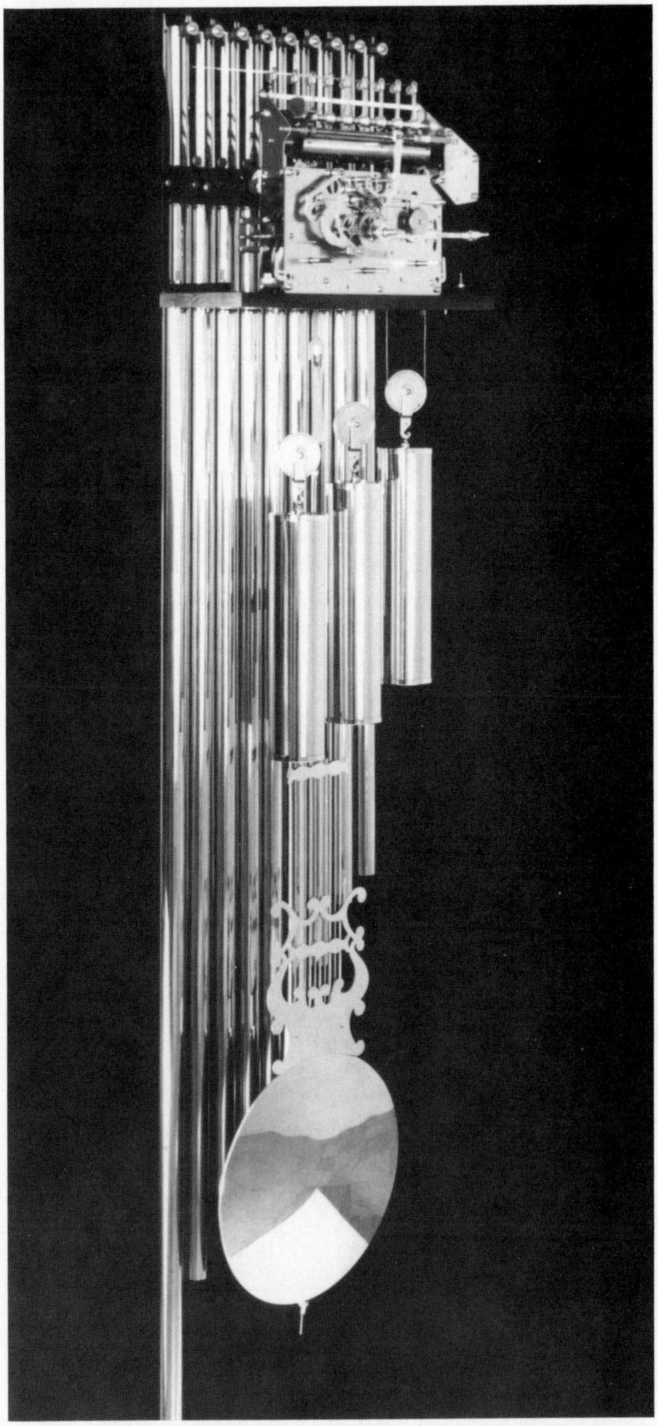

There are companies that sell clock movements and parts. Also check your local crafts store for clock parts.

CHAIRS

Chairs are difficult to build if they involve compound leg angles. Few chairs are stable if the legs are perpendicular to the seat. In addition, front leg angles typically differ from back leg angles.

The Captain's chair shown in Fig. 50-5 is an example of a permanent spindle leg assembly. Drill the leg sockets while the seat still has square corners. Build a fixture to let you drill compound angles. Set the side angle at 12 degrees with a T-bevel. Raise the fixture. Set the front or back angles at 8 degrees with the T-bevel. Use a Forstner bit centered over the drill press table to drill the holes.

Fig. 50-4. Triple chime movement for a grandfather or grandmother clock. (Craft Products)

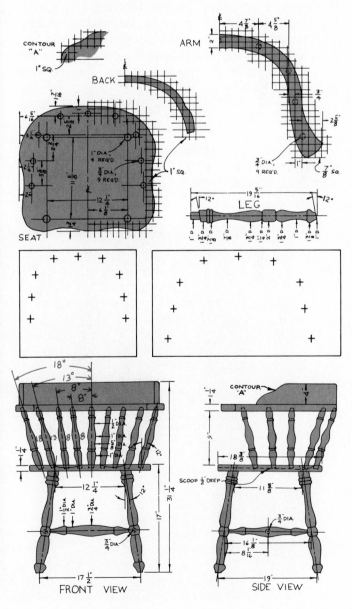

Fig. 50-5. Design for a Captain's chair. (Stanley)

Next, drill the arm and back rest spindles. Start with the center spindle in the back. Set your compound angle fixture to the 18 degree back angle. Drill the back row of holes. Then, drill the holes in the left side of the seat top. Finally, drill the holes in the right side of the seat top. Follow this same procedure to drill the holes in the arm rest.

BEDS

Beds are an integral part of the cabinetmaking field. In fact, they are usually only one part of a bedroom set containing dressers, nightstands, and possibly, a desk or chest, Fig. 50-6.

A typical bed contains several parts, including the frame, headboard, and, sometimes, a footboard. Some styles might include posts and, possibly, a canopy.

The box springs and mattress rest in the frame. *Box springs* are wood frames separated by spring coils, and enclosed in a cover material. *Standard mattresses* contain foam and/or coils under padding in a cloth cover material. *Water-filled mattresses* are much like vinyl inner tubes. They can be soft-side or hard-side.

FRAMES

Bed frames support the box springs and mattress. Visible frames are usually made of wood and finished to match the headboard and footboard. Hidden frames are typically made of angle iron and are adjustable to mattress size.

Frames must be sized or adjusted to various mattress dimensions. There are king, queen, full, twin, and single sizes, Fig. 50-7. The dimensions differ slightly for standard and water-filled mattresses.

Frames for cotton mattresses

Support for a cotton mattress frame is the headboard, two rails, and a footboard, Fig. 50-8. The inside dimensions are slightly larger than the box springs. On wood rail frames, cleats are glued and screwed inside. Three or four slats, in turn, support the box springs and mattress.

Frames should not be permanently assembled. Special two-piece bed rail fasteners for wood frames allow you to assemble and disassemble the frame easily, Fig. 50-9. One piece fits in a recess routed in the headboard and footboard. The other is bolted, screwed, or pinned to the side rail.

Another style, the platform frame, has become common in contemporary furniture, Fig. 50-10. It resembles the frame for a water bed, but requires less support since the mattress is relatively light.

Frames for water-filled mattresses

The mattress for a water bed is very heavy. A king size water-filled mattress can weigh close to a ton. Strong, well supported frames are required. The weight is supported by a plain or cabinet-type *platform* beneath the mattress, Fig. 50-11.

Fig. 50-6. A typical bedroom set. The wood bed frame is hidden by the bedspread. (Thomasville)

Type	Cotton or foam mattresses and box springs	Water bed	
		Hard-side	Soft-side
Super Single		48 x 84 1 220 x 2 130	
Twin	36 x 74 915 x 1 880		36 x 74 915 x 1 880
Full	54 x 74 1 370 x 1 880		54 x 74 1 370 x 1 880
Queen	60 x 80 1 524 x 2 032	60 x 84 1 524 x 2 134	60 x 80 1 524 x 2 032
King	76 x 80 1 930 x 2 032	72 x 84 1 830 x 2 134	76 x 80 1 930 x 2 032
Bassinet	18 x 36 457 x 915		
	22 x 39 559 x 990		
Junior Crib	23 x 46 584 x 1 168		
	25 x 51 559 x 1295		
6-Year Crib	27 x 51 686 x 1 295		
	31 x 57 788 x 1 448		
Youth Bed	33 x 66 838 x 1 676		
	36 x 76 915 x 1 930		

BEDDING SIZES
(In inches and millimeters)

Fig. 50-7. Standard mattress sizes.

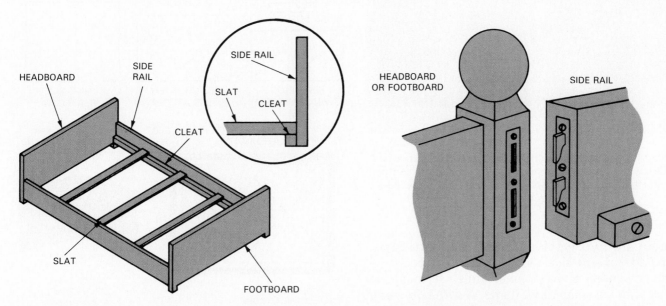

Fig. 50-8. A standard mattress is held in a frame formed by the headboard, footboard, and two side rails.

Fig. 50-9. Bed rail fasteners connect the rails to the headboard and footboard. (Woodworkers' Store)

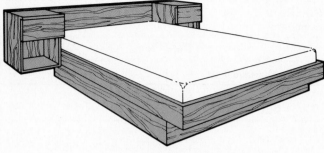

Fig. 50-10. Platform bed made with oak veneer over pine. This model is shipped disassembled. (Unfinished Furniture)

A

B

Fig. 50-11. A—Water bed with plain platform. B—Cabinet-type platform with drawers underneath. At the end of the bed you can see that the drawer cases were made in three parts. (Trendwest)

There are two types of water bed mattresses: hard-side and soft-side. A *hard-side water bed mattress* is simply a vinyl inner tube. It must be placed within a solid (hard) frame. A *soft-side water bed mattress* requires no frame. The edges of the mattress include firm, but soft, foam edges that pro-

vide support and contain the water. A soft-side mattress can be used with most any frame as long as an extra supportive platform is placed underneath. This discussion will focus on making a hard-side mattress frame.

The mattress itself sits inside a *plastic liner* which holds the water should the mattress leak. The liner fits inside the rails. Refer to the details in Fig. 50-12. Panels inside the side rails, headboard, and footboard hold the liner in place. Most liners today have hardboard panels attached with a 1/4 in. spacer to the edges to hold it in place inside the frame. The liner stops 1 in. below the top edge of the side rails and should lie flat on the platform and in the corners.

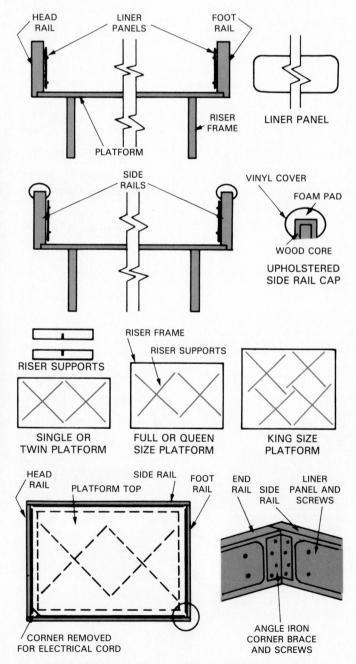

Fig. 50-12. Details for a plain platform, hard-side water bed.

The mattress rails rest on the platform with a 1/2 in. plywood or 5/8 in. particleboard top. The rails, usually 2 x 10 lumber, are rabbeted 3/4 in. by 3/4 in. along the inside bottom edge. The platform fits inside this rabbet to support the rails and keep them square. The side rails should have blind rabbets so that the cuts are not seen. The rails are joined at the corners with 1/8 x 1 1/4 x 7 in. angle iron or angle braces and wood screws. See the construction dimensions given in Fig. 50-13. People who prefer not to have a hard edge on the side rails can install upholstered side rail caps.

Platforms

You can support water bed platforms one of two ways. A simple platform merely sits on several vertical supports. A cabinet-type platform makes efficient use of the area below the bed with doors and/or drawers for storage.

Plain platforms. *Plain platforms* consist of a riser frame, interior riser supports, and a top. The riser supports are 1/2 in. plywood or 5/8 in. particleboard about 9 to 12 in. high. Corner blocks, corner irons, or metal clips are needed to hold the riser frame together. These are fastened with screws to allow for easy disassembly.

Make the platform support about 8 in. shorter and somewhat narrower than the mattress frame. Finish the riser frame with black paint so that it is not readily visible, or finish it to match the headboard and mattress frame.

The inside riser supports are assembled with lap joints to form several "X" shapes under the platform top. Try to have no more than 18 in. of unsupported area under the platform. Use more interior risers for a king size bed than for smaller sizes.

The platform top consists of two or three pieces of 1/2 in. plywood or 5/8 in. particleboard. Size the platform top accurately since it must fit the rabbet cut in the mattress frame. This keeps the mattress frame square. Cut about 1 in. off one corner of the platform top to allow for the electrical cord that powers the mattress heater.

Cabinet platforms. *Cabinet platforms* support the mattress and provide doors or drawers for access to storage. Size the platform about 2 to 3 in. less than the mattress length and width. Then you are less likely to kick or trip on the door and drawer pulls.

It is best to build two or more separate cases that combine to form the cabinet platform. This makes the platform easier to move. There is no need to put a top on the cases since the platform top will serve that purpose. Remember, use sturdy case construction techniques since the cases must support an immense amount of weight.

HEADBOARD

The *headboard* protects the wall, provides decoration, and sometimes offers storage. The simplest type, a *flat headboard,* usually is a frame and spindle or frame and panel assembly. The headboard connects to metal frames with a bolt. It usually is a part of wood frames. Flat headboards are often accompanied by nightstands to store books, clocks,

BILL OF MATERIALS FOR PLAIN WATERBED FRAMES					
MATTRESS RAIL	Single	Twin	Full	Queen	King
LENGTHS Sides (2 x 10)	87	87	87	87	87
Ends (2 x 10)	36	39	54	60	72
LINER LENGTHS Sides	81	81	81	81	81
Ends	33	36	51	57	69
PLATFORM Top Widths	37 1/2	40 1/2	55 1/2	61 1/2	73 1/2
Top Lengths	85 1/2	85 1/2	85 1/2	85 1/2	85 1/2
Riser Frame Lengths (Foot and Head)	31	32	46	52	64
Riser Frame Widths	9	9	9	9	9
Riser Frame Lengths	79	79	79	79	79
Inside Supports Widths	9	9	9	9	9
Inside Supports Lengths			variable		
RAIL CORNER BRACES 1/8 x 1 1/4 x 1 1/4 angle iron 7 in. long					
PLATFORM RISER CORNER BRACES 2 x 2 in. wood variable length or angle iron					

Fig. 50-13. Dimensions for constructing a plain platform for various mattress sizes.

radios, or other items, Fig. 50-14.

Bookcase headboards have depth for storage areas, Fig. 50-15. Often, they replace nightstands when space around the bed is limited. The headboard can hold a bed lamp, clock radio, books, or other items. The storage areas could be open shelves or have sliding doors.

FOOTBOARDS

Footboards prevent bedspreads from slipping off the bed and often provide decoration. They are usually frame and spindle or frame and panel assemblies. When wood rails are used, the footboard becomes part of the frame.

CANOPY/POSTER BEDS

Canopy beds are very decorative. Some have an arch shaped, fringed cloth canopy or cover, Fig. 50-16. They can provide privacy with the addition of curtains. Beneath the cloth is a wooden frame with canopy support slats. The two side frames may be segment glued or bent wood. Corners are joined with lap joints. A finial with a dowel under it fits through the frame and into the corner post. This holds the cloth-covered frame in place about 7 ft. above the floor. By removing the canopy and installing the finials, you have a tall poster bed, Fig. 50-17. Shorter poster beds are available. On these, the finial shape is turned on the post. Corner posts are 4 to 4 1/2 ft. from the floor.

Fig. 50-14. Nightstands are typically found with a flat headboard. (Thomasville)

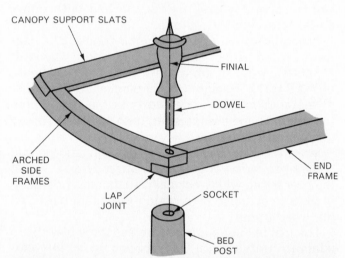

Fig. 50-15. Bookcase headboard with a cabinet-type platform. (Trendwest)

Fig. 50-16. Arched canopy bed with finials. (Ethan Allen)

Fig. 50-17. Poster bed. (Ethan Allen)

Some canopy beds have a visible wooden tester frame mounted on the corner posts, Fig. 50-18. There may be a cloth canopy inside the frame. The tester is also connected to the corner posts with dowels. Curtains or drapes often are added for decoration and privacy.

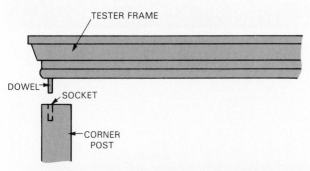

Fig. 50-18. Tester canopy bed. (Ethan Allen)

CASTERS

Beds with cotton mattresses can have casters installed in the headboard and footboard. The bed can then be moved for cleaning and arranging furniture. Barrel-shaped roller casters are recommended.

MIRROR FRAMES

Mirrors are attached to walls, dresser backs, and closet doors. They also can be supported in a stand, called a *cheval mirror,* Fig. 50-19. The size will vary according to your needs.

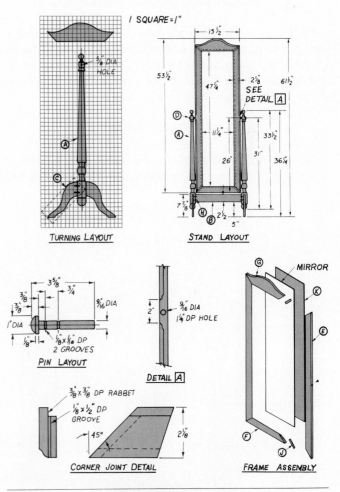

Bill of Materials
(finished dimensions in inches)

A	Spindles (2)	2 x 2 x 34
B	Stretcher	3/4 x 2-1/2 x 16
C	Legs (4)	3/4 x 3-1/2 x 10-1/2
D	Pivot pins (2)	1" dia. x 3-5/8
E	Stiles (2)	3/4 x 2-1/8 x 51-3/8
F	Bottom rail	3/4 x 2-1/8 x 15-1/2
G	Top rail	3/4 x 4-1/4 x 15-1/2
H	Dowel pins (12)	5/16" dia. x 2
J	Splines (4)	1/8 x 1 x 3-1/2
K	Mirror back	1/8 x 12 x 48

Hardware

1/8" x 12" x 48" Mirror
8 Mirror retainer clips
4 3/8" I.D. O-ring
2 #8 x 3/4" Flathead wood screws

Fig. 50-19. This elegant cheval mirror tilts to adjust for a full view. (Shopsmith, Inc.)

The stand is quite simple. The spindles may be round or square and tapered. Round spindles may be difficult to turn if the lathe bed is too short. Then, turn the spindles in two parts.

ROOM DIVIDERS

Room dividers are used to separate work areas, reduce drafts, or provide privacy. They may be solid, part wall and part open, or contain glass or plastic panels. Dividers can be flat, or resemble case goods, with shelves and possibly doors or drawers, Fig. 50-20. Case-type dividers should be flexible and have adjustable shelving.

FOLDAWAY WORK BENCH

Work benches are valuable to the do-it-yourself person. In apartments and other areas where space is limited, a foldup tabletop provides adequate surface but folds away for convenient storage. Refer to the drawings in Fig. 50-21.

DUAL-PURPOSE FURNITURE

Apartments and small rooms allow only a limited selection of furniture. Dual-purpose furniture comes

A

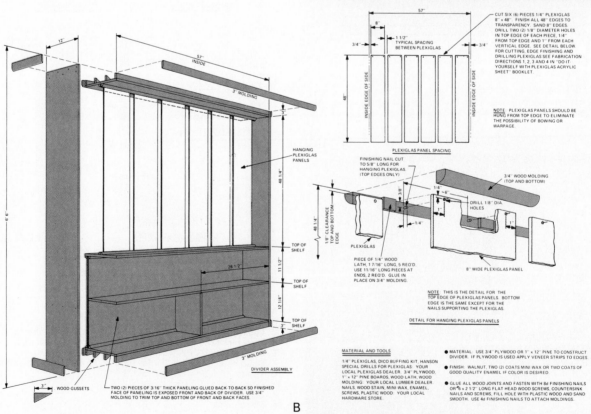

B

Fig. 50-20. Room dividers set off entries and separate large areas. A—Flat room divider. B—Plans for a case-type room divider. (Rohm and Haas)

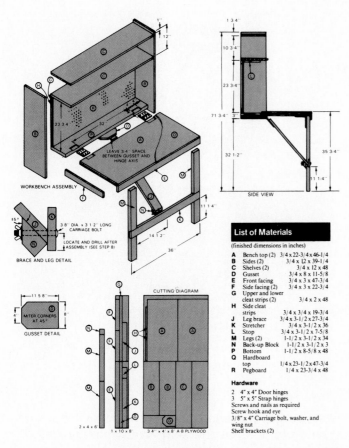

WORKBENCH ASSEMBLY

BRACE AND LEG DETAIL

3/8" DIA. x 3 1/2" LONG CARRIAGE BOLT

LOCATE AND DRILL AFTER ASSEMBLY (SEE STEP 8)

GUSSET DETAIL

MITER CORNERS AT 45°

LEAVE 3/4" SPACE BETWEEN GUSSET AND HINGE AXIS

SIDE VIEW

CUTTING DIAGRAM

List of Materials

(finished dimensions in inches)

A	Bench top (2)	3/4 x 22-3/4 x 46-1/4
B	Sides (2)	3/4 x 12 x 39-1/4
C	Shelves (2)	3/4 x 12 x 48
D	Gusset	3/4 x 8 x 11-5/8
E	Front facing	3/4 x 3 x 47-3/4
F	Side facing (2)	3/4 x 3 x 22-3/4
G	Upper and lower cleat strips (2)	3/4 x 2 x 48
H	Side cleat strips	3/4 x 3/4 x 19-3/4
J	Leg brace	3/4 x 3-1/2 x 27-3/4
K	Stretcher	3/4 x 3-1/2 x 36
L	Stop	3/4 x 3-1/2 x 7-5/8
M	Legs (2)	1-1/2 x 3-1/2 x 34
N	Back-up Block	1-1/2 x 3-1/2 x 3
P	Bottom	1-1/2 x 8-5/8 x 48
Q	Hardboard top	1/4 x 23-1/2 x 47-3/4
R	Pegboard	1/4 x 23-3/4 x 48

Hardware

2 4" x 4" Door hinges
3 5" x 5" Strap hinges
Screws and nails as required
Screw hook and eye
3/8" x 4" Carriage bolt, washer, and wing nut
Shelf brackets (2)

Fig. 50-21. A foldup workbench provides convenience in small spaces. (Shopsmith, Inc.)

in handy where space is limited. The example in Fig. 50-22 is a table when the top is horizontal, but provides sitting space with the top vertical. The seat also contains a drawer.

An alternative to the example in Fig. 50-23 is to make the top square. The seat might have a lid for

Fig. 50-22. This piece of furniture serves as a table and bench. It also has a storage area under the seat. (Unfinished Furniture)

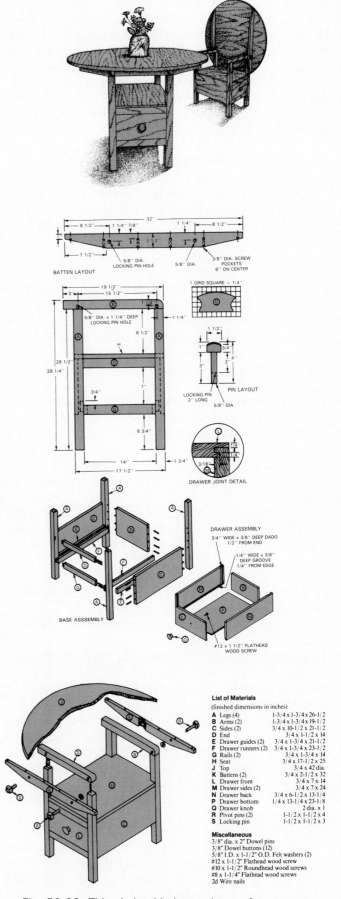

BATTEN LAYOUT

5/8" DIA. LOCKING PIN HOLE

3/8" DIA. SCREW POCKETS 6" ON CENTER

5/8" DIA.

1 GRID SQUARE = 1/4"

5/8" DIA. x 1 1/4" DEEP LOCKING PIN HOLE

LOCKING PIN 2" LONG 5/8" DIA.

PIN LAYOUT

DRAWER JOINT DETAIL

BASE ASSEMBLY

DRAWER ASSEMBLY
3/4" WIDE x 3/8" DEEP DADO 1/2" FROM END
1/4" WIDE x 3/8" DEEP GROOVE 1/4" FROM EDGE

#12 x 1 1/2" FLATHEAD WOOD SCREW

List of Materials

(finished dimensions in inches)

A	Legs (4)	1-3/4 x 1-3/4 x 26-1/2
B	Arms (2)	1-3/4 x 1-3/4 x 19-1/2
C	Sides (2)	3/4 x 10-1/2 x 21-1/2
D	End	3/4 x 1-1/2 x 14
E	Drawer guides (2)	3/4 x 1-3/4 x 21-1/2
F	Drawer runners (2)	3/4 x 1-3/4 x 23-1/2
G	Rails (2)	3/4 x 1-3/4 x 14
H	Seat	3/4 x 17-1/2 x 25
J	Top	3/4 x 42 dia.
K	Battens (2)	3/4 x 2-1/2 x 32
L	Drawer front	3/4 x 7 x 14
M	Drawer sides (2)	3/4 x 7 x 24
N	Drawer back	3/4 x 6-1/2 x 13-1/4
P	Drawer bottom	1/4 x 13-1/4 x 23-1/8
Q	Drawer knob	2 dia. x 1
R	Pivot pins (2)	1-1/2 x 1-1/2 x 4
S	Locking pin	1-1/2 x 1-1/2 x 3

Miscellaneous

3/8" dia. x 2" Dowel pins
3/8" Dowel buttons (12)
5/8" I.D. x 1-1/2" O.D. Felt washers (2)
#12 x 1-1/2" Flathead wood screw
#10 x 1-1/2" Roundhead wood screws
#8 x 1-1/4" Flathead wood screws
2d Wire nails

Fig. 50-23. This chair-table has a drawer for storage. (Shopsmith, Inc.)

access to storage. Select a strong positioning or locking joint to provide the greatest stability. Start by making a box with a lid that is slightly short. This keeps the lid from rubbing when it is raised. Any of several positioning or locking joints can be used. They provide the greatest stability yet are not visible from the outside. The pivot pin position for the lid is critical. Drill holes in matching sides at the same time.

PRODUCT IDEAS

Illustrations throughout this book have presented various products. To show all types and styles would be impossible. The following list should help you select products to design and build.

Beds
Bunk: one bed over another, usually twin size. You reach the upper bed with a ladder.
Canopy, arched: poster bed with a cloth-covered straight or arch-shaped metal or laminated wood frame overhead. Often includes curtains on the sides for privacy. A wood finial (cap) tops each corner.
Canopy, tester: a bed with a visible straight wood frame, that may have curtains or drapes.
Platform: bed with mattress on a platform rather than legs.
Poster: bed with corner posts much higher than the headboard. Tall ones could support a canopy or tester.
Trundle: nested beds, usually twin size, where the lower bed rolls out on casters from storage under the other bed.

Chairs
Captain's: type of Windsor chair with saddle seat and low bent wood back and arms.
Comb back: chair with parallel vertical, comblike spindles.
Ladder back: back with ladder, or steplike, horizontal slats.
Mate's: same as captain's style but slightly smaller, with shorter arms or no arms, Fig. 50-24.
Saddle seat: shaped, rather than flat, seat for added comfort. May be found on several other chair styles.
Windsor: chair style characterized by thin spindles, wooden saddle seat, and slanted legs usually joined with a stretcher at the bottom.
In addition, chair backs usually have many descriptors:
Balloon back: open circles on the chair back.
Comb: wide board across the top of the back with parallel dowel-like spindles to the seat.
Fan: dowel-like spindles spread out from the seat to the top on the chair back.
Fiddle: shape of the back resembles a violin.

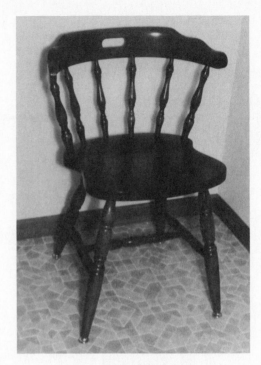

Fig. 50-24. Mate's chair.

Hoop: square shaped bent wood chair back that starts and ends at the seat, with fan spindles.
Spoon: curved to fit the human body.

Clocks
Grandfather: tall (over 80 in.) floor-standing case clock with enclosed pendulum.
Grandmother: tall (72 to 80 in.) floor-standing case clock with enclosed pendulum.
Granddaughter: tall (60 to 72 in.) floor-standing case clock with enclosed pendulum.
Jewelers: rectangular wall clock with enclosed pendulum.
Railroad: rectangular wall clock with a shelf beneath the pendulum.
Schoolhouse: octagon shaped wall clock with enclosed pendulum.
Mantel: short, wide clock with large base for stability. Also known as a table clock.
The word REGULATOR often is visible on wall and mantel clocks. Historically, this indicates the most accurate timepiece in the store, station, or school building. Other clocks are set according to it.

Desks
Executive: large desk with top that extends over two drawer sections. Another drawer extends across the knee space. The knee space desk is closed in the front with a panel.
Pedestal: smaller than executive desk with drawers on two sides and across the knee space. The desk usually is open over the knee space. However, it could be paneled.

Rolltop: pedestal desk with a tambour door section on top containing open shelves and/or small drawers and doors.

Secretary: small desk, usually with at least one drawer and a drop-front door or lid that covers the desk top much like a rolltop desk, Fig. 50-25. Many secretaries have glass doors or an open bookcase above.

Fig. 50-25. Secretary.

Filing cabinets

Filing cabinets provide storage space for letter (8 1/2 x 11 in.) and legal size (8 1/2 x 14 in.) paper. The cabinet may have from one to four drawers. Some cabinets have casters. The depth ranges from 12 to 24 in. Tall and deep units tend to tip if more than one heavy upper drawer is open.

Mirrors

Wall: size varies from small to full length and attaches like a heavy picture.

Dresser: mounts to the back of a dresser.

Cheval: tilting full length mirror on a stand. There are smaller versions with a drawer in a base. These sit on tables or chests.

Storage

Armoire: a cupboard-over-drawer combination case on legs or a plinth. Used for storing clothing.

Bachelor chest: small-scale chest of table height with two or three drawers. May have an added hinged top that folds down against the side.

Bench: chest with hinged lid and padded or upholstered cover. Typically used for out-of-season storage of blankets and clothes.

Buffet: table height cabinet with a row of drawers and doors one or both sides. The drawers may be hidden behind a central door. Often used to store dinnerware and linens in a dining room.

Chest of drawers: set of five or six drawers in a case that rests on a plinth or legs.

Chest-on-chest: two chests, one mounted on top of the other. The top section of drawers is slightly smaller. When on cabriole legs, this becomes a highboy.

China cabinet: tall cabinet with glass doors often used to display dinnerware or collectibles.

Commode: originally, a boxlike structure holding a chamber pot under an open seat. Later combined with a washstand and cupboard underneath. Now refers to a low chest of drawers, often highly decorated.

Corner cupboard: narrow, three-sided hutchlike cupboard cabinet that fits in a corner.

Credenza: buffetlike or sideboard-like storage unit on a plinth or larger base.

Cupboard: Standing storage unit with shelves hidden behind doors.

Curio cabinet: transparent cabinet, often lighted inside, for displaying collectible items. May be on legs, base, or wall mounted. May also be a corner cabinet, Fig. 50-26.

Fig. 50-26. Corner curio.

Fig. 50-27. Dry sink.

Fig. 50-28. Sweater or lingerie chest.

Dry sink: low cupboard with a frame several inches wide attached around the edges or the top, Fig. 50-27. Typically has an open well lined with a copper tray. Originally, water was added to wash dishes.

Etagere: narrow, tall, open set of shelves held by shelf supports, rather than the case. May have an enclosed cabinet as a base.

Hope chest: benchlike storage for linens, keepsakes, and personal items. Can have a lift-out or mechanical lift-up tray. Usually not upholstered.

Hutch: open shelved storage above with cupboard below. May also be called a Chiffonier or Welch Cupboard.

Nightstand: Small case that usually sits beside a bed, often with a drawer and storage shelf. May be on legs, base, or a plinth.

Sweater or lingerie chest: chest of five or six narrow drawers, Fig. 50-28.

Sideboard: buffet-height cabinet, usually on legs, with drawers, compartments, and/or shelves. Typically a piece of dining room furniture for holding articles of table service.

Wardrobe: cabinet like an armoire, typically with only one drawer underneath a large storage area behind doors.

Tables

Butterfly table: table with rounded table leaves that drop when not in use, Fig. 50-29. Table is named after its butterfly wing-shaped support.

Fig. 50-29. Butterfly table. (Ethan Allen)

Candlestand: small table with tripod or pedestal originally made to hold candles. Now used mostly for decorative plants and collectibles.

Chair table: one piece of furniture with seat and writing surface. Often holds a telephone.

Coffee: low and narrow table at about seat height for use with living room furniture.

Console: table typically placed against a wall under a mirror. It sometimes contains a drawer, transparent door, or open shelf. Often found in entry-ways. Sometimes called pier table.

Dining: term generally given to tables designed at a comfortable height for eating. Encompasses a wide range of styles.

Dough box: table with sloping sides and hinged door covering a storage compartment, once used for raising bread, Fig. 50-30.

Fig. 50-31. Gateleg table.

Fig. 50-30. Dough box.

Drop leaf table: table with one or two hinged sections (leaves) that hang when the table is not in use.

End: table placed beside living room furniture to support a lamp, reading materials, or other items. The height is usually no higher than that of a chair arm.

Gateleg table: table with two drop leaves and legs attached to a fly rail with stretchers that swing out to support the leaves, Fig. 50-31.

Lowboy: occasional table with drawer located beneath the top.

Nested: small size tables where one fits under the other for convenient storage, Fig. 50-32.

Occasional: small to medium size tables in various sizes and shapes. Designed to be used as the occasion demands.

Pedestal: table with one or two column supports with legs that spread from it.

Refectory: long narrow occasional table with heavy legs.

Step: table with more than one top at different levels. Now often used as an end table, it originally was made to reach high bookshelves.

Trestle: table with long rectangular top where leaves

Fig. 50-32. Nested tables.

are added on the ends rather than in the middle, as opposed to an extension table where leaves are added in the middle.

SUMMARY

Creating furniture is a challenging activity. This chapter has illustrated a number of pieces you might build. Your design skills are important when planning furniture. If the piece should replicate a certain style, make sure you research the wood species, dimensions, and finishes of that period.

Being able to analyze joinery is another important skill. Keep in mind that there are usually several joints that will assemble the product. Select those that can be made with available equipment, machines, supplies, and tools.

CABINETMAKING TERMS

Movement, box springs, standard mattress, water-filled mattress, frames, platform, hard-side water bed mattress, soft-side water bed mattress, plastic liner, plain platform, cabinet platform, headboard, flat headboard, bookcase headboard, footboard, canopy bed, poster bead, cheval mirror, room divider.

TEST YOUR KNOWLEDGE

1. A clock movement is a mechanism that keeps time. True or False?
2. Quartz movements are battery operated. True or False?
3. Two kinds of mattresses are _____ and _____ _____.
4. What supports the cotton and water-filled mattresses?
5. The sizes are the same for cotton and water-filled mattresses. True or False?
6. Describe how you can make long spindles on a short-bed lathe?
7. List two uses of room dividers.
8. What features might you find in dual purpose furniture?

Chapter 51
BUILT-IN CABINETRY AND PANELING

After studying this chapter, you will be able to:
☐ *Meet various storage needs with built-in cabinets.*
☐ *Locate available areas for built-in cabinets.*
☐ *Install built-in storage and workspaces.*
☐ *Select lumber and wood products for paneling.*
☐ *Plan and estimate a paneling job.*
☐ *Install tongue and groove lumber paneling.*
☐ *Install sheet paneling.*
☐ *Install millwork over paneling.*

The chapters up to now have focused mainly on freestanding casework and kitchen cabinets. There is another equally important area—*built-in cabinets.* These are storage units often custom-made to fit special space restrictions.

In addition, this chapter covers selecting and installing paneling. Paneling has found wide acceptance as wall covering because it is easy to install, yet very attractive. There are several types of paneling from which you might choose.

BUILT-IN CABINETS

Built-in cabinets help solve storage and workspace problems as an alternative to freestanding cabinets. They make use of otherwise idle space. Built-in cabinets must be designed and built with the same care taken to construct other products. Typical needs for added storage are:
1. Towels and wash cloths.
2. Toiletries.
3. Bedding.
4. Laundry supplies.
5. Books and magazines.
6. Car care products.
7. Sporting goods.
8. Out-of-season clothing.
  Workspace needs might be:
1. Utility room.
2. Home office.
3. Workshop.
4. Photography darkroom.
  The needs people have for storage and workspace are almost endless. As you design products to meet these needs, strive for convenience, efficiency, and flexibility. Refer to chapters dealing with case goods, doors, drawers, and tops for design options. Also review information about solid plastic tops, laminates, and hardware that will make the installation easier.

LOCATING SPACE

After you decide that you need more storage space, search for areas that can adapt to built-in cabinetry. Look for so-called *dead space*—those unused areas of floors and walls. You will find this in bathrooms, closets, stairwells, and attics. Fig. 51-1 suggests some typical home storage areas.

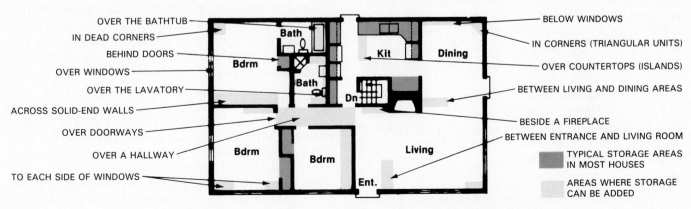

Fig. 51-1. Look for "dead space" as possible storage areas.

DESIGNING BUILT-IN STORAGE

When designing built-in cabinetry, follow four general rules.
1. Know what it is you want to store.
2. Measure items to be stored, if possible.
3. Decide how you want to store them.
4. Identify where the items will be used. This suggests where to look for storage space.

In many instances, existing cabinets and closets can be made more efficient. For example, cups are awkward to store. You might attach cup hooks to permanent shelves to hang them. Adjustable shelving also helps solve problems of storing odd size items or items that will not stack safely, Fig. 51-2.

Adding storage areas involves building open or closed cabinetry. Open shelves and racks tend to collect dust. Enclosed cases allow you to hide items when solid doors or drawers are used. They can also be used to display collections and trophies behind glass doors.

Storage cabinets may be installed several ways. You can place them on the floor, anchor them to the wall, or hang them from the ceiling.

Plan for the weight of the filled cabinet. Select positioning or locking joints that will support the items. This is especially important for wall-mounted cabinets. Using frame and panel assemblies will lighten the cabinet somewhat yet maintain its strength. Design the cabinet using the techniques you learned for constructing case goods and kitchen cabinets.

Bathrooms

Bathrooms typically contain vanities and related cabinetry. There may be base, wall, and utility units. Vanities usually support one or more sinks and provide storage for toiletries. Wall and tall cabinets hold towels, wash cloths, and other supplies.

Custom-made vanities can follow the guidelines and standard sizes given for kitchen cabinets, but are lower. Some differences might be the material of the countertop and the style of fixtures. When planning the vanity, take into account color, style, and space restrictions of the room.

Be aware that some bathroom items and medicine may be harmful. Keep these out of the reach of small children. Consider installing locks or safety latches on the doors.

A clothes hamper or chute to a basement laundry area is convenient. Select your materials carefully since hampers may be filled with damp towels and clothing. The container at the end of the chute will require the same treatment.

Closets

Closets often can be made more efficient. For example, you could add lights, adjustable rods, and

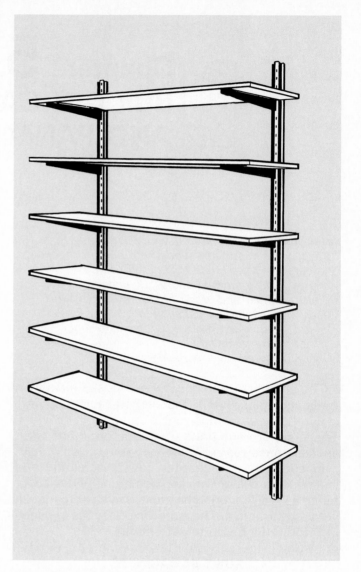

Fig. 51-2. Adjustable shelving makes closets more effective storage areas.

slide-out trays. With added drawers and shelving, closets can store folded clothes, appliances, and cleaning supplies, Fig. 51-3.

General storage

General storage usually is hidden, possibly in a garage or an enclosed basement area. As with other storage space, you must know the sizes of the objects to be stored, and then design the method to contain them, Fig. 51-4.

Wall units

Walls need not simply enclose a room or house. Instead, they can serve a number of purposes. Many times, a built-in wall unit provides startling character to an otherwise uninteresting room. Most are anchored to the wall, Fig. 51-5. Units as little as 15 in. deep provide an amazing amount of display and storage area.

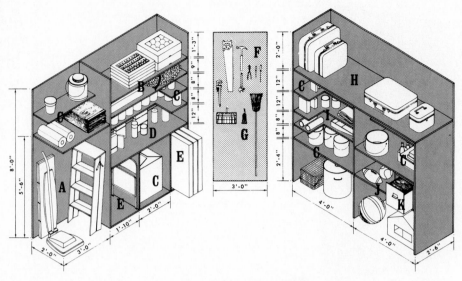

GENERAL STORAGE ITEMS

A. Cleaning Equipment and Table Leaves. The main items include broom, dust mop, vacuum cleaner, step stool, dining table leaves, and possibly an ironing board. This space is near the door for convenience.

B. Christmas Ornaments.

C. Miscellaneous Items.

D. Cleaning Products.

E. Card Tables and Chairs. Space for three tables and eight folding chairs.

F. Small Tools. Tools for minor household repairs —

workshop or hobby shop requires separate space.

G. Cleaning Items. Small cleaning tools can also be hung on the wall panel hangers.

H. Hand Luggage.

I. Paints and Supplies. Only water-base paints and supplies are shown. A metal cabinet in basement or garage is recommended for storing flammable paints and supplies.

J. Toys. Other toys may be stored in a toy box in the child's bedroom.

K. Office File. A single-drawer file is shown.

Fig. 51-3. Drawers, trays, shelving, and pegboard make storage space more efficient. (University of Illinois)

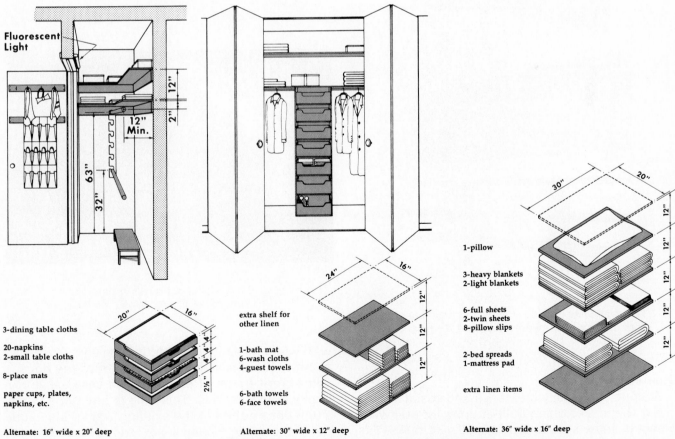

Fig. 51-4. General household storage should be well planned. (University of Illinois)

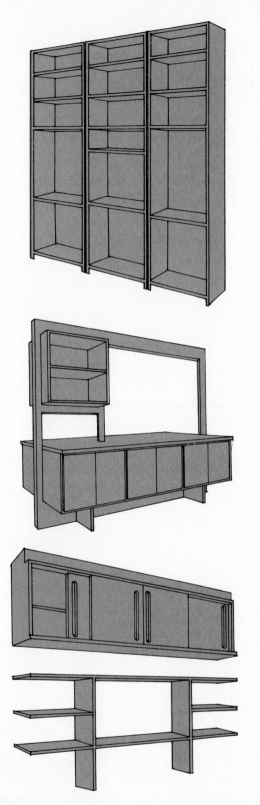

Fig. 51-5. Wall units provide storage and may make a room more attractive. (American Plywood Association)

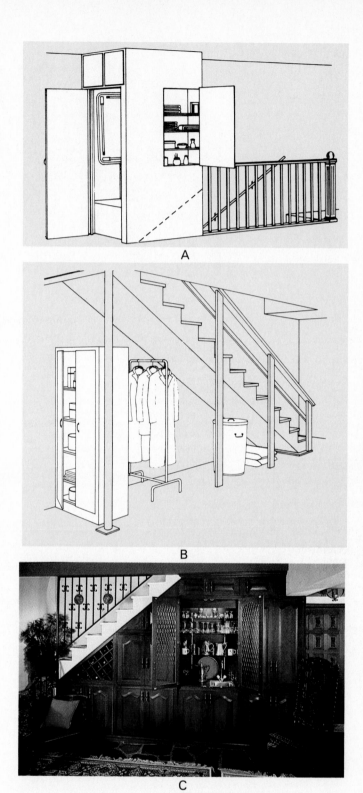

Fig. 51-6. Utilize stairwells for storage.
(University of Illinois, Wood-Mode)

Stairwells

Stairwells typically create wasted space over or under them. Designing built-in units for stairwells presents some special problem-solving tasks, Fig. 51-6. There are allowances for headroom to deal with when measuring and fitting the unit. To create a unit that looks like an integral part of the house, add a front frame after sliding the case assembly in place, Fig. 51-6C. This covers any gaps when a unit does not meet the existing wall or stair support accurately. Finally, install trim over the joints, hang the doors, and install the drawers.

Attics

An attic is often valuable for out-of-season storage. The units you build may have to fit odd angles created by the rafters, Fig. 51-7.

INSTALLING ACTIVITY AREAS

Finding space for activities can be more difficult than locating storage areas. It might involve con-

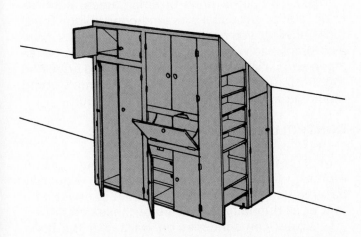

Fig. 51-7. Although attics adapt to many kinds of storage, you must deal with odd angles.

verting and remodeling some areas currently used for storage. This could include an extra room, basement, attic, or other area.

Your design must take into account several factors. First, it must accommodate one or more people, either standing or seated. Full height walls should allow for plenty of head room, as discussed in Chapter 5. Second, your design must make room for equipment. Depending on the activity, this could include a table saw, photo enlarger, computer, sewing machine, or typewriter. Measure the components and also decide how much space is needed between them. Items that are often used should be centrally located. Supplies should be close at hand.

When adding built-in activity areas, rough in utilities first. You may want hot and cold water, sewer connections, electrical service, and maybe gas. Utilities are essential for a wet bar, darkroom, or utility room.

EXTRA ROOM OR BASEMENT

People participate in many social and leisure time activities that require a large area. Families who entertain may find need for a bar, Fig. 51-8. A wet bar has all the utilities. Dry bars have electrical service, or no utilities at all.

QTY.	MATERIAL LIST
3	Sheets ¾″ × 4′ × 8′ plywood (Interior or MDO)
1	Sheet ½″ × 4′ × 4′ plywood (Interior)
7	1 × 2 × 45″ (trim)
2	1 × 2 × 57¾″ (top supports)
4	1 × 2 × 12″ (end shelf supports)
1	1 × 2 × 60″ (front edging)
1	1 × 2 × 24″ (end edging)
2	2 × 4 × 57¾″ (base)
2 pr.	Hinges (flush door type)
2	Cabinet knobs
2	Magnetic catches

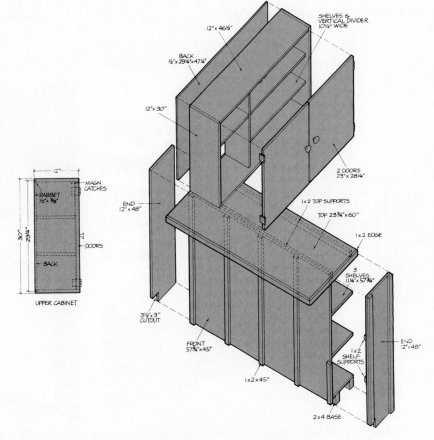

Fig. 51-8. A wet or dry bar may be desired in activity areas. (Weyerhauser)

A hobby that also requires adequate space and utilities is photography. The photographic darkroom for developing film and making prints requires hot and cold water. A light table, timer, and enlarger require electrical service, Fig. 51-9. A small refrigerator stores chemicals and film.

Some people are ''do-it-yourselfers'' and need a workshop area equipped with tools, a workbench, and storage. Stationary power machines will occupy floor space all the time while portable items can be stored when not in use.

An extra room or portion of the basement can also support laundry activities, Fig. 51-10. Take into account the following utility and storage factors:
1. Electricity.
2. Hot and cold water.
3. Sewer drains.
4. Gas (if appropriate to the appliance).
5. Ventilation and vent duct for the dryer.
6. Hanger space for washed items.
7. Supply storage.

ATTIC

Creating attic activity areas can involve odd-shaped restrictions, Fig. 51-11. However, with a proper design, an attic can support a studio, home office, computer center, or sewing room. You can plan for activities that occupy the same space.

ROUGH-IN AND FINISH WORK

Installing built-ins involves rough-in and finish work. *Rough-in work* includes building walls and in-stalling utilities. *Finish work* involves installing a face frame, attaching trim, installing fixtures, and possibly placing paneling.

Walls are made with 2 x 4 studs nailed between a sole and top plate. Cover the walls with plasterboard or wood paneling. After installing plasterboard sheets, tape and cover the joints with compound. Paneling must be installed accurately since you do not cover the joints. Review a good carpentry book before tackling any rough-in work.

Installing built-in units in small areas, such as under stairs, will usually be time-consuming. To attach paneling, you need to precut many pieces, each a different size with various angles. Place the paneling in such a way that you can cover the edges on top, bottom, and in corners with moulding. Cutting moulding is discussed later in the chapter.

CONTROLLING MOISTURE PROBLEMS

Moisture can be a problem in kitchens, bathrooms, utility rooms, garages, and especially basements. The moisture can come in direct contact or as humidity. Be aware of these conditions:
1. Water can condense on walls near the floor. This occurs frequently in basements and garages.
2. Water and steam contact cabinets in the bathroom around a tub, shower, or vanity.
3. In the kitchen around the sink cabinet and dishwasher, water and steam directly contact cabinets.

Fig. 51-9. A typical darkroom requires ample storage and counter space. (Wood-Mode)

Fig. 51-10. Laundry and utility rooms need storage around appliances. (International Paper Co.)

Fig. 51-11. Attics will support many activities. (Wood-Mode)

4. In utility and laundry rooms, water problems can be wet clothing or leaking appliance connections.

Plan for air circulation to prevent moisture buildup. Otherwise, mildew or mold will form. Be aware of possible water leaks around supply lines, drains, hose connections, and spray hoses. A wet basement wall may need outside waterproofing or a vapor barrier inside. It is also wise to hang louver doors on cabinets in areas exposed to moisture. For workspaces and activity areas, you might increase air circulation and reduce moisture problems by adding heating and air conditioning ductwork, or installing a dehumidifier.

PANELING

Paneling is an alternative to plastered or plasterboard-covered walls. It is available as lumber millwork and manufactured sheet products. The surface texture can range from smooth to very rough.

Paneling can cover the entire wall or only a portion of it. Paneling placed partway up from the floor is called wainscoting and is topped with a cap, Fig. 51-12. The cap prevents chair backs from damaging the wall.

Fig. 51-12. A wainscot extends from the floor partially up the wall. (Georgia Pacific)

MATERIALS

Millwork paneling is either planed smooth or rough sawn. Smooth faces are often milled with decorative grooves. The edges may be chamfered or rounded to help hide the joint. The individual slats generally fit together with a tongue and groove joint. It helps align the panel while reducing warpage. The joint you see may be a butt, channel, or V-groove. See Fig. 51-13.

You will find millwork paneling in set widths—4, 6, and 8 in. It is also available in variable widths since using slats all the same width can look repetitious. Millwork paneling is 1/2 to 3/4 in. thick and installed on furring strips or directly to the wall studs. *Furring strips* are 1 x 3 or 1 x 4 nailing strips attached to studs with cement coating 6d or 8d nails. They can be attached to concrete with adhesive and masonry nails.

Manufactured *sheet paneling* usually comes in 4 x 8 sheets and is textured or grooved. (Metric sheets are somewhat smaller, 1200 x 2400 mm.) Sheet paneling installs easily and covers quickly. The paneling might be made from tempered or untempered hardboard, fiberboard, and plywood. The surface can be paper, vinyl, plastic laminate, or wood veneer with wood grain, solid color, floral, or other patterns, Fig. 51-14. Real wood veneers can be prefinished or ready for staining and topcoating.

Most sheeting is 1/8 to 1/4 in. thick. Install it over a plasterboard, waferboard, particleboard, or plywood covered surface. It is too weak and flexible for direct installation to wall studs. Grooves cut in the paneling help hide the colored nails you use to attach the sheet. Some high gloss surfaces may be grooved along and across the panel to resemble ceramic tile. Install thicker sheets like millwork.

INSTALLATION TOOLS AND SUPPLIES

When paneling, first decide on the desired decorative effects you want in the room. Then purchase the needed materials and supplies. Paneling may be bundled. Separate the packages and allow the material to sit for about 48 hours to reach room temperature. Sort the veneer panel pieces if you intend to match the grain.

Add mouldings in corners, over joints, and covering exposed edges after paneling walls. Select moulding the same specie as millwork paneling or use matching stain. You can usually find plastic moulding to match manufactured sheet paneling.

BUTT

CHANNEL

V-GROOVE

Fig. 51-13. Millwork paneling may be butted, channeled, or V-grooved. (California Redwood Association)

WOOD VENEER   PHOTO PAPER   PLASTIC LAMINATE   VINYL LAMINATE

Fig. 51-14. There are many kinds of panel products. (Weyerhaeuser)

Supplies include mechanical fasteners, construction adhesive, and a fine tooth saw blade to reduce splintering. A line level, plumb bob, and chalk line are also needed to help align sheet panels and millwork, Fig. 51-15. In addition, obtain wood shims and wedges when needed to straighten paneling on irregular walls. You can purchase shims or make them from narrow strips of tapered wood shingles.

Obtain plywood, waferboard, or plasterboard to install beneath thin sheet panels. Use 1 x 3 or 1 x 4 horizontal strips nailed behind vertical millwork paneling. Horizontal millwork can attach directly to wall studs.

PLANNING

When you begin a paneling job, first rough in all electrical, plumbing, heating, telephone lines, and other utilities. They must conform to building codes. Use 2 x 4 studs and standard framing practices to add new walls. Attach horizontal furring strips if you will be installing vertical millwork paneling. See illustrations in Fig. 51-16.

Paneling with sheets is generally done on a modular basis of 48 in. (1200 mm) distances. Place studs 16 in. (400 mm) on-center. Estimate four studs or furring strips for every 48 in. of wall surface to cover. The extra stud or strip will be used in a corner, next to a door, or elsewhere.

When purchasing millwork paneling, buy lengths that will be economical to install. Reduce the need for mid-wall butt joints. Lengths are available in 2 ft. increments. Protect the tongue and groove during storage and cut them off only when placing the panels in corners.

Fig. 51-15. Levels, chalk lines, and plumb bobs help align paneling. (Columbian, Stanley)

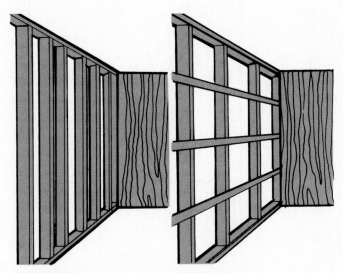

Fig. 51-16. Horizontal millwork paneling attaches directly to studs. Place horizontal furring strips if you will be installing vertical millwork paneling.

When the location of doorways and built-in cabinets is flexible, place them so that the edge of a full panel will be under the trim. This is easier than sawing a door opening in a panel. Measure from one side of doorways rather than toward them.

To estimate the number of sheets needed, follow this procedure:

1. Sketch the floor plan and wall elevations on graph paper, Fig. 51-17.
2. Count the number of squares to calculate the perimeter of the room.
3. Locate all door, windows, and other openings or areas where paneling will not be installed.
4. Make allowances for openings as follows.
   Window—1/2 panel
   Fireplace—1/2 panel
   Hinged door—2/3 panel
   Patio door— 1 1/3 panel
5. Divide the perimeter by the width of your paneling, usually 48 in., to find the number of sheets.
6. Subtract the allowances from the total number of sheets to arrive at the estimated total number of sheets.

When possible, plan your paneling so that the only place you have to cut sheets is at the room's inside corners. The raw or unfinished edge will be hidden by corner trim. When you have to cut across a panel, place the cut edge at the floor. It will be hidden by base trim.

If the cut edge might be visible, place the good face down when cutting with a portable circular saw. Place the good face up with using a table saw. This, along with a sharp, fine-toothed blade, will reduce splintering. Another method to prevent splintering is cutting through the panel surface with a utility knife or scribing tool, Fig. 51-18.

INSTALLING MILLWORK PANELING

Millwork panels may be installed vertically, horizontally, or diagonally, Fig. 51-19. Nail horizontal or diagonal paneling directly into wall studs. Attach vertical millwork to furring strips. Also add short furring strips around window and door openings where there is no stud to nail into.

Vertical paneling

Install 1 x 3 or 1 x 4 furring strips with cement coating 6d or 8d nails. Nail one against the ceiling and another near the floor. Between these two, place three more horizontally. Check the wall surface with a 4 to 8 ft. straightedge. Drive wood shims between the studs and furring strips where the wall is not straight.

Do not wedge paneling between the floor and ceiling. Leave about 1/2 in. at the floor. The baseboard will cover this. If you do not plan to install ceiling moulding, raise the squared panel snugly against the ceiling before nailing it.

Normally, you start installing vertical panels in a corner. If there is a fireplace or other unpaneled floor to ceiling area, start there. Make the cutouts for switches, outlets, and plumbing as necessary.

Position the first panel with the grooved edge in the corner. Place a level on the tongue edge. If

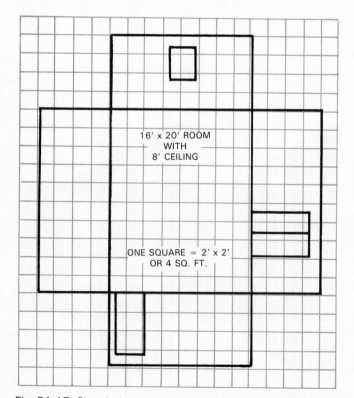

Fig. 51-17. Sketch the room on grid paper to help you calculate the number of sheet or millwork panels for the job.

16' x 20' ROOM
WITH
8' CEILING

ONE SQUARE = 2' x 2'
OR 4 SQ. FT.

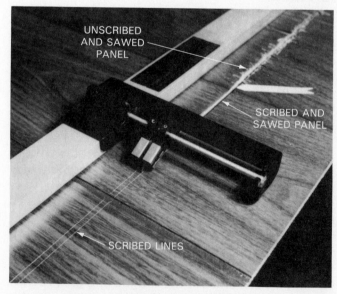

UNSCRIBED AND SAWED PANEL

SCRIBED AND SAWED PANEL

SCRIBED LINES

Fig. 51-18. Use a scribing tool or utility knife to prevent splintering. (Penn-Scarf)

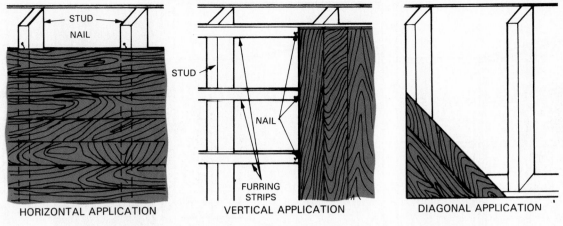

Fig. 51-19. Install millwork panels horizontally, vertically, or diagonally.

necessary, cope the groove edge with a compass and plane it to fit. With the panel plumb (vertical), toenail the tongue edge into a furring strip temporarily. Fasten the panels with finishing nails.

After placing a second panel, inspect the tongue and groove joint. If it is open, place a short scrap of grooved edge paneling over the tongue. Drive the panel joint closed with a hammer, Fig. 51-20.

Toenail the tongue edges at each furring strip. You can drive finishing nails through the face where ceiling moulding, corner moulding, baseboard, or trim will hide them. If you need to face-nail where moulding will not cover, set the nails and cover them with the proper color of stick putty.

Horizontal paneling

Begin installing horizontal paneling at the floor with the tongue edge up. Level and face-nail the panel near the floor. Use a carpenter's level or line level and chalk line. Make necessary cutouts and install the material as described for vertical paneling. Do not wedge the panels between walls.

Diagonal paneling

Begin installing diagonal panels in a corner. Establish a diagonal guide line and use a framing square to determine the vertical and horizontal miter cuts. Lay out these distances on the paneling. Saw the miter on each end of the panel. Install the first panel in a lower corner and work diagonally across the wall. You should be able to nail the panels securely to wall studs. Face-nail only where moulding will cover the nails.

INSTALLING SHEET PANELING

Sheet paneling is generally much easier to install than millwork. The sheets are often flexible and should be fastened to a backing. If furring strips are installed, locate them on 12 in. centers. Be sure there is a nailing groove or apply panel adhesive.

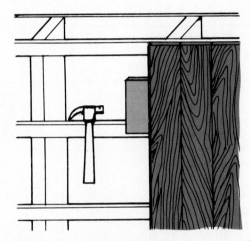

Fig. 51-20. Close any joint gaps with a hammer and block of paneling.

With panels in place, install base, trim, and corners to cover gaps.

Panel backing

Use plasterboard, waferboard, or plywood for a backing. Install the backing horizontally for vertical paneling since the panel joints should not be parallel to the backing joints. When installing backing, make chalk marks on the floor or ceiling to locate studs for nailing. Use marks and a plumb line. Work toward corners, fastening material with ring shank nails or plasterboard screws every 8 in.

Installation

Steps for installing sheet paneling are given in Fig. 51-21. Hang sheets with colored panel nails. Use brown or black ones in recessed nailing grooves. Drive panel-colored nails only if you face nail.

Leave some space at the floor so the panel is not wedged between the floor and ceiling. Finish the panel backing black where panels join. This will hide the joint. Leave a narrow space between panels, (about the thickness of a panel nail). This will keep the paneling from buckling should it expand.

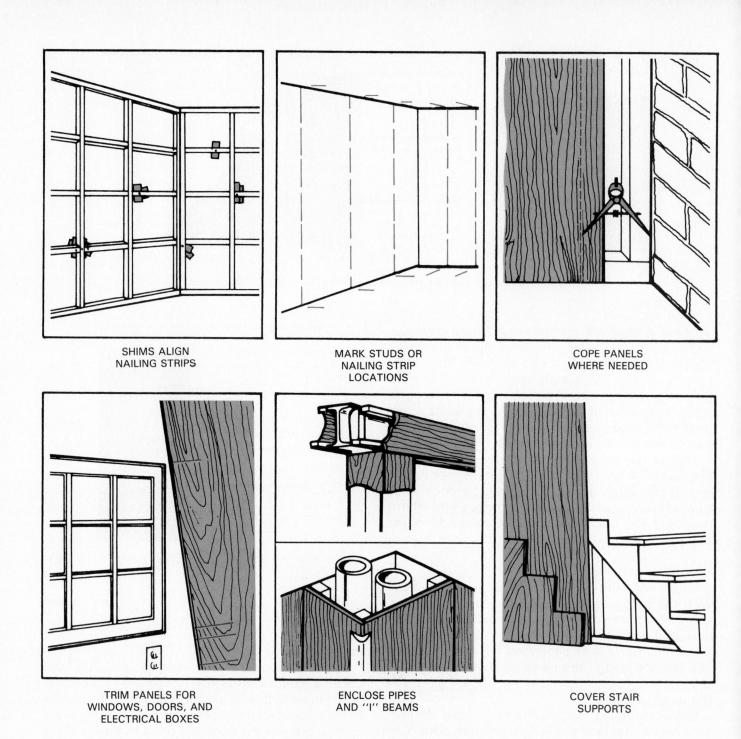

SHIMS ALIGN
NAILING STRIPS

MARK STUDS OR
NAILING STRIP
LOCATIONS

COPE PANELS
WHERE NEEDED

TRIM PANELS FOR
WINDOWS, DOORS, AND
ELECTRICAL BOXES

ENCLOSE PIPES
AND "I" BEAMS

COVER STAIR
SUPPORTS

Fig. 51-21. Series of steps taken to install sheet paneling. (Weyerhaeuser)

Begin by installing full sheets and working toward corners. Plumb the first panel. Cope the edge to fit an existing surface or corner if necessary. Make cutouts for switches, outlets, and plumbing with a saber saw as needed. Do so with the layout marks on the back side of the panel.

You can install panels with adhesive and/or nails. Panels with a smooth face are best attached using adhesive. Apply a bead of adhesive about 1/4 in. wide in two "X" patterns on the back of the panel. Apply a bead 1 to 2 in. from the panel edges. If at-

taching the panel to furring strips, apply the adhesive to the strips.

After pressing the panel against the backing, pull it away. Inspect the wall for adhesive spread. If adequate, press the panel to the wall. This movement helps adhesive to set. Then, fasten the sheets with colored panel nails.

Paneling with grooves can be nailed. Use 1 in. panel nails the same color as the panel grooves. If the panel was laid out properly, the grooves should align with furring strips or studs behind the backing.

Metal caps, flat joints, and corners

Some installations call for metal or plastic caps, joint strips, and corners, Fig. 51-22. Use them where moisture could be a problem, such as around a shower. With a bead of caulk or sealant in the panel groove, these pieces help prevent moisture penetration. Select rustproof nails. Buy mouldings to match panel thickness.

Begin by installing one corner piece. Work from there around the walls in one direction. Where panels meet, install a divider. Slip one groove over an installed panel. Nail the visible back edge to the wall. In the same manner, slip outside corners over one panel and nail the visible edge. Installing the panel that hides the nails in the last strip may be difficult. Fit one side and trim the other. Bend the panel slightly and slide it into the moulding groove. It will spring back in place.

WORKING WITH CONCRETE WALLS

It is difficult to attach materials to concrete walls. When raising a wall, apply construction adhesive on the concrete floor where the wall will stand. Raise the wall into position. Use shims between the wall and overhead joists for a tight fit as needed at the floor. Anchor the top to ceiling joists with cement-coated nails. The adhesive minimizes, and often eliminates, the need for masonry nails to secure the wall to the floor. These nails can crack concrete floors and block walls.

To attach paneling to concrete walls, first install 1 x 2 or 2 x 2 furring strips to the wall with adhesive. Install a masonry nail at each end and at about 4 ft. intervals. Add shims when needed to correct for an irregular wall.

Installations over concrete often occur below

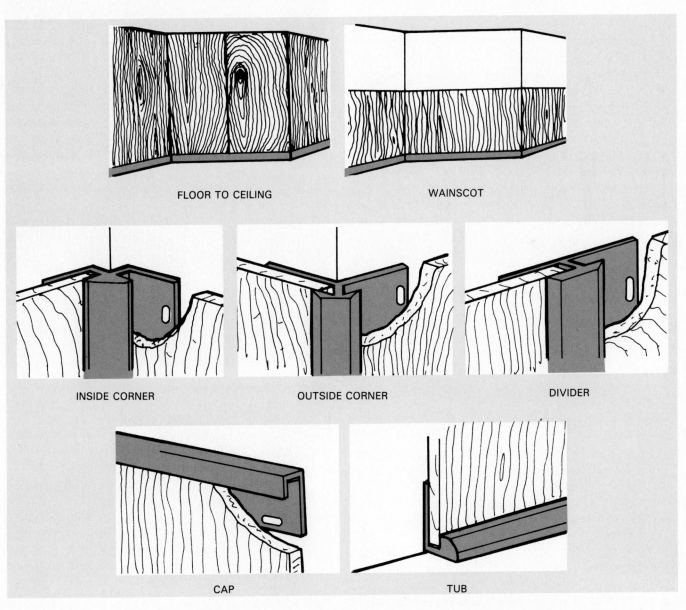

FLOOR TO CEILING   WAINSCOT

INSIDE CORNER   OUTSIDE CORNER   DIVIDER

CAP   TUB

Fig. 51-22. Some panel installations, especially laminated panels in the bathroom, fit into metal or plastic trim.

grade where moisture and heat loss are problems. Waterproofing, vapor barrier materials, and insulation may be necessary. Consult a carpentry text for these topics.

INSTALLING MOULDING AND TRIM

Once paneling is in place, you may install window and door trim, chair railing, and wainscot caps, baseboard, ceiling moulding, and corner moulding, Fig. 51-23. Where moulding, baseboard, and trim are face-nailed, set the nails and fill the holes later with colored wood dough or stick putty.

While trim around windows and doors usually is mitered on the corners, most inside baseboard and corner pieces are not. They are coped to fit. Install trim and moulding with finishing nails. Set and cover nail heads.

Install mouldings in this order:
1. Door trim. This trim is mitered at the upper corners. Door trim extends from the floor up. Window and door trim are usually the same design. Door trim is generally set back 1/4 to 3/8 in. to reveal the door jamb.
2. Window trim. Window trim starts from the sill and is mitered at the upper corners. The sill usually has an apron piece under it.
3. Baseboard. Start at a corner and use a bevel joint where any lengths meet. Edge miter the outside corners. For inside joints, cope one side. See Fig. 51-24. Butt the baseboard against the edge of door trim.

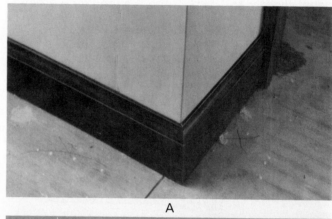

A

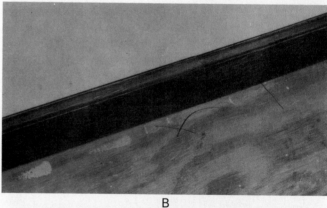

B

C

Fig. 51-24. Cutting base trim. A—Outside corners are mitered. B—Join long lengths with a bevel joint. C—Cope inside corners.

Fig. 51-23. Plan for the moulding before you start to work. (Council of Forest Industries of British Columbia)

INSIDE CORNER

PAINT

4. Inside corners. Select cove moulding for inside corners. Cope it over the baseboard and ceiling mouldings.
5. Outside corners. Select caps for outside moulding and cope the ends where they meet other moulding.
6. Ceiling moulding. Ceiling moulding typically is coped in the corners and joined with a bevel joint where long lengths meet.
7. Chair railing. Varies according to chair height, but should be about 36 in. starting at corner moulding. May extend to another corner, door, or window. Butt against window/door trim.
8. Wainscoting cap. Decorative trim generally is used to cover the wainscot ends and edges.

SUMMARY

Built-in cabinets make use of otherwise idle space. They also help solve storage and workspace problems not solved with freestanding cabinets.

When planning for built-ins, know what you want to store and the sizes. Decide how to store it, and identify where the items will be used. After you decide that you need more storage area, search for so-called "dead space" in bathrooms, closets, stairwells, and attics.

You might also look for space for activity areas. This could involve converting and remodeling an extra room, basement, attic, or area under a stairway. When roughing in new areas, always install utilities first. Hot and cold water, sewer connections, and electrical service all run through the walls.

Paneling is an alternative to plaster or drywall. It is available as millwork lumber in various widths and as manufactured 4 x 8 sheet products. The surface texture can range from smooth to very rough. It may also be covered with plastic laminate or photo paper. Paneling can be installed horizontally, vertically, or diagonally.

A sound backing is necessary beneath paneling. Millwork is installed easily over furring strips or all studs. Sheet products are too flexible and need plywood, particleboard, or waferboard backing.

CABINETMAKING TERMS

Built-in cabinets, dead space, rough-in work, finish work, paneling, millwork paneling, furring strips, sheet paneling.

TEST YOUR KNOWLEDGE

1. Begin planning built-in cabinets by:
   a. Measuring items to be stored.
   b. Establishing activity and storage needs.
   c. Locating space to be used.
   d. Making working drawings.

2. An often overlooked concern for bathroom planning is:
   a. Where to store items.
   b. Size of the lavatory to be mounted.
   c. Protecting children from medicine and chemicals.
   d. Selecting base, wall, or tall cabinets.
3. Explain how you might make a closet more efficient.
4. Headroom is a problem only above doors. True or False?
5. The difference between a wet and dry bar is:
   a. Ventilation.
   b. Location.
   c. Size.
   d. Water and sewer connections.
6. List several ways you might control moisture in built-in storage or activity areas.
7. Paneling comes as _____ in various widths or 4 x 8 _____.
8. Wainscoting partially covers a wall, beginning at the floor. True or False?
9. Metric sheet paneling is smaller than customary paneling. True or False?
10. Sheet paneling requires backing because:
    a. Furring strips are not used.
    b. It is too flexible.
    c. Nails are not required.
    d. Construction adhesive will not adhere to concrete.
11. Diagonal millwork paneling can be nailed directly to furring strips. True or False?
12. Sheet paneling is up to _____ in. thick.
13. Make full length cuts for fitting sheet panels only:
    a. Over windows.
    b. Over doorways.
    c. When installing millwork.
    d. In corners.
14. Adhesives reduce or eliminate the need for face-nailing. True or False?
15. Toenail millwork:
    a. At an angle near the tongue.
    b. At an angle near the groove.
    c. Vertical to the tongue.
    d. Vertical to the groove.
16. When is a plumb bob and chalk line needed for paneling?
17. Use aluminum nails to attach furring strips to studs. True or False?
18. A good average adhesive bead is _____ in. in diameter.
19. Colored nails are used to fasten sheet paneling because they will not rust. True or False?
20. In what order should these mouldings be installed? Place the letters in the proper order.
    a. Wainscot caps.   c. Inside corners.
    b. Door trim.   d. Baseboard.

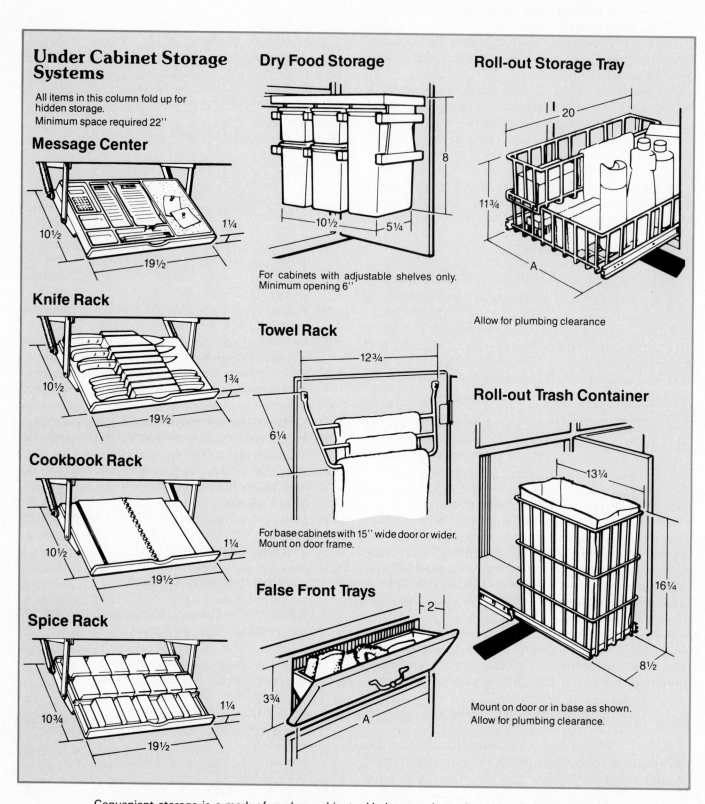

Under Cabinet Storage Systems

All items in this column fold up for hidden storage.
Minimum space required 22''

Message Center

10½
1¼
19½

Knife Rack

10½
1¾
19½

Cookbook Rack

10½
1¼
19½

Spice Rack

10¾
1¼
19½

Dry Food Storage

8
10½
5¼

For cabinets with adjustable shelves only.
Minimum opening 6''

Towel Rack

12¾
6¼

For base cabinets with 15'' wide door or wider.
Mount on door frame.

False Front Trays

2
3¾
A

Roll-out Storage Tray

20
11¾
A

Allow for plumbing clearance

Roll-out Trash Container

13¼
16¼
8½

Mount on door or in base as shown.
Allow for plumbing clearance.

Convenient storage is a mark of modern cabinets. Various ready-made applications are available.
(American Woodmark Corp.)

Chapter 52
INDUSTRIAL PRODUCTION CABINETMAKING

After studying this chapter, you will be able to:
☐ Discuss custom and batch production.
☐ Understand facility layout problems of the cabinetmaking industry.
☐ Identify a typical departmentally organized industry.
☐ Describe the work of aftermarket personnel.

The main purpose for producing cabinets is to meet the changing needs and wants of people. Cabinetmaking serves home and commercial markets, both wanting quality products at an affordable price. Advancements in technology now allow firms to produce quality products with reasonable material and labor costs.

Cabinetmaking has changed over the years, Fig. 52-1. In earlier times, cabinets were assembled and completed individually on a custom basis. Now, all but a few are mass produced.

CUSTOM PRODUCTION

Custom production refers to making one-of-a-kind products. There are at least two forms of custom production. The first involves creating a single finished product for yourself or someone else. The item could be a bookcase, table, or trophy case. Once that item is done, you move on to another project. This process reflects the tasks of a home woodworker.

The second type of custom production, often called contract cabinetmaking, is specialized processing. Here, you would be contracted by another company to make components or subassemblies. You might agree to provide a set of assembled frame and panel doors. In this way, companies rely on your skill in a particular area of cabinetmaking. By having contracts with several companies, you can keep busy.

This book has discussed both products and processes, and decision-making concerning tools, materials, and operations. These decisions relate to design and production. For some operations, you use jigs, fixtures, and templates to duplicate dimensions, maintain accuracy, and increase efficiency. Machines are set up once and operated for a period of time. Each dimension is not measured or marked on the material independently. These devices let you work alone for the most part. Only if something large and heavy or awkward must be handled will more than one person be necessary.

Fig. 52-1. Technology for cabinetmaking production has changed over the years. (Columbus Show Case)

BATCH PRODUCTION

Batch production, a form of mass production, is a standard practice in the cabinetmaking industry for filling most orders. Company managers predict consumer needs for a period of time. An inventory of furniture or cabinets is built and stored in a warehouse. From there, the products are sold to wholesalers, who deal with retailers, who sell to consumers.

Batch production must be timely. Having items in storage too long is undesirable. They may not remain marketable. They no longer meet the cabinetmaker's main goal—producing products that meet customer needs.

Successful batch or mass production requires teamwork. Without it, industries fail. Working together begins at the executive level. The board of directors makes decisions about financing the company operations and product lines. Product ideas, as sketches and drawings, illustrate what will be built. Working drawings become guidelines for production operations and schedules. People in research and development work constantly to improve products, increase productivity, and attain high standards of quality.

There is much competition in the cabinetmaking industry. Patents protect the entrepreneurs who improve existing processes or invent new products and technologies. Consumer awareness depends on effective advertising. Maintaining quality products at an affordable price keeps a company on the leading edge. If production costs rise or product quality falls, customers will buy from other manufacturers.

Successful mass production relies on effective and efficient decision-making. A well organized factory, educated managers, trained production personnel, dedicated support people, and reliable equipment all contribute to success.

A mass production cabinetmaking shop consists of two areas. One is quiet, and the other usually noisy and active.

The quiet zone includes company executives, buyers, accountants, sales personnel, secretaries, and production engineers. These are people who do not actually work on the production line. Buyers purchase materials at competitive prices. Accountants monitor company finances. Business personnel prepare payrolls for management, production, and support personnel.

The active zone is the focus of this chapter. It includes receiving, processing, storing, assembling, finishing, packaging, warehousing, and shipping activities. People from the receiving to shipping docks are considered the backbone of the company. They turn ideas into products.

For departments to work together smoothly,

safety and maintenance are important. Time lost through accidents reduces production and may increase insurance costs. Heavy equipment, such as movable carts, forklifts, or hydraulic tables reduce material handling yet are a frequent cause of accidents and injuries. Likewise, expensive equipment that is idle because of poor maintenance occupies space that should be active.

Automated production lines increase yields and lower costs both in materials and labor. For example, in an automated line, production personnel rarely measure lengths or check for squareness on each part. Machines are set up to perform those repetitive operations. After sampling just a few parts for quality, the machinery can be adjusted to maintain accuracy.

DEPARTMENTS

Meeting market demands requires teamwook, Fig. 52-2. Satisfied people are more likely to be reliable and concerned about producing quality products. This is essential in any industrial department.

The departments on the production side of cabinetmaking include receiving, processing, assembly, finishing, packaging, and warehousing.

A

B

Fig. 52-2. Production requires teamwork. A—Supervisors discuss production problems. (Formitex) B—Working together in production. (Riviera Cabinets)

RECEIVING

The receiving department makes sure that ordered materials and supplies are received and stored. Panel products, lumber, adhesives, abrasives, finishes, hardware, and tools, are only a few. These items must be inventoried by a person in the receiving department. Often, shipments are on pallets and transported with heavy equipment, Fig. 52-3. The number of items can vary from a single piece to a truck load.

Much of the equipment used today is for multiple operations. Panel saws, Fig. 52-4, cut up panel products. Some machines operate in one direction, Fig. 52-4A. Long rectangular workpieces are made from standard stock with a single pass. Notice the adjustable table in the forefront that reduces lifting by the worker. Other equipment can make cuts two ways without moving the panel. The worker in Fig. 52-4B stands at the console of such a machine. The cuts that can be made using panel saws are shown in Fig. 52-4C.

Fig. 52-3. Receiving involves handling and storing standard stock items. (Riviera Cabinets)

PROCESSING

The material processing, or production department occupies a major portion of a cabinetmaking factory. Materials, such as panel products and lumber, must be cut to size, surfaced, shaped, and prepared for assembly. Most firms have relatively large equipment, able to make multiple cuts at a single pass.

Sawing

Most production systems begin with sawing operations. Single operation machines, such as the table saw, can be the bottleneck in a production schedule. If several machines are added to reduce the problem, they might occupy valuable factory space.

Fig. 52-4. Panel sawing. A—Several cuts in one direction. B—Several cuts in both directions. (Formitex) C—Sequence of cuts that can be made.

There are similar saws, called gang saws, for lumber. In Fig. 52-5, you see the equipment and process for making multiple cuts through lumber.

Surfacing

Lumber is typically surfaced after being sawn, Fig. 52-6. Some industries, depending on available space and personnel, saw and surface their own materials. Others buy lumber already surfaced and cut to size. This might be done under contract with a custom production facility. A smaller company often purchases prepared lumber to avoid buying equipment that is not needed regularly.

Drilling

Production firms often use multiple spindle drilling and boring machines, Fig. 52-7. One or more holes may be drilled at the same time. This is especially important when drilling rows of holes for the 32 mm system, discussed in Chapter 38. Programmable automatic machines further simplify multiple drilling operations.

Shaping

Industries either make or buy the moulding they use. Moulding machines like that shown in Fig. 52-8 will process lumber on both the top and bottom surfaces.

Other kinds of shaping are done with production shapers and routers. Production shapers set up with a template can make cutouts and perform internal shaping, Fig. 52-9.

Combination machines

Customized machines are often designed and manufactured for specific needs. For example, the machine shown in Fig. 52-10 drills holes for dowels.

Fig. 52-5. Gang sawing lumber. (SFPA)

Fig. 52-7. Multiple spindle drill press creates rows of holes for 32 mm cabinet construction. (Riviera Cabinets)

Fig. 52-6. Surfacing with industrial equipment. (SFPA)

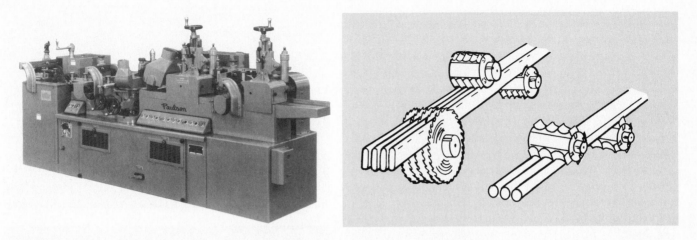

Fig. 52-8. Moulding machine. Note that 2-head and 3-head moulders create the entire piece of millwork in one pass. (Paulson Machines)

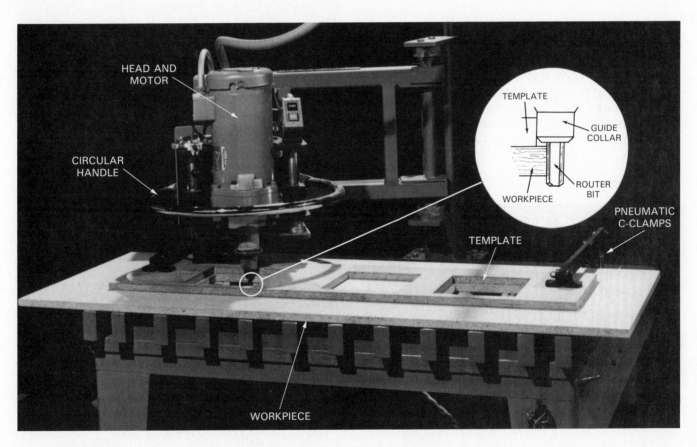

HEAD AND MOTOR

CIRCULAR HANDLE

TEMPLATE

GUIDE COLLAR

ROUTER BIT

WORKPIECE

TEMPLATE

PNEUMATIC C-CLAMPS

WORKPIECE

Fig. 52-9. Production template routing. (Evans-Rotork)

It also shapes edges for tongue and groove type joints. You can see the short dowels and tongues on the stacked workpieces.

Joinery

A number of lightweight and heavy duty pieces of equipment cut joints. Chapter 29 discussed some of these machines. In addition, Fig. 52-11A shows a table saw adapted to spline joinery. The double power miter saw, Fig. 52-11B, cuts to length and miters both ends of a board at the same time. A double-ended tenoner will cut tenons on both ends of a part at the same time, Fig. 52-11C. There are also programmable dovetail machines. The one shown in Fig. 52-11D cuts the sockets in drawer fronts.

Fig. 52-10. Drilling and edge jointing on custom equipment. (Formitex)

COMPONENT STORAGE

Storage is always a concern. The whereabouts of partially completed products must be monitored. They might be individual workpieces or assembled components, Fig. 52-12. Sometimes these items are marked with bar codes and read with a scanner to take inventory.

A

B

Fig. 52-12. A—Parts stored for further processing. (Formitex) B—Cases stored before finishing. (Fox Cabinets)

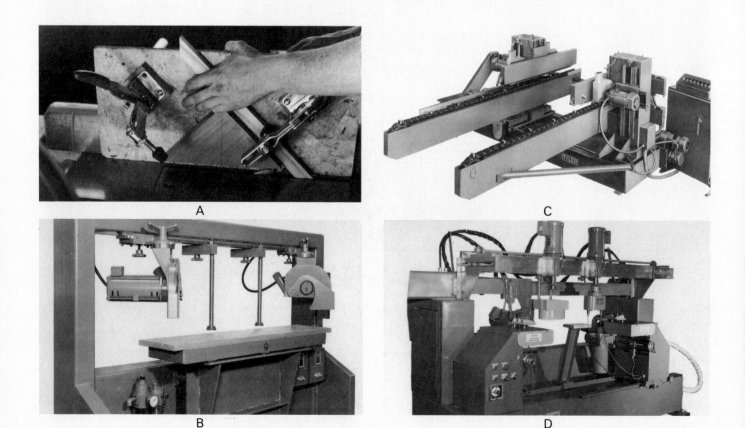

Fig. 52-11. Joinery machines. A—Spline cutting on a table saw. B—Mitering and cutting to length both ends in one pass. C—Double-ended tenoner. D—Programmable dovetailing machine. (Tyler)

ASSEMBLY

Assembling a product involves adhesives and mechanical fasteners. Among items called for on working drawings are glue, screws, staples, nails, and RTA fasteners.

Bonding

A bonding operation could involve assembling parts or attaching veneer. Fig. 52-13 shows machines involved in bonding veneer to lower quality softwood core stock. The veneer passes through a glue spreader. It is placed on the core and clamped under pressure until the adhesive sets.

Bonding with heat

Heat can be used to shorten an adhesive's set time. On the machine shown in Fig. 52-14A, laminates comes through the system starting from the left. The roller spreads glue on the lower surface of cores and veneers. From the glue spreader, laminates are aligned on the indexing table. Then they proceed through the heat tunnel and are pressed together. When they exit the machine on the right, they are completely cured.

In another machine, Fig. 52-14B, bent laminates are coated with adhesive and pressurized between two electric hot plates. The heat cures the adhesive faster.

A

A

B

Fig. 52-13. Adhesive bonding. A—Glue spread on core stock and veneer. (Forest Products Laboratory) B—A press for applying pressure to laminated products while the adhesive sets. (Tyler)

B

Fig. 52-14. Electric heat cures adhesives. A—This machine preheats and cleans the core and veneer, spreads glue, and cures the assembled layers with heat. (Evans-Rotork) B—Heat pads to cure bent laminate products. (Forest Products Laboratory)

Another heat bonding process deals with edge banding plastic onto particleboard. Not only are the surfaces covered with laminate, but the edges also receive a similar treatment. In Fig. 52-15, the worker at the right feeds a panel door into the edge banding machine. The door panel moves along the table. Adhesive is applied to edges from behind the machine. Strips of laminate are fed from a roll, cut, and pressed against the particleboard. The door then passes a heat plate to cure the adhesive. In front is a roller conveyor system. The worker at the left places the doors on the conveyor. They return to the right for another pass. The process is repeated four times for each door.

Another edge banding technique makes use of hot-melt adhesive. The adhesive can be applied to the particleboard or comes preapplied to the laminate.

Fig. 52-16. RF gluing presses for bonding laminates. (L & L Industries)

Fig. 52-15. Edge banding particleboard panels with plastic laminate. (Riviera Cabinets)

RF bonding

Another modern glue system involves RF (radio frequency) bonding. This technique is often used in bonding laminates, Fig 52-16. A stack of laminate, spread with adhesive, is placed on the machine. The platen lowers and applies pressure. The RF circuit is turned on to cure the adhesive by heating the glue with high-frequency radio waves. With two machines, you alternate so that neither is idle.

Assemblies, such as frames or frames and panels, are often RF glued. Adhesive is spread on the joints. The assemblies, with glue still wet, are placed in the press. Pressure applied with hydraulic clamps

closes the joints and aligns the components, Fig. 52-17. Closing the lid provides downward pressure. Finally, the RF generator is turned on to cure the adhesive.

Mechanical fasteners

On a production line, assembling components with screws, staples, and other fasteners often involves a clamping machine. Fig. 52-18 shows a frame, case, and drawer held in a clamp.

Fig. 52-19A shows a screw gun being used to drive screws to attach door hinges. The doors had

Fig. 52-17. RF bonding with edge and top clamping pressure. (L & L Industries)

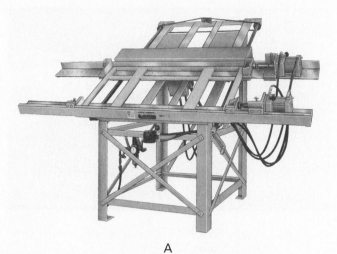

A

B

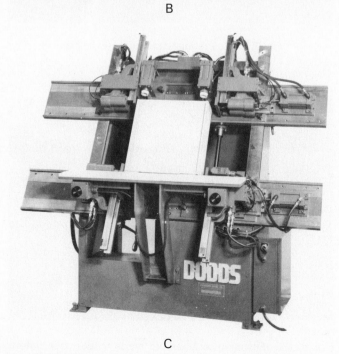

C

Fig. 52-18. Clamping with air pressure. A—Frame. B—Case goods. (J.M. Lancaster) C—Drawer. (Alexander Dodds)

already been edge banded. In Fig. 52-19B, frame clamps are holding cabinet fronts while staples are installed with a pneumatic stapler.

FINISHING

Finishing involves preparation, staining, filling, sealing and topcoating. In a production setting, most finishes are applied by spraying.

A

B

Fig. 52-19. A—Attaching door hinges with a screw gun. B—Assembling face frames with a pneumatic stapler. (Formitex)

Hand spray finishing

Cabinets on a conveyer system pass through the spray booth area where the worker sprays a quick-drying film, such as lacquer. The cabinets continue on the conveyer to the packaging area, Fig. 52-20.

A

B

Fig. 52-20. Spraying completed products. A—The finish is applied in a ventilated spray booth. B—Dried cabinets roll out ready for packaging. (Riviera Cabinets)

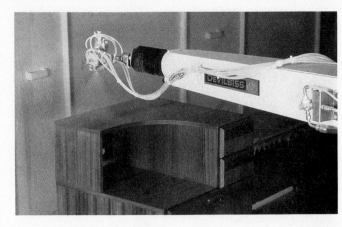

Fig. 52-21. Spraying with a robot. (Devilbiss)

Fig. 52-22. Prefinishing doors. (Devilbiss)

Fig. 52-23. Finishing touches are made to the case before prefinished doors are installed. The case sides are covered with laminate. (Formitex)

Robot spray finishing

Companies which produce one model of cabinet in large numbers often use an automated finishing system. The spraying is done by a robot, Fig. 52-21. Robots are especially important when the finish is very toxic or flammable.

Prefinished cabinets

Some cabinets are finished before assembly. This might include laminating and edge banding, or spraying on a coating. Fig. 52-22 shows stain being preapplied to frame and panel doors. In Fig. 52-23, the finished case awaits door installation. The doors are being installed in Fig. 52-24. Ready-to-assemble cabinets are also prefinished. They are shipped much like a kit and assembled by the consumer.

Fig. 52-24. The prefinished doors and catches are installed last on laminate covered cabinets. (Formitex)

PACKAGING

After a final inspection, cabinets are packaged for warehousing or direct shipment, Fig. 52-25. They are usually sealed in corrugated cardboard with foam, cardboard, or other packing material. Cabinet corners often have added protection. While being handled, the package might be dropped or bumped on its corners.

WAREHOUSING

Warehousing is the storage of packaged cabinets. They may be kept on inventory in a warehouse ready for customer orders. A skilled managing team determines how many of each cabinet model can

Fig. 52-25. Packaging prepares products for safe storage and shipment. (Columbus Show Case)

be expected to be ordered and delivered within a given time. As a result, a minimum number of products can be kept on hand and still meet market demands, Fig. 52-26.

As you learned in Chapter 38, ready-to-assemble (RTA) cabinets are less costly to store. Because the products assemble easily, they are shipped disassembled to save space during transportation. Several disassembled cabinets can be stored in the same amount of space as one assembled item.

Another type of production system minimizes warehousing. The cabinets are manufactured after the order arrives. This usually delays delivery until the order can be scheduled into the production system. However, this plan reduces costs since a large warehouse is less essential.

Fig. 52-26. Products stacked on crates in the warehouse. (Columbus Show Case)

AFTERMARKET PRODUCTIVITY

The *aftermarket* is the sale of parts and service, possibly covered under warranty. The aftermarket is a top priority of companies that wish to remain competitive. They issue guarantees on their product lines and follow up with prompt, courteous service. If lumber or veneer cracks, wood joints separate, or finishes peel off, a service person fixes it.

Meeting aftermarket demands for retaining product value and company integrity is a constant concern. A company may employ people to service their products. It also may contract with others to provide maintenance. In either case, these individuals are typically called *factory representatives.*

People working in the aftermarket are confronted by two problems. They should know how the product was originally manufactured. This includes types of lumber, wood products, adhesives, and mechanical fasteners used. Also, they must be able to deal with people having problems with their products. This requires thoughtfulness. Serve your customers as you would like to be served. They are more likely to buy your products in the future. Not meeting aftermarket needs certainly discourages repeat purchases.

SUMMARY

Throughout this book, you learned how to make cabinets productively. An efficient cabinetmaking shop has the right people, with the right materials, in the right place, at the right time. Without a concerned marketing staff, you cannot identify customer needs. Without trained and satisfied workers, you cannot produce. And, with good aftermarket representatives, a customer feels you support your products. The point is that teamwork is essential to satisfy both market and aftermarket demands. Companies without teamwork fail.

CABINETMAKING TERMS

Custom production, batch production, factory representative, aftermarket.

TEST YOUR KNOWLEDGE

1. Making one-of-a-kind products is called _____ production.
2. Mass producing large numbers of cabinets is called _____ production.
3. Lost time accidents reduce _____ and may increase _____ _____.
4. List the departments involved with producing cabinets.
5. Machines which cut sheet products in one or two directions are _____ _____.
6. Why might a small company purchase sawn and surfaced lumber?
7. To help keep track of inventoried items, you might mark parts with a _____ _____.
8. List three bonding processes found in a production cabinetmaking firm.
9. In a production setting, most finishes are applied by _____ or _____.
10. One of the most protected areas of a packaged cabinet is its _____.
11. Servicing installed cabinets is called _____, and is done by _____ _____.

Chapter 53
EMPLOYMENT IN CABINETMAKING

After studying this chapter, you will be able to:
☐ *Recognize employment opportunities in cabinetmaking.*
☐ *Identify what it takes to succeed at a job.*
☐ *Explain the alternatives for career advancement.*
☐ *Describe the role of an entrepreneur.*

Employment in the cabinetmaking industry can be compared to many other sectors of the economy. Cabinetmaking is a relatively stable field because homes and businesses always need new or replacement furnishings. The market trends for furniture and cabinets are set by the needs and wants of consumers. There is also an important aftermarket in the industry. The skill of rebuilding, repairing, and refinishing is often in demand.

Your job in a cabinetmaking company, as in other fields, may lead to a career in the industry. Each position you hold offers challenge and rewards. Moving ahead requires knowledge, skill, and a positive attitude. Showing concern for quality in the product you build or the service you provide is part of attitude. If you do not take pride in the tasks you perform, you may be in the wrong field.

Pursuing a career in cabinetmaking is a long-term investment of time and energy. While working your daily job, you plan the steps to advance in the field. Ambitious individuals do more than just their job. They search for answers to questions like:
1. Is this the best procedure to use?
2. How can I improve this operation?
3. What would improve product quality?

AVAILABLE EMPLOYMENT

There are many jobs available to you. Two government publications, the *Occupational Outlook Handbook* and the *Dictionary of Occupational Titles* (DOT), list occupations, availability, average salary, skill, and general description. Opportunities exist in management, design, production, and support personnel. Select the areas you want to pursue based on your knowledge and skills.

Within management are company executives, office managers, and supervisors. These individuals are generally the decision-makers. The design area includes engineers, designers, drafters, and quality assurance persons. The production area includes laborers, helpers, machine operators, machine attendants, assemblers, laminate installers, and spray finishers, to name a few. Many of these job titles sound familiar, except, perhaps, for an attendant. This person customarily operates automated equipment. Support personnel usually do not work directly in production. They perform all the tasks that make management, design, and production more efficient. Among these people are forklift operators, timekeepers, inventory control clerks, and secretaries.

This book gives information to help you develop the skills needed to secure a job. In addition, consider your attitude. Strive to become the best worker you can be. In doing so, you will find the tasks more challenging and satisfying. Your job should give you self-satisfaction, in addition to a paycheck.

Unfortunately, there are people who do only what is needed to keep from being fired. They push the "green START button" at the beginning of the shift and the "red STOP button" at the end of the shift. In between, they take a work break and stop for lunch. These individuals who do not seek a challenge or self-satisfaction are probably unhappy with their job.

FINDING EMPLOYMENT

How do you find a job that is "right" for you? You have to begin somewhere. First, identify your knowledge and skill levels. Then search for companies that need people with your qualifications.

To find job openings in your area, read the classified ads in the newspaper, Fig. 53-1. Also listen to other people in the field. Most jobs are located by word of mouth. Another source of job openings is magazines such as *Business Employ-*

Fig. 53-1. Classified ads in your local newspaper advertise job openings.

ment Weekly. Most of these positions are for managers and engineers.

More formal search methods involve using library resources. The *Thomas Register* of manufacturers, *National Trade and Professional Association* guide, and Standard and Poor's *Directory of Corporations* are all examples. They classify companies by product and give addresses. Many wood-related jobs are found in the south and northwest where major forests are located. Finding the right position for you might mean relocating to another part of the country.

Contact the personnel departments of potential employers or send a short letter of inquiry. Find out if they are hiring people with your qualifications. If so, submit a letter of application and a resume, if requested. The application letter should state what you can do for the organization, not what you expect from it. Keep the resume short. It should highlight and reinforce what you stated in the letter of application. Any company is in business to satisfy its market first, and employees second. Without a satisfied market, there would be no jobs.

There are also job-finding agencies that contract with employers to locate workers. These organizations advertise in newspapers according to job titles describing required experience and education. The agency may also perform an initial interview to screen applicants. Only the top candidates are referred to the potential employer.

At the company, there will likely be more interviews. Make sure that you have done your homework first. Research the company, study it, and learn the nature of their service or product, Fig.

53-2. Be able to ask questions and make informed comments about production procedures, standards, and markets. If you meet their qualifications and are selected from among the candidates, the company will make an offer.

This sounds like a lot of work. It is! However, your future is at stake. Consult your local library for information on all these steps for your job search. This includes writing letters, developing a resume, and tips when interviewing.

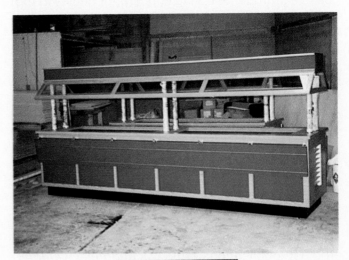

FORMICA CRAFTSPERSON—
With 3 years experience. We offer
piece work, flex time, insurance,
shop privileges. Longterm relationship desired. Salary open.

Fig. 53-2. Do you know the products made by the company? The ad doesn't say, but you should find out before interviewing. (Columbus Show Case)

STARTING A JOB

Most employment begins with some training, usually done on the job. In a relatively short time, you learn all about the company. Items covered include: expectations, potential risks and hazards, pay scale (hourly, piecework, salary), company benefits, advancement, and company procedures. Pay close attention to your duties and responsibilities.

WORKING

What *you do* on the job speaks louder than what you *say you do. Employees want to see results.* They do not expect 100 percent productivity when you start, but they want to see steady progress. This could be measured in concern for safety, tasks completed per hour, number of scraps, or other benchmarks.

Quality work is most important to the employer. This includes product appearance, tool maintenance, and holding to the production schedule. It makes you, your department, and the company's product or service all look good. Remember, the purpose of your company is to serve a market. By building quality products, you are satisfying the customer, who will return and tell others about your organization.

ADVANCING

Some people are content to work a single job all their life. Others seek new challenges and advancement. Over time, you advance in pay and responsibility as your skill and knowledge increase. Obviously, this relates to experience and your willingness to work. Have you taken on new assignments offered you? Did you say "NO" when asked to complete a more difficult task?

What does a company mean when they do not offer the raise you felt you deserved? Being overlooked might say that you are not as productive as you thought, or the company expected. In such a case, either meet the company needs or look for new employment that fits your skills better. Otherwise, you may never advance.

ENDING A JOB

People leave jobs willingly or by being fired. If you plan to leave one employer, give notice several weeks ahead of time. Make your plans known as a courtesy and do not leave unannounced. However, you need only to report that you are leaving, not where you will go. Leaving on good terms might result in a letter of recommendation from your employer. Also, your new employer may contact the former one for a work history report.

If you are fired, there may be little or no warning. Yet, you often can sense that the end is near. A supervisor will observe your poor work habits, absenteeism, or bad attitude. Rarely do people lose their jobs because of a single incident. Continuing personal disagreements with coworkers and supervisors are a much greater cause. Workers with good work ethic, displayed as professionalism, can solve these differences.

CAREERS

A *career* is a decision to dedicate yourself to a particular field. People looking for a career in cabinetmaking seek jobs with the potential for advancement. A career person hopes that someday they will be the decision-maker. More pay is associated with higher level of responsibility.

The potential for advancing in responsibility, job title, and pay is often called a *career ladder.* Each rung demands additional knowledge, skill, and positive attitude. A career person may begin with an entry level job, but knows how and when to climb the corporate ladder. For example, a laborer could become a machine attendant, then an engineer, a production manager, and, finally, company president. Don't think this is impossible.

Career-minded individuals find answers to "Why do I do this?" or "Is there a better way?" Their actions reflect a positive attitude toward the product they make *and* the people around them. Both are traits of leadership in any successful enterprise. These individuals are professionals, tuned in to production requirements and needs of the workers who produce, Fig. 53-3.

KITCHEN PROFESSIONAL
Immediate opening for experienced kitchen designer with established east side cabinet company. Call

Fig. 53-3. Pursuing a career means being a professional. (Formica)

STARTING A CAREER

Personal confidence and a positive corporate attitude are essential to career planning. You cannot build a successful career with selfish, self-centered motives. Join a professional organization to witness the characteristics of people whose shoes you want to fill. Also determine how your background and potential can assist the employer. As you develop competence, the company likely will move you to a higher rung on the career ladder.

BECOME THE BEST

Learn your duties well and become as competent as you can. For example, if you assemble doors, strive to be the top producer week after week. Your work will receive recognition. Let your actions, not your words, speak for your talents.

UPWARD MOBILITY

Always look for advancement opportunities. Moving up the career ladder usually occurs one step at a time. Each step offers new challenges, and the chance to improve your skills. Along the way, you will find that a single person cannot provide quality products or services. It takes a team. Realize that you must help others, and seek their aid, to meet company goals. There is much more to a career than dealing with the materials in the factory.

With upward mobility comes professional and public relations. Telling people what to do, as a parent does a child, gains little. However, you can drop hints to coworkers and supervisors when you feel you have the solution to a problem. They should be receptive. If they are not, consider that they feel threatened by your ideas, and maybe feel you are trying to occupy their rungs on the ladder.

To lessen office politics and increase cooperation, companies often adopt a participative management program. Workers actually have a chance to help make decisions. Some companies reward workers with a bonus for suggestions that increase productivity or reduce safety hazards.

People tend to resist change because they see it as a threat to their sense of security and stability. Yet, you must remember that the market is highly competitive. Some small improvement can mean the difference between profit and loss. The change you initiate, and prove profitable, will draw the attention of decision-makers. At this point, you are reaching the people-centered phases of industry known as management.

CAREER LEVELS

Every ladder has a limit to its length. When you reach the top, take time to establish yourself. At this point, you are not standing on a rung. The ladder you just left may have elevated you to a supervisory position, often called lower management. Note the other people who have also reached this level. What knowledge and experience do they have that you lack? Do what is necessary to be competitive. Become an example, not by criticizing others, but by making wise decisions and following up on your word.

The further you rise in a career, the more competition there will be. If necessary, further your education, formally or informally. As you do, another ladder will confront you. It leads to another level, likely a mid-management position such as manufacturing planner, Fig. 53-4, personnel

Manufacturing Planner

The Worthington Plant of Toledo Scale Corporation/Reliance Electric is looking for an aggressive individual to assume the position of Manufacturing Planner. The ideal candidate for this entry-level position will have a degree in industrial engineering or manufacturing operations. Duties would include assistance to insure all material is properly planned, ordered, statused and made available for all new products being introduced at the Worthington plant.

If you are ready to join a people-oriented company committed to quality and excellence, please send your resume

Fig. 53-4. A manufacturing planner may have to make decisions about protecting products during shipment. (Columbus Show Case)

manager, or a position in research and development, Fig 54-5. Remember, your actions speak so loudly that others cannot hear what you say.

Sometimes your career ladder leads to another company. Make your change for good reason, not for just a small pay increase at the company down the street. Sometimes, a competitor interested in your knowledge and skill will come looking for you. This interest puts you in a better position to bargain for salary and benefits.

Success at the mid-management level becomes the ground on which your next ladder rests. This ladder leads to upper management. Here you find vice-presidents in charge of various operations, factories, and people. At the very top is the organization's CEO (chief executive officer).

DESIGNERS

Several immediate openings in the Delaware, OH area. Long term assignments. Minimum 3 years on-the-job experience required. CAD experience helpful. CALL or send resume to:

Fig. 53-5. Research and development work leads to new products. (Columbus Show Case)

FROM MARKET TO AFTERMARKET

Most people do not seek to take over the top job. In fact, there are a large number of cabinetmakers who do not even work in the shop. They serve the aftermarket.

Suppose your interests lie in service rather than production. Products might come back to the factory for repair, or you may go to the customer. On-site service requires knowing how the product was built and being able to deal with the public. These people may be dissatisfied or angry when you arrive.

While servicing products, you might learn that customers need modified or new products. Take

these suggestions to the company managers. Doing so shows your interest in the future.

There are times when your employer is not interested in new products or services. The company could be working to capacity. If you see opportunities for meeting consumer needs, consider starting a business of your own.

ON YOUR OWN

An *entrepreneur* is someone who starts a business. This person has gained experience and skill working with and for others. Many entrepreneurs move out of companies that resist change to products or production. On your own, you can pursue the ideas you developed. Acquiring an ongoing business has an advantage. There are current customer contacts along with material and equipment in place. Starting "from scratch" requires a great deal of capital investment.

THE MARKET

Is finding a market easy? You might believe you have the market identified. Unfortunately, too many people find that the rest of the world does not share their feelings. Finding a market means research. Contact potential customers and test your ideas on the real world.

FINANCIAL BACKING

Even if the market indicates a need, you still must convince partners, lending institutions, and investors. Financial support will come only after you appraise the existing products or services. Small business loans are available if you study the market and present documentation. Who will be the customers? What are they willing to pay? How much will it cost to provide the goods or service? How much of your own assets are you willing to invest? Do you have a growth plan? These are by no means the extent of the questions. However, they will start you thinking.

A cost analysis is essential. It is not a matter of seeing how much profit can be made. The analysis tells how soon there will be *any* profit, based on projected sales. Reaching the *break-even point* takes time, even years. As a cabinetmaker, note that you must invest money for equipment, rent, utilities, materials, supplies, advertising, and taxes. This is only the beginning.

INDIVIDUAL TRAITS

Many factors help determine potential of a product or service. Most begin with the individual. Are you totally committed with personal finances, energy, and time to this enterprise? What experience do you have? Are you in contact with the anticipated market? Are you easily discouraged? Working for yourself generally is extremely time-consuming. You could be away from home 40 to 80 hours per week. Are you prepared to rent a building?

A business is located either in the home or in its own building. Be familiar with local zoning codes. It usually is illegal to operate a business in a residential zone.

NEW BUSINESSES

Most new cabinetmaking businesses begin with some form of custom production through contract or consignment agreements. There are also aftermarket services.

Contract production

Contract businesses start with one or more contracts for completed products or subassemblies, Fig. 53-6. Your first contract might be to manufactured drawers at a savings to your current employer. The work is done evenings and on weekends.

Contract work begins with one customer while you make proposals to other companies for your product or service. Impress these people with a convincing, successful track record. If your business is new, display your own custom products or services you worked at previously.

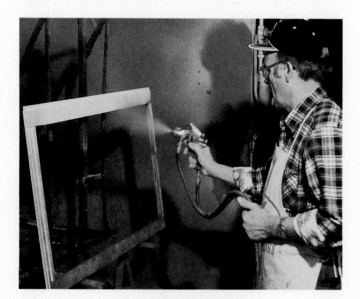

Fig. 53-6. This entrepreneur has started a business making frames under contract with a mirror company.
(Columbus Show Case)

As your company becomes better known and credible, the customer base will grow. This expansion leads to the need for more space and workers. At some point, you have to stop working and start managing. The larger the facility, the more workers and managers you need.

Consignment production

Another way to start a business is with consignment production. Approach a department store or specialty shop with sample products. Unique and interesting toys or gadgets sell to this market. Most items are usually not what people intend to buy, but do so on impulse.

The consignment agreement works like this: for each product sold, the shop owner will retain a percentage of the selling price and hand the rest to you. In turn, you keep the store stocked with a small inventory of products. At regular intervals, return to determine the sales and replenish those items that have sold out. Spend time producing what customers will buy, not what you like.

Aftermarket services

So far, this discussion has centered on the market. There are also places for the entrepreneur in the aftermarket. Businesses that reupholster, rebuild, and finish furniture are but a few aftermarket services. Some companies come to the customer's house and reface kitchen cabinets. Your ideas are limited only by the market.

NOT EVERYONE SUCCEEDS

Many resources—books, magazines, newspapers, videos, seminars—tell you about succeeding. However, there is another side to the story. Some entrepreneurs start on too large a scale. They overspend and wind up with debts they cannot overcome. Money lenders expect to be paid. Missing payments can result in loan foreclosure, and bankruptcy. You, personally, may not lose large amounts of money. However, your credibility is damaged for years to come.

About one-fourth of all new businesses go bankrupt within three years. Why? Most experts feel that the entrepreneur overlooked minute details or showed poor judgment. As you start on your own, spend adequate time testing the market, and plan each step. This forethought will lead to success.

SUMMARY

This last chapter is a capstone to the book's many pages of information and skill development. It leads you from a world of study to the world of work. You may make cabinetmaking your career, or just a stepping stone to another field.

Jobs related to cabinetmaking can provide challenge and job satisfaction. If you are a person who looks to improve cabinetmaking processes and products, this may be a career.

As a decision-maker, your responsibility will be to meet the consumer's needs. When quality slips, or your products are no longer needed, buyers do business elsewhere.

Advancement up a career ladder can lead to even greater satisfaction. Accepting responsibility means you have been trusted to handle people. Changes you make can affect the entire company.

Individuals with knowledge, experience, and a desire to be their own boss, acquire or start a business. It might be to create a product or provide a service. Although a market demand is the key to starting a business, it is not the only factor for success. There must be financial backing that supports the company until it turns a profit. With the strength of your ideas, and a good proposal, money will become available.

CABINETMAKING TERMS

Career, career ladder, market, aftermarket, contract production, consignment production, entrepreneur.

TEST YOUR KNOWLEDGE

1. The market is set by the products cabinetmaking companies produce. True or False?
2. All employees have career goals. True or False?
3. List steps taken to secure a job.
4. Most people are fired because of a single incident. True or False?
5. In addition to knowledge and skill, pursuing a successful career requires a _____ _____.
6. People climbing a career ladder:
   a. Tell supervisors what they do wrong.
   b. Have public relations skills.
   c. Possess self-centered attitudes.
   d. Tell the boss how good they are.
7. Give three reasons for becoming an entrepreneur.
8. Entrepreneurs are likely to start businesses with _____ or _____ production.
9. Why is the break-even point important to a business or industry?

INDEX-GLOSSARY REFERENCE

This section serves two purposes. As an index, it will help you locate topics anywhere in the book. As a glossary, the bold-faced entries show you where to find definitions for unfamiliar technical terms.

The Index-Glossary is more useful than either the conventional index or the conventional glossary of terms. It gives you access to more detailed information about terms being questioned. At the same time, you can read the definition in context with its related information. You can also read more about the subject as the need arises. Also, referring to related illustrations will make the new term more understandable.

Half-blind dovetail joint, **453**
Half-lap miter, **444**
Half-round cutting, **168**
Hammer drill, **364**
Hand drill, **361**
Hand plane surfacing, 342-347
Hand planes, squaring a board, 345, 346
Hand sanders, **475**
Hand sanding, 475-477
Hand sawing, 310-312
Hand scraper, **346**
Hand scrapers, sharpening, 350
Hand screws, **503**
Hand tool, shaping, 397-400
Hand tool surfacing safety, 347
Hand tools, drilling and boring holes, 364-366
Hand tools for drilling, 360, 361
  brace, **360**
  hand drill, **361**
  push drill, **361**
Handedness, **271**
Handling materials, 238, 239
Handsaw blades, sharpening, 319
Handsaws, 307-310
  sawing curved lines, 309, 310
  sawing straight lines, 307-309
  selecting, 310
Hard maple, 135
Hard mock-up, **82**
Hardboard, **161**
Hardboard types, 161
Hardware, 218-236
  bed, 233
  casters, **232**
  corner protectors, **232**
  door, 220
  door hinges, 221-229
  drawer, 229-231
  furniture, glides, **234**
  furniture, levelers, **234**
  hinges for wood doors, 220
  lid and drop leaf, 233, 234
  locks, 232
  pulls and knobs, **218**
  shelf supports, **231**, 232
Hardwood, **94**, **124**
Hardwood cells, **96**
Hardwood cell structure, **96**
  fibers, **96**
  parenchyma cells, **96**
  vessels, **96**
  wood rays, **96**
Hardwood grading, 112, 113
  dimension grades, **112**
  factory grades, **112**, 113
  moulding grades, **112**
Hardwood plywood, **150**, **158**, 159
  face veneer, **158**

grading, 158, 159
ordering, 159
Harmony, **40**, 41
Harvesting,
  sawing, 104
  sectional felling, **103**
  systematic felling, **103**
Hazardous conditions, **239**-248
  compressed air, 245, 246
  electrical, 244, 245
  exhaust and ventilation, 241
  finishing room hazards, 241, 242
  fire protection, **239**
  flammable liquids, **239**, 240
  material storage, 244
  mechanical guarding, 246-248
  personal protective equipment, 242
  substances, 241
  walking and working surfaces, 239
Hazardous substances, 241
Headboard, **727**, 728
Headstock, **405**
Health and safety, 237-248
  hazardous conditions, **239**-248
  unsafe acts, **238**, 239
Heartrot, peck, and grub holes, **108**
Heartwood, **124**
Hepplewhite, **21**, **22**
Hickory, 133
Hidden lines, **74**
Hidden tops, 624
Hide glue, **491**
High density fiberboard, **161**
High frequency heating, **498**
Highboy, **19**, **20**
High-build coatings, **679**
Hinged door catches, 228, 229
Hinged door mounts, 591
  flush front, **591**
  flush overlay, **591**
  lip-edge, **591**
  reveal overlay, **591**
Hinged tops, 624
Hinged wood doors, 591-597
  flush mount, 592
  lip-edge mount, 595
  mounting, 592-595
  overlay mount, 595
Hinged wood lids, 596
Hinges, door, 221-229
Hinges for wood doors, 220
Hold-down clamps, **507**
Hole saw, **359**
Honeycomb, **110**
Horizontal and vertical resin ducts, **95**
Horizontal division, **39**
Hot melt glue, **173**, 527
Hot melt gluing, 498

Metal and plastic edging, manufactured, 617, 618
Metal edging, **617**
Metal finishing decisions, 632
Metric kitchen cabinet measurements, 717
Metric scales, **86**
Microberlinia, 144
Millwork, **117**-120
  moulding and trim, **117, 118**
  moulding grades, 118-120
  paneling, **744** 746
Mirror frames, 729, 773
Mirror glass, **178**
Mirrors, product ideas, 733
Miter clamps, **505**
Miter gauge, **272**
Miter jig, **431**
Miter joint, **443**, 444
Miter trimmer, **433**
Mitering, **279**
Mock-ups, **48, 77, 81**
Modern, **26**
Modern cabinetmaking, 19
Moisture content, **98**, 99
  equilibrium moisture content, **98**
  removing water, 98
  testing moisture content, 98
Moisture meter, **98**
Moisture problems, controlling, 742, 743
Molded glass, plastic, and ceramic, 177, 178
Mortise, **444**
Mortise and tenon joints, **444**
  blind, **448**, 449
  decorative, 451
  making with hand tools, 450
  variations, 449
Mortising and tenoning equipment, 445-447
Mortising chisel, **445**
Mortising machine, **447**
Mosaics, **193**
Mottling, **674**
Moulding and trim, **117, 118**
Moulding grades, **112, 114,** 118-120
Mounting, **182**
  hinged wood doors, 592-595
  legs, 574-580
  stock, 409, 410
  the glass assembly, grouting, 185
  the glass assembly, stabilizing, 184, 185
  tripod legs, 579, 580
Mullion, **565**
Multioperational bits, 359
Multiple rooms, 28, 29
Multipurpose machine, **433, 434**
Multispur bit, **357**
Multi-view drawing, **72**
  three-view drawing, **73**
  two-view drawing, **73**

N

Nail coatings, 200
  cement, **200**
  zinc, **200**
Nails, 198-201
Nails, sizes, 199, 200
Natural abrasives, 466
Natural defects, 106-108
  bark pocket, **108**
  heartrot, peck, and grub holes, **108**
  knots, **106**
  other, 108
  peck, **108**
  pitch pocket, **108**
  white pockets, **108**
Natural finishes, 676-678
  linseed oil, **677**
  penetrating wax, **667**, 668
  tung oil, **677**
Natural penetrating finishes, **676**
Natural varnish, **681**
New businesses, 770
N-grade, **118**
No. 1 Common grade, **113**
No. 2 Common grade, **113**
No. 3 Common grade, **113**
Nonbleeder guns, **648**
Non-grain-raising (NGR) stain, **666**
Nonpositioned joint, **437**
Nonscratch surfaces, 686, 687
Nonvolatile materials, **676**

O

Oak, 136
Oblique lap, **442**
Offset dovetail saw, **309**
Ogee bracket foot, **573**
Oil spots, removing, 638
Oil stains, **666**
Oleoresinous varnish, **681**
One-piece anchors, **213**
One-piece connectors, **208**
One-piece tops,
  hardware, 618
  joinery, 619
  securing, 618, 619
Opaque finishes, **40**
Open grain, **98, 124**
Open mortise and tenon joint, **449**
Orange shellac, **679**
Ordering abrasives, 254
Ordering adhesives, 254
Ordering finishing products, 253, 254
Ordering glass, plastics, ceramics, and laminates, 252
Ordering hardware, 253, 254

Workbench vises, 505
Working drawings, **50, 68**
Working qualities, **100**, 101
  cell structure, 101
  dulling effect, **100**
  reaction wood, **100**, 101
Working with panel products, 162-164
  applying edge treatment, 163
  machining, 163
  planing, 163
  sanding, 163

sawing, 162, 163
storing, 162
using screws or nails, 163

Y

Yard lumber, **114**

Z

Zebrawood, 144, 145